FOURTH ANNUAL EDITION

The Antique Trader

ANTIQUES & COLLECTIBLES PRICE GUIDE

Edited by

Catherine Murphy & Kyle Husfloen

A comprehensive price guide to the entire field of antiques and collectibles for 1988 market.

Illustrated

The Babka Publishing Co.

P.O. Box 1050

Dubuque, Iowa 52001

ISBN: 0-930625-03-X

Library of Congress Catalog Card No. 85-648650

Additional copies of this book may be ordered from:

THE BABKA PUBLISHING CO.
P.O. Box 1050
Dubuque, Iowa 52001

$11.95 plus $1.00 postage and handling.

A WORD TO THE READER

For seventeen years The Antique Trader has been publishing a Price Guide. *The Antique Trader Price Guide to Antiques and Collectors' Items* has been available by subscription and on newsstands across the country, first as a semi-annual and then as a quarterly publication and, since 1984, it has been published on a bi-monthly basis.

In 1985, in response to numerous requests for a publication combining the material from the bi-monthly issues to provide a large, single price guide volume, the first edition of *The Antique Trader Antiques & Collectibles Price Guide* was issued. The book you now hold is the 1988 guide, our Fourth Annual Edition.

We feel this book is the most current price listing available and the most reliable book for dealers and collectors to refer to when seeking realistic values for antiques and collectibles. Prices listed here have not been unrealistically set by the editor or staff but are methodically compiled using an extensive system of sources including antique shops, shows, advertisements, auctions and an in-house staff of experts to help analyze prices and trends. Items are fully described and listings are carefully examined by the staff who discard unreasonable exceptions to bring you the most well-balanced and authoritative Price Guide available.

Our format enables us to maintain a wide range of both antique and collectible items in a running tabulation to which we are continually adding information and prices. As new avenues of collecting interest develop, new categories are added and, if a definite market is established, this material becomes a part of the Price Guide. A number of new categories have been added this year and include: Aluminum (under Metals), Bakelite, Bicycles, Gibson Artwork, Gutmann Artwork, Homer (Winslow) Engravings, Ice Skates, Juke Boxes, Napoli (under Glass), Perfume Bottles, Pyrography, Rose Bowls (under Glass), Statue of Liberty Collectibles, Steamship Memorabilia and Steiff Toys. In the Ceramics section we have added the categories of Abingdon Pottery, Alcock China, Carlton Wares and Watt Pottery.

During the past year six popular areas of collecting were highlighted in well-illustrated "Special Focus" segments which provided background material and tips on collecting. The focuses included in this edition are: American Games, Children's Furniture, Tea Leaf Ironstone, Teddy Bears, Tinplate Trains and Wine Advertising.

This book should be used only as a *guide* to prices and is not intended to set prices. Prices do vary from one section of the country to another and auction prices, which are incorporated into this guide, often have an even wider variation. Though prices have been double-checked and every effort has been made to assure accuracy, neither the compilers, editor or publisher can assume responsibility for any losses that might be incurred as a result of consulting this guide, or of errors, typographical or otherwise.

This guide follows an alphabetical format. All categories are listed in alphabetical order. Under the category of Ceramics, you will find all types of pottery, porcelain, earthenware china, parian and stoneware listed in alphabetical order. All types of glass, including Art, Carnival, Custard, Depression, Pattern and so on, will be found listed alphabetically under the category of Glass. A complete Index and cross-references in the text have also been provided.

We wish to express sincere appreciation to the following authorities who help in selecting material to be used in this guide: Robert T. Matthews, West Friendship, Maryland; Connie Morningstar, Salt Lake City, Utah; Cecil Munsey, Poway, California; J. Michael and Dorothy T. Pearson, Miami Beach, Florida; Bob Rau, Portland, Oregon; Jane Rosenow, Galva, Illinois; Ruth Schinestuhl, Absecon, New Jersey and Vera Tiger, Colorado Springs, Colorado.

The authors of our "Special Focus" segments deserve special recognition: "American Games" by Bruce Whitehall, Bedminster, New Jersey; "Children's Furniture" by Connie Morningstar, Salt Lake City, Utah; "Tea Leaf Ironstone" by Jean Wetherbee, Hillsboro, New Hampshire and Adele Armbruster, Dearborn, Michigan; "Teddy Bears" by Sybill McFadden, Lakewood, New York; "Tinplate Trains" by Susan and Al Bagdade, Northbrook, Illinois and "Wine Advertising" by Cecil Munsey, Poway, California.

Photographers who have contributed to this issue include: E.A. Babka, Dubuque, Iowa; Susan and Al Bagdade, Northbrook, Illinois; Stanley Baker, Minneapolis, Minnesota; Dorothy Beckwith, Platteville, Wisconsin; Donna Bruun, Galena, Illinois; Marie Bush, Amsterdam, New York; Carter Photographers, Tulsa, Oklahoma; Joseph P. Chalala, Willow Street, Pennsylvania; J.D. Dalessandro, Cincinnati, Ohio; Bill Freeman, Birmingham, Alabama; Mary Frank Gaston, Bryan, Texas; Vicki Gross, Hillsboro, Oregon; Jeff Grunewald, Chicago, Illinois; William Heacock, Marietta, Ohio; Beverly Kubesheski, Dubuque, Iowa; Joan C. LeVine, New York, New York; M.M. Mahan, Mayfield, Kentucky; Jim Martin, Monmouth, Illinois; Robert T. Matthews, West Friendship, Maryland; Sybill McFadden, Lakewood, New York; James Measell, Berkley, Michigan; John Mebane, Mableton, Georgia; Donald Moore, Alameda, California; Gale E. Morningstar, Salt Lake City, Utah; Jan Rebner, Oxford, Connecticut; Tammy Roth, East Dubuque, Illinois; Ruth Schinestuhl, Absecon, New Jersey; John Schumann III, Pottstown, Pennsylvania; Leslie A. Sorenson, Muskego, Wisconsin; Robert B. Taylor, Richmond, Virginia; Rose Mary Taylor, Pecatonica, Illinois and Doris Virtue, Galena, Illinois.

For other photographs, artwork, data or permission to photograph in their shops, we sincerely express appreciation to the following auctioneers, galleries, museums, individuals and shops: Neal Alford Company, New Orleans, Louisiana; American Graniteware Association, Downers Grove, Illinois; Andover Antiques, Brimfield, Illinois; Anker Expo, Copenhagen, Denmark; The Antiquer, Salt Lake City, Utah; Bear Cat Antiques, Salt Lake City, Utah; Bell Tower Antique Mall, Covington, Kentucky; Boehm Porcelain Studios, Trenton, New Jersey; Richard A. Bourne Co., Inc., Hyannis, Massachusetts; The Brass Key, Salt Lake City, Utah; Bruhn Auction Gallery, Wheatridge, Colorado; Butterfield & Butterfield, San Francisco, California; Carole's Coach House Antiques, Glen Ellyn, Illinois; Norm & Diana Charles, Hagerstown, Indiana; Christie's, New York, New York; Mrs. J. Ciparchia, Norwood, New Jersey; Clark's Antiques, St. Louis, Missouri; Country House Antiques, Salt Lake City, Utah; Mrs. James Craig, Washington, Pennsylvania; D. & L. Antiques, North Berwick, Maine; The Doll Shoppe, Salt Lake City, Utah; Doyle's Auctioneers & Appraisers, Fishkill, New York; Edith Dragowick, Dubuque, Iowa; Mary Duncan's, Anaheim, California; Dunning's Auction Service, Elgin, Illinois; Early Auction Company, Milford,

Ohio; T. Emert, Cincinnati, Ohio; Frasher's Doll Auction Service, Kansas City, Missouri; Garth's Auctions, Delaware, Ohio; Glass-Works Auctions, East Greenville, Pennsylvania; Glick's Antiques, Galena, Illinois; Grunewald Antiques, Hillsborough, North Carolina; Gene Harris Auction Center, Marshalltown, Iowa; Kenneth Hayes & Associates, Louisville, Kentucky; Hills House Gallery, Salt Lake City, Utah; Jane's Antiques, Galva, Illinois; Jeanne & Keith Antiques, Cassville, Wisconsin; James D. Julia Auction Service, Fairfield, Maine.

Also to the Klinger Collection at Bix, Anamosa, Iowa; Lenawee County Antique Show, Adrian, Michigan; Leo & Sons, Elyria; Ohio; Mariann Marks, Honesdale, Pennsylvania; J. Martin, Mount Orab, Ohio; Hanna Mebane Enterprises, Atlanta, Georgia; Rosemary Meyer, Dubuque, Iowa; Virginia Mills, Peabody, Massachusetts; The Nippon Room, Rexford, New York; Lloyd Ralston Toy Auctions, Fairfield, Connecticut; Rich Man, Poor Man, Fresh Meadows, New York; Daniel Ruthenbur, Jamestown, New York; Scheikel Antiques, Milwaukee, Wisconsin; Sellner Auctions, Scottsdale, Arizona; Robert W. Skinner, Inc., Bolton, Massachusetts; Sotheby's, New York, New York; Doris Spahn, East Dubuque, Illinois; Speck's Auction, Perrysburg, Ohio; Stein Collectors International, Kingston, New Jersey; Sybill's Museum of Antique Dolls and Toys, Lakewood, New York; Temple's Antiques, Minneapolis, Minnesota; Theriault's, Annapolis, Maryland; Time Was Museum, Mendota, Illinois; Don Treadway Auction Service, Cincinnati, Ohio; Trunzo Auction, Salt Lake City, Utah; Village Antiques Show, Dearborn, Michigan; Lee Vines, Hewlett, New York; Walcott Antique Show, Maumee, Ohio; Walker Auctions, Potosi, Wisconsin; Westchester Auction Galleries, Mahopac, New York; Whalen Antiques Auction, Neapolis, Ohio; Wilson House Antiques, Mineral Point, Wisconsin and Woody Auction Company, Douglass, Kansas.

The staff of *The Antique Trader Antiques & Collectibles Price Guide* welcomes all letters from readers, especially those of constructive critique, and we make every effort to respond personally.

The Editors

ABC PLATES

These children's plates were popular in the late 19th and early 20th centuries. An alphabet border was incorporated with nursery rhymes, maxims, scenes or figures in an apparent attempt to "spoon feed" a bit of knowledge at meal time. They were made of ceramics, glass and metal. A recent boon to collectors is the fine book, "A Collectors Guide to ABC Plates, Mugs and Things" by Mildred L. and Joseph P. Chalala.

CERAMIC

"Prince of Wales" ABC Plate

4½" d., transfer of merchant selling clothes, hanging hames, another stall w/sign "To Let," Staffordshire $125.00

5" d., animals & alphabet multi-colored transfer border, American, 20th c. 45.00

5¼" d., children's activities & games, transfer scene of boy goat herder w/horn, dog & goat, highlighted w/multicolor enameling, embossed alphabet border, Staffordshire 75.00

5½" d., "Hide & Seek," black transfer center, embossed alphabet border, Staffordshire, 1840-60 .... 75.00

5½" d., religious theme, black transfer of "All-Seeing-Eye" & 4-line verse w/child singing & angels overhead highlighted w/polychrome enameling, embossed alphabet border 110.00

6" d., donkey, green transfer scene 65.00

6" d., Franklin Maxim, "He That Hath A Trade Hath An Estate," green transfer scene center highlighted w/polychrome enameling, embossed alphabet border, Staffordshire (stains) 50.00

6" d., pink transfer of lady selling bakery goods & little girl peeking in basket, Staffordshire 75.00

6½" d., nursery rhyme, "Higgledy Piggledy---," gold alphabet border, Thompson mark 45.00

6 11/16" d., Indian series, "A Sioux Indian Chief," brown transfer scene center, embossed alphabet border, C.A. & Sons, England, 1890 .... 85.00

6 15/16" d., "England's Hope - Prince of Wales," black transfer of young boy on pony, Staffordshire, ca. 1859 (ILLUS.) 60.00

6 15/16" d., occupations, "The Village Blacksmith" black transfer scene center highlighted w/polychrome enameling, embossed alphabet border 85.00

7" d., children's activities & games, "Playing at Lovers," transfer scene of boy & girl wearing adult's hats & dog looking on at center, embossed alphabet border, unmarked Staffordshire, 19th c...... 38.00

7" d., children's activities & games, transfer scene of 2 little girls leaving house under umbrella, smaller children & mother in background, highlighted w/polychrome enameling, embossed alphabet border, Edge Malkin & Co., 1871-1903 .... 85.00

7" d., children's activities & games, transfer scene of Greenaway-type girls wearing large hats standing beside gate center, embossed alphabet border, Staffordshire, late 19th c. 75.00

7" d., nursery rhyme, "Hey Diddle Diddle," multicolored transfer scene of cow jumping over moon center, printed alphabet border, unmarked, early 20th c. 32.00

7" d., feeding dish type, "Baby Bunting and Little Dog Bunch," multicolored transfer print scene center, embossed alphabet border, American, 20th c. .... 45.00 to 55.00

7 3/16" d., children's activities & games, "The Guardian," transfer scene of dog watching girl sleeping highlighted w/polychrome enameling, embossed alphabet border, Elsmore & Foster, 1853-71...................... 95.00

7¼" d., American President, brown transfer bust portrait of George Washington center, embossed alphabet border, unmarked Staffordshire, 19th c. (crow's foot & stains) 85.00

7¼" d., children's games & activi-

ties, black transfer of piper followed by pigs highlighted
w/polychrome enameling 35.00

7¼" d., hunting scene, green transfer scene of dogs & hunters at the
hunt start, embossed alphabet
border, unmarked Staffordshire . . 60.00

7¼" d., wild animals, "A Fishing Elephant," pink transfer of elephant
fishing beside 2 little girls center,
embossed alphabet border,
Charles Allerton & Sons,
1890-1912 . . . . 85.00

7 3/8" d., famous places & buildings, "Evening Bathing Scene at
Manhatton Beach," transfer scene
center, embossed alphabet
border 85.00

7 3/8" d., famous places & buildings, "Niagara From the Edge of
the American Fall," transfer scene
center, embossed alphabet
border 85.00

7 3/8" d., famous places & buildings, "Oriental Hotel," hotel, people on beach & ocean, transfer
scene center, embossed alphabet
border 75.00

7½" d., wild animals, "The Leopard," brown & green transfer
scene center & alphabet border,
Brown Hills Pottery Co., 1882 . . . . . 75.00

8" d., "American Sports - Base Ball -
Pitcher," green transfer scene of
man ready to throw a ball, em-
bossed alphabet border 110.00

"Little Red Riding Hood" ABC Plate

8 3/16" d., nursery rhyme, "Little
Red Riding Hood," multicolored
transfer in reserve with scattered
alphabet to the side, Stafford-
shire, ca. 1887 (ILLUS.) 85.00

GLASS

5½" d., Little Boy Blue center scene,
etched, ornate open bordered
edge 42.00

5½" d., Little Miss Muffet center
scene, etched, ornate, open bor-
dered edge 42.00

5½" d., Mary Had A Little Lamb
center scene, etched, ornate,
open bordered edge 42.00

Clock Face ABC Plate

6" d., clock face center w/Arabic &
Roman numerals, alphabet bor-
der, frosted & clear (ILLUS.) 50.00

6" d., deer & tree center, clear 50.00

6" d., dog center, clear 50.00

6" d., rabbit in meadow center
scene, alphabet border 45.00

6" d., milk white, alphabet border . . 55.00

6" d., stag center, clear &
frosted 125.00

6 1/16" d., Santa center, clear &
frosted 50.00

"Christmas Eve" ABC Plate

6¼" d., "Christmas Eve," Santa
w/tree & toys descending chimney
center, alphabet border, clear
(ILLUS.) 165.00

TIN

3" d., boy & girl w/hoops 72.50

3½" d., girl swinging center,
alphabet border 35.00

8" d., "Who Killed Cock Robin" 47.00

Girl on Swing ABC Plate

8½" d., Girl on Swing lithographed
scene center, printed alphabet
border (ILLUS.) 45.00

ADVERTISING CARDS

"Empire" Cream Separator Card

The Victorian trade card evolved from informal calling cards and hand decorated notes. From the 1850's through the 1890's, the American home was saturated with these black-and-white and chromolithographed advertising cards given away with various products.

Assorted animals, various advertising, colorful frogs, monkeys, dogs, horses, etc., 19th c., set of 39 .... $95.00
Baby food, hold-to-light, "Mellons Food for Infants" 17.50
Cleanser, "Bon Ami," chromolithograph of chicks & slogan 8.00
Coffee, "Lion Coffee," chromolithograph of covered wagon scene ... 6.00

Coffee, "Lion Coffee," chromolithograph of old sleigh 2.00
Coffee, "Lion Coffee," chromolithograph of sleeping child in winter scene 5.00
Cologne, "Hoyt's German Cologne," chromolithograph of 3 children on tree trunk 4.00
Cologne, "Hoyt's German Cologne," chromolithograph of gentleman & lady in garden setting 2.00
Cologne, "Hoyt's German Cologne," chromolithograph of girl w/head resting on chair, 1891 calendar reverse 3.00
Cologne, various advertising, chromolithograph, assorted set of 50.. 60.00
Cream separator, "Empire," die-cut chromolithograph of young girl beside separator, holding rose in one hand & turning crank w/other, "I can turn the Empire," 5¼ x 3½" (ILLUS.) 10.00
Farm machinery, "McCormick," chromolithograph of early mower, ca. 1885 .... 40.00
Graniteware, "Agate Iron Ware," colorful scene, "Father Time can't destroy these wares." 20.00
Graniteware, "Granite Iron Ware," chromolithograph of 3 ladies at tea - "All the Gossip" 20.00
Hair products, "Ayers Hair Vigor," chromolithograph of 4 mermaids 5.00
Hair products, "Best Tonic," portrait of Mrs. Grover Cleveland 5.00

Metamorphic Card

Patent medicine, metamorphic, "Scovill's Sarsaparilla," folded shows lady w/unseemly blotches hiding her beauty & extended reveals her fair complexion after dose of Scovill's, 5½" l. extended (ILLUS.) 12.00

Sewing machine, "Singer," Costumes of All Nations series, souvenir of 1893, Chicago World's Fair, set of 32 .... 55.00

Soap, "Soapine," chromolithograph of State of Liberty 12.00

Soap, "Soapine," colorful die-cut whale-shaped card w/sailor washing whale 15.00

"Garland Stoves & Ranges"

Stoves, "Garland Stoves & Ranges," chromolithograph of girl, slippers by window w/candle & quarter moon visible, "I have come to stay," Michigan Stove Co. on reverse, 6 x 4½" (ILLUS.) 4.00

Thread, various companies, chromolithograph, assorted set of 80.. 100.00

Tobacco, "James C. Butler Tobacco Co.," chromolithograph of man & woman 12.00

ADVERTISING ITEMS

"Firestone" Ash Tray

Thousands of objects made in various materials, some intended as gifts with purchases, others used for display or given away for publicity, are now being collected. They range from ash and drink trays to toys. Also see ADVERTISING CARDS, ALMANACS, AUTOMOBILE ACCESSORIES & LITERATURE, BANKS, BASEBALL MEMORABILIA, BOOKMARKS, BOTTLE OPENERS, BOTTLES & FLASKS, BREWERIANA, BUSTER BROWN COLLECTIBLES, BUTTON HOOKS, CAMPBELL KID COLLECTIBLES, CANS & CONTAINERS, CARNIVAL GLASS, CIGAR & CIGARETTE CASES, HOLDERS & LIGHTERS, CIGAR & TOBACCO CUTTERS, COCA-COLA ITEMS, COOKBOOKS, COUNTRY STORE COLLECTIBLES, KNIVES, MATCH SAFES & CONTAINERS, MUCHA ARTWORK, PAPER DOLLS, PARRISH ARTWORK, POSTCARDS, POSTERS, SALESMAN'S SAMPLES, SCALES, SIGNS & SIGNBOARDS and SPOOL, DYE & ALLIED CABINETS.

Angel food cake pan, "Swans Down," tin, 1923 patent $12.50

Apple corer, "Baye Needle Co.," metal implement w/wooden handle, ca. 1915.................... 6.00

Ash tray, "Doe-Wah-Jack (Dowagiac, Michigan) Stoves," copper, arrowhead shape, 1905 .... 45.00

Ash tray, "Fidelity Mutual Life Insurance," Pennsbury pottery, grey glaze, "75th Anniversary," 1953 .. 28.00

Ash tray, "Firestone Tires," rubber tire shape w/amber glass insert, 6½" d. (ILLUS.) 22.50

Ash tray, "Goodyear Tires," rubber tire shape w/amber glass insert .. 20.00

Ash tray, "Greyhound Bus Lines," copper 7.00

Ash tray, "John Deere," galvanized metal, deer jumping over log, "Sample of Material Used in John Deer Van Brunt Drill," 3¼" d. 25.00

Ash tray, "Kelly-Springfield Tires," rubber tire shape w/green glass insert 24.00

Ash tray, "Mack Truck," chrome, model of bulldog center 36.00

Ash tray, "Mercedes Benz," aluminum, free form 5-point star-shaped base w/matchbox holder center inset w/enameled emblem 65.00

Ash tray, "Monarch Stoves," cast iron, dated 1905, 6 x 3½"....... 22.00

Ash tray, "Mountain States Telephone & Telegraph Co.," blue graniteware w/bellhop holding advertisement for "Yellow Pages" center, 4¾" d. (ILLUS.) 45.00

Ash tray, "Pyrene Fire Extinguishers," metal ....12.00 to 18.00

"Mountain States Telephone & Telegraph"

Ash tray, "Oakland Automobiles,"
copper 45.00
Ash tray, "Red Cab," blue glass,
"25-cent fare taxi" & telephone
number 15.00
**Ash tray, "Roebling Wire Rope,
Trenton, New Jersey," Lenox
china, ivory w/gold trim,
5¼" d.** 26.00
Banner, "Arbuckles Coffee," muslin
cloth, mother & child w/camera &
premiums pictured, 58 x 24" (edge
stain) 125.00
Banner, "Lowney's Chocolates," canvas, 54 x 22" 40.00
Banner, "Mobil Oil," canvas, "Calling All Cars," ca. 1930, 72" l..... 78.00
Banner, "Prince Albert Tobacco,"
muslin cloth, 2 men & pocket tin
pictured, 1939, 94 x 42"......... 65.00
Banner, "Smith Brothers Cough
Drops," canvas, portraits of
brothers & box of cough drops &
"For Health Sake" 275.00
Baseball bat, "Peter's Weatherbird
Shoes," wooden, 32" l. 45.00
Bean pot, "Heinz 57," brown-glazed
pottery 110.00
Beater jar, "Babers Mercantile, Hansel, Ia.," utilitarian crockery, grey
w/blue bands 65.00
Bench, "Red Goose Shoes," wooden,
3-seat 650.00
Bill hook, "Ceresota Flour," metal
w/chromolithographed cardboard
insert of boy.................. 30.00
Biscuit cutter, "Davis Baking Powder," tin...................... 7.50
Biscuit cutter, "Gold Medal Flour,"
tin 5.00
Blotter, "Goodyear Tires," colorful
picture of wife beside Model T
w/flat tire & husband telephoning
for service, 1920's 10.00
Book, "American Oil Co.," entitled
"Houdini's Big Little Book of Magic," 1927...................... 32.50

Book, "Burma Shave," jingles,
1939 .... 16.00
Book, "DeLaval Cream Separators,"
golden anniversary issue, "First in
1878 - Best in 1928," 36 pp. 13.00
Book, "Educator Shoes," entitled
"Peter Rabbit," from a series illus-
trated by Harrison Cady, 1922,
3 x 2½"...................... 10.00
Book, "Jewel Tea," entitled "Peter
Rabbit the Magician Magic Show,"
1942 .... 18.50
Book, "Kellogg's," entitled "Farm-
yard Favorites," 1917 .... 20.00
Book, "Pebeco Toothpaste," entitled
"The Gumps in Radio Land,"
1937 .... 25.00
Booklet, "California Perfume Com-
pany," entitled "Baby Mine," artist
Fanny Y. Cory, 1920, 16 pp. 17.50
Booklet, "Dr. Daniels Veterinary
Medicines," 1904, color
advertisements 39.00
Booklet, "Hanford Mfg. Co.," enti-
tled "ABC Jingles," 1920 .... 10.00
Booklet, "Jell-O," Maxfield Parrish
full color cover illustration, 1924 .. 40.00
Booklet, "Little Boy Blue Fairy
Soap," series 19, entitled "Fuzzy
Wuzzy Bears Out Camping" 12.00
Booklet, "Metropolitan Insurance,"
entitled "Mother Goose," color il-
lustrations by Emma Clark 15.00
Booklet, "Pied Piper Shoes," w/two
pages of paper dolls, 1930's 55.00
Booklet, "Tetley Tea," illustrated for
children, early 1900's 7.00
Bottle crate, "Pepsi-Cola," wooden,
24-bottle, 1920's................ 20.00
Bowl, cereal, "Baltimore Dairy
Lunch, J.A. Whitcomb," china,
cow decor, Grindley, England
mark........................ 30.00
Bowl, cereal, "Ford" in script,
china 30.00
Bowl, cereal, "Pettijohn's Flaked
Breakfast Food," china, bear on
rocky crag decor, wheat trim,
5¾" d....................... 80.00

"Ralston Purina" Cereal Bowl

Bowl, cereal, "Ralston Purina," china, green checkered edge, rabbit w/spoon, "Um-m All Gone" & "Find the Bottom" center, 5½" d. (ILLUS.) 37.50

Box opener & nail puller, "Cornbread Tobacco," cast iron 50.00

Bridge score pad, "Chesterfield Cigarettes," pretty lady, 1930's ... 15.00

Brochure, "Larkin Soap," die-cut desk-shaped booklet w/information about "The Chautauqua Desk," 7 x 4" 22.00

Brochure, "Schrader Tire Pressure Gauge," balloon tires & product, "The Air You Ride On," 1926 ..... 4.00

Broom rack, wall-type, "Garland Stoves" 65.00

Bucket, "Aardappelin Potatoes," graniteware, grey marbleized swirls 45.00

Butter crock, "Dentel's Store, Ackley, Iowa," utilitarian crockery, blue & grey 67.50

Cake pan, "Calumet Baking Powder," tin, round 7.50

Calendar, 1881, "Wm. Deering," farm machinery 25.00

Calendar, 1889, "Alexander Medicines," 4 little girls w/trumpets ... 32.00

Calendar, 1893, "Anchor Pain Expeller," sailor & girls pictured, pocket-type 30.00

Calendar, 1893, "Hood's Sarsaparilla," little girl ....32.00 to 45.00

Calendar, 1898, "Cutler & Grinder Barber Supplies," chromolithograph of Victorian girl & cat, 8¼ x 6" 15.00

Calendar, 1898, "John Hancock Life Insurance," "Liberty Tree," framed 150.00

Calendar with Buster Brown

Calendar, 1902, "Prucha, Son & Richtarik - Farm Implement Dealers, Wilber, Nebraska," w/Buster Brown & Tige illustration (ILLUS.) 300.00

Calendar, 1904, "Dr. Miles Patent Medicines," chromolithograph of child in white w/red tie 20.00

Calendar, 1906, "Wales Goodyear Rubbers," beautifully dressed ladies in fold-out scroll borders 45.00

Calendar, 1907, "Grand Union Tea Co.," cardboard, young girl holding puppy & seated in wheelbarrow filled w/flowers 55.00

Calendar, 1907, "Merrill & Bangs Pharmacist, Linden, N.H.," small boy & girl riding on barrel w/pr. puppies hitched to harness while mother dog oversees all 35.00

Calendar, 1910, "Empire Cream Separator Company," chromolithograph of smiling mother & child, by American Litho Co., N.Y., 25 x 12" 65.00

Calendar, 1914, "Continental Fire Insurance," scene of "First Shot at Yorktown" 35.00

Calendar, 1916, "Prudential Insurance Co.," entitled "The Prudential Girl" & signed Haskell Coffin, framed 35.00

Calendar, 1924, "Winchester Arms," lake scene.................... 302.50

Calendar, 1925, "Remington Arms," old hunter painting his decoys, framed, 33 x 21" 675.00

Calendar, 1925, "DeLaval Cream Separators," sleeping barefoot boy & Airedale dog w/fishing pole alongside, signed Price, 24 x 12" 65.00

Calendar, 1925, "Peters Cartridge," mallards flying above marsh, framed, 35 x 20" 350.00

Calendar, 1927, "Doe-Wah-Jack (Dowagiac, Michigan) Round Oak Stoves," in original envelope w/sales pamphlet 175.00

Calendar, 1930, "Western Ammunition," scene of hunter & Indian in canoe, full pad................. 275.00

Calendar, 1934, "Sieberling Tires," with 9 x 7" Rolf Armstrong print entitled "Irish Eyes," overall 16¼ x 10¼" 32.00

Calendar, 1940, "Pepsi-Cola," sportsman's scene 29.50

Chair, "Gravely Tobacco Co.," wooden, folding-type 190.00

Chair, "Piedmont Cigarettes," wooden folding-type w/blue & white graniteware back 120.00

Chair, "Sargent Floor and Furniture Enamel," wooden, various shades of bright paint overall, 20th c. 155.00

Change tray, "Newsweek Magazine," cast iron 22.00

Charm bracelet, "Planters Peanuts," chain w/plastic Mr. Peanut & peanut charms 16.00

Cigarette case-match safe combination, "Gillenwaters Coffee," celluloid 50.00

Cigarette silk, sport series, Babe Zira..................... 35.00

Clipboard, "Sperry Surveying Co., New Haven, Conn.," brass, scene of surveyor looking through transit, under blue enamel, 1920's, 7½ x 3¼"..................... 75.00

Clock, animated electric, "Trixy Root Beer," Pickaninny face w/blinking eyes, Lux Clock Co. 150.00

Clock, electric wall model, "Cat's Paw Soles & Heels," black cat on dial 135.00

"None Such" Clock

Clock, electric wall model, "None Such Mince Meat & Pumpkin Squash," tin, orange pumpkin-shaped face w/numerals, "Like Mother Used to Make" in black, 12" d. (ILLUS.) 300.00

Clock, electric wall model, "Poll Parrot Shoes," colorful parrot on dial 575.00

Advertising Clock with Crate

Clock, mantel or shelf, "Reed's Tonic," in original shipping crate (ILLUS.)........................ 625.00

Clock, wall regulator, "Hostetter's Stomach Bitters," Ingraham Clock Co., Bristol, Connecticut, oak case 1,100.00

Clothes pins, "Diamond Match Co.," wooden pin w/iron wire banding, 1920's, set of 20 in colorful box ... 10.00

Clothes rack, "Horseshoe Brand (laundry) Wringers," wooden folding-type 40.00

Coffee cup, "Dickinson's Pine Tree Seeds," graniteware 52.00

Compact, "Djer Kiss," silverplate, Art Nouveau style.............. 22.00

Counter display, "Borden's," papier mache bust of Elsie the Cow 120.00

Counter display, "Clayton's Dog Remedy's," papier mache model of a bulldog 775.00

Counter display, "Feenamint Gum," tin, easel-type, woman & product 145.00

Counter display, "Kiss-Me-Gum," cardboard die-cut of lady w/tambourine, boy & girl dancing 200.00

Counter display, "Oak-Hytex Toy Balloons," papier mache figure of a clown holding wooden sticks w/miniature balloons in each hand, w/extra balloons, 15½" h....................... 375.00

Counter display, "Red Goose Shoes," papier mache model of goose, 12" h. 475.00

Counter display, "Snow King Baking Powder," die-cut cardboard foldout, Santa Claus in sleigh w/reindeer, bag w/toys & Snow King can, colorful 275.00

Counter display, "White King Soap," cardboard, easel-type, little girl, pirate ship & dog, 1930's, 36 x 26"...................... 85.00

Counter display bin, "Beech-Nut Gum," tin, little girl pictured, 1916, 15 x 6 x 6"............... 225.00

Counter display box, "H.B. Turkey Red Embroidery Cotton," wooden, 10½ x 5"..................... 17.50

Counter display case, "Arrow Handkerchiefs," wooden box w/framed glass lid, 11½ x 10½" 55.00

Counter display case, "Eveready Shaving Brushes," tin case w/marquee, man shaving 700.00

Counter display case, "Fern Brand Confectionery," wooden box w/framed glass lid 135.00

Counter display case, "Gem Razor & Blade," tin, w/marquee, baby & father sitting on razor 850.00

Counter display case, "Natural Tip Shoe Laces," corner-type, wood & glass 125.00

Counter display case, "Shrade Pocket Knives," oak, glass lid w/gold lettering, 22¾ x 10¾", 10½" h. . . 250.00

Counter display figure, "Dutch Boy Paint," papier mache figure of Dutch boy, 15" h. 255.00

Counter display figure, "Red Man Tobacco," die-cut cardboard figure of an Indian, easel-type, 36" h. . . . 150.00

Counter display jar, cov., "Adams Pepsin Chewing Gum," clear glass, paper label "Pepsin" . . . . .85.00 to 100.00

Counter display jar, cov., "Buffalo Nuts," clear glass 150.00

Counter display jar, "Bunte" (candies), clear glass, lid w/ground stopper 60.00

Counter display jar, cov., "Carnation Malted Milk," milk white glass w/green lettering 38.00

Counter display jar, "Horlick's Malted Milk," aqua glass, original lid, 1-gal. 28.00

Counter display jar, "Lutted S.P. Cough Drops," clear glass model of a log cabin w/roof as lid 260.00

Counter display jar, cov., "Nut House," clear glass, embossed lettering . . . . .85.00 to 100.00

Counter display jar, cov., "Walla Walla Gum Co.," clear glass, embossed Indian head. 155.00

Counter display jar, cov., "W & S Cough Drops," clear glass. 200.00

"Chief Watta Pop"

Counter display penny sucker holder, "Chief Watta Pop," bust of Indian Chief w/suckers forming feathers in headdress, 9" h. (ILLUS.). 125.00

Cream whip, "Rumford Baking Powder," 1908 . . . . 12.00

Door guard bar, "Hires," metal, "Ask for Hires" & bottle front & "Thank You - Call Again" reverse, 18 x 5" 42.00

Door pull, "Colonial Bread," tin, loaf-shaped, 24" 75.00

Door push plate, "Dr. Caldwell's Syrup Pepsin," graniteware, black & yellow 50.00

Door push plate, "Domino Cigarettes," tin 60.00

Door push plate, "Hires Root Beer," tin, bottle, 1930's, 3½ x 11" 35.00

Door push plate, "Holsom Bread," graniteware, parrots decor 60.00

Egg separator, "Shulls Pure Extracts," tin. 18.00

Fan, folding-type, "Nyal Drug Store" 8.00

Fan, folding-type, "Opal Coffee" 15.00

Fan, "Kool Cigarettes," cardboard, colorful scene of Willie the Penguin using ice tongs to carry pack of "Kools" front & several housewares premiums reverse, wooden handle, 1927 . . . . 25.00

Fan, "Moxie," cardboard, colorful scene each side w/Frank Archer, wooden handle, 1922 . . . . 42.50

Fan, "Putnam Dyes," cardboard, colorful Art Nouveau scene w/butterflies & fairies, wooden handle 11.00

Fan, "Tube Rose Snuff," die-cut cardboard snuff can shape, wooden handle 20.00

Feeding dish, "Borden's Dairy," ceramic, "Elsie the Cow" & family decor 75.00

Feed sack, "Narragansett Intermediate Chick Feed," cotton cloth, Indian in full headdress center, red & black on white, 100-lb. size, 20 x 33" 8.00

Figure, "Planters Peanuts," Mr. Peanut w/blinking eye, cast iron, square base, 42" h. 1,750.00

First aid kit, "Mobilgas," tin, Flying Red Horse, cars & gas station on lid, 1940's 24.00

Flask, "Dayton Tire Co.," cigar-shaped, glass insert holds a shot 35.00

Flour sack, "Chanticleer Red Cock Flour," cloth, 100-lb. 20.00

Flour sack, "Larabee's Airy Fairy Flour," cloth, 10-lb. 17.00

Flour sack, "Top Hat Flour," cloth, 24-lb. 9.00

Flour sifter, "The Albion Center Creamery," tin w/wooden handle, 2-cup, 3½" d., 3" h. (ILLUS.) 15.00

Tin Flour Sifter

Flour sifter, "Mother Hubbard
    Flour" 13.00
Food mold, "Jello," aluminum 2.00
Gasoline pump top globe, "Elreco,"
    milk white glass w/two inserts,
    "Buy Miles Not Gallons" 225.00
Gasoline pump top globe, "Kool Mo-
    tor," milk white glass cloverleaf
    shape 400.00
Gasoline pump top globe, "Skelley
    Keotane," plastic 75.00
Gasoline pump top globe, "Tydol,"
    milk white glass, 15" 375.00
Grain sack, "Yaeger's Roller Mills,"
    paper, Indian Maid on
    horseback 19.00
Horse collar measurer, "Gall Cure
    Collars, Hess & Hopkins Leather
    Co.," wood & iron 65.00
Ice pick, "Holt-Brandon Ice & Coal
    Co.," iron 5.00
Jigsaw puzzle, "Coco-Malt," wind-
    mills, 65 pcs. in original envelope 10.00
Jigsaw puzzle, "Olivilo Soap," Setter
    dog & puppies, 9 x 7" 10.00
Jigsaw puzzle, "Pan Am Gasoline &
    Motor Oil," speedboat at marina,
    pretty girls, 100 pcs. 28.00
Jigsaw puzzle, "Pepsodent," Molly
    Goldberg, 1932, original mailer ... 20.00
Key chain, "Bull Durham Tobacco,"
    gold-plated, w/model of a bull ... 30.00
Knife, pocket-type, "Star Brand
    Shoes," figural shoe 65.00
Letter opener, "Oakland, The Sensi-
    ble Six," celluloid, automobile
    pictured 30.00
Mask, "Gilette Blades," paper,
    Gepetto, Pinocchio or Jiminy
    Cricket, copyright 1939, each 10.00
Match holder, wall-type, "Solarine
    Metal Polish," tin 55.00
Measuring cup, "Barrington Hall-
    Baker-ized Coffee," tin 8.00
Measuring cup, "Borden's," glass,
    Elsie the Cow 16.00
Mirror, pocket-type, "The Elite Pet-
    ticoat, Kennedy Gardner Co.,
    Iowa Falls," woman in turn-of-the-
    century petticoat 35.00

"Aunt Jemima's Pancake Flour"

Needle book, "Aunt Jemima's Pan-
    cake Flour," cardboard, red
    w/black & white printing, w/nee-
    dles, 3½ x 5¼" (ILLUS.) 30.00
Pamphlet, "Pacific Coast Borax Co.,"
    200 uses for Borax, 1896 .... 15.00
Paper clip, "The Pennsylvania Fire
    Insurance Co., Philadelphia,"
    brass, bust of William Penn, dark
    blue w/gold border, 2½ x 2½"... 25.00
Paperweight, "Glauber Water
    Valve," brass, embossed nude girl
    in waves, "They Never Leak,"
    3 1/8 x 5" oval 35.00
Paperweight, "Social Tea Biscuit,"
    glass, Japanese Geisha Girl...... 15.00
Perpetual calendar, "Springfield Fire
    & Marine Insurance Company,"
    lithographed tin over cardboard,
    cowboys & covered wagon, 13 x
    19" 75.00
Razor blade holder, "Listerine,"
    china, figural elephant 25.00
Rolling pin, "Joseph Reuter, General
    Merchandise, Gilbertville, Iowa,"
    utilitarian crockery, w/wooden
    handles 190.00
Salt & pepper shakers, "RCA Vic-
    tor," Lenox china, models of Nip-
    per, "His Master's Voice,"
    pr. ....20.00 to 35.00
Tape measure, "Lydia Pinkham,"
    celluloid 35.00
Toy clicker, "Poll Parrot Shoes," tin,
    1 7/8" l. 9.00
Toy doll, "Kellogg's," rag-stuffed
    Tom the Piper's Son, 1928 .... 85.00
Tumbler, "Welch's Grape Juice,"
    glass, etched grapes & lettering .. 25.00
Whet stone, "Bagley's Sweet Tips
    Tobacco," oval 30.00
Whistle, "Auto-Matic Washer,"
    wooden, "A Copper Washer For
    Every Home" 12.00

WINE HISTORY AND ADVERTISING

the well-kept secret!

by Cecil Munsey

No one knows when wine was first made. Paleontologists have found evidence of wine making by prehistoric man. Phoenician traders introduced grape vines into Europe and later the Roman Legions carried them into France, Germany, and England. (Interestingly, England is one of the best wine markets but the English have never been able to produce wine successfully in commercial quantities. Thus, collectible advertising from England promotes wines from other countries.)

The greatest single influence upon wine has been the Church. The development of winegrowing and making has accompanied the spread of Christianity.

The grape vine has played an important part in America as well as throughout the world. In the year 1000, a small band of Vikings discovered America and dubbed it "Vineland the Good" because of the wild profusion of grape vines they found on our shores. For 600 years thereafter the country was referred to in Icelandic literature as Vineland.

Formally, or "officially," American wine history covers some four hundred years, at least forty-one states, and a thousand historic vineyards. As we watch Bartles & Jaymes cavort on our television sets promoting wine coolers, how many of us understand that although winegrowing has had significant influence on the economy and culture of many states, it is unlikely that wine is even mentioned in their histories because the Prohibitionists erased it? Like dictators who rewrite their nations' histories to blot out other ideologies, the fanatical forces responsible for Prohibition spent years of zealous effort obliterating references to wine in printed texts. As a result, few of us now associate winegrowing with such historic figures as

Lord Delaware, John Winthrop, William Penn, Thomas Jefferson, Padre Junipero Serra, General Vallejo, Captain John Sutter, or Leland Stanford. And hardly anyone now living in Cincinnati, St. Louis, Pittsburgh, or Los Angeles realizes that these cities were winemaking centers a century ago. Even in California, where the oldest industry is winegrowing, the official textbook from which school children were taught California history discussed every product of the state's farms and factories, but until the 1970's it never once mentioned wine.

Collectors of wine advertising have long noticed and lamented a lack of specific promotional memorabilia to which they aspire. On the other hand, the value of those items which were produced and are still extant is at least double for comparable items promoting other products. Available historic items advertising wineries and their products seem to date back no more than one hundred years.

The first American wines were made in the mid-1500's by the French Huguenots from Scuppernong grapes they found growing near what is now Jacksonville, Florida. The Jamestown colonists in Virginia fermented local grapes to make wine in 1609, as did the Mayflower Pilgrims at Plymouth in 1623 for the first Thanksgiving.

For three centuries attempts were made to grow the fragile Old World wine grapes in the East. Lord Delaware in 1619; Governor John Winthrop of Massachusetts in 1632; John Printa, governor of New Sweden, in 1643; Lord Baltimore in 1662; William Penn in 1683; Thomas Jefferson in 1773 -- they all tried but failed. Father Serra successfully transplanted Mission Grapes from Mexico as he established his California Missions.

The beginning of commercial winegrowing in North America dates from before the Revolution when the native red Alexander was cultivated in Thomas Penn's (a son of William Penn) garden by James Alexander. Soon extensive vineyards of Alexander grapes were planted in Pennsylvania, Ohio, and Indiana. By the mid-1800's scores of native grape varieties were found and cultivated. By 1840 winegrowing ventures had begun in Alabama, Missouri, Maryland, New York, and North Carolina. By 1880 Georgia, Illinois, Iowa, Kansas, Michigan, Mississippi, New Jersey, New Mexico, Tennessee, Virginia, and West Virginia could be added to the list.

California began to successfully do what couldn't be done in the East -- by the 1850's Californians were growing grapes from Old World stock and shipping wine to England, Germany, Russia, Australia, and China. Then, in 1869, the first transcontinental railroad was completed and California wines were shipped to the East and Midwest. Trade wars and fierce competition forced firms to begin advertising their wines more heavily.

As serious wine advertising began to appear in the last quarter of the 19th century, the advertising industry, bolstered a lot by patent and proprietory medicine revenues, became one of the nation's large industries. It is from the late 1800's and early 1900's that much of the most sought after wine advertising pieces come.

A great deal of collectible advertising promoting wine is for "champagne." In the Champagne region of France, in the mid-to-late 1600's, a Benedictine monk named Dom Perignon discovered secondary fermentation that takes place in a tightly sealed bottle creates sparkling wine. A story handed down by tradition has it that the pious monk exclaimed, "Oh, come quickly! I'm drinking stars" as he first made his discovery. Dom Perignon also perfected the art of blending wines from various vineyards for a more balanced and uniform wine. He also was the first to use the bark of the cork tree as a stopper for Champagne bottles. Although cork bark had been used in other wine regions, Dom Perignon introduced it in the Champagne region to replace the bits of tow soaked in oil as a stopper, making it possible to retain the sparkle in the wine for a much longer period of time.

As a result of Dom Perignon's discovery it became a law in France that only sparkling wine from the Champagne region could be called "Champagne." Other countries, notably the United States, do not feel bound by French law so sparkling wine made in this country is called "Champagne." This is almost without exception historically. In recent times some of the Champagne firms of France have opened wineries in other countries -- they call their products "Sparkling Wine." It is, therefore, important for collectors to understand that a product advertised as "Champagne" did (does) not necessarily come from France. Around the turn of the century champagne (sparkling wine) was a very popular beverage and there were a great many brands, both domestic and imported. The resulting advertising was mostly in English with a smattering of French mixed in with those truly from France.

The quantity of wine advertising memorabilia for collectors to amass today is truly limited. This is caused mostly by the success of the early temperance advocates. Indiana had the first American Dry Law in 1816. Gradually towns and counties in other states voted themselves dry. Then whole states began going dry starting with Kansas in 1880. By 1914, when the First World War broke out in Europe, thirty-three American states had gone dry. With that many states dry, wine advertising needed for both domestic and imported wines was quite limited and did, of course, have an effect on the wine memorabilia available today.

With Wartime Prohibition in 1919, followed by the Eighteenth Amendment and the Volstead National Prohibition Act in 1920, the need for most wine advertising during the 1920-1933 Prohibition period was for nonalcoholic wine. After 1933, wine and its accompanying advertising once again proliferated. Since there are relatively few collectors of wine advertising memorabilia today the interest remains limited to pre-Prohibition items for the most part. A collector with an eye to the future would take note of the fact and act accordingly.

(**Editor's Note:** *The appeal of early wine advertising becomes apparent in this well-researched article by teacher-author Cecil Munsey who follows the various aspects of the collectors' market closely. An educator with a Ph. D., he serves as the Coordinator for Planning, Research and Evaluation of the San Diego County Office of Education, San Diego, California. Through the years, Dr. Munsey has researched and written several books for collectors, including:* The Illustrated Guide to the Collectibles of Coca-Cola (1972); Disneyana - Walt Disney Collectibles (1974); *and* The Illustrated Guide to Collecting Bottles (1970), *all published by Hawthorn Books, Inc., New York City. He has authored books related to the education field and contributed numerous articles to a wide variety of magazines and journals.* The Illustrated Guide to Collecting Bottles, *a widely used reference for the beginning bottle collector, has been kept in print by E.P. Dutton, Inc. (2 Park Ave., New York), and may be ordered through any book store.*)

Wherever possible, historical information or interesting sidelights about the various wineries or brands has been included in our listings.

"G.H. Mumm & Co." Ash Tray

Ash tray, "Extra Day Champagne, G.H. Mumm & Co., Société Vinicole De Champagne-Successeur" (the latter name adopted in 1920 after the firm was confiscated by the French Government from its German owners during World War I). China, made by Haviland & Co., Limoges, France, ca. 1925, 5 1/8 x 4 1/8" (ILLUS.) $40.00

Ash tray - match box holder, "Gold Seal Champagne," Nippon china . . 55.00

"California Old Sherry"

Bottle (empty) w/label "Los Hermanos Vineyards California Old Sherry" of 1888. Los Hermanos (the brothers) brand was owned by Jacob & Frederick Berringer, St. Helena, California & the winery was established in 1876. 9½" h. bottle (ILLUS.) 25.00

Pewter Bottle Stopper

Bottle stopper, "Gundlach-Bundchu Wine Company" of Sonoma, California. This vineyard was founded as the Rhinefarm in 1853 and renamed Gundlach-Bundchu Wine Co. in 1895. Pewter stopper, ca. 1910, 2½" h. (ILLUS.) 50.00

1898 Calendar

Calendar, 1898, "Gold Seal Champagne" by Urbana Wine Co., Steuben County, New York. Chromolithograph calendar (complete) by Rock Folding Box Co., Rock, New York, 22 x 12" (ILLUS.) 300.00

Catalogue advertisement, "Great Western Champagne," by Pleasant Valley Wine Co. in the wholesale price list of Weeks & Potter Co., Boston, Massachusetts, dealers in "drugs, sundries, wines & spirits for medicinal purposes." Until 1970 Great Western advertised they were located in Rheims, New

GREAT WESTERN CHAMPAGNE

IS MORE ACCEPTABLE TO PALATE AND
STOMACH THAN IMPORTED WINES
BECAUSE OF ITS

Unquestioned Purity

TOUCHES THE POCKET
LIGHTLY—YET FILLS
THE BILL.

Served at all first-class Clubs, Cafes and Buffets, everywhere.
The vintage now marketed is especially pleasing and very dry.

Pleasant Valley Wine Co,,
Sole Makers,   RHEIMS, N. Y.
Sold by Wine Dealers Everywhere.

Catalogue Advertisement

York. Rheims (taken from the famous champagne region of France) was just a post office at the winery. Pleasant Valley Wine Company was actually located in Hammondsport, New York. The neighboring Taylor Winery (see history of company below) purchased Pleasant Valley Winery & its famous Great Western Champagne brand in 1961. Inside page black-and-white advertisement, February, 1900, 5 x 3½" (ILLUS.).. 10.00

Catalogue back cover, "Gold Seal Champagne" by Urbana Wine Co., New York. Black-and-white back cover ad on Weeks & Potter Company catalogue, ca. 1900, 7 7/8 x 5¼" 20.00

Cigarette Lighter

Cigarette lighter, "Golden State Extra Dry Champagne" (sparkling wine by Italian Swiss Colony), bottle-shaped lighter w/pull-out top revealing striker, ca. 1935, 2¾" h. (ILLUS.) 35.00

Corkscrew, "Moët & Chandon," a firm founded in France in 1743 and famous as producers of the following champagnes: Brut Im-

"Moet & Chandon" Corkscrew

perial, White Star extra dry & Dom Pérignon. This corkscrew, patented in England in 1903 by Georg Hausmann of Cassel, Germany, is usually found with its name "Goliath." Because this example is considered a rarer version the value is higher. (ILLUS.).. 150.00

"Taylor's Muscatel" Decanter

Decanter w/stopper, "Taylor's Muscatel" by Taylor Wine Company (see history below). Clear glass w/enameled lettering, ca. 1910, 10¼" h. (ILLUS.) .... ·50.00

TAYLOR WINE COMPANY

At Hammondsport, New York in 1880 Walter Taylor began the Taylor Wine Company on a seven-acre vineyard. Taylor was a master cooper and came to the area to make barrels for the thriving wineries, including Pleasant Valley Winery, producers of Great Western Champagne, which was right next door. In 1882

Taylor added 70 more acres to his holdings. He brought his father George to the growing winery to help with the development. Walter and his wife Addie soon had five children. Born between 1883 and 1903, sons Fred, Clarence,a nd Greyton; and daughters Flora and Lucy all grew up in the business and helped it grow.

Taylor wines were popular in several states before Prohibition began. The Taylors switched from making wine to making grape juice. They did well and expanded their operation by buying the nearby Columbia Winery (established 1886). They modernized their holding and were among the first to have wine on the market after Repeal. Their wines were uncomplicated, consisting of port, sherry, sauterne, rhine, burgundy, claret, rosé champagnes, muscatel, and vermouth.

In 1961 when the Taylors bought out their neighbors at Pleasant Valley Winery, they "went public" thus becoming the first American winery to put its stock on the open market. The Taylors managed their own company until all three sons had died: Fred in 1968, Greyton in 1970, and Clarence in 1976.

In 1977, a year after the death of the last Taylor, The Coca-Cola Company bought Taylor and Pleasant Valley Wine Companies for an exchange of stock worth $93 million. In 1983 The Coca-Cola Company sold these and their other wine holdings to the Seagram empire. (Seagram, by the way, had already acquired the Gold Seal winery of New York in 1979.)

"Champagne Monopole" Ice Bucket

Ice bucket, "Champagne Monopole," the premier champagne of Heidsieck & Company, founded by Florence-Louis Heidsieck in 1785 in the area of Reims, France. The company is now owned by H.G. Mumm & Co. Nickel-plated brass ice bucket, ca. 1920, 7½" d., 7¾" h. (ILLUS.) 125.00

Invoice from R. Arnhold & Co., Inc. of San Francisco, agent of Inglenook Vineyard of Napa, California. Inglenook was founded in

1903 Invoice of Inglenook Agent

1879. 8½ x 9 3/8" invoice dated 1903 (ILLUS.) 25.00

"Los Hermanos Burgundy" Label

Label, "Los Hermanos Vineyards California Burgundy" by Beringer Bros., St. Helena, California. The "Los Hermanos" brand is now owned by Nestlé, the multinational Swiss chocolate maker, who bought the winery in 1970. 5 3/8 x 3 3/8" label of 1900 (ILLUS.) 10.00

"Los Hermanos Zinfandel" Label

Label, "Los Hermanos Vineyards California Zinfandel" by Beringer Bros., St. Helena, California. This winery which opened in 1876 has made wine in every vintage since 1879 allowing the title "oldest Napa Valley winegrower." 4 5/8 x 3 3/8" label of 1890 (ILLUS.) 10.00

Labels from the Kenwood Vineyards

Labels, "Kenwood Vineyards," established by Julius Pagani in 1905. Producer of bulk wines until purchased by John Sheela & Martin & Michael Lee in 1970. To commemorate the 1977 "Special Cabernet," Michael Lee commissioned artist David Lance Goines to make the first label in the winery's "artist series." Goines designed a label featuring a naked woman (left) which was rejected by the Bureau of Alcohol, Tobacco & Firearms (BATF). Goines, in anger, designed the label next with a skeleton of the former naked woman (center). BATF rejected it as well. The final label & the one used on the wine featured merely a landscape (right). One a few of the first two labels "escaped" the winery, hence the complete set has a value of (ILLUS.) 350.00

1903 Magazine Advertisement

Magazine advertisement, "Great Western Champagne," by Pleasant Valley Wine Co., New York, featuring waiter serving champagne to party couple & extolling "Brut Special 1900 - Special Reserve, Extra Dry" & claiming the Pleasant Valley Wine Company as the "oldest & largest producers of champagne in America." Indeed, the firm was established in 1860 by Charles Davenport Champlin. Full-color 1903 magazine advertisement, framed, 8½ x 11½" (ILLUS.)....................... 70.00

"Jerezcona Wine" Advertisement

Magazine advertisement, "Jerezcona Wine for Influenza, Neuralgia & Headache," from 1895 Christmas edition of *The Illustrated London News*, promoting Jerezcona Wine as both a beverage & remedy, black-and-white 5 x 7½" advertisement (ILLUS.) 10.00

Champagne Advertisment

Magazine advertisment, "Laurent - Perrier's Sans-Sucre (without sugar) Champagne" from 1895 Christmas edition of *The Illustrated London News*. Laurent-Perrier & Co., Vve was established in Tours-sur-Marne, France, in 1812. The firm is also noted for its brandy. Black-and-white 7½ x 5" advertisement (ILLUS.) 10.00

1912 Magazine Advertisement

Magazine advertisement, "E. La
Montagne's Sons of New York,"
from December 5, 1912 issue of
Life Magazine, listing the various
imported wines. Among the most
popular of the products listed is
Louis Roederer Champagne (pictured at right) first made in
Reims, France in 1760. Black-and-
white 11 x 18" 2-page (double
truck) advertisement (ILLUS.) 20.00

Pocket Match Safe

Match safe, pocket-type, "Drink the
Only Original Edouard Dubonnet &
Labussiere," the famous French
apéritif (wine to "open the meal"
or whet the appetite). Dubonnet
is classified as an aromatized
wine made bitter by the addition
of quinine (used in the treatment
of malaria). Metal match safe
w/celluloid inset, ca. 1910,
2¾ x 2" (ILLUS.) 65.00

Paperweight, "Cook's Imperial Extra
Dry Champagne - American Wine
Co., St. Louis," the latter having
become the successor to Cook's
Champagne Cellar. Adolf Heck,
Sr., father of the Heck Brothers
who later came to own Korbel
Vineyard & Winery in California,
was undercapitalized when he re-

"Cook's Imperial Extra Dry" Paperweight

opened Cook's Champagne Cellar
as The American Wine Co. after
Repeal. A Swiss firm invested in
the company in 1939. Five years
later, in 1944 during World War II,
government investigators discovered that the secret owner of the
winery was Hitler's foreign minister, Joachim von Ribbentrop and
the firm was seized and sold. Today Cook's brand is owned by the
Guild Winery, Lodi, California and
Cook's Imperial Champagnes are
still being produced. 3" d.
(ILLUS.)........................ 65.00

Poster with American Theme

Poster, "American Extra Dry Champagne," produced by Marschall &
Co. (whose company history &
brand have eluded rigorous research). Figure of patriotic lady
accepting glass of champagne as
she is draped with American flag
while other figures, representative of the various continents,
look on, ca. 1870, 14 x 12"
(ILLUS.)........................ 250.00

"Big Tree" Brand California Wines

Poster, "Big Tree Brand California
Wines." "Big Tree" was the name
of bulk wines of the California
Wine Association. The same wines
in bottles were sold under the
"Calwa" label. Both wines were
for export. The "Big Tree" is "Wa-
wona" (275 ft. high 28 ft. d.), one
of 80 similar trees in a grove in
Mariposa, California. This poster
was printed by Sharpe & Co. of
Queen Victoria St., London, ca.
1910, 29 x 23" (ILLUS.) 275.00

"Winehaven" Poster

Poster, "California Wine Association's *Winehaven* Winery," built
by Percy Morgan on San Francisco
Bay near Richmond, California after the 1906 San Francisco earthquake which destroyed 15 million
gallons of the Association's wine
inventory & all but one of its
several cellars. Winehaven was,
at the time, the largest winery in
the world with a capacity of 10
million gallons. Wine was shipped
in ocean vessels, from its own
pier, to most countries of the
world. In the late 1930's, the
structure was obtained by the
U.S. Government and is still part

of a naval fuel depot today. Poster, ca. 1910, 21¼ x 14¼"
(ILLUS.) 350.00

"M. Hommel" Poster

Poster, "M. Hommel Champagnes,
Vermouth & Brandy" by Michael
Hommel Winery of Sandusky,
Ohio. Founded in 1878, this win-
ery operated until 1967 when it
burned. Lithograph poster by
Wittemann Litho Co., New York,
ca. 1910, framed, 26½ x 20¾"
(ILLUS.) 275.00

"The Diamond Wine Co." Poster

Poster, "San Pareil & Gold Top
Champagne" by the Diamond
Wine Co., Sandusky, Ohio. This
firm was established in 1857, near
the time that Ohio was the premier wine state, producing more
than one-third of the national to-
tal of wine. By Gray Lithograph
Co., New York, w/copyright of
1896, 27 3/8 x 19", framed
(ILLUS.) 750.00
Poster, "Wente Bros. Brut," by
Wente Bros. Winery, Livermore,

"Wente Bros. Brut" Poster

California, first established in 1883 by Carl Heinrich Wente of Hanover, Germany. Before Prohibition wine was sold in bulk but since the late 1930's Wente table wines have become popular under their own name. The Art Deco full-color poster by artist Stephen Haines Hall was issued in 1983 to commemorate the 100th year of business & to celebrate the release of their first champagne "Wente Bros. Brut 1980," 24 x 18" poster, w/autograph of Carolyn Wente (ILLUS.) 50.00

"Beehive Brandy" Sign

Sign, "Beehive Brandy by the Associated Vineyard Cultivators Company," a firm managed by J.B. Laurent (Laurent-Perrier & Co. Vve, Tours, France). This brandy was "produced in Cognac, France" & won a gold medal at the Calcutta Exhibition of 1884. Self-framed

lithograph-on-tin, ca. 1890 (ILLUS.) 350.00

"Brotherhood Champagne" Sign

Sign, "Brotherhood Champagne" by Brotherhood Corporation Winery, Washingtonville, New York (the oldest active winery in the United States, having been established in 1839). Lithograph-on-tin over cardboard sign by Hauserman Litho of New York & Chicago, featuring bottles of "Extra Dry Champagne" & "Sparkling Burgundy," ca. 1905, 13 3/8 x 6 1/8" (ILLUS.) 175.00

"Cook's Imperial Champagne Extra Dry"

Sign, "Cook's Imperial Champagne Extra Dry," by American Wine Co., St. Louis, a firm originally founded as the Missouri Wine Co. in 1832 & renamed Cook's Champagne Cellar when purchased by Chicago political leader Isaac Cook in 1859 (see the paperweight listing). Artwork signed "Woelfe," an artist known to have created similar work for the rival firm of Garrett & Co. about 1920). Self-framed lithograph-on-tin, ca. 1910, 24¼ x 20¼" (ILLUS.) 500.00
Sign, "Cook's Imperial Champagne Extra Dry - The American Wine Co., St. Louis, Missouri." Lithograph-on-tin oval made by H.D. Beach of Coshocton, Ohio, w/patent date October 10, 1905, 28½ x 22½" oval 750.00
Sign, "Cresta Blanca Sparkling Wines" (champagnes) by Cresta

"Cresta Blanca Sparkling Wines"

Blanca Winery, Livermore, California. Wine bottle labels mention "Wetmore-Bowen Co." Charles Wetmore started Cresta Blanca winery in the early 1880's on 480 acres of land purchased for $200 in gold coin. The winery was ultimately sold to the Guild Wine Co. in 1971. Self-framed lithograph-on-tin, ca. 1915, 19¼ x 16¼" (ILLUS.)........................ 350.00

"Great Western Champagne"

Sign, "Great Western Champagne," by Pleasant Valley Wine Co., Hammondsport, New York, featuring bottle of non-vintage Great Western Extra Dry Champagne, lithograph-on-tin, ca. 1905, 19 x 13¼" (ILLUS.).............. 325.00

Sign, "Korbel Sec California Champagne," by Korbel Vineyards & Champagne Cellars, founded about 1886 near Guerneville,

Daring Sign

California on the Russian River. Of this lithograph-on-tin sign, circa 1910, the authors of *The Promise and the Product* (Macmillan Publishing Co., Inc., 1979) indicate: "A daring attempt at conveying sexuality; the poster turned upside down changes the model's arms to legs." (Identical artwork was used on a poster that today is valued at $200). 24 x 18" (ILLUS.) 150.00

"G.H. Mumm & Co. Extra Dry Champagne"

Sign, "G.H. Mumm & Co. Extra Dry Champagne," issued by deBary & Co., New York, sole agents for G.H. Mumm & Co. Originally a German firm from Frankfort, the Mumm firm opened in France in 1827. Self-framed lithograph-on-tin, ca. 1900, 28¼ x 22¼" (ILLUS.)...................... 450.00

Sign, "Virginia Dare," by Garrett & Company which had operations in North Carolina, Virginia, Ohio, Missouri, New York and California when this sign was issued in 1915. Lithograph-on-tin featuring the legendary Paul & Virginia, 40 x 30" 900.00

Tip tray, "Doniphan Vineyards Wine Co., Atchison, Kansas," featuring bottle of "Brenner's Pure Grape Wines." The history of this firm is

"Doniphan Vineyards" Tip Tray

sketchy but since Kansas was a "dry" state from 1880 until 1948, it is safe to assume that Brenner's wines were non-alcoholic grape juices and since the tray was made by Charles N. Shonk Manufacturing & Lithograph Co. (Chicago), the tray was issued between 1890 and 1935, while that firm was in business, 4¼" d. (ILLUS.)........................ 125.00

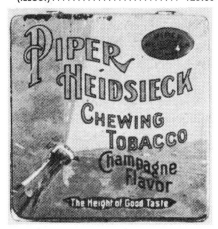

Tobacco with "Champagne" Flavor

Tobacco can, "Piper Heidsieck Champagne Flavor Tobacco." Piper Heidsieck was part of the original Heidsieck & Co. formed in 1785 in France but split up in 1834. In 1880, Kunkelmann & Co. became the name of the firm making Piper Heidsieck Champagnes and still does today. 3" square hinged box featuring bottle of champagne on lid, ca. 1935 (ILLUS.)........................ 20.00

Trade card, "Champagne," by New Urbana Wine Company, Urbana, Steuben County, New York. Chromolithograph w/champagne glass & grape clusters front & printed promotion for various wines & "Pure Brandy" reverse, ca. 1900, 5 5/8 x 3½"..................... 20.00

"Paul and Virginia" Tray

Tray, "Virginia Dare Wine - Paul Garrett Champagne," by Garrett & Company, founded by Paul Garrett in 1900. This tin tray featuring the legendary Paul & Virginia was lithographed by American Art Works, Coshocton, Ohio and a virtually identical tray was made by H.D. Beach Company, also of Coshocton, ca. 1915, 13" d. (ILLUS.)........................ 300.00

Prohibition Tray

Tray, "Virginia Dare Wine," by Garrett & Company, Brooklyn, New York, claiming "less than ½ of

1% alcohol" in Virginia Dare Wine & promoting that it was "non-intoxicating." A close examination of the bottle label indicates the firm was "established in 1835" when, in fact, Paul Garrett founded the firm in 1900 when he was 37 years old. Artwork on tray signed "A. Woelfe," ca. 1920, 13¼" d. (ILLUS.) 325.00

Wilson's Invalids' Port Wine

Tray, "Wilson's Invalid's Port Wine - A Big Bracing Tonic." Not much is known about the product or its producers but careful study deduces facts about the tray itself. The wine was aromatized with quinine from Peru as stated by "A La Quina Du Perou," a French statement pointing to the probability of that country as being the country of origin for the tray. The artwork gives validity to dating the tray about 1920 (during Prohibition) when only medicinal or sacramental wine could be made or imported to the United States. 14¼ x 10½" (ILLUS.)...... 250.00

"Tipo Red & White Wine" Waiter's Knife

Waiter's knife & corkscrew, "Tipo Red & White Wine," by Italian Swiss Colony, ca. 1915. The same wines were called "Tipo Chiantis" before 1910. Rafia-covered Italian *fiaschi* were the firm's most popu-

lar wines before Prohibition. Tipo red was revived in the 1970's but because the bottles cost more than the wine, it was discontinued as unprofitable. 4¼" l. knife w/corkscrew (ILLUS.) 35.00

(End of Special Focus)

ALMANACS

Dr. Kilmer's Swamp-Root Almanac

Almanacs have been published for decades. Commonplace ones are available at $4 to $12; those representing early printings or scarce ones are higher.

Agricultural Almanac, 1884-1923, Lancaster, Pennsylvania, 39 issues $48.00
American Telephone & Telegraph Almanac, 1934 .... 10.00
Arm & Hammer Baking Soda Almanac, 1921 .... 5.00
Ayer's American Almanac, 1887 .... 6.00
Ayer's American Almanac, 1899 .... 8.00
Christian Almanac for New England, 1832 .... 15.00
Dr. O. Phelps Brown's Shakespearian Annual Almanac, 1872 .... 10.00
Dr. O. Phelps Brown's Shakespearian Almanac, 1890 .... 8.50
Dr. Jayne's Medical Almanac and Guide to Health, 1862, 56 pp. 10.00
Dr. Jayne's Medical Almanac, 1912 .... 4.00
Dr. Kilmer's Swamp-Root Almanac, 1938 (ILLUS.) 10.00
Dr. Kilmer's Swamp-Root Almanac, 1940 .... 5.00
Dr. J.H. McLean's Almanac, 1890 or 1895, each.................... 8.00
Dr. Miles Almanac, 1926 .... 8.00
Farmer's Almanack, 1852 .... 5.00
Ford Almanac, 1937 .... 8.00
Gilbert's Squaw Vine Compound Almanac, 1901 .... 10.00

Healthway Almanac, 1960, Illinois
   Herb Co. 6.00
Hostetter's Illustrated United States
   Almanac, 1899 .... 10.00
Kansas City Daily Journal Almanac,
   1884 .... 3.00
Lum & Abner's Family Almanac,
   1936 .... 20.00
Mobil Flying Red Horse Almanac,
   1952 or 1954, each 8.00
Neuer Calendar fur Nord-Amerika,
   1847 .... 12.50
Phinney's Western Almanac,
   1816 .... 12.00
Planters Almanac, 1891, published
   by Lippman Bros. Wholesale Drug-
   gists, Savannah, Georgia 5.00
The Practical Farmer's Almanac,
   1899 .... 20.00
Rawleigh's Almanac, 1913 .... 15.00
Shaker Almanac, 1886 .... 45.00
Velvet Joe's Almanac, 1920 .... 2.50
Western Farmer's Almanac, 1831 ... 10.00

ART DECO

Sterling Silver Cocktail Set

Interest in Art Deco, a name given an art movement stemming from the Paris International Exhibition of 1925, is at an all-time high and continues to grow. This style flowered in the 1930's and actually continued into the 1940's. A mood of flippancy is found in its varied characteristics-zigzag lines resembling the lightning bolt, sometimes steppes, often the use of sharply contrasting colors such as black and white and others. Look for Art Deco prices to continue to rise. Also see BOOKENDS, CANDLESTICKS & CANDLE HOLDERS, CLARICE CLIFF DESIGNS and FURNITURE.

Ash tray, bronze, figural nude lady
   on base $150.00
Bar pin, black Bakelite, carved
   design 12.00
Bookends, chrome female figure on
   black base, pr. 42.00
Bracelet, bangle-type, ivory &
   chrome...................... 295.00
Bracelet, bangle-type, yellow marbleized Bakelite, 7/8" w. 18.00
Bust of Art Deco lady wearing floppy hat, porcelain, 6" h. 75.00
Candy dish, cov., green frosted
   glass, kneeling female nudes (2)
   at base, overall 8" h. 58.00
Cigarette lighter, table model, stainless steel, model of airplane,
   6" l., 3" h. 50.00
Cocktail set: shaker & 6 goblets; sterling silver, cylindrical shaker w/fit-
   ted strainer, fitted double-spouted
   cover & petaled domed foot,
   conical goblets w/matching feet,
   Georg Jensen, 7 pcs. (ILLUS.) 1,320.00
Cocktail shaker, Pigeon Blood enamel on sterling silver, geometric
   cover w/rooster finial, removable
   strainer, 9" h. 300.00
Coin purse, compact-type, "Mad
   Money," sterling silver, w/long
   sterling silver mesh handle 95.00
Cuff links, sterling silver, wheat
   sheaves, Georg Jensen, pr. 95.00
Dresser set: hand mirror & hair
   brush; sterling silver, 2 pcs. 75.00
Figure of an Art Deco girl & her
   Greyhound dog, chalkware,
   10" h. 25.00
Flower holder, porcelain, figural Art
   Deco nude lady w/arms out-
   stretched, impressed "Germany,"
   8" h. 65.00
Lamp base, chrome, seated nude
   holding marble ball, 15" 395.00

Frosted Glass Art Deco Lamp Base

Lamp base, frosted glass, dancing couple on domed circular base, 7½" h. (ILLUS.) 55.00

Lamp, spelter figure of lady kneeling & holding yellow-amber glass shade above her head 75.00

Lamp, green glass cylindrical shade w/inner celluloid revolving cylinder painted w/goldfish that swim around when lighted 135.00

Manicure set: nail file, cuticle knife & implement on stand; English silver, engine-turned handles w/pyramidal ends, suspended from rectangular stand applied w/stepped devices & mounted on oblong base w/engine-turned top, Birmingham, 1935, 4 pcs. 165.00

Mirror, hand-type, deep orange Bakelite w/rayed design, 10" l. 20.00

Mirror, vanity table top model, circular mirror centered in octagonal blue mirrored glass frame, on 4 Lucite ball feet, ca. 1935, 24" d. ... 66.00

Model of penguin, chalkware, 11" h. 50.00

Necklace, graduated marbled brown Bakelite beads 20.00

Perfume bottle w/matching stopper, lavender glass w/cut panels 30.00

Pin, celluloid bust of Art Deco lady w/h.p. features, on metal backing, 1920's 15.00

Pin, rhinestone, red & white sunburst design in sterling silver..... 48.00

Pin, sterling silver, 3 bells in silhouette 15.00

Powder box & cover, green glass, sailboat finial 20.00

Art Deco Powder Box

Powder box & cover, pink frosted glass, figural Art Deco lady & dogs finial, 4½" d. (ILLUS.)....... 37.50

Powder box & cover, porcelain, kneeling lady in 1930's bathing suit finial, lavender ground, black trim, overall 7¼" h. 37.50

Rug, wool, woven black, red, yellow

& beige geometric design, ca. 1930, 60 x 36" 110.00

Silent butler, gold-toned metal pan w/Bakelite handle, marked "Chase" 35.00

Talcum powder bottle, cov., jade green glass bottle w/embossed elephants, brass lid 25.00

Wall sconces, gilt bronze, ca. 1927, 7" w., 18" l., pr. 185.00

Whisk Broom

Whisk broom, porcelain half doll handle, marked "Germany," overall 8½" h. (ILLUS.) 35.00

ART NOUVEAU

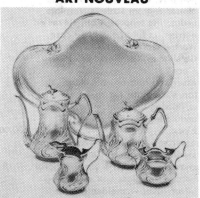

Art Nouveau Coffee & Tea Service

Art Nouveau's primary thrust was between 1890 and 1905 but commercial Art Nouveau productions continued until about World War I. This style was a rebellion against historic tradition in art. Using natural forms as inspiration, it is primarily characterized by un-

dulating or wave-like lines. Many objects were made in materials ranging from glass to metals. While interest in Art Nouveau still remains high, especially for jewelry in the Nouveau taste, prices appear to be leveling off. Also see BUTTONS and FURNITURE.

Ash tray, pewter, hammered relief undulating vines, "Liberty & Co.," 6½" d. $55.00

Bon bon, pewter, shell-shaped, w/full figure Art Nouveau nude woman, signed "Kayserzinn," 8 x 6¾" 175.00

Bowl, pewter, hammered & paneled, open flowing beaded handles, signed "Nekrassoff," 14½ x 4" . . . 75.00

Bowl, sterling silver, "repousse" Art Nouveau women's heads, 5" d. 130.00

Card tray, bronze, shell-shaped, cast w/nude Art Nouveau maiden amidst swirling waves 85.00

Card tray, silver finish metal, cast w/figure of a woman w/large fan, 6¼ x 4½" 65.00

Coffee & tea service: cov. coffee pot, cov. teapot, creamer, 2-handled sugar bowl & tray; silver, pear-shape embossed & chased w/undulating foliage, tendril handles & finials (one repaired), shaped oblong tray w/border of embossed & chased undulating stems & water lilies, Heimburger, Denmark, 1901, 5 pcs. (ILLUS.) . . .3,300.00

Cuff links, 10k gold, Art Nouveau lady w/flowing hair, set w/mine cut diamond, oval, pr. 125.00

Desk set: ink stand, chamberstick, pen tray, letter opener, roller blotter & gram scale; silverplate, undulating tendrils & gilt clover or berries, in fitted silk-lined case, Wurttembergische Metallwarenfabrik, Geislingen, Germany, ca. 1900, 6 pcs. 1,210.00

Dresser set: hair brush & hand mirror; silverplate Art Nouveau lady w/flowing hair amidst poppies & undulating vines in relief, 2 pcs. 100.00

Dresser set: hand mirror & cov. box; sterling silver mirror embossed & chased w/maiden & birds w/floral border, cut glass box w/sterling silver cover w/maiden & birds, 2 pcs. 310.00

Dresser set, silverplate, lady's head w/flowing hair, 10 pcs. 400.00

Figure of an Art Nouveau woman wearing long flowing gown & chignon hair style, throwing a ball, bronze, oblong base, signed "Burger," 5¼" h. 325.00

Glove stretcher, sterling silver, Art Nouveau lady on handles 95.00

Hair comb, celluloid, deep yellow, 7 x 7½" 75.00

Inkwell, pewter, embossed florals & leaves, "Kayserzinn," 5" w., 8" l. 115.00

Lamp, gilt-bronze, figure of Loie Fuller, her dress swirling about her body, tossing her veils up overhead to conceal 2 light sockets, signed "Raoul Larche" & numbered, Paris France, ca. 1900, 18" h. . . .11,500.00

Letter rack, brass, ladies' heads w/flowing hair 43.00

Locket, gilt-brass, embossed head of an Art Nouveau maiden, 1¾" d. locket w/32" double-twist chain . . 58.00

Mirror, child's, gilt metal, lovely lady w/flowing hair on back, 4" l., 2" d. 45.00

Mirror, beveled edge, easel type frame, embossed w/cupids, flowers & filigree, 10¾ x 8½" 65.00

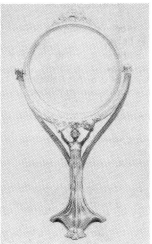

Art Nouveau Table Mirror

Mirror, table-type, pewter, circular mirror swiveling in frame cast w/flowers supported by a column in the form of a standing woman in a flowing gown, impressed "Wurttembergische Metallwarenfabrik," Germany, 19¾" h. (ILLUS.) 2,310.00

Panel from a fire back or stove, cast iron, woman's face w/flowing tresses & rays, 23¼ x 31" 290.00

Pendant, sterling silver, Art Nouveau lady's head 195.00

Perfume bottle, silverplate, embossed lady playing harp on each side, screw-on top, chain for hanging, 1 5/8 x 2 1/8" 89.00

Brass Water Lily Pin

Pin, brass, relief molded water lily
inside rope-twist frame, 2½" l.
(ILLUS.)........................ 30.00
Pin, sterling silver, gold-washed
grapes, accent stones 35.00
Pin, sterling silver, lady & poppies
decor 25.00

Silver and Ivory Pitcher

Pitcher, sterling silver & ivory, ivory
tusk body mounted with silver
neck & foot rims decorated
w/elaborate "repousse" design of
morning glories, Martele silver by
Gorham, "Sterling 9722," 14" h.
(ILLUS.) 17,600.00
Plaque, wall-type, bisque, Art Nouveau lady w/brown hair, holding
lavender Iris decor on green
ground, Ernst Wahliss company,
10" d....................... 250.00
Ring box, brass, cherubs & flowers
decor, red silk lining, marked
JB289, 2½ x 2" 65.00
Tea set: kettle on stand, cov. coffee
pot, cov. teapot, cov. sugar bowl,
creamer, waste bowl & 2-handled
tray; silver, Martele, baluster-
shaped, "repousse" & chased w/flo-
rals, rims & footrims serpentine,
curved handles w/ivory insulating

rings, Gorham Mfg. Co., Providence, Rhode Island, 7 pcs......16,500.00
Teaspoon, sterling silver, full figural
nude lady handle 125.00
Tea strainer, sterling silver, fits over
the cup........................ 60.00
Vase, pewter, impressed coins in
relief, "Kayserzinn," 8½" h....... 100.00
Vase, silver, elongated pear form on
shaped square base w/four curling
panel supports, everted lip, undulating rims, Martele, embossed
& chased florals & foliage overlapping strapwork panels, Gorham
Mfg. Co., Providence, Rhode
Island, retailed by Chester Billings
& Son, New York, 1905-12,
17¾" h. 7,150.00
Vase, sterling silver, ovoid,
applied w/semi-nude woman
w/cupids, dragonflies & leaves,
base modeled as water w/a mer-
maid, ca. 1900, 22" h. ....,2,090.00
Vase, pottery, peacock feather design in deep blue, white & ochre
on green ground, iridescent glaze,
signed Firenze & initialed 295.00
Vase, berry laden branches decor,
triangular chunky feet, fall colors,
Ernst Wahliss company 160.00

AUDUBON PRINTS

Black Warrior

*John James Audubon, American ornithol-
ogist and artist, is considered the finest nature artist in history. About 1820 he conceived the idea of having a full color book published portraying every known species of*

American bird in its natural habitat. He spent years in the wilderness capturing the beauty in vivid color only to have great difficulty finding a publisher. In 1826 he visited England, received immediate acclaim, and selected Robert Havell as his engraver. "Birds of America," when completed, consisted of four volumes of 435 individual plates, double-elephant folio size, which are a combination of aquatint, etching and line engraving. W.H. Lizars of Edinburgh engraved the first ten plates of this four volume series. These were later retouched by Havell who produced the complete set between 1827 and early 1839. In the early 1840's, another definitive work, "Viviparous Quadrupeds of North America," containing 150 plates, was published in America. Prices for Audubon's original double-elephant folio size prints are very high and beyond the means of the average collector. Subsequent editions of "Birds of America," especially the chromolithographs done by Julius Bien in New York (1859-60) and the smaller octavo (7 x 10½") edition of prints done by J.T. Bowen of Philadelphia in the 1840's are those that are most frequently offered for sale.

American Goldfinch - Plate XXXIII (33), hand-colored engraving & aquatint plate from "The Birds of America," engraved, printed & colored by Robert Havell, Jr., London, 1827-38, 19½ x 12 3/8" $2,640.00

Black Tern - Plate CCLXXX (280), hand-colored engraving & aquatint plate from "The Birds of America," engraved, printed & colored by Robert Havell, Jr., London, 1827-38, 19¾ x 12 3/8" 990.00

Black Warrior - Plate LXXXVI (86), hand-colored engraving & aquatint plate from "The Birds of America," engraved, printed & colored by Robert Havell, Jr., London, 1827-38, 38¾ x 25½" (ILLUS.) 1,540.00

Black & White Creeper - Plate XC (90), hand-colored engraving & aquatint plate from "The Birds of America," engraved, printed & colored by Robert Havell, Jr., London, 1827-38, 19 3/8 x 12¼" 1,055.00

Broad-Winged Hawk - Plate XCI (91), hand-colored engraving & aquatint plate from "The Birds of America," engraved, printed & colored by Robert Havell, Jr., London, 1827-38, 37 x 25¾" .. 4,125.00 to 7,975.00

Carolina Parrot - Plate XXVI (26), Amsterdam Edition (exact facsimile of the Havell Edition, printed in 1971 on rag paper & limited to 250), 26½ x 39½" 900.00

Chestnut-Coloured Finch, Black-Headed Siskin, Black Crown Bunt-ing & Arctic Ground-Finch - Plate CCCXCIV (394), hand-colored engraving & aquatint plate from "The Birds of America," engraved, printed & colored by Robert Havell, Jr., London, 1827-38, 19½ x 12¼" ...1,210.00

Chestnut-Sided Warbler - Plate LIX (59), hand-colored engraving & aquatint plate from "The Birds of America," engraved, printed & colored by Robert Havell, Jr., London, 1827-38, 19½ x 12¼" ....1,210.00 to 1,375.00

Chuck-Will's Widow - Plate LII (52), hand-colored engraving & aquatint plate from "The Birds of America," engraved, printed & colored by Robert Havell, Jr., London, 1827-38, 26 7/8 x 20¾" 3,740.00

Florida Cormorant

Florida Cormorant - Plate CCLII (252), hand-colored engraving & aquatint plate from "The Birds of America," engraved, printed & colored by Robert Havell, Jr., London, 1827-38, 19¾ x 26 1/8" (ILLUS.) 2,860.00

Golden Eagle - Plate CLXXXI (181), hand-colored engraving & aquatint plate from "The Birds of America," engraved, printed & colored by Robert Havell, Jr., London, 1827-38, 38 1/8 x 25½" 5,225.00

Great Cinereous Owl - Plate CCCLI (351), hand-colored engraving & aquatint plate from "The Birds of America," engraved, printed & colored by Robert Havell, Jr., London, 1827-38, 38 1/8 x 25¼" ..3,740.00

Harlequin Duck - Plate CCXCVII (297) hand-colored engraving & aquatint plate from "The Birds of America," engraved, printed & colored by Robert Havell, Jr., London, 1827-38, 20 5/8 x 30 3/8" 1,760.00

Mocking Bird - Plate XXI (21), hand-colored engraving & aquatint plate from "The Birds of America," engraved, printed & colored by Robert Havell, Jr., London, 1827-38, 33 1/8 x 23½" 7,560.00

Nashville Warbler - Plate LXXXIX (89), hand-colored engraving & aquatint plate from "The Birds of America," engraved, printed & colored by Robert Havell, Jr., London, 1827-38, 19 3/8 x 12¼" 1,615.00

Pigeon Hawk - Plate XCII (92), hand-colored engraving & aquatint plate from "The Birds of America," engraved, printed & colored by Robert Havell, Jr., London, 1827-38, 25 7/8 x 20¾" ......1,870.00 to 5,060.00

Pileated Woodpecker - Plate CXI (111), hand-colored engraving & aquatint plate from "The Birds of America," engraved, printed & colored by Robert Havell, Jr., London, 1827-38, 38 3/8 x 25¼" .....12,100.00 to 14,850.00

Purple Gallinule - Plate CCCV (305), hand-colored engraving & aquatint plate from "The Birds of America," engraved, printed & colored by Robert Havell, Jr., London, 1827-38, 12 3/8 x 19½"........660.00 to 1,540.00

Purple Grackle - Plate VII (7), hand-colored etching & engraved plate from "The Birds of America," engraved by W. H. Lizars, printed & colored by Robert Havell, Sr., London, on paper w/watermark "J. Whatman Turkey Mill 1827," 26¼ x 20¾".........1,870.00 to 3,960.00

Rathbone Warbler - Plate LXV (65), hand-colored engraving & aquatint plate from "The Birds of America," engraved, printed & colored by Robert Havell, Jr., London, 1827-38, 19 3/8 x 12¼" ....1,760.00 to 1,870.00

Red-Breasted Merganser - Plate CCCCI (401), hand-colored engraving & aquatint plate from "The Birds of America," engraved, printed & colored by Robert Havell, Jr., London, 1827-38, 26 5/8 x 39½" ......6,600.00 to 11,550.00

Rice Bunting - Plate LIV (54), hand-colored engraving & aquatint plate from "The Birds of America," engraved, printed & colored by Robert Havell, Jr., London, 1827-38, 19 3/8 x 12¼" ....1,210.00 to 2,200.00

Richardson's Jager - Plate CCLXXII (272), hand-colored engraving & aquatint plate from "The Birds of America," engraved, printed & colored by Robert Havell, Jr., London, 1827-38, 20 5/8 x 25 7/8" .....1,155.00 to 1,320.00

Ruff-Necked Humming-Bird - Plate CCCLXXIX (379), hand-colored engraving & aquatint plate from "The Birds of America," engraved, printed & colored by Robert Havell,

Jr., London, 1827-38, 19¾ x 12¼" ....4,070.00 to 6,600.00

Summer Red Bird - Plate XLIV (44), hand-colored engraving & aquatint plate from "The Birds of America," engraved, printed & colored by Robert Havell, Jr., London, 1827-38, 19½ x 12 3/8" ....3,080.00 to 3,850.00

Swamp Sparrow - Plate LXIV (64), hand-colored engraving & aquatint plate from "The Birds of America," engraved, printed & colored by Robert Havell, Jr., London, 1827-38, 19¼ x 12¼" ....880.00 to 1,045.00

Tyrant Flycatcher - Plate LXXIX (79), hand-colored engraving & aquatint plate from "The Birds of America," engraved, printed & colored by Robert Havell, Jr., London, 1827-38, 19 3/8 x 12¼" ....2,090.00 to 2,200.00

Wild Turkey. . .Female and Young - Plate VI (6), hand-colored etching & engraved plate from "The Birds of America," engraved by W. H. Lizars, colored by Robert Havell, Sr., London, on paper w/watermark "J. Whatman Turkey Mill 1827," 38¼ x 25 5/8" .....11,500.00 to 14,300.00

Wild Turkey. . .Female and Young - Plate VI (6), Amsterdam Edition (exact facsimile of the Havell Edition, printed in 1971 on rag paper & limited to 250), 39½ x 26½" 1,200.00

Winter Hawk - Plate LXXI (71), hand-colored engraving & aquatint plate from "The Birds of America," engraved, printed & colored by Robert Havell, Jr., London, 1827-38, 25¾ x 37" 4,810.00

Yellow Billed Magpie, Stellers Jay, Ultramarine Jay & Clark's Crow - Plate CCCLXII (362), hand-colored engraving & aquatint plate from "The Birds of America," engraved, printed & colored by Robert Havell, Jr., London, 1827-38, 26 x 21 5/8" 3,520.00

AUTOGRAPHS

Values of autographs and autograph letters depend on such factors as content, scarcity and the fame of the writer. Values of good autograph material continue to rise. A.L.S. stands for "autographed letter signed"; L.S. for "letter signed."

Adams, John Quincy, (1767-1848) 6th President of the United States, document signed, December 5, 1797, appointment of Samuel Williams as United States Consul at London, 1 p. $2,250.00

Arthur, Chester A., (1830-86) General during the Civil War & 21st President of the United States, A.L.S., New York, November 4, 1862, written as a General to a fellow officer, 2 pp. 750.00

Barnum, Phineas Taylor, (1810-91) circus producer, card signed, December 3, 1885 . . . . 75.00

Burbank, Luther, (1849-1926) American horticulturist, autographed card, "With the best wishes of Luther Burbank, Santa Rosa, Calif. Feb. 12, 1923," 5 x 7" 25.00

Cobb, Tyrus Raymond, (1886-1961) baseball player, signature on letter to him requesting his autograph 75.00

Cooper, James Fenimore, (1789-1851) American author, A.L.S., Rome, ca. 1829, to Mr. Duby, 1 p. 350.00

Davis, Jefferson, (1808-89) President of the Confederate States, document signed, Richmond, December 6, 1864, to the Secretary of the Treasury, 1 p. 1,800.00

Edward VIII, (1894-1972) King of England, black & white photograph signed as Prince of Wales, Edward standing in the woods, apparently on a golf course as he is in golfing attire, 5 x 7" 250.00

Franklin, Benjamin, (1706-90) American Statesman, inventor, diplomat & Signer of the Declaration of Independence, A.L.S., Philadelphia, February 12, 1756, to his sister in Boston after the death of their eldest brother, 1 p. 6,500.00

Gielgud, Sir John, actor, typed L.S., November 30, 1959, to Mrs. McAneny at the Princeton Theater, 1 p. 20.00

Grant, Ulysses S., (1822-85) Commander of Union Armies at the Close of the Civil War & 18th President of the United States, A.L.S., Galena, Illinois, April 23, 1880, to publisher George W. Childs, 3 pp. 875.00

Harding, Warren G., (1865-1923) 29th President of the United States, sepia photograph signed, 11 x 14" 350.00

Johnson, Andrew, (1808-75) 17th President of the United States, document signed, June 1, 1865, appointing George R. Vernon as 1st Lieutenant in the Army 685.00

Key, Francis Scott, (1779-1843) author of "The Star Spangled Banner" & lawyer, A.L.S., Georgetown, October 8, 1819, to William Meade (later Episcopal Bishop of Virginia), 3 pp. 2,500.00

Kilmer, Joyce, (1886-1918) American poet, A.L.S., New York Times letterhead, no date, to poet Edwin Markham, 1 p. 350.00

Lincoln, Abraham, (1809-1865) 16th President of the United States, document signed, November 4, 1861, appointing John S. Clark of New York as United States Consul at Singapore, countersigned by the Acting Secretary of State, 1 p. 2,250.00

Madison, Dolley P., (1768-1849) wife of President James Madison, A.L.S., Montpellier, September 20, 1840, to Mrs. Wingate, 1 p. 1,250.00

McKinley, William, (1843-1901) 25th President of the United States, document signed, June 24, 1901, appointing George F. Brady a 2nd Lt. of Infantry, 1 p. 375.00

Presley, Elvis, (1935-1977) American rock & roll singer, black & white photograph signed, dated 1956 . . . 150.00

Roosevelt, Theodore, (1858-1919) 26th President of the United States, typed L.S., White House letterhead, October 27, 1908, to William Addoms, 1 p. 575.00

Sargent, John Singer, (1865-1925) American artist, A.L.S., Boston, May 1, 1921, to Sir Phillip Sassoon, 4 pp. 235.00

Taylor, Zachary, (1784-1850), 12th President of the United States, L.S., Washington, June 11, 1849, to author Brantz Mayer, 1 p. 3,900.00

Tyler, John, (1790-1862) 10th President of the United States, document signed, September 14, 1841, appointing James N. Baker Acting Comptroller of the U.S. Treasury Department, 1 p. 775.00

Victoria, (1819-1901) Queen of England, A.L.S., Buckingham Palace, London, March 17, 1850, to an unidentified Duchess, 3 pp. 475.00

Wilson, Woodrow, (1856-1924) 28th President of the United States, A.L.S., October 19, 1901, to Charles Talcott, a Princeton classmate, 2 pp. .2,500.00

Wright, Frank Lloyd, (1869-1959) American architect, typed L.S., Taliesin letterhead, November 4, 1952, to artist Dale Nichols, 1 p. . . . 475.00

AUTOMOBILE ACCESSORIES

"Pontiac" Hood Ornament

Chauffeur's badge, 1927, Vermont .. $18.00
Chauffeur's badge, 1930, Missouri .. 15.00
Chauffeur's badges, 1930-40, Minnesota, nickel-plated, set of 10 ... 75.00
Chauffeur's badge, 1931, Maine 18.00
Chauffeur's badge, 1935, Indiana ... 10.00
Chauffeur's badge, 1937, Oregon ... 10.00
Chauffeur's badge, 1940, Illinois 15.00
Chauffeur's badge, 1940, Iowa 12.50
Chauffeur's badge, 1940, Ohio 18.00
Clock, "Chevrolet," Delco, w/box & instructions, 1950's 15.00
Clock, Waltham, 8-day, w/original ornate swivel bracket 55.00
Coils, "Ford Model T," set of 4 ..... 45.00
Duster, lady's, linen ....55.00 to 75.00
Gas pump nozzle, brass 35.00
Gasoline gauge, "Ford," wooden ... 22.00
Gear shift knob, Akro Agate glass .. 68.00
Gear shift knob, clear glass w/pin-up girl inside, ca. 1940 .... 25.00
Gear shift knob, marbleized blue & white graniteware, 2" d. 35.00
Gear shift knob, swirled red & white glass 35.00
Head lamp, "Winton," brass 175.00
Headlights, "Ford Model A," 1928, pr. 50.00
Headlight, "Ford Model T," kerosene-type, brass 50.00
Hood ornament, bust of lady w/long flowing hair, glass 75.00
Hood ornament, "Ford," greyhound, 1933 .... 65.00
Hood ornament, model of a red goose, advertising Red Goose Shoes, for Ford Model T 350.00
Hood ornament, "Packard" 95.00
Hood ornament, "Pontiac," white metal w/copper face, 1930's, 3½" h. (ILLUS.) 50.00
Horn, "Ford Model A," 1930 .... 14.00
Horn, "Ooga," brass w/original bulb, 16" 45.00

Horn, "Rolls Royce," brass, 1927 .... 125.00
Hub caps, "Cadillac," chrome, 1940, set of 4 .... 25.00
Hub cap, "Ford Model A" 10.00
Hub cap, "Plymouth," 1930-50 ...... 12.00
License plate, 1909, Massachusetts.. 60.00
License plate, 1912, Wisconsin 100.00
License plate, 1913, New Jersey 15.00
License plate, 1913, Wisconsin 80.00
License plate, 1915, California, graniteware 77.00
License plate, 1915, Vermont, graniteware 65.00
License plate, 1917, Wisconsin 40.00
License plates, 1920, Illinois dealer, pr. 48.00
License plate, 1925, Wisconsin 15.00
License plate, 1931, Ohio 20.00
License plate, 1933, Arizona, copper 50.00
License plates, 1933, North Dakota, w/original wrappers, pr. 14.00
License plate, 1934, Pennsylvania ... 40.00
License plate, 1942, Florida 8.00
License plates, 1943, Illinois, pr. 20.00
License plate, 1945, Illinois 17.50
Mirror, side-view, "Rolls Royce," late 1920's 65.00
Motometer, "Packard," w/crossbar, 1923 .... 60.00
Piston rings, "Dodge," 1935-40, original box, set 10.00
Pliers, "Ford" in script 7.00
Radiator cap, "Ford Model T" 10.00
Radiator cap, "Paige," brass 17.00

Radiator Emblem Plate

Radiator emblem plate, "Oldsmobile," Art Deco style, chrome & black, 5" l. (ILLUS.) 22.00
Spare tire lock, "Johnson" 30.00
Tire pressure gauge, "Ford Model A," brass 8.50
Tire pressure gauge, "Ford Model T," brass 9.00
Tire pressure gauge, "Peerless," automatic dial 50.00
Tire pressure gauge for balloon tires, "Schrader," dated 1923 ..... 10.00
Tire pump, "Ford," original red rubber hose 27.00
Tire pump, cast iron 16.00
Vase, "Buick," marigold Carnival glass, w/metal bracket, 1928 ..... 35.00
Vase, clear glass, molded arched

panels engraved w/roses & foliage, serrated rim, 8¼" h. 30.00
Vases, gold lustre glass, signed Quezal, w/original bronze brackets, 7" h., pr. 275.00
Vase, vaseline glass, Fine Cut & Daisy patt., w/original metal bracket 32.50
Wrench, 6-point, "Ford No. 35," in original box 24.00
Wrench, "Pierce Arrow" 25.00

AUTOMOBILE LITERATURE

Auto Kinks, 1934, auto repair manual, illustrated, 192 pp. $12.50
Auto Trade Journal, November, 1917, special commercial car issue, 390 pp. 25.00
Buick owner's manual, 1941 .... 15.00
Buick "Six" Motor Cars catalog, 1925, 47 pp. 50.00
Cadillac instruction manual, 1913, 4th edition, 80 pp. 35.00
Chevrolet sales brochure, 1938 or 1939, each.................... 25.00
Chevrolet "Six" book, 1932, car & truck construction, operation & repair, hardbound 37.50
Chevrolet owner's manual, 1955 .... 30.00
Dodge trucks sales brochure, 1936, die-cut, large 25.00
Flint sales brochure, 1924 .... 30.00
Ford owner's manual, 1922 .... 12.50
Ford sales brochure, "26 Reasons to Buy a Model T," 1911 (first edition), die-cut Model T shape, color-illustrated cover, 20 pp. 32.50
General Motors Automobile Buyer's Guide, 1934, illustrated, 80 pp. ... 40.00
Hudson sales brochure, 1946, original envelope.................. 15.00
Kaiser sales brochure, 1949 .... 10.00
Lee's American Automobile Annual for 1900, illustrations of steam, electric, compressed gas & internal combustion propelled vehicles, 275 pp. 75.00
Maxwell owner's manual, 1918 ..... 35.00
Oakland owner's manual, 1915 ..... 25.00
Packard brochure, 1946, original envelope 25.00
Tucker Motor Car showroom brochure, color illustrations 30.00
Willys-Overland Model 60 parts & price list 22.50

AUTOMOBILES

1927 Model T Ford

Buick, 1955 4-door hardtop, restorable condition $450.00
Chevrolet, 1941 pickup truck, restorable condition 1,495.00
Chevrolet, 1946 Fleetmaster 4-door sedan 1,200.00
Chevrolet, 1955 Bel Air 4-door sedan, 8-cylinder, 265 engine, automatic transmission, coral & charcoal ...3,700.00
Chevrolet, 1959 Parkwood station wagon, power steering, radio, all original, 14,500 actual miles 3,300.00
Edsel, 1959 Ranger 4-door hardtop...................... 2,000.00
Ford, 1926 Model T coupe 4,500.00
Ford, 1927 Model T touring car (ILLUS.) .... 9,000.00 to 11,000.00
Ford, 1936 fire truck, tanker 2,900.00
Ford, 1950 pickup truck, 8-cylinder flathead, new tires, 51,000 actual miles 1,800.00
Ford, 1960 Fairlane 4-door sedan, 8-cylinder, 292 engine, standard transmission (needs engine rings) 325.00
Ford, 1966 Mustang hardtop, 8-cylinder, burgundy 3,500.00
Frazer, 1951 4-door sedan 1,750.00
Nash, 1960 Metropolitan convertible, white w/black top, 81,450 actual miles 1,800.00
Oldsmobile, 1930 sport coupe, dual fender mount spare tires, trunk rack, rebuilt engine & transmission 7,000.00
Oldsmobile, 1941 4-door sedan, restorable condition 550.00
Oldsmobile, 1949 4-door sedan, 8-cylinder, 303 rocket engine, automatic transmission, restorable condition 750.00
Oldsmobile, 1960 Super Rocket Eighty-Eight 4-door hardtop, air conditioning, ruby red & white ... 950.00
Packard, 1941 limousine, 120 engine, 2-tone green (needs some exterior & interior restoration) 10,500.00
Studebaker, 1952 Commander convertible, restored 7,500.00

Triumph, 1968 convertible, 250
  engine, ice blue, 85% restored . . 4,600.00
Volkswagen, 1969 Karmann Ghia
  convertible, blue w/new white
  top 2,200.00

AVIATION COLLECTIBLES

Lindbergh Bookends

Recently much interest has been shown in collecting items associated with the early days of the "flying machine." In addition to relics, flying adjuncts and literature relating to the early days of flight, collectors also seek out items that picture the more renowned early pilots, some of whom became folk-heroes in their own lifetime, as well as the early planes themselves.

Admission tickets, "Lindbergh Day,"
  Baltimore, Maryland, pr. $15.00
Book, child's, "Air Babies," Kalep,
  forward by Amelia Earhart, 1936,
  w/dust jacket 12.50
Book, "Boy's Story of Lindbergh the
  Lone Eagle," 1928 . . . . 15.00
Book, "The Fun of It," by Amelia
  Earhart, 1932, 31 photos (ex-
  library copy) 15.00
Book, "Over the Ocean To Paris," by
  Franklin W. Dixon, 1927, Grosset
  & Dunlop publishers 5.00
Book, "Search for Amelia Earhart,"
  by Goener, first edition, 1966 . . . . 10.00
Bookends, bronze finish cast iron,
  bust of Lindbergh, "Lindy," 1927,
  6¼" h., pr. 52.50
Bookends, bronze finish cast iron,
  Lindy in cockpit of "Spirit of St.
  Louis," w/chrome propeller that
  can be spun by hand, 2 x 4¼"
  base, 7" h., pr. (ILLUS.) 60.00
Bookends, bronze finish pot metal,
  bust of Lindbergh wearing flight
  jacket, leather helmet & goggles,
  pr. 49.00

Calendar, 1934, "Lindbergh Flight by
  Ripley's Believe It or Not," color-
  ful, 9 x 4" 14.00
Commemorative ribbon, "Lindbergh,
  1927," woven silk, 7" l. 45.00
Model of "Spirit of St. Louis" air-
  plane, by Metal Craft, original
  box 140.00
Pencil box, tin, Lindy & the "Spirit of
  St. Louis" plane pictured 35.00
Pinback button, Lindbergh portrait,
  advertising "Bond Bread" 16.00
Pinback button, "Welcome Lindy" . . . 18.00
Plate, commemorative, 1927 Lind-
  bergh New York to Paris flight,
  Limoges china, 8½" d. 45.00
Pocket watch & fob, Lindbergh's
  "New York to Paris," Ingraham . . . 215.00
Poster, Inman Bros. Flying Circus,
  full-color pictures of Boeing &
  Ford trimotor planes, para-
  chutists, etc., autographed by Wil-
  son Inman, 1930, 39 x 25" 425.00
Program, "Lindbergh Day," Fargo,
  North Dakota, dated 35.00
Quilt, appliqued Lindbergh com-
  memorative, 36 colorful planes &
  geometrics on white, 1930's 450.00
Sheet music, "Like an Angel You
  Flew into Everyone's Heart," dedi-
  cated to Charles Lindbergh 8.00
Tapestry, woven w/Lindbergh por-
  trait & "Spirit of St. Louis" air-
  plane center & scenes of New
  York & Paris each end, 55 x 20" . . 75.00
Token, bronze, "Qantas Airline, 10th
  Anniversary of 1st Pacific Jet
  Flight," 1 5/8" d. 10.00
Token, metal, "1st Non-Stop New
  York to Paris," plane on reverse. . 35.00
Token, metal, "Lucky Lindbergh
  Coin," 1927 . . . . 12.00

BABY MEMENTOES

Everyone dotes on the new baby and through many generations some exquisite and unique gifts have been carefully select- ed with a special infant in mind. Collectors now seek items from a varied assortment of baby mementoes, once tokens of affection to the newborn babe. Also see ABC PLATES, CHILDREN'S MUGS, NURSING BOT- TLES, QUILTS under Textiles, ROSE- VILLE POTTERY JUVENILE LINE and the "Special Focus" on FURNITURE FOR CHILDREN.

Baby's record book, embossed leather cover, color illustrations by

Melcena Burns Denny, 1915, entries begin 1933 .... $16.00

Baby's record book, color illustrations by Frances Brundage, published by Raphael Tuck 65.00

Bowl, earthenware china, yellow lustre exterior w/gold-stenciled rim design, cream interior transfer-printed w/wicker basket of foliage & baby chicks, "Their First Day," 7" d. 30.00

Carriage (or buggy), leather-covered carriage & collapsible hood, metal spoke wheels w/white hard rubber tires, 1920's, 24" w., 52" l. 100.00

Silver Nursing Nipple

Feeder, silver, circular nipple attached to straw designed to fit in round bottle top, marked "E. Lownes" on bottle cap, Philadelphia, 1815-30, 6¾" l. (ILLUS.) 1,760.00

Feeding dish, earthenware china, rolled edge, boy w/bunnies decor, D.E. McNicol Pottery 45.00

Feeding dish, earthenware china, rolled edge, girl on horse decor, D.E. McNicol Pottery 36.00

Feeding dish, earthenware china, rolled edge, Little Bo Peep decor, D.E. McNicol Pottery 35.00

Feeding dish, earthenware china, "The House that Jack Built" verse & decal on creamy yellow, red trim, marked Roma, 5¼" d. 28.00

Feeding dish, earthenware china, children (4), dolls & numbers decor, marked Germany 125.00

Feeding dish, earthenware china, jointed Teddy Bears at various sports decor 75.00

Feeding dish, earthenware china, chicks hatching from eggs decal, marked Germany 30.00

Feeding spoon, silverplate, advertising "Gerber" 10.00

Feeding spoon, sterling silver, curved handle ....15.00 to 26.00

Food pusher, sterling silver, Cordis patt., Tiffany 25.00

Food pusher, sterling silver, hoe-shaped, alphabet on handle ....40.00 to 50.00

Hot water bottle, pink rubber, Old Mother Hubbard & other nursery rhymes in relief, terry cloth cover w/bunny, 1920's 22.50

Mug, earthenware china, lettered "Baby" on green & yellow, 2½" h. 22.00

Mug, silverplate, scene of Little Boy Blue in relief, Rogers ......20.00 to 30.00

Mug, sterling silver, "repousse" florals, marked Shiebler 125.00

Mug, sterling silver, engraved scene of children, Tiffany & Co. 295.00

Plate, graniteware, transfer-printed nursery rhyme, "There was an Old Woman lived under a Hill" & scene of old woman feeding chicks before hill, 8" d. 35.00

Plate, sterling silver, relief-molded wide border of child, squirrel, grasshoppers, birds, ducks, frogs, etc., Tiffany & Co., New York, 6½" d. 185.00

Rattle, celluloid, "Peter Rabbit," pre-war sticker, 9" l. 95.00

"Plackie" Rattle

Rattle, plastic, boy w/bow tie, pink & white, marked "Plackie - Youngstown, Ohio," 6¼" h. (ILLUS.)...................... 25.00

Rattle, sterling silver, dumbbell form, 4½" l. ....36.00 to 50.00

Rattle, sterling silver, round disc hung w/bells, mother of pearl handle w/teether end 95.00

Rattle, sterling silver disc, "Who Killed Cock Robin" & bird one side, "Bow Wow Wow" dog oppo-

site, mother-of-pearl handle,
3½" l. 135.00
Rattle, sterling silver, "repousse"
florals & bust portrait of baby
holding basket of flowers, 5" l. 85.00
Rattle, sterling silver, figural policeman w/English Bobby's hat,
w/ivory teether 135.00
Rattle, wooden, puzzle-type of interlocking key design, hand-carved
half-moons & hearts, patinated
finish, ca. 1830 .... 85.00
Rattle-whistle, sterling silver, "Little
Bo Peep," hung w/bells,
w/mother-of-pearl handle 195.00
Teething ring, ivory 45.00
Teething ring, mother-of-pearl ring
w/sterling silver bell inscribed
w/birth record 85.00
Teething ring, mother-of-pearl ring
hung w/sterling silver figure of
boy wearing cap & overalls &
w/hands in pockets, marked
Unger Bros., 4" l. 185.00

BAKELITE

Bakelite is the trademark for a group of thermoplastics invented by Leo Hendrik Baekeland, an American chemist who invented this early form of plastic in 1909, only twenty years after immigrating to New York City from his native Belgium where he had taught at the University of Ghent. Bakelite opened the door to modern plastics and was widely used as an electrical insulating material replacing the flammable celluloid. Jewelry designers of the 1920's considered Bakelite the perfect medium to create pieces in the Art Deco style and today Bakelite bracelets, earrings and pins of this period are finding favor with another generation of modish women. Also see ART DECO and RADIOS.

Bar pin, etched, navy blue $5.00
Belt buckle & 6 large buttons,
green, carved, set 32.00
Bracelet, bangle-type, green & yel-
low, carved, ¼" w. ....12.00 to 20.00
Bracelet, bangle-type, 2-tone green
marbleized, 1" w. 25.00
Bracelet, bangle-type, black edged
in aluminum, 1" w. 20.00
Bracelet, bangle-type, orange,
carved, 1" w. 25.00
Bracelet, bangle-type, burgundy,
carved, 1 1/8" w. 12.50
Bracelet, hinged, red, carved 45.00
Cigarette holder, black w/silver
wire decor, 9" l. ....60.00 to 75.00

Earrings, clip-on type, green,
carved, 1¼" l., pr. 12.00
Napkin ring, ivory 15.00
Necklace, red cubes w/chrome
spacers 50.00
Necklace, bracelet & earrings, red,
set............................ 45.00
Pencil sharpener, model of a Scottie
dog, red........................ 22.00
Pin, rose, carved 25.00
Pin, model of bird, colorful inlaid
stones 35.00
Pin, model of elephant, grey 20.00

BANKS

Original early mechanical and cast iron still banks are in great demand with collectors and their scarcity has caused numerous reproductions of both types and the novice collector is urged to exercise caution. The early mechanical banks are especially scarce and some versions are seldom offered for sale but, rather, are traded with fellow collectors attempting to upgrade an existing collection. Prices for all bank toys continue to rise as interest expands to more collectors and auctions within the past year have caused some mechanical bank prices to soar. In past years, our standard reference for cast iron still banks was Hubert B. Whiting's book Old Iron Still Banks, *but because this work is out of print and a beautiful new book,* The Penny Bank Book - Collecting Still Banks, *by Andy and Susan Moore pictures and describes numerous additional banks, we will use the Moore numbers as a reference preceeding each listing and indicate the Whiting reference in parenthesis at the end. The still banks listed are old and in good original condition with good paint and no repairs unless otherwise noted. An asterisk (*) indicates this bank has been reproduced at some time. Also see CANDY CONTAINERS and DISNEY COLLECTIBLES.*

MECHANICAL
4   Always Did 'Spise a Mule
(on bench)...............$450.00
5   Always Did 'Spise a Mule
(riding mule)......400.00 to 775.00
6   Artillery - Square Block
House ....500.00 to 1,300.00
7   Artillery - 8-sided Block House,
no soldier................$3,200.00
8   Atlas - "Money Moves the
World" 2,300.00
20 Boy Robbing Bird's Nest 2,600.00
22 Boys - Stealing Water-
melons 1,800.00

23	Boy on Trapeze	2,200.00
24	Bread Winner	17,000.00
26	Buffalo - Bucking	3,000.00
33	Cabin	325.00 to 385.00
34	Calamity (restored)	2,500.00
	Calumet - printed tin & cardboard	195.00
45	Chinaman - Reclining	2,600.00

Clown on Globe Mechanical Bank

49	Clown on Globe (ILLUS.)	900.00
52	Cow - Milking or Kicking	3,000.00
53	Creedmore - Soldier aims Rifle at Target in Tree Trunk	400.00
54	Creedmore - New (Tyrolese Bank)	600.00
56	Darktown Battery	1,500.00
57	Dentist	2,400.00
58	Dinah	250.00
61	Dog - Barking (Watch Dog Safe)	950.00
62	Dog - Bull Savings Bank	2,600.00
67	Dog on Turntable	275.00
69	Dog - Speaking	650.00 to 850.00
71	Dog - Trick	250.00 to 550.00
72	Dog - Trick, modern w/one-piece base	325.00
73	Doll's Head - Projecting from Egg	425.00
75	Eagle & Eaglets	450.00 to 700.00
76	Education & Economy (Bank of) - Patented April 30, 1895	850.00

Elephant with Three Stars

79	Elephant - Three Stars - replaced tail & white paint (ILLUS.)	200.00

82	Elephant with Man in Howdah	200.00 to 300.00
83	Elephant with Locked Howdah	425.00
86	Elephant - Small Jumbo	1,000.00 to 1,200.00
88	Elephant & Three Clowns on Tub	600.00 to 800.00
93	Football Player	1,600.00
95	Fortune Teller Safe	550.00
97	Fowler	2,800.00
99	Frogs - Two	785.00 to 950.00
103	Frog on Stump	500.00
105	Gem - Dog & Building	450.00
108	Girl in Victorian Chair	4,400.00

Girl Skipping Rope Mechanical Bank

109	Girl Skipping Rope (ILLUS.)	15,500.00
117	Guessing Bank	2,200.00
121	Hen - Setting	3,000.00
122	Hindu (some touchup)	800.00
126	Horse Race	5,000.00
129	Indian Shooting Bear	1,500.00
130	Initiating Bank - First Degree	8,200.00
137	Jolly Nigger - Starkie Patent, red coat, white collar, blue tie (aluminum)	255.00
138	Jonah and the Whale	950.00
145	Lighthouse	1,000.00
147	Lion and Monkeys	450.00 to 550.00
151	Locomotive (repaired & restored)	1,200.00
154	Magician	2,600.00
155	Mammy and Child	1,900.00 to 2,450.00
156	Mason and Hod Carrier	1,800.00
160	Minstrel, tin	400.00
163	Monkey and Coconut	2,100.00
164	Monkey and Organ Grinder	450.00
168	Mosque	600.00
171	Multiplying Bank	400.00
176	Novelty	600.00
177	Organ Bank - with Monkey, Cat and Dog	350.00 to 500.00

179 Organ Bank - with Monkey on
    Top 375.00
181 Organ Grinder and Dancing
    Bear .2,300.00
184 Owl with Book - Slot in
    Book .550.00
187 Patronize the Blind Man and
    His Dog 2,200.00

Picture Gallery Bank

192 Picture Gallery (ILLUS.) 7,600.00

Pony Trick Bank

196 Pony - Trick (ILLUS.) 485.00

Popeye Knockout Bank

Popeye Knockout Bank, tin
    (ILLUS.) 400.00
199 Presto - Building . . . .150.00 to 300.00
211 Roller Skating 7,600.00
222 Stump Speaker 1,100.00
226 Teddy and the Bear in Tree . . .950.00
227 Telephone - "Pay Phone
    Bank" 300.00
230 Uncle Remus 5,800.00
237 William Tell . . . . .350.00 to 595.00
244 World's Fair Bank - with
    Columbus and Indian 700.00

STILL

1063 Administration Building 1893
    World's Fair, cast iron, com-
    bination trap, Magic Intro-
    duction Co., 1893 patent
    5 x 5¼" .95.00
1604 Alphabet - 26 Facets with let-
    ter on each, cast iron,
    3 7/8" d. (W. 227) 1,500.00
217 Andy Gump - Seated, cast
    iron, Arcade, 1928,
    4½" h. * 850.00
219 "Andy Gump Savings Bank,"
    lead, General Thrift Pro-
    ducts, 1920's, 5¾ x 5¾" 275.00
800 Apollo 8 Rocket, cast iron,
    John Wright, 1968, 3" d.,
    4¼" h. .45.00
1621 Apple on Twig & Leaf -
    with Bumblebee on face of
    apple, cast iron, Kyser &
    Rex, 1882, 5¼" w.
    (W. 299) 675.00
1424 Armored Car - World War I
    mobile army unit, cast iron,
    A.C. Williams Co., 1914-27,
    6¾" l. (W. 160) 875.00
1484 Auto - Model T Ford, cast
    iron, Arcade, 1923-25, 6¼" l.
    (W. 157) 350.00
1487 Auto - early 4-passenger model
    w/large wheels, cast iron,
    A.C. Williams Co., 1910,
    6¾" l., 3½" h. 450.00
52 Baby in Cradle w/Rosettes,
    cast iron, 1890's, 4" l.
    (W. 231) 1,260.00
807 "Bailey's Centennial Money
    Bank," cast iron, "Proclaim
    1776 Liberty - Centennial
    Money 1876 Bank," on square
    marble base, 4¼" w. base,
    overall 4½" h. (W. 280) 67.50
906 "Bank of Columbia" safe, cast
    iron, Arcade, 1891-1913,
    3¾ x 3 3/8" sq., 4 7/8" h. . .150.00
1608 Baseball on Three Bats -
    "American and National League
    Ball" & "Official League Ball,"
    cast iron, Hubley Mfg. Co.,
    1914, 5" h. (W. 220) 525.00

Baseball Player

18　Baseball Player, cast iron,
　　　A.C. Williams Co., 1909-39,
　　　5¾" h., W. 10 (ILLUS.) 145.00

1450　Battleship "Oregon" - small,
　　　cast iron, J. & E. Stevens Co.,
　　　1891-1906, 5 1/16" l.
　　　(W. 144) 225.00

698　Bear - variant, without "Teddy"
　　　on side, cast iron, 4" l.
　　　(W. 331 variant) 210.00

711　Bear on Hing Legs, aluminum,
　　　John Harper Ltd., England,
　　　6" h. 45.00

710　Bear on Hind Legs, cast iron,
　　　John Harper Ltd., England,
　　　ca. 1911, 6 1/8" h. * 75.00

122　"Ben Franklin" bust, lead,
　　　Preferred Bank Service Co.,
　　　1920's, 5¼" h. (W. 313) 80.00

1196　Bethel College Administration
　　　Building, cast iron, Service
　　　Foundry, ca. 1935, 2 7/8 x
　　　5¼", 3 7/8" h. 45.00

81　Billiken on Throne - "Good
　　　Luck," cast iron, A.C. Wil-
　　　liams Co., 1909-19, 6½" h.
　　　(W. 48) 95.00

927　Bird Cage Bank (Crystal Bank),
　　　iron wire mesh cylinder
　　　w/cast iron base & top,
　　　3" d., 3½" h. (W. 242) 60.00

560　Buffalo - small, cast iron,
　　　Arcade, 1920-25 & A.C. Wil-
　　　liams Co., 1920-34, 4½" l.
　　　(W. 208) 85.00

770　Camel Kneeling with Pack,
　　　cast iron, Kyser & Rex, 1889,
　　　4 7/8" l., 2½" h. (W. 256) ...450.00

1425　Cannon on Wheels, cast iron,
　　　Hubley Mfg. Co., ca. 1914,
　　　6 7/8" l. (W. 165) 1,850.00

38　Captain Kidd - with shovel be-
　　　side tree, cast iron, ca. 1910,
　　　5½" h., W. 38 (ILLUS.) 265.00

Captain Kidd

1114　Castle with Two Towers, cast
　　　iron, John Harper, Ltd.,
　　　England, 1908-11, 4 5/8 x
　　　3 1/8", 7" h. 375.00

1355　"Champion" Heater w/com-
　　　bination lock on door, cast
　　　iron, 2 3/8 x 2¾", 4 1/8" h. ...65.00

124　Charles Lindbergh Bust - "Lindy
　　　Bank" on back, aluminum,
　　　Grannis & Tolton, 1928,
　　　6¼" h. 135.00

892　Church Window Safe, cast
　　　iron, Shimer Toy Co., 1890's,
　　　2¼ x 2¼", 3 1/8" h. 40.00

462　Circus Elephant - seated &
　　　wearing child's straw sailor
　　　hat w/ribbon, cast iron,
　　　Hubley Mfg. Co., 1930-40,
　　　4" h. 160.00

1111　"City Bank" with Directors
　　　Room on Top, cast iron, John
　　　Harper, Ltd. & Chamberlain
　　　& Hill, England, ca. 1902,
　　　3½ x 2½", 4 1/8" h.
　　　(W. 380) 85.50

1099　"City Bank" with Teller, cast
　　　iron, Judd Co., 3 x 2",
　　　5¼" h. (W. 400) 125.00

1095　"City Bank" with "Crown" on
　　　roof, cast iron, Thomas
　　　Swan designer, 1873 patent,
　　　5½" h. 360.00

1101　"City Bank" with Tiered Base
　　　& Chimney on Roof, cast
　　　iron, Thomas Swan designer,
　　　1873 patent, 6¾" h.,
　　　(W. 436) 465.00

1544　Clock - "A Money Saver" on
　　　face, cast iron & steel, Ar-
　　　cade, 1909-20's, 3½" d.
　　　(W. 224) * ....50.00 to 67.50

1545　Clock - Gold Dollar face em-

bossed "Save Your Pennies to
Make Dollars," cast iron &
steel, Arcade, 1910-13,
3½" d. (W. 226) 210.00

1541 Clock - "Grandfather's Clock,"
cast iron, possibly English,
1890's, 5½" h. (W. 222) 450.00

1540 Clock - Hall Clock with Pendulum, cast iron, Arcade, ca.
1923, 5¾" h. (W. 217) 350.00

211 Clown - Standing, cast iron,
A.C. Williams Co., 1908,
6¼" h. (W. 29) * 115.00

210 Clown with Crooked Hat, cast
iron, 6¾" h. (W. 28) 750.00

1558 "Coin Registering Bank," metal,
Kingsbury Mfg. Co., 1932,
5 1/8" w., 7" h. 31.50

993 Colonial House with Porch -
small, cast iron, A.C. Williams Co., 1910-31, 2½ x
2 1/8", 3" h. (W. 404) 55.00

783 Columbia Savings Bank (Globe
with Eagle atop), cast iron,
wood & paperboard, 1889,
3" d. globe, 5½" h.
(W. 240) 270.00

1118 "Columbia Tower," cast iron
Columbia Grey Iron Casting
Co., 1897, 3 1/8" d.,
6 7/8" h. (W. 378) 450.00

1311 Coronation (Elizabeth II) Crown,
"Made in England," 1953,
3¼ x 3" 25.00

1319 "Coronation (George V) Bank,"
bust portraits of Queen Mary
& British flags, cast iron,
possibly by Sydenham &
McOustra, England, ca. 1911,
6¼" h. (W. 361) 375.00

1110 "County Bank," cast iron,
John Harper, Ltd., England,
ca. 1892, 4¼ x 5 x 2¾" 95.00

926 "Crystal Bank" - clear glass
cylinder w/iron base & top,
3" d., 3½" h. (W. 243) 70.00

1147 Cupolo Bank (Bank Building) -
small, cast iron, J. & E.
Stevens Co., ca. 1872,
2½" w., 3¼" h. (W. 307) 78.50

414 "Cutie" (Puppy Dog) with ribbon at neck, cast iron, Hubley Mfg. Co., ca. 1914,
3 7/8" h. (W. 334) . .80.00 to 100.00

865 "The Daisy" Safe, cast iron,
Shimer Toy Co., 1899, 2 1/8 x
1¾ x 1½" (W. 319) 85.50

1381 Derby Hat - "Pass Around the
Hat" on top, cast iron,
3 1/8" d., 1 5/8" h.
(W. 260) . . . . .135.00 to 180.00

921 "Dime Registering Coin Barrel," cast iron, Kyser &
Rex, 1889, 2½" d., 4" h. 80.00

413 Dog - Boston Bulldog, seated,
cast iron, Hubley Mfg. Co.,
1930's, 5½" l. (W. 114) 112.50

403 Dog - Bulldog, standing, cast
iron (converted paper-
weight), Arcade, 1910-13,
2¼" h. 320.00

396 Dog - English Bulldog, seated,
Hubley Mfg. Co., ca. 1928,
3¾" h. (W. 102) 115.00

411 Dog - Husky, cast iron, possibly by Grey Iron Casting
Co., ca. 1910, 5" l. 250.00

405 Dog - Pugdog seated, cast
iron, Kyser & Rex, 1880,
3" l., 3½" h. (W. 111) 82.50

St. Bernard with Pack

439 Dog - St. Bernard with Pack,
small, cast iron, A.C. Williams Co., 1905-30, W. 106
(ILLUS.) 55.00

428 Dog - Tiny Scottie, cast iron,
3 1/8" h. 325.00

435 Dog - Scottie, standing, cast
iron, 4¾" l., 3¼" h.
(W. 108) 95.00

418 Dog - Spaniel, cast iron, Hubley Mfg. Co., 1930's, 6" l.
(W. 109) 135.00

417 Dog (Puppy Dog) - "Fido"
on collar, cast iron, Hubley
Mfg. Co., 1914-46, 5" h.
(W. 337) * . . . . .70.00 to 110.00

407 Dog - "Lost Dog," cast
iron, possibly by Judd Mfg.
Co., 1890's, 5½" h.
(W. 115) . . . . .350.00 to 535.00

1183 Domed "Bank" Building -
large, cast iron, A.C. Williams Co., 1899-1934,
4 x 2 3/8", 4¾" h.
(W. 421) 42.50

1314 "Dreadnaught Bank" - "United
We Stand," w/clasped hands
& English flags, cast iron,
probably by Sydenham &
McOustra, England, ca.
1911, 7" h. (W. 363) 510.00

615 Duck, cast iron, A.C. Williams

Co., 1909-35, 4 7/8" h.
(W. 211) 100.00

450 Elephant (Art Deco) -
"G.O.P." on side, cast iron,
5½" l., 4" h. (W. 72) 125.00

483 Elephant on Tub - no blanket,
cast iron, A.C. Williams
Co., 1920's, 5¼" h.
(W. 59) . . . . .95.00 to 155.00

484 Elephant with Blanket on Tub,
cast iron, A.C. Williams
Co., 1920-34, 5½" h. *
(W. 60) 85.00

430 Fala (President Franklin
Roosevelt's dog), cast iron,
metal trap, 1930's, 2¾" 85.00

863 "Fidelity Safe" - faithful dog
guarding keyhole, large,
cast iron, Kyser & Rex,
ca. 1880, 2 5/8" sq.,
3 5/8" h. . . . . .45.00 to 60.00

"Fidelity Trust Vault"

903 "Fidelity Trust Vault" with
Lord Fauntleroy, cast
iron, J. Barton Smith
Co., Chicago, ca. 1890,
5 7/8" x 5 3/8", 6½" h.
(ILLUS.) 400.00

1160 "Flat Iron Building Bank" -
small trap, cast iron,
Kenton Hardware Mfg.
Co., 4¾ x 4½", 5¾" h. 115.00

**320 Foxy Grandpa, cast iron,
Wing Mfg. Co. (ca. 1900),**
Hubley Mfg. Co. (1920's),
5½" h. * (W. 23) 145.00

1485 Gas Pump, cast iron,
2 1/8" sq., 6" h. 200.00

1349 Gas Stove - "Save Your
Money & Buy a Gas Stove"
on top & "Pat App'd For"
on base, cast iron & sheet
metal, S. Bernstein Co.,
New York City,
1901 . . . . .75.00 to 100.00

50 General Sheridan - astride
cavalry horse on base, cast
iron, Arcade, 1910-25,

4 x 2 3/8" base, 6" h.
(W. 88) 467.50

1330 G.E. Refrigerator - small, cast
iron, Hubley Mfg. Co.,
1930-36, 3¾" h.
(W. 237) 75.00

1331 G.E. Refrigerator - large, cast
iron, Hubley Mfg. Co.,
1930-36, 2 1/8" w.,
4¼" h. 175.00

808 Globe Combination Bank with
Swivel Door - on tripod,
cast iron, ca. 1889, 4" d.
globe, 5 3/16" h. 112.50

791 Globe on Wood Base, metal
w/lithograph paper-covered
globe, Miller Bank Service
Co., 1930's, 4¼" h. 75.00

812 Globe Safe with Hinged
Door - on tripod, cast
iron, Kenton Hardware
Mfg. Co., 1911-31, 5"h. 110.00

614 Goose, cast iron, 3¾" h.
(W. 214) . . . . .125.00 to 175.00

1428 "Graf Zeppelin" Airship, cast
iron, A.C. Williams Co.,
1920-34, 6¾" l.
(W. 171) . . . . .110.00 to 195.00

1430 "Goodyear Zeppelin" Hangar,
duralumin, Ferrosteel,
1930, 2¼" h., 7 3/8" l. 135.00

1534 Hall Clock with Paper Face,
cast iron, Hubley Mfg. Co.,
1914-20, 2 3/16" w., 5¼" h.
(W. 221) 337.50

1217 High Rise (Multi-Windowed
Bank Building), cast iron,
Kenton Hardware Mfg. Co.,
2¾" sq., 5½" h. (W. 418) . . 99.00

1215 High Rise with Tiered Roof
(Multi-Windowed Bank
Building), cast iron, Kenton
Hardware Mfg. Co., 5¾" h.
(W. 419) 115.00

1201 Home Savings - "Property of
the Peoples Savings Bank,
Grand Rapids, Mich." over
door, cast iron, 8 1/8 x
6¼", 10½" h. 295.00

532 Horse - "Beauty," cast iron,
Arcade, 1910-32, 4¾" l.,
4 1/8" h. (W. 82) 60.00

509 Horse on Tub, cast iron, A.C.
Williams Co., 1920's,
5¼" h. * (W. 56) . .200.00 to 250.00

517 Horse Prancing, cast iron, Arcade, A.C. Williams Co. &
Dent Hardware Co.,
1910-37, 4¼ x 4 7/8"
(W. 77) 37.50

520 Horse Prancing on Oblong
Base - large, cast iron,
Arcade & A.C. Williams
Co., 1910-34 * (W. 78) 65.00

521 Horse Prancing on Pebbled
Base, cast iron,
7¼ x 6½" * 55.00

507 Horse with Saddle, cast iron,
Grey Iron Casting Co.,
1928, 5½" l., 4¼" h.
(W. 79) 265.00

Horseshoe "Good Luck" with Buster & Tige

508 Horseshoe with "Good Luck"
horse, Buster Brown &
Tige, cast iron, Arcade,
1908-32, 4¼" h. (ILLUS.) ... 145.00

1371 Ice Cream Freezer (North
Pole Bank) - "Save Your
Money and Freeze It,"
nickeled cast iron, Grey
Iron Casting Co., 1922-28,
2½" d., 4" h.
(W. 156) ....150.00 to 375.00

1211 Independence Hall - replica of
building, cast iron, ca.
1876, 11 x 3", 6 3/8" h.
(W. 449) 725.00

1243 Independence Hall - complete
with side wings, cast iron,
overall 15½" w., 8 1/8" h.
(W. 452) ......1,650.00 to 2,300.00

1202 Independence Hall Tower,
cast iron, Enterprise Mfg.
Co., 1876, 3 7/8 x 3 7/8",
9½" h. ....235.00 to 300.00

228 Indian with Tomahawk, cast
iron, Hubley Mfg. Co.,
1915-30, 6" h. * (W. 39) 195.00

1404 Japanese Helmet with Star,
tin, ca. World War II era,
Japan 75.00

883 "Japanese Safe" - embossed
dragon guarding keyhole,
Kyser & Rex, ca. 1880,
4½" sq., 5 3/8" h.
(W. 349) ....65.00 to 85.00

896 "Jewel Safe" with Guard Bars
over Keyhole, cast iron,
J. & E. Stevens Co., 1907,
3¾ x 3¼", 5 3/8" h. 200.00

259 Jimmy Durante - "Schnozzola,"
white metal, Abbot Wares,
6¾" h. 135.00

1616 Key, cast iron, Wm. J. Som-
merville designer, 5½" l. .. 450.00

349 Kitty with Ribbon at Neck,
cast iron, Hubley Mfg. Co.,
1930-46, 4¾" h. (W. 335)... 65.00

595 Lamb - small, cast iron, ca.
1880, 4" l., 3" h.
(W. 192) 105.00

Lamb Bank

601 Lamb - large, cast iron, Grey
Iron Casting Co., 1928,
5½" l. (ILLUS.) .....80.00 to 110.00

792 Liberty Bell - miniature, cast
iron, Penncraft (modern),
3½" h. 22.50

780 Liberty Bell - "Proclaim Liberty Throughout All the
Land Unto All the In-
habitants There Of," cast
iron, J.M. Harper, 1905,
3¾" h. (W. 273) 350.00

809 Liberty Bell with Yoke - "Proclaim Liberty Throughout
the Land," cast iron,
Arcade, 1925-34, 3½" h.
(W. 279) 45.00

1482 Limousine with Driver, cast
iron w/steel wheels, Arcade
(No. 05 model), ca. 1920,
4½" l. 1,215.00

1380 Lincoln High Hat - "Pass
Around the Hat" on top,
cast iron, ca. 1882,
3" d., 2 3/8" h. (W. 259) ... 80.00

757 Lion - ears up, cast iron, A.C.
Williams Co. (1934), Arcade
(1932), 3 5/8 x 4½" 45.00

758 Lion - "Quilted," cast iron,
3¾" h., 4¾" l............. 360.00

764 Lion - tail between legs
(spread-legged stance),
cast iron, 3" h., 5¼" l.
(W. 92) 75.00

755 Lion - tail right, cast iron,
5" l. * (W. 90) ......30.00 to 48.00

747 Lion on Tub - small, cast iron,
A.C. Williams Co., 1920-34,
4¼" h. (W. 61)............ 76.00

746 Lion on Tub with Cord in
Mouth, cast iron, A.C.
Williams Co., 1920-34,
5½" h. * (W. 57) 90.00

760 Lion on Wheels, cast iron,
A.C. Williams Co., 1920's,
4½" h., 4 5/8" l. (W. 95)... 175.00

37 Man on Bale of Cotton (Coon
Bank), cast iron, U.S. Hard-
ware Co., 4 7/8" h.
(W. 37) 1,400.00

1246 Marietta Silo - "Saves You
Money," cast iron, 5½" h.
(W. 154) 435.00

164 Mary & Little Lamb, cast iron,
1901, 4½" h. * (W. 1) 400.00

1611 Merry-Go-Round, nickel-
plated cast iron, Grey Iron
Casting Co., 1925-28,
4 5/8" d., 4 3/8" h. * 215.00

36 Middy Bank - English Ad-
miralty character, cast
iron, 5¼"h. * (W. 26) 120.00

327 Minuteman, white metal, key-
locked trap, Banthrico,
1941, 8 1/8" h............ 140.00

1262 Money Bag - "100,000" on
side, cast iron, key-
locked trap, 4¼" w.,
3½" h. (W. 295) 475.00

1228 Moody & Sankey - "Hold the
Fort," w/portraits in ovals,
cast iron, Smith & Egge,
patented 1870, 4¼ x 3½",
5" h. (W. 266) 790.00

1636 Mosque, cast iron, 2½" w.,
3" h. (W. 341) 47.50

Three-Story Mosque

1175 Mosque - three-story, cast
iron, A.C. Williams Co.,
1920's, 2½ x 1 5/8", 3½" h.
(ILLUS.)................. 36.00

1177 Mosque with Dome "Bank"
medium, cast iron, Grey
Iron Casting Co., 1903-28,
4 1/8" w., 4¼" h.
(W. 416) 55.00

1176 Mosque with Dome & Combination Door - large, cast
iron, Grey Iron Casting Co.,
1903-28, 5 1/8" h.
(W. 417) 185.00

177 Mulligan the Cop, cast iron,
A.C. Williams Co., 1905-32,
5½" h. * (W. 8) ...100.00 to 137.50

55 Old Beggar Man, white

metal, key-locked trap,
Germany, 19th c., 7½" h... 125.00

30 Old Doc Yak (conversion),
cast iron, Arcade, 1911-17,
4½" h.................. 475.00

186 Oriental Boy on Pillow (conversion), cast iron, Hubley
Mfg. Co., 1920's, 5½ x
6¼ x 5¼"............... 250.00

769 "Oriental" Camel - on
rockers, cast iron, 3¾" h.,
5 3/8" l.
(W. 263).........500.00 to 700.00

1313 "Our Kitchener" - bust portrait of Lord Kitchener
within wreath, cast iron,
Sydenham & McLoustra,
England, ca. 1915, 6½" h... 135.00

597 Owl - square base, cast iron,
Vindex, ca. 1936, 4¼" h.
(W. 203)................ 215.00

598 Owl (on Stump) - "Be Wise -
Save Money" on stump,
4 7/8" h. (W. 204) 90.00

1153 Pagoda Bank (Building on
Stilts) - with stairs leading
to door, cast iron, England,
1889, 3" sq., 5" h.
(W. 288) 225.00

679 Pelican, cast iron, Hubley
Mfg. Co., 1930's, 4¾" h.... 475.00

912 "Penny Register" Pail, cast
iron, Kyser & Rex, ca. 1889,
2¾" top d., 2¾" h. 70.00

840 Piano - "R.L. Berry's Piano
Bank," steel, key-locked
trap, 5 1/8 x 5 7/8" 120.00

608 Pig - "Bismark," cast iron,
1880's, 7 3/8" l. (W. 176)... 90.00

579 Pig - Grinning, lead, key-
locked trap, Europe,
2 5/8 x 5 1/16" 78.00

625 Pig - "Osborn," cast iron,
4" l., 2" h. 255.00

609 Pig "Thrifty" - "The Wise Pig -
Save A Penny Yesterday,"
etc., cast iron, 6½" h.
* (W. 175) ....65.00 to 85.00

606 Pig with Bow at Neck - seat-
ed, cast iron, Shimer Toy
Co., 1899, 5" l.
(W. 178).........75.00 to 95.00

182 Policeman (Fireman), cast
iron, Arcade, 1920-34,
5½" h. (W. 9)............ 255.00

263 Porky Pig at Tree Trunk,
white metal, Metal Moss
Mfg. Co., late 1930's,
4 7/16 x 5¾" 55.00

845 "Postal Savings Mailbox," cast
iron, Nicol & Co., 1920's,
3¾" w., 6¾" h........... 35.00

1612 Potato (without Pingree), cast
iron, Mary A. Martin

designer, 1897, 2 1/8" d.,
5¼" l. (W. 301 variant) 550.00

1348 Pot Bellied Stove, cast iron,
George C. Knerr, 1968,
2¼" d., 5¾" h. 30.00

1169 Presto "Bank" - medium, cast
iron, A.C. Williams Co.,
1905-34, 2¾ x 1 7/8",
3¼" h. 40.00

1167 Presto Still - large, cast iron,
A.C. Williams Co., 1911-13,
3½" w., 4" h. (W. 425) 42.50

311 Professor Pug Frog (Frog
Bank), cast iron, A.C. Wil-
liams Co., 1905-12, 3¼" h.
* (W. 230) ....225.00 to 315.00

1266 Purse - "Put Money in Thy
Purse," cast iron, ca. 1886,
3½" w., 2¾" h.
(W. 296).........500.00 to 650.00

565 Rabbit - lying down, cast iron,
5" l., 2¼" h. (W. 101) 390.00

566 Rabbit - sitting upright begging, cast iron, A.C. Williams Co., 5¼" h. *
(W. 98) 90.00

821 "Radio Bank" - 2 dials, cast
iron, Hubley Mfg. Co.,
1928, 3½" h. (W. 136) 100.00

829 Radio Bank - 3 dials, cast iron
w/sheet iron sides & back,
Kenton Hardware Mfg. Co.,
1927-32, 3" h., 4½" l.
(W. 137)..........65.00 to 100.00

827 Radio "Majestic" - cabinet-
style, cast iron w/steel
back, Arcade, 1932-34,
4½" h. 80.00

825 Record Player (Victrola) -
"Brunswick" floor model,
bronze, 5" h. 75.00

330 Republic Pig - standing in suit
& tie, "Bank on Republic
Pig Iron," cast iron,
1970 .... 85.00

778 Rhesus Monkey - long curly
tail, cast iron (doorstop
conversion), 8½" h. 75.00

721 Rhino, cast iron, Arcade,
1910-25, 5" l.
(W. 252) ....250.00 to 325.00

148 Roosevelt (Franklin D.) bust -
"New Deal" on base, white
metal, Kenton Hardware
Mfg. Co., 1933-36.
5" h. ....175.00 to 210.00

548 Rooster - silver w/red comb &
wattles, cast iron, Hubley
Mfg. Co. & A.C. Williams
Co., 1910-34, 4¾" h. *
(W. 187) 75.00

619 "Round" Duck, cast iron,
original paint, large Ken-
ton-type trap, Kenton Hard-

ware Mfg. Co., 5" d., 4" h.
(W. 325).........245.00 to 300.00

75 Rumplestiltskin - "Do You
Know Me" on feet & base,
cast iron, ca. 1910, 2¼" w.,
6" h. (W. 49) ....200.00 to 325.00

848 "U.S. Airmail" Box - on pedestal, cast iron, Dent Hardware Co., 1920, 6½" h.
(W. 118) 330.00

859 "U.S. Bank" Mail Box
w/American Eagle Finial -
pedestal base, cast iron,
1890's, overall 9¼" h.
(W. 119).........135.00 to 275.00

835 "U.S. Mail Bank" - with combination trap, cast iron,
Kenton Hardware Mfg. Co.,
early 1900's, 3¼ x 2",
4¾" h. (W. 128) 60.00

Mail Box Bank

838 "U.S. Mail" Box - small, cast
iron, Kenton Hardware
Mfg. Co. (1904-10) & A.C.
Williams Co. (1912-31),
2¾" w., 3½" h. (ILLUS.) ... 26.50

837 "U.S. Mail" Box - narrow
w/hinged slot, cast iron,
Kenton Hardware Mfg. Co.
& A.C. Williams Co.,
1912-31, 2¼" w.,
4 3/8" h. 42.50

851 "U.S. Mail" Box with Eagle -
"Pull Down" on flap &
"Letters" below, cast iron,
Kenton Hardware Mfg. Co.,
1932-34, 3¼" w., 4 1/8" h.
(W. 121) 40.00

GLASS

Baseball, clear glass w/white-
painted interior & Mobil
"flying red horse" Pegasus,
w/tin screw-on closure,
Heffelfinger Publications,
N.Y., 3" d., 3½" h......... 40.00
Cat, clear figure w/metal cap,

container for "Grapette"
drink 18.00
298 Charlie Chaplin beside ash
barrel, clear barrel, painted
figure, Borgfeldt & Co.,
1920's 225.00

Charlie Chaplin & Barrel Bank

299 Charlie Chaplin beside barrel,
clear barrel, painted figure,
L.E. Smith Co., 1920's
(ILLUS.) 165.00
Elephant, clear standing figure,
container for "Grapette"
drink 16.50
Glass block, advertising
"Corning Glass,"
clear . . . . 18.00 to 25.00
1207 Independence Hall, clear replica
of building, 7" h. 165.00
301 Kewpie beside barrel, clear
barrel, painted figure, George
Borgfeldt & Co., 1919,
3" h. 125.00
Liberty Bell, amber, original
tin closure 52.50
Log cabin, milk white glass
w/brown paint, opening in
chimney for coins 126.00
"Lucky Joe," man's head, con-
tainer for Nash's Mustard,
clear 22.00
Milk bottle, clear, w/lock &
key, ½ pt. 20.00
Penguin, clear figure w/slotted
tin closure 20.00
Pig, clear figure, container for
"New England Syrup" marked
"Piggy Bank Bottle" 10.00
Pig, clear figure embossed
"Brother Can You Spare A
Dime" 15.00

POTTERY
Advertising, "Acorn Stoves Saves
Money," model of an acorn,
glazed earthenware pottery . . 35.00

Advertising, "Sun Life Insurance," book-shaped, glazed
earthenware pottery, dated
"7/3/23" 17.50
Bear, seated w/hands clasped,
white clay pottery, brown
glaze, 5¾" h. (minor base
flakes) 35.00
Bell-shaped, souvenir of 1936
German Olympics, glazed
earthenware pottery 75.00
Bust of dog, earthenware pottery
w/sponge-daubed black, yellow-ochre & green decor, clear
glaze, 3½" h. (crazed) 55.00
Casper the Ghost, ceramic
white w/black trim 35.00
Cottage, mottled brown Rockingham-glazed pottery,
3¼" h. 60.00
Eagle w/shield, Staffordshire
pottery, green, yellow & blue
highlights, ca.1840 . . . . 225.00
Monkey w/coin marked "Mon-
key Business," glazed
pottery 20.00
Pig, white clay pottery, 2-tone
white & amber glazed
w/brown drips, 3½" l. 30.00
Pig, earthenware pottery,
mottled glaze, 4" l. 45.00

Spongeware Pig

Pig, yellowware pottery w/dark
blue & brown sponge-daubed
circle designs, 6" l.
(ILLUS.) 125.00
Pig standing, mottled brown
Rockingham-glazed pottery,
19th c. 70.00
Pig in suitcase, china, pink pig's
head & 1 foot protruding from
one side of green suitcase &
tail & hindquarters on side
opposite, gold trim, coin slot
on suitcase 65.00
Santa Claus standing, china,
colorful souvenir of Santa
Claus, Indiana, 1960,
6¼" h. 60.00

TIN
Advertising, "B. & M. Baked
Beans," lithographed, 1935 . . . 30.00
Advertising, "Cities Service 5-D
Koolmotor Oil," oil can
shape 6.00

Advertising, "National Canners
Association," printed picture
of robots making soup,
"Canny Cook" 35.00
Advertising, "Old Dutch
Cleanser" 40.00
Advertising, "Red Circle (A & P)
Coffee," red 9.50
592 Advertising, "Red Goose Sav-
ings Bank," red on yellow,
2 x 1¾" sq., 1 3/8"h.........20.00
Advertising, "Rival Dog Food,"
1940 ....9.00
Baseball, "Compliments of
Your Atlantic Dealer - Phila-
delphia Athletics - Connie
Mack," 4½" h. 55.00
Baseball on stand, "Official
League Ball," Ohio Art Co. ...18.00

Ten Dollar Register

Cash register, "Registers
Ten Dollars" (ILLUS.) 28.00
Cash register, "Uncle Sam's
Register Bank," original
black w/brass trim, 6" h. 45.00
1576 "Children's Crusade for Children," cylinder, w/artwork by
Norman Rockwell, 1940's,
2 7/8" d., 4" h. 27.00
987 Church on base, painted &
stenciled decor, George W.
Brown, 1870's, 6½ x 5 3/8",
12½" h. 1,300.00
Combination safe, "National
Bank," w/combination for
lock.......................25.00
Cylinder w/pierced sides, dome
top lid w/slot, 2½" h. 42.50
1565 Dime register, "Jackie Robinson," square w/cut corners,
portrait of Jackie and "Save
& Win" 75.00
Mail box, rural-type w/flag,
7" l. 15.00
Monkey on base, semi-mechan-
ical, tips hat, J. Chein & Co.,
ca. 1900, 5" h. 75.00
Pirate chest w/domed top......32.50
Rabbit Uncle Wiggily, J. Chein
& Co. 95.00
Trunk, patented 1888 ....22.50

WOODEN

Wooden Heart Bank

Advertising, "Armour's Quality
Products," model of a truck ..50.00
1488 Automobile, 4-passenger,
5 1/8" l...................405.00
Barrel, depositer's enticement,
Minnesota or New Hampshire,
each 10.00
Beehive, 2-section, lathe-
turned 45.00
Bullet (or shell), turned,
w/paper lithograph of Ad-
miral Dewey 25.00
Heart flanked by smaller
hearts, laminated light &
dark wood layers, w/coin
slot in top, 19th c., 8½" h.
(ILLUS.) 550.00

BAROMETERS

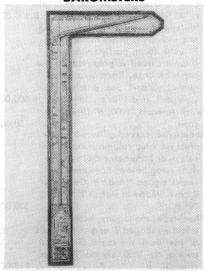

Queen Anne Angle-Tube Barometer

Aneroid, brass, signed E.E. Bausch &
Son, 5½" d. $260.00

Angle-tube, gilt-decorated japanned,
tube set in a molded back plate,
painted Oriental scenes, Queen
Anne, late 17th/early 18th c.,
36½" h., 17" w. (ILLUS.) 6,600.00

Stick-type, aneroid, architectural
cornice w/brass urn finial, case
w/shell rosette inlay, silvered dial
marked "G. Camoto & Co.," prob-
ably England, 19th c., 37" h. 330.00

Stick-type, mahogany, arched case
of typical form, w/thermometer,
George III period, late 18th c.,
36¾" h. 1,100.00

Stick-type, mahogany, molded support carved w/egg & dart, tube
enclosed within pierced treillage,
silver indicators, George III period,
3rd quarter 18th c., 36¾" h. 3,575.00

Stick-type, mahogany, broken arch
pediment, case of typical form &
edged w/rope twist lines, w/ther-
mometer, signed "B. Gatty, Reading," George III period, late
18th c., 38½" h. 1,210.00

Stick-type, mahogany inlaid w/ebony,
molded top above an etched bone
barometer panel, long straight
case set w/a thermometer,
Andrew Ross, London, mid-19th c.,
39½" h. 1,650.00

Stick-type, mahogany, elaborately
carved acanthus crest above a
hygrometer over 2 brass panels
w/a thermometer & barometer indicator flanked by canted fluted
corners above a shaped beaded
body ending in a shell-carved
cistern, George III period, mid-18th
c., 43¾" h. 8,800.00

Stick-type, ship's instrument, mahogany w/ivory & brass mountings,
baluster form, partly reeded
column carved w/palmettes at the
capital & base, fitted w/a brass
gimbal support, Jas. Bassnet,
Liverpool, mid-19th c., 38" h. 6,600.00

Veitch Aneroid, 1900, 6" fitted
case 150.00

Wheel-type, carved giltwood, eagle
crest on Ionic column hung w/tas-
sels over barometer dial w/pen-
dant swag below, barometer
works signed "Made in Germany"
& case "Made in Italy," 20th c.,
38" h. 330.00

Wheel-type, mahogany, banjo-form,
inlaid w/shaded & engraved shells
& rosettes at the crest, George III
period, ca. 1800, signed "A.D. Sol-
cha," 38" h. 715.00

Wheel-type, inlaid mahogany banjo-

form, broken arch pediment
w/eagle finial, thermometer on
throat, circular silvered dial
w/maker's name "Josh. Riboldi,"
star inlays top & bottom, shell inlays on sides, England, ca. 1800,
39" h. 605.00

Wheel-type, inlaid mahogany, cross-
banded case of baluster form
w/tapered cresting, indicator dial
w/black roman numerals, signed
"C.A. Canti, Town Malling, Kent,"
mid-19th c., 42" h. 412.00

BASEBALL MEMORABILIA

Whitey Ford Baseball Card

*Baseball was named by Abner Doubleday
as he laid out a diamond-shaped field with
four bases at Cooperstown, New York, in
1839. A popular game from its inception, by
1869 it was able to support its first all-
professional team, the Cincinnati Red Stockings. The National League was organized in
1876 and though the American League was
first formed in 1900, it was not officially
recognized until 1903. Today, the "national
pastime" has millions of fans and collecting
baseball memorabilia has become a major
hobby with enthusiastic collectors seeking
out items associated with players such as
Babe Ruth, Lou Gehrig, and others, who became legends in their own lifetimes. Though
baseball cards, issued as advertising premiums for bubble gum and other products, seem
to dominate the field there are numerous other items available. Also see BANKS.*

Ash tray, 1965 World Series, marked
Red Wing. **$55.00**

Baseball, autographed by Babe
Ruth 300.00

Baseball, autographed by Hank
Greenberg & "School Boy" Rowe,
1934 . . . . 90.00

Baseball card, 1880's, "Old Judge
Cigarettes," Brown of New York . . 40.00

Baseball card, 1880's, "Old Judge
Cigarettes," S.S. Fuller of
St. Louis 45.00
Baseball card, 1880's, "Old Judge
Cigarettes," C.F. Johnson of
Boston 45.00
Baseball card, 1952, Red Man Chew-
ing Tobacco, Gil McDougald 6.00
Baseball card, 1955, Topps Gum,
Ted Williams (No. 2) 22.50
Baseball card, 1956, Topps Gum,
Willie Mays 32.00
Baseball card, 1960, Topps Gum,
Whitey Ford, No. 35 (ILLUS.) 3.00
Baseball cards, 1953, Topps Gum,
assorted set of 35 . . . . 30.00
Baseball cards, 1954, Topps Gum,
assorted set of 50 . . . . 40.00
Baseball cards, 1955, Topps Gum,
assorted set of 40 . . . . 20.00
Bat, wooden miniature, inscribed
"Louisville Slugger" & "Mickey
Mantle," 16" l. 15.00
Bat, wooden miniature, inscribed
"Louisville Slugger" & "Pete Rose,"
1950's, 16½" l. 45.00
Book, "Baseball in Cincinnati," by
Harry Ellard, 1908 . . . . 55.00
Book, "Boy of the Sandlots," by Lou
Gehrig, w/dust jacket 15.00
Book, "Courtney of the Center Gar-
den," 1915 Big League baseball
story 9.00
Book, "Dizzy Baseball," amusing
baseball terms of Dizzy Dean,
1952 . . . . 15.00
Book, "Greatest World Series
Thrillers," by Ray Robinson,
1965 . . . . 10.00
Book, "Major League Baseball - 1941
Facts & Figures" 20.00
Book, "The Science of Baseball,"
published by Wilson Co., photo-
graphs of Babe Ruth, Mattewson
& others, 1922, 190 pp. 25.00
Coloring book, "New York Mets,"
1965, unused 15.00
Hat, Baltimore Orioles, advertising
"Tip Top Bread" 25.00
Knife, pocket-type, bat-shaped,
"Babe Ruth," by Camillus
Cutlery 110.00
Pennant, 1965 World Series - Dod-
gers vs. Twins, felt 10.00
Photograph of Lou Boudreau,
autographed 29.00
Pinback button, "Brooklyn Dodgers"
& ball & bat, w/ribbon 18.00
Pinback button, Bill Dickey of the
New York Yankees, 1938, w/rib-
bon & rabbit's foot 75.00
Pinback button, Ted Williams,
1 5/8" 17.50
Plaque, Hank Aaron in Atlanta

Braves uniform, chalkware,
bronze finish, 12 x 9" 35.00
Program, 1935 World Series, Cubs
vs. Tigers, pitchers Warneke &
Rowe penciled in w/other line-up
changes 75.00

1947 All Star Program

Program, 1947 All Star Game,
Wrigley Field, Chicago, 10¾ x
8¼" (ILLUS.) 65.00
Program, 1959 All Star Game 55.00
Program, 1965 World Series, Dodg-
ers vs. Twins 12.00
Ring, metal, Chicago Cubs logo 25.00
Scorecard, celluloid, advertising,
"The Dallas News," 4 x 2" 6.00
Watch, pocket-type, Dizzy Dean,
Ingersoll, 1933 . . . . 175.00
Watch fob-scorekeeper, Babe Ruth
pictured, celluloid & tin 130.00
Yearbook, 1957 Detroit Tigers 20.00
Yearbook, 1963 Baltimore Orioles . . 12.00
Yearbook, 1965 Los Angeles Dodg-
ers or 1965 Pittsburgh Pirates,
each 5.00
Yearbook, 1969 New York Mets 18.00

BASKETS

*The American Indians were the first bas-
ket weavers on this continent, and, of necessity, the early Colonial settlers and their
descendents pursued this artistic handicraft
to provide essential containers for berries,
eggs and endless other items to be carried or
stored. Rye straw, split willow and reeds are
but a few of the wide variety of materials
used. The Nantucket baskets, plainly and
sturdily constructed, along with the baskets
woven by American Indians and at the Shaker settlements, would seem to draw the*

greatest attention in an area of collecting where interest has stablized because of the wide availability of fine baskets by contemporary basketweavers for art and craft shows across the country.

Papago Indian Coilwork Basket

American Indian cov. basket, Nootka, brown, red & green design, 4½" l. $90.00

American Indian cov. basket, Woodland tribes, woven splint, domed lid w/handle, brown & blue designs, 18½" d., 14" h. (minor damage) 500.00

American Indian basket, Hupa, twined, woven steps to the mountain design, 1910, 5" d. 160.00

American Indian basket, Pima, straight sides, woven coilwork construction, polychrome & natural design, 6¾" d., 4" h. 130.00

American Indian basket, Papago, woven Yucca coilwork construction, dark brown & natural design, 9½" h. (ILLUS.) 160.00

American Indian basket-tray, Pima, woven coilwork construction, dark brown "devil's claw" design on natural, 18½" d. 475.00

American Indian burden basket, Apache, woven geometric design, trimmed w/fringe & tin cone dangles, buckskin carrying strap, 9½ x 7½" 195.00

American Indian fish basket, North Carolina Cherokee, woven oak splint, 12" 135.00

American Indian "wedding" basket, Navajo, woven coilwork construction, woven in black, (faded) red & natural, 1900-30, 13½" d., 3¼" h. 85.00

Beehive, woven splint & rye straw, 18th c., 11 x 8" 110.00

"Buttocks" basket, 16-rib construc-

tion, woven splint, 5½ x 5¼", 3" h. plus bentwood handle 250.00

"Buttocks" basket, 26-rib construction, woven white oak splint, 8 x 7", 4" h. plus bentwood handle ... 195.00

"Buttocks" basket, 20-rib construction, woven natural & brown splint, 8½ x 7½", 4½" h. plus bentwood handle 115.00

"Buttocks" basket, woven oak splint, 11½ x 8", 4½" h. plus bentwood handle .... 135.00 to 150.00

Cheese basket, woven oak splint, traces of early blue paint exterior, 22½" d. (minor damage) 185.00

Egg gathering basket, tightly woven splint w/"kick-up" center, double-wrapped rim, carved handle, 7½" d., overall 8¾" h. 150.00

Egg gathering basket, tightly woven splint, radiating ribs w/design in faded dark green, 12 x 10", 5¾" h. plus bentwood handle 200.00

Egg gathering basket, tightly woven hickory splint, melon-ribbed, arched bentwood handle, 12" d. ... 190.00

Egg gathering basket, tightly woven splint, melon-ribbed, 18 x 13½", 8" h. plus bentwood handle 400.00

Field (or gathering) basket, woven natural & tan splint, 12" d. top, square base, w/swinging bentwood handle, 10" h. 65.00

Field (or gathering) basket, woven splint & cane, old green paint, 14" d., 7¾" h. plus handle 185.00

Oak Splint Field Basket

Field (or gathering) basket, woven oak splint, w/bentwood rim & handles, round, bushel size (ILLUS.)........................ 160.00

Fishing creel basket w/hinged slant lid, woven wicker, w/carrying strap 35.00

Half-buttocks basket, woven oak splint, radiating ribs w/"god's eye" design at handle, 10½" w., 5½" deep, plus handle 135.00

Laundry basket, woven split wood, bentwood rim w/handles at sides, 1940's, 26 x 17", 12½" h. ...45.00 to 75.00

Market (or utility) basket, woven
  oak splint, ring-like foot,
  elaborate "god's eye" design at
  handle, 7" d., 3¾" h. plus bent-
  wood handle 140.00
Market (or utility) basket, woven
  hickory splint, w/bentwood swivel
  handle, 10" d., 7" h. 275.00
Market (or utility) basket, tightly
  woven splint, cane-woven bottom
  w/kick-up & radiating splint
  staves, carved swivel handle,
  12½" d., 7¼" h. 625.00
Market (or utility) basket, woven
  oak splint, old red paint, 16" d.,
  10" h. plus handle 770.00
Melon basket, 18-rib construction,
  woven splint, woven "god's eye"
  design at handle, 9 x 8" warped
  d., 4¼" h. plus bentwood
  handle 175.00
Melon basket, 22-rib construction,
  woven hickory splint w/"god's
  eye" design at handle, 10 x 8¾"
  oval, 4¾" h. plus handle 175.00
Melon basket, 30-rib construction,
  tightly woven hickory splint, good
  patina w/red-painted "god's eye"
  design at handle, 11 x 10½" top
  d., 6" h. plus bentwood handle . . . 135.00

Nantucket Lightship Baskets

Nantucket lightship basket, tightly
  woven rattan sides, penciled
  "Made by Samuel Cobman, etc."
  on wooden bottom, Nantucket,
  Massachusetts, 19th c., 7" d.,
  3¾" h. (ILLUS. left) 605.00
Nantucket lightship basket, tightly
  woven rattan sides, turned wood-
  en base, bentwood swivel handle
  w/brass rivets, 11½" d., 6¾" h.
  plus handle 1,200.00
Nantucket lightship basket, tightly
  woven rattan sides, w/partial
  handwritten red-bordered label of
  Ferdin & Sylvaro, 1920-30, 14" d.,
  7" h. plus handle (ILLUS.
  right) 660.00
Picnic (or storage) hamper, woven
  willow, hinged dome lid, 1930's,
  16 x 11½ x 8½" 30.00

Picnic Basket with Lid

Picnic (or storage) hamper & cover,
  woven splint, w/double swivel
  handles, 22 x 16", 13" h.
  (ILLUS.) 145.00
Rye straw (bread) basket, coilwork
  construction, 12" d., 4" h. 50.00
Rye straw (bread) baskets, coilwork
  construction, 11 x 8" oval &
  12" d., pr. 60.00
Sewing basket, cov., woven reed,
  w/Peking glass beads, Chinese
  coins & silk tassels, 9" d. . . 22.00 to 35.00
Shaker berry basket, metal rim at
  top & bottom, signed & dated,
  1859, 3¼" d., 3" h. 150.00

Shaker Laundry Basket

Shaker laundry (or open storage)
  baskets, woven splint, flaring cylinder, carved wood handles at
  rim, late 19th/early 20th c., each
  17" d., pr. (ILLUS. of one) 467.50
Storage basket, cov., woven wide &
  narrow splint, w/faded orange &
  green watercolor floral designs,
  20 x 13" oblong, 9" h. 150.00
Storage basket, cov., woven oak
  splint, lid attached w/slides on
  uprights at bentwood handles,
  12" d., 9¾" h. plus handle 135.00
Storage basket, open, tightly woven
  hickory splint, painted blue,
  9¼" d., 3¾" h. 605.00
Storage basket, open, woven ash
  splint w/heart-shaped fixed han-

dles, early red paint, 11½" oval,
4" h. 1,100.00
Storage basket, open, woven wide
& narrow splint in black, orange &
natural, bentwood rim handles,
19 x 12½" oblong, 7½" h. 415.00
Wall-hanging basket, 3-tier, finely
woven oblong splint trays w/sides
attached to tapering backplate,
ca. 1900 . . . . 605.00
Winnowing basket, loosely woven
splint bottom & tightly woven
sides, bentwood frame & rim handles, traces of old blue paint,
35 x 24" 265.00
Wool rinsing basket, woven splint,
square base, footed, bentwood
frame & rim handles, 2-tone patinated splint, ca. 1840,
12½ x 12" 340.00

BEADED & MESH BAGS

Beaded Bag

*Beaded and mesh bags, popular earlier in
this century, are now in great demand. Ladies have found them to be the perfect acces-
sory to the casual long gowns now so fashionable. Sterling silver bags and those set
with precious stones bring high prices, but
the average glass beaded bag is much lower.*

Beaded, black beading on mesh fabric w/silver beaded border,
small $28.00
Beaded, black & grey beading,
clutch-type, Czechoslovakia,
1930's 45.00
Beaded, blue & amber beading
forming floral & geometric designs
on gold beaded ground, ornate
embossed frame w/chain handle,
marked "Made in France,"
5¾" w., 6½" l. (ILLUS.) 65.00
Beaded, brown, red & green bead-

ing, scene of 2 equestrian figures,
ornate brass frame 50.00
Beaded, gold beading, ornate gold-
finish metal frame 75.00
Beaded, marcasite beading on black
satin fabric 75.00
Beaded, marigold Carnival glass
beading on dark brown beaded
ground 40.00
Beaded, multicolored beading form-
ing a house & floral design,
6½" l. 38.00
Beaded, multicolored floral design
beading on dark blue beaded
ground, beaded monogram re-
verse, 12 x 7" 55.00
Beaded, multicolored beading, over-
all rose design, ca. 1890,
12 x 7" 85.00
Beaded, multicolored beading on
black velvet fabric, w/beaded tassel, tortoise shell celluloid
frame 45.00
Beaded, multicolored beading, flow-
er basket design, ornate brass
frame 49.00
Beaded, multicolored beading, bird
design, dated 1919 . . . .   30.00
Beaded, multicolored beading in
muted tones, castle scene,
Germany 125.00
Beaded, orange blending to brown
beading forming thumbprint design on bag & handle, envelope
clutch-type w/gilt bronze over-
flap applied w/three oval
enameled portraits of beautiful
women, each oval within ormolu
fishscale frame set w/pearls, satin lined double pocket interior,
signed Marabito, Paris, 8 x 7". . . . 275.00
Beaded, pink, blue & yellow beaded
stripes, silverplate frame & chain
handle, 6 x 5" 40.00
Beaded, red & yellow beading, flo-
ral design on blue beaded
ground, drawstring-type 65.00
Beaded, yellow & pink beading, butterfly & floral design on green
beaded ground, 9" l. 48.00
Enameled mesh, beige & brown de-
sign, Whiting-Davis, 1920's 38.00
Enameled mesh, beige, turquoise
blue & brown floral design, elongated points at base, blue
jeweled clasp, Mandalian Mfg.
Co., 8 x 4¾" 55.00
Enameled mesh, black & white Art
Deco style design on silver finish
mesh, chain handle 30.00
Enameled mesh, blue & white de-
sign, chain handle, 1920's 35.00
Enameled mesh, blue, brown &
white design, fringed base, silver-

plate frame & chain handle, 1920,
6 x 4" 50.00
Enameled mesh, red, white, black &
gold geometric design, w/chain
handle, Mandalian Mfg. Co. 60.00
Gold finish mesh, base w/tassels,
Whiting-Davis 52.00
Gold finish mesh, rhinestone clasp,
Whiting-Davis 60.00

Gun Metal Mesh Bag

Gun metal mesh, marked "Real Gun
Metal France," chain handle,
9½" w., 5½" l. (ILLUS.) 60.00
Silver mesh, England, hallmarks for
1919 .... 125.00
Sterling silver mesh, beaded drops
at base, frame chased w/florals .. 75.00

BELLS

Cast Iron Door Bell

Altar sanctuary bell, brass,
large $250.00
Animal bell, billy goat, brass,
w/wooden clapper, leather
thong 32.00
Animal bell, cow, brass, embossed
designs, large 70.00
Animal bell, cow, hand-carved walnut, 8" w., 4" h. 65.00
Animal bell, sheep, brass, arched
loop for neck strap, 4 x 4" 32.00
Animal bell, sheep, cast iron,
arched loop for neck strap 3.50
Animal bell, turkey, brass, neck-
type to be worn on leather strap
or thong...................... 45.00
China, Royal Bayreuth w/blue Tettau
mark, Little Jack Horner & verse
decor 225.00

China, Royal Bayreuth w/blue Tettau
mark, "tapestry" finish, pastoral
scene decor 385.00
Dinner gong, brass, 2 graduated
bells in crane-decorated framework, marked "China" 110.00
Door bell, cast iron, 2-section, geometric designs & marked "Con-
nel's Patent 1874," pull-down to
ring (ILLUS.) 65.00
Figural bell, brass, Welsh lady,
w/spinning wheel as clapper,
1¾" d., 3¼" h. 69.00
Figural bell, brass, Victorian lady
wearing hat w/plume, full skirt,
2" d., 4¼" h. 70.00
Figural bell, brass, Lucy Locket,
w/clapper feet, 3 3/8" d.,
4¾" h. 80.00
Figural bell, brass, lady wearing
powdered wig & hoop skirt &
holding a fan, 3½" d., 5½" h. 75.00
Figural bell, brass, old lady wearing
cap & apron, 2¾" d., 5¾" h. 115.00
Figural bell, brass, Colonial lady
wearing tiered skirt & shawl,
3¼" d., 6½" h. 110.00
Figural bell, brass, Mary Queen of
Scots, w/feet as clapper,
3 3/8" d., 7¼" h. 175.00
Figural bell, porcelain, doll in full-
length skirt, marked Germany &
numbered, 3¾" h. 145.00
Glass bell, clear cut glass, Brilliant
Period cutting, original clapper,
5¾" h. 255.00
Glass bell, clear cut glass attributed
to Dorflinger, strawberry diamond, fan & other cutting 375.00
Glass bell, cranberry w/applied
clear swirl-ribbed handle,
10" h. 125.00
Glass bell, cranberry w/applied
clear handle w/white opaque
figural hand finial, clear glass
clapper, 6" d., 10½" h. 215.00
Glass bell, cranberry w/green spatter & gold mica spangles, clear
handle w/cranberry rigaree 145.00
Glass bell, Nailsea-type, light topaz
w/opaque white & amethyst loopings, conforming handle,
ca. 1860 .... 340.00
Hand bell, brass, figural handle of
comic cat seated, marked "Registered Applied For," 2" d.,
4¾" h. 45.00
Hand bell, brass, figural Napoleon
handle, relief-molded scenes of
"Battle of Waterloo" around body,
3" d., 6¼" h. 75.00
Hand bell, cast iron, figural bust of
African Woman w/gilt earrings on
handle, cream & black stripe-

painted body, England, 1930's,
2¼" d., 5 3/8" h. 45.00
Hemony bell, "Sad-Faced Queen,"
w/deeply carved band of cherubs
w/instruments on body & inscription "F. Hemony Me Fecit Anno
1569" on body, 4½" d., 6½" h. . . .   185.00
Locomotive bell, bronze, w/yoke &
cradle, 17" d. 875.00
School teacher's hand bell, brass
w/turned wood handle,
7½" h. . . . . .40.00 to 55.00
Serke bell, bell metal, embossed
"Jacob Serke Has Cast Me In the
Year 1370" etc., embossed scenes
on body 295.00

Sleigh Shaft Bells

Sleigh cutter shaft bells, 3 nickel-
plated shaft chimes w/multiple
clappers on iron strap
(ILLUS.). . . . . .55.00 to 70.00
Sleigh bells, 9 graduated crotal-type
brass bells on (worn) leather
strap w/cotter keys, 41" l. 75.00
Sleigh bells, 17 small brass crotal-
type bells riveted on 27" l. leather
strap 100.00
Sleigh bells, 26 graduated brass
crotal-type bells on leather strap
w/cotter keys. 225.00
Sleigh bells, 30 small nickel-plated
bells riveted to leather strap 100.00

Russian Silver Table Bell

Table bell, Russian silver, w/mono-
gram of Grand Duke Michael
Nicholaevich (son of Nicholas I)

one side & crowned Imperial
Eagle reverse, baroque handle &
border chased w/strapwork, workmaster Carl Tegelston, St. Peters-
burg, 1839, 4½" h. (ILLUS.) 1,100.00
Tap bell, silverplate dome w/lever
to depress, marble base, overall
6" h. 40.00
Trolley car bell, brass 45.00

BICYCLES

High-Wheeler Bicycle

*The early rotary-pedal bicycles of the 19th
century were known as "velocipedes" to the
French but the English dubbed them
"boneshakers" because of their affect on the
riders who rode them on the rough unpaved
roads of the day. Gradually the front wheels
of these early bicycles were enlarged to increase the distance gained by each revolution
of the pedal. To offset the weight added to
the front wheel, the rear wheel was made
smaller and the term "high-wheeler" came
into use. All bicycles made before 1900 are
desirable but the early high-wheelers are
scarce because their popularity was so short-
lived for they were difficult to mount, to dis-
mount and quite dangerous to ride. In this
listing, we include only high-wheeler bicycles
but intend to broaden this listing in future
years.*

High-wheeler, 38" d. front wheel,
15" d. rear wheel, overall 53" l.,
47" h. $1,150.00
High-wheeler, 42" d. front wheel,
all wood w/wire spoke wheels
(needs work) 900.00
High-wheeler, 48" d. front wheel,
dark green w/pinstriping 1,950.00
High-wheeler, 52" d. front wheel,
brass brake, restored 2,400.00

BIG LITTLE BOOKS

Flash Gordon Big Little Book

The original "Big Little Books" series of small format was originated in the mid-30's by Whitman Publishing Co., Racine, Wis., and covered a variety of subjects from adventure stories to tales based on comic strip characters and movie and radio stars. The publisher originally assigned each book a serial number. Most prices are now in the $8.00-$20.00 range with scarce ones bringing more.

Andy Panda's Vacation, No. 1485,
  1946 . . . . $40.00
Arizona Kid on the Bandit Trail,
  No. 1192, 1936 . . . . 12.50
Big Chief Wahoo and the Lost
  Pioneers, "movie flip" page
  corners, No. 1432, 1942 . . . . 9.00
Blondie and Dagwood in Hot Water,
  No. 1410, 1946 . . . . 17.00
Blondie, The Bumsteads Carry On,
  No. 1419, 1941 . . . . 14.00
Brick Bradford with Brocco the Mod-
  ern Buccaneer, No. 1468, 1938 . . . . 7.50
Bringing Up Father, No. 1133,
  1936 . . . . 20.00
Bronc Peeler, The Lone Cowboy,
  No. 1417, 1937 . . . . 11.00
Buck Jones and the Rough Riders in
  Forbidden Trails, "movie flip"
  page corners, No. 1486, 1943 . . . . . 22.00
Buck Rogers and the Doom Comet,
  No. 1175, 1936 . . . . 36.00
Buck Rogers and the Planetoid Plot,
  No. 1197, 1936 . . . . 17.00
Buck Rogers in the 25th Century
  A.D., 1933, Cocomalt premium . . . 39.00
Buck Rogers on the Moons of
  Saturn, No. 1143, 1934 . . . . 50.00
Bugs Bunny, No. 1435, 1943 . . . . 16.00
Captain Easy, Behind Enemy Lines,
  No. 1474, 1943 . . . . 20.00
Captain Midnight and the Moon
  Woman, No. 1452, 1943 . . . . 14.00

Charlie Chan, Inspector of the Hono-
  lulu Police, No. 1478, 1939 . . . . 20.00
Dan Dunn Secret Operative 48,
  No. 1116, 1934 . . . . 30.00
Dan Dunn Secret Operative 48 and
  the Border Smugglers, No. 1481,
  1938 . . . . 10.00
David Copperfield, No. 1148, 1934 . . 20.00
Dick Tracy (Adventures of), No. 707,
  1932 . . . . 45.00
Dick Tracy and the Bicycle Gang,
  No. 1445, 1948 . . . . 15.00
Doctor Doom Faces Death at Dawn,
  International Spy, No. 1148,
  1937 . . . . 9.00
Donald Duck and Ghost Morgan's
  Treasure, No. 1411, 1946 . . . . 25.00
Donald Duck and the Green Ser-
  pent, No. 1432, 1947 . . . . 30.00
Draftie of the U.S. Army, No. 1416,
  1943 . . . . 9.00
Erik Noble and the Forty-Niners,
  No. 772, 1934 . . . . 7.00
Flash Gordon and the Perils of Mon-
  go, No. 1423, 1940 . . . . 51.00
Flash Gordon and the Red Sword In-
  vaders, No. 1479, 1945 . . . . 30.00
Flash Gordon and the Tournaments
  of Mongo, No. 1171, 1935
  (ILLUS.) 52.00
Flash Gordon in the Forest Kingdom
  of Mongo, No. 1492, 1938 . . . . 30.00
G-Man on the Crime Trail, No. 1118,
  1936 . . . . 10.00
G-Man vs. the Red X, No. 1147,
  1936 . . . . 10.00
Gene Autry Cowboy Detective,
  No. 1494, 1940 . . . . 17.00
Gene Autry in Law of the Range,
  No. 1483, 1939 . . . . 25.00
Ghost Avenger, "movie flip" page
  corners, No. 1462, 1943 . . . . 30.00
Green Hornet Cracks Down, "movie
  flip" page corners, No. 1480,
  1942 . . . . 40.00
Hairbreadth Harry in Department
  Q.T., No. 1101, 1935 . . . . 12.00
Jackie Cooper, Movie Star of Skippy
  and Sooky, No. 714, 1933 . . . . 11.00
Jane Arden, The Vanished Princess,
  No. 1490, 1938 . . . . 8.00
Joe Louis, The Brown Bomber,
  No. 1105, 1936 . . . . 38.00
Joe Palooka, The Heavyweight Box-
  ing Champ, No. 1123, 1934 . . . . 22.50
King of the Royal Mounted and the
  Great Jewel Mystery, No. 1486,
  1939 . . . . 23.00
Li'l Abner in New York, No. 1198,
  1936 . . . . 28.00
Little Orphan Annie and Sandy,
  No. 716, 1933 . . . . 36.00
Little Orphan Annie and the Ghost
  Gang, No. 1154, 1935 . . . . 15.00

Little Women, No. 757, 1934 . . . . 10.00

Lone Ranger and the Black Shirt
Highwayman, No. 1450, 1939 . . . . . 15.00

Lone Ranger and the Menace of
Murder Valley, No. 1465, 1937 . . . . 15.00

Lone Ranger and the Vanishing
Herd, No. 1196, 1936 . . . . 16.00

Mandrake the Magician, No. 1167,
1935 . . . . 27.00

Mickey Mouse, No. 717, 1933 . . . . . . 95.00

Mickey Mouse & the Bat Bandit,
No. 1153, 1935 . . . . 45.00

Mickey Mouse & the Desert Palace,
No. 1451, 1948 . . . . 30.00

Mickey Mouse Big Little Books

Mickey Mouse & the 'Lectro Box,
No. 1413, 1946 (ILLUS. right) 27.00

Mickey Mouse & the Magic Lamp,
"movie flip" page corners,
No. 1429, 1942 (ILLUS. left) 20.00

Mickey Mouse & the Sacred Jewel,
No. 1187, 1936 (ILLUS. center) 33.00

Mickey Mouse & the Seven Ghosts,
No. 1475, 1940 . . . . 8.00

Mickey Mouse in the Race for Rich-
es, "movie flip" page corners,
No. 1476, 1938 . . . . 20.00

Mickey Mouse in the Treasure Hunt,
"movie flip" page corners,
No. 1401, 1941 . . . . 20.00

Moon Mullins & Kayo, No. 746,
1933 . . . . 11.50

My Life & Times, Shirley Temple,
No. 1596, 1936 . . . . 22.50

New Adventures of Tarzan,
No. 1180, 1935 . . . . 20.00

Oswald, The Lucky Rabbit, No. 1109,
1934 . . . . 30.00

Pinocchio & Jiminy Cricket,
No. 1435, 1940 . . . . 25.00

Plainsman, No. 1123, 1936 . . . . 14.00

Popeye, No. 1301, 1934 . . . . 55.00

Secret Agent X-9, No. 1144, 1936 . . . 10.50

Tailspin Tommy in the Famous Pay-
roll Mystery, No. 747, 1933 . . . . . . 25.00

Tarzan & the Ant Men, No. 1444,
1945 . . . . 7.50

Tarzan & the Land of Giant Apes,
No. 1467, 1949 . . . . 20.00

Tarzan & the Lost Empire, No. 1442,
1948 . . . . 9.50

Tarzan of the Apes, No. 744, 1933 . . 45.00

Tarzan Twins, No. 770, 1934 . . . . 60.00

Tarzan's Revenge, No. 1488, 1938 . . . 20.00

Terry & War in the Jungle, No. 1420,
1946 . . . . 14.00

Tim McCoy in The Westerner,
No. 1193, 1936 . . . . 13.00

Tom Mix and the Hoard of Montezu-
ma, No. 1462, 1937 . . . . 25.00

Tom Mix and the Stranger from the
South, No. 1183, 1936 . . . . 17.50

Tom Mix and Tony, Jr. in Terror
Trail, No. 762, 1935 . . . . 25.00

Tom Mix in the Fighting Cowboy,
No. 1144, 1935 . . . . 25.00

Tom Swift and His Giant Telescope,
No. 1485, 1939 . . . . 25.00

Uncle Wiggily's Adventures,
No. 1405, 1946 . . . . 12.50

Wells Fargo, No. 1471, 1938 . . . . 12.00

Will Rogers, No. 1576, 1935 . . . . 16.00

Wyatt Earp, No. 1644, 1958 . . . . 15.00

BILLIKEN COLLECTIBLES

Billiken Bank

The Billiken craze swept this country in the early years of this century. A symbolic good luck figure was created in the form of an Oriental-type pixie with slanting eyebrows and a pointed head. A doll, copyrighted in 1909 by the Billiken Company and produced by Horsman Company of New York, was an immediate success and soon stamp boxes, tape measures, bridge pads, blotters, picture frames and other items with Billiken decoration began to appear on merchant's shelves. Today these celluloid, leather, china and paper items are attracting collectors.

Bank, cast iron, figure of seated Billiken, marked "Billiken" on base,
4¼" h. (ILLUS.) $60.00

Brooch, brass, 2½" 25.00

Chocolate mold, pewter 68.00
Figure, bisque, hand-painted fea-
tures, 6" h. 265.00
Figure, chalkware, Billiken seated
on throne w/metal medallion
"God of Good Luck" attached to
base, Billiken Co., Chicago, 1908,
7" h. ....30.00 to 45.00
Figure, composition head, stuffed
body, original label, 12" 35.00
Figure, Frankoma pottery, large 75.00
Mug, silverplate, 5 Billiken figures
in relief 50.00
Pillow cover, hand-painted silk,
1908 .... 57.50
Pinback button, Billiken center, 1910
trademark 40.00
Plate, dated 1909, 7½" d. 40.00
Print, colorful Billiken scene 25.00
Salt & pepper shakers, chalkware,
pr. 12.00
Tape measure, brass, full figure
Billiken, windup tape return,
2½" h. 145.00
Vase, Limoges china, Billiken decor,
2½" h. 35.00
Wall pocket, ceramic, 7" h. 50.00
Watch fob, advertising "Dr.
Pepper" 65.00

BOOKENDS

Bronze Bookends

*Also see AVIATION COLLECTIBLES,
ANIMALS under Glass, ROOKWOOD and
TECO POTTERY.*

Brass, bust of an Indian, pr. $45.00
Brass, model of German Shepherd
dog, pr. 35.00
Bronze, Bookmark patt., border set
w/green & blue glass cabochons,
signed Tiffany Studios, New York
& numbered, 6 1/8" h., pr. 430.00
Bronze, figure of old gentleman in
chair reading book, signed J.
Ruhl, 4 x 6", pr. 225.00
Bronze, model of a Greyhound dog,
"A Sportsman's Friend," 7" h.,
pr. 68.00
Bronze, model of teepee, artist-
signed, pr. 125.00
Bronze, model of a walking tiger &
walking lion, brown patina,

Antoine-Louis Barye, inscribed
Barye/F. Barbedienne, Fondeur,
late 19th-early 20th c., on ma-
hogany base stamped Tiffany &
Co., 10" l., pr. (ILLUS.) 2,090.00
Bronze-finish pot metal, bust of
Abraham Lincoln on plinth,
marked Parsons Casket Hdw. Co.,
Belvidere, Illinois, pr. 55.00
Bronze-finish pot metal, figure of a
nude male discus thrower, Jennings Bros., 7" h., pr. 65.00
Bronze-finish pot metal, model of an
Art Deco leaping fox, pr. 50.00
Cast iron, basket of flowers, pr. 55.00
Cast iron, figure of Art Deco semi-
nude woman dancer w/tambou-
rine, pr. 35.00
Cast iron, model of eagle w/wings
spread & head turned, standing
on mound base w/band of impressed stars around base,
marked Hamilton Foundry Inc.,
6½" h., pr. 55.00
Ceramic, model of stylized Art Deco
polar bears on black base,
marked Germany, pr. 30.00
Chalkware, model of Scottie dogs,
marked Melillo, N.Y., pr. 50.00
Copper, model of Russell-type Indian
teepee & kneeling Indian w/bow
& arrow, pr. 295.00
Pot metal, figure of Art Deco man &
woman musicians, greenish-gold
finish, green onyx base, pr. 125.00
Pot metal, figure of knight w/lance
astride horse, marked M.B., 7" h.,
pr. 75.00
Pressed glass, model of Pouter
pigeons, clear, 6¼" h., pr. 30.00
Pressed glass, model of squirrel,
clear, etched & polished, signed
Josef Hoffman, pr. 450.00
Soapstone, variegated beige, tan &
russet, pr. 60.00
Wooden, semi-circular, hand-carved
walnut w/Art Nouveau florals &
monogram, hammered copper
base, 5" h., pr. 27.00

BOOKMARKS

Advertising, "Cunningham Piano,"
celluloid $10.00
Advertising, "Heinz," die-cut pickle,
little girl pictured 8.00
Advertising, "Maltene," celluloid,
model of an owl 15.00
Advertising, "Planters Peanuts," die-

cut Mr. Peanut w/top hat &
  cane 15.00
Advertising, "Texaco," celluloid 15.00
Advertising, "Velvet Candy," tin,
  die-cut & color-printed monkey ... 20.00
Advertising, "Winter Pianos, James
  Abrams, Jacksonville, Florida,"
  paper, child pianist pictured,
  1900's 2.00
Brass, model of the Empire State
  Building, Art Deco style, black
  inlay 8.00

Celluloid Bookmark

Celluloid, pansy, crossed flags &
  spread-winged American eagle,
  3½ x 1¾" (ILLUS.) 5.00
Celluloid, roses decor, 5" l. 2.50
Paper, embossed & lithographed
  Spaniel dog.................... 12.00
Silk, "National Geographic Balloon
  Society," from fabric of Explorer II
  that set world's altitude record
  Nov. 11, 1935, 7 x 2½",
  w/authentication from National
  Geographic Society 98.00
Sterling silver, enameled colorful
  maple leaf & "Canada,"
  4 x 5/8"...................... 25.00
Sterling silver, embossed ship 32.00
Woven silk, American flag w/thir-
  teen stars, w/advertising 22.50

BOOTJACKS

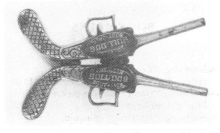

"American Bull Dog" Bootjack

Cast iron, folding-type, cast in the
  form of a revolver, "The American
  Bull Dog Boot Jack," 8¼" l.
  (ILLUS.)...................... $75.00
Cast iron, model of a beetle, worn
  paint......................... 45.00
Cast iron, model of deer head...... 90.00
Cast iron, model of a ladybug 25.00
Cast iron, "Naughty Nellie," Alton,
  Illinois Screw Co................ 50.00
Cast iron, "Try Me"............... 42.50
Wooden, painted blue, ca. 1875 .... 35.00

BOTTLE OPENERS

Cast Iron Bottle Openers

Corkscrews were actually the first bottle openers and these may date back to the mid-18th century, but bottle openers, as we know them today, are strictly a 20th century item and come into use only after Michael J. Owens invented the automatic bottle machine in 1903. Avid collectors have spurred this relatively new area of collector interest that requires only a modest investment. Our listing, by type of metal, encompasses the four basic types sought by collectors: advertising openers; full figure openers which stand alone or hang on the wall; flat figural openers such as the lady's leg shape; and openers with embossed, engraved or chased handles. Also see BREWERIANA and COCA-COLA ITEMS.

Advertising, "Caton Ale," flat figural
  nude female $8.00
Advertising, "Dr. Pepper - Drink A
  Bite to Eat" 11.00
Advertising, "Iroquois Beer, Buffalo,
  New York," aluminum, figural
  Indian........................ 48.00
Advertising, "Old Crow," bottle-
  shaped, opener springs out from
  bottom when top is pressed 25.00
Advertising, "Pepsi," bottle-
  shaped 11.00
Aluminum, full figure pheasant..... 10.00
Aluminum, full figure shark 15.00
Brass, full figure Amish boy, paint-
  ed, Wilton Products 40.00
Brass, full figure Dachshund dog,
  4½" 60.00
Brass, model of a padlock, Wilton
  Products...................... 22.00
Brass, wall-type, black man, "Cappy
  the Bottle Butler" 32.00

Brass, wall-type, lobster, John
  Wright Co...................... 20.00
Cast iron, full figure bull.......... 20.00
Cast iron, full figure cowboy playing
  guitar 75.00
Cast iron, full figure donkey
  seated & braying, Wilton
  Products..................19.00 to 27.00
Cast iron, full figure drunk at palm
  tree......................... 32.00
Cast iron, full figure "Freddie
  Frosh," L & L Favors 50.00
Cast iron, full figure goat, worn
  original paint, 4¼" h. 32.00
Cast iron, full figure goose, original
  polychrome paint, 3 5/8" l. (ILLUS.
  left)......................... 80.00
Cast iron, full figure Mademoiselle
  by lamppost 35.00
Cast iron, full figure parrot w/fold-
  ing corkscrew in tail............ 22.00
Cast iron, full figure rooster, original polychrome paint, 3¼" h. 45.00
Cast iron, full figure sailor, John
  Wright Co..................... 45.00
Cast iron, full figure sea gull stand-
  ing on piling, worn original paint,
  3 1/8" h. 40.00
Cast iron, full figure trout, original
  polychrome paint, 5" l. (ILLUS.
  right) 50.00
Cast iron, wall-type, laughing clown,
  original white paint w/red,
  orange, black & blue details,
  4½" h. ....60.00 to 75.00
Cast iron, wall-type, hanging drunk,
  Wilton Products 27.00
Cast iron, wall-type, four-eyed lady,
  John Wright Co................. 50.00
Sterling silver, Acorn patt., Georg
  Jensen, 4¾" l.................. 65.00
Sterling silver, beaded trim, Georg
  Jensen 85.00
Sterling silver w/mother-of-pearl in-
  lay, full figure fish, 9" l. 65.00

BOTTLES & FLASKS

Glass bottles and flasks have been made since ancient times and the first attempt to manufacture glass in the new world took place at the Jamestown, Virginia settlement, probably between 1609 and 1617. Over one-hundred years passed before another glass factory could survive more than a decade. Caspar Wistar and subsequently his son, operated a glasshouse, from 1739 to 1779, in New Jersey where bottles and other utilitarian wares were produced from ordinary win-

dow glass and green, or bottle, glass. Henry William Stiegel, whose glass factory opened in Manheim, Pennsylvania in 1763, produced a fine quality glass in the European tradition by employing German, Venetian and English glass blowers. The quality of Stiegel's glass was so fine that today it is difficult to distinguish from the Continental glasswares produced during the same time span. Today, almost all early glass made in colonial America is categorized as being either Jersey-type or Stiegel-type though few pieces can be positively identified.

Bottles and flasks were either free-blown or pattern-molded and expanded. Stiegel bottles are typically pattern-molded. The Pitkin glasshouse, near Hartford, Connecticut produced bottles of all kinds, but "pitkin" has become a generic term for a flask that is fine-ribbed vertically or spirally, or possibly in a combination of both. A "chestnut" bottle is a globular or ovoid bottle with a tapered neck, somewhat resembling the American chestnut and can be free-blown or pattern-molded and expanded.

"Ludlow," a term often applied to chestnut bottles, is derived from the fact that early bottle collectors assumed all chestnut-form bottles were made at a glassworks that operated at Ludlow, Massachusetts about 1815. Carboys are large bottles that usually held corosive liquids and often were encased in wooden crates, while demijohns are usually large narrow-necked wine bottles often originally encased in wicker.

"Bitters" were merely a means of evading a tax on gin imposed by George II of England. Gin merchants added herbs to the gin and sold it for medicinal purposes, evading the tax levy and retaining their margin of profit. For the same reason, Bitters became popular in colonial America. Case bottles are square-bodied bottles that are sometimes tapered. Case gin bottles and other early bottles before the mid-19th century will have pontil scars and applied lips. Sometimes gin and wine bottles have an applied "seal," a glob of molten glass applied to the shoulder or body that is subsequently stamped with a seal. These are referred to as "seal" bottles.

Historical flasks have national themes with portraits of national heroes, prominent people and presidents or patriotic themes. Historical and pictorial flasks constitute a well-researched area of bottle collecting. Figural, ink and nursing bottles represent still other aspects of the overall bottle collecting hobby.

J. Michael Owens patented his automatic bottle making machine in 1891 and, by the very early 1900's, hand blowing of bottles gave way to this automated procedure. Bottles do not have to be hand-blown to be collectible and many of the beer, soda and whiskey bottles that are avidly collected to-day are those made by machine. A good reference for the beginning bottle collector is Cecil Munsey's "The Illustrated Guide to Collectible Bottles." Collectors of historical flasks will find invaluable material in George and Helen McKearin's comprehensive work, "American Glass." Also see PERFUME, SCENT & COLOGNE BOTTLES.

BARBER

Cranberry Opalescent Hobnail Pattern

Amber, enameled coral pink &
   white beading (no stopper) $85.00
Amethyst, enameled decor, original
   stopper, 8¼" h. 120.00
Apple green, enameled decor (no
   stopper) 65.00
Black opaque, enameled white bird
   & leaf decor (no stopper) 65.00
Blue, enameled orange & white
   beading (no stopper) 85.00
Blue opalescent, Hobnail patt. (no
   stopper) 125.00
Clambroth, paneled sides, black
   borders & burnt orange script lettering, set of 4 (no stoppers) 72.00
Clear to opalescent, square, original
   stopper 145.00
Cobalt blue, bulbous bottoms, long-
   stemmed slender necks,
   enameled white decor, pr. (no
   stoppers) 250.00
Cobalt blue, enameled white florals
   & gold leaves (no stopper) 100.00
Cranberry, Drape patt., 7" h. (no
   stopper) 90.00
Cranberry opalescent, Daisy & Fern
   patt., original stopper 100.00
Cranberry opalescent, Hobnail patt.
   (ILLUS.) 145.00
Cranberry opalescent, Stripe patt.
   (no stopper) 80.00

Emerald green, bell-shaped,
   enameled white scrolls & florals,
   6¾" h. (no stopper) 125.00
Mary Gregory type, amethyst, white
   enameled boy on one & girl on
   other, pr. (no stopper) 350.00
Mary Gregory type, cobalt blue,
   white enameled figure (no
   stopper) 185.00
Milk white, Basketweave patt., gold
   trim (no stopper) 30.00
Milk white, octagonal, original
   stopper 65.00

BITTERS

Augauer Bitters

Allen's (Williams) Congress, rectangular, aqua, ¾ qt. 325.00
Arabian Bitters, Lawrence & Weich-
   selbaum, Savannah, Ga., square,
   amber, 9¾" h. 325.00
Atwood's Jaundice Bitters, Formerly
   Made By Moses Atwood, Geor-
   getown, Mass., 12-sided, aqua,
   screw-top threading, 6¼" h. 14.00
Augauer, rectangular, green, origi-
   nal label each side, 8" h.
   (ILLUS.) 150.00
Ayer (Dr. M.C.) Restorative Bitters,
   Boston, Mass., rectangular, aqua,
   8 7/8" h. 125.00
Baker's Orange Grove, square
   w/roped corners, orange-amber,
   ¾ qt. 135.00
Barber's Indian Vegetable Jaundice,
   Olive Johnson & Co., Providence,
   R.I., 12-sided, aqua, 6 1/8" h. 105.00
Baxter's (Dr.) Mandrake, Lord Bro's
   Proprietors, Burlington, Vt., 12-
   sided, smooth base, aqua,
   6½" h. 16.50
Beggs Dandelion, amber, ½ pt. 55.00
Berlin Magin Bitters, Pat. Applied
   For, S.B. Rothenberg, Sole Agent,
   square, milk white, 9" h. 135.00
Big Bill Best, square, orange-amber,
   12 1/8" h. 85.00

Blue Mountain, rectangular, aqua,
7 7/8" h. 32.50

Boerhaves Holland Bitters, B. Page
Jr. & Co., Pittsburgh, Pa., rectan-
gular, aqua, 8" h. . . . . .75.00 to 125.00

Bourbon Whiskey, barrel-shaped,
pink-amber, 9¼" h. 350.00

Boyce's (Dr.) Tonic, 12-sided, aqua,
7¾" h. . . . . .50.00 to 60.00

Brown (F.) Sarsaparilla & Tomato,
oval, pontil, aqua,
9½" h. . . . . .110.00 to 160.00

Brown's Celebrated Indian Herb,
Patented Feb. 11, 1868, figural Indian Queen, yellow-amber,
12¼" h. . . . . .350.00 to 595.00

Brown's Iron, square, applied top,
amber, pt. 17.50

Brown's Iron, square, applied top,
citron yellow, pt. 35.00

Bulls' (Dr. John) Compound Cedron
Bitters, Louisville, Ky., square,
amber, 10" h. 195.00

Burdock Blood Bitters, Buffalo, N.Y.,
Foster, Milburn & Co., rectangu-
lar, aqua, 8 3/8" h. 15.00

Caldwell's (The Great Dr.) Herb Tonic, triangular, amber, 12¾" h. 165.00

California Fig, California Extract of
Fig Co., San Francisco, Cal.,
square, amber, 10" h. 85.00

Campbell's (Dr.) Scotch Bitters,
strap-sided flask, amber, ¼ pt.
(dug) 60.00

Carmeliter For All Kidney & Liver
Complaints, Carmeliter Stomach
Bitters Co., New York, square,
amber, 10¼" h. 35.00

Caroni, cylindrical, olive green,
½ pt. 22.00

Clarke's Compound Mandrake, oval,
aqua, 7 5/8" h. 47.50

Clarke's (E.R.) Sarsaparilla Bitters,
Sharon, Mass., rectangular, pon-
til, aqua, 7 3/8" h. 500.00

Cole Brothers Vegetable, rectangu-
lar, aqua, 8½" h. 40.00

Columbo Peptic, L.E. Jung, New
Orleans, square, amber, 9" h. 30.00

Copp's (Dr.) White Mountain, J.
Copp & Co., Manchester, N.H..,
w/"JHC" monogram, oval, tooled
mouth w/collar, pt. 85.00

Damaiana, Baja, California, round,
aqua, 11¾" h. 55.00

Deutenhoffs Swiss Bitters, G.M.
Heidt, Savannah, Ga., square,
amber, 9¼" h. 475.00

Devil-Cert Stomach, round, clear,
8" h. 55.00

DeWitt's Stomach, square, amber,
label only, 8¾" h. 35.00

DeWitt's Stomach, square, yellow-
amber, label only, 8¾" h. 49.00

Dingens Napoleon Cocktail, Dingen
Brothers, Buffalo, N.Y., banjo
shape w/lady's leg neck & portrait
of Napoleon on side, yellow-green,
10½" h. 2,000.00

Doyle's Hop, 1872, square, amber,
9 5/8" h. 26.50

Drake's Plantation, cabin-shaped,
4-log, amber. . . . . .55.00 to 70.00

Drake's Plantation, cabin-shaped,
4-log, yellow. 80.00

Drake's Plantation, cabin-shaped,
5-log, light golden yellow 275.00

Drake's Plantation, cabin-shaped,
6-log, amber. 65.00

Drake's Plantation, cabin-shaped,
6-log, salmon pink (apricot) 150.00

Drake's Plantation, cabin-shaped,
6-log, yellow-green. 325.00

Eagle Angostura Bark, Eagle Liqueur
Distilleries, Patented Feb. 4th,
1902, globe-shaped, amber, 7" h. . 225.00

Fenner's (Dr. M.M.) Capitol, rectangular, aqua, 9 1/8" h. 48.50

Fisch's (Dr.), W.H. Ware, Patented
1866, figural fish, amber,
11¾" h. . . . . .90.00 to 150.00

Fish (The), W.H. Ware, Patented
1866, figural fish, amber,
11½" h. . . . . .135.00 to 155.00

Garry Owen Strengthening, square,
amber 85.00

Gates & Co. Life of Man, rectangu-
lar, aqua, w/labels. 46.50

Globe (The) Tonic, square, amber,
w/labels 65.00

Goff's (S.B.) Herb, Camden, N.J.,
rectangular, aqua, 7¾" h. 10.00

Granger Bitters

Granger, flask-shaped, tooled lip,
amber, original label, ½ pt.
(ILLUS.). 70.00

Greeley's Bourbon, barrel-shaped
w/ten hoops above & below cen-
ter band, amber 225.00

Green Mountain Cider w/"HJ & L"

monogram, round, aqua,
10¼" h. 295.00

Greer's Eclipse, square, amber,
9½" h. 60.00

Gregory's (Dr.) Scotch Bitters,
square, amber, label only,
9½" h. 65.00

Harter's (Dr.) Wild Cherry, rectangu-
lar, amber 25.00

Hartwig Kantorowicz, 8-sided, milk
white, miniature,
4 1/8" h. . . . . .50.00 to 65.00

Holtzerman's Patent Stomach, cabin-
shaped, amber . . . . .140.00 to 175.00

Home, Jas. A. Jackson & Co. Proprietors, Saint Louis, square, amber,
9" h. 70.00

Hooflands's (Dr.) German, aqua,
pt. 57.50

Hop & Iron, Utica, N.Y., square,
amber, 8½" h. 160.00

Hopkin's (Dr. A.S.) Union Stomach,
Hartford, Conn., square, amber,
9¾" h. 45.00

Dr. Hostetter's Bitters

Hostetter's (Dr. J.) Stomach, square,
amber, 9½" h. (ILLUS.) 32.50

Indian Vegetable & Sarsaparilla,
Geo. C. Goodwin, Boston, rectan-
gular, pontil, aqua, 8 3/8" h. 600.00

Jewett's (Dr. Stephen) Celebrated
Health Restoring, Rindge, N.H.,
rectangular, pontil, amber 230.00

Jewett's (Dr. Stephen) Celebrated
Health Restoring, Rindge, N.H.,
rectangular, pontil, aqua 85.00

John's (Dr. Herbert) Indian Bitters -
Great Indian Discoveries, square
w/beveled corners, amber,
8½" h. 185.00

Kaiser Wilhelm Bitters Co., Sandusky, Ohio, round, clear,
10 1/8" h. 45.00

Kelly's Old Cabin, cabin-shaped,
amber . . . . .450.00 to 600.00

Kimball's Jaundice, Troy, N.H., rectangular, olive amber 250.00

Lash's Bitters Co., N.Y.-Chicago,
S.F., round, amber 45.00

Lash's Kidney & Liver, square,
amber, w/label, 9½" h. 22.50

Lippman's Great German, Savannah,
Georgia, square, collared mouth
w/ring, amber 300.00

Malt Company, Boston, U.S.A.,
round, smooth base, green, pt.,
9" h. 20.00

Mansfield's New Style Highland
Stomach Bitters, Scotch Tonic,
Memphis, Tenn., square, amber,
8 7/8" h. 400.00

Mishler's Herb, square, golden
amber, 9" h. 30.00

Mist of the Morning, barrel-shaped,
yellow-amber 225.00

Moonseed Bitters Co., Swindon, rectangular, aqua, 4¼" h. 35.00

Moxie, square, amber, 9½" h. 125.00

National, figural ear of corn, amber,
¾ qt. . . . . .170.00 to 275.00

National, figural ear of corn, cherry-
red to puce, ¾ qt. 850.00

National, figural ear of corn, light
yellow-amber, ¾ qt. . . . .300.00 to 335.00

National, figural ear of corn, puce,
¾ qt. 600.00

National, Patent 1867, figural ear of
corn, amber, 12 5/8" h. 275.00

National Tonic, square w/roped
corners, aqua, 9½" h. 450.00

O.K. Plantation 1840, Patented 1868,
triangular, smooth base, amber,
¾ qt. 435.00

Old Homestead Wild Cherry, cabin-
shaped, amber, 9 7/8" h. 165.00

Old Sachem Bitters & Wigwam
Tonic, barrel-shaped, amber 185.00

Parker's Celebrated Stomach,
amber 80.00

Peruvian, square, smooth base,
amber 48.00

Petzold's (Dr.) Genuine German,
Incpt. 1862, figural beehive,
amber, 10 5/8" h. 120.00

Peychaud's Bitter Cordial, cylindri-
cal, amber. 15.00

Phoenix, John Moffat, New York,
rectangular w/wide beveled cor-
ners, aqua, ½ pt. 52.50

Phoenix, Price 1 Dollar, John
Moffat, New York, rectangular
w/wide beveled corners, olive
green, ½ pt. 225.00

Pierce's (Dr.) Indian Restorative, rectangular, pontil, aqua 57.50

Pineapple, J.C. & Co., pineapple-
shaped, amber, ¾ qt. 165.00

Prickley Ash, square, amber,
¾ qt. 22.50

Prickley Ash, square, green,
¾ qt. 100.00
Ratttinger's (Dr.) Herb & Root, St.
Louis, Mo., square, amber,
9 1/8" h. 140.00
Red Cloud, Vowinkle & Theller,
square, amber, 9½" h. (light stain
one panel)...................... 200.00
Reed's, lady's leg shape, amber,
12½" h........................ 165.00
Rex Kidney & Liver, amber 27.50
Richardson's (S.O.), rectangular
w/wide beveled corners, aqua,
pt............................. 60.00
Richardson's (S.O.), rectangular
w/wide beveled corners, green,
pt............................. 30.00
Roback's (Dr. C.W.) Stomach, barrel-
shaped, golden amber, ¾ qt. 140.00
Romaine's Crimean, golden amber .. 175.00
Royal Italian, cylindrical, light to
medium amethyst 325.00
Royal Pepsin Stomach, amber,
8¾" h........................ 70.00
Rush's, amber.................... 35.00
Sanborn's Kidney & Liver, amber,
10" h......................... 85.00
Sanitarium Bitters, Hi-Hi Bitters Co.,
Rock Island, Ill., triangular,
yellow-green, 9 11/16" h. 275.00
Sazarac Aromatic, lady's leg shape,
milk white...................... 375.00
Severa (W.F.) Stomach, square,
amber 85.00
Simon's Centennial, bust of
Washington, amber, ¾ qt.,
9¾" h. 1,450.00
Simon's Centennial, bust of
Washington, aqua, ¾ qt.,
9¾" h......................... 425.00
Sims' (Dr.) Anti-Constipation Bitters,
square, amber, 7" h. 60.00
Skinner's (Dr.) Celebrated 25 cent
Bitters, So. Reading, Mass., rec-
tangular, aqua, 8½" h. 125.00
Smith's Druid, barrel-shaped, deep
red-amber 450.00
Solomon's Strengthening & Invigorat-
ing, cobalt blue (dug)........... 350.00
Soule's (Dr.) Hop, cabin-shaped,
amber 40.00
Sperry's (Dr.) Rheumatic Bitters,
Hartford, Ct., rectangular, aqua,
10 1/8" h. 95.00
Steketee's Blood Purifying, square,
amber, 6 5/8" h. 135.00
Suffolk, figural pig, pontil, canary
yellow 500.00
Sunny Castle Stomach, amber,
w/label 125.00
Tippecanoe, H.H. Warner Co., tree
bark design w/canoe, golden
amber, ¾ qt.................... 68.00
Toneco, clear 45.00

Wahoo (Dr. E. Dexter Loveridge),
cabin-shaped, DWD, Patd, XXX,
1863 on roofed shoulders,
green 2,475.00
Walker's Tonic, lady's leg shape,
amber, 11½" h................. 300.00
Walker's Vinegar, round, aqua,
8½" h......................... 38.50
Walkinshaw's (Dr.) Curative Bitters,
Batavia, N.Y., square, embossed
& w/label, amber, 9 7/8" h....... 140.00
Wallace's Tonic Stomach, amber 75.00
Wampoo Bitters, Blum Siegel & Bro.,
New York, square, amber,
9¾" h......................... 60.00
Warner's Safe Tonic, oval, amber,
7 3/8" h. 275.00
West India Stomach, square, yellow,
8½" h......................... 50.00
Whitwell's Temperance, pontil, light
green (base flake) 100.00
Wilder's (Edw.) Stomach, building
shape, clear 130.00
Wilson's (Dr.) Herbine, aqua 20.00
Winter's Stomach, square, amber,
9½" h......................... 60.00
Wonne's (Dr.) Gesundheits, square,
amber, w/three labels, 9" h. 225.00
Wonser's (Dr.) U.S.A. Indian Root,
dark amber, ¾ qt. 1,600.00
Wood's (Dr.) Sarsaparilla & Wild
Cherry, pontil, aqua 115.00
Woodcock Pepsin, Schroeder's Med.
Co., amber 77.50
Zingari, amber...........170.00 to 245.00

DRUG STORE BOTTLES & JARS

Apothecary Jars

Amber pressed glass bottle, embossed "Dickey Chemist, S.F." &
mortar & pestle 5.00
Aqua mold-blown glass bottle, embossed "R. & J. Adams Druggists,
St. Louis, Superior Mineral
Waters," cylinder, applied lip 110.00
Aqua mold-blown glass bottle, embossed "Hecht & Fleming Apothecaries, Easton, Pa.," open pontil,
5½" h......................... 40.00
Aqua mold-blown glass bottle, embossed "Laughlins Bushfield Druggists, Wheeling, Va.," open
pontil 25.00
Aqua mold-blown glass bottle, em-

bossed "Wilsons Botonic Drug-
gists, Boston" 65.00
Clear blown glass apothecary jar
w/ground glass stopper, cylinder
w/label under glass intact,
12" h. 55.00
Clear pressed glass bottle, "Jones
Drug Co. Druggists, Under Hotel
Plazza, Vicksburg, Miss." 15.00
Clear pressed glass bottle, em-
bossed "Owl Drug Co.," rectangu-
lar, 8" h. 10.00
Clear pressed glass bottle, applied
lip, "Pure Drugs" on embossed
mortar & pestle, "Warren Toppan
Pharmacist, Lynn, Mass." 25.00
Cobalt blue blown apothecary bot-
tle, gilt label intact, signed "W.N.
Walton" & dated 1862, 6½" h. 85.00
Green mold-blown glass bottle, em-
bossed "G.W. Merchant
Chemist" 50.00
Green (olive) mold-blown glass jar,
cylinder w/full label "From A.
Peizley Fitch, Wholesale & Retail
Druggist, Cowerd, N.H.," 7" h. . . . 75.00
Milk white pressed glass bottle, embossed "John Sullivan Pharmacist,
Boston" 15.00
Porcelain apothecary jars & covers,
cylindrical, each w/central symbol
of medical ointment within colorful cartouche on sky blue ground,
gilt trim, late 19th c., 11" h., set
of 10 (ILLUS. of part right) 770.00
Porcelain apothecary jars & covers,
cylindrical, each w/central cartouche enclosing named drugs
within polychrome reserve of
snakes, symbols & palm-tree
trunks on white ground, late
19th c., 11¼" h., pr. (ILLUS.
left) 247.00

FIGURAL

Child Emerging from Egg

Bear, Kummel-type, black-amethyst
glass 65.00
Bear, Kummel-type, milk white
glass 135.00
Billy club, amber glass, 10" l. 90.00
Boot, clear glass, applied top,
3½" h. 15.00
Bunch of cigars, amber glass, metal
cap 36.00
Bust of Benjamin Harrison, frosted
glass bust on black glass column,
1880-1920, 16" h. 310.00
Bust of George Washington, amber
glass partial paper label,
9 7/8" h. 65.00
Bust of Grover Cleveland, frosted &
clear glass, 10" h. 125.00
Carrie Nation, clear glass, 8¾" h. . . 36.00
Castle, clear glass, 6-sided building
w/stone walls, doors, windows &
roof, 11½" h. 12.50
Child emerging from egg, frosted
glass, head as stopper, 1880-1920,
12½" h. (ILLUS.) 330.00
Coachman, "Van Dunck's," amber
glass 110.00
Coachman, "Van Dunck's Genever,"
puce glass 275.00
Elk's tooth, milk white glass 80.00
Grant's tomb, milk white glass 300.00

Negro Waiter

Negro waiter, frosted glass w/black
glass head-stopper, 1880-1920,
12¼" h. (ILLUS.) 160.00
Pig, clear glass, "Something Good In
a Hog's," 4¼" l. 70.00
Pig, salt-glazed stoneware, incised
"Find Old Bourbon in a Hogs...
Cairo Mounds, Chicago, St. Louis,
Cincinnati," cobalt blue-highlighted
eyes, midwestern, ca. 1860,
7" l. 1,320.00
Pineapple, amber glass,
9" h. 125.00 to 200.00

Potato, sponge-daubed earthenware
pottery, blue daubing on white,
7" l. 345.00

Powder horn, Nailsea-type glass,
applied clear foot, clear w/red
loopings, 2 applied rings,
11¼" h. 250.00

Powder horn, Nailsea-type glass,
clear w/white loopings & deep cobalt blue stripes, applied clear
glass base, w/pouring ring & lip,
pontil, 13¾" l. 165.00

Pretzel, earthenware pottery, typical
twisted form, pebbled bisque
shards "salted" on translucent
mottled brown glaze, Staffordshire (repaired) 45.00

Violin, ears or tabs each side of
neck, cobalt blue glass,
8" h. .... 12.00 to 18.00

Violin, clear glass, marked "De-
pose" on front & back & "B. & D."
on front, w/original stopper,
17" h. 425.00

FLASKS

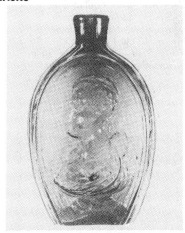

Byron - Scott Flask

*(Numbers used below refer to those used in
the McKearin's "American Glass.")*

American Eagle w/shield on oval
frame w/"Zanesville" - Cornucopia w/produce, plain lip, vertically ribbed edges, pontil, yellow-amber, ½ pt. (GII-18) 2,100.00

American Eagle w/shield & 13
stars - Bunch of Grapes, plain lip,
vertically ribbed edges, pontil,
aqua, ½ pt. (GII-56) 200.00

American Eagle w/shield on laurel
wreath & "LIBERTY" above - "Willington Glass Co. West Willington
Conn.," plain lip, smooth edges,
pontil, amber, pt. (GII-64) 60.00

American Eagle - Cornucopia, plain

lip, vertically ribbed edges, aqua,
pt. (GII-73) 100.00

"Baltimore" Monument - "Corn For
The World," ear of corn, plain lip,
smooth edges, pontil, clear green,
½ pt. (GVI-7) 750.00

"Baltimore" Monument - "Corn For
The World, " ear of corn, smooth
edges, amber, qt. (GVI-4) 335.00

Byron - Scott, plain lip, vertically
ribbed edges, olive amber, ½ pt.
(ILLUS.) 140.00

Chestnut, 16 swirled ribs, pale
green, Mantua, Ohio, 6" h. 150.00

Chestnut, 24 ribs swirled to left,
pale green, Zanesville, Ohio,
6¼" h. 105.00

Cornucopia - Urn, plain lip, vertically ribbed edges, pontil, olive
green, ½ pt. (GIII-7) 50.00

Cornucopia - Urn, plain lip, vertically ribbed edges, pontil, olive
green, pt. (GIII-4) 80.00

Double American Eagle lengthwise,
plain lip, vertically ribbed edges,
pontil, olvie amber, ½ pt.
(GII-71) 135.00

Double American Eagle w/banner &
14 stars, plain lip, horizontally
corrugated edges, pontil, aqua,
pt. (GII-24) 110.00

Double American Eagle w/shield &
banner above stellar motif, plain
lip, horizontally corrugated edges,
pontil, peacock green, qt.
(GII-26) 225.00

Double Scroll w/fleur-de-lis &
8-point star, plain lip, vertical
medial rib, pontil, strawbery
puce, ½ pt. (GIX-34) 1,250.00

Double Scroll w/two stars, plain lip,
vertical medial rib, pontil, aqua,
pt. (GIX-13) 80.00

Double Scroll w/two stars, plain lip,
vertical medial rib, pontil, green,
pt. (GIX-41) 350.00

Double Scroll w/two 6-point stars,
plain lip, vertical medial rib, pontil, dark blue aqua, qt. (GIX-2) ... 40.00

Double "Success to the Railroad"
w/horse pulling cart on rail, plain
lip, vertically ribbed edges, pontil,
olive, pt. (GV-3) 100.00

Double (elongated) Sunburst
w/twelve rays in small sunken
oval panel w/ornamental banding
at edge on vertically ribbed body,
plain lip, pontil, blue-green, ¾ pt.
(GVIII-29) 250.00

"General Jackson" above bust -
American Eagle w/shield on oval
frame w/"J.R.," plain lip, horizontally beaded edges, pontil, clear
w/amethyst tint, pt. (GI-66) 3,300.00

Hunter - Fisherman calabash, plain
lip, 4 shallow fluted edges, pontil,
amber, qt. (GXIII-4) 225.00
Hunter - Fisherman calabash, plain
lip, 4 shallow fluted edges, pontil,
blue-green, qt. (GXIII-4) 200.00

Jenny Lind Calabash Flask

"Jenny Lind" calabash, View of
Glasshouse w/plain roof, rounded
collar, heavy vertical ribbing, pon-
til, sapphire blue, qt. (ILLUS.) 2,100.00
Kossuth facing right w/"Bridgeton"
right & "New Jersey" left - Sloop
sailing left w/flying pennant,
plain lip, vertically ribbed edges,
pontil, aqua, pt. (GI-111) 200.00
"La Fayette" above bust, "T.S." below
horizontal bar - Masonic Emblems,
plain lip, horizontally corrugated
edges, pontil, light olive amber,
½ pt. (GI-84) 1,400.00
"La Fayette" above bust, horizontal
bar & "T.S." below - "De Witt Clin-
ton" above bust & "Coventry C -
T" below, plain lip, horizontally
corrugated edges, light olive am-
ber, pt. (GI-80) 650.00
"La Fayette" above bust & "Coventry
C-T" below - French Liberty Cap
on pole w/semicircle of eleven 5-
pointed stars above & "S & S" below, plain lip, finely ribbed vertical edges, pontil, olive amber, pt.
(GI-85) 325.00
"Louis Kossuth" above bust - Frig-
ate, "U.S. Steam Frigate Mississippi S. Huffsey" calabash, sloping
collar, fluted edges, pontil, emerald green olive tone, qt.
(GI-112) 1,500.00
Masonic Emblems - American Eagle
above plain oval, plain lip,
smooth edges w/single medial
rib, pontil, olive green, ½ pt.
(GIV-24) 220.00

Pitkin, 36 vertical ribs in broken
swirl to the right, sheared mouth,
pontil, clear green, 5 1/8" h. 110.00
Pitkin, 36 vertical ribs in broken
swirl to the left, sheared mouth,
pontil, clear green, 5 5/8" h. 110.00
Pitkin, 32 ribs in broken swirl to the
left, sheared mouth, pontil, grass
green, 6 5/8" h. (interior stain) . . . 210.00
Pitkin, 38 ribs in broken swirl,
blown, green, 7½" h. 250.00
Sheaf of Grain - Tree in Foliage calabash, double round collar, 4
wide vertical flutes on edges,
aqua, qt. (GXIII-46) 100.00
Sheaf of Grain - "Westford Glass
Co., Westford Conn.," plain lip,
smooth edges, olive amber, ½ pt.
(GXIII-37) 75.00
Sloop w/pennant - 8-pointed star,
plain lip, smooth edges, pontil,
deep aqua, ½ pt. (GX-9) 275.00
Sloop w/pennant - 8-pointed star,
plain lip, smooth edges, pontil,
medium green, ½ pt. (GX-9) 350.00
Soldier, "Balt. Md." - Ballet dancer,
"Chapman," plain lip, smooth
edges, pontil, deep cornflower
blue, pt. (GXIII-11) 625.00
"Summer" tree - "Winter" tree, plain
lip, smooth edges, pontil, aqua,
pt. (GX-15) 79.00
Taylor, "Rough and Ready" - Ameri-
can Eagle w/shield, "Masterson"
in semicircle above group of 13
stars, plain lip, horizontally corrugated edges w/vertical medial
rib, pontil, aqua, qt. (GI-77) 650.00
"Traveler's" above & "Companion"
below center star formed by circle
of 8 triangles, smooth edges, dark
amber, qt. (GXIV-1) 100.00
Tree in full foliage w/buds - Tree in
full foliage without buds, plain
lip, smooth edges, pontil, aqua,
qt. (GX-18) 175.00
Tree in full foliage w/buds - Tree in
full foliage without buds, plain
lip, smooth edges, pontil, cobalt
blue, qt. (GX-18) 2,600.00
"Union" above clasped hands & "L.F.
& CO" below - Eagle w/pennant
above frame w/"Pittsburgh,"
smooth edges, yellow-amber, qt.
(GXII-13) 325.00
"Union" above clasped hands - Ea-
gle flying right w/pennant w/"A &
CO," smooth edges, honey amber,
pt. (GXII-22) 300.00
"Union" above clasped hands & "F A
& Co." below - Cannon facing
right, smooth edges, aqua, ½ pt.
(GXII-42) 75.00
U.S. Army dragoon - Hound walking

right, plain lip, smooth edges, pontil, yellow, qt. (GXIII-16) 155.00

Washington - American Eagle w/shield & stars, plain lip, heavy vertical medial rib w/narrow rib each side, pontil, aqua, qt. (GI-26) 100.00

"Washington" above bust - "Jackson" above bust, plain lip, vertically ribbed edges, pontil, olive amber, ½ pt. (GI-34) 125.00

"Washington" above bust - Taylor, "Bridgeton (star) New Jersey" above, plain lip, vertically ribbed edges, pontil, yellow-green, pt. (GI-24) 500.00

Washington, "Bridgetown New Jersey" - Taylor, "Bridgetown New Jersey," plain lip, heavy vertical medial rib w/narrow rib each side & 2 narrow ribs forming outer edge of each panel, pontil, aqua, qt. (GI-25) 133.00

Washington, "The Father of His Country" - Taylor, "Gen. Taylor Never Surrenders," plain lip, smooth edges, pontil, bright green, qt. (GI-39) 138.00

Washington, "The Father of His Country" - Taylor, "A Little More Grape Captain Brass," plain neck, smooth edges, pontil, deep sapphire blue, qt. (GI-42) 1,100.00

Washington, "The Father of His Country" - Taylor, "I Have Endeavor.d To Do My Duty," plain lip, smooth edges, pontil, deep blue-green (GI-43) 415.00

INKS

"Petroleum P B & Co Writing Fluid"

Barrel-shaped, aqua mold-blown glass, embossed "Petroleum P B & Co Writing Fluid" on sides, applied lip, 2¼" l., 2½" h. (ILLUS.)........................ 155.00

Barrel-shaped, aqua mold-blown glass, embossed "W.E. Bonney" on side, tooled lip, 2½" h. 70.00

Blown-three-mold glass, olive amber, 2¼" d. (McKearin No. GIII-29) 85.00

Blown-three-mold glass, dark olive amber, 2¼" d. (McKearin No. GII-2) 95.00

Blown-Three-Mold Ink Bottles

Blown-three-mold glass, olive amber, 2¾" d., McKearin No. GII-18, each (ILLUS. of pair) 145.00

Cone-shaped, olive amber mold-blown glass, sheared lip, open pontil, 2¼" h. ....55.00 to 85.00

Cone-shaped, aqua mold-blown glass, embossed "Dovell's Patent" on sides, 2 7/8" d., 2½" h. 20.00

Cone-shaped, aqua mold-blown glass, embossed "Wood's Black Ink Portland" on sides, open pontil, 2¼" d., 2½" h. 165.00

Cottage-shaped, amber mold-blown glass, impressed "Leveson's Inks St. Louis," tooled lip, 2½" h. 185.00

Cottage-shaped, aqua mold-blown glass, tooled lip, smooth base, 2½" h. 225.00

Cylindrical, sapphire blue mold-blown glass, embossed "Harrison's Columbian Ink" on sides, rolled lip, open pontil, original label on back, 1 7/8" h. 420.00

Cylindrical, aqua mold-blown glass, embossed "W.E. Bonney" on sides, tooled lip, smooth base, 2 1/8" h. 30.00

Cylindrical, aqua mold-blown glass, embossed "J.J. Butler, Cin. O." on shoulder, rolled lip, open pontil, 2 5/8" h. 75.00

Cylindrical, aqua mold-blown glass, embossed "E. Waters Troy, NY" below fluted shoulders, applied wide flaring lip, open pontil, 2 7/8" h. 165.00

Cylindrical, blue-green mold-blown glass, embossed "Davids & Black, New York" on shoulder, applied lip, open pontil, 4 15/16" h. 85.00

Domed w/offset neck (igloo), teal blue mold-blown glass, tooled lip, 1¾" h. 160.00

Figural "Ma" & "Pa" Carter, porcelain, marked "Carter's Inx" on base, pr. ....100.00 to 130.00

Funnel-type, clear mold-blown glass,

25 vertical ribs, pontil-scarred base, 1 7/8" h. (slight wear on shoulder) 90.00

Funnel-type, amethyst mold-blown glass, 2 3/8" h. (missing rubber stopper for hole in base)........ 75.00

Master size, automatic bottle machine-made cobalt blue glass, "Carter's" cathedral w/Gothic arch "windows," ½ pt. 75.00

Master size, automatic bottle machine-made cobalt blue glass, "Carter's" cathedral w/Gothic arch "windows," qt. ....45.00 to 80.00

Master size, aqua mold-blown glass octagon, embossed "Estes N.Y. Ink" on side, applied wide lip, open pontil, 6¾" h. 160.00

Master size, aqua mold-blown glass, embossed "Barnes National Ink" on base, 8¼" h. 5.00

Master size, stoneware pottery cylinder w/pouring spout, full label "Arnold's Writing Fluid," 9" h. 75.00

Octagonal, aqua mold-blown glass, embossed "Harrison's Columbian Ink" on sides, rolled lip, open pontil, 1¾" h. 60.00

Octagonal, olive amber mold-blown glass, embossed "Farley's Ink" on sides, sheared lip, open pontil, 1¾" h. 350.00

Patented, aqua mold-blown glass, model of locomotive, embossed "Pat. Oct. 1874" on side & "Trade Mark" reverse, sheared lip, 2" h. (pinhead flake at wheel)........ 600.00

Square, aqua mold-blown glass, embossed "J.J. Butler, Cin. Ohio" on side, rolled lip, open pontil, 2½" h. ....45.00 to 95.00

Teakettle Ink

Teakettle-type fountain inkwell w/neck extending up at angle from base, brilliant green mold-blown glass 8-panel body, spout w/original cap, 1 7/8" h. (ILLUS.)........................ 925.00

Teakettle-type fountain inkwell w/neck extending up at angle from base, amethyst mold-blown glass 8-panel body, original

hinged cap on spout, 2 1/16" h. 525.00

Teakettle-type fountain inkwell w/neck extending up at angle from base, deep sapphire blue mold-blown glass, 2 5/16" h. (faint inside haze) 275.00

Triangular, aqua mold-blown glass, embossed "Allings Patent Apl. 25 1871" on side, 2 3/8 x 2½", 1 7/8" h. 40.00

Twelve-sided, aqua mold-blown glass, embossed "Butlers Ink, Cincinnati" on sides, rolled lip, open pontil, 2 3/8" h. ....120.00 to 170.00

Umbrella-type (paneled cone shape), aqua mold-blown glass, embossed "S.O. Dunbar Taunton" on side, rolled lip, open pontil, 2 3/8" h. 100.00

Umbrella-type (paneled cone shape), aqua mold-blown glass, rolled lip, open pontil, original label "National Ink Co., New York Ink.," 2 3/8" h. 65.00

MEDICINES

Carter's Spanish Mixture

Alexander's Sure Cure for Malaria, Kidney & Liver Tonic, amber...... 12.00

Allen's (Mrs.) World Hair Restorer, light strawberry puce 260.00

Anderson's (Prof: H.) Dermador, round, pontil, aqua, 5½" h. 35.00

Anti Apoplectine Paralysis Cure, aqua 25.00

Ayer's (Dr. J.C.) Ague Cure, rectangular, aqua, 7" h. 9.00

Ayer's (Dr. J.C.) Cherry Pectoral, rectangular, aqua, 7" h. 30.00

Ayer's Hair Vigor, peacock blue, 6½" h. 27.50

Barry's Tricopherous for the Skin and Hair, aqua................. 20.00

Bear Oil, pontil, aqua 10.00

Blackman's (Dr.) Genuine Healing Balsam, 8-sided, clear 35.00

Brinkerhoff's Health Restorative, New York, rectangular, pontil, olive green, 7" h. 255.00

Buchan's Hungarian Balsam of Life, London, round, aqua, 6" h. 12.00

Carter's Spanish Mixture, round, iron pontil, medium olive green (ILLUS.) 175.00

Christie's (Dr.) Magnetic Fluid, rectangular, aqua, 4 7/8" h. 25.00

Clarke's World Famed Blood Mixture, blue 18.00

Corbin's German Drops, pontil, aqua 135.00

Craig's Kidney Cure, amber, 9½" h. 145.00

Curtis' (J.L.) Compound Syrup of Sassafras, rectangular, aqua, 5" h. (dug) 35.00

Curtis' Hygeana or Inhaling Hygean Vapor and Cherry Syrup, rectangular, clear 75.00

Dalby's Carminative Indian Vegetable Specific, round, tapering towards top, pontil, aqua, 3 5/8" h. 20.00

Davenport's Eye Water, pontil, aqua 35.00

Davis (Dr. W.A.) Depurative, bluegreen 150.00

Deschens Hemoglobine, cobalt blue, 8¼" h. 20.00

DeWitt's Colic & Cholera Cure 9.00

Dodge Brothers Melanine Hair Tonic, amethyst 275.00

Dubois Pain Specific Balm, New York, 6-sided, aqua 25.00

Duncan's (Dr.) Expectorant Remedy, rectangular w/beveled edges, deep aqua-blue, 6½" h. 170.00

Elepizone, A Certain Cure For Fits & Epilepsy, rectangular w/rounded corners, aqua, 9¾" h. 40.00

Fahnestock's Vermifuge, round, open pontil, aqua, 4" h. 20.00

Fenner's (Dr. M.M.) Kidney & Backache Cure, oval, amber, 95% label, 10" h. ....20.00 to 35.00

Fenner's (Dr. M.M.) St. Vitus Dance Specific, round, aqua, 4½" h. 25.00

Foley's Kidney & Bladder Cure, Chicago, U.S.A., rectangular, amber, 4¼" h. 10.00

Foley's Kidney & Bladder Cure, Chicago, U.S.A., rectangular, amber, 7½" h. 25.00

Foord's (Dr. A.) Tonic Cordial, Cazenovia, N.Y., rectangular, pontil, aqua, 4¼" h. 85.00

Forsha's Alterative Balm, rectangular w/rounded shoulders, deep blue-aqua, 5½" h. 125.00

Franklin's Eagle Hair Restorer, Columbus, Ohio, medium amber.. 45.00

Fulham's Habits of Drink, labeled stoneware bottle, 1800, 6" h. 65.00

Glover's Imperial Blood Purifier, amber 12.00

Glover's Imperial Mange Cure, amber 12.50

Goff's (S.B.) Indian Vegetable Cough Syrup & Blood Purifier, rectangular, aqua, 5¾" h. 10.00

Graefenberg Children's Panacea 75.00

Graefenberg Dysentary Syrup 20.00

Graham's (S. Grover) Dyspepsia Cure, rectangular, clear, 6 5/8" h. 4.00

Gray's Balsam, Best Cough Cure, rectangular, aqua, 6½" h. 18.00

Graydon (Dr. T.W.), Cincinnati, O., Diseases of the Lungs, square, amber, 7¼" h. 20.00

Gregg's Constitution Life Syrup, deep aqua 15.00

Gregory's Instant Cure, open pontil, aqua 150.00

Grove's (Dr.) Anodyne for Infants, Philada., rectangular, clear, 5" h. 25.00

Guinn's Pioneer Blood Purifier, Macon, Georgia, amber, w/label 65.00

Hadlock's Celebrated Vegetable Syrup, 6-sided, aqua, 6½" h. 350.00

Hampton's Vegetable Tincture, applied mouth, tubular pontil, deep golden amber, 6 3/8" h. 225.00

Healy & Bigelow's Kickapoo Indian Sagwa, rectangular, embossed Indian, amber, 8" h. 22.50

Henry's Calcined Magnesia, clear ... 15.00

Hobson's (Dr.) Baby Cough Syrup, bimal, aqua 12.00

Hooker's (Dr.) Cough and Croup Syrup, round, aqua, 5 5/8" h. 55.00

Hunt's Remedy, Wm. E. Clarke Pharmacist, Providence, R.I., rectangular, aqua, 7¼" h. 15.00

Hunter's Pulmonary Balsam or Cough Syrup, J. Curtis Prop., Bangor, Me., rectangular, aqua, 6" h. 65.00

Hurds Cough Balsam, partial label, open pontil, aqua 37.50

Hutchinson (Dr. F.S.) Apoplexy Preventive and Paralysis Cure, aqua 45.00

Indian Cough Syrup, Warme Springs, Oregon, rectangular, clear, 7" h. 20.00

Irish's (Dr.) Indian Bone Ointment, aqua, 6½" h. 80.00

Jackson's (Dr.) Rheumatic Liniment, Philada., oval, aqua, 5¼" h. 58.00

Jayne's (Dr. D.) Alterative, rectangular, aqua, 7" h. 24.00

Jayne's (Dr. D.) Carminative Balsam,
round, aqua, 5¼" h. 10.00

Jefferson's Hair Renewer, cobalt
blue, 9" h...................... 150.00

Jones' Drops For Humors, square
w/thin flared lip 85.00

Keeley's (Dr. L.E.) Gold Cure for
Drunkenness, flat-paneled oval,
clear, 5½" h. 70.00

Kendall's (Dr. B.J.) Spavin Cure, 12-
sided, amber, 5½" h. 15.00

Kennedy's Salt Rheum Ointment,
2" h........................... 75.00

Kidder's (Mrs. E.) Cordial, Boston,
aqua 100.00

Kier (S.M.) Petroleum, Pittsburgh,
Pa., rectangular, aqua, full label,
6½" h......................... 95.00

Kilmer's (Dr.) Ocean Weed Heart
Remedy, The Blood Specific, rectangular, embossed heart, aqua,
8½" h......................... 28.00

Kitchen & Henderson's Hair Preser-
vative, rectangular, applied lip,
open pontil, clear, 6 1/8" h....... 45.00

Kodol Dyspepsia Cure, rectangular,
aqua, 6¾" h. 15.00

Lake's Indian Specific, rectangular
w/deeply beveled corners &
raised frame around embossing,
aqua-green, 8¼" h. 325.00

Laxol, A.J. White, New York, odd
triangular shape, cobalt blue,
7" h.......................... 8.00

Lindsay's Blood Searcher, aqua 32.50

McEckron's R.B. Liniment, oval,
aqua, 5 7/8" h. 67.50

McLean's (Dr. J.H.) Strengthening
Cordial & Blood Purifier, aqua 16.50

McMunn's Elixir of Opium, round,
aqua, 4½" h. 17.00

Merchant's (G.W.) Gargling Oil, rectangular, open pontil, green,
5" h.......................... 82.00

Mexican Mustang Liniment, round,
pontil, aqua, 4" h. 12.00

Miles (Dr.) New Heart Cure, rectangular, aqua, 8 3/8" h. 17.00

Miles' (Dr.) Restorative Nervine,
aqua, 8½" h. 5.00

Miller's (Dr. J.R.) Magnetic Balm,
rectangular, aqua, 4¾" h. 22.50

Moxie Nerve Food, round, aqua,
9¾" h......................... 11.00

Newton's Panacea or Purifier of the
Blood, 6-panel, pontil, olive
amber 1,500.00

One Minute Cough Cure, rectangular, aqua, 5½" h. 10.50

Osgood's India Cholagogue, New
York, rectangular, pontil, aqua,
5 3/8" h. 30.00

Packard & James Paregoric Elixir,
New York, aqua, w/label 27.50

Paine's Celery Compound, square,
aqua 16.00

Pareira's (Dr.) Great Italian Remedy,
rectangular, 5½" h. 130.00

Pinkham's (Lydia) Blood Purifier,
oval, aqua, 8½" h. 6.00

Radway's Ready Relief (R.R.R. No.
1), rectangular, aqua, 6½" h. 45.00

Roger's (Dr. A.) Liverwort, Tar and
Canchalagua, rectangular, aqua,
7½" h. 30.00

Rohrer's Wild Cherry Tonic Expectoral

Rohrer's Wild Cherry Tonic Expectoral, Lancaster, Pa., tapered square
w/roped corners, collared mouth,
iron pontil, amber, 10½" h.
(ILLUS.)...................... 175.00

Rowand's Tonic Mixture, 6-sided,
pontil, aqua, 6" h. 100.00

Sanborn's (Dr.) Celebrated Croup
Syrup, Pat. 1862, w/label 35.00

Sanford's (Dr.) Liver Invigorator, rectangular, aqua, 7¼" h. 10.00

Sanford's Radical Cure, rectangular,
cobalt blue, 7 5/8" h........... 26.00

Schenck's (J.H.) Sea Weed Tonic,
square, iron pontil, aqua,
8 3/8" h. 110.00

Scott's Emulsion of Cod Liver Oil,
rectangular, aqua, 9¼" h. 8.00

Shiloh's Consumption Cure, S.C.
Wells, Leroy, N.Y., rectangular,
aqua, 5½" h. 12.00

Sutherland Sisters Hair Tonic,
w/separate early 1900's photo of
sisters, each w/floor-length hair .. 45.00

Swaim's Panacea, sloping collared
mouth, scarred base, deep olive
amber, 7¾" h. 155.00

Thomson's Compound Syrup of Tar
and Wood Naphtha, rectangular,
aqua, 5¾" h. 67.50

Tom's Russian Liniment, square,
aqua, 4½" h. 90.00

Turlington's Balsam of Life, flared
lip, open pontil, aqua 35.00

Vaughn's Vegetable Lithontriptic Mixture

Vaughn's (Dr. G.C.) Vegetable
Lithontriptic Mixture, aqua, small
size (ILLUS.) 36.00
Warner's Safe Cure Co., round, am-
ber, 4¼" h. 24.00
Warner's Safe Cure, Melbourne,
amber, pt...................... 40.00
Warner's Safe Diabetes Cure, oval,
amber, 9¾" h.................. 42.00
Warner's Safe Kidney & Liver Cure,
oval, amber, 9¾" h. 17.00
Weaver's (Dr. S.A.) Canker & Salt
Rheum Syrup & Cerate, oval,
aqua, 9" h. 72.00
Winans Brothers' Indian Cure, em-
bossed & full label, 9¼" h. 130.00
Wishart's (Dr. L.Q.C.) Pine Tree Tar
Cordial, square, amber, w/label .. 64.00
Wishart's (Dr. L.Q.C.) Pine Tree Tar
Cordial, square, emerald green,
9½" h. 54.00
Wistar's Balsam of Wild Cherry, Cin-
cinnati, O., 8-sided, deep aqua ... 22.00
Woodward's Vegetable Tincture,
rectangular, aqua, 5¾" h. 163.00

MINERAL WATERS
Alburg Springs, Vt................. 265.00
CG & Co. Mineral Water, Lancaster,
Pa., single tapered top, iron pon-
til, green 35.00
Casper (J & H) Mineral Water, Lan-
caster, Pa., aqua, ca. 1860 .... 7.00
Champlain Spring, Highgate, Vt..... 245.00
Chemung Spring Water, embossed
Indian, clear, ½ gal. 16.00
Clarke & White, N.Y., olive green,
pt............................. 36.00
Clarke & White "C," olive green,
qt............................. 40.00
Congress & Empire "E," Saratoga,
N.Y., olive green, qt............ 32.00
Congress & Empire Spring Co.,
Saratoga, N.Y., olive green, qt. .. 27.00

Congress Spring Bottle

Congress Spring Co., "C" mono-
gram, Saratoga, N.Y., green, pt.
(ILLUS.)........................ 80.00
Congress Spring Co., Saratoga,
N.Y., dark green, qt. 40.00
Crawford (M.T.), Springfield, Union
Glass Works, Phila., Superior
Mineral Water, round w/"mug"
base, applied top, iron pontil,
deep cobalt blue 425.00
Crook (Albert) Paradise Spring
Saratoga Co., N.Y., olive green,
qt............................. 850.00
Edwards (J.B.) Mineral Water,
Columbia, Pa., single tapered top,
iron pontil, deep aqua, 1848 ..... 45.00
Gettysburg Katalysine Water, green,
qt............................. 33.00
Hathorn Spring, Saratoga, New
York, deep black amber, pt. 27.00
Highrock Congress Spring, without
twigs, citron green 48.00
Hotchkiss & Son, Saratoga, olive
green, ½ pt. 100.00
Iodine Spring Water, South Hero,
Vt............................. 225.00

Mineral Water Bottles

J. Lamppins Mineral Water, Utica
Bottling Establishment, New York,
iron pontil, light blue, ½ pt.
(ILLUS. right)................... 165.00
"Mineral Waters," light cobalt blue,
½ pt. (ILLUS. left).............. 104.50
Oak Orchard, Acid Springs, C.W.
Merchant, Lockport, N.Y.,
saratoga-type, emerald green,
qt............................. 35.00
Poland (Moses) Water, figural, milk
white glass.................... 325.00
Reiners Improved Mineral Water,
San Francisco, Cal., blob top,
smiling moon trademark, light
green......................... 37.00
Rockbridge Alum Water, Rockbridge
County, Va., blue green, ½ gal... 69.50
St. Catherine's Mineral Water, C.L.
Mather Agent, Astor House, New
York, glob top, olive brown...... 325.00
Saratoga Mineral Waters, Saratoga
Seltzer Spring Co., Saratoga, N.Y.,
olive green, qt. 875.00
Schurr (J.J.) Superior Mineral Water,
round w/"mug" base, applied top,
iron pontil, deep green......... 185.00
Stirlings Magnetic Mineral Water,
Eaton Rapids, Michigan, Saratoga,
deep amber, qt. 118.00
Thornton (Dr.), Lewisburg, Pa., Su-
perior Mineral Water, cobalt
blue.......................... 388.00
Veronica Medicinal Spring Water,
amber 8.00
Veronica Mineral Water, square
w/round shoulder, clear,
10¼" h....................... 9.00
Washington Spring Co., w/embossed
bust of Washington............. 400.00

NURSING

Aqua, mold-blown, 20 vertical ribs,
6¼" l. 45.00
Aqua, mold-blown, 24 vertical ribs,
Zanesville, 7" l. (traces of sick-
ness)......................... 95.00
Aqua (light), 18 vertical ribs,
sheared mouth, pontil, 8 7/8" l. ... 45.00
Clear, double-ended oval, embossed
"Griptite" 27.50
Clear, pressed glass, embossed
"Happy Baby" & baby each side,
8 oz.......................... 16.00
Clear, pressed glass, embossed
"Hygeia," 4 oz. 3.50
Clear, pressed glass, embossed kit-
tens, dogs & bunnies, 8 oz., set of
3 .... 30.00
Clear, pressed glass, embossed
"Sunny Boy" 17.00
Clear, pressed glass, embossed
"Temp Guard," w/thermometer in
bottle 25.00

Clear, shoe-shaped w/extended
neck, embossed "N. Wood &
Sons" 25.00
Clear, turtle-shaped, embossed
"Acme Nursing Bottle" & mono-
gram within 8-point star,
6" oval ....20.00 to 32.50
Clear, turtle-shaped, embossed "The
Alexandra Feeding Bottle" 35.00
Green (light), mold-blown, 18 verti-
cal ribs, 8 5/8" l. (minor wear &
flake on lip).................. 47.50

PEPPERSAUCES

Cathedral & Fluted Peppersauces

Cathedral arches, 4-sided, applied
mouth, smooth base, apple green,
8½" h........................ 60.00
Cathedral arches, square, "W.K.L. &
Co." vertically on one side, open
pontil, aqua 265.00
Cathedral arches, 6-sided, open
pontil, aqua 62.50
Cathedral arches, 6-sided, smooth
base, applied mouth, light to
medium green, 8¼" h. (ILLUS.
left)......................... 70.00
Fluted sides (8), applied collar, open
pontil, medium green, rare color,
8⅓" (ILLUS. right) 350.00
Medium emerald green, "E.R. Dur-
kee & Co., N.Y." & "Pat'd Feb. 17,
1874," 7¾" h.................. 30.00
Paneled sides, embossed "C.L. Stick-
ney," aqua 75.00
Ribbed, open pontil, aqua......... 22.50
Ridge-sided tapering square, rounded mouth, smooth base, deep
sage green, 8" h. 30.00
Round, long reinforced neck, cobalt
blue, 7¼" 16.00
Swirl, teal green 30.00

PICKLE BOTTLES & JARS

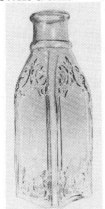

Cathedral Pickle Jar

Amber, square, embossed "Bunker
Hill" 20.00
Aqua, 4-sided, cathedral-type
w/gothic arch windows, embossed
"S.T.G.," 7½" h. 65.00
Aqua, draped shoulder effect, rolled
lip, smooth base, 8 7/8" h. 70.00
Aqua, 4-sided, cathedral-type
w/gothic arch windows, pontil,
9½" h. (flake on lip) 155.00
Aqua, round w/rounded panels, em-
bossed "Wm. Underwood & Co.
Boston" around bottom, rolled lip,
open pontil, 11½" h. (faint inside
haze) 140.00
Aqua, 4-sided, cathedral-type
w/gothic arch windows & embossed fleur-de-lis & vines,
smooth base, 11¾" h. (ILLUS.) 250.00
Aqua, 5 rounded panels, embossed
"W.K. Lewis & Co., Boston," iron
pontil 265.00
Blue-green, cathedral type w/gothic
arch windows, rolled lip, iron
pontil, 8¾" h. 170.00
Deep aqua, cathedral-type w/gothic
arch windows, rolled lip, smooth
base, 9¼" h. 55.00
Deep green, 4-sided, cathedral-type
w/gothic arch windows 150.00
Light blue-green, round w/rounded
panels, embossed "W.K. Lewis &
Co. Boston" on shoulder, rolled
lip, iron pontil 215.00
Light green, 4-sided, cathedral-type
w/gothic arch windows, pontil,
11¾" h. (minor sickness) 105.00
Light to medium green, 4-sided,
cathedral-type w/gothic arch windows, rolled lip, smooth base,
original lead label "W.H. Davis &
Co., Boston, Gerkins, Pickles,
Sauces," 11¾" h. 170.00
Medium green, 4-sided, cathedral-

type w/gothic arch windows,
rolled lip, smooth base, 6¼" h. . . 90.00
Medium green, 4-sided, cathedral-
type w/gothic arch windows,
polished pontil, 13¾" h. 525.00
Teal blue, 4-sided, cathedral-type
w/gothic arch windows,
13½" h. 185.00

"Shaker Brand" Pickle Jar

Yellow tinged w/olive tones, embossed "Shaker Brand, E.D. Pet-
tengill & Co., Portland, Me,"
heavy folded lip, smooth base,
slight wear inside mouth,
5 1/8" h. (ILLUS.) 325.00

POISONS
Amber, triangular, embossed "Poi-
son" in 1½" letters, 3" h. 15.00
Blue, embossed "Not To Be
Taken" 7.50
Cobalt blue, embossed "Not To Be
Taken," 4 1/16" rectangle 10.00
Cobalt blue, irregular hexagon, 4
point stars, embossed "Not To Be
Taken," 5¼" 18.00
Cobalt blue, triangular, embossed
"Owl Drug Company" 52.00
Cobalt blue, 3-sided 10.00
Green, embossed "Not To Be
Taken" 27.50

SODAS & SARSAPARILLAS
Albuquerque Bottling Works, soda,
Hutchinson stopper (rough lip &
cloudy) 70.00
Allen (The) Sarsparilla Co., rectan-
gular, aqua, 7½" h. 30.00
Arizona Bottling Works, Phoenix,
Arizona, soda, Hutchinson
stopper 90.00
Babb & Co., San Francisco, Cal.,
soda, blob top, green 60.00
Babcock (J.V.) Gold Medal Sar-
saparilla, embossed in indented
panels, amber, 9" h. 32.50
Bakers (Dr. Ira) Honduras Sar-
saparillas, aqua . . . . 75.00 to 95.00

Bay City Soda Water, San Francisco,
blob top, cobalt blue 70.00
Biedenharn Candy Co., soda, aqua.. 30.00
Bristols Sarsaparilla, rectangular,
aqua 45.50
Buffum Sarsaparilla & Lemon Mineral Water, Pittsburg, 10-sided, applied lip, iron pontil, deep cobalt
blue 725.00
Buffum Sarsaparilla & Lemon Mineral Water, Pittsburg, 10-sided, applied lip, iron pontil, yellow-
green 1,100.00
C. & K. Eagle Works, Sac City, soda,
blob top, blue 69.00
California Soda Works, H. Ficken,
San Francisco, soda, light green .. 250.00
Canada Dry, marigold Carnival
glass.....................5.00 to 10.00
Canada Dry Sparkling Orangeade,
marigold Carnival glass 28.00
City Ice & Bottling Works,
Georgetown, Texas, soda, Hutch-
inson stopper, light green....... 18.00
Coburn Lange & Co. XX Boston,
soda, cobalt blue.............. 85.00
Coca-Cola, Biedenharn Candy Co.,
Vicksburg, Miss., Hutchinson
stopper 150.00
Coca-Cola, Biedenharn Candy Co.,
Vicksburg, Miss., crown top
type 100.00
Coca-Cola, Chattanooga, Hutchinson
stopper 425.00
Coca-Cola, Cleveland, Ohio, straight
sides, amber 25.00
Coca-Cola, Dayton, Ohio, "Act of
Congress," amber 70.00
Coca-Cola, Greenwood, Miss.,
straight sides, amber 41.00
Coca-Cola, Norfolk, Va., straight
sides, amber 30.00
Coca-Cola, Rockwood, Tenn.,
straight sides, amber 60.00
Coca-Cola, Williamsport, Pennsylva-
nia, straight sides, amber 150.00
Codd-stoppered (internal marble
stopper), amber............... 22.00
Codd-stoppered, green 50.00
Denhalter Bottling Co., Salt Lake
City, Utah, soda, Hutchinson
stopper 15.00
Dennis (S.C.) & Co., Hilton Head,
S.C., soda, green 175.00
Distilled Soda Water Co. of Alaska,
Hutchinson stopper 375.00
Dixon Soda Works, soda, Hutchinson
stopper, aqua................. 17.50
Dr. Pepper, Good For Life, 10-2-4,
Baltimore, Maryland, soda 4.00
Empire Soda Works, San Francisco,
soda, blob top, aqua 50.00
Finkler, LaSalle, Ill., soda, cobalt
blue 225.00

Foleys Sarsaparilla, amber 45.00
Gillette (T.W.), New Haven, soda,
iron pontil, emerald green 125.00
Henry Kuck, Savannah, Ga., soda,
blob top, green (dug)........... 24.00
Hoffman Bros., Chicago, soda,
Hutchinson stopper, ice blue 14.00
J.N., Boise, Idaho, soda, Hutchinson
stopper 58.00
Knauss & Lichtenwallner, Allentown,
Pa., soda, squat, smooth base,
double tapered top, blue (dug) ... 40.00

Knicker Bocker Soda Water

Knicker Bocker (S.S.) Soda Water,
164 18th St., N.Y. 184, 10-sided,
applied lip, iron pontil, cobalt
blue, slight wear & burst bubble
one panel (ILLUS.) 95.00
Krause Bottling Co., Baltimore,
Maryland in slug plate, soda,
eagle 6.00
Leon's Sarsaparilla, aqua 55.00
Lester Soda Water, St. Louis, pontil,
green (dug)................... 75.00
Marble-stoppered, embossed,
aqua 11.00
McGrann (Michel), soda, squat,
olive green, ca. 1860 .... 17.00
McLaughlin (J.), soda, iron pontil,
green (small lip bruise) 20.00
Northrup Sturgis Company, Portland,
Oregon, soda, Hutchinson
stopper 15.00
Owens (J.R.), Parkesburg, Pa.,
soda, deep blue-green.......... 35.00
Pacific Bottling Works, Tacoma,
Washington, soda, Hutchinson
stopper, aqua, 6 7/8" h. 16.00
Palliser (D.), Mobile, Ala., soda,
tombstone slug plate, Hutchinson
stopper 18.00
Pepsi Cola, New Bern, amber, 8" h.
(dug)...................... 40.00
Pioneer Soda Works, San Francisco,
soda, blob top, aqua 15.00
Queen Bottling Works, Sioux City, S.

Dak. in slug plate, soda, Hutchinson stopper, aqua 20.00

Queen City Bottling Works, Marion, Indiana, soda, Hutchinson stopper 7.00

Rocky Mountain Bottling Co., Butte, Mont., soda, Hutchinson stopper, aqua 40.00

Ryan (John), soda, dark strawberry red (polished w/lip chip - first of its type found in 1964) 3,000.00

Ryan (John), 1866, Augusta, Ga., soda, cobalt blue 125.00

Ryan (John) Cider, light olive green 625.00

Ryan (John) Excelsior Ginger Ale, 1852, Savannah, Ga. 50.00

Schille (P.), Columbus, Ohio in arch, P.O.C. on reverse, soda, honey amber, w/bail, qt. 40.00

Scammon Bottling Works, Scammon, Kansas, soda, Hutchinson stopper 20.00

Schmidt (F.), Leadville, Colorado, soda, Hutchinson stopper 20.00

Seitz & Bro., Easton, Pa., soda, 8-sided, smooth base, blue (dug) 22.50

Seitz & Bro., Easton, Pa., soda, squat, 7-Up green 25.00

Seven-Up, Salt Lake City, Utah, swimsuit girl 5.00

Smexey & Brandt, soda, slug plate, iron pontil (dug) 17.00

H.S. Smith Soda Bottle

Smith (H.S.), Auburn, N.Y., ten-pin shape, applied lip, smooth base, cobalt blue (ILLUS.) 475.00

Smith (H.T.) Soda Water Mfg., Toronto, blob top, dated 1867 . . . . 100.00

Smith & Forheringham Soda Water,

St. Louis, This Bottle Is Never Sold, 10-sided, applied lip, iron pontil, cobalt blue 550.00

Southwestern Bottling Co., Tulsa, I.T. (Indian Territory), soda, Hutchinson stopper, clear 175.00

Sprenger (J.J.), Lancaster, Pa., soda, iron pontil, green 40.00

Tampa Bottling Works, Tampa, Fla., soda, applied crown top, aqua . . . 4.00

Twitchell, soda, emerald green (dug) 35.00

Walter & Brother, Reading, Pa., soda, squat, blue-green 32.00

Wise (James), Allentown, Pa., soda, cobalt blue 85.00

WHISKEY & OTHER SPIRITS

Picnic Beer Bottle

Beer, "ABCM Co. 2, Belleville, Ill.," blob top, cobalt blue 50.00

Beer, "Albert Stoehr Milwaukee Lager, Manchester, N.H.," blob top, amber 13.50

Beer, "Bayview Brewing Co., Seattle, Wash.," blob top, olive green, qt. (dug) 75.00

Beer, "Budweiser," patent No. 6376, aqua, pt. (dug) 20.00

Beer, "Columbus Weiss Beer, Chicago," 10-paneled sides, amber, w/Lightning stopper 11.00

Beer, "Des Moines Brewing Co., Des Moines, Iowa," picnic size, amber, w/Lightning stopper . . . . . . 16.00 to 30.00

Beer, "Dr. Cronks Sarsaparilla Beer," stoneware pottery, qt. 25.00

Beer, "Elgin National Brewery," amber, w/original Lightning stopper 10.00

Beer, "Fredericksburg Brewery, San Jose," blob top, red-amber, qt. . . . 50.00

Beer, "Fredericksburg, San Francisco," blob top, green, pt. 20.00

Beer, "Gambrinus Bottling Co., San
Francisco," blob top, amber, qt. . .   10.00
Beer, "Gerst Brewing Co., Nashville,
Tn.," stoneware pottery 60.00
Beer, "Ironwood Brewing, Ironwood,
Mich.," picnic size, amber,
w/Lightning stopper (ILLUS.) 30.00
Beer, "James Kane, Wilkesbarre
Hill, Pa.," blob top, deep cobalt
blue, tall 750.00
Beer, "John Stanton Brewing Co.,
Troy, N.Y.," blob top, emerald
green 25.00
**Beer, "Kings," embossed, original
paper labels, picnic size, amber,
20" h.** 90.00
Beer, "Los Angeles Brewing Co.,"
eagle on shield, blob top, amber,
qt. 15.00

Beer Bottle of 1940's

Beer, "Red Stripe Lager," amber,
w/labels (ILLUS.) 12.00
Beer, "Rochester N.Y. Glass Works,"
amber, 9½" h. 10.00
Beer, "Rolling Rock," embossed
horse, green, dated 1939 . . . .   18.00
Beer, "Sandkyhlers Weiss," amber . .   22.00
Beer, "Schlitz," royal ruby,
32 oz. . . . . .22.50 to 30.00
Beer, "Tacoma Bottling Co., San
Francisco, Cal.," blob top, amber,
qt. 8.00
Beer, "Tahoe Beer" 15.00
Beer, "Western Brewery," w/label,
64 oz. 22.00
Case gin, "African," olive amber . . .   18.00
Case gin, embossed, dark amber . . .   24.00
Case gin, "V. Hoytema & Co.," ta-
pered, dark olive green, whittled,
9¼" h. 32.50
Case gin, "E. Kiderlen," tapered,
dark olive green, whittled,
9¼" h. 42.50
Case gin, "P. Loopuyt & Co., Dis-
tillers, Schiedam," dark olive
green, 9" h. 20.00

Case gin, "S" on base, green,
10" h. 15.00
Case gin, "A. Van Hoboken, Rotter-
dam," olive green, 9" h. 15.00
Case gin, free-blown, olive amber,
9½" h. 52.50
Gin, "Elbart Dry Gin," cork stopper,
aqua 6.00
Gin, "Van Den Bergh & Co.," ap-
plied seal w/bell, olive green,
10½" h. 75.00
Liqueur, "White Seal Blackberry Li-
queur, T. J. Pendergast Wholesale
Liquor Co., Kansas City, Missouri,"
half-pint 60.00

Early Rum Bottle

Rum (beer or ale), blown in 3-part
mold, applied lip, dark olive
green, ca. 1860, 8¾" h. (ILLUS.) . .   70.00
Schnapps, "Schiedam Aromatic,"
ground pontil, yellow-green,
8" h. 60.00
Schnapps, "Udolpho Wolfe's," pontil,
olive green 50.00
Schnapps, "Udolpho Wolfe's," straw-
berry orange, 8" h. 30.00
Schnapps, "Udolpho Wolfe's,"
yellow-amber 30.00
Whiskey, "Belle of Anderson," em-
bossed "Old Fashion Handmade
Sour Mash" within 6-point star,
milk white 67.00
Whiskey, "Beiser & Fishler," figural
pig, golden amber, 9¾" l. 375.00
Whiskey, "E. & B. Beven IXL Valley
Whiskey," double collared mouth,
golden amber, 7½" h. 1,100.00
Whiskey, "A.M. Bininger & Co., 38
Broadway, N.Y., Old Kentucky
Bourbon," barrel-shaped w/rings
above marked center band, gold-
en amber, 8" h. 186.00
Whiskey, "A.M. Bininger & Co.,"
handled urn, golden amber,
9" h. 900.00

Whiskey, "Bininger Old London Dock Gin," amber, pt. 42.50

Whiskey, "Buchanan's Absolutely Pure Malt Whiskey," cannon barrel shape, light golden amber 9 1/8" h. 350.00

Whiskey, "The Campus, Gossler Bros. Prop's, Columbus Av., N.Y.," applied handle, collared mouth, smooth base, amber, 9½" h. 45.00

Whiskey, "Chapin & Gore," embossed "Hawley Glass Co." on base, inside-threaded top, amber, 4/5 qt. 75.00

Whiskey, "The F. Chevalier Castle Whiskey, San Francisco, Cal.," amber, 4/5 qt. 42.50

Whiskey, "J.F. Cutter, San Francisco, Cal.," embossed shield, amber ... 9.50

Whiskey, "Cutty Sark," green, 18" .. 27.50

Whiskey, "Dallemand & Co. Inc. Brandy," blob neck, amber, 11¼" h. 9.00

"Deer Lick Whiskey" Bottle

Whiskey, "Deer Lick," clear flask w/paper label, pt. (ILLUS.) 12.00

Whiskey, "Delmonico Club Rye Whiskey, Jos Myers Sons, 1868, Philadelphia," squat cylinder, honey amber, qt. 75.00

Whiskey, "Duffy Malt," golden amber, pt. 10.00

Whiskey, "Duffy Malt - Rochester," amber, qt. 8.50

Whiskey, "J.H. Duker & Bro., Quincy, Ill.," pumpkin seed w/web design, clear, ½ pt. 40.00

Whiskey, "Evans & Ragland Old Ingledew Whiskey, LaGrange, Ga.," amber 250.00

Whiskey, "J.T. Gayen, Altona,"

cannon-shaped, collared mouth, smooth base, amber, ¾ qt. 695.00

Whiskey, "Golden Wedding," marigold Carnival Glass, 1/10 pt. 54.00

Whiskey, "I.W. Harper Gold Medal Whiskey," cream-glazed pottery, square 37.50

Whiskey, "J.F.T. & Co., Philad.," vertical ribbed melon shape, applied handle, collared mouth, open pontil, yellow-amber, 6 7/8" h. 315.00

Whiskey, "Julius May Fine Whiskey and Wine, Brunswick, Ga.," strap flask, aqua 130.00

Whiskey, "McQuade's M.D. Whiskey, Utica, N.Y.," cylinder, amber, qt. 35.00

Whiskey, "Millionaires Club, Philadelphia," olive green, qt. 20.00

Whiskey, "Mount Vernon Rye," amber, dated 1890, fifth 19.00

Whiskey, "Ricketts & Co. Glassworks Bristol," seal bottle, seal w/horse head & initials "A.G.C.," scarred base, dark olive amber, 11" h. ... 85.00

Whiskey, "J. Rieger & Co., Kansas City," cylinder, fluted neck, clear 10.00

Whiskey, "Roth & Co., San Francisco," cylinder, aqua, fifth 20.00

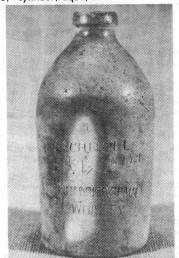

"J.C. Schnell" Pottery Jug

Whiskey, "J.C. Schnell Sour Mash Kiln Dried Grain Whiskey," stoneware pottery jug, 8" h. (ILLUS.) ... 80.00

Whiskey, "U.S.A. Hosp. Dept.," collared mouth, smooth base, yellow olive, qt. 75.00

Whiskey, "Whartons Whiskey 1850 Chestnut Grove," flask, slug plate, cobalt blue 250.00

Whiskey, "Wilson, Fairbanks & Co.
Old Bourbon," aqua, pt. 35.00
Wine, "Duroy Port Wine, Sandusky,
Ohio," jug-shaped, qt. 80.00
Wine, squat onion form, free-blown
dark amber, ca. 1730, 7½" h. 350.00
Wine demijohn, apple-shaped, open
pontil, sea green, 4-gal. 98.00

(End of Bottle Section)

BOY & GIRL SCOUT ITEMS

*Scout rules and regulations, handbooks and
accouterments have changed with the times.
Early items associated with these movements
are now being collected. A sampling follows.*

BOY SCOUT

Boy Scout Telescope

Axe, hand-type, "Bridgeport Boy
Scout" model $30.00
Book, "The Boy Scouts at the Pana-
ma Canal," by Lt. Howard Payson,
published by Hurst & Co., 1913 ... 10.00
Book, "The Boy Scouts Hike Book,"
illustrated by Norman Rockwell,
1913 .... 30.00
Book, "The Boy Scouts in a Trapper's
Camp," by Thornton W. Burgess,
Penn Publishing Company, 1915 .. 10.00
Bugle, brass, "Conn" 35.00
Calendar, 1931, Norman Rockwell
illustration.................... 90.00
Camera, Seneca Model 2A, original
box 70.00
Compass, silver, pocket watch
shape, ca. 1930 .... 17.50
Flashlight, brass, "Eveready" 15.00
Handbook, 1911, August, 400 pp. ... 150.00
Handbook, 1926, 512 pp. 45.00
Handbook for Patrol Leaders, 1949.. 8.00
Handbook for Scoutmasters,
1920 ....20.00 to 35.00
Knife, pocket-type, Remington No.
RS 4233, 4-blade, scalloped bolster
ends (minor rust)............... 135.00
Lamp, clip-on type, polished brass,
shade engraved "Scouts 1928" 40.00

Magazine, "Scouting," 1930,
August 6.00
Mess kit........................ 15.00
Neckerchief, "1939 New York
World's Fair"................... 50.00
Neckerchief, "1950 Jamboree,"
silk 22.50
Neckerchief slide, metal 5.00
Paperweight, cast iron, Boy Scout
logo 22.00
Pocket patch, "1953 Jamboree" 25.00
Ring, sterling silver............... 20.00
Signal set, battery-operated, ca.
1948, original box ....15.00 to 20.00
Stationery, "1937 Jamboree," origi-
nal box 24.00
Sun watch, "Ansonia," original
box 125.00
Telescope, metal, gold finish
w/black bands & emblem, 6x
lens, opens to 14", original box
(ILLUS.)...................... 18.00
Tie rack, wooden 20.00
Vest, w/"1935 Jamboree" patch & 18
miscellaneous patches 125.00
Wrist watch, "Ingersoll,"
1930's ....75.00 to 150.00

GIRL SCOUT
Badge, Proficiency Badge series,
"Horsewoman," square, khaki 10.00
Book, "Campward Ho," 1920,
hardbound..................... 18.00
Book, "Girl Scout Game Book,"
1929 .... 10.00
Bracelet, gold-plated 6.00
Catalogue, "Girl Scout Equipment,"
1934, 34 pages (some cover
wear) 12.00
Compass, blue Bakelite case,
1930's 12.00
Game, card-type, "Trupe," 1939 .... 20.00
Handbook, 1921, light brown soft
cover 20.00
Handbook for "Brownie" leaders,
1930, "Brown Book for Brown
Owls" 15.00
Patch, "First Class," grey & green on
red ground 10.00
Pin, "Brownie" leader, enameled
brown owl 50.00
Pin, "Brownie" wings, multi-
colored....................... 12.50
Pin, badge-type, "Community Serv-
ice," 1930 .... 10.00
Pin, "Golden Eaglet," 10k gold 250.00
Poster, Girl Scout w/puppy, ca.
1935, 17 x 22" 35.00
Ring, gold-filled 18.00
Uniform, "Brownie," w/insignia &
hat, 1930, 2 pcs. 50.00

BREWERIANA

"Miller High Life" Bottle Opener

Beer is still popular in this country but the number of breweries has greatly diminished. More than 1,900 breweries were in operation in the 1870's but we find fewer than 40 supplying the demands of the country a century later. The small local brewery has either been absorbed by a larger company or forced to close, unable to meet the competition. Advertising items used to promote the various breweries, especially those issued prior to prohibition, now attract an ever growing number of collectors. The breweriana items listed are a sampling of the many items available. Also see BOTTLE OPENERS and BOTTLES.

Ale set: 12½" h. tankard pitcher & 6 mugs; pottery, "Leisey Brewing Co., Peoria, Ill." on green glazed ground, 7 pcs. $350.00

Ash tray, "Jax Beer," ceramic, brown........................ 18.00

Booklet, "Pictorial Trip Through Anheuser-Busch Brewery, 1937," 28 pp......................... 20.00

Bottle opener, "Ballentine Ale," metal, 3 ring logo at end of handle 4.00

Bottle opener, "Gilt Top Beer, Spokane, Wash.," metal, leg-shaped 25.00

Bottle opener, "Gold Nugget Beer," brass 75.00

Bottle opener, "Miller High Life Beverages," metal (ILLUS.) 4.00

Calendar, 1897, "Iroquois Brewing Co.," Indian pictured 250.00

Calendar, 1907, "Pabst Extract," beautiful lady in red pictured..... 175.00

Can, cone-top, "Bavarian Beer," 12 oz....................... 52.00

Can, cone-top, "Carling's Black Label," 12 oz.................... 32.00

Can, cone-top, "Eslinger's Premium Ale," 32 oz. 78.00

Can, cone-top, "Iroquois Beer," 12 oz...................... 45.00

Can, cone-top, "Piel's," blue & gold, 16 oz....................... 48.00

Can, cone-top, "Schmidt's Tiger Brand Ale," qt. 75.00

Can, flat-top, "Krueger Beer," 12 oz........................... 16.00

Can, flat-top, "Schaefer," 12 oz. 10.00

Can, flat-top, "Westover," 12 oz. ... 68.00

Card case, "Anheuser-Busch," leather, early 1900's 5.00

Coaster, "A.B.C. Beer," cardboard, 4" 12.00

Coaster, "Dick's Beer," cardboard... 12.00

Coaster, "Eblings" 20.00

Coaster, "Yuengling," 3¾" sq. 22.00

Corkscrew, "Anheuser-Busch," bottle-shaped w/corkscrew inside, ca. 1892 ....25.00 to 35.00

Corkscrew, "Lemp Beer," bullet-shaped 25.00

Counter display, "Apache Beer," chalkware model of an Indian w/full headdress, 12" h. 100.00

Counter display, "Argonaut Beer," cardboard, easel-type w/bottle, prospector, mule & Golden Gate Bridge pictured, 1930's 55.00

Counter display, "Blatz Beer," chalkware figure of a Bavarian waitress dancing on beer keg, 19" h. 200.00

Fan, "Schlitz," cardboard 18.00

Foam scraper, "American Brewing Co., N.Y." 28.00

Foam scraper, "Burkhardt's"........ 30.00

Foam scraper, "Rheingold" 10.00

Foam scraper, "Trommer's," aluminum 23.00

Knife, pocket-type, "West End Brewing Co., leg-shaped, 2-blade 75.00

Match holder, "Goebel Brewing Co.," stoneware pottery 245.00

Match holder, "Greensburg Brewing Co.," earthenware pottery 150.00

Match holder, "Joliet Citizens Brewing Co.," mug shape, factory pictured 95.00

Match safe, "Anheuser-Busch," brass, "A" w/eagle ......65.00 to 80.00

Match safe, "Schlitz," leather-covered metal w/chrome trim 65.00

Mortar & pestle, "Coors, U.S.A.," ironstone, miniature............ 25.00

Mug, "Arrow Beer," stoneware pottery, tan 14.00

Mug, "Hamm's," Red Wing pottery .. 35.00

Mug, "Royal Pilsener Kansas City," stoneware pottery.............. 125.00

Mug, "Waukesha Old Ale," pewter 125.00

Pennant, "Dick & Brothers, Bock Beer, Quincy, Ill.," felt 60.00

Pilsener glass, "Good Old Leisey's," annniversary issue, clear glass w/enameled lettering 95.00

Pilsener glass, "Old Tavern Lager Beer, Warsaw, Illinois," clear glass w/red enameled lettering .. 7.00

Pilsener glass, "Washington Beer," clear glass w/frosted shell & bust of George Washington........... 150.00

Postcard, "Budweiser," Clydesdale
  horses pictured, 1940-50, double-
  size 15.00
Sign, "A.B.C. Beer," self-framed tin,
  bulldog staring at bottle, 1900,
  24 x 20" 475.00
Sign, "Falstaff," tin, "The Peace-
  maker," 1910, 31 x 23" 450.00
Sign, "Hamm's Beer," graniteware,
  eagle pictured, 1910, 14" 235.00

"Imported Pilsener" Tin Sign

Sign, "Imported Pilsener," lithographed tin, young woman carrying steins of beer, embossed-
  curled corners, Meek Company
  lithographers, 1901-09 (ILLUS.) 350.00
Sign, "Lemp Beer," self-framed tin,
  Sir John Falstaff seated at desk
  w/factory visible through
  window 1,750.00
Sign, "Schlitz," self-framed tin,
  Statue of Liberty pictured, 1941 . . . 250.00
Sign, "Yuengling's," tin, eagle on
  keg pictured, 13½ x 6" 105.00

Mettlach Stein

Stein, "Anheuser-Busch Brewing
  Assn.," etched & printed under
  glaze, inlaid pewter lid w/inscrip-
  tion, Mettlach, ½ liter (ILLUS.) . . . 2,310.00
Stein, "Citizens Brewery, Joliet,"
  embossed mountain scene w/peo-
  ple & animals, Germany,
  1½ liter 175.00
Tap knob, "Budweiser Light,"
  plastic 7.00
Tap knob, "Fitzgerald Bros. Brewing
  Co. Burgomaster Beer" 15.00
Tap knob, "Old
  Griesedieck" . . . . .45.00 to 60.00
Tap knob, "Pabst," wooden,
  12" h. 10.00
Tap knob, "Schlitz," figural semi-
  nude woman seated on world
  globe, 12" h. 20.00
Tap knob & pump, "Fredericksburg,
  San Jose" on knob, nickel-plated
  brass, pre-prohibition 175.00
Vienna Art tin plate, "Anheuser-
  Busch Malt Nutrine," beautiful
  woman pictured 49.00
Vienna Art tin plate, "Frank Jones,
  Portsmouth, N.H." 65.00
Watch fob, "Phoenix Brewery" 37.50

BRONZES

Nude Maiden after Carrier-Belleuse

*Small bronzes, used as decorative adjuncts
in today's homes, continue to attract interest.
Particularly appealing to collectors today are
works by "Les Animaliers," the 19th century French school of sculptors who turned to
animals for their subject-matter. These, to-*

gether with figures in the Art Deco and Art Nouveau taste, are very popular with collectors and available in a wide price range.

Alonzo, Dominique, figure of a Dutch flowerseller wearing a bonnet, her arms filled w/flowers, gilt-bronze & ivory, early 20th c., 8¼" h. $412.50

Barrias, Louis-Ernest, figure of a female cellist in full-length low-cut gown w/cello in hand, brown patina, late 19th c., 38" h. 3,300.00

Bartholdi, Frederic-Auguste, figure of a peasant girl w/ribbon-tied long braid reaching upward & presenting flowers to the carved oak memorial "France," on bronze base, brown patina, late 19th c., 19" h. 1,760.00

Barye, Antoine-Louis, model of a fawn, medium brown patina, late 19th c., 8¾" h. 770.00

Barye, Antoine-Louis, model of a lion walking, rectangular base w/detailed rocky terrain, black-green patina, late 19th c., 12" l. . . 770.00

Bonheur, Isidore Jules, model of a stag on rocky ground, golden brown patina, late 19th c., 9¾" l. 440.00

Boucher, Alfred, figure of a nude woman reclining against a pillow, green patina, ca. 1900, 24" l. 880.00

Carrier-Belleuse, Albert Ernest, figure of a nude maiden walking through bullrushes, an overturned amphora at her feet, brown patina, ca. 1880, 30" h. (ILLUS.) 3,520.00

Chapu, Henri Michel Antoine, figure of Joan of Arc seated on naturalistic ground, dark brown patina, 19th c., 18 5/8" h. 1,100.00

Chiparus, Demetre, figure of a woman frolicking, gilt-bronze & ivory, mottled & striated green & orange marble stand w/metal base, ca. 1930, 15¼" h. 2,530.00

Silvered Bronze Panthers

Decour, group of 2 menacing panthers, silvered bronze, cast from a model by Decour & inscribed Decour, black onyx base trimmed in green onyx, 19½" l. (ILLUS.) 1,320.00

Dubois, Paul, figure of Harlequin w/left leg forward & back arched, holding slapstick in his right hand,

a mandolin slung over his shoulder, on rectangular plank-cast base w/perpendicular supports, brown patina, late 19th c., 32" h. 1,100.00

Gardet, Georges, models of Great Danes reclining, each w/studded collar, rectangular base, dark brown patina, early 20th c., 17¼" l., pr. 2,200.00

Russian Bronze Group after Lanceray

Lanceray, Evgenie, group of a goatherd pursuing a goat, Chopin factory mark & Finance Ministry stamp, late 19th c., 10" l. (ILLUS.) 1,210.00

Mene, Pierre-Jules, model of an Arabian stallion, brown patina, late 19th c., 15¼" l., 12¼" h. . . .2,200.00

Moigniez, Jules, model of a Bloodhound on the scent, brown patina, late 19th c., 22" l. 1,650.00

Moigniez, Jules, model of a pheasant standing upon a rocky base, coppery patina, late 19th c., 13" l. 440.00

Moreau, Mathurin, figure of a farm girl holding basket of flowers over one arm & rooster in the other, standing on rocky base, brown patina, on bronze revolving base, late 19th c., overall 16 3/8" h. 605.00

Pautrot, Ferdinand, group of a partridge feeding her chick, golden patina, late 19th c. 770.00

Ple, Henri-Honore, figure group, lady & gentleman dancing, she in bodice dress w/fan in her right hand, he wearing breeches, each w/arm held high & embracing the other, brown patina, early 20th c., 26" h. 2,310.00

Preiss, Fritz, figure of an autumn dancer in short blue-green waisted tunic w/long sweeping train & turbaned cap, leaping into the air as she dances, cold-painted bronze & ivory, green & black onyx socle

& octagonal base, ca. 1930, overall
14¾" h. 4,400.00
Vidal, Louis, model of a snarling lion
　stalking, rectangular base, brown-
　ish green patina, late 19th-early
　20th c., 25¼" l. 1,045.00

Bust of "Phryne"

Villanis, Emmanuele, bust of
　"Phryne," young girl w/her hair
　caught up en chignon & a band
　encircling her brow, socle base,
　brown patina, impressed Societe
　des Bronzes de Paris seal, ca.
　1900, 25" h. (ILLUS.) 990.00

BROWNIE COLLECTIBLES

Illustration with Brownies

*The Brownies were creatures of fantasy
created by Palmer Cox, artist-author, in 1887.
Early in this century, numerous articles with
depictions of or in the shape of Brownies appeared.*

Basket, silverplate, Brownies decor,
　w/chocolate advertising, James
　W. Tufts $140.00
Book, "The Adventures of a Brown-
　ie," by Palmer Cox, published by
　Mulock, 1893, 6½ x 8½",
　168 pp. 22.50
Book, "The Brownie Clown of
　Brownie Town," published by
　Century Co. 50.00
Book, "The Brownie Primer," by
　Palmer Cox, color illustrations,
　1901, 7 x 10", 74 pp. 35.00
Book, "The Brownies at Home," by
　Palmer Cox, 1st edition 87.00
Book, "The Brownies in the Philip-
　pines," published by Century
　Co. 75.00
Book, "The Brownies Latest Adven-
　ture," published by Century Co. . . 75.00
Butter pat, china, Brownies (2) danc-
　ing decor, gold lustre trim,
　2¾" d. 15.00
Cup, silverplate, engraved Brownies
　decor 95.00
Demitasse spoons, sterling silver,
　Brownies decor, set of 6 in
　presentation box 100.00
Dolls, printed cloth, uncut, 1892, set
　of 6 . . . . 475.00
Napkin ring, silverplate, figural
　Brownie beside ring engraved
　w/florals, ornate 155.00
Needles, "1893 Columbian Exposi-
　tion," w/Palmer Cox Brownie
　Policeman on package 45.00
Paper doll, w/Lion Coffee advertis-
　ing reverse 15.00
Paperweight, mushroom-shaped, 3
　intaglio Brownies molded in frost-
　ed base, 2¾" d. 135.00
Plate, china, Brownies decor, Cook
　& Hancock, Trenton, New Jersey,
　7" d. 55.00
Plate, silverplate, Brownies decor
　border, 8½" d. 42.00
Stein, relief Brownies (12) at various
　pursuits, figural Brownie Police-
　man finial, multicolored, ½ liter . . 600.00
Thermometer, silverplate, full figure
　Brownie standing beside oak leaf
　trimmed thermometer on domed
　base, Pairpoint Mfg. Co., 4 x 3" . . 75.00
Toothpick holder, silverplate, full
　figure Brownie standing beside
　holder, Pairpoint Mfg. Co. 145.00

BUSTER BROWN COLLECTIBLES

Buster Brown Book

Buster Brown was a comic strip created by Richard Outcault in the New York Herald in 1902. It was subsequently syndicated and numerous objects depicting Buster (and often his dog, Tige) were produced.

Advertising card, "Buster Brown Shoes," Halloween scene w/Buster & Tige, 1909 . . . . $35.00

Book, "Buster Brown's Amusing Capers," by Richard Outcault, 1906, published by Cupples & Leon (ILLUS.) 45.00

Book, "Buster Brown - My Resolutions," by Richard F. Outcault, 1906, published by Frederick A. Stokes Co., 68 pp. 60.00

Camera, Anthony Scovill Co., in original lithographed cardboard box 290.00

Compact, Buster Brown & Tige decor 50.00

Creamer, china, Buster Brown & Tige decor 38.00

Cup, china, Buster Brown decor 65.00

Fork, silverplate, figural Buster Brown handle 18.00

Knife, pocket-type, bone handle, advertising "Buster Brown Shoes" . . . 45.00

Mask, paper, Buster Brown 10.00

Mug, china, Buster Brown & Tige decor 95.00

Mustard can, "Buster Brown Mustard," w/lithographed paper label of Buster & Tige, 2½" h. 65.00

Paint book, 1916, published by Cupples & Leon 20.00

Perfume bottle, glass, figural Buster Brown, 3" h. 48.00

Pillow cover, printed fabric, w/verses, signed Outcault 75.00

Pinback button, advertising "Buster Brown Bread" 12.00

Pinback button, advertising "Buster Brown Hose Supporters" 25.00

Pitcher, china, Buster Brown, Tige & Mary Jane at tea decor 75.00

Plate, china, Buster, Tiger & balloons decor 85.00

Playing cards, 1913, each card different scene 32.00

Postcard, Valentine Greetings, signed Outcault . . . . 6.00 to 8.00

Ring, brass 50.00

Stockings, w/original paper labels, 6 pr. in original box 65.00

Toy clicker, tin, Buster & Tige 7.00

Toy whistle, tin, advertising "Buster Brown Shoes," w/picture of Buster & Tige. 18.00

Valentine, hanging-type, heart-shaped, signed Richard F. Outcault, published by Raphael Tuck 15.00

BUTTER MOLDS & STAMPS

Eagle Butter Stamp

While they are sometimes found made of other materials, it is primarily the two-piece wooden butter mold and one-piece butter stamp that attracts collectors. The molds are found in two basic styles, rounded cup form and rectangular box form. Butter stamps are usually round with a protruding knob handle on the back. Many are factory made items with the print design made by forcing a metal die into the wood under great pressure, while others have the design chiseled out by hand.

Acorn mold, double, wooden, hand-carved, miniature $50.00

Compass star "lollypop" double-sided stamp, wooden, hand-carved 330.00

Cow mold, wooden, hand-carved, minature, 2" d. 160.00

Cow stamp, wooden, hand-carved, grey scrubbed finish, 4 7/8" d. . . . 155.00

Cow stamp, wooden, deeply hand-

carved cow, fence, grass &
bough 245.00
Eagle stamp, wooden, hand-carved,
1-piece w/carved wood handle,
4¼" d. (ILLUS.) 355.00
Fern fronds & monogram stamp,
cherrywood, hand-carved, 1-piece
w/knob handle, 4½" sq. 350.00
Flower stamp, wooden, hand-
carved, turned wood handle,
4" d. 175.00
Flower & leaves mold, wooden,
hand-carved, mortised case, 6 x
4¼" 75.00
Fruits (4) mold, wooden, hand-
carved, 1-lb. 95.00
Lily-of-the-Valley mold, wooden,
hand-carved, oblong case, 2-lb. . . 185.00
Peacock mold, wooden, hand-
carved, half-lb. 375.00
Pineapple mold, wooden, die-
stamped, round, 1-lb 70.00

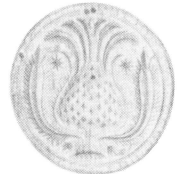

Pineapple Butter Stamp

Pineapple stamp, wooden, hand-
carved fruit & foliage, turned
wood handle, 4" d. (ILLUS.) 135.00
Pineapple & foliage half-circle stamp
(made to stamp half the top of a
5 lb. crock), wooden, hand-
carved, 6 7/8" w. 275.00
Pine tree "lollypop" stamp, wooden,
hand-carved, square, carved handle w/cut-out heart at end, over-
all 7¾" l. 825.00
Rooster mold, wooden, hand-carved,
round 75.00
Sheaf of barley mold, wooden,
hand-carved, round, 1-lb. 85.00
Sheaf of wheat stamp, burl, hand-
carved, 1-piece w/turned handle,
4¾" d. 625.00
Starflower w/hearts, tulips & other
flowers stamp, wooden, hand-
carved w/rope-carved edge,
turned wood handle, 4 5/8" d. . . . 275.00
Strawberry stamp, wooden, hand-
carved, white scrubbed finish,
5" d. 75.00

Sunflower stamp, wooden, hand-
carved, round 45.00
Swan mold, wooden, hand-carved . . 110.00
Tulip "lollypop" stamp, wooden,
hand-carved stylized blossom,
scrubbed finish, 8¾" l. 425.00

BUTTON HOOKS

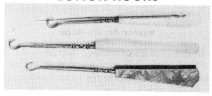

Button Hooks

*From the 1860's through the early years of
the 20th century, people buttoned up their
shoes, along with many layers of garments
and gloves and the button hook was an in-
dispensable part of everyday life. Produced
in a variety of forms and materials, this once
useful gadget is now a popular collector's
item.*

Advertising, "Hurd Shoes" $2.50
Advertising, "J.C. Penney" 18.00
Advertising, "Lowenthals Shoe
House" 8.00
Bone handle, plain (ILLUS. top) 4.00
Celluloid handle, end modelled as a
jockey's cap, pearlized green 45.00
Celluloid handle, green (ILLUS.
bottom) 4.00
Celluloid handle, mottled "tortoise
shell," 6" l. 12.00
Glass, whimsey 5.00
Mother-of-pearl handle 23.00
Silver handle, engraved decor,
hallmarked 24.00
Silver handle, English hallmark for
1909, 10½" l. 30.00
Sterling silver handle, folding-type,
"repousse" scrolled edge, 3" l. . . . 26.00
Sterling silver handle, Heraldic
patt., Whiting, 3" l. 32.00
Sterling silver handle, Art Nouveau
bust of long haired maiden amidst
calla lilies in relief both sides,
7¾" l. 75.00
Sterling silver handle, engraved
florals, Gorham, 8" l. 22.00
Sterling silver handle, Art Nouveau
style, Shiebler, 8½" l. 125.00
Sterling silver handle, ornate
"repousse" floral decor . . . . 22.00 to 30.00

BUTTONS

Art Nouveau Sterling Silver Button

Brass, Art Nouveau floral decor,
large $20.00
Brass, Civil War, Union Army,
large 3.50
Brass, "Police," 5/8" d. 1.00
Brass, "Washington Huntsman,"
Paris, France, 19th c. 25.00
Carnival glass, Fox & Crow, ¾" d. . . . 8.00
Celluloid, Art Deco geometric de-
sign, 1 1/8" d. 1.00
China, Satsuma, colorful bird &
hanging wisteria blossoms, heavy
gold trim, ca. 1900, ¾" d. 20.00
China, Satsuma, mother & child,
speckled gold ground, ca. 1922,
¾" d. 17.00
China, Satsuma, Arhats (elderly
male disciples of Buddha, usually
w/haloes about head), set of 4 in
original box 85.00
Enamel, English hunting scenes, Bir-
mingham, England, ca. 1760,
1½" d., set of 12, now mounted
under glass in small carved wood
case 850.00
Gilt metal, Arab leading camel to
oasis, set of 8 . . . . 15.00
Gilt metal, birds & tree 5.00
Gilt metal, scene of boy & girl 5.00
Glass, daisy, 2-tone green, set
of 4 . . . . 20.00
Glass, paperweight-type, mul-
ticolored millefiori canes, set of
14 . . . . 200.00
Jasper ware, white relief bust of
Christ on black ground 35.00
Mother-of-pearl, bluebird 2.00
Silver, Art Nouveau lady in relief,
¾" d. 24.00
Silver, hunt buttons: 12 coat & 6 cuff
or waistcoat; each modeled in high
relief w/heads of horses, fox &
bloodhounds, wolf, foxes, hare,
boar, stag & antelope, on matted
grounds, 1 1/8" & ¾" d., now
mounted on velvet rectangular
plaque w/gilt rim 1,980.00
Sterling silver, Art Nouveau lady's
head (ILLUS.) 45.00

CALENDAR PLATES

1909 Gibson Girl Calendar Plate

Calendar plates have been produced in this country since the turn of the century, primarily of porcelain and earthenwares but also of glass and tin. They were made earlier in England. The majority were issued after 1909, largely intended as advertising items.

1909, beautiful woman center,
calendar months border, Nebras-
ka advertising $22.00
1909, Gibson-type girl center, calen-
dar months, fruit & floral border,
Wisconsin advertising, 9½" d.
(ILLUS.) 25.00
1909, poppies center, calendar
months border 27.50
1910, beautiful woman center,
Maine advertising 32.00
1910, beautiful woman in garden
center, calendar months border,
10" d. 29.00
1910, bust of beautiful woman wear-
ing large hat center, calendar
months, fruit & floral border,
9½" d. 52.00
1910, calendar months & "Ingle-
wood, California" center, floral
garland border 22.50
1910, cherubs ringing in New Year
center 34.00
1910, horse center, calendar months
border 25.00
1910, Mt. Vernon center, calendar
months, border, Wisconsin
advertising 25.00
1910, Niagara Falls center 24.00
1910, "The Old Swimming Hole,"
scene of young boy swimming in
secluded pond center, Nebraska
advertising 45.00
1910, violets center, calendar
months border 25.00
1912, airplane center 42.00

1912, angel ringing bell center,
Canadian advertising 25.00
1912, Indian maiden w/corn center,
Maine advertising, 8¼" d. 42.00
1912, Zeppelin & "Merry Christmas"
center, calendar months border . .   55.00
1913, calendar months center,
garlands of roses & holly border . .   20.00
1914, Liberty Bell & "Philadelphia"
center 32.50
1915, boy eating watermelon center,
"Souvenir of Pittsburg" 125.00

CAMPBELL KID COLLECTIBLES

Campbell Kids Mug

*The Campbell Kids were created by Grace
Weiderseim (Drayton) at the turn of this century and their first use is said to have been
on street car cards. They have been used for
years by the Campbell Soup Company in its
advertisements and various objects were
produced graced with illustrations of them.
Also see DOLLS.*

Alphabet blocks, paper-covered
wood, chromolithographed paper
Campbell Kids w/letter of alphabet centered on wooden cut-
out figure, set of 13 . . . .$225.00
Feeding dish, pottery, Campbell Kids
decor, signed Drayton, Buffalo
Pottery 100.00
Greeting card w/envelope, "Camp-
bell Kid" pictured 8.00
Mug, plastic, thermal-type, white
w/"Campbell Up!" & Campbell Kid
each side, 4" h. (ILLUS.) 6.00
Print, scene of Campbell Kids,
signed Grace Drayton, by Campbell Art Co., Elizabeth, New Jer-
sey, No. 2505 . . . . 180.00
Print, "Skinnydipping," by Grace
Drayton 65.00
Salt & pepper shakers, plastic,
figural Campbell Kids,
pr. . . . . .14.00 to 18.00

Soup spoons, silverplate, figural
Campbell boy & girl handles,
pr. 16.00
Teaspoon, silverplate, figural Camp-
bell boy or girl handle,
each .10.00 to 15.00

CANDLESTICKS & CANDLE HOLDERS

Tiffany Candelabrum

*Also see CUT GLASS and LIGHTING
DEVICES.*

Candelabrum, bronze & Favrile glass,
4-branch, oval base, central floriform handle enclosing a snuffer
receptacle (snuffer missing) flanked by 4 candle cups cased in amber iridescent glass, impressed
Tiffany Studios, New York, 1899-
1920, 15" h. (ILLUS.) $1,870.00
Candelabra, silver, 5-light, shaped
oval base, baluster form stem
chased w/shells, leaf tips & pendants, w/detachable 4-light branches & central socket, Gorham & Co.,
16" h., pr. 1,210.00
Candelabra, Sheffield plate, 3-light,
vase form w/borders of shells,
scrolls & flowers, reeded arms,
campana-shaped sconces, detachable nozzles & finials, ca. 1825,
24½" h., pr. (one sconce
repaired) 2,750.00
Candle holder, brass, chamberstick-
type, circular saucer base w/ring
handle, cylindrical stem
w/pushup, 4" h. 90.00
Candle holder, silver, chamberstick-
type, circular saucer base en-

graved w/a crest, vase form
stem, beaded borders, w/conical
snuffer, Smith & Sharp, London,
George III period, 1785, 5½" d. .. 990.00
Candle holder, tin, chamberstick-
type, circular saucer base w/ring
handle, painted decor, 3" d.,
1" h. 95.00
Candlestick, art glass, pink over
white cased base & top, clear
twisted stem, 8" h. (single) 275.00

Art Deco Style Candlestick

Candlestick, bronze, stem cast in
the form of an Art Deco style owl,
5" h., single (ILLUS.) 95.00
Candlestick, bronze, cast as a saxi-
frage plant w/pierced flowering
upper cluster enclosing the candle
holder above a tall stem & band of
openwork leaves at the foot, impressed Tiffany Studios, New York,
18¼" h. (single) 3,850.00
Candlestick, cast iron, "hogscraper"
w/pushup marked "Bill" & hang-
ing lip, 7 7/8" h. (single) 135.00

Irish Silver Candlestick

Candlestick, silver, 17th c. style from
brass or pewter prototype, spreading circular base, tapering cylindrical stem molded w/wavy ridges
& applied w/projecting midband &
fixed nozzle, gadroon borders,

John Craig, Dublin, George III
period, ca. 1760, 11" h., single
(ILLUS.) 2,475.00
Candlestick, tin, "capstan," flaring
weighted base, pushup w/brass
knob, 9¾" h. (single) 260.00
Candlesticks, bell metal, stepped
base, baluster stem w/shaped
knob, 17½" h., pr. 135.00
Candlesticks, brass, scalloped domed
base, ring- and baluster-turned
stem, flaring candle nozzle, Queen
Anne period, early 18th c., 9½" h.,
pr. 1,475.00
Candlesticks, brass, circular base,
turned standard w/circular mid-
drip pan, Continental, 17th c.,
11" h., pr. 2,090.00
Candlesticks, brass, octagonal
stepped base, Diamond Prince
patt., English registry mark, Vic-
torian, 11¾" h., pr. 230.00
Candlesticks, ormolu, fluted beaded
circular base, baluster-shaped stem
w/laurel leaf garlands, beaded
drip pan above fluted & reeded
bobeche, Louis XVI, 3rd quarter
18th c., 11" h., pr. 1,980.00
Candlesticks, pewter, circular base,
ring-turned stem, urn-shaped candle cup w/flared bobeche, Flagg
& Homan, Cincinnati, Ohio,
19th c., 9" h., pr. 605.00
Candlesticks, rock crystal & silver,
Renaissance style, hexagonal cut
rock crystal base w/beaded silver
rim & ball feet, faceted baluster-
shaped stem, 8" h., pr. 2,200.00
Candlesticks, silver, Cactus patt.,
Georg Jensen, Denmark, 1¾" h.,
set of 4 . . . . 605.00
Candlesticks, silverplate, Art Nou-
veau style, floral & whiplash de-
cor, Pairpoint, 11" h., pr. 155.00
Candlesticks, sterling silver, pierced
dome base, baluster stem decorated w/panels of trailing flowers
& laurel swags, conforming vase-
shaped candle cup w/detachable
nozzle, Graff, Washbourne & Dunn,
New York, ca. 1910, retailed by
Black, Starr & Gorham, set
of 6 . . . . .3,575.00

CANDY CONTAINERS (Glass)

*Indicates the container might not have
held candy originally. +Indicates this container might also be found as a reproduction.*

‡*Indicates this container was also made as a bank. All containers are clear glass unless otherwise indicated. Any candy container that retains the original paint is very desirable and readers should follow descriptions carefully realizing that an identical candy container that lacks the original paint will be less valuable.*

Miniature Battleship

Airplane - "Army Bomber 15-P-7," J.H. Millstein, 1940's, 4 1/8" l..... $22.50

Airplane - w/left side rear door, metal screw cap & tin propeller, painted wing & wheels, probably 1930's, 4 5/8" l. 190.00

Airplane - "Spirit of Goodwill," w/screw cap & propeller, Victory Glass Co., ca. 1930, 4 5/8" l. 95.00

Automobile - little sedan w/stippled wheels & top, 3" l. 22.50

Automobile - electric coupe marked "Patented Feb. 18, 1913" on bottom, straight hood, w/closure, 3 3/8" l. 89.00

Automobile - sedan, 2-door, w/radiator cap, open top w/tin slide-on cover, 4¼" l. 120.00

Automobile - sedan w/twelve vents, w/closure, 4 5/16" l. 75.00

Automobile - coupe w/long hood, "U.S.A.," 5¼" l. 85.00

Autombile - electric coupe w/patent of Feb. 18, 1913, w/closure 65.00

Bell - Liberty Bell w/hanger & original closure, clear, 3 3/8" h. 47.00

Boat - miniature Battleship, paper closure, 5½" l. (ILLUS.) 23.00

Bus - "Victory Lines Special," painted, w/closure, 4 7/8" l. 67.50

Chicken on Nest - "Manufactured by J.H. Millstein Co." on rim of base, 4 5/8" h. (no closure) 22.50

Clock - round top shelf model, milk white glass w/painted decoration, w/tin closure, ca. 1908, 3 3/16" h. .... 125.00 to 165.00

Dog - Hound Pup, w/paper & metal hat, 3 5/8" h. 13.00

Dog - "Scotty" w/head down, 2 7/8 x 1½", 2¼" h. 21.00

Dog by Barrel - painted dog, marked "L.E. Smith Co., etc." on base of barrel, w/tin closure on barrel slotted for use as bank, ca. 1915, 3¼" h. 150.00

Drum - milk white, original closure, 2 15/16" d. 295.00

Duck on plain top basket, painted, w/closure, 3" l., 2¾" h. 96.00

Duck on rope top basket, marked "V.G. Co.," w/tin closure, 1920's, 3 1/8" h. 68.50

Elephant - marked "G.O.P." on side, painted grey, marked "V.G. Co.," w/tin closure, ca. 1925, 2 7/8" l., 2¾" h. 120.00

Fire Engine - large boiler, flat radiator cap, 5¼" l................. 50.00

*Girl w/two geese, 5¾" h. 30.00

*Gun - Round Butt Revolver No. 1, 7 7/8" l. 23.00

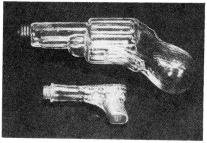

Gun Candy Containers

Gun - Stough's "Three Dot," w/whistle closure, 3½" l. (ILLUS. bottom) 20.00

Gun - marked "Kolt" on grip & "V.G." on barrel, w/round tin closure on handle grip, ca. 1925, 4¼" l. ....45.00 to 65.00

*Gun - Round Butt Revolver No. 1, 7 7/8" l. (ILLUS. top) 23.00

Horn - trumpet-shaped but no valves, milk white glass w/gilt trim & souvenir lettering, color decal of either bears or Dutch children decor, ca. 1908, 5½" l. ... 110.00

House - one-story bungalow w/dormer in roof, painted, w/tin closure, early 1900's, 2¾ x 2 1/8", 2 3/8" h. 150.00

Independence Hall

‡Independence Hall - replica of historic building, all glass w/coin slots in roof, marked "Bank of Independence" & "1776-1876," original tin closure on base, 7 3/16" h. (ILLUS.) 300.00

Iron - electric-type w/string as cord, 4½" l. (no closure) 35.00

Jeep with Driver - w/original cardboard closure, J.H. Millstein Co., ca. 1944, 4 3/8" l. 25.00

+Kewpie by Barrel - painted figure, marked "Geo. Borgfeldt & Co." etc., under barrel, w/tin closure slotted for use as bank, ca. 1915 . . . . 110.00

Lantern - tiny, plain model, marked "J.C. Crosetti Co." on base, metal screw-on cap & bail handle, 2¼" h. 10.00

Lantern - all glass w/six vertical ribs, marked "Pat. Dec. 20, '04" on base, metal screw-on cap pierced as shaker, 3¼" h. 21.00

Lantern - red-stained glass globe w/flared metal base & metal cap closure, w/wire bail handle, Victory Glass Co., 3¾" h. 25.00

Lantern - clear glass globe w/flared metal base & metal cap closure, w/wire bail handle, Victory Glass Co., 3¾" h. 26.00

Lantern - T.H. Stough Co. "No. 81 Large Railroad Lantern," clear glass globe w/enameled red screw-on metal cap w/reflector & metal base, wire bail handle, 1957, 4 3/8" h. 22.00

Lantern - barn-type enclosed in glass frame w/wire bail handle attached through top of glass frame, clear, metal screw-on closure at base, West Bros. Co., ca. 1913, 4½" h. 75.00

Lantern - barn-type enclosed in glass frame w/wire bail handle attached through top of glass frame, ruby-stained, marked "West Bro's Co., Grapeville, Pa." on base, original tin closure, ca. 1913, 4½" h. 80.00

*Lantern - "Bond Mono Cell," w/battery in hanger & light bulb that switches on as handle is raised, 4½" h. 25.00

*Light House Night Light - frosted glass lighthouse (battery-operated) in metal holder, 5" h. . . . 30.00

Locomotive - Stough's "E 3 S" engine w/narrow cab, marked "E3S" on boiler below stack & "1028" below window on cab, 4" l. 25.00

Locomotive Candy Container

Locomotive - American-type engine w/lithographed tin closure, ca. 1924, 4 3/16" l. (ILLUS.) 85.00

+Locomotive - single window in engine cab marked "888" below, American-type locomotive, painted wheels, 4 7/8" l. 25.00

+Locomotive - double window in engine cab marked "888" below, American-type locomotive, glass wheels, 4 7/8" l. 29.00

Locomotive - with man in window of engine cab, marked "999" below, w/original closure in back of cab, Cambridge Glass Co., ca. 1916, 4 7/16" l. 150.00

+Locomotive - engine marked "1028" below windows on cab, w/cow-catcher at front, marked "Victory Glass Co." on cardboard closure, 5 1/8" l. 20.00

Milk Bottle - "Dolly's Milk" & "V.G." monogram on side, Victory Glass Co., 3" h. 27.50

Milk Bottles in Carrier - clear bottles w/cardboard closures in metal carrier, 2¼" h. bottles, 3¼" sq. carrier, overall 3½" h. 125.00

Mug - "Kiddies Drinking Mug," w/cardboard closure, ca. 1943, 3 7/16" 23.00

+Mule Pulling Two-Wheeled Barrel with Driver - painted, some examples marked "Victory Glass Co.," w/tin cap closure on back of barrel, 4½" l. 80.00

Nursing Bottle - waisted-type w/red rubber nipple, 2¼" h. 10.00

Nursing Bottle - plain cylinder, 2 5/8" h. 12.50

Pencil - marked "Baby Jumbo," 5½" l. 49.00

Phonograph - w/glass record & gilt tin horn, w/tin closure on base, early 1920's, 2 7/8" w., 1¾" h. plus tin horn (ILLUS.) 197.00

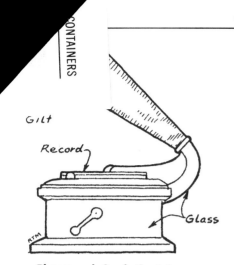

Gilt
Record
Glass

Phonograph Candy Container

Phonograph - w/tin horn & tin record, w/inkwell-type depression,
tin closure on base, 2 7/8" w.,
4 5/8" to top of tin horn 225.00
+Piano - upright model, painted in
gilt, w/tin slide on back & also
slotted for use as bank, early
1920's, 2 13/16" h. ......110.00 to 160.00
*Pipe - Bavarian-type w/wicker
bowl, 10¼" l.................... 80.00
Powder Horn - w/hanger & metal
closure, 8¾" l.................. 47.00
Pump - for "Candy," red plastic over
glass, Millstein, complete,
6 1/8" h. 85.00
Pumpkin Head Witch - original
paint, w/closure, 4½" h. 329.00
Purse - alligator skin design,
4 1/8" l., 3 5/8" h. 175.00

Rabbit with Wheelbarrow

+Rabbit with Wheelbarrow - originally painted, unmarked, w/tin
closure, 1920's, 3¾" l. (ILLUS.) ... 130.00
Rabbit Mother with Daughter,
5 1/8" h. 330.00

Rabbit - wearing hat, pants & suspenders, 2" base d., 5 3/8" h..... 650.00
+Safe - "Penny Trust Co." in upper
panel of door, w/tin closure,
2 7/8" h. 79.00
Safety First - baby w/oversized safety pin on diapers standing beside
barrel, 3¾" h. 475.00

Santa Claus Candy Container

Santa Claus - descending brick chimney, marked "V.G." monogram on
side, Santa originally painted, ca.
1927, 5" h. (ILLUS.) 85.00
Santa Claus - paneled coat, w/clo-
sure, 5¼" h..................... 105.00
Santa Claus - "Sears" (1967),
9½" h......................... 12.50
Skookum by Tree Stump - w/bank
slot, 3 5/8" h. 170.00
Suitcase - milk white glass, decal
type "Roosevelt Bears,"
w/closure 90.00
Telephone - musical toy w/plastic
screw cap closure & tin whistle
attached, 4 5/8" h. 21.50
Telephone - "Redlich's Screw Top,"
wood receiver "Redlich-Chicago-
Serial No. - Patent 852242," early,
2" base d., 6¼" h. 135.00
Toonerville Depot Line - replica of
Toonerville Trolley, no paint,
some chips, 2 7/8" l., 3½" h. 525.00
Top - spinning type w/winding disc,
overall 3¾" h. 70.00
Train Engine & Coach - marked
"New York Central" on coach &
"N.Y.C." on engine, w/glass couplers to attach units, lithographed
tin closure on engine & tin roof
closure on coach, Westmoreland
Specialty Co., ca. 1923, 4 7/8" l.
engine & 5 1/8" l. coach 540.00
Turkey - gobbler, 3½" h. 85.00

Village Building - "Bank," painted tin shell w/red roof, red upper trim, green doors & windows, w/glass liner 125.00

Village Railroad Station - tin shell w/green roof, red upper trim & grey brick base, w/glass liner, 2½" h. 130.00

*Washing Machine - glass tub on metal base, metal screw top closure, printed "Little Miss Washing Machine," 2 3/8" w., 4¾" h. 30.00

World Globe on metal stand, all original, 4¼" h. 325.00

CANS & CONTAINERS

Calumet Baking Powder Can

The collecting of tin containers has become quite popular within the past several years. Air-tight tins were at first produced by hand to keep foods fresh, and after the invention of the tin-printing machine in the 1870's, containers were manufactured in a wide variety of shapes and sizes with colorful designs.

Adding machine ribbon, Burroughs $4.00

Anti-freeze, Eveready, early auto scene, 1929, 1-gal. 11.50

Automobile polish, Wonder Mist, pt. 12.00

Axle grease, Mica 1-gal. pail 48.00

Axle grease, Nourse miniature pail 8.50

Axle grease, Sambo 10-lb. pail 95.00

Axle grease, Scholl's, terrified blacks in wagon w/runaway horse 60.00

Baking powder, Calumet 5-lb. can, Indian (ILLUS.) 10.00

Baking powder, Good Luck, 4-leaf clover & horseshoe on red ground, dated 1901-02 .... 15.00

Baking powder, Rough Rider, Teddy Roosevelt on horseback 28.00

Baking powder, Rumford 4-oz. can .. 15.00

Baking powder, Schilling 2-lb. 8-oz. can 8.00

Baking powder, Snow King 3-oz. sample size, paper label w/Snow King pictured 18.00

Baking powder, Watkins, lady w/platter of biscuits 15.00

Biscuit, Crawford's "Sundial," pseudo brick base inscribed "No Man Can Tether Time," 1926, 9½" h. .. 200.00

Biscuit, Huntley & Palmers "Artist," palette-shaped w/scene of boy & lute before fence, 1900, 9 7/8 x 7½", 2" h. 165.00

Biscuit, Huntley & Palmers "Athletic" triangular box, scenes of various sporting activities on top & sides, 1892 .... 200.00

Biscuit, Huntley & Palmers "Bell," inscribed "When Ye Doe Ringe," etc., 1912..................... 145.00

Biscuit, Huntley & Palmers "Books" ("Gardens Old and New", "Poems of John Keats," etc.) between Georgian bookends, 1909, 9 x 4", 4" h. 220.00

Biscuit, Huntley & Palmers "Bookstand," books in case, 1905, 4¼" w., 6¼" h................. 220.00

Biscuit, Huntley & Palmers "Buhl Locket," simulated brass & tortoise shell inlay, 1907-09, 7 x 5" oval 150.00

Biscuit, Huntley & Palmers "Cabinet," china closet replica, 1911, 3½" w., 7½" h................. 375.00

Biscuit, Huntley & Palmers "Egyptian Urn," embossed relief scenes & stylized geometric papyrus plants & birds, 1924, 8 4/5" h. 145.00

Biscuit, Huntley & Palmers "Fame" casket w/roll-top in the "Sevres" version, 1907-10, 9¼ x 6¼", 8½" h. 750.00

Biscuit, Huntley & Palmers "Farmhouse" w/garden wall, 1931-38, 6" w., 4" h.................... 400.00

Biscuit, Huntley & Palmers "Holiday Haunts," w/scenes of England, 1926-29, 3" sq., 7½" h. 50.00

Biscuit, Huntley & Palmers "Ink Stand," reserve scene of fox hunting on lid flanked by hunting horns & fox tails, 1928, 9½" l..... 175.00

Biscuit, Huntley & Palmers "Jubilee," Queen Victoria diamond jubilee w/portrait of Queen & Albert, 1897 .... 120.00

Biscuit, Huntley & Palmers "Lantern," 1911-13................... 145.00

Biscuit, Huntley & Palmers "Library"

books, red volumes in book strap,
1900, 6¼" h. 145.00
Biscuit, Huntley & Palmers "Litera-
ture" books ("History of England",
"Pilgrim's Progress," etc.) bound
in leather strap, 1901-02,
6¼ x 4¾ x 6¼" 450.00
Biscuit, Huntley & Palmers "Syrian
Table," 6-sided table in the far
Eastern taste, 1903-06, 6½" hex-
agonal top, 7¼" h. 135.00
Biscuit, Huntley & Palmers "Wedg-
wood," blue-and-white jasper
ware round 25.00

Ivin's Biscuit Box

Biscuit, Ivin's box, girl & parrot on
black ground, "Say Ivin's," 1910,
5 x 5 x 5" (ILLUS.) 45.00
Biscuit, W. & R. Jacobs "Humming
Top," replica of spinning top 480.00
Biscuit, Loose-Wiles "Hiawatha's
Wedding Journey" 2 lb. 8 oz. box
w/bail handle, Hiawatha & Indian
maiden by waterfall, w/poem 150.00
Biscuit, Sheldon & Pearson, Ltd.,
Puffed Rice Biscuit Toffee canister,
elephants & Indians wearing tur-
bans, 5½" h. 67.50
Biscuit, Sunshine box, Washington
D.C. cherry blossom scene on lid,
11 x 12½" 25.00
Biscuit, Uneeda box, pastoral coun-
try scenes w/sheep in sepia tones
on all sides, 1920's, 11 x 8",
2¾" h. 190.00
Biscuit, Vanderueer & Holmes or-
nate trunk shape w/latch & han-
dle, realistic lithograph 375.00
Blasting caps, Hercules 25.00
Boot polish, Wren can, bird 20.00
Candy, "Compliments of Santa
Claus" pail, 1898 . . . . 185.00
Candy, Gazette Candy Co. box,
Lindbergh waving to spectators on
lid, 1920's, 12½ x 9½" 35.00
Candy, Kandies for Kiddies pail. 85.00
Candy, Lamb's Nursery Rhyme lunch
box, Mother Goose characters . . . 165.00

Candy, Licorice Pellets store box
w/hinged lid, glass window at
front, Young & Smylie, Brooklyn,
N.Y., 7½" h. 145.00
Candy, Merry Christmas pail, baby &
Santa cameo silhouettes,
1900 . . . . .145.00 to 185.00
Candy, Monarch Toffee store canis-
ter, portrait of lion in center roundel flanked by Teenie Weenies,
15" h. 475.00
Candy, Norris, Atlanta 2-lb. box,
cotton bale-shaped 75.00
Candy, Nutrine Higher Quality 25-lb.
store canister, knight in armor on
battlefield 125.00
Candy, Peter Rabbit oval box 70.00
Candy, Peter Rabbit lunch box,
oblong 55.00
Candy, Queen of Hearts pail, Lovell
& Covel . . . . .75.00 to 145.00
Candy, Riley's Toffee box, Royal
Family (Elizabeth II & Margaret
Rose as children) 25.00
Candy, Satin Sanders Candies pail,
children, 1920's, 5½" h. 55.00
Chocolate, Runkels Essence of
Chocolate square can w/round
screw-on lid, 6" sq., 9" h. 350.00
Cigarettes, Ardath Cork Tip Virginia
flat fifties 8.00
Cigarettes, Camel round one-
hundreds . . . . .20.00 to 32.00
Cigarettes, Chesterfield round
fifties 22.50

Lucky Strike Flat Fifties

Cigarettes, Lucky Strike flat fifties,
green, red & gold (ILLUS.). . .8.00 to 12.50
Cigarettes, Lucky Strike flat fifties
"Christmas" box. **35.00**
Cigarettes, McDonald's flat fifties . . . 12.00
Cigarettes, Murad Turkish box 15.00
Cigarettes, Old Gold flat
fifties . . . . .12.00 to 20.00
Cigarettes, Pall Mall box, Christmas
holly trim, 8 x 7 x 2" 30.00
Cigarettes, Parliament flat fifties . . . 25.00
**Cigarettes, Phillip Morris one-
hundreds oval box** **20.00**
Cigarettes, Player's flat fifties 17.50
Cigarettes, Queen Gold box, Arabi-
an cigarette girl offering smokes
to Sultan astride horse 35.00

Schinasi Bros. Flat Fifties

Cigarettes, Schinasi Bros. flat fifties,
5 x 2" (ILLUS.) 20.00
Cigarettes, State Empress flat
fifties 8.00
Cigars, Bank Note canister, 4¼" d.,
5½" h. 18.00
Cigars, Bayuk Philadelphia Phillies
box 11.50
Cigars, Belfast box 10.00
Cigars, Ben Bey Box, Arabian horse
w/Arab rider on cover, 9 x 6½",
3" h. 65.00
Cigars, Black Fox box .....500.00 to 850.00
Cigars, Check box, monetary check
of Rock City Cigar Co. 75.00
Cigars, Court Royal container, wom-
an & factory scene 50.00
Cigars, Cremo counter bin, 13¾ x
6¼", 6" h. 75.00
Cigars, Dutch Masters container 15.00
Cigars, El Producto box 35.00
Cigars, El Roi Tan canister 17.50
Cigars, El Verso box, shepherdess &
sheep, 5 x 3½ x 1" 22.50
Cigars, Flor de Melba round box ... 35.00
Cigars, Key Clips canister 10.00
Cigars, King Midas box, portrait of
king, 6¼ x 4¼ x 5½" 45.00
Cigars, Lady Churchill small box 8.00
Cigars, LaFendrich canister 22.00
Cigars, LaPalina box, Spanish
senorita 25.00
Cigars, Mohawk canister 1,815.00
Cigars, Muriel canister, lady's por-
trait, 5¼" d., 5¼" h. 13.50
Cigars, Niles & Moser container 25.00
Cigars, Orcico (2 for 5c) box, Indian
portrait, 6 x 4¼", 5½" h. 110.00
Cigars, Popper's Ace box, World
War I biplane 100.00
Cigars, Possum canister, "Am Good
and Sweet," possom, 5¼" d.,
5¼" h. 75.00
Cigars, Reas Habana container 28.00
Cigars, Red Dot Jr. box, 4¾ x 3",
1½" h. 18.00
Cigars, Rose of Cuba canister 75.00
Cigars, Tango box 45.00
Cigars, Tom Moore flat box 15.00
Cigars, Vanko oval canister, horse,
stirrup, trotters & sulky, green &
gold, 6½" l., 5½" h. 45.00

Cigars, Washington's Cabinet
container 50.00
Cigars, Webster canister 20.00
Cigars, White Hen lunch box 175.00
Cigars, Wm. Penn Perfectos box
w/hinged lid, 5 x 4" 10.00
Cleanser, Bon Ami sample size, lady
washing windows & chick, 6½"... 20.00
Cleanser, Gold Dust 14-oz. can,
twins (unopened)................ 22.00
Cleanser, Lighthouse canister 10.00
Cleanser, Watch Dog 14-oz. can 5.00
Cocoa, American Stores oval con-
tainer, Dutch boy & girl w/wind-
mill, 1920's 25.00
Cocoa, Baker's sample size, round .. 95.00
Cocoa, Droste's square 8 oz. con-
tainer, Dutch boy & girl 18.00
Cocoa, Klein's sample size 65.00
Cocoa, Laxo container, Brownies
decor 65.00
Cocoa, McNess sample size 12.00
Cocoa, Monarch sample size, lions.. 24.50
Cocoa, Monarch square container,
lions, 3" h. 15.00
Cocoa, National container......... 45.00
Cocoa, Rawleigh's sample size 40.00
Cocoa, Sexton Breakfast 4-lb.
container 10.00
Coconut, Creaoles box, black
woman 35.00
Coconut, IGA pail 16.00
Coconut, San Blas square container
w/round lid, monkeys, 1890's 125.00
Coconut, Schepp's "cake box,"
1-shelf 165.00
Coconut, Schepp's "cake box,"
2-shelf 95.00
Coconut, Schepp's 1-lb. pail, mon-
keys playng, black & green 195.00
Coconut, Schepp's square container,
green 38.00

After Glow Coffee Pail

Coffee, After Glow 4-lb. pail
(ILLUS.)..................35.00 to 50.00
Coffee, Batavia 5-lb. container
w/side lock................... 50.00

Coffee, Battleship 3-lb. container,
battleship 35.00
Coffe, Blackhawk Coffee & Spice Co.
store bin, 32 x 20" 110.00
Coffee, Blanke's Defy cream can
w/lid & bail handle 375.00
Coffee, Blue Bird pail 185.00
Coffee, Bokar 1-lb. container
w/screw-on lid 12.50
Coffee, Camel 4-lb. can 34.00
Coffee, Campfire can 150.00

Central Union Cut Plug Lunch Box

Tobacco, Central Union lunch box
(ILLUS.) 30.00
Tobacco, Century Lorillard pocket
tin 55.00
Tobacco, Checkers pocket tin 320.00
Tobacco, Chesapeake pocket tin 395.00
Tobacco, Cinco Londres pocket tin . . 15.00
Tobacco, City Club pocket tin 60.00
Tobacco, Coach & Four pocket tin . . . 54.00
Tobacco, Country Life canister 85.00
Tobacco, Crow-Mo-Smokers lunch
box 150.00
Tobacco, Dial pocket tin 28.00
Tobacco, Dixie Cup Chop barrel,
Ginna, 1880's 175.00
Tobacco, Donniford pocket tin 70.00
Tobacco, Duke's Mixture bin 450.00

Wak-Em-Up Coffee

Coffee, Wak-Em-Up 5-lb. pail, Indian
profile in round medallion
(ILLUS.) 90.00
Coffee, WGY 1-lb. can, 4¼" d.,
6" h. 20.00
Coffee, White Bear square contain-
er, polar bear in oval, 4½ x 3",
6" h. 60.00
Coffee, Wishbone 4-lb. pail 24.50
Coffee, Wood's Boston pail 14.00
Tobacco, Abbey pocket tin 133.00
Tobacco, Acme Extra Mild pocket
tin 10.00
Tobacco, Allen & Ginter Dixie Chop
barrel, Ginna, 1880's 250.00
Tobacco, Beech-Nut store bin 145.00
Tobacco, Belfast canister 20.00
Tobacco, Belfast lunch box 14.50
Tobacco, Big Ben pocket tin, horse
pictured 28.00
Tobacco, Boar's Head box 72.50
Tobacco, Boar's Head store bin 65.00
Tobacco, Bob White box,
4 x 2½ x 3" 600.00
Tobacco, Briggs pocket tin 9.50
Tobacco, Brotherhood lunch box 130.00
Tobacco, Buckhorn pocket tin 12.00
Tobacco, Bugler pocket tin 15.00
Tobacco, Burley Boy (Bagley's) lunch
box 1,750.00
Tobacco, California Nugget pocket
tin 108.00
Tobacco, Canadian Club pocket tin,
McHies 450.00
Tobacco, Catcher canister 34.00

Edgeworth and Tuxedo Tobacco Pocket Tins

Tobacco, Edgeworth Jr. pocket tin
(ILLUS. left) 22.50
Tobacco, Ensign box 175.00
Tobacco, Epicure pocket tin 79.00
Tobacco, Estabrook & Eaton's Slice
pocket tin, 3¾ x 4½ x 1¼" 45.00
Tobacco, Fairmount pocket tin 110.00
Tobacco, Fast Mail (J. Bagley & Co.)
pail, black steam engine locomo-
tive on red-orange 5,060.00
Tobacco, Forest & Stream pocket tin,
canoe 170.00
Tobacco, Four Roses pocket tin,
green 556.00
Tobacco, Game Fine Cut store bin . . 275.00
Tobacco, George Washington Cut
Plug lunch box 35.00
Tobacco, George Washington pocket
tin 27.50

Tobacco, Granger pocket tin 335.00
Tobacco, Granulated 54 pocket tin,
single leaf 42.50
Tobacco, Guide pocket tin 133.00
Tobacco, Half & Half pocket tin 6.00
Tobacco, Hand Bag Cut Plug lunch
box 40.00
Tobacco, Hickey's Perique Mixture
box 12.00
Tobacco, Hugh Campbell's Shag
pocket tin 120.00
Tobacco, Jewel of Virginia box 32.00
Tobacco, King Edward pocket tin . . . 600.00
Tobacco, Kipling pocket tin 45.00
Tobacco, Lucky Tiger lunch box,
red 35.00
Tobacco, Maryland Club box, round
corners 17.00
Tobacco, Maryland Club pocket tin,
roll top 695.00
Tobacco, Matador box, square
corners 29.00
Tobacco, Matoaka pocket tin 600.00
Tobacco, Mayo's Roly Poly Mammy . . 410.00
Tobacco, Mellow Sweet store
bin 1,486.00
Tobacco, Model canister 35.00
Tobacco, Morse's Duchess Brand
5-lb. canister, Victorian woman
pictured 35.00
Tobacco, Nigger Hair canister 150.00
Tobacco, North Star pocket tin 188.00
Tobacco, Okeh box 25.00
Tobacco, Old Gold (Kimball Bros.)
box, 4½ x 3 x 2" 11.50
Tobacco, Old Squire pocket tin, por-
trait of old squire 100.00
Tobacco, Palmy Days pocket tin 118.00
Tobacco, Pastime store bin, red 143.00
Tobacco, Patterson's Seal Cut Plug
pail, basketweave 27.00
Tobacco, Paul Jones pocket tin,
blue 900.00
Tobacco, Penny Post lunch box 259.00
Tobacco, Pipe Major pocket tin 240.00
Tobacco, Player's Navy Cut box,
square corners, sailor &
seascape 22.50

Tobacco, Plow Boy canister, farmer
by plow (ILLUS.) 42.50
Tobacco, Plow Boy lunch pail 43.00
Tobacco, Postmaster round contain-
er, "Postmaster Smokers 2 for 5
cents" 24.00
Tobacco, Queed pocket tin 55.00
Tobacco, Red Indian canister 250.00
Tobacco, Regal pocket tin 300.00
Tobacco, Revalation pocket tin, sam-
ple size 40.00
Tobacco, Richmond Club (Columbian)
box, square corners 40.00
Tobacco, Roosevelt horizontal box
(Canadian) 110.00
Tobacco, Round Trip lunch box 185.00
Tobacco, Saratoga Chips box,
3 3/16 x 2 7/16 x 1" 14.00
Tobacco, Seal of North Carolina can-
ister, small top 175.00
Tobacco, Senator lunch box, small . . 30.00

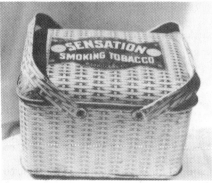

Sensation Tobacco Lunch Pail

Tobacco, Sensation lunch pail,
basketweave, 7½ x 5 x 5"
(ILLUS.) 40.00
Tobacco, Spearhead Plug box 7.50
Tobacco, Staghorn pocket tin 15.00
Tobacco, Stanwix pocket tin 800.00
Tobacco, Sterling Dark store canis-
ter, green, 16" h. 99.00

Plow Boy Tobacco Canister

Sterling Tobacco Canister

Tobacco, Sterling Light 5-lb. canister
(ILLUS.)......................... 45.00
Tobacco, Summer Time pail 40.00
Tobacco, Sweet Cuba lunch pail 27.50
Tobacco, Sweet Cuba store bin,
blue 750.00
Tobacco, Sweet Cuba store bin,
green, slant front 147.50
Tobacco, Tam O'Shanter pocket
tin 15.00
Tobacco, Tiger box, 4 x 6" 55.00

Tiger Tobacco Lunch Pail

Tobacco, Tiger lunch pail (ILLUS.) ...   32.00
Tobacco, Tiger pocket tin 182.00
Tobacco, Troost pocket tin, man in
stocks........................   40.00
Tobacco, Tuxedo canister, paper
band w/"Fresh Wherever You Get
It, etc.," unopened 65.00
Tobacco, Tuxedo pocket tin (ILLUS.
right) 24.00
Tobacco, Uncle Daniel Dark pie-
shaped container................   75.00
Tobacco, Uniform canister 1,250.00
Tobacco, Union Leader box, 3" 30.00
Tobacco, Velvet canister, pull-off
top, pipe & cigar decor, 5 x 6" ...   15.00
Tobacco, Virginia Dare box, bare
breasted woman w/goose, Hasker
& Marcuse, late 1800's 50.00
Tobacco, Wild Fruit (Bagley's) pail ..   45.00
Tobacco, Willoughby Taylor
canister 15.00
Tobacco, Yale Mixture box 17.50
Tobacco, Yale Mixture pocket tin,
3¾ x 2½ x 1½" 35.00
Tobacco, Yale Smoking Tobacco box,
green & gold, 2" 15.00
Tobacco, Yosemite box 85.00
Tooth tablet, Avon's California Per-
fume Company 25.00
Typewriters, Chesapeake, sailboat
on bay, Baltimore Co. 20.00
Typewriter ribbon, Miller Line Elk ...   8.00

Veterinary medicine, Bickmore Gall
Salve, paper seal & contents,
3" d.......................... 12.00
Watch dials, Breivogel, Tom Thumb
size man window washing oversized watch face 10.00
Watches, Waltham Watch Co. Main
Springs, 1888, Waltham factory,
horse & buggy & trolley.......... 25.00

CARD CASES

Sterling Silver Card Case

*In a more leisurely and sociable era, ladies
made a ritual of "calling" on new neighbors
and friends. Calling card cases held the small
cards engraved or lettered with the owner's
name and sometimes additionally decorated.
The cases were turned out in a wide variety
of styles and material which included gold,
silver, ivory, tortoise shell and leather. A sampling of collectible calling card cases is listed below.*

Coin silver, Philadelphia, Pennsylvania, ca. 1860...................$225.00
Ivory, carved scene of figures in an
elaborate garden setting, 3 3/8 x
1¾" 120.00
Mother-of-pearl shell, carved florals
& birds, Victorian 85.00
Silver, chased scrolling & florals
front, engine-turned design
reverse, hallmarked,
3 1/8 x 2 1/8" 125.00
Silver, chatelaine-type, basketweave
ground applied w/well-detailed
gold bird on a branch, hinged lid,
Continental, 3¾ x 2 3/8", w/long
double chain................... 145.00
Silver, filigree w/wire framing, applied w/butterfly, florals & foliage
within a circle of beading, lift-off
top, 3 7/8 x 2 5/8" 155.00

Sterling silver, bright-cut insects &
florals, engraved name, hinged
lid, chain handle, 2½ x 4½"
(ILLUS.)........................ 140.00
Sterling silver, Japanese patt., gold-
washed, chain handle, Gorham... 265.00
Sterling silver, embossed Moose
Lodge insignia 45.00

CASH REGISTERS

"National" Cash Register

*James Ritty of Dayton, Ohio, is credited
with inventing the first cash register. In 1882,
he sold the business to a Cincinnati salesman,
Jacob H. Eckert, who subsequently invited
others into the business by selling stock. One
of the purchasers of an early cash register,
John J. Patterson, was so impressed with the
savings his model brought to his company,
he bought 25 shares of stock and became a
director of the company in 1884, eventually
buying a controlling interest in the National
Manufacturing Company. Patterson thor-
oughly organized the company, conducted
sales classes, prepared sales manuals and established salesman's territories. The success
of the National Cash Register Company is
due as much to these well organized origins
as to the efficiency of its machines. Early
"National" cash registers, as well as other
models, are deemed highly collectible today.*

Brass, "National," Model 0, candy
store model, original etched glass
"Amount Purchased" marquee &
clock, restored $2,400.00
Brass, "National," Model 188 ... 950.00
Brass, "National," Model 250, candy
store model, restored 1,250.00
Brass, "National," Model 311,
restored 1,150.00
Brass, "National," Model 313,
registers up to $1.95 ....750.00 to 950.00
Brass, "National," Model 317, candy
store model 440.00

Brass, "National," Model 367,
registers up to $50.00 .... 490.00
Brass, "National," Model 442, wooden
base, ca. 1912, restored.........1,250.00
Brass, "National," Model 563-6F,
floor model 690.00
Brass, "National," Model 578-C,
2-drawer w/marble coin shelf,
w/cleaning & parts kit 1,500.00
Brass, "National," Model 592-A,
floor model on oak 10-drawer
base 975.00
Brass, "National," Model 597-C 550.00
Brass, "National," Model 657 ..... 850.00
Brass, "National," Model 711, candy
store model 200.00
Brass, "National," Model 852-E, last
patent date March 2, 1920,
registers to $99.99, 25" w., 23" h.,
on oak base 775.00
Bronze, "National," Model 522-El-2C,
bar model, side-by-side drawers,
tape reel & electric
sign ....1,650.00 to 1,900.00
Nickel-plated brass, "National," on
8-drawer oak base, dated 1913,
restored 2,000.00
Oak, "Hough," dated 1897 .... 425.00
Oak, "National," Model 45, ornate
rose bronze trim, hinged front
cover, w/original operating instructions & 1909 bill of sale 775.00
Rosewood w/inlay, "National," last
patent date July 6, 1886
(ILLUS.) 1,300.00
Wooden, "The Seymour," Detroit,
Michigan, paper roll model 875.00

CASTORS & CASTOR SETS

Cut Glass Castor Set

Castor bottles were made to hold condiments for table use. Some were produced in sets of several bottles housed in silverplated frames. The word also is sometimes spelled "Caster."

Castor set, 3-bottle, clear glass Daisy & Button patt. bottles, toothpick holder in center, pressed glass holder $95.00

Castor set, 4-bottle, clear cut glass square bottles, square silverplate stand w/center handle (ILLUS.) ... 200.00

Castor set, 4-bottle, clear glass King's Crown patt. bottles, glass stand w/metal center handle 100.00

Castor set, 4-bottle, cranberry glass Inverted Thumbprint patt. bottles w/enameled floral decor, silverplate stand, marked Meriden 395.00

Castor set, 4-bottle, green cut to clear square glass bottles, square silverplate stand, 8¼" h. 335.00

Castor set, 4-bottle, Rubina Crystal glass bottles, silverplate stand ... 495.00

Castor set, 5-bottle, Blue Willow patt. china bottles, matching china stand 112.00

Castor set, 5-bottle, clear glass bottles w/cut Honeycomb patt. & etched florals, silverplate stand, marked Tufts, 18" h. 185.00

Castor set, 5-bottle, ruby cut to clear glass bottles, silverplate stand 190.00

Castor set, 5-bottle, vaseline glass Daisy & Button patt. bottles, silverplate stand, marked Middletown Silverplate Co. 375.00

Pickle castor, amber glass insert w/enameled white florals, small blue forget-me-nots & green & yellow leaves, silverplate frame, cover & fork, marked Pairpoint, 4½" d., 10¾" h. 225.00

Pickle castor, Amberina glass melon-ribbed Inverted Thumbprint patt. insert, silverplate frame engraved w/storks, marked Wilcox 395.00

Pickle castor, blue glass Daisy & Button with "V" Ornament patt. insert, ornate silverplate frame, cover & tongs, marked Wilcox 195.00

Pickle castor, clear glass Bull's Eye patt. insert, ornate footed silverplate frame & tongs, marked Aurora 120.00

Pickle castor, clear glass Mardi Gras (Duncan & Miller No. 42) patt. insert, silverplate frame & tongs ... 110.00

Pickle castor, cranberry glass insert, figural cherubs & birds on silverplate frame, marked Meriden 215.00

Pickle castor, cranberry glass insert w/enameled floral decor, goldwashed silverplate frame & tongs 330.00

Cranberry Glass Pickle Castor

Pickle castor, cranberry glass Inverted Thumbprint patt. insert, ornate silverplate frame, cover & fork (ILLUS.) 110.00

Pickle castor, cranberry opalescent glass Daisy & Fern patt. insert, silverplate frame, cover & tongs 375.00

Pickle castor, Pigeon Blood glass insert, silverplate frame 200.00

Pickle castor, pink to raspberry mother-of-pearl Satin glass Diamond Quilted patt. insert w/enameled gold & white branches, florals & dotting, ornate footed silverplate frame & cover, marked Wilcox 495.00

Pickle castor, Pomona 1st grind glass insert w/blue cornflower decor, silverplate frame & cover, 11¾" h. 480.00

Pickle castor, purple marble glass insert, footed silverplate frame, cover & tongs, marked Tufts 145.00

Pickle castor, Royal Flemish matte finish glass insert w/yellow & white enameled spider chrysanthemums & pebbled gold band at top & base, ornate silverplate rim, base & frame, marked Pairpoint 1,265.00

Pickle castor, Rubina Crystal glass Medallion Sprig patt. insert, footed silverplate frame 275.00

CAT COLLECTIBLES

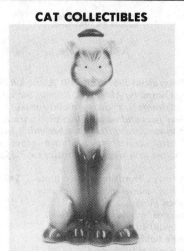

Cat Clothes Sprinkler

Cats–love them or hate them–you have to respect the fact that today cats are pets in almost one-fourth of all households in the United States. Proud, aloof and indifferent, their haughty poses have been recaptured in artwork in a variety of materials through the years. Other representatives catch the inquisitive, cuddly and playful mood of the domestic cat. Both have brought a delightful area of collecting to cat lovers across the country. Also see DOORSTOPS.

Ash tray, bronze Art Deco cat on
   green onyx oval tray, overall
   4½ x 3½"..................... $55.00
Clothes sprinkler, ceramic, figural
   cat, brown to ivory, brass screw-
   on cap pierced as sprinkler, impressed "Cardinal U.S.A.," 8½" h.
   (ILLUS.) 15.00
Creamer w/figural cat handle,
   iridescent black glass,
   Czechoslovakia 95.00
Door stop, brown-glazed redware
   pottery, model of a sleeping cat,
   Ohio origins, 19th c., 13" l. (some
   chips) 260.00
Door stop, chalkware, model of a
   cat w/glass eyes, ca. 1900,
   14" l. 75.00
Model of a cat seated, Chelsea porcelain, auburn & white cat on
   green & gold cushion, 1¾" h. 105.00
Model of a cat in stretching position, china, blue & white, Russian,
   7" l. 140.00
Model of a cat seated, bisque, black
   & white coat, blue eyes, excellent
   fur details, impressed "D" on
   base, 8¼" h. 85.00
Model of a cat in reclining position,
   chalkware, ca. 1860, 11" l. 150.00
Pitcher w/figural cat handle, majoli-

ca, cobalt blue ground w/colorful
   blackberries & florals in relief 185.00
Plate, portrait of white Persian cat,
   souvenir or "Rhinelander, Wisc.,"
   5½" d....................... 26.00
Print, "My Little White Kittens -
   Playing Dominoes," small folio by
   Currier & Ives, beveled mahogany
   veneer frame, 16¼" w.,
   12¼" h....................... 85.00
Print, "My Little White Kittens - Taking the Cake," small folio by Currier & Ives, slightly trimmed
   margins, smoke-grained beveled
   pine frame, overall
   16¼ x 12¼"................... 125.00
Soap dish, blue-and-white utilitarian
   stoneware crockery, Cat Head
   patt. 90.00

Delft Tile Picture

Tile pictures, each composed of six
   Delft tiles, one w/cat painted in
   manganese & other w/cat painted
   in blue, Dutch, 18th/19th c.,
   15 x 9¾", framed, pr. (ILLUS.
   of one)...................... 605.00
Toothpick holder, papier mache, 3
   brown cats, 4 x 5" 28.00

CELLULOID

Celluloid was our first commercial plastic and early examples are now "antique" in their own right, having been produced as early as 1868 after the perfection of celluloid by John Wesley Hyatt. Also see ADVERTISING ITEMS, BOOKMARKS and BUTTON HOOKS.

Address book, clamp-on type for
   candlestick telephone, embossed
   telephone decor on cover $24.00

Collar box, creamy ivory & green, w/portrait of Victorian lady on lid 30.00

Collar & cuff box, creamy ivory, scenic decor on lid, lined interior 35.00

Curling iron, creamy ivory handle... 19.00

Dresser set: cov. hair receiver, cov. powder box & tray; creamy ivory, h.p. doves decor, 3 pcs. 27.00

Dresser set, Art Deco style, mottled tortoise shell brown, 4 pcs. 22.00

Dresser set, pearlized green w/amber trim, 7 pcs. 25.00

Dresser set: hairbrush, cov. hair receiver, cov. powder box, cov. jewelry box, ring box, nail buffer, 2 trinket boxes, button hook, perfume tube w/three triangular bottles w/faceted stoppers & razor box w/razor; creamy ivory, 15 pcs. 55.00

Glove box, creamy ivory, embossed plumes decor 24.00

Glove casket, camel back lid, overall pink & mauve roses & buds, purple & yellow pansies & green foliage on pale green ground, gold latticework design on sides & base, 18 x 11½", 6" h. 275.00

Hair comb, creamy ivory 20.00

Mirror, hand-type, w/beveled mirror plate, creamy ivory, 13" oval 22.00

Mustache comb, creamy ivory, w/silver case 30.00

Mustache scissors, creamy ivory handles 16.00

Nail Buffer and Rouge Jar

Nail buffer & cov. rouge jar, creamy ivory, 4½" l. & 1½" d., pr. (ILLUS.)....................... 12.00

Nail grooming set, creamy ivory w/coral trim, 5 pcs. 20.00

Napkin ring, creamy ivory, "Niagara Falls" & embossed Indian bust 15.00

Necktie box, creamy ivory 35.00

Powder jar, cov., creamy ivory 10.00

Shoe horn, creamy ivory 10.00

Talcum powder shaker, creamy ivory........................... 18.00

Thermometer, easel-type, creamy ivory, Wilder Co. 45.00

CERAMICS

ABINGDON

From about 1934 until 1950, Abingdon Pottery Company, Abingdon, Illinois, manufactured decorative pottery, mainly cookie jars, flower pots and vases. Decorated with various glazes, these items are becoming popular with collectors who are especially attracted to Abingdon's novelty cookie jars.

Ash tray, advertising, brown glaze.. $40.00

Ash tray, model of donkey at side, black glaze 60.00

Bookends, molded as an inkwell w/quill, 10", pr................. 45.00

Candle holders, Fern Leaf line w/vertical feathering in relief, turquoise glaze, 8" h., pr......... 68.00

Console set: 14" l. console bowl & pr. 2-light candle holders; rose glaze, 3 pcs.................... 20.00

Cookie jar, "Choo Choo".....42.00 to 65.00

Cookie jar, "Cookie Time Clock" ....30.00 to 48.00

Cookie jar, "Daisy," yellow & brown...................... 20.00

Cookie jar, "Humpty Dumpty" 50.00

Cookie jar, "Jack-O-Lantern"..................50.00 to 75.00

Cookie jar, "Jack-in-the-Box"....... 90.00

Cookie jar, "Little Bo Peep" ..50.00 to 95.00

Cookie jar, "Money Bag," white ....30.00 to 45.00

Cookie jar, "Rocking Horse"........ 125.00

Cornucopia-vase, blue glaze........ 12.00

Cornucopia-vase, pink glaze........ 20.00

Dish, shell-shaped, iridescent white glaze, 12" l. 10.00

Flower pot, h.p. cattails decor...... 10.00

Inkwell, advertising "First State & Savings, Abingdon, Illinois" 59.00

Model of a penguin 28.00

Planter, model of a peacock ....25.00 to 40.00

Vase, 6 3/8" h., yellow tulip each side, creamy ivory ground 18.00

Vase, 7" h., 2-handled, white daisies & leaves decor, celadon green ground 24.50

Vase, 10" h., steel blue glaze 14.00

Wall pocket, sunflower, red glaze .. 30.00

ADAMS

The Adams family has been potters in England since 1650. Three William Adamses made pottery all of it collectible. Most Adams pottery easily accessible today was made in the 19th century and is impressed or marked variously ADAMS, W. ADAMS, ADAMS TUNSTALL, W. ADAMS & SONS, and W. ADAMS & CO. with the word "England" or the phrase "made in England" added after 1891. Wm. Adams & Son, Ltd. continues in operation today. Also see FLOW BLUE and HISTORICAL & COMMEMORATIVE CHINA.

Adams "Oliver Twist" Mug

Cup & saucer, farmer size, Cries of
    London series...........$70.00 to 90.00
Cup & saucer, Sower patt., pink
    transfer...................... 47.50
Mug, Dickensware series - "Oliver
    Twist," scene of "Oliver Recap-
    tured by Fagin and the Boys" on
    side, creamy ivory w/green trim,
    4" h. (ILLUS.)................... 40.00
Pitcher, tankard, 7" h., black
    transfer-printed American eagle
    highlighted w/polychrome
    enameling...................... 60.00
Plate, 9½" d., Spanish Convent
    patt., brown transfer........... 25.00
Plate, 9 3/8" d., "The Sea," black
    transfer....................... 45.00

Columbus Series Plate

Plate, 9½" d., Landing of Columbus
    series - Indian scene, pink trans-
    fer (ILLUS.).................... 60.00

Plate, 10" d., Cries of London
    series - "Knives, Scissors & Razors
    to Grind"....................... 30.00
Plate, 10" d., Cries of London
    series - "Orange Seller"......... 32.00
Plate, 10" d., Dr. Syntax series -
    "Dr. Syntax Pays the Rent," blue
    transfer....................... 65.00
Plate, 10½" d., Caledonia patt.,
    purple-black transfer........... 75.00
Plate, 10 5/8" d., Caledonia patt.,
    red transfer................... 35.00
Plate, 11 7/8" d., black transfer-
    printed American eagle highlight-
    ed w/polychrome enameling,
    marked "Patriotic Ware - Adams
    Tunstall"....................... 60.00
Plate, Dr. Syntax series - "Bound to
    a Tree by Highway Men"......... 135.00
Platter, Caledonia patt., purple
    transfer....................... 150.00
Platter, Cattle Scenery patt., blue
    transfer, small................. 28.50
Soup plate w/flange rim, late
    Adam's Rose patt................ 55.00
Teapot, cov., dark blue transfer,
    1810-25........................ 250.00

ALCOCK (Samuel & Co.)

Parian "Distin Family" Jug

The Staffordshire potteries of Samuel Alcock & Co. operated from 1828 to 1859 at two
locations, Cobridge and Burslem. Their output included fine bone china, semi-porcelain,
blue-printed earthenwares, parian and bisque,
a sampling of which follows in our listing.

Cup & saucer, handleless, Tyrol
    patt., blue-printed earthenware,
    1839-46........................ $40.00
Dessert service: fruit stand, pr. cake
    stands & 8 plates (1 cracked); bone
    china, center w/realistic floral

sprigs on white, claret-ground rim
heightened w/"cracked ice" &
wrigglework gilding on yellow
shaded twig-edged panels, 1845-50,
11 pcs. 1,100.00

Pitcher, 8" h., ironstone, h.p. florals
& presentation inscription, dated
1851 . . . . 75.00

Pitcher, 9" h., jug-type, relief portraits of the Distin Family of "Sax
Horn Performers," each of 5
w/gentleman holding musical instrument within scrolling borders
on lilac ground, ca. 1850
(ILLUS.) 220.00

Plate, 9¼" d., Moselle patt., semi-
porcelain, purple transfer 20.00

Plates: 10 dessert & 8 dinner; bone
china, h.p. floral spray on white
center, cobalt blue-ground rim reserved w/yellow fan-shaped
panels feathered in gilding &
w/white floral sprays & gilt foli-
age, ca. 1844, set of 18 . . . . 275.00

Vases, 7¾" h., bone china, applied
sprays of colorful florals around
center bordering panels of open
basketwork, painted green leaf-
shaped foot & rim highlighted in
gilt w/vermicule designs over
shaded coral edges, ca. 1830,
pr. 300.00

AUSTRIAN

Fish Platter

*Numerous potteries in Austria produced
good-quality ceramic wares over many years.
Some factories were established by American
entrepreneurs, particularly in the Carlsbad
area, and other factories made china under
special brand names for American importers.
Marks on various pieces are indicated in
many listings. Also see KAUFFMANN
(Angelique) CHINA and ROYAL VIENNA
PORCELAIN.*

Bowl, 4¼" d., h.p. pansies & butter-
fly decor (Victoria-Carlsbad) $42.00

Box w/hinged lid, h.p. angels (2) on
green ground w/gold overlay,
2¾" h. (Victoria-Carlsbad) 235.00

Chocolate set: cov. chocolate pot &
6 c/s; pink tea roses decor, gold
handles, artist-signed, 13 pcs.
(M.Z.) 245.00

Creamer & cov. sugar bowl, ball-
shaped, Bluebird patt.,
(Victoria-Carlsbad) 42.00

Cup & saucer, demitasse, decal portrait of Louis XIV & Madame Pompadour on cobalt blue ground,
ornate gold trim (Victoria-
Carlsbad) 65.00

Cup & saucer, rooster & chicks decor
(Victoria-Carlsbad) 25.00

Dresser set: 14 x 9½" tray
w/pierced handles, ring tree, cov.
trinket bowl, handled perfume
ewer w/stopper & 7" h. candlestick; large floral sprays on white
ground, deeply scalloped & embossed rococo rims w/gilt high-
lights, 5 pcs. 85.00

Fish set: 16½" l. platter, gravy boat
w/attached underplate & eight
9" d. plates w/scalloped rims;
multicolored fish decor center,
10 pcs. (M.Z.) 115.00

Fish set: 11 x 8" platter & twelve
8½" d. plates; colorful fish in natural habitat center, greenish-blue
borders w/floral decals, 13 pcs.
(ILLUS. of part) 270.00

Hair receiver, cov., tall gold feet,
h.p. pink floral decor 42.00

Mug, h.p. ear of corn decor,
6" h. 59.00

Mustard jar, cover & attached underplate, Art Deco decor 38.00

Plaque, pierced to hang, bust portrait of Philippe d'Orleans the Regent, Madame Pompadour, the
Grand Dauphin, Montespan &
Count Mars reserved on cobalt
blue ground, heavy gold border,
12" d. (Victoria-Carlsbad) 150.00

Plate, 8" d., h.p. white grapes
w/red & green leaves, gold trim
(Imperial) 75.00

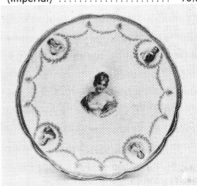

Austrian China Portrait Plate

Plate, 8½" d., decal bust portrait of
Madame Recamier center, Napo-
leon, Josephine & others at bor-
der, gold trim (ILLUS.) 45.00
Plate, 8½" d., decal portrait of
Queen Louise 18.00
Plate, 9" sq., reticulated rim, Blue-
bird patt. (Victoria-Carlsbad) 35.00
Plate, 9" d., h.p. red & pink roses .. 37.00
Plate, 9¼" d., portrait of lady w/au-
burn hair, green border 75.00
Plate, 10" d., h.p. yellow roses
decor 35.00
Relish tray, Bluebird patt., 8½" l.
(Victoria-Carlsbad) 38.00
Rose bowl, h.p. yellow roses on
cream ground, scalloped gold rim
(Carlsbad) 75.00
Salt & pepper shakers, ribbed body,
rose w/gold trim, pr. (O & E.G.,
1899-1913) 24.00
Sugar shaker, Bluebird patt.
(Victoria-Carlsbad) 48.00
Teapot & cover w/flower finial, h.p.
roses decor, 6½" h. (M.Z.) 120.00
Tea set: cov. teapot, creamer &
sugar bowl; mother-of-pearl finish
w/decal portrait on each, 3 pcs.
(pseudo beehive mark) 125.00
Tea set: cov. teapot, creamer, cov.
sugar bowl & tray; double ring
handles, holly decor, 4 pcs. 150.00
Urns, cov., metal pedestal base &
metal finial, multicolored decal
portrait front & reverse reserved
on maroon ground, gold trim,
11½" h., pr. 135.00
Vase, 7¾" h., 3 3/8" d., 3-footed
pedestal base w/relief-molded &
gilt lion masks, h.p. pink florals &
green leaves decor outlined in
gold 130.00
Vases, 13½" h., reserve portrait
medallion w/two ladies & cupid
front & h.p. scene reverse, pr. ... 325.00
Wine jug w/gilt stopper & gilt handles, h.p. pale green florals on
darker green ground, 7" h. 65.00

BAVARIAN

*Ceramics have been produced by various
potteries in Bavaria for many years. Those
appearing for sale in greatest frequency
today having been produced in the 19th and
early 20th centuries. Also see HUTSCHEN-
REUTHER, NYMPHENBURG and
ROSENTHAL.*

Ash tray, full figure Art Deco bisque
finish nude figure w/beige hair

seated on rim, white w/gold trim,
6 x 3½" $65.00
Basket w/overhead handle, roses
decor, small, Z.S. & Co. (Zeh,
Scherzer & Co.) 65.00
Bowl, 10" d., scalloped rim, decal
portrait decor 55.00

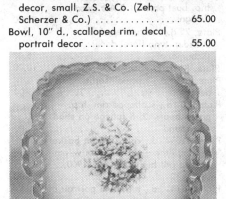

Bavarian Cake Plate

Cake plate, pierced handles, garden
flowers decal center, shaded
green rococo-embossed rim,
10½" sq. (ILLUS.)............... 40.00
Cake plate, pierced handles, scalloped rim, h.p. chrysanthemums
decor, satin finish, 11" d. 75.00
Candlesticks, h.p. forget-me-nots
decor, pr. 55.00
Cup & saucer, large pink roses on
pink lustre ground 35.00

Bavarian China with Gold Trim

Dinner service for 6: 6 dinner, salad, bread & butter plates & 6 c/s;
white w/gold rims & monogram,
30 pcs. (ILLUS. of part) 150.00
Dresser set: pr. perfume bottles &
cov. powder box; Art Deco decor,
3 pcs. 125.00
Game plate, pheasants center, wide
gold band & soft rose border 75.00
Hair receiver, cov., enameled white
& pastel roses, gold trim 27.00

Humidor & cover w/pipe finial, floral decor 68.00

Marmalade jar, cover & underplate, h.p. bust portrait & Art Deco designs 75.00

Plate, 7" d., reticulated rim, Dresden-type floral decor (Schumann).................... 75.00

Plate, 8" d., fruit decal 18.00

Plate, 8½" d., h.p. poinsettia decor 45.00

Plate, 10" d., scalloped rim, h.p. green pears (2) & foliage on shaded ground 45.00

Plates, 10¾" d., colorful fruit basket center, lime green borders w/embossed gilt highlights, ca. 1900, set of 12 .... 165.00

Plates, 11¼" d., h.p. bust portrait of Art Nouveau lady within daisy surrounds on cobalt blue ground, scalloped & gilt edge, pr. 312.00

Plate, h.p. porfile portrait of beautiful lady (R.C.).................. 70.00

Punch bowl, h.p. interior & exterior roses overall, gold pedestal base (H. & C.) 250.00

Salt & pepper shakers, pink apple blossom sprays on white ground, reticulated gold tops, pr. 25.00

Vase, 9½" h., portrait of gypsy woman on brown shaded to gold ground 95.00

Vase, 10" h., h.p. roses decor, gold trim......................... 75.00

Vase, 10" h., 4-footed cylinder, red poppies on green & red ground, gold trim, artist-signed 95.00

BELLEEK

Belleek china has been made in Ireland's County Fermanagh for many years. It is exceedingly thin porcelain. Several marks were used, including a hound and harp (1865-1880), and a hound, harp and castle (1863-1891). A printed hound, harp and castle with the words "Co. Fermanagh Ireland" constitutes the mark from 1891. Belleek-type china also was made in the United States last century by several firms, including Ceramic Art China Works, Columbian Art Pottery, Lenox Inc., Ott & Brewer and Willets Manufacturing Co. Also see COMMEMORATIVE PLATES.

AMERICAN
Bouillon cup, ornate gold-encrusted trim, 1924 (Morgan Belleek China Co.)........................... $25.00

Bowl, 7" d., 4" h., scalloped &

crimped rim, h.p. pink wild roses & green leaves decor on sides, heavy gold interior & gold-edged handles (Willets) 169.00

Bowl, 7½" d., h.p. portrait decor (Willets)....................... 275.00

Bowl, 8½" d., 4½" h., creamy ivory (Willets)....................... 75.00

Chalice, blended burgundy to red currant clusters & variegated green leaves decor, gilt interior, artist-signed, 11¼" h. (Willets) ... 285.00

Coffee set: cov. coffee pot, creamer & cov. sugar bowl; gold spout, square base w/decorated corners, h.p. V-shaped pink rose garlands w/green foliage, 3 pcs.......... 225.00

Creamer, gold handle & wide lip, overall h.p. pansies, other florals & leaves decor, 3" h. (Ott & Brewer)........................... 175.00

Cup & saucer, demitasse, Art Deco decor (Coxon).................. 90.00

Willets Belleek Desk Set

Desk set: rocker-type blotter & stamp moistener; Delft-type decor w/h.p. blue windmill & water scene on white, 6" l. blotter & 3" w. moistener, Willets, 2 pcs. (ILLUS.)........................ 285.00

Ewer, shell-molded w/twig handle, shaded pink, heavy gold trim, 8½" h. (Willets)............... 675.00

Ewer, twig handle, encrusted gold trim, 10½" h. (Ott & Brewer) 1,000.00

Mug, h.p. scene of 2 monks seated & drinking, 5½" h. (Ceramic Art Co.)............................ 160.00

Mug, h.p. bust portrait of man, green tones (Lenox) 125.00

Mug, tankard w/applied lizard form handle, St. Bernard dog decor, signed "G. Houghton" (Willets) ... 450.00

Pitcher, 6" h., cherry motif (Ott & Brewer) 110.00

Pitcher, tankard, 11" h., 6½" base d., branches w/hanging lemons, blossoms & leaves decor on shaded cream to green ground, artist-signed (Lenox Palette mark) 275.00

Pitcher, 15" h., gold dragon handle, green & purple grape clusters on cream ground, artist-signed & dated 1910 (Willets) 250.00

Pitcher, tankard, lizard handle, St. Bernard decor, artist-signed (Willets) 650.00

Plate, 8½" d., scalloped, poly-
chrome florals & gold paste foli-
age (Ott & Brewer) 110.00
Plate, 10" d., "Canada Goose in
Flight," artist-signed (Lenox) 140.00
Plate, 10" d., "Orchids," artist-
signed (Lenox) 140.00
Plate, 11" d., handled, Art Nouveau
gold rim, h.p. decor, 1912 (green
Palette mark) 65.00
Rose bowl-vase, h.p. roses w/gold
tracery 125.00
Salt dip, open, gold rim & legs, "C"
monogram, 2¼" d. (Willets)...... 20.00
Salt dips, 3-footed, pastel interiors,
pink roses exterior, 2" d., set of 6
(Willets) 60.00

Ceramic Art Company Stein

Stein, h.p. silver lid, dated 1898,
faint line on underside of base,
Ceramic Art Company (ILLUS.) 340.00
Sugar bowl, cov., silver overlay Art
Deco design around inverted
heart (Lenox) 55.00
Toothpick holder, urn-shaped, foot-
ed, gold band (Lenox) 48.00
Tray, ruffled gold rim, gold paste
floral decor, 6" sq. (Ceramic Art
Company) 140.00

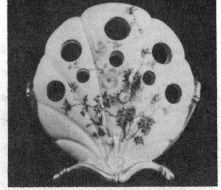

Ceramic Art Company Vase

Vase, 5" h., pierced shell design,
h.p. florals, ca. 1890, Ceramic Art
Company Palette mark (ILLUS.) ... 300.00
Vase, 7 7/8" h., 2¼" d., cylindrical,
h.p. wide pastel blue bands
w/trailing roses top & bottom,
ivory ground (Willets)........... 65.00
Vase, 8" h., h.p. magenta roses on
green ground (Willets) 100.00
Vase, 9" h., blue floral decor
(Lenox)....................... 125.00
Vase, 12" h., swans swimming in
pond decor (Lenox Palette
mark) 160.00
Vase, 12½" h., autumn leaves
decor, ca. 1879 (Ceramic Art Com-
pany) 145.00
Vase, 15" h., h.p. green ferns decor
(Willets) 295.00
Vase, 15" h., pedestal base, white &
red roses decor (Ceramic Art
Company) 295.00
Vase, 16" h., 2 white cranes w/or-
ange trim on black, grey & cream
ground (Willets) 255.00
Vase, slender neck, gold griffin handles, lilac decor (Ceramic Art
Company) 295.00

IRISH

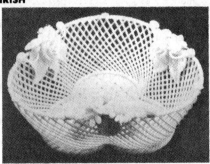

Shamrock Basket Ware

Basket-dish, Basket Ware, 3-strand,
shamrock (trefoil) shape, applied
florals at rim, small size, 1st black
mark (ILLUS.) 325.00
Bowl, 4½" d., Tridacna patt., 1st
black mark 90.00
Bread plate, Harp Shamrock patt.,
3rd black mark 105.00
Bread plate, Hawthorne patt.,
9½" d., 1st black mark 372.00
Brush tray, scalloped rim, Hawthorne patt., center w/blue spider
web, 1st black mark 325.00
Creamer, Echinus patt., gold trim,
3 7/8" h., 1st black mark 175.00
Creamer, Mask patt., large, 3rd
black mark 85.00
Creamer & sugar bowl, Lotus patt.,
green, 2nd black mark, pr........ 125.00

Creamer & sugar bowl, Toy Shell
patt., 2nd black mark, pr......... 115.00
Cup & saucer, demitasse, Mask
patt., 3rd black mark 95.00
Cup & saucer, Cone patt., green
trim, 2nd black mark .....95.00 to 140.00
Cup & saucer, Echinus patt., 1st
black mark 97.50
Cup & saucer, Erne patt., green
trim, 2nd black mark 195.00
Cup & saucer, Harp Shamrock patt.,
2nd black mark 70.00
Cup & saucer, Hexagon patt., green
trim, 2nd black mark 70.00
Cup & saucer, Mask patt., 1st black
mark........................ 110.00
Cup & saucer, Shamrock-
Basketweavae patt., 2nd black
mark........................ 45.00
Cup & saucer, Tridacna patt., pink
trim, 2nd black mark 65.00
Dish, Sycamore Leaf patt., 4½", 3rd
black mark 50.00
Dish, 12-point star-shaped Hexagon
patt., 6" w., 2nd black mark 60.00
Dish, Shell patt., white w/pink trim
decor, 6½" d., 1st black mark.... 125.00
Egg cup, Shamrock-Basketweave
patt., 2nd black mark 70.00
Egg cup, Tridacna patt., 1st black
mark........................ 99.00
Flower holders, model of seahorse
on base, 1st black mark, pr. 800.00
Flower pot, Diamond patt., 3½" h.,
1st green mark 55.00
Holy water font, cherub's head &
wings in full relief over basin, 3rd
black mark 250.00
Lithophane panel, scene of barefoot
priest & alcolyte, shoes in hand,
crossing stream 2,400.00
Model of seahorse w/shell, 5" l., 1st
black mark 450.00
Model of Greyhound dog, 6" h., 3rd
black mark 615.00
Model of swan, 1st black mark 225.00
Model of Prince Charles' dog on
cushion, 1st black mark......... 800.00
Mug, Shamrock patt., 3", 2nd black
mark........................ 48.00
Mustard jar w/lid, Shamrock patt.,
3rd black mark 50.00
Pitcher, milk, 6" h., Shamrock patt.,
3rd black mark 125.00
Pitcher, milk, 6" h., green handle,
white berries w/green & white
leaves, 1st green mark 120.00
Pitcher, Nautilus patt., 1st black
mark........................ 175.00
Placecard holder, carnation blossoms & leaves on front, reverse
w/smaller applied flowers &
leaves, lustre ground, 2nd black
mark........................ 231.00
Plate, 6" d., Ivy patt., gold berries &

shaded green leaves, gold trim,
2nd black mark 57.00
Plate, 6" d., Tridacna patt., coral
rim, 1st black mark 100.00
Plate, 6½" d., Limpet patt., gold
trim, 3rd black mark 36.00
Plate, 6½" d., Shamrock-
Basketweave patt., 1st black
mark........................ 35.00
Plate, 6¾" d., Thistle patt., pink
trim, 2nd black mark 75.00
Plate, 7½" d., Tridacna patt., 3rd
black mark 190.00
Plate, 8" d., Grasses patt., 1st black
mark........................ 70.00
Plate, 8" d., Harp-Shamrock patt.,
1st green mark 35.00
Plate, 8" d., Limpet patt., 3rd black
mark........................ 37.00
Plate, 10" d., crimped irregular
edge trimmed in pink w/gold
band, green factory scene center,
2nd black mark 550.00
Salt dip, fluted, star-shaped, 3rd
black mark 35.00
Salt dip, Limpet patt., white w/lus-
tre, 2nd black mark 75.00
Salt dip, Shell patt., 2nd black
mark........................ 48.00

Rock Spillholder

Spillholder, cornucopia on rock form
base, 9½" h., 1st black mark
(ILLUS.)..................... 410.00
Salt & pepper shakers, Tridacna
patt., yellow trim, pr. 75.00
Spillholder, Cleary patt., 5" h., 1st
black mark 112.00
Spillholder, Indian Corn patt., 1st
black mark 340.00
Spillholder, Nautilus Shell on Flying
Fish, 1st black mark 275.00
Sugar bowl, cov., Hexagon patt.,
2nd black mark 52.00
Sugar bowl, open, Neptune patt.,
green, 2nd black mark 100.00

Sugar bowl, open, Shell & Shamrock
patt., 3rd black mark 32.00
Tea kettle, cov., Hexagon patt.,
pink trim, small, 2nd black
mark......................... 394.00
Tea kettle, cov., Shamrock patt., 3rd
black mark 205.00
Tea kettle, cov., Tridacna patt.,
green trim, 6" d., 5½" h., 2nd
black mark & also impressed 1st
black mark 383.00
Teapot, cov., Cone patt., rust trim &
gilt, 2nd black mark 495.00
Teapot, cov., Erne patt., green trim,
2nd black mark 495.00
Teapot, cov., Grasses patt., 2nd
black mark 275.00
Teapot, cov., Neptune patt., yellow
trim, medium size, 2nd black
mark......................... 290.00
Teapot, cov., Shell patt., pale green
trim, 2nd black mark 360.00

Shamrock-Basketweave Tea Set

Tea set: cov. teapot, creamer & cov.
sugar bowl; Shamrock-Basketweave patt., 3rd black mark,
3 pcs. (ILLUS.).................. 160.00
Tea set: cov. teapot, creamer &
open sugar bowl; Shell patt.,
w/shell feet, 2nd black mark,
3 pcs. 450.00
Tea set: 4¾" d., 4" h. cov. teapot,
open sugar bowl, creamer, cup &
saucer & 12¼ x 15" tray; Echinus
patt., pink trim, 1st black mark,
6 pcs. 1,750.00
Tea set: cov. teapot, cov. sugar
bowl, creamer, 6 c/s & six 7¼" d.
plates; Limpet patt., 3rd black
mark, 21 pcs................... 665.00
Tray, Tridacna patt., green trim, 2nd
black mark 475.00
Trinket box, cov., Shamrock patt.,
3¾" oval 50.00
Tumbler, ribbed, Shamrock patt.,
large, 2nd black mark 114.00
Vase, 3½" h., model of seahorse on
rectangular base, all white, 1st
black mark 333.00
Vase, 4 x 4", Nautilus patt., trellis &
roses decor, 2nd black mark 135.00

Vase, 4 3/8" h., 2¾ x 4¼", flying
fish below shell cornucopia, pink
trim, 2nd black mark 480.00
Vase, 6" h., formed as an ear of
corn, green, yellow & pearl, 1st
black mark 350.00
Vase, 7" h., yellow & cream Grape
patt., 3rd green mark 54.00
Vase, 8½" h., Nautilus Shell on coral branches, pink trim, 2nd black
mark......................... 765.00

Nile Pattern Vase

Vase, 13" h., 6½" d., Nile patt.,
white, 2nd black mark (ILLUS.) ... 495.00
Vase, 13" h., 8½" d., Hoof Tripod,
1st black mark 675.00
Vase, Nautilus patt., white, 1st
black mark 325.00
Vase, Rathburn patt., 3rd black
mark......................... 210.00

BENNINGTON

Bennington Lion

*Bennington wares, which ranged from
stonewares to parian and porcelain, were*

made in Bennington, Vt., primarily in two potteries, one in which Captain John Norton and his descendants were principals, and the other in which Christopher Webber Fenton (also once associated with the Nortons) was a principal. Various marks are found on the wares made in the two major potteries, including J. & E. Norton, E. & L. P. Norton, L. Norton & Co., Norton & Fenton, Edward Norton, Lyman Fenton & Co., Fenton's Works, United States Pottery Co., U.S.P. and others.

The popular pottery with the mottled brown on yellowware glaze was also produced in Bennington, but such wares should be referred to as "Rockingham" or "Bennington-type" unless they can be specifically attributed to a Bennington, Vermont factory. Also see HOUND HANDLED PITCHERS and ROCKINGHAM.

Book flask, mottled brown Rock-
   ingham glaze . . . . $250.00 to 400.00
Book flask, mottled brown Rock-
   ingham glaze w/yellow flecks,
   5 5/8" h. (minor glaze chips at 2
   corners) 225.00
Candlestick, mottled brown Rock-
   ingham glaze, 6 3/8" h.
   (single) 250.00
Candlestick, domed base, cylindrical
   stem w/ring, plain nozzle, mottled
   brown Rockingham glaze, 9½" h.
   (single) 200.00
Coachman bottle, figural coachman
   w/bottle in hand, tassels, mustache & protruding feet, impressed "1849" mark on base,
   10" h. (base hairline) 292.50
Crock, cobalt blue leaf on grey, im-
   pressed "E. & L.P. Norton, Bennington, Vt.," 7¼" h. 175.00
Crock, blue florals on grey, im-
   pressed "E. & L.P. Norton," 11" d.,
   10½" h. 165.00
Cuspidor w/side vent, Shell patt.,
   Rockingham glaze, 8½ x 3½" 112.00
Cuspidor, Diamond pattern, Flint Enamel glaze, w/olive green, faintly
   impressed "1849" mark, 9½" d. . . 115.00
Jug, semi-ovoid, strap handle,
   brushed cobalt blue foliage on
   grey, impressed "E. Norton & Co.,
   Bennington, Vt.," 10¼" h. 185.00
Jug, straight sides, applied handle,
   cobalt blue slip-quilled floral
   spray on grey, impressed "E. &
   L.P. Norton, Bennington," 11¼" h.
   (minor hairline in bottom) 275.00
Jug, stoneware, cobalt blue bird on
   branch on grey, J.E. Norton,
   1½-gal. 495.00
Model of a lion standing, w/front
   left paw resting on a ball, tex-

tured string mane, mottled brown
   Rockingham glaze, 1849-58,
   7½" h. (restored) 495.00
Model of a lion standing, w/one
   paw resting on a ball, rectangular
   base, 19th c., 9" h. (ILLUS.) 352.00
Vase, Heron patt., Flint Enamel
   glaze 575.00

Bennington Gothic Water Cooler

Water cooler, Gothic pattern, octagonal form with double arched
panels in each section, brick-style
base, spigot hole at one corner,
light grey-green Flint Enamel glaze
with green splashes, impressed,
"Bennington 1849" on base,
cover missing, 16½" h. (ILLUS.) . . 1,100.00

BENNINGTON-TYPE
Bowl, 6" d., 3" h., mottled brown
   Rockingham glaze 75.00
Foot warmer, mottled brown Rock-
   ingham glaze 400.00
Goblet, mottled brown Rockingham
   glaze, 4 5/8" h. 215.00
Jug, fox handle, Rockingham
   glaze 125.00

Bennington-type Mixing Bowl

Mixing bowl, Rockingham glaze,
   8½" d. 85.00
Mug, mottled brown Rockingham
   glaze, 3 1/8" h. 100.00
Mug, mottled brown Rockingham
   glaze, early 19th c., 4½" h. 265.00

Pitcher, 8" h., Basketweave patt. on brown stoneware, bunches of grapes & leaves decor 125.00

Pitcher, 10" h., hen on nest w/rooster fighting off hawk 190.00

Soap dish, mottled brown Rockingham glaze 75.00

Pitcher, 6½" h., relief-molded grapes & leaves on sides, dark brown glaze 85.00

BERLIN (KPM)

Painting of "Ruth"

The mark, KPM, was used at Meissen from 1723 to 1725, and was later adopted by the Royal Factory, Konigliche Porzellan Manufaktur, in Berlin. At various periods it has been incorporated with the Brandenburg sceptre, the Prussian eagle or the crowned globe. The same letters were also adopted by other factories in Germany in the late 19th and 20th centuries. With the end of the German monarchy in 1918, the name of the firm was changed to Staatliche Porzellan Manufaktur and though production was halted during World War II, the factory was rebuilt and is still in business. The exquisite paintings on porcelain produced at the close of the 19th century and eagerly sought by collectors today.

Candelabra, 2-light, figural girl in a tree, all white, ca. 1887 ....$250.00

Jug, figural seated court jester (or devil) w/hat stopper, mouth pour, gold trim, ca. 1830, 4½" h. 145.00

Painting on porcelain, girl holding candle, 5¼ x 3¾", ornate frame 250.00

Painting on porcelain, entitled "Der Grossvater's Liebling," after Myers, grandfather & granddaughter scene, 8 x 7", framed ..1,500.00

Painting on porcelain, entitled "Flora," signed A. Wickner, 9 x 6" oblong, framed...........1,100.00

Painting on porcelain, Ruth (after Landelle), wearing a flowing grey garment, her brown tresses covered by a white kerchief, holding a sheaf of wheat, late 19th c., 9¼ x 6¼" (ILLUS.) 1,100.00

Painting of "Shamrock"

Painting on porcelain, "Shamrock," portrait of maiden w/long hair wearing classical costume against leaf-patterned ground, artist-signed, ca. 1910, 9¼ x 6¼" (ILLUS.) 2,090.00

Painting on porcelain, entitled "The Penitent Magdalene," reading the book of Scriptures & wearing a flowing blue garment, a skull nearby, late 19th c., 9¼ x 6 3/8" 3,025.00

Painting on porcelain, entitled "Expectation," young gypsy girl wearing an exotic flowing blue garment standing beside a stone fountain w/one hand raised to her forehead & gazing into the distance, 3rd quarter 19th c., 9 3/8 x 6¼" 880.00

Painting on porcelain, "Card Players" (after Teniers, 1610-95), velvet matt & giltwood frame, overall 10 x 8".................. 225.00

Painting on porcelain, entitled "Innocence," bust-length portrait of brown-haired maiden wearing a blue & diaphanous white shawl about her shoulders, signed

Wagner, late 19th c.,
13 5/8" oval....................4,510.00
Painting on porcelain, cloudy landscape w/August fir trees in foreground, green, blue & white,
artist-signed, early 20th c.,
framed, overall 14 1/8 x 14 1/8".. 660.00

BILOXI (George Ohr) POTTERY

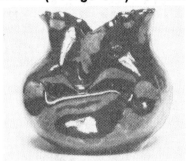

George E. Ohr Vase

*George Ohr, the eccentric potter of Biloxi,
Mississippi, worked from about 1883 to 1906.
Some think him to be one of the most expert
throwers the craft will ever see. The majority of his works were hand thrown, exceedingly thin-walled items, some of which have a
crushed or folded appearance. He considered
himself the foremost potter in the world and
declined to sell much of his production, instead accumulated a great horde to leave as
a legacy to his children. In 1972, this collection was purchased for resale by an antique
dealer.*

Bowl, brown glaze, signed $145.00
Bowl, crimped edges, light green
glaze w/mottled brown spots,
signed 225.00
Pitcher, 7½" h., ribbed handle, rol-
licking cherubs in relief one side
& incised flowering tree opposite,
black crystalline glaze 990.00
Vase, 3½" h., pinched sides, mottled glaze, signed 255.00
Vase, 4" h., bulbous, unglazed, 1
large handle one side & 2 attached handles opposite, marked
"Expo Clay 1904" & signed 295.00
Vase, 5½" h., dark green matte
glaze 480.00
Vase, 7¾" h., elongated double
gourd shape, streaked red, green,
light blue & gun-metal glaze,
signed......................1,045.00
Vase, 8" h., ruffled & crinkled body,
oil-splashed deep green glaze,
signed (ILLUS.) 695.00

BISQUE

Bust of Apollo

*Bisque is biscuit china, fired a single time
but not glazed. Some bisque is decorated with
colors. Most abundant from the Victorian era
are figurines and groups, but other pieces
from busts to vases were made by numerous
potteries in the U.S. and abroad. Also see
KEWPIE COLLECTIBLES and TOBACCO
JARS.*

Animal covered dish, dog w/bone
on basketweave base, brown &
white dog lying on his side on
green blanket, white & gilt
basketweave base, 9 x 6½",
5½" h. $495.00
Basket-vase, barefoot boy wearing
wide-brimmed hat seated on rim,
marked Germany & numbered,
8" h. 45.00
Bust of Apollo, mythological Greek
god of sun, on waisted socle base,
France, late 19th c., restored,
28½" h. (ILLUS.) 1,760.00
Candlestick, double, girl w/blonde
hair wearing blue & white dress
seated on swing suspended between columns, gilt trim, 5¾ x
2½", 8¾" h..................... 190.00
Figure of a young black boy wearing
orange shorts & turban seated in
tan & green chair, 2¾" d.,
4¾" h. 85.00
Figure of a bathing beauty lying on
her stomach, wearing green bathing suit & red floppy hat, marked
Germany & numbered, 5" l. 125.00
Figure of a young blond boy seated
on a swing & holding a harlequin
doll, wearing light blue hat &
clothing w/gold trim, 3" d.,
5½" h. 100.00
Figure of a girl dancing, wearing
green dress w/white collar & pink

bow, marked Heubach, 3¼ x
2¼", 6½" h.................... 75.00

Figure of a peasant girl w/black
hair & red headdress, green skirt,
white blouse & white apron
w/green & red trim, tan peanut-
shaped basket at her feet,
Heubach, 5¾" d., 8½" h........ 195.00

Figure of girl holding rabbit, pastel
coloring, Heubach mark (France),
9½" h. 150.00

Figure of boy seated on wicker
chair, wearing eyeglasses &
smoking a cigar, pastel coloring,
Heubach, 14½" h 380.00

Figures, boy & girl wearing wire-
rimmed glasses & fur-trimmed
costumes, holding school books,
late 19th c., 7" h., pr. 195.00

Figures, man & woman holding
(removable) brooms w/wooden
handles, pastel shades of cream
w/pink florals on skirt & pants &
tan & pink trim overall, France,
13½" h., pr. 407.00

Model of a dog seated, long-haired
white coat, brown intaglio eyes,
rust collar, Heubach, 3½ x 2½"
base, 6" h. 75.00

Model of a dog dressed as a drummer, wearing ornate hat
w/plume, red, white & blue jacket
& blue & white striped trousers,
marked "Bibi Tapin" & numbered
on base, 3½ x 4½", 10¼" h. 175.00

Nodding figure, seated man in
jester's costume w/helmet-like
headgear & holding a pipe, pastel
peach & white w/gold trim,
2½" d., 3½" h. 70.00

Nodding figures, Turkish lady & gentleman, she dressed in pink
w/gold dot trim, gold necklace &
bracelet, he in green & lavender,
blue turban w/gold trim, holding
pipe, w/moving tongues, 2½" d.,
4½" h., pr. 245.00

Nodding Figures

Nodding figures, Oriental lady &
gentleman, wearing pink robes
enriched w/gilding & seated before a keyboard centered w/music

book, Continental, 19th c. (one
w/repairs), 8¾" h., pr. (ILLUS.)... 495.00

Piano Babies

Piano baby, black boy wearing polka dot rompers, Heubach, 5" h. .. 800.00

Piano baby, seated w/hands on 1
foot, wearing white gown w/blue
trim, Heubach, 7¼" h........... 275.00

Piano baby, boy seated, wearing
blue hat & holding a drum, Royal
Rudolstadt, Germany, 8" 350.00

Piano baby, kneeling boy holding
pig trying to drink from chamber
pot, 8½" h.................... 400.00

Piano baby, boy wearing blue shift
& white apron, throwing ball,
Heubach, 12" h................. 495.00

Snow baby w/camera, 1¾" h....... 125.00

Snow baby "Santa," red & white
Santa sitting in front of green
sleigh, brown reindeer, marked
Germany & numbered, 3½" l. 225.00

Snow baby w/banjo or saxophone,
pebbled bisque garments, Germany, each 75.00

Snow baby on skis, pebbled bisque
garments, marked Germany 75.00

"Swinging" figures, black boy & girl,
each wearing blue outfit & hat,
2¾" d., 5¾" h., pr. 225.00

Vase, 3½" h., 1 7/8" d., figural
"googlie" eyed girl w/blonde hair,
blue skirt, orange top, white
apron & hat, w/small brown teddy
bear, marked Shafer & Vater..... 75.00

BLUE WILLOW

Blue Willow Pattern

This pseudo-Chinese pattern has been used by numerous firms throughout the years. The original design is attributed to Thomas Minton about 1780 and Thomas Turner is believed to have first produced the ware during his tenure at the Caughley works. The blue underglaze transfer print pattern has never been out of production since that time. An oriental landscape incorporating a bridge, pagoda, trees, figures and birds, supposedly tells the story of lovers fleeing a cruel father who wished to prevent their marriage. The gods, having pity on them, changed them into birds enabling them to fly away and seek their happiness together. Also see BUFFALO POTTERY.

Bacon rasher, Allertons $35.00
Bone dish, Wedgwood 16.00
Bowl, 6" d., scalloped rim,
   Allertons 15.00
Bowl, 9" d., Ridgway 40.00
Butter dish, cov., round, Booths 60.00
Butter pat, Allertons, 3" d. 18.00
Canister, cov., Ridgway, qt. 75.00
Coffee pot, cover & warming stand,
   Japan 150.00
Creamer, individual size,
   Shenango 7.00
Creamer, Buffalo Pottery 55.00
Creamer & cov. sugar bowl,
   Allertons, pr. 50.00
Creamer & cov. sugar bowl, Japan,
   pr. 39.00
Cup & saucer, demitasse, Burleigh
   Ware 22.50
Cup & saucer, handleless, Buffalo
   Pottery 18.00
Cup & saucer, Allertons 20.00
Cup & saucer, Homer Laughlin 10.00
Dish, shell-shaped w/closed handle,
   Ridgway, 7" w. 35.00
Egg coddler, w/original metal
   screw-on lid, Royal Worcester,
   1912 .... 68.00
Gravy boat, Buffalo Pottery, 1911 ... 50.00
Gravy boat w/underplate,
   England 60.00
Horseradish dish, Doulton & Co. 30.00
Horseradish dish, Japan 50.00
Mixing bowls, nest-type, 4" to
   8½" d., Villeroy & Boch, set
   of 4 .... 350.00
Mug, Shenango Pottery 12.50
Mustard jar, cover & ladle 49.00
Pickle dish, Buffalo Pottery, 1911 ... 22.00
Pitcher, milk, 7" h., w/metal lid,
   Booths, 1880's 135.00
Pitcher, tankard, Allertons 95.00
Plate, 6" d., Japan 3.00
Plate, 7" d., scalloped rim,
   Allertons 10.00
Plate, 7" d., Ridgway 20.00
Plate, 7¼" d., Buffalo Pottery,
   1911 .... 10.00

Plate, 8" d., Adams 12.00
Plate, 8" d., Buffalo Pottery, 1911 ... 13.00
Plate, 9" d., Occupied Japan 8.00
Plate, 9" d., Ridgway 15.00
Plate, 9" d., Shenango Pottery 10.00
Plate, 9¼" d., Japan 6.00
Plate, 9½" d., Allertons 12.00
Plate, 10" d., Allertons 14.00
Plate, 10" d., Japan 5.00
Plate, 10" d., Ridgway 12.50
Plate, chop, 13" d., Allertons 40.00
Plate, dinner, Johnson Bros. 7.00
Platter, 9½" l., Allertons 25.00
Platter, 10½ x 8½", Buffalo Pottery,
   1911 .... 22.00
Platter, 11¼ x 9", Allertons 36.00
Platter, 12 x 9" oval, Ridgway 23.00
Platter, 13½ x 10¾", deep,
   Ridgway 55.00
Platter, 16 x 12", Johnson Bros. 32.00
Platter, 16¾ x 13½", Andrew
   Stevenson, pre-1818 .... 175.00
Platter w/well & tree, 18½ x 14",
   unmarked England 275.00
Relish dish, Allertons, 8½ x 4¾" ... 35.00
Relish dish, Buffalo Pottery, 1909,
   4½ x 5½" 18.00
Salt & pepper shakers, Japan, pr. .. 12.00
Salt & pepper shakers, pr. 26.00
Salt box, cov., Japan 45.00
Sauce dish, Allertons, 4¾" d. 6.00
Sauce dish, Japan 6.00
Soup plate w/flange rim, Ridgway,
   8" d. 8.00
Sugar bowl, cov., Allertons 35.00
Sugar bowl, cov., large, Buffalo Pot-
   tery, 1911 .... 35.00
Sugar bowl, cov., Ridgway 52.00
Teacups, handleless, Buffalo Pot-
   tery, set of 4 .... 18.00
Teapot, cov., child's, Occupied
   Japan 35.00
Teapot, cov., Japan, 1-cup individual
   size 25.00
Teapot, cov., small, Sadler 17.00
Teapot, cov., Woods 85.00
Tea set, child's, cov. teapot,
   creamer & sugar bowl, 3 pcs. 45.00
Tea set, cov. teapot, creamer, cov.
   sugar bowl & 2 c/s, 7 pcs. 62.00
Tea set, cov. teapot, creamer, cov.
   sugar bowl & 6 c/s, 15 pcs. 125.00

Blue Willow Child's Tureen

Tureen, cover & underplate, child's,
  5" l., 3¼" h. (ILLUS.) 45.00
Tureen, cov., ornate handles, Royal
  Worcester, 1902 .... 95.00

Blue Willow Copeland Tureen

Tureen, open, Copeland, 15" l.
  (ILLUS.) 150.00
Tureen, pedestal base, unmarked,
  11" oval 150.00
Vegetable dish, cov., large,
  Allertons 87.00
Vegetable dish, cov., square, large,
  Ridgway 75.00
Vegetable dish, open, Buffalo Pot-
  tery, 6¼ x 5" 35.00
Vegetable dish, open, Ridgway, 9".. 45.00
Wall pocket, Samovar-shaped,
  Japan 65.00

BOCH FRERES

Boch Freres Vases

   *This Belgium firm, founded in 1841 and still
in production, first produced stoneware art
pottery of mediocre quality, attempting to upgrade their wares through the years. In 1907,
Charles Catteau became the art director of the
pottery and slowly the influence of his work
was absorbed by the artisans surrounding
him. All through the 1920's, wares were decorated in a distinctive Art Deco motif that is
now eagerly sought along with the hand-
thrown gourd form vessels coated with earth-
tone glazes that were produced during the
same time. Almost all Boch Freres pottery
is marked, but the finest wares also carry the
signature of Charles Catteau in addition to
the pottery mark.*

Plaques, pierced to hang, elderly
  lady reading by window on one &
  elderly gentleman smoking clay
  pipe on second, each w/house &
  ship in background, blue & white
  w/floral borders, small, pr. $90.00
Vase, 9½" h., tiered conical form,
  black & orange-brown rectangles
  on crazed white ground 770.00
Vase, 10" h., ovoid, blue, yellow,
  lime green & turquoise birds
  amidst yellow, brown & fuchsia
  flowers (ILLUS. left) 715.00
Vase, 11" h., elongated oviform, incised dark brown stylized storks
  on pale yellow-speckled tan &
  brown ground 770.00
Vases, 11½" h., swollen cylinder,
  central band of mustard, navy
  blue & white spirals & yellow,
  navy blue, brown & light orange
  stars on black ground, pr. 990.00
Vase, 11¾" h., swollen cylinder,
  brown & yellow monkeys amidst
  ochre & brown palm trees on light
  blue crazed ground (ILLUS.
  right) 528.00
Vase, 12½" h., footed hexagon,
  three stepped rectangular handles, alternating sides w/navy
  blue, aquamarine & white geometric pattern 418.00

Boch Freres Vases

Vase, 13¼" h., ovoid, green-spotted
  black, navy blue & turquoise deer
  amidst stylized navy blue & turquoise foliage, designed by
  Charles Catteau (ILLUS. right) 715.00
Vase, 14½" h., tiered baluster form,
  central band of black, grey, light
  blue & brown stylized storks on a
  pale yellow, blue, grey & black
  ground, designed by Charles
  Catteau 1,650.00
Vase, 16" h., ovoid w/short cylindrical neck, incised & enameled
  black trelliswork embellished in
  yellow & orange w/clusters &

panels of stylized fruit & leaves
on a crackled grey & white
ground, ca. 1925 .... 302.50

Vase, 16" h., tiered baluster form,
broad central band of mottled
brown & pastel green elephants &
palm trees bordered by angular
pastel green bands on a mottled
brown ground, designed by Charles
Catteau, ca. 1928 ....2,860.00

Vase, 19½" h., ovoid, broad central
crazed white band w/green-spot-
ted turquoise, black & navy blue
deer amongst green & navy
foliage 1,320.00

Vase, 20" h., ovoid, bright orange,
green & pale blue birds on lavender trees bordered by large scar-
let & turquoise flowers 1,430.00

Vase, 20" h., ovoid, crazed blue
glaze (ILLUS. left) 550.00

BOEHM PORCELAINS

Road Runner by Boehm

*Although not antique, Boehm porcelain
sculptures have attracted much interest, Edward Marshall Boehm excelled in hard porcelain sculptures. His finest creations,
inspired by the beauties of nature, are in the
forms of birds and flowers. Since his death
in 1969, his work has been carried on by his
wife at the Boehm Studios in Trenton, New
Jersey. In 1971, an additional studio was
opened in Malvern, England, where bone porcelain sculptures are produced. We list both
limited and non-limited editions of the Boehm
Studios.*

Black-Capped Chickadee (Male on
Holly Leaves), bisque, decorated,
1957, 9" h. $750.00

Black-Headed Grosbeak (Male on
Vine Maple), bisque, decorated,
1969, 10 x 14½" 1,600.00

Blue Grosbeak with Fall Foliage,
bisque, decorated, 1967, 11" h. ...1,300.00

Bob White Quail, bisque, 1953,
7½" h. male & 6" h. female,
pr. 2,300.00

Brown Pelican, bisque, decorated,
1972, 25 x 18" 14,500.00

Canada Geese, bisque, decorated,
1953, 7½ x 7½", pr. 800.00

Common Tern, bisque, decorated,
1968, 16 x 12" 4,750.00

Eastern Kingbird, bisque, decorated,
1975, 18 x 16" 4,000.00

Green Jays with Black Persimmon,
bisque, decorated, 1966, 18" h.
male & 14" h. female, pr. 3,500.00

Hooded Mergansers, bisque, decorated, 1968, 10½" h., pr..........3,000.00

Indigo Bunting (Male on Wild Rose),
bisque, decorated, 1957, 10" h. 750.00

Kingfishers, English bone porcelain,
decorated, 1976, 9¼ x 9¾".....2,000.00

Lapwing with Dandelions, English
bone porcelain, decorated, 1973,
18 x 19" 2,800.00

Long-Tail Tits with Gorse, English
bone porcelain, decorated, 1975,
14 x 10½" 2,800.00

Mearns Quail with Cactus, bisque,
decorated, 1963, 15" h. male &
7" h. female, pr. 2,800.00

Mute Swans (Bird of Peace), bisque,
white, 1972, 17 x 17" 6,000.00

Nonpareil Buntings on Flowering
Raspberry, bisque, decorated,
1958, 8½ x 5"................1,400.00

Nuthatch, English bone porcelain,
decorated, 1971, 8 x 8" 1,100.00

Oven Bird with Indian Pipe, bisque,
decorated, 1970, 11 x 7" 1,800.00

Owls, bisque, decorated eyes &
beak only, 1960, 9" h., pr. 750.00

Prothonotary Warbler, Female
w/Eggs & Fledglings, bisque,
decorated, 5½" 500.00

Road Runner with Horned Toad,
bisque, decorated, 1968, 14 x 20½"
(ILLUS.) 3,500.00

Ruffed Grouse, bisque, decorated,
1960, 12" h., pr. 4,500.00

Rufous Hummingbirds on Icelandic
Poppy, bisque, decorated, 1966,
14 x 9" 2,500.00

Song Sparrows with Tulips, bisque,
decorated, 1953, 17 x 9" 42,000.00

Stonechats with Blackberry & Bram-
ble, English bone porcelain, decorated, 1974, 12 x 8½"..........2,800.00

Sugarbirds, bisque, decorated, 1961,
25½ x 11" 15,000.00

White-Throated Sparrow on Cherokee Rose, bisque, decorated,
1957, 9½" h. 750.00

Yellow-Throated Warbler on
Crimson-Eye Mallow, bisque,
decorated, 1957, 10" h. 750.00

BUFFALO POTTERY

Buffalo Pottery was established in 1902 in Buffalo, N.Y., to supply pottery for the Larkin Company. Most desirable today is Deldare Ware, introduced in 1908 in two patterns, "The Fallowfield Hunt" and "Ye Olden Times," which featured central English scenes and a continuous border. Emerald Deldare, introduced in 1911, was banded with stylized flowers & geometric designs and had varied central scenes, the most popular being from "The Tours of Dr. Syntax." Reorganized in 1940, the company now specializes in hotel china. Also see BLUE WILLOW.

DELDARE

Deldare Mug and Vase

Bowl, fruit, 9" d., The Fallowfield
Hunt - Breaking Cover . . $395.00 to 450.00
Bowl, fruit, Ye Village
Tavern . . . . 375.00 to 450.00
Candlestick, shield-back, Village
Scenes (single) . . . . 500.00 to 675.00
Candlesticks, Village Scenes,
9½" h., pr. 650.00
Card tray, The Fallowfield Hunt -
The Return, 7¾" d. 275.00
Card tray, Ye Lion Inn, 7¾" d 250.00
Creamer, The Fallowfield Hunt -
Breaking Cover 150.00
Creamer, Scenes of Village Life in
Ye Olden Days 175.00
Creamer & cov. sugar bowl, octagonal, Scenes of Village Life in
Ye Olden Days, pr. 350.00
Cup & saucer, The Fallowfield Hunt -
The Return 195.00
Dresser tray, Dancing Ye Minuet,
12 x 9" 450.00
Humidor, cov., bulbous, There was
an Old Sailor, etc., 8" h. 750.00
Matchbox holder w/ash tray, Scenes
of Village Life in Ye Olden Days,
6½" w., 3¼" h. 375.00
Mug, Breakfast at the Three
Pigeons, 4½" h. 235.00
Mug, The Fallowfield Hunt,
2½" h. 350.00

Mug, The Fallowfield Hunt - Breaking Cover, 3½" h. (ILLUS. left) 225.00
Mug, Ye Lion Inn, 3½" h. 210.00
Pitcher, 6" h., octagonal, Their Manner of Telling Stories - Which He
Returned with a Curtsy 400.00
Pitcher, 7" h., The Fallowfield Hunt -
Breaking Cover 375.00
Pitcher, 7" h., octagonal, "To Spare
an Old Broken Soldier - To Advise
Me in Whisper," 1923 . . . . 450.00
Pitcher, 8" h., octagonal, The Fallowfield Hunt - The Return 450.00
Pitcher, 8" h., octagonal, To Demand my Annual Rent - Welcome
Me, 1908 . . . . 450.00 to 600.00
Pitcher, 9" h., octagonal, With a
Cane Superior Air - This Amazed
Me 525.00
Pitcher, tankard, 12½" h., All You
Have To Do Is Teach the Dutchman English - The Great
Controversy 720.00
Pitcher, tankard, 12½" h., The Hunt
Supper 800.00

An Evening at Ye Lion Inn

Plaque, pierced to hang, An Evening
at Ye Lion Inn, 1908, 12" d.
(ILLUS.) 475.00
Plaque, pierced to hang, The Fallowfield Hunt - Breakfast at the
Three Pigeons, 12" d. 475.00
Plaques, pierced to hang, "Thursday" - Monks fishing or "Friday" -
Monks dining on fish caught the
day before, 12" d., each 1,200.00
Plate, 6¼" d., At Ye Lion Inn 110.00
Plate, 7¼" d., Ye Village Street,
1908 . . . . 100.00
Plate, 8½" d., The Fallowfield
Hunt - The Death, 1909 . . . . 170.00
Plate, 8½" d., Ye Town
Crier . . . . 125.00 to 175.00
Plate, 9½" d., The Fallowfield
Hunt - The Start, artist-signed 160.00

Plate, 9½" d., Ye Olden
Times ....125.00 to 165.00
Plate, chop, 14" d., An Evening at
Ye Lion Inn, pierced to hang,
artist-signed 475.00
Plate, chop, 14" d., The Fallowfield
Hunt - The Start 495.00
Soup plate w/flange rim, The Fal-
lowfield Hunt - Breaking Cover,
9" d. 190.00

Deldare Stein

Stein, The Fallowfield Hunt, 1908,
inlaid lid marked "Seattle Hotel
Burley & Company Chicago" in-
side, ½ liter (ILLUS.) 577.50
Sugar bowl, cov., Scenes of Village
Life in Ye Olden Days 180.00
Teapot, cov., Scenes of Village
Life in Ye Olden Days,
4¾" h. ....175.00 to 235.00
Teapot, cov., Scenes of Village
Life in Ye Olden Days,
5¾" h. ....285.00 to 375.00
Tea tile, The Fallowfield Hunt -
Breaking Cover, artist-signed,
6" d. 200.00
Tea tray, Heirlooms, 13¾ x 10¼" .. 560.00
Vase, 9¼" h., hourglass shape, Ye
Olden Village Scenes (ILLUS. with
Mug) ....250.00 to 325.00

EMERALD DELDARE
Card tray, handled,, Dr. Syntax
Robbed of his Property, 7" d...... 450.00
Cup & saucer, Dr. Syntax
scenes ....350.00 to 400.00
Hair receiver, cov. 295.00
Pin tray, Dr. Syntax Received by the
Maid 535.00
Plaque, pierced to hang, Dr. Syntax
Sketching the Lake, 12" d........1,000.00
Plate, 7¼" d., Dr. Syntax
Soliloquising 425.00
Plate, 8½" d., Dr. Syntax Reading
his Tour 365.00
Plate, 10" d., Dr. Syntax Disputing
his Bill with the Land-
lady ....195.00 to 350.00

Plate, 10½" d., Dr. Syntax and the
Bees ....195.00 to 400.00
Plate, 10½" d., Dr. Syntax Drawing
after Nature ....150.00 to 400.00
Plate, 10½" d., Dr. Syntax Mistakes
a Gentleman's House for an
Inn ....150.00 to 400.00
Plate, 10½" d., Dr. Syntax Taking
Possession of his Living 450.00
Powder jar, cov. 395.00
Salt & peppers shakers, Art Nou-
veau geometric & florals, 3" h.,
pr. 370.00
Vase, 8" h., Art Nouveau geometric
& florals, 1911 .... 750.00
Vase, 13½" h., cylindrical, "American Beauty," typical borders
w/frieze of butterflies above
flowering plants................ 680.00

MISCELLANEOUS
Batter jug, cov., Blue Willow patt.,
1909, 5" h. 75.00
Bowl, 7¼" d., Blue Willow patt. 15.00
Bowl, 9½" d., Gaudy Willow patt. .. 100.00
Butter dish, cover & drain insert,
Blue Willow patt., 3 pcs. 115.00
Butter tub, 2-handled, w/drain in-
sert, pink Apple Blossom patt.,
1915, 2 pcs. 18.00
Christmas plate, 1951 .... 52.50
Christmas plate, 1953 .... 35.00
Christmas plate, 1956 .... 45.00
Christmas plate, 1956 .... 36.00
Feeding dish, Campbell Kids decor.,
7¾" d. ....55.00 to 75.00
Game plate, Mallard Ducks, green
ground, 9" d. 42.50
Game platter, Buffalo Hunt,
14 x 11" 160.00
Game set: 15" platter & four 9" d.
plates; various deer species,
signed R.K. Beck, 5 pcs. 300.00
Jug, Cinderella, 6" h......275.00 to 375.00
Jug, Landing of Roger Williams,
6" h. 345.00
Jug, Dutch, h.p. windmill scene,
6½" h. 245.00
Jug, Geranium, blue & white,
6½" h. 255.00
Jug, Hounds & Stag, dated 1906,
6½" h. 245.00
Jug, George Washington, blue
decor, gold trim,
7½" h. ....295.00 to 450.00
Jug, Mason, Neopolitan fisherman &
Roman ruins at top, conventional
fruit & florals below, 1907,
8¼" h. 625.00
Jug, Robin Hood, 8¼" h............ 375.00
Mug, Abino Ware, windmill decor,
3½" h. 350.00
Pitcher, 7" h., Bluebird patt., 6 birds
in formation 125.00

Pitcher, Gaudy Willow patt., dated
1907 .... 300.00
**Plaque, pierced to hang, Abino
Ware, sailing ships & windmill
scene, dated 1911, artist-signed
"Stuart," 12½" d.** 750.00
Plate, 6" d., Blue Willow patt. 12.00
Plate, 7½" d., commemorative,
"State Capitol, Helena, Mont.,"
1909 .... 80.00
Plate, 7½" d., commemorative,
Trinity Church, New York City,
blue-green 60.00
Plate, 7½" d., commemorative, U.S.
Capitol, Washington, D.C., blue-
green 52.50
Plate, 9" d., Dr. Syntax Disputing
His Bill with the Landlady, blue &
white 150.00
Plate, 9½" d., Abino Ware, windmill
scene w/sailboats off the
shoreline 500.00
Plate, 10" d., Blue Willow patt. 150.00
Plate, 10" d., Gaudy Willow patt. 85.00
Plate, 10" d., historical series, The
Capitol Building, Washington,
D.C., blue-green 32.50
Plate, 10" d., historical series,
Washington's Home, Mount Ver-
non, blue-green on white 27.50
Platter, 10½ x 8½", Blue Willow
patt. 35.00
Platter, 10½ x 8½", Gaudy Willow
patt., ca. 1911 .... 145.00

Blue Willow Relish

Relish, Blue Willow patt., 9¾" l.
(ILLUS.) 30.00
Sauce dish, Gaudy Willow patt.,
5" d. 30.00
Teapot, cov., Blue Willow patt. 75.00

CALIFORNIA FAIENCE

*Chauncey R. Thomas and William V.
Bragdon organized what was to become the
California Faience pottery in 1916, in
Berkeley, California. Originally named after
its owners, it later became The Tile Shop, fi-
nally adopting the California Faience name*

*about 1924. Always a small operation whose
output was a simple style of art pottery,
primarily designed for the florist shop trade,
it also made colorfully decorated tiles. During the mid-1920's, California Porcelain was
produced by this firm for the West Coast Porcelain Manufacturers of Millbrae, California.
The great Depression halted art pottery
production and none was produced after 1930
although some tiles were made for the Chicago World's Fair about 1932. Collectors now
seek out these somewhat scarce pieces that
always bear the incised mark of California
Faience. Also see TILES.*

California Faience Mark

Bowl, 15 x 12", shell-shaped, blue
glaze $95.00
Console bowl, green matte finish ... 125.00
Console bowl w/flower frog, footed,
black matte exterior glaze, glossy
turquoise interior, 10½" d. bowl,
2 pcs. 125.00
Console bowl w/flower frog
modeled as pr. ducks, glossy blue
glaze, 2 pcs. 175.00
Flower holder, figural Chinese laundry woman, colorful, 6" h. 195.00
Pitcher, 8½" h., green glaze 145.00
Vase, 9½" h., 5½" w., classic
shape, runny light tan over rust
glaze 375.00

CANTON

Canton Punch Bowl

*This ware has been produced for nearly two
centuries in potteries near Canton, China. Intended for export sale, much of it was origi-*

nally inexpensive blue-and-white hand decorated ware. Late 18th and early 19th century pieces are superior to later ones and fetch higher prices.

Creamer, w/long spout, blue-and-white, late 19th c. $55.00

Dish, cov., boar's head handles, blue-and-white, 7½" l., 4¾" h. (minor damage) 300.00

Dish, leaf-shaped, blue-and-white, 7" l. 125.00

Dish, footed, lobed sides, "famille-rose" decor, w/numerous insects, ca. 1875, 11" l. 90.00

Fish bowls, "famille-rose" decor, panels of nobles in gardens in landscapes, reserved on light brown ground of flowers & scrolls, rim border of floral medallions painted in pink, blue & yellow beneath a row of bats, interior w/iron-red fish swimming amidst waterweeds, w/wooden stands, 21" d., pr. 2,475.00

Platter, 14½" l., pagoda scene, blue-and-white, "lemon peel" glaze 145.00

Punch bowl, "famille-rose" decor, enameled w/two large & 2 small panels of Mandarin figures in shades of blue, green, turquoise, rose, purple, iron-red, yellow, black & gold on exterior & w/central roundel w/figures surrounded by continuous figural frieze beneath gilt-ground border of lush florals & fruits, mid-19th c., 21" d. (ILLUS.) 4,950.00

Wall pocket, cone-shaped, 13" 250.00

CAPO DI MONTE

Capo-di-Monte Jewel Box

Production of porcelain and faience began in 1736 at the Capo-di-Monte factory in Naples. In 1743 King Charles of Naples established a factory there that made wares with relief decoration. In 1759 the factory was moved to Buen Retiro near Madrid, operat-

ing until 1808. Another Naples pottery was opened in 1771 and operated until 1806 when its molds were acquired by the Doccia factory of Florence, which has since made reproductions of original Capo-di-Monte pieces with the "N" mark beneath a crown. Some very early pieces are valued in the thousands of dollars but the subsequent productions are considerably lower.

Bowl, cov., colorful allegorical scene w/goddesses in relief $125.00

Box w/hinged lid, relief-molded & enameled cherub scenes on lid & sides, ormolu fittings, 6" oval 295.00

Ferner, relief-molded & enameled allegorical figures on sides & full relief female mask at each end, 11" oval 95.00

Figure of a woman wearing an elegant Empire-style gown of the 1840's, 21" h. 575.00

Figures, hunchback dwarf musicians (4) & 3½" h. conductor, 1860's, set of 5 .... 250.00

Figure group, chestnut vendors, old woman w/small copper stove & urchin selling chestnuts, artist-signed, 7 x 8 x 10" 225.00

Jewel box w/hinged lid, relief-molded & brightly painted frieze of drunken putti being carried away by mischievous baby satyrs on sides & domed cover w/group depicting Venus at her toilette within entwined rose garland & feather borders, 19th c., shaped 9¾" oval 330.00

Jewel box w/hinged lid, relief-molded & enameled putti on frieze & cover, 14 x 9½" oval (ILLUS.) 2,750.00

Model of a crowned crane standing on one leg in water, realistic colors, signed, 14" h. 150.00

Capo-di-Monte Snuff Box

Snuff box w/hinged lid, cartouche-
shaped, molded basketweave &
flowerhead exterior, inside lid
painted w/court lady & her page
examining portrait of gentleman,
gold mountings, ca. 1740, restored,
3¼" w. (ILLUS.) 1,650.00

Tazza, 5 relief-molded medallions on
top, full figure cherubs playing
French horns on base, 14½" w.,
7½" h........................... 200.00

Urns & covers, relief-molded continuous frieze scene of putti & tri-
tons, base w/intertwined putti,
polychrome enameling, cover
w/applied putti, 19th c., 14" h.,
pr............................ 440.00

Vases & covers w/bird finials,
11¾" h., applied w/ram's heads,
their horns wrapping around the
corners on 3 sides, pr........... 850.00

CARLTON WARE

*The Staffordshire firm of Wiltshaw &
Robinson, Stoke-on-Trent, operated the
Carlton Works from about 1890 until 1958,
producing both earthenwares and porcelain.
Specializing in decorative items like vases
and teapots, they became well known for their
lustre-finished wares, often decorated in the
oriental taste. The trademark* Carlton Ware
*was incorporated into their printed mark.
Since 1958, a new company, Carlton Ware
Ltd., has operated the Carlton Works at
Stoke.*

Ash tray, maroon "Rouge Royale"
lustre finish, 5" d.............. $40.00

Bowl, 4½" d., 3½" h., rose bowl
shape, maroon "Rouge Royale"
lustre finish w/enameled & gilt
decor, 1920's.................. 85.00

Bowl, 8½" d., 3½" h., deep red
w/enameled & gilt "chinoiserie"
scene w/pagoda 185.00

Bowl, 9½" d., glossy blue
w/enameled gilt birds decor 85.00

Candy dish, maroon "Rouge Royale"
w/gilt spider web decor, 8½" l. ... 48.00

Cookie jar, rich pink w/panels of
white enriched w/enameled
florals & small birds, silverplate
rim, cover & bail handle, 5½" d.,
6½" h......................... 115.00

Cookie jar, soft pink shaded to
cream w/enameled mauve orchid
& green & tan leaves decor, silverplate rim, cover & bail handle,
1890's, 5½" d., 6½" h. 98.00

Cookie jar, cream bisque finish
w/multicolored florals & green

leaves decor, gold trim, silverplate rim, cover & bail handle,
5½" d., 7" h.................. 110.00

Cup & saucer, demitasse, deep
glossy blue w/enameled & gilt
"chinoiserie" decor 60.00

Ginger jar, cov., maroon "Rouge
Royale" w/raised enamel & gilt
decor, 10½" h. 225.00

Mustard jar, cov., deep cobalt blue
w/enameled "chinoiserie" decor .. 65.00

Pin dish, pink w/lavender & deep
pink floral decor, 4" l.......... 18.00

Pitcher w/pewter lid, 6¼" h.,
creamy ivory w/enameled floral
decor, 1890's.................. 75.00

Teapot, cov., creamy ivory
w/enameled floral decor,
5½" h......................... 85.00

Tray, single handle, scalloped edge,
maroon "Rouge Royale"
w/enameled pond lilies, cattails &
dragonflies highlighted in gilt 115.00

Wash basin & pitcher, cobalt blue
lustre finish w/enameled florals
& butterflies outlined in gilt,
12½" h. tankard pitcher &
15" d. basin, pr. 345.00

CATALINA ISLAND POTTERY

Catalina Island Candlesticks

*The Clay Products Division of the Santa
Catalina Island Co. produced a variety of
wares during their brief ten-year operation.
The brainchild of chewing-gum magnate, William Wrigley, Jr., owner of Catalina Island
at the time, and his business associate D.M.
Retton, the plant was established at Pebbly
Beach, near Avalon in 1927. Its two-fold goal
was to provide year-round work for the island's residents and building material for
Wrigley's ongoing development of a major
tourist attraction at Avalon. Early production consisted of brick, roof and patio tiles.
Later, art pottery, including vases, flower
bowls, lamps and home accessories, were
made from a local brown-based clay and,
about 1930, tablewares were introduced.*

These early wares carried vivid glazes but had a tendency to chip readily and a white-bodied, more chip-resistant clay, imported from the mainland was used after 1932. The costs associated with importing clay eventually caused the Catalina pottery to be sold to a California mainland competitor in 1937. These wares were molded and are not hand-thrown but some pieces have handpainted decoration.

Bowl, 9½" d., purple glaze interior,
aqua exterior $30.00
Candlesticks, yellow glaze on
brown-based clay, 4" base d.,
5¼" h., pr. (ILLUS.) 40.00
Candlesticks, dark green glaze,
pr. 25.00
Charger, swordfish decor on light
blue ground, 14" d. 175.00
Model of a nautilus shell, white,
7" l. 12.00
Plate, 10" d., h.p. moose head center decor, artist-signed 75.00
Vase, 5" h., cream glaze 27.00
Vase, 6" h., blue "crackled" glaze . . 9.00
Vase, 6" h., robin's egg blue interior glaze, "Sang de boeuf" exterior . . 75.00
Vase, 6" h., bulbous, Chinese red
glaze 35.00
Vase, 10" h., blue interior glaze,
white exterior 35.00
Vase, 11" h., side handles, sky blue
high glaze 25.00
Water set: cov. carafe & 4 mugs;
burnt orange carafe, 2 orange & 2
yellow mugs w/wood & metal
handles, 5 pcs. 145.00

CAUGHLEY

Bowl with "S" Mark

Thomas Turner produced fine quality porcelain at the Caughley Works near Broseley, Shropshire, England, from 1775 until 1799, when the factory was taken over by the Coalport works. Much of the ware was impressed "salopian" in lower case letters, or maked "S" in underglaze blue, indicating that it had been produced in Salop, another name for Shropshire county. While most of the porcelain was painted or printed in underglaze-blue, some was finely decorated in enamel and gilt. Turner's Salopian Warehouse in London was a great outlet for the wares.

Bowl, 7" d., blue transfer-printed
floral decor $85.00
Bowl, 7 5/8" d., underglaze-blue
transfer-printed Fisherman patt.,
diapered borders & central rock
cluster interior, "S" mark in
underglaze-blue, 1785-90
(ILLUS.) 385.00
Creamer, White Stag patt. 385.00
Cup, black transfer-printed rural
scene highlighted w/polychrome
enameling, marked "Salopian,"
large size (no saucer) 145.00
Pitcher, jug-type, Tobacco Leaf
mold, underglaze-blue "chinoiserie" decor, marked "Salopian"
(tiny professional repair inside
pouring spout) 350.00
Teabowls & saucers, miniature,
underglaze-blue transfer-printed
Fence patt. within blue line borders, ca. 1775, set of 4 . . . . 1,760.00
Teapot w/high domed cover, slightly
ovoid, black transfer-printed birds
& florals highlighted w/a blue
band, early 19th c., 9¾" h. (small
chip on spout & glaze chips on inside cover rim) 220.00

CELADON

Korean Celadon Cup

Celadon is the name given a highly-fired Oriental porcelain featuring a glaze that ranges from olive through tones of green, blue-green and greys. These wares have been made for centuries in China, Korea and Japan. Fine early Celadon wares are costly, later pieces are far less expensive.

Bottle-vase, globular w/tapered
faceted neck applied w/small
ring, sea green glaze, Korea,
13th c., 12 7/8" h. $4,125.00
Bowl, 4½" d., deep, glazed rim, exterior carved w/lotus, olive glaze,
Northern Song Dynasty 1,650.00
Bowl, 5 3/8" d., interior carved
w/central floral spray encircled by

combed waves within a single line border, bubble-suffused sea green glaze, Jin Dynasty 4,070.00

Bowl, 7" d., conical w/notched rim, interior w/floral medallion beneath 2 open lotus blossoms, greyish green glaze, Korea, Koryo Dynasty (some firing faults) 330.00

Bowl, 8" d., deep flared sides, interior carved w/large leafy sprig bearing 1 peony blossom & serrated leaves, bubble-suffused glaze of olive green, Song Dynasty 2,750.00

Bowl, 13" d., shallow, molded w/eight trigrams between borders of florettes, raised on 3 animal mask feet, China, Ming Dynasty. 4,675.00

Cup, fluted sides w/rows of vertical florettes rising to scalloped petal rim, splayed flower-form foot, Korea, Koryo Dynasty, 2¾" h. (ILLUS.) 7,700.00

Dish, deep w/everted lip, interior molded w/two small fish, exterior w/overlapping chrysanthemum petals, bluish green glaze, Southern Song/Yuan Dynasty, 5 1/8" d. 935.00

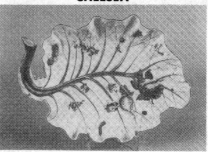

Celadon Jar

Jar, broad body molded w/scrolling blossoming lotus between bands of lappets at mouth & stiff leaves at foot, pale green glaze, probably 18th c., 9½" h. (ILLUS.) 1,430.00

Platter, 13" oval, large blue peacock w/chrysanthemums border, 19th c. 135.00

Rose petal jar w/inner lid, bulbous shoulders, deep pink, red & blue florals w/green leaves in relief & ornate gold trim on green ground, China, early 20th c., 6" h. 75.00

Vase, 7½" h., embossed flowers & bluebird in relief decor, 1880's . . . 95.00

Vase, 14½" h., slender ovoid, carved lotus meander, crackled olive green glaze, China, Ming Dynasty 990.00

CHELSEA

Chelsea Leaf Dish

This ware was made in London from 1754 to 1770 in England's second porcelain factory. From 1770 to 1783 it was operated as a branch of the Derby Factory. Its equipment was then moved to Derby. It has been reproduced and ceramics made elsewhere are often erroneously called Chelsea.

Bonbonniere in the form of a boy & boar: the boy wearing a green hat, puce jacket, turquoise breeches & w/fur satchel over his shoulder w/inscription on strap, kneeling on a green mound molded w/colorful florettes & green leaves while shearing the mane of a brownish grey boar; the interior painted w/three iron-red, yellow & puce floral sprigs within a shaded green leaf border; hinged gold mount at rim & white cover painted w/colorful floral sprigs on exterior & single rose sprig interior, red anchor mark, 2 1/8" h. $1,980.00

Dish, leaf-shaped w/stalk-form handle, painted puce veining, turnip, insects & pr. figs & floral sprays, gold anchor period, ca. 1760, 11" l. (ILLUS.) 1,650.00

Dishes, molded as a peony flower between 2 leaves enriched in puce, iron-red & green, stalk forming the handle, 9" l., pr. (1 cracked). 1,100.00

Chelsea Botanical Plate

Plate, 8" d., Hans Sloane botanical
type, painted large flowering
branch, insects, flower spray &
brown rim edge, red anchor period,
ca. 1775 (ILLUS.) 1,320.00

Plate, 9½" d., painted w/large sprig
of yellow-centered purple blossoms
w/pale blue-shaded petals & bright
green leaves, 2 yellow, grey &
blue insects & 3 small sprigs of
red berries, blue blossoms or
maroon-centered yellow flowers,
rim edged in brown, red anchor
period, ca. 1755 . . . . .1,760.00

Scent bottle w/stopper, realistically
modeled as a white head of cauliflower within pink-ribbed green
leaves issuing from a thick olive
green stem, stopper in the form
of a white cauliflower florette in
gold mounts, red anchor period,
ca. 1756, 2½" h. 3,410.00

Soup plate, octagonal, center
painted w/iron-red & gold phoenix
in flight above a yellow-breasted
blue & iron-red pheasant perched
on a turquoise rock before an iron-
red, blue, turquoise & gold flowering tree, ridged rim w/gilt-height-
ened iron-red floral vine border,
red anchor period, ca. 1753,
9 3/8" w. .1,980.00

CHINESE EXPORT

Chinese Export Barber's Basin

*Large quantities of porcelain have been
made in China for export to America from the
1780's, much of it shipped from the ports of
Canton and Nanking. A major source of this
porcelain was Ching-te-Chen in the Kiangsi
province but the wares were also made elsewhere. The largest quantities were blue and
white. Prices fluctuate considerably depend-
ing on age, condition, decoration, etc. Also see
CANTON and ROSE MEDALLION.*

Barber's bowl, "famille-verte" decor,
painted w/pr. exotic birds amidst

peonies within fenced garden of
grapevines & bamboo center &
w/peonies & pomegranates reserved w/fan-shaped landscape
panels on black-stippled green
ground at rim, 1700-20, 14½" oval
(ILLUS.) $2,200.00

Basin & covered jug, green Fitzhugh
patt., 1820-40, 12 7/8" d. basin &
11" h. jug, 2 pcs. 3,520.00

Bowl, 11 3/8" d., "Mandarin Palette,"
exterior w/iron-red, black & gold
Y-diaper ground reserved on the
front & reverse w/underglaze-
blue scroll-bordered panels of
Oriental figures at various pursuits
in garden, sides w/small panels of
birds, interior w/central figural
medallion & elaborate border of
foliate-edged diaper, scalework
& other patterned panels below a
band of underglaze-blue cell
diaperwork, ca. 1785. . . . . .1,320.00

Cup & saucer, handleless, Medallion
patt., blue & white 75.00

Garniture set: 3 baluster-shaped
vases, 1 cover & 2 beakers; lobed
oval forms, iron-red cell diaper
ground embellished w/rose, yellow
& green floral vines surrounding
leaf-shaped reserves of peony
sprigs, shoulder or rim w/black-
edged turquoise lappet border
w/pink peonies & yellow scrolls,
base w/pink, green, yellow &
white "ruyi" sceptre border &
neck w/pink swastika diaper band,
late 18th-early 19th c., 11 3/8"
to 9¾" h., 5 pcs. 3,080.00

Chinese Export Mug

Mug, molded dragon handle, painted w/genre scenes of family &
home beside lake reserved on
orange fishscale ground,
7½" h. (ILLUS.) 605.00

Plate, 8 7/8" d., "Crucifixion,"
painted "en grisaille" & heightened
in gilding w/scene of centurians
casting dice before the crucified
Christ flanked by 2 thieves on
crosses, ca. 1745 ....1,045.00

Plate, 9" d., "famille-rose" decor,
lady holding basket & watching
another standing on a stool by a
tea tree & handing to a third a
a basket of leaves while 2 other
ladies inside a pavillion cut the
leaves & place them in a bowl,
cavetto w/gilt spearhead border,
rim w/four gilt-edged panels
depicting at the top & bottom a
river scene w/two men in a skiff
& at sides a pr. of grey billing
doves on the branches of a rose
bush, ca. 1745.................1,870.00

Plate, 9" d., "In the Arbour" after
Cornelis Pronk, painted in shades
of underglaze-blue w/six chinoiserie figures by a pond & an arbor
within a wide patterned border
reserved w/panels of flowers,
fruit & butterflies flanked by
shells & plumes, underside of
brown-edged rim w/tassel border,
ca. 1740............1,540.00 to 1,760.00

Plates, 9 1/8" d., painted rose,
green, iron-red, blue, yellow,
"grisaille" & gold branches of
flowering tree peonies growing
behind stylized rockwork, ca.
1740, set of 6 ....1,210.00

"La Dame au Parasol" Plate

Plates, 9¼" d., "La Dame au Parasol" after Cornelis Pronk, painted
Imari palette in underglaze-blue,
iron-red, light brown & gold depicting an Oriental lady standing
beneath a parasol held by her
attendant & watching 4 waterbirds
within a floral border on the ca-

vetto & w/diapered rim border interrupted by alternating panels of
ladies & birds, underside of rim
w/seven underglaze-blue insects,
1736-45, pr. 7,700.00

Platters, 15½" oval, painted in a
Mandarin palette of rose, purple,
brown, iron-red, yellow & green
& heightened in gilding w/central
ribbon-tied bouquet surrounded on
the cavetto & molded rim w/floral
sprigs between gold & iron-red
spearhead borders, ca. 1780,
pr. 1,540.00

Punch ladle, fluted lozenge-shaped
bowl painted in purple mono-
chrome on exterior w/four floral
clusters beneath an iron-red-
edged gilt band border repeated
around the handle fitting, interior
w/small purple sprig & rim edged
in worn gilding, affixed w/turned
& carved wood handle showing
traces of lacquer & gilt decor, ca.
1770, 3¾" w. bowl, overall
8½" l. 825.00

Tea bowl & saucer, "famille-rose"
decor, painted in blue, turquoise,
green, aubergine, yellow, pink &
black w/two fishermen holding or
casting their nets center, fluted
rim or sides lightly molded
w/bamboo & w/alternating panels
of turquoise or pink diaperwork &
gold zones of blossoms on a black
ground, 1730-40 .... 880.00

Teapot Circa 1740

Teapot, cov., globular body painted
"en grisaille" & heightened
w/shades of brown & gilding
w/scene of young woman seated
at table stringing beads while
older lady leans on chair to super-
vise, rim & cover w/"grisaille"
scroll panel & blue floral panels
in border & cover w/lavender-
ground roundel centering gilt-
tipped knop, ca. 1740, 5" h.
(ILLUS.) 2,310.00

Teapot, cov., "famille-rose" decor,
large........................... 175.00

Tureens, covers & stands, painted in shades of underglaze-blue w/oriental river landscape depicting a Chinaman crossing an arched bridge between pagodas & pavilions on both banks, cover & stand rims w/border of variously patterned & diapered panels & floral sprigs, footrim & stand cavetto w/cell diaper band, ca. 1785, 10 7/8" to 11¼" l., pr. 2,750.00

Vegetable tureen, cover w/strawberry finial & deep stand, brown Fitzhugh patt., early 19th c., 11" oval 990.00

Wig stands, blue & white w/"orange peel" glaze, 11" h., pr. (each w/stress marks at same location) 550.00

CLARICE CLIFF DESIGNS

"Bizarre" Vase

Clarice Cliff was a designer for A.J. Wilkinson, Ltd., Royal Staffordshire Pottery, Burslem, England when they acquired the adjoining Newport Pottery Company whose warehouses were filled with undecorated bowls and vases. About 1925, her flair with the Art Deco style was incorporated into designs appropriately named "Bizarre" and "Fantasque" and the warehouse stockpile was decorated in vivid colors. These hand-painted earthenwares, all bearing the signature of designer Clarice Cliff, were produced until World War II and are now finding enormous favor with collectors.

Beaker, "Bizarre," Crocus patt., 3¾" h....................... $45.00
Bone dish, Tonquin patt., green or plum, each 17.00
Bowl, 8" octagon, "Fantasque," houses & trees decor 170.00

Bowl, 10" d., "Bizarre," Sea & Landscape patt. 150.00
Coffee set: cov. coffee pot, creamer & 2 c/s; "Bizarre," bold geometric design, 6 pcs. 120.00
Cookie jar, cov., "Bizarre," Nasturtium patt., Art Deco orange & yellow florals w/green leaves & brown spatter trim, yellow & orange bands on lid, original wicker handle, 5 3/8" d., 6" h. 282.00
Cup & saucer, "Bizarre," Gay Day patt., Art Deco orange, rust & lavender flowers w/yellow, brown & green trim..................... 79.00
Egg cup, "Bizarre," Islands Moderne patt. 38.00
Honey pot & cover w/bee finial, Delicia patt. 65.00
Marmalade jar, Celtic Harvest patt. 125.00
Pitcher, 5¾" h., 5¼" d., jug-type, "Fantasque," Art Deco landscape w/house in bright orange, yellow, brown & black, orange top band.. 225.00
Pitcher, 7" h., 8" w., Pineapple patt. 65.00
Pitcher, 8" h., "Bizarre," Crocus patt. 95.00
Plaque, pierced to hang, slightly convex form, "Bizarre," molded in high relief w/flowerheads & leafage, brightly painted in orange, yellow, blue, green, brown & black on a pierced black & cream ground, ca. 1930, 13¼" d. 385.00
Plate, 8" d., "Bizarre," Delicia patt., fruit decor 40.00
Plate, 10" sq., "Bizarre," bold geometric design 90.00
Platter, 12" oval, "Bizarre," Water Lily patt. ....50.00 to 65.00
Sugar shaker, cone-shaped, "Bizarrre," Tiger Tree patt., green, orange, yellow, puce, brown & black trees & hilly landscape on cream ground, black, green & cream border bands, ca. 1930, 5½" h.......................... 302.50
Teapot, cov., "Bizarre," Islands Moderne patt. 165.00
Tumbler, water, "Bizarre," Art Deco orange, brown & gold trees & florals w/gold lines, 3 3/8" d., 4 1/8" h. 125.00
Vase, 4" h., "Bizarre," My Garden patt. 150.00
Vase, 7" h., flaring cylinder, "Bizarre," Delicia patt., broad border of alternating oranges, lemons & green leaves, cream ground streaked w/green & black, ca. 1930 .... 275.00
Vase, 9" h., ovoid w/short neck,

"Bizarre," hilly landscape, w/trees interrupted by views of water, beneath cloud-bordered sky in shades of orange, yellow, brown, blue & green between border bands of brown, yellow & grey-blue, ca. 1930 (ILLUS.) 440.00

Vase, 18" h., ovoid w/flaring neck & flattened conical foot, "Bizarre," cottage at the edge of the woods scene, flame-streaked interior & exterior neck 1,430.00

CLEWELL WARES

Though Charles W. Clewell of Canton, Ohio, didn't operate a pottery, he is responsible for a category of fine art pottery through his development of a unique metal coating placed on pottery blanks obtained from Owens, Weller and others. By encasing objects in a thin metal shell, he produced copper and bronze finish ceramics. Later experiments led him to chemically treat the metal coating to attain the blue-green patinated effect associated with copper and bronze. Although he produced metal-coated pottery from 1902 until the mid-1950's, Clewell production was quite limited for he felt no one else could competently re-create his artwork and, therefore, operated a small shop with little help.

Mug, copper-covered w/riveted seams & green patinated finish, dated 1914, 4¼" h. ....$100.00 to 125.00

Tea cup, copper-covered w/riveted seams (inside w/stained crazing) 58.00

Vase, 3½" h., copper-covered w/green patinated finish......... 70.00

Vase, 5" h., copper-covered w/green patinated finish......... 140.00

Vase, 6" h., bulbous, copper-covered w/riveted seams & green patinated finish 230.00

Vase, 6¼" h., copper-covered w/green patinated finish......... 250.00

Vase, 7" h., semi-ovoid w/narrow neck, copper-covered w/patinated finish 115.00

Vase, 11" h., copper-covered w/riveted seams & patinated finish 265.00

CLEWS, J. & R.

James and Ralph Clews established this pottery in Cobridge, England in 1814 and operated it until 1836 when it was taken over by Wood & Brownfield. Some of the wares have been reproduced. Also see HISTORICAL & COMMEMORATIVE CHINA.

"Christmas Eve" Tea Bowl & Saucer

Plate, 9" d., Wilkie series, dark blue transfer "Christmas Eve" ....$135.00 to 155.00

Plate, 9" d., Wilkie series, dark blue transfer "The Valentine" 160.00

Plate, 10" d., blue transfer "Playing at Draughts".................... 210.00

Plate, 10" d., Wilkie series, dark blue transfer "The Valentine" 225.00

Platter, 17 x 13" oblong w/cut corners, dark blue transfer scene of "Fonthill Abbey, Wiltshire," ca. 1830 .... 330.00

Platter, 17¾" oval, shaped & scalloped rim, black transfer Chinese landscape center & floral border (pinpoint rim flakes)............. 85.00

Tea bowl & saucer, Wilkie series, dark blue transfer "Christmas Eve" (ILLUS.) 160.00

Vegetable bowl, open, Wilkie series, dark blue transfer "Letter of Introduction - Errand Boy," 12" l. 395.00

Wash basin & pitcher, dark blue transfer Basket & Flora Vase patt., pr. 550.00

CLIFTON ART POTTERY

Clifton Art Pottery Mark

William A. Long, an organizer of the Lonhuda Pottery, and Fred Tschirner, a chemist, established the Clifton Art Pottery in Newark, New Jersey, in 1905. The first art pottery produced was designated the Crystal Patina line and was decorated with a subdued pale green crystalline glaze which was later also made in shades of yellow and tan. Indian Ware, introduced in 1906, was patterned after the the pottery made by the American Indians. These two lines are the most notable in the pottery's production though Tirrube and Robin's-egg Blue lines were also produced. After 1911, production shifted to floor and wall tiles and by 1914 the pottery's name was changed to Clifton Porcelain Tile Company to better reflect this production.

Coffee pot, cov., swollen body
w/flaring base, short tube-like
spout, shaded mottled gold glaze,
7½" h. $75.00

Coffee pot, cov., waisted form
w/flaring top & base, short tube-
like spout, incised geometric designs, mottled yellow glaze 75.00

Humidor, cov., Indian Ware, red
clay w/black & cream geometric
designs, 5½" h. 30.00

Pitcher, 6½" h., 4½" d., Indian
Ware 45.00

Teapot, cov., Crystal Patina line,
green patinated glaze, 7" h. 125.00

Vase, 5" h., Crystal Patina line,
green patinated glaze,
1903 .95.00 to 125.00

Vase, 5½" h., 3½" w., Indian Ware,
red clay w/black & cream
designs 57.00

Vase, 8" h., Crystal Patina line 170.00

Vase, 8" d., Indian Ware, incised
"Little Colo., Ariz., No. 226". 155.00

Vase, 8" h., 5" top d., 11" widest
d., Indian Ware, red clay w/buff,
terra cotta & black designs exteri-
or, black-glazed interior 200.00

COALPORT

Coalport Dessert Set

Coalport Porcelain Works operated at Coal-port, Shropshire, England, from about 1795 to 1926 and has operated at Stoke-on-Trent as Coalport China, Ltd., making bone china since then.

Box, cov., pomegranate form, h.p.
multicolored rosettes
w/"jewelled" trim on pale yellow
ground, miniature $150.00

Cup & saucer, Sevres-style, reserved
w/exotic birds on salmon pink
ground, by John Randall, ca.
1835 . . . . 175.00

Dessert service: 11½" oval compote,
pr. oval dishes, pr. shaped square
dishes & nine 7¾" d. plates; h.p.
floral bouquets & scattered flower
sprays, scroll-molded borders enriched in gilding, ca. 1830, 14 pcs.
(ILLUS.). 880.00

Dessert service: fruit stand, pr.
quatrefoil dishes, lozenge-shaped
dish & 11 plates; each w/pastel
floral cluster center within wide
pale peach border edged in gilt
foliate scrolls & molded at scalloped rim edge w/further white &
gold foliate scrolls, ca. 1835,
15 pcs. .1,210.00

Figure of "Christine," dark blue
dress, brown hair, w/fan in right
hand, 7¼" h. 85.00

Plate, 9" d., h.p. cherub amidst a
profusion of garden flowers on
shaded pastel ground within a relief gold floral garland, ornate
gold scrolled trim, artist-signed,
dated 1893 . . . . 405.00

Plate, 9½" d., h.p. gold snowflake
decor center, deeply scalloped rim
w/embossed gold-trimmed shells
& tiny turquoise blue flowers on
cream shaded to beige ground . . . 75.00

Plates, 9½" d., scalloped shell-
molded rim, fruit & floral medallion center, ornate gold trim, ca.
1895, pr. 165.00

Coalport Solitaire Set

Solitaire set: cov. teapot, cov. sugar
bowl, cream jug, c/s & 10½" w.
tray w/gilt scroll handles; painted
in colors w/butterflies within ovals
outlined in gilding reserved on yellow ground, ca. 1820, 6 pcs.
(ILLUS.) 3,960.00

COPELAND & SPODE

Spode Jardiniere

W.T. Copeland & Sons, Ltd., have operated the Spode Works at Stoke, England, from 1847 to the present. The name Spode was used on some of its productions. Its predecessor, Spode, was founded by Josiah Spode about 1784 and became Copeland & Garrett in 1843, continuing under that name until 1847. Listings dated prior to 1843 should be attributed to Spode. Also see COMMEMORATIVE PLATES.

Bouillon cup & saucer, Mayflower patt. $70.00
Butter pat, hunt scene, blue transfer 20.00
Cup & saucer, crested birds transfer decor 35.00
Cup & saucer, Italian patt., blue transfer 25.00
Cup plate, Spode's Tower patt., blue transfer 12.00
Dessert service: 2-handled compote, shell-shaped dish, 2 oval sauce tureens w/covers, stands & 1 ladle, 2 pierced basket stands & 15 plates; transfer-printed & painted in colors & gilt w/overall scrolling fruiting vine, ca. 1785, 24 pcs. 3,740.00
Jardinieres & pierced covers, gilt crocodile handles, white relief playful putti below band of stylized foliage on pink ground, pierced cover w/similar foliate band, Spode, ca. 1820, repairs to one cover & one jardiniere, 7¾" h., pr. (ILLUS. of one) 935.00
Mug, Spode's Fortuna patt., white relief figures of golfer & caddy on greyish green ground, white handle, 4¼" d., 6 7/8" h. 130.00
Pitcher, 4" h., Spode's Tower patt., blue transfer. 25.00

Pitcher, water, hunting scene, blue transfer 125.00
Plate, 6" d., bird amidst florals & foliage decor, heavy gold trim, Spode 105.00
Plate, 7½" d., Spode's Tower patt., red transfer 12.00
Plates, 8¾" d., creamware, printed & painted in colors, center w/shell motif in pink surrounded by flowering foliage enriched in gilding on a brown net pattern ground, gilt rims, Spode, ca. 1820, set of 4 . . . .   330.00
Plate, 9¼" d., Spode's Tower patt., blue transfer. 45.00
Plate, 9½" d., bird perched on snowy branch w/holly leaves & berries 100.00
Plate, 9¾" d., Imari patt., cobalt blue, iron-red & gilt, ca. 1860 . . . .   125.00
Plates, 10" d., Egyptian tombs scene center, elephant & wild animal border, light blue transfer, Spode, pr. 130.00
Plate, 10" d., Spode's Christmas Tree patt., ca. 1890 . . . .   20.00
Plate, 10½" d., Spanish Festivities patt. 30.00

Spode's Tower Pattern Platter

Platter, 8 x 6¼" oblong, Spode's Tower patt., blue transfer (ILLUS.) 30.00
Platter, 20¼" oval, shaped rim w/floral border, Italian ruins scene center, light blue transfer, Spode 175.00
Punch bowl, Spode's Tower patt., blue transfer, 15½" d. 140.00
Serving dish, center handle, 2-compartment, rose decor on cobalt blue ground, gold edge, ca. 1906, 15½" l. 75.00
Tea set: cov. teapot, creamer, cov. sugar bowl & footed compote; Copeland's Ruins patt. w/acorn & oak leaves border, sepia transfer, ca. 1860, 4 pcs. 185.00
Tumbler, blue transfer 60.00

Tureen, cover & stand, stoneware, Japan patt., iron-red, cobalt blue & gilt stylized flower-filled urns & scrolling foliage w/blossoms, twig-shaped handles w/leaf terminals, ca. 1820, 17" l. 1,100.00

Urn, Spode's Tower patt., blue transfer, 17" h. 695.00

Wine cooler, 2 scroll handles enriched in gilding, transfer-printed & painted in iron-red & black on both sides w/classical figures, rim w/band of diamond patt., Spode, ca. 1820, 7½" h. 242.00

CORDEY

Bust of a Lady

Founded by Boleslaw Cybis in Trenton, New Jersey, the Cordey China Company was the forerunner of the Cybis Studio, renowned for its fine porcelain sculptures. A native of Poland, Boleslaw Cybis was commissioned by his government to paint "el fresco" murals for the 1939 New York World's Fair. Already a renowned sculptor and painter, he elected to remain and become a citizen of this country. In 1942, under his guidance, Cordey China Company began producing appealing busts and figurines, some decorated by applying real lace dipped in liquid clay prior to firing in the kiln. Cordey figures were assigned numbers that were printed or pressed on the base. The Cordey line was eventually phased out of production during the 1950's as the porcelain sculptures of the Cybis Studios became widely acclaimed.

Bust of a girl wearing net hat, hair in ringlets, roses on dress, 6¾" h. $50.00

Bust of a girl wearing Napoleon-type hat, hair in long ringlets, No. 40136, 7" h. 50.00

Bust of a lady, much lace, No. 4048Q, 14¼" h. (ILLUS.)...... 200.00

Bust of Madame DuBarry, roses in hair styled w/elaborate ringlets, wearing lace-trimmed capelet, scrolled base, blue, No. 8038, 14¼" h. 185.00

Bust of a lady, No. 5010 .... 65.00

Busts: lady (No. 3006) & gentleman (No. 3007), pr. 75.00

Figure of a ballerina dancing, flower festooned lace outfit, 11½" h..... 250.00

Figure of a boy, casually carrying coat & hat w/large plume, bisque, 11" h....................... 100.00

Figure of Empress Eugenie, 14" h. .. 150.00

Figure of a girl w/jug on her shoulder, No. 5047, 10" h. 125.00

Figure of a grape harvestor (lady) w/basket of grapes, No. 304, 16" h....................... 125.00

Figure of a grape harvestor (man), No. 305, 16" h. 90.00

Figure of a lady dressed in lace, No. 3031, 10¾" h. 125.00

Figure of a man dressed in lace, No. 3032, 10¾" h. 125.00

Figure of a man w/grey ringlet pompadour, lace & roses in greens & pinks, No. 4072, 13½" h....................... 120.00

Figure of a man w/bouquet of flowers, green shades, 15½" h. 69.00

Figures: lady, Colonial attire (No. 5088) & gentleman, Colonial attire (No. 5043); 10½" h., pr..... 225.00

Lamp, full-figure lady, No. 5061, 14" 85.00

Lamp, figure of a girl holding bouquet 175.00

Lamps: figure of Madame (No. 5084) & Monsieur (No. 5041); dressed in lace & roses, original paper labels, pr. 150.00

Model of a seated cat, white fluffy fur, tail curls to paws, pink collar w/rose, blue eyes, 8¾" h. 148.00

Plaque, pierced to hang, lady's face decor, No. 902, 10"............. 135.00

Wall shelf, cornucopia-shaped, nude lady entwining side, No. 7028 .... 110.00

COWAN

R. Guy Cowan first opened a studio pottery in 1913 in Cleveland, Ohio. The pottery continued to operate almost continuously, at various locations in the Cleveland area, until it was forced to close in 1931, due to financial problems. This fine art pottery, which was gradually expanded into a full line of commercial productions, is now sought out by collectors.

Ash tray, gazelle in bottom, flame & brown ground $55.00
Bowl, 10" d., 2½" h., grey swirls on blue ground 60.00
Bowl, 15" l., 6" h., seahorse handles, ivory glaze w/green interior 135.00
Bowl, 15 x 11½", Chinese red glaze 115.00
Bowl, 17" w., 4¾" h., pterodactyl decor, blue lustre finish 210.00
Bowl, oblong, green velour glaze exterior, yellow glaze interior 75.00

Cowan Candle Holders

Candle holders, ivory glaze, 5" l., 3" h., pr. (ILLUS.) 45.00
Candle holders, 3-light, 8" h., pr. 65.00
Candlesticks, green velour glaze, pr. 55.00
Candlesticks, black matte finish, silver trim, pr. 80.00
Candlesticks, pierced handle, Art Deco style in the oriental taste, red glaze, pr. 60.00
Centerpiece, model of a flamingo in bowl-base, mottled orange & brown glaze 250.00
Cigarette holder, model of a seahorse, ivory finish 18.00
Console set: console bowl w/flower frog & pr. matching candlesticks; blue lustre finish, 4 pcs. 29.00
Flower frog, figural dancing nude lady w/scarf, ivory glaze, 6½" h. ....130.00 to 165.00
Flower frog, figural dancing nude lady bent backwards w/one knee raised & flowing scarf held in her outstretched hands, ivory glaze, 7" h. 225.00
Flower frog, figural dancing nude ladies (2), 7½" h. 200.00
Flower frog, figural dancing nude lady w/one hand on hip, the other raised & holding a flowing scarf, ivory glaze, 8" h. ....160.00 to 200.00
Flower frog, model of a gazelle standing on leafy base, 8½" 145.00
Flower holder, narrow base, flaring mouth, ivory glaze, 5½" h. 25.00

Paperweight, model of an elephant, black glaze, 4½" 150.00

Cowan Punch Bowl by Schreckengost

Punch bowl, sgraffito abstract cocktail & skyscraper motifs glazed in black over turquoise, ca. 1931, impressed Cowan mark & signed Viktor/Schreckengost (designer) in underglaze black, 13 7/8" d. (ILLUS.) 6,875.00
Teapot, cov., cream glaze, 6" h. 85.00
Tea tile, silhouette profile of young girl on dark blue ground, green wreath border, 6½" d. 175.00
Trivet, hexagonal, molded foliage, ivory glaze, 6" w. 55.00
Vase, 5¼" h., green crystalline glaze 55.00
Vase, 5½" h., bulbous, matte green & rose glaze 45.00
Vase, 6" h., fan-shaped on seahorse base, ivory glaze 22.00
Vase, 7" h., Chinese orange glaze 60.00
Vase, 7" h., flowing brown glaze over orange 50.00
Vase, 8" h., Art Deco geometric shape, bronze & green glaze 125.00
Vase, 10" h., blue lustre finish 100.00
Vase, 12" h., cocoa green matte finish 18.00

Cowan Vase

Vase, 12" h., 12" widest d., 2-handled, Chinese red glaze (ILLUS.) 175.00

CUP PLATES (Staffordshire)

Like their glass counterparts, these small plates were designed to hold a cup while the tea or coffee was allowed to cool in a saucer before it was sipped from the saucer, a practice that would now be considered in poor taste. The forerunner of the glass cup plates, those listed below were produced in various Staffordshire potteries in England. Their popularity waned after the introduction of the glass cup plate in the 1820's. Also see CUP PLATES under Glass.

Alcock, Seaweed & Shell patt.,
green transfer $30.00
Davenport, Amoy patt., flow blue,
ca. 1844 .... 65.00
Furnival (Jacob & Thomas), Indian
Jar patt., flow blue, ca. 1843 ..... 75.00
Mayer, Canova patt., green transfer, ca. 1830 .... 30.00
Salopian (Thomas Turner's Caughley
Works), transfer of birds, florals &
fruit highlighted w/polychrome
enameling, 3¾" d. (minor hairline) 85.00
Staffordshire (unmarked), park
scene, brown transfer 45.00
Wedgwood, red transfer "An Only
Son" scene center, floral-
embossed border highlighted
w/polychrome enameling,
4¼" d. 65.00

DAVENPORT

The Davenport factory operated under various names at Longport, England, from about 1794 to 1887. Various marks were used, including an anchor. Also see FLOW BLUE, IRONSTONE and the "Special Focus" on TEA LEAF IRONSTONE.

Bowl, 11½" d., oriental decor,
green transfer (professional
repair) $125.00
Cookie jar, cov., Imari-type decor,
silverplate rim, cover & bail
handle 125.00
Cup & saucer, ornate gold handle,
central medallion w/large rose on
blue fishscale ground, gold trim .. 75.00
Mug, black transfer "Victoria Girls
For Ever" & polychrome enamel
floral decor, 4 5/8" h. (stains) 85.00
Plate, 7" d., Cyprus patt., mulberry-
sepia transfer, ca. 1850 .... 30.00
Plate, 8½" d., daffodils decor, scalloped edge w/brown trim,
1790-1810..................... 40.00

Plate, 8½" d., roses decor, scalloped edge w/brown trim,
1790-1810..................... 40.00
Plate, 8½" d., tulips decor, scalloped edge w/brown trim,
1790-1810..................... 40.00
Plate, 9" d., large gold medallion
center, maroon & gold border,
ca. 1850 .... 25.00

DEDHAM

Vase with Volcanic Glaze

This pottery was organized in 1866 by Alexander W. Robertson in Chelsea, Mass., and became A. W. & H. Robertson in 1868. In 1872, the name was changed to Chelsea Keramic Art Works and in 1891 to Chelsea Pottery, U.S.A. About 1895, the pottery was moved to Dedham, Mass., and was renamed Dedham Pottery. Production ceased in 1943. High-fired colored wares and crackle ware were specialities. The rabbit is said to have been the most popular decoration on crackle ware in blue.

Bowl, 6" d., Rabbit $130.00
Bowl, 7 5/8" d., Rabbit 285.00
Bowl, 9" d., 4" deep, 2" wide border
on outside rim, Rabbit (hairline) .. 445.00
Creamer, Rabbit, 3¼" h. ..225.00 to 265.00
Cup, Snow Tree 95.00
Cup & saucer, Elephant ....330.00 to 440.00
Cup & saucer, Rabbit ......145.00 to 225.00
Mug, Rabbit 195.00
Mush cup & saucer, Rabbit,
3½" h....................... 265.00
Paperweight, model of a rabbit,
2¾" 260.00
Pitcher, Morning & Evening (rooster,
hens & sun)................... 575.00
Plate, 6" d., Iris 65.00
Plate, 6" d., Pond Lily ....55.00 to 95.00
Plate, 6" d., Rabbit ....60.00 to 85.00
Plate, 6" d., Turtle 265.00
Plate, 7¾" d., Turkey 175.00
Plate, 8½" d., Grape 140.00
Plate, 8½" d., Lobster 575.00
Plate, 8½" d., Rabbit......100.00 to 115.00

Plate, 8½" d., Turtle 395.00
Plate, 8¾" d., Rabbit 155.00
Plate, 9½" d., Turkey 125.00
Plate, 10" d., Duck ....175.00 to 235.00
Plate, 10" d., Pineapple........... 540.00
Plate, 10" d., Pond Lily 265.00
Plate, 10" d., Rabbit 175.00
Salt shaker, Rabbit, 2¾" h.
  (single)........................ 135.00
Sugar bowl, cov., 2-handled,
  Rabbit......................... 225.00
Tray, Lobster, 9 x 5¼"............ 295.00
Vase, 7¾" h., baluster-shaped, ir-
  regular brown, black & blue vol-
  canic glaze (ILLUS.) 5,280.00
Vase, 8" h., bulbous tapering to-
  wards base, Poppies on "crackle-
  ware" 2,310.00

Dedham Cylindrical Vase

Vase, 11½" h., cylindrical, amber,
  coffee & brown drip glaze, signed
  H.C.R. (Hugh C. Robertson) &
  numbered (ILLUS.) 1,540.00

DELFT

Dutch Delft Wall Plaque

*Delft, a tin-glazed pottery, is of a type that
originated in Belgium and Italy centuries*

*ago. Because Dutch traders made the city of
Delft the center of their world-wide trade on
these items, the term "delft" became synonymous with "tin-glazed pottery." The use of
delft to indicate only blue and white is in er-
ror since all potters worked in polychrome as
well. Delft, faience, and majolica are all tin-
glazed pottery. Also see CAT COLLECTI-
BLES and TILES.*

Dish, painted in the oriental style
  w/pagodas amidst trees on islands, band enclosing trellis pattern & scrolls at the well, blue &
  white, English, ca. 1740,
  13¾" d......................$110.00
Dish, painted in the oriental style
  w/flowering chrysanthemum &
  bamboo issuing from rockwork,
  border w/flower sprays, blue &
  white, Dutch, ca. 1760, 14½" d. ... 132.00
Inkstand, cov., shaped lid painted
  w/scene of figures at a harbor,
  opening to a removable well &
  quill holder, blue & white, Dutch,
  4" h........................... 132.00
Pitcher, windmill by spout w/letter-
  ing "A 1575 & Erven Lucas Bols-
  Amsterdam," ornate florals & water scene w/boat, blue & white,
  19th c. 285.00
Plaque, polychrome, painted blue
  cellist & flautist within a scroll-
  molded border, enriched in iron-
  red, manganese, green & yellow,
  Dutch, ca. 1740, 9½" l. (small
  repair to top, minor chips).......1,650.00
Plaque, quatrefoil, painted w/chil-
  dren (2) playing musical instruments in pastoral setting w/build-
  ings & windmills in the distance,
  raised border w/band of stylized
  foliage, blue & white, Dutch, ca.
  1740, 9¾" w. (ILLUS.) 1,320.00
Plaque, polychrome, center painted
  w/blue canal scene, buildings &
  figures within elaborate scroll &
  foliate cartouche, enriched w/iron-
  red trellis patt. panels on a yellow
  ground supporting 2 birds & a shell
  motif, raised border w/band of
  scrolls in iron-red on a yellow
  ground, Dutch, ca. 1750, 13" h. ...1,980.00
Plates, 8¾" d., underglaze-blue
  landscape scene within diapered
  borders interspersed w/leaftips,
  rim w/stylized foliate scroll band,
  yellow edge, Dutch, 19th c., pr.
  (rim chips)..................... 137.50
Plate, 9" d., blue & white, floral decor (minor edge chips)........... 255.00
Plate, 9" d., shaped rim w/scalloped
  edge, polychrome, painted scene
  of boy & bird on river bank center, floral sprays border, under-

glaze blue w/yellow & green,
Dutch, 18th c.................. 137.50
Plate, 9 1/8" d., polychrome, painted
blue center scene of two boys in
rowboat before distant castles &
church within cartouche edged in
yellow, iron-red, green & yellow
scrolls, conforming rim decorated
in same palette w/elaborate border of diapered & stippled panels,
blossoms & foliate scrolls, Dutch,
ca. 1765 ....1,210.00
Plate, 12 1/8" d., polychrome, center painted w/vase of flowers before spread "peacock tail," blue &
white, ochre-edged rim w/border
of butterflies alternating
w/flowerheads on a tight-scroll
ground, 19th c. 165.00

18th Century Dutch Delft

Strawberry strainer dish & stand,
blue & white, 3-footed dish w/cen-
tral blue medallion pierced w/pat-
tern of diamonds & scrolls, center
of stand w/painted floral sprigs,
each piece w/wide fluted border of
alternating blue & white tulip &
rose panels about husk-edged herringbone band below border of
molded leafage, Dutch, De Twee
Scheepjes, 1755-70, "IP" monogram
for Jan Pennis (ILLUS.) 1,045.00
Tankard, painted w/three panels of
flowering plants between tight-
scroll & leafage borders, blue &
white, "AK" monogram & "7"
for Albertus Kiell, Dutch, De Witte
Starre, ca. 1765, w/Dutch silver
mounts of later date, 9¼" h. (rim
& footrim chips) 1,540.00

**Tile pictures, each 6-tile, manganese,
figures, buildings & cattle in canal
landscapes, Dutch, 18th c., 15½ x
10¼", pr. (minor repair) 1,960.00**

Tile picture, 6 center tiles, depicting
a green parrot on a perch enriched
in yellow & manganese, manganese border tiles of scrolling flowering foliage, in wooden frame,
Dutch, 18th c., 20½ x 15¼"
(damage to border) 1,430.00
Tile picture, 12-tile, depicting a cat
& dog seated on their haunches
within an interior w/drapes, in
wooden frame, Dutch, 18th c.,
21 x 16" (damage & repair) 1,650.00

Delft Tulip Vase

Tulip vase, 5-finger, oval body
painted w/musical putti admist
flowers on front & reverse, flower
nozzles, borders & sides painted
w/floral sprays, blue scroll handles, blue & white, Dutch, De.
Grieksche A., ca. 1700, repaired,
10½" h. (ILLUS.) 2,090.00
Tyg, 3-handled, blue & white 150.00
Wine cooler w/pewter-mounted rims,
polychrome, painted iron-red, blue
& gold oriental floral sprays between molded blue borders heightened w/gilding, molded bearded
lion's mask & ring handles, Dutch,
De Grieksche A, 1705-20, "PAK"
monogram for Pieter Adriaensz
Kochs, 7 7/8" d. 2,530.00

DERBY & ROYAL CROWN DERBY

*William Duesbury, in partnership with
John and Christopher Heath, established the
Derby Porcelain Works in Derby, England,
about 1750. Duesbury soon bought out his
partners and in 1770 purchased the Chelsea
factory and six years later, the Bow works.
Duesbury was succeeded by his son and
grandson. Robert Bloor purchased the business about 1814 and managed successfully
until illness in 1828 left him unable to exer-*

cise control. The "Bloor" Period, however, extends from 1814 until 1848, when the factory closed. Former Derby workmen then resumed porcelain manufacture in another factory and this nucleus eventually united with a new and distinct venture, Derby Crown Porcelain, Ltd., 1890.

Derby "Apple" Box

Box, cov., realistically modeled as
   an apple, applied flowerheads &
   foliage (w/minute chips) on oblong base, ca. 1800, 3" h.
   (ILLUS.)........................$275.00
Cup & saucer, demitasse, Imari
   patt., cobalt blue, iron-red & gilt
   on white, dated 1889............ 65.00
Dinner service: 2-handled oval soup
   tureen & cover, pr. cov. vegetable
   tureens, pr. cov. sauce tureens
   w/stands, 6 oval dishes, nineteen
   10" d. plates, 17 soup plates & 16
   side plates; King's patt., iron-red,
   blue & gilt, ca. 1820, 63 pcs......5,720.00
Figure of Mansion House Dwarf,
   1780, 7" h..................... 600.00
Figures, sportsman & a companion:
   he in black tricorn hat, fur-lined
   turquoise coat & iron-red
   breeches, holding his gun; his
   companion in turquoise hat, pink
   fur-lined coat & iron-red &
   turquoise-striped skirt, holding a
   bird; both w/a dog by their sides,
   on circular scroll-molded bases
   enriched in turquoise & gilt & applied w/flowerheads & foliage,
   ca. 1760, 9" h., pr. (minor chips to
   flowerheads & repairs)..........1,210.00
Figures, shepherd & a companion:
   he holding a basket of flowers,
   wearing colorful costume, w/dog
   by his side; companion holding
   flowers in her apron, w/lamb by
   her side; each on shaped scroll-
   molded base enriched in puce,
   turquoise & gilt, ca. 1755, 9¼" h.,
   pr. (repairs & chips)............ 880.00
Figures, "Autumn" & "Spring": Au-

tumn depicted as a young girl
   w/white kerchief & turquoise-
   lined pink dress over a cream-
   colored skirt patterned w/iron-
   red, blue & rose floral sprays &
   carrying a basket of green & purple grapes; Spring as a youth
   w/black hat, turquoise-lined pink
   jacket over a purple-sprigged
   waistcoat & cream-colored
   breeches & holding a floral garland; each on pierced scroll-
   molded base heightened in turquoise & gilding, ca. 1775, 11¾" &
   11 3/8" h., pr. (restoration to basket handle & neck of Spring)..... 990.00

"Europa & Bull" and "Leda & Swan"

Figures, "Leda & the Swan" &
   "Europa & the Bull": Leda in flowered dress & iron-red sandals seated
   on rockwork base w/swan by her
   side; Europa seated on a bull
   w/floral garland about his head
   & neck; each on scroll-molded
   base enriched in green & gilt,
   ca. 1765, w/repairs to bull's leg
   & Leda's neck, 11½" h., pr.
   (ILLUS.).......................8,800.00
Ginger jar, cov., overall enameled
   florals & gilt decor, 9" h........ 395.00
Model of a squirrel seated on its
   haunches, holding a nut in its
   front paws, bushy tail, enriched in
   iron-red & wearing gilt collar, on
   circular grassy mound base enriched in green, ca. 1780, 3¼" h.
   (repair to base)................ 825.00
Mug, cylindrical, Japan patt.,
   underglaze-blue, iron-red, green
   & gilt stylized oriental florals &
   foliate scrolls on cobalt blue or
   white ground, within borders of
   alternating diamond & flowerhead
   panels, ca. 1810, 4½" h......... 495.00
Plate, 9¾" d., center w/sepia
   figures in a lake landscape within
   a foliate entwined gilt band, border w/trailing husks suspended by
   ribbons, ca. 1785............... 440.00

Plates, 10" d., center painted w/coat-of-arms within gilt scroll borders, surmounted by a unicorn & suspending a scroll w/inscription, borders w/elaborate gilt scroll & foliage on blue ground, Bloor period, ca. 1820, pr......................1,100.00

Derby Sauceboat

Sauceboat, molded as overlapping leaves w/curling stalk handle & bud & flowerhead terminal, painted scattered floral sprays on body, green rims & puce bud at handle, ca. 1756, minor footrim chip on one, 7¾" w., pr. (ILLUS. of one).......................1,210.00
Vases, 6" h., modeled as a tulip, petals enriched in iron-red on one & puce on other, supported by foliate stem, brown base applied w/flowerheads & foliage, ca. 1810, pr...........................4,950.00
Vases, 7½" h., modeled as an iris, petals enriched in blue, pink, burgundy & yellow, green leaves, on shaped circular rockwork base, ca. 1825, pr. 6,380.00

DOULTON & ROYAL DOULTON

Doulton & Co., Ltd., was founded in Lambeth, London, about 1858. It was operated there till 1956 and often incorporated the words "Doulton" and "Lambeth" in its marks. Pinder Bourne & Co., Burslem, was purchased by the Doultons in 1878 and in 1882 became Doulton & Co., Ltd. It added porcelain to its earthenware production in 1884. The "Royal Doulton" mark has been used by this factory, which is still in production. Character jugs and figurines are commanding great attention from collectors at the present time. Also see FLOW BLUE, GIBSON GIRL PLATES and TOBY MUGS & JUGS.

DICKENSWARE

Dickensware Cookie Jar

Ash pot, Old Charley $95.00
Bowl, 7½" d., shallow, Sam Weller 40.00
Bowl, 8½" sq., shallow, Little Nell .. 95.00
Bowl, 9" octagon, Sam Weller in low relief ....85.00 to 100.00
Bust of Mr. Micawber, small 75.00
Bust of Sam Weller, brown hat, yellow vest, cream shirt & brown tie, 2½" h....................... 60.00
Candlestick, The Artful Dodger, bulbous, 7" h. (single) 100.00
Charger, Alfred Jingle & Bill Sykes, signed Noke, 13" d. 125.00
Charger, Fagin, 13" d. 110.00
Charger, Tony Weller, 13" d. 188.00
Charger, Trotty Veck, 13" d. 110.00
Coffee pot, cov., Tony Weller, 7¼" h....................... 195.00
Cookie jar, Old Peggoty, silverplate rim, cover & bail handle (ILLUS.).. 300.00
Cup & saucer, Barnaby Rudge 65.00
Cup & saucer, cup w/Fagin & saucer w/Mr. Micawber 55.00
Cup & saucer, Tony Weller 65.00
Figurine, Tiny Tim, 3¼" h. 35.00
Match holder, bombe form, Sam Weller 95.00
Mug, Mark Tapley, 6" h............. 85.00
Pitcher, 4 7/8" h., 2¾" d., Cap'n Cuttle 95.00
Pitcher, 5½" h., jug-type, Pickwick Papers - White Hart Inn 145.00
Pitcher, 8 7/8" h., 4¼" d., Sydney Carton 156.00
Plate, 6" d., Old Peggoty 45.00
Plate, 7½" d., Mr. Squeers......... 55.00
Plate, 7½" d., Sydney Carton 55.00
Plate, 8½" d., Sam Weller 60.00
Plate, 10" d., The Artful Dodger & Sydney Carton 70.00
Plate, 10" d., Little Nell........... 80.00
Plate, 10" d., Sydney Carton 85.00

Teapot, cov., Bill Sykes,
6" h. . . . . .195.00 to 235.00
Teapot, cov., Fat Boy, large 225.00
Tea tile, Mr. Micawber, 6" d. 60.00
Tray, Bill Sykes, 8½" sq. 200.00
Vase, 3½" h., 1 7/8" d., Bill
Sykes 79.00
Vase, 5" h., square, Artful
Dodger . . . . .80.00 to 95.00
Vase, 5" h., Tony Weller 70.00
Vase, 7½" h., 4¼" d., 2-handled,
Sam Weller 155.00
Vase, 7¾" h., 3½" d., 2-handled,
Mr. Squeers 160.00

MISCELLANEOUS

Drake Character Jugs

Bowl, 3¾" d., scrolled feet w/gold
beading, floral decor outlined in
gold 95.00
Bowl, 7½" d., pedestal base, Rustic
England series w/rural scene
decor 75.00
Cake plate, Robin Hood series 89.00
Candlesticks, white Grecian figures
on black ground, 4" h., pr. 65.00
Character jug, 'Ard of 'Earing,
miniature, 2¼" h. . . . . .1,000.00 to 1,200.00
Character jug, 'Ard of 'Earing, large,
6" h. . . . . .875.00 to 1,200.00
Character jug, 'Arriet, tiny,
1¼" h. 190.00
Character jug, 'Arriet, miniature,
2¼" h. 60.00
Character jug, 'Arriet, small,
3½" h. 76.50
Character jug, 'Arry, miniature,
2¼" h. 62.50
Character jug, 'Arry, large,
6¾" h. 170.00
Character jug, Auld Mac, tiny,
1¼" h. 200.00
Character jug, (Sergeant) Buz Fuz,
small, 3½" h. 100.00
Character jug, Captain Hook, small,
3½" h. 300.00
Character jug, Captain Hook, large,
6" h. 335.00
Character jug, Cardinal, tiny,
1¼" h. 180.00
Character jug, Cardinal, miniature,
2¼" h. 45.00
Character jug, Cavalier, w/goatee,
1940-50, large 5,450.00

Character jug, Dick Turpin, mask on
face, horse handle, miniature,
2¼" h. 40.00
Character jug, Drake, small,
3½" h. 70.00
Character jug, Drake, large,
5 5/8" h. (ILLUS.) 135.00
Character jug, Drake, early version
without hat, large (ILLUS.
right) . . . . .4,000.00 to 5,000.00
Character jug, Farmer John, small,
3½" h. 70.00
Character jug, Farmer John, large,
6" h. 137.50
Character jug, Fat Boy, tiny,
1¼" h. 95.00
Character jug, Fat Boy, miniature,
2¼" h. 55.00
Character jug, Fat Boy, "A" mark,
small, 3½" h. 75.00
Character jug, Field Marshall Smuts,
large . . . . .1,650.00 to 2,150.00
Character jug, Fortune Teller, minia-
ture, 2¼" h. 290.00
Character jug, Fortune Teller, small,
3½" h. 325.00
Character jug, Fortune Teller, large,
6" h. 395.00
Character jug, Friar Tuck, large,
6" h. 335.00
Character jug, Gladiator, miniature,
2¼" h. 325.00
Character jug, Gladiator, small,
3½" h. 335.00
Character jug, Gladiator, large,
6" h. 485.00
Character jug, Gondolier, large 490.00
Character jug, Granny, early version
without tooth, large 995.00
Character jug, Gulliver, miniature,
2¼" h. 360.00
Character jug, Gulliver, small,
3½" h. 335.00
Character jug, Jarge, small,
3½" h. 155.00
Character jug, Jockey, large, 6" h. . . . 230.00
Character jug, John Barleycorn,
miniature, 2¼" h. 60.00
Character jug, John Peel, tiny,
1¼" h. 215.00
Character jug, John Peel, large 120.00
Character jug, Johnny Appleseed,
large, 6" h. 265.00
Character jug, Lord Nelson, large . . . 300.00
Character jug, Mephistopheles,
large . . . . .2,250.00 to 3,000.00
Character jug, Mikado, miniature,
2¼" h. 250.00
Character jug, Mikado, large,
6" h. 380.00
Character jug, Mr. Micawber, tiny,
1¼" h. 90.00
Character jug, Mr. Micawber, minia-
ture, 2¼" h. 50.00

Character jug, Mr. Pickwick, tiny,
1¼" h. 215.00
Character jug, Mr. Pickwick, miniature, 2¼" h. 52.50
Character jug, Mr. Pickwick, large .. 145.00
Character jug, Old Charley, tiny,
1¼" h. 95.00

Poacher Character Jug

Character jug, Poacher, large
(ILLUS.) 55.00
Character jug, Punch & Judy, minia-
ture, 2¼" h. 365.00
Character jug, Punch & Judy,
large 550.00
Character jug, Regency Beau, minia-
ture, 2¼" h. 500.00
Character jug, Sairey Gamp, tiny,
1¼" h. ....85.00 to 100.00
Character jug, Sam Johnson, large,
6" h. 245.00
Character jug, Sam Weller, tiny,
1¼" h. 95.00
Character jug, Sam Weller, large,
6" h. 135.00
Character jug, Scaramouche, minia-
ture, 2¼" h. 400.00
Character jug, Tony Weller, small,
3½" h. 55.00
Character jug, Tony Weller,
large 120.00
Character jug, Town Crier, minia-
ture, 2¼" h. 135.00
Character jug, Ugly Duchess, minia-
ture, 2¼" h. 235.00
Charger, flow blue, mother & child
w/foliage ground, 14" 325.00
Charger, Jackdaw of Rheims series,
dated 1943, 15" d. 225.00
Cheese dish, cov., Robin Hood se-
ries - "Under the Greenwood
Tree" 325.00
Chess piece, model of mouse,
signed Tinworth 250.00
Chocolate pot, cov., stoneware, Lit-
tle Bo Peep & Queen of Hearts in
relief, 10" h. 100.00
Cigarette lighter, Long John Silver .. 90.00
Cigarette lighter, Poacher 90.00

Coffee pot, cov., Gnomes series 180.00
Coffee pot, cov., Art Deco shape,
Robin Hood series - "Robin Hood
The King of Archers," 3¼" d.,
8¼" h. 230.00
Coffee set: coffee pot w/red knob
finial on cover, creamer & open
sugar bowl; Reynard the Fox series, riding crop forms handles,
h.p. fox in relief decor, 3 pcs. 225.00
Compote, 5 3/8" d., 3½" h., autumn
colors trees, grassland & mountains decor, artist-signed 175.00
Cookie jar, overall floral decor on
cream & green tapestry ground,
embossed pink & brown flowers
w/green leaves, gold trim, silverplated rim, cover & handle, 5" d.,
6" h. 145.00
Cookie jar, Tony Weller, w/silver-
plate rim, cover & bail handle,
7" h. 395.00
Cookie jar, florals w/rust & gold foliage decor on cobalt blue base
w/pink top rim, gold trim, silverplate rim, cover & handle, Doul-
ton-Burslem, 6" d., 7¼" h. 100.00
Cookie jar, pottery, ribbed cream
ground w/gold trim, wide sky
blue center band w/panels of
animals & birds in color, silverplate rim, cover & handle, Doulton-
Burslem, 5¾" d., 7½" h. 148.00
Cookie jar, h.p. multicolored florals
w/gold leaf floral overlay on cobalt blue ground, silverplate cover, Doulton Burslem 195.00
Cookie jar, cov., Nursery Rhyme
patt., "Cat & Fiddle," for Huntley
Palmer 400.00
Cookie jar, cov., stoneware, etched
deer & fox decor, signed Hannah
Barlow, 1883 .... 340.00
Creamer, Welsh Ladies series,
5" w., 4½" h. 165.00
Creamer, King's Ware, "Old Woman
at Hearth," signed Noke 95.00
Creamer & sugar bowl, stoneware,
white figures, dogs, trees, horses
& man smoking pipe in relief on
brown & tan ground, pr. 225.00
Cup, King's Ware, portrait of Bill
Sykes, 2½" h. 130.00
Cup & saucer, demitasse, landscape
decor, "flambe" glaze 75.00
Cuspidor, stoneware, ornately beaded decor on blue ground 70.00
Dish, 3-section, Zunday Zmocks
series, head of man in tall black
hat by hollyhocks & brick wall decor, 6 7/8 x 11 5/8" oval 100.00
Ewer, stoneware, applied lizard
handle, frog spout, incised fish
decor, artist-signed, 14" h. 260.00

Figurine, "A 'Courting," HN 2004 .... 435.00
Figurine, "A Gentlewoman,"
  HN 1632, lavender dress 475.00
Figurine, "A Jester," HN 1702,
  brown, purple & red costume 545.00
Figurine, "Adrienne," HN 2152, rose-
  red dress 135.00
Figurine, "Afternoon Tea," HN 1747,
  pink dress 280.00
Figurine, "Aileen," HN 1645, green
  dress 1,500.00
Figurine, "Alison," HN 2336, blue
  overdress 103.00
Figurine, "Angela," HN 1303, blue
  fan, spotted costume 750.00
Figurine, "Annabella," HN 1871,
  peach skirt, green bodice 293.00
Figurine, "Annabella," HN 1872,
  green skirt 408.00
Figurine, "Bachelor" (The),
  HN 2319 .... 255.00
Figurine, "Balinese Dancer,"
  HN 2808, red, yellow & green
  costume 340.00
Figurine, "Ballad Seller," HN 2266 .. 245.00
Figurine, "Balloon Man," HN 1954,
  dark jacket, green pants 125.00
Figurine, "Belle," HN 754, pastel
  multicolored dress 550.00
Figurine, "Bernice," HN 2071 ...... 800.00
Figurine, "Blacksmith of Williams-
  burg," HN 2240, white skirt,
  brown hat 125.00
Figurine, "Bluebeard," HN 2105,
  dark cloak, orange & green
  costume 240.00
Figurine, "Bon Appetit," HN 2444 ... 156.00
Figurine, "Bon Jour," HN 1888, red
  dress 585.00
Figurine, "Boy from Williamsburg,"
  HN 2183, purple jacket, red vest .. 97.00
Figurine, "Bride" (The), HN 2166,
  pale pink dress 190.00
Figurine, "Broken Lance" (The),
  HN 2041 .... 440.00
Figurine, "Cello," HN 2331, yellow
  dress 950.00
Figurine, "Charley's Aunt," HN 35,
  black dress 470.00
Figurine, "Charley's Aunt," HN 1703,
  white dress, no base 520.00
Figurine, "Child from Williamsburg,"
  HN 2154, blue dress 100.00
Figurine, "Christine," HN 1839, lilac
  dress, blue shawl 700.00
Figurine, "Christmas Time,"
  HN 2110 .... 337.00
Figurine, "Clarinda," HN 2724 ...... 145.00
Figurine, "Clarissa," HN 1525, green
  dress, red shawl 625.00
Figurine, "Clemency," HN 1643,
  green trim on dress, red top 575.00
Figurine, "Coachman" (The),
  HN 2282 .... 425.00

Figurine, "Cobbler" (The), HN 1706,
  green & blue striped shirt & hat
  w/yellow 218.00
Figurine, "Deidre," HN 2020 .... 298.00
Figurine, "Delphine," HN 2136,
  1954-67 .... 225.00
Figurine, "Derrick," HN 1398 ...... 452.00
Figurine, "Dimity," HN 2169 .... 312.00
Figurine, "Easter Day," HN 1976,
  white dress, blue flowers 390.00
Figurine, "Eugene," HN 1521, red &
  white dress 650.00
Figurine, "Fair Maiden," HN 2211,
  green dress, yellow sleeves,
  5¼" h. 60.00
Figurine, "Family Album,"
  HN 2321 .... 320.00
Figurine, "Folly," HN 1335, green
  hat, pink dress 1,300.00
Figurine, "Four O'Clock," HN 1760 .. 733.00
Figurine, "Gainsboro Hat" (The),
  HN 47, light green dress 1,950.00

"Gay Morning"

Figurine, "Gay Morning," HN 2135,
  1954-67 (ILLUS.) 215.00
Figurine, "Gentleman from Williams-
  burg," HN 2227, green costume,
  black shoes, white stockings,
  black hat, seated on wooden
  bench, 6¼" h. 137.00
Figurine, "Good Catch," HN 2258,
  dark green suit 114.00
Figurine, "Gretchen," HN 1397, blue
  & white dress 588.00
Figurine, "Gwendolen," HN 1494,
  green & pink dress .....375.00 to 495.00
Figurines, "He Loves Me" & "She
  Loves Me Not," HN 2046 &
  HN 2045, pr. 300.00
Figurine, "Heart to Heart,"
  HN 2276 ....250.00 to 375.00
Figurine, "Helen," HN 1509, white,
  blue & red dress 950.00

"Her Ladyship"

Figurine, "Her Ladyship," HN 1977,
1945-59 (ILLUS.) . . . . 240.00 to 300.00
Figurine, "Herminia," HN 1644,
white flower-printed dress 1,050.00
Figurine, "Herminia," HN 1704,
red dress, green purse 1,050.00
Figurine, "Hermione," HN 2058,
1950-52 . . . . 1,550.00
Figurine, "Kate Hardcastle,"
HN 1734, white & green dress,
pink flower 155.00
Figurine, "Kate Hardcastle,"
HN 1919, red overskirt, green
dress, black base 650.00
Figurine, "Kate Hardcastle,"
HN 2028, 1949-52 . . . . 500.00
Figurine, "Kathleen," HN 1357, pink,
orange & yellow skirt 550.00

"La Sylphide"

Figurine, "La Sylphide," HN 2138,
1954-65 (ILLUS.) 330.00
Figurine, "Lady April," HN 1958, red
dress, 1940-59 . . . . 275.00
Figurine, "Lady Betty," HN 1967 . . . . 275.00
Figurine, "Lady Clare," HN 1465 . . . . 650.00
Figurine, "Lady of the Georgian
Period," HN 331, brown & yellow
dress 2,100.00
Figurine, "Lady Pamela,"
HN 2718 . . . . 110.00 to 185.00
Figurine, "Lido Lady," HN 1220,
flowered blue costume . . 500.00 to 850.00
Figurine, "Lisette," HN 1523, white &
red dress 900.00
Figurine, "Little Land" (The), HN 67,
blue costume 1,750.00
Figurine, "Little Mistress" (The),
HN 1449 . . . . 310.00
Figurine, "Lizana," HN 1756, pink
dress, green cloak 950.00
Figurine, "London Cry, Strawber-
ries," HN 749, cream overdress,
red skirt 1,050.00
Figurine, "London Cry, Turnips and
Carrots," HN 752 . . . . 800.00
Figurine, "Margery," HN 1413 . . . . . . 365.00
Figurine, "Margot," HN 1653, white
& red dress, red hat 750.00
Figurine, "Marguerite," HN 1946,
red dress, green hat 225.00
Figurine, "Marietta," HN 1341, black
costume, red cape . . . . . . 550.00 to 900.00
Figurine, "Marietta," HN 1446, lilac
costume, green cape 635.00
Figurine, "Marion," HN 1583, blue
skirt 1,400.00
Figurine, "Mask," HN 657, black &
white costume 775.00
Figurine, "Mendicant" (The),
HN 1365 . . . . 230.00
Figurine, "Meriel," HN 1932,
green dress 1,650.00
Figurine, "Midsummer Noon,"
HN 1899, red dress,
1939-49 . . . . 425.00 to 525.00
Figurine, "Millicent," HN 1714,
pink shawl 1,000.00
Figurine, "Miranda," HN 1818, red
skirt 1,550.00
Figurine, "Mirror," HN 1852 . . . . 1,750.00
Figurine, "Miss Fortune," HN 1897,
blue & white shawl, pink
dress 750.00
Figurine, "Modena," HN 1846, red
dress 2,250.00
Figurine, "Modern Piper" (The),
HN 756 . . . . 2,000.00
Figurine, "My Pretty Maid,"
HN 2064 . . . . 450.00
Figurine, "Nana," HN 1767, lilac
dress 325.00
Figurine, "Noelle," HN 2179 . . . . 350.00
Figurine, "Old King," HN 1801 . . . . . . 350.00

Figurine, "Olga," HN 2463 . . . . 195.00

Figurine, "Omar Khayyam,"
HN 2247 . . . . 120.00

Figurine, "One of the Forty,"
HN 712, checkered red robes 900.00

Figurine, "Orange Seller,"
HN 1325 . . . . 850.00

Figurine, "Parson's Daughter" (The),
HN 564, multicolored skirt 265.00

Figurine, "Pauline," HN 1444 . . . . . . 375.00

Figurine, "Perfect Pair" (The),
HN 581 . . . . 650.00 to 950.00

Figurine, "Philippa of Hainault,"
HN 2008 . . . . 400.00

Figurine, "Pied Piper" (The),
HN 2102, brown cloak, grey hat &
boots 215.00

Figurine, "Poacher" (The),
HN 2043 . . . . 220.00 to 265.00

Figurine, "Potter" (The), HN 1493,
dark brown & red robe & hood,
multicolored jugs & jars, 7" h. 225.00

Figurine, "Premiere,"
HN 2343 . . . . 120.00 to 175.00

Figurine, "Primroses," HN 1617 . . . . . 600.00

Figurine, "Prized Possessions,"
HN 2942 . . . . 255.00

Figurine, "Professor" (The),
HN 2281 . . . . 115.00 to 150.00

Figurine, "Promenade," HN 2076,
blue overdress, peach skirt 1,295.00

Figurine, "Queen Elizabeth II,"
HN 2502 . . . . 1,633.00

Figurine, "Queen Elizabeth II,"
HN 2878, blue & crimson robes,
white gown 294.00

Figurine, "Rendezvous," HN 2212 . . . 315.00

Figurine, "Repose," HN 2272 . . . . 160.00

Figurine, "Rocking Horse" (The),
HN 2072 . . . . 1,500.00

Figurine, "Rose," HN 1416, blue-
purple dress 90.00

Figurine, "Rosemary," HN 2091 . . . . . 344.00

Figurine, "Rosina," HN 1358, red
dress, ermine trim 650.00

Figurine, "Ruth," HN 2799 . . . . 68.00

Figurine, "Santa Claus," HN 2725,
red & white suit, pack of toys 138.00

Figurine, "Schoolmarm," HN 2223 . . . 140.00

Figurine, "Scotties," HN 1281, red
dress 1,100.00

Figurine, "Sea Harvest," HN 2257 . . . 160.00

Figurine, "Seashore," HN 2263 . . . . . . 216.00

Figurine, "She Loves Me Not,"
HN 2045 . . . . 133.00

Figurine, "Sir Walter Raleigh,"
HN 2015, orange costume, dark
cloak 538.00

Figurine, "Sleepy Darling,"
HN 2953 . . . . 166.00

Figurine, "Sonia," HN 1692, pink
bodice, white skirt 650.00

Figurine, "Spanish Lady," HN 1294,
red mottled dress 790.00

Figurine, "Spring Flowers," HN 1807,
green skirt, grey-blue overskirt . . . 292.00

Figurine, "Stayed at Home,"
HN 2207 . . . . 142.00

"Summer's Day"

Figurine, "Summer's Day," HN 2181,
1957-62 (ILLUS.) 320.00

Figurine, "Susanna," HN 1233, pink
robe 808.00

Figurine, "Sweet Anne," HN 1318,
blue jacket, pale green skirt 209.00

Figurine, "Sweet Anne," HN 1496,
pink & purple dress & hat 180.00

Figurine, "Sweet Seventeen,"
HN 2734 . . . . 124.00

Figurine, "Sweet Sixteen,"
HN 2231 . . . . 182.00

Figurine, "Sweet Suzy," HN 1918 . . . . 563.00

Figurine, "Sweet & Fair," HN 1865,
green dress 1,100.00

Figurine, "Sweet & Twenty,"
HN 1298, red & pink dress, Potted
by Doulton 200.00

Figurine, "Sweet & Twenty,"
HN 1549, multicolored dress &
couch 414.00

Figurine, "Sweet & Twenty,"
HN 1610, red dress, yellow
couch 223.00

Figurine, "Swimmer" (The), HN 1270,
black, floral print bathing suit . . . 1,100.00

Figurine, "Sylvia," HN 1478 . . . . 488.00

Figurine, "Tete a Tete," HN 798,
mottled pink & blue dress, Potted
by Doulton 1,100.00

Figurine, "To Bed," HN 1805, green
shirt & shorts 113.00

Figurine, "Tom," HN 2864 . . . . 85.00

Figurine, "Town Crier," HN 2119 . . . . 225.00

Figurine, "Uncle Ned," HN 2094,
1952-65 . . . . 357.00

Figurine, "Viking" (The), HN 2375 . . . 246.00

Figurine, "Votes For Women,"
HN 2816 . . . . 168.00

Figurine, "Willy Won't He," HN 2150,
1955-59 . . . . 245.00
Figurine, "Winter," HN 2088 . . . . 305.00
Figurine, "Young Widow,"
HN 1399 . . . . 1,575.00
Fish plates, each w/different fish
swimming amongst aquatic
weeds, scalloped rim edged in
gilding, artist-signed, late 19th c.,
9" d., set of 12 . . . . 440.00
Flask, "Seagram's," stoneware,
9" h. 125.00
Flask w/stopper, "DeWar's," Kings-
ware, "George the Guard,"
10" h. 350.00
Hot water pitcher, cov., Zunday
Zmocks series, 3 7/8" d., 7" h. . . . 160.00
Inkwell, footed, owls (3) decor,
marked "Faience" & dated 1876,
5" d. 275.00
Jardiniere, flow blue Babes in
Woods series, 2 little girls under
tree scene, 8" h. 650.00
Loving cup, basaltes, "The Pilgrim
Fathers" in relief front & "The
Mayflower" reverse, 1970 limited
edition in original box, 8¼" h. 210.00
Loving cup, "The Three Musketeers,"
1936, 10" h. 600.00
Marmalade jar, cov., Gaffers
series 125.00
Match holder, stoneware, blue
leaves in relief around collar &
blue florals in relief on tan sides,
hallmarked silver rim, 2¾" d.,
2 3/8" h. 60.00
Match holder w/striker, diamonds,
hearts, spades & clubs decor,
cream w/orange & black designs,
3¼ x 3 5/8", 2 5/8" h. 65.00
Match holder w/striker, stoneware,
tan w/raised white figures of men
& dogs, 4 3/8" d., 3¾" h. 90.00
Pitcher, 2¾" h., 1¾" d., Welsh La-
dies series, front & reverse
w/Welsh ladies (2) in colorful
dress on tan ground w/blue-
trimmed top 90.00
Pitcher, 4" h., 6" d., Gaffers series,
signed Noke 125.00
Pitcher, 4½" h., beige hunting
scene in relief on brown 85.00
Pitcher, 5" h., "Northwind" mask
spout, Worcester-type florals out-
lined in gilding. 175.00
Pitcher, 5¼" h., Gallant Fishers
series 95.00
Pitcher, 7¼" h., jug-type, stone-
ware, figures of cherubs amidst
grapes in relief on sides, brown
lettering "Good is Not Good
Enough - The Best is Not too
Good" on light tan w/rich brown
rim 160.00

Plate, 10" d., Automobile series -
"Blood Money," 1906-07 . . . . 195.00
Plate, 10" d., Golfers series 135.00

Hiawatha Portrait Plate

Plate, 10" d., Indian series, Hia-
watha, w/quote, wigwam border
(ILLUS.) 135.00
Plate, 10½" d., rack-type, Night
Watchman series - "Town Offi-
cials," w/pike & lantern 70.00
Sauce dish, Robin Hood series -
"Under the Greenwood Tree" 35.00
Sugar bowl, 3-handled, lavender
scenic decor on blue ground
w/gold, 7½" d. 115.00
Tazza, 2-handled, footed, stone-
ware, signed George Tinworth,
11" 250.00
Tazza, footed, Harlem Dutch scene
decor 108.00
Teapot, cov., Robin Hood series -
"Under the Greenwood Tree,"
8½" d., 4¾" h. 295.00
Tea tile, Gleaners series, 6½" d. 65.00
Toothpick holder, Robin Hood
series - "Under the Greenwood
Tree" 75.00

Doulton Vases

Vases, 11" h., frieze of fruit, florals
& foliage at shoulders, blue
ground, pr. (ILLUS.)............. 225.00

Vase, 12" h., 5" d., cobalt blue iris
decor on off white ground, gold
trim...................... 255.00

Vase, 12" h., stoneware, incised
donkeys decor, signed Hannah
Barlow 375.00

Vase, 12" h., stoneware, incised
horses & sheep decor, signed
Hannah Barlow 365.00

Vase, 12" h., stoneware, incised
frieze of sheep decor, signed
Hannah Barlow ....315.00 to 425.00

Vase, 12¼" h., relief-molded multicolored leaves & fruit on cream
ground 180.00

Vase, 12 3/8" h., 4½" d., stoneware, incised black circus horses
on tan ground, blue leaves border, signed Hannah Barlow 575.00

Vase, 13¾" h., 6 1/8" d., flow blue
Babes in Wood series, scene of
lady w/large hat standing behind
little girl 500.00

DRESDEN

Dresden Mantel Garniture

*Dresden porcelain has been produced since
the type now termed Dresden was made at
the nearby Meissen Porcelain Works early in
the 18th century. "Dresden" and "Meissen"
are often used interchangeably for later
wares. "Dresden" has become a generic name
for the kind of porcelains produced in Dresden and certain other areas of Germany but
perhaps should be confined to the wares made
in the city of Dresden. Also see MEISSEN.*

Bread tray, reticulated ends, roses
decor, ornate gold trim, 12 x 7"
oval $85.00

Compote, 9" d., 9" h., open latticework sides w/applied pastel
roses, 19th c. 695.00

Cups & saucers, young lovers in
landscapes within quatrefoil
panels outlined in gilding & reserved on blue ground enriched
w/trailing foliage, ca. 1900, set
of 20 ....2,640.00

Ecuelle, cover & leaf-molded stand,
applied w/scattered flower sprays
enriched in colors, scroll-molded
handles enriched in gilding, stand
w/branch handle, gilt rims, 9" w.
stand 165.00

Figure of a ballerina seated & ad-
miring bouquet, pink & white
"lace" costume adorned w/ap-
plied florettes, 10" d., 9" h. 140.00

Figure group, lady & gentleman at
dining table, w/dogs, 17" l. 385.00

Garniture set: mantel clock & pr.
candlesticks; clock case w/applied
emblematic figures & florettes,
3 pcs. (ILLUS.) 2,450.00

Jardinieres, bucket-shaped, landscapes within roundels on overall
green & gilt foliate ground,
ground divided by puce dots between rope twist bands, 8¾" h.,
pr. 2,750.00

Models of King Charles spaniels,
grey hair markings, flesh-colored
faces, each in playful attitude,
12" l., pr. 1,045.00

Model of a cat seated on its
haunches, busy tail & thick fur enriched in brown, Dresden Pot-
schappel mark, 12¾" h. 330.00

Plates, 8¼" d., cupid center, cobalt
blue blue border w/heavy gold
floral decor, pr.................. 330.00

Salt dip, master size, model of a
wheelbarrow w/movable wheel,
overall applied blue forget-me-
nots & pink buds, matching
shovel-shaped spoon, 4½ x
1 7/8", 2" h., 2 pcs. 123.00

Tete a tete: cov. coffee pot, cov.
sugar bowl, cov. cream jug, 2 coffee cans & saucers & 11½" octagonal tray; puce birds on
branches within gilt & blue foliage
surrounds reserved on blue & gilt
flowerhead ground, Dresden Pot-
schappel marks, 8 pcs. 330.00

Tureens, cov., modeled as ducks
looking to the left & right respectively, incised feather markings
enriched in green, purple, brown
& grey, 9½" w., pr. 495.00

Vase, 7½" h., 5¾" d., 3-handled,
overall multicolored floral decor
w/ornate gold trim 125.00

FAIRINGS, GOSS & CREST

Pitcher with Crest of Launceston

Fairings are brightly-colored small porcelain objects, largely groups and boxes, that were made in molds in Germany and Bohemia and painted in the late 19th and early 20th centuries. Most related to courtship and marriage, family life, children, animals and the like and bore captions. They were originally sold at fairs and bazaars and as souvenir pieces. In much the same category were the Goss and Crest miniature pieces, made by W.H. Goss at Stoke-on-Trent, England, and other factories, and many bearing crests. All are now widely sought.

Cup & saucer, Bagware, in the form of a tied bag gathered by blue cord w/gilded tassels, Goss	$35.00
Ewer, w/crest of Arundel, Goss, 4½" h.	25.00
Ewer, w/crest of Shrewsbury, Goss, 4" h.	25.00
"Five O'Clock Tea," w/five cats (fairing)	95.00
"Married for Money" (fairing)	175.00
Model of First & Last House in England, Goss	145.00
Model of Jersey fish basket, Goss, 4" l. (crest)	30.00
Model of Look-out House, Newquay, Goss	150.00
Model of Rufus Stone, Goss	39.00
Model of St. Nicholas Chapel, Goss	225.00
Model of a shoe, w/crests of Bath & Winchester, Goss, 3" h.	24.00
Pitcher, 3" h., w/crest of Launceston (ILLUS.)	28.00
"Returning at One O'Clock in the Morning" (fairing)	95.00
"Twelve Months after Marriage" (fairing)	120.00
Vase, 4" h., 5" d., rose bowl shape w/ruffled rim, Belleek-type porcelain, h.p. w/crests of England, Wales, Ireland & Scotland, Goss	40.00
Vase, 6" h., w/crest of Southwold, Goss	45.00

"Wedding Night" (fairing)	125.00
"When a Man is Married His Troubles Begin" (fairing)	65.00

FIESTA WARE

Fiesta Ware Casserole

Fiesta dinnerware was made by the Homer Laughlin China Company of Newell, West Virginia, from the 1930's until the early 1970's. The brilliant colors of this inexpensive pottery have attracted numerous collectors and though it is not even out of production for a decade, it merits inclusion in our price guide. On February 28, 1986, Laughlin reintroduced the popular Fiesta line with minor changes in the shapes of a few pieces and a contemporary color range. The effect of this new production on the Fiesta collecting market is yet to be determined.

Ash tray, cobalt blue, forest green or red, each	$30.00 to 35.00
Ash tray, ivory or light green, each	20.00
Bowl, 6" d., forest green, ivory or rose, each	12.00 to 16.00
Bowl, individual salad, 7½" d., medium green	55.00
Bowl, individual salad, 7½" d., yellow	35.00
Bowl, nappy, 8½" d., grey, light green, turquoise or yellow, each	12.00 to 16.00
Bowl, salad, 9½" d., ivory or turquoise, each	18.00 to 24.00
Bowl, fruit, 11¾" d., cobalt blue, light green or turquoise, each	95.00
Bowl, fruit, 11¾" d., red	155.00
Bowl, 12" d., low foot, ivory, light green or yellow, each	37.00 to 45.00
Bowl, cream soup, cobalt blue, grey, ivory, medium green, turquoise or yellow, each	18.00 to 25.00
Bowl, cream soup, forest green or light green, each	12.50
Cake plate, cobalt blue, 10" d.	35.00
Candle holders, bulb-type, ivory, light green or red, each pr.	45.00
Candle holders, tripod-type, medium green or yellow, each pr.	155.00
Carafe, cov., cobalt blue, light green or turquoise, each	75.00

Casserole, cov., 2-handled, chartreuse or cobalt blue, 10" d.,
each 70.00
Casserole, cov., stick handle, yellow
(ILLUS.)....................... 115.00

Fiesta Ware Demitasse Pot

Coffee pot, cov., demitasse, stick
handle, ivory (ILLUS.) 95.00
Coffee pot, cov., cobalt blue or forest green, each 80.00
Compote, sweetmeat, high stand,
cobalt blue, ivory, medium green
or yellow, each 30.00
Creamer, stick handle, red......... 17.00
Creamer, chartreuse, forest green,
grey or red, each ....11.00 to 15.00
Creamer & cov. sugar bowl, red,
pr................................ 35.00
Cup & saucer, demitasse, stick handle, chartreuse, light green or turquoise, each.................... 25.00
Cup & saucer, ring handle, grey or
medium green, each 23.00
Egg cup, cobalt blue, ivory or red,
each ....25.00 to 32.00
Egg cup, forest green or grey,
each 40.00
Gravy boat, chartreuse 24.00
Marmalade jar, cov., cobalt blue or
yellow, each.................... 95.00
Mixing bowl, nest-type, light green,
size No. 1 .... 15.00
Mixing bowl, nest-type, cobalt blue,
size No. 2 .... 39.00
Mixing bowl, nest-type, light green,
size No. 3 .... 25.00
Mixing bowl, nest-type, turquoise or
yellow, size No. 4, each 30.00
Mixing bowl, nest-type, light green,
size No. 6 .... 55.00
Mixing bowl, nest-type, cobalt blue,
size No. 7 .... 87.50
Mug, forest green, medium green or
rose, each...............35.00 to 40.00
Mug, red 45.00

Mustard jar, cov., cobalt blue or
ivory, each 80.00
Mustard jar, cov., light green or turquoise, each...............45.00 to 50.00
Onion soup bowl, cov., cobalt blue,
ivory or medium green,
each .... 175.00 to 185.00
Pitcher, jug-type, cobalt blue or
rose, qt., each 40.00
Pitcher, jug-type, yellow, qt. 22.00
Pitcher, juice, disc-type, forest
green or rose, 30 oz., each 46.00
Pitcher, juice, disc-type, grey,
30 oz.......................... 70.00
Pitcher w/ice lip, globular, ivory,
2-qt. 42.50
Pitcher w/ice lip, globular, red,
2-qt. 85.00
Pitcher, water, disc-type, chartreuse
or grey, each 80.00
Pitcher, water, disc-type, cobalt
blue, ivory, turquoise or yellow,
each ....32.00 to 40.00
Plate, 6" d., cobalt blue, grey or
red, each.................6.00 to 8.00
Plate, 7" d., chartreuse, cobalt blue,
ivory or yellow, each 6.00
Plate, 9" d., cobalt blue, forest
green, ivory or yellow,
each ....7.00 to 9.00
Plate, 10" d., chartreuse, forest
green or red, each 16.00
Plate, grill, 10½" d., medium green,
turquoise or yellow, each 12.50
Plate, grill, 11½" d., ivory or yellow, each 25.00
Plate, chop, 13" d., ivory, light
green or red, each 15.00
Plate, chop, 15" d., cobalt blue, red
or rose, each ....25.00 to 30.00
Platter, 12" oval, ivory, medium
green, turquoise or yellow,
each ....10.50 to 13.00
Platter, 13" oval, forest green, ivory
or yellow, each ....12.00 to 14.00
Relish tray, w/five inserts, ivory,
light green or yellow,
each ....75.00 to 85.00
Salt & pepper shakers, cobalt blue,
forest green or red pr...... 13.00
Sauce dish, cobalt blue, ivory, medium green or rose, 4¾" d.
each ....10.00 to 13.00
Soup plate w/flange rim, chartreuse, ivory, light green, turquoise or yellow, 8" d.,
each ....12.00 to 14.00
Soup plate w/flange rim, forest
green or rose, 8" d.,
each ....24.00 to 26.00
Sugar bowl, cov., red or rose,
each 20.00
Syrup pitcher w/original lid,
red 135.00

Teapot, cov., chartreuse or rose,
medium, each 120.00
Teapot, cov., cobalt blue, medium
green or turquoise, large, each... 65.00

Fiesta Ware Tidbit Tray

Tidbit tray, 3-tier, yellow
(ILLUS.)........................ 85.00
Tom & Jerry set: master bowl
& 12 mugs; ivory, "Tom &
Jerry" in gold lettering,
13 pcs................500.00 to 545.00
Tumbler, juice, medium green, turquoise or yellow, 5 oz.,
each ....13.00 to 15.00
Tumbler, water, red, 10 oz. 30.00
Utility tray, cobalt blue, ivory or
light green, each 17.00
Vase, bud, 6½" h., cobalt blue,
ivory, light green, or turquoise,
each ....26.00 to 32.00
Vase, 8" h., ivory, light green or
red, each ....150.00 to 185.00
Vase, 10" h., cobalt blue, ivory or
red, each..................... 230.00

FLOW BLUE

*Flowing Blue wares, usually shortened to
Flow Blue, were made at numerous potteries
in Staffordshire, England, and elsewhere.
They are decorated with a blue that smudged
lightly or ran in the firing. The same type of
color flow is also found in certain wares decorated in green, purple and sepia. Patterns
were given specific names, which accom-
pany the listings here.*

ABBEY (George Jones & Sons, ca. 1900)
Bowl, 7" oblong $50.00

Bowl, fruit, 9½" d.,
5¼" h..................160.00 to 180.00
Cake plate, 10" oval.............. 37.00
Compote 150.00
Creamer, 3" h.................... 46.00
Cup & saucer, twig or ring handle .. 45.00
Jardiniere 285.00
Plate, 7½" to 8½" d........20.00 to 32.00
Plate, 10" d..................... 40.00

ALASKA (W. H. Grindley, ca. 1891)
Bowl, 10" d. 50.00
Butter pats, set of 6 .... 75.00
Dinner service for 12 w/serving
pieces, 92 pcs. 3,500.00
Egg cup 50.00
Plate, 7" to 8" d............15.00 to 23.00
Plate, 9" to 10" d...........30.00 to 45.00
Platter, 10 x 7½" 75.00
Platter, 14 x 10" 85.00
Saucer 18.00

ALBANY (W. H. Grindley, ca. 1899)
Bowl, cereal 45.00
Gravy boat 35.00
Plate, 6½" to 7½" d........12.00 to 17.00
Saucer 10.00

ALBANY (Johnson Bros., ca. 1900)
Bowl, soup 22.50
Plate, 9" d...................... 47.00
Plate, 10" d..................... 55.00
Sauce dish...................... 15.00

ALTON (W. H. Grindley, ca. 1891)
Bowl, 10" d. 65.00
Plate, 7" d...................... 34.00
Plate, 10" d..................... 52.00
Platter, 16" l.................... 125.00
Platter, 18" l.................... 165.00

AMOY (Davenport, dated 1844)

Amoy Plate

Creamer & cov. sugar bowl, pr.
(professional repair to finial) 375.00

Cup & saucer	115.00
Cup plate	62.00
Plate, 7" d.	43.00
Plate, 9" d. (ILLUS.)	76.00
Plate, 10" d.	95.00
Sauce dish, 5½" d.	48.00
Teapot, cov. (professional repair to finial)	500.00
Vegetable bowl, open, 9½" l.	80.00

ARGYLE (Ford & Sons, ca. 1895)

Gravy boat	55.00
Plate, 10½" d.	30.00
Sauce tureen, cover, underplate & ladle	175.00
Vegetable tureen, cov., hexagonal	130.00

ARGYLE (W. H. Grindley, ca. 1896)

Argyle Cup and Saucer

Cup & saucer (ILLUS.)	48.00
Gravy boat w/attached underplate	150.00
Plate, 10" d.	42.00
Platter, 13" to 15" l.	45.00 to 65.00
Platter, 17" l.	210.00
Vegetable bowl, cov., oval	145.00 to 185.00

ASHBURTON (W. H. Grindley, ca. 1891)

Cup & saucer, demitasse	45.00
Plate, 7" d.	30.00
Plate, 9" to 10" d.	45.00 to 55.00
Saucer	15.00
Soup tureen, cov.	195.00

ATALANTA (Wedgwood & Co., ca. 1900)

Plate, 8" d.	25.00
Platter, 10" l.	50.00
Vegetable bowl, cov.	200.00

BEAUFORT (W. H. Grindley, ca. 1903)

Butter pat	25.00
Creamer	80.00
Gravy boat	50.00 to 65.00
Plate, 10" d.	50.00
Sauce dish	20.00
Sugar bowl, cov.	95.00

BELMONT (J. H. Weatherby & Sons, ca. 1892)

Plate, 8" d.	42.00
Plate, 9" to 10" d.	50.00 to 60.00
Platter, 10½" to 11½" l.	82.00
Platter, 13" to 14" l.	90.00
Sauce tureen, underplate & ladle	165.00

BENTICK (Cauldon, ca. 1905)

Bentick Plate

Creamer	85.00
Plate, 6½" d.	28.00
Plate, 8½" d. (ILLUS.)	45.00
Platter, 10" l.	80.00
Vegetable bowl, cov., 10" to 11" oval	130.00 to 150.00
Vegetable bowl, open, 8½" oval	75.00

BLUE DANUBE, THE (Johnson Bros., ca. 1900)

Butter pat	22.00
Plate, 6" d.	25.00
Plate, 8" to 10" d.	30.00 to 45.00
Sauce dish, 5" d.	20.00

BLUE ROSE (W. H. Grindley, ca. 1900)

Bowl, cereal, 6" d.	28.00
Cup & saucer	35.00 to 50.00
Gravy boat	77.50
Plate, 6" to 7" d.	22.00 to 30.00
Plate, 8" to 9" d.	35.00 to 40.00
Platter, 12" to 14" l.	75.00
Sauce dish, 5" d.	18.00
Soup plate w/flange rim	35.00
Vegetable bowl, open, 9" to 10" oval	65.00 to 75.00

BURLEIGH (Burgess & Leigh, ca. 1903)

Plate, 9½" d.	25.00
Platter, 13½" l.	90.00
Soup plate w/flange rim, 8" d.	20.00
Vegetable bowl, cov., 8½" d.	145.00

CAMBRIDGE (New Wharf Pottery, ca. 1891)

Bowl, 9" d.	40.00
Cup	25.00
Vegetable bowl, cov.	250.00 to 275.00

CANDIA (Cauldon Ltd., ca. 1910)
Cake plate, open handled, 8½"
  oblong 60.00
Platter, 17 x 14" 155.00
Sauce dish.................8.00 to 12.00

CANTON (John Maddock, ca. 1850)
Cup & saucer 120.00
Plate, 7½" d. 35.00
Platter, 14" l. 95.00

CARLTON (Samuel Alcock, 1850)
Cup & saucer 85.00
Plate, 8" to 10" d...........55.00 to 65.00
Waste bowl...................... 140.00

CASHMERE (Ridgway & Morley, G. L. Ashworth, et al., 1840's on)
Cup & saucer ....100.00 to 125.00
Plate, 8" d. 70.00
Plate, 9" d. 95.00
Sugar bowl, cov. 350.00

CAVENDISH (Keeling & Co., ca. 1910)
Fruit bowl, 10½" w., 3¾" h. 190.00
Vase, 11" h. ....135.00 to 150.00
Vases, 13" h., urn-shaped, pr...... 450.00

CELTIC (Unknown, English, ca. 1900)
Bone dish 40.00
Cup & saucer 80.00
Platter, 19" l. 130.00
Sauce dish...................... 12.00

CHAPOO (John Wedge Wood, ca. 1850)
Cup & saucer ....95.00 to 115.00
Plate, 7½" d. 60.00
Plate, 9½" d. 85.00
Plate, 10½" d. 95.00
Platter, 12 x 9½" 135.00
Platter, 14 x 10½" ....195.00 to 225.00
Sauce tureen, cov., 7¼" l. 160.00

CHISWICK (Ridgways, ca. 1900)
Cup & saucer 40.00
Gravy boat w/underplate 85.00
Plate, 7½" d. 100.00
Plate, 8½" to 9½" d.......125.00 to 140.00
Platter, 20 x 18", w/well & tree 310.00
Sugar bowl, open 35.00

CLARENCE (W. H. Grindley, ca. 1900)

Clarence Pattern

Bone dish 30.00
Butter pat 27.00
Pitcher, water, 8" h. 125.00
Plate, 6" to 7" d...........23.00 to 30.00
Plate, 9" to 10" d...........35.00 to 50.00
Platter, 14" l. 95.00
Sauce dish...................... 15.00
Soup plate w/flange rim 35.00
Vegetable bowl, cov., 8" d. 150.00

CLIFTON (W. H. Grindley, ca. 1891)
Cup & saucer 25.00
Pitcher, water 205.00
Plate, 6½" d. 15.00
Plate, 8½" d. 37.00

CLOVER (W. H. Grindley, ca. 1910)
Cup............................ 65.00
Plate, 10" d. 22.50
Platter, 10" 35.00
Soup plate w/flange rim, 8" d. 20.00

COBURG (John Edwards, ca. 1860)
Creamer 145.00
Plate, 7" d. 40.00
Plate, 8½" d. 48.00
Sugar bowl 145.00
Syllabub cup (pedestal base &
  handle) 75.00
Vegetable bowl, cov., 10 x 7"
  oblong 395.00

COLONIAL (J. & G. Meakin, ca. 1891)
Butter dish, cover & drain insert 90.00
Plate, 9" d. 37.00
Sugar bowl, cov. 75.00

CONWAY (New Wharf Pottery, ca. 1891)
Bowl, 7¼" d., 2¼" h. 46.00
Butter pat 30.00
Creamer 130.00
Plate, 8½" d. 40.00
Plate, 9½" to 10½" d.......45.00 to 55.00
Platter, 10½" l. 50.00
Sauce dish...................... 30.00
Soup plate w/flange rim, 9" d. 52.50
Vegetable bowl, open, 9" d. 50.00
Wash basin & pitcher, 2 pcs. 325.00

CORAL (Johnson Bros., ca. 1900)
Plate, 10" d. 30.00
Relish dish...................... 45.00
Vegetable tureen, cov., handled,
  oval 130.00

DAHLIA (Maker unknown, brush-painted)
Cup, demitasse 65.00
Mug 85.00
Plate, 8½" d. 65.00
Vegetable bowl, cov. 285.00

DAINTY (John Maddock & Son, ca. 1896)
Butter pat 26.00
Cup & saucer, demitasse 62.00

Vegetable bowl, cov., 9½ x 7¼"
oval 145.00

DAISY (Burgess & Leigh, ca. 1897)
Bowl, soup 24.50
Cake stand 195.00
Creamer & cov. sugar bowl, pr. 190.00
Cup, demitasse 45.00
Plate, 9" to 10" d...........25.00 to 35.00
Waste bowl...................... 50.00

DAVENPORT (Wood & Sons, ca. 1907)
Gravy boat 80.00
Soup plate w/flange rim, 9" d. 25.00
Vegetable bowl, cov. 130.00

DELFT (Mintons, ca. 1871)
Gravy boat 75.00
Ladle, 10" l. 65.00
Platter, 13½ x 10" 75.00

DELPH (Wood & Sons, ca. 1907)
Bowl, 10½" d. 75.00
Platter, 14 x 11" 52.00
Platter, 16 x 12½" 75.00
Vegetable bowl, oval 45.00

DENTON (W. H. Grindley, ca. 1891)
Butter dish, cover & drain insert 100.00
Butter pat 18.00
Platter, 14" l. 105.00

DERBY (W. H. Grindley, ca. 1891)
Gravy boat 55.00
Platter, 14" l. 95.00
Sugar bowl, cov. 65.00

DEVON (Ford & Son, Ltd., ca. 1908)
Gravy boat, 8" oval 24.00
Plate, 7½" d. 20.00
Plate, 9" d. 42.00
Vegetable bowl, cov. 110.00

DOROTHY (Johnson Bros., ca. 1900)

Dorothy Pattern Plate

Bone dish 35.00
Gravy boat w/undertray 86.00
Plate, 8" d. (ILLUS.) 55.00

DRESDEN (Villeroy & Boch, ca. 1900)
Butter pats, set of 6 .... 75.00
Plate, 7" d. 20.00
Sauce tureen, cover & underplate ... 155.00

DUCHESS (W. H. Grindley, ca. 1891)
Bowl, 9½" d. 60.00
Butter pat 22.00
Gravy boat w/underplate 100.00
Pitcher, water, 2-qt. 125.00
Plate, 10" d. 35.00
Platter, 16" l. 95.00
Soup plate w/flange rim 35.00
Sugar bowl 85.00
Vegetable bowl, cov., oval 88.00
Vegetable bowl, open, 9¾" oval ... 50.00

DUDLEY (Ford & Sons, ca. 1890)
Dish, 9" oval.................... 25.00
Gravy boat, 8" oval 52.50
Platter, 12" l. 55.00

DUNDEE (Ridgways, ca. 1910)
Bone dish 27.50
Creamer 105.00
Cup & saucer, demitasse 65.00
Cup & saucer 55.00
Platter, 15 x 10" 60.00

EBOR (Ridgways, ca. 1910)
Creamer 125.00
Platter, 12½ x 8½" 62.00
Sauce dish...................... 15.00

FAIRY VILLAS - 3 styles (W. Adams, ca. 1891)

Fairy Villas III Plate

Bowl, 10½" d., 2½" h. 55.00
Bowl, cereal ....28.00 to 35.00
Butter pat 24.00
Creamer 75.00
Cup & saucer 62.00
Plate, 7½" d. 35.00
Plate, 9" d. 45.00
Plate, 10" d. (ILLUS.) 65.00

Soup plate w/flange rim, 9" d. 40.00
Vegetable bowl, cov. 185.00
Vegetable bowl, open, 9½"
   oval . . . . 55.00 to 65.00

FLORA (Thomas Walker, ca. 1845)
Creamer 165.00
Pitcher, 2-qt. 225.00
Plate, 6½" to 7½" d. . . . . 45.00 to 55.00
Plate, 9½" d. 85.00
Sugar bowl, cov. 175.00

FLORAL (Thomas Hughes & Son, ca. 1895)
Bowl, 9" d. 45.00
Butter pat 18.00
Cheese dish, cov. 195.00
Compote 175.00
Pitcher, 7" h. 155.00
Wash basin w/scalloped rim & bul-
   bous pitcher, 2 pcs. 1,850.00

FLORIDA (W. H. Grindley, ca. 1891)
Butter pat 25.00
Cup & saucer, demitasse 45.00
Gravy boat 65.00
Platter, 14" l. 110.00

FORMOSA (Thos., John & Joseph Mayer, ca. 1850)
Plate, 9½" d. 80.00
Platter, 16 x 12" 275.00
Saucer, 6" d. 40.00
Vegetable bowl, open, 13 x 10" 185.00

GEISHA (Upper Hanley Potteries, Ltd., ca. 1901)
Plate, 7" d. 12.00
Sauce dish, 5" d. 10.00
Soup plate w/flange rim, 8" d. 15.00
Soup tureen, cov. 250.00

GEM (John Maddock & Sons, Ltd., ca. 1896)
Butter pat . . . . 12.00 to 16.00
Cups & saucers, set of 6 . . . 270.00 to 325.00
Gravy boat w/undertray 40.00
Plate, 8" d. 82.50
Plate, 10" d. 140.00
Soup plate w/flange rim, 9" d. 145.00

GENEVA (Royal Doulton, dated 1906, 1907)
Creamer, 4½" h. 112.50
Jardiniere, 9½" d. 175.00
Pitcher, 5½" h. 125.00
Pitcher, 6½" h. 185.00
Pitcher, 7½" h. 225.00
Plate, 6½" d. 28.00

GEORGIA (Johnson Bros., ca. 1903)
Bone dish 20.00
Bowl, 9" d. 45.00
Cup & saucer, large 85.00
Plate, 10" d. . . . . 45.00 to 55.00
Sugar bowl, cov. 115.00

GIRONDE (W. H. Grindley, ca. 1891)

Gironde Pattern Cup & Saucer

Bone dish . . . . 25.00 to 30.00
Cup & saucer (ILLUS.) 45.00
Plate, 7" d. 25.00
Plate, 9" d. 38.00
Platter, 15" l. 80.00
Sauce dish 20.00
Soup plate w/flange rim 35.00

GOTHIC (Jacob Furnival, ca. 1850)
Pitcher, 6½" h. 125.00
Plate, 7" d. 30.00
Soup plate w/flange rim, 10½" d. . . . 95.00

GRACE (W. H. Grindley, ca. 1897)
Cup & saucer, demitasse 58.00
Gravy boat 62.50
Pitcher, milk, 7" h. 135.00
Plate, 6" d. 25.00
Platter, 13" l. 75.00
Soup plate w/flange rim 35.00
Sugar bowl, cov., helmet-shaped,
   ornate scroll handles 175.00
Vegetable bowl, open, 10" sq. 85.00

GRENADA (Henry Alcock & Co., ca. 1891)
Creamer 92.50
Dinner service for 6 w/cov. butter
   dish, gravy boat, 2 cov. vegetable
   bowls, 2 open vegetable bowls &
   2 platters, 32 pcs. 1,250.00
Pitcher, milk 75.00
Plate, 9" d. 55.00
Vegetable bowl, open, ruffled
   edge 75.00

HAMILTON (John Maddock & Sons, ca. 1896)
Bowl, 10" d. 30.00
Egg cup 24.00
Plate, 9" d. 23.00
Platter, 15 x 13" 95.00
Sauce dish 10.00
Soup plate w/flange rim 22.00
Vegetable bowl, open, 2-handled,
   footed, 9 x 7" 65.00

HINDUSTAN (John Maddock, ca. 1855)
Cup & saucer, handleless	70.00
Plate, 10" d.	48.00
Platter, 13½"	85.00
Syllabub cup (pedestal base & handle)	75.00
Teapot, cov.	450.00

HOLLAND (Johnson Bros., ca. 1891)
Compote, 8" d., 4" h.	135.00
Plate, 7" d.	35.00
Platter, 8" l.	24.00
Platter, 12½ x 9½"	50.00
Sugar bowl, cov.	105.00

HONG KONG (Charles Meigh, ca. 1845)
Plate, 9" d.	80.00
Platter, 16" l.	325.00
Platter, 20" l.	365.00
Soup plate w/flange rim	85.00
Sugar bowl, cov.	260.00

HUDSON (J. & G. Meakin, ca. 1890)
Bowl, 5" d.	27.50
Plate, 7" d.	29.00
Plate, 8" d.	35.00
Plate, 9" d.	39.00
Platter, 10½" l.	30.00

IDRIS (W. H. Grindley, ca. 1910)
Egg cup, double	30.00
Plate, 9" d.	18.00
Plate, 10" d.	28.00
Vegetable bowl, open	72.50

INDIAN (possibly F. & R. Pratt, ca. 1840)
Cup & saucer, handleless	90.00
Honey dish, 4" d.	75.00
Plate, 7" d.	35.00
Plate, 9" d.	65.00
Plate, 10½" d.	95.00
Platter, 13½ x 10½"	185.00
Sauce tureen & ladle	200.00
Soup plate w/flange rim, 10¾" d.	85.00

INDIAN JAR (Jacob & Thos. Furnival, ca. 1843)
Cup & saucer	75.00
Cup plate	75.00
Gravy boat	95.00
Pitcher, milk	200.00 to 225.00
Plate, 7" d.	30.00
Plate, 9½" to 10½" d.	60.00 to 80.00
Platter, 11" l.	135.00 to 150.00
Platter, 18 x 14"	295.00

IRIS (Arthur Wilkinson-Royal Staffordshire Potteries, ca. 1907)
Celery	150.00
Custard cup	25.00
Plate, 5" to 6" d.	55.00 to 65.00
Plate, 9" d.	125.00

KAOLIN (Podmore & Walker, ca. 1850)
Plate, 9½" d.	48.00
Platter, 13 x 10½"	165.00
Sugar bowl, cov.	100.00

KEELE (W. H. Grindley, ca. 1891)
Bowl, 10" d.	40.00
Butter dish, cov.	115.00
Cup & saucer	35.00
Plate, 7" to 8" d.	15.00 to 20.00
Plate, 9" d.	25.00
Platter, 14 x 10"	80.00
Platter, 16½" l.	140.00
Sauce dish, 5" d.	15.00
Soup plate w/flange rim, 8½" d.	25.00
Vegetable bowl, cov., oval	110.00
Waste bowl	50.00

KENWORTH (Johnson Bros., ca. 1900)
Butter dish, cov.	135.00
Butter pat	25.00
Cup & saucer	55.00
Dinner service for eight, w/serving pieces, 65 pcs.	2,200.00
Relish tray, 8" l.	55.00
Soup plate w/flange rim	45.00
Vegetable bowl, open, 9" oval	50.00

KNOX (New Wharf Potteries, ca. 1891)
Plate, 9" to 10" d.	40.00 to 45.00
Platter, 11½ x 8½"	80.00
Sauce dish, 5" d.	20.00

KYBER (John Meir & Son, ca. 1870; W. Adams & Son, ca. 1891)

Kyber Plate

Bouillon cup (Adams)	85.00
Bowl, 9" d., shallow	60.00
Charger, 12" d. (Adams)	130.00
Cup & saucer, handleless (Meir)	125.00
Gravy boat (Adams)	125.00
Plate, 8" to 9" d. (Adams)	35.00 to 50.00
Plate, 10" d., Adams (ILLUS.)	55.00 to 70.00
Platter, 10 x 7½" (Adams)	90.00 to 110.00
Platter, 17" l. (Adams)	230.00 to 280.00

Soup plate w/flange rim, 9" d.
(Adams) 50.00
Vegetable bowl, open, 10½ x 7¾"
oblong (Adams) 165.00
Waste bowl, 6¼" (Adams) 95.00

LA BELLE (Wheeling Pottery, ca. 1900)

La Belle Creamer

Bon bon dish, 5 x 5" 30.00
Bone dish 45.00
Bowl, 11½" d., loop handle 185.00
Butter pat 22.00
Cake plate, 10" d. 45.00
Celery tray, 13 x 4½" 115.00
Creamer (ILLUS.) 140.00
Cup & saucer 65.00
Dinner set, child's, 32 pcs. 300.00
Game set, 19½ x 13" platter & six
10" d. plates, 7 pcs. 350.00
Pitcher, 6" to 7" h. . . . . .150.00 to 185.00
Pitcher, 2-qt. 220.00
Plate, 7" d. 35.00
Plate, 9" to 10" d. . . . . .45.00 to 65.00
Plate, chop, 14½" d. 95.00
Platter, 13" l. 85.00
Platter, 16" l 175.00
Soup plate w/flange rim, 7" d. 45.00
Sugar bowl, cov. 135.00
Vegetable bowl, open 95.00
Waste bowl 60.00

LA FRANCAIS (French China Co., ca. 1890)

Butter pat 18.00
Creamer 18.00
Dinner service for 4, w/serving
pieces, 26 pcs. 500.00
Platter, 13" l. 60.00

LAHORE (Thos. Phillips & Son, ca. 1840)

Creamer 175.00
Cup plate, 4" d. 65.00
Plate, 7½" d. 40.00
Plate, 9" d. 55.00
Platter, 16½ x 12½" 275.00

LANCASTER (New Wharf Pottery, ca. 1891)

Butter dish, cov. 55.00

Cup & saucer 50.00
Gravy boat 70.00
Plate, 9" d. 45.00
Relish 45.00
Saucer 20.00
Soup plate w/flange rim 38.00

LEICESTER (Sampson Hancock, ca. 1906)

Gravy boat w/underplate 80.00
Plate, 7½" d. 36.00
Platter, 10 x 8" 45.00
Platter, 12 x 9" 60.00
Platter, 15 x 12" 115.00
Soup plate w/flange rim 30.00
Vegetable bowl, cov. 150.00

LE PAVOT (W. H. Grindley, ca. 1896)

Butter dish w/cover & drain insert . . 175.00
Platter, 8½ x 4" 28.00
Platter, 12½" oval 60.00
Platter, 14½" oval 75.00
Vegetable bowl, cov., oval 135.00

LINDA (John Maddock & Sons Ltd., ca. 1896)

Bowl, 9" d. 48.00
Butter pat 15.00
Creamer & cov. sugar bowl, pr. 195.00
Cup & saucer, demitasse 50.00
Gravy boat w/underplate 85.00
Plate, 9" d. 45.00
Platter, 17" l. 90.00
Platter, 21" l. 135.00
Soup tureen, cover & ladle 135.00
Teapot, cov. 150.00
Vegetable bowl, cov., round 95.00

LOBELIA (G. Phillips, dated June 19, 1845)

Coffee pot, cov. 265.00
Sugar bowl, cov. 150.00
Teapot, cov. (professional repair to
lid) 290.00
Wash basin & pitcher, pr. . . .475.00 to 600.00

LONSDALE (Ridgways, ca. 1910)

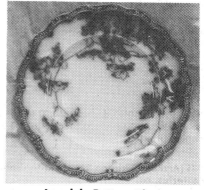

Lonsdale Pattern Plate

Gravy boat 78.00
Plate, 10" d. (ILLUS.) 60.00

Platter, 13½ x 11" 105.00
Relish dish......................... 44.00
Sauce dish......................... 12.50
Sugar bowl, cov. 95.00

LORNE (W. H. Grindley, ca. 1900)
Bone dishes, set of 6 .... 175.00
Bowl, soup, 8" d. 35.00
Butter pat 18.00
Creamer 115.00
Plate, 8" d. 30.00
Plate, 9" to 10" d. ....45.00 to 55.00
Platter, 14" l. ....75.00 to 85.00
Platter, 16" l. 100.00
Relish dish....................... 70.00
Sauce dish, 5½" d. 20.00
Saucer 10.00
Vegetable bowl, cov., oval 115.00

MADRAS (Doulton & Co., ca. 1900)
Creamer, 6" h. ....85.00 to 100.00
Cup & saucer 55.00
Egg cup 50.00
Gravy boat 75.00
Pitcher, 2-qt...................... 145.00
Plate, 9½" to 10½" d. ....45.00 to 65.00
Platter, 15" l. (small back chip)..... 100.00
Relish dish, handled 65.00
Sauce dish........................ 20.00
Vegetable bowl, cov. 175.00

MANDARIN (Pountney, ca. 1900)
Platter, 18 x 13½" 215.00
Sauce tureen, cover & underplate,
  9 x 7"......................... 340.00

MANHATTAN (Henry Alcock, ca. 1900)
Butter pat, 3 3/8" d............... 20.00
Creamer, individual size 60.00
Plate, 7½" d. 32.00
Sugar bowl, cov. 75.00
Teapot, cov. 225.00
Vegetable bowl, cov., 10"
  oval ....125.00 to 145.00

MANILLA (Podmore Walker, ca. 1845)
Bowl, 12¼" oval (minor stains) 150.00
Creamer 275.00
Cup & saucer, handleless 130.00
Gravy boat ....110.00 to 125.00
Plate, 7½" d. 55.00
Plate, 9" to 10" d................. 75.00
Platter, 18" l. 400.00

MARECHAL NIEL (W. H. Grindley, ca. 1895)
Butter pat ....19.00 to 25.00
Gravy boat 53.00
Plate, 6½" d. 27.50
Plate, 10" d. 49.00
Platter, 14½" l. 90.00
Teapot, cov. 350.00
Vegetable bowl, cov., oval 145.00

MARIE (W. H. Grindley, ca. 1891)
Compote 150.00
Platter, 16 x 11" 130.00
Sauce dish........................ 23.00
Vegetable dish, individual size,
  oval 35.00

MELBOURNE (W. H. Grindley, ca. 1900)
Butter pat, 3¼" d. 30.00
Gravy boat 75.00
Plate, 6½" d. 30.00
Plate, 8" to 9" d. ....32.00 to 45.00
Plate, 10" d. 58.00
Platter, 11" to 12" l. ....70.00 to 80.00
Platter, 14" l. 95.00
Platter, 16" to 17" l. ......100.00 to 135.00
Sauce dish........................ 24.00
Saucer 15.00
Soup plate w/flange rim, 8" d. 35.00
Vegetable bowl, cov. 125.00

MELROSE (Doulton, ca. 1891)
Bowl, soup 39.00
Sauce tureen, cov. 100.00
Vegetable bowl, cov. 135.00
Vegetable bowl, open 55.00

MONARCH (Myott, Son & Co., ca. 1907)
Creamer & cov. sugar bowl, pr.
  (finial reset) 75.00
Cup & saucer 39.00
Sauce dish........................ 16.00
Teapot, cov. 135.00

MONTANA (Johnson Bros., ca. 1900)
Gravy boat w/underplate 135.00
Pitcher, 7" h. 130.00
Pitcher, milk, 9" h. 150.00
Soup tureen, cov. 195.00

NON PAREIL (Burgess & Leigh, ca. 1891)

Non Pareil Pattern Plate

Bone dish 40.00
Butter pat 25.00
Cake plate, 11" d................. 65.00
Dinner service for 12 w/serving
  pieces, 95 pcs........3,500.00 to 3,750.00
Gravy boat 100.00

d. 30.00	
Plate, 7½" to 8½" d. . . . . . . .35.00 to 45.00	
Plate, 9½" d. (ILLUS.) 53.00	
Platter, 12" l. 125.00	
Platter, 15½" l. 145.00	
Sauce dish 18.00	
Soup plate w/flange rim 55.00	
Vegetable bowl, 9½" oval 95.00	

OREGON (T. J. & J. Mayer, ca. 1845)

Oregon Pattern Sauce Tureen

Cup & saucer, handleless 60.00
Plate, 8" d. 57.50
Plate, 9½" to 10½" d. . . . . . . .70.00 to 85.00
Soup plate w/flange rim, large 110.00
Teapot, cov. 400.00
Sauce tureen, cover, underplate &
 ladle, 6" l., 3 pcs. (ILLUS.) 435.00

ORIENTAL (Ridgways, ca. 1891)
Bowl, 10" d., footed, pierced
 handles 175.00
Butter dish, cov. 225.00
Butter pat, 3¼" d. 20.00
Pitcher, 6" h. 125.00
Plate, 8" d. 48.00
Platter, 11 x 9" 90.00
Platter, 13" l. 140.00

OSBORNE (W. H. Grindley, ca. 1900)
Plate, 7" d. 27.00
Plate, 9" d. 40.00
Plate, 10" d. 45.00
Platter, 16 x 11¾" 148.00
Sauce dish, 5½" d. 15.00
Saucer 10.00

OSBORNE (Ridgways, ca. 1905)
Butter pat 18.00
Creamer, 5" h. 50.00
Gravy boat 60.00
Soup plate w/flange rim, 8¾" d. . . . 38.00
Vegetable bowl, cov., cloverleaf-
 shaped 185.00

OXFORD (Johnson Bros., ca. 1900)
Bowl, 7¾" oval 20.00
Bowl, 9" oval 37.50
Butter pat 18.00
Creamer & cov. sugar bowl, pr. 140.00

Plate, 6¾" d. 20.00
Plate, 8" d. 25.00
Plate, 9" d. 30.00
Platter, 14" l. 90.00
Sauce dish 20.00
Vegetable bowl, cov., round 125.00

PEACH or PEACH ROYAL (Johnson Bros., ca. 1891)
Bowl, cereal 45.00
Butter pat 18.00
Creamer 65.00
Pitcher, water 150.00
Plate, 7" to 8" d. . . . . .20.00 to 25.00
Plate, 9" d. 37.00
Plate, 10" d. 45.00
Platter, 14" l. 100.00
Platter, 16" l. 125.00
Sauce dish, 4¾" d. 20.00
Saucer 10.00
Vegetable bowl, cov., individual
 size, 6½" d. 65.00
Vegetable bowl, cov., 11" oval 135.00

PERSIAN MOSS (Utzschneider & Co., ca. 1891)
Bowl, cereal, 6" d. 30.00
Bowl, 8½" d. 38.00
Cup & saucer 43.00
Sauce dish 14.00
Vegetable bowl, open, 8" d. 35.00

PORTLAND (W. H. Grindley, ca. 1891)
Bowl, berry 18.00
Butter pat 20.00
Cup & saucer 60.00
Plate, 8" d. 42.00
Relish dish, 8¾" 35.00
Soup plate w/flange rim, 8" d. 38.00
Vegetable bowl, cov., 12 x 7½"
 oval 210.00

PRINCETON (Johnson Bros., ca. 1900)
Butter pat 16.00
Cup & saucer . . . . .38.00 to 45.00
Pitcher, milk, 9" h. 155.00
Sauce dish 16.00
Soup plate w/flange rim, 9" d. 32.00
Vegetable bowl, open, oval 90.00

REGENT (Alfred Meakin Ltd., ca. 1897)
Cup & saucer 75.00
Plate, 9" d. 30.00
Plate, 10" d. 35.00
Platter, 12 x 9¼" 65.00
Sauce tureen, cov., oval 115.00

ROSE (W. H. Grindley, ca. 1893)
Butter dish, cov. (rim flakes) 85.00
Creamer . . . . .55.00 to 65.00
Cup & saucer . . . . .25.00 to 30.00
Gravy boat w/underplate 75.00
Plate, 6½" d. 15.00
Plate, 7½" d. 25.00

Plate, 10" d. 35.00
Platter, 10 x 7¼" 40.00
Platter, 16" l. .... 55.00 to 65.00
Sauce dish........................ 14.00
Sauce tureen, cover, undertray &
　ladle 160.00
Sugar bowl, cov. 90.00
Vegetable bowl, cov., 9¾" d. 95.00

ROSEVILLE (John Maddocks, ca. 1891)

Roseville Soup Plate

Cup & saucer 35.00
Plate, 9" d. .... 25.00 to 30.00
Plate, 10" d. 45.00
Platter, 16 x 11½" 115.00
Sauce dish....................... 15.00
Soup plate w/flange rim, 8½" d.
　(ILLUS.)........................ 40.00
Soup tureen, cover & ladle 450.00
Sugar bowl, cov. 50.00
Vegetable tureen, cov. 195.00

SABRAON (Maker unknown, probably English, ca. 1845)

Creamer 195.00
Gravy boat 175.00
Plate, 8½" to 9½" d........ 60.00 to 70.00
Platter, 10" l. 130.00
Platter, 12½ x 10½" 160.00
Soup plate w/flange rim 75.00

ST. LOUIS (Johnson Bros., ca. 1900)

St. Louis Sugar Bowl

Bone dish 35.00
Bowl, 9½" d. 44.50
Pitcher, 8" h. 75.00
Plate, 10" d. 65.00
Platter, 16" l. 110.00
Sugar bowl, cov. (ILLUS.).......... 65.00
Vegetable bowl, cov. 125.00

SAVOY (Johnson Bros., ca. 1900)

Savoy Plate

Gravy boat 45.00
Plate, 10" d. (ILLUS.) 42.50
Platter, 14½ x 10½" 120.00
Soup plate w/flange rim 35.00

SCINDE (J. & G. Alcock, ca. 1840 and Thomas Walker, ca. 1847)

Scinde Relish Dish

Bowl, 12" d., low 195.00
Creamer, 5½" h. 250.00
Cup & saucer, handleless ...90.00 to 125.00
Cup plate 70.00
Gravy boat, 8 x 3½" 125.00
Honey dish, 5" d. 75.00
Pitcher, milk............. 130.00 to 145.00
Plate, 7" d. .... 45.00 to 55.00
Plate, 9" d. 75.00
Plate, 10½" d. .... 95.00 to 125.00
Platter, 11" l. 150.00
Platter, 16 x 12½" 250.00
Relish dish, shell-shaped (ILLUS.) ... 95.00
Sauce dish....................... 55.00
Soup plate w/flange rim 75.00

Soup tureen, cov. ....550.00 to 650.00
Sugar bowl 175.00
Tray, 16" l. 280.00
Vegetable bowl, cov., 8-sided 350.00

SEVILLE (New Wharf Pottery, ca. 1891 and Wood & Son)
Bowl, 6" d. 23.00
Gravy boat 45.00
Plate, 9" d. 52.00
Plate, 10" d. 75.00
Platter, 12½ x 9" 125.00
Vegetable bowl, cov. 205.00

SHANGHAE (J. Furnival, ca. 1860)
Cup, large 25.00
Pitcher, 6½" h. 145.00
Plate, 7" d. ....17.00 to 25.00
Plate, 9" d. 80.00
Plate, 10" d. 95.00
Platter, 13½" l. 165.00

SHANGHAI (W. H. Grindley, ca. 1891)
Bouillon cup & underplate 75.00
Bowl, soup, 7¾" d. 40.00
Plate, 5¾" d. 30.00
Plate, 8" d. 40.00
Plate, 10" d. 55.00
Platter, 16 x 11½" 150.00
Soup plate w/flange rim, 9" d. 37.00
Teacup & saucer 55.00

SPINACH (Libertas, ca. 1900, brush-painted)

Spinach Pattern Bowl

Bowl, 8" d. (ILLUS.).........40.00 to 50.00
Creamer 60.00
Cup & saucer 55.00
Dinner service, 4 each 7½" d.
  plates, sauce dishes, soup bowls
  & c/s plus creamer & sugar bowl,
  22 pcs. 650.00
Oyster bowl 85.00
Plate, 6" d. 35.00
Plate, 7½" d. 40.00
Vegetable bowl, 10" d. 60.00

TEMPLE, THE (Podmore Walker, ca. 1850)
Creamer 250.00
Cup & saucer, handleless 95.00
Dinner service, four each 10" d.,
  9" d., 8" d. & 7" d. plates & c/s
  plus 13½" l. platter, 25 pcs. 1,600.00
Ladle 85.00
Pitcher, 6" h. 265.00
Pitcher, 7½" h. 275.00
Plate, 7" d. 55.00
Plate, 8" to 9" d. ....60.00 to 75.00
Plate, 10" d. ....80.00 to 90.00
Platter, 13" l. 165.00
Saucer 28.00
Tureen & cover w/flower finial,
  footed, octagonal 395.00
Waste bowl 175.00

TONQUIN (Joseph Heath, ca. 1850)
Platter, 12" l. 175.00
Platter, 15" l. 295.00
Soup plate w/flange rim 75.00
Sugar bowl, cov. (finial professional-
  ly reset) 245.00

TOURAINE (Henry Alcock, ca. 1898 and Stanley Pottery, ca. 1898)
Bowl, 5" d. 25.00
Bowl, 7" d. 32.00
Butter dish, cov. 265.00
Butter pat 28.00
Creamer, 4½" h. ....135.00 to 165.00
Cup & saucer, demitasse 55.00
Cup & saucer 65.00
Gravy boat 110.00
Pitcher, 3 pt. 295.00
Plate, 6½" d. 30.00
Plate, 7½" d. 35.00
Plate, 8½" d. 43.00
Plate, 9" d. 54.00
Plate, dinner, 10" d. 60.00
Platter, 10" l. 75.00
Platter, 12" l. 100.00
Platter, 15" l. 135.00
Sauce dish, 4½" d. 17.00
Soup plate w/flange rim, 10" d. 50.00
Sugar bowl, cov. 145.00
Sugar bowl, open 100.00
Teacup & saucer 55.00
Vegetable bowl, cov.,
  9" oval ....245.00 to 275.00
Vegetable bowl, open, 9½" oval ... 85.00

TRENT (Ford & Son, ca. 1900)
Plate, 10½" d. 50.00
Platter, 14 x 9¾" oval, scalloped
  rim 65.00
Vegetable tureen, 11 x 8". 175.00

TROY (Charles Meigh, ca. 1840)
Creamer 250.00
Plate, 9¼" d. 70.00
Plate, 10¼" d. 85.00
Sauce dish, 6" d. 40.00

VERMONT (Burgess & Leigh, ca. 1895)
Cup & saucer (tiny rim nick) 65.00
Plate, 10" d. 45.00
Soup plate w/flange rim, 9" d. 60.00
Vegetable bowl, cov., oval 85.00

WALDORF (New Wharf Pottery, ca. 1892)

Waldorf Pattern Cup & Saucer

Bowl, 9" d. 65.00
Creamer 130.00
Cup & saucer (ILLUS.) 55.00
Dinner service for nine w/serving
    pieces, 90 pcs. 2,500.00
Plate, 7" d. 25.00
Plate, 9" d. 50.00
Plate, 10" d. 60.00
Platter, 11" l. 80.00
Platter, 14" oval 125.00
Sauce dish 25.00
Soup plate w/flange rim, 9" d. 50.00
Vegetable bowl, cov., oval 285.00
Vegetable bowl, open, 9" oval 75.00

WARWICK (Johnson Bros., ca. 1900)
Gravy boat 70.00
Plate, 8" d. . : 38.00
Plate, 12" d. 75.00
Vegetable bowl, open 57.50

WATTEAU (Doulton, ca. 1900)
Bowl, 9" d. 145.00
Loving cup 245.00
Plate, 7" d. 30.00
Plate, 8½" d. 40.00
Plate, 10" d. 70.00
Platter, 17 x 14" 265.00
Soup plate w/flange rim 50.00
Teapot, cov. 145.00
Vegetable bowl, cov. 215.00

WHAMPOA (Mellor and Venables, ca. 1840)
Gravy boat 150.00
Mug, 3" h. 100.00
Sauce tureen 235.00

WHEEL (Maker unknown, early, brush painted)
Creamer 150.00
Mug 145.00
Tea set, child's, cov. teapot, sugar
    bowl & waste bowl, 3 pcs. 450.00

FRANKENTHAL

Frankenthal Cup & Saucer

Porcelain was made in Frankenthal, Germany, from 1755 until 1800. One of the more successful porcelain manufactories of the 18th century, it produced finely modeled figures and exquisitely painted tablewares. It is very scarce today.

Cup & saucer, painted panels of
    trailing florals & foliage on seed-
    ed gilt ground, ca. 1775 (ILLUS.) . . $605.00

Venus on Dolphin

Figure of Venus, scantily draped,
    seated on a dolphin emerging from
    a shell, holding a string of pearls

and, enriched in
circular base, 1780,
ot, 8" h. (ILLUS.)...1,100.00
Figure group, "Discord in Marriage,"
irate woman raising her hand to
strike her cowering husband, on
green moss-encrusted base molded w/scrollwork, 1766-70 ,
7 3/8" h. (some chips on
clothing)....................... 990.00
Needle case, painted hunting scenes
& floral sprays outlined w/gilt
scrolls, gilt-metal mounts, ca.
1775, 5¼" l. 1,100.00
Plate, 9½" d., deep, painted exotic
birds perched on a tree in a landscape, basketwork-molded border
w/scattered flower sprays,
ca. 1770 .... 220.00
Platter, 15¼" oval, painted puce,
purple, blue, iron-red, yellow &
green floral spray & small sprigs,
brown-edged paneled rim w/al-
ternating painted & molded floral
sprays, ca. 1765 .... 385.00

FRANKOMA POTTERY

Frankoma Cowboy Boots

*John Frank began producing and selling
pottery on a part-time basis during the summer of 1933 while he was still teaching art and
pottery classes at the University of Oklahoma. In 1934, Frankoma Pottery became an incorporated business that was successful
enough to allow him to leave his teaching position, in 1936, and devote full time to its
growth. The pottery was moved to Sapulpa,
Oklahoma in 1938 and a full range of art pottery and dinner wares were eventually
offered. Since John Frank's death in 1973, the
pottery has been directed by his daughter,
Joniece. The early wares and limited editions
are becoming increasingly popular with collectors today. Also see COMMEMORATIVE
PLATES.*

Ash tray, seated figure of an Indian
bowl maker $42.50
Bean pot, cov., Plainsmen patt.,
desert gold glaze, 2-qt. 14.00

Bookends, model of Irish Setter dog,
brown or green glaze, each
pr.......................50.00 to 65.00
Bottle-vase, 1969, prairie green
glaze w/black base, 15" h. 75.00
Bowl, 10" d., low, desert gold
glaze 17.50
Candle holder, 3-light, prairie green
glaze (single) 7.50
Candle holders, Wagon Wheel patt.,
desert gold glaze, pr. 15.00
Christmas card, 1956, cloverleaf
tray, black glaze, 4" 95.00
Christmas card, 1962, shell tray 65.00
Christmas card, 1971, "Grace Lee
and John," 3" d. 27.50
Christmas card, 1975, "Year of the
Potter," 3" d. 13.00
Figure, "Flower Girl," prairie green
dress, white bandana & brown
basket, 5½" h. 60.00
Figure of a fan dancer, tan & rust
glaze, 13" l., 8½" h. 145.00
Honey jar & cover w/bee finial,
brown glaze 10.00
Mask, Indian Chief wearing
2-feathered headdress,
5" h. 50.00
Mask, Peter Pan, black glaze,
6" h. 35.00
Masks, Oriental man & woman, sil-
ver sage glaze, ca. 1936, 5½" &
4¾" h., pr. 200.00
Model of a circus horse, green
glaze, 4½" h. 25.00
Models of cowboy boots, light
brown & green glaze, 7" h., pr.
(ILLUS.)....................... 20.00
Model of a puma, 3" h. 25.00
Mug, 1969 (Republican) elephant,
"Nixon-Agnew," flame red
glaze 38.50
Mug, 1972 elephant, prairie green
glaze 36.00
Mug, 1974 elephant, coffee brown
glaze 12.00
Mug, 1981 elephant, "Reagan-Bush,"
celery green glaze 11.00
Planter, Madonna of Grace, marked
"Gracetone," 6" h. 45.00
Plate, 7" d., 1972, limited edition
Wildlife series, Bobwhite Quail,
prairie green glaze 27.00
Plate, 7" d., 1975, limited edition
Wildlife series, Largemouth Bass,
prairie green glaze 27.00
Plate, 9" d., Aztec patt., green 4.00
Salt & pepper shakers, figural bull,
1942, pr. 45.00
Teapot, cov., Plainsman patt.,
brown satin glaze, 12-cup 30.00
Trivet, rooster 20.00
Vase, 4" h., cobalt blue glaze,
1936-38....................... 26.00

Vase, 5" h., celadon green glaze ...	60.00
Wall pocket, model of a cactus, prairie green glaze	15.00
Water set: pitcher & 6 mugs; Barrel patt., desert gold glaze, 7 pcs.	30.00

FROG MUGS

The potter's sense of humor comes to the front in these mugs made in England and elsewhere in the 18th and 19th centuries and frequently decorated with copper lustre. The realistically modeled frog contained in the cup's interior is revealed only after the liquid has been drunk. Early frog mugs are scarce and a collector's delight.

Copper lustre china, 2-handled, enameled multicolor florals & 2 applied frogs exterior, molded frog applied to side of interior, 5" d., 5" h.	$250.00
Earthenware, branch handle, figures on sides, molded frog inside	55.00
Pratt ware, molded in the form of a Satyr's head, ochre, brown, blue & green, molded frog inside, pedestal base, 4 7/8" h.	210.00
Staffordshire pottery, 2-handled, h.p. hunting dogs & pheasants in relief exterior, molded frog inside, 1840, 6" d., 9" h.	170.00
Sunderland pink lustre china, transfer-printed in black & enameled in iron-red, blue, yellow & green w/classical profiles of Victoria & Napoleon within cartouches below "May They Ever Be United" above the Royal Arms within pink lustre squiggles, rim & base w/pink lustre band, interior applied w/a large green frog, ca. 1856, 4 5/8" h.	280.00

FULPER

FULPER BROS.
FLEMINGTON, N.J.

F U L P E R

Fulper Pottery Marks

The Fulper Pottery was founded in Flemington, N.J., in 1805 and operated until

1935, *although operations were curtailed in 1929 when its main plant was destroyed by fire. The name was changed in 1929 to Stangl Pottery, which continued in operation until July of 1978, when Pfaltzgraff, a division of Susquehanna Broadcasting Company of York, Pennsylvania, purchased the assets of the Stangl Pottery, including the name. Also see DOLLS.*

Ash tray, matte green glaze	$85.00
Bookends, lion's mask, "verte antique" green glaze, pr. ...150.00 to	185.00
Bowl, 7" d., 2" h., 2-handled, blue crystalline glaze	70.00
Bowl, 9" d., green to earth-toned glaze	70.00
Bowl, 9" w., 10-sided, mustard yellow drip glaze over white	60.00
Bowl, 12" oblong, butterscotch over black crystalline glaze	65.00
Candle holder, pinched form, white glaze (single)	55.00
Candlesticks, blue glaze, 3½" h., pr.	80.00
Candlesticks, Art Deco style, green crystalline glaze, pr.	85.00
Chamberstick, lavender "flambe." glaze	40.00
Chamberstick, hooded-type w/handle	125.00
Console bowl w/mushroom-shaped flower frog, aqua glaze, 9" d. ...65.00 to	80.00
Console bowl, green crystalline glaze, 16" d.	110.00
Creamer, rose drip glaze over green	55.00
Decanter w/stopper, pinched lip, glossy green w/crystalline highlights, 9¾" h.	120.00
"Effigy" bowl, shallow circular bowl supported by 3 seated figures raised on tiered circular platform, speckled blue-grey glaze, 7½" h. ...400.00 to	550.00
Ewer, blue crystalline glaze, 5" h.	40.00
Flower frog, model of a frog, metallic green glaze over brown, 4¾" h.	45.00
Flower frog, model of a swan, ivory drip glaze over blue, 6"	65.00
Jardiniere, 2-handled, blue & green glaze	75.00
Lamp base, 2 flapper-type women attired in bathing suits & seated back-to-back, 8" h.	165.00
Perfume night lamp, figural ballerina, blonde hair, blue dress	250.00
Perfume night lamp, figural ballerina, black hair, pink dress	155.00
Perfume night lamp, figural parrot, blue w/orange-tipped wings ...325.00 to	775.00

Vase, 8½" h., mottled green, yellow & brown glaze 125.00
Vase, 9¼" h., 2-handled, turquoise
crystalline glaze................. 67.50
Vase, 11¼" h., 2-handled, tapering
cylinder w/long oblong handles,
green crystalline glaze.......... 275.00

Vase by Fulper

Vase, 12" h., broad baluster form,
2-handled, textured blue-streaked
pastel green glaze (ILLUS.) 440.00
Vase, 13" h., baluster-shaped,
earred handles, black "flambe"
glaze w/grey crystalline highlights 396.00
Vase, 13" h., baluster-shaped, ochre
shaded to turquoise crystalline
glaze 185.00
Vase, 16" h., baluster-shaped, 4
partially-glazed feet, tan-streaked
blue "flambe" glaze, ca. 1915 .... 495.00
Wall pocket, acorn-shaped, molded
design at shoulder, blue "flambe"
glaze, 5" w., 7" h. 80.00
Wall pocket, model of a Scissor-
tailed Flycatcher, green glaze 110.00
Wall pocket, bird decor on green
ground, vertical mark 65.00
Wall pocket, matte blue glaze 145.00
Wall pocket, green "leopard skin"
glaze 150.00

GEISHA GIRL WARES

   *The beautiful geisha, a Japanese girl spe-
cifically trained to entertain with singing or
dancing, is the featured decoration on this
Japanese china which was cheaply made and
mass-produced for export. Now finding favor
with collectors across the United States, the
ware varies in quality. The geisha pattern is
not uniform-Butterfly, Paper Lanterns, Parasol, Sedan Chair and other variations are
found in this pattern that is usually colored*

*in shades of red through orange but is also
found in blue and green tones. Collectors try
to garner the same design in approximately
the same color tones.*

Bowl, 4" d., footed, scalloped rim,
red trim $6.00
Bowl, 7" d., scalloped rim, red
trim.......................... 9.00
Cake plate, pierced handles, red
trim, 10" d................... 28.00
Chocolate pot, cov., orange trim,
9½" h........................ 45.00
Chocolate set: cov. chocolate pot &
3 cups & saucers; red trim,
7 pcs......................... 95.00
Cookie jar, cov., red trim 45.00

Creamer with Geisha Girls

Creamer, Geishas before tea house,
orange trim, Nippon mark
(ILLUS.)...................... 18.00
Creamer & sugar bowl, red trim,
pr............................ 15.00
Cup & saucer, demitasse, blue
trim.....................12.00 to 20.00
Cup & saucer, demitasse, green or
red trim 5.50
Cup & saucer, blue trim ......8.00 to 15.00
Cup & saucer, red trim ....7.00 to 10.00
Dessert set: cake plate & 4 c/s; red
trim, 9 pcs................... 125.00
Dish, 3-section w/center handle, red
trim, 8½" d.................. 22.00
Hatpin holder, orange trim, 4" h. ... 32.00
Pin tray, red trim 9.50
Powder box, cov., red trim, original
box 37.50
Plate, 5½" d., red trim 6.00
Plate, 6" d., green trim 4.00
Plate, 7" d., red trim 6.00
Salt & pepper shakers, red trim,
pr............................ 10.00
Sauce dish, red trim 5.00
Teapot, cov., rust trim, individual
size 22.50
Tea set: creamer, sugar bowl &
4 c/s; Parasol patt., 10 pcs. 120.00
Tea set: cov. teapot, creamer, cov.
sugar bowl & 4 c/s; red trim,
11 pcs..................60.00 to 75.00
Toothpick holder, orange trim 15.00
Toothpick holder, 3-handled, red
trim.......................... 30.00

GIBSON GIRL PLATES

"And Here Winning New Friends"

The artist Charles Dana Gibson produced a series of 24 drawings entitled "The Widow and Her Friends," and these were reproduced on plates by the Royal Doulton works at Lambeth, England. The plates were copyrighted by Life Publishing Company in 1900 and 1901. The majority of these plates usually sell within a price range of $70.00 to $85.00 today. Also see GIBSON ARTWORK.

A Message from the Outside World
(No. 1) $70.00
And Here Winning New Friends,
No. 2 (ILLUS.) 75.00
A Quiet Dinner with Dr. Bottles
(No. 3) 85.00
Failing to Find Rest and Quiet in the
Country She Decides to Return
Home (No. 4) 70.00
Miss Babbles Brings a Copy of the
Morning Paper (No. 5) 75.00
Miss Babbles, the Authoress, Calls
and Reads Aloud (No. 6) 82.50
Mrs. Diggs is Alarmed at Discover-
ing...(No. 7) 72.50
Mr. Waddles Arrives Late and Finds
Her Card Filled (No. 8) 90.00
She Becomes a Trained Nurse
(No. 9) 76.50
She Contemplates the Cloister
(No. 10) 85.00
She Decides to Die in Spite of Dr.
Bottles (No. 11) 80.00
She Finds Some Consolation in Her
Mirror (No. 12)................. 87.50
She Finds That Exercise Does Not
Improve Her Spirits (No. 13)...... 76.00
She Goes into Colors (No. 14) 67.50
She Goes to the Fancy Dress Ball as
"Juliet" (No. 15)................ 85.00
She is Disturbed by a Vision
(No. 16) 75.00
She is Subject to More Hostile Criti-
cism (No. 17) 80.00

She Longs for Seclusion (No. 18) 85.00
She Looks for Relief Among Some of
the Old Ones (No. 19) 72.50
Some Think that She has Remained
in Retirement Too Long (No. 20) .. 77.50
The Day After Arriving at Her Jour-
ney's End (No. 21) 77.50
They All Go Skating (No. 22) 75.00
They All Go Fishing (No. 23) 85.00
They Take a Morning Run (No. 24) .. 70.00

GOLDSCHEIDER

Goldscheider Bust of Smiling Boy

The Goldscheider firm manufactured porcelain and faience in Austria between 1885 and 1953. Founded by Friedrich Goldscheider and carried on by his widow, the firm came under the control of his sons, Walter and Marcell, in 1920. Fleeing their native Austria at the time of World War II, the Goldscheiders set up an operation in the United States. They were listed in the Trenton, New Jersey, City Directory from 1943 through 1950 and their main production seems to have been art pottery figurines.

Ash tray, model of German Shepherd dog on tray, 7 3/8" d.,
5½" h. $25.00
Ash tray, model of Russian Wolfhound on tray 38.00
Bust of a smiling boy, wearing black
cap, jacket & neckerchief tied in
bow, early 20th c., 11½" h.
(ILLUS.)....................... 225.00
Bust of an Art Deco lady, 12" h. 275.00
Bust of an African lady, her wild
curls in turquoise blue 295.00
Candlestick, figural Art Deco couple
kissing, 11" h. (single) 300.00
Candy box & cover w/English Setter
dog finial, blue 75.00

Figure of a Southern belle, wearing
off-shoulder beige & green dress
& holding straw hat filled
w/roses, marked "U.S.A.,"
8½" h. 65.00

Figure of Madonna, w/hands folded
in prayer, 9" h. 55.00

Figure of a Spanish lady w/fan,
10" h. 200.00

Figure of a lady wearing a yellow
hat, 10½" h. 80.00

Figure of an Oriental man,
13" h. 85.00

Figure of "Madonna in the Clouds,"
15" h. 195.00

Figure of a woman standing, wearing
a navy blue & red-spotted blue-
grey dress w/matching hat & lavender shoes, 1926-38, 18¾" h. 1,650.00

Figure of a butterfly dancer, posed
on tip-toe, w/outstretched arms &
spread wings, black, yellow,
amber & flesh tones, ca. 1930,
19 3/8" h. 467.50

Figure group, couple embracing,
woman wearing a flamboyant yellow, blue, green, purple & red
dress, man wearing grey tights,
w/brown-grey gondola on navy
blue base, 1926-38, 15½" h. 2,090.00

Lamp Base by Goldscheider

Lamp base, figures of 3 butterfly
dancers, w/hands joined, encircling a maypole, wearing robes of
pink, lavender, blue & green, on
black circular base, 19" h.
(ILLUS.) 2,860.00

Wall mask, bust profile silhouette of
woman w/flaming orange hair,
green collar, 11" h. 585.00

GOUDA

Gouda Toothpick Holder

*While tin-enameled earthenware has been
made in Gouda, Holland, since the early
1600's, the productions of modern factories
are attracting increasing collector attention.
The art pottery of Gouda is easily recognized
by its brightly colored peasant-style decoration with some types having achieved a
"cloisonne" effect. Pottery workshops located in, or near, Gouda include Regina, Zenith,
Plazuid, Schoonhoven, Arnhem and others.
Their wide range of production included
utilitarian wares, as well as vases, miniatures
and large outdoor garden ornaments.*

Bowl, 8" d., 2¾" h., turned-in rim,
vibrant colors on black, house
mark $55.00

Bowl, 9" d., peacock decor on black
matte finish 50.00

Bowl, fruit, 12½" d., pedestal base,
colorful decor 110.00

Candlestick, flaring foot, swirl-
ribbed black stem, artist-signed,
house mark, 9½" h. (single) 58.00

Dish, h.p. geometric designs on
blue-white pebbled ground, artist-
signed, 8½ x 4½" oval, 2" h. 20.00

Pitcher, 3½" h., mottled decor on
black matte, Zenith mark 35.00

Pitcher, 5½" h., stylized multicolored decor, artist-signed,
Schoonhoven 45.00

Smoking set: 4½ x 3¾" cov. cigarette box & 4" d. ash tray; vibrant
colors on border of lid & tray,
Metz Royal & house mark, pr. 60.00

Toothpick holder, colorful decor
(ILLUS.) 50.00

Vase, 4" h., bulbous, Art Nouveau
raindrop, wave & cloud designs
on high gloss finish, Plazuid
mark 50.00

Vase, 4" h., hexagonal, floral decor
on black ground 55.00

Vase, 5¼" h., boat & windmill
scene, Zuid mark 55.00

Vase, 7½" h., Art Nouveau irises &
leaves on high glaze, Zuid mark .. 100.00

Vase, 9" h., 4½" w., Art Nouveau

florals & leaves in ochre, mauve,
blue, orange, yellow & green
above off-white center section
highlighted w/orange dots &
green base, artist-signed 395.00
Whimsey, model of a shoe, colorful
decor, artist-signed, house mark &
Royal Zuid paper label........... 85.00

GRUEBY

Double Gourd Form Vase

Some fine art pottery was produced by the
Grueby Faience and Tile Company, established in Boston in 1891. Choice pieces were
created with molded designs on a semi-
porcelain body. The ware is marked and often bears the initials of the decorators. The
pottery closed in 1907. Also see TILES.

Bowl, 8" d., 1½" h., swirl-molded,
  high green glaze $250.00
Paperweight, model of a scarab, cu-
  cumber green glaze, 4" l. 350.00
Vase, 3½" h., 6" d., squat bulbous
  shape w/rolled rim, incised lines
  circling shoulder, matte green elephant skin glaze 340.00
Vase, 4¼" h., bulbous w/short
  neck, molded cream-colored fleur-
  de-lis, florals & leaves on pale
  green ground, ca. 1905 .... 770.00
Vase, 7" h., bulbous base w/molded
  leaves, flaring elongated neck
  w/cream-colored buds, green
  glaze, paper label.............. 605.00
Vase, 7" h., swollen cylinder
  w/rounded shoulders, molded
  feathering, textured matte green
  glaze 270.00
Vase, 7¾" h., fluted rim, molded
  leaves & florals, mottled light to
  dark green high glaze, impressed
  mark........................ 350.00

Vase, 7 7/8" h., double gourd form,
molded wide petals around rim
continuing to form vertical rib
(ILLUS.) 1,100.00

HAMPSHIRE POTTERY

*Hampshire Pottery was made in Keene,
N.H., where several potteries operated as far
back as the late 18th century. The pottery
now known as Hampshire Pottery was established by J.S. Taft shortly after 1870. Various types of wares, including Art Pottery,
were produced through the years. Taft's
brother-in-law, Cadmon Robertson, joined the
firm in 1904 and was responsible for developing over 900 glaze formulas while in charge
of all manufacturing. His death in 1914 created problems for the firm and Taft sold out to
George Morton in 1916. Closed during part
of World War I, the pottery was later reopened by Morton for a short time and
manufactured white hotel china. From 1919
to 1921, mosaic floor tiles became the main
production. All production ceased in 1923.*

Chamberstick, handled, matte green
  finish, 7" h.....................$110.00
Chamberstick, shield-back type,
  green glaze, 7" h............... 95.00
Creamer, dark green high glaze, impressed "J.S.T. & Co.," 2¾" base,
  4" h.......................... 30.00
Ewer, green glaze, 10" h. 95.00
Fruit bowl, Royal Worcester-type
  finish 110.00
Jug, stoneware, cobalt blue floral
  on grey, impressed "J.S. Taft &
  Co., Keene, N.H.," 1-gal. 165.00
Peanut jug, center handle, green
  high glaze, 2¼" base, 4¼" h..... 35.00
Pitcher, 7" h., model of pumpkin,
  stem forms handle, colorful leaves
  molded around top 65.00
Pitcher, cov., inscribed "Old Point
  Comfort" 65.00
Teapot, cov., butterfly decor 150.00
Tea set: cov. teapot, creamer &
  sugar bowl; olive green glaze,
  "Tampa, Fla." in gold, 3 pcs. 68.00
Urn, turned top, blue glaze,
  4½" h. 45.00
Vase, 1½" h., 4¼" w., 1½" open-
  ing, maroon high glaze, marked
  "J.S.T. & Co.".................. 25.00
Vase, 4½" h., green glaze 37.50
Vase, 4½" h., handled, green
  glaze 55.00
Vase, 7" h., blue matte finish 85.00
Vase, 9" h., tulip decor, green
  glaze 245.00

HAVILAND

Haviland Bone Dish

Haviland porcelain was originated by Americans in Limoges, France, shortly before mid-19th century and continues in production. Some Haviland was made by Theodore Haviland in the United States during the last World War. Numerous other factories also made china in Limoges. Also see COMMEMORATIVE PLATES.

Bone dish, multicolored florals,
  Haviland & Co., 6" l. (ILLUS.) $40.00
Bone dish, Princess patt., Haviland
  & Co. 30.00
Bowl, 10 x 8½", Old Carnation
  patt. 22.50
Candle holder, delicate yellow floral
  decor, Charles Field Haviland,
  6¼" h. 45.00
Chocolate pot, cov., bright pink &
  blue floral decor, one color
  dominating each side, 9" h. 115.00
Chocolate pot, cov., pink floral
  decor, Ranson blank, 10" h. 135.00
Chocolate pot, cov., molded stalk
  handle, relief-molded grapes
  brushed w/gold, dainty rose
  garlands, blue ribbons & gold
  scrollwork decor, ca. 1895 .... 175.00
Coffee pot, cov., Moss Rose decor .. 65.00
Coffee set: cov. coffee pot, creamer
  & cov. sugar bowl; Ranson patt.,
  white w/gold trim, 3 pcs. 135.00
Cookie jar & cover w/openwork
  handle, h.p. strawberries decor,
  gold trim 75.00

Creamer & Open Sugar Bowl

Creamer & open sugar bowl, h.p.
  florals & bows decor, Haviland &
  Co. blank, American decoration
  signed by artist & dated 1906, pr.
  (ILLUS.)...................... 50.00
Cup & saucer, demitasse, pink roses
  within pink & blue rose wreath,
  gold rococo rim 16.00
Cup & saucer, Chrysanthemum
  patt. 55.00
Cup & saucer, Silver Anniversary
  patt. 30.00
Dinner service: six 6-piece place
  settings, platter, serving bowl,
  gravy boat, creamer & cov. sugar
  bowl; Pauline patt., Theo.
  Haviland, Limoges, 41 pcs. 850.00
Dish, scalloped rim, white Ranson
  blank, undecorated, 12 x 5½".... 35.00
Dish, leaf-shaped w/underplate, tiny
  pink florals, gold sponge-daubed
  rim, 2 pcs..................... 55.00
Dresser tray, scalloped rim, lavender floral spray decor, 16½ x8" .. 75.00
Egg cup w/attached saucer base,
  overall pink florals, 3½" h. 30.00
Ewer, h.p. berries & leaves decor on
  pink shaded to russet ground,
  9" h.......................... 675.00
Fish set: 24 x 9" platter & twelve
  8½" d. plates; each piece depicting various fish species, 13 pcs. .. 550.00
Gravy boat w/attached underplate,
  Ranson patt., 6½ x 3½" 40.00
Ice cream set: 14 x 8½" master
  bowl & twelve 7" sq. serving
  plates; Napkin Fold blank w/wide
  coral pink borders & varying h.p.
  winter scenes center, Haviland &
  Co., Limoges, 1876-89, 13 pcs..... 850.00
Marmalade jar, cover & underplate,
  heavy gold trim, Haviland & Co.,
  Limoges 150.00
Oyster plate, Ranson blank, blue &
  white forget-me-nots & green
  foliage 50.00
Pitcher, 9" h., 6" d., scalloped base,
  melon-ribbed, pink floral sprays
  decor, gold trim............... 70.00
Pitcher, milk, Ranson blank 75.00
Plate, 5" d., Princess patt., Haviland
  & Co. 14.00
Plate, 8" d., Field Flowers patt. 13.00
Plate, 8½" d., h.p. pink dogwood
  blossoms & shaded brown
  branches highlighted in gold on
  pale blue ground............... 25.00
Plate, 8½" d., Drop Rose patt.,
  Theodore Haviland ....45.00 to 55.00
Plate, 8¾" d., Rosalinde patt.,
  Theodore Haviland, Limoges 20.00
Plate, 9" w., octagonal scalloped
  edge, birds in flight over native
  foliage center, blue border
  w/gold birds & florals 40.00

Plate, 9½" d., Old Carnation
patt. 16.00
Plates, 10½" d., Apple Blossom
patt., Theodore Haviland, set
of 6 .... 66.00
Plate, 11" d., sparrow decor, artist-
signed & dated 1889 .... 65.00
Plate, chop, 12½" d., Princess patt.,
Star blank, Haviland, France 70.00
Plate, chop, 13" d., Ranson blank,
pink floral decor 55.00
Platter, 9¼ x 6½" oval, Princess
patt., Haviland & Co. 35.00
Platter, 11 x 9", w/well & tree,
Montreux patt., Theodore
Haviland 39.50
Platter, 13½" l., Moss Rose patt. 35.00
Platter, 14" l., Silver Anniversary
patt. 65.00
Platter, 15½ x 9½", Old Blackberry
patt. 45.00
Platter, 18 x 13", overall pink carna-
tions decor, Theodore Haviland ... 45.00
Ramekin & underplate, shaded blue
& pink floral sprays decor 45.00
Salad set: 10" d. bowl & six 8" d.
plates; h.p. multicolored pastel
seashells & blue water against
delicate peach ground, scalloped
gold rims, 7 pcs. 385.00
Soup tureen, cov., ribbon handles,
Ranson blank, blue florals &
green leaves, Haviland & Co.,
14" oval 200.00

Princess Pattern Teapot

Teapot, cov., Princess patt., 6½" h.
(ILLUS.) 75.00
Tea set: cov. teapot, creamer, sugar
bowl & 2 serving plates; h.p. butterflies, Charles Field Haviland,
5 pcs. 185.00
Vase, 5¼" h., 3¾" d., h.p. bust
portraits of ladies wearing large
hats alternating w/multicolored
floral panels on shaded rose &
beige ground, Charles Field
Haviland, Limoges............... 335.00
Vegetable dish, cov., Ranson blank,
undecorated, 8" d. 75.00

Vegetable dish, cov., Princess patt.,
11" oval 56.00
Vegetable dish, open, Old Carnation
patt., Diana blank, ca. 1880,
10 x 8¼" 20.00
Vegetable dish, open, Ranson patt.,
10" oval 55.00
Vegetable dish, open, Varenne
patt., oval 40.00
Waste bowl, Princess patt. 50.00

HISTORICAL & COMMEMORATIVE

Inclined Plane Railroad Plate

*Numerous potteries, especially in England
and the United States, made various porcelain and earthenware pieces to commemorate persons, places and events. Scarce
English historical wares with American
views command high prices. Objects listed
here are alphabetically by title of views.*

Arms of New York plate, flowers &
vines border w/spoked wheels
equidistant around, dark blue,
10" d. (Mayer) $507.00
The Baltimore & Ohio Railroad (In-
cline) plate, shells border, circular
center w/trailing vines around
outer edge of center, dark blue,
9" d., Wood (ILLUS.) 475.00
Battery & C, New York plate, long-
stemmed roses border, pink, 8" d.
(Jackson) 115.00
Battle Monument, Baltimore plate,
long-stemmed roses border, red,
9" d. (Jackson) 115.00
Battle of Bunker Hill plate, fruits &
flowers border, dark blue
(Rowland & Marsellus) 65.00
Castle w/flags, boats in foreground
pitcher, States patt. border w/rib-
bon naming states at neck, dark
blue, 10" h., Clews, 1818-34, crack
to handle (ILLUS. left) 880.00

Early Historical Staffordshire Wares

City Hall, New York plate, long-
stemmed roses border, sepia,
10½" d. (Jackson) 62.50

Columbian Star, Oct. 28th, 1840 -
Log Cabin (side view of man
plowing w/two horse team) plate,
star border, blue, 10¼" d. (Ridg-
way) 85.00

Columbian Star, Oct. 28th, 1840 -
Log Cabin (side view) cov. sugar
bowl, star border, violet, 5¾" h.
(Ridgway) 185.00

Fair Mount Near Philadelphia plate,
spread eagles amid flowers &
scrolls border, dark blue, 10" d.
(Stubbs) 285.00

Fair Mount Near Philadelphia plate,
spread eagles amid flowers &
scrolls border, medium blue,
10" d. (Stubbs) . . . . 135.00 to 175.00

Lake George, U.S. platter, flowers,
shells & scrolls border, red,
13¼" l. (Adams) 200.00

Miles Standish Monument plate,
rolled edge, vignettes border,
dark blue, 10" d. (Rowland &
Marsellus) . . . . 38.00 to 45.00

Nahant Hotel, Near Boston plate,
spread eagles amid flowers &
scrolls border, blue, 8½" d.
(Stubbs) 275.00

Near Fishkill, Hudson River plate,
birds, flowers & scrolls border,
light blue, 7½" d. (Clews) 95.00

Old Chicago plate, rolled edge, vignettes border, dark blue, 10½" d.
(Rowland & Marsellus) 65.00

Plymouth Rock plate, fruits & flowers border, dark blue, 10" d.
(Rowland & Marsellus) 39.00

Schuylkill Water Works sugar bowl,
small flowers & moss border, light
blue, 7¾" h. (Charles Meigh) 140.00

State House, Boston plate, long-
stemmed roses border, red,
10½" d. (Jackson) 115.00

Table Rock, Niagara soup plate,
shells border, circular center
w/trailing vines around outer

edge of center, dark blue, 10" d.
(Wood) 340.00

Upper Ferry Bridge over the River
Schuylkill platter, spread eagle
amid flowers & scrolls border,
dark blue, 19" l. (Stubbs) 825.00

Upper Ferry Bridge over the River
Schuylkill sauceboat, ladle & tray,
spread eagle amid flowers &
scrolls border, dark blue, 8" l.,
6½" h. boat & 9" l. tray, Stubbs
(ILLUS. right) 1,320.00

View Near Conway, N. Hampshire,
U.S. plate, flowers, shells &
scrolls border, pink, 9" d.
(Adams) 75.00

The Water Works, Philadelphia
plate, long-stemmed roses border,
red, 9" d. (Jackson) 45.00

West Point, Military School, New
York, U.S. platter, flowers, shells
& scrolls border, red, 17½" l.
(Adams) 175.00

Wilkes-Barre, Vale of Wyoming
pitcher, narrow lace border
w/three small flowers bunched together, blue, 8" h. (Ridgway) 150.00

HOUND HANDLED PITCHERS

Pitcher by Harker, Taylor & Co.

*Pitchers and jugs with handles formed as
hunting hounds comprise a unique collecting
category. For the most part, these pitchers
had a hunting scene molded in relief on the
body. Listed below by maker or type of glaze,
these pitchers usually command a high price.*

Bennington Pottery, Bennington,
Vermont, hound w/nose resting
on paws & chain link collar, stag
scene in relief on body, mottled
brown Flint Enamel glaze w/green
streaks, 8¾" h. (spout & base
chips & hairlines) $185.00

Harker, Taylor & Co., East Liverpool,
Ohio, fruiting vine border & stag
hunting scene in relief on body,
impressed label on base, hairlines
in foot, 8 1/8" h. (ILLUS.) 300.00
Majolica, pedestal base, multicolored hanging game birds, fox,
rabbit, game bag & cartridge belt
in relief on green ground,
9¾" h. 175.00
Majolica, woman feeding dogs in
relief on body 210.00
Parian, hanging game & hunting
scene in relief on grey, 8" h. 90.00
Rockingham glaze, hanging game in
relief, 8¼" h. 95.00
Salt-glazed stoneware, hanging
game in relief, light green 75.00
Vance Faience Co., Wheeling, West
Virginia or Tiltonville, Ohio, molded after the Daniel Greatbach
model w/continuous scene of
hounds attacking a stag in relief
on sides & w/vintage neck &
shoulders, matte green glaze,
10" h. 185.00
Wedgwood, John Peel scene
w/horses & riders in relief,
5" h. 125.00

HULL

Magnolia Pattern Cornucopia-Vase

*This pottery was made by the Hull Pottery
Company, Crooksville, O., beginning in 1905.
Art Pottery was made until 1950 when the
company was converted to utilitarian wares.
All production ceased in 1986.*

Ale set: 9½" h. tankard pitcher &
five 6½" h. steins; stoneware,
relief-molded drinking scenes,
brown & cream glaze, 6 pcs. $175.00
Bank, Little Red Riding Hood patt. ... 185.00
Basket, Fiesta patt., deep rose han-

dle & sides w/relief-molded foliage & squirrels, white ruffled
body & interior, 6½" h. 38.00
Basket, Parchment & Pine patt.,
16½" l., 9½" h. 62.50
Basket, Serenade patt., matte blue
exterior, glossy yellow interior,
12 x 11½" 52.00
Basket, hanging-type, Woodland
patt., shaded pink matte finish,
7½" 45.00
Bookends, Orchid patt., blue matte
finish, 7", pr. 200.00
Bowl, fruit, 11½ x 10", 7" h.,
footed, Serenade patt., blue
matte finish 30.00
Butter dish, cov., Little Red Riding
Hood patt. ....100.00 to 140.00
Candle holders, Blossom Flite patt.,
black on glossy pink ground, pr... 35.00
Candle holders, Woodland patt.,
green shaded to cream matte
finish, 3½" h., pr. 25.00
Casserole, cov., Serenade patt., yel-
low matte finish, 9" d. 20.00
Console bowl, 3-footed, Butterfly
patt., ivory w/turquoise interior,
12" d. 35.00
Console bowl, bird handles, Open
Rose patt., shaded pink matte fin-
ish, 11" l. 75.00
Console set: 12" l. console bowl &
pr. candlesticks; Wildflower patt.,
pink shaded to blue matte finish,
3 pcs. 70.00
Cookie jar, cov., Floral patt. 22.00
Cookie jar, cov., Little Red Riding
Hood patt. ....70.00 to 95.00
Cornucopia-vase, Magnolia Gloss
patt., pink, 8½" (ILLUS.) 22.00
Creamer & sugar bowl, Little Red
Riding Hood patt., pr. 70.00
Ewer, Iris patt., yellow shaded to
rose matte finish, 8" h. 50.00
Feeding dish, Little Red Riding Hood
patt. 75.00

Water Lily Pattern Flower Pot

Flower pot w/attached saucer,
Water Lily patt., pink shaded to
turquoise, 5½" h. (ILLUS.) 35.00
Jardiniere, Bow Knot patt., 5¾" 42.00
Jardiniere, Tulip patt., blue, 5" 25.00
Lamp base, 2-handled, Poppy patt.,
9" h. 110.00
Match holder, Little Red Riding Hood
patt. 325.00
Model of a duck w/bandana 7.50
Model of a swan, yellow & green,
8½" h. 8.00
Mustard jar w/cover & spoon, Little
Red Riding Hood patt., 5¼" h. ... 135.00
Pitcher, 6" h., Bow Knot patt. 40.00
Pitcher, 10½" h., Serenade patt.,
blue 30.00
Planter, figural Madonna, 11½" h... 17.00
Planter, twin geese, green 35.00
Rose bowl, Poppy patt., 4¾" 45.00
Salt & pepper shakers, Little Red
Riding Hood patt., small, pr. 22.00
Sugar bowl, open, Little Red Riding
Hood patt. 35.00
Sugar bowl, cov., Serenade patt.,
blue 10.00
Teapot, cov., Blossom Flite patt. 35.00
Teapot, cov., Bow Knot patt.,
6" h. 100.00
Teapot, cov., Magnolia patt., matte
finish, 6½" h. 55.00
Teapot, cov., Parchment & Pine
patt., 12" h. 45.00
Tea set: cov. teapot, creamer & cov.
sugar bowl; Butterfly patt.,
3 pcs. 65.00
Tea set: cov. teapot, creamer & cov.
sugar bowl; Parchment & Pine
patt., 3 pcs. 50.00
Tray w/center handle, Butterfly
patt. 28.00
Vase, 5½" h., Magnolia Gloss
patt. 22.00

Vase, 5" h., Bow Knot patt.
(ILLUS.) 30.00
Vase, 5½" h., Wildflower patt. 14.00
Vase, 6" h., Orchid patt. 27.00
Vase, 6" h., Sueno Tulip patt. 30.00
Vase, 8" h., Calla Lily patt. 54.00
Vase, 8¼" h., Tokay patt., green &
white 20.00
Vase, 9½" h., handled, Wildflower
patt., pink & blue decor 40.00
Vase, 10" h., Tulip patt. 35.00
Vase, 12½" h., Magnolia Gloss
patt. 43.00
Vase, 15" h., Magnolia patt., shad-
ed yellow & rose 125.00
Vase, 15½" h., Wildflower patt.,
pink & blue 185.00
Wall pocket, Bow Knot patt. 45.00

HUMMEL FIGURINES

"Duet"

The Goebel Company of Oeslau, Germany, first produced these porcelain figurines in 1934 having obtained the rights to adapt the beautiful pastel sketches of children by Sister Maria Innocentia (Berta) Hummel. Every design by the Goebel artisans was approved by the nun until her death in 1946. Though not antique, these figurines, with the "M.I. Hummel" signature, especially those bearing the Goebel Company factory mark used from 1934 and into the early 1940's, are being sought by collectors though interest may have peaked about 1980.

"Adoration," last bee mark used,
1972-79, 6¼" h. $120.00
"Adventure Bound," last bee mark
used, 1972-79, 7½" h. 1,000.00
"A Fair Measure," last bee mark
used, 1972-79, 5½" h. 90.00

Bow Knot Vase

"Angel Duet," last bee mark used,
1972-79, 5" h. 67.50
"Angel Duet," three line mark,
1963-71, 5" h. 100.00
"Angelic Song," stylized bee mark,
1956-68, 4" h. 90.00
"Angelic Song," crown mark,
1934-49, 4" h. 225.00
"Auf Wiedersehen," last bee mark
used, 1972-79, 5" h. 75.00
"Band Leader," stylized bee mark,
1956-68, 5" h. 95.00
"Band Leader," full bee mark,
1940-57, 5" h. 125.00
"Barnyard Hero," 1956-68, 5½" h. . . . 180.00
"Big Housecleaning," 1972-79,
4" h. 90.00
"Bird Duet," 1940-57, 4" h. 110.00
"Book Worm," 1956-68, 4" h. 120.00
"Book Worm," 1972-79, 9" h. 825.00
"Book Worm" bookends, 1940-57,
5½" h. 320.00
"Boots," 1972-79, 6½" h. 82.50
"Brother," 1972-79, 5½" h. 52.50
"Candlelight," 1972-79, 6¾" h. 60.00
"Carnival," 1972-79, 5¾" h. 60.00
"Chef, Hello," 1972-79, 6¼" h. 55.00
"Chicken-Licken," 1972-79, 4¾" h. . . 95.00
"Chimney Sweep," 1972-79, 4" h. . . . 30.00
"Chimney Sweep," 1956-68, 4" h. . . . 40.00
"Chimney Sweep," 1940-57, 4" h. . . . 55.00
"Chimney Sweep," 1972-79,
5½" h. 55.00
"Chimney Sweep," 1956-68,
5½" h. 95.00
"Christ Child," 1940-57, 2 x 6" 80.00
"Cinderella," 1972-79, 4½" h. 92.50
"Close Harmony," 1963-71, 5½" h. . . 160.00
"Confidentially," 1972-79, 5½" h. . . . 72.50
"Congratulations" (no socks),
1956-68, 6" h. 99.00
"Coquettes," 1972-79, 5" h. 82.50
"Coquettes," 1956-68, 5" h. 115.00
"Coquettes," 1940-57,
5" h. . . . . 200.00 to 225.00
"Crossroads," 1972-79, 6¾" h. 140.00
"Culprits," 1956-68, 6¼" h. 120.00
"Culprits," 1940-57, 6¼" h. 170.00
"Doctor," 1972-79, 4¾" h. 52.50
"Doctor," 1956-68, 4¾" h. 82.50
"Doctor," 1940-57, 4¾" h. 125.00
"Doll Mother," 1940-57, 4¾" h. 200.00
"Drummer," 1956-68, 4¼" h. 75.00
"Duet," 1972-79, 5" h. 80.00
"Duet," 1956-68, 5" h. 125.00
"Duet," 1940-57, 5" h. (ILLUS.) 150.00
"Duet," 1934-49, 5" h. 350.00
"Easter Time," 1972-79, 4" h. 95.00
"Eventide," 1972-79, 4¾ x 4¼" 92.00
"Feathered Friends," 1972-79,
4¾" h. 100.00
"Feeding Time," 1963-71, 5½" h. . . . 105.00
"Festival Harmony," w/flute,
1963-71, 8" h. 130.00

"Flower Madonna," white, 1940-57,
11½" h. 300.00
"Forest Shrine," 1956-68,
9" h. . . . . 425.00 to 1,000.00

"For Mother"

"For Mother," 1972-79, 5" h.
(ILLUS.) 50.00
"Girl with Doll," 1972-79, 3½" h. . . . 20.00
"Globe Trotter," 1972-79, 5" h. 60.00
"Goose Girl," 1963-71, 4" h. 80.00
"Group of Children," 1972-79,
3 x 4¾" 50.00
"Happy Days," 1956-68, 4¼" h. 85.00
"Happy Days," 1972-79, 5¼" h. 105.00
"Happy Days," 1940-57, 5¼" h. 275.00
"Hear Ye, Hear Ye," 1956-68,
6" h. 130.00
"Hear Ye, Hear Ye," 1940-57,
6" h. 110.00
"Heavenly Angel," 1940-57,
4¾" h. 100.00
"Heavenly Angel," 1956-68,
8¾" h. 230.00
"Heavenly Protection," 1956-68,
6¾" h. 220.00
"Holy Child," 1972-79, 6¾" h. 50.00
"Home From Market," 1972-79,
4¼" h. 50.00
"Home From Market," 1963-71,
4¼" h. 52.50
"Home From Market," 1956-68,
5½" h. 95.00
"Home From Market," 1940-57,
5½" h. 200.00
"Homeward Bound," w/post,
1963-71, 5¼" h. 425.00
"Joyful," 1934-49, 4" h. 150.00
"Just Resting," 1972-79, 4" h. 48.00
"Just Resting," 1956-68, 4" h. 85.00
"Just Resting," 1972-79, 5" h. 70.00
"Just Resting," 1963-71, 5" h. 80.00
"Just Resting," 1940-57, 5" h. 175.00
"Kiss Me," 1972-79, 6" h. 75.00
"Latest News," 1934-49, 5" h. 300.00
"Latest News," 1972-79, 5" h. 92.50
"Let's Sing," 1940-57, 3" h. 115.00

"Let's Sing," 1963-71, 4" h. 110.00
"Letter to Santa Claus," 1963-71,
    7¼" h. 300.00
"Little Cellist," 1972-79, 7½" h. 138.00
"Little Cellist," 1934-49, 7½" h. 1,000.00
"Little Fiddler," 1972-79, 4¾" h. 55.00
"Little Fiddler," 1940-57, 4¾" h. 140.00
"Little Fiddler," 1956-68, 6" h. 80.00
"Little Fiddler," 1940-57, 6" h. 148.00
"Little Gardener," 1940-57, 4" h. 125.00
"Little Gardener," 1934-49, 4" h. 130.00
"Little Goat Herder," 1963-71,
    4¾" h. 90.00
"Little Goat Herder," 1956-68,
    4½" h. 100.00
"Little Goat Herder," 1963-71,
    5½" h. 90.00
"Little Guardian," 1940-57, 4" h. 175.00
"Little Helper," 1972-79, 4" h. 54.00
"Little Helper," 1956-68, 4" h. 72.50
"Little Hiker," 1972-79, 4½" h. 40.00
"Little Hiker," 1956-68, 4½" h. 55.00
"Little Pharmacist," 1972-79, 6" h. . . . 80.00
"Little Pharmacist," 1956-68, 6" h. . . . 90.00
"Little Shopper," 1972-79, 4¾" h. . . . 45.00
"Little Sweeper," 1956-68, 4¼" h. . . . 80.00
"Little Sweeper," 1940-57, 4¼" h. . . . 97.50
"Little Sweeper," 1934-49, 4¼" h. . . . 180.00
"Little Tailor," 1963-71, 5½" h. 120.00
"Little Thrifty,"1940-57, 5" h. 300.00
"Lost Stocking," 1972-79, 4¼" h. 50.00
"Madonna," w/halo, standing, white
    w/colored halo, 1956-68,
    10½" h. 65.00
"March Winds," 1956-68, 5½" h. 62.50
"March Winds," 1940-57, 5½" h. 110.00
"Max & Moritz," 1963-71, 5" h. 70.00
"Meditation," 1963-71, 4¼" h. 58.00
"Merry Wanderer," 1940-57,
    4¾" h. . . . . .150.00 to 175.00
"Mischief Maker," 1972-79, 5" h. 85.00
"Mother's Helper," 1940-57, 5" h. . . . 195.00
"Not For You," 1963-71, 6" h. 85.00
"Postman," 1940-57, 6¾" h. 190.00
"Prayer Before Battle," 1940-57,
    4¼" h. 165.00
"Ring Around the Rosie," 1963-71,
    6¾" h. 1,245.00
"Prayer Before Battle," 1940-57,
    4¼" h. 165.00
"Puppy Love," 1963-71, 5" h. 70.00
"Schoolboys," 1956-68, 7½" h. 450.00
"School Girl," 1972-79, 5" h. 76.00
"Schoolgirls," 1972-79, 7½" h. 435.00
"Schoolgirls," 1956-68, 7½" h. 600.00
"Sensitive Hunter," 1972-79,
    5½" h. 78.00
"Serenade," 1972-79, 4¾" h. 44.00
"Serenade," 1940-57, 4¾" h. 110.00
"She Loves Me," 1934-49, 4¼" h. . . . 250.00
"Shepherd's Boy," 1956-68, 5½" h. . . 142.00
"Shepherd's Boy," 1940-57, 5½" h. . . 202.00
"Silent Night," 1956-68, 5½ x 4¾" . . 282.00
"Silent Night," 1934-49, 5½ x 4¾" . . 350.00

"Singing Lesson"

"Singing Lesson," 1972-79, 2¾" h.
    (ILLUS.). 48.00
"Sister," 1956-68, 4¾" h. 60.00
"Skier," 1972-79, 5" h. 76.00
"Skier," 1934-49, wooden poles,
    5" h. 350.00
"Skier," 1940-57, 6" h. 200.00
"Spring Cheer," 1972-79, 5" h. 42.00
"Spring Cheer," 1963-71, 5" h. 65.00
"Spring Cheer," 1934-49, 5" h. 395.00
"Star Gazer," 1940-57, 4¾" h. 174.00
"Street Singer," 1934-49, 5" h. 185.00
"Surprise," 1972-79, 5½" h. 85.00

"Telling Her Secret"

"Telling Her Secret," 1956-68,
    6½" h. (ILLUS.) 428.00
"To Market," 1934-49, 4" h. 75.00
"To Market," 1963-71, 5½" h. 64.00
"Tuneful Goodnight," 1956-68,
    4¾" h. 750.00
"Umbrella Boy," 1940-57, 4¾" h 425.00
"Umbrella Boy" & "Umbrella Girl,"
    1956-68, 4¾" h., pr. 672.00

"Umbrella Boy" & "Umbrella Girl,"
1956-68, 8" h., pr. 775.00
"Umbrella Boy" & "Umbrella Girl,"
1940-57, 8" h., pr. 679.00
"Umbrella Boy" & "Umbrella Girl,"
1934-49, 8" h., pr. 1,000.00
"Umbrella Girl," 1940-57, 4¾" h. ... 350.00
"Village Boy," 1972-79, 4" h. 39.50
"Village Boy," 1940-57, 4" h. 89.00
"Village Boy," 1956-68, 7¼" h. 225.00
"Village Boy," 1940-57, 7¼" h. 600.00
"Volunteers," 1934-49, 5½" h. 450.00
"Volunteers," 1972-79, 6½" h. 144.00
"Volunteers," 1940-57, 6½" h. 275.00
"Watchful Angel," 1956-68, 6¾" h. ... 225.00
"Wayside Devotion," 1972-79,
8¾" h. 172.00
"Wayside Devotion," 1956-68,
8¾" h. 225.00
"Wayside Harmony" lamp, 1940-57,
9½" h. 950.00

"Which Hand?"

"Which Hand?," 1972-79, 5½" h.
(ILLUS.)........................ 47.50
"Whitsuntide," 1956-68, 7" h. 1,000.00
"Worship," 1972-79, 12¾" h. 750.00
"Worship," 1956-68, 12¾" h. 1,695.00

HUTSCHENREUTHER

The Hutschenreuther family name is associated with fine German porcelains. Carl Magnus Hutschenreuther established a factory at Hohenberg, Bavaria and was succeeded in this business by his widow and sons, Christian and Lorenz. Lorenz later established a factory in Selb, Bavaria (1857) which was managed by Christian and his son, Albert. The family later purchased factories near Carlsbad (1909), Altwasser, Silesia (1918) and

Arzberg, Bavaria and, between 1917 and 1927, acquired at least two additional factories. The firm, noted for the fine quality wares produced, united all these branches in 1969 and continues in production today.

Figure of girl w/butterfly, 6½" $95.00
Figure of a nude woman, dancing,
8" h. 275.00
Figure of Columbine seated on
stump holding gold ball, multicolored Art Deco style, 1920's,
13" h. 286.00
Figure of a nude woman on gold
ball, all white, 1930 .... 185.00
Figure group, naked Putti (2)
w/pipes, 1920, 5" 137.00
Figure group, cavorting cherubs (3)
on base, artist-signed, 13" l.,
7½" h. 365.00
Figure group, girl w/deer, all white,
artist-signed, 8" h. 150.00
Garniture set: 4" d. bowl & pr. bird
figures, white, Selb, artist-signed,
3 pcs. 85.00
Model of an elephant, 8½" h. 80.00
Model of an English bulldog in seat-
ed position, tan & brown, artist-
signed, 4 x 3½" 110.00
Model of a fawn, Selb, 5 x 4" 425.00
Model of jungle cat, 9½" 250.00
Model of Mallard ducks, brilliant
colors, on white base, 3" d.,
3" h. 50.00
Model of a parakeet, yellow, 6" 115.00
Model of a Pekingese, signed &
w/paper label, 3¼ x 4¼" 145.00
Model of a penguin, 5" 45.00
Plate, 10½" d., "Favorite," artist-
signed 75.00
Tray, floral decor on blue ground,
gold trim, 9" l.................. 32.00
Tray, full figure Art Deco Pan play-
ing flute, sitting across tray 125.00

IMARI

This is a multicolor ware that originated in China but was imitated and made famous by the Japanese and subsequently copied by English and European potteries. It was decorated in overglaze enamel. Made in the Hizen and Arita areas of Japan, much of it was exported through the port of Imari. Arita Imari often has brocade patterns. Imitative wares made elsewhere are now usually lumped together under the generic term Imari. It is currently being reproduced.

Bowl, 9" w., fluted, underglaze-
blue, red & gold panels of birds &
diaperwork, ca. 1800 ....$385.00

Unusual Imari Bowl

Bowl, 11" d., deep, scalloped edge border molded on the interior rim into 12 leaf-shaped depressions painted w/alternating cloud scrolls & scrolling tendrils suspending jeweled tassels & tama above a large foreign sailing vessel designed in underglaze-blue w/three crew men on deck, exterior w/double band of sailing vessels separated by stylized waves, fritting, early 19th c. (ILLUS.) 1,045.00

Bowl, 12 3/8" d., 5" h., underglaze-blue & iron-red overglaze floral decor 205.00

Bowl, 14¼" d., 3¼" h., underglaze-blue turtles & water fowl decor . . . 255.00

Charger, underglaze-blue, iron-red, gold & green decor, early 20th c., 10½" d. 69.00

Chargers, center reserve w/stylized florals, paneled border, 20th c., 13½" d., pr. 192.50

Charger, underglaze-blue w/alternating multicolored overglaze enameled panels & medallions of florals, 16" d. 285.00

Dish, shell-shaped, underglaze-blue & iron-red flying birds & cherry blossoms decor, ca. 1800 . . . . 250.00

Fish bowl, squat spherical form, underglaze-blue continuous scene of geese in landscape between patterned borders, 19th c., 19½" d., 13¼" h. 605.00

Jardiniere, large shaped cartouches of lush garden flowers reserved on a field of further flowers, painted below everted rim w/band of blue set w/red floral medallions & above foot w/wide band of foliate patterns in underglaze-blue, late 19th c., 17" d., 16" h. 2,200.00

Pitcher, 9" h., vertical florals & diapering decor, ca. 1885 . . . . 425.00

Plate, 8½" d., brown border, blue & white landscape scenes within

rectangles in center, impressed seal 65.00

Umbrella stand, underglaze-blue & iron-red designs, late 19th c., 8¾" d., 24" h. 385.00

Vase, 14" h., square, white dragon handles, underglaze-blue decor. . . 185.00

Vases, 14¼" h., ovoid, fluted, painted in underglaze-blue, iron-red & gold w/alternating floral & formal patterns, border of floral scrollwork at the waist, upper flutes pinched in & then flaring to a wide mouth, early 20th c., pr. 1,320.00

IRONSTONE

The first successful ironstone was patented in 1813 by C.J. Mason in England. The body contains iron slag incorporated with the clay. Other potters imitated Mason's ware and today much hard, thick ware is lumped under the term ironstone. Earlier it was called by various names, including graniteware. Both plain white and decorated wares were made throughout the 19th century. Also see FOOD MOLDS.

GENERAL

Ironstone Gravy Boat

Cake stand, all white, Meakin, 14¼" d., 6" h. $195.00

Chocolate cup, President shape, all white, J. Edwards, 1855-56 . . . . 16.00

Coffee pot, cov., Ceres shape, Wheat patt., all white w/copper lustre trim, Elsmore & Forster, 1853-71 . . . . 275.00

Coffee pot, cov., Prize Puritan patt., all white, T. J. & J. Mayer, registered 1851 . . . . 85.00

Coffee pot, cov., Wheat & Blackberry patt., all white 95.00

Coffee pot, cov., Wheat & Clover patt., all white 195.00

Coffee pot & high domed cover, all white, J.W. Pankhurst & Co., 1852-82 . . . . 75.00

Compote, Sydenham shape, all
white, Meakin 165.00
Creamer, Columbia shape, all white
w/copper lustre trim, Livesley &
Powell, 1851-66 .... 55.00
Creamer, Grenade shape, all white,
T. & R. Boote, 1850's 60.00
Creamer, Potomac shape, all white,
W. Baker & Co., 1862 .... 75.00
Creamer, Wheat patt., all white,
Elsmore & Forster, 1853-71 .... 135.00
Creamer, Wheat & Clover patt., all
white 60.00
Cup & saucer, demitasse, Tiny Oak
& Acorn patt., all white, J.W.
Pankhurst 25.00
Cup & saucer, demitasse, Vista
patt., brown transfer 18.00
Cup & saucer, handleless, "gaudy,"
5-petal flowers outlined in copper
lustre 125.00
Cup & saucer, Bordered Hyacinth
patt., W. Baker & Co............. 30.00
Cup & saucer, Ceres shape, all
white, Elsmore & Forster,
1853-71....................... 38.00
Gravy boat, Ceres shape, all white,
Elsmore & Forster, 1853-71 ...... 75.00
Gravy boat, Fuchsia patt., all white,
Meakin 30.00
Gravy boat, Gothic shape, all white
(ILLUS.)....................... 18.00
Gravy boat, Hyacinth patt., all
white, Wedgwood & Co. 22.00
Nappy, Fig shape, all white 16.00
Nappy, Greek Key patt., all white,
J.W. Pankhurst................. 9.00
Nappy, Prairie Flowers patt., all
white, Livesley, Powell & Co...... 15.00

Plate by Ford & Challinor

Plate, 8½" d., Rosa patt., purple
transfer, Ford & Challinor, 1865-80
(ILLUS.)....................... 20.00
Soup tureen, cov., Tulip patt. handles, Wedgwood & Co., 10"
octagon 225.00

Toddy cup, blue decor on white,
Mason's, ca. 1840 .... 40.00
Toddy cups, Trumpet Vine patt., all
white, Liddle, Elliot & Son, 1865,
set of 4 .... 80.00

"Blinking Eye" Toddy Plate

Toddy plate, "gaudy," Blinking Eye
patt., 1856, 5" d. (ILLUS.) 225.00
Toothbrush holder, horizontal shape,
Fuchsia patt., all white 28.00
Toothbrush holder, horizontal shape,
Wheat Harvest patt., all white,
Alcock 45.00
Toothbrush holder, cov., vertical
form, President shape, all white,
James Edwards 50.00
Toothbrush holder w/drain, vertical
form, all white................. 40.00
Toothbrush holder, vertical form, all
white w/copper lustre trim....... 65.00
Toothbrush holder w/underplate,
vertical form, Wheat, Clover &
Bow Knot patt., all white, Turner
Tomkinson, 1860-72............. 60.00
Tray, shells & seaweed in relief at
border highlighted w/copper lus-
tre & blue, 8½" sq. 100.00
Urn, 8-panel body, Imari-type decor,
Mason's, 19th c., 15" h. 650.00
Vegetable dish, cov., Berlin Swirl
patt., all white, Mayer & Elliot,
1856-58....................... 115.00
Vegetable dish, cov., octagonal, all
white, T. & R. Boote 110.00
Vegetable dish, cov., Savoy patt.,
all white, T. & R. Boote 40.00
Vegetable dish, cov., Sydenham
shape, all white, round, T. & R.
Boote 60.00
Waste bowl, Columbia shape, all
white 70.00
Waste bowl, Morning Glory patt.,
all white, Elsmore & Forster,
1853-71....................... 60.00
Waste bowl, Wheat & Clover patt.,
all white, small 45.00
Waste bowl, "gaudy" decor,
5" d.......................... 145.00

Tea Leaf Ironstone

by Jean Wetherbee

In the history of ceramics, seldom has a particular pattern held its popularity for more than a decade or two. An exception is the very collectible copper lustre tea leaf motif on white ironstone blanks. After the mid-19th century and on through the turn of the 20th century, Staffordshire potters from England and their American imitators supplied these copper lustred sets. American housewives clamored for the sprig-decorated sets and the ambitious potters kept filling the orders.

Around 1940, American collectors searched for pieces to supplement Grandma's wedding china; the popularity waned for a period but for the past dozen years or so, the Tea Leaf enthusiasts have been out in full force. Prices have shot up accordingly. We'll purchase anyway!

Several Americana museums are today displaying the Copper Tea Leaf earthenwares. The Firestone Farm at Greenfield Village in Dearborn, Michigan, for instance, sets a table with this popular pattern and echoes the copper-lustred look in a full corner cupboard.

Old advertisements mention *Lustre Band with Sprig* or *Lustre Spray*. Nobody seems to know just how the nickname "tea leaf" was conceived, but 20th century collectors may have been the innovators. The little three-leaved twig and bud certainly looks nothing like a real tea leaf. It reminds me of one of the wild strawberry plants that rim our pastures and hedges. Nevertheless, the now-familiar name — *Copper Tea Leaf* or *Tea Leaf Lustre* — is here to stay.

Collectors have agreed to credit Anthony Shaw with the first use of this well-known three-leaved stem with bud. His early shapes thus decorated were probably used in the 1850's and the 1860's. They included *Shaw's Fan, Shaw's Hanging Leaves, Gothic, Wrapped Sydenham, Bordered Fuchsia, Chinese Shape* and *Lily-of-the-Valley*. These earlier pieces are rarer than his later, plainer shapes. At least thirteen separate Shaw blanks have been located with the Tea Leaf emblazoned on centers and sides. Just before the century turned, Shaw marketed a plain, lighter-weight set of this ware, marked "Anthony Shaw & Co."

About twenty-two English potters applied Copper Tea Leaf to their white ironstone as did several native United States potters. For years these competitive companies, on both sides of the Atlantic, vied for the Copper Tea Leaf market. An American company offered china sets as "underglaze Lustre Band and Sprig," suggesting that some former offerings had been marketed with the lustre added over the glaze. In the early 1880's, J. & E. Mayer of Beaver Falls, Pennsylvania stated that their copper lustre trim on white granite was as "Indestructible as the Rock of Ages." Other native manufacturers of Tea Leaf were the Cartright Bros., Wm. Brunt Jr. & Co., Goodwin Bros. Pottery Co., Knowles, Taylor & Knowles Co., C.C. Thompson Co., among others.

The most unusual Copper Tea Leaf treatment was executed by Davenport on a *Fig Cousin* white body. He coppered the usual sprig motifs and the bands around the edges, but then continued with copper outlines on the foliage around the handles, finials and spouts of the larger serving pieces. An added pink lustre on all the leaves make these items modern treasures, rare and beautiful.

The majority of today's collectors look for pieces by their favorite potters who generally worked with round, oval or square shapes during the last quarter of the 19th century. Many patterns are available and variations occur on finials, handles or ribs.

Most difficult for collectors to unearth are the shaving mugs, butter dishes with covers and liners, pedestalled servers, and four-piece sauce or soup tureens. Of course, any collector would scream for a coppered ladle or a huge toilet waste jar, and even dance for a Shaw's reticulated fruit bowl — that is, if each one was emblazoned with that familiar three-leaved sprig.

Names for popular Tea Leaf Lustre patterns have evolved in several ways. The copper lustre trim on certain body styles was applied with lines that suggest a name: *Bullet, Fish Hook, Daisy, Sunburst* or *Dolphin.* A name which already identifies the white ironstone blank is sometimes used: *Square Ridged, Basketweave, Shaw's Hanging Leaves, Shaw's Fan, Shaw's Lily-of-the-Valley,* etc. Other names combine a shape name impressed with the potter's mark and the nickname for the copper motif: *Teaberry* on *New York Shape* and *Prairie Shape, Morning Glory* on *Portland Shape, Chinese Shape* from a similar Boote set, *Royal, Peerless,* and *Victory* (Dolphin). There is some overlap in nomenclature as enthusiasts use nicknames to discuss patterns. Any method is acceptable as long as we communicate.

Several companies experimented with copper bands and a center motif different from the popular tea leaf. Pieces with variant motifs are very desirable today and these dishes have become part of the Copper Tea Leaf story.

Joseph Clementson, subsequently Clementson Bros., utilized copper bands with a teaberry motif on sets impressed with the words "New York Shape, reg'd 1858." Similar pieces, marked "Clementson Bros.," included the familiar phoenix bird in the backstamp. Today, some of the added decor looks dark green or black, most of the copper lustre having worn away over the years. *New York Shape, Prairie Shape, Medallion Scroll,* a *Plain Round,* and a simple *Square* were endowed with this *Teaberry* sprig. Some collectors call this treatment a *coffeeberry* decoration.

On certain sets, Elsmore and Forster chose to embellish with copper lustre a *Morning Glory* bloom on the popular white *Portland Shape* and *Pepper Leaf* (Tobacco Leaf) on the *Little Scroll Shape* and also on a plain shape. This company covered the molded heads and stalks of their famous *Ceres* wheat pattern, registered in 1859, and the wreaths on their *Laurel Wreath,* registered in 1867, with, of course, the shining copper lustre.

Elsmore and Forster also used a reverse teaberry motif on the *Portland Shape;* the branch was covered with green, edged with lustre, and both lustre and forest green bands edged the pieces.

Other copper lustre designs that are featured on white ironstone are *Thistle* on a *Washington Shape, Seaweed* on the *New York Shape, Cinquefoil* on *Panelled Grape*

Shape, Pinwheel on a *Gothic Shape,* and a few others. These last patterns were not as prolifically produced as was the Copper Tea Leaf. The green clover that rests on the sides of Walley's *Niagara Shape* is often discussed as a pre-Tea Leaf treatment.

Some collectors use the under-lustre base colors (such as black, green or purple) as a clue to origin since some manufacturers consistently used the same base color. Others read the diamond-shaped marks that recorded the registry date of the blank. Remember this date is a record only of the day, month and year that the blank was registered. It is *not* necessarily the date the added decor was applied.

Copper Tea Leaf collectors have an organization which compiles a membership list, distributes newsletters, and gathers annually for a Tea Leaf convention. Enthusiastic fans cheer for their favorite twig at "show and tell" sessions, lid exchanges, slide shows, auctions, and informative seminars. More information can be secured by writing to Tea Leaf Club International, P.O. Box 904, Mount Prospect, Illinois 60056.

Now, collectors, make sure that the gleam in your eye is copper lustred!

(Editor's Note: *Jean Wetherbee is a well-known writer and authority in the field of ironstone chinawares and Tea Leaf Lustre. Her first book,* White Ironstone, *was self-published in 1974 and was followed by an expanded work,* A Look at White Ironstone, *which is now revised as* A Second Look at White Ironstone.

For further reading on the subject of Tea Leaf Lustre, the best single reference, and the standard for all serious collectors, is Grandma's Tea Leaf Ironstone, *by Annise Doring Heaivilin. This well-illustrated and comprehensive study of producers of early Tea Leaf china is published by The Wallace-Homestead Book Company, P.O. Box 6500, Dept. 27, Chicago, IL 60680. This publisher also produces Mrs. Wetherbee's book.)*

GUIDE TO DATING TEA LEAF IRONSTONE

by Adele Armbruster

"How old is Tea Leaf?" This often-asked question may be answered in a variety of different ways. One popular answer is that Tea Leaf was manufactured for approximately 50 years beginning with the decade of the 1850's. This answer leads to the next question, however, "When during that 50-year span was this piece of Tea Leaf made?" To answer that question, several factors must be considered:

The white ironstone body style on which the Tea Leaf motif is found provides a valuable clue to dating a piece of Tea Leaf. Body styles may be associated with specific decades.

— The 1850's concentrated on designs which were more geometric in nature. Finials were often fashioned to resemble gourds, apples, cones, or pears. Walley's **Gothic** and **Niagara Shape,** Shaw's **Wrapped Sydenham, Fan, Chinese Shape,** and Elsmore & Forster's **Portland Shape** are all endowed with similar characteristics.

— The 1860's brought grains and flowers. **Prairie Shape** (wheat and poppy) by Clementson, and **Lily-of-the-Valley** are typical examples of this decade.

— The 1870's and 1880's respected simplicity. The heavy embossments of the 1850's and 1860's were replaced with plain round and square shapes. Adornments were for the most part limited to ridges or scallops or tiny flowers in the ironstone body. Heads of animals such as the dolphin or lion were included in finials and handles. The **Bamboo, Square Ridged, Favorite Shape,** and **Victory** patterns exemplify the 1870's and 1880's.

Potters' marks may be used to determine the dates a manufacturer used specific marks. Reference materials on marks often provide examples of various marks used by a potter as well as the dates the marks were used. The registry mark, if present, will provide the date the white ironstone pattern was registered. These marks were either printed or impressed.

— A diamond-shaped registry mark was used between 1842 and 1883.

— An "Rd. No." designation followed by a number indicates the item was registered between 1884 and 1909.

Under the McKinley Tariff Act, the term "England" had to be incorporated into marks beginning in 1891. Caution should be exercised as some potters were incorporating this word into their marks prior to this act. The Trade-Mark Act of 1862 resulted in the inclusion of the words "Trade Mark" in marks after 1862. This notation was more widely used after 1875. "Made in England" indicates the item was produced after 1900.

The following is an alphabetical listing of some of the more well-known ironstone potters and the approximate dates they would have applied the Tea Leaf motif or such variations as Morning Glory, Teaberry, Pepper Leaf, Tobacco Leaf, and Reverse Teaberry to their ironstone wares. Specific names of popular patterns and their respective dates of manufacture are also included for each potter.

Potter/Popular Patterns	Dates of Tea Leaf Manufacture
Adams & Sons, W.	Late 1850's
Popular Pattern:	
Huron Shape	Reg. 1858
Alcock	1875-?
Popular Pattern:	
Blanket Stitch (Pie Crust)	1870's
Baker & Co., W.	1860's-?
Popular Pattern:	
Plain Round with Leaves (Morning Glory)	1860's
Burgess, Henry	1864-1892
Popular Patterns:	
Cable and Ring	Late 1870's
Plain Square	1880's
Plain Uplift	1880's
Square Ridged	Reg. 1886
Clementson, J.	1858-1864
Clementson Bros.	1865-1900
Popular Patterns:	
Medallion Scroll (Teaberry)	1870's
New York Shape (Teaberry)	Reg. 1858
Plain Round (Teaberry)	1870's+
Prairie Shape (Teaberry)	Reg. 1862
Square (Teaberry)	1880's
Davenport	1871-1880's
Popular Patterns:	
Fig Cousin (Pink Lustre)	1871-1873
Plain Round	1870's
East End Pottery - East Liverpool, Ohio	1894-1909
Edge Malkin & Co.	1871-1903
Edwards, John	1880-1900
Popular Patterns:	
Peerless (Feather)	Reg. 1887
Victory (Dolphin)	Reg. 1884
Elsmore & Forster	1853-1871
Elsmore & Son	1872-1887
Popular Patterns:	
Little Scroll (Pepper Leaf, Tobacco Leaf)	Reg. 1862
Portland Shape (Morning Glory and Reverse Teaberry)	Late 1850's
Furnival & Sons, Thomas	1871-1890
Popular Patterns:	
Cable and Ring	Late 1870's
Plain Uplift	Reg. 1883
Rooster (Gentle Square)	Reg. 1876
Grindley & Co., W.H.	1880-1914
Popular Patterns:	
Bamboo	1880's
Favorite Shape (Similar to Square Ridged)	Reg. 1886
Johnson Bros.	1883-1913
Popular Pattern:	
Chelsea	1880's
Mayer, J. & E. - Beaver Falls, Pennsylvania	1881-1890's
Meakin, Alfred (England)	1875-1897

Meakin, Alfred (Ltd., England)	1897-1913
Popular Patterns:	
Bamboo	1870's
Chelsea	1880's
Fish Hook	1870's
Powell & Bishop	1866-1878
(Formerly Livesley	
Powell & Co.)	1851-1866
Powell, Bishop & Stonier	1878-1891
Bishop & Stonier	1891-1900
Popular Patterns:	
Square Ridged (Tea Leaf)	1870's
Washington Shape (Thistle)	Reg. 1863
Shaw, Anthony (Tunstall)	1851-1856
Shaw, Anthony (Burslem)	1860-1882
Shaw, Anthony (and Son)	1882-1898
Shaw, Anthony (and Co.)	1898-1900
Popular Patterns:	
Basketweave	Reg. 1887
Bordered Fuchsia	1860's
Bullet (square shaped	
body)	1880's
Cable and Ring	Late 1870's
Chinese Shape	Late 1850's
Daisy (square shaped	
body)	1880's
Gothic Shape (marked	
Tunstall)	1850's
Lily-of-the-Valley	1860's
Plain Uplift (bulbous body)	1870's+
Shaw's Fan	1860's
Shaw's Hanging Leaves	1860's
Sunburst (hexagonal	
shaped body)	1880's
Wrapped Sydenham	
(marked Tunstall)	1850's
Walley, Edward	? - 1856
Popular Patterns:	
Gothic Shape (Pre-Tea	
Leaf)	1850's
Niagara Shape (Pre-Tea	
Leaf)	Reg. 1856
Wedgwood & Co.	1862-1900
Popular Patterns:	
Plain Square	1870's
Mild Scallop	1880's
Square Ridged	1880's
Wileman, James F.	1864-1892
Popular Pattern:	
Richelieu Shape	
(Morning Glory)	1870's
Wilkinson, Arthur J.,	
Late R. Alcock	1879-1881
Wilkinson & Hulme	1881-1885
Wilkinson, Arthur J.	1885-1896
Wilkinson, Arthur J. (Limited)	1896-?
Popular Patterns:	
Bullet (square shaped	
body)	1880's
Daisy (square shaped	
body)	1880's
Plain Round	1880's
Sunburst	1880's

Mellor, Taylor & Co.	1880-1904
Popular Patterns:	
Lion's Head	1880's
Square Ridged	1880's

About this Article and the Price Guide

The above article, as well as the Tea Leaf pricing guide, were prepared by Adele Armbruster, who also did the black and white photography for the guide and the color transparency for the cover of this issue of "The Antique Trader Price Guide to Antiques and Collectors' Items." She and her husband, Dick Armbruster, reside in Michigan, where they have been collecting Tea Leaf and its variations for the past 11 years.

The dating of Tea Leaf has been of particular interest to the Armbrusters. Their research has resulted in the compilation of this listing of popular Tea Leaf manufacturers and their better known Tea Leaf patterns.

The following price guide is alphabetically organized by type of item. The only exceptions occur with "Assorted Individual Serving Dishes" and "Toilet Articles" which have been dealt with as categories rather than as a type of item. The last section of this guide is devoted to the Tea Leaf variants known as Morning Glory, Pepper Leaf, Pre-Tea Leaf, Teaberry and Thistle.

Price ranges have been provided for each article listed. These ranges apply to items which are in overall excellent condition and free of major chips, cracks, hairlines, discoloration, and repair. They should only be used as a guide and should not be used to establish prices. Price ranges will vary in different parts of the country.

In addition to collecting, the Armbrusters also conduct a mail-order ironstone matching service for Tea Leaf as well as embossed white ironstone, Mulberry and Flow Blue. They exhibit at antiques shows in Michigan, Ohio, Indiana, and Illinois. For further information, please write to them at Dorian House, P.O. Box 2430, Dearborn, Michigan 48123.

ASSORTED INDIVIDUAL SERVING DISHES

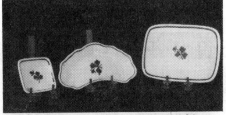

Meakin Square Butter Pat, Meakin Scalloped Bone Dish, Wilkinson Rectangular Bacon Rasher

Bacon rashers - rectangular, oval,
rectangle w/cut corners, 5 5/8 x
3 7/8" to 6 5/8 x 4 5/8", any mak-
er (ILLUS.) . . . .$28.00 to 38.00
Bone dishes - crescent & scalloped -
6 5/8 x 4 5/8", any maker
(ILLUS.). . . . . .40.00 to 50.00
Butter pats - round, square, square
w/cut corners, hexagonal - 2 3/8"
to 3 3/8" d., any maker
(ILLUS.). . . . . .8.00 to 10.00
Cup plates - 3½" to 4½" d.
Plain, any maker . . . . .40.00 to 50.00
Chinese Shape, Shaw, late
1850's . . . . .45.00 to 55.00
Shaw's Fan, 1856 . . . . .45.00 to 55.00

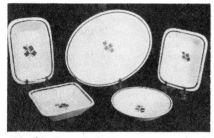

**Meakin Rect. Ind. Veg., Burgess Oval
Open Veg., Shaw Rect. Ind. Veg.,
Meakin Sq. Ind. Veg., and
Meakin Rd. Ind. Veg.**

Individual vegetable or sauce dishes
(nappies)
Oval, 5¾ x 4 1/8", plain or scal-
loped rim, any maker . . . .18.00 to 22.00
Rectangular
5 5/8 x 3 7/8", any maker
(ILLUS.) . . . . .18.00 to 22.00
6¼ x 4 3/8", any
maker . . . . .24.00 to 28.00
Round - 4¾" to 5¼" d.
Plain, Shaw . . . . .22.00 to 25.00
Chinese Shape, Shaw,
late 1850's . . . . .25.00 to 30.00
Hanging Leaves, Shaw
1860's . . . . .25.00 to 30.00
Lily-of-the-Valley, Shaw
1860's . . . . .25.00 to 30.00
All other, plain
(ILLUS.) . . . . .15.00 to 18.00
Square, 4 7/8", plain or scal-
loped edge, any maker
(ILLUS.) . . . . .15.00 to 18.00

**Meakin Mush Bowl and
Unmarked Oyster Bowl**

Mush bowl, Meakin (ILLUS.) . .40.00 to 50.00
Oyster bowl, unmarked
(ILLUS.) . . . . .45.00 to 55.00

BREAD OR CAKE PLATES

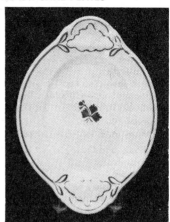

**Mellor Taylor Oval Bread or
Cake Plate**

Bamboo, square, 8¼ x 9" handle to
handle, Meakin . . . . .40.00 to 45.00
Fish Hook, square, 8½ x 10" handle
to handle, Meakin . . . . .40.00 to 45.00
Round with scalloped rim, 9¾" d.,
Meakin. . . . . .50.00 to 60.00
Oval with handles, Mellor Taylor
(ILLUS.). . . . . .60.00 to 70.00

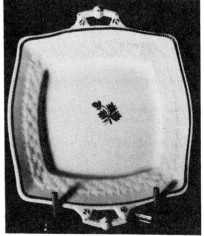

**Shaw Basketweave Bread or
Cake Plate**

Basketweave, 8 5/8 x 10½" handle
to handle, Shaw, 1887
(ILLUS.). . . . . .80.00 to 90.00
Cable and Ring with reticulated han-
dles, oval, Shaw . . . . .75.00 to 85.00
Daisy, square w/handles,
Shaw . . . . .60.00 to 70.00

Sunburst, hexagonal w/handles,
8 7/8 x 11 7/8", Shaw .....70.00 to 80.00
Plain Square w/handles, 8½ x 9"
handle to handle,
Wedgwood ....50.00 to 60.00
Daisy, square w/handles,
Wilkinson ....50.00 to 60.00

COVERED BUTTER DISHES - 3-PIECE

**Wedgwood Plain Square
3-Piece Butter Dish**

Cable and Ring, round,
Shaw ....140.00 to 160.00
Fish Hook, square,
Meakin ....125.00 to 145.00
Lily-of-the-Valley, round, Shaw,
1860's, two sizes ....200.00 to 225.00
Plain Square, Wedgwood
(ILLUS.) ....110.00 to 130.00
Square Ridged, Wedgwood,
1880's ....110.00 to 130.00
Sunburst, hexagonal,
Shaw ....165.00 to 185.00

COVERED VEGETABLE DISHES

**Shaw Cable and Ring Covered
Vegetable Dish**

Bamboo, rectangular, Meakin, two
sizes ....70.00 to 80.00
Bamboo, square, Meakin, two
sizes ....85.00 to 95.00
Cable and Ring, oval, Shaw, several
sizes (ILLUS.) ....100.00 to 120.00
Cable and Ring, round,
Shaw ....125.00 to 150.00
Chelsea, oval, Meakin,
1880's ....110.00 to 120.00

Chinese Shape, oval, Shaw, late
1850's, two sizes ....175.00 to 225.00
Daisy, square,
Shaw ....100.00 to 110.00
Feather (Peerless), rectangular,
Edwards, 1887 ....115.00 to 125.00
Fish Hook, rectangular, Meakin, two
sizes ....70.00 to 80.00
Fish Hook, square, Meakin...85.00 to 95.00
Lily-of-the-Valley, oval, Shaw,
1860's, several sizes .....175.00 to 195.00
Plain Square, rectangular, Wedg-
wood, two sizes ....80.00 to 90.00
Rooster (Gentle Square), Furnival,
1876, two sizes ....80.00 to 90.00
Sunburst, hexagonal, Shaw, several
sizes ....125.00 to 140.00
Sunburst, Wilkinson, several
sizes ....80.00 to 90.00

CREAMERS

Shaw Bullet Creamer

Bamboo, Meakin, two sizes ..75.00 to 95.00
Bullet, Shaw (ILLUS.) ......115.00 to 125.00
Bullet (squatty shape),
Shaw ....75.00 to 85.00
Cable and Ring, Burgess ....95.00 to 105.00
Cable and Ring, Furnival .....85.00 to 95.00
Cable and Ring, Shaw, two
sizes ....115.00 to 135.00
Chelsea, Meakin ....95.00 to 105.00
Chinese Shape, Shaw, two sizes,
late 1850's (ILLUS. w/Shaw
Chinese teapot & sugar
bowl) ....200.00 to 225.00
Feather (Peerless), Edwards,
1887 ....85.00 to 95.00
Fish Hook, Meakin, two
sizes ....75.00 to 95.00
Lily-of-the-Valley, Shaw, 1860's, two
sizes ....150.00 to 175.00
Mild Scallop, bulbous,
Wedgwood ....65.00 to 75.00
Plain Square, Wedgwood ....85.00 to 95.00
Plain Round, Wilkinson ......85.00 to 95.00

Shaw's Fan Creamer

Shaw, Fan, 1856 (ILLUS.) ...200.00 to 225.00

CUPS (HANDLED) WITH SAUCERS

**Handled Cups with Saucers -
Wedgwood Square Ridged, Meakin
Barrel, Meakin Squatty**

Barrel shape, plain, any maker
(ILLUS.)..................45.00 to 55.00
Cable and Ring, Shaw ....75.00 to 85.00
Chelsea, Meakin ....55.00 to 65.00
Cone shape, plain, any
maker ....45.00 to 55.00
Square Ridged, Wedgwood, 1880's
(ILLUS.)..................50.00 to 60.00
Squatty shape, plain, any maker
(ILLUS.)..................45.00 to 55.00

CUPS (HANDLELESS) WITH SAUCERS

**Shaw Chinese Shape Handleless
Cups with Saucers**

Barrel shape, plain, Shaw....75.00 to 85.00
Bordered Fuchsia, Shaw,
1860's ....100.00 to 110.00

Chinese Shape, Shaw, late 1850's
(ILLUS.)..................75.00 to 85.00
Hanging Leaves, Shaw,
1860's ....90.00 to 100.00
Lily-of-the-Valley, Shaw,
1860's ....70.00 to 80.00
Shaw's Fan, 1856..........95.00 to 105.00

GRAVY BOATS

Meakin Fish Hook Gravy Boat

Bamboo, Meakin ....28.00 to 32.00
Cable and Ring, Shaw ......40.00 to 45.00
Fish Hook, Meakin
(ILLUS.)..................28.00 to 32.00
Plain Square, Wedgwood ....28.00 to 32.00

OPEN VEGETABLE DISHES (BAKERS)

Oval shape
Plain, any maker, small, medium,
large..................30.00 to 55.00
Lily-of-the-Valley, Shaw, small,
medium, large ....40.00 to 75.00
Rectangular shape
Plain, any maker, small, medium,
large, extra large ....20.00 to 60.00
Square Ridged, Wedgwood, small,
medium, large ....25.00 to 50.00
Gentle Square, Furnival, small,
1876 ....18.00 to 20.00

OPEN VEGETABLE DISHES OR FRUIT BOWLS

Round w/melon-ribbed exterior surface, any maker, small, medium,
large....................45.00 to 85.00
Round w/pie crust edge & smooth
exterior surface, any maker,
small, medium, large......35.00 to 80.00
Square w/melon-ribbed exterior surface, any maker, several
sizes ....15.00 to 45.00

PEDESTAL SERVING DISHES

Shaw Apple Bowl on Low Pedestal

Apple bowl on low pedestal, any
maker (ILLUS.) . . . . .225.00 to 275.00
Apple bowl on tall pedestal, any
maker . . . . .275.00 to 325.00
Doughnut stand, round on short
pedestal, any maker . . . .225.00 to 275.00

**Shaw Round Doughnut Stand
on Tall Pedestal**

Doughnut stand, round on tall
pedestal, any maker
(ILLUS.) . . . . .250.00 to 295.00

**Shaw Square Doughnut Stand
on Tall Pedestal**

Doughnut stand, square on tall
pedestal, any maker
(ILLUS.) . . . . .260.00 to 310.00

PITCHERS

**Alcock Blanket Stitch
(Pie Crust) Milk Pitcher**

Bamboo, Meakin
7¼" h. . . . . .150.00 to 165.00
8" h. . . . . .165.00 to 185.00
9" h. . . . . .225.00 to 250.00
Blanket Stitch (Pie Crust), Alcock,
8 3/8" h. (ILLUS.) . . . . . . .120.00 to 130.00
Cable and Ring, Shaw
7¼" h. . . . . .160.00 to 175.00
8" h. . . . . .175.00 to 195.00
Chelsea, Johnson Bros.
9¾" h. . . . . 240.00 to 260.00
Daisy, Wilkinson
8" h. . . . . .135.00 to 150.00
Plain Square, Wedgwood
7¼" h. . . . . .120.00 to 135.00

**Edwards Victory (Dolphin)
Milk Pitcher**

Victory (Dolphin), Edwards, 1884
8 1/8" h. (ILLUS.) . . . . .175.00 to 195.00
9¼" h. . . . . .225.00 to 250.00

PLATES

**Meakin Dinner, Luncheon, Bread and
Butter, and Dessert Plates**

Bread & butter plates
Plain, any maker, 7¾" d.
(ILLUS.) . . . . .8.00 to 10.00
Dessert plates
Chinese Shape, Shaw, late 1850's
7¾" d. . . . . .14.00 to 16.00
Fig Cousin, Davenport, 1871-1873
6½" d. . . . . .12.00 to 14.00
Plain, any maker, 6¾" d.
(ILLUS.) . . . . .6.00 to 8.00
Dinner plates
Bordered Fuchsia, Shaw, 1860's,
9 5/8" d. . . . . .25.00 to 27.00

Chinese Shape, Shaw, late 1850's,
  9 5/8" d. . . . . .20.00 to 22.00
Fig Cousin, Davenport, 1871-1873,
  10" d. . . . . .16.00 to 18.00
Plain, any maker, 9¾" to 10" d.
  (ILLUS.) . . . . .16.00 to 18.00
Luncheon plates
Plain, any maker, 8¾" d.
  (ILLUS.) . . . . .6.00 to 8.00
Shaw's Fan, 1856, 8¾" d. . . .14.00 to 16.00
Soup plates
Fig Counsin, Davenport, 1871-1873,
  10 1/8" d. . . . . .18.00 to 20.00
Lily-of-the-Valley, Shaw, 1860's,
  8¾" d. . . . . .25.00 to 27.00
Plain, any maker,
  Small. . . . . .14.00 to 16.00
  Large . . . . .16.00 to 18.00

PLATTERS
Lily-of-the-Valley, oval, Shaw,
  1860's, medium . . . . .25.00 to 30.00
Oval, plain, any maker, small,
  medium, large . . . . .20.00 to 30.00
  Extra large . . . . .35.00 to 40.00
Rectangular, plain, any maker,
  small, medium, large . . . .15.00 to 20.00
  Extra large . . . . .25.00 to 30.00
Square Ridged, Mellor
  Taylor, medium . . . . .15.00 to 20.00

RELISH DISHES/GRAVY BOAT UNDERPLATES

**Wedgwood Square Ridged Relish Dish
or Gravy Boat Underplate**

Bamboo, rectangular,
  Grindley . . . . .20.00 to 25.00
Cable and Ring, oval w/impression
  for gravy boat foot, Shaw . .22.00 to 28.00
Fish Hook, rectangular,
  Meakin. . . . . .20.00 to 25.00
Lily-of-the-Valley, oval shape cluster
  of three leaves w/lilies at narrow
  end, Shaw, 1860's . . . . .50.00 to 60.00
Plain, mitten shape w/reticulated
  handle, 9 x 5½",
  Wilkinson . . . . .50.00 to 60.00
Plain Square, rectangular, Wedg-
  wood . . . . .20.00 to 25.00
Square Ridged, rectangular, Wedg-
  wood (ILLUS.) . . . . .25.00 to 30.00

SAUCE TUREENS
Bamboo w/liner and ladle, rectangular, Meakin (ILLUS.) . . .325.00 to 375.00

**Meakin Bamboo Sauce Tureen
with Liner and Ladle**

Cable and Ring w/liner, oval,
  Shaw . . . . .185.00 to 205.00
Daisy without liner or ladle, rectan-
  gular, Wilkinson . . . . .100.00 to 125.00
Fish Hook w/liner, rectangular,
  Meakin (ILLUS. w/Meakin Fish
  Hook soup tureen) . . . . . .150.00 to 175.00
Fish Hook w/liner & ladle, rectangu-
  lar, Meakin. . . . . .325.00 to 370.00
Plain Square, rectangular, Wedg-
  wood . . . . .325.00 to 375.00
Sauce ladle. . . . . .125.00 to 175.00

SOUP TUREENS

**Meakin Fish Hook
Soup Tureen with Liner and
Sauce Tureen with Liner**

Bamboo w/liner, rectangular,
  Meakin . . . . .450.00 to 550.00
Fish Hook w/liner, rectangular,
  Meakin (ILLUS.) . . . . .450.00 to 550.00
Soup ladle. . . . . .175.00 to 225.00

SPOONERS

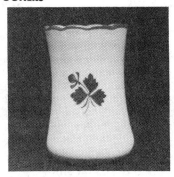

Meakin Spooner

Scalloped 2" d. lip, Meakin
(ILLUS.) ....150.00 to 175.00
Scalloped 3½" d. lip,
Meakin ....195.00 to 225.00

SUGAR BOWLS

Shaw Chinese Shape Teapot, Sugar Bowl, and Creamer

Bamboo, Meakin, two
sizes ....55.00 to 65.00
Cable and Ring, bulbous, Shaw, two
sizes ....80.00 to 90.00
Chinese Shape, Shaw, late 1850's
(ILLUS.) ....115.00 to 125.00
Favorite Shape, rope handles w/rib-
bing, Grindley ....80.00 to 90.00
Fish Hook, Meakin, two
sizes ....55.00 to 65.00

Shaw Hanging Leaves Teapot and Sugar Bowl

Hanging Leaves, Shaw, 1860's,
two sizes (ILLUS.) ....125.00 to 145.00
Lily-of-the-Valley, Shaw,
1860's ....125.00 to 140.00
Plain Square,
Wedgwood ....55.00 to 60.00

TEAPOTS

Bamboo, Meakin,
8 7/8" h. ....115.00 to 125.00
Cable and Ring, Burgess,
9¾" h. ....165.00 to 185.00
Chelsea, Johnson Bros.,
squatty.................145.00 to 165.00
Chinese Shape, Shaw, 9½" h., late
1850's (ILLUS. w/Shaw Chinese
sugar bowl & creamer) ..240.00 to 260.00
Fish Hook, Meakin, two sizes,
8½" h. & 8¾" h.........110.00 to 135.00

Hanging Leaves, Shaw, 1860's
(ILLUS. w/Shaw Hanging Leaves
sugar bowl) ....240.00 to 260.00
Lion's Head, Mellor
Taylor..................115.00 to 125.00

Mellor-Taylor Square Ridged Teapot

Square Ridged, Mellor Taylor
(ILLUS.) ....110.00 to 120.00

Wilkinson Plain Round Teapot

Plain Round, Wilkinson
(ILLUS.) ....140.00 to 150.00

WASTE BOWLS

Chinese Shape, Shaw, late 1850's,
5½" d., 3 5/8" h. ....110.00 to 120.00
Lily-of-the-Valley, Shaw, 1860's,
5 3/8" d., 3½" h. ....75.00 to 85.00
Plain bulbous shape, any
maker ....50.00 to 60.00
Plain cone shape, any
maker ....50.00 to 60.00

TOILET ARTICLES

Bowl & pitcher sets
Bamboo, Meakin ....325.00 to 350.00
Fish Hook, Meakin ......325.00 to 350.00
Lily-of-the-Valley, Shaw, 1860's
(ILLUS.) ....425.00 to 475.00

**Shaw Lily-of-the-Valley
Bowl and Pitcher**

Square Ridged, Burgess . .335.00 to 365.00
Chamber pots (base and lid)
Cable and Ring, Shaw ...185.00 to 205.00
Daisy, Wilkinson ....175.00 to 195.00
Fish Hook, Meakin ......145.00 to 165.00
Sunburst, Shaw ....200.00 to 225.00

**Shaw Cable and Ring
Covered Soap Dish with Liner**

Covered soap dishes - 3-piece
Bamboo, rectangular,
Meakin ....115.00 to 125.00
Cable and Ring, Shaw
(ILLUS.) ....165.00 to 185.00
Fish Hook, rectangular,
Meakin ....115.00 to 125.00
Square Ridged,
Burgess ....165.00 to 185.00
Square Ridged, Mellor
Taylor ....165.00 to 185.00
Shaving mugs
Bullet, Shaw ....85.00 to 95.00
Cable and Ring,
Shaw................115.00 to 125.00
Chinese Shape, Shaw
late 1850's, 3¼" d.,
3 1/8" h. ....95.00 to 105.00
Chinese Shape, Shaw,
late 1850's, 3¾" d.,
3 5/8" h. ....145.00 to 155.00
Fish Hook, Meakin ......90.00 to 100.00

Lily-of-the-Valley,
Shaw, 1860's ....115.00 to 125.00
Plain Round,
Wilkinson.............90.00 to 100.00
Square Ridged,
Burgess ....95.00 to 105.00

**Shaw Conical Shape
Vertical Toothbrush Holder**

Toothbrush holders
Bamboo, vertical,
Meakin ....135.00 to 145.00
Conical shape, vertical,
Shaw (ILLUS.) ....150.00 to 175.00
Fish Hook, vertical,
Meakin ....150.00 to 160.00
Lily-of-the-Valley w/lid,
horizontal, Shaw,
1860's ....165.00 to 185.00

TEA LEAF VARIANTS

Baker Morning Glory Creamer

Morning Glory by W. Baker & Co.
Creamer, bulbous, 1860's, 5 5/8" h.
(!LLUS.)..................70.00 to 80.00

Morning Glory by Elsmore & Forster
Portland Shape, late 1850's
Coffee pot ....215.00 to 235.00

Creamer...............150.00 to 175.00
Sugar bowl ....100.00 to 125.00
Teapot ....175.00 to 195.00
Waste bowl.............65.00 to 75.00

Morning Glory by J. F. Wileman
Richelieu Shape covered butter dish
    w/liner, 1860's..........140.00 to 160.00

Pepper Leaf (Tobacco Leaf, Coffee Bean) by Elsmore & Forster, 1860's

**Elsmore & Forster Pepper Leaf
Covered Butter Dish with Liner**

Chamber pot w/lid........175.00 to 195.00
Covered butter dish
    w/liner (ILLUS.) ....150.00 to 175.00
Covered vegetable dish....100.00 to 125.00
Cups w/saucers, handled or handle-
    less, two sizes ....50.00 to 60.00
Plates
    Bread & butter, 7½" d. ....12.00 to 14.00
    Dessert, 6½" d. ....12.00 to 14.00
    Luncheon, 8¾"d ....14.00 to 16.00
    Dinner, 9 5/8" d. ....18.00 to 20.00
Platters, oval, several sizes ..25.00 to 45.00
Spittoon..................500.00 to 550.00
Sugar bowl ....90.00 to 100.00
Teapot ....150.00 to 175.00
Waste bowl................65.00 to 75.00

Pre-Tea Leaf by Walley, 1850's

**Walley Pre-Tea Leaf
Niagara Shape Handleless
Cups with Saucers**

Gothic Shape or Niagara Shape
    Cups with saucers, handled or
        handleless, two sizes
        (ILLUS.).................55.00 to 65.00
    Platter, oval, 14½ x
        11½"..................55.00 to 65.00
    Teapot ....175.00 to 195.00

Teaberry by Clementson, Late 1850's through 1880's

**Clementson Teaberry
New York Shape Milk Pitcher**

New York Shape, 1858
    Individual vegetable or sauce
        dishes (nappies), round,
        5 5/16" d. ....22.00 to 25.00
    Milk pitcher, 8½" h.
        (ILLUS.)................175.00 to 195.00
Plain, 1870's
    Relish dish, pear-
        shaped ....50.00 to 60.00
    Sugar bowl, bulbous .....110.00 to 120.00
    Teapot, bulbous ....200.00 to 225.00

Thistle

**Powell and Bishop Thistle
Washington Shape Covered
Vegetable Dish**

Covered vegetable dish, Washington
    Shape, 1863 ....110.00 to 125.00

(End of Special Focus)

JACKFIELD POTTERY

Jackfield Pottery Dogs & Hen Dish

Jackfield pottery originated in England in the early 17th century. It is black-glazed and is found both plain and decorated. Pieces most frequently available today are 19th century black-glazed objects that are generally termed Jackfield.

Animal covered dish, hen on nest, black glaze hen, white nest, gilt accents & white enameled eye, 3½" l. $130.00

Animal covered dish, hen on nest, black glaze hen, white nest (ILLUS. center) 300.00

Creamer, figural cow on oval base, black glaze w/gilt trim (chips) 85.00

Models of Spaniel dogs in seated position, black glaze, glass eyes, pr. (ILLUS.) 700.00

Pitcher, 11" h., jug-type, black glaze, gilt scene of horse & hounds in landscape, "I + A" & "True Blue" within gilt scrollwork & foliage suspended from chains, spout w/gilt foliate scrolls, ca. 1760 .... 770.00

Pitcher w/pewter lid, black glaze, enameled decor................. 60.00

Tea set: cov. teapot, creamer & sugar bowl; black glaze, miniature, 3 pcs. 125.00

JASPER WARE

Wedgwood Jardiniere

Jasper ware is fine-grained exceedingly hard stoneware made by including barium sulphate in the clay and was first devised by Josiah Wedgwood, who utilized it for the body of many of his fine cameo blue-and-white and green-and-white pieces. It was subsequently produced by other potters, notably William Adams & Sons, and is in production at the present. The following is a listing of Wedgwood items only.

Candlesticks, white relief classical design on olive green, 7½" h., pr..............................$375.00

Cookie jar, white relief mythological figures & garlands on center lavender band w/sage green top & bottom border bands, silverplate cover, rim & handle, marked Wedgwood only, 4¾" d., 6" h. 695.00

Cookie jar, white relief panels of classical figures above stiff leaf base border on sage green, silverplate cover, rim & bail handle, marked Wedgwood only, 5" d., 6" h........................... 235.00

Cookie jar, white relief classical ladies & cupids on dark blue, silverplate cover, rim & handle, marked Wedgwood only, 5 1/8" d., 6" h. 425.00

Cookie jar, white relief classical ladies on green, silverplate cover, rim & handle, marked Wedgwood only, 5" d., 6½" h. 225.00

Cookie jar, light blue, dark blue & white relief classical figures on center dark blue band, resilvered cover, rim, ball-footed base & handle, marked Wedgwood, England, ca. 1910, 5" d., 7" h..... 383.00

Cookie jar, barrel-shaped, white relief classical figures on dark blue, silverplate cover, rim & handle, marked Wedgwood only, 5½" d., 7½" h 190.00

Dresser tray, oblong w/cut corners, white relief classical figures at each corner & oak leaf & acorn border on light blue, marked Wedgwood, England, ca. 1910, 19½ x 7¾" 110.00

Jardiniere, white relief grape garlands pendant from lion's mask & rings over classical figures on dark blue, ca. 1910 (ILLUS.) 156.00

Marmalade jar, white relief classical ladies on cobalt blue, silverplate lid, 3¼" d., 4¼" h. 100.00

Marmalade jar w/attached underplate, black & white relief on yellow, silverplate lid, 18th c., overall 3½" h. 285.00

Match box, white relief classical lady & cupids on lid, cobalt blue

ground, marked Wedgwood only,
3¾ x 2" oval, 7/8" h. 80.00

Mug, white relief classical figures &
medallion on dark blue, marked
Wedgwood only on base &
marked Elkington & Co. Ltd. on
silverplate rim, 4 7/8" h. 135.00

Pitcher, tankard, 6¼" h., white relief classical figures (4), tree,
flowers, bird, deer & cherub on
dark blue, signed Wedgwood
only 130.00

Plaque, white relief cherubs playing
blind man's buff on blue, marked
Wedgwood only, 11¾ x 5¾" oblong plaque in black & gilt frame,
overall 13¾ x 7½" 495.00

Spill vase, white relief classical
figures on dark blue, marked
Wedgwood only, 4" h. 125.00

Teacup & saucer, twisted rope handle, white relief classical ladies
on dark blue, marked Wedgwood
only 145.00

Teapot, cov., white relief classical
figures & borders on dark blue,
marked Wedgwood only,
ca. 1910 .... 185.00

JEWEL TEA AUTUMN LEAF PATTERN

Autumn Leaf Gravy Boat

*Though not antique, this ware has a devot-
ed following. The Hall China Company of
East Liverpool, Ohio, made the first pieces
of Autumn Leaf pattern ware to be given as
premiums by the Jewel Tea Company in 1933.
The premiums were an immediate success
and thousands of new customers, all eager to
acquire a piece of the durable Autumn Leaf
pattern ware, began purchasing Jewel Tea
products. Though the pattern was eventually used to decorate linens, glasswares and tin-
wares, we include only the Hall China
Company items in our listing.*

Baking dish, swirl form, 7½" d. $18.00

Bean pot, cov., single
handle ....250.00 to 300.00

Bean pot, cov., 2-handled 75.00

Bowl, 8" d., shallow 15.00

Bowl, salad, 9" d. 15.00

Butter dish, cov., squared-off handles, ¼-lb. ....345.00 to 390.00

Butter dish & cover w/scalloped
handle, ¼-lb. 110.00

Cake plate w/"Goldenray" metal
base 170.00

Casserole, cov., 8½" d. 22.00

Clock, electric, wall model,
9½" d. ....260.00 to 400.00

Coffee percolator, electric, 8-cup ... 295.00

Coffee pot, cov., drip-type, w/metal
insert, 1937 & on, 8-cup 40.00

Coffee pot, cov., drip-type, w/metal
insert, 1934-41, 9-cup 235.00

Coffee pot (or casserole) warmer,
round 105.00

Creamer, ruffled, 1940 .... 7.50

Creamer & cov. sugar bowl, pre-
1940, pr. 50.00

Cup & saucer 12.50

Drippings bowl, cov., 5" d. 13.00

Gravy boat w/underplate (ILLUS.)... 26.00

Irish coffee mug 72.50

Mixing bowl, nest-type, 6" d. 10.00

Mixing bowl, nest-type, 8½" d. 18.00

Mustard jar w/ladle, 2 pcs. 25.00

Mustard jar, cover, ladle & underplate, 3 pcs. 35.00

Pitcher, 6" h. 16.00

Pitcher, globular jug-type 16.00

Pitcher w/ice lip 15.00

Plate, 7" d. 4.50

Plate, 9" d. 9.50

Plate, 10" d. 10.00

Platter, 11" 16.00

Platter, 13½" l. 17.00

Range top set, cov. grease jar & salt
& pepper shakers, 3 pcs. 30.00

Salt & pepper shakers, handled,
pr. 12.00

Autumn Leaf Salt & Pepper Shakers

Salt & pepper shakers, small, pr.
(ILLUS.)....................... 12.00

Sauce dish...................... 5.00

Snack bowl 15.00

Souffle-casserole, 10 oz. individual
size 16.00

Soup bowl, coupe, 8¼" d. 11.00

Sugar bowl, cov. 19.00

Teapot, cov., Aladdin lamp shape
w/long spout 42.00

Teapot, cov., "Autumn Leaf Club
New York" 225.00

Tidbit tray, 3-tier 45.00

Vegetable bowl, cov., 10½" oval ... 40.00

Vegetabel bowl, open, divided,
10½ x 8" oval 65.00

JUGTOWN POTTERY

Jugtown Pottery Teapot

This pottery was established by Jacques and Juliana Busbee in Jugtown, North Carolina, in the early 1920's in an attempt to revive the skills of the diminishing North Carolina potter's art as Prohibition ended the need for locally crafted stoneware whiskey jugs. During the early years, Juliana Busbee opened a shop in Greenwich Village in New York City to promote the North Carolina wares that her husband, Jacques, was designing and a local youth, Ben Owen, was producing under his direction. Owen continued to work with Busbee from 1922 until Busbee's death in 1947 at which time Juliana took over management of the pottery for the next decade until her illness (or mental fatique) caused the pottery to be closed in 1958. At that time, Owen opened his own pottery a few miles away, marking his wares "Ben Owen - Master Potter." The pottery begun by the Busbee's was reopened in 1960, under new management, and still operates today using the identical impressed mark of the early Jugtown pottery the Busbee's managed from 1922 until 1958.

Bowl, 5" d., blue & grey $25.00
Bowl, 5" d., 3" h., frog's skin
  glaze 55.00
Cookie jar, cov., ovoid, strap han-
  dles, 12" h. 75.00
Cup, green frog's skin glaze. 15.00
Finger bowl, "Chinese
  Translation" 100.00
Jar, cov., bulbous w/flaring rim,
  earred handles, redware, bright
  orange glaze, 6¾" h. (edge
  chips) 45.00
Jar, cov., ear strap handles, orange
  & brown, 11" 95.00
Pie plate, orange w/black concentric
  circles interior decor, 9½" d. 65.00
Pitcher, 3½" h., yellow glaze
  (dings) 30.00
Pitcher, 5" h., grey & cobalt blue
  salt glaze. 70.00
Rose jar, cov., blended olive drab
  glaze, 4½" h. 45.00
Teapot, "tobacco spit" glaze, signed,
  1930's, 5¼" h. (ILLUS.) 40.00

Vase, 6½" h., bulbous, open han-
  dles, Chinese white glaze 150.00
Vase, 8" h., embossed handles, Chi-
  nese blue-green glaze 175.00

KAUFFMANN, ANGELIQUE

Angelica Kauffmann (Marie Angelique Catherine Kauffmann) was an accomplished Swiss artist, who lived from 1741 until 1807. Paintings copied from her original work often embellish porcelain and those signed with her name have attracted collectors.

Bowl, 10" sq., scene of maidens (3)
  & cupid after Kauffmann reserved
  on cranberry ground w/gold border, Austrian beehive mark
  blank $120.00
Charger, scene of classical ladies &
  cupid on portico after Kauffmann
  reserved on tan shaded to white
  ground, dark green border
  w/(worn) gold design, Victoria,
  Austria blank, 13½" d. 145.00
Chocolate pot, cover & underplate,
  "Kauffmann" signed scene of
  cherub w/wings outlined in gold,
  cobalt blue ground w/gold tracery, Victoria, Carlsbad, Austria
  marks 165.00
Chocolate set: cov. chocolate pot &
  2 c/s; Kauffmann-type figures reserved on powder blue ground,
  Royal Vienna blanks, 5 pcs. 200.00
Cookie jar, cov., Kauffmann-type
  portrait reserved on cobalt blue
  ground 85.00
Cup & saucer, classical scene after
  Kauffmann reserved on cobalt
  blue ground, Royal Vienna
  blanks 70.00
Plaque, pierced to hang, allegorical
  scene of maidens after Kauffmann, maroon border w/gold,
  12" 125.00
Plate, 10" d., scene of 4 classical
  maidens & cupid after
  Kauffmann 150.00

LEEDS

The Leeds Pottery in Yorkshire, England, began production about 1758. It made, among other things, creamware that was highly competitive with Wedgwood's. In the 1780's it began production of reticulated and punched wares. Little of its production was marked.

Most readily available Leeds ware is that of the 19th century during which time the pottery was operated by several firms.

Leeds Model of a Horse

Creamer, creamware, "gaudy"
flowering foliage decor, 4½" h. . .$325.00
Cup & saucer, handleless, 4-color
floral decor 200.00
Model of a horse, pearlware, black-
sponged coat, black mane, tail,
ears (left chipped) & hooves, standing on an olive green rectangular
base edged w/a border of cobalt
blue molded leafage, 2 left ankles
hair cracked, 1810-20, 11 7/8" h.
(ILLUS.) 9,075.00
Mug, applied handle, 5-color floral
decor, 6" h. (short rim
hairline). 295.00
Plate, 6 3/8" d., 5-color scene of
house & sponged trees, blue
feather edge. 325.00
Platter, 19¼" l., blue flowers &
leaves, blue feather edge (stains
& crack) 235.00
Platter, creamware, reticulated rim,
small 125.00

Leeds Creamware Teapot

Teapot, cov., creamware, cylindrical, entwined rope-twist handle,
curved spout molded w/foliage,
body decorated w/scattered gilt
flowering plants, cover w/flower-
head finial, stained, ca. 1775,
7½" w. (ILLUS.) 605.00

LENOX

Lenox Mug

The Ceramic Art Company was established at Trenton, New Jersey, in 1889 by Jonathan Coxon and Walter Scott Lenox. In addition to true porcelain, it also made a Belleek-type ware. Re-named Lenox Company in 1906, it is still in operation today. Also see BELLEEK - AMERICAN and TOBY MUGS & JUGS.

Box & cover w/bird finial, floral
decor, 6" d. $80.00
Bust of Art Deco woman, wearing
plumed & feathered headdress, on
2-tier pedestal base 600.00
Butter pats, stylized pale purple
florals & foliage decor, gold edge,
3½" d., set of 8. . . . . 45.00
Creamer, Ming patt.. . . . . 60.00
Cup & saucer, demitasse, fluted
w/flaring rim, coral pink handle &
footrim. 60.00
Cup & saucer, wheat decor on
cobalt blue ground 50.00
Decanter w/original stopper, brown
w/sterling silver overlay & reserved h.p. scene on stopper
w/chain, artist-signed & dated . . . 450.00
Demitasse pot, cov., cobalt blue
w/sterling silver overlay 150.00
Dinner service for 12, Wheat patt.,
92 pcs. 1,012.00
Dish, leaf-shaped, bright green ex-
terior, ivory interior, 5¼" l.. . . . . . 50.00
Egg cup, Ming patt. 25.00

Figure of a ballerina, white dress,
1906-24, 6" h. 450.00
Figure of "Natchez" southern belle. . 225.00
Game plate, partridge center,
10½" d. 150.00
Marmalade jar, cover & attached
underplate, Fairmont patt. 50.00
Mayonnaise bowl & underplate,
Autumn patt., gold trim, 2 pcs. . . . 80.00
Model of an elephant standing
w/trunk down, black w/white
tusks, 9 x 6½" 275.00
Model of a swan, pink w/gold
edges, 4½" h. 15.00
Mug, cobalt blue w/sterling silver
overlay, 4¾" h. (Ceramic Art
Company mark) 100.00
Mug, smiling monk holding up glass
of wine on shaded brown ground,
sterling silver rim, 6¼" h.
(ILLUS.) 150.00
Perfume lamp, figural Marie An-
toinette, bisque finish, dated
1929, 9" h. 650.00
Salt & pepper shakers, h.p. green &
gold bird decor, pr. 60.00
Salt dips, h.p. pink roses w/green
leaves & blue forget-me-nots de-
cor, set of 8 . . . . 80.00

Lenox Steins

Stein, h.p. portrait of monk with upraised glass on green ground,
sterling silver lid, ½ liter (ILLUS.
left). 253.00
Stein, h.p. scene of monks by wine
barrel on black ground, copper &
silver lid, ½ liter (ILLUS.
right) 467.00
Tea set: cov. teapot, creamer & cov.
sugar bowl; cobalt blue w/sterling
silver overlay, 3 pcs. 350.00
Tea strainer, h.p. small roses
decor 65.00
Vase, 7" h., embossed morning
glories, creamy ivory glaze, gold
rim & base trim 45.00
Vase, 9¼" h., h.p. woodland scene
on shaded brown ground (Ceramic
Art Company mark) 95.00

LIMOGES

Limoges Game Plaques

Numerous factories produced china in
Limoges, France, with major production in
the 19th century. Some pieces listed below are
identified by the name of the maker or the
mark of the factory. Although the famed
Haviland Company was located in Limoges,
wares bearing their marks are not included
in this listing. Also see HAVILAND.

Bowl, 6¾" d., 3" h., 3-footed, center floral & blue scrolls on pastel
ground, artist-signed $45.00
Bowl, fruit, footed, h.p. grapes on
rose ground, T. & V. (Tressemann
& Vogt) 100.00
Box, cov., h.p. cupids on lid, cobalt
blue & white ground, 4¼" sq. 179.00
Box, cov., h.p. portrait on lid,
8½" w. 325.00
Cache pot, h.p. ferns decor, 5" w.,
7" h., W.G. & Co. (Wm. Guerin &
Co.). 125.00
Charger, overall yellow roses decor,
gold & black rim, artist-signed,
12¼" d., Coronet (George Borg-
feldt Importer) 85.00
Charger, garlands of pink roses
decor, scalloped gold rim,
12½" d. 70.00
Charger, scene after "The Angelus"
center w/peasant couple in field
w/heads bowed, 14½" d., D. & C.
(R. Delinieres) 160.00
Chocolate pot, cov., large h.p. roses
& ornate gold trim on green
ground, 9½" h. 159.00
Chocolate pot, cov., elegant pink &
yellow florals on pale green
ground, 11" h. 95.00
Chocolate pot, cov., Thistle patt. on
green ground, J.P.L. (J. Pouyat,
Limoges) 85.00
Chocolate set: cov. chocolate pot &
5 c/s; tiny roses decor, 6 pcs. 190.00
Cookie jar, cov., h.p. orange & vio-
let poppies decor, gold trim 150.00
Creamer & handled sugar basket,
h.p. purple violets decor, pr.,
T. & V. 95.00
Dessert set: 10" h. cov. teapot,
creamer, cov. sugar bowl, 6 c/s &
six 7 3/8" d. plates; h.p. plush
roses on shaded blue ground,
21 pcs. 500.00

Dish, 3-section w/center handle & irregular gold-trimmed edge, sprays of lavender florals & lily-of-the-valley on shaded pink to white ground, 13" d., 4" h. 140.00

Dresser set: oval tray, pr. cov. oval boxes, cov. round box, ring tree & candlestick; deep cobalt blue w/gold tracery decor on cream ground, 6 pcs. 450.00

Fish plaque, pierced to hang, carp swimming amidst morning glories, ornate rococo gold border, artist-signed, 14" d. 265.00

Fish set: 24" l. platter, 4 plates, sauceboat & underplate; sea shells & marine life decor, 7 pcs., A.L. (A. Lanternier) 425.00

Fish set: 24" l. platter, eight 9" d. plates & sauceboat; h.p. varied fish species, pink borders, gold rims, 10 pcs. 550.00

Game plaques, pierced to hang, h.p. quail in natural woodland setting, heavy gold rococo edge, 10½" d., pr. (ILLUS.) 375.00

Game plate, deer in forest land-scape, artist-signed, 9" d. 165.00

Game plate, fighting boars (2) decor, artist-signed, 10" d., Coronet 110.00

Game plate, h.p. hunting dog fer-ring out pheasant, realistic colors, 12" d. 175.00

Humidor, cov., h.p. scene of Indians smoking peace pipe decor, orange ground, gold trim 275.00

Ice cream set: 16" l. platter & 12 in-dividual plates; h.p. floral decor, 13 pcs. 275.00

Mug, serpent handle, h.p. iris de-cor, JP France (J. Pouyat) 40.00

Mustache cup & saucer, roses w/green leaves & gold 48.00

Nappy, curved gold handle inside dish, gold scalloped edge, soft pink blossoms on blue-green ground, 6" d. 30.00

Perfume tray, pierced handles, h.p. apple blossoms on blue shaded to pink to grey ground, 9½" d. 48.00

Pitcher, cider, 6½" h., apples decor, gold trim, artist-signed 110.00

Pitcher, cider, 7" d., apple blossoms decor, artist-signed 145.00

Pitcher, milk, 7" h., 4¾" d., h.p. pink florals w/gold trim decor 70.00

Pitcher, cider, 8 x 6½", beaded han-dle, russet-yellow apples overall decor, multi-shaded ground, artist-signed J.P.L. (J. Pouyat, Limoges) 110.00

Pitcher, tankard, 11" h., h.p. black-berries decor, J.P.L. 125.00

Limoges Tankard Pitcher

Pitcher, tankard, 12" h., 6½" at base, hanging grape bunches on variegated ground, J.P.L. (ILLUS.) 185.00

Pitcher, cider, pond lily decor w/gold 95.00

Pitcher, figural court jester handle, rococo base, J.P.L. 275.00

Plaque, pierced to hang, strutting cockatoo rooster decor, artist-signed, 9¾" 60.00

Plaque, pierced to hang, gold roco-co border, h.p. rose & pink roses w/green leaves on pastel ground, 13½" d. 250.00

Plaque, pierced to hang, gentleman holding yarn, lady winding it, 13½" d. 325.00

Plaque, pierced to hang, h.p. por-trait of beautiful young lady, 18" d., J.P.L. 475.00

Plaques, pierced to hang, North African birds in monotone of rose-brown on white ground, heavy rococo borders, 13¼" d., pr. 485.00

Plaques, pierced to hang, gold roco-co scalloped border, one w/young couple in garden & other w/young couple standing, pastel decor, 13¾" d., pr. 550.00

Plate, 7" d., h.p. columbines decor 25.00

Plate, 8½" d., scalloped rim, h.p. pink roses, leaves & gold trim decor 22.00

Plate, 9" d., ornate gold scalloped rim, h.p. pastel florals & Art Nou-veau enameled gold decor 27.00

Plate, 9" d., scalloped rim, h.p. roses, ornate gold border 47.00

Plate, 12¼" d., h.p. large pink

hydrangeas w/multicolored leaves
& ornate gold trim decor 115.00
Platter, h.p. turkey, white w/feathered gold trim, made for Marshall
Fields & Company 70.00
Punch bowl, Daisy Chain patt., gold
ground w/gold trim, T. & V. (Tressemann & Vogt) 175.00

Limoges Punch Set

Punch set: 12½" d. bowl w/threefooted pedestal & 5 cups; grapes
decor, 8 pcs., T & V (ILLUS.) 425.00
Tea set: bulbous cov. teapot, cov.
sugar bowl, creamer & tile; pink
roses on pale blue shaded to
beige ground, gilt trim, 4 pcs.
W.G. & Co. (Wm. Guerin & Co.) . . 150.00
Tray, h.p. center scene of thatched
cottages w/bridge & stream, two
people walking down path, embossed leaves border w/pink &
gold trim, unmarked, 14 1/8" d. . . 232.00
Tray, h.p. pink, lavender & green
grapes w/gold netting, ½" rim,
15¼" 175.00
Vase, 6" h., deep red & pink roses,
vines & leaves on shaded blue to
green ground, artist-signed,
J.P.L. 68.00
Vase, 10" h., cylindrical, birds (2) on
a tree limb w/beaded flowers &
blue rim 150.00

Limoges Vase

Vase, 13" h., h.p. pale lavender
irises & green leaves on shaded
blue ground, T. & V. (ILLUS.) 300.00
Vase, 16" h., roses one side, ladies
reverse 350.00
Vegetable dish, pink roses on white
ground w/gold trim, made for
"Vorenbergs Boston," 9½" d.,
J.P.L. 28.00

LIVERPOOL

*Liverpool is often used as a generic term
for wares made by numerous potteries in this
English city during the 18th century. Many
wares are unmarked.*

Bowl, 4¼" d., iron-red, blue &
green pagoda in a river landscape
one side, reverse w/trees by a
fence, interior w/flower spray, ca.
1765 . . . . $275.00
Jug, creamware, ovoid, transferprinted in black one side w/maiden leaning on an anchor, a ship
sailing in the distance, reverse
w/central scene of 2 clasped
hands centered by a heart surrounded by inscription, within
rose & grapevine borders flanked
by ewers, a medallion depicting a
ship at sea below, ca. 1800,
7" h. 825.00
Jug, creamware, transfer-printed in
black w/figures of "Peace" &
"Plenty," green enamel rim, 7" h.
(rim & spout chips & crow's foot in
bottom) 325.00
Jug, creamware, transfer-printed in
black w/scene of sailing ship
within an oval surmounted by Liberty cap & crossed flags w/American eagle, 13 stars, "Independence" & "E Pluribus Unum" at
bottom, 7 7/8" h. (stains, edge
wear & spout chip) 725.00
Jug, creamware, transfer-printed in
black w/scene of musicians
w/harpsichord, initials & an
eagle, highlighted in polychrome
enamel, 9 7/8" h. 600.00
Jug, creamware, transfer-printed in
black one side w/clipper ship flying American flag w/sixteen stars
highlighted in polychrome enamel, reverse w/black eagle & shield
w/"E Pluribus Unum," empty oval
wreath beneath spout, 11" h.
(edge chips, discoloration & short
hairline) 800.00
Jug, creamware, transfer-printed in
black w/scene of American sailing

ship one side & oval scene of
Washington's tomb ringed w/names
of the 13 states reverse, initials
"MR" under spout, 11½" h. (hairlines & chips on table ring) 1,200.00
Jug, creamware, transfer-printed in
black w/Farmer's Arms & inscribed
below "In God our Trust," flanked
by various vignettes & subjects
w/animals, harvesters, seasons &
sportsmen within oval & shaped
cartouches, rim & foot rim w/brown
line, strap handle enriched
w/brown stylized foliage, ca. 1800,
13¼" h. (chips & crack) 2,640.00
Mug, twined handle, transfer-
printed in black w/American
eagle w/fifteen stars & "James
Leech," brown & black enamel
trim, 4 7/8" h. (small chips on
handle) 104.00
Mug, transfer-printed in black &
heightened in enamel w/Farmer's
Arms, inscribed "God Speed the
Plough" & "Peace and Plenty,"
5½" h. (stains & short hairline in
base) 175.00

LLADRO

Lladro Figures

Spain's famed Lladro porcelain manufactory creates both limited and non-limited edition figurines as well as other porcelains. The
classic simple beauty of the figures and their
subdued coloring makes them readily recog-
nizable and they have an enthusiastic following of collectors.

Angel with Horn, No. 4540 .... $37.00
Boy Soccer Player, No. 5135 .... 89.00
Dutch Boy, No. 4811 .... 69.00
Fairy, No. 4595 .... 65.00
Girl Clown, No. 4924 .... 315.00
Girl Soccer Player, No. 5134 .... 89.00

Girl with Lamb, No. 1010 .... 100.00
Good Book, No. 5084 ......135.00 to 190.00
Hamlet & Yorik, No. 1254 .... 440.00
Japanese Girl with Fan, No. 4990 ... 150.00
Lady Golfer, No. 4851 (ILLUS. left) .. 95.00
Lady Tennis Player, No. 4798 (ILLUS.
right) 95.00
Matrimony, No. 1404 ......250.00 to 320.00
Mother with Child, No. 4575........ 195.00
Nude, No. 4511 .... 100.00
Pottery Seller with Donkey,
No. 4859 ....250.00 to 350.00
Rabbit in Forest, No. 4773.......... 60.00
Roaring 20's, No. 5174 .....129.00 to 173.00
Sewing a Trousseau,
No. 5126 ....135.00 to 185.00
Toast by Sancho, No. 5165 ..75.00 to 100.00

LONGWY

Longwy Jungle Scene Plaque

This faience factory was established in 1798
in the town of Longwy, France and is noted
for its enameled pottery which resembles
cloisonne. Utilitarian wares were the first
production here but by the 1870's, an Oriental style art pottery that imitated "cloisonne"
was created through the use of heavy enamels
in relief. By 1912, a modern Art Deco style
became part of Longwy's production and
these wares, together with the Oriental style
pieces, have made this art pottery popular
with collectors today. As interest in Art Deco
has soared in recent years, values of
Longwy's modern style wares have risen
sharply. Also see TILES.

Box, cov., enameled multicolored
florals on blue ground, 2 7/8" w.,
3½" l. $45.00
Charger, enameled cranes (3) center
amidst colorful stylized vegeta-
tion, 12" d. 360.00
Pilgrim flask, enameled nude female & 2 peacocks one side, sin-

gle peacock reverse, shades of
blue & cream on azure blue
ground, signed, ca. 1925 . . . . 375.00
Plaque, jungle scene w/blue ele-
phants & a woman plucking coco-
nuts from palm trees, enameled in
shades of blue, brown, green &
mauve on "crackle" ground,
retailed by Bon Marche, 15" d.
(ILLUS.) 1,100.00
Platter, 11" l., enameled blue,
green & red florals, 1880's 95.00
Tray, enameled yellow & black Art
Deco design, 11" l. 200.00
Trivet, scene of woman w/stylized
foliage on "crackle" ground,
Primavera, after Matisse, 8" sq. . . 425.00
Vase, 4¾" h., cylindrical, footed,
enameled nude females reclining
on beach w/birds overhead on
yellow "crackle" ground, black
borders 550.00
Vase, 14½" h., octagonal baluster
form, enameled blue & green
leaves amongst gold flower-
heads 418.00

LOTUS WARE

Lotus Ware Rose Bowl

*Avidly sought by many collectors are these
exquisite bone china wares made by Knowles,
Taylor & Knowles, of East Liverpool, Ohio,
in the last decade of the 19th century. The
firm also produced ironstone and hotel china.*

Bowl, 5" d., 4" h., h.p. pink, green
& gold floral decor $525.00
Bowl, 6 x 4¾" oval, 4¼" h., pierced
design at ends, relief florals on
sides, all white 650.00
Bowl, oval, high sides, reticulated
ends, embossed medallions w/gilt
highlights on creamy white 275.00
Creamer, fishnet design on green
shaded to white ground 250.00
Rose bowl, ruffled rim, h.p. pink
roses w/gold highlights, 5"
widest d., 4¼" h. 225.00

Rose bowl, scalloped & crimped rim
w/beaded edge, cupids riding in a
shell chariot drawn by doves, reverse w/delicate purple violets,
artist-signed (ILLUS.) 400.00
Vase, 7 x 4", pillow-shaped, ornate
gold handles, crimped rim, h.p.
pink floral decor, gold beading &
trim 595.00

LUSTRE WARES

*Lustred wares in imitation of copper, gold,
silver and other colors were produced in
England in the early 19th century and onward. Gold, copper or platinum oxides were
painted on glazed objects which were then
fired, giving them a lustred effect. Various
forms of lustre wares include plain lustre—
with the entire object coated to obtain a
metallic effect, bands of lustre decoration and
painted lustre designs. Particularly appealing is the pink or purple "splash lustre" sometimes referred to as "Sunderland" lustre in
the mistaken belief it was confined to the
production of Sunderland area potteries. Objects decorated in silver lustre by the "resist"
process, wherein parts of the objects to be left
free from lustre decoration were treated with
wax, are referred to as "silver resist." Also
see FROG MUGS.*

COPPER

Copper Lustre Goblet

Coffee pot, cov., pedestal base,
Georgian style, copper lustre
body w/embossed vertical ribbing
& beaded trim, 10½" h. $375.00
Crocus pot, copper lustre body
w/enameled blue, green & white
florals, 7½" h. (edge chips) 155.00
Goblet, copper lustre body, creamy
white band w/pink lustre spots,
4½" h. 45.00
Goblet, copper lustre body, wide
blue center band embossed
w/rose blossoms highlighted
w/red enamel & copper lustre,
4¾" h. 30.00

Goblet, copper lustre body
w/enameled pink, green, yellow
& white florals (ILLUS.) 75.00
Pitcher, 3" h., copper lustre body
w/enameled pink florals 38.00
Pitcher, 4½" h., bulbous, copper
lustre body, wide white band
transfer-printed in red w/scene of
youth & maiden, white rim band
w/purple lustre & red enamel
trim 47.50
Pitcher, 5" h., copper lustre body,
canary yellow band w/enameled
florals 75.00
Pitcher, 5" h., jug-type, copper lustre body w/white embossed
cherubs & vintage decor, pink lustre trim 125.00
Pitcher, 5¼" h., copper lustre body
w/polychrome stylized florals 125.00
Pitchers, 5¾" & 5" h., first pair baluster form w/squared handle &
curving spout, copper lustre body
w/horizontal reeding, band of
pink lustre resist & pale blue
flowers & vines at shoulder, second pair baluster form, copper
lustre body, blue midband w/ap-
plied ornament heightened
w/overglaze enamels, Staffordshire, ca. 1820, set of 4 .... 308.00
Pitcher, 6" h., copper lustre body,
blue band w/embossed cherub
musicians 75.00
Pitcher, 6¼" h., mask spout, copper
lustre body, wide blue band
w/embossed & enameled florals .. 65.00
Pitcher, 7½" h., mask spout, copper
lustre body, blue bands
w/enameled florals 75.00

19th Century Copper Lustre Pitcher

Pitchers, 7¾" h., copper lustre body
w/embossed beading around rim
& bordering wide blue center
band decorated w/embossed &
polychrome enameled scenes of
cupids in chariots & floral sprays,
England, early 19th c., pr. (ILLUS.
of one) 264.00

Teapot, cov., griffin handle, copper
lustre body 175.00
Waste bowl, copper lustre w/em-
bossed & enameled girl & dog
scene, 1840, 5½" h. 75.00

SUNDERLAND PINK & OTHERS

Pitchers with Pink Lustre Decor

Cup & saucer, handleless, h.p. pink
lustre foliage & trim 48.00
Mug, pink lustre, House patt., ca.
1820, 3" h. 75.00
Pitcher, 7½" h., jug-type, transfer-
printed in black w/a standing figure of a man & woman flanking
an armorial, beneath banners inscribed "We unite to maintain our
Rights Inviolate/Prosperity attend
ye Justness of our Cause," banner
below inscribed "The Friendly Society of Cordwainers of England,"
reverse inscribed "Success to the
Fleece/To the Plough and the
Sail./May our Taxes Grow
Less/And our Commerce ne'er
Fail," decorated on the interior,
exterior & base w/pink splash lustre, 2nd quarter, 19th c. (ILLUS.
right) 330.00
Pitcher, 7½" h., pink splash lustre .. 35.00
Pitcher, 7¾" h., jug-type, transfer-
printed in black & enameled in
green, yellow & pink w/two sailing ships behind large circular
compass, reverse w/inscription
"The Lord is my Shepherd my
guardian and guide,....." within
flowering vine borders, decorated
overall w/meandering pink lustre
scrollwork, rim & handle w/pink
lustre foliate vines, 2nd quarter,
19th c., hairline crack at rim
(ILLUS. left) 715.00
Pitcher, 8½" h., transfer-printed in
black w/scenes & "A Mist view of
the cast iron Bridge over the River
Wear...," a sailor returning home
& "The sweet little cherub that
sits up aloft, will look out a good
berth for poor Jack" & a poem by
Byron on pink splash lustre
ground (crow's foot in bottom) ... 375.00

Pitcher, 8½" h., transfer-printed in black w/scene of "Weirmouth Bridge," reverse w/mariner's compass & verse under spout, on white ground within pink splash lustre borders (spout restoration)...................... 330.00

Plaque, pierced to hang, transfer-printed in copper lustre w/ship scene & trading verse center, pink splash lustre borders, ca. 1810, 8¼ x 10"...................... 125.00

Plate, 7¾" d., "Shepherd Boy," transfer-printed in black w/scene of boy, dog & lamb center, pink lustre border, 1820-40 .... 46.00

Punch bowl, transfer-printed medallions of hunt scenes interior & exterior, pink lustre ground, Staffordshire, 1800-10, 11½" d., 5½" h........................ 450.00

MAJOLICA

Majolica, a tin-enameled-glazed pottery, has been produced for centuries. It originally took its name from the island of Majorca, a source of figuline (potter's clay). Subsequently it was widely produced in England, Europe and the United States. Etruscan majolica, now avidly sought, was made by Griffen, Smith & Hill, Phoenixville, Pa., in the last quarter of the 19th century. Most majolica advertised today is 19th or 20th century. Once scorned by most collectors, interest in this colorful ware so popular during the Victorian era has now revived and prices have risen dramatically in the past two years. Also see HOUND HANDLED PITCHERS, SARREGUEMINES, TOBY MUGS & JUGS and WEDGWOOD.

ETRUSCAN

Small Shell & Seaweed Bowl

Bowl, 5½" d., Shell & Seaweed patt., lavender lining (ILLUS.).....$125.00

Bowl, 9¾" d., Classical series, Pegasus center, vintage grape border, sepia 80.00

Butter pat, Pansy patt., 3" d....................35.00 to 45.00

Butter pat, Shell & Seaweed patt.... 95.00

Cake stand, Classical series, Pegasus center, vintage grape border, sepia 65.00

Coffee pot, cov., Bamboo patt. (hairline on bottom) 175.00

Compote, Grape Leaf patt., 1879 GSH mark 115.00

Creamer, Cauliflower patt......... 150.00

Creamer, Hawthorne patt., tan, unsigned, 5¼" h.............. 48.00

Creamer, Pineapple patt. 85.00

Cup & saucer, Pineapple patt., cup w/lilac lining 125.00

Cup & saucer, Shell & Seaweed patt. 176.00

Shell & Seaweed Humidor

Humidor, cov., Shell & Seaweed patt. (ILLUS.)................... 295.00

Mug, Acorn patt................... 160.00

Pitcher, 5¾" h., Shell & Seaweed patt......................... 195.00

Pitcher, 7" h., w/butterfly spout, Wild Rose patt. 85.00

Pitcher, 8½" h., bulbous, Rustic patt., brown body w/green & lavender leaves................... 190.00

Plates, 5¼" d., Shell & Seaweed patt., pr. 60.00

Plate, 6" d., Cauliflower patt. 65.00

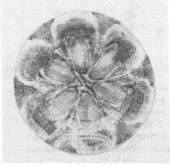

Shell & Seaweed Pattern Plate

Plate, 7¼" d., Shell & Seaweed
patt. (ILLUS.)..............80.00 to 95.00
Plate, 8" d., Bamboo patt. 75.00
Plate, 9" d., Cauliflower patt. 120.00
Serving dish, molded acorns & oak
leaves, green & brown on pale
lavender ground, 1876-90, 12¼"
oval 175.00
Spooner, Bamboo patt. 125.00
Sugar bowl, cov., Bamboo patt.,
6" 95.00
Sugar bowl, cov., Pineapple patt... 150.00
Syrup jug w/original top, Sunflower
patt., realistic sunflower on cobalt
blue ground 245.00
Teapot, cov., Pineapple patt....... 150.00
Teapot, cov., Shell & Seaweed
patt.......................... 275.00
Teapot stand, molded floral medallion center, quill-molded border,
small tab feet underside, pink &
white, 7" d. 175.00
Tray, Begonia Leaf patt.,
9" l.....................60.00 to 95.00
Tray, Oak Leaf patt.,
12" l..................90.00 to 115.00

GENERAL

Majolica Humidor

Ash tray, figural snake charmer
seated on Persian rug w/coiled
snake, 5 x 4 x 3" 55.00
Basket, twig-molded handle, colorful
florals & leaves on sides,
7" l........................... 75.00
Bowl, 8" d., strawberries decor,
marked Wedgwood.............. 110.00
Bowl, 9½" d., leaf-molded rim,
green & cream center 65.00
Bowl, 10¾" d., footed, pierced handles, white & yellow florals &
leaves on red, pink, blue, yellow,
brown & green ground.......... 115.00

Bread tray, Basketweave patt.,
14 x 10½"..................... 189.00
Butter dish, cov., Strawberry patt.
(short hairline) 185.00
Butter pat, Strawberry patt. on grey
& green ground, 3½"........... 12.00
Compote, 9" d., figural crane pedes-
tal, lily pad bowl.............. 325.00
Compote, low, Bird & Fan patt.,
Wedgwood 225.00
Compote, Sunflower & Classical Urn
patt., Samuel Lear, Hanley,
England, 1881 Registry mark 295.00
Creamer, Blackberry patt.,
Chesapeake Pottery mark, 1880's,
4" h.......................... 55.00
Creamer, Corn (or Maize) patt.,
4½" h......................... 70.00
Creamer & sugar bowl, Bird & Fan
patt., cobalt blue ground, pr...... 185.00
Cup & saucer, Blackberry & Basketweave patt. 110.00
Cup & saucer, Wardle Bird & Fan
patt., English Registry mark 55.00
Cuspidor, Corn patt., white kernels
& green stalks, mottled blue
lining 215.00
Cuspidor, lady's, pink & lavender
rose w/dark green leaves on yellow exterior, deep fuchsia pink
lining 225.00
Fish plate, blue fish & white pond
lily within blue border on brown
ground, impressed J. Holdcroft,
1865-1906, 8½" d.............. 110.00
Goblet, entwining multicolored sea
monsters, sirens & centaurs,
England, 10" h. 115.00
Humidor, cov., figural bulldog holding mug of beer, 7" h. (ILLUS.) ... 145.00
Ice cream tray, Fielding Fan patt., 4
shell feet, turquoise bow handles,
magenta cherry blossoms, yellow
& brown scrolls, dragonfly, bird &
butterfly fan on sharkskin ground,
brown ribbed edge, English Registry mark, 14½" l. 250.00
Ink stand, grey inkwell & shell-
shaped pen holder on cobalt blue
base, 6¾ x 5" 125.00
Jardiniere, 3 pedestal feet, deer,
fawn & green leafage on mottled
green & brown ground, pink lining, 8½" w., 9¾" h. 140.00
Match holder, hanging-type, model
of a woven basket w/pendant
acorns & oak leaves, 4 x 3" 195.00
Match holder, figural boy w/basket
of fish standing beside pool 85.00
Models of recumbent deer, each
realistically modeled & colored:
one w/head turned to side & one
w/head erect; both on grassy
mound bases, attributed to Sar-

Recumbent Deer

reguemines, late 19th c., 11¼" l.,
   pr. (ILLUS. of one) 935.00
Mug, Fielding Shell & Fishnet patt...   90.00
Mug, brown handle, tan tree bark
   w/green leaves 45.00
Pitcher, 6¼" h., Wild Rose on Tree
   Bark patt., England.............   65.00
Pitcher, 6½" h., Pineapple patt. 90.00
Pitcher, 7" h., Basketweave & Apple
   Blossom patt., pink lining 60.00
Pitcher, 7½" h., Banks & Thorley
   Basketweave & Bamboo patt.,
   English Registry mark...........   95.00
Pitcher, 8½" h., Fish on Waves
   patt. 130.00
Pitcher, 10" h., figural owl, by
   Morley & Co., Wellsville, Ohio,
   unsigned 165.00
Pitcher, 11" h., figural parrot, pours
   from beak, France 85.00

Owl Planter

Planter, modeled as an owl perched
   on an oblong wooden box w/acorns
   & oak leaves at sides, realistically
   colored owl w/glass eyes, Brown,
   Westhead, Moore & Co., England,
   13" h. (ILLUS.) 2,392.00

Plate, 6" d., cherries & tulips decor,
   Germany 20.00
Plate, 8" d., Bird in Flight patt., turquoise ground, impressed Holdcroft monogram mark, England,
   1865-1906......................   65.00
Plate, 9" d., Pond Lily patt. 65.00
Plate, 9½" d., green asparagus
   spears centered on yellow basketweave ground 82.50

Dog & Doghouse Plate

Plate, 11" d., Shaggy Dog & Doghouse patt., scalloped edge
   (ILLUS.) ....85.00 to 145.00
Platter, 13½" oblong, pale blue center w/segmented lines, waterlily
   buds & lily pad leaves border, J.
   Holdcroft impressed mark 180.00
Sardine box, cov., brown twig handles, pink florals & green leaves
   on white ground, "Sardines" on
   cover 225.00
Spooner, Water Lily patt. 95.00
Sugar bowl, Bird & Fan patt., cobalt
   blue ground 110.00
Syrup pitcher, Maple Leaf patt., roy-
   al blue ground, 7½" h. 165.00
Syrup pitcher w/pewter lid, Hold-
   croft Lily patt., 4¾" h............ 135.00
Syrup pitcher w/pewter lid, Ben-
   nett's Sunflower patt., marked
   "Bennett's Jan. 28, 1873, Patent,"
   7¾" h. 170.00
Syrup pitcher w/original pewter lid,
   barrel-form, grape clusters at
   handle, brown ground 85.00
Teapot, cov., Bamboo patt., English
   Registry mark for 1884 .... 128.00
Teapot, cov., Bamboo & Bow patt.,
   Hampshire Pottery 135.00
Teapot, cov., Bird & Fan patt.,
   large......................... 175.00
Tea tile in wire mesh holder, green,
   brown & yellow puppy & frog on
   white ground, fleur-de-lis border,
   5½" sq. 145.00

MARBLEHEAD

This pottery was organized in 1904 by Dr. Herbert J. Hall as a therapeutic aid to patients in a santarium he ran in Marblehead, Massachusetts. It was later separated from the sanitarium and directed by Arthur E. Baggs, a fine artist and designer, who bought out the factory in 1916 and operated it until its closing in 1936. Most wares were hand-thrown and decorated and carry the company mark of a stylized sailing vessel flanked by the letters "M" and "P." Also see TILES.

Bowl, 8½" d., green matte exterior,
   blue-grey interior $90.00
Bulb bowl, slate grey glaze,
   ca. 1915, 6" d. 77.00

Marblehead Pottery Vase

Vase, 3½" h., squat bulbous form,
   incised leaves & berries, dark
   blue on slate blue ground,
   ca. 1919 (ILLUS.) 522.50
Vase, 4" h., bulbous, lavender
   glaze 125.00
Vase, 4" h., pink glaze 58.00
Vase, 4¼" h., 5" d., inverted bell
   shape, wide neck border of incised red & orange berries &
   green leaves on dark blue exteri-
   or, light blue lining 675.00
Vase, 4½" h., 4 1/8" d., squat cylin-
   der w/wide mouth, incised blue
   berries & green leaves & brown
   tree trunk on oatmeal yellow
   ground, ca. 1915 . . . . 990.00
Vase, 5¼" h., flaring cylinder, grey
   glaze 90.00
Vase, 5¼" h., 3¼" d., wide-
   mouthed expanding cylinder, incised blue flowering trees on
   slate blue, ca. 1915 . . . . 770.00
Wall pocket, acorn-shaped, light
   brown matte glaze 85.00
Wall pocket, cobalt blue glaze,
   large. 100.00

MARTIN BROTHERS POTTERY

Martinware, the term used for this pottery, dates from 1873 and is the product of the Martin brothers-Robert, Wallace, Edwin, Walter and Charles Martin, often considered the first British studio potters. From first to final stages, their hand-thrown pottery was completely the work of the team. The early wares may be simple and conventional, but the Martin brothers built up their reputation by producing ornately engraved, incised or carved designs on their wares. The amusing face-jugs are considered some of their finest work. After 1910, the work of the pottery declined and can be considered finished by 1915, though some attempts were made to fire pottery as late as the 1920's.

Inkwell, birds decor $150.00
Pitcher, 5" h., blue foliage decor . . . 54.00
Pitcher, 5" h., snake handle 80.00
Pitcher, 11" h., incised peacock
   decor 325.00
Tile, fish decor, 3" 125.00
Tobacco jar, incised birds decor,
   ca. 1880 . . . . 185.00
Vase, 2" h., bald crow decor 165.00
Vase, 2" h., smiling crow decor 135.00
Vase, 5" h., grotesque fish decor . . . 200.00
Vase, 7" w., squash decor on red
   lustre ground 165.00
Vase, 10" h., incised palmettes
   decor 155.00
Vase, fish decor, unglazed,
   miniature. 75.00
Vase, frog decor, unglazed,
   miniature. 75.00

MC COY

Coffee Grinder Cookie Jar

Collectors are now beginning to seek the art wares of two McCoy potteries. One was founded in Roseville, O., in the late 19th century as the J.W. McCoy Pottery, subsequently becoming Brush-McCoy Pottery Co., later Brush Pottery. The other was founded also in Roseville in 1910 as Nelson McCoy Sanitary Stoneware Co., later becoming Nelson McCoy Pottery. In 1967 the pottery was sold to D.T. Chase of the Mount Clemens Pottery Co., who sold his interest to the Lancaster Colony Corp. in 1974. Productions of this company are still marked McCoy and Nelson McCoy, Jr. is President of the company known yet as the Nelson McCoy Pottery Co.

Ale set: tankard pitcher & 6 mugs; Corn line, 7 pcs.	$140.00
Bank, barrel-shaped, "Drydock Savings Bank, That's my Bank"	10.00
Cookie jar, Bear w/Cookies in Vest, 1943-45	35.00
Cookie jar, Christmas Tree, 1959	155.00
Cookie jar, Clown in Barrel, 1953-56	30.00
Cookie jar, Clown bust, 1943-49	19.00
Cookie jar, Coffee Grinder, brown, 1961-64 (ILLUS.)	18.00
Cookie jar, Cookie Bank, 1962	37.00
Cookie jar, Cookie Cabin (log cabin), 1957-60	31.00
Cookie jar, Cookstove, black, 1962-64	19.00
Cookie jar, Frog on Stump, 1971	18.00
Cookie jar, Frontier Family, 1970-71	22.00
Cookie jar, Gingerbread Boy, 1961	33.00
Cookie jar, Hobby Horse, 1950-51	42.00
Cookie jar, Kangaroo, 1965	76.00
Cookie jar, Mammy with Cauliflowers, 1939	325.00
Cookie jar, Mr. & Mrs. Owl, 1953-55	28.00
Cookie jar, Pear, yellow, 1952-57	30.00
Cookie jar, Pelican, turquoise or white, 1940-43, each	37.50
Cookie jar, Sad Clown, 1970-71	25.00
Cookie jar, Strawberry, 1955-57	21.00
Cookie jar, Tea Kettle, w/moveable bail handle, antique bronze finish, 1963-64	21.00
Cookie jar, Teepee, 1957-59	97.50
Cookie jar, Woodsy Owl, 1973-74	44.00
Decanter, train engine	35.00
Dog feeding dish, embossed dog figures (3), green, 6" d., 2½" h.	25.00
Jardiniere, floral decor, marked Loy-Nel-Art, 4½ x 6"	40.00
Jardiniere, Pine Cone patt. w/pine cones in relief, green, 6½" h.	30.00
Jardiniere, embossed ferns, cobalt blue glaze, marked Sanitary Stoneware	32.00
Jug, doughnut-shaped, Onyx patt., blue	15.00
Lamp, model of a boot	35.00

Model of frogs, h.p. "Big Daddy," "Mama" & "Baby Frog," set of 3	40.00
Mug, barrel-shaped, green glaze, ca. 1926	7.00
Mug, tankard, stoneware, green	27.50
Novelty dish w/bird, green & brown	15.00
Pitcher, ball jug-type w/ice lip, 3-leaf clover decor on yellow ground	10.00
Pitcher, brown swastika decor	36.00
Pitcher, stoneware, green	60.00
Planter, Aladdin lamp, Olympia patt.	120.00
Planter, model of a bird bath w/yellow bird	7.50
Planter, Scottie dogs (5)	15.00
Planter, Spinning Wheel, 1930's	125.00
Sugar bowl, Pine Cone patt.	8.00
Teapot, cov., daisy decor	25.00
Vase, 9" h., handled, Grecian	25.00
Vase, 10" h., impressed leaf decor, white glaze	10.00

Cuckoo Clock Wall Pocket

Wall pocket, Cuckcoo Clock, 1952 (ILLUS.)	20.00

MEISSEN

Meissen Oval Basket

The secret of true hard-paste porcelain, known long before to the Chinese, was "discovered" accidently in Meissen, Germany, by J.F. Bottger, an alchemist, working with E.W. Tschirnhausen, and the first European true porcelain was made in the Meissen Porcelain Works organized about 1709. Meissen marks have been widely copied by other factories. Some pieces listed here are recent.

Basket, 2-handled, Schmetterling patt. interior, basketwork-molded exterior, handles w/mask terminals enriched in colors, ca. 1735, 10¾" l. (ILLUS.) \$990.00

Bowl, 9" d., deep, scalloped corners & shaped sides, Blue Onion patt., 19th c. ....165.00 to 200.00

Bowl, 12" d., h.p. multicolored center florals & gold-encrusted florals overall 195.00

Bowl, 12 x 8" oval, 2 areas of deep cobalt blue fading to white, overall gold-encrusted floral decor 175.00

Boxes, cov., modeled as chickens, one w/head turned to the back, incised feather markings enriched in brown & grey tones, iron-red wattles, ca. 1740, 3¾" l., pr. (one cover w/hairline crack) 935.00

Butter pat, leaf-shaped, Blue Onion patt., early 20th c. 25.00

Candelabra, 2-light, one w/figure of 5¼" h. boy & other w/girl at stem, overall 8½" h., pr. 425.00

Meissen Chocolate Set

Chocolate set: cov. chocolate pot, cov. sugar bowl, spill vase, 6 plates & 6 c/s; h.p. roses & gilt rims, late 19th c., 21 pcs. (ILLUS.). 850.00

Cologne bottle w/stopper, Blue Onion patt., 4 1/8" h. 165.00

Compote, 5½" d., h.p. florals interior, applied colorful florettes exterior 275.00

Cream jug, cov., h.p. Chinoiserie figures on terraces among flowering plants & palm trees, cover w/birds on branches & knob finial,

scroll handle entirely gilt, ca. 1730, 6¼" h. 3,080.00

Cup & saucer, Imari patt., late 19th c. 110.00

Dish, 5-sided, h.p. blue, brown, green, grey, yellow, iron-red & puce center scene of fishermen (3) in a dory on a river w/large building on the far bank within a brown-heightened worn gilt cartouche, rim w/floral sprigs & a gilt Laub-und-Bandelwerk border, 1745-50, 6" w. 550.00

Dish, h.p. center scene of European & Turkish merchants in an extensive harbor landscape w/trading vessels within an iron-red, puce & gilt Laub-und-Bandelwerk cartouche enriched w/"Boettger Lustre," border w/foliate scrolls in gilt & underside w/three flower sprays in the Kakiemon palette, ca. 1730, 7" d. 2,090.00

Dishes, 1 painted w/goldfinch & woodpecker & other w/two finches perched on a small tree, late 18th c., 11¾" d., pr. 825.00

Dishes, triangular, h.p. birds on branches center, Ozier-molded borders enriched w/insects & butterflies, gilt rims, ca. 1765, 12" w., pr. 660.00

Figure of a Putto seated beside a brown cage containing a hen peeping from between its bars, wearing yellow-lined white drapery pattern w/indianische Blumen, edged in gold & fastened w/a blue strap, on scroll-molded low mound base heightened in gilding & applied w/a florette & green leaves, ca. 1755, 5¼" l. 715.00

Figure of young girl child, wearing a white Empire-style dress & dragging a doll wearing a deep mauve blouse & blue, red & yellow-printed skirt, 6½" h. 275.00

Figures, allegorical depiction of "Africa" & "America:" Africa wearing a grey elephant-head headdress, yellow-lined puce cape & gold-belted skirt of puce, yellow, turquoise blue & iron-red feathers, a wheat sheaf at her left hip; America wearing a headdress, cape & skirt of puce, iron-red, yellow, blue, turquoise & green feathers affixed to "jeweled" gold straps, holding a parrot on her right hand & supporting a bow, a jewel-filled cornucopia & quiver in her left hand; each standing on a mound base molded w/a lion or a crocodile &

gilt-heightened scrolls, ca. 1755 &
1775, 5 7/8" & 6 1/8" h., assembled, pr. (some restoration,
repairs & chips) 1,045.00
Figure group, "Harlequin und Columbine," stylized figures from the
Italian Comedy, Columbine wearing
a ruffled white dress, her companion a brightly-colored diamond-
patterned costume & mask,
10 5/8" h. (minor chips) 1,540.00
Fish platter w/2-piece drain, Blue
Onion patt., ca. 1900,
22½ x 11¼".................... 475.00
Model of a monkey playing the con-
certina, wearing white & blue
trimmed pajamas, seated on a
stool, circular base, 7" h. 935.00

Monkey Band Figures

Monkey band: conductor wearing a
deep claret coat & flowered waistcoat, violinist wearing a straw hat
& pale blue coat, mandolin player
wearing a black hat w/a feather &
a white ruff, female hurdy-gurdy
player wearing a patterned-laven-
der dress sprigged w/pansies, a
trumpeter, a French horn player,
bassoonist wearing a feathered turban, a drummer also playing a
fife, a drummer carrying his kettle
drums on his back, a bagpiper, a
pianist w/his instrument supported
on the back of another monkey, a
flautist, a triangle player, a female
harpist, 3 female vocalists, a bass
fiddle player & a fifer; after
models by J.J. Kaendler, 19th c.,
4¾" to 7 1/8" h., set of 19 (ILLUS.
of bass fiddle player, violinist &
conductor) 4,620.00
Mustache cup, Blue Onion patt. 65.00
Mustard pot w/attached underplate,
cover & ladle, Blue Onion patt.,
2 pcs. 125.00
Pitcher 6" h., Blue Onion patt. 75.00
Plate, 7" d., Little Tables.......... 35.00

Plates, 7" d., various courting
scenes center, reticulated border,
set of 8 .... 345.00
Plate, 9" d., scalloped & fluted rim,
gold encircled medallions of flowers on green ground 150.00
Plate, 9½" d., Blue Onion patt.,
19th c. 52.00
Plate, 10" triangle, high rim, Blue
Onion patt..................... 160.00
Platters, 15 1/8" & 22" l., each
painted w/"deutsche Blumen," &
central floral spray in shades of
pink, rose, orange, blue & green,
rim edged w/various floral sprays
within a gilded border, ca. 1870,
pr. 1,045.00

Meissen Blue Onion Platter

Platter, 21" l., Blue Onion patt.,
mid-19th c. (ILLUS.) 425.00
Sweetmeats, figures in yellow robes
w/"indianische Blumen," seated
on shell-shaped containers on circular bases, 1 w/hinged cover,
8" h., pr. 770.00
Tankard, strap handle w/scroll terminals enriched in puce, bouquets
of "deutsche Blumen" & scattered
flower sprays, gilt metal lid
embossed w/scrolls & flowerheads,
scroll thumbpiece, ca. 1755,
5½" h. 1,430.00
Tankard, cylindrical, Chinoiserie figures on a terrace making tea & at
other pastimes among palm trees
& flowering plants supported by
an elaborate gilt net, trellis &
diamond cartouche enclosing an
oval painted "en camaïeu rose"
w/figures in an extensive river
landscape, scroll & foliage border
outlined in iron-red & suspending
puce trellis panels w/iron-red &
puce foliage, sides w/large sprays
of "indianische Blumen" issuing
from rockwork, rim w/band of gilt
Bandelwerk enclosing net panels,
scroll handle w/foliage terminal
enriched in gilding, hinged silver-

gilt lid w/spiral gadroons & folige
motif inset w/an inscribed gold
coin, thumbpiece w/a mask, ca.
1730, 6¾" h. 17,600.00
Teabowl & saucer, Chinoiserie figures
on terraces among flowering plants
within elaborate iron-red, gilt &
puce "Laub und Bandelwerk" cartouches enriched in Bottger Lustre,
rims w/foliage scrolls in gilt, interior of teabowl w/flowering prunus
issuing from rockwork, ca. 1728
(slight wear to saucer) 1,045.00
Tea caddy, cov., baluster-shaped,
bouquets of scattered flower
sprays, rim of cover & shoulder
enriched in puce, cover w/flower-
head finial, ca. 1765, 4½" h. 715.00
Teacups & saucers, specimen birds
perched on branches, butterflies
& insects, gilt rims, ca. 1740,
pr. 1,155.00
Teapot, cov., painted in colors
w/"indianische Blumen" within
shaped panels reserved on turquoise ground, angular handle &
bird's head spout enriched in iron-
red, yellow & puce, cover similarly painted w/knob finial, ca. 1735,
7½" w. (small chip to interior
rim). 770.00
Vases, 19" h., campana-shaped,
snake handles, wide band of full-
blown seasonal flowers beneath
cobalt blue border, whole en-
riched w/gilding, pr. 3,300.00
Vegetable dish, open, Blue Onion
patt., 7 x 5½" 85.00

METTLACH

Mettlach Plaque

*Ceramics with the name Mettlach were
produced by Villeroy & Boch and other pot-*
*teries in the Mettlach area of Germany. Ville-
roy and Boch's finest years of production are
thought to be from about 1890 to 1910. Also
see STEINS.*

Beaker, printed under glaze man
playing violin, No. 1023/2327,
¼ liter $78.00
Beaker, printed under glaze flute
player, No. 1024/2327, ¼ liter . . . 75.00
Beaker, printed under glaze bar-
maid scene, No. 1025/2327,
¼ liter 65.00
Beaker, printed under glaze scene
of fisherman w/net on beach,
No. 1192/2327, ¼ liter 38.00
Beaker w/handle, advertising,
w/legend "Join Health and Cheer"
over toasting lad & "Hires Root
Beer" below, No. 2327 . . . . 85.00
Pitcher, bulbous, gargoyle mask
spout, cameo relief white bowling
figures on blue ground, No. 2210,
3-liter 585.00
Plaque, pierced to hang, phanolith
cameo relief scene of Cupid
standing on an ornate fountain,
being held by Venus, green
ground, No. 7074, 8" sq. 408.00
Plaque, pierced to hang, etched
barefoot girl carrying basket
depicting Autumn, No. 1607,
11" d. 550.00
Plaque, pierced to hang, etched
scene of the opening of the crypt
of Carl the Great, No.
1048/3036II, 16" d. 575.00
Plaques, etched bust portraits of
bearded man wearing plumed hat
on one & young woman in plumed
hat other, No. 1168 & No. 1411,
17" d., pr. (ILLUS. of No. 1411). . .1,760.00
Plaque, pierced to hang, cameo relief figures of classical man &
women depicting industry on
bluish green ground, No. 2875,
18" d. 775.00

Mettlach Plaque

Plaque, pierced to hang, etched bird
perched on a branch amidst cluster
of budding flowers & foliage,
No. 1676, 19" d. (ILLUS.) 1,320.00
Plaque, pierced to hang, cameo
relief of Trojan warriors on boat,
No. 2442, 19" d. 1,150.00
Plaque, pierced to hang, etched &
relief depiction of "Germania"
center, border of medallions containing arms of German cities,
No. 1386, 20" d. 2,800.00
Punch bowl, cov., pedestal base, re-
lief woman's head under handles,
Oriental lady within relief medallion one side, Grecian lady reverse, tan, brown, green & light
grey ground, light pink interior,
No. 1978, 9½" d., 13" h., 4 liter . . 750.00
Punch bowl w/lid & underplate,
neptune handles, relief dancing
figures on blue ground, No. 2087,
8 liter 585.00

Vase, 11" h., footed, mosaic geo-
metric designs, No. 1289 . . . . 235.00
Vase, 13" h., etched maidens
w/flowers, No. 1749 . . . . 255.00
Vase, 14" h., etched Art Nouveau
leaves, No. 2414 . . . . 275.00
Vase, 14" h., incised seated figures
of Grecian (or Classical) women,
No. 2242 . . . . 395.00
Vases, 14" h., 5½" d., etched
panels of cherubs depicting the
Four Seasons, soft pink lining,
No. 1537, pr. 650.00

MOCHA

Mocha Chamber Pot

*Mocha decoration is found on basically
utilitarian creamware or yellowware articles
and is achieved by a simple chemical reaction.
A color pigment of brown, blue, green or black
is given an acid nature by infusion of tobacco or hops. When this acid nature colorant is
applied in blobs to an alkaline ground color,
it reacts by spreading in feathery seaplant designs. This type of decoration is usually accompanied by horizontal bands of light color*

*slip. Produced in numerous Staffordshire pot-
teries from the late 18th until the late 19th
centuries, its name is derived from the similar markings found on mocha quartz.*

Bowl, 4" h., straight sides w/wide
white band w/blue feathering
seaplants on yellowware $195.00
Bowl, 5" h., Earthworm patt. in
blue, brown & white on pearl-
ware 285.00
Bowl, 6 1/8" d., 2 7/8" h., mar-
bleized blue, white, brown &
green w/feathering seaplants &
brown rim on yellowware (short
internal hairlines) 425.00
Chamber pot, exterior w/white slip
band w/blue feathering seaplants
& brown striping on yellowware
(ILLUS.) 85.00
Creamer, wide white slip band
w/blue feathering seaplants &
brown bands on yellowware,
4 x 5½" 195.00
Mixing bowl, exterior w/wide white
band w/green feathering seaplants & brown striping on yellow-
ware, 14¾" d., 6¾" h. 155.00
Mug, straight sides w/white slip
band w/brown dashes & striping,
2 5/8" h. 235.00
Mug, ovoid, leaf-molded handle,
brown feathering seaplants &
striping on orange, 2 7/8" h. 175.00
Mug, brown feathering seaplants &
brown striping on beige,
3½" h. 225.00
Mug, leaf-molded handle, straight
sides w/wide white slip band
w/embossed design of stripes of
orange, green & chocolate brown,
3½" h. (minor edge wear) 275.00
Mug, dark brown dashes & zigzags,
embossed green bands w/choco-
late brown striping, 5 5/8" h.
(short edge hairline) 335.00

Mocha Mug

Mug, straight sides, wide light blue
band w/black feathering

seaplants & white slip & black
band borders (ILLUS.) 195.00
Mustard pot w/hinged metal lid,
brown marbleized, 3 1/8" d. 85.00
Pepper pot, embossed checkerboard
design in brown, orange & green
on white, 3¼" h. (small flakes on
dome, repair to top rim) 425.00
Pepper pot, black feathering
seaplants & orange striping on
cream, 4" h. (repair to dome
top) 275.00
Pitcher, 5¾" h., embossed dots &
dashes w/white, green, grey,
orangish tan & chocolate brown
striping 550.00
Pitcher, 6 1/8" h., leaf-molded handle, Earthworm patt., bands of
white, light blue & cream
w/chocolate brown design & striping (short hairline in base & spout
repair) 325.00
Sugar bowl, cov., Earthworm patt. &
white striping on yellowware,
4" h. (old chip on lid) 265.00
Tumbler, brown marbleized,
4 1/8" h. 85.00

MOORCROFT

Moorcroft Vase

*This ware is made in a pottery established
at Cobridge, England, in 1913, by William
Moorcroft and now headed by his son Walter.
Several marks have been used through the
years. Earlier pieces bring the higher prices.*

Candlesticks, yellow, purple & pink
fruit on dark blue ground, 4¾" h.,
pr. $110.00
Candlesticks, trees decor, "flambe"
glaze, 6½" h., pr. 475.00
Compote, 5¼" d., 5½" h., high loop
handles at sides, pedestal base,

Florian Ware, stylized florals out-
lined in slip on light ground,
Moorcroft-Mcintyre, 1897-1913 .... 295.00
Cookie jar, crocus decor, silverplate
rim, cover & bail handle 300.00
Dish, rose & blue poppies on green
ground, 11" w., 2" h. 205.00
Pitcher, 8" h., Florian Ware, silver
rim 500.00
Tazza, pomegranate decor on flat
surface, silverplate stem 190.00
Vase, 3¾" h., hibiscus decor, dark
lustre ground 75.00
Vase, 4" h., squat-form, Hazledene
Ware, olive green glaze,
ca. 1914 .... 450.00
Vase, 5½" h., bulbous, fruit decor
on blue ground, 1913-22 .... 150.00
Vase, 7" h., 3½" w., ochre & red
poppies on midnight blue ground,
1921-30 .... 360.00
Vase, 7¾" h., pansies & foliage decor in shades of rose to plum red,
1930-45 (ILLUS.) 175.00
Vase, 8" h., Florian Ware, lilac decor on blue & violet ground 500.00
Vase, 9" h., rolled rim, orchids &
small blue florals on cobalt blue
ground, original sticker, 1930-45 .. 165.00
Vase, 10" h., bulbous, pink hibiscus
decor on dark blue ground,
1916-21 .... 350.00
Vase, 10" h., Florian Ware, ruffled
rim, dark blue florals on light
blue ground, Moorcroft-Macintyre,
1897-1913 .... 350.00
Vase, 10" h., 5¼" w., mottled yellow trees & blue & green hills
w/dark blue highlights on midnight blue ground shaded to
mottled blue & green at rim,
1922-28 ....1,050.00
Vase, 10" h., oviform, large crimson
pomegranate, purple berries &
green-streaked brown leaves
decor, ca. 1918 .... 550.00

Moorcroft Vases

Vases, 10¼" & 9" h., each w/rose,
orange, brown & purple peaches
& grapes & foliage frieze outlined
in sage green slip on cobalt blue
ground, 1921-30, pr. (ILLUS.) 357.00
Vase, 14½" h., 7½" d., yellow, purple, pink & red Wisteria & green
leaves on mottled green top
shaded to deep midnight blue ...2,200.00

NEWCOMB COLLEGE POTTERY

Vase with Moonlit Spanish Moss

*This pottery was established in the art
department of Newcomb College, New
Orleans, La., in 1897. Each piece was hand-
thrown and bore the potter's mark and decorator's monogram on the base. It was always
a studio business and never operated as a factory and its pieces are therefore scarce, with
the early wares being eagerly sought. The pottery closed in 1940. Also see TILES.*

Candle holder, chamberstick-type
w/saucer base & candle nozzle
w/handled drip-pan top, inscribed
"Days Turn is Over - Now Arrives
the Night," signed M.G.S. (Mary
Sheerer) & dated 1903, 5¼" h...$2,310.00
Tile, oak tree w/hanging Spanish
moss decor, shaded blue glaze,
signed A.F.S. (Anna Frances Simp-
son) & dated 1917, 3½" sq.,
framed 800.00
Vase, 3" h., glossy blue glaze 160.00
Vase, 3½" h., blue, green & ivory
swirls, matte finish, signed J.H.
(Julia Hoerner), ca. 1916 .... 300.00
Vase, 4½" h., iris in relief at shoulder, blue matte glaze 875.00
Vase, 5" h., 6½" d., squat bulbous
form, floral band w/touch of yellow around shoulders, matte blue-
green glaze, artist-signed &
dated 715.00

Vase, 5½" h., scenic decor, signed
Sadie Irvine.................... 650.00
Vase, 6" h., black semi-glossy finish, signed A.F.S. & dated
1927 .... 365.00
Vase, 6" h., moonlit scene of trees
covered w/hanging Spanish moss,
ca. 1932...............800.00 to 935.00
Vase, 6½" h., cylindrical, wooded
landscape scene in blue-green,
signed A.F.S 715.00
Vase, 6½" h., 8" d., 2" band of
daffodils & leaves in relief on
medium blue ground, signed
Sadie Irvine.................... 975.00
Vase, 9" h., incised decor, dark
green glaze, signed A.F.S. 700.00
Vase, 9 1/8" h., expanding cylinder,
incised dogwood blossoms at
shoulder, matte blue glaze, artist-
signed 1,045.00
Vase, 10" h., moonlit scene w/oak
trees laden w/Spanish moss,
shades of blue, green & yellow,
signed Sadie Irvine (ILLUS.) 1,525.00

NILOAK

Planter with Pan

*This pottery was made in Benton, Arkan-
sas, and featured hand-thrown vari-colored
swirled clay decoration in objects of classic
forms. Designated Mission Ware, this line is
the most desirable of Niloak's production
which was begun early in this century. Less
expensive to produce, the cast Hywood line,
finished with either high gloss or semi-matte
glazes, was introduced during the economic
depression of the 1930's. The pottery ceased
operation about 1946.*

Ash tray, Mission Ware, tan, rouge,
cream & grey marbleized swirls .. $80.00

Basket, Hywood line, blue glaze,
3½" h. 19.00
Bowl, 5" d., 1½" h., Mission Ware,
marbleized swirls 35.00
Bowl, 5½ x 4", scalloped rim, Hywood line, purple-rose glaze 12.00
Bowl, 8¼" d., low, Mission Ware,
brown, tan & rouge marbleized
swirls 40.00
Candlesticks, marbleized swirls,
9" h., pr. 350.00
Creamer, Hywood line, yellow matte
glaze, 3¼" h. 12.00
Ewer, Hywood line, eagle in relief,
yellow glaze, 10" h. 25.00
Pitcher, 7½" h., Hywood line, geometric florals in relief, white
glaze 35.00
Planter, Hywood line, figure of
young Pan seated on edge of
melon-ribbed bowl, powder blue
glaze, impressed mark on base,
overall 7" h. (ILLUS.) 17.50
Planter, Hywood line, model of a
bullfrog, white matte glaze,
4½ x 5" 20.00
Planter, Hywood line, model of an
elephant, pink or white glaze,
6" h., each 18.00
Planter, Hywood line, model of a
fox, soft rose glaze 12.00
Planter, Hywood line, model of a
polar bear, white glaze 22.00
Planter, Hywood line, model of a
squirrel, blue glaze............. 14.50
Planter, Hywood line, model of a
swan, green glaze, 5" l. 20.00
Toothpick holder, Mission Ware,
marbleized swirls 95.00
Urn, Mission Ware, brown & blue
marbleized swirls, 4½" h. 29.00
Vase, 3" h., Mission Ware, mar-
bleized swirls 37.00
Vase, 4½" h., Mission Ware, red &
brown marbleized swirls 55.00
Vase, 5" h., bulbous, Hywood line,
matte green glaze.............. 35.00
Vase, 5½" h., bulbous, Mission
Ware, rust, blue & cream marbleized swirls 55.00
Vase, 6" h., Hywood line, matte
grey or matte rose glaze, each ... 25.00
Vase, 6" h., Mission Ware, cream,
turquoise blue, rust & brown marbleized swirls ....45.00 to 70.00
Vase, 7" h., 6" d., bulbous, flaring
neck, Mission Ware, brown, blue
& rust marbleized swirls ...70.00 to 90.00
Vase, 8" h., Hywood line, aqua-
green glaze, w/paper label 20.00
Vase, 8" h., waisted, Mission Ware,
orange, brown & grey marbleized
swirls 80.00
Vase, 9" h., Mission Ware, grey,

Niloak Mission Ware

rouge, tan & cream marbleized
swirls (ILLUS.) ....90.00 to 150.00
Vase, 12" h., 5" d., Mission Ware,
marbleized swirls 175.00
Vase, 16½" h., Mission Ware, marbleized swirls 400.00
Wall pocket, Mission Ware, marbleized swirls 250.00
Water bottle, Hywood line, pink
glaze 65.00

NIPPON

Comic Ash Tray

*This colorful porcelain was produced by
numerous factories in Japan late last century and until about 1921. There are numerous
marks on this ware, identifying the producers
or decorating studios. The hand-painted
pieces of good quality have shown a dramat-
ic price increase with the past three years.*

Ale set: 11½" h. tankard pitcher & 4
mugs; relief-molded & h.p. deer
in forest scene decor, applied ant-
ler form handles, 5 pcs. (green
"M" in Wreath mark) $2,150.00
Ale set: 11" h. tankard pitcher & 6
mugs; h.p. owl on branch on
shaded grey to blue bisque finish,
acorn & oak leaf borders, 7 pcs.
(green "M" in Wreath mark)......975.00

Ash tray, relief-molded & h.p. comic
faces, 4" d., each (ILLUS.) 95.00
Ash tray, relief-molded cigar & box
of matches on brown & yellow
ground, 6" 200.00
Ash tray, round w/figural kingfisher
bird perched on edge, 6½" d. 600.00
Berry set: master berry bowl & 6
sauce dishes; h.p. lavender, black
& green florals, gold-beaded rim,
7 pcs. (green "M" in Wreath
mark) 125.00
Berry set: 8" d. master berry bowl &
6 sauce dishes; cobalt blue bor-
der, heavy gold trim, 7 pcs. 135.00
Bowl, 7" octagon, souvenir-type
w/center decal scene of Washing-
ton, D.C., h.p. gold trim 35.00
Bowl, 9" d., h.p. pink strawberries,
wide gold edge 95.00
Bowl, 9¾" d., 2¾" h., scalloped
rim, white enameled beading &
green trim on deep red & overall
gold ground 170.00

Bowl with Raised Gold Decor

Bowl, 11" d., scalloped rim, h.p.
center roundel & floral border
outlined in raised gold &
w/enameled gold beading
(ILLUS.) 235.00
Bread tray, h.p. pink roses on green
border, gold trim, 14" l. 45.00
Cake plate, "gaudy," h.p. lush roses
on cobalt blue ground, gold trim,
11" d. 135.00
Candlestick, square base, tapering
cylindrical stem, raised gold beading on base & candle nozzle, h.p.
scene on stem, 10½" h. (single) . . 235.00
Chocolate pot, cov., "gaudy," red,
pink & green florals on shaded
ground, heavy gold borders
w/raised beading 125.00
Chocolate set: cov. chocolate pot &
5 c/s; h.p. yellow florals & brown
leaves outlined in gold on shaded
brown ground, 11 pcs. 195.00
Coaster, h.p. scene of Dutch man

standing at water's edge & smok-
ing a pipe 25.00
Condensed milk can holder, cover &
underplate, h.p. orange blossom
decor, 3 pcs. 75.00
Condensed milk can holder, cover &
underplate, h.p. pink roses, green
trim, enameled gold beading &
gold finial, 3 pcs. 115.00
Condiment set: cov. mustard pot,
toothpick holder, salt & pepper
shakers & 7" d. tray; h.p. yellow
& blue florals & black diapered
stripes decor, gold trim, 5 pcs. . . . 75.00
Creamer, child's, relief-molded &
h.p. comic face (Rising Sun
mark) . . . . 45.00 to 70.00

Nippon Creamer & Sugar Bowl

Creamer & cov. sugar bowl, h.p.
lush roses on cobalt blue shoulders & lid, raised gold trim, pr.
(ILLUS.) 125.00
Dish, souvenir-type, figural Nipper
seated beside horn, "Colorado
Springs," 4½" d. 185.00
Dish w/gold center handle, h.p. pur-
ple violets decor, gold trim, 8½"
oval (Rising Sun mark) 45.00
Dresser set: 10 x 7" tray, footed
hair receiver & footed powder box
& cover; h.p. pink & yellow blossoms & blue bands decor, gold
trim, 3 pcs. (Rising Sun
mark) . . . . 85.00 to 110.00
Ferner, footed, h.p. red roses &
pink flowers on dark green
ground, ornate gold trim, 7½" d.,
4" h. (Maple Leaf mark) 130.00
Ferner, 4 gold feet, "moriage,"
overall raised green & white slip
beading on soft green blending to
tan & white ground . . . . . . 90.00 to 120.00
Hair receiver, cov., h.p. red & yellow roses decor, gold band at top
& base 110.00
Humidor, cov., h.p. desert scene
w/Arab on camel, palm trees &
village in distance, geometric motif borders, 5½" h. (green "M" in
Wreath mark) 395.00
Humidor, cov., relief-molded & h.p.
Indian on horse decor on tortoise

shell ground, 6" h. (green "M" in
Wreath mark)................... 850.00
Humidor, cov., relief-molded & h.p.
crouching lions decor, 7¼" h.
(green "M" in Wreath mark) 850.00
Humidor, cov., h.p. pink & fuchsia
azaleas w/ornate gold trim,
8½" h...................... 300.00
Ice cream set: 12¼ x 7" platter &
six 5¼" sq. serving dishes; pink,
green & yellow design center &
border, gold trim, 7 pcs. (magenta
"M" in Wreath mark) 110.00
Lemonade set: 8½" h. cov. pitcher &
six 3¾" h. mugs; h.p. white
geese in flight w/gold highlights
on aqua ground, 7 pcs. 600.00

Matchbox Holder - Ash Tray

Matchbox holder & ash tray combination, advertising "Fatima Turkish Blend Cigarettes," 4¼" l. tray,
3¼" h. (ILLUS.) 100.00
Mug, h.p. desert scene w/Arab on
camel in an oasis setting, "moriage" trim, 4¾" h. (green "M" in
Wreath mark)................. 250.00
Mug, "moriage" dragon decor on
shaded brown & tan ground,
5½" h. (green "M" in Wreath
mark) 195.00
Napkin ring, h.p. butterfly & floral
decor, 2" w. (green "M" in Wreath
mark) 65.00
Nut bowl, hexagonal, 2-handled,
relief-molded & h.p. chestnuts &
foliage decor w/"moriage" trim,
8½" w. (green "M" in Wreath
mark) 175.00
Pancake dish & dome cover, h.p.
floral decor, lavish gold trim 150.00
Pitcher, water, 7" h., h.p. red roses
decor on pale green ground, lavish gold tracery (Maple Leaf
mark)........................ 175.00
Pitcher, lemonade, h.p. pink blossoms & green leaves w/"moriage"
trim.......................... 150.00
Pitcher, tankard, "gaudy," h.p. roses
w/ornate gold trim on cobalt blue
ground 350.00
Plaque, pierced to hang, h.p. hunt

scene w/red-coated riders & dogs
crossing a stream in shades of
tan, green & blue, 9" d. (green
"M" in Wreath mark) 200.00
Plaque, pierced to hang, h.p. brilliant blue parrot on a flowering
branch against a green shaded to
white ground, 10" d. (green "M"
in Wreath mark) 250.00
Plaque, pierced to hang, h.p. scene
of Dutch woman & child beside
canal, 10" d. (green "M" in
Wreath mark)................. 275.00
Plaque, pierced to hang, relief-
molded & h.p. moose in forest
landscape setting, 10" d. (green
"M" in Wreath mark) 245.00
Plaque, pierced to hang, relief-
molded & h.p. stag in forest landscape setting, 10½" d. (green "M"
in Wreath mark) 535.00
Plate, 6¾" d., relief-molded & h.p.
child's face 60.00
Plate, 9½" d., open handles, h.p.
florals outlined in gold, raised
gold border (green "M" in Wreath
mark) 120.00
Plate, 11½" d., h.p. red & blue
grapes, ornate gold border
w/beading 115.00
Powder jar, cov., h.p. "googlie-
eyed" Doll Face mold........... 65.00
Punch bowl & base, scenic decor
w/ornate gold trim, 16" d. bowl,
2 pcs........................ 650.00
Rose bowl, 4 gold feet, overall pink
coralene blossoms & green
leaves, gold trim 195.00
Salt & pepper shakers, footed, h.p.
bull in pasture setting, pr. (green
"M" in Wreath mark) 60.00
Smoking set: 7¾" d. tray, cov. humidor w/pipe finial, matchbox
holder & ash tray; h.p. pipe, cigar
& cigarette decor, 4 pcs. (green
"M" in Wreath mark) 385.00
Stamp box, cov., h.p. sailboat scene
(green "M" in Wreath mark) 75.00
Stein, h.p. landscape scene
w/flowering trees & house, 7" h.
(green "M" in Wreath mark) 475.00
Stein, h.p. landscape scene w/coun-
try road, river & cottage, owl &
pine cone borders, 7" h. (blue Maple Leaf mark) 295.00
Sugar shaker, h.p. shaded pink
florals & green leaves w/gold
tracery on deep pink ground,
4½" h. (Maple Leaf mark) 65.00
Sugar shaker, hexagonal, handled,
h.p. gold florals, bows, bells &
beaded swags decor on cobalt
blue shaded to white ground,
5" h. (RC mark) 75.00

Syrup pitcher w/octagonal underplate, h.p. gold grapes & vining
leaves decor, gold trim, 4¼" h.
pitcher, 5¼" w. underplate, 2 pcs.
(green "M" in Wreath mark) 75.00

Tea set: cov. teapot, creamer & cov.
sugar bowl; h.p. violets within
maroon scrollwork highlighted
w/white "moriage" dots & gold
trim, cobalt blue pedestal bases,
handles & borders, 3 pcs. 215.00

Tea set: 4" h. cov. teapot, creamer,
cov. sugar bowl & 6 c/s; figural
red tomato w/green leaves &
brown handles, finials & spout,
15 pcs. (green "M" in Wreath
mark) 485.00

Toothpick holder, h.p. desert scene
w/pyramids & palm trees 45.00

Tray, octagonal, woodland scene
w/pine trees, mill wheel & swans
in pond (green "M" in Wreath
mark) 125.00

Nippon Vase

Vase, 4" h., 2-handled, h.p. airplane
decor, green "M" in Wreath mark
(ILLUS.)....................... 125.00

Vase, 5" h., 2-handled, h.p. scene
of lake, inlet & island w/"moriage" trim, cobalt blue bands
w/lavish gold scrollwork &
jeweled medallions, bisque finish
(blue Maple Leaf mark) 120.00

Vase, 5¼" h., h.p. roses w/gold
trim against "tapestry" textured
ground 525.00

Vase, 6¼" h., 3 gold elephant handles, h.p. shaded orange hibiscus
blossoms & green leaves w/Art
Nouveau style gold crosshatching,
network, bands & beading 165.00

Wine jug w/knob stopper, baluster
form, handled, portrait of monk
drinking, encrusted w/brown
"moriage" grape clusters & vines
on variegated green ground, ca.
1900, 9½" h. 412.50

NORTH DAKOTA SCHOOL OF MINES POTTERY

All pottery produced at the University of North Dakota School of Mines was made from North Dakota clay. In 1910, the University hired Margaret Kelly Cable to teach pottery making and she remained at the school until her retirement. Julia Mattson and Margaret Pachl were other instructors between 1923 and 1970. Designs and glazes varied through the years ranging from the Art Nouveau to modern styles. Pieces were marked "University of North Dakota - Grand Forks, N.D. - Made at School of Mines, N.D." within a circle and also signed by the students until 1963. Since that time, the pieces bear only the students' signatures. Items signed "Huck" are by the artist Flora Huckfield and were made between 1923 and 1949. We list only those pieces made prior to 1963.

Bowl, 3½" w., 1 3/8" h., incised arrows decor $75.00

Bowl, 4½" d., 2" h., light green
glossy glaze, signed Cable (Margaret Kelly Cable) 60.00

Bowl, 7 x 4", incised band of leaves,
2-tone green, artist-signed 410.00

Creamer, rose decor, glossy cream
ground, artist-signed, dated
1956 ....   26.00

Creamer & sugar bowl, glossy black
glaze, pr. 30.00

Figure of cowboy toting gun, 3
colors, signed Julia Mattson 230.00

Honey pot, cover w/bee finial & 3
incised green bands, signed Cable, 4½" h..................... 120.00

Paperweight, turquoise glaze, artist-
signed 65.00

Pitcher, 8½" h., incised flower on
maroon ground 125.00

Teapot, cov., Art Deco style, matte
finish 75.00

Tile, incised leaping gazelle, signed
Julia Mattson, 5" d. 130.00

Tile, incised thunderbird, red &
brown glaze 95.00

Vase, 3" h., deep blue............   70.00

Vase, 4" h., incised tulips decor 110.00

Vase, 5" h., incised pansies decor
on pink matte finish 135.00

Vase, 5" h., mushroom cloud decor
on burnt orange ground, signed
"Huck" (Flora Huckfield) 85.00

Vase, 6" h., cobalt blue glaze,
signed J. Mattson 95.00

Vase, 6¼" h., 2" d., light green
matte finish, signed Cable, dated
Apr. 1929.....................   75.00

Vase, 7¼" h., Art Deco style, red
glaze, signed Julia Mattson 140.00

Vase, 8" h., multiple rows of alter-

nating angular lines, glossy glaze,
artist-signed, 1950 . . . . 295.00
Vase, 9" h., incised Indians on
horseback decor, green glaze,
signed Julia Mattson 300.00

NYMPHENBURG

*A hard-paste porcelain factory that was to
become world-famous was founded in Nymphenburg, Bavaria, Germany, in 1753,
flourished under royal patronage until the late
18th century when it was taken over by the
state, and was leased again to private interests in 1862. This factory is still in production making modern porcelains. The early
productions are quite high-priced.*

Figure of Andromeda, scantily
draped figure clasping a flower
spray to her bosom & w/a flower
in her hair, drapes striped in puce,
gilt & blue, standing on baluster
pedestal marbleized in puce &
ochre, ca. 1763, 6" h. (repair to
rim of pedestal) $1,320.00
Figure of lady in regional costume,
ca. 1946, 8" h. 100.00
Model of a flamingo, w/wings out-
stretched, cream colored, 3¼"
wing span, 6" h. 150.00
Model of German Shepherd dog
reclining, white, 9" l., 5" h. 195.00
Plates, 7½" d., each painted in the
center w/different ripened fruit
reserved on a white ground, within lightly molded narrow green
band edged w/gilding, ca. 1900,
set of 17 (1 chipped) 770.00

OLD IVORY

Old Ivory Pattern No. 28

*Old Ivory china was produced in a great
diversity of table pieces, most of which bear
pattern stock numbers.*

Berry set: master bowl & 4 sauce
dishes; No. 16, 5 pcs. $150.00
Berry set: master bowl & 6 sauce
dishes; No. 75, 7 pcs. 195.00
Bowl, 6½ x 4½" oval, No. 16 . . . . . . 45.00
Bowl, 9½" d., No. 11 . . . . 85.00
Bowl, 10" d., No. 84 . . . . 85.00
Butter pat, No. 16 . . . . 42.00
Cake plate, pierced handles, No. 16,
10" d. 82.50
Cake set: 11" d. master plate
w/pierced handles & four 6" d.
serving plates; No. 75, 5 pcs. 150.00
Cake set: 10" d. master plate
w/pierced handles & twelve
6¾" d. serving plates; No. 16,
13 pcs. 310.00
Celery tray, No. 15 . . . . 75.00
Celery tray, No. 200, 11¼ x 5½" . . . 65.00
Chocolate cup & saucer, No. 11 . . . . . 50.00
Chocolate cup & saucer, No. 33 . . . . . 62.50
Chocolate pot, cov., No. 75 . . . . 275.00
Chocolate set: cov. chocolate pot &
4 c/s; No. 84, 9 pcs. 400.00
Chocolate set: cov. chocolate pot &
5 c/s; No. 16, 11 pcs. 450.00
Cookie jar, cov., No. 11 . . . . 225.00
Cookie jar, cov., No. 15 . . . . 295.00
Creamer & cov. sugar bowl, No. 16,
pr. 140.00
Creamer & cov. sugar bowl,
No. 200, pr. 120.00
Cup & saucer, No. 28 (ILLUS.) 45.00
Cup & saucer, No. 122 . . . . 25.00
Cup & saucer, No. 200 . . . . 37.50
Mustard pot, No. 16 . . . . 90.00
Nappy, No. 16 . . . . 40.00
Nappy, No. 84 . . . . 110.00
Oyster bowl, No.16, 5¾" d. 95.00
Plate, 6" d., No. 10 . . . . 25.00
Plate, 6" d., No. 16 . . . . 23.50
Plate, 6" d., No. 82 . . . . 24.00
Plate, 6" d., No. 200 . . . . 20.00
Plate, 7" d., No. 16 . . . . 25.00
Plate, 7½" d., No. 11 . . . . 23.00
Plate, 7½" d., No. 15 . . . . 30.00

Old Ivory Pattern No. 16

Plate, 7½" d., No. 16 (ILLUS.) 30.00
Plate, 7½" d., No. 75 .... 25.00
Plate, 7½" d., No. 84 .... 33.50
Plate, 8" d., No. 15 .... 25.00
Plate, 8" d., No. 16 .... 37.50
Plate, 8" d., fluted, No. 28 .... 32.50
Plate, 8" d., No. 200 .... 25.00
Plate, 8½" d., No. 16 .... 35.50
Plate, 8½" d., No. 75 .... 45.00
Plate, 8½" d., No. 82 .... 45.00
Plate, 8½" d., No. 84 .... 37.50
Plate, 8½" d., No. 200 .... 35.00
Plate, 12½" d., No. 15 .... 100.00
Platter, 11 x 8", No. 16 .... 40.00
Platter, 11½" l., No. 84 .... 130.00
Relish or pickle dish, No. 15 .... 35.00
Relish or pickle dish, No. 84 .... 34.50
Relish tray, No. 200 .... 52.50
Salt shaker, No. 75 (single) 38.00
Salt & pepper shakers, No. 15, pr... 110.00
Salt & pepper shakers, No. 16, pr... 90.00
Salt & pepper shakers, No. 84, pr... 85.00
Sauce dish, No. 16, 5" d. 15.00
Saucer, No. 84 .... 10.00
Sugar bowl, cov., No. 11 .... 65.00
Sugar bowl, cov., No. 33 .... 35.00
Sugar bowl, cov., No. 84 .... 55.00
Sugar shaker, No. 84 .....165.00 to 195.00
Teacup & saucer, No. 15 .... 40.00
Teacup & saucer, No. 75 .... 40.00
Teapot, cov., No. 84 .... 250.00
Tea set: cov. teapot, creamer, sugar
  bowl & 4 c/s; No. 84, 11 pcs...... 650.00
Toothpick holder, No. 75 .... 100.00
Vegetable dish, No. 16, 10¼" d. ... 60.00

OLD SLEEPY EYE

1952 Steins

Sleepy Eye, Minn., was named after an Indian Chief. The Sleepy Eye Milling Co. had stoneware and pottery premiums made at the turn of the century first by the Weir Pottery Company and subsquently by Western Stoneware Co., Monmouth, Ill. On these items the trademark Indian head was signed beneath "Old Sleepy Eye." The colors were Flemish blue on grey. Later pieces by Western Stone-

ware to 1937 were not made for Sleepy Eye Milling Co. but for other businesses. They bear the same Indian head but "Old Sleepy Eye" does not appear below. They have a reverse design of teepees and trees and may or may not be marked Western Stoneware on the base. These items are usually found in cobalt blue on cream and are rarer in other colors.

Bowl (salt bowl), 6½" d., 4" h.,
  Flemish blue on grey stoneware,
  Weir Pottery, 1903 .... $425.00
Butter jar, Flemish blue on grey
  stoneware, Weir Pottery,
  1903 .... 350.00 to 400.00
Mug, cobalt blue on grey, small In-
  dian head on handle, Western
  Stoneware Co., World War I era,
  1914-18, 4¼" h........ 350.00 to 400.00
Mug, 2 blue bands at top & base,
  printed w/picture of Old Sleepy
  Eye & verse "Here's to the Brave
  Brown Warrior," etc., Red Wing
  Pottery, 5¼" h. 1,200.00
Mug, cobalt blue on white, small Indian head on handle, Western
  Stoneware Co., 1906-37 .... 180.00
Pitcher, 4" h., cobalt blue on white,
  w/small Indian head on handle,
  Western Stoneware Co., 1906-37
  (half-pint) 175.00
Pitcher, 5¼" h., cobalt blue on
  white, w/small Indian head on
  handle, Western Stoneware Co.,
  1906-37 (pint) .... 185.00 to 275.00
Pitcher, 6¼" h., cobalt blue on
  white, w/small Indian head on
  handle, Western Stoneware Co.,
  1906-37 (quart) 215.00
Pitcher, 6¼" h., all yellow, w/small
  Indian head on handle, Western
  Stoneware Co., World War I era,
  1914-18 (quart) .... 750.00 to 950.00
Pitcher, 7¾" h., cobalt blue on
  white, w/small Indian head on
  handle, Western Stoneware Co.,
  1906-37 (half-gallon) .....175.00 to 250.00
Pitcher, 8½" h., cobalt blue on
  white, w/small Indian head on
  handle, Western Stoneware Co.,
  1907-37 (gallon) 265.00
Pitcher, "Standing Indian," w/wig-
  wams, Flemish blue on grey
  stoneware ....850.00 to 1,000.00
Stein, all blue, Western Stoneware,
  7¾" h. .... 500.00 to 750.00
Stein, brown on white, Western
  Stoneware Co., 7¾" h. ..600.00 to 850.00
Stein, brown on yellow, Western
  Stoneware Co., 7¾" h. 600.00
Stein, chestnut brown, 1952, 22 oz.
  size (ILLUS. right) ....275.00 to 350.00
Stein, chestnut brown, 1952, 40 oz.
  size (ILLUS. left) 450.00

Steins made for Board of Directors
of Western Stoneware, 1968 to
1973, each 275.00
Sugar bowl, cobalt blue on white,
Western Stoneware Co., 1906-37,
4" h. . . . . .275.00 to 400.00
Vase, 9" h., Flemish blue on grey
stoneware, Indian head signed,
dragonfly, frog & bullrushes reverse, Weir Pottery Co., 1903 . . . . 265.00
Vase, 9" h., grey stoneware, mold-
ed cattails & dragonfly each
side. 225.00

OWENS

Owens Utopian Vases

*Owens pottery is the product of the J.B.
Owens Pottery Company, which operated in
Ohio from 1890 to 1929. In 1891 it located in
Zanesville and produced art pottery from
1896, introducing "Utopian" wares as its first
art pottery. The company switched to tile
after 1907. Efforts to rebuild after the factory burned in 1928 failed and the company
closed in 1929.*

Ewer, Matt Utopian line, light color
matte finish, artist-signed,
10½" h. $195.00
Humidor, cov., Matt Utopian line,
flattened globular form, light
color matte finish 105.00
Mug, Aborigine line, American
Indian designs 60.00
Mug, Utopian, underglaze slip-
painted cherries, standard brown
glaze, 4" h. . . . . 90.00 to 130.00
Pitcher, tankard, 12" h., Utopian,
underglaze slip-painted florals,
standard brown glaze 185.00
Pitcher, Lotus line, underglaze slip-
painted sandpiper standing on
one leg on light shaded
ground . . . . .185.00 to 250.00

Vase, 3" h., Utopian, 3-footed cuspidor shape, underglaze slip-
painted pansies, standard brown
glaze 75.00
Vase, 4" h., Utopian, 2-handled,
underglaze slip-painted florals,
standard brown glaze, artist-
signed 110.00
Vase, 5" h., Matt Utopian line,
twisted form, artist-signed 140.00
Vase, 8¼" h., Utopian, underglaze
slip-painted large fish (2) on front
& single large fish reverse,
standard brown glaze 650.00
Vase, 10" h., Utopian, corset-
shaped, underglaze slip-painted
pansies, standard brown glaze . . . 120.00
Vase, 10½" h., Utopian, underglaze
slip-painted daisies, standard
brown glaze, signed T.S. (Tot
Steele) 185.00
Vase, 10½" h., Utopian, straight-
sided cylinder w/narrow neck,
underglaze slip-painted kittens,
standard brown glaze, signed
M.T. (Mae Timberlake) 2,500.00
Vase, 12" h., Opalesce Inlaid line,
wavy olive green lines w/gold
outlined in black on light
ground 325.00
Vase, 12½" h., Utopian, ribbed
neck, underglaze slip-painted
orange roses, standard brown
glaze 245.00
Vase, 15" h., Utopian, underglaze
slip-painted autumn leaves,
standard brown glaze 95.00

PAIRPOINT - LIMOGES

*The Pairpoint Manufacturing Company of
New Bedford, Massachusetts, producers of
fine plated silver, as well as glass items, had
china especially made in Limoges, France for
a short period of time. These tastefully decorated porcelains, often enhanced with plated
silver, are in short supply.*

Bowl & cover w/fish finial, 8" w.
across handles, 6½" h., lavish
raised gold chrysanthemum blossoms & foliage on eggshell white
ground, handles highlighted
w/gold striping, signed &
numbered $550.00
Cookie jar w/silverplate rim, cover
& bail handle, h.p. daisy decor on
apricot ground, molded bulbous
base, signed & numbered, 7" d.,
6" h. 295.00
Ewer, football-shaped w/wide trian-

gular spout, applied gold lotus branch handle w/lotus bud & small leaves at junction of upper handle & body, ridged body w/relief-molded & h.p. shaded green lotus leaves outlined in gold enameling, signed & numbered, 9" across handle, 6¼" h. . . . 775.00

Platter, 12 x 8½", Mallard ducks (2) in shades of blue, grey & white in flight across a blazing gold sun on white ground w/gold highlights, further embellished w/a framework of gold tracery around the scene, wide cobalt blue border w/lavish gold trim 485.00

Salt & pepper shakers, h.p. floral decor, 4¾" h., pr. 42.50

Vase, 15" h., applied cobalt blue openwork handles, front w/winged cherub partially clad in a flowing pink drape & carrying a large tray of peonies, reverse w/spray of colorful poppies, each scene within an ornate gold border, whole reserved on a cobalt blue ground shading to powder blue at the rim 1,250.00

PARIAN

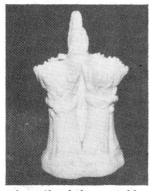

Wheat Sheaf Flower Holder

Parian is unglazed porcelain in the biscuit stage, and takes its name from its resemblance to Parian marble used for statuary. Parian wares were made in this country and abroad through much of the last century and continue to be made. Also see HOUND HANDLED PITCHERS.

Bust of Henry Wadsworth Longfellow, Robinson & Leadbeater, late 19th c., 8" h. $60.00

Bust of Pope Leo XIII, Robinson & Leadbeater, early 20th c., 8" h. 95.00

Bust of beautiful woman on plinth

base, marked "Crystal Palace Art Union - Copeland" & dated 1869, 13" h. 265.00

Bust of a beautiful lady, wearing flowers in her hair, enriched in colors & gilt, draped in pale blue cloak w/flowered sheath, on flaring pedestal base enriched in gilding, impressed Copeland & dated 1881, 18" h. 825.00

Dish, footed, scalloped edge, overall low relief vintage grapes against stippled ground, T. J. & J. Mayer, Dale Hall Pottery, Longport Prize Medal 1851, 8½" d. 90.00

Figure of a boy reading newspaper, wearing oversized coat, glasses & slippers, impressed initials, 10" h. 125.00

Figure of a nude woman w/drapery over her left arm and a turtle at her right foot, oval base, unmarked, 15¾" h. 150.00

Figure of "The Greek Slave," classical nude woman w/one hand resting on a draped pillar, chain of silver metal connecting both wrists, circular base, unmarked copy of Hiram Powers figure, 21" h. 185.00

Flower holder, molded as 3 sheaves of wheat (ILLUS.) 115.00

Pin box, cov., girl w/hen & chicks in relief on lid, 3 5/8" h. 70.00

Pitcher, 5" h., panels of relief-molded hanging game below latticework 55.00

Pitcher, 6½" h., white relief figures on brown ground, Mayer, Dale Hall Pottery, Longport, w/July 2, 1850 English Registry mark 75.00

Pitcher, 7½" h., jug-type, white relief of boy climbing tree one side & boy holding bird's nest reverse, deep rose ground, T. J. Mayer, dated 1850 . . . . 232.50

Pitcher, 7 5/8" h., 5¼" d., jug-type, relief-molded bark & ivy vines on lavender ground, white interior, dated 1847 . . . . 151.00

Vase, 7" h., ovoid, 4 panels of low relief designs, applied grape clusters at shoulder 70.00

PARIS & OLD PARIS

China known by the generic name of Paris and Old Paris was made by several Parisian factories from the 18th through the 19th century; some of it is marked and some is not. Much of it was handsomely decorated.

Paris Vase-on-Stand

Cache pots, square, 4 swan-shaped
feet, painted on 2 sides in polychrome enamel w/view of a
French battle scene or the Place
Vendome or the Place de la Con-
corde, further painted w/two
panels w/military trophies reserved on a "rose Pompadour"
ground, gilt dentil rim, 3rd quarter 19th c., 6¼" h., pr.
(repairs).............................$660.00
Coffee can, golden maidens on deep
blue ground 150.00
Coffee can & saucer, h.p. doe in
landscape decor (hidden hairline
in saucer) 165.00
Dinner service: oval 2-handled cov.
tureen, cov. butter dish, tazza,
10¾" salad bowl, 2 each cov.
round tureens, 2-handled cov.
vegetable tureens, sauceboats
w/stands, cov. mustard pots on
stands, round footed dishes, octagonal footed dishes, 4 round
dishes in sizes, six 10¾" d. plates,
10 oval dishes in sizes, eighteen
8¾" d. side plates & forty-eight
9¼" d. plates; white, enriched
w/band of gilt, ca. 1820,
102 pcs. 7,150.00
Fruit dish, 2-handled, Fuchsia patt.,
gold trim 45.00
Pitcher, 7 1/8" h., ornate handle,
footed, deep magenta ground reserved w/floral bouquet medallion, gold trim 40.00
Soup tureen & cover w/finial, ornate
handles, emerald green bands,
floral cartouche decor 160.00
Tea set: oviform cov. hot water jug,
oviform cov. teapot, oviform milk
jug, 2-handled cov. sugar bowl,
slop bowl & 12 teacups & saucers;
in the Empire taste, sepia vases of

fruit flanked by putti seated on
foliage scrolls & anthemion on
wide bands on salmon pink
ground, beneath gilt borders,
ca. 1820, 29 pcs.................4,147.00
Tureen, cov., 2-handled, gold decor
w/panels of little gold beads,
19th c., 15" wide, 13" h. 300.00
Vase, 6" h., pink, blue & gold
florals........................ 40.00
Vase, 12¾" h., painted w/continu-
ous frieze of couples strolling on
the grounds of a park or a young
boy fishing, applied either side
w/mask handles, ca. 1820 (repairs
to gilding & now mounted as a table lamp)...................... 990.00
Vase-on-stand, flattened ovoid,
satyr's mask handles between
pierced panels, each side w/panels
of brightly colored summer flowers
within scroll-molded borders, on
conformingly shaped base supported on 8 scroll feet, whole enriched
in gilding, 3rd quarter 19th c.,
overall 15¾" h. (ILLUS.) 1,430.00

PATE-SUR-PATE

George Jones Pate-Sur-Pate Vase

*Taking its name from the French phrase
meaning "paste on paste," this type of ware
features designs in relief, obtained by succes-
sive layers of thin pottery paste, painted one
on top of the other. Much of this work was
done in France and England, and perhaps the
best-known wares of this type from England
are those made by Minton.*

Box, cov., white relief cupids on cobalt blue ground, artist-signed,
marked Limoges, 4¼" sq........$185.00
Plaque, pierced to hang, white relief lovely maiden in filmy gown
holding basket in one hand while
picking flowers from a tree w/the

other on deep blue ground,
marked Limoges, 10¼ x 6¼" 250.00
Vase, 4½" h., white relief medallion of a woman in flowing gown
on cobalt blue ground, gold
borders 180.00
Vase, 7" h., 7¾" widest d., white
relief figures of maidens (2) wearing diaphanous gowns on deep olive green ground, George Jones.. 530.00
Vase, 10" h., pilgrim bottle shape,
white relief cupids, one armed
w/a large net & the other w/an
arrow, frolicking amongst tall
weeds & flowers while attempting
to capture butterflies, neck, shoulder, handles & base enriched
w/gilding, Mintons, ca. 1880 ..... 880.00
Vase, 10 3/8" h., white relief maid-
en seated in a swing formed of
entwined vines suspended from
the limbs of a tree on deep brown
ground, rims edged in gilding,
George Jones, ca. 1880 (ILLUS.) .. 935.00
Vase, 25 3/8" h., white relief cupid
judge & court of maidens front,
reverse w/cupids surrounding
trophies of justice, shoulder & base
w/polychrome relief flowerheads &
foliate devices, the whole on a
deep olive green ground, mask
handles, rim & base w/gilt & silvered details, Mintons, dated 1887
& gilt-printed w/plume mark &
"Paris Exhibition 1878" 1,980.00

PAUL REVERE POTTERY

Plate with Dancing Rabbit

*This pottery was established in Boston,
Mass., in 1906, by a group of philanthropists
seeking to establish better conditions for un-
derprivileged young girls of the area. Edith
Brown served as supervisor of the small*

*"Saturday Evening Girls Club" pottery oper-
ation which was moved, in 1912, to a house
close to the Old North Church where Paul Revere's signal lanterns had been placed. The
wares were mostly hand decorated in mineral colors and both sgraffito and molded decorations were employed. Although it became
popular, it was never a profitable operation
and always depended on financial contributions to operate. After the death of Edith
Brown in 1932, the pottery foundered and finally closed in 1942.*

Bookends, rectangular, concave
scene of owls on branch, turquoise blue ground, marked
"S.E.G." (Saturday Evening Girls),
5" w., 3¾" h., pr. (some glaze
crawl).........................$385.00
Bowl, 5" d., blue, marked "S.E.G." &
dated 1921 .... 75.00
Creamer, blue bands & squirrels decor, 2" h...................... 155.00
Creamer, mountains, trees & sky
decor on beige ground, marked
"S.E.G.," 3½" h. 265.00
Creamer, yellow, marked "S.E.G.,"
4" h.......................... 75.00
Egg cup w/underplate, chick decor
on blue ground, marked
"S.E.G." 155.00
Mug, trees around top, yellow
ground, aritst-signed & dated
1915, 4" 700.00
Paperweight, hexagonal shape,
Norse sailing ship decor, artist-
signed & marked "S.E.G." 195.00
Plate, 6" d., green splatter on dark
blue 30.00
Plate, 6½" d., chick border decor,
marked "S.E.G." 88.00
Plate, 6½" d., geese (10) border
outlined in black on deep green-
blue, artist-signed 155.00
Plate, 7½" d., inscribed "Barbara -
Her Plate" on white band, blue
w/white center 240.00
Plate, 7½" d., central roundel
w/dancing rabbit on blue ground
& border inscribed "In the Night
at the Right Time - So I've Under-
stood - It is the Habit of Sir Rabbit
to Dance in the Wood," ca. 1914
(ILLUS.) 4,070.00
Plate, 8" d., dancing chicks & blue
band decor, marked "S.E.G.".... 325.00
Plate, 8½" d., floral border, 3-color
decor, marked "S.E.G." 140.00
Plate, 10" d., green glossy finish,
marked "S.E.G." 48.00
Vase, 7½" h., black & white drip
over dark blue 110.00
Vase, cylindrical, incised stylized
cypress trees against blue & green

Vase by Saturday Evening Girls

landscape, marked "S.E.G." &
dated 1913 (ILLUS.) 3,850.00
Wall pocket, turquoise, 6" h........ 69.00

PETERS & REED

Peters & Reed Tankard Pitcher

In 1897, John D. Peters and Adam Reed
formed a partnership to produce flower pots
in Zanesville, Ohio. Formally incorporated as
Peters and Reed in 1901, this type of production was the mainstay until after 1907 when
they gradually expanded into the art pottery
field. Frank Ferrell, a former designer at the
Weller Pottery, developed the "Moss Aztec"
line while associated with Peters and Reed
and other art lines followed. Though unmarked, attribution is not difficult once
familiar with the various lines. In 1921, Peters
and Reed became Zane Pottery which continued in production until 1941.

Candle holders, Pereco line, green
   semi-matte finish, pr............. $30.00
Jug, single handle, bulbous,
   sprigged on grape clusters & vine
decor, standard glossy brown
   glaze 52.50
Loving cup, 3-handled, sprigged on
   lion's head & florals, standard
   glossy brown glaze............. 165.00
Mug, sprigged on grape clusters &
   leaves decor, standard glossy
   brown glaze, 5½" h. 35.00
Pitcher, 4" h., sprigged on man
   w/banjo decor, standard glossy
   brown glaze 35.00
Pitcher, tankard, 13½" h., sprigged
   on grapevine & grape clusters,
   standard glossy brown glaze
   (ILLUS.)....................... 140.00
Rose bowl, 3-footed, sprigged on
   wreath decor, standard glossy
   brown glaze 40.00
Vase, 4" h., 6" w., hexagonal
   w/pinched sides, sprigged on floral medallion decor, standard
   glossy brown glaze............. 60.00
Vase, 5½" h., wide mouth, Landsun
   line, blended glaze............. 40.00
Vase, 8½" h., Shadow ware, blue &
   cream drip glaze on olive green .. 38.00
Wall pocket, Moss Aztec line,
   grapes decor, signed Ferrell,
   7½" h..................40.00 to 55.00

PEWABIC POTTERY

Mary Chase Perry (Stratton) and Horace J.
Caulkins were partners in this Detroit, Michigan pottery. Established in 1903, Pewabic
Pottery evolved from their Revelation Pottery – "Pewabic" meaning "clay with copper
color" in the language of Michigan's Chippe-
wa Indians. Caulkins attended to the clay formulas and Mary Perry Stratton was the
artistic creator of forms & glaze formulas,
eventually developing a wide range of colors
for her finely textured glazes. The pottery's
reputation for fine wares and architectural
tiles enabled it to survive the depression
years of the 1930's. After Caulkins died in
1923, Mrs. Stratton continued to be active in
the pottery until her death, at age ninety-four,
in 1961. Her contributions to the art pottery
field are numerous.

Ash tray, iridescent glaze $110.00
Bowl, 4" d., 2" h., iridescent glaze.. 150.00
Tile, embossed fish, 3" sq. 100.00
Vase, 12" h., light green leaves in
   relief on green ground, Maple Leaf
   mark, probably by Mary Chase
   Perry 2,500.00
Vase, 12¼" h., paneled ovoid, stiff
   upright acanthus leaves in relief
   on sides, iridescent glaze 4,950.00

PHOENIX BIRD or FLYING TURKEY

Phoenix Bird Bowl

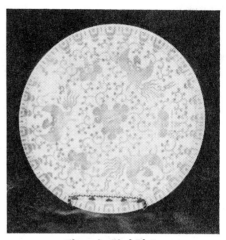

Phoenix Bird Plate

The phoenix bird, a symbol of immortality and spiritual rebirth, has been handed down through Egyptian mythology as a bird that consumed itself by fire after 500 years and then rose again, renewed from its ashes. This bird has been used to decorate Japanese porcelain, designed for export, for more than 100 years. The pattern incorporates a blue design of the bird, variously known as the "Flying Phoenix," the "Flying Turkey" or the "Ho-o," stamped on a white ground. It became popular with collectors because there was an abundant supply since the ware was produced for a long period of time. Pieces can be found marked with Japanese characters, with a "Nippon" mark, or a "Made in Japan" or "Occupied Japan" mark. Though there are several variations to the pattern and border, we have lumped them together since values seem to be quite comparable. A word of caution to collectors, Phoenix Bird pattern is still being produced.

Bowl, 4½" w., Phoenix Bird	$6.00
Bowl, 5" d., Phoenix Bird, marked "Made in Japan" (ILLUS.)	7.00
Bowl, soup, 7" d., Phoenix Bird	15.00
Bowl, 8" d., Phoenix Bird	8.00
Butter pat, Phoenix Bird	13.00
Casserole, cov., Phoenix Bird, 6¼ x 4½" oval, 2½" h.	47.50
Chocolate pot, cov., Flying Turkey . .	85.00
Coffee pot, cov., Flying Turkey, unmarked, 7½"	45.00
Creamer, Phoenix Bird	10.00
Creamer, Phoenix Bird, marked "Nippon"	24.00
Creamer, Flying Turkey	15.00
Creamer & cov. sugar bowl, Phoenix Bird, pr.	30.00
Cup & saucer, Flying Turkey	9.00
Cup & saucer, Phoenix Bird	12.00
Egg cup, Phoenix Bird, 2¼" h.	7.50
Egg cup, double, Flying Turkey	12.50
Pitcher, milk, 4 5/8" h., Flying Turkey	25.00
Plate, 7¼" d., Flying Turkey	5.50

Plate, 8¼" d., Phoenix Bird, marked "Made in Japan" (ILLUS.)	20.00
Plate, dinner, 10" d., Phoenix Bird . .	35.00
Platter, 12", Phoenix Bird	25.00
Salt & pepper shakers, Phoenix Bird, pr.	12.50
Salt tub, handled, Flying Turkey	15.00
Sugar bowl, cov., loop handles, Phoenix Bird, 4" h.	15.00
Teapot, cov., Flying Turkey, individual size	35.00
Tumbler, Flying Turkey	10.50
Tumbler, Phoenix Bird, 3" h.	12.00
Vegetable dish, cov., Flying Turkey, marked "Noritake"	55.00

PICKARD

Pickard Marks

Pickard, Inc., making fine hand-decorated china today in Antioch, Ill., was founded in Chicago in 1894 by Wilder A. Pickard. The company now makes its own blanks but once bought them from other potteries, primarily from the Havilands and others in Limoges, France.

Bowl, 7" d., 2" h., gold scalloped rim & footed base, strawberry decor, artist-signed, Haviland blank	$135.00
Bowl, 8¼" d., footed, h.p. hazelnut decor, ca. 1898	175.00
Bowl, 9" d., acorns on rust ground, heavy gold trim, artist-signed	92.50

Bowl, 9¾" d., 3" h., interior & exterior decor of purple berries w/green & gold leaves on shaded creamy yellow to rust & green ground, wide gold interior band, artist-signed, 1898-1904 mark 180.00

Bowl, fruit, 10" d., poppies & leaves decor, artist-signed, 1898 mark ... 135.00

Bowl, 10" d., yellow & lavender grapes w/green, lavender & aqua tendrils & leaves on lemon yellow to lavender ground, scalloped gold edges outlined in red, artist-signed & dated 1905 .... 200.00

Celery tray, boat-shaped, clusters of grapes & leaves decor, gold trim, signed Challinor, T. & V. Limoges blank, 13½" l. 130.00

Creamer & open sugar bowl, large h.p. roses w/gold trim on brown ground, pr. 90.00

Creamer & open sugar bowl, birds & florals w/gold trim, artist-signed, pr. 70.00

Dish, heart-shaped, orchids & leaves w/gold stems & wide gold border, artist-signed, 1905 mark, 5½ x 4" 110.00

Marmalade jar, cov., h.p. blackberries decor, 7" h. 78.00

Mayonnaise bowl & underplate, h.p. butterflies interior, peach & gold pearlized exterior, 1912 mark 95.00

Mug, berries decor, gold handle & rim, artist-signed, 5½" h. 150.00

Perfume bottle w/gold stopper, yellow primroses on shaded ground, Limoges blank, artist-signed, 1905 .... 195.00

Pitcher, milk, 4½" h., gold handle, pansies decor, artist-signed 195.00

Pitcher, lemonade, 7¼" h., cherry clusters w/gold trim, artist-signed 195.00

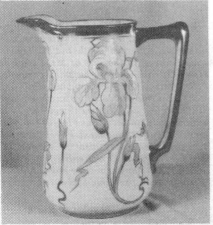

Pickard Pitcher

Pitcher, 7¾" h., gold rim & handle, h.p. stylized yellow iris on iridescent shell pink ground, 1905-10 mark (ILLUS.) 235.00

Pitcher, 10" h., tulips decor, artist-signed 265.00

Plate, 7½" d., h.p. currants decor, 1898 mark 75.00

Plate, 8½" d., moonlight pavilion scene, artist-signed, 1912-19 ..... 145.00

Plate, 8½" d., gold rim, poppies w/gold tracery, signed Challinor .. 159.00

Plate, 8¾" d., stylized leaf decor on gold ground, artist-signed 95.00

Plates, 11" d., each w/a different 7" d. garden scene center, ornate gold border, signed E. Challinor, set of 12 ....3,500.00

Powder box, cov., roses decor, artist-signed, 4" d. 95.00

Salt & pepper shakers, overall gold-etched design, pr. 26.00

Salt & pepper shakers, h.p. florals on pearlized ground, 1905 mark, pr. 110.00

Stein, light russet grapes, leaves & shadowy figures on shaded deep russet ground, heavy gold trim on handle, rim & flared base, artist-signed & dated 1898, 4½" d., 6" h. 195.00

Teapot, cov., tapered body, overall gold-etched design, 9" h. 135.00

Tea set: cov. teapot, creamer & cov. sugar bowl; h.p. florals w/ornate gold & silver trim, 1912-19, 3 pcs. 185.00

Tea set: cov. footed teapot w/dolphin's head spout, tankard creamer, cov. sugar bowl & 11" d. tray; turquoise blue, pink & rose stylized tulips & gold tracery on pearlized ground, gold trim at rims, handles & feet, artist-signed, 4 pcs. 650.00

Vase, 6" h., 2-handled, lake scene on matte finish ground, Nippon blank, signed Challinor 265.00

Vase, 7 1/8" h., 2 gold handles, moon & palm tree scene, artist-signed 375.00

Vase, 7½" h., band of brilliant blue peacocks within gold beading on gold textured ground, aritst-signed & dated 1912 .... 200.00

Vase, 7¾" h., cylindrical, moonlit lake & pine trees scene, Nippon blank, signed Challinor 245.00

Vase, 9" h., large golden chrysanthemums & green leaves on soft turquoise blue shaded to green, golden yellow, pink & deep rose, gold trim, artist-signed, 1898 ..... 295.00

Vase, 11" h., cylindrical, Art Nouveau style partially-clad beautiful maiden w/long red hair dancing w/butterfly poised on one out-stretched hand on creamy white ground, artist-signed 235.00

Vase, 11½" h., scene of birch trees, lake & roses bushes in matte pastels, signed Challinor 400.00

Vase, 12" h., Phoenix birds & ornate gold decor on cobalt blue ground, artist-signed 225.00

PICTORIAL SOUVENIRS

These small ceramic wares, expressly made to be sold as a souvenir of a town or resort, are decorated with a pictorial scene which is usually titled. Made in profusion in Germany, Austria, Bavaria, and England, they were distributed by several American firms including C.E. Wheelock & Co., John H. Roth (Jonroth), Jones, McDuffee & Co., Stratton Co., and others. Because people seldom traveled in the early years of this century, a small souvenir tray or dish, picturing the resort or a town scene, afforded an excellent, inexpensive gift for family or friends when returning from a vacation trip. Seldom used and carefully packed away later, there is an abundant supply of these small wares available today at moderate prices. Their values are likely to rise.

Creamer, "Court House, Medina, Ohio" scene on cobalt blue ground $18.00

Creamer, "Savin Rock, Lighthouse Ferry," cobalt blue, Germany, 2 x 3 x 4¼" 25.00

Creamer, "State Normal School, DeKalb, Ill.," 4½" h. 19.00

Model of a boot w/curled toes, "Public Library of Canton, Ohio," w/view of Canton, ornate, 4" h. ... 27.00

Model of a teddy bear w/bean pot & another teddy bear alongside, "Souvenir of Savin Rock," 2¼ x 2¼ x 4" 65.00

Mug, "State Capitol, Helena, Montana" 21.00

Pitcher, 3½" h., "Washington Hotel, Seattle, Washington" transfer scene, Wheelock-Dresden 22.00

Plate, 8¼" d., "Independence Hall, Philadelphia," openwork rim w/gilt floral swags all around, Bavarian blank 18.00

Plate, 8¼" d., "Prospect Point, Ni-agara Falls," openwork border w/heavy gilt, Germany, made for N.M. Kirshner, Buffalo, N.Y. 18.00

Plate, 10" d., "Williamsburg" scene, pink, Adams-Jonroth 22.50

Plate, 10¼" d., "White House" center scene, 2" border features White House rooms 12.00

Plate, 10½" d.,"1949 Easter Fires of Fredericksburg, Texas," Vernon Kilns 24.50

Plate, 10¾" d., "State Capitol, Virginia" scene, green & yellow transfer, 2" border features historical sites 12.00

Plate, 11" d., "St. Louis Cathedral, New Orleans, Louisiana" scene, blue & white, Crown Ducal 14.00

Plate, "Cottage Sanitarium, Saranec Lake, New York" scene, Hampshire Pottery.................... 30.00

Plate, "Iowa State Capitol" scene ... 22.00

Plate, "Niagara Falls" scene........ 39.00

Plate, "Normal School, Newark, N.J.," pierced border for ribbon .. 22.50

Plate, "Sailing Close, Clarendon, New York," centennial 1910, scene by Christy, Dresden 27.50

Sugar bowl, open, "Barbeton High School & Grammer School," cobalt blue, 1906 .... 38.00

Teapot, cov., "Jasper Park Lodge, Canadian National Railways," w/picture of lodge 125.00

Toothpick holder, "High School, Watertown, S.D.," Wheelock 35.00

Tray, "Capitol Building Washington, D.C.," Nippon Spoke mark, 12¾" 40.00

Whimsey, model of a canoe, "St. Petersburg, Florida," fishing dock scene, cobalt blue ground, Germany, 5" l. 12.00

PISGAH FOREST

Walter Stephen experimented with making pottery shortly after 1900 with his parents in Tennessee. After their deaths in 1910, he eventually moved to the foot of Mt. Pisgah in North Carolina where he became a partner of C.P. Ryman. Together they built a kiln and a shop but this partnership was dissolved in 1916. During 1920, Stephen again began to experiment with pottery and by 1926, had his own pottery and equipment. Pieces are usually marked and may also be signed "W. Stephen" and dated. Walter Stephen died in 1961 but work at the pottery still continues, although on a part-time basis.

Ash tray, crystalline glaze $165.00

Beaker, pink & blue matte finish, 4¼" h........................... 40.00

Cup & saucer, yellow glaze, dated
1940 .... 100.00
Flower pot, turquoise & purple
glaze, dated 1942, 6" h. 40.00
Jar, cov., blue glaze, signed
"Stephen - 1946," 4" h. 28.00
Jug, cobalt blue glaze, signed
"Stephen - 1934," 14" h..........1,100.00
Mug, cameo-like white relief cov-
ered wagon scene on blue, signed
"Stephen" 100.00
Mug, cameo-like white relief scene
of fiddler, etc., on green......... 180.00
Pitcher, 4" h., bulbous, turquoise
crackle glaze exterior, pink
interior......................... 30.00
Pitcher, 8" h., green glaze 35.00
Pitcher, 8¾" h., turquoise shaded to
maroon glaze, dated 1940........ 65.00
Teapot, cov., cameo-like white relief
scene of covered wagon, Indians
& teepee, dated 1930 .... 710.00
Tea set: cov. teapot, creamer & cov.
sugar bowl; mottled blue & green
glaze exterior, orchid interior,
3 pcs. 95.00
Vase, 4¾" h., pink glaze, dated
1940 .... 48.00
Vase, 5¼" h., blue crystalline
glaze 215.00
Vase, 5½" h., 3-handled, green
glaze, dated 1928 .... 65.00
Vase, 5½" h., flared top, turquoise
crackle glaze exterior, ivory
interior........................ 40.00
Vase, 6½" h., 4½" d., turquoise
glaze, exterior, pink interior, dated 1940 .... 30.00
Vase, 7" h., turquoise crackle glaze,
dated 1942 .... 30.00
Vase, 8" h., cameo-type white relief
covered wagon scene around collared neck, mottled light green,
signed "Stephen"................ 500.00
Vase, 8¾" h:, baluster form, blue &
green crystalline glaze, dated
1943 .... 187.00

PRATT WARES

*The earliest ware now classified as Pratt
wares was made by Felix Pratt at his pottery
in Fenton, England from about 1810. He
made earthenware with bright glazes, relief
sporting jugs, toby mugs and commercial
pots and jars whose lids bore multicolored
transfer prints. The F. & R. Pratt mark is mid-
19th century. The name Pratt ware is also applied today to mid and late 19th century
English ware of the same general type as that
made by Felix Pratt.*

Pratt Ware Plaque

Compote, oval, handled, "Highland
Music," acorn border $275.00
Cup plate, relief-molded Dalmation
dog w/black enameled spots, blue
& green border stripes,
3 1/8" d. 55.00
Figure of Flora, Staffordshire, 1790,
8" 190.00
Pitcher, 8" h., relief-molded boys (2)
playing cards, Staffordshire,
1820 .... 105.00
Pitcher, milk, relief-molded & painted vintage & fishscale design
(chip on handle) 175.00
Plaque, circular, molded in relief
w/Bacchus drinking from a glass,
Venus caressing Cupid, Ceres
seated in the background wearing
feather headdress & holding a
cornucopia filled w/fruit & flowers, scantily draped figures seated
on grass mound, enriched in blue,
brown & ochre, raised border
molded w/foliage & enriched in
brown, yellow & blue, top surmounted by an urn suspending foliage swags, base w/foliage, ca.
1800, 11" l. (ILLUS.).............. 605.00
Plate, 8½" d., lavender, blue &
green multiscenic view of 1876
Philadelphia Exposition, marked
"Keer's China Hall, 1218 Chestnut
St., Philadelphia" & "Philadelphia
Exhibition 1876" 90.00
Plates, 8¾" d., color-printed scenes
of knife grinder & checker game,
typical border, pr............... 110.00
Plate, 9" d., color-printed scene of
"Haddon Hall" center, classical
figures border 65.00

Plate, 9½" d., 2-handled, center
scene of rural landscape w/castle
in background, deep plum & gold
stencil-work border.............. 70.00
Plate, 9½" d. plus tab handles,
plum colored band surrounding
center scene of cattle by a
stream, gold stenciled border,
gold rim....................... 75.00
Tazza, "Spanish Dancers," scrolled
gold border, 1850, 11".......... 160.00
Tea caddy, embossed comic figures
of men & women, 4 5/8" h. (lid
missing, short hairline)......... 130.00
Vase, 6½" h., modeled as 5 fingers,
slender necks molded w/foliage,
lower part painted w/stylized
flowers in brown, blue & ochre,
ca. 1790 (small chip repair to
base)......................... 550.00

QUIMPER

Henriot Quimper Tray

*This French earthenware pottery has been
made in France since the end of the 17th century and is still in production today. Because
the colorful decoration on this ware, predomi-
nently of Breton peasant figures, is all hand
painted and each piece is unique, it has become increasingly popular with collectors in
recent years. Most pieces offered today date
from about the mid-19th century to the
present. Modern potteries continue to operate today and contemporary examples are
available in gift shops.*

Bowl, footed oval, 10-scallop rim,
reverse panel of Breton peasants
front & floral panel reverse,
scrolling floral & foliate sprays
overall, H.B. Quimper, early
20th c. $500.00
Cake stand, pedestal base, Breton
peasant man decor, blue trim,
Henriot Quimper, after 1922,
9½" d., 4½" h. 140.00
Console bowl, dolphin handles, Breton peasant man & woman decor,
Porquier Beau mark, 17" l....... 750.00
Cup & saucer, 6-sided, Breton peas-

ant woman & foliage decor, Henriot Quimper, after 1922........ 55.00
Cup plate, Breton peasant woman
decor, yellow ground w/blue &
red-orange trim, H.B. Quimper,
1883-1910.................... 27.50
Egg cup w/attached underplate,
Henriot Quimper 48.00
Figure, peasant woman bent under
heavy burden, Grand Maisson certificate, early 20th c., 5 x 5½"
base, 8" h. 475.00
Figure of peasant girl w/umbrella,
by the artist J. Bachelet, H.R.
Quimper, 1904-22, 10" h. 285.00
Figure group, Breton nuns (3) carry-
ing banner, by the artist J.E.
Sevellec, Henriot Quimper,
4 x 6"........................ 800.00
Figure group, "Les Trois Commeres"
(three gossiping women), by the
artist L.H. Nicot, 1920-30, Henriot
Quimper 800.00
Inkwell & cover w/acorn finial, hat
shape w/rolled rim, Henriot
Quimper, after 1922............ 95.00
Pitcher, 7½" h., blue & brown
florals on pale blue ground
w/blue, pink & yellow bands,
Henriot Quimper, after 1922 ..... 125.00
Pitcher, 8" h., dusty blue florals al-
ternating w/red & blue petals,
H.B. Quimper, late 19th c. 210.00
Plate, 5¼" d., blue florals & green
fern-like stems on yellow, H.B.
Quimper 45.00
Plate, 6½" hexagon, blue & red
florals, Henriot Quimper 45.00
Plate, 7¼" d., geometric design in
dark blues on yellow ochre, H.B.
Quimper 45.00
Plate, 8¼" d., peasant man on yel-
low ground w/blue bands, Henriot
Quimper 40.00
Plate, 9¼" d., peasant man decor,
H.B. Quimper, before 1913....... 85.00
Plate, naive decor & "Smoke Drifts -
Friendship Stays" in French
script 75.00
Salt dip, figural peasant man
flanked by baskets, H.B. Quimper,
6½" h........................ 120.00
Teapot, cov., long spout, peasant
man w/hat & flowing scarf, green
pants & staff one side & geometric
florals reverse, Henriot Quimper,
8" h. 235.00
Teapot, cov., short spout, peasant
man wearing orange jacket decor,
Henriot Quimper 145.00
Tray, pierced handles, peasant
woman holding basket & umbrella
decor, blue & green trim, H.B.
Quimper, 9¾ x 6½" 110.00

Tray, cut corners, peasant man &
  woman decor, red, blue & green
  trim, Henriot Quimper, 9¾ x 6½"
  (ILLUS.)......................... 95.00
Vase, 15¼" h., long side handles,
  Odetta line, portrait decor,
  Henriot Quimper 165.00
Wall pocket, peasant woman hold-
  ing bouquet, H.R. Quimper,
  10½" h......................... 355.00

REDWARE

Redware Covered Jar

*Red earthenware pottery was made in the
American colonies from the late 1600's.
Bowls, crocks and all types of utilitarian
wares were turned out in great abundance to
supplement the pewter and handmade treenware. The ready availability of the clay, the
same used in making bricks and roof tiles, ac-
counted for the vast production. The lead-
glazed redware retained its reddish color,
though a variety of colors could be obtained
by adding various metals to the glaze. Interesting effects occurred accidentally
through unsuspected impurities in the clay
or uneven temperatures in the firing kiln
which sometimes resulted in streaks or mottled splotches. Also see SHENANDOAH
VALLEY POTTERY and SLIP WARE.*

Bean pot, bulbous, w/handle, unglazed outside, rust glaze on handle & interior, ca. 1830 .... $45.00
Bowl & domed cover w/knob finial,
  3 7/8" h., earred side handles,
  greenish glaze 280.00
Bowl, 15" d., 6" h., flaring sides,
  applied rim handles, clear glaze
  w/yellow slip wavy lines & brown
  & green splotches 195.00
Bundt pan, green glaze over mottled
  light rust, 7" d. 130.00
Bundt pan, manganese decorated
  sponge top & border, 7" d. 85.00

Charger, coggled edge, yellow slip
  wavy lines & "Plump," clear glaze
  w/brown flecks, 12" d..........1,850.00
Charger, coggled edge, mottled
  brownish amber glaze w/yellow
  slip chicken, dots, wavy lines &
  date "1808," 12" d. 2,200.00
Collander, 3 applied feet & rim handles, clear glaze w/running brown
  flecks, 9¾" d., 7" h. 30.00
Cookie mold, stylized bird & flowers, reverse w/incised compass
  design & dated "1701," worn clear
  glaze, Pennsylvania, 6½" d. (old
  edge chips) 550.00
Cup, brown glaze, 2 x 2½" 75.00
Flower pot, flaring sides, tooled
  bands & stripes of yellow slip,
  6" h........................... 160.00
Jar, semi-ovoid, green glaze
  w/orange spots, 4¼" h. 75.00
Jar, cov., applied rope-twist handles, brownish red glaze, 8¼" d.,
  6" h........................... 200.00
Jar, cov., ovoid, amber glaze
  w/running brown, minor lid chips,
  10¼" h. (ILLUS.) 375.00
Jug, ovoid, applied strap handle,
  (indistinct) incised inscription at
  shoulder, greenish amber glaze,
  4 1/8" h. 75.00
Jug, ovoid, applied handle, protruding lip, incised line at shoulder,
  brownish black metallic glaze,
  6¼" h......................... 200.00
Jug, ovoid, ribbed strap handle,
  tooled lines at shoulder, dark
  brown glaze, bottom incised "18,"
  8½" h......................... 165.00
Jug, slightly ovoid w/standing
  straight sided collar, orange
  splotches on olive green, Gonic,
  New Hampshire, early 19th c.,
  4½" base d., 9" h. 605.00
Jug, ovoid body w/rolled rim,
  applied ribbed handle, mottled
  brown under clear glaze, early
  19th c., 10½" h................1,540.00
Model of a Spaniel-type dog in seated position on oblong base, free-
  standing front legs, dark reddish
  brown glaze, Greensboro/New
  Geneva, 9" h. (in the making
  hairline between dog & base) 100.00
Mug, ovoid w/slightly flaring rim,
  applied handle, clear glaze
  w/brown sponging, 2 5/8" h...... 185.00
Pie plate, coggled edge, sgraffito
  bird, flowers & "Drawn by T.B.,"
  Telford, Pa.," clear glaze
  w/brown sponging, 8¾" d. (minor
  edge chips) 500.00
Pie plate, coggled edge, 3 line yellow slip decor, 9¾" d........... 450.00

Pitcher, 4½" h., ovoid, dark brown
glaze 85.00
Pitcher, 6 3/8" h., bulbous body
w/high flaring spout, clear lead
glaze w/black speckling 300.00
Pitcher, 7 7/8" h., strap handle,
tooled line at shoulder, brown
flecks, amber dots & running
black w/greenish highlights
(minor edge chips) 375.00
Preserving jar, cream slip w/brown
& rust marbleizing below clear
glaze, white slip interior,
6¼" h........................ 350.00
Sugar bowl & domed cover w/flat-
tened ball finial, slightly flared
rim, applied handles, marbleized
white w/black slip on a red
ground, Pennsylvania, 1st half
19th c., 12" h................. 3,400.00

RED WING

Red Wing Union Stoneware Crock

*Various potteries operated in Red Wing,
Minnesota, from 1868, the most successful being the Red Wing Stoneware Co., organized
in 1878. Merged with other local potteries
through the years, it became known as Red
Wing Union Stoneware Co. in 1894, and was
one of the largest producers of utilitarian
stoneware items in the United States. After
a decline in the popularity of stoneware
products, an art pottery line was introduced
to compensate for the loss and this was
reflected in a new name for the company, Red
Wing Potteries, Inc., in 1930. Stoneware
production ceased entirely in 1947, but vases,
planters, cookie jars and dinnerwares of art
pottery quality continued in production until 1967 when the pottery ceased operation al-
together.*

Ale set: tankard pitcher & 5 mugs;
embossed transportation decor,
made for 1933 Chicago World's

Fair, "A Century of Progress,"
white glaze, 6 pcs. $375.00
Bean crock, cov., brown glaze...... 75.00
Bowl, 6" d., Greek Key patt., stoneware, light blue around top fading
to grey 40.00
Bowl, 7" d., Grey Line stoneware
w/Spongeband decor ...... 65.00 to 85.00
Bowl, 7" d., spongeware, blue &
rust daubing on grey stoneware .. 67.00
Bowl, 8" d., paneled sides, spongeware, blue & rust daubing on tan
stoneware, unmarked 75.00
Bowl, 9" d., ribbed sides, Grey Line
stoneware w/Spongeband
decor .... 85.00 to 95.00
Bowl, 9½" d., Saffron ware, blue &
rust daubing on yellowware 50.00
Bowl, 10" d., paneled sides, spongeware, blue & rust daubing on
cream, unmarked .... 75.00 to 85.00
Butter churn, cov., stoneware, 3-
gal.................... 110.00 to 155.00
Butter churn, white glaze stoneware, large (4") red wing decal
signature, 3-gal. (no lid) 85.00
Butter churn, salt-glazed stoneware,
cobalt blue slip-quilled birch leaf,
4-gal. 190.00
Butter crock, salt-glazed stoneware,
10-lb. 60.00
Butter crock, white glaze stoneware,
large (4") red wing decal signature, 20-lb. .... 225.00 to 285.00
Casserole, cov. Grey Line
w/Spongeband decor, qt. 250.00
Casserole, cov., spongeware, blue &
rust daubing on white,
1½ qt. .... 140.00 to 160.00
Chamber pot, cov., white w/blue
striping (chip in lid) 95.00
Cookie jar, cov., art pottery line,
figural Katrina (or Dutch Girl),
blue glaze 36.50
Cookie jar, cov., art pottery line,
figural monk, "Thou Shalt Not
Steal" 37.50
Cookie jar, cov., cattails in relief on
blue fading to grey stoneware.... 165.00
Cookie jar, cov., spongeware, blue
& rust daubing on grey stoneware.................... 95.00 to 120.00
Crock, straight sides, stoneware,
large (4") red wing decal signature, 1-gal. 265.00
Crock, straight sides, salt-glazed
stoneware, "Lazy 8" & "target,"
2-gal. 75.00
Crock, straight sides, stoneware,
cobalt blue slip-quilled birch
leaves & "2" w/oval stamp "Red
Wing Union Stoneware," 2-gal.
(ILLUS.)...................... 35.00
Crock, straight sides, stoneware,

embossed "Minnesota Stoneware"
on bottom, 3-gal. .... 30.00 to 45.00

Crock, straight sides, stoneware,
large (4") red wing decal signature, w/wire bail handles & wood-
en grips at sides, dated 1915,
15-gal. 200.00

Custard cup, Grey Line stoneware
w/Spongeband decor 110.00

Fruit jar w/screw-on zinc lid,
"Stone Mason Fruit Jar, Union
Stoneware Co., Red Wing, Minn."
printed in black on stoneware,
1-gal. .... 260.00 to 300.00

Jug, brown-glazed stoneware, molded w/middle seam, signed "Red
Wing Stoneware Co." w/"bird"
mark, half-gal. 150.00

Jug, stoneware, brown-glazed
shoulder, white-glazed base, w/Il-
linois advertising, 1-gal. 95.00

Red Wing Beehive Jug

Jug, beehive shape, white glaze,
red "wing" decal & oval "Red
Wing Union Stoneware Co." mark,
4-gal. (ILLUS.) 200.00

Jug, beehive shape, salt-glazed
stoneware, cobalt blue "Lazy 8" &
"5," impressed "Red Wing Union
Stoneware" on bottom, 5-gal. 300.00

Jug, beehive shape, white-glazed
stoneware, w/Iowa advertising,
5-gal. .... 400.00 to 450.00

"Koverwate" (crock cover-weight
designed to hold pickles under
brine), stoneware, 1-gal (crock
size) 165.00

Mixing bowl, spongeware, blue &
orange daubing on grey stoneware, w/advertising, 8" d. 79.00

Mixing bowl, white-glazed stoneware, signed "Red Wing,"
11" d. 35.00

Mug, Saffron Ware, cattails decor,
4½" h. 45.00

Pie plate, stoneware, spongeband
decor, 8" d. 100.00

Pitcher, 8" h., Min-
nesota adv...

Planter, art p...
Dachshund, ...

Planter, brushe...
low relief, gre...
7" l. ....

Poultry feeder (or...
ware, "KoRec Fe...					...00

Refrigerator jar, cov...
w/Spongeband de... d.,
3½" h. 350.00

Refrigerator jar, stacking-type,
white-glazed stoneware w/blue
bands, 4¾" d. 98.00

Salt box, cov., hanging-type, Gray
Line w/Spongeband decor, Minnesota advertising, dated 1934 ... 275.00

Salt shaker, Gray Line w/Sponge-
band decor (single) 185.00

Snuff jar, cov., brown-glazed stoneware, 1-gal. 40.00

Vase, 10" h., art pottery line, brown
panels on green ground 20.00

Vase, 15½" h., art pottery line,
Egyptian decor 48.00

Water cooler, cov., white-glazed
stoneware w/blue bands, 3-gal. ... 185.00

Water cooler, cov., white-glazed
stoneware, red "wing" decal, "15"
& oval "Red Wing Union Stoneware Co.," 15-gal................ 285.00

RIDGWAY

Ridgway Dessert Set

*There were numerous Ridgways among
English potters. The firm J. & W. Ridgway
operated in Shelton from 1814 to 1930 and
produced many pieces with scenes of historical interest. William Ridgway operated in
Shelton from 1830 to 1865. Most wares
marked Ridgway that have been offered in
this country were made by one of these two
firms, or by Ridgway Potteries, Ltd., still in
operation. Also see FLOW BLUE and
HISTORICAL & COMMEMORATIVE
CHINA.*

barrel-shaped
4" h. mugs & 12½" d.
tray; Coaching Days &
series, black transfer on
caramel ground, silver lustre trim,
8 pcs. $275.00

Coffee pot, cov., Coaching Days &
Ways series, silver lustre trim,
7½" h. 85.00

Cookie jar, cov., wicker handle, Mr.
Pickwick series, black transfer on
caramel ground, silver lustre trim,
5¼" d., 6" h. 116.00

Cup & saucer, Oriental patt. 35.00

Dessert set: 13" oval 2-handled compote, 2 shaped square dishes; 2
oval dishes, 2 circular dishes &
sixteen 9" d. plates; each painted
& printed in colors w/floral specimens within shaped borders enriched in gilding w/scrolling foliage on blue ground, shaped rims
molded w/scrolls & shell motifs
enriched in gilding, ca. 1830,
23 pcs. (ILLUS. of part) 1,980.00

Mug, straight sides, Coaching Days
& Ways series, black transfer on
caramel ground, silver lustre rim
& handle, 3" d., 4¾" h. 44.00

Pitcher, 7¼" h., 5" d., jug-type, Mr.
Pickwick series, black transfer on
caramel ground, silver lustre rim,
base & handle 75.00

Pitcher, 9" h., jug-type, rope handle, bamboo caneware form
w/rope bandings, William Ridgway, dated 1835 .... 150.00

Pitcher, 11" h., salt glaze stoneware, Jousting Knights patt., dated Sept. 1, 1840................. 175.00

Pitcher, tankard, 12½" h., 6¼" d.,
Mr. Pickwick series, black transfer
on caramel ground, silver lustre
trim......................... 132.00

Plate, 7¾" d., Royal Vista patt.,
sailing scene, gold lustre rim 37.00

Plate, 8" d., Coaching Days & Ways
series - "A Clandestine Inter-
view..." 25.00

Plate, 9" d., Coaching Days & Ways
series - "Eloped," silver lustre
rim 45.00

Plate, chop, 13½" d., Coaching Days
& Ways series 110.00

Tumbler, Coaching Days & Ways
series, black transfer on caramel
ground, silver lustre top band,
2 7/8" d., 4" h. 33.00

Vase, 5" h., 3½" d., ovoid, 2-
handled, Coaching Days & Ways
series, black transfer on caramel
ground, silver lustre top band &
handles 60.00

ROCKINGHAM

"Tulip" Inkwell

*An earthenware pottery was first estab-
lished on the estate of the Marquis of Rockingham in England's Yorkshire district about
1745 and occupied by a succession of potters.
The famous Rockingham glaze of mottled
brown, somewhat resembling tortoise shell,
was introduced about 1788 by the Brameld
Brothers, and was well received. During the
1820's, porcelain manufacture was added to
the production and fine quality china was
turned out until the pottery closed in 1842.
The popular Rockingham glaze was subsequently produced elsewhere, including Bennington, Vt., and at numerous other U.S.
potteries. We list herein not only wares
produced at the Rockingham potteries in
England, distinguishing porcelain wares from
the more plentiful earthenware productions,
but also include items from other potteries
with the Rockingham glaze. Also see BEN-
NINGTON, HOUND HANDLED PITCH-
ERS and TOBY MUGS & JUGS.*

Bowl, 6¾" d., 3¼" h., mottled
brown glaze $45.00

Bowl, 12" d., mottled brown glaze .. 65.00

Box, cov., porcelain, butterfly-
shaped, wings enriched in puce &
blue, box enriched in green w/gilt
lines, ca. 1830, 3½" w. 1,320.00

Creamer, paneled sides, mottled
brown glaze, 4¼" h. 95.00

Creamer, embossed foliage on
sides, 4¾" h. 80.00

Cup & saucer, mottled brown
glaze 125.00

Cuspidor, paneled sides w/scrolls in
relief, 8" d., 4" h. 95.00

Dish, tub-shaped w/handles at rim,
mottled brown glaze, 3½" d...... 85.00

Dish, embossed foliate scrolls on
sides, mottled brown glaze,
8½" d., 2¼" h. 70.00

Furniture rests, model of lion's
head, 1830, 5", set of 4 . . . . 155.00
Inkwell, cov., porcelain, modeled as
a central tulip w/three buds,
enriched w/puce striations & supported on green foliage on mound
base, w/liner, ca. 1825, 4¾" h.
(ILLUS.) 2,860.00
Jar, cov., cylindrical, mottled brown
glaze, 2 7/8" h. 75.00
Jar & cover w/flower finial, paneled
sides, mottled brown glaze,
8 1/8" h. 110.00

Milk Cooling Basin

Milk cooling basin, canted sides,
mottled brown glaze, 13½" d.,
3¾" h. (ILLUS.) 135.00
Mixing bowl, embossed arch panels
on sides, mottled brown glaze,
14¾" d., 7¼" h. (short rim
hairline) 125.00

Rockingham Glazed Spaniel

Model of a dog in seated position,
well-detailed tooling, free-
standing front legs, irregular oblong base, mottled brown glaze,
11" h. (ILLUS.) . . . . 200.00 to 350.00
Mug, double-faced satyr, early
19th c., 4½" 165.00
Pitcher, 8" h., hanging game in
relief, mottled brown glaze 115.00
Pitcher, 8" h., wide-paneled body,
mottled brown glaze 145.00

Pitcher, 8½" h., embossed anchor
each side, mottled brown
glaze . . . . 75.00 to 95.00
Pitcher, 9 5/8" h., Tulip patt., tulips
in relief, mottled brown glaze 95.00
Plaques, porcelain, double-sided,
painted one side w/colorful
baskets & vases of flowers in formal garden setting, reverse
w/fruit & flowers in landscapes
within shaped panels outlined in
gilding reserved on green ground,
in giltwood frame, early 19th c.,
11½ x 8¼", pr. 550.00
Platter, 13½" l., mottled brown
glaze 105.00
Sauce dish, mottled brown glaze,
4 3/8" d. 42.50
Soap dish, embossed acanthus leaf
designs, 6" l. 85.00
Soap dish, round, footed, mottled
brown glaze 55.00
Teapot, cov., Rebecca at the Well
patt., mottled brown glaze,
7¼" h. . . . . 85.00 to 125.00
Vase, 5" h., porcelain, modeled as
a tulip, enriched w/iron-red striations & yellow interior, supported
on green foliate & stem w/applied
bud, on shaped base applied
w/flowerheads, ca. 1825 (minor
repairs) 1,980.00

ROOKWOOD

Rookwood Bowl of 1881

*Considered America's foremost art pottery,
the Rookwood Pottery Company was established in Cincinnati, Ohio in 1880, by Mrs.
Maria Longworth Storer. To accurately
record its development, each piece carried the
Rookwood insignia, or mark, was dated, and,
if individually decorated, was usually signed
by the artist. The pottery remained in Cincinnati until 1959 when it was sold to Her-
schede Hall Clock Company and moved to
Starkville, Mississippi, where it continued in
operation until 1967. Also see TILES.*

Ash tray, advertising, "General Electric" logo on double electric light
bulb shape, maroon glaze, 1949 . . $90.00

Ash tray, oblong, celadon green
high glaze, 1953 .... 25.00
Ash tray, round w/squared rim,
grey glaze, 1955 .... 25.00
Ash tray, model of a fish, white
matte finish, 1942 .... 42.50
Ash tray, model of a rook perched
at one side, green high glaze,
shape No. 1139 .... 80.00
Basket, 4-footed, 2-handled w/up-
folded sides, underglaze-slip-
painted florals, standard brown
glaze, Edith Regina Felton, 1887,
7" l., 4" w., 4" h. 400.00
Basket, footed, 2-handled, floral decor, standard glaze, 1897, Edith R.
Felten, 6¾" l. 350.00
Bookend, model of an elephant
walking, white glaze, 1921
(single)....................... 85.00
Bookends, figure of girl seated &
reading book on oblong base,
1929, pr. 200.00
Bookends, model of Dachshund,
brown w/tan highlights, 1927,
Louise Abel, pr................. 200.00
Bookends, model of rook, chocolate
brown glaze, William McDonald,
pr............................. 165.00
Bookends, model of tree on base,
multicolored, William McDonald,
pr............................. 250.00
Bowl, 5½" d., 4" h., underglaze
slip-painted purple florals & dark
green leaves on light green
ground, 1915, Charles Stewart
Todd 100.00
Bowl, 7" d., 3" h., incised decor on
gold matte glaze, 1919 .... 35.00
Bowl, 10" w., 4" h., flared, high
black glaze w/turquoise interior,
1921 .... 60.00
Bowl, 16" d., footed, underglaze
slip-painted blue fish, olive green
frogs & blue & scarlet-berried
black trees outlined in gilt, 1881
(ILLUS.) 1,100.00
Candlestick, triangular, molded
figural seahorses decor, 1911,
Sara Toohey (single) 85.00
Creamer, underglaze slip-painted
leaf & berry decor, standard
glaze, shape No. 655, 1903, Sallie
E. Coyne, 3" h. 245.00
Cup & saucer, Albino florals on
salmon ground, 1888, Harriet
Wilcox 350.00
Ewer, floral decor, standard brown
glaze, 1902, Lena E. Hanscom,
8" h. 350.00
Ewer, underglaze slip-painted ber-
ries & leaves, standard shaded
brown glaze, 1900, Elizabeth
Neave Lincoln, 9¼" h. 425.00

Ewer, handled, tri-foil top, underglaze slip-painted maple leaves &
buds decor, standard glaze, 1897,
Constance A. Baker, 10" h. 475.00
Flower frog, model of a raven,
black glaze, 1923, 6" h.......... 200.00
Humidor & cover w/butterfly finial,
floral decor, Cameo smear glaze
w/gilt highlights, 1887, 6½" d.
6" h........................... 425.00
Model of a cat, green high glaze,
1946, Louise Abel 195.00
Model of a panther, green glaze,
1945 .... 125.00
Model of a rooster, green glaze,
1928, William McDonald, 5¼" h... 110.00
Mug, molded floral decor, matte fin-
ish, 1909, Cecil A. Duell 175.00
Paperweight, model of a chick, yellow matte glaze, 1937, Louise
Abel 110.00
Paperweight, model of a frog,
greenish purple glaze, 1929,
large......................... 120.00
Paperweight, model of rooster, 4-
color glaze, shape No. 6030, 1943,
William Purcell McDonald, 5" h. .. 140.00
Paperweight, model of a rose, yellow matte glaze, 1940 .... 65.00
Pitcher, 4" h., berries decor, 1908,
Katherine Van Horne 295.00
Pitcher, 9½" h., narrow tapering
cylinder, angular handle, shaded
green spray of ferns on muted
mustard ground streaked w/dark
brown & black, standard glaze,
1890, Kataro Shirayamadani 440.00
Plaque, underglaze slip-painted pink,
grey, green & slate blue view of a
river bend w/mature trees on both
shores, Vellum glaze, 1927, Edward
Timothy Hurley, framed,
7 7/8 x 6" 1,100.00
Plaque, blue, green, rose & ivory
waterscape w/grassy shoreline &
trees in distance silhouetted
against skyline at dusk, 1918,
Carl Schmidt, 12¼ x 9¼",
framed 2,200.00

Rookwood Scenic Plaque

Plaque, underglaze slip-painted mountain landscape scene w/trees in foreground & snow-covered mountain range w/one massive peak in the distance in deeply shaded russet, brown, forest green, blue & white, Vellum glaze, 1913, Sadie Markland, 14½ x 9¼", framed (ILLUS.) 2,090.00

Smoking set, sectioned cigarette & match holder w/reclining nude on cover & 2 oblong ash trays, blue high glaze, 1928, 3 pcs.......... 130.00

Tobacco jar, cov., skull & cigarette decor, 1898, Ed Diers 1,650.00

Trivet, lady w/bucket decor, 1922... 100.00

Trivet, model of a rook, black glaze 125.00

Rookwood Urn by Sara Sax

Urn, footed, 2-handled, Persian scroll motif in pastel glazes, Sara Sax (1896-1931), 11¾" h. (ILLUS.)........................ 770.00

Vase, 3" h., slightly bulbous, aqua unevenly brushed over yellow & tan, high glaze finish, 1930....... 150.00

Vase, 4" h., pink florals on grey-green ground, Iris glaze, Olga Reed......................... 550.00

Vase, 4" h., underglaze slip-painted pastel florals on beige-grey ground, Iris glaze, Lorinda Epply (1904-48) 550.00

Vase, 4½" h., 2-handled, under-glaze slip-painted brown shaded to yellow florals, standard glaze, 1905, Lorinda Epply 345.00

Vase, 5½" h., 5" d., Tiger Eye glaze, 1892, Olga Geneva Reed .. 650.00

Vase, 5½" h., cylindrical, purple, yellow & plum iris blossoms w/olive green leaves on white ground, 1919, Lorinda Epply 2,420.00

Vase, 5½" h., thistle decor, stand-ard glaze, 1904, Jeanette Swing 295.00

Vase, 6" h., 4½" d., overall brown & lavender stylized florals & foliage, orange-beige Wax Matte glaze, shape No. 2917, 1930, Jens Jensen 850.00

Vase, 6¼" h., underglaze slip-painted orange poppies, standard glaze, 1903, Edith Regina Felton .. 325.00

Vase, 6½" h., etched green sea-horses (3) in high relief "floating" in midnight blue water, 1905 ..... 295.00

Vase, 6½" h., stenciled border of flying geese, blue matte w/lime green glaze, 1908, Lenore Asbury 475.00

Vase, 6¾" h., ovoid, underglaze slip-painted olive green leaves & blue pansies, standard glaze, 1905, Clara Christian Lindeman ..1,430.00

Vase, 7" h., 3-handled, portrait of Indian brave, standard brown glaze, 1898, Harriet Elizabeth Wilcox........................2,700.00

Vase, 7½" h., baluster-shaped, underglaze slip-painted blue, mauve & orange pumpkins amongst pink flowers & green vines, Vellum glaze, 1924, Lenore Asbury 1,870.00

Vase, 8" h., cranes (2) in flight over cattails on sea green ground, 1895, Olga Geneva Reed 2,750.00

Vase, 8" h., swollen cylinder, slender dark blue & green trees against pale rose sky, Vellum glaze, 1912, Kataro Shirayamadani...........4,400.00

Vase, 8½" h., night scene w/trees & hills in distance, dark green base & top, Iris glaze, 1909, Sarah Elizabeth (Sallie) Coyne 1,600.00

Vase, 8½" h., mistletoe decor on shaded brown, Vellum glaze, 1910, Olga Geneva Reed........ 695.00

Vase, 9½" h., scenic decor, Vellum glaze, 1913, E.T. Hurley.......... 950.00

Vase, 9¾" h., underglaze slip-painted pink & turquoise dawn forest scene, Vellum glaze, 1913, Edward T. Hurley............... 975.00

Vase, 10" h., 2-handled, incised sty-lized florals & leaves decor, salm-on glaze, 1924, William E. Hentschell 525.00

Vase, 11 1/8" h., angled shoulder on footed tapering cylinder, un-derglaze slip-painted scene of 2 boats under sail, pale blue, pink & cream, Vellum glaze, 1924, Charles Schmidt 3,300.00

Vase, 14" h., purple flower & green leaves on light green, Iris glaze, 1900, Matt Daly 900.00

Vase, 14" h., cream & apricot tulips & olive blue leaves & stems, Sea Foam glaze, 1910, Carl Schmidt .3,850.00

19th Century Rookwood Vase

Vase, 18¾" h., ovoid w/cylindrical neck, underglaze slip-painted yellow magnolias amongst olive green & brown leaves & branches, standard glaze, 1889, Matthew Andrew Daly (ILLUS.) 2,640.00

ROSEMEADE

Replica of Mount Rushmore

Laura Taylor was a ceramic artist who supervised Federal Works Projects in her native North Dakota during the Depression era and later demonstrated at the potter's wheel during the 1939 New York World's Fair. In 1940, Laura Taylor and Robert J. Hughes opened the Rosemeade-Wahpeton Pottery, naming it after the county and town of Wahpeton where it was located. Rosemeade Pottery was made on a small scale for only about twelve years with Laura Taylor designing the items and perfecting colors. Wildlife animals and birds are popular among collectors. Hughes and Taylor married in 1943 and the pottery did a thriving business until her death in 1959. The pottery closed in 1961 but stock was sold from the factory salesroom until 1964.

Ash tray w/figural pheasant at side, large $31.00
Ash tray, souvenir-type, "Tennessee," yellow glaze 14.00
Basket, pale powder blue glaze, 3" h. 17.00
Console bowl w/figural leaping fawn flower frog, black glaze, 2 pcs. 36.00
Figure of Indian, "God of Peace," 9" h. 80.00
Flower frog, figural leaping fawn, 6" 25.00
Model of pheasant, 7" h., 13" l. 125.00
Pitcher, ball-shaped, small 15.50
Planter, model of elephant, brown glaze 20.00
Planter, model of swan, powder blue glaze 20.00
Salt & pepper shakers, model of dog's head, black finish, original paper label, pr. 22.50
Salt & pepper shakers, model of kangaroo, original labels, pr. 13.50
Spoon rest, model of lady's slipper, pink glaze 40.00
Vase, 5" h., pink glaze, original paper label 8.00
Whimsey, model of boot, black glaze, 4" h. 18.50
Whimsey, model of boot, green glaze, 6½" 33.00
Whimsey, model of "Mount Rushmore," grey-washed tan finish, 5" w., 4" h. (ILLUS.) 18.50

ROSE MEDALLION - ROSE CANTON

Rose Medallion Wares

This Chinese ware, made through last century and in the present one, features alternating panels of people and of flowers, birds or insects. Most pieces have four to six medallions, and colors utilized are appealing. The ware is called Rose Canton if flowers fill all the panels. Unless otherwise noted, our listing is for Rose Medallion wares.

Basins, panels of figures & florals
  interior, widely spaced floral
  sprays exterior, 19" d., pr. $1,760.00
Bouillon cup & saucer, unmarked ...   38.00
Bowl, 6¼" d., 2½" h., marked
  "Made in China," 1920-30 ....   45.00
Bowl, 7" d., 3" h., ca. 1850 ....   90.00
Bowl, 7¾" d., scalloped rim, 4
  panels, interior & exterior decor,
  ca. 1890 .... 100.00
Bowl, 14", Rose Canton, 19th c. 325.00
Bowl, cover & underplate, 1920's,
  3 pcs. 65.00
Butter pat 25.00
Candlestick, 7½" h. (single) 125.00
Creamer, marked "Made in China,"
  1920-30, 4" h. 55.00
Creamer, helmet-shaped, 19th c. ... 120.00
Cup & saucer, demitasse, unmarked,
  ca. 1850 ....   60.00
Cup & saucer, ca. 1850 .....45.00 to 65.00
Cup & saucer, marked "China,"
  ca. 1891 ....   50.00
Cup & saucer, marked "Made in
  China," 1920-30 ....   35.00
Cup & saucer, octagonal 55.00
Cup & saucer, fluted, scalloped
  rim ....45.00 to 60.00
Cup & saucer, handleless cup
  w/cover 70.00
Dish, shaped oval, "orange peel"
  glaze underside, 10½" l. 180.00

Rose Medallion Garden Seats

Garden seats, barrel-shaped w/raised
  knob bands, reticulated designs on
  top & sides, unglazed interior,
  China, 19th c., 19" h., pr.
  (ILLUS.) 5,775.00
Pitcher, 3 7/8" h., 7¼" d., helmet-
  shaped, unmarked (tiny chips on
  spout) 185.00
Pitcher, milk, bulbous 98.00
Plate, 5½" d. 27.00
Plate, 6" d., unmarked 45.00
Plate, 7½" d. 55.00
Plate, 8" d. 75.00
Plate, 9½" d. ....65.00 to 80.00
Plate, 10" d. ....40.00 to 55.00
Platter, 18 x 13" oval, "orange peel"
  glaze underside, marked "China,"
  19th c. 275.00

Platter, oval, ca. 1840 .... 165.00
Punch bowl, 19th c., 14" d.,
  6" h. 1,072.00
Punch bowl, slightly flaring sides,
  ca. 1820, 23" d. 5,280.00
Saucer, octagonal 32.00
Soap dish, cover & drain insert,
  5½" l. (chip on edge of insert) ... 155.00
Soup tureen, w/stand, 19th c.,
  2 pcs. 250.00
Tazza, Rose Canton, 1830, 9" h. 100.00
Tea cup & saucer.................   65.00
Teapot, child's, bulbous, 3" h. 235.00
Teapot, cov., cylindrical, Rose Can-
  ton, 7" h. 90.00
Teapot, cov., woven reed handle,
  ca. 1830 .... 150.00
Tea set, cov. teapot & 2 cups in
  fitted wicker basket w/brass
  hardware, ca. 1895, 4 pcs. 310.00
Tea set, cov. teapot, 4 cups & 10" d.
  tray, marked, 6 pcs. 285.00
Vase, 3" h., ca. 1850 ....   50.00
Vases, 6" h., ca. 1860, pr. 120.00
Vase, 8" h., gilt dragon in relief at
  top 145.00
Vase, 10¼" h., 5" d., flaring mouth,
  applied foo dog handles, 1800-
  1900 (small nick on handle) 350.00
Vases, 12" h., Rose Canton, pr. 450.00
Vase, 14" h., hexagonal 245.00
Vase, 23" h., Rose Canton,
  ca. 1850 .... 350.00
Water bottle, spherical body, long
  tapering neck, 19th c., 13" h. 550.00

ROSENTHAL

*The Rosenthal porcelain manufactory has
been in operation since 1880 when it was established by P. Rosenthal in Selb, Bavaria.
Tablewares and figure groups are among its
specialities. Also see COMMEMORATIVE
PLATES.*

Chocolate set: cov. chocolate pot,
  10" d. handled plate & 4 c/s;
  brown shaded to beige transitional Art Deco/Nouveau decor on
  cream ground, gold trim, artist-
  signed & dated, 1922, 10 pcs. $135.00
Cup & saucer, portrait of a beautiful
  woman, gold trim, artist-signed ..   50.00
Figure of a young boy frolicking
  w/lamb, artist-signed, 6" h. 190.00
Figure of a female harlequin wearing a black, purple & green costume & playing a gilt-stringed
  guitar, 14½" h. 1,650.00
Figure of an Oriental dancer w/her
  right leg upraised, wearing an

ornate yellow, blue, mauve, green,
black & gilt costume, w/gilded
Oriental man seated on the base,
15¾" h. 1,210.00
Model of a Dachshund dog in seated
position, 6" h. 150.00
Model of a deer reclining,
10 x 6 x 5" 350.00
Model of a Pointer dog, black &
white, 8 x 6" 125.00
Model of a Poodle dog standing,
white w/green collar, artist-
signed, 8 x 8" 230.00
Model of a Springer Spaniel dog
w/bird in mouth, white w/brown
markings, 9 x 5½" 150.00
Mug, grapes decor, artist-signed &
dated 35.00
Plate, 8¾" d., bearded Dutch fisherman wearing lavender trousers &
cap on pale blue ground 35.00
Plate, 10" d., daisies decor........ 30.00
Vase, 7" h., shaded tan & rust foliage, crackle glaze, artist-signed &
dated 1946 .... 90.00

ROSEVILLE

*Roseville Pottery Company operated in
Zanesville, O., from 1898 to 1954 after having been in business for six years prior to that
in Muskingum County, Ohio. Art wares similar to those of the Owens and Weller Potteries were produced. Items listed here are by
patterns or lines.*

APPLE BLOSSOM (1948)

Apple Blossom Vase

Basket w/overhead handle, apple
blossoms in relief on green or
rose, 8" h., each $60.00

Basket, hanging-type, apple blossoms in relief on blue or rose,
each 70.00
Bookends, apple blossoms in relief
on green, pr. 57.50
Bowl, 6½" d., 2½" h., apple blossoms in relief on blue 35.00
Candle holders, apple blossoms in
relief on green, 2" h., pr........ 25.00
Console bowl, apple blossoms in
relief on rose, 12" l............. 42.00
Cornucopia-vase, apple blossoms in
relief on rose, 8" h. 33.00
Ewer, apple blossoms in relief on
rose, 8" h..................... 50.00
Jardiniere & pedestal base, apple
blossoms in relief on rose, overall
24½" h., 2 pcs. ....435.00 to 475.00
Vase, 10" h., branch handles rising
from flat bulbous base, apple
blossoms in relief on green 60.00
Vase, 12" h., branch handles at
base, apple blossoms in relief on
rose (ILLUS.) 45.00
Wall pocket, apple blossoms in relief on rose, 8" h. ....50.00 to 70.00

ARTWOOD (1951)

Artwood Planter

Planter, Ming tree framed within
oblong cut-out, mottled green
shading to brown, 8" h.
(ILLUS.)....................... 35.00
Planter, woody branch framed within oblong cut-out, mottled grey
shading to wine, 8½" l., 6½" h... 30.00
Planter, woody branch & foliage
framed within oblong cut-out,
mottled yellow shading to deep
brown, 9½" l., 7" h............. 30.00

BANEDA (1933)
Bowl, 10" d., 3½" h., 2-handled,
band of embossed pods, blossoms

& leaves on green or raspberry
pink, each.............100.00 to 115.00
Jardiniere, band of embossed pods,
blossoms & leaves on green,
7½" h........................ 150.00
Vase, 4½" h., tab handles at rim,
band of embossed pods, blossoms
& leaves on green.............. 52.00
Vase, 5½" h., 2-handled, band of
embossed pods, blossoms &
leaves on raspberry pink 65.00
Vase, 7" h., 2-handled, cylindrical,
band of embossed pods, blossoms
& leaves on raspberry pink....... 62.00
Vase, 9" h., handles rising from
mid-section to rim, band of embossed pods, blossoms & leaves
on raspberry pink 225.00
Vase, 12" h., base handles, band of
embossed pods, blossoms &
leaves on green or raspberry
pink, each..............155.00 to 195.00
Vase, 15" h., band of embossed
pods, blossoms & leaves on raspberry pink.............300.00 to 350.00

BITTERSWEET (1940)
Bookends, orange bittersweet pods
& green leaves on grey bark-
textured ground, pr............. 73.00
Candle holders, handles rising from
cone-shaped base, orange bittersweet pods & green leaves on yellow bark-textured ground, 3" h.,
pr........................... 45.00
Ewer, branch handle, orange bittersweet pods & green leaves on yellow bark-textured ground, 8" h. ... 52.00
Planter, pointed end handles, oval
w/shaped sides, orange bittersweet pods & green leaves on yellow bark-textured ground, 8" l.... 38.00
Teapot, cov., orange bittersweet
pods & green leaves on green
bark-textured ground 55.00
Vase, double bud, 6" h., 2 columns
rising from stepped base joined
by spray of relief-molded leaves,
orange bittersweet pods on green
bark-textured ground 39.00
Vase, 14" to 16" h., orange bittersweet pods & green leaves on
green bark-textured ground,
each ....125.00 to 145.00
Wall pocket, overhead & side
branch handles, orange bittersweet pods & green leaves on
grey bark-textured ground,
7½" h........................ 47.00

BLACKBERRY (1933)
Basket, hanging-type, band of blackberries & leaves in relief on green
textured ground ....265.00 to 300.00

Bowl, 6½" d., 2-handled, band of
blackberries & leaves in relief on
green textured ground.......... 100.00
Console set: 13" l. bowl & pr.
4½" h. candlesticks; band of
blackberries & leaves in relief on
green textured ground, 3 pcs..... 425.00
Jardiniere, band of blackberries &
leaves in relief on green textured
ground, 4" h. 105.00
Vase, 4" h., angular handles, conical base, short neck, band of
blackberries & leaves in relief on
green textured ground.......... 100.00
Vase, 8" h., band of blackberries &
leaves in relief on green textured
ground 155.00
Vase, 12½" h., handles rising from
shoulder to rim, band of blackberries & leaves in relief on green
textured ground................ 410.00
Wall pocket, cluster of blackberries
& leaves in relief on green textured ground, 8½" h............ 300.00

BLEEDING HEART (1938)

Bleeding Heart Vase

Basket w/pointed overhead handle,
pedestal base, pink blossoms &
green leaves on shaded green,
12" h......................... 100.00
Bowl, 8" d., shallow, pink blossoms
& green leaves on shaded
green 40.00
Ewer, pink blossoms & green leaves
on shaded blue, 10" h. 55.00
Pitcher, water, asymmetrical w/high
arched handle, pink blossoms &
green leaves on shaded green,
w/matching underplate, 2 pcs. ... 120.00
Vase, 4" h., pink blossoms & green
leaves on shaded green or pink,
each 26.00
Vase, 6½" h., base handles, hexagonal petal-form mouth, pink
blossoms & green leaves on shaded green 40.00

Vase, 9½" h., pink blossoms & green leaves on shaded pink (ILLUS.) 58.00

Vase, 18" h., 2-handled, pink blossoms & green leaves on shaded blue 190.00

Wall pocket, angular overhead handle, pink blossoms & green leaves on shaded blue or pink, 8½" h., each 75.00

BURMESE (1950's)

Candle holder-bookends, figural bust of Burmese woman, green glaze, pr. 125.00

Candle holders, square tapering base, white glaze, 3" h., pr. 28.00

Planter, green glaze, 10" l. 25.00

Plaque, pierced to hang, figural bust of Burmese man, black or white glaze, 7½" h., each ..... 110.00 to 145.00

Plaque, pierced to hang, figural bust of Burmese woman, black or green glaze, 7½" h., each 150.00

BUSHBERRY (1948)

Bushberry Double Bud Vase

Basket w/overhead handle, berries & leaves on blue or russet bark-textured ground, 10" h., each 75.00

Basket, hanging-type, berries & leaves on blue bark-textured ground 115.00

Bookends, berries & leaves on blue, green or russet bark-textured ground, each pr. .... 85.00 to 125.00

Bowl, 4" d., berries & leaves on russet bark-textured ground 40.00

Cider set: pitcher & 6 mugs; berries & leaves on blue or russet bark-textured ground, 7 pcs., each set 380.00

Console bowl, 2-handled, berries & leaves on blue bark-textured ground, 13" l. 38.00

Cornucopia-vase, berries & leaves on blue, green or russet bark-textured ground, 6" h., each .... 35.00 to 45.00

Ewer, berries & leaves on blue or russet bark-textured ground, 10" h., each .... 70.00 to 85.00

Tea set: cov. teapot, creamer & sugar bowl; berries & leaves on green bark-textured ground, 3 pcs. 145.00

Vase, double bud, 4½" h., 8½" l., 2 low-footed green bark-textured cylinders joined by spray of relief-molded berries & leaves (ILLUS.).. 45.00

Vase, 14½" h., asymmetrical handles, berries & leaves on russet bark-textured ground 165.00

Wall pocket, high-low handles, berries & leaves on blue dark-textured ground, 8" h. 75.00

CARNELIAN II (1915)

Carnelian II Wall Pocket

Flower frog, rock form, blue-grey shading to grey glaze, 6 x 4" 30.00

Planter, angular side handles, intermingled shades of green & grey glaze, 8" l. oval, 3" h. 25.00

Vase, 5" h., fan-shaped, intermingled shades of turquoise blue 20.00

Vase, 8" h., 2-handled, ovoid w/short neck, intermingled shades of raspberry 40.00

Vase, 15" h., tab handles, intermingled shades of rose & ivory glaze 145.00

Wall pocket, intermingled shades of rose, blue & rust glaze, 8" h. (ILLUS.) 45.00

CHERRY BLOSSOM (1933)

Bowl, 6" d., cherry blossoms & ivory fencework against brown combed ground 145.00

Candlesticks, flared base, earred handles at midsection, cherry blossoms & ivory fencework against brown combed ground, 4" h., pr. 175.00

Jardiniere, cherry blossoms & ivory fencework against brown combed ground, 5" h. 105.00

Jardiniere & pedestal base, cherry

blossoms & ivory fencework agaisnt brown combed ground, overall 25½" h., 2 pcs...........1,050.00

Urn-vase, cherry blossoms & ivory fencework against brown combed ground, 8" h................... 235.00

Vase, 10" h., cherry blossoms & pink fencework against blue combed ground 165.00

Wall pocket, cherry blossoms & ivory fencework against brown combed ground, 8" h. 325.00

CHLORON (1907)

Bowl, 6½" d., green matte finish ... 50.00

Vase, 4½" h., green matte finish ... 175.00

Vase, 7" h., 2-handled, pillow-shaped, green matte finish....... 210.00

Wall pocket, relief-molded figure of a nude woman, green matte finish, 8½" h..................... 450.00

CLEMANA (1934)

Bowl, 4½" d., low foot, stylized blossoms & embossed latticework on green ground 55.00

Bowl, 6" d., stylized blossoms & embossed latticework on brown ground....................... 50.00

Vase, 6" h., pierced handles, stylized blossoms & embossed latticework on green ground 55.00

Vase, 7" h., stylized blossoms & embossed latticework on blue ground....................... 100.00

Vase, 9½" h., stylized blossoms & embossed latticework on brown ground....................... 140.00

CLEMATIS (1944)

Clematis Vase

Basket w/overhead handle, clematis blossoms on blue textured ground, 10" h. 55.00

Basket, hanging-type, clematis blos-

soms on blue or green textured ground, each ....60.00 to 75.00

Bookends, clematis blossoms on blue textured ground, pr......... 75.00

Candle holders, clematis blossoms on green textured ground, 2" h., pr............................. 30.00

Console bowl, clematis blossoms on green textured ground, 10" d..... 34.00

Cookie jar, cov., angular side handles, clematis blossoms on blue or green textured ground, 10" h., each....................85.00 to 115.00

Ewer, clematis blossoms on brown or green textured ground, 15" h., each 150.00

Flower arranger, 3-prong, clematis blossoms on green textured ground, 4½" h. 32.50

Pedestal base, clematis blossoms on blue textured ground, 17" h. 125.00

Tea set: cov. teapot, creamer & sugar bowl; clematis blossoms on green textured ground, 3 pcs....................95.00 to 125.00

Vase, 7" h., clematis blossoms on blue textured ground (ILLUS.) 38.00

Vase, 12" h., 2-handled, clematis blossoms on green textured ground 125.00

Wall pocket, angular side handles, clematis blossoms on textured blue or brown ground, each ....50.00 to 65.00

COLUMBINE (1940's)

Columbine Vase

Basket, antular handle rising from footed base, columbine blossoms in relief on shaded tan ground, 7" h......................... 55.00

Basket, hanging-type, columbine blossoms in relief on shaded blue ground 60.00

Bowl, 3" d., 2-handled, columbine blossoms in relief on shaded blue ground 21.00

Jardiniere & pedestal base, columbine blossoms in relief on shaded tan ground, 2 pcs............... 525.00

Vases, bud, 7" h., columbine blossom in relief on shaded tan ground, pr..................... 45.00

Vase, 7½" h., columbine blossoms in relief on shaded pink ground (ILLUS.)......................... 40.00

Vase, 14" h., columbine blossoms in relief on shaded pink ground..... 155.00

Wall pocket, square mouth, columbine blossoms in relief on shaded pink ground, 8½" h. 82.50

CORINTHIAN (1923)

Corinthian Vase

Basket, hanging-type, fluted body w/embossed band of grapevine, fruit, foliage & florals at shoulder, green & ivory, 8" d. 70.00

Bowl, 7" d., fluted body w/embossed band of grapevine, fruit, foliage & florals at rim, green & ivory........................... 40.00

Compote, 8½" d., low foot, fluted body w/embossed band of grapevine, fruit, foliage & florals at rim, green & ivory 40.00

Console set: 10" d. bowl & pr. 8" h. candlesticks; fluted body w/band of grapevine, fruit, foliage & florals, 3 pcs................... 150.00

Jardiniere & pedestal base, fluted body w/band of grapevine, fruit, foliage & florals, overall 32" h., 2 pcs........................... 350.00

Vase, 7" h., bulbous, fluted body w/band of grapevine, fruit, foliage & florals (ILLUS.) 47.50

Vase, double bud, 7" h., 2-fluted columns joined by a reticulated gate w/diagonal spray of grapevine, fruit, foliage & florals 35.00

Wall pocket, fluted body w/wide band of grapevine, fruit, foliage & florals at rim, 8½" h............. 55.00

Wall pocket, fluted body w/bands of grapevine, fruit, foliage & florals, 12" h......................... 85.00

CORNELIAN (early 1900's)

Pitcher, 5" h., embossed ear of corn, dark blue sponge-daubed decor on light blue 55.00

Pitcher, tankard, 9½" h., embossed wild roses, blue & russet sponge-daubed decor on yellow 240.00

Shaving mug, yellow & brown sponge-daubed decor 35.00

Wash basin, green sponge-daubed decor on ivory, 15½" d. 85.00

COSMOS (1940)

Cosmos Vase

Basket w/overhead handle, footed, realistic cosmos blossoms in relief on ivory band, shaded blue ground, 12" h. 95.00

Candle holders, base handles, realistic cosmos blossoms in relief on green band, shaded tan ground, 2½" h., pr. 28.00

Console set: 10" l. oval bowl & pr. candle holders; realistic cosmos blossoms in relief on ivory band, shaded blue ground, 3 pcs. 65.00

Flower pot w/saucer, realistic cosmos blossoms in relief on ivory band, shaded blue ground, 5" h......................... 40.00

Vase, bud, 7" h., cosmos blossoms in relief on blue band, shaded green ground 32.50

Vase, 10" h., cosmos blossoms in relief on blue band, shaded green ground 75.00

Vase, 12½" h., cosmos blossoms in relief on ivory band, shaded blue ground (ILLUS.)................. 128.00

Window box, cosmos blossoms in

relief on blue band, shaded green
ground, 9 x 3", 3¼" h. 42.50

CREMONA (1927)
Bowl, 8" sq., relief-molded small
floral cluster & arrowhead leaves,
mottled pink 30.00
Bowl, 9" sq., cut corners, relief-
molded small floral cluster & arrowhead leaves, mottled pink 32.00
Cornucopia-vase, relief-molded
small floral cluster & arrowhead
leaves, mottled green, 8" h. 32.50
Vase, 10" h., angular handles,
ovoid, relief-molded small floral
cluster & arrowhead leaves, mottled pink 68.00
Vase, 12½" h., relief-molded small
floral cluster & arrowhead leaves,
mottled green 75.00

DAHLROSE (1924-28)

Dahlrose Vase

Basket, hanging-type, ivory blossoms in relief on mottled tan
shaded to green, 8" d. 110.00
Bowl, 7" d., angular rim handles,
ivory blossoms in relief on mottled tan shaded to green 24.00
Candlesticks, shaped base w/angu-
lar handles, ivory blossoms in relief on mottled tan shaded to
green, 3½" h., pr. 48.00
Jardiniere, ivory blossoms in relief
on mottled tan shaded to green,
8" h. 165.00
Vase, 6" h. (ILLUS.) 35.00
Vase, double bud, 6½" h., 8" w.,
gate form 32.00
Vase, 8" h., angular rim handles ... 60.00
Vase, 12" h., angular rim handles .. 75.00
Wall pocket, long angular handles,
10" h. 80.00

DAWN (1937)
Centerpiece, rose bowl w/candle
holders attached to elongated tab

handles, incised florals w/slender
petals, green matte finish, 6" d.
bowl 85.00
Rose bowl, square base, tab handles, incised florals w/slender
petals, pink matte finish, 4" d. ... 44.00
Rose bowl, square base, tab handles, incised florals w/slender
petals, green matte finish,
6" d. 55.00
Vase, 6" h., square base, tab handles, incised florals w/slender
petals, yellow matte finish 32.00
Vase, 8" h., slender cylinder, incised florals w/slender petals,
green matte finish 37.50

DOGWOOD I (1916-18)
Basket, dogwood blossoms on tex-
tured green ground, 10" h. 140.00
Basket, hanging-type, dogwood
blossoms on textured green
ground, 7" d. 90.00
Jardiniere, dogwood blossoms on
textured green ground, 4½" h. 49.00
Vase, 6" h., bulbous, dogwood blos-
soms on textured green ground .. 55.00
Vase, bud, 9" h. 30.00
Vase, 9" h. 48.00
Wall pocket, conical, 9½" h. 95.00
Window box 125.00

DOGWOOD II (1928)
Basket w/overhead handle, bulbous,
dogwood blossoms on matte
green ground, 8" h. 45.00
Jardiniere, dogwood blossoms on
matte green ground, 8" h. 65.00
Planter, boat-shaped, dogwood blossoms on matte green ground,
6" h. 55.00
Vase, double bud, 8" h., 2 trumpet-
shaped holders joined by flowering dogwood branch 40.00
Vase, 8" h., cylindrical 40.00
Wall pocket, double, 9" h. 70.00

DONATELLO (1915)

Donatello Jardiniere

Ash tray, cherubs in light relief on
tan band, green & ivory fluted
body, 2" h. ....80.00 to 95.00

Basket w/tall pointed handle, cherubs in light relief on tan band, green & ivory fluted body, 14" h. 225.00

Basket, hanging-type, cherubs in light relief on tan band, green & ivory fluted body, 7" h. ....95.00 to 125.00

Compote, 6" d., cherubs in light relief on tan bowl, green & ivory fluted flaring foot 47.50

Console bowl w/flower frog, 8" d. ... 65.00

Cuspidor, 5½" h. 185.00

Jardiniere, 4½" d., 3" h. (ILLUS.) ... 42.00

Jardiniere, 10" h. 225.00

Umbrella stand 310.00

Vase, double bud, 7" h., 2 square fluted columns w/angular side handles joined from base to mid-section by oblong plaque w/cherub in light relief 300.00

Vase, 10" h., expanding cylinder, footed 55.00

Wall pocket, 10" h.......... 75.00 to 90.00

DUTCH (pre-1916)

Ale set: tankard pitcher & 6 mugs; creamware w/varied Dutch decals, 7 pcs. 395.00

Humidor, cov., creamware w/Dutch decal, 6" h. ....120.00 to 150.00

Mug, creamware w/decal of Dutch children ....60.00 to 75.00

Pitcher, 9½" h., creamware w/decal of Dutch children............... 130.00

Pitcher, tankard, 11½" h., creamware w/Dutch decal......95.00 to 125.00

Tray for smoking set, turned in rim, creamware w/decal of 2 Dutchmen, 11 d. 87.50

EARLAM (1930)

Jardiniere, mottled green glaze, 6" 85.00

Planter, 2-handled, shaped rim, mottled green & blue glaze, 10½ x 5½".................... 32.00

Vase, 5½" h., handles rising from mid-section to rim, bulbous w/wide collared mouth, mottled green glaze.................... 32.50

Vase, 7" h., angular handles, ovoid, mottled blue & green glaze 60.00

Vase, 8" h., 2-handled, bulbous, mottled green glaze 65.00

EARLY EMBOSSED PITCHERS (pre-1916)

"The Bridge," 6" h. 45.00

"The Cow," 7½" h. 120.00

"Landscape," 7½" h. 55.00

"The Owl," 6½" h. 140.00

"Poppy," 9" h. 175.00

"Tulip," 7½" h. (ILLUS.) 65.00

"Wild Rose," 9½"h 80.00

Embossed Tulip Pitcher

EGYPTO (1905)

Creamer, triple spout, shades of deep green matte glaze, 3½" h... 155.00

Pitcher, 12" h., ovoid melon-ribbed body w/narrow neck & flaring rim, w/applied ceramic seal, shades of deep green matte glaze......................... 275.00

Vase, 12½" h., square w/canted sides, w/applied ceramic seal, shades of dark green matte glaze......................... 265.00

FALLINE (1933)

Bowl, 11" d., impressed triangles at rim, peapod decor at base, tan ... 250.00

Vase, 6" h., 2-handled, swollen cylinder, impressed triangles & peapod decor, blue shaded to green & tan 135.00

Vase, 7" h., 2-handled, bulbous bottom, graduated rings at top, impressed triangles & peapod decor, browns shaded to tan 135.00

Vase, 8" h., 2-handled, expanding cylinder, low foot, impressed triangles below rim, peapod decor on body, blue shaded to green & tan 175.00

FERRELLA (1930)

Bowl, 12" d., 7" h., reticulated base w/molded shells, flaring sides & pierced rim w/impressed shell design, mottled brown 205.00

Console bowl w/attached flower frog, reticulated low footed base w/molded shells, pierced rim, mottled red & turquoise, 9" d., 4" h.................200.00 to 235.00

Urn-vase, small handles at shoulder, pierced shell-molded base & rim, mottled red & turquoise, 6" h..... 200.00

Vase, 5" h., handles rising from pierced shell-molded base to flaring reticulated rim, mottled brown......................... 125.00

Wall pocket, pierced, shell-molded
rim, mottled red & turquoise,
6½" h. 315.00

FLORENTINE (1924-28)

Florentine Wall Pocket

Basket, hanging-type, bark-textured
panels alternating w/embossed
garlands of cascading fruit &
florals, dark brown
tones ....110.00 to 130.00
Bowl, 6" to 8" d., bark-textured
panels alternating w/embossed
garlands of cascading fruit &
florals, dark brown tones,
each ....30.00 to 45.00
Candlesticks, flaring base, bark-
textured panels alternating w/em-
bossed pendant garlands of fruit
& florals, brown tones, 8½" h.,
pr............................ 85.00
Jardiniere, 2-handled, bark-textured
panels alternating w/berries & foliage, ivory, tan & green, 6" h. 80.00
Jardiniere, bark-textured panels alternating w/garlands of cascading
florals & fruit, brown tones,
12 x 10¼" 200.00
Vase, 6½" h., bark-textured panels
alternating w/garlands of cascading florals & fruit, brown tones ... 35.00
Vase, 11" h., bark-textured panels
alternating w/pendant garlands of
fruit & florals, ivory, tan &
green 65.00
Wall pocket w/overhead handle,
central bark-textured panel
flanked by pendant floral
garlands, ivory, green & tan,
8½" h. 65.00
Wall pocket, central bark-textured
panel flanked by pendant floral
garlands, brown tones, 9½" h.
(ILLUS.)...................... 60.00

FOXGLOVE (1940's)
Basket w/overhead handle rising
from base, white foxglove spray
on shaded blue or green ground,
8" h., each 58.00

Basket, hanging-type, white foxglove spray on shaded blue
ground 115.00
Bowl, 14" d., white foxglove spray
on shaded pink ground 60.00
Candle holders, white foxglove
spray on shaded blue ground,
1½" h., pr.................... 22.50

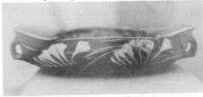

Foxglove Cornucopia-Vase

Cornucopia-vase, white foxglove
spray on shaded blue ground,
6½" h. (ILLUS.) 35.00
Ewer, white foxglove spray on shaded blue ground, 6½" h. ...60.00 to 75.00
Ewer, white foxglove spray on shaded blue or green ground, 10" h.,
each ....75.00 to 95.00
Jardiniere, white foxglove spray on
shaded pink ground, 6" d. 65.00
Model of a conch shell, white foxglove spray on shaded blue
ground, 6" l................... 35.00
Tray, single handle, leaf-shaped,
white foxglove spray on shaded
green ground, 8½" l............ 50.00
Vase, 6" h., white foxglove spray on
shaded pink ground 30.00
Vase, 14" h., 4 handles at base,
white foxglove spray on shaded
green ground 110.00

FREESIA (1945)

Freesia Console Bowl

Basket w/low overhead handle,
white to yellow blossoms & green
leaves in relief on shaded blue
textured ground, 7" h........... 42.50
Basket, hanging-type, white blossoms & green leaves in relief on
shaded green textured
ground.................53.00 to 65.00
Bowl, 8½" d., 2-handled, white to
yellow blossoms & green leaves in

relief on shaded blue or tangerine
textured ground, each . . . . . 25.00 to 30.00

Candle holders, domed base supporting angular side handles,
white blossoms & green leaves on
shaded green textured ground,
2" h., pr. 30.00

Console bowl, 2-handled, white to
yellow blossoms & green leaves
on shaded tangerine textured
ground, 14" l. (ILLUS.) . . . . . 55.00 to 65.00

Ewer, white blossoms & green
leaves on shaded green textured
ground, 15" h. 125.00

Flower pot w/attached saucer,
white to yellow blossoms & green
leaves on shaded tangerine tex-
tured ground, 5" h. 40.00

Jardiniere & pedestal base, white
blossoms & green leaves on shad-
ed blue textured ground, 2 pcs. . .   450.00

Pitcher, 10" h., white blossoms &
green leaves on shaded blue or
green textured ground,
each . . . . 55.00 to 65.00

Vase, 6" h., pillow-shaped, white to
yellow blossoms & green leaves
on shaded tangerine textured
ground 40.00

Vase, 8" h., 2 handles rising from
bulbous base to mid-section, flaring mouth, white blossoms &
green leaves on shaded blue tex-
tured ground 45.00

Vase, 10" h., bulbous base, white
blossoms & green leaves on shad-
ed green textured ground . . 42.00 to 50.00

Vase, 15" h., white blossoms &
green leaves on shaded green
ground 150.00

Wall pocket, white to yellow blossoms & green leaves on shaded
tangerine ground, 8½" h. 55.00

FUCHSIA (1939)

Basket w/overhead handle, footed,
pendant fuchsia blossoms on blue
w/cream highlights, 8" h. 50.00

Basket, hanging-type, pendant fuchsia blossoms on brown w/gold
highlights . . . . 95.00 to 135.00

Candlesticks, domed base, tubular
form raised on ring, pendant fuchsia blossoms on blue w/cream
highlights, 5½" h., pr. 95.00

Jardiniere & pedestal base, pendant
fuchsia blossoms on blue w/cream
highlights, 2 pcs. 525.00

Vase, 7" h., 2-handled, pendant
fuchsia blossoms on blue w/cream
highlights 50.00

Vase, 8" h., pendant fuchsia blossoms on blue w/cream highlights
(ILLUS.) 55.00

Fuchsia Vase

Vase, 10" h., pendant fuchsia blossoms on brown w/gold high-
lights . . . . 75.00 to 85.00

Wall pocket, pendant fuchsia blossoms on green w/terra cotta high-
lights, 8½" h. 125.00

FUTURA (1928)

Bowl, 4½" h., footed, sharply cant-
ed sided, blended earth tones 125.00

Candlestick, shaped square base
rising to square candle nozzle,
relief-molded stylized green vine
& foliage on sandy beige ground,
4" h. (single) 80.00

Vase, 6" h., twisted square body
w/tapering sides, square mouth,
blended tan & green
glaze . . . . 95.00 to 125.00

Vase, 7" h., globular w/short narrow neck, square base, relief-
molded stylized tapering blue-
green leaf design rising from base
to shoulder against light blue-
green ground 200.00

Vase, bud, 10" h., disc base,
stacked tapering sections, relief-
molded green foliage on terra
cotta glaze 155.00

Wall pocket, canted sides, angular
rim handles, geometric design in
creamy white & grey-green on
blended terra cotta glaze,
8" h. . . . . 165.00 to 215.00

GARDENIA (1940's)

Basket, circular handle rising from
base, white gardenia blossom on
shaded green or grey, 10" h.,
each . . . . 65.00 to 85.00

Bookends, white gardenia blossom
on shaded tan, 5 x 4½ x 5", pr. . . .   85.00

Candle holders, white gardenia

blossom on shaded green, 2" h.,
pr. . . . . .25.00 to 32.50
Cornucopia-vase, white gardenia
blossom on shaded green, 6" h. . . 35.00
Ewer, ovoid w/long slender neck,
white gardenia blossom on shad-
ed green, 10" h. . . . . .65.00 to 75.00
Tray, lobed form, white gardenia
blossom on shaded tan, 15" l. 55.00
Vase, 6" h., white gardenia blossom
on shaded grey 30.00
Vase, 10" h., base handles, white
gardenia blossom on shaded
tan 65.00

Gardenia Vase

Vase, 16" h., 2-handled, white
gardenia blossom on shaded tan
(ILLUS.) 125.00
Window box, white gardenia blos-
som on shaded grey or tan,
8 x 3¼", each . . . . .20.00 to 28.00

IMPERIAL I (1916)

Imperial I Basket

Basket w/overhead handle, pretzel
twisted vine & grape leaves in relief on green & brown textured
ground, 6" h. (ILLUS.) 50.00
Basket w/overhead handle, pretzel-
twisted vine & grape leaves in re-

lief on green & brown textured
ground, 10" h. . . . . .60.00 to 75.00
Basket, hanging-type, pretzel-
twisted vine & grape leaves in relief on green & brown textured
ground 80.00
Bowl, 7" d., 2-handled, pretzel-
twisted vine & grape leaves in relief on green & brown textured
ground 30.00
Jardiniere, pretzel-twisted vine &
grape leaves in relief on green &
brown textured ground, 9 x 9" . . . 90.00
Vase, 8" h., 2-handled, bulbous,
pretzel-twisted vine & grape
leaves in relief on green & brown
textured ground 65.00
Vase, 10" h., pierced handles,
pretzel-twisted vine & grape
leaves in relief on green & brown
textured ground 75.00
Wall pocket, curved body w/con-
forming handle, pretzel-twisted
vine & grape leaf in relief on
green & brown textured ground,
8" h. 75.00

IMPERIAL II (1924)
Ash tray, mottled blue & gold glaze,
6½ x 2" 95.00
Bowl, 9" d., mottled green & russet
glaze 125.00
Vase, 8" h., 2½" base d. flaring to
7" at top, mottled brown glaze . . . 120.00
Vase, 8½" d., semi-ovoid, short
horizontally ribbed neck w/relief
floral decor, beige textured matte
finish 115.00
Vase, 8½" h., 7½" widest d.,
pierced rim handles, horizontally
ridged lower section, mottled
brown glaze 225.00
Wall pocket, 3-prong, horizontal
ridges, mottled orange & green
glaze, 6½" h. 200.00

IRIS (1938)
Basket w/pointed overhead handle,
iris & leaves on shaded tan
ground, 8" h. 85.00
Candlesticks, pierced handles rising
from flared base, iris & leaves on
shaded pink ground, 4½" h.,
pr. 50.00
Console bowl, iris & leaves on shad-
ed blue or pink ground, 10" l.,
3" h., each . . . . .40.00 to 55.00
Vase, 4" h., urn-shaped, iris &
leaves on shaded pink ground 26.00
Vase, 6" h., iris & leaves on shaded
pink ground 35.00
Vase, 8" h., iris & leaves on shaded
tan ground 40.00

Vase, 12½" h., 2-handled, iris &
leaves on shaded blue ground 95.00
Wall pocket, 2 handles rising from
base to below flaring mouth, iris
& leaves on shaded pink ground,
8" h.......................... 125.00

IXIA (1930's)

Basket, hanging-type, lavender floral cluster on shaded green 45.00
Bowl, 9" d., lavender floral cluster
on shaded green 30.00
Candle holders, 2-light, white floral
cluster on shaded pink, 3" h.,
pr............................. 55.00
Vase, 6" h., pointed closed handles
at shoulder, lavender floral cluster on shaded yellow 32.00
Vase, 9" h., white floral cluster on
shaded pink 53.00
Vase, 10" d., lavender floral cluster
on shaded green 65.00
Vase, 12" h., white floral cluster on
shaded pink 95.00

JONQUIL (1931)

Basket w/elongated pointed overhead handle, jonquil blossoms &
leaves in relief against textured
tan ground, 9" h. 150.00
Basket, hanging-type, jonquil blossoms & leaves in relief against
textured tan ground 170.00
Bowl, 4" d., 2-handled, jonquil blossoms & leaves in relief against
textured tan ground .... 35.00 to 45.00
Jardiniere, jonquil blossoms &
leaves in relief against textured
tan ground, 10" h. 300.00
Vase, 4½" h., handles at mid-
section, jonquil blossoms & leaves
in relief against textured tan
ground 32.50
Vase, bud, 6" h., 2 handles rising
from slightly bulbous base to slender mid-section, jonquil blossoms
& leaves in relief against textured
tan ground .... 60.00 to 70.00
Vase, 8" h., elongated side handles,
jonquil blossoms & leaves in relief
against textured tan ground 95.00
Wall pocket, jonquil blossoms &
leaves in relief against textured
tan ground, 8½" h. .....195.00 to 210.00

JUVENILE (1916 on)

Bowl, 6½" d., sitting rabbits
decor 80.00
Chamber pot, sitting rabbits decor,
6" d., 3½" h. 225.00
Egg cup, sitting rabbits decor,
3½" h.......................... 110.00
Feeding dish w/rolled edge, ducks
decor, 8" d. 40.00

Feeding dish w/rolled edge, duck
w/hat decor, 8" d. 85.00
Feeding dish w/rolled edge, nursery
rhyme "Little Bo Peep," 8" d...... 45.00

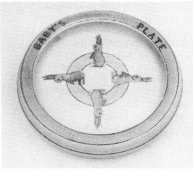

Feeding Dish

Feeding dish w/rolled edge, sitting
rabbits decor center, 8" d.
(ILLUS.).................45.00 to 60.00
Feeding dish w/rolled edge &
pitcher, Sunbonnet Girl decor,
2 pcs. 95.00
Mug, 2-handled, seated dog decor,
3" h.......................... 55.00
Mug, rabbits decor, 3" h. 45.00
Mug, 2-handled, Sunbonnet Girl
decor, 3" h. 45.00
Pitcher, 3½" h., sitting rabbits
decor ....50.00 to 60.00
Pitcher, 5½" h., chicks decor...... 48.00
Plate, 7" d., sitting rabbits decor ... 45.00
Plate, 8" d., standing rabbits
decor ....35.00 to 45.00
Plate & mug, standing rabbits decor,
green border, pr. 65.00
Pudding dish, chicks decor,
3½" d. 35.00

LAUREL (1934)

Laurel Vase

Bowl, 6" d., 2½" h., laurel branch &
berries in low relief, reeded
panels at sides, green 15.00
Bowl, 8" d., laurel branch & berries

in low relief, reeded panels at
sides, terra cotta 30.00
Console bowl, laurel branch & ber-
ries in low relief, reeded panels
at sides, deep yellow, 13" 60.00
Vase, 6" h., laurel branch & berries
in low relief, reeded panels at
sides, deep yellow 35.00
Vase, 7" h., laurel branch & berries
in low relief, reeded panels at
sides, green 40.00
Vase, 8" h., footed, laurel branch &
berries in low relief, reeded
panels at sides, green (ILLUS.) 70.00
Vase, 8" h., tapering cylinder
w/pierced angular handles at
mid-section, laurel branch & berries in low relief, reeded panels
at sides, terra cotta 75.00

LOMBARDY (1924)
Bowl, 7" d., 3-footed, melon-ribbed,
blue matt glaze 75.00
Jardiniere, 3-footed, melon-ribbed,
blue-grey matte glaze,
6½" h. . . . . .95.00 to 125.00
Vase, 6" h., 3-footed, acorn-shaped,
melon-ribbed, green, grey-blue or
white high-gloss finish,
each . . . . .95.00 to 110.00
Wall pocket, melon-ribbed, tur-
quoise blue matt glaze, 8½" h. . . .   110.00

LOTUS (1952)
Bowl, 9" d., 3" h., stylized lotus petals in relief, blue & white or
brown & yellow high-gloss finish,
each . . . . 65.00 to 75.00
Candle holders, footed, stylized lo-
tus petals in relief, blue & white
high-gloss finish, 2½" h., pr. 52.00
Planter, stylized lotus petals in relief, turquoise & tan high-gloss
finish, 4" sq.   50.00
Planter, stylized lotus petals in re-
lief, green & yellow high-gloss fin-
ish, 10½" l. 65.00
Wall pocket, stylized lotus petals in
relief, tan & green high-gloss fin-
ish, 7½" h. 130.00

LUFFA (1934)
Candlestick, high domed base, angular handles at mid-section,
relief-molded ivy leaves & blossoms on shaded green wavy
horizontal ridges, 5" h. (single) . . .   37.00
Vase, 6" h., relief-molded ivy leaves
& blossoms on shaded green wavy
horizontal ridges 40.00
Vase, 7" h., angular rim handles,
relief-molded ivy leaves & blossoms on shaded green wavy
horizontal ridges (ILLUS.) 55.00

Luffa Vase

Vase, 15½" h., footed, relief-
molded ivy leaves & blossoms on
shaded brown & green wavy
horizontal ridges 295.00
Wall pocket, angular rim handles,
relief-molded ivy leaves & blossoms on shaded green wavy
ridges, 8½" h. 225.00

LUSTRE (1921)
Bowl, 7" d., 2½" h., glossy
orange 20.00
Bowl, 8" d., glossy pink 40.00
Candlesticks, flaring base rising to
baluster-shaped stem, glossy or-
ange, 10" h., pr. 60.00
Console bowl, footed, glossy silver
grey, 12" d., 5" h. 35.00
Vase, 9" h., tapering cylinder,
glossy orange 55.00

MAGNOLIA (1943)

Magnolia Cookie Jar

Ash tray, angular side handles,
magnolia blossoms on textured
green ground, 7" d. 55.00

Basket w/low overhead handle,
footed, magnolia blossoms on textured blue or green ground,
10" h., each ....65.00 to 85.00
Basket, hanging-type, magnolia
blossoms on textured blue or tan
ground, 5", each 75.00
Bowl, 6" d., 2-handled, magnolia
blossoms on textured green
ground 16.00
Bowl, 14" d., magnolia blossoms on
textured green ground.......... 65.00
Candle holders, angular handles rising from circular base to rim,
magnolia blossoms on textured
green ground, 2½" h., pr. 30.00
Cider set: pitcher & 6 mugs; magnolia blossoms on textured blue
ground, 7 pcs. 290.00
Cookie jar, cov., magnolia blossoms
on textured tan ground, 10" h.
(ILLUS.) ....95.00 to 115.00
Ewer, magnolia blossoms on textured green or tan ground, 6" h.,
each 42.50
Flower holder, 2-handled, magnolia
blossoms on textured green
ground, 4" h. 30.00
Jardiniere & pedestal base, magnolia blossoms on textured blue or
green ground, overall 25" h.,
2 pcs., each set ....325.00 to 475.00
Tea set: cov. teapot, creamer & sugar bowl; magnolia blossoms on
textured tan ground, 3 pcs. 115.00
Vase, bud, 7" h., magnolia blossoms
on textured green ground 35.00
Vase, 15" h., magnolia blossoms on
textured green ground.......... 135.00
Wall pocket w/overhead handle,
magnolia blossom on textured tan
ground, 8½" h. 55.00

MATT GREEN (pre-1916)
Basket, hanging-type, dark green
matt finish..................... 60.00
Console bowl w/flower frog, dark
green matte finish, 2½" h........ 50.00
Vase, double bud, 5" h., 8" w., fluted columns joined by gate, dark
green matt finish............... 30.00
Wall pocket, dark green matt finish,
10" h. 75.00
Wall pocket, dark green matt finish,
12" h. 145.00

MAYFAIR (late 1940's)
Basket, buff glaze, 10" h. 35.00
Candle holders, brown glaze, low,
pr.............................. 23.00
Pitcher, 6" h.,, buff or dark green
glaze, each 28.00
Pitcher, 8" h., ball-shaped, brown
glaze 45.00

Pitcher, tankard, 12" h., brown
glaze 50.00
Wall pocket, corner-type, green
glaze, 8" h..................... 50.00

MEDALLION (pre-1916)
Creamer, oval cameo decal decor
w/gold floral swags on creamware, 3½" h. 40.00
Dresser set: 10" d. tray, cov. powder box, cov. hair receiver & ring
tree; oval cameo decal decor
w/gold floral swags on creamware, 4 pcs.............225.00 to 300.00
Sugar bowl, oval cameo decal decor
w/gold floral swags on
creamware 55.00

MING TREE (1949)

Ming Tree Vase

Basket w/overhead branch handle,
oriental branches in relief on blue
or green ground, 13" h.,
each ....95.00 to 125.00
Basket w/overhead branch handle,
undulating form, oriental
branches in relief on green
ground, 14½" h. 115.00
Candle holders, branch handles, bulbous melon-ribbed base, oriental
branches in relief on blue, green
or white ground, 2" h., each
pr...................... 30.00 to 45.00
Console bowl, branch handles,
asymmetrical sides, oriental
branches in relief on white
ground, 10" l.................. 45.00
Model of a conch shell, oriental
branches in relief on green
ground, 8½" l.................. 30.00
Planter, oriental branches in relief
on green or white ground, 8½" l.,
4" h., each 30.00
Vase, 6" h., asymmetrical branch
handles, oriental branches in relief on blue ground (ILLUS.) 45.00

Wall pocket w/overhead branch
handle, oriental branches in relief
on blue ground, 8½" h.......... 125.00

MOCK ORANGE (1950)

Basket w/overhead handle, white
blossoms & green leaves on pink
ground, 6" h. 40.00
Basket w/overhead handle, white
blossoms & green leaves on green
ground, 10" h. 55.00
Bowl, 6" d., white blossoms & green
leaves on green or pink ground,
each 25.00
Candle holders, white blossoms &
green leaves on pink ground,
2" h., pr...................... 32.00
Coffee pot, cov., white blossoms &
green leaves on green ground.... 65.00
Ewer, white blossoms & green
leaves on yellow ground, 6" h. ... 45.00
Vase, 7" h., pillow-shaped, 3-footed,
white blossoms & green leaves on
pink ground 42.50

MONTACELLO (1931)

Montacello Vase

Bowl, 4" d., white stylized trumpet
flowers w/black accents on band,
mottled tan ground............. 55.00
Console bowl w/attached flower
frog, white stylized trumpet flowers w/black accents on band,
mottled turquoise shaded to tan
ground, 13" d. 85.00
Vase, 4" h., 2 handles rising from
shoulder to rim, white stylized
trumpet flowers w/black accents
on band, mottled blue & tan
ground 55.00
Vase, 7" h., 2-handled, white stylized trumpet flowers w/black accents on band, mottled tan
ground (ILLUS.)................. 60.00

MORNING GLORY (1935)

Bowl-vase, 2-handled, stylized pas-

tel morning glories in low relief
on green or white ground, 7"
widest d., 4" h., each 165.00
Urn-vase, pointed shoulder handles,
stylized pastel morning glories in
low relief on white ground,
6" h. 125.00
Vase, 7" h., angular handles rising
from low foot to mid-section, stylized pastel morning glories in
low relief on white ground....... 125.00
Vase, 8½" h., 2-handled, stylized
pastel morning glories in low relief on white ground............ 170.00
Wall pocket, double, stylized pastel
morning glories in low relief on
white ground, 8½" h. ...350.00 to 425.00

MOSS (1930's)

Moss Wall Pocket

Basket, hanging-type, pendant moss
on pink shaded to green ground,
5" 125.00
Bowl, 8" d., pendant moss on pink
shaded to blue ground.......... 40.00
Console set: 10" d. bowl & pr. 2" h.
candle holders; pendant moss on
pink shaded to blue ground,
3 pcs......................... 95.00
Flower pot w/attached underplate,
pendant moss on pink shaded to
green ground, 5" h. 75.00
Vase, 6" h., angular side handles,
pendant moss on pink shaded to
green ground 35.00
Vase, 8" h., pillow-shaped, pendant
moss on pink shaded to blue
ground 45.00
Wall pocket, pendant moss on pink
shaded to blue ground, 8½" h.
(ILLUS.) ....85.00 to 120.00

MOSTIQUE (1915)

Basket, hanging-type, glossy geometric design on pebbled grey
ground, 9" d. 85.00

Bowl, 5½" to 6½" d., glossy multicolored floral designs on pebbled brown ground, each . .22.00 to 30.00

Mostique Bowl

Bowl, 8" widest d., 3" h., blue, green, yellow & brown glossy designs on pebbled grey ground, glossy green interior (ILLUS.) 35.00
Jardiniere, glossy stylized floral designs on pebbled tan ground, 8" to 9" d., each . . . . 40.00 to 50.00
Vase, 6" h., glossy geometric design on pebbled grey ground 27.50
Vase, 12" to 14" h., glossy arrowhead motif on pebbled tan ground, each . . . . 60.00 to 80.00
Wall pocket, glossy stylized floral design on pebbled grey ground, 10½" h. 50.00

NORMANDY (1924)

Normandy Hanging Basket

Basket, hanging-type w/original chains, ribbed body & band of grapevines & clusters, green & ivory w/brown ground band, 7" d. (ILLUS.) . . . . 150.00 to 170.00
Jardiniere, ribbed body & band of grapevines & clusters, green & ivory w/brown ground band, 7" d. 95.00
Jardiniere, ribbed body & band of grapevines & clusters, green & ivory w/brown ground band, 11" d., 9" h. 250.00

ORIAN (1935)

Compote, 10½" d., 4½" h., glossy yellow w/green lining 65.00
Rose bowl, slender side handles, glossy turquoise w/brown lining, 6" h. 40.00
Vase, 7" h., side handles to base, glossy burgundy w/turquoise lining 60.00
Vase, 6" h., slender handles rising from foot to shoulder, glossy yellow w/green lining 60.00
Vase, 7½" h., glossy pale brown w/green lining & handles 70.00
Vase, 10½" h., glossy yellow w/turquoise lining 135.00
Vase, 12½" h., glossy burgundy w/turquoise lining. 145.00
Wall pocket, double, pale brown w/turquoise lining, 8" h. 175.00
Window box, glossy burgundy w/turquoise lining, 15" l. 100.00

PANEL (1920)

Bowl, 5" d., panels of florals on deep green ground 35.00
Candlesticks, square flaring base, panels of florals on deep green ground, 8½" h., pr. 125.00
Vase, double bud, 5½" h., waisted cylinders joined by floral panel, brown-black ground 45.00
Vase, 6" h., 7" w., pillow-shaped, panels of florals on brown-black ground . . . . 95.00 to 125.00
Vase, 6" h., slightly swollen cylinder, panels of naturalistic leaves on dark green ground 45.00
Vase, 8" h., fan-shaped, flaring base, panels w/nude lady on dark green ground 185.00
Vase, 10½" h., cylindrical, panels w/nude lady on brown-black ground 250.00

PEONY (1930's)

Peony Double Candle Holders

Basket w/asymmetrical angular overhead handle, peony blossoms in relief against textured gold ground, 7" h. 52.50
Basket, hanging-type, peony blossoms in relief against textured gold or green ground, 5", each . . . 85.00
Bookends, peony blossoms in relief

against textured green shaded to
pink ground, 5½" h., pr......... 65.00
Candle holders, double, peony blossom & foliage between candle
nozzles, textured gold ground,
5" h., pr. (ILLUS.) 65.00
Ewer, peony blossoms in relief
against textured gold ground,
6" h.......................... 32.00
Ewer, peony blossoms in relief
against textured green or pink
ground, 15" h., each 140.00
Jardiniere & pedestal base, peony
blossoms in relief against textured green shaded to pink
ground, overall 24½" h., 2 pcs. .. 450.00
Lemonade set: pitcher & 6 mugs; peony blossoms in relief against textured green ground, 7 pcs........ 235.00
Model of a conch shell, peony blossoms in relief against textured
green ground, 9½" l............. 60.00
Vase, 6" h., peony blossoms against
textured green ground........... 25.00
Vase, 12" h., peony blossoms
against textured gold ground..... 75.00
Vase, 14" h., angular handles at
mid-section, peony blossoms
against textured green ground ... 105.00
Wall pocket, peony blossoms
against textured pink ground,
8" h.......................... 65.00

PERSIAN (1916)
Bulb bowl, 3-handled, red & yellow
waterlily motif w/green foliage on
creamware, 3½" h. 95.00
Candlestick, pierced base, colorful
geometric motif on creamware,
9" h. (single) 65.00
Jardiniere, colorful stylized floral
motif on creamware,
5" h...................110.00 to 125.00
Jardiniere, stylized green & yellow
foliate motif on creamware,
6" h.......................... 150.00
Jardiniere, stylized orange poppy
blossoms & green ivy-type foliage
on creamware, 10" d., 8" h....... 235.00
Window box, colorful geometric
motif on creamware............. 200.00

PINE CONE (1931)
Ash tray, realistic pine cones in relief on shaded brown or green
ground, 4½" l., each 45.00
Basket w/overhead branch handle,
realistic pine cones in relief on
shaded blue, brown or green
ground, 10" h., each ....120.00 to 155.00
Basket, hanging-type w/original
chains, pine cones in relief on
shaded blue ground, 5"..185.00 to 225.00
Bowl, 6" d., pine cones in relief on
green ground 27.00

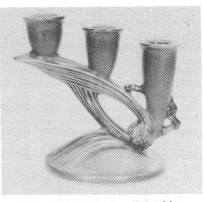

Pine Cone Triple Candle Holder

Candle holders, triple, domed base,
pine cones in relief on blue
ground, 5½" h., pr. (ILLUS. of
one) 200.00
Console set: 12" l. bowl & pr.
2½" h. candle holders; pine cones
in relief on brown ground,
3 pcs. 150.00
Cornucopia-vase, pine cones in relief on brown ground, 6" h. 40.00
Flower pot w/saucer, pine cones in
relief on green ground, 4" h...... 60.00
Mug, pine cones in relief on brown
ground, 4" h. 60.00
Pitcher w/ice lip, 8" h., bulbous,
pine cones in relief on brown
ground 170.00
Planter, pine cones in relief on
brown ground, 9" l., 3½" h. 50.00
Rose bowl, pine cones in relief on
blue ground, 4" d. 125.00
Tumbler, pine cones in relief on
blue ground, 5" h. ....95.00 to 125.00
Umbrella stand, pine cones in relief
on brown ground ......600.00 to 700.00
Urn-vase, pine cones in relief on
blue or brown ground, 7" h.,
each 50.00
Vase, 6" h., fan-shaped, pine cones
in relief on green ground 40.00
Vase, 8" h., branch handle at base
& rim, pine cones in relief on
brown ground.................. 110.00
Vase, 14½" h., 2-handled, pine
cones on blue or brown ground,
each ....175.00 to 235.00
Wall pocket, pine cones in relief on
blue or brown ground, 9" h.,
each ....135.00 to 160.00
Wall shelf, pine cones in relief on
brown ground.................. 145.00

POPPY (1930's)
Basket w/rounded overhead handle,
poppies on turquoise blue shaded
to white ground, 10" h. 95.00

Ewer, yellow poppies on turquoise
blue shaded to white ground,
10" h. 90.00
Jardiniere, poppies on shaded pink
or turquoise blue ground, 3" h.,
each 25.00
Jardiniere & pedestal base, poppies
on shaded pink ground, overall
26" h., 2 pcs. 670.00
Vase, 6" h., trumpet-shaped, pop-
pies on shaded turquoise blue
ground 40.00

Poppy Vase

Vase, 7" h., 2-handled, poppies on
yellow shaded to pink ground
(ILLUS.) 40.00
Wall pocket, triple, pink poppies on
yellow shaded to pink ground,
8½" h. . . . . 125.00 to 150.00

PRIMROSE (1932)

Bowl, 6" d., 2-handled, cluster of
long-stemmed blossoms & pad-
like leaves in relief on tan
ground 40.00
Jardiniere & pedestal base, cluster
of long-stemmed blossoms & pad-
like leaves in relief on pink
ground, 2 pcs. 225.00
Vase, 6" h., angular side handles,
cluster of long-stemmed blossoms
& pad-like leaves on blue
ground 40.00
Vase, 7" h., 2-handled, long-
stemmed blossoms & pad-like
leaves on blue or pink
ground, each . . . . 35.00 to 50.00
Vase, 10" h., 2-handled, long-
stemmed blossoms & pad-like
leaves on tan ground 90.00

RAYMOR (1952)

Bean pot, cov., long handles, dark
green dull finish, 2-qt. 35.00
Bun warmer, cov., side opening,
black or brown dull
finish, each . . . . 100.00 to 135.00

Butter dish, cov., white dull finish . . 45.00
Casserole, cov., terra cotta dull fin-
ish, 11" d. 40.00
Coffee pot, cov., w/swinging-type
stand, grey dull finish . . . 150.00 to 175.00
Creamer, cov., terra cotta dull
finish 30.00
Cruet w/original stopper, terra cotta
dull finish 35.00
Dinner service for 4: dinner plates,
bread & butter plates & c/s; dark
green dull finish, 16 pcs. 120.00
Ramekin, cov., dark green dull fin-
ish, 6½" d. 25.00
Salt & pepper shakers, ovoid, white
dull finish, pr. 20.00
Sugar bowl, cov., terra cotta dull
finish 30.00

ROSECRAFT (1916-19)

Bowl, 8" d., 3" h., glossy blue 45.00
Candlesticks, glossy black, 8½" h.,
pr. 80.00
Jardiniere & pedestal base, glossy
black, overall 30½" h., 2 pcs. 850.00
Vase, 5¼" h., 2-handled, squatty,
glossy black 40.00
Vase, 6" h., 2-handled, glossy
black 60.00
Vase, 8" h., rim handles, cylindrical,
glossy black 120.00
Wall pocket, glossy yellow, 10" h. . . 165.00
Wall pocket, 2-handled, glossy blue,
10½" h. 125.00

ROSECRAFT VINTAGE (1924)

Rosecraft Vintage Vase

Bowl, 4½" d., 2½" h., curving band
of brown & yellow grapevine
w/fruit & foliage below rim, dark
brown matte ground 32.00
Bowl, 8" d., curving band of brown
& yellow grapevine w/fruit & foliage, dark brown matte ground . . . 75.00
Vase, 5" h., curving band of brown
& yellow grapevine w/fruit & foliage at shoulder, dark brown
matte ground (ILLUS.) . . . . . 30.00 to 40.00

Vase, 6" h., globular w/short neck
& small mouth, curving band of
brown & yellow grapevine w/fruit
& foliage at shoulder, dark brown
matte ground 55.00

Wall pocket, tapered form, brown &
yellow grapevine w/fruit & foliage, dark brown matte ground,
9" h. 95.00

Wall pocket, 2-handled, cluster of
grapevine w/fruit & foliage, dark
brown matte ground, 9" h. 135.00

ROZANE (1900's)

Rozane Tankard Pitcher

Bowl, 2½" d., underglaze slip-
painted delicate florals, standard
brown glaze 85.00

Bowl, 5" d., 3-toed, underglaze slip-
painted yellow daffodils, standard
brown glaze 120.00

Dresser tray, underglaze slip-
painted yellow roses, standard
brown glaze, artist-signed,
13 x 8½" 395.00

Ewer, underglaze slip-painted yellow pansies, standard brown
glaze, 8" h. 130.00

Jardiniere & pedestal base, underglaze slip-painted florals, standard brown glaze, overall 30" h.,
2 pcs. .... 500.00 to 600.00

Letter holder, underglaze slip-
painted florals, standard brown
glaze, artist-signed 125.00

Mug, underglaze slip-painted cluster
of cherries & foliage, standard
brown glaze, artist-signed,
4½" h. 190.00

Pitcher, tankard, 10½" h., underglaze slip-painted wild roses,
shaded tan to dark brown stand-
ard glaze, artist-signed 300.00

Pitcher, tankard, 13" h., underglaze
slip-painted cluster of red cherries, standard brown glaze, artist-
signed (ILLUS.) 500.00

Vase, 4" h., 2-handled, underglaze
slip-painted daisies, standard
brown glaze 125.00

Vase, 6½" h., 2-handled, everted
rim, underglaze slip-painted gold
berries & green foliage, standard
brown glaze 165.00

Vase, 7½" h., underglaze slip-
painted yellow roses, standard
brown glaze 110.00

Vase, 8½" h., underglaze slip-
painted yellow florals & shaded
green foliage, standard brown
glaze, artist-signed 185.00

Vase, 9" h., underglaze slip-painted
portrait of a majestic buck w/full
rack of antlers, standard brown
glaze, artist-signed 1,450.00

Vase, 10½" h., underglaze slip-
painted yellow florals, standard
brown glaze, artist-signed 525.00

SILHOUETTE (1940's)

Silhouette Vase

Ash tray, silhouette floral panel
center, shaded tan 22.00

Basket w/pointed overhead handle,
silhouette floral panel, white
w/turquoise blue, 6" h. 30.00

Basket w/overhead handle rising
from base to opposite rim, silhouette floral panel, shaded tan,
8" h. 40.00

Basket, hanging-type, silhouette floral panel, shaded rose or tan, 4",
each .... 45.00 to 60.00

Cigarette box, cov., silhouette floral
panel on lid, shaded turquoise
blue 48.00

Ewer, angular side handle & body,
silhouette floral panel, white
w/turquoise, 10" h. 40.00

Planter, low foot, silhouette foliate
panel, shaded rose, 14" l. 50.00

Vase, 7" h., 8" w., fan-shaped, silhouette panel of a nude, shaded tan (ILLUS.) 125.00

Vase, 7" h., leaf-shaped base handles, silhouette floral panel, shaded tan 30.00

Vase, 8" h., bulbous, silhouette panel of a nude, shaded rose or white w/turquoise blue, each .... 120.00 to 150.00

Wall pocket, silhouette foliate panel, shaded turquoise blue, 8" h. ... 55.00

SNOWBERRY (1946)

Snowberry Pillow-Shaped Vase

Basket w/pointed overhead handle, snowberry branch in relief on shaded green ground, 7" h. 53.00

Basket, hanging-type, snowberry branch in relief on shaded green or rose ground, 5", each ... 65.00 to 85.00

Bookends, snowberry branch in relief on shaded blue or rose ground, each pr. .... 55.00 to 65.00

Bowl, 6" d., low, snowberry branch in relief on shaded blue ground .. 27.50

Candle holders, 2-handled, bulbous, snowberry branch in relief on shaded green ground, 2" h., pr. ... 25.00

Cornucopia-vase, snowberry branch in relief on shaded blue ground, 6" h. 18.00

Ewer, snowberry branch in relief on shaded green ground, 15" h. 150.00

Jardiniere, snowberry branch in low relief on shaded blue or green ground, 6" h., each 65.00

Tea set: cov. teapot, creamer & sugar bowl; snowberry branch in relief on shaded rose ground, 3 pcs. 135.00

Vase, 6½" h., pillow-shaped, snowberry branch in relief on shaded rose ground (ILLUS.) 35.00

Vase, bud, 7" h., angular handle rising from base, snowberry branch in relief on shaded rose ground .. 30.00

Vase, 9" h., snowberry branch in relief on shaded rose ground 47.50

Vase, 12½" h., ovoid w/flaring mouth, angular handles at midsection, snowberry branch in relief on shaded rose ground 75.00

Wall pocket, angular handles rising from base, snowberry branch in relief on shaded blue ground, 8" w., 5½" h. 55.00

SUNFLOWER (1930)

Sunflower Vase

Basket, hanging-type w/original chains, chrysanthemum-type yellow sunflowers on mottled green ground 175.00

Bowl, 8" d., 6½" h., chrysanthemum-type yellow sunflowers on mottled green ground 150.00

Planter, chrysanthemum-type yellow sunflowers on mottled green ground, 9 x 7½" 140.00

Urn, chrysanthemum-type yellow sunflowers on mottled green ground, 4" h. 62.50

Urn, chrysanthemum-type yellow sunflowers on mottled green ground, 6½" h. 100.00

Vase, 5" h., 2-handled, chrysanthemum-type yellow sunflowers on mottled green ground (ILLUS.) 75.00

Vase, 6" h., small rim handles, chrysanthemum-type yellow sunflowers on mottled green ground 55.00

Vase, 8" h., 7" widest d., bulbous base, wide neck, chrysanthemum-type yellow sunflowers on mottled green ground 100.00

Vase, 10" h., cylindrical, small rim handles, chrysanthemum-type yellow sunflowers on mottled green ground 145.00

Wall pocket, curved openwork double handle, chrysanthemum-type

yellow sunflowers on mottled
green ground, 7½" h. 205.00

SYLVAN (1918)
Jardiniere, molded squirrel w/nut
amidst oak leaves & acorns
against bark-textured ground,
9" h. 325.00
Jardiniere, molded deer against
bark-textured ground 700.00
Umbrella stand, molded foliage
against bark-textured ground 200.00

TEASEL (1936)
Bowl, 4" d., small closed side handles, footed, embossed teasel
spray, beige shaded to tan 40.00
Bowl-vase, small closed handles at
rim, footed, embossed teasel
spray, medium blue highlighted
w/gold, 6" h. 65.00
Flower holder, small side handles,
footed, pierced top, embossed
teasel spray, shaded blue 25.00
Vase, 7" h., embossed teasel spray,
beige shaded to tan 25.00
Vase, 8" h., bulbous, embossed tea-
sel spray, cream highlighted
w/terra cotta 45.00
Vase, 9" h., embossed teasel spray,
rose shaded to pink 35.00
Vase, 12" h., conical foot, embossed
teasel spray, blue crystalline
glaze over mint green 85.00

THORN APPLE (1930's)
Basket w/overhead handle,
trumpet-like flower one side &
prickly burr reverse on shaded
pink ground, 7" h. 50.00
Candle holders, single burr resting
on leaf, pink shading to green
ground, 2½" h., pr. 45.00
Jardiniere, trumpet-like flower one
side & prickly burr reverse on
shaded brown ground, 4" h. 42.00
Jardiniere, trumpet-like flower one
side & prickly burr reverse on
shaded brown ground, 7" h. 135.00
Urn-vase, trumpet-like flower one
side & prickly burr reverse on
shaded blue ground, 6" h. 33.00
Vase, 9" h., trumpet-like flower one
side & prickly burr reverse on
pink shading to green ground 65.00
Vase, 15" h., trumpet-like flower
one side & prickly burr reverse on
shaded blue or brown ground,
each . . . . 210.00 to 260.00
Wall pocket, 2 handles above flaring
rim, trumpet-like flowers & prickly
burrs on shaded brown ground,
8½" h. 125.00

TOPEO (1934)
Bowl, 11½" d., 3" h., 4 areas of
relief-molded beading, glossy
deep red glaze 85.00
Urn, 4 areas of relief-molded bead-
ing, glossy deep red glaze,
6" h. 125.00
Vase, 5" h., 4 areas of relief-molded
beading, green shaded to blue
glaze 110.00
Vase, 6" h., 4 areas of relief-molded
beading, glossy deep red glaze . . . 68.00
Vase, 9½" h., 6" widest d., 4 areas
of relief-molded beading from rim
to above mid-section, green shaded to blue or glossy deep red
glaze, each . . . . 100.00 to 140.00
Vase, 11" h., 4 areas of relief-
molded beading, glossy deep red
glaze 150.00

TOURMALINE (1933)
Cornucopia-vase, mottled turquoise
blue, 9" h. 55.00
Urn, hemispherical, embossed de-
sign around short neck, mottled
turquoise blue, 4½" h. 45.00
Vase, 5½" h., handles rising from
mid-section of bulbous base to
rim, streaked powder blue 37.50
Vase, 7" h., semi-ovoid w/sloping
shoulders, streaked powder
blue 42.00
Vase, 8" h., bulbous base, wide
flaring neck, handles rising from
base to mid-section, mottled terra
cotta & yellow 45.00
Vase, 8" h., pedestal base, ribbed
bulbous base, narrow handles rising from mid-section to rim,
streaked powder blue 30.00

TUSCANY (1924-28)
Bowl, 10" d., open handles terminating in embossed clusters of
blue grapes & green leaves, mot-
tled pink 40.00
Candle holders, conical base
w/open handles rising from embossed clusters of grapes &
leaves, mottled grey, 4" h., pr. . . . 30.00
Flower arranger, pedestal base,
flaring body, open handles terminating in clusters of grapes &
leaves, mottled grey, 5" h. 45.00
Flower arranger, baluster form, flaring base w/open handles rising
from clusters of grapes & leaves,
mottled grey, 5½" h. 35.00
Vase, 5" h., open handles terminat-
ing in clusters of grapes & leaves,
mottled grey or pink, each 30.00
Vase, 6" h., low footed, square
w/cut corners, everted rim, open

handles terminating in clusters of
grapes & leaves, mottled pink 35.00
Vase, 8" h., ovoid w/short wide
neck, open handles rising from
clusters of grapes & leaves at
shoulder, mottled grey 36.00
Wall pocket, conical, open handles
terminating in clusters of grapes
& leaves, mottled grey, 7" h...... 57.00
Wall pocket, flaring rim, elongated
open handles rising from clusters
of grapes & leaves, mottled grey
or pink, 8" h., each ...... 50.00 to 60.00

VELMOSS (1935)

Velmoss Vase

Bowl-vase, 2-handled, band of wavy
horizontal lines w/cluster of pendant leaves on mottled green,
5¼" h. 50.00
Vase, 6½" h., 3½" d., band of
wavy horizontal lines w/cluster of
pendant leaves on mint green 33.00
Vase, 8" h., expanding cylinder
w/sloping shoulders, angular handles, band of wavy horizontal
lines w/cluster of pendant leaves
on mottled raspberry red 62.00
Vase, 9" h., 2-handled, band of
wavy horizontal lines w/cluster of
pendant leaves on mottled green
(ILLUS.)...................... 68.00
Vase, 14½" h., expanding cylinder,
footed, 2-handled, band of wavy
lines w/cluster of pendant leaves
on mottled raspberry red 125.00
Wall pocket, double, bands of wavy
lines w/cluster of leaves rising to
form overhead handle, mottled
green, 8½" h. .... 250.00 to 275.00

VISTA (1920's)

Basket w/overhead handle, footed,
flaring rim, embossed green coconut palm trees & lavender-blue
pool against grey ground,
9½" h. 135.00
Bowl, 7½" d., 3½" h., embossed
green coconut palm trees &

lavender-blue pool against grey
ground 90.00
Vase, 12" h., embossed green coconut palm trees & lavender-blue
pool against grey ground 165.00
Vase, 15" h., 2-handled, slightly expanding cylinder, small open handles at rim, embossed green
coconut palm trees & lavender-
blue pool against grey ground.... 225.00

WATER LILY (1943)

Water Lily Cornucopia-Vase

Basket w/asymmetrical overhead
handle, curved & sharply scalloped rim, water lilies in relief on
textured brown shaded to tan or
pink shaded to green ground,
12" h., each .... 70.00 to 80.00
Basket, hanging-type w/original
chains, angular rim handles, water lilies in relief on textured blue
ground, 9"...................... 75.00
Console bowl, angular handles, water lilies in relief on textured
brown shaded to tan ground,
10" l. 32.00
Console bowl, angular handles, water lilies in relief on textured blue
or brown shaded to tan ground,
14" l., each .... 40.00 to 48.00
Cornucopia-vase, water lilies in relief on textured brown shaded to
tan ground, 8" h. (ILLUS.) 55.00
Ewer, bulbous base, water lilies in
relief on textured brown shaded
to tan ground, 10" h 70.00
Ewer, ovoid body, water lilies in relief on textured blue or brown
shaded to tan ground, 15" h.,
each .... 135.00 to 175.00
Model of a conch shell, water lilies
in relief on textured pink shaded
to green ground, 8" 60.00
Vase, 6" h., cylindrical, large angu-

lar handles rising from base, water lilies in relief on textured brown shaded to tan or pink shaded to green ground, each.... 30.00

Vase, 10" h., cylindrical w/flaring base & mouth, water lilies in relief on pink shaded to green ground 60.00

Vase, 14" h., water lilies in relief on blue or pink shaded to green ground, each ....135.00 to 175.00

Vase, 18" h., ovoid, angular handles, water lilies in relief on blue or pink shaded to green ground, each 235.00

WHITE ROSE (1940)

White Rose Console Set

Basket w/pointed circular handle, white roses in relief on brown shaded to green ground, 10" h. .. 67.00

Basket, hanging-type, white roses in relief on shaded blue ground, 5" 65.00

Bowl, 4" d., loop handles at rim, white roses in relief on shaded blue ground 25.00

Console set: 10" l. bowl & pr. candle holders; white roses in relief on pink shaded to green ground, 3 pcs. (ILLUS.)................... 65.00

Cornucopia-vase, white roses in relief on shaded blue ground, 6" h. 20.00

Cornucopia-vase, double, white roses in relief on shaded blue ground, 8" h. 55.00

Flower frog w/asymmetrical overhead handle, white roses in relief on pink shaded to green ground.. 25.00

Jardiniere, white roses in relief on brown shaded to green ground, 9" d., 6" h...................... 47.50

Pedestal base, white roses in relief on shaded blue ground 150.00

Tea set: cov. teapot, creamer & sugar bowl; white roses in relief on pink shaded to green ground, 3 pcs...................115.00 to 145.00

Vase, double bud, 4½" h., 2 columns joined by gate w/applied white rose blossoms & curving overhead handle, pink shaded to green ground 40.00

Vase, 7" h., side handles, one rising from base to rim & the other from mid-section to rim, white roses in relief on shaded blue ground..... 42.50

Vase, 8" h., pillow-shaped, angular rim handles, white roses in relief on brown shaded to green ground 47.50

Vase, 18" h., white roses in relief on shaded blue ground 250.00

Wall pocket, conical w/flaring rim, curving handle rising from base to mid-section of opposite side, white roses in relief on pink shaded to green ground, 6½" h....... 75.00

Wall pocket, fan-shaped, asymmetrical handles, white roses in relief on pink shaded to green ground, 8½" h........................ 60.00

WINCRAFT (1948)

Wincraft Basket

Basket w/overhead handle, berries & leaves in relief on glossy shaded blue ground, 12" l., overall 8" h. (ILLUS.) 60.00

Bowl, 8" d., florals in relief on glossy shaded tan ground 22.00

Bowl, 10" d., florals in relief on glossy lime green ground 32.00

Candle holders, mottled glossy blue or green ground, 2½" h., each pr......................25.00 to 30.00

Cigarette box & ash tray, berries & leaves in relief on glossy shaded green ground, 2 pcs. 55.00

Cornucopia-vase, berries & leaves in relief on glossy shaded blue ground, 9" l., 5" h............. 32.00

Ewer, branch handle, glossy mottled tan ground, 6" h. 30.00

Ewer, maple leaves & acorns in relief on glossy shaded green ground, 19" h. 245.00

Planter set, 6" h. flaring square container w/molded florals & foliage in open center, flanked by low outward curving containers w/florals in relief, glossy shaded yellow ground, 3 pcs............ 40.00

Tea set: cov. teapot, creamer & sugar bowl; florals in relief on

glossy shaded green ground,
3 pcs. . . . . .75.00 to 85.00
Vase, 6" h., asymmetrical fan
shape, pine cones & needles in
relief on glossy shaded blue
ground 35.00
Vase, 7" h., square, paneled sides
w/swirled Art Deco style design
in relief on glossy shaded green
ground 45.00
Vase, 10" h., ovoid base, straight
neck, Art Deco style handles,
geranium blossoms & leaves in relief on glossy shaded blue
ground 60.00
Vase, 14" h., berries & leaves in re-
lief on glossy shaded green
ground 150.00
Wall pocket, globular, ivy vine in re-
lief on glossy shaded tan ground,
5" h. 85.00

WINDSOR (1931)
Bowl, 10" l., diamond-shaped,
2-handled, stylized vines against
mottled blue ground 85.00
Planter, diamond-shaped, 2-handled,
band of yellow & green squares &
rectangles against mottled terra
cotta ground, 16" l. 165.00
Vase, 5" h., handles rising from
mid-section to rim, stylized florals
against mottled blue ground 50.00
Vase, 6" h., band of yellow & green
squares & rectangles against mot-
tled terra cotta ground 90.00
Vase, 7" h., large side handles, stylized florals against mottled terra
cotta ground 185.00
Vase, 7" h., globular w/collared
neck, 2-handled, stylized ferns
against mottled terra cotta
ground 270.00
Vase, 8" h., expanding cylinder,
2-handled, band of yellow &
green squares & rectangles
against mottled blue ground 225.00

WISTERIA (1933)
Bowl-vase, canted sides, small angular rim handles, lavender
wisteria & vines on textured blue
to brown ground, 4" h. 65.00
Bowl-vase, angular rim handles, lavender wisteria & vines on tex-
tured brown ground, 6½" h. 110.00
Candlesticks, lavender wisteria &
vines on textured blue to brown
ground, 4" h., pr. 110.00
Console bowl, oblong, angular rim
handles at each end, lavender
wisteria & vines on textured blue
to brown ground, 12" l. 85.00
Vase, 5" h., 2-handled, wisteria &

vines on textured blue to brown
ground 82.50
Vase, 5" h., angular handles at
shoulder, wisteria & vines on textured blue to brown ground 65.00
Vase, 6" h., ovoid w/wide neck,
loop handles at shoulder, wisteria
& vines on textured blue to brown
ground 75.00
Vase, 8" h., expanding cylinder,
2-handled, wisteria & vines on
textured blue to brown ground . . . 135.00
Vase, 8½" h., conical, curving handles rising from base, wisteria &
vines on textured blue to brown
ground 85.00
Vase, 8½" h., bulbous, angular han-
dles, wisteria & vines on textured
brown ground. 110.00

Wisteria Vase

Vase, 9½" h., angular handles,
wisteria & vines on textured blue
to brown ground (ILLUS.) 170.00
Wall pocket, flaring rim, wisteria &
vines on textured blue to brown
ground, 8" h. 175.00

WOODLAND (1905)
Lamp base, incised floral decor on
stippled bisque ground, 14" h. 435.00
Vase, 7" h., incised florals & foliage
enameled in orange, gold, brown
& dark green on stippled bisque
ground 395.00
Vase, 7½" h., incised dogwood-type
blossoms & foliage enameled in
white, dark green & tan on stip-
pled bisque ground 425.00
Vase, 10" h., square twisted body,
incised florals & foliage on stippled bisque ground (1" hairline at
rim) 400.00

ZEPHYR LILY (1946)
Ash tray, yellow lilies on brown
shaded to green ground w/im-
pressed oval swirls 33.00

Basket w/overhead handle, footed, white & yellow lilies on blue ground w/impressed oval swirls, 7" h. 45.00

Bookends, yellow lilies on brown shaded to green ground w/impressed oval swirls, pr. 62.00

Bowl, 8" l., 2-handled, white & yellow lilies on blue ground w/imprssed oval swirls 42.00

Bowl, 10" l., boat-shaped, rose & yellow lilies on green ground w/impressed oval swirls 50.00

Candle holders, 2-handled, yellow lilies on brown shaded to green ground, 2" h., pr. 19.00

Console bowl, 2-handled, white & yellow lilies on blue ground, 16" l. 45.00

Cornucopia-vase, white & yellow lilies on blue ground, 6" h. 30.00

Ewer, rose & yellow lilies on green ground, 6" h. 35.00

Ewer, yellow lilies on brown shaded to green ground, 10" h. 65.00

Planter, rose & yellow lilies on green ground, 8" l. 35.00

Tea set: cov. teapot, creamer & sugar bowl; white & yellow lilies on blue ground, 3 pcs. .....80.00 to 95.00

Urn-vase, white & yellow lilies on blue ground, 8" h. 45.00

Vase, 7" h., pillow-shaped, 2 handles above base, rose & yellow lilies on green ground 40.00

Vase, 9½" h., long handles at midsection, slanted rim, rose & yellow lilies on green ground 35.00

Vase, 10" h., bulbous base, long neck w/flaring mouth, 2 handles at mid-section, white & yellow lilies on blue ground 55.00

Zephyr Lily Wall Pocket

Wall pocket, 2-handled, yellow lily on blue ground, 8" h. (ILLUS.) 45.00

ROYAL BAYREUTH

Good china in numerous patterns and designs has been made at the Royal Bayreuth factory in Tettau, Germany, since 1794. Listings below are by the company's lines, plus miscellaneous pieces. Interest in this china remains at a peak and prices continue to rise. Pieces listed carry the company's blue mark except where noted otherwise.

CORINTHIAN

Corinthian Pitcher

Chamberstick, serpent handle, green $110.00

Pitcher, 6" h., classical figures on black ground, yellow bands w/leaf decor around neck & base, (ILLUS.) 125.00

Toothpick holder, 3-handled 65.00

DEVIL & CARDS

Devil & Cards Humidor

Ash tray 125.00

Creamer, 4" h. 132.00

Cup & saucer, demitasse 135.00

Humidor, winged devil finial,
7¾" h. (ILLUS.) 675.00
Match holder, hanging-type 195.00
Pitcher, 5" h., devil & 6 cards 235.00
Pitcher, water, 7½" h., figural red
devil handle 500.00
Wall pocket, figural devil 200.00

MOTHER-OF-PEARL FINISH
Bowl, 8" d., footed, pansy molded,
pearlized white 150.00
Bowl, large, oak leaf molded....... 275.00
Celery, oak leaf molded,
13 x 5½"..................... 125.00
Cookie jar, cov., Murex Shell patt... 250.00
Cookie jar, cov., figural grape clus-
ter, pearlized yellow 375.00
Creamer, grape cluster mold,
pearlized white 87.00
Creamer, Murex Shell patt. 45.00
Creamer, poppy molded, pink-
tinged......................... 125.00
Marmalade jar, cov., Murex Shell
patt., large 100.00
Mustard jar, poppy molded, pink
highlights 110.00
Mustard jar, cover & spoon, grape
cluster mold 110.00
Pitcher, milk, 5 x 7", Murex Shell
patt.......................... 75.00
Pitcher, milk, grape cluster mold,
pearlized white 168.00
Pitcher, water, Murex Shell patt. ... 295.00
Pitcher, water, poppy molded,
pearlized white 375.00
Salt & pepper shakers, Murex Shell
patt., pr...................... 50.00
Sugar bowl, cov., grape cluster
mold, pearlized lavender 65.00
Sugar bowl, cov., Oyster & Pearl
patt.......................... 100.00
Teapot, cov., grape cluster mold,
white satin finish............... 275.00
Toothpick holder, Murex Shell
patt.......................... 75.00

ROSE TAPESTRY

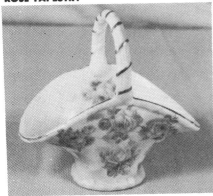

Rose Tapestry Basket

Basket, single rope handle, 3-color
roses, 4¼" w., 4" h. (ILLUS.) 275.00
Basket, 3-color roses, 8 x 4",
3½" h......................... 165.00
Bowl, 6" d., 3-color roses 155.00
Box, cov., pink & yellow roses,
4" d., 1¾" h. 285.00
Cake plate, pink roses,
10½" d.................195.00 to 300.00
Creamer & sugar bowl, 3-color
roses, gold handles, pr. 350.00
Dish, leaf-shaped, pink roses....... 178.00
Dresser set: dresser tray, hair receiver, powder box, hatpin holder
& oval box; 3-color roses,
5 pcs......................... 945.00
Hair receiver, 3 gold feet, 3-color
roses ....,...... 150.00
Mustard jar w/ladle, pink & white
roses 225.00
Nut set: master bowl & 4 individual
nut dishes; gold feet, 3-color
roses, 5 pcs................... 795.00
Pitcher, 3½" h., roses w/gold
trim.......................... 155.00
Pitcher, 6" h., 3-color roses 295.00
Planter, 2-handled, 3-color roses,
w/original insert 210.00
Plate, 6" d., 3-color roses, molded
gold rim...................... 148.00
Powder box, cov., 3-footed, pink &
white roses, 4½" d. 200.00
Powder box, cov., 3-footed, 3-color
roses 185.00
Salt dip, 3-color roses 135.00
Sauce dish, pink roses, 6" d. 135.00
Teapot, cov., pink roses, 6¾" l.,
3½" h........................ 350.00
Vase, 3" h., 2 squared handles, pink
roses 125.00
Vase, 6½" h., reverse cone shape,
3-color roses 275.00
Whimsey, lady's low-cut shoe
w/eyelets, 3-color roses, 5" 325.00

SNOW BABIES
Creamer & sugar bowl, pr......... 185.00
Plaque, pierced to hang, 9" d....... 165.00
Plate, babies on ice 75.00
Flower pot (no liner) 60.00

SUNBONNET BABIES

Sunbonnet Babies Items

Bell, babies washing ......285.00 to 350.00
Bon bon dish, 3-toed, babies
   sewing 125.00
Box, cov., oval, babies fishing,
   4½ x 2½" 245.00
Box, cov., heart-shaped, babies
   sewing ....145.00 to 195.00
Cake plate w/pierced handles,
   babies ironing, 10" d. 275.00
Candlestick, babies cleaning, 4½" h.
   (single)....................... 225.00
Chamberstick, shield-back type,
   babies fishing, 3½" d.,
   4¾" h. ....275.00 to 345.00
Creamer, babies cleaning, 4" h. 155.00
Creamer & sugar bowl, rectangular,
   babies washing, gold handles,
   pr......................250.00 to 310.00
Feeding dish, babies cleaning 290.00
Model of a Dutch shoe............. 385.00
Plate, 6" d., babies fishing 120.00
Plate, 7½" d., babies
   ironing ....100.00 to 135.00
Salt shaker, babies washing
   (single)....................... 145.00
Teapot, cov., babies ironing........ 275.00
Tea tile, babies cleaning, 6" d. 225.00
Toothpick holder, coal scuttle shape
   w/gold handle, babies mending .. 395.00

TOMATO ITEMS

Tomato Mustard Pot

Tomato bowl w/green lettuce leaf
   underplate 72.00
Tomato covered box w/leaf insert .. 50.00
Tomato cookie jar, cov............. 135.00
Tomato creamer & cov. sugar bowl,
   pr............................. 130.00
Tomato dish, cov., large 40.00
Tomato gravy boat 55.00
Tomato mustard pot, cover & spoon,
   3" d. (ILLUS.) 38.00
Tomato plate, 7½" d. 30.00
Tomato salt & pepper shakers, pr. ... 30.00
Tomato sugar bowl, cov............ 32.00
Tomato teapot, cov. 150.00

MISCELLANEOUS

Fish Head Creamer

Ash tray, open inset handle, 2 men
   in rowboat fishing scene, 5¾" l.,
   3¼" w. 43.00
Ash tray, figural elk's head 95.00
Ash tray, figural pine cones, black
   w/gold 58.00
Basket, "tapestry," Cavalier scene .. 288.00
Basket, "tapestry," violets decor.... 195.00
Bowl, 7¾ x 6", figural lobster 150.00
Bowl, 9½" d., deep, Goose Girl
   decor 135.00
Box, cov., "tapestry," Dixon
   Cavaliers tavern scene, un-
   marked, 4" 70.00
Bread tray, figural oak leaf, white
   satin finish 175.00
Candlesticks, fox hunt scene decor,
   4½" h., pr. 260.00
Chamberstick, saucer base, ring
   handle, scenic decor w/cattle
   grazing amidst trees on dark
   green shaded to yellow ground,
   6" h. 135.00
Chamberstick, shield-back type,
   Little Boy Blue decor on ginger
   brown ground.................. 150.00
Chocolate pot, dome-shaped lid, or-
   nate handle, floral & fruit decor .. 175.00
Cigarette set: cigarette box & match
   holder; musicians decor, 2 pcs. 150.00
Creamer, cows grazing & trees,
   beige ground, gold rim 69.00
Creamer, Old Man in the Mountain
   patt. 75.00
Creamer, figural beagle dog,
   unmarked 125.00
Creamer, figural bear 295.00
Creamer, figural Bo Peep 55.00
Creamer, figural bull, black 150.00
Creamer, figural conch shell, red,
   blue & cinnamon 60.00
Creamer, figural duck 108.00
Creamer, figural fish head (ILLUS.).. 93.00
Creamer, figural frog, green & or-
   ange, unmarked 75.00
Creamer, figural geranium 130.00
Creamer, figural goat head 90.00
Creamer, figural hound dog,
   brown........................ 85.00

arked 290.00
.... 650.00
er 160.00
.... 70.00
af 75.00
ed 46.00

Monkey Creamer

Creamer, figural monkey, green, 5"
(ILLUS.)......................... 215.00
Creamer, figural moose head 182.00
Creamer, figural mountain goat 225.00
Creamer, figural pansy 140.00
Creamer, figural peach 135.00
Creamer, figural pelican,
    unmarked 95.00
Creamer, figural pig.............. 195.00
Creamer, figural robin 135.00
Creamer, figural seashell 72.00
Creamer, figural strawberry....... 100.00
Creamer, figural sunflower........ 175.00
Creamer, Little Jack Horner decor .. 53.00
Creamer & cov. sugar bowl, demi-
    tasse, figural poppy, red, pr...... 150.00
Cup & saucer, demitasse, figural
    rose, pink ....185.00 to 225.00
Dresser tray, "tapestry," gold rim,
    shaded pink roses, white daisies
    & green leaves on shaded
    lavender ground, 11 x 8" 325.00
Gravy boat w/underplate, red pop-
    py decor 75.00
Humidor, cov., figural elk.......... 350.00
Jug, handled, w/pouring spout,
    Babes in Wood series, little girls
    (2) talking to troll, 4" across bot-
    tom, 6½" h. 295.00
Marmalade jar, cov., figural straw-
    berry, 6" h..................... 175.00
Match holder, figural reclining
    clown ....240.00 to 300.00
Match holder, girl & dog decor 200.00
Match holder, hanging-type, figural
    red poppy 110.00
Mug, long-horned steers scene 75.00
Mustard jar, cov., figural rose 195.00
Nappy, cloverleaf-shaped, ring han-
    dle, "tapestry," Arab horseman &
    palm tree decor................ 175.00
Pin box, lilacs decor, 3½" l., 2" h... 150.00
Pin tray, w/handle, penguin decor
    on yellow ground 75.00

Pipe rest, figural Basset Hound
    dog 295.00
Pitcher, 5½" h., Arab & camel
    decor 45.00
Pitcher, 6" h., cow & calf scene on
    shaded blue ground 118.00
Pitcher, milk, 6" h., 5" d., man
    tending turkeys decor 150.00
Pitcher, water, 7" h., figural
    elk ....235.00 to 295.00
Pitcher, water, 8½" h., fox hunt
    scene on green ground 115.00
Pitcher, milk, figural pansy 235.00
Pitcher, water, figural eagle 595.00
Plate, 6" d., Little Miss Muffet
    decor 54.00
Plate, 7" d., Jack & the Beanstalk
    decor 135.00
Plate, chop, 13" d., scenic decor
    w/boy & donkey 120.00
Powder box, cov., figural elk....... 85.00
Relish, figural poinsettia, 7½" l..... 105.00
Rose bowl, footed, floral decor 50.00
Salt & pepper shakers, figural
    poppy, pr...................... 150.00
Salt & pepper shakers, figural rose,
    yellow w/pink center, pr......... 75.00

Elk Stein

Stein, figural elk (ILLUS.).......... 225.00

Rooster's Head String Holder

String holder, figural rooster's head
(ILLUS.) ....175.00 to 225.00
Table set: creamer, sugar bowl &
salt & pepper shakers; figural
grape cluster, 4 pcs............. 225.00
Teapot, cov., figural pansy 350.00
Tea strainer, figural sunflower 145.00
Toothpick holder, 2-handled, footed,
"tapestry," courting scene........ 350.00
Toothpick holder, coachman decor .. 170.00
Toothpick holder, figural moose
head 67.50
Vase, 2¾" h., 2½" d., 2-handled,
hunt scene 60.00
Vase, 3 3/8" h., 2 3/8" d.,
2-handled, Dutch girl & boats
scene, hallmarked silver top
rim 44.00
Vase, 3½" h., ball form, flow blue
portrait of 2 children 150.00
Vase, 3¾" h., castle w/waterfall
scene 35.00
Vase, 4" h., "tapestry," chrysanthe-
mums decor 350.00
Vase, 4¾" h., double portrait
decor 172.00
Vase, 6¼" h., "tapestry," portrait of
lady wearing a bonnet........... 275.00
Vase, 8" h., "tapestry," 2-handled,
tavern scene.................. 235.00
Wall pocket, figural strawberry 225.00
Whimsey, model of a man's high
Oxford shoe, w/original lace, tan,
unmarked 82.00

ROYAL COPENHAGEN

Royal Copenhagen Fish Plate

This porcelain has been made in Copenhagen, Denmark, since 1715. The ware is hard-paste. Also see COMMEMORATIVE PLATES.

Basket, reticulated sides applied
w/pastel florettes, Flora Danica
patt. interior, botanical specimen

within border heightened w/pink
enamel & gilding, 9 7/8" oval ...$1,320.00
Candle bobeches, Full Lace patt.,
blue, 3½" d., pr................. 65.00
Candlesticks, circular columns molded w/foliate swags suspended
from tied ribbons enriched in gilding, lower & upper parts w/shal-
low grooves & stylized foliage on
flaring bases, white & gilt, 7" h.,
set of 4 .... 990.00
Compote, 8 1/8" d., reticulated, Flora
Danica patt., botanical specimen
within border heightened w/pink
enamel & gilding 1,210.00
Creamer & cov. sugar bowl, Flora
Danica patt., named botanical
specimen within border, branch
handles, pr. 880.00
Cup & saucer, fluted, Half Lace
patt., blue 25.00
Egg cups, Flora Danica patt., botanical specimen within border
heightened w/pink enamel & gilding, set of 4 .... 385.00
Figure of Pan, seated w/hands in
lap, 3½" h.................... 130.00
Figure of Pan, seated & playing
w/snake, 4¼" h. ....230.00 to 315.00
Figure of Wee Willie Winkie, artist-
signed, 6½" h................. 125.00
Figure of Pan, riding a white goat,
8½ x 8½" 575.00
Figure of a little girl, holding water
jug & covered pail, w/sheaf of
wheat on back, artist-signed,
9" h......................... 195.00
Figure group, man & woman in
colonial dress, 1920's, 11" h.,
pr............................ 275.00
Fish plates, each fish named on
reverse, borders enriched in pale
green & gilt, 10" d., set of 16
(ILLUS. of one) 4,400.00
Plates, dessert, 7¾" d., Flora
Danica patt., botanical specimen
within border heightened w/pink
enamel & gilding, set of 14 ......3,025.00
Platters, 14¼" oval, Flora Danica
patt., botanical specimen within
border heightened by pink enamel
& gilding, pr. 880.00

ROYAL DUX

These wares were made in Bohemia and many were imported to the United States around the turn of the century. Although numerous pieces were originally inexpensive, collectors have taken a fancy to the ware and the prices of the better pieces continue to rise.

Royal Dux Vase

Bust of a young Roman man wearing laurel wreath crown, green toga & salmon pink tunic, 8½" h. $275.00

Centerpiece, shell-form bowl raised on swelling wave awash w/seaweed & foliage, one side w/semi-draped maiden w/musical instrument, single calla lily at base, green, pink & beige tones burnished in gold, pink triangle mark, early 20th c., 12¼" w., 14¾" h. 575.00

Figure of a nude lady seated w/butterfly on her knee, 8" h. 150.00

Figure of a nude Art Nouveau maiden on a curling wave base, 9 x 7" 300.00

Figure of a woman carrying a basket of fish, matte finish, 15½" h. 345.00

Figure of "Rebecca at the Well," 16¼" h. 600.00

Figure of a peasant boy carrying goose, ducks & rabbit, pre-1918, 21" h. 425.00

Figures, peasant man & woman, pink, green & gold w/satin finish flesh tones, 4" d., 11½" h., pr.... 562.00

Figures, lady & gentleman in 18th c. attire, he playing the violin & she dancing, pink triangle mark, 16" h., pr. 455.00

Figures, young couple in Victorian attire carrying water, 24" h. figures on hand-carved wooden bases, pr. 1,250.00

Figures, Hindu water carriers, 27¾" h., pr. 950.00

Figure group, lady & gentleman wearing rose Grecian togas, she playing the lyre & standing attentively as he plays a mandolin while seated on a marble Doric column decorated w/flowers & vines, 14" h. 400.00

Figure group, woman wearing flowing gown leaning against column & watching potter at his work, 6 x 6" base, 15½" h. 880.00

Figure group, peasant couple binding sheaves of wheat, he standing & she kneeling at her work, pink, green & gold w/flesh tones, pink triangle mark, 19" h. 825.00

Model of a monkey w/horn, pink triangle mark, 4" h. 55.00

Model of a stalking tiger, 15" l. 150.00

Vases, 11¾" h., woman holding jug in relief against a seahorse scene, shades of avocado, brown & cream, pr. (ILLUS. of one) 545.00

Vase, 14" h., blue-green lustre glaze w/applied white relief figure of an Art Nouveau lady, pink triangle mark 350.00

ROYAL RUDOLSTADT

Royal Rudolstadt Cake Plate

This factory's wares came from Thuringia, Germany, where a faience factory was established in 1720. E. Bohne made hard paste porcelain here from 1854, and most wares found today date from the late 19th century. Also see KEWPIE COLLECTIBLES.

Bowl, 9½" d., windmills decor on blue ground, irregular rolled rim $70.00

Bust of Queen Louise, 8½" h. 195.00

Cake plate, gold rim, h.p. roses decor, 11" d. (ILLUS.) 50.00

Chocolate pot, cov., h.p. clusters of pink roses, white florals & foliage on white ground, gold trim, 10" h. 150.00

Cups & saucers, pedestal bases, h.p. roses on blue ground, set of 8.... 150.00

Dresser tray, roses decor, 10 x 7½" 62.00

Ewer, brown serpentine handle,

pebbled shell mold body, shaded
pale pink & cream, 13½" h. 175.00
Hair receiver, pink roses decor, gold
trim 50.00
Plate, 8" d., h.p. grapes decor 60.00
Plate, chop, 13" d., h.p. poppies
decor 100.00
Sweetmeat jar, cov., overall pink
florals w/green & rust leaves on
cream ground, w/silverplate
holder marked "Middletown" 135.00
Urn, cov., scene of Hector & An-
dromache on cobalt blue ground,
gold trim, artist-signed, 19th c.,
10" h. 250.00
Vase, 6½" h., gold handles,
enameled florals & gold beading
on cobalt blue ground 165.00
Vase, 12" h., Art Nouveau style
florals on yellow shaded to beige
ground w/relief-molded leaves &
fronds 85.00
Vase, 16" h., 10" d., dragon's head
handles, 4 salamander feet, front
w/scene of bird awakening at
dawn, reverse w/night scene of
sleeping bird, earth tones 540.00

ROYAL VIENNA

Royal Vienna Portrait Plate

The second factory in Europe to make hard-paste porcelain was established in Vienna in 1719 by Claud Innocentius de Paquier. The factory underwent various changes of administration through the years and finally closed in 1865. Since then, however, the porcelain has been reproduced by various factories in Austria and Germany, many of which have reproduced also the early beehive mark. Early pieces, naturally, bring far higher prices than the later ones or the reproductions.

Compote, portrait decor on plum
ground w/gold relief details, on
ornate 2-handled gilded metal
stand $215.00

Paintings on porcelain, one depicting Christ on the cross & the other
the Virgin Mary, ornate silver
easel frames, dated 1854, 4 x
2½" plus frame, pr. 275.00
Plate, 9½" d., center scene of 2
ladies feeding birds in a formal
garden setting, magenta, pink,
yellow & turquoise border w/or-
nate gold relief 650.00
Plates, 9½" d., "Toufe des Achilles"
& "Samson & Delilah," scene of
woman bathing child w/other
women around her on one &
Delilah & warriors on other, each
within deep iridescent maroon
border w/intricate gold relief
designs, artist-signed, pr. 750.00
Plate, 9 7/8" d., bust portrait of
dark-haired lady, emerald green
border heightened w/gilt details
(ILLUS.) 300.00
Plate, 10" d., portrait of Juliet
reserved on cobalt blue ground
heightened w/gilding, artist-
signed 265.00
Plate, 13" d., portrait of "Musik" . . . 350.00
Vase, 4¼" h., beehive-shaped, portrait of beautiful young girl
reserved on blue ground w/ornate
beading, signed Wagner 325.00
Vase, 6½" h., portrait of Madam
LeBrun, signed Wagner 550.00
Vase, 7¾" h., 2-handled, portrait of
a lovely lady within ornate gilt
bands, reverse w/florals & foliage
on maroon ground, signed
Wagner 350.00
Vase, cov., 8½" h., 4½" w., gilt
handles, center portrait of young
woman w/dark blonde long wavy
hair wearing a pastel orange
dress reserved on dark green
ground enriched w/gold relief
floral motifs, artist-signed 775.00
Vase, 15" h., h.p. green shaded to
peach floral decor 195.00
Vase, cov., 23¼" h., neck w/con-
tinuous frieze w/maiden disarm-
ing cupid who attempts to re-
trieve his bow or a cupid weeping at the feet of a forlorn maid-
en gazing despondently toward a
ship sailing out to sea, mid-
section w/procession of allegorical figures reserved on a beaded
gilt ground, whole reserved between lustrous pale yellow or
pink borders & enriched by gild-
ing, on stand, late 19th c. 2,750.00
Vase-on-stand, cov., 33½" h., ovoid
w/flaring mouth, "Liebesbotschaft,"
scene of classical maiden regard-
ing a pink rose while her lover

looks on within gilt border, reserved on streaky blue & green
iridescent ground enriched in
gilding w/various floral motifs,
signed Wagner 3,025.00

ROYAL WORCESTER

Royal Worcester Figure

*This porcelain has been made by the Roy-
al Worcester Porcelain Co. at Worcester,
England, from 1862 to the present. For earlier porcelain made in Worcester, see WOR-
CESTER. Royal Worcester is distinguished
from those wares made at Worcester between
1751 and 1862 that are referred to as only
Worcester by collectors. Also see TOBY
MUGS & JUGS.*

Bowl, 4½" d., 2-handled, h.p.
  florals w/burnished gold trim on
  glossy cream ground $125.00
Candle snuffer, "Confidence," figure
  of Jenny Lind (the Swedish Night-
  ingale) w/bird's head, ca. 1888 ... 160.00
Candlesticks, figure of a classical
  lady wearing gold laurel wreath,
  creamy white w/burnished gold
  trim, satin finish, 3¾" d.,
  11 3/8" h., pr. 900.00
Coffee pot, cov., moonlit scene in
  shades of purple, gold trim,
  8½" h. 550.00
Compote, 9½" d., footed, gold
  cranes in flight on cobalt blue
  ground 175.00
Cookie jar, swirl-molded body, pink,
  yellow & blue florals on beige satin ground, silverplate rim, cover &
  bail handle, 1899, 5½" d., 7" h. .. 300.00
Cup & saucer, h.p. castle scenes on
  yellow ground, artist-signed, ca.
  1920 .... 250.00

Demitasse set: 8" h. cov. coffee pot,
  creamer, cov. sugar bowl & 4 c/s;
  white handles, embossed gold
  geometric band around tops, blue
  mottled exteriors, white interiors
  w/gold trim, 11 pcs............. 275.00
Ewer, molded stag's horn handle,
  h.p. scene of barn owls, 1887,
  7½" h........................ 420.00
Ewer, burnished gold salamander
  handle, blue florals & tan foliage
  outlined in gold on cream satin
  finish ground, 1887, 4 3/8" d.,
  9" h......................... 460.00
Figure of "The Yankee," beige, soft
  green, tan & burnished gold, satin
  finish, 1906, 2 5/8" d., 6¾" h..... 398.00
Figure of a fisher woman, burnished
  gold, green & orange vest over
  gold clothing, carrying a fishing
  basket, satin finish, 2¾" d.,
  7¾" h........................ 415.00
Figure of "Peter Pan," ca. 1930,
  8" h. (ILLUS.) 260.00
Figure of a Kate Greenaway type
  boy carrying basket, cream &
  beige w/blue details & gold trim,
  satin finish, 1893, 4" d., 8½" h. .. 515.00
Figures, Welsh man & woman, beige
  & burnished gold, satin finish,
  1896, 8" h., pr. 595.00
Figures, "Joy" & "Sorrow," each
  wearing pale yellow gown
  w/overall dainty floral decor &
  gold trim, one holding live bird &
  the other holding dead bird, satin
  finish, 1896, 3½" d., 9½" h.,
  pr............................ 865.00
Figure group, "In the Ring," 3 circus
  horses in the ring w/rider,
  1937 ....1,850.00
Gravy boat w/underplate, burnished
  gold elephant head handle, brown
  & blue florals on cream ground,
  gold trim 145.00
Jardiniere & stand, parian, 2-
  paneled body pierced & carved in
  the Japanese style w/cranes,
  stand w/frieze of faces w/gaping
  mouths, ca. 1873, 2 pcs.........1,750.00
Jug, chrysanthemums decor, artist-
  signed & dated 1889, 7½" h. 145.00
Jug, gold serpent handle, owl on
  branch before moonlit sky decor,
  ca. 1885, 11¼" h. 925.00
Match holder, h.p. floral decor on
  beige ground 78.00
Model of goldfinch, No. 2667,
  6" h......................... 125.00
Model of Nautilus shell supported
  by coral branches 450.00
Pitcher, 4¼" h., 3" d., multicolored
  flowers on beige satin finish, teal
  blue & gold handle, 1899........ 180.00

Pitcher, 4¼" h., 2 5/8" d., dainty pink, yellow & blue flowers w/green leaves outlined in gold on beige satin finish, gold ribbed handle & gold trim 92.00

Royal Worcester Pitcher

Pitcher, 6" h., pink flowers & smaller yellow ones outlined in gold on beige satin finish, ornate handle, gold trim, 1903 (ILLUS.) ... 130.00

Pitcher, 6½" h., 4¾ x 11", basket-shaped w/spout at each end, Roman style man & woman's head protruding at sides, beige satin finish w/gold trim, 1902 .... 562.00

Pitcher, 8" h., gold beaded mask spout & handle, peach shaded to cream base & border, gold floral w/gold trim relief decor on deep pink ground 230.00

Pitcher, 8¼" h., overlapping gold leaves rim w/extending spout, ornate handle, multicolored floral decor on beige ground 240.00

Pitcher, 9" h., h.p. florals on cream matte ground, 1888 .... 145.00

Pitcher, tankard, 10" h., gold bands & floral decor, 1884 .... 285.00

Planter, figural lizard around side, round, 1852 .... 195.00

Plate, 8¾" d., floral decor w/gold band at rim.................... 65.00

Pot, cov., woman's head spout, gold basketweave handle, overall multicolored Persian decor, tall 750.00

Sugar shaker, girl wearing hat w/gold trim on beige satin ground, 2¾" d., 7½" h. 410.00

Sweetmeat jar, pineapple shape, peach & cream satin finish, silverplate rim, lid & handle w/ornate leaf trim, 5" d., 4¼" h.......... 115.00

Tea caddy, gold trimmed cover, collar & foot, oval shape, blending pale orangy pink to yellow decor,

artist-signed inside cover, 3¼ x 3 x 4¾" 75.00

Vase, 3½" h., 3 turtles in relief crawling around body, canary yellow ground 130.00

Vases, 4 1/8" h., 2¾" d., "Sabrina Ware," fish & seaweed decor on rich blue ground, pr. 282.00

Vase, 4½" h., 8" l., bamboo form, gilded handle, raised leaves, ca. 1886 .... 175.00

Vase, 6" h., egg-shaped, 3 hoofed feet, reticulated, ca. 1908 .... 560.00

Vases, cov., 6¾" h., ovoid, 2-handled, fruit decor obverse & reverse, artist-signed, pr.......... 525.00

Vase, 10" h., 2-handled, enameled fernery & leaves w/gold trim decor on beige ground 387.00

Vase, 13" h., 7½" w., footed stand w/gaping-mouthed faces, reticulated, cranes w/trees & bamboo decor, ca. 1873 ....1,750.00

Wall pocket, shell form, coral handle, ca. 1885, 10½" 65.00

SARREGUEMINES

Sarreguemines Character Jug

This factory was established in Lorraine, France, about 1770. Subsequently, Wedgwood-type pieces were produced as was Mocha ware. In the 19th century, the factory turned to pottery and stoneware.

Character jug, majolica, shaded beige flesh tones w/ruddy cheeks, 6" h.......................... $65.00

Character jug, majolica, jolly man w/ruddy complexion, turquoise blue interior, 6¾" h. 60.00

Character jug, majolica, flesh tones w/ruddy cheeks & nose, dark eyebrows & hair, 8½" h. (ILLUS.) 98.00

Pitcher, water, 7" h., bulbous, soft

green w/underglaze random silver circles & lacy patches 65.00

Pitcher, 12" h., pink blossoms & vining leaves in relief on white ground 45.00

Plates, 7½" d., majolica, scalloped rim, various fruits on gold leafy ground, set of 4 .... 80.00

Plate, 7¾" d., majolica, apples or strawberries decor, each 17.50

Plate, 8" d., boy & girl at play decor 25.00

Plate, 8" d., majolica, shaded purple, green & white floral decor ... 17.00

Plates, 8" d., wide etched lacy gold border & center design on cobalt blue ground, set of 6 ......65.00 to 80.00

Plates, 9¾" d., majolica, red cherries & strawberries on gold ground, set of 6 .... 145.00

Wall pocket, beetle decor, iridescent ground, 9½" h. 95.00

SATSUMA

Satsuma Teapot

These wares have been made in Japan for centuries, and the early pieces are scarce and high-priced. But mass-produced Satsuma-type ware is plentiful and has been turned out for the past century and a quarter. The so-called "Thousand Faces" design is considered desirable by collectors and all Satsuma prices have escalated in the last decade. Also see BUTTONS.

Bowl, 4" d., Arhats (elderly male disciples of Buddha, usually w/haloes about head) & dragon decor, Meiji period, ca. 1890 ....$100.00

Bowl, 8" d., 6" h., scalloped rim, bird & leaf decor on diapered ground 225.00

Box, cov., drum-shaped, floral decor, Edo period, ca. 1850, 2¾" d. 375.00

Box, cov., floral decor, gosu blue & red w/heavy gold trim, Edo period, ca. 1840, 2¾" d. 650.00

Egg cup, floral decor, gold trim, Kinkozan 45.00

Figure of Hotei (deity of contentment) w/sack, squirrel perched in his lap, Meiji period, 1875, 6½" w., 6" h................. 950.00

Jar, cov., Samurai warriors decor, 18" h.......................... 300.00

Koro (incense burner), reticulated brass cover w/chrysanthemum finial, ball-shaped, 14 seated Arhats wearing garments enameled in gosu blue, red, turquoise & black diapering, beneath a cloud-filled sky, lavish gold trim, Edo period, ca. 1860, 5½" d....................... 700.00

Model of a camel, overall gold & enameling, 7 x 7½" 250.00

Mug, scene w/gold pagoda on dull black ground, signed w/Oriental characters in burntorange, 6½" w., 4 5/8" h. 48.00

Plaque, pierced to hang, red & gold rim, multicolored scene w/two water fowl, florals & pond, ornate gold hanging wisteria & peonies, Meiji period, ca. 1900, 9¾" d..... 225.00

Plate, 8½" d., butterfly decor 150.00

Salt dip, red & blue chrysanthemum decor, signed 34.00

Tea bowl, Arhats wearing gosu blue, red & black garments, Edo period, ca. 1850, 3" h. 300.00

Tea bowl, straight sides, large maple trees w/red & green branches exterior & continuing to interior, gilt rim, Meiji period, late 19th c., 4 7/8" d. 825.00

Teapot, cov., gosu blue & colorful Shishi decor, gosu cross & circle, early 19th c. 695.00

Teapot, cov., gold Tokugawa mon decor, ca. 1850, 3" h............. 375.00

Teapot, cov., finely detailed reserves of women, children & scholars, colorful flowers, much gold, Meiji Period, ca. 1900, 3½" h........................ 255.00

Teapot, cov., reserve of large group of seated women w/wisteria border along top, blue ground, gold handle, spout & finial, early 20th c., 6" h. (ILLUS.) 225.00

Tea set: 8" h. cov. teapot, creamer & cov. sugar bowl; gold dragon in relief around top, dragon head finials, gold & green ground, red dragon on white ground at base, 3 pcs. 85.00

Tea set, flying cranes decor, Kinkozan, 9 pcs. 95.00

Tray, cranes in relief & floral decor, early 19th c., 7" w............. 595.00

Vase, 2½" h., bulbous, Geisha &
florals within panels front & reverse, overall gold floral decor on
cobalt blue ground, Taisho period,
ca. 1920 .... 65.00

Vase, 3" h., tapestry designs in red,
turquoise & brown in relief on
brown ground.................. 325.00

Vase, 3½" h., 2 scenic panels
w/ladies & children, gilt on
cobalt blue 78.00

Vase, 5" h., mallet handles, floral
panels, gosu cross & circle, ca.
1830 .... 875.00

Vase, 5" h., 2" d., front panel of
numerous women in group, floral
decor all around body, children
playing ball near river in background at bottom, intricate work
around neck 675.00

Vase, 6" h., Thousand Butterflies
patt. 375.00

Vase, 6½" h., bulbous, tapered top,
2-paneled, figures on front,
chrysanthemums reverse,
19th c. 150.00

Vase, 7¼" h., 4" d., orange, lavender & blue flowers outlined in
gold, 2 pheasants, trees, streams
& hill, cobalt blue collar & base
w/lavender florals outlined in
gold, gold trim................ 325.00

Vase, 8" h., dragon around neck &
body, 28 Arhats with & without
haloes, Mon Crest on bottom &
neck 392.00

Vases, 8½" h., handled, double
bases w/five-petaled flower cut
into each lower base, each panel
depicts a varying array of seasonal flowers enameled in colors &
gilt, Edo period, ca. 1820, pr. 600.00

Vase, 9½" h., bottle-shaped, floral
decor, Tozan, ca. 1870 .... 385.00

Vase, 9½" h:, 3 Oriental figures,
many Arhats & recumbant tiger in
relief 190.00

Vase, 9½" h., ring handles,
enameled warlord & servant on
both sides, ca. 1890 .... 75.00

Vase, 11¾" h., tapering cylinder,
2-handled, footed, multicolored
florals on gold ground within
scrolling borders, enameled
repetitive design around top on
green ground 140.00

Vase, 12" h., coil construction,
"moriage" vertical gold bamboo &
diagonal bands of florals decor,
mid-19th c. 500.00

Vase, 12" h., pr. of quail in flight
against cloud-filled sky front, reverse w/overall enameled floral
decor 550.00

Late 19th Century Satsuma Vases

Vases, 14½" h., urn-shaped, figures
in high relief on brown ground,
polychrome & gilt floral borders,
Meiji period, ca. 1880, pr.
(ILLUS.)...................... 330.00

Vase, 15" h., 2-handled, pear-
shaped, overall multicolored floral
motif against blue ground, Edo
period, ca. 1830 ....2,200.00

Vase, 15" h., red, purple & turquoise leaves w/relief beaded &
gold outlining on cobalt blue
ground, ca. 1915 .... 110.00

Vase, 18" h., varied motifs including
Phoenix on gosu blue, green &
gold ground, on Japanese bronze
base ground 800.00

Vase, 20" h., 2-handled, front &
back floral enameling, relief
molded decor, flared 175.00

Vase, 24½" h., warlords in court-
yard decor..................... 950.00

SCHLEGELMILCH

*Handpainted china marked "RS Germany"
and "RS Prussia" continues to grow in
popularity. According to Clifford J. Schlegelmilch in his book, "Handbook of Erdmann
and Reinhold Schlegelmilch—Prussia—
Germany and Oscar Schlegelmilch—Germany," Erdmann Schlegelmilch established
a porcelain factory in the Germanic provinces
at Suhl, in 1861. Reinhold, his younger
brother, worked with him until 1869 when he
established another porcelain factory in Tillowitz, upper Silesia. China bearing the name
of this town is credited to Reinhold Schlegelmilch. It customarily bears also the phrase
"R.S. Germany." Now collectors seek additional marks including E.S. Germany, R.S.
Poland and R.S. Suhl. Prices are high and collectors should be aware of the forgeries that
sometimes find their way to the market.*

R.S. GERMANY

R.S. Germany Relish

Bowl, 7½" w. across handles, floral
  decor on lavender ground $55.00
Bowl, 8" sq., 2-handled, large robin
  on blossom branch decor on
  bright blue ground 145.00
Bowl, 10" d., fuchsia decor on shaded ground .... 90.00 to 115.00
Bowl, 11" d., carnation mold, roses
  & lilacs decor 150.00
Cake plate, pierced handles, white
  florals on green ground, gold
  trim 55.00
Chocolate cup & saucer, roses
  decor 30.00
Cookie jar, cov., Sheepherder scene
  w/cottage & water wheel 225.00
Game plate, Golden Pheasant
  decor 169.00
Nappy, triangular Art Deco shape
  w/three handles, hydrangeas on
  shaded green ground, gold trim,
  7" w. 30.00
Pitcher, milk, 5¾" h., roses &
  chrysanthemums decor 65.00
Plate, 6" d., sweetpeas decor 7.00
Plate, 8½" d., hydrangea decor on
  soft green & white ground, gold
  trim 25.00
Ramekin, pink roses on satin
  finish 29.00
Relish tray, pierced handle, dark
  purple violets decor, 7" oval 30.00
Relish tray, pierced handles, white
  daisies on soft yellow-green, gold
  trim, 7" l. (ILLUS.) 30.00
Relish tray, pink tulips highlighted
  in white enamel on purple lustre
  shaded to cream ground 26.00
Tea set: cov. teapot, creamer & cov.
  sugar bowl; white tulip decor on
  soft green ground, gold trim,
  3 pcs. 135.00
Toothpick holder, 2-handled, oak
  leaf w/peach trim & gold beading
  on ivory ground, 2" h. 35.00
Toothpick holder, 3 gold handles,
  azalea decor 55.00

R.S. PRUSSIA

Berry set: master bowl & 6 sauce
  dishes; poppies on cream shaded
  to blue ground, 7 pcs. 295.00

Berry set: master berry bowl & 6
  sauce dishes; snowballs decor,
  lustre finish, 7 pcs. 285.00
Bowl, 6¼" d., 3-footed, Castle
  scene 260.00
Bowl, 7" d., footed, icicle mold,
  carnation decor 250.00
Bowl, 7" d., footed, medallion-type
  mold, Snowbird scene
  w/cottage 470.00
Bowl, 7½" d., cabbage mold, pink &
  white roses interior, shaded green
  exterior 200.00
Bowl, 8½" d., poppy mold, mauve &
  crimson roses decor 125.00
Bowl, 9¼" d., 2¼" h., tassel mold,
  Pheasant scene, cobalt blue
  trim 710.00
Bowl, 9¼" d., beaded rim, pink,
  yellow & white poppies on dark
  pink ground 160.00
Bowl, 9½" d., iris mold, Winter Season portrait 695.00
Bowl, 10" d., icicle mold, Pond Lilies
  reflecting in Water 135.00
Bowl, 10 3/8" d., iris mold, red to
  pink roses decor, high lustre
  finish 200.00

Fruit Bowl

Bowl, 10½" d., bowl-in-bowl mold,
  fruit decor (ILLUS.) 375.00
Bowl, 10½" d., medallion mold,
  Flora portrait center, Madame
  Lebrun & Madame Recamier &
  Princess Potocka portraits in
  medallions 750.00
Bowl, 10½" d., 6-point floral mold,
  garden flowers on shaded cream
  to soft blue 175.00
Bowl, 10½" d., Quiet Cove (or Old
  Man in Mountain) scene 350.00
Bowl, 11" d., leaf scroll & bead
  mold, Turkey & Evergreen Trees
  scene 350.00
Bowl, 11" d., 6-point plume & floral
  mold, poppies & daisies reflecting
  in water, shaded cream to light
  blue 200.00

Spring Season Bun Tray

Bun tray, iris mold, Spring Season
  portrait (ILLUS.) 1,200.00
Cake plate, pierced handles, scalloped rim, carnations on ivory to
  green ground, gold trim,
  9½" d........................ 145.00
Cake plate, pierced handles, plume
  mold, poppies decor, 10" d...... 110.00
Cake plate, pierced handles, Mill
  scene on shaded brown ground,
  10" d........................ 275.00
Cake plate, pierced handles, Quiet
  Cove (Old Man in the Mountain)
  scene, blue tint, 11" d. 750.00
Cake plate, pierced handles, Swan
  scene 325.00
Candy dish, pierced handles, Bluebirds & Cottage scene, pearlized
  finish, 8 x 4" 150.00
Celery tray, icicle mold, Sheepherder scene, 12" l. (unmarked) .. 195.00
Celery tray, medallion mold, basket
  of roses on pearlized ground,
  12" l. 165.00
Celery tray, Dice Players (after
  Murillo) on brown ground,
  12½" l. 410.00

Dice Players Chocolate Set

Chocolate set: cov. chocolate pot &
  4 c/s; jewel mold, Dice Players
  (after Murillo) scene, 9 pcs.
  (ILLUS.) 3,100.00

Madame Lebrun Chocolate Set

Chocolate set: cov. chocolate pot &
  6 c/s; Madame Lebrun portrait
  decor, 13 pcs. (ILLUS.)..........2,800.00
Coffee pot, cov., ripple mold, roses
  decor 325.00
Coffee pot, cov., pink roses on blue
  ground 525.00
Compote, 5½" d., 3¼" h., pedestal
  w/five bluebirds in flight decor, 6
  bluebirds & roses interior & 6
  bluebirds in flight exterior
  decor 295.00
Compote, 7" d., 4" h., scalloped
  edge alternating beige points &
  gold design, center lilies, white,
  purple, blue pods & green leaves,
  satin finish 350.00
Compote, Christmas roses & holly
  on white pearlized ground 195.00
Cookie jar, cov., h.p. daisies decor,
  6" d., 4½" h. 250.00
Cookie jar, cov., 4-scallop mold,
  Swans w/Temple scene, blues,
  greens & cream, 9½" d.,
  5" h............................ 750.00
Cookie jar, cov., scalloped rim &
  base, pink roses decor, 6" h...... 225.00
Cookie jar, cov., Countess Potocka
  portrait 1,350.00
Creamer, delicate pink mums w/soft
  blue petals 85.00
Creamer & cov. sugar bowl, icicle
  mold, Swans (3) on Lake decor,
  dark & light blue & tan ground,
  pr............................ 675.00
Creamer & cov. sugar bowl, Mill &
  Cottage scene, green & white,
  pr............................ 350.00
Creamer & cov. sugar bowl, Snow
  scene, pr.....................1,400.00
Cup & saucer, demitasse, purple
  blossoms on light green & orange
  ground, relief-molded upper
  body 105.00

Cup & saucer, demitasse, roses
w/gold trim decor 54.00
Dish, scalloped edge, pink & white
roses on lustre pearl finish,
w/gilding & floral border, 7" d.... 40.00
Dish, feather mold, poppies &
daisies reflected in water decor,
8½" 185.00
Dish, shell-shaped, pink roses on
tinted green & beige ground,
10" 135.00
Dresser tray, feather & plume mold,
pink & white poppies decor,
w/gold, 11¾ x 7½" 168.00
Ewer, footed, brown & tan roses decor, gold trim, 7½" h. 250.00
Ferner w/original insert, scalloped
top, pink & white roses decor 395.00
Hair receiver, roses on shaded grey
satin finish, cover w/blue border,
4" sq. 120.00
Hair receiver, pink roses w/gold
trim decor 167.00
Hair receiver, white flowers on pale
green ground, darker green
around opening 132.00
Ice cream bowl, pierced handles,
floral mold, roses & daisies on
green ground, 12½ x 7¾" 225.00
Mustard jar, cov., roses w/ornate
gold trim decor 300.00
Pitcher, milk, 8½" h., scalloped rim,
embossed tinted lady one side,
white lady reverse, overall floral
decor embossed star mark 795.00
Pitcher, tankard, 11" h., carnation
mold, pink & yellow roses decor
on blue-green ground 500.00
Plaque, wall-type, bisque, "tapestry," Mill scene, 8¾" d.......... 600.00
Plaque, wall-type, lady w/dog
decor, large, relief-molded frame,
Steeple mark 1,400.00
Plate, 7¾" d., icicle mold, turkeys &
ducks decor 375.00
Plate, 8½" d., keyhole mold, Spring
Season portrait 825.00
Plates, 9" d., floral decor, satin finish, set of 4 .... 295.00
Plate, 10" d., portrait of beautiful
lady center, dark green border
w/gold trim, Crown mark 275.00
Plate, 11" d., shell mold, pink &
white carnations on light green
ground 177.00
Plate, 11" d., pierced handles,
medallion mold, pink poppies &
small daisies on orange shaded to
bluish green ground, gold
trim.......................... 143.00
Relish dish, pines & pheasant decor,
12 x 6" 300.00
Sugar shaker, colonial figures
decor 300.00

Tea set: cov. teapot, creamer & cov.
sugar bowl; roses within medallions, lilacs, green swirling & gold
trim decor, 3 pcs. 450.00
Tray, pierced handles, carnation
mold, lavender carnations & open
poppies, satin finish 350.00
Vase, 4" h., church on tinted green
ground 188.00
Vase, 6" h., handled, roses w/pearl
jewels on shaded lavender satin
ground 275.00
Vase, 8" h., Belles of Linden portrait
(unmarked) 2,400.00
Vase, 8" h., Sheepherder scene 415.00
Vase, 8¾" h., 2-handled, double
paneled, Melon Eaters 1,050.00
Vase, 9¼" h., 2-handled, Easter
lilies & clustering small flowers on
olive to light green ground, gold
trim.......................... 260.00

OTHER MARKS

Wheelock Creamer & Sugar Bowl

Berry set: master bowl & 6 sauce
dishes; Poinsettia decor, 7 pcs.
(R.S. Tillowitz) 95.00
Bowl, 5½" d., 2-handled, roses
decor (E.S. Prov. Saxe) 30.00
Bowl, portrait of lovely lady w/roses
& twining gold floral decor on co-
balt blue ground (E.S. Germany).. 295.00
Bowl, floral decor, satin finish (R.S.
Poland) 230.00
Bowl-vase, pink poppies & green
leaves on white, brass openwork
top, 4 5/8" d., 4 3/8" h. (R.S.
Poland & R.S. Germany) 100.00
Cake plate, pierced handles, floral
decor, 10½" d. (Wheelock
Prussia) 95.00

Creamer & cov. sugar bowl, Barnyard scene, cobalt blue & gold
trim, Wheelock, pr. (ILLUS.) 725.00
Dish, gold handle, white flowers
w/pink edge, green & brown
leaves on cream ground, gold
border, 4¾ x 9¼", 2¾" h. (R.S.
Poland) 100.00
Dish, pierced handles, Dogwood
blossoms on green ground, 10" l.
(R.S. Tillowitz Silesia) 35.00

Ewer, lady holding conch shell to
ear within gold medallion, 7" h.
(E.S. Germany Prov. Saxe.) 85.00
Flower arranger, 2-part, mother of
pearl (R.S. Tillowitz) 42.00
Plaque, pierced to hang, daisies de-
cor, 10½" d. (R.S. Suhl).......... 60.00
Plate, 11" d., h.p. floral decor (R.S.
Tillowitz) 38.00
Salt & pepper shakers, vertically
ribbed, variegated pink & white
rose blossom & green leaves, gold
trim, pr. (R.S. Suhl).............. 58.00
Tankard, pears & white flowers on
shaded pale blue ground, 12½" h.
(E.S. Prussia)...................1,000.00
Vase, 4¾ x 3¾", 4 portraits decor,
green Tiffany-type finish (E.S.
Germany) 185.00
Vase, 5" h., bulbous base tapering
to narrow neck, gold handles,
bust portrait of young lady
w/flowers in her hair, Tiffany-type
finish (E.S. Germany-Royal
Saxe) 95.00
Vases, 5¼" h., 3" d., blue & green
peacock on one & orange, brown
& yellow pheasant on other,
cream, brown & gold ground,fac-
ing pr. (R.S. Poland) 145.00
Vase, 7½" h., swans, lake & woods
scene (R.S. Poland) 285.00
Vase, 8" h., 4 women decor (R.S.
Poland) 235.00
Vase, 8¾" h., 4½" d., top gold
band w/garlands of gold roses &
leaves, pink & white roses decor
on cream ground (R.S. Poland) ... 168.00
Vase, 12" h., daisies decor on grey
ground (R.S. Suhl) 110.00

SEVRES

Bust of Marie Antoinette

*Some of the most desirable porcelain ever
produced was made at the Sevres factory,
originally established at Vincennes, France,
and transferred through permission of Madame de Pompadour, to Sevres as the Royal
Manufactory about the middle of the 18th
century. King Louis XV took sole responsibility for the works in 1759 when production
of hard paste began. Between 1850 and 1900,
many biscuit and soft-paste porcelains were
again made. Fine early pieces are scarce and
high-priced. Many of those available today
are late productions. The various Sevres
marks have been copied.*

Bust of Marie Antoinette, bisque,
her head slightly turned to the
right, wearing a diadem & pearls
in her hair, her shoulders draped
in a loose cloak, on square base
(chip to one corner), 1770-1800,
16¾" h. (ILLUS.)..............$1,7600.00
Centerpiece bowl, 10-sided, exterior
w/panels of flowers within gilt
borders reserved on apple green
ground, interior w/colorful birds
below an apple green lappet border, now on a gilt-bronze base &
"Rose Pompadour" (salmon pink)
ground pedestal reserving fruit &
flower panels within apple green
borders edged in gilding, late
19th c., 10¾" h. .... 440.00·
Coffee can & saucer, cylindrical,
urns & floral swags within a border of blue dots enclosed w/gilt
ribbon, lower part w/band of berried foliage, 1771 .... 660.00
Coffee can & saucer, profile portrait
of Louis XVI within a jeweled &
gilt oval cartouche surmounted by
a royal blue & gilt crown flanked
by laurel, reverse enameled
w/white fleur-de-lis enriched
w/gilding, saucer enameled
w/various amatory trophies, gilt
dentil rims, ca. 1865 .... 400.00

Sevres Jardiniere

Jardiniere, white body molded w/play-
ful putti carrying floral garlands,
rim band of grotesques on gilt
ground w/four gilt ram's head handles (some chips, 1 horn repaired),
ca. 1820, 19" h. (ILLUS.) 5,720.00

Plate, 6¾" d., Whippet dog center
decor, gold border 40.00

Plate, 9" d., Duchesse de Bourgogne
portrait, artist-signed 200.00

Plate, 9½" d., center w/rose, purple,
blue, yellow & green cluster of
fruit & flowers, "Bleu Lapis" rim
w/three floral garlands within oval
cartouches edged in tooled gilt
foliate scrolls & floral clusters,
lightly feather-molded edge,
1759 ....2,200.00

Plate, 9½" d., center painted in colors w/Lory de Gueby bird, border
w/green & gilt "oeil-de-perdrix,"
shaped gilt rim, artist-signed,
1793 ....1,320.00

Plate, 9½" d., Mme. De Montespan
portrait, yellow & white, heavily
gold encrusted w/scalloped rim,
"Chateau des Tuileries" mark,
artist-signed 135.00

Plates, 9½" d., one with center
scene of rustic woman churning
butter w/her small son & dog
watching, second with maiden
carrying young child in basket on
her back while another tugs at
her skirt, within a "Bleu Celeste"
(sky blue) border enriched w/gilt
latticework w/rosettes at the
junctions & enclosing enameled
fleur-de-lis, artist-signed, 19th c.,
pr..................... 522.00

Plates, 9 5/8" d., center w/sprays of
flowers repeated on rim within 3
gilt floral & foliate scroll-edged
panels reserved on later-
decorated "Bleu Celeste" ground,
edge w/gilt dentil border, 18th c.,
pr..................... 440.00

Plates, 10" d., center w/fruit &
flower sprays, border w/three gilt
scroll & flowering foliage cartouches enclosing exotic birds in
landscapes reserved on "Bleu
Celeste" ground, 1757-72, set
of 9 ....1,760.00

Plate, romantic center scene, scalloped rim w/doves, florals & blue
ribbon border, "Chateau des
Tuileries" mark, 1846 .... 210.00

Platter, 21½" oval, center scene of
2 maidens relaxing in a landscape
near a monument w/a suitor playing a mandolin, within a "bleu-du-
roi" border w/gilding, mounted in
gilt-metal frame w/two handles &

supported on 4 scrolling feet,
artist-signed 950.00

Sauce dishes, center painted w/scat-
tered rose sprays, royal blue border enriched w/flower sprays &
gilt circles, artist-signed, 1771,
8¼" d., pr. 2,860.00

Soup plates, bouquets & scattered
flower sprays, blue line & gilt
dash border, shaped rim, ca.
1762, set of 6 .... 440.00

Sugar bowl, cov., exotic birds on
branches in landscapes within gilt
scroll & foliage surrounds reserved on "Bleu Celeste" ground,
cover w/flowering branch finial,
gilt dentil rim, 1771, 3¼" h. 880.00

Sevres Teapot

Teapot, cov., bouquets & scattered
flower sprays, 1765, minor wear
to gilding, 4" h. (ILLUS.) 330.00

Urn, cov., woman w/flowing hair
amidst gold relief lily pads on
blue ground, artist-signed,
10" h. 425.00

Vase, cov., 22½" h., pastoral scene
of a boy & donkey collecting
wood, a shepherdess w/her flock
& a milkmaid & cow in a distant
wooded landscape & floral bouquet reverse within gilt foliage
surrounds tied w/ribbons on "bleu
du-roi" (cobalt blue) ground, relief
foliate swags at shoulder, folded
strap handles w/gilt bosses,
domed cover w/radiating gilt
panels & knob finial, flaring gilt-
mounted foot on square ormolu
base w/band of fruiting foliage
tied w/ribbons, C-scroll motif on
sides, 4 paw feet w/foliate terminals, ca. 1770 ....46,200.00

Vase, cov., 30½" h., continuous
frieze depicting the battleground
at Rivoli & the young Napoleon on
horseback w/his men within
"Bleu Celeste" borders heightened
w/gilt laurel branches & other
foliate devices, the cover w/a
crowned "N," gilt-bronze mounts,
artist-signed, late 19th c. 5,500.00

Vase, 32¾" h., frieze depicting a
maiden descending a grand staircase to join her lover who waits
below in a gondola on a tranquil
woodland stream, whole between
wide "Bleu Celeste" (sky blue)
borders w/gilt details, artist-
signed, late 19th c. 1,870.00

SHAWNEE

Clown Cookie Jar

*The Shawnee Pottery operated in Zanes-
ville, Ohio, from 1937 until 1961. Much of the
early production was sold to chain stores and
mail order houses including Sears Roebuck,
Woolworth and others. Planters, cookie jars
and vases, along with the popular "Corn
King" oven ware line, are among the collectible items which are plentiful and still
reasonably priced.*

Bank-cookie jar combination,
   figural Winnie Pig, dark
   brown ....$80.00 to 100.00
Bowl, 6" oval, "Corn King" line 16.00
Bowl, soup, "Corn King" line 13.50
Butter dish, cov., "Corn Queen"
   line 36.00
Casserole, cov., Fruit Basket 18.50
Casserole, cov., "Corn King" line,
   individual size 27.00
Cookie jar, cov., "Corn King" line... 60.00
Cookie jar, cov., figural Clown
   w/seal (ILLUS.) 65.00
Cookie jar, figural Elephant 43.00
Cookie jar, figural Owl, gold trim .. 57.50
Cookie jar, figural Sailor Boy 32.50
Creamer, "Corn King" line 14.00
Creamer, "Corn Queen" line 13.50
Creamer, figural Elephant 13.00
Cup & saucer, "Corn King" line 20.00
Mixing bowl, "Corn King" line,
   5" d. 11.50
Mixing bowl, "Corn King" line,
   6½" d. 16.00

Mixing bowl, "Corn King" line,
   8" d. 20.00
Mug, "Corn King" line, 8 oz. 17.00
Pitcher, milk, 8½" h., "Corn King"
   line 26.00
Pitcher, figural Little Boy Blue 17.00
Pitcher, figural Puss 'n Boots 12.00
Pitcher, figural Smiley Pig 35.00
Planter, figural Oriental lady 14.00
Planter, model of a bull, black 35.00
Planter, model of a fish 45.00
Planter, model of a flying goose 8.00
Planter, model of stag, brown 16.00
Planter, model of a train w/blue
   locomotive engine, yellow tender,
   green hopper & tan caboose,
   marked "SRR," overall 17½" l.,
   4 pcs. 30.00
Planter, model of a wishing well
   w/Dutch boy & Dutch girl 15.00
Plate, 10" oval, "Corn King" line 10.00
Platter, "Corn Queen" line 15.00
Salt & pepper shakers, figural Chan-
   ticleer Rooster, large, pr. 18.00
Salt & pepper shakers, figural Farmer Pig, pr. 17.00
Salt & pepper shakers, figural Mug-
   sey dog, gold trim, 5" h., pr. 18.00
Salt & pepper shakers, figural Owl,
   3" h., pr. 11.50
Salt & pepper shakers, figural Win-
   nie Pig, pr. 16.00
Salt & pepper shakers, model of a
   watering can, pr. 6.00
Sauce dish, "Corn King" line,
   6" oval 15.00
Sugar bowl, cov., "Corn King"
   line 18.00
Sugar bowl, cov., "Corn Queen"
   line 10.00
Teapot, cov., figural Granny Ann,
   blue 40.00
Teapot, cov., figural Tom the Piper's
   Son 35.00
Vegetable bowl, open, "Corn King"
   line, 9" oval 22.00

SHENANDOAH VALLEY POTTERY

Shenandoah Pitcher

*The pottery of the Shenandoah Valley in
Maryland and Virginia, turned out an earth-*

enware pottery of a distinctive type. It was the first earthenware pottery made in America with a varied, brightly colored glaze. The most notable of these potters, Peter Bell, Jr., operated a pottery at Hagerstown, Maryland and later at Winchester, Virginia, from about 1800 until 1845. His sons and grandsons carried on the tradition. One son, John Bell, established a pottery at Waynesboro, Pennsylvania in 1833, working until his death in 1880, along with his sons who subsequently operated the pottery a few years longer. Two other sons of Peter Bell, Jr., Solomon and Samuel, operated a pottery in Strasburg, Virginia, a town sometimes referred to as "pot town" for six potteries were in operation there in the 1880's. Their work was also continued by descendants. Shenandoah Valley redware pottery, with its colorful glazes in green, yellow, brown and other colors, and the stoneware pottery produced in the area, is eagerly sought by collectors. Some of the more unique forms can be considered true American folk art and will fetch fantastic prices.

Dish, redware w/white slip & clear glaze splashed w/green, old gilt paint exterior, 6¾" d., 2" h. $175.00
Flower pot, ovoid body w/incised rings & serrated rim, redware w/green glaze on white slip, attached serrated rimmed pan, S. Bell & Sons, 9" h. 440.00
Jar, semi-ovoid, earred handles, brushed cobalt blue stylized florals on greyish brown, impressed "John Bell, Waynesboro," 5-gal., 14 x 13" warped d., 12½" h. 600.00
Pitcher, 4¼" h., redware w/white slip & mottled green & clear glaze (ILLUS.). 525.00
Pitcher, 5 5/8" h., ribbed strap handle, white slip w/running brown & green (short hairline in rim & old edge & surface flakes). 550.00
Preserving jar, yellowware, impressed "John Bell, Waynesboro," 7¼" h. 300.00
Salt dip, cylindrical w/stepped base, redware w/white slip & clear glaze streaked w/running brown, 1¾" h. 550.00
Vase, 8" h., redware w/colorful glaze decor 67.50

SLIP WARE

This term refers to ceramics, primarily redware, decorated by the application of slip, or semi-liquid paste made of clay. Such wares were made for decades in England and Ger-

many and elsewhere on the Continent, and in the Pennsylvania Dutch country and elsewhere in the United States. Today, contemporary copies of early Slip Ware items are featured in numerous decorator magazines and offered for sale in gift catalogues. These reproductions hurt dealers who handle authentic old pieces of Slip Ware.

19th Century Slip Ware Plate

Bowl, 8¼" d., 3 1/8" h., rolled rim, yellow slip on redware, Pennsylvania $155.00
Bowl, 13" d., shallow, coggled edge, yellow-ivory slip design on redware w/manganese splotches through the clear glaze 412.50
Loaf pan, coggled edge, yellow slip 4-line design on redware, 15¾ x 11½", 3" h. 475.00
Loaf pan, coggled edge, yellow slip 3-line designs on redware, 17" l. (small edge chips) 775.00
Pie plate, yellow slip straight & curved lines on redware, 7½" d. 210.00
Pie plate, coggled edge, yellow slip crow's foot design on redware, 7¾" d. (minor surface wear) 200.00
Pie plate, coggled edge, yellow slip 3-line & crow's foot designs on redware, 8" d. 475.00
Pie plate, green & yellow slip "S" curves on redware, back impressed "W. Smith Womelsdorf," 8" d. (stain, wear & short hairlines) 400.00
Pie plate, yellow slip 2-line designs on redware, 8 3/8" d. 195.00
Pie plate, coggled edge, yellow slip 3-line design on redware, 8 3/8" d. 185.00
Pie plate, coggled edge, yellow slip crow's foot design on redware, 11½" d. 650.00
Plate, 6" d., coggled edge, yellow

slip wavy line design on redware, green & clear glaze (rim chips) ... 500.00

Plate, 8 5/8" d., coggled edge, yellow slip 3-line design on redware (ILLUS.) 200.00

Plate, 10 7/8" d., coggled edge, yellow slip 3-line design on redware 285.00

Plate, 11¼" d., yellow slip w/sgraffito tulips, double-headed eagle & foliate border heightened in green on redware, Pennsylvania, probably late 19th c. 250.00

SPATTERWARE

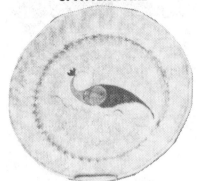

Peafowl Plate

This ceramic wares takes its name from the "spattering" of designs on it in color with rustic decor and flowers, houses and eagles and the like. Much of that now available in this country was imported from potteries in England last century.

Bowl, 11" d., free-hand red & green florals, spatter rim $65.00

Creamer, red & blue rainbow spatter, 4" h. 275.00

Creamer, paneled body, black & purple rainbow spatter, embossed fan detail at spout, 4 5/8" h. 375.00

Cup, Schoolhouse patt., blue spatter 245.00

Cup & saucer, handleless, blue transfer of eagle & shield w/"E Pluribus Unum," blue stick spatter on white, marked "R. Hamersley" 100.00

Cup & saucer, handleless, red & blue rainbow spatter on white.... 175.00

Cup & saucer, handleless, Peafowl patt., free-hand red, blue, yellow, red & black peafowl on green spatter ground 400.00

Cup & saucer, handleless, Rose patt., free-hand red, green & black rose, rainbow spatter borders 250.00

Cup & saucer, handleless, free-hand red, green & black vining design, red spatter border 205.00

Cup & saucer, handleless, black & purple rainbow spatter, miniature size 95.00

Dessert dish, Peafowl patt., free-hand blue, red & yellow peafowl on red spatter ground, 4" d. 145.00

Pitcher, 6 5/8" h., paneled body, red & blue striped rainbow spatter (chip on rim near spout) 375.00

Plate, 7½" d., Peafowl patt., free-hand green, blue, yellow & black peafowl on red spatter ground (ILLUS.) 290.00

Plate, 8¼" d., Bull's Eye patt., black & purple spattered bull's eye center, rainbow spatter border 310.00

Plate, 9" d., gaudy stick spatter florals, marked "Villeroy & Boch" 55.00

Plate, 9½" d., purple & brown rainbow spatter 275.00

Plate, 9¾" d., Rose patt., free-hand red, green & black rose, blue spatter border 235.00

Plate, 10" d., Tulip patt., free-hand red, green & black tulip, blue spatter border 175.00

Platter, 12 3/8" l., cut corners, blue spatter on white 175.00

Saucer, Peafowl patt., free-hand red, blue, yellow & black peafowl on green spatter ground 150.00

Sugar bowl, cov., black & purple rainbow spatter, 4 3/8" h. 250.00

Teapot, cov., paneled, red & blue rainbow spatter on white, 8¾" h. 525.00

Toddy plate, Rose patt., free-hand red, green & black rose on blue spatter ground, 5¼" d. 115.00

Rose Pattern Bowl & Pitcher

Wash bowl & pitcher, paneled, Rose patt., free-hand red rose & green leaves on side of pitcher & in bot-

tom of bowl, blue spatter trim
(ILLUS.). 650.00
Waste bowl, Peafowl patt., free-
hand red, blue, yellow & black
peafowl on green spatter ground,
4½" d., 2 5/8" h. 345.00
Waste bowl, red & blue rainbow
spatter, 5 3/8" d., 3½" h. 250.00

SPONGEWARE

Spongeware Bowl

*Spongeware's designs were spattered or
daubed on in colors, sometimes with a piece
of cloth. Blue and blue-and-white ware
predominated. Some collectors lump Spatterware and Spongeware into a single category,
but dealers offer them as separate wares. Also
see RED WING POTTERY.*

Batter bowl, w/pour spout, blue
daubing on yellowware, 7½ x
4¼" (replaced wire bail handle) . . $120.00
Batter pitcher, blue daubing on
white, extra large 265.00
Bowl, 6" d., blue daubing on
white 55.00
Bowl, 6" d., brown daubing on
yellowware 45.00
Bowl, 6½" d., blue & rust daubing
on cream, w/Iowa advertising 50.00
Bowl, 6½" d., scalloped scroll-
molded rim, green daubing on
cream 65.00
Bowl, 6¾" d., 3" h., brown & green
daubing on cream 37.50
Bowl, 7" d., blue & rust daubing on
cream 50.00
Bowl, 8½" d., 3½" h., blue daubing
on white (ILLUS.) 95.00
Bowl, 9½" d., 4 7/8" h., brown,
blue & red daubing on cream 65.00
Bowl, 10¾" d., 4 1/8" h., arch-
molded sides, light blue daubing
on tan 210.00
Bowl, fruit, blue daubing on yellow-
ware, ornate molded design 95.00
Chamber pot, blue daubing on
white 135.00
Cuspidor, molded basketweave de-
sign, blue daubing on white 150.00
Custard cup, brown daubing on
yellowware 25.00
Jug, blue daubing on cream,
1-gal. 250.00

Mixing bowl, blue daubing on
white, 11" d. 135.00
Pitcher, milk, 4½" h., red, white &
blue daubing, Morton Pottery, ca.
1940 . . . . 47.50
Pitcher, 4 5/8" h., brown & green
daubing on yellowware 50.00
Pitcher, milk, 5" h., brown & green
daubing on yellowware 95.00
Pitcher, 5½" h., squatty, brown &
green daubing on cream 60.00
Pitcher, 6" h., fluted sides, brown &
green daubing on yellowware 75.00
Pitcher, 6½" h., square handle, blue
daubing on white 200.00

Spongeware Pitcher

Pitcher, 7" h., green & brown daub-
ing on cream (ILLUS.) 90.00
Pitcher, 7 3/8" h., blue daubing on
white (hairline at rim & base, mi-
nor rim chips) 170.00
Pitcher, 8 3/8" h., blue daubing on
white 185.00
Pitcher, 9½" h., blue daubing on
white 245.00
Pitcher, brown daubing on blue 85.00
Pitcher, embossed duck, blue daub-
ing on white, tall 165.00
Pitcher, light green & brown daub-
ing on cream, large 80.00
Pitcher, milk, blue daubing on
white 195.00
Pitcher, tankard, green & rust daub-
ing on yellowware 125.00
Plate, 9½" d., green daubing on
cream 45.00
Platter, 10 x 9", deep daubing blue
on white 175.00
Soup bowl, blue daubing on white,
7½" d., 2½" h. 125.00
Syrup jug, blue daubing on grey,
8½" h. 165.00
Vase, 10¾" h., blue daubing on
white 225.00
Water cooler w/cover & spigot, blue
daubing on white, Western Stone-
ware Co., 4-gal. 435.00

STAFFORDSHIRE FIGURES

Figure of Scottish Lady

Small figures and groups made of pottery were produced by the majority of the Staffordshire, England, potters in the 19th century and were used as mantel decorations or "chimney ornaments," as they were sometimes called. Pairs of dogs were favorites and were turned out by the carloads, and 19th century pieces are still available. Well-painted reproductions also abound and collectors are urged to exercise caution before investing.

Bust of George Washington, looking
to the left, blue coat, raised on
"faux" marble socle, 19th c.,
8½" h. $286.00
Dog, Dalmation in seated position,
oval blue base, 1850, 5" h. 105.00
Dogs, Greyhound, reclining on blue
oval base, front legs crossed,
6" l., pr. 220.00
Dog, Greyhound w/hare in mouth,
1860, 7" h. 95.00
Dog, Poodle, begging, red base,
3" h. 75.00
Dog, Spaniel in seated position,
white "sanded" coat, black muz-
zle, copper lustre collar, 6" h. 85.00
Dog, Spaniel, facing left, gold locket
& chain, 6" base, 9½" h. 60.00
Dogs, Spaniel in seated position,
white coat w/russet spots & col-
lar, 9 5/8" h., pr. 230.00
Dog, Spaniel, white w/rust spots,
facing left, 10¼" 95.00
Equestrian figure, actor Mr. Wells
on horse as "John Gilpin," 7" h. . . 423.00
Equestrian figure, Prince Royal on
horseback, w/drum, 1845, 8" h. . . 140.00
Equestrian figure, Princess Royal on
horseback, w/flag, 1845, 8" h. . . . 140.00
Equestrian figures, Dick Turpin on

black horse, Tom King on white
horse, each w/blue jacket & or-
ange scarf, 9¾" h., pr. 192.50
Figure of a boy on elephant, 4" h. . . 65.00
Figure of Napoleon, 1850, 4" h. 70.00
Figure of Little Red Riding Hood,
4½" h. 55.00
Figure of boy as "Summer," 1850,
6" h. 115.00
Figure of fat snuff taker, 1850,
6" h. 100.00
Figure of Mr. Pickwick beside chair,
6" h. 165.00
Figure of a peasant, carrying a bas-
ket of fruit in his right hand,
wearing pale blue jacket & green
breeches, standing on a circular
tree stump base, on square plinth,
Ralph Wood, ca. 1770, 6¾" h. . . .1,870.00
Figure of Faith, 1800, 7" h. 120.00
Figure of "The Woman of Samaria,"
1850, 7" h. 95.00
Figure of John Wesley, wearing
white robe, 1850, 8" h. 100.00
Figure of Longshoreman w/barrel,
1875, 8" h. 120.00
Figure of Toby Philpots w/hat, 1850,
8" h. 150.00
Figure of actress Sarah Eggerton as
Helen MacGregor, tartan skirt,
blue bodice, plumed hat, holding
an axe & shield, gilt-lined oval
base, 9" h. 310.00
Figure of a Scottish lady w/bowl in
right hand, 9" h. (ILLUS.) 150.00
Figure of "Charlotte at Tomb of
Werther," 1800, 10" h. 150.00
Figure of "Widow of Zarapeth,"
1810, John Walton, 10" h. 132.00
Figure of Hope w/anchor,
ca. 1810 . . . . 132.00
Figure group, couple sleeping in
bower, 4" h. 65.00
Figure group, Tam O'Shanter & Sou-
ter Johnny, 1850, 5½" h. 140.00

Staffordshire Figure Group

Figure group, lady seated on the
back of a goat, 4½" w., 6" h.
(ILLUS.) 150.00
Figure group, boy, girl, bridge &
swan, 1805, 7" 115.00
Figure group, sailor & lass by an ar-
bor, 1850, 7" h. 125.00
Figure group, Napoleon III, Eugenie
& Prince, 1856, 8" h. 125.00
Figure group, Romeo & Juliet under
arbor, 1850, 8" h. 185.00
Figure group, Vicar & Moses, 1800,
9" h. 190.00
Figure group, boy, girl, sheep & dog
w/spillholder vase, 1850, 9" h. . . . 160.00
Figure group, Neptune w/dolphin,
1800, 9" h. 225.00
Figure group, gardening country
couple, gentleman seated among
tree branches w/woman below
holding a rake, on naturalistic
base raised on a square plinth,
late 18th c., 11¼" h. 330.00
Figure group, Robert Burns & High-
land Mary, w/spillholder vase,
1850, 12" h. 200.00
Figure group, archers (2) & dog,
w/spill-vase, 1850, 13" h. 135.00
Figure group, bagpiper & lady seat-
ed above clock, dressed in traditional Scottish attire, bagpipes
resting in his lap, 19th c.,
13¾" h. 165.00
Figure group, lady & gentleman un-
der an arbor, 14 x 9" 150.00
Lion in standing position, yellow &
brown, 3½ x 3" 110.00
Lions in recumbent position, shaded
brown, 12 x 5", pr. 195.00

Staffordshire Lion

Lion, beige hair markings, his
mouth open to reveal teeth, his
left front paw resting on a yellow
ball, standing on oblong black
marbleized base w/yellow line
border, damage to tongue, ca.
1780, 12½" l. (ILLUS.) 1,100.00
Pastille burner, model of a house,
1850, 5" h. 125.00
Sheep w/spillholder vase, 1850,
5" h. 85.00

STANGL POTTERY BIRDS

Shoveler Duck

*Johann Martin Stangl, who first came to
work for the Fulper Pottery in 1910 as a ceramic chemist and plant superintendent, acquired a financial interest and became
president of the company in 1926. The name
of the firm was changed to Stangl Pottery in
1929 and at this time much of the production
was devoted to a high grade dinnerware to
enable the company to survive the depression
years. Around 1940 a very limited edition of
porcelain birds, patterned after the illustrations in John James Audubon's "Birds of
America," were issued. Stangl subsequently
began production of less expensive ceramic
birds and these proved to be popular during
the war years, 1940-46. Each bird was hand-
painted and each was well marked with impressed, painted or stamped numerals which
indicated the species and the size. Collectors
are now seeking these ceramic birds which we
list below.*

Black-Throated Warbler, No. 3814 . . $62.50
Blackpoll Warbler, No. 3810 . . . . 50.00
Blue Bird, No. 3276, 5" h. 62.50
Bluebird, No. 3726-S, 5" h. 50.00
Blue-Headed Vireo, No. 3448,
4¼" h. 45.00
Broadbill Hummingbird, No. 3629,
6½" l., 4½" h. 90.00
Broadtail Hummingbird, No. 3626,
6" h. 90.00
Cardinal, No. 3444, 6" h. 65.00
Cerulean Warbler, No. 3456,
4¼" h. 55.00
Chat, No. 3590, 4¼" h. 62.50
Chestnut-Backed Chickadee,
No. 3811, 5" h. 65.00
Chestnut-Sided Warbler, No. 3812 . . 67.50
Cockatoo, No. 3405, 6" h. 45.00
Cockatoo, No. 3405-S, 6" h. 37.50
Cockatoo, medium, No. 3580,
8 7/8" h. 92.50
Cockatoo, No. 3584, 15" h. 185.00
Drinking Duck, No. 3250-E, 3¾" h. . . 25.00
Feeding Duck, No. 3250-C, 1¾" h. . . 35.00

Gazing Duck, No. 3250-D, 3¾" h. . . . 30.00
Golden Crowned Kinglet, No. 3848,
4" h. 45.00
Goldfinch, No. 3849 . . . . 75.00
Grey Cardinal, No. 3596, 4¾" h. . . . 40.00
Grosbeak, No. 3813, 5" h. 80.00
Group of Kinglets, No. 3853 . . . . 325.00
Nuthatch, No. 3593, 2½" h. 32.50
Painted Bunting, No. 3452, 5" h. 85.00
Pair of Cockatoos, No. 3405-D,
9½" h. 80.00
Pair of Love Birds, No. 3404-D,
4½" h. 90.00
Pair of Orioles, No. 3402-D,
5½" h. 75.00
Pair of Redstarts, No. 3490-D,
9" h. 135.00
Paraquet, No. 3449, 5½" h. 95.00
Parula Warbler, No. 3583, 4¼" h. . . 37.50
Red-Faced Warbler, No. 3594,
3" h. 38.00
Rieffers Hummingbird, No. 3628,
4½" h. 87.50
Rivoli Hummingbird, No. 3627,
6" h. 87.50
Rufous Hummingbird, No. 3585,
3" h. 40.00
Shoveler (Duck), No. 3455, 12¼ x
14" (ILLUS.) 245.00
Standing Duck, No. 3431, 8" h. 300.00
White Headed Pigeon (Double),
No. 3518-D, 12½ x
7½" . . . . .375.00 to 450.00
White-Wing Crossbill, No. 3754-D,
8¾" h. 275.00
Wren, No. 3401-S, 3½" h. 35.00
Yellow Warbler, No. 3850 . . . . 62.50

STONEWARE

Crock by Burger & Lang

Stoneware is essentially a vitreous pottery, impervious to water even in its unglazed state, that has been produced by potteries all over the world for centuries. Utilitarian wares such as crocks, jugs, churns and the like, were

the most common productions in the numerous potteries that sprung into existence in the United States during the 19th century. These items were often enhanced by the application of a cobalt blue oxide decoration. In addition to the coarse, primarily salt-glazed stonewares, there are other categories of stoneware known by such special names as basaltes, jasper and others. Also see BENNINGTON and RED WING POTTERY.

Butter churn, slightly ovoid, molded
rim, earred handles, brushed cobalt blue stylized florals & "6" on
grey, 6-gal., 19½" h. (rim hairline
& small lip chips) $250.00
Butter crock, straight sides, sten-
ciled cobalt blue label "D.L. Rat-
cliff & Co., Wheeling, W. Va." on
grey, 5¾" h. 120.00
Crock, stenciled cobalt blue "A.P.
Donaghho" on grey-tan, 1-gal. . . . 60.00
Crock, straight sides, stenciled cobalt blue "Hamilton & Jones,
Greensboro, Pa." on grey, 7" h. . . 160.00
Crock, straight sides, earred handles, slip-quilled cobalt blue
striped dog & "2" on grey, impressed "S. Hart, Fulton," 2-gal.,
10" d., 8¾" h., w/turned wood
cover 1,150.00
Crock, straight sides, earred han-
dles, slip-quilled medium blue
polka-dot pecking chicken on
grey, impressed "2," unmarked,
2-gal., 9 3/8" h. 350.00
Crock, straight sides, earred han-
dles, slip-quilled cobalt blue flower, leaves & "2" on grey,
impressed "Burger & Lang, Rochester, N.Y.," 1871-78, 2-gal.,
9½" h. (ILLUS.) 250.00
Crock, ovoid, brushed cobalt blue
design on grey, marked "Lewis &
Cady, Fairfax, Vt.," 2-gal., 9" d.,
9½" h. 450.00
Crock, straight sides, earred han-
dles, slip-quilled cobalt blue stylized sprig on grey, impressed
"White's, Utica, N.Y." & "2,"
19th c., 2-gal., 10¾" h. 192.50
Crock, ovoid, earred handles, slip-
quilled cobalt blue "1833" on
grey, impressed "E.S. Fox,
Athens" & "2" brushed over in
cobalt blue, 1838-43, 2-gal.,
11" h. 225.00
Crock, straight sides, earred han-
dles, slip-quilled cobalt blue
flowerhead on grey, impressed
"Satterlee & Mory, Fort Edward,
New York," 1861-85, 2-gal. 242.00
Crock, straight sides, earred handles, slip-quilled stylized leaf de-
cor, unmarked, 2-gal. 125.00

Crock, straight sides, stenciled & brushed "Williams & Reppert" on tan-grey, 2-gal. 195.00

Crock, cylindrical w/projecting rim, applied handles, cobalt blue full-length figure of a farmer w/wide brim hat holding a rake & sickle on grey, impressed "WM-A-MAQUOID & Co. LITTLE Wst 12th St. 3," ca. 1860, 3-gal., 10" h. 7,150.00

Crock, straight sides, earred handles, slip-quilled cobalt blue design on grey, impressed "J. Burger, Rochester, N.Y." & "3," ca. 1860, 3-gal., 10" h. 175.00

Crock, ovoid, earred handles, slip-quilled cobalt blue swags around shoulders & "3" above scrolling spray on grey, impressed "John B. Caire & Co., Po'Keepsie," 1840-42, 3-gal., 10" h. 350.00

Crock, straight sides, earred handles, brushed cobalt blue florals & "3" on grey, impressed "T. Harrington, Lyons," 1852-72, 3-gal., 10¼" h. 550.00

Crock, straight sides, earred handles, slip-quilled light blue bird & branch on grey, impressed "Ottman Bro's. Co. Fort Edward, N.Y." & "3," 3-gal., 10 5/8" h. 400.00

Crock, straight sides, earred handles, slip-quilled cobalt blue double fish on grey, impressed "R.O. Whittemore, Havanna, N.Y." & "3," 1860-80, 3-gal. 4,600.00

Crock, straight sides, earred handles, 8 stenciled cobalt blue stars encircling large blue "3," unmarked, 3-gal. 90.00

Crock, straight sides, earred handles, brushed cobalt blue double-headed flower & folige on grey, impressed "N. Clark, Athens, N.Y." & "4," 1842-93, 4-gal., 11¼" h. 250.00

Crock, ovoid, applied shallow handles, underglaze-blue stylized bird perched on a branch on grey, impressed "New York Stoneware Co., Fort Edward, New York," late 19th c., 11½" h. 302.50

Crock, straight sides, earred handles, brushed cobalt blue floral design & "5" on grey, impressed "Wm. Rowley, Middlebury, O.," 19th c., 5-gal., 13" h. 200.00

Flask, flattened ovoid, grey, 5½" h. 85.00

Flower pot, cylindrical w/strap handles, brushed cobalt blue florals around center reserve inscribed in flourishing script, "James Hamilton So like the sun should i fullfill the

Stoneware Flower Pot

Business of the day beginn mi work betimes and still march on mi hevenly way (sic)," inscribed under 1 handle, "Baltimore," ca. 1835 (cracked), 12" h. (ILLUS.) . . .2,970.00

Jar, cov., semi-ovoid, brushed cobalt blue double flower & "½" on grey, unmarked, ½ gal., 7 3/8" h. 325.00

Jar, ovoid, earred handles, impressed swags & single flower washed over in cobalt blue on grey, impressed label "C. Crolius Manufactured, Manhattan-Wells, New York," 7½" h. (hairlines in base & small rim chips) 1,100.00

Jar, slightly ovoid, brushed cobalt blue 3-part flower on grey, impressed "1," unmarked, 1-gal., 9½" h., w/wooden lid 130.00

Jar, slightly ovoid, stenciled & slip-quilled cobalt blue label "R.T. Williams, New Geneva, Pa." & "1½" on dark grey, 1½-gal., 9 1/8" h. 170.00

Jar, ovoid, brushed cobalt blue short lines & large "2" on grey, 2-gal., 9 5/8" h. 175.00

Jar, straight sides, earred handles, collared rim, slip-quilled cobalt blue bowl of fruit & flowers on grey, impressed "White's Utica" & "2," 2-gal., 10½" h. (some firing bubbles & small edge chip) 300.00

Jar, earred handles, brushed cobalt blue tulip blossoms & foliage on grey, impressed "A. & W. Bouchner" & "4," 4-gal., 12¼" h. 725.00

Jar, ovoid, earred handles, brushed cobalt blue trumpet flowers, stripes & "III" on grey, 13¼" h. 275.00

Jar, stenciled & free-hand cobalt blue label "Hamilton & Jones, Greensboro, Pa." & "3" on grey, 3-gal., 14¼" h. 200.00

Unmarked Stoneware Jar

Jar, semi-ovoid, earred handles,
slip-quilled cobalt blue sunflower
& leaves on grey, unmarked,
3-gal. (ILLUS.) 250.00

Jar, ovoid, earred handles, impressed "S. Purdy, Ohio" & "4"
washed over in cobalt blue on
grey, 4-gal., 13½" h. (minor edge
flakes & interior hairline at handle) 175.00

Jar, earred handles, stenciled cobalt
blue "T. F. Reppert, Eagle Pottery,
Greensboro, Pa." w/spread-
winged eagle & brushed "4" &
wavy lines on grey, 14½" h. 625.00

Jar, straight sides, earred handles,
stenciled cobalt blue eagle,
"Hamilton & Jones, Greensboro,
Pa." & "4" w/brushed stripes,
wavy lines & foliate scrolls on
grey, 4-gal., 14¾" h. 325.00

Jar, earred handles, brushed cobalt
blue florals & wavy lines on grey,
stenciled cobalt blue label
"Samuel Booker, Louisville, Ky." &
"8", 18½" h. 450.00

Jar, earred handles, stenciled cobalt
blue label w/eagle & "Williams
and Reppert, Greensboro, Pa." &
"6," w/freehand brushed stripes,
wavy lines & scrolling foliage on
dark grey, 6-gal., 24½" h. 350.00

Jug, cobalt blue bird w/single sprouting flower to the left & continuous
curving line w/dots on the right on
grey, impressed "W.H. Farrar &
Co., Geddes, N.Y.," 1841-58,
1-gal., 11" h. 4,620.00

Jug, slip-quilled cobalt blue florals &
leaves on grey, impressed "Fort
Edward Pottery Co., Fort Edward,
N.Y.," 1870-80, 1-gal. 190.00

Jug, semi-ovoid, cobalt blue splashes on grey, impressed "White's,
Utica, N.Y." (Noah White,
1828-40), 1-gal. 165.00

Jugs by White's of Utica, N.Y.

Jug, straight sides, slip-quilled cobalt blue bird on grey, impressed
"White's, Utica" & "1," 1880's,
1-gal. (ILLUS. left) 330.00

Jug, straight sides, slip-quilled
cobalt blue long-necked bird looking backwards from crooked branch
on grey, impressed "White's, Utica," N.Y." ca. 1880, 1-gal. (ILLUS.
right) 1,430.00

Jug, cobalt blue stenciled griffins on
grey, impressed label "Webster &
Berge," brushed "2," 2-gal.,
13¼" h. 135.00

Jug, semi-ovoid, strap handle,
brushed cobalt blue floral design,
impressed "Whites, Utica,"
13½" h. 275.00

Jug, semi-ovoid, slip-quilled cobalt
blue foliage on grey, impressed
"Edmands & Co." (Charlestown,
Massachusetts) & "2" on grey,
1850-65, 2-gal., 13¾" h. 75.00

Jug, slightly ovoid, stenciled cobalt
blue label "Jas. Hamilton & Co.,
Greensboro, Pa." & "2" on grey,
1850-80, 2-gal., 14¼" h. (lip
chip) 285.00

Jug, semi-ovoid, slip-quilled cobalt
blue flower & "2" on grey, impressed "John Burger, Rochester,"
ca. 1860, 2-gal., 14½" h. 400.00

Jug, semi-ovoid, stenciled cobalt
blue label "Hamilton & Jones,
Greensboro, Pa." & "2" on grey,
ca. 1870, 2-gal., 14½" h. 175.00

Jug, straight sides, slip-quilled
cobalt blue fantail peacock
w/turned head & crude tree
stump on grey, impressed
"White's Utica," ca. 1885, 3-gal.,
15" h. 1,760.00

Jug, semi-ovoid, slip-quilled medium
blue long-tailed bird & foliage on
grey, impressed "Fort Edward Pottery Co." & "3", 1870-80, 3-gal.,
15¼" h. 375.00

Jug, straight sides, slip-quilled cobalt blue scrolling foliage on grey, impressed "L. & B.G. Chace, Somerset" (Pottersville & Boston, Massachusetts) & "3" washed over in blue, 1882-1909, 3-gal., 16" h... 250.00

Jug, ovoid, cobalt blue slip flower & "3" on grey, impressed label "Burger Bro's & Co., Rochester, N.Y.," 3-gal., 16¾" h. (hairlines in base) 130.00

Jug, semi-ovoid, slip-quilled cobalt blue label "S. F. Eagan 133E. Senica St, Buffalo, N.Y." on grey, impressed label "C. W. Braun, Buffalo, N.Y.," 11½" h.......... 85.00

Jug, ovoid, brushed cobalt blue drapery swag on grey over impressed mark "Commeraws Stoneware" (New York City), 1795-1820 ....1,575.00

Pitcher, 10¼" h., ovoid w/wide straight neck, brushed cobalt blue florals & foliage on grey 375.00

Preserving jar, brushed cobalt blue decorative vertical lines of varying lengths on dark grey, 6¼" h. 150.00

Preserving jar, brushed medium blue lines & stenciled stars on grey, unmarked, 6½" h. 400.00

Preserving jar, stenciled cobalt blue label "Palatine Pottery Co., Palatine W. Va." & grey on grey, 6½" h. (minor lip flakes)......... 200.00

Preserving jar, stenciled cobalt blue label "Hamilton & Jones" (Greensboro, Pennsylvania) & cherries on grey, ca. 1870, 7 7/8" h. 550.00

Preserving jar, stenciled cobalt blue "McCarthey & Hayless, Louisville, Ky." on grey, 8" h. 200.00

Preserving jar, brushed cobalt blue single tulip blossom & line at top & bottom on grey, unmarked, 8 1/8" h. 250.00

Preserving jar, stenciled cobalt blue "Janson Bros. Pure French Mustard, Cinti., O." on grey, 9½" h....................... 150.00

Preserving jar, stenciled cobalt blue pears & brushed straight & wavy lines on grey, unmarked, 10" h. ... 850.00

Salt dip, brushed cobalt blue swatch w/running drips on grey, 2 5/8" d., 1 1/8" h. (small rim flakes) 500.00

Water cooler, stenciled cobalt blue label "Fort Dodge Stoneware Co." on grey, 4-gal. 250.00

Water cooler & domed cover, ovoid, applied loop handles incised florals highlighted w/cobalt blue, impressed "Cyrus Felton," 24½" h. (hairline in base, lid chipped)...................... 650.00

TECO POTTERY

Teco Pottery Vase

Teco Pottery was actually the line of art pottery introduced by the American Terra Cotta and Ceramic Company of Terra Cotta (Crystal Lake), Illinois in 1902. Founded by William D. Gates in 1881, American Terra Cotta originally produced only bricks and drain tile. Because of superior facilities for experimentation, including a chemical laboratory, the company was able to develop an art pottery line, favoring a matte green glaze in the earlier years but eventually achieving a wide range of colors including a metallic lustre glaze and a crystalline glaze. Though some hand-thrown pottery was made, Gates favored a molded ware because it was less expensive to produce. By 1923, Teco Pottery was no longer being made and in 1930 American Terra Cotta and Ceramic Company was sold.

Bookend, "Rebecca at Well," model of girl w/jug, 2 colors (single) $450.00

Bowl, 7" d., low, indented upper rim, green glaze 95.00

Bowl, 8" d., 2½" h., wide flattened form swelling at base, molded stylized roots, ca. 1910 .... 385.00

Bowl, 9" d., berries & leaves decor, green glaze, No. 136 (partial sticker)...................... 395.00

Mug, "Mac" inscribed on handle, dark green glaze, 3½" h......... 95.00

Vase, 4" h., melon ribbed, classic shape, green glaze 120.00

Vase, 5¼" h., bulbous, flared rim, medium green glaze............ 100.00

Vase, 6¾" w., 4 baluster handles, green glaze, No. 405 .... 165.00

Vase, 6¾" h., ovoid, 2 angular handles, matte green glaze 385.00

Vase, 8" h., baluster form, green glaze 4,180.00

Vase, 9" h., square, 4 broad handles at shoulder, matte green glaze 660.00

Vase, 10½" h., tapered cylinder

w/everted rim & 4 long L-shaped handles, green glaze, impressed "TECO 444" (ILLUS.) ....950.00 to 1,100.00

Wall pocket, square top, circular bottom, Arts & Crafts style design 485.00

TEPLITZ

Teplitz Bust of Woman

This ware was produced in numerous potteries in the vicinity of Teplitz in the Bohemian area of what is now Czechoslovakia during the late 19th and early 20th centuries. Vases and figures, of varying quality, were the primary productions and most were hand decorated. These items originally retailed in gift shops at prices from 25 cents to around $2. Now collectors are searching out these marked items and prices for finer examples are soaring.

Bust of a woman, turquoise & white gown w/gold trim, marked "RSTK Turn Teplitz," 8¼" h. $285.00

Bust of a woman, dressed in revealing Regency-inspired costume, elaborately curled in beribboned coif, on circular flower-molded socle, colored in pale earth tones w/mauve, mint green & w/gilt details, marked "R.S. & K Teplitz," ca. 1900, 19" h. 605.00

Bust of a woman, dressed in elaborate gown w/lace-edged collar, elaborately curled coif arranged w/flowers, on flower-encrusted socle, colored in pale earth tones w/realistic florals & gilt details on gown, ca. 1900, 21" h. (ILLUS.) 825.00

Creamer, cobalt blue w/blue, ivory

& heavy gold decor, marked "Stellmacher-Teplitz," 4" h........ 30.00

Ewer, applied stalk handle, relief-molded & h.p. variegated purple poppies & bulbs w/enameled gold details on cream ground, 9" h. ... 135.00

Vase, 3¼" h., 6¾" d., 2-handled, h.p. scene of farm girl pulling rooster's tail reserved on mottled green ground 75.00

Vase, 5½" h., 2-handled, large enameled orchid w/gold beading on cobalt blue ground highlighted w/overall enameled florettes..... 70.00

Vase, 6" h., 5" widest d., Art Nouveau profile of Alphonse Mucha type lady, marked "Amphora Turn Teplitz" 350.00

Vase, 6" h., gold handles, pedestal base, relief-molded & h.p. green, pink & blue florals, marked "Teplitz-Amphora"............... 125.00

Vase, 7½" h., h.p. scene of child blowing horn reserved on grey-speckled ground, marked "Stellmacher" 115.00

Vase, 12" h., 2-handled, cobalt blue neck w/speckled gold, h.p. florals w/enameled gold outlining on pale pink body.................. 225.00

TERRA COTTA

This is redware or reddish stoneware, usually unglazed. All kinds of utilitarian objects have been made for centuries as have statuettes and large architectural pieces.

Figure of a partially reclining nude woman, raised on low circular plinth, ca. 1920, 9" h.............$330.00

Figure of a nude woman w/coiled tresses, seated on a stepped base w/length of cloth about her waist, posed to set an arrow in bow, 20¾" h. 715.00

Match box & cover w/dog finial 40.00

Medallion, Benjamin Franklin in profile to the left, wearing fur cap, inscribed "B. Franklin American" (sic), dated 1777, 4½" d......... 385.00

Model of an owl on leafy branch, deeply molded feathers & talons, buff shading to dark brown, oblong base impressed "Evans & Howard," 28" h., together w/framed copy of "Clayworker" magazine from 1897 picturing similar owl by same maker 350.00

Syrup pitcher w/Sheffield pewter lid, center band enameled

w/busts of Elizabethan characters,
"Millars: Pat.," "Atkin Bros." 60.00
Umbrella stand, figural girl,
Germany, 36" h. 2,000.00

TILES

Bristol Tiles

*Tiles have been made by potteries in the
United States and abroad for many years.
Apart from small tea tiles used on tables,
there are also decorative tiles for fireplace,
floors and walls and this is where present col-
lector interest lies, especially in the late 19th
century American-made art pottery tiles.
Also see CAT COLLECTIBLES and
NORTH DAKOTA SCHOOL OF MINES
POTTERY.*

American Encaustic Tiling Co.,
Zanesville, Ohio, h.p. sailing ves-
sel & crew, framed, 6 x 3" $85.00
American Encaustic Tiling Co.,
Zanesville, Ohio, Simple Simon,
6 x 6" 50.00
American Encaustic Tiling Co.,
Zanesville, Ohio, draped lady
blowing horn on cream ground,
18 x 6" 275.00
American Encaustic Tiling Co.,
Zanesville, Ohio, full-figure of
woman 225.00
American Encaustic Tiling Co.,
Zanesville, Ohio, lion decor 65.00
Bristol, variously painted w/animals,
one w/tiger, one w/lion, one
w/goat, one w/sheep & two
w/two mountain goats, manganese, English, ca. 1760, mounted in frame, 5 x 5," set of 6
(ILLUS.) 418.00

California Faience Company, Berkeley, California, Viking ship in
stormy ocean decor, brown, gold
& 3 shaded blue ground,
5¼ x 5¼" 300.00
Cambridge Art Pottery, Cambridge,
Ohio, "Night" & "Morning," pr. ... 350.00
Delft faience, scene of Noah's ark &
the flood, purple & white, Holland, 5 x 5" (minor edge chips) ... 75.00
Delft faience, cat sits on book,
5 x 9" 225.00
Grueby Faience & Tile Company,
Boston, Massachusetts, cherub
playing tambourine decor, blue &
brown, 6 x 6" 185.00
Grueby Faience & Tile Company,
Boston, Massachusetts, sailing
ship, 4-color, artist-signed 385.00
Longwy Pottery, Longwy, France,
bird on flowering branch w/rocks
& lake, 6" sq. 110.00
Low (J. & G.) Art Tile Works, Chelsea, Massachusetts, green geometric design, dated 1881,
4¼ x 4¼" 7.00
Marblehead Pottery, Marblehead,
Massachusetts, multicolored
waves & ship decor, 4 x 4" 400.00
Minton Hollins & Co., Stoke-on-
Trent, Staffordshire, England, dog
by beehive, protecting himself
from surging bees, ca. 1880,
6 x 6" 45.00
Minton Hollins & Co., Stoke-on-
Trent, Staffordshire, England,
transfer scene w/dog seated by
beehive & protecting himself from
buzzing bee, 8 x 6 x 6" 75.00
Mintons China Works, Stoke-on-
Trent, Staffordshire, England, tan
transfer scene on brown of Inter-
state Industrial Building, Chicago
Exposition of 1880, 6 x 6" 110.00
Mintons China Works, Stoke-on-
Trent, Staffordshire, England,
hunting dog & foliage scene on
turquoise ground, 8 x 8", pr. 100.00
Mintons China Works, Stoke-on-
Trent, Staffordshire, England,
scenes entitled "Jeanie & the
Queen" & "Bonthein Accuses Roth-
say," 8 x 8", pr. 100.00
Mintons China Works, Stoke-on-
Trent, Staffordshire, England,
each w/a representation of the
seasons, blue glaze, framed,
8½ x 8½", set of 4 (some
wear) 110.00
Mosaic Tile Co., Zanesville, Ohio,
German Shepherd dog on cream
matte, 9½ x 9½" 90.00
Mosaic Tile Co., Zanesville, Ohio,
portrait of Lincoln 25.00

Mosaic Tile Co., Zanesville, Ohio, white turtle box, small 50.00

Newcomb College Pottery, New Orleans, Louisiana, floral decor, 6" d. 450.00

Pardee (C.) Works, Perth Amboy, New Jersey, baby's face 95.00

Pilkington's Tile & Pottery Co., Lancashire, England, street scene, framed, 8 x 8" 50.00

Rookwood Pottery Co., Cincinnati, Ohio, river scene, signed Sarah Coyne, 5 x 9½" 850.00

Rookwood Pottery Co., Cincinnati, Ohio, 12-sided, blue ships on white ground, 6" w. 125.00

Rookwood Pottery Co., Cincinnati, Ohio, Dutch scene 125.00

Rookwood Pottery Co., Cincinnati, Ohio, grapes decor, 1950 .... 95.00

Rookwood Pottery Co., Cincinnati, Ohio, faience, shaded green, blue, yellow & brown oak leaf & acorn decor on coppery deep green, 1908, Craftsman Fireplace, set of 180 .... 3,950.00

Rookwood Pottery Co., Cincinnati, Ohio, rose color, "Veritas" Harvard 99, second Triennial 1905 .... 125.00

Trent Art Tile Co., Trenton, New Jersey, bearded man, attributed to Broome 250.00

Wheatley Tile and Pottery Company, Covington, Kentucky, good luck symbol, 2-color, 4 1/8 x 4 1/8" ... 90.00

TOBY MUGS & JUGS

"Napoleon" Toby Jug

The Toby is a figural jug or mug usually delineating a robust, genial drinking man. The name has been used in England since the mid-18th century. Copies of the English mugs and jugs were made in America.

American Pottery "Indian Boy Head" Toby, glazed in tortoise shell brown w/green feather head-dress, ca. 1860 .... $125.00

Evans "Napoleon" Toby, standing figure, Philadelphia, Pennsylvania, 5½" h. 230.00

Lenox "William Penn" Toby, white handle, green decor 255.00

Morris and Willmore (attributed) "Napoleon" Toby, standing figure wearing black hat & yellow & blue waistcoat w/gilt trim, Trenton, New Jersey, ca. 1895, 10" h. (ILLUS.) 242.00

Occupied Japan "General MacArthur" Toby 45.00

Rockingham glaze "Ben Franklin" Toby, w/stopper, ca. 1840, 9" h. ... 225.00

Royal Doulton "Cliff Cornell" Toby, blue, 1956, 5½" h. 298.00

Royal Doulton "Dick Turpin" Toby, "A" mark, 1940-60, 2¼" h. 42.00

Royal Doulton "Falstaff" Toby, 1939 to present, 8½" h. 95.00

Royal Doulton "Old Charley" Toby, full seated figure, 1939-60, 8¾" h. 195.00

Royal Doulton "Parson Brown" Toby, full seated figure, "A" mark, 1935-60 .... 110.00

Royal Doulton "Sairy Gamp" Toby, No. 6263, 1948-60 .... 185.00

Royal Doulton "Toby Philpots" Toby, full seated figure, "A" mark, 1937-69 .... 110.00

Royal Doulton "Tony Weller" Toby, full seated figure, "A" mark, 1936-60 .... 110.00

Royal Doulton "Touchstone" Toby, 1936-60, large 300.00

Royal Worcester "Toby Philpot" Toby, blue coat, red vest & black trousers & hat, 1929, 1" d., 1¾" h. 99.00

Sampson & Hancock "Derby" Tobies, ca. 1880, each different, 1" h., set of 4 .... 800.00

Shorter & Son "Beefeater" Toby, 8" h. 75.00

Shorter & Son "Cavalier" Toby, 7" h. 35.00

Staffordshire "Judy" Toby, w/hat stopper, ca. 1850, 10" h. 165.00

Staffordshire "Martha Gun" Toby, seated woman w/black tricorn hat wearing green & brown dress, 10½" h. 155.00

Staffordshire "Monk" Toby, ca. 1860, 10" h. 150.00

Staffordshire "Nelson" Toby, standing, by W. Kent, 1850, 11" h. 275.00

Staffordshire "Snuff Taker" Toby, ca. 1900, 9½" h. 85.00

Staffordshire "Toby Philpots" Toby,
w/ship head handle, ca. 1850,
10" h. 175.00
Wain (M.) & Sons "Punch" Toby,
6" h. 85.00
Whieldon-type Toby, seated gentle-
man in a tricorn hat drinking from
toby jug similarly modeled, enriched in blue, yellow & green
glazes, late 18th c., 10" h. 605.00

VAN BRIGGLE

Hopi Indian Maiden

*The Van Briggle Pottery was established
by Artus Van Briggle, who formerly worked
for Rookwood Pottery, in Colorado Springs,
Colo., at the turn of the century. He died in
1904 but the pottery was carried on by his
widow and others. From 1900 until 1920, the
pottery was dated. It remains in production
today, specializing in Art Pottery.*

Ash tray, figure of Hopi Indian
maiden kneeling & grinding corn,
Persian Rose (maroon to blue-
green) glaze, 8" l., 6" h.
(ILLUS.) $125.00
Bookends, model of bear on tree
trunk, mulberry glaze, pr. 295.00
Bookends, model of dog, blue glaze,
pr. 145.00
Bookends, model of owl w/spread
wings, green matte finish, ca.
1910, pr. 135.00
Bowl, 4" d., mistletoe in relief, Tur-
quoise Ming (royal blue over tur-
quoise) glaze, 1908-11 . . . . 250.00
Bowl, 4½" d., relief-molded leaves,
green glaze, 1908-11 . . . . 110.00
Bowl, 6" d., 3¼" h., relief-molded
dragonflies, dark plum glaze,
pre-1920 . . . . 65.00
Bulb vase, relief-molded moths, Tur-
quoise Ming glaze, 9" d. 110.00
Candle holder-night light combina-
tion, brown glaze, 1914 . . . . 55.00

Console bowl w/flower frog insert,
Siren of the Sea, blue glaze,
2 pcs. 295.00
Cup, Turquoise Ming glaze,
2½" h. 20.00
Flower holder, three-frog, Mountain
Craig (blended brown & green)
glaze, 1915 . . . . 70.00
Lamp, large relief-molded leaves,
Turquoise Ming glaze, 12" h.,
w/original shade 95.00
Lamp, boudoir, swirl-molded, Per-
sian Rose glaze, w/original shade,
overall 14¼" h. 55.00
Lamp base, "Damsel of Damascus,"
Persian Rose glaze . . . . . .150.00 to 175.00
Model of an elephant, Turquoise
Ming glaze, 7" l. 45.00
Planter, model of a conch shell,
Persian Rose glaze, 12½" l. 40.00
Plaques, pierced to hang, bust of In-
dian "Big Buffalo" & bust of Indian
Maiden "Little Star" in full relief,
Turquoise Ming glaze, 5" oval,
pr. 175.00
Vase, 3" h., relief-molded butterfly,
blue glaze, 1919 . . . . 75.00
Vase, 3 3/4" h., top w/four puffed-
out points & relief-molded florals,
Turqouise Ming glaze 40.00
Vase, 4" h., Mountain Craig glaze,
ca. 1920 . . . . 70.00

WARWICK

Warwick Mug with Indian Portrait

*Numerous collectors have turned their at-
tention to the productions of the Warwick
China Manufacturing Company that operated in Wheeling, West Virginia, from 1887 until 1951. Prime interest would seem to lie in
items produced before 1914 that were decorated with decal portraits of beautiful wom-
en, monks and Indians. Fraternal Order
items, as well as floral and fruit decorated
items are also popular with collectors.*

Cuspidor, floral decor $105.00
Ewer, portrait of monk looking
upward 175.00

Humidor, cov., portrait of "old salt"
fisherman smoking pipe on brown
shaded to tan ground, gold trim,
bisque finish, 4½" d., 6½" h. 215.00
Humidor, cov., portrait of monk 95.00
Mug, fraternal souvenir, portrait of
Indian front, "2 K.T. Wash. D.C.
Apr. 1905" reverse, 5" h.
(ILLUS.) 75.00
Mug, "B.P.O.E." & Elk decor 35.00
Mug, Bulldog decor 85.00
Mug, portrait of monk singing 49.00
Pitcher, 9" h., overall small florals
on blue & white ground, gold
trim 98.00
Pitcher, 12" h., poinsettias decor on
brown ground 95.00
Pitcher, tankard, portrait of Indian .. 150.00
Plate, 9½" d., catfish decor 75.00
Plate, 9½" d., portrait of monk
drinking from wine bottle 96.00
Vase, 8" h., pillow-shaped, portrait
of beautiful woman on red
ground 135.00
Vase, 9" h., obelisk form, bust portrait of Gibson-type girl on pink
shaded to green ground 75.00
Vase, 9½" h., twig handles, poinsettias decor on red ground 95.00
Vase, 10½" h., twig handles, portrait of lady smelling rose on
brown ground 140.00
Vase, 12" h., creamy white florals
on brown ground 85.00

WATT POTTERY

*Founded in 1922, in Crooksville, Ohio, this
pottery continued in operation until the factory was destroyed by fire in 1965. Although
stoneware crocks and jugs were the first
wares produced, by 1935 sturdy kitchen items
in yellowware were the mainstay of production. Attractive lines like Kitch-N-Queen
(banded) wares and the hand-painted Red Apple, Cherry and Dutch (tulip) lines were popular throughout the country. Today these
hand-painted utilitarian wares are "hot" with
collectors.*

Bean pot, Red Apple patt. $55.00
Bean pot w/domed lid, yellowware
w/brown slip accents,
8½ x 6½" 30.00
Bowl, 5" d., Star Flower patt. 18.00
Bowl, 8" d., Star Flower patt. 25.00
Bowl, 8¼" d., 3½" h., Red Apple
patt. 35.00
Casserole, cov., Red Apple patt..... 47.50
Cookie jar, cov., Red Apple patt. 75.00
Cookie jar, cov., relief-molded
Morning Glory 95.00

Creamer, Cherry patt. 32.00
Creamer, Cherry patt.,
w/advertising 38.00
Creamer, Dutch (tulip) patt., 5" h. .. 45.00
Creamer, Red Apple patt., 5" h. 25.00
Creamer, Red Apple patt., w/adver-
tising, 5" h..................... 40.00
Grease jar, cov., Red Apple patt.... 95.00
Ice bucket, Red Apple patt. 77.00
Mixing bowl, Kitch-N-Queen, striped
bands, 7" d. 25.00
Mixing bowl, Red Apple patt.,
8" d. 28.00
Mixing bowl, Dutch (tulip) patt.,
8½" d., 5½" h. 65.00
Mixing bowl, Red Apple patt.,
14" d. 40.00
Mug, Star Flower patt. 48.00
Nappy, Red Apple patt., long
handle 40.00
Pepper shaker, hourglass shape,
Rooster patt., w/advertising
(single) 40.00
Pie plate, Red Apple patt. 65.00
Pitcher, 15" h., Rooster patt. 39.00
Pitcher, water, Dutch (tulip) patt. ... 36.00
Salt shaker, Cherry patt. (single) ... 33.00
Salt & pepper shakers, Star Flower
patt., pr. 50.00
Spaghetti bowl, Red Apple patt.,
13" d. 50.00
Spooner, 2-handled, Red Apple
patt., w/advertising 20.00
Sugar bowl, cov., Red Apple patt.,
w/advertising 80.00
Sugar bowl, cov., relief-molded
Morning Glory 75.00

WEDGWOOD

*Reference here is to the famous pottery es-
tablished by Josiah Wedgwood in 1759 in
England. Numerous types of wares have been
produced through the years to the present.
Also see COMMEMORATIVE PLATES,
HISTORICAL & COMMEMORATIVE
CHINA (Rowland & Marsellus) and JASPER
WARE.*

BASALTES

Bust of Aristophanes, marked Wedgwood only, 2 1/8" d., 4¼" h..... $395.00
Bust of Sir Walter Raleigh, 1920,
6" h............................ 75.00
Bust of Venus, marked Wedgwood
only, 7 5/8" d., 14 3/8" h. 895.00
Figures of Psyche & Cupid, modeled
after Falconet, Psyche w/bow &
Cupid w/arrows, circular bases
w/bands of anthemion, ca. 1860,
8" h., pr. (ILLUS.) 605.00

Psyche & Cupid

Figure of Cleopatra seated nude on rock w/asp curled around her wrist, marked Wedgwood only, 5¾" d., 9¼" h. 607.00

Model of a raven w/glass eyes, ca. 1915, marked Wedgwood only, 5" d., 4½" h. 460.00

Plaque, pierced to hang, young man feeding a lion in relief, marked Wedgwood only, 5¾ x 7½" 484.00

Teapot, cov., enameled rose, white, yellow & blue flowers & green leaves decor, marked Wedgwood only, 6" d., 4½" h. 343.00

Urn, satyr mask handles, dated 1800, 7" h. 115.00

Vase, 4" h., presentation-type, engine-turned, 1920 . . . . 90.00

CANEWARE

Wedgwood Caneware Mug

Cup & saucer, cup molded in relief w/nude putti above a band of shallow flutes, cane-molded handle, saucer molded w/shallow flutes, ca. 1785 . . . . 286.00

Cup & saucer, cup molded in relief w/nude children above band of molded cane, cane branch handle, ca. 1790 . . . . 330.00

Custard cup, cover & cream jug, custard cup w/shallow grooves & arrow handle, cover w/disc finial, cream jug applied in drab w/fern & stars, ca. 1820, 3" h. cream jug, 2 pcs. 385.00

Game pie dish & cover w/rabbit finial 350.00

Mug, body molded w/two nude children holding a stag's head w/dog by their side, handle & foot rim simulating cane & enriched in blue, rim w/band of stylized blue lappets, silver mounted, ca. 1790, 3¾" h. 1,650.00

Mugs, one molded w/two nude children holding a stag's head w/a dog at their side, the other w/three nude children, lower parts & handles (one repaired) simulating cane, silver mounted, ca. 1780, 5" h., pr. (ILLUS. of one) 935.00

Plate, basalt vine in relief, 18th c. 200.00

CREAMWARE

Creamware Jelly Mold

Bowl, 10½" d., footed, embossed grape clusters & vines in shades of blue 155.00

Box, cov., white berries & vines in relief on light blue, 4 x 5" 90.00

Cache pot, classical figures w/pink garlands decor 85.00

Cup & saucer, birds & feathers decor, marked Aaron Steele, ca. 1814 . . . . 975.00

Jelly mold, cov., conical, painted in colors w/trailing flowers, cover molded w/ridges, ca. 1800, 10" h. (ILLUS.) 2,640.00

Pitcher, milk, 7" h., embossed grape clusters & vines in shades of blue 125.00

Tazza, the Presentation of Christ in the Temple w/numerous figures, 1 holding a banner, lower right incised Hironimus, ca. 1870, 15" d. 1,320.00

Vases, 13¾" h., oviform w/short neck w/band of turquoise & ochre, flaring trellis pattern feet enriched in deep red & ochre, Mercury mask handles, playful putti & mermaids among dolphin fountains in continuous mountainous river landscapes on turquoise scale pattern ground, one signed Emile Lessore, 1861, pr. (both w/repair to shoulders & 1 to foot) 770.00

ROSSO ANTICO

Rosso Antico Teapot & Plate

Jug, pinched spout, redware w/applied black formal foliage & bellflowers, ca. 1820, 6" h. 198.00

Potpourri vase, cov., globular, 2 loop handles, redware painted in the famille rose palette w/pheasants among flowering shrubs issuing from rockwork, between black line rims, ca. 1820, 8¼" h. 660.00

Teapot & cover w/crocodile finial, depressed form, redware w/band of hieroglyphs at shoulder, 1810, 10½" w. 418.00

Teapot, cover w/crocodile finial & plate, redware decorated in black relief w/Egyptian motifs & band of stylized key patt. on side, angular handle & spout w/foliage motifs, plate similarly applied in black w/Egyptian motifs, ca. 1810, teapot 7¼" w., 2 pcs. (ILLUS.) 660.00

Tea set, enameled Capri ware, ca. 1920, large, 3 pcs. 600.00

MISCELLANEOUS

Bottle w/original stopper, blue, Ferrara patt., made for Humphrey Taylor and Co., 7" h. 118.00

Bowl, 6 3/8" d., 3" h., Fairyland Lustre, exterior ruby lustre w/green-eyed black Firbolgs outlined in gold, interior greenish lustre w/center scene of Thumbelina

talking to 2 frogs in water, Portland Vase mark, Patt. No. Z 5200 .... 995.00

Bowl, 8" d., 3¾" h., Flame Daventry Lustre, exterior lavender lustre panels w/scene of Oriental man alternating w/florals, interior mottled flame red & crimson lustre w/scene of Oriental bridge & temple 1,250.00

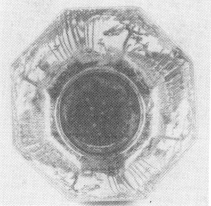

Fairyland Lustre Bowl

Bowl, 10¾" octagon, Fairyland Lustre, exterior outline-printed in gold & lustred in colors w/trees & minaret-topped buildings in river landscapes within gilt surrounds, interior w/continuous wooded landscape w/pixies, fairies, goblins & elves, Portland Vase mark, Patt. No. Z 5125i, 1920's (ILLUS.) 2,200.00

Box & cover w/maroon lustre widow finial, Dragon Luster, mottled green lustre exterior w/gold dragons & ornate gold bands, mother-of-pearl lustre interior w/three jewels in base, Portland Vase mark, 5¾" d., 4 7/8" h. 450.00

Cheese dish, cov., majolica, basketwork molded dish on 3 stump feet covered in a brown glaze, domed cover molded w/continuous band of flowering primula enriched in yellow, green & brown on a dark blue ground, branch finial w/foliate terminals enriched in green & brown, impressed mark & date code for 1873, 10" h. (repair to 1 side) 825.00

Compote, 5 5/8" d., 4" h., 2-handled, pedestal base, yellow lustre exterior w/green lustre scrollwork, interior w/scrollwork, copper lustre trim, 1920's 105.00

Cup & saucer, jasper, Diced Ware, green, yellow & white checkered design, 1780-1800 .... 850.00

Flower pot w/attached saucer, khaki relief classical figures of men & women on tan satin finish, marked Wedgwood only, 3¼" d., 3 1/8" h. 235.00

Smear-Glazed Honey Pot

Garniture set: 11" h. center vase & pr. 8" h. squared vases; Dragon Lustre, flying cranes & dragon breathing flames, 3 pcs. 900.00

Honey pot & cover, realistically modeled as a beehive, translucent smear-glazed stoneware, ca. 1820, 3¾" h. (ILLUS.) 220.00

Pepper pot, bulbous, grapes & leaves in relief, white, impressed Wedgwood, 3½" h. 95.00

Pitcher, 6½" h., Ferrara patt., blue & white 75.00

Pitcher, 8½" h., jug-type, majolica, jeweled designs, turquoise lining, ca. 1860 .... 350.00

Pitcher, brown transfer on Ivory ground, English Registry mark of 1878 .... 90.00

Plaque by Emile Lessore

Plaque, painted in color w/two children & 3 rabbits, signed Emile Lessore, 6¾ x 5¼" (ILLUS.) 770.00

Plate, 6½" d., majolica, butterflies, florals & fans decor 65.00

Plate, 9¼" d., commemorative, "Memorial Hall, Washington, D.C.," blue transfer on white, ca. 1890 .... 45.00

Plate, 9¼" d., commemorative, "Washington's Headquarters," blue transfer on white, ca. 1890 .. 65.00

Plate, 9¼" d., commemorative, "Wellesley College," blue transfer on white, ca. 1890 .... 75.00

Plate, 9½" d., mottled brown & green glaze, Wedgwood-Whieldon, 1760-70 .... 440.00

Plate, 9¾" d., Moonlight Lustre, purple lustre splotches front & back, ca. 1810 .... 201.00

Plate, 10" d., Ivanhoe series, "Friar Tuck Entertains Black Knight" 65.00

Plate, 10¾" d., Fairyland Lustre, imps on bridge outlined in gold center, lacy gold fairies & florals on gold border, mottled blue underside 1,695.00

Plate, "The Wendell Hotel," blue & white, dated 1900 .... 85.00

Platter, 12½", majolica, basket-weave center w/bamboo edge ... 100.00

Platter, commemorative, "Historic America," Barnum's Museum, Broadway, New York, acorn & leaf border, blue transfer on white 120.00

Salt dip, Dragon Lustre, blue exterior, orange dog's head in bowl, 2¼" 130.00

Teapot, cov., foliage-molded spout & double-scroll handle w/horizontal engine-turning, bright yellow & green stripes, cover w/flower-head finial, Whieldon period, ca. 1760, 4¾" h. 4,180.00

Urn, cobalt blue w/scrolled gold rim, ca. 1875, 8½" h............. 325.00

Vase, 5 1/8" h., 2½" d., Humming-bird Lustre, mottled blue lustre ground w/colorful hummingbirds finely outlined in gold, mottled flame lustre top interior 200.00

Vase, 7 7/8" h., 3 7/8" d., trumpet-shaped, Fairyland Lustre, midnight blue lustre w/fairy in hawthorne branches either side, pixies & birds inside top rim, Portland Vase mark, Patt. No. Z 4968 ..... 1,150.00 to 1,295.00

Vase, 8 1/8" h., 3¼" d., Moonlight Fairyland Lustre, "Boys on Bridge," Portland Vase mark, Patt. No. Z 5462 .... 1,150.00

Vase, 9¾" h., 4¾" d., Dragon Lustre, mottled powder blue lustre exterior w/dragon breathing flames, outlined in gold, ornate gold designs at top, base & inside top rim....................... 450.00

Water bottle, majolica, colorful florals between horizontal blue stripes on cream ground, dated 1879, 10" h. 300.00

WELLER

Weller

Weller Pottery

Incised Weller Marks - 1927-1930's

This pottery was made from 1872 to 1945 at a pottery established originally by Samuel A. Weller at Fultonham, Ohio, and moved in 1882 to Zanesville. Numerous lines were produced and listings below are by the pattern or lines. Most desirable is the Sicardo line.

ARDSLEY (1920-28)
Bulb bowl, sword-shaped green
leaves forming overhead handles,
water lily form, 5" $55.00
Console bowl & "Kingfisher" flower
frog, 16½" d., 3½" h. bowl molded w/cattails & grasses & 9½" h.
flower frog, 2 pcs. . . . . . .200.00 to 235.00
Vase, bud, 7½" h., expanding cylin-
der, molded water lilies at base,
cattails & grasses body, green
matte glaze. 25.00
Vase, double, 9½" h., expanding
cylinders joined by overhead handle, molded water lilies at base,
cattails & grasses body, green
matte glaze . . . . .45.00 to 55.00
Vase, 11½" h., molded water lilies
at base, cattails & grasses body,
green matte glaze. 55.00

AURELIAN (1898-1910)
Jardiniere & pedestal base, slip-
painted florals, glossy brown glaze,
artist-signed, 2 pcs. 1,250.00
Pitcher, tankard, 6" h., slip-painted
berries & green leaves, glossy
brown glaze, artist-signed 250.00
Pitcher, tankard, 12" h., slip-painted
berries, glossy brown glaze,
artist-signed 350.00
Vase, 3½" h., 2-handled, squatty,
slip-painted yellow florals, glossy
brown glaze, artist-signed 135.00
Vase, 9" h., slip-painted florals,
glossy brown glaze 255.00
Vase, 12 x 10", pillow-shaped, slip-
painted blackberries, glossy
brown glaze, artist-signed 360.00

BALDIN (1915-20)
Bowl, 6½ x 6", realistically painted
apples & branches molded in low
relief against earth tones 95.00

Bowl, 7" d., low, realistically painted apples & branches molded in
low relief against earth tones 70.00
Jardiniere & pedestal base, realistically painted apples & branches
molded in low relief against earth
tones, overall 34" h. . . . .450.00 to 550.00
Vase, 6" h., stick-type, realistically
painted apples & branches molded
in low relief against earth tones . . 35.00
Vase, 7" h., stick-type, realistically
painted apples & branches molded
in low relief against earth tones . . 40.00
Vase, 11" h., conical, realistically
painted apples & branches molded
in low relief against midnight
blue 175.00

BARCELONA (1920's)

Barcelona Vase

Candle holders, ridged body w/sten-
ciled stylized florals, pr. . . .55.00 to 65.00
Pitcher, 6" h., ridged body w/color-
ful stenciled floral medallion
decor 125.00
Vase, 6½" h., 2-handled, ridged
body w/colorful stenciled floral
medallion decor 60.00
Vase, 9" h., 2-handled, ridged body
w/colorful stenciled floral medal-
lion decor (ILLUS.) . . . . .85.00 to 95.00

BLOSSOM (mid-late 1930's)

Blossom Vase

Basket, overhead handle, rounded
sides, irregular scalloped rim,
molded pink flowers & green
leaves, blue matte glaze, 6" h. ...   25.00
Cornucopia-vase, molded pink flowers & green leaves, blue or green
matte glaze, 8½" h.,
each . . . . 20.00 to 28.00
Vase, 5½" h., molded pink flowers
& green leaves, blue matte glaze
(ILLUS.) 32.00
Vase, 9½" h., 2-handled, low foot,
cylindrical, molded pink flowers &
green leaves, green matte
glaze 30.00

BLUE DRAPERY (1915-20)
Bowl, 5½" d., low, clusters of roses
pendant from rim, vertical folded
blue matte drapery
ground . . . . 18.00 to 24.00
Candlestick, double gourd form,
clusters of roses pendant from
nozzle, vertical folded blue matte
drapery ground, 9" h., pr. 85.00
Vase, 8" h., clusters of roses pen-
dant from rim, vertical folded
blue matte drapery ground 50.00
Wall pocket, clusters of roses pendant from rim, vertical folded
blue matte drapery ground,
9" h. 45.00 to 57.00

BLUE WARE (pre-1920)
Jardiniere, 3-footed, ivory relief of
classical lady against deep blue
ground, 6½" h. 85.00
Jardiniere, 3-footed, ivory relief of
classical ladies against deep blue
ground, 7½" h. . . . . 100.00 to 125.00
Vase, 8½" h., ivory relief of classi-
cal lady holding cluster of grapes
against deep blue ground 85.00
Vase, 10" h., ivory relief of classical
ladies dancing against deep blue
ground 130.00

BONITO (1927-33)
Bowl, 5" d., low, h.p. florals & foliage on cream ground . . . . . . 35.00 to 45.00
Flower pot w/saucer, h.p. multicolored floral decor on cream
ground 55.00
Vase, 4" h., small rim handles, h.p.
brown, blue & green floral decor
on cream ground 20.00
Vase, 6" h., urn-shaped, brown &
green floral decor on cream
ground, artist-signed 40.00
Vase, 6½" h., 2-handled, floral de-
cor on cream ground, green in-
terior, artist-signed 55.00

BOUQUET (1930's)

Bouquet Vase

Bowl-vase, white dogwood blossoms
in relief on soft matte green
matte finish ground,
4½" h. 14.00 to 18.00
Pitcher, 9½" h., yellow jonquil blos-
som & bud in relief on white
matte finish ground 55.00
Vase, 5½" h., white dogwood blos-
soms in relief on soft matte green
finish ground (ILLUS.) 40.00
Vase, 8" h., white dogwood blos-
soms in relief on slate blue matte
finish ground 34.00

BRIGHTON (1915)
Flower frog, model of a Flamingo in
preening position on leafy base,
6" h. 95.00 to 110.00
Flower frog, model of a Kingfisher
on a tree stump, 9" h. . . . 125.00 to 150.00
Flower frog, model of a Swan,
4½" 70.00
Model of Canaries (2) on textured
base, 4" h.   160.00
Model of a Woodpecker, 5" h. 65.00

BURNTWOOD (1910)

Burntwood Vase

Humidor, cov., etched stylized
florals on creamy tan to brown,
5½" h. 150.00
Jardiniere, etched chickens, creamy
tan to brown w/brown border
bands, 8" h. 250.00
Vase, 8" h., etched stylized florals
on stippled creamy tan to brown
w/brown border bands 65.00
Vase, 12" h., etched grape clusters,
vines & leaves on stippled creamy
tan to brown w/brown border
bands (ILLUS.) . . . . .85.00 to 100.00

CAMEO (1935-39)
Basket w/asymmetrical overhead
handle, white relief florals on
matte coral or powder blue,
7½" h., each 26.00
Basket w/double overhead handle,
white relief florals on matte coral
or powder blue, 7½" h.,
each .28.00 to 32.00
Ewer, white relief florals on matte
coral, powder blue or soft green,
10" h., each 35.00
Vase, 5" h., 2-handled, white relief
florals on matte powder blue 23.00
Vase, 10" h., white relief florals on
matte powder blue 35.00

CHASE (late 1920's)
Vase, 6" h., white relief fox hunt
scene on deep blue 120.00
Vase, 10" h., footed, white relief
fox hunt scene on deep blue 150.00
Vase, 11" h., white relief fox hunt
scene on deep blue 200.00

CLAYWOOD (1910)
Bowl, 6½" d., 2½" h., canted sides,
incised stylized floral panels, tan
& dark brown matte finish 36.00
Cuspidor, incised stylized floral
panels, tan & dark brown matte
finish, 7" d., 4½" h. 60.00
Vase, 3½" h., panels of incised
star-shaped florals against stippled ground, tan & dark brown . . . 30.00
Vase, 6½" h., cylindrical w/flaring
base, creamy tan pine cone &
branch against dark brown matte
finish 75.00

COPPERTONE (late 1920's)
Candle holder, model of a turtle
w/pond lily candle nozzle on
back, blotchy semi-gloss green
over brown glaze, 3" h. . .95.00 to 125.00
Console bowl, irregular rim
w/figural frog seated at end,
blotchy semi-gloss green over
brown glaze, 10½" w., 2" h. 115.00

Coppertone Flower Holder

Flower holder, figural frog w/pond
lily (ILLUS.) 70.00
Model of a frog, 2" h. 50.00
Model of a frog, 4" h. 70.00
Model of a frog, gardenware
w/hole for water tube, 6 x 5½" . . 300.00
Model of a turtle, 4½" l. 60.00
Pitcher, 7½" h., fish handle, blotchy
semi-gloss green over brown
glaze 265.00
Vase, 6" to 7" h., blotchy semi-gloss
green over brown glaze,
each .32.00 to 40.00

CORNISH (1933)
Bowl, 4" d., molded spray of leaves
w/pendant berries, brown semi-
gloss finish 48.00
Vase, 3½" h., globular, molded
spray of leaves w/pendant ber-
ries, green semi-gloss finish 15.00
Vase, 10" h., small closed handles,
cylindrical w/flaring base, molded
spray of leaves w/pendant ber-
ries, blue semi-gloss finish 52.50
Vase, 12" h., small closed handles,
ovoid, molded spray of leaves
w/pendant berries, tan semi-gloss
finish 55.00

DELSA (1930's)
Basket, embossed florals on stippled
white ground, 6" h. 29.00
Ewer, embossed florals on stippled
green ground, 12" h. 50.00
Vase, 6" h., embossed pansies on
stippled blue ground 13.00
Vase, 9½" h., embossed florals on
stippled white ground 30.00
Vase, 13" h., embossed yellow
florals on stippled white
ground 52.00

DICKENSWARE 1ST LINE (1897-98)
Ewer, slip-painted florals, glossy
brown glaze, 12" h. 595.00
Jardinere, slip-painted florals & foli-
age, glossy brown glaze, 7" h. . . . 250.00
Vase, 11½" h., double gourd form,

slip-painted thistle decor, glossy brown glaze, artist-signed ....375.00 to 425.00

DICKENSWARE 2ND LINE (1900-05)

2nd Line Dickensware Mug

Jug, sgraffito portrait of Indian "Blackhawk," 5¾".............. 475.00

Mug, sgraffito bust portrait of Indian, 5½" h. (ILLUS.) 225.00

Mug, tankard, street scene from David Copperfield front, reverse w/inscription "Mr. Micawber impressing the names of streets upon me....," 6" h. 525.00

Plate, 12½" d., advertising, sgraffito scene & "Pickwick Papers, Dickens Pottery, S. A. Weller" in shades of brown & tan 3,500.00

Vase, 7½" h., flask-shaped, sgraffito full-length portrait of lady golfer 400.00

Vase, 11" h., sgraffito portrait of Indian "Jack Red Cloud"........1,295.00

Vase, 14" h., sgraffito bust portrait of Indian, artist-signed 1,200.00

EOCEAN (1898-1918)

Eocean & Etna Line Vases

Pitcher, 6½" h., 5" d., slip-painted pansy decor on grey shaded to eggshell ground................. 100.00

Vase, bud, 5½" h., slip-painted flo-ral decor on grey shaded to white ground 65.00

Vase, 8" h., slip-painted pansy decor on grey shaded to white ground 135.00

Vase, 8" h., slip-painted pink roses decor on brown shading to white then blue ground (ILLUS. right) ... 145.00

Vase, 10" h., slip-painted floral decor on cream shaded to grey-green ground 225.00

ETNA (1906)

Mug, relief-molded & painted realistic grape cluster on shaded grey, 5½" h........................ 145.00

Pitcher, 10" h., relief-molded & painted realistic maroon florals on shaded light to dark grey 110.00

Pitcher, tankard, 14" h., relief-molded & painted realistic grape cluster on shaded light to dark grey 185.00

Vase, 4½" h., hourglass-shaped, relief-molded & painted realistic florals on shaded grey 80.00

Vase, 7" h., baluster form, relief-molded & painted realistic pink apple blossoms on shaded light to dark grey 85.00

Vase, 8¼" h., relief-molded & painted realistic thistles on shaded light to dark grey (ILLUS. with Eocean vase) 120.00

Vase, 9" h., relief-molded & painted realistic orange dandelions on shaded grey 100.00

Vase, 9" h., 2-handled, bulbous, relief-molded & painted realistic pink wild roses on shaded light to dark grey 195.00

Vase, 11" h., relief-molded & painted realistic long-stemmed red roses on shaded light grey 125.00

FLORETTA (1904)

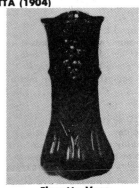

Floretta Vase

Ewer, slip-painted purple grapes in low relief, shaded brown glaze ... 55.00

Mug, slip-painted grapes in low relief, shaded brown glaze......... 95.00
Pitcher, tankard, 10" h., slip-painted
purple grapes in low relief, shaded brown glaze 100.00
Vase, 9" h., slip-painted cascading
purple grape clusters in low relief
on shaded oatmeal grey ground .. 110.00
Vase, 10" h., slip-painted pink
florals in low relief on cream
shaded to grey ground 175.00
Vase, 12" h., slip-painted cluster of
green grapes in low relief, shaded brown glaze (ILLUS.)......... 110.00

FOREST (1915)

Forest Planter

Basket w/overhead handle, realistically molded & painted forest
scene, 8½" h. 165.00
Basket, hanging-type, realistically
molded & painted forest scene,
10" d.................. 80.00 to 125.00
Jardiniere, realistically molded
& painted forest scene,
4½" h.................. 85.00 to 100.00
Pedestal base, realistically molded &
painted forest scene, 17" h....... 200.00
Pitcher, 6½" h., realistically molded
& painted forest scene, high-gloss
glaze 100.00
Planter, realistically molded & painted forest scene, 22" l., 11" w.,
11" h. (ILLUS.) .... 625.00 to 680.00
Umbrella stand, realistically molded
& painted forest scene, 19¾" h. ... 600.00
Vase, 8" h., waisted cylinder,
realistically molded & painted forest scene................ 55.00 to 65.00

GLENDALE (1920's)

Candle holder, 2-light, bird & nest
w/eggs in low relief, shades of
russet, blue & grey 150.00
Centerpiece bowl & flower frog,
shallow rolled edge bowl w/birds
& nest of eggs in low relief, flower frog in the form of a bird's
nest w/eggs, shades of yellow,
tan, blue & beige, signed Timberlake, 15" d., 2 pcs. 395.00
Vase, 6½" h., marsh birds standing
amidst tall grasses in low relief,
shades of tan & green 145.00
Vase, double bud, 7" h., 2 flower

holders in the form of tree trunks
flanking plaque w/bird & nest of
eggs in low relief, shades of blue,
tan & russet 140.00
Vase, 8½" h., love birds on branch
in low relief, shades of pink, yellow, blue, russet & beige 200.00
Wall pocket, mother birds & babies
(3) on branch, sky blue &
yellow .... 150.00 to 195.00

GLORIA (after 1936)

Basket w/overhead handle, branch
w/blackberries & white blossoms
in relief on caramel matte finish
ground, 7" h. 50.00
Vase, 4½" h., double, ruffled rims,
creamy white flower & green foliage on caramel matte finish
ground 30.00
Vase, 5½" h., 2-handled, yellow
flower & green foliage on green
matte finish ground 20.00

HOBART (1920's)

Candle holder, figure of a partially
draped nude lady kneeling beside
candle nozzle, turquoise blue
matte finish, 6" h............... 60.00
Flower frog, figure of a nude boy &
swan, turquoise blue matte finish,
6½" h. 55.00
Flower frog, figure of a partially
draped nude lady holding bouquet
of flowers on circular base
pierced for flowers, turquoise
blue matte finish, 8½" h. 45.00

HUDSON (1920's-1935)

Hudson Line Vases

Bulb bowl, underglaze slip-painted
florals, 9½" d. 65.00
Planter, underglaze slip-painted
pink & blue dogwood blossoms,
artist-signed, 6½" h. 165.00
Vase, 5½" h., double, underglaze

slip-painted chrysanthemums,
signed Hester Pillsbury 155.00
Vase, 6" h., underglaze slip-painted
white daisies, artist-signed 145.00
Vase, 7" h., underglaze slip-painted
berries & foliage, deep blue matte
glaze, signed Ruth Axline 195.00
Vase, 7¾" h., 4¼" d., underglaze
slip-painted pink & blue florals &
green leaves, deep blue matte
glaze, artist-signed 120.00
Vase, 8" h., underglaze slip-painted
soft brown birds & aster blossoms
w/trailing stems, creamy ivory
matte glaze..................... 225.00
Vase, 8" h., cylindrical, underglaze
slip-painted iris & leaves 150.00
Vase, 9" h., underglaze slip-painted
florals, deep blue matte glaze.... 185.00
Vase, 9" h., underglaze slip-painted
purple vining florals, white matte
glaze 195.00
Vase, 9½" h., underglaze slip-
painted rose & large nasturtiums,
deep blue matte glaze 105.00
Vase, 9½" h., underglaze slip-
painted trumpet vines, white
matte glaze, signed Hester
Pillsbury...................... 285.00
Vase, 10" h., underglaze slip-
painted red roses, green shaded
to rose matte glaze, signed
Hester Pillsbury (ILLUS. right)..... 180.00
Vase, 11" h., underglaze slip-
painted bluebird on branch 475.00
Vase, 11½" h., hexagonal, underglaze slip-painted band of florals,
buds & foliage, white matte glaze
(ILLUS. left) 60.00
Vase, 12" h., underglaze slip-
painted florals, blue matte glaze,
artist-signed 550.00
Vase, 12" h., 7" d., underglaze slip-
painted roses, grey shaded to
pink matte glaze, signed Hester
Pillsbury...................... 375.00
Vase, 13" h., 5" d., underglaze slip-
painted wild roses, artist-signed .. 350.00

HUNTER (1904)
Mug, dolphin handle, underglaze
slip-painted band of dolphins
around rim, large fish on each
side, shaded standard brown
glaze, artist-signed 295.00
Vase, 5½" h., 5½" w., underglaze
slip-painted butterflies, shaded
standard brown glaze, artist-
signed 425.00

IVORY (pre-1914)
Jardiniere, panels of florals & foli-
age in low relief, 9" d. 45.00
Jardiniere, squirrels seated in oak

tree nibbling acorns in low relief,
10" d., 8½" h. 100.00
Umbrella stand, scrollwork & florals
in low relief, 19½" h. ...115.00 to 175.00
Window box, grazing sheep in low
relief, 11 x 7".................. 95.00

KNIFEWOOD (1915-20)
Tobacco jar, cov., hunting dog
amidst forest scene in low relief.. 300.00
Jardiniere & pedestal base, overall
daisies in low relief, 10½" d. 265.00
Vase, 8¼" h., owls in low relief.... 145.00

L'ART NOUVEAU (1903-04)

L'Art Nouveau Ewer

Ewer, relief-molded figure of a
woman in flowing gown & pink
florals w/trailing green stems,
purple matte finish, 10" h.
(ILLUS.)....................... 75.00
Mug, relief-molded trailing floral
rim, matte finish, 5" h. 75.00
Pitcher, tankard, 13½" h., relief-
molded grape clusters, shaded
deep brown glossy finish 275.00
Vase, 8" h., bulbous base, long
cylindrical neck, relief-molded
pink florals & trailing green
stems, matte finish 65.00

LA SA (1920-25)
Lamp base, scenic decor w/palm
trees, iridescent glaze, 14½" h.,
w/shade 1,200.00
Vase, 4" h., bulbous, scenic decor
w/trees & mountains, iridescent
pink & gold glaze, unsigned 125.00
Vase, bud, 5½" h., tapering cylinder, scenic decor w/palm trees,
gold, red & copper iridescent
glaze 125.00
Vase, 12" h., baluster-shaped, scenic decor w/trees, water & mountains, iridescent glaze (ILLUS.) 375.00

La Sa Vase

Vase, 13½" h., tapering cylinder,
scenic decor, iridescent glaze 350.00

LONHUDA (1894)
Bowl, 4" d., 3-footed, floral decor,
shaded brown glaze, artist-
signed 180.00
Bowl-vase, berries & leaf decor,
shaded brown glaze, artist-signed
& dated 1895, 6" d.............. 350.00
Vase, 6" h., 9" w., 2-handled, roses
decor, shaded brown glaze, artist-
signed 285.00
Vase, 8 x 8", swimming fish decor,
shaded brown glaze, artist-
signed........................1,200.00

LOUWELSA (1896-1924)

Louwelsa Portrait Vase

Bowl, 6" d., 4" h., slip-painted
florals, standard brown glaze 125.00
Clock, mantel-type, slip-painted
florals, standard brown glaze,
12" h......................... 750.00
Ewer, squatty, slip-painted orange
nasturtiums & green foliage, standard brown glaze, 4" h. 150.00

Jardiniere, slip-painted yellow
daffodils, standard brown glaze,
13" d......................... 250.00
Jug, slip-painted brown & orange
berries, standard brown glaze,
4½" d., 5½" h. 175.00
Pedestal, hourglass shape, slip-
painted chrysanthemums, standard brown glaze, 22" h.......... 275.00
Pitcher, 3" h., 4" d., squatty, slip-
painted pansies, standard brown
glaze 75.00
Pitcher, 5" h., 3-footed, slip-painted
florals, standard brown glaze 150.00
Pitcher, tankard, 12" h., slip-painted
portrait of Indian in full headdress, standard brown glaze,
artist-signed 795.00
Pitcher, tankard, 12½" h., slip-
painted blackberries & foliage,
standard brown glaze, artist-
signed 495.00
Pitcher, tankard, 17" h., slip-painted
grape clusters, standard brown
glaze, artist-signed 650.00
Vase, 2" h., 2-handled, slip-painted
pansies, standard brown glaze ... 90.00
Vase, 4" h., pillow-shaped, slip-
painted sweet peas, standard
brown glaze, artist-signed 160.00
Vase, 5" h., 3-footed, 3-handled,
slip-painted florals, standard
brown glaze, artist-signed 250.00
Vase, 6" h., slip-painted pansies,
shaded blue glaze.............. 400.00
Vase, 7" h., baluster-shaped, slip-
painted daffodils, standard brown
shaded to orange glaze.......... 140.00
Vase, 9½" h., cylindrical, slip-
painted yellow florals, standard
brown glaze, artist-signed 175.00
Vase, 12" h., 2-handled, slip-painted
berries & foliage, standard brown
glaze 195.00
Vase, 16" h., slip-painted bust portrait of an Indian in full headdress, standard brown glaze,
artist-signed (ILLUS.)............ 605.00

LUSTRE (1920)
Powder jar, cov., blue lustre
glaze 45.00
Vase, 5" h., 2 handles rising from
mid-section of bulbous body to
rim of narrow neck, blue lustre
glaze 30.00
Vase, 8½" h., bulbous, green lustre
glaze 60.00
Vase, 11" h., pink lustre glaze 65.00

MALVERN (late 1920's)
Console set: 11" oval console bowl
w/flower frog & pr. 2" h. candle
holders; relief-molded leaf & bud

forming bowl edge, swirl-textured green body w/mauve interior, 4 pcs. 90.00

Vase, 5½" h., relief-molded leaf & bud on swirl-textured green to ochre-brown ground 30.00

Vase, 6½" h., pillow-shaped, relief-molded leaf & bud on swirl-textured green to ochre-brown ground 40.00

Vase, 8" h., circular, relief-molded leaf & bud on swirl-textured green to ochre-brown ground 40.00

MAMMY LINE (1935)

Creamer, figural nude boy handle ....150.00 to 185.00

Sugar bowl, cov., figural boy handles 300.00

Syrup pitcher, cov., figural Mammy, 6" h. 325.00

Teapot, cov., figural Mammy, 8" h. 450.00

MARVO (mid-1920's)

Marvo Wall Pocket

Bowl, 5" d., molded ferns & fronds, tan matte finish 35.00

Candle holders, molded leaves & berries, green matte finish, 2½" h., pr. 25.00

Console bowl, molded palm leaves & fronds, tan matte finish, 11" d., 3" h. 37.00

Flower frog, molded ferns & fronds, green matte finish, 5" d. 12.00

Pitcher, 8" h., molded palm leaves & fronds, green or tan matte finish ....80.00 to 88.00

Umbrella stand, molded palm leaves & fronds, green matte finish 150.00

Vase, bud, 9" h., molded leaves & berries, tan matte finish 21.00

Vase, 9" h., molded leaves & berries, green matte finish 35.00

Wall pocket, molded leaves & berries, green matte finish, 8½" h. (ILLUS.) 40.00

NOVAL (1920's)

Bowl, 10" d., 3½" h., canted sides, applied realistically colored fruit on front & reverse, white high-gloss glaze piped in black 35.00

Candlestick, domed base, narrow cylindrical body w/rounded nozzle, applied realistically colored fruit & roses, white high-gloss glaze piped in black, 9½" h. (single) 25.00

Compote, 5½" h., flaring base, shallow bowl, applied realistically colored fruit at sides, white high-gloss glaze piped in black 45.00

Vase, 8" h., applied realistically colored roses, white high-gloss glaze piped in black 60.00

NOVELTY LINE (1930's)

Ash tray, model of 3 pigs, white.... 65.00

Planter, model of a Dachshund, 6" l., 3" h. 45.00

Planter, model of a Dachshund, 8½" l., 4½" h. 35.00

PANELLA (mid to late 1930's)

Panella Bowl

Bowl, 6½" d., 3-footed, pansies in relief within panels, shaded tan matte finish (ILLUS.) 30.00

Cornucopia-vase, pansies in relief within panels, shaded tan matte finish, 5½" h. 16.00

Ginger jar, cov., pansies in relief within panels, shaded blue or green matte finish, 6½" h., each 38.00

Vase, 5½" h., body raised on 3 curving pierced feet, pansies in relief within panels, shaded blue matte finish 45.00

Vase, 6½" h., bulbous base w/flaring cylindrical neck, handles at mid-section, pansies in relief within panels, shaded blue matte finish 25.00

Wall pocket, undulating rim, pansies in relief within panels, shaded green matte finish, 8" h. 35.00

ROBA (mid to late 1930's)

Bowl, 7" w., 3-footed, tri-cornered,

molded swirls w/floral sprigs in
relief, shaded blue ground 40.00
Bowl, 10½" l., footed, molded
swirls w/floral sprigs in relief,
green shaded to white ground. . . . 65.00
Ewer, molded swirls w/floral sprigs
in relief, shaded tan ground,
6" h. 50.00
Vase, 6" h., draped leaf foot, un-
dulating rim, molded swirls w/flo-
ral sprigs in relief, shaded tan
ground 30.00
Vase, 6½" h., bulbous base, 2 han-
dles rising from mid-section to
rim, molded swirls w/floral
sprigs, shaded tan ground 30.00
Vase, 8" h., closed handles at mid-
section, molded swirls w/floral
sprigs, shaded blue or tan
ground, each 50.00

ROMA (1914 - late 1920's)

Roma Wall Pocket

Basket, hanging-type, relief-molded
& tinted deep purple grapes
w/green & tan vine on ivory
ground 65.00
Bowl, 5" d., relief-molded & tinted
red & green floral band on ivory
ground 18.00
Compote, 5½" h., 3 handles rising
from foot to base of bowl, relief-
molded & tinted tan geometric
leaf design on ivory ground 35.00
Jardiniere & pedestal base, relief-
molded & tinted red roses & green
foliage on ivory ground, 2 pcs. . . . 275.00
Vases, double bud, 8½" h., footed
base, square columns of unequal
height joined by pierced disc,
relief-molded & tinted bands of
red roses & green foliage on ivory
ground, pr. 85.00
Vase, 10" h., square w/canted
sides, relief-molded & tinted pink

grapes & green foliage on ivory
ground 60.00
Wall pocket, relief-molded & tinted
red roses & green foliage on ivory
ground, 7" h. (ILLUS.) 40.00
Wall pocket, ribbed, cluster of
relief-molded & tinted red roses,
purple grapes & green foliage on
ivory ground, 8" h. 45.00

SICARDO (1902-07)

Sicardo Vase

Vase, 5" h., 5" d., overall orchid
blossom design on iridescent
ground 525.00
Vase, 6" h., gold orchids design on
iridescent blue-green shaded to
rose ground, signed 395.00
Vase, 6½" h., thistle design on
iridescent ground 400.00
Vase, 7" h., rolled lip, berries &
vine design on iridescent ground,
signed 625.00
Vase, 7" h., 5" widest d., tapered,
iridescent green trailing floral design on spotted iridescent reddish
bronze ground 350.00
Vase, 7" h., cylindrical, maple leaf
design on iridescent ground 375.00
Vase, 8½" h., floral design on
iridescent ground 650.00
Vase, 10½" h., rolled lip, iridescent
blue-green flowing poppies on
shaded purple ground, signed
(ILLUS.) 500.00
Vase, 13" h., cylindrical, iridescent
blue-green to emerald green
glaze 350.00
Vase, 15" h., berries & vine design
on iridescent blue-green to crim-
son glaze 800.00

SILVERTONE (1925-29)

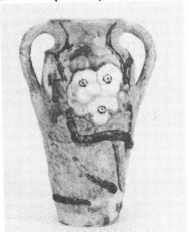

Silvertone Vase

Console set: 12" d., 3" h. bowl & pr. 3" h. candle holders; relief-molded florals against textured ground, shaded pastel blue & grey, 3 pcs..................... 175.00
Vase, 7" h., twisted handles, relief-molded sunflower-type blossoms against textured ground, shaded pastel lavender & blue.......... 65.00
Vase, 8½" h., 2-handled, bulbous w/ruffled rim, relief-molded florals against textured ground, shaded pastel lavender & blue ... 145.00
Vase, 9" h., baluster form, relief-molded lily-type blossoms against textured ground, shaded pastel lavender & blue 80.00
Vase, 9½" h., 2-handled, relief-molded florals against textured ground, shaded pastel tones (ILLUS.)........................ 110.00
Vase, 10" h., stick-type w/long angular handles, relief-molded lily-type blossoms against textured ground, shaded blue & grey 90.00
Vase, 11" h., 6" widest d., relief-molded morning glory blossoms against textured ground, shaded blue & grey.................... 110.00
Vase, 12" h., 2-handled, relief-molded pink poppy blossoms & yellow butterfly against textured grey ground 140.00
Vase, 16" h., relief-molded florals against textured ground, shaded pastel blue & grey 165.00

SOUEVO (1910)

Basket, hanging-type w/chains, red-ware w/cream band of black geometric Indian motifs, 11" d. 85.00

Bowl, sloping shoulders & narrow mouth, redware w/tan band of chocolate brown Indian motifs 75.00
Jardiniere, redware w/cream band of chocolate brown arrowheads, 9" d., 8½" h. 140.00
Vase, 4¼" h., ovoid, redware w/tan band of geometric Indian motifs .. 75.00
Vase, 6" h., bulbous base, flaring neck, redware w/cream band of black geometric Indian motifs 85.00
Vase, 9" h., ovoid, wide mouth, red-ware w/chocolate brown band of cream geometric Indian motifs at mid-section 130.00

TURADA (1897-98)

Bowl, 4½" d., 2½" h., blue & tan lace-like trim on glossy brown.... 110.00
Humidor, cov., blue & white lace-like trim on glossy butterscotch & brown......................... 160.00
Mug, white lace-like trim on glossy cobalt blue 125.00

WARWICK (late 1920's)

Planter, branch molded feet & handles, molded tree bark ground w/branch of green leaves & red florals in relief, 3½" h. 45.00
Vase, bud, 7" h., molded tree bark ground w/branch of green leaves & red florals in relief 30.00
Vase, 7" h., pillow-shaped, footed, 2-handled, molded tree bark ground w/branch of leaves & florals in relief, tan matte finish .. 35.00
Wall pocket, molded tree bark ground w/branch of green leaves & red florals in relief, 11½" h. 60.00

WILD ROSE (1930's)

Wild Rose Ewer

Basket w/double overhead handle, globular, open wild rose decor, shaded green matte finish, 5½" h. 22.00

Basket, hanging-type, open wild rose decor, shaded pink matte finish 34.00

Bowl, 8" d., low, open wild rose decor, shaded green matte finish . . . 21.00

Console set: 18" l. low-footed console bowl & pr. 3-light candle holders; open wild rose decor, shaded pink matte finish, 3 pcs. . . 90.00

Ewer, open wild rose decor, shaded pink matte finish, 7" h. (ILLUS.). . . 22.00

Vase, 6½" h., open wild rose decor, shaded green matte finish 20.00

Vase, 7½" h., 4-footed, open wild rose decor, shaded green or pink matte finish, each 24.00

Vase, 8½" h., deeply scalloped rim, curving handles rising from foot to mid-section, open wild rose decor, shaded pink matte finish 34.00

Vase, 10½" h., cylindrical, double ring handles, open wild rose decor, shaded green matte finish . . . 38.00

WOODCRAFT (1920-33)

Woodcraft Planter

Ash tray, bark-textured ground w/oak leaves in low relief, 3" 80.00

Basket, hanging-type w/original chains, bark-textured ground w/fox head, red fruit & green leaves in relief, 9" d., 4½" h. . . . . 130.00 to 150.00

Bowl, 7" d., 3½" h., panels (5) depicting squirrel seated on a branch eating a nut amidst oak leaves in low relief, brown earthtones . . . . 75.00 to 95.00

Bowl, 7" l., 5½" h. overall, soft green oak leaves w/tan acorns & branch in low relief on creamy white ground w/figural squirrel perched at one end 100.00

Bowl, 9" sq., 4" h., footed, pierced woven twig sides, brown earthtones 48.00

Candlesticks, tree trunk w/spreading branches supporting candle

nozzle, brown earthtones, 8½" h., pr. 80.00

Humidor & cover w/squirrel finial, model of an acorn w/textured rim & smooth body, brown earthtones, 9 x 6" 300.00

Planter, bark-textured ground w/leaves in low relief & 3 foxes peering from den on side, 5½" h. (ILLUS.) . . . . 125.00 to 150.00

Planter, log-shaped w/stump feet, bark-textured ground w/oak leaves in low relief, 9" l. 50.00

Vase, 5" h., fan-shaped, fruit-laden tree in low relief 35.00

Vase, 7" h., tree trunk w/figural owl perched on small limb, brown earthtones 200.00

Vase, 8½" h., cylindrical, bark-textured ground w/branches of pink florals in low relief 50.00

Vase, 9" h., bark-textured ground w/red fruit & green leaves in low relief 58.00

Vase, bud, 10" h., tree trunk w/open limbs, red fruit & green leaves in low relief 37.50

Wall pocket, bark-textured ground w/branches & fruit in low relief & figural squirrel at base, 9" h. . . . . 110.00 to 135.00

Wall pocket, bark-textured ground w/small branches of pink florals extending from body, 9½" h. 45.00

WOODROSE (pre-1920)

Jardiniere, model of an oaken bucket w/pendant red roses & green leaves on brown matte ground, 3½" h. 25.00

Vase, 9" h., model of an oaken bucket w/pendant red roses & green leaves on brown matte ground 40.00

Vase, 10" h., model of an oaken bucket w/pendant red roses & green leaves on brown matte ground 49.00

Wall pocket, fan-shaped, model of an oaken bucket w/pendant florals on brown matte ground, 5½" h. . . . . 55.00 to 70.00

ZONA (1915-20)

Bowl, cereal, tinted red apples w/green leaves & tan branches on creamy white ground 25.00

Compote, 5½" h., incised pink flowers & grey-green leaves against a stippled grey-green ground, creamy white foot 45.00

Pitcher, 6" h., tinted red apples w/green leaves & tan branches on creamy white ground 55.00

Zona Pitcher

Pitcher, 7" h., tinted red apples &
stems in panels on creamy white
ground (ILLUS.) . . . . 70.00 to 85.00
Pitcher, 7" h., dancing duck & grass-
es in low relief on sides, white &
olive green 70.00
Pitcher, 7" h., molded branch han-
dle, kingfisher & cattails in low
relief on sides, deep
rose . . . . 85.00 to 95.00
Pitcher, 8" h., molded branch han-
dle, kingfisher & cattails in low
relief on sides, blue, white & tan
bird 145.00
Pitcher, 8" h., molded branch han-
dle, kingfisher & cattails in low
relief on sides, deep green 130.00
Plate, 7½" d., tinted red apples
w/green leaves & tan branches on
creamy white ground 10.00

WHIELDON-TYPE WARES

Whieldon-Type Ewer

The Staffordshire potter, Thomas Whieldon, first established a pottery at Fenton in

1740. Though he made all types of wares
generally in production in the 18th century,
he is best known for his attractive, warm-
colored green, yellow and brown mottled
wares molded in the form of vegetables, fruit
and leaves. He employed Josiah Spode as an
apprentice and was briefly in partnership
with Josiah Wedgwood. The term Whieldon
ware is, however, a generic one since his
wares were unmarked and are virtually in-
distinguishable from other similar wares
produced by other potters during the same
period. Also see COW CREAMERS and
TOBY MUGS & JUGS.

Dish, leaf-shaped, molded veins,
leaves & flower-heads enriched in
green, manganese & yellow, serrated rim, stalk handle, ca. 1755,
7" w. (minor chip to rim) $1,540.00
Dish, border molded w/barley corn
panels, shaped rim, striated manganese glaze, ca. 1765, 14¾" d. . . 550.00
Ewer, body molded as a bearded
mask w/animal's ears & horns
wearing fruiting vine, molded
mask spout between 2 goat's heads,
female caryatid-molded handle,
flaring foot molded w/fruit, masks
& bands of lappets, overall decoration in brown, blue, green & yellow glazes (crack at rim), ca.
1765, 10¼" h. (ILLUS.) 2,200.00
Model of a cat seated on its
haunches, looking to the right,
sponged manganese glaze, ca.
1750, 5¼" h. 3,190.00
Mug, cylindrical, splashed in man-
ganese w/green & ochre vertical
stripes, entwined strap handle
w/foliage terminals, ca. 1755,
6¼" h. (star crack to base, minor
foot rim chips) 1,760.00
Plates, 7½" octagon, splashed in
brown, ochre & green, borders
w/band of circlets, ca. 1760, pr. . . 495.00
Plate, 8¼" d., molded scrolls enclosing trellis patterned panels,
center w/basketwork, pierced
border w/lappet panels & foliage
scrolls, green glaze, ca. 1755 . . . . . 660.00
Plate, 8½" octagon, raised rope
twist rim, entirely splashed in
manganese, ca. 1755, pr. (1 w/mi-
nor rim chip) 990.00
Plate, 9" d., splotches of green, yel-
low & brown on a grey-green
spotted ground, late 18th c. 220.00
Plate, 9½" d., molded in the center
w/scroll motif on basketwork
ground, entwined basketwork border suspending clusters of fruit
enriched in manganese, yellow &
cream on apple green ground, ca.
1755 . . . . 1,870.00

Plates, 9½" d., splashed in manganese, blue, green & ochre within feather-molded edge, ca. 1755,
pr. 605.00
Plate, 9¾" d., lobed, center molded
w/foliage branch enriched in manganese & pale blue, border w/for-
mal foliage suspending anthemion
on molded trellis pattern ground
enriched in green, ca. 1755 (minor
rim chip repair) 1,210.00

Whieldon-Type Dolphin Sauceboat

Sauceboat, modeled as a dolphin,
enriched in pale green & brown
(star crack in base), ca. 1755,
6¾" l. (ILLUS.) 330.00
Tea caddy, rectangular w/canted
corners & flat shoulder, splashed
in brown glazes, ca. 1755,
5½" h. 418.00
Teapot, cov., applied scrolling fruited
vine issuing from branch handle,
branch spout, cover w/branch finial, brown & greyish-blue tortoise
shell glaze, ca. 1760, 7" w. 2,200.00

WORCESTER

Early Chamberlains Worcester Vases

*The famed English Worcester factory was
established in 1751 and produced porcelains.
Earthenwares were made in the 19th century. Its first period is known as the "Dr. Wall"
period; that from 1783 to 1792 as the "Flight"
period; that from 1792 to 1807 as the "Barr
and Flight & Barr" period. The firm became
Barr, Flight & Barr from 1807 to 1813; Flight,*

*Barr & Barr from 1813 to 1840; Chamberlain
& Co. from 1840 to 1852, and Kerr and Binns
from 1852 to 1862. After 1862, the company
became the Worcester Royal Porcelain Company, Ltd., known familiarly as Royal
Worcester, which see. Also included in the following listing are examples of wares from the
early Chamberlains and Grainger factories in
Worcester.*

Basket, reticulated sides, rose, iron-
red, purple, yellow & green central
floral spray surrounded by small
sprigs on lightly fluted sides & at
gilt-edged rim, yellow exterior
molded as open basketwork applied
at the intersections w/green-cen-
tered rose florettes & w/iron-red,
yellow & rose rope-twist handles
issuing iron-red & purple floral
sprays w/green leaves at ends,
Dr. Wall period, ca. 1765,
8 3/8" oval $1,870.00
Baskets, Pine Cone patt., transfer-
printed in underglaze-blue in center w/cluster of flowers, fruit &
pine cones, & on the rim w/a trellis diaper & floral paneled border,
exterior applied at the intersections of interlocking open circlets
w/blue-heightened florettes, Dr.
Wall period, ca. 1775, 9 1/8" &
8 7/8", pr. 990.00
Cup & saucer, 2-handled, cup re-
served w/a gilt-edged chamfered
rectangular panel painted in
shades of green, brown, yellow &
grey w/two figures in a Sussex
river scene, gilt handles & rim,
each w/shaded brown ground
marbleized in pastel shades of
green, blue, pink, mauve, iron-
red & white, Barr, Flight & Barr,
ca. 1805, 5" w. cup, 5 3/8" d.
saucer 410.00
Dessert set: rectangular fruit stand,
pr. lozenge-shaped dishes, pr. kidney-shaped dishes & pr. square
dishes; each w/different botanical
specimen center, gilt-edged wide
cobalt blue border within gilt gadrooned edge interrupted by shells
& palmettes, early Chamberlains,
ca. 1830, 7 pcs. 2,860.00
Dish, circular, Blind Earl patt., center
w/three chinoiserie figures, stalk
handle enriched in brown, yellow
& green, ca. 1760, 6¼" w. 1,320.00
Dish, modeled as 2 overlapping
leaves w/puce veins & green serrated rims, center w/three butterflies, branch handle, ca. 1755,
7¼" l. (small firing crack to
foot rim) 1,210.00
Dish, Bengal Tiger patt., shaped gilt

line rim, Chamberlain period, ca.
1840, 20¾" d. 770.00
Fruit dish, center w/berried foliage
within an oval puce hatch pattern
panel outlined in gilding, pierced
border suspending trailing foliage
divided by gilt scrolls, feather-
molded rim enriched in gilding,
ca. 1770, 11¾" oval 1,760.00
Garniture, "Warwick Vases," each
w/pale blue ground reserved on
the front w/a gilt-edged rectangular panel painted "en grisaille"
against a yellow ground w/a Wor-
cestershire view above a white
beadwork band & gold & white foliate border repeated on the
reverse beneath gilt gadrooned rim
& around the circular foot, gilt
entwined grapevine handles, gilded square foot, one painted w/a
cornet reverse, Barr, Flight & Barr,
ca. 1810, 7" & 7 1/8" h., set
of 3 ....4,290.00
Plates, 8" d., bouquets of flowers to
the center within gilt surround,
borders w/four diamond-shaped
panels enclosing strawberry
sprays reserved on bright yellow
ground, shaped rim gilt, ca. 1780,
pr.......................... 770.00
Plates, 8¼" to 8½" d., Dragon in
Compartments patt., painted in
iron-red, green, blue, yellow, rose
& gold w/four fan-shaped panels
of fabulous beasts or vases on
tables surrounding central rose
chrysanthemum blossoms & reserved on a grey stippled ground,
gilt-edge rim w/iron-red & green
cell diaper border interrupted
w/four panels of flowerheads,
early Chamberlains, ca. 1795-1805,
set of 12.....................1,980.00
Plate, 8½" d., 6 reserves w/insects
border, 3 large reserves w/birds,
3 small reserves w/insects, gold
trim on blue scale ground, Dr.
Wall period, late 18th c. 488.00
Plates, 10" d., Kings patt., iron-red,
blue & gilt, Chamberlain period,
set of 19 .... 990.00
Soup plate, cobalt blue scalloped
border w/floral swags extending
to flowers center, gold edge
around border, Dr. Wall period,
late 18th c. 245.00
Spill vases, panels enclosing feathers
on an orange & gilt marbleized
ground, flaring rims w/bands of
stylized foliage, early Chamberlains, ca. 1800, 5¾" h., pr. (ILLUS.
sides) 1,430.00

Dr. Wall Period Teapot

Teapot, cov., spherical body painted
in 'Japan' pattern in a Kakiemon
palette heightened in gilding
w/Oriental flowering plants, some
beside fences, within panels divided by underglaze-blue zones reserved w/small cartouches of
floral sprigs within gilt scrollwork
& floral sprays, similarly decorated cover w/floral sprig knob,
pseudo seal mark, Dr. Wall
Period, 1765-70, 5¾" h.
(ILLUS.)....................... 990.00
Teapot, cov., Queen Charlotte patt.,
pink, blue, gilt & iron-red, flowerhead finial, ca. 1770, 7" w. 605.00
Teapot, cov., buildings in Oriental
landscapes within borders of trellis, cone finial, blue & white, ca.
1765, 7¼" w. (minor interior cover chip) 440.00
Vase, 8½" h., urn-form, feathers
within gilt surround on a gilt &
orange net pattern ground, shoulder applied w/two rams' heads
enriched in gilding & bands of
stylized foliage, on flaring foot &
marbleized base, early Chamber-
lains, ca. 1800 (ILLUS. center) 2,200.00

YELLOWWARE

Yellowware Custard Cups

*Yellowware is a form of utilitarian ware
produced in the United States from the 1850's
onward. Its body texture is less dense and
vitreous (impervious to water) than stoneware. Most, but not all, yellowware is unmarked and its color varies from deep yellow
to pale buff. In the late 19th and early 20th*

centuries, bowls in graduated sizes were widely advertised. Still in production, yellowware is plentiful and still reasonably priced. Also see FOOD MOLDS and SPONGEWARE.

Batter bowl w/pouring lip & handle,
  10" d. . . . .$50.00 to 85.00
Bedpan. 22.50
Bowl, 5" d., blue & white pin
  stripes 42.00
Bowl, 6" d., brown & white pin
  stripes 22.50
Bowl, 6¼" d., 3¼" h., three blue
  pin stripes 35.00
Bowl, 7¼" d., 3¾" h., three blue
  pin stripes 35.00
Bowl, 8" d., brown bands &
  stripes 33.50
Bowl, 9½" d., brown pin stripes &
  white slip band . . . . .35.00 to 45.00
Bowl, 10" d., 3 white pin stripes 32.00
Bowl, 10" d., Cottage patt., girl
  watering flowers 115.00
Bowl, 12" d., brown & white pin
  stripes 50.00
Chamber pot, white band w/brown
  pin stripes, 2¾" d., 1 7/8" h. 55.00
Cookie jar, cov. 75.00
Custard cup, 3 blue bands decor,
  each (ILLUS.) 25.00
Custard cup, pink band 35.00
Mixing bowl, brown & white pin
  stripe bands on subtle 2-tone
  glaze, 13" d., 5¾" h. 45.00
Mixing bowl, embossed bands &
  brown pin stripes, 14½" d.,
  8½" h. 95.00
Mug, barrel-shaped, white interior,
  16 oz. 35.00
Mug, "Compliments of Retail
  Grocer's Assoc., Davenport, Iowa"
  on front 38.00
Pitcher, 9½" h., spurred handle,
  ringed base, 1-gal. 65.00
Rolling pin, turned wood handles,
  15" l. . . . . .200.00 to 275.00
Salt box, wall-type w/wooden lid . . . 45.00
Sugar bowl, open, small 65.00
Syrup jug w/pewter top, attributed
  to Ridgway 145.00

ZSOLNAY

This pottery was made in Pecs, Hungary, in a factory founded in 1855 by Vilmos Zsolnay. Currently Zsolnay pieces are being made in a new factory.

Bowl, 7" d., reticulated, animals
  decor on iridescent green glaze . .$200.00
Ewer, iridescent green glaze,
  11½" h. 137.00

Jug, handled, overall multicolored
  enameled florals on iridescent
  cream ground, 9" h. 195.00
Model of Russian bears (2) playing
  on round plinth, "Max & Beba -
  1911," 8½" d., 11½" h. 175.00
Plate, 8½" d., Art Nouveau style
  decor 90.00
Puzzle jug, handled, 2 reticulated
  roundels & 3 looped protrusions,
  multicolored jeweling & iridescent
  florals on beige ground, 6¾" h. . . . 175.00
Puzzle jug, colorful Persian-style
  decor, 7½" h. 135.00
Urn, 2-handled, floral decor,
  11" h. 225.00
Vase, 6" h., iridescent green
  glaze 60.00

Zsolnay Vase

Vase, 18¼" h., elongated ovoid,
  scene of a shepherd, child &
  cloaked man standing against a
  wide open field w/tall trees &
  grasses in foreground in shades
  of iridescent burgundy, cranberry
  red & copper, ca. 1900 (ILLUS.) . . .1,650.00

(End of Ceramics Section)

CHALKWARE

So-called chalkware available today is actually made of plaster-of-paris, much of it decorated in color and primarily in the form of busts, figurines and ornaments. It was produced through most of the 19th century and the majority of pieces were originally quite inexpensive when made. Today even 20th century "carnival" pieces are collectible but we do not include any of them in this listing.

Bust of "Sunny Jim," signed "Morel-
li," ca. 1898, 14" h. $425.00
Doorstop, model of a bulldog, Vic-
torian, 10½" h. 135.00
Figure group, child & Collie dog,
"Can't You Talk?" 7½ x 4",
6" h. 80.00
Mantel garnitures, fruit arrange-
ment in footed compote, white
compote & polychrome-decorated
fruit, 13½" h., pr. (one w/dam-
age to back & repair on base) 900.00
Mantel garniture, fruit & foliage arrangement on low standard, original red, yellow & black paint
w/wear, 13¾" h. 475.00
Model of a cat in seated position,
original worn red, black & yellow
paint, 5¼" h. 295.00

Chalkware Cat

Model of cat in seated position,
original red, black & yellow paint,
9½" h. (ILLUS.) 700.00
Model of a Spaniel dog in seated
position, original worn grey &
black-painted coat, yellow eyes &
features picked out in black &
red, 8½" h. . . . . .105.00 to 175.00
Models of doves perched on square
leaf-molded bases, original (worn)
paint, 10¾" h. 550.00
Model of a pig on grassy mound
base, original (worn) black &
green paint, 6" l. 295.00
Model of a rabbit on oval base,
original red paint on ears & col-
lar, 5" h. 250.00
Model of a rabbit w/open basket,
8¾" h. 185.00
Model of a ram, original (worn)
paint, 3½" h. (old base repairs) . .   85.00
Model of a squirrel seated on
stump, original (worn) paint,
6¼" h. 200.00

CHARACTER COLLECTIBLES

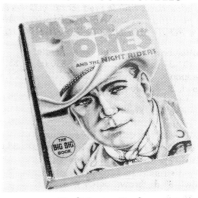

Buck Jones Book

*Numerous objects made in the likeness of
or named after movie, radio, television, com-
ic strip and comic book personalties or charac-
ters abounded from the 1920's through the
1940's. Scores of these are now being eager-
ly collected and prices still vary widely. Also
see BANKS, BIG LITTLE BOOKS,
BROWNIE COLLECTIBLES, BUSTER
BROWN COLLECTIBLES, CAMPBELL
KIDS, CHRISTMAS TREE LIGHTS,
COMIC BOOKS, DISNEY ITEMS, DOLLS,
KEWPIE COLLECTIBLES, SHEET
MUSIC and the "Special Focus" on AMERI-
CAN GAMES.*

Adams Family bank, "Thing" $15.00
Amos & Andy book, "All About
Amos 'n Andy," Carroll & Gosden,
1930, 127 pp. 35.00
Amos & Andy jigsaw puzzle, Pepso-
dent premium, 1932 copyright 100.00
Amos & Andy map of Weber City,
Pepsodent premium, 1935 . . . .   30.00
Andy Gump ash tray stand, wooden
floor-standing model of Andy
holding metal ash tray w/glass in-
set, 1930's, 28" h. 145.00
Andy Gump book, "The Gumps in
Radio Land," Pebeco Toothpaste
premium, 1937 . . . .   20.00
Andy Gump face mask, advertising
premium 65.00
Andy Gump planter, ceramic 65.00
Andy Gump ring, Post Toasties
premium, 1949 . . . .   12.00
Andy Gump toy car, Tootsietoy 150.00
Barney Google figure, wood-jointed,
Schoenhut, ca. 1922, 8½" h. 325.00
Batman ring, flicker-type, The
Penguin 15.00
Beatles book, "Hard Day's Night,"
paperback, 1964 . . . .   16.00
Beatles coin purse, plastic, red,
white or yellow, each 27.50
Beatles magazine, Vol. I, No. 6,
1965 . . . .   14.50

Beatles plate, china, w/portraits, Washington Pottery Ltd., 1960's, 7" d.................................. 47.50

Beatles press pass, for 1966 tour, "This Pass Card Issued by Nems, Identifies Holder as Official Authorized Member of Beatles Touring Party" 65.00

Beatles wig, synthetic hair 35.00

Betty Boop doll quilt, full figure of Betty, machine-quilted fabric, 16 x 12"........................ 50.00

Betty Boop figure, celluloid, playing violin, 3" h....................... 45.00

Betty Boop wall pocket, china, Betty w/cat on front, stamped on back "Betty Boop by Fleischer Studios, Japan"........................... 100.00

Betty Boop & Bimbo bridge set: tally cards & score pad; dated 1932 .... 85.00

Blondie action figure, "hingie," cardboard, 1940's, original envelope .. 20.00

Blondie cookbook, 1st edition, w/dust jacket................. 20.00

Blondie paint & coloring book, Whitman, 1945 .... 17.50

Blondie paint box, tin, American Crayon Co., 1946, 5¾ x 4½" 18.00

Blondie ring, Post Toasties premium, 1949 .... 12.00

Buck Jones "Big Big" book, "Buck Jones and the Night Riders," Whitman, 1937, 316 pp., 9½ x 7½" (ILLUS.) 10.00

Buck Jones cowboy outfit 85.00

Buck Jones guitar 55.00

Buck Jones pinback button, "Rangers' Club of America," w/photo, 1" d.................. 25.00

Buck Rogers badge, "Solar Scout," Cream of Wheat premium, 1934 .. 45.00

Buck Rogers "Big Big" book, "The Adventures of Buck Rogers," 1934 .... 75.00

Buck Rogers book, pop-up type, "A Dangerous Mission" 130.00

Buck Rogers flying saucer, 1930's .. 55.00

Buck Rogers handbook, "Space Patrol".......................... 100.00

Buck Rogers helmet 85.00

Buck Rogers paint book, 1935, 11 x 18", unused 85.00

Buck Rogers pin, "Solar Scout" 30.00

Buck Rogers pinback button, 1940's ....35.00 to 65.00

Buck Rogers pocket watch, Buck & Wilma on face, E. Ingraham Co., 1935 .... 215.00

Buck Rogers "signal" flashlight, gun-shaped, 1952 .... 50.00

Buck Rogers Space Ranger kit, Sylvania T.V. premium, 1952........ 125.00

Bugs Bunny soap figure............ 20.00

Captain Kangaroo mug 5.00

Captain Marvel puppet, paper, 1944 .... 20.00

Captain Midnight book, "Trick & Riddle," 1939 .... 18.00

Captain Midnight decoder, 1945, Magni-Magic Code-O-Graph, Ovaltine premium ....20.00 to 35.00

Captain Midnight decoder, 1946, Mirro-Flash Code-O-Graph, Ovaltine premium 32.50

Captain Midnight decoder manual, 1941 .... 110.00

Captain Midnight decoder manual, 1946 .... 95.00

Captain Midnight, "Flight Commander" flyer's cross, 1942........ 105.00

Captain Midnight ring, sliding secret compartment 60.00

Captain Video "Galaxy Rocket," painted pressed steel & plastic w/decals, Roberts Toy, 26" l...... 125.00

Captain Video ring, "Secret Seal".......................... 75.00

Charlie Chaplin book, "Charlie Chaplin in the Movies," copyright 1917 by Keeley.................. 200.00

Charlie Chaplin figure, chalkware, Statue Arts, 11" h. 50.00

Charlie McCarthy book, "Charlie McCarthy Meets Snow White," soft cover, Whitman, 1938............ 55.00

Charlie McCarthy card game, "Rummy," Whitman Publishing Co., 1939 .... 20.00

Charlie McCarthy coloring book, 1938 .... 14.00

Charlie McCarthy doll, rubber, wearing tuxedo & monicle w/string, unmarked, 9" h. 30.00

Charlie McCarthy game, "Radio Party," 21 pcs. complete w/spinner & envelope, Chase & Sanborn Coffee premium, 1938 .... 32.50

Charlie McCarthy game, "Topper," 1938 .... 30.00

Charlie McCarthy paint book, Whitman Publishing, 1938 .... 20.00

Charlie McCarthy pencil sharpener .. 27.50

Charlie McCarthy pinback button ... 10.00

Charlie McCarthy radio, "Majestic," 1930's 250.00

Charlie McCarthy soap figure, original box 35.00

Chester Gump pinback button, Kellogg's "Pep" Cereal premium 4.00

Chester Gump toy, Chester figure in cart pulled by horse, cast iron, 1905 .... 295.00

Cisco Kid mask, advertising premium 12.00

Cisco Kid & Poncho masks, Tip Top Bread premium, 1953, pr. 25.00

Daddy Warbucks nodding figure, bisque 150.00

Dale Evans cowgirl outfit & hat,
w/picture of Dale & horse, in
original box 65.00
Dale Evans wrist watch, Ingraham,
1951 .... 45.00
Daniel Boone rifle, Flintlock Model
196, Louis Marx & Co., on original
cardboard 50.00
Dick Tracy badge, "Inspector
General" 350.00
Dick Tracy "Big Big" book, "Dick
Tracy and the Mystery of the Purple Cross," 1938............... 85.00
Dick Tracy book, "Ace Detective,"
by Chester Gould, autographed &
w/dust jacket 12.00
Dick Tracy cap gun, cast iron 20.00
Dick Tracy "Crimestopper" kit,
w/badge, whistle, flashlight, etc.,
1961 .... 22.50
Dick Tracy game, "Target,"
lithographed tin w/gun & 2 darts,
Louis Marx & Co., original
box .... 32.50 to 50.00
Dick Tracy salt & pepper shakers,
pr............................. 25.00
Dick Tracy suspenders, from Detec-
tive set, boxed................. 30.00
Dick Tracy wrist radio, 1940's....... 32.50
Dionne Quintuplets book, "Pictorial
Story of the Dionne Quintuplets,"
Whitman, 1935 .... 20.00
Dionne Quintuplets calendar, 1938,
"The Five Little Sweethearts of the
World" dressed as nursery rhyme
characters 16.50
Dionne Quintuplets calendar, 1939,
"This Year They are Five,"
11 x 16"....................... 22.50
Dionne Quintuplets calendar, 1940,
"Quints in School Days".......... 17.50
Dionne Quintuplets calendar, 1942,
"Springtime," painting by Andrew
Loomis 20.00
Dionne Quintuplets calendar, 1943,
"Sunny Days," painting by Andrew
Loomis, 12 x 15" 12.50
Dionne Quintuplets photograph al-
bum, Dell Products, 1936........ 20.00
Dionne Quintuplets plate, Annette,
Cecile & Yvonne as babies,
7" d.......................... 30.00
Dionne Quintuplets scrapbook,
272 pp........................ 55.00
Dionne Quintuplets teaspoon,
"Annette," silverplate 12.50
Dionne Quintuplets teaspoon,
"Cecile," silverplate 14.00
Felix the Cat doorstop,
wooden .... 45.00 to 60.00
Felix the Cat feeding dish, Royal
Rudolstadt china, 12 poses on bot-
tom & sides, yellow & black rim,
7" d.......................... 78.00

Felix the Cat figure, wood-jointed,
copyright 1922-24 by Pat Sullivan,
pat. June 23, 1925, Schoenhut,
6" h.......................... 130.00
Felix the Cat figure, chalkware,
"Felix the Fullback," holding football, 11" h. 75.00

Felix the Cat Figure

Felix the Cat figure, composition,
13" h. (ILLUS.) .... 165.00 to 180.00
Felix the Cat pencil box, 1931 ...... 27.50
Felix the Cat perfume bottle, glass,
6" h..................... 65.00 to 95.00
Felix the Cat pitcher, ceramic 35.00
Felix the Cat pull toy, lithographed
tin, Felix in pursuit of 2 red & yel-
low mice, on orange 4-wheeled
base, Nifty, 1920's, 8" l. 400.00
Felix the Cat ring, Post Toasties
premium, 1949 .... 20.00
Felix the Cat "sparkler" toy, Nifty,
1925-35....................... 120.00
Felix the Cat valentine, celluloid
Felix attached to card 75.00
Flash Gordon book, "Caverns of
Mongo," 1936, hardcover, G & D,
w/dust jacket 50.00
Flash Gordon figure, Syrocco
(pressed wood pulp), 1944 .... 225.00
Flash Gordon jigsaw puzzle,
15 x 10"....................... 28.00
Flash Gordon kite 32.50
Flash Gordon pistol, "Radio Repeat-
er," lithographed tin, original
box 80.00
Flash Gordon space suit, 1930-40 ... 225.00
Flash Gordon toy, windup tin "Rock-
et Fighter No. 5," Louis Marx &
Co., 1930's .... 250.00 to 330.00
Foxy Grandpa book, "The Merry
Pranks of Foxy Grandpa," by
Bunny, copyright 1902 .... 150.00
Frank Buck book, "Bring 'em Back
Alive," hardcover, 1930, 316 pp. ... 45.00

Frank Buck pinback button, "Adventure Club" 25.00
Gene Autry book, "Thief River Outlaws," 1944 .... 7.00
Gene Autry cap gun, cast iron, Kenton 40.00
Gene Autry cap gun, cast iron, ivory grips, "Kenton Hardware" 55.00
Gene Autry chaps ....30.00 to 45.00
Gene Autry pinback button, pistol-boot 18.00
Happy Hooligan game 125.00
Happy Hooligan postcard 12.00
Happy Hooligan roly-poly toy, wood & composition, Schoenhut 150.00
Happy Hooligan smoker's set, figural match, cigar & cigarette holder & ash tray w/striker, majolica, set 80.00
Happy Hooligan vase, majolica 135.00
Harold Teen "Bat-o-Ball" game, 1938 .... 40.00
Herbie mask, Famous Artists Syndicate, 1933 .... 7.50
Hopalong Cassidy alarm clock, U.S. Time 120.00
Hopalong Cassidy birthday card, w/rope......................... 18.00
Hopalong Cassidy book, "Coming of Hopalong Cassidy," hardbound, colorful dust cover, ca. 1913 ...... 10.00

Hopalong Cassidy Cap Gun

Hopalong Cassidy cap gun, gold finish metal, black plastic hand grip, 7½" l. (ILLUS.) 25.00
Hopalong Cassidy cookie jar, cov., "Bar 20 Cookie Corral," pottery, decal & embossed designs, 8" d., 6½" h. 175.00
Hopalong Cassidy cowgirl outfit, original box ....80.00 to 100.00
Hopalong Cassidy crayon & stencil set, dated 1950 ....35.00 to 70.00
Hopalong Cassidy flashlight 15.00
Hopalong Cassidy fountain pen 40.00
Hopalong Cassidy game, "Dominoes," Milton Bradley, 1950 ...... 75.00
Hopalong Cassidy "Bunkhouse Clothes Corral" hat rack, 3-hook, Northland Milk premium, 22" l.... 45.00
Hopalong Cassidy movie theatre lobby card, "The Dead Don't Dream," 1947, 14 x 36" 75.00
Hopalong Cassidy neckerchief, cot-

ton, black w/white & gold ....20.00 to 30.00
Hopalong Cassidy neckerchief slide, steer's head 16.00
Hopalong Cassidy night light, figural bullet, Aladdin Alacite glass 125.00
Hopalong Cassidy pinback button, Raisin Bran Cereal premium 5.00

Hopalong Cassidy Plate

Hopalong Cassidy plate, milk white glass w/black decal of Hoppy & Topper, Anchor Hocking, 7" d. (ILLUS.)........................ 14.00
Hopalong Cassidy plate, china, signed "To My Friend, Hoppy," marked W.S. George Mfg., 10" d. 20.00
Hopalong Cassidy record album, "Singing Bandit"................. 22.50
Hopalong Cassidy ring, "Good Luck Bar 20," Post Cereal premium, 1949 .... 29.00
Hopalong Cassidy roller skates, original box 95.00
Hopalong Cassidy tie clasp, "Bar 20 Ranch," on card 12.50
Hopalong Cassidy waste basket, simulated leather cover 53.50
Hopalong Cassidy whistle, tin 15.00
Howdy Doody baby spoon, silverplate 14.00
Howdy Doody costume, size 8 ...... 90.00
Howdy Doody doll, plastic, 3¾" ... 20.00
Howdy Doody paint set, 1950's 40.00
Howdy Doody pencil, 1950's 15.00
Howdy Doody pinback button, National Broadcasting Co., large 9.00
Howdy Doody record player, "Phono Doodle," 1950's 135.00
Howdy Doody shake-up mug, Ovaltine premium 60.00
Howdy Doody shoe polish 12.50
Howdy Doody tool box, metal 22.50
Howdy Doody "spinning" top, tin ... 25.00
Jack Armstrong airplane kit, "P-40 Zero," w/original mailer 30.00
Jack Webb (Dragnet) badge, "714".. 10.00
Jack Webb (Dragnet) whistle 5.00

Jackie Coogan figure of "The Kid,"
chalkware, brown, 7½" h. 25.00
Jiggs doorstop, wooden, large 185.00
Jiggs figure, wood-jointed,
Schoenhut 375.00

Jiggs, Maggie & Rosie Figures

Jiggs, Maggie & Rosie figures,
bisque, King Features Syndicate,
4" h., each (ILLUS.) 25.00
Joe Palooka lunch box, 1946 .... 45.00
Joe Palooka lunch box, 1948 .... 45.00
Joe Palooka wrist watch, Joe in
boxing gear on face, brown leath-
er band, New Haven Clock &
Watch Co., 1947 .... 110.00
Krazy Kat pinback button 30.00
Lil Abner cigarette lighter, "Dog-
patch U.S.A.," 1968 Capp
Enterprises 40.00
Lil Abner tumbler, clear glass
w/enameled Abner 7.00
Lil King book, "The Little King," O.
Soglow, hardcover w/dust jacket,
1945, 32 pp. 15.00
Lil King figure, wood & composition,
Ideal, 12" h. 70.00
Little Lulu coloring book, Whitman
No. 1258, 1955 .... 25.00
Little Lulu purse, plastic, 1944 ...... 20.00
Lone Ranger belt, "glow-in-the-
dark," 1941 .... 55.00
Lone Ranger blanket, cotton, alter-
nating rows of Lone Ranger &
Tonto, red, brown & beige 62.00
Lone Ranger blotter, Bond Bread
premium 15.00

Lone Ranger bookbag, leatherette,
multicolored picture on tan,
12 x 10" (ILLUS.) 30.00
Lone Ranger certificate, "Silvercup
Bread Safety Club," 1938 .... 35.00
Lone Ranger figure, chalkware,
15" h. 55.00
Lone Ranger flashlight, "signal
siren," w/silver bullet
code .... 25.00 to 55.00
Lone Ranger paint box, complete ... 15.00
Lone Ranger pen, silver bullet 22.50
Lone Ranger tumbler, clear glass
w/white enameled Lone Ranger &
Silver, dated 1938 .... 32.00
Looney Tunes tea set: cov. teapot,
2 c/s & 4½" l. tray; tin, 6 pcs. ... 38.50
Mae West boudoir doll, ca. 1920,
30" h. 215.00
Mama Katzenjammer "roly-poly"
toy, papier mache 50.00
Mandrake the Magician magic kit,
King Features Syndicate, 1949 .... 55.00
Mandrake the Magician pin, "Magic
Club" 45.00
Min Gump pinback button, Kellogg's
Pep Cereal premium 4.00
Moon Mullins bottle, frosted glass,
figural, 3" h. 95.00
Moon Mullins drawing & tracing
book, McLoughlin, 1932 .... 30.00
Mutt & Jeff book, "Adventures of
Mutt & Jeff," Cupples & Leon,
1920, 11 x 16" 40.00
Mutt & Jeff figures, composition
heads & hands, ball-jointed metal
bodies, late 1920's, made in
Switzerland, 8" & 6½" h.,
pr. 650.00
Mutt & Jeff song book, tunes from
the Broadway musical, 1911,
20 pp. 25.00
Olive Oyl puppet, King Features
Syndicate, late 1940's 25.00
Olive Oyl ring, 1949 .... 12.00

Lone Ranger Bookbag   **Olive Oyl "Squeaker" Toy**

Olive Oyl toy, rubber figure w/squeaker, King Features Syndicate, 8" h. (ILLUS.) 45.00

Orphan Annie ash tray, glazed ceramic 80.00

Orphan Annie bank, dime register ....50.00 to 100.00

Orphan Annie book, "Little Orphan Annie & Jumbo," pop-up type, 1935 .... 85.00

Orphan Annie book, "Little Orphan Annie & The Gila Monster Gang," 1944 .... 10.00

Orphan Annie book, "Little Orphan Annie & The Pinchpenny," 1934 ... 16.00

Orphan Annie book, "Little Orphan Annie Ship Wrecked," 1931 ...... 25.00

Orphan Annie circus set, cardboard cut-outs, complete.............. 175.00

Orphan Annie coloring book, 1930 .. 30.00

Orphan Annie decoder, 1937, Ovaltine premium, w/manual ....65.00 to 80.00

Orphan Annie decoder, 1942, Whirlomatic 115.00

Orphan Annie decoder manual, 1934 .... 35.00

Orphan Annie decoder manual, 1936 .... 42.50

Orphan Annie decoder manual, 1938 .... 45.00

Orphan Annie decoder manual, 1939 .... 40.00

Orphan Annie figure, wood-jointed, stamped Harold Gray............ 55.00

Orphan Annie game, "Jacks," complete w/rubber ball & metal jacks, 1930's 55.00

Orphan Annie game, "Little Orphan Annie Travel Game," Milton Bradley, original box 35.00

Orphan Annie "hingee," paper assembly toy by King, Larson, McMahon of Chicago, Ill., 1944 ... 22.50

Orphan Annie jigsaw puzzle, by Stephens & Kindred Company, New York, distributed by Novelty Distributing of Newark, New Jersey 22.00

Orphan Annie map of Simmons Corners, Tucker County, 1936, 24 x 19" 85.00

Orphan Annie mug, creamware pottery, w/decal picture of Annie & Sandy, Ovaltine premium, signed Harold Gray 35.00

Orphan Annie pinback button, "Secret Society" 20.00

Orphan Annie planter, bisque, 1930's 65.00

Orphan Annie puppet, in original box 150.00

Orphan Annie ring, radio premium 32.50

Orphan Annie sun dial-compass (sun watch), 1938 .... 50.00

Orphan Annie telephone, plastic, red 40.00

Orphan Annie toy laundry set, clothes pins, wash line & pulleys, on card, 1938 .... 45.00

Orphan Annie Stove

Orphan Annie toy stove, tin, blue, 4½" h., 4¾" w. (ILLUS.) 38.00

Orphan Annie whistle, tin, 1942 .... 30.00

Orphan Annie wrist watch, original red leather band, New Haven, ca. 1934 .... 85.00

Orphan Annie & Sandy planter, bisque, marked "Orphan Annie and Sandy, - F.A.S., S4," 3" w., 5" h. 60.00

Paladin lunch box, 1960............ 10.00

Perry Winkle figure, bisque, movable arms, 3¾" h. 85.00

Pinky Lee pull-toy, Pinky dancing, Nabisco premium, original box ... 30.00

Popeye ash tray, chalkware, 1929, 6" h. 150.00

Popeye belt, leather w/brass buckle, 1929 .... 50.00

Popeye blocks, nesting-type, cylinders 85.00

Popeye book, "Adventures of Popeye," 1934, Saalfield 35.00

Popeye book, "Popeye & The Pirates," animated, illustrated by Sagendorf, 1945, spiral-bound 65.00

Popeye book, "Popeye in Puddleburg," 1934, hard cover 28.00

Popeye book, "Popeye With the Hag of the Seven Seas," pop-up type, 1935 .... 75.00

Popeye bubble blowing set, Transogram, in original box, dated, 1936 .... 25.00

Popeye card game, 1929-34 .... 18.00

Popeye change tray, wooden, 1930's 200.00

Popeye cookie jar, cov., 1965 ....65.00 to 100.00

Popeye doorstop, cast iron, painted, Hubley Mfg. Co. for King Features Syndicate, 1929, 9" h. 650.00

Popeye figure, celluloid, jointed, King Features Syndicate, 1940's, 6" h. 65.00

Popeye figure, composition, King Features Syndicate, dated 1944, 5" h. 25.00

Popeye figure, rubber, King Features Syndicate, 1940's, 13" h. 125.00

Popeye figure, wood-jointed, J. Chein & Co. for King Features Syndicate, Inc., 1932, 11" h. 250.00

Popeye game, "Bingo," 1929 .... 37.50

Popeye game, "Popeye the Juggler," 1929 copyright 47.50

Popeye game, "Sling Dart," 1958 ... 22.00

Popeye game, "Target" 28.00

Popeye hairbrush 18.00

Popeye "hingee," cardboard action figure, 1940's, original envelope .. 20.00

Popeye jack-in-box, Popeye in spinach can, lithographed tin w/plastic head, Mattel, 1957 copyright ....27.00 to 60.00

Popeye kazoo, tin & cardboard, 1934, 3" l. 20.00

Popeye lamp, metal, figure of Popeye, paint worn to pewter finish, King Features Syndicate, 1935, overall 14" h. .....145.00 to 225.00

Popeye lantern, tin & glass, Linemar Toys, 1950's, original box 125.00

Popeye marble pouch, 1937 .... 20.00

Popeye mirror, metal w/iron wire handle & 3" l. decal, 1929 .... 45.00

Popeye Night Light

Popeye night light, vinyl, King Features Syndicate, 1959, Alan Jay, 8" h. (ILLUS.) 30.00

Popeye paint book, 1930's, 12 x 10" 65.00

Popeye pencil, extra large, dated 1929 .... 27.50

Popeye pinback button, enameled picture, 1930's 30.00

Popeye pipe, ivory-like pseudo Meerschaum material .....20.00 to 45.00

Popeye pocket knife, celluloid, 2-blade, red 60.00

Popeye punching bag, inflatable-type, original box 25.00

Popeye sailboat, wooden, King Features Syndicate, 1929 .... 230.00

Popeye sailor's cap, blue cloth 35.00

Popeye tie clasp, metal, enameled character 30.00

Popeye toothbrush holder, bisque, movable right arm & wooden pipe, 1920's, 5" h. 150.00

Popeye toy, friction-type, Popeye in roadster, Linemar 650.00

Popeye & Olive Oyl Figures

Popeye & Olive Oyl figures, wood-jointed, King Features Syndicate, 5½" h., pr. (ILLUS.) 130.00

Popeye & Olive Oyl fountain pen ... 45.00

Popeye, Olive Oyl & Wimpy soap figures, set of 3 in original box... 110.00

Porky Pig bank, bisque, 4½" 100.00

Porky Pig bank, pot metal, Porky beside tree trunk, Metal Moss Mfg. Co., 1930's, 4½" h. (Moore Bank No. 263) 55.00

Porky Pig mug, ceramic, decal on turquoise blue 25.00

Porky Pig wrist watch, 1949 .... 175.00

Princess Summer-Fall/Winter-Spring marionette 60.00

Raggedy Ann & Andy mug, ceramic, 1941 .... 27.50

Red Ryder book, "Red Ryder & the Adventure at Chimney Rock" 12.00

Red Ryder book, "Riddle of Roaring Range," 1951 .... 9.00

Red Ryder game, table model pin-ball by Gotham, signed Fred Harman 38.00

Rin Tin Tin button, "Official Club Member," Nabisco premium 15.00

Rin Tin Tin & Rusty (child's) necktie, colorful 15.00

Robin (Batman series) "flicker" ring, 1960's 15.00

Roy Rogers Book Bag

Roy Rogers book bag, brown
  leatherette, 13" w., 10" h.
  (ILLUS.)........................ 35.00
Roy Rogers game, "Horseshoes,"
  complete in original box 50.00

Roy Rogers "Lucky" Horseshoe

Roy Rogers "lucky" horseshoe, hard
  rubber (ILLUS.) 15.00
Roy Rogers pencil box, w/contents,
  7 x 4"......................... 14.00
Roy Rogers pocket watch 85.00
Roy Rogers pull-toy, Roy & Trigger,
  wooden 225.00
Roy Rogers raincoat, yellow slicker
  w/black trim, original tag........ 80.00
Roy Rogers ring, sterling silver,
  w/saddle 40.00
Roy Rogers "Song Folio No. 1," pic-
  tures, music & stories, 1943,
  59 pp.......................... 27.50
Roy Rogers spurs, George Schmidt
  Co., 1949, pr. 20.00
Roy Rogers toy village, "Mineral
  City" (frontier town), metal, cow-
  boys, Indians, furniture & horses,
  27 x 8 x 6" deep, 128 pcs. 85.00
Roy Rogers yo-yo................. 45.00
Rudolph the Red-Nosed Reindeer
  wrist watch, Ingraham 35.00
Sandy (Orphan Annie) nodding fig-
  ure, bisque 45.00

Schmoo (Lil Abner) alarm clock, Lux
  Clock Co....................... 250.00
Sergeant Preston cards, "Challenge
  of the Yukon," set 65.00
Sergeant Preston signal light 12.00
Sergeant Preston totem pole set,
  w/instructions 87.50
The Shadow blotter, Blue Coal ink .. 20.00
The Shadow "Club Membership" pin,
  metal 200.00
The Shadow ring, glow-in-the-dark
  w/"Blue Coal" jewel on white
  ring 200.00
Shield G-Man badge.............. 47.00
Shield G-Man pencil sharpener, cel-
  luloid, gun-shaped 29.00
Shirley Temple "beauty bar" set,
  w/atomizer, cologne, bubble
  bath, soap, etc., in original
  "clear" box 80.00
Shirley Temple book, "Captain Janu-
  ary & The Little Colonel," Random
  House edition 15.00
Shirley Temple book, "Little
  Princess" 24.00
Shirley Temple book, "Little Star -
  Her Life in Pictures," published by
  Saalfield Publishing Co., 1936 .... 45.00
Shirley Temple book, "My Young
  Life," 1945 .... 35.00
Shirley Temple book, "The Story of
  Shirley Temple," 1934........... 20.00
Shirley Temple book, "Twinkletoes,"
  1936 .... 16.00
Shirley Temple book, "Wee Willie
  Winkie," authorized soft cover
  edition w/pictures, 1937 .... 22.50
Shirley Temple coloring book,
  Shirley holding blackboard "This is
  my Crayon Book," 1935 .... 25.00
Shirley Temple fountain pen........ 75.00
Shirley Temple hair bow, original
  card 85.00

Shirley Temple Mug

Shirley Temple mug, cobalt blue
  glass w/decal portrait of Shirley
  (ILLUS.)...................35.00 to 55.00
Shirley Temple paper dolls, cut,

Saalfield No. 4435 or No. 5110,
each 30.00
Shirley Temple paperweight, glass,
3" w., 2½" h. 75.00
Shirley Temple playing cards, Shirley
as "The Little Colonel" 60.00
Shirley Temple pocket watch 145.00
Shirley Temple sheet music, "On the
Good Ship Lollipop," Shirley on
cover 10.00
Shirley Temple song book, "Shirley's
Favorite Songs," 1937 .... 20.00
Shirley Temple valentine, paper
fold-out type.................. 12.00
Skeezix coloring book, 1929 .... 21.00
Skeezix figure, bisque, 2½" h. 35.00
Skippy pencil box, dated 1933 ...... 35.00
Skippy teaspoon, silverplate, figural
Skippy handle.................. 8.00
Skippy toothbrush holder, bisque,
movable arms, 5¾" h........... 60.00
Sky King ring, "Navajo Treasure" ... 175.00
Smitty figure, bisque, Japan, 1930's,
3½" h. 20.00
Smokey Stover "hingee," cardboard
action figure, 1940's, original
envelope 20.00
Sonja Henie coloring book, 1939 .... 25.00
Superman badge, "Junior Defense
League," ca. 1943 .... 110.00
Superman belt buckle 18.00
Superman game, "Quoits" (ring
toss), complete 8 pc. set w/in-
structions, 1940's .... 95.00 to 140.00
Superman pencil box 25.00
Superman pinback button, Kelloggs
premium 15.00

Superman Wrist Watch

Superman wrist watch, round dial,
metal band, 1966 (ILLUS.) 100.00
Terry & the Pirates book, "Ship-
wrecked," pop-up type, 1935 ..... 80.00
Terry & the Pirates coloring book,
1945 .... 25.00
Three Stooges ring, flicker-type, "I'm
Curly"........................ 20.00
Tom Corbett Space Cadet flashlight,
original box 42.50

Tom Corbett Space Cadet lunch box,
w/thermos, 1952 ....30.00 to 45.00
Tom Corbett Space Cadet (Atomic
Ray) rifle, Louis Marx & Co., origi-
nal box 100.00
Tom Mix bracelet, "Straight Shoot-
er," Ralston Cereal premium 55.00
Tom Mix lariat, wooden handle, Ral-
ston Cereal premium, 1933 ...... 50.00
Tom Mix song book, "Western
Songs," 1935, 68 pp. 35.00
Tom Mix spurs, "Glow in Dark,"
pr.......................... 75.00
Uncle Walt, Skeezix, Smitty & Herby
figures, bisque, distributed by N.
Shure Co. of Chicago, 2¼" to
3½" h., set of 4 .... 75.00
Uncle Wiggily book, "Uncle Wiggily's
Auto Sled," 1931 .... 15.00
Uncle Wiggily (cereal) bowl,
ceramic 70.00
Uncle Willie bottle, ceramic, figural,
6½" h. 45.00
Uncle Willie & Emma planter,
ceramic 45.00
Wimpy toy, "musical hamburger,"
dated 1936 .... 40.00
Wyatt Earp gun, Buntline by Hubley,
1959 .... 35.00
Yellow Kid pinback button No. 16 or
32, each..................... 30.00
Yellow Kid sheet music, "Yellow Kid
on Parade," matted & framed,
1886 .... 85.00
Zorro billfold, 1957 .... 9.00
Zorro costume 30.00
Zorro fountain pen 12.50
Zorro postcard 3.00
Zorro rifle, Flintlock Model 196/Z,
on original cardboard........... 50.00
Zorro ring, plastic 12.00
Zorro thermos bottle 10.00

Zorro Wrist Watch

Zorro wrist watch, original box
(ILLUS.)...................... 62.50

CHILDREN'S BOOKS

Child's Miniature Book

The most collectible children's books today tend to be those printed after the 1850's and while age is not completely irrelevant, illustrations play a far more important role in determining the values. While first editions are highly esteemed, it is the beautifully illustrated books that most collectors seek. The following books, all in good to fine condition, were sold within the past twelve months. Also see BIG LITTLE BOOKS, BROWNIE COLLECTIBLES, BUSTER BROWN COLLECTIBLES, CHARACTER COLLECTIBLES, COMIC BOOKS, DISNEY COLLECTIBLES and GREENAWAY ITEMS.

"A Christmas Carol," by Charles Dickens, illustrated by Arthur Rackham, published by Lippincott, 1935 .... $17.50

"The Adventures of Mr. Mocker," by Thornton Burgess, illustrated by Cady, 1925 .... 10.00

"Boys & Girls of Bookland," illustrated by Jessie Wilcox Smith, 1923 .. 55.00

"The Children of Dickens," by Samuel Crothers, 10 color illustrations by Jessie Wilcox Smith, published by Scribner's, 1932 .... 35.00

"The Cowardly Lion of Oz," by L. Frank Baum, 1923 .... 25.00

"Doctor Doolittle's Caravan," by Hugh Lofting, 1926, 1st edition ... 28.50

"Dolly-Land," 3 x 2½" (ILLUS.) 10.00

"Dr. Boners," by Dr. Seuss (Theodor Geisel), 1931, 1st edition 50.00

"Eagle Blood," by James Creelman, 6 illustrations by Rose O'Neill, 1902 .... 15.00

"The Emerald City of Oz," by L. Frank Baum, illustrated by John Neill, published by Reilly & Britton, 1910, 1st edition 125.00

"Fairy Tales Far & Near," by Sir Arthur Quiller-Couch, illustrated by

H. R. Miller, published by Frederick R. Stokes Co., 1895 .... 20.00

"Girl of the Limberlost," by Gene Stratton Porter, published by Grosset & Dunlap, 1909 .... 12.00

"Goldilocks," color illustrations by Frances Brundage, 1919.......... 25.00

"Hansel & Gretel," illustrated by Margaret Evans Price, published by Stecher Litho Co., 1920....... 25.00

"Jo's Boys," by Louisa May Alcott, 1909 .... 20.00

"Jungle Girl," by Edgar Rice Burroughs, 1932 .... 65.00

"Kidnapped," by Robert Louis Stevenson, 10 color illustrations by N. C. Wyeth, Classics edition, published by Scribner's, pictorial cover, 1940 .... 22.50

"The Last of the Mohicans," by James Fennimore Cooper, illustrated by N. C. Wyeth, 1945...... 65.00

"The Life & Adventures of Santa Claus," by L. Frank Baum, 12 pages color illustrations, published by M. A. Donahue & Co.... 90.00

"Little Black Sambo & the Tiger Kitten," 1926 .... 30.00

"Moths of the Limberlost," by Gene Stratton Porter, published by Doubleday, 1916, in original box.. 100.00

"Mysterious Island," by Jules Verne, 12 color illustrations by N. C. Wyeth, 1920 .... 15.00

"The Night Before Christmas," by Clement Moore, illustrated by Arthur Rackham, 1931 .... 175.00

"The Old Woman & Her Pig," published by McLoughlin, 1903 .... 12.00

"Ozma of Oz," by L. Frank Baum, 1907, w/dust jacket 45.00

"Patches, A Wyoming Cowpony," by Hawkes, illustrated by Jessie Wilcox Smith, published by Milton Bradley, 1928, 1st edition 15.00

"Penrod & Sam," by Booth Tarkington, 1916, 1st edition 40.00

"Pinocchio," illustrated by Frances Brundage, published by Saalfield, 1924 .... 20.00

"Raggedy Ann in the Deep Deep Woods," by Johnny Gruelle, 1930 .... 20.00

"Rebecca of Sunnybrook Farm," by Kate Douglas Wiggin, published by Grosset & Dunlop, 1903, 1st edition ....45.00 to 65.00

"Rich Mrs. Duck," illustrated, published by McLoughlin, 1899 .... 10.00

"Robinson Crusoe," by Daniel Defoe, published by Hubbard Bros., gilt-edged pages, embossed cover, 1872 .... 45.00

"Romances of Charlie Rabbit," by

Uncle Milton, 11 color plates, published by Ullman Co., 1908, 4 x 5" 20.00

"Santa Visits Mother Goose," pop-up type, 1953, 9 x 11", original box .. 15.00

"The Scarecrow of Oz," by L. Frank Baum, illustrated by J.R. Neill, 1915 .... 30.00

"The Second Froggy Fairy," by Anthony Biddle, illustrated, 1900 .... 10.00

"Sleeping Beauty," illustrated by H. Lentz, pop-up type, 1933 .... 55.00

"Snowman's Christmas," by Mary Bird, 1908 .... 8.00

"The Story of the Three Little Kittens," published by McLoughlin Bros., 1892 .... 25.00

"The Tale of the Squirrel Nutkin," by Beatrix Potter, published by Warne, 1903, 1st edition 110.00

"Uncle Tom's Cabin," by Harriet Beecher Stowe, 1886 .... 45.00

"Wood's Natural History"

"Wood's Natural History," by Rev. J. C. Wood, published by M. A. Donohue & Company, 1908 (ILLUS.)...................... 12.00

"Zig Zag Journey's in Europe," illustrated, 1882, 311 pp. 15.00

CHILDREN'S DISHES

During the reign of Queen Victoria, doll houses and accessories became more popular and as the century progressed, there was greater demand for toys which would subtly train a little girl in the art of homemaking. Also see ABC PLATES, AKRO AGATE GLASS, BLUE WILLOW, BROWNIE

COLLECTIBLES, BUSTER BROWN, DEPRESSION GLASS, DISNEY COLLECTIBLES, GRANITEWARE, GREENAWAY ITEMS, KEWPIE COLLECTIBLES, PATTERN GLASS and SUNBONNET BABIES.

Blue Willow Pattern Plate

Banana bowl, pedestal base, pressed glass, Little Ladders patt., clear $45.00

Berry set: master bowl & 4 sauce dishes; pressed glass, Inverted Strawberry patt., clear, 5 pcs..... 120.00

Berry set: master bowl & 6 sauce dishes; pressed glass, Nursery Rhymes patt., clear, 7 pcs....... 135.00

Butter dish, cov., pressed glass, Button Arches patt., ruby-stained w/enameled florals, souvenir 165.00

Butter dish, cov., pressed glass, Drum patt., clear............... 115.00

Butter dish, cov., pressed glass, Frosted Lion patt., clear & frosted 140.00

Butter dish, cov., pressed glass, Wee Branches patt., clear........ 130.00

Cake stand, pressed glass, Hawaiian Lei patt., clear 35.00

Candlesticks, pressed glass, Star patt., Cambridge Glass Co., light blue, pr. 25.00

Castor set, 4-bottle, pressed glass, Ribbon Band patt., clear bottles .. 95.00

Chamber set: wash basin & pitcher, cov. toothbrush holder, cov. soap dish & tumbler; china, light blue band w/dark blue ivy decor on white ground, 5 pcs. 135.00

Compote, open, pressed glass, Little Ladders patt., clear 35.00

Creamer, pressed glass, Cloud Band patt., milk white 50.00

Creamer, pressed glass, Menagerie patt., owl, clear................ 110.00

Creamer, pressed glass, Pert patt., clear 55.00

Creamer & cov. sugar bowl, pressed glass, Mardi Gras patt., Duncan & Miller Glass Co., clear, pr. 75.00

Cruet w/original stopper, pressed glass, English Hobnail patt., green 25.00

Cup & saucer, handleless, china, blue spatter 65.00

Cup & saucer, china, Capering Elves patt., pink lustre trim, ca. 1900 ... 18.00

Cup & saucer, tin, Red Riding Hood decor, marked "Ohio Art Co." 15.00

Dinner service for 5, china, Happifats decor, w/red trim, marked "Royal Rudolstadt," 20 pcs. 365.00

Goblet, pressed glass, Vine patt., cobalt blue 60.00

Horseradish dish, pressed glass, Menagerie patt., bear, clear 120.00

Ice cream set: platter & 5 plates; pressed glass, Patt. No. 44 (Button & Panel patt.), Duncan & Miller Glass Co., clear, 6 pcs. 295.00

Mush set: bowl, underplate & pitcher; china, Little Bo Peep decor, pink lustre trim, marked "Germany," 3 pcs. 50.00

Pitcher, water, blown glass, Hobb's Hobnail patt., clear 45.00

Pitcher, water, pressed glass, Oval Star patt., Northwood Glass Co., clear w/gold trim 40.00

Plate, china, Blue Willow patt., 3½" d. (ILLUS.) 8.50

Plate, graniteware, green & white swirls, 2½" d. 8.50

Plate, pressed glass, snowflake center, "Present For Good Children" border, clear, 6" d. 125.00

Plate, Staffordshire pottery, "The Favourite," brown transfer scene of girl & cat center highlighted w/colorful enameling, embossed daisy border, 7½" d. 70.00

Punch set: bowl & 5 cups; pressed glass, Inverted Strawberry patt., clear, 6 pcs. 150.00

Sauce dish, pressed glass, Flute patt., clear 6.00

Soup set: 6 x 3½" tureen w/cover, underplate & ladle & six 4½" d. bowls; Staffordshire pottery, blue acorn decor, 9 pcs. 130.00

Spooner, pressed glass, Balder patt., clear 15.00

Spooner, pressed glass, Doyle's 500 patt., amber 35.00

Spooner, pressed glass, Lion patt., clear 75.00

Spooner, pressed glass, Twist patt., vaseline opalescent 75.00

Sugar bowl, cov., pressed glass, Liberty Bell patt., clear 135.00

Table set: cov. butter dish; cov. sugar bowl, creamer & spooner; pressed glass, Bead & Scroll patt., clear, 4 pcs. 335.00

Hawaiian Lei Pattern Spooner

Table set: cov. butter dish, sugar bowl, creamer & spooner; pressed glass, Hawaiian Lei patt., clear, 4 pcs. (ILLUS. of spooner) 135.00

Table set: cov. butter dish, open sugar bowl, creamer, spooner & tray; pressed glass, Doyle's 500 patt., blue, 5 pcs. 200.00

Teapot, cov., china, Blue Willow patt., 5½" sq., 3½" h. 35.00

Teapot, cov., china, children playing w/kitten & ball of twine, rabbit & dog, ca. 1900, marked "Germany" 55.00

Teapot, cov., graniteware, dark blue 16.00

Tea set: cov. teapot, creamer, waste bowl & 4 handleless c/s; majolica, pink interior, cobalt blue exterior, rosebud finials, 11 pcs. 495.00

Tea set: cov. teapot, creamer, cov. sugar bowl, 3 c/s, cake plate & 3 plates; china, Tree in Meadow patt., marked "Noritake," 13 pcs. 195.00

Tea set: cov. teapot, 4 c/s, 4 plates & serving tray; tin, Dutch children decor, Ohio Art Co., 1939, 14 pcs. 49.00

Tumbler, pressed glass, Hobnail patt., milk white, 1½" d., 2" h. .. 18.00

Tumbler, pressed glass, Patee Cross patt., clear 8.00

Vegetable bowl, graniteware, blue & white swirls 40.00

Water set: pitcher & 2 tumblers; pressed glass, Flute patt., clear, 3 pcs. 40.00

Water set: pitcher & 4 tumblers; blown glass, enameled bearded elves & floral decor, 5 pcs. 65.00

Water set: pitcher & 6 tumblers; pressed glass, Nursery Rhymes patt., clear, 7 pcs. 235.00

CHILDREN'S MUGS

Souvenir Mug

The small size mug used by children first attempting to drink from a cup, appeals to many collectors. Because they were made of china, glass, pottery, graniteware, plated silver and silver, the collector is given the opportunity to assemble a diversified collection or to single out one particular type of decoration, such as Franklin Maxims, or a specific material, such as glass, around which to base his collection.

China, baby crawling toward dog's
feeding dish decal, ca. 1900 ...... $40.00
China, Blue Willow patt.,
England 65.00
China, copper lustre body w/wide
blue band 40.00
China, Little Red Riding Hood decal,
early 20th c. 25.00
China, monkey & clown riding pigs
decor 40.00
China, polychrome transfer print of
family at table 140.00
China, polychrome transfer print of
girl feeding kitten 140.00
China, "St. Paul" in gilt on white,
gilt trim, 3" h. (ILLUS.) 15.00
China, ironstone, "Crystal Palace,
1851" 80.00
Pressed glass, Beaded Circle patt.,
blue 15.00
Pressed glass, "By Jingo," clear 35.00
Pressed glass, Cupid & Venus patt.,
clear, 3½" h. 23.00
Pressed glass, Doyle's 500 patt.,
clear 30.00
Pressed glass, Grapevine patt.,
clear 28.00
Pressed glass, Heron & Peacock
patt., blue 45.00
Pressed glass, Heron & Peacock
patt., vaseline, 2¾" h. 34.00
Pressed glass, "Humpty Dumpty"
patt., w/"Tom the Piper's Son" reverse, amber ....40.00 to 48.00
Pressed glass, Liberty Bell patt.,
clear 115.00
Pressed glass, Pointing Dog patt.,
clear, 2 5/8" 30.00

Pressed glass, Robin patt., amber,
2 5/8" h. 42.00
Pressed glass, Sawtooth patt.,
amber or clear, 2" h., each 25.00
Pressed glass, Stippled Arrow patt.,
clear 22.00
Silver, engraved scene, Russia,
1891 .... 135.00
Silverplate, Little Boy Blue w/cow &
sheep decor 22.00
Silverplate, embossed kitten wearing overalls & holding umbrella,
interior center engraved w/scene
of children playing, E. Dragsted,
Denmark 30.00
Staffordshire pottery, brown transfer
of alphabet & "Little Jack Horner"
(minor stains) 55.00
Staffordshire pottery, "I (sic) Diddle
Diddle, The Cat and the Fiddle,"
brown transfer of performing cat,
2 7/8" h. 65.00
Staffordshire pottery, red transfer
"S" & "T" w/appropriate scenes,
2 3/8" h. 55.00
Tin, embossed ABCs around rim,
1¾" h. 75.00
Tin, gilt stenciled "Daisy" w/flowers
& scrolling design, blue japanned
handle, 2" h 48.00

CHRISTMAS TREE LIGHTS

Along with a host of other Christmas-related items, early Christmas tree lights are attracting a growing number of collectors. Comic characters seem to be the most popular form among the wide variety of figural lights available, most of which were manufactured between 1920 and World War II in Germany, Japan and the United States. Figural bulbs listed are painted clear glass unless otherwise noted.

BULBS
Andy Gump, milk white $45.00
Baby in stocking 27.00
Barney Google 175.00
Bell ....12.00 to 20.00
Bell, w/embossed Santa Claus face
each side................15.00 to 22.00
Betty Boop, milk white 85.00
Bird, milk white................. 14.00
Bird cage w/two red birds 12.00
Bubble-type.................... 18.00
Bulldog..................15.00 to 22.00
Cat & the fiddle, milk
white ....20.00 to 30.00
Clown's head 30.00
Cross 10.00

Dick Tracy, milk white 55.00
Dirigible, milk white . . . . .40.00 to 47.00
Doll, milk white 25.00
Duck 12.00
Ear of corn 35.00
Fish 9.00
Floral basket, milk white 25.00
Fruit (apple, orange or pear),
    each .10.00 to 15.00
Girl w/muff 35.00
House, snow-covered 6-sided cot-
    tage, yellow, 2¾" . . . . .15.00 to 20.00
Humpty Dumpty, standing 45.00
Ice cream cone . . . . .10.00 to 19.00
Japanese lantern, milk white 15.00
Jiminy Cricket, milk white 30.00
Kayo, milk white, 2½" h. 50.00
Lion wearing suit & holding pipe 40.00
Little Miss Muffet 27.00
Man w/bow tie 35.00
Minnie Mouse, milk white 38.00
Mother Goose 35.00
Orphan Annie 45.00
Parakeet 14.00
Parrot . . . . .11.00 to 17.00
Pigeon 25.00
Pinocchio, milk white 30.00
Sandy (Orphan Annie's dog), milk
    white, 3" h. 45.00
Santa Claus' head, double sided,
    milk white, 3" h. . . . . .15.00 to 24.00
Santa Claus bust in oval medallion,
    milk white, 3¾" h. 20.00
Santa Claus, full figure, milk
    white . . . . .25.00 to 35.00
Ship 45.00
Smitty .45.00 to 55.00
Snowman, large . . . . .15.00 to 22.00
Watch, milk white 25.00

STRINGS

Japanese lanterns, original paint,
    set of 9 . . . . 28.00
NOMA (National Outfit Manufac-
    turers Association) "Bubble-Lites,"
    original box 25.00
NOMA "Dresden" (painted glass
    figural shell that screwed on over
    a plain bulb), fruit, flowers, cat,
    lantern, etc., 1927 patent date,
    set of 11 . . . . 250.00
Walt Disney characters, Mickey
    Mouse & Friends at Christmas,
    standard-series bulbs, each
    w/bell-shaped plastic shade deco-
    rated w/decal, NOMA, 1936, set
    of 8 . . . . .75.00 to 130.00
Walt Disney characters: Mickey
    Mouse, Minnie Mouse, Jiminy
    Crickett, Pluto, Donald Duck,
    Pinocchio, Dwarf & Pig; figural,
    Paramount, set of 8 in original
    box 135.00
Walt Disney characters, Silly Sym-

phony, standard-series bulbs,
    each w/bell-shaped plastic shade
    decorated w/decal, NOMA, set
    of 8 . . . . 70.00
Walt Disney characters, Three Little
    Pigs, standard-series bulbs, each
    w/bell-shaped plastic shade deco-
    rated w/decal, NOMA 85.00

CHRISTMAS TREE ORNAMENTS

Blown Glass Christmas Tree Ornaments

    *The German blown glass Christmas or-
naments and other commercially-made ornaments of wax, cardboard and cotton batting,
were popular from the time they were first
offered for sale in the United States in the
1870's. Prior to that time, Christmas trees had
been decorated with homemade ornaments
that usually were edible. Now nostalgic collectors who seek out ornaments that sold for
pennies in stores across the country in the early years of this century, are willing to pay
some rather hefty prices for unusual or early
ornaments.*

Airplane, Dresden-type cardboard . .$175.00
Angel, tree-top figure, papier
    mache, 19th c. 94.00
Baby in shoe, blown glass, each
    (ILLUS.) 220.00
Basket of roses, blown glass 8.00
Bear, cotton batting 75.00
Bust of Chinaman, blown glass 525.00
Butterfly, blown glass body, spun
    glass wings 125.00
Camel, Dresden-type cardboard 150.00
Carrot, blown glass, orange,
    4¼" l. 85.00
Cat, blown glass, black 80.00
Cat, Dresden-type cardboard 125.00
Charlie Chaplin, blown glass 260.00
Chick w/bonnet, blown glass 230.00

Child holding teddy bear, 1920's,
3" h. 150.00
Cockatoo, blown glass, spring clip . . 12.00
Cuckoo clock w/paper face, blown
glass, silver w/polychrome detail,
3 7/8" h. 25.00
Dog, Scottie, blown glass, gold
w/white trim, 3¾" h. 45.00
Duck swimming, blown glass, blue. . 50.00
Frog, blown glass, silver, 4" l. 45.00
Grape cluster, blown glass, green,
2¾" l. 350.00
Guitar, blown glass 15.00
Gun, revolver, Dresden-type card-
board, pink & blue 125.00
Happy Hooligan, blown glass, spring
clip . . . . .120.00 to 150.00
Heart, blown glass 12.00
Horse, blown glass, blue. 80.00
Keystone cop, blown glass 250.00
Kugel (blown glass ball), reddish
pink w/silvered interior, brass
top, 5½" d. 85.00
Man-in-the-moon, blown glass,
green 30.00
Mouse, blown glass 475.00

Dresden-type Christmas Tree Ornament

Paddle wheel boat, Dresden-type
cardboard, silver, late 19th c.,
3¾" l. (ILLUS.) 495.00
Pear, blown glass, 3¾" l. 65.00
Pineapple, Dresden-type
cardboard 97.50

Blown Glass Christmas Tree Ornament

Pinecone, blown glass, red w/white
"snow," 2¾" l. (ILLUS.) . . . . .8.00 to 10.00

Pipe w/jeweled bowl, Dresden-type
cardboard, 7½" l. 125.00
Prussian soldier, blown
glass . . . . .250.00 to 275.00
Pumpkin head, blown glass 350.00
Rabbit w/lettuce, cotton batting 50.00
Sailor boy w/accordion, blown
glass 55.00
Santa Claus holding tree, blown
glass, 3¾" h. 38.00
Sheep, cotton batting 75.00
Snowman, blown glass . . . . . .28.00 to 35.00
Squirrel, blown glass, red & white,
2¾" h. 55.00
Stag leaping, blown glass, silver
w/amber ears & antlers,
Germany 35.00
Stork standing, blown glass, blue,
5" h. 50.00
Stork flying, cotton batting 100.00
Strawberry, Dresden-type card-
board 97.50
Swan, blown glass, pink 50.00
Trumpet, blown glass 10.00
Violin, blown glass, pink & gold
w/wire mesh, 6" l. 40.00
Watermelon slice, blown glass,
4½" l. 85.00
Zeppelin, "Los Angeles," Dresden-
type cardboard. 135.00

CIGAR & CIGARETTE CASES, HOLDERS & LIGHTERS

Faberge Gold Cigarette Case

Cigar case, silverplate, engraving on
both sides, gold-washed interior,
holds 3 cigars, 2½" w., 5" l. $38.00
Cigar holder, ivory, in original case,
3¾" 10.00
Cigar holder, meerschaum, carved
baby in garland, w/case,
7" l 75.00
Cigar holder, meerschaum, amber
stem, full figure of buxom lady

seated on lounge chair w/arm over back holding fan (no case) .. 65.00

Cigar lighter, bronze, devil figure... 375.00

Cigarette case, black enamel w/engraved Siamese dancers, Siam ... 95.00

Cigarette case, black matte enamel w/silver, copper & gold inlay forming scene of ships, mountains, trees, bridge, hinged & marked "K24," 6¼ x 3¼" 105.00

Cigarette case, brass, Egyptian motif front & back 35.00

Cigarette case, gold, hinged cover w/alternating reeded & polished panels, cabochon sapphire thumbpiece, Riga, Latvia, ca. 1910, 3 5/8" l. 1,320.00

Cigarette case, 14k gold, rectangular shape w/rounded sides, stippled finish, applied w/two-color gold monogram, cabochon sapphire thumbpiece, Faberge, Moscow, Russia, ca. 1900, 3 5/8" l. (ILLUS.) 2,640.00

Cigarette case, gold, reeded in a diagonal pattern, w/match compartment & tinder slide, cabochon sapphire thumbpiece, engraved w/armorials, pseudo-Faberge mark, ca. 1910, 4" l. 3,300.00

Cigarette case, gold & translucent enamel, curved, enameled translucent rose pink over a "guilloche" ground, w/green & white enamel borders, diamond-set thumbpiece, France, ca. 1910, 3¾" l.........4,125.00

Platinum Cigarette Case

Cigarette case, platinum, rectangular w/rounded sides, reeded overall w/"invisible" hinge, interior of cover w/monogram below a coronet, Continental, ca. 1910, 3 1/8" l. (ILLUS.) 3,850.00

Cigarette case, silver & enamel, hinged cover enameled w/scene of 2 dueling bare-breasted ladies, reverse mounted w/various gold monograms, cabochon sapphire thumbpiece, Gustav Klingert, Moscow, 1891, 3¼" l. 3,410.00

Cigarette case, silver, square, hinged cover enameled w/a nude young woman reclining amidst pillows, Austrian, 3¼" 550.00

Cigarette case, silver, lid engraved w/Art Deco lady w/a mask, large dog & monogram "C.J.H.," gilt interior, stamped "Cartier," 5 x 6".. 180.00

Cigarette case, silver, embossed chariot & horses cover, 1882 ..... 39.00

Cigarette case, silver-gilt & enamel, hinged cover enameled w/three armoured mounted warriors pausing by a river, the surround enameled w/foliage, reverse w/stylized trees, red cabochon thumbpiece, Khlebnikov, Moscow, ca. 1910, 4 1/8" l. 2,970.00

Cigarette case, silverplate, semi-nude woman on cover, 1920's 7.50

Cigarette case, sterling silver, w/initials "WJF," Elgin American, 3 x 5"......................... 34.00

Cigarette case, sterling silver, face of mailed letter w/stamp & postmark dated 1939, gold-washed interior......................... 110.00

Cigarette holder, 18k gold band w/mother-of-pearl section & black gutta percha, w/screw-off sections, stamped "Cartier," 14" l.... 180.00

Cigarette holder, carved ivory, finely detailed claw 43.00

Cigarette lighter, advertising, "Dr. Pepper" 20.00

Cigarette lighter, brass, advertising, "Demley Surelite," Austria 20.00

Cigarette lighter, advertising, "Pepsi Cola" 15.00

Cigarette lighter, advertising, "Skelly-Skelgas," Ronson 17.50

Cigarette lighter, cast iron, model of German Shepherd dog, 5" 60.00

Cigarette lighter, model of luxury steamship liner, "Queen of Esquimalt"...................... 15.00

Cigarette lighters, table model, silverplate, Mayfair patt., Ronson, pr............................ 22.00

CIGAR & TOBACCO CUTTERS

Both counter-type and individual cigar and plug tobacco cutters were in widespread use last century and earlier in this century. Some counter types were made in combination with lighters and vending machines and were used to promote various tobacco packaging companies.

Counter-type, brass, bottle-shaped, Art Deco style, 6" $55.00

Counter-type, brass, advertising,
"Battle Axe" 175.00

Counter-type, brass, model of a
dog, "Paraflint" engraved each
side, 4 x 7" 230.00

Counter-type, cast iron, advertising,
"Arrow-Cupples Co." 36.00

Counter-type, cast iron, advertising,
"Blackstone Cigars," keywind-
spring cutter 350.00

Counter-type, cast iron, advertising,
"Spearhead Brand Tobacco, J.P.
Sorg Co." 190.00

"Star" Tobacco Cutter

Counter-type, cast iron, advertising,
"Star Brand Tobacco," 1885
(ILLUS.) 53.00

Counter-type, cast iron, figural imp
thumbing his nose 125.00

Counter-type, cast iron, "Griswold
No. 3" 100.00

Counter-type, cast iron, "Master
Workman," w/original label 95.00

Counter-type, sterling silver cutter
mounted on 9" carved boar tusk .. 225.00

Desk model, cast iron, model of a
bulldog 38.00

Desk model, silverplate, model of a
horse's head w/bridle & flowing
mane, 5¾" l. 90.00

Desk model, guillotine, wooden,
10" h. 90.00

Pocket-type, advertising, "5th Ave.
Cigar," key-wind 22.00

Pocket-type, brass w/pearl inlay,
scissors-type 45.00

Pocket-type, 14k gold, engraved
horseshoe & florals 70.00

Pocket-type, ivory boar tusk w/ster-
ling mount 195.00

Pocket-type, Little Imp "Brighton,"
3" 68.00

Pocket-type, metal, advertising,
"Climax Plug" 35.00

Pocket-type, sterling silver,
repousse Art Nouveau full figure
nude on waves, ring at end 40.00

Pocket-type, sterling silver,
repousse decor both sides 32.00

CLOCKS

China Case Clock

*Also see ADVERTISING ITEMS,
CHARACTER COLLECTIBLES, COCA-
COLA ITEMS and DISNEY COL-
LECTIBLES.*

Alarm, Westclox "Big Ben," Western
Clock Company, LaSalle, Illinois,
white dial, nickel-plated case
w/two front feet, 1914 patent $50.00

Animated, Lux Clock Co., Waterbury, Connecticut, "Spinning
Wheel" 75.00

Animated, United Electric Co.,
Brooklyn, New York, metal case
w/figure of cowboy whirling lariat
over horseshoe-framed clock,
marble base, 10 x 12 x 5" 62.50

Banjo, attributed to Howard & Davis, Boston, Massachusetts, drum
clock w/white-painted dial, rosewood case w/black & gilt
"eglomise" panel in throat & conforming panel in lower door,
mid-19th c., 29" h. 770.00

Banjo, Aaron Willard Jr., Boston,
Massachusetts, drum clock
w/white-painted dial surmounted
by brass urn finial, mahogany
case w/"eglomise" geometric panel in door flanked by brass fillets
& "eglomise" panel of spread-
winged American eagle & maker's
name in lower door, ca. 1825,
34" h. 6,600.00

Banjo, Simon Willard, Roxbury, Massachusetts, drum clock w/white-
painted dial surmounted by metal
eagle finial, mahogany case
w/cross-banding & "eglomise" panel in throat flanked by brass fillets
& "eglomise" panel in lower door,
ca. 1820, 34½" h. (some restoration to painted panels) 1,320.00

Banjo, John Sawin, Boston, Massachusetts, drum clock w/white-

painted dial w/alarm register &
signed by maker surmounted by
bell, mahogany & giltwood case
w/"eglomise" panel of leaves in
throat flanked by brass fillets &
w/"eglomise" panel in lower door
depicting various American symbols including an Eagle & Indian,
spherule-molded acorn pendant
below, ca. 1820, 39" h..........6,050.00

Banjo, The E. Ingraham & Co.,
Bristol, Connecticut, "Treasure Island" model, 8-day time & strike
movement, walnut case, 20th c. .. 450.00

"Blinking Eye," Bradley & Hubbard
Manufacturing Co. w/Chauncey
Jerome 30-hour movement, cast
iron figural "John Bull" case
w/"blinking eyes," ca. 1860 .....1,550.00

"Blinking Eye," Bradley & Hubbard
Manufacturing Co. w/Chauncey
Jerome 30-hour movement, cast
iron figural "Topsy" case w/"blinking eyes" 1,800.00

China case, Ansonia Clock Co., Ansonia, Connecticut, blue sailing
vessels & cobalt blue & gilt trim
(ILLUS.)...................... 600.00

China case, "La Plata" model w/ex-
posed escapement, Royal Bonn
case w/yellow & rose florals on
shaded green ground & lion's
head in full relief on molded lion's
mask feet, 13½" w., 12½" h. 525.00

Crystal regulator, Boston Clock Co.,
Chelsea, Massachusetts, "Del-
phus" model, gold-plated metal &
glass case, 1888-97 .... 750.00

Crystal regulator, Seth Thomas,
Thomaston, Connecticut, Empire
Model No. 65, bowed front
w/columns 450.00

Double dial calendar, Seth Thomas,
Thomaston, Connecticut, 8-day
movement, mahogany case......1,250.00

Grandfather, William Cummins, Roxbury, Massachusetts, white-painted
dial w/minute & date registers
above maker's name & surmounted
by painted urn, mahogany hooded
Federal-style case w/arched top
centering 3 brass ball & steeple
finials, waist w/molded fan-inlaid
door flanked by fluted quarter columns fitted w/brass caps, base
w/line-and-fan inlaid corners, ball
feet, ca. 1800, 94" h. (restoration to painted dial) 7,700.00

Grandfather, Daniel Oyster, Reading,
Pennsylvania, white-painted dial
w/minute & date registers &
maker's name surmounted by
phases of the moon dial, cherrywood hooded Federal-style case

w/swan's neck cresting ending in
sunburst-inlaid terminals centering
3 urn finial & w/floral-inlaid
frieze, waist w/inlaid eagle & florals on molded door, base w/ap-
plied scalloped panel centering inlaid star, bird cut-out bracket
feet, ca. 1810, 94" h..........13,200.00

Grandfather, George Miller, German-
town, Pennsylvania, engraved
brass dial inscribed w/maker's
name, walnut hooded Chippendale-
style case w/swan's neck cresting
& arched door opening to dial
flanked by free-standing columns,
waist w/molded arched door flanked by fluted quarter columns, conforming base on short ogee-molded
bracket feet, ca. 1780, 18" w.,
96" h. (restoration to rosettes
on hood & feet) 6,050.00

Grandfather, Daniel Porter, Williamstown, Massachusetts, white-painted
dial w/date register & maker's
name, Federal-style maple case
w/swan's neck cresting on hood
w/arched door flanked by colonettes, waist w/incised door inlaid w/patera flanked by fluted
quarter columns, molded base inlaid w/conforming patera, turned
feet, ca. 1810, 108½" h.........4,675.00

Grandfather Clock from Scotland

Grandfather, Rob T. Gillies, Leith,
Scotland, white-painted dial w/flo-
ral spandrels, inlaid mahogany
case w/free-standing columns
flanking arched door opening to
dial, waist w/inlaid door flanked
by fluted quarter columns, inlaid
base w/molded edge, Scotland,
late 18th c. (ILLUS.) 1,375.00

Jeweler's wall regulator, Gilbert
Clock Co., Bristol & Winsted,
Connecticut, Model No. 12, porcelain dial, lyre-form brass pendulum, oak case 4,000.00

Jeweler's wall regulator, Gilbert
Clock Co., Bristol & Winsted, Connecticut, Model No. 12, iron pendulum, oak case 3,300.00

Jeweler's wall regulator, Waterbury
Clock Co., Waterbury, Connecticut,
Model No. 41, 8-day movement,
enameled dial w/sweep seconds
hand, walnut case w/glass
sides 3,950.00

Kitchen, Ansonia Clock Co., Ansonia, Connecticut, 8-day time &
strike movement, gingerbread-
carved oak case 120.00

Kitchen, Seth Thomas, Thomaston,
Connecticut, gingerbread-carved
oak case 150.00

Kitchen, Waterbury Clock Co.,
Waterbury, Connecticut, 8-day
movement, gingerbread-carved
golden oak case 250.00

Kitchen, Waterbury Clock Co.,
Waterbury, Connecticut, white-
painted dial, time & strike movement, original Sandwich glass
pendulum, walnut case 195.00

Schoolhouse, Ingraham Clock Co.,
Bristol, Connecticut, 30-hour
movement, round-top oak case,
short drop 180.00

Schoolhouse, Seth Thomas Clock
Co., Thomaston, Connecticut,
octagon-top walnut case, short
drop 180.00

Shelf, or mantel, Beehive case, New
Haven Clock Co., New Haven,
Connecticut, 8-day time, strike &
alarm movement, mahogany
case 185.00

Shelf, or mantel, Case-on-Case,
Aaron Willard, Boston, Massachusetts, white-painted dial,
mahogany & "eglomise" case
w/shaped cresting surmounted by
metal eagle finial above hinged
door centering white-painted dial
w/"eglomise" foliate & lyre motifs
centering maker's name & "Boston"
in oval reserve, lower case w/"eglomise" corner lyre motifs centering a mirror, brass ball feet,
12" w., 34½" h. 9,350.00

Shelf, or mantel, Case-on-Case,
David Wood, Newburyport, Massachusetts, white-painted dial w/flo-
ral spandrels signed by maker,
cherrywood Federal-style case
w/shaped crest centering an eagle
flanked by brass urn finials above

Case-on-Case Clock

arched door flanked by applied
pilasters & lower door w/applied
fluted pilasters & keystone arch
flanked by fluted corner pilasters,
cove-molded base, ca. 1800
(ILLUS.) 7,150.00

Shelf, or mantel, Pillar-and-Scroll
case, Eli Terry & Son, Plymouth,
Connnecticut, white-painted dial
w/floral spandrels, mahogany veneer case w/swan's neck cresting
centering 3 brass urn finials
above bird's eye maple veneer
plinths, door w/"eglomise" panel
depicting a mourning scene in
lower section flanked by turned
columns, base w/shaped skirt &
bracket feet, ca. 1830, 31½" h.
(some restoration to plinth &
feet) 880.00

Pillar-and-Scroll Clock

Shelf, or mantel, Pillar-and-Scroll
case, white-painted dial w/floral

spandrels, 30-hour weight driven
movement, mahogany case
w/swan's neck cresting centering
3 urn finials & lower door w/"eglomise" panel depicting a rural
scene, base w/shaped skirt &
bracket feet, ca. 1835 (ILLUS.) ...1,320.00
Shelf, or mantel, Steeple case,
Waterbury Clock Co., Waterbury,
Connecticut, 30-hour time & strike
movement, rosewood veneer
"Gothic" top case, 15" h. 165.00
Shelf, or mantel, Steeple case, E.N.
Welch, Forestville, Connecticut,
8-day time, strike & alarm movement, mahogany case 195.00

Triple Decker Clock

Shelf, or mantel, Triple Decker case,
Forestville Manufacturing Co.,
Forestville, Connecticut, 8-day
brass weight-driven movement,
white-painted wooden dial w/flo-
ral spandrels, mahogany veneer
American Empire style case
w/projecting ogee-molded cornice
over door w/stenciled compass
design in tablet, stenciled snowflake design in lower door
flanked by turned columns over
C-scrolls, ca. 1830, 32" h.
(ILLUS.)........................ 357.00
Shelf, or mantel, Triple Decker case,
Birge & Peck, Bristol, Connecticut,
8-day movement, white-painted
dial w/floral spandrels, rosewood
veneer case w/lithographed scene
in tablet & lower door, ca. 1849 .. 675.00
Shelf, or mantel, Ansonia Clock Co.,
Ansonia, Connecticut, time &
strike movement, porcelain dial,
case iron case w/bust of beautiful
lady at top & brass lion's mask &
rings at sides, Empire columns at
front 350.00

Shelf, or mantel, Seth Thomas Clock
Co., Thomaston, Connecticut, 8-
day movement, 1876 Centennial
model, walnut case w/color-
printed transfer of Main Hall,
"1876" flags & American eagle in
door, 14½" h. 600.00
Ship's, Chelsea Clock Co., Boston,
Massachusetts, brass case,
marked "U.S. Maritime Commission Serv." 275.00
Statue, Florence Kroeber, New
York, New York, 8-day brass
movement, white-enameled dial,
cast iron case w/gilt figure standing alongside on plinth base, ca.
1890, 17" w., 20" h. figure 450.00
Statue, E.N. Welch Manufacturing
Co., Bristol, Connecticut, 8-day
time & strike movement, cast iron
case w/figure atop case & urns
flanking dial 235.00
Wag-on-wall, unknown maker,
white-painted wooden dial
w/colorful floral spandrels & Roman numerals, wooden & brass
works, w/weights & pendulum,
12" w., 17" h................... 425.00

CLOISONNE

Cloisonne Charger

*Cloisonne work features enameled designs
on a metal ground. There are several types
of this work, the best-known utilizing cells of
wire on the body of the object into which the
enamel is placed. In the plique-a-jour form of
cloisonne, the base is removed leaving translucent enamel windows. "Pigeon Blood"
cloisonne is a pseudo-cloisonne with foil enclosed within clear glass walls. Cloisonne is
said to have been invented by the Chinese and
brought to perfection by the Japanese.*

Bowl, florals on blue, green & red
ground, 4" d. $75.00
Bowl, yellow dragons w/flaming
pearl around rim & interior on
black ground, 8" d., 2½" h.,
w/brass stand 130.00
Brush pot, asters & butterfly decor
on light blue ground, signed
Takeuchi, ca. 1875, Japanese,
5" h. 195.00
Charger, geometric border, red
roses, pink daisies, blue flowers,
butterflies & green foliage on turquoise ground, 10¾" d. 335.00
Charger, scalloped edge, pink &
rose florals & green leaves w/two
grey birds in flight & 1 sitting on
branch on turquoise blue ground,
12" d. (ILLUS.) 398.00
Ginger jar, cov., yellow scaly dragon on dark blue ground, marked
"China," on ornate carved wooden
base, 6¾" h. 275.00
Humidor, cov., colorful flowers on a
brick red ground, light blue border, double "T" fret cloisons,
figural brass Foo dog finial, ornate teakwood base, 5¾" d.,
8" h. 225.00
Incense burner, 3 cobalt blue round
feet, cut-out butterflies on brass
lid, multicolored floral decor on
cobalt blue ground 225.00
Models of elephants, each enameled
in white w/multicolored harness &
howdah blanket, supporting beribboned double gourd vase resting
on the raised saddle, Jiaqing,
11¾" h., pr. (minor repairs) 7,150.00
Plique-a-jour beaker, enameled blue,
red & yellow between engraved
flowers, scrolls & foliage, on circular foot, Russian, Anton Kuz-
michev, Moscow, ca. 1890,
3¼" h. 1,100.00
Rose petal jar, cov., panels around
top in white, blue, green & rust
w/flowers & butterflies, black,
gold & blue panels below w/flow-
ers, 4 1/8" d., 4½" h. 290.00
Salt & pepper shakers, one w/mul-
ticolored dragon, other w/cranes,
both on pale blue fishscale
ground, Japanese, 2" d., 2½" h.,
pr. 225.00
Sauceboat, green handle, turquoise
artichoke decor, marked
"China" 110.00
Teapot, cov., double gourd shape,
diagonal bands of flowers & butterflies against white & green interspersed w/black & goldstone,
Japanese, 3½" h. 245.00
Tumbler, flared beaker shape, iron-

red serpentine dragon on sky blue
ground, 3¾" h. 110.00
Vase, multicolored peacock on
white foil ground, silver wire
flowers at bottom, Japanese,
1¾" d., 3½" h. 650.00
Vases, white & purple flowers
w/green leaves on black ground,
Japanese, 2" d., 4¾" h., pr. 258.00
Vase, shield-like panels w/exotic
dragons, blue ground & green
w/goldstone, small butterflies
around top, Japanese, 3¾" d.,
9¾" h. 395.00

Cloisonne Vase

Vases, compressed ovoid, continuous
scene of birds in flight near cluster
of blossoming peony & chrysanthemum below a shoulder of elaborate floral meanders framing reserves of bird & flower subjects set
off by lotus & foliate tendril
ground, 31½" h., pr. (ILLUS.
of one) 1,650.00
Vases, cov., double-gourd form,
overall design of leafy vines bearing numerous double gourds in
aubergine, green, yellow & white
amidst white & aubergine flowers
on reddish-brown ground, conforming covers w/applied gilt bronze
stalks, Chinese, 19th c., 40½" h.,
pr. 8,800.00

COCA-COLA ITEMS

*Coca-Cola promotion has been achieved
through the issuance of scores of small objects through the years. These, together with
trays, signs, and other articles bearing the
name of this soft drink, are now sought by
many collectors. Also see BOTTLES.*

1942 Coca-Cola Blotter

Ash tray set, 4 card-shaped (diamond, heart, spade & club) metal trays, in original box, 1940's, set .... $85.00 to 100.00

Baseball scorekeeper, "Perpetual Calendar," for runs, hits & errors, 1906 .... 65.00

Beach ball, inflatable vinyl, 6" d. 10.00

Billfold, pigskin, gold-stamped bottle & "Have a Coke," 1950's 25.00

Billfold, tri-fold, black leather, w/small calendar, 1919-22 .... 60.00

Billfold, black leather, gold-stamped "Drink Coca-Cola Delicious-Refreshing," 1928 .... 45.00

Billfold, brown leather, embossed bottle & gold-stamped "Drink Coca-Cola," 1970 .... 15.00

Blotter, 1920's, "Refresh Yourself," gentleman in white hat raising bottle of Coke 16.50

Blotter, 1920's, couple leaning on open ice box 15.00

Blotter, 1928, "A Pure Drink of Natural Flavors," black & white, pretty lady 38.00

Blotter, 1935, railroadman drinking from bottle 30.00

Blotter, 1936, 50th Anniversary 28.50

Blotter, 1942 (ILLUS.) 5.00

Blotter, 1951, Sprite Boy behind bottle 4.50

Books, "Flower Arranging," Vols. 1, 2 & 3, soft bound, 1941-42, set of 3 .... 16.00 to 25.00

Bottle carrying case, aluminum, 6-pack, 1950's 18.50

Bottle carrying case, masonite, 6-pack, 1940's 65.00

Bottle carrying case, wooden w/rope handle, 6-pack, 1940's 35.00

Bottle opener, flat brass finnish wrench-form, embossed "Drink Coca-Cola in Bottles," 1910 .... 10.00

Bottle opener & can punch, flat steel bar, "Have a Coke" 3.50

Bottle opener & ice pick combination, cast iron 16.00

Bottle opener w/corkscrew, nickel-plated 27.50

Calendar, 1916, Constance (ILLUS. left) 400.00

Coca-Cola Calendars

Calendar, 1919, Knitting Girl 450.00

Calendar, 1922, Autumn Girl 200.00

Calendar, 1923, Flapper Girl 375.00

Calendar, 1925, Girl at Party (ILLUS. right) 250.00

Calendar, 1939, Girl in Black Dress (holding bottle & unmarked glass), lithographed by Forbes of Boston 165.00

Calendar, 1960, Ski Couple 25.00

Calendar, 1962, Prom Scene 25.00

Calendar, 1965, Couple beside Log Cabin 12.00

Calendar, 1974 .... 8.00

Calendar holder, round metal disc w/hook, white lettering on red ground, 1950.................... 30.00

Cigar cutter, souvenir "1915 Panama-Pacific Exposition, San Francisco," brass, "Drink Coca-Cola" front & lady's exposecd bosom reverse when open 175.00

Cigars, "Havatampa," wrapped in "Coca-Cola" advertising bands, pr............................. 30.00

Cigarette lighter, "Coke" can replica 20.00

Clock, wall regulator, Edward P. Baird Clock Co., Chicago, 30-day movement, tin face embossed "Drink Coca-Cola 5c - Delicious & Refreshing," 1896-1900 .... 4,500.00 to 6,000.00

Clock, wall-type gallery clock, Ingraham time & strike movement, oak circular frame, dial w/Roman numerals & "Coca-Cola Delicious, Refreshing Drink," 15½" d. 600.00

Clock, wall-type, electric, maroon outer edge w/numerals, 1951, 17½" d........................ 90.00

Cooler, salesman's sample, metal "open front" model, white letter-

Salesman's Sample Cooler

ing on red, 11 x 9 x 8½"
(ILLUS.) 57.50
Cooler, Glascock ice chest type,
double case model, 1929-32,
67 x 24" 425.00
Counter display bottle, "Dec. 25,
1923," blue-tinted clear glass,
20" h. .... 85.00 to 125.00
Counter display bottle, white rubber, embossed & painted, 1942,
42" h. 650.00
Counter display sign, die-cut Santa
w/Coke trying to hush barking
dog, signed Sundblom, 1950's,
24 x 14" 55.00
Counter jar, cov., "Coca-Cola Chewing Gum," clear glass, 1915 ...... 170.00
Door pull plate, bottle-shaped,
metal 125.00
Door push plate, graniteware, red
lettering "Ice Cold in Bottles" on
white & white on red "Coca-Cola"
emblem center, 1940's,
29¾ x 4" .... 60.00 to 80.00
Door push plate, graniteware, embossed white "Coca-Cola" & yellow "Iced Here" letters on red
ground, 1940's, 31½ x 3" 95.00
Fan, cardboard, hand holding bottle,
"Quality Carries On," 1940's 18.50
Fan, cardboard, Sprite Boy & "Have
a Coke," 1950's 25.00
Game, Chinese Checkers, wood &
heavy paperboard playing board,
1940's .... 35.00 to 50.00
Gum wrapper, "Coca-Cola Spear-
mint Flavor Gum," Franklin-Caro
Co., ca. 1906 .... 45.00 to 65.00
Seltzer bottle, paneled sides, trans-
lucent green glass etched "Coca-
Cola - Denver, Colorado" in
script 300.00
Sewing kit, World War I, "Every
soldier's friend, Coca-Cola Bottling
Co., San Antonio, Texas, Coca-
Cola in bottles," nickel-plated
brass cylinder w/khaki thread 30.00
Sheet music, "Rum & Coca-Cola,"
Andrews Sisters on cover 15.00

Shipping crate, wooden, "Drink
Coca-Cola in Bottles" on sides 65.00
Sign, cardboard, girl w/ping pong
paddle, 1938 .... 90.00
Sign, cardboard, girl getting off airplane, 1942 .... 65.00
Sign, cardboard, self-framed, lady
wearing broad-brimmed hat & frilly blouse, 1930's 125.00
Sign, graniteware, small Coca-Cola
bottle, 1930's, 6" d. ......70.00 to 150.00
Sign, graniteware, bottle w/"Dec.
25th, 1923" date on red ground,
18" d. 200.00
Sign, graniteware, "Coca-Cola - Sign
of Good Taste," 43 x 16" 75.00

1940's Plastic Sign

Sign, plastic, bottle on red ground,
1940's, 9" d. (ILLUS.) 40.00
Sign, tin, red & green, "Gas Today -
Drink Coca-Cola While You Wait,"
dated 1929, 27 x 20" 135.00
Sign, tin, "Take a Case Home To-
day - $1 plus deposit," 28 x 20" .. 55.00
Sign, tin, pictures "6 bottles for
25c," 1939, 29 x 23" 95.00
Street "Safety" marker, cast brass,
ca. 1900, 4" d. 200.00
Syrup bottle, clear glass, "Drink
Coca-Cola" within wreath, 1910
(no cap) 210.00
Thermometer, bottle-shaped, 1930's,
17" .... 75.00 to 100.00
Thermometer, metal, "Drink Coca-
Cola Delicious and Refreshing" on
red ground circle above thermometer & black-on-white silhouette
of girl drinking from bottle in circle below, 1939 ....48.00 to 60.00
Thermometer, tin, twin bottles,
1941-42, 7" w., 16" h. 65.00
Thermometer, tin, bottle-shaped,
1950's, 17" h. 22.50
Thermometer, gold-finish metal,
bottle-shaped, 1958, 7" h. ...20.00 to 30.00

Thimble, aluminum, dated 1920..... 23.00
Toy truck, "Buddy L," yellow metal, 1960, 10½" l. 50.00
Toy truck, "Buddy L," yellow metal, w/open rack back & plastic bottle cases, 1970's.................... 35.00
Toy truck, "Marx," yellow metal w/pseudo bottle cases each side, 1950's........................ 90.00
Toy truck, "Marx," yellow metal, w/horn on cab, 1950 (no bottles) ....45.00 to 80.00
Toy truck, "Marx," yellow plastic, w/six cases, 1950's 19.00
Toy truck, yellow plastic, w/cardboard cases, Hong Kong, 1960's .. 22.00
Tray, change, 1920, glass change receiver w/Art Nouveau scrolls & "Drink Coca-Cola," 7" d. 380.00
Tray, 1912, Hamilton King girl, 13¼ x 10½" oblong ....300.00 to 375.00
Tray, 1921, Summer Girl, 13¼ x 10½" oblong ....280.00 to 400.00
Tray, 1922, Autumn Girl, 13¼ x 10½" oblong................... 300.00
Tray, 1923, Flapper Girl, 13¼ x 10½" oblong ....135.00 to 200.00
Tray, 1924, Smiling Girl, 13¼ x 10½" oblong ....250.00 to 400.00
Tray, 1929, Girl in Yellow Swimsuit w/Bottle, red border, 13¼ x 10½" oblong................... 295.00
Tray, 1950, Girl with Menu, 13¼ x 10½" oblong ....30.00 to 45.00
Tray, 1958, Picnic Basket, 11¼ x 10½" oblong................... 20.00
Tray, 1972, Duster Girl reproduction, 14¾ x 10¾" oblong 12.00
Vienna Art tin plate, "Topless," issued by Western Reserve, original ornate giltwood frame........... 550.00
Wall sconce, cardboard, green, silver & red, 9" w., 12" h.......... 150.00

COFFEE GRINDERS

Most coffee grinders collected are lap or table and wall types used in many homes in the late 19th and early 20th centuries. However, large store-sized grinders have recently been traded.

Lap-type, cast iron & brass, "Izons & Co." $90.00
Lap-type, cherrywood base w/machine dovetailing & drawer, pewter hopper, cast iron handle w/wooden knob, 9¼" h.......... 135.00
Lap-type, maple base w/machine dovetailing & drawer, cast iron hopper & handle w/wooden knob......................... 85.00
Lap-type, oak base w/machine dovetailing, tin drawer, cast iron hopper & handle, "Delmar 97, Double Grinder, H. M. Meier, St. Louis"...................... 85.00
Lap-type, pine base w/machine dovetailing & drawer, cast iron hopper & handle, 12½" h. 45.00
Lap-type, tin base w/drawer, original black japanned finish, "Brighton," 6" sq. 30.00
Lap-type, tin base w/drawer, "Elma" 55.00
Lap-type, wooden base w/machine dovetailing & drawer, cast iron hopper & handle ....55.00 to 85.00
Store counter model, 2-wheel, cast iron, "Elgin National Coffee Mill, Woodruff & Edwards Co., Elgin, Ill.," 29" d. wheels 225.00
Store counter model w/crank handle, cast iron, "Enterprise No. 1," 12½" h...............135.00 to 230.00

"Landers, Frary & Clark No. 20"

Store counter model, 2-wheel, cast iron, "Landers, Frary & Clark No. 20," original porcelain knob on drawer (ILLUS.) 325.00
Store counter model, 2-wheel, cast iron, "Star Model No. 10" 300.00
Store floor model, 2-wheel, cast iron, "Fairbanks Morse," painted white, brass hopper w/ornate finial, overall 38" h. 350.00
Table model, cast iron, octagonal column base, 6" d. wheels, "A.K. & Sons" 185.00
Table model, clamp-on type, cast iron, embossed top & crank handle, "Imperial" by Arcade 50.00
Table model, walnut base w/machine dovetailing & drawer, brass hopper, wrought iron handle w/turned wood knob, bottom

board w/geometric inlay extending to form working surface, 12½ x 29", 15" h. 325.00

Wall-type, advertising, "Golden Rule Coffee the finest Blend in the World," cast iron, wood & tin, overall 17" h. ....145.00 to 175.00

Wall-type, cast iron w/clear glass jar, "Alexander Werk," 14" h. 125.00

Wall-type, cast iron, "Enterprise," large....................65.00 to 85.00

Wall-type, cast iron, "Landers, Frary & Clark," pat. 1905-9 .... 40.00

Wall-type, cast iron w/copper finish, "C. Parker Co.," w/patent date of 1876, V-shaped 40.00

Wall-type, cast iron, "Regal No. 44" 38.00

COMIC BOOKS

Assorted Comic Books

Comic books, especially first, or early issues of a series, are avidly collected today. Prices for some of the scarce ones have reached extremely high levels. Prices listed below are for copies in fine to mint condition.

Animal Comics (Walt Kelly),
No. 104 .... $20.00
Batman, No. 9 .... 125.00
Batman, No. 64 .... 37.50
Beatles Yellow Submarine, w/pull-out poster, 1969................ 25.00
Blackstone, Master Magician, Vol. 1, No. 1, 1946 .... 20.00
Bonanza, No. 27 .... 1.50
Boy Comics, No. 17............... 10.00
Brave & the Bold (The), No. 36 ..... 9.00
Captain Science, No. 2, 1951 ...... 10.00
Charlie Chaplin in the Army, No. 316, 1917 .... 35.00
Charlie McCarthy in the Haunted Hideout, 1948 ....15.00 to 20.00

Cisco Kid, No. 3, 1945 .... 13.00
Contact, No. 5 .... 10.00
Crime & Punishment, No. 1, 1948 ... 10.00
Crime Suspenstories, No. 17, 1953 .. 100.00
Detective Comics, No. 23, 1939 (taped spine) 50.00
Donald Duck in Trick or Treat, No. 26, 1952 .... 25.00
Donald Duck in the Old Castle's Secret, No. 189, 1948 .... 60.00
Felix the Cat, No. 46, 1944 .... 99.00
Flying Saucers, No. 1, 1950........ 25.00
Gabby Hayes, No. 1, 1948 .... 6.50
Gene Autry, Dell No. 11, 1943..... 93.00
Gene Autry, No. 23 .... 18.00
Green Hornet, No. 24 .... 10.00
Hopalong Cassidy, No. 24 .... 12.00
Lone Ranger, No. 27.............. 38.00
Looney Tunes, Dell No. 223 .... 35.00
Major Hoople, No. 1, 1942 .... 20.00
March of Comics, Donald Duck in Darkest Africa, No. 20, 1948 ..... 250.00
Marge's Little Lulu, Dell No. 40 ..... 39.50
Marvel Mystery Comics, No. 54 ..... 20.00
Miss Liberty, No. 1, 1945.......... 10.00
Modern, No. 56 .... 10.00
Mutt & Jeff Cartoons, No. 6 .... 78.00
Police, No. 44.................... 10.00
Popeye, No. 26, 1939 .... 30.00
Popeye & Wimpy, No. 17, 1940 ... 35.00
Queen of the West, Dale Evans, Dell No. 10, 1956 .... 4.00
Real Fact, No. 1, 1946 .... 10.00
Roy Rogers, No. 82 .... 12.00
Roy Rogers, No. 166 .... 42.50
Rudolph, the Red-Nosed Reindeer, Montgomery Ward premium, 1939 .... 35.00
Secret Agent, No. 2, 1968 .... 2.75
Shock Suspenstories, No. 1, 1952 ... 75.00
Startling, No. 34 .... 10.00
Sub-Mariner, No. 18 .... 10.00
Superman, No. 10 .... 250.00
Superman's Christmas Adventure, Nehi premium, 1944......50.00 to 125.00
Tarzan, Dell No. 1, 1948 .... 125.00
Tom Mix, Ralston premium, No. 2, 1940 .... 36.00
Tom Mix, No. 59 .... 6.00
Uncle Scrooge, No. 4 .... 14.00
Uncle Scrooge, No. 21, 1958........ 10.00
Uncle Scrooge in Back to the Klondike, No. 456, 1953........20.00 to 30.00
Underworld, No. 2, 1948 .... 10.00
Walt Disney's Comics & Stories, Vol. 1, No. 3, 1940 .... 350.00
Walt Disney's Comics & Stories, No. 69, 1946 .... 43.00
Weird Science, No. 13, 1950........ 35.00
Young Allies, No. 13 .... 15.00
Zago, Jungle Prince, No. 2, 1948 ... 10.00

COMMEMORATIVE PLATES

Limited edition commemorative and collector plates rank high on the list of collectible items. The oldest and best-known of these plates, those of Bing & Grondahl and Royal Copenhagen, retain leadership in the field, but other companies are turning out a variety of designs, some of which have been widely embraced by the growing numbers who have made plate collecting a hobby. Plates listed below are a representative selection of the fine porcelain and glass plates available to collectors.

ANRI

1971 Anri Christmas Plate

1971 Christmas, St. Jakob In Groden (ILLUS.)	$61.00
1972 Christmas, Pipers At Alberobello	80.00
1973 Christmas, Alpine Horn	305.00
1974 Christmas, Young Man & Girl	77.00
1975 Christmas, Christmas in Ireland	60.00
1976 Christmas, Alpine Christmas	175.00
1977 Christmas, Legend Of Heiligenblut	125.00
1978 Christmas, The Klocker Singers	53.00
1979 Christmas, The Moss Gatherers of Villnoess	54.00
1980 Christmas, Wintry Churchgoing in Santa Christina	102.00
1981 Christmas, Santa Claus in Tyrol	95.00
1982 Christmas	125.00
1983 Christmas	110.00
1984 Christmas	112.00
1972 Father's Day, Alpine Father & Children	40.00
1973 Father's Day, Father Playing Fiddle	85.00
1974 Father's Day, Cliff Gazing	35.00
1975 Father's Day, Sailing	125.00
1972 Mother's Day, Alpine Mother & Children	42.00
1973 Mother's Day, Alpine Mother & Children	36.00
1974 Mother's Day, Alpine Mother & Children	51.00
1975 Mother's Day, Alpine Mother & Children	41.00
1976 Mother's Day, Knitting	48.00

BAREUTHER

1970 Bareuther Mother's Day Plate

1967 Christmas, Stiftskirche	144.00
1968 Christmas, Kappelkirche	35.00
1969 Christmas, Christkindlesmarkt	22.00
1970 Christmas, Chapel in Oberndorf	17.00
1971 Christmas, Toys for Sale	31.00
1972 Christmas, Christmas in Munich	47.00
1973 Christmas, Sleigh Ride	32.00
1974 Christmas, Black Forest Church	45.00
1975 Christmas, Snowman	36.50
1976 Christmas, Chapel in the Hills	28.00
1977 Christmas, Story Time	33.50
1978 Christmas, Mittenwald	29.00
1979 Christmas, Winter Day	27.50
1980 Christmas, Mittenberg	28.00
1981 Christmas, Walk in the Forest	21.00
1982 Christmas, Bad Wimpfen	22.00
1983 Christmas, The Night Before Christmas	23.00
1984 Christmas, Zeil on the River Man	21.00
1969 Father's Day, Castle Neuschwanstein	36.50
1970 Father's Day, Castle Pfalz	16.00
1971 Father's Day, Castle Heidelberg	22.00
1972 Father's Day, Castle Hohenschwangau	25.00

1973 Father's Day, Castle Katz......	27.00
1974 Father's Day, Castle Wurzburg......................	25.00
1975 Father's Day, Castle Lichtenstein...................	25.50
1976 Father's Day, Castle Hohenzollern	24.00
1977 Father's Day, Castle Eltz	24.00
1978 Father's Day, Castle Falkenstein...................	25.00
1979 Father's Day, Castle Rheinstein...................	28.00
1980 Father's Day, Castle Cochum ..	27.00
1981 Father's Day, Castle Gutenfels	29.00
1982 Father's Day, Castle Zwingenberg	26.00
1983 Father's Day, Castle Lauenstein...................	25.00
1984 Father's Day	28.00
1969 Mother's Day, Dancing	28.00
1970 Mother's Day, Mother & Children (ILLUS.)..................	19.00
1971 Mother's Day, Doing the Laundry	26.00
1972 Mother's Day, Baby's First Step	22.50
1973 Mother's Day, Mother Kissing Baby	26.00
1974 Mother's Day, Musical Children.......................	26.00
1975 Mother's Day, Spring Outing...	23.00
1976 Mother's Day................	20.00
1977 Mother's Day................	20.00
1978 Mother's Day................	19.00
1979 Mother's Day................	19.00
1980 Mother's Day................	20.00
1981 Mother's Day................	19.00
1982 Mother's Day................	21.00
1983 Mother's Day................	22.00
1984 Mother's Day................	25.00

BELLEEK

1970 Christmas, Castle Caldwell	87.00
1971 Christmas, Celtic Cross.......	35.00
1972 Christmas, Flight of the Earls ..	37.00
1973 Christmas, Tribute to Yeats....	52.00
1974 Christmas, Devenish Island	185.00
1975 Christmas, The Celtic Cross....	50.00
1976 Christmas, Dove of Peace	45.00
1977 Christmas, Wren	52.00
1978 Wildlife Christmas, A Leaping Salmon......................	62.00
1979 Wildlife Christmas, Hare at Rest	49.00
1980 Wildlife Christmas, The Hedgehog	62.00
1981 Wildlife Christmas, Red Squirrel	69.00
1982 Wildlife Christmas, Irish Seal ..	78.00
1983 Wildlife Christmas, Red Fox ...	72.50

BING & GRONDAHL

1895 Christmas 2,250.00	
1896............................1,081.00	

1897	610.00
1898	405.00
1899	872.00
1900	646.00
1901	200.00
1902	188.00
1903	162.00
1904	79.00
1905	90.00
1906	50.00
1907	62.00
1908	35.00
1909	46.00
1910	40.00

1911 Bing & Grondahl Christmas Plate

1911 (ILLUS.)....................	39.00
1912	37.00
1913	41.00
1914	34.00
1915	76.00
1916	35.00
1917	37.00
1918	40.00
1919	35.00
1920	38.00
1921	31.00
1922	28.00
1923	30.00
1924	29.00
1925	30.00
1926	30.00
1927	43.00
1928	28.00
1929	35.00
1930	47.00
1931	37.00
1932	40.00
1933	35.00
1934	34.00
1935	36.00
1936	38.00
1937	41.00
1938	58.00
1939	85.00
1940	86.00
1941	133.00

1942	89.00
1943	91.00
1944	53.00
1945	64.00
1946	38.00
1947	47.00
1948	32.00
1949	37.00
1950	58.00
1951	46.00
1952	35.00
1953	39.00
1954	43.00
1955	47.00
1956	61.00
1957	69.00
1958	51.00
1959	65.00
1960	101.00
1961	62.00
1962	39.00
1963	67.00
1964	32.00
1965	37.00
1966	30.00
1967	27.00
1968	21.00
1969	15.00
1970	13.00
1971	11.00
1972	10.00
1973	14.00
1974	12.50
1975	12.00
1976	13.00
1977	12.00
1978	16.00
1979	15.00
1980	16.00
1981	20.00
1982	23.00
1969 Mother's Day, Dog & Puppies	306.00
1970 Mother's Day, Birds & Chicks	25.00
1971 Mother's Day, Cat & Kitten	8.00
1972 Mother's Day, Mare & Foal	11.00
1973 Mother's Day, Duck & Ducklings	11.00
1974 Mother's Day, Bear & Cubs	14.00
1975 Mother's Day, Doe & Fawn	12.00
1976 Mother's Day, Swan Family	13.00
1977 Mother's Day, Squirrel & Young	14.00
1978 Mother's Day, Heron	14.00
1979 Mother's Day, Fox & Cubs	16.00
1980 Mother's Day, Woodpecker & Young	17.00
1981 Mother's Day, Hare & Young	21.00
1982 Mother's Day, Lioness & Cubs	30.00
1960 Jubilee, Kronborg Castle	96.00
1965 Jubilee, Churchgoers	57.00
1970 Jubilee, Amalienborg Castle	13.00
1975 Jubilee, Horses Enjoying Meal	24.00
1980 Jubilee, Yule Tree	20.00

FRANKOMA

1965 Christmas, Goodwill Towards Men	222.00
1966 Christmas, Bethlehem Shepherds	113.00
1967 Christmas, Gifts for the Christ Child	84.00
1968 Christmas, Flight into Egypt	14.00
1969 Christmas, Laid in a Manger	11.00
1970 Christmas, King of Kings	11.00
1971 Christmas, No Room in the Inn	13.50
1972 Christmas, Seeking the Christ Child	9.00
1973 Christmas, The Annunciation	9.00
1974 Christmas	9.00
1975 Christmas	10.00
1976 Christmas	9.00
1977 Christmas	10.00
1978 Christmas	9.50
1979 Christmas	10.00
1980 Christmas	10.00
1981 Christmas	9.50
1982 Christmas	10.00

Teenagers of the Bible Series:

1973 Jesus the Carpenter	18.00
1974 David the Musician	9.00
1975 Jonathan the Archer	9.00
1976 Dorcas the Seamstress	16.00
1977 Peter the Fisherman	12.00
1978 All Nature Rejoices	9.00
1979 Daniel	9.00
1980 Ruth	9.00
1981 Joseph	10.00
1982 Mary	11.50

GORHAM - NORMAN ROCKWELL

1971 Four Seasons, Boy & His Dog, set of 4	308.00
1972 Four Seasons, Young Love, set of 4	114.00
1973 Four Seasons, Ages of Love, set of 4	188.00
1973 Buttergirl	130.00
1974 Four Seasons, Grandpa & Me, set of 4	114.50
1974 Streakers	27.00
1974 Truth About Santa	31.00
1975 Four Seasons, Me & My Pal, set of 4	104.00
1976 Four Seasons, Grand Pals, set of 4	235.00
1976 Christmas Trio	21.00
1977 Four Seasons, Going on Sixteen, set of 4	140.00
1978 Four Seasons, The Tender Years, set of 4	82.00
1979 Four Seasons, A Helping Hand, set of 4	55.00
1979 Reflections	15.00
1980 Four Seasons, Dad's Boy, set of 4	81.50
1981 Four Seasons, Old Timers, set of 4	76.50

1981 Music Maker 17.00
1982 Four Seasons, Life with Father,
set of 4 .... 60.00

HAVILAND & CO.

1970 Haviland Christmas Plate

1970 Christmas, Partridge in a Pear
Tree (ILLUS.) 113.00
1971 Christmas, Two Turtle Doves .. 23.00
1972 Christmas, Three French
Hens 17.00
1973 Christmas, Four Colly Birds 19.00
1974 Christmas, Five Golden Rings .. 17.50
1975 Christmas, Six Geese A'
Laying 17.00
1976 Christmas, Seven Swans A'
Swimming 21.00
1977 Christmas, Eight Maids A'
Milking........................ 30.00
1978 Christmas, Nine Ladies
Dancing 31.00
1979 Christmas, Ten Lords A'
Leaping 30.00
1980 Christmas, Eleven Pipers
Piping......................... 41.00
1981 Christmas, Twelve Drummers
Drumming 49.00
1973 Mother's Day................. 9.00
1974 Mother's Day................. 10.50
1975 Mother's Day................. 10.50
1976 Mother's Day................. 13.50
1977 Mother's Day................. 12.00
1978 Mother's Day................. 14.50
1979 Mother's Day................. 18.00
1980 Mother's Day................. 9.00

HUMMEL (GOEBEL WORKS)

1971 Christmas................... 525.00
1972 Christmas................... 44.00
1973 Christmas................... 103.00
1974 Christmas (ILLUS.) 46.00
1975 Christmas................... 46.00
1976 Christmas................... 45.00
1977 Christmas................... 62.00
1978 Christmas................... 38.00

1974 Goebel Hummel Christmas Plate

1979 Christmas.................... 25.00
1980 Christmas.................... 39.00
1981 Christmas.................... 43.00
1982 Christmas.................... 84.00
1983 Christmas.................... 114.00
1975 Anniversary................. 104.00
1980 Anniversary................. 55.00

LALIQUE (GLASS)

1968 Lalique Annual Plate

1965 Annual 1,170.00
1966 Annual 168.00
1967 Annual 115.00
1968 Annual (ILLUS.).............. 61.00
1969 Annual 65.00
1970 Annual 52.00
1971 Annual 50.00
1972 Annual 51.00
1973 Annual 44.00
1974 Annual 47.00
1975 Annual 53.00
1976 Annual 86.00

PORSGRUND

1968 Christmas, Church Scene 175.00
1969 Christmas, Three Kings 12.00

1970 Christmas, Road to
Bethlehem 9.00

1971 Porsgrund Christmas Plate

1971 Christmas, A Child is Born
(ILLUS.) 8.00
1972 Christmas, Hark the Herald
Angels Sing................... 12.00
1973 Christmas, Promise of the
Savior....................... 12.00
1974 Christmas, The Shepherds 35.00
1975 Christmas, Road to Temple 21.00
1976 Christmas, Jesus & the Elders.. 22.00
1977 Christmas, Draught of the
Fish......................... 15.00
1978 Christmas, Guests are
Coming 13.00
1979 Christmas, Home for
Christmas 14.50
1980 Christmas, Preparing for
Christmas 15.00
1981 Christmas, Christmas Skating .. 17.50
1982 Christmas, White Christmas ... 21.00
1983 Christmas.................... 21.00
1984 Christmas.................... 25.00
1971 Father's Day, Fishing 4.00
1972 Father's Day, Cookout 4.00
1973 Father's Day, Sledding 4.00
1974 Father's Day, Father & Son with
Wheelbarrow 4.00
1975 Father's Day, Skating 4.00
1976 Father's Day, Skiing 4.00
1977 Father's Day, Soccer 5.00
1978 Father's Day, Canoeing 5.00
1979 Father's Day, Father &
Daughter 11.00
1980 Father's Day, Sailing 8.00
1981 Father's Day 8.50
1982 Father's Day 9.00
1983 Father's Day 10.00
1970 Mother's Day, Mare & Foal 4.00
1971 Mother's Day, Boy & Geese 4.00
1972 Mother's Day, Doe & Fawn 4.00
1973 Mother's Day, Cat & Kittens ... 5.00
1974 Mother's Day, Boy & Goats 5.00
1975 Mother's Day, Dog & Puppies .. 5.00
1976 Mother's Day, Girl & Calf 5.00
1977 Mother's Day, Boy &
Chickens 8.00

1978 Mother's Day, Girl & Pigs 8.00
1979 Mother's Day, Boy &
Reindeer 8.00
1980 Mother's Day, Girl & Lambs ... 8.00
1981 Mother's Day, Boy & Birds 8.50
1982 Mother's Day, Child with
Rabbit........................ 8.50
1983 Mother's Day, Mother &
Kittens 17.00
1984 Mother's Day................. 14.50

RED SKELTON PLATES
1976 Freddie..................... 360.00
1977 W.C. Fields 57.00
1978 Happy 50.00
1979 Freddie in the Bath Tub 190.00
1979 The Pledge 55.50
1980 Freddie's Shack 68.50
1981 Freddie on the Green 44.00
1982 Love That Freddie 47.00
1982 Bronco Freddie 36.00
1982 Captain Freddie 41.00
1983 Sir Freddie................. 37.00
1983 70 Years Young 58.00
1984 Torchbearer................. 43.00

RORSTRAND

1970 Rorstrand Christmas Plate

1968 Christmas, Bringing Home the
Tree 338.00
1969 Christmas, Fisherman Sailing
Home 53.00
1970 Christmas, Nils with His Geese
(ILLUS.)...................... 19.00
1971 Christmas, Nils in Lapland..... 18.50
1972 Christmas, Dalecarlian
Fiddler 15.00
1973 Christmas, Farm in Smaland ... 50.00
1974 Christmas, Vadstena.......... 47.00
1975 Christmas, Nils in
Vastmanland 11.50
1976 Christmas, Nils in Uppland 10.50
1977 Christmas, Nils in Varmland ... 11.00
1978 Christmas, Nils in Fjallbacka... 16.00
1979 Christmas, Nils in
Vaestergoetland 17.50

1980 Christmas, Nils in Holland	20.00
1981 Christmas, Nils in Gotland	20.00
1982 Christmas, Nils in Skansen	26.00
1983 Christmas, Nils in Oland	28.50
1984 Christmas, Angerman Land	31.00
1971 Mother's Day	7.00
1972 Mother's Day	7.00
1973 Mother's Day	24.00
1974 Mother's Day	13.00
1975 Mother's Day	5.00
1976 Mother's Day	6.50
1977 Mother's Day	6.50
1978 Mother's Day	17.50
1979 Mother's Day	17.50
1980 Mother's Day	22.00
1981 Mother's Day	23.00
1982 Mother's Day	24.00
1983 Mother's Day	25.00
1984 Mother's Day	27.50

ROSENTHAL

1971 Wiinblad Christmas, Maria & Child	1,193.00
1972 Wiinblad Christmas, King Caspar	454.00
1973 Wiinblad Christmas, King Melchior	361.00
1974 Wiinblad Christmas, King Balthazar	237.00
1975 Wiinblad Christmas, The Annuciation	134.00
1976 Wiinblad Christmas, Angel with Trumpet	119.00
1977 Wiinblad Christmas, Adoration of the Shepherd	158.00
1978 Wiinblad Christmas, Angel with Harp	110.00
1979 Wiinblad Christmas, Exodus from Egypt	114.00
1980 Wiinblad Christmas, Angel with Glockenspiel	119.00
1981 Wiinblad Christmas, Christ Child Visits Temple	152.00
1982 Wiinblad Christmas, Christening of Christ	122.00
1983 Wiinblad Christmas	141.00
1984 Wiinblad Christmas	129.00

ROYAL COPENHAGEN

1908	1,336.00
1909	88.00
1910	78.00
1911	86.00
1912	90.00
1913	74.00
1914	77.00
1915	77.00
1916	55.00
1917	50.00
1918	51.00
1919	51.00
1920	48.00
1921	41.00
1922	38.00

1923	39.00
1924	60.00
1925	52.00
1926	49.00
1927	82.00
1928	47.00
1929	48.00
1930	56.00
1931	59.00
1932	52.00
1933	76.00
1934	69.00

1935 Royal Copenhagen Christmas Plate

1935 (ILLUS.)	94.00
1936	86.00
1937	92.00
1938	153.00
1939	170.00
1940	228.00
1941	204.00
1942	208.00
1943	285.00
1944	118.00
1945	212.00
1946	101.00
1947	133.00
1948	110.00
1949	115.00
1950	118.00
1951	217.00
1952	78.00
1953	75.00
1954	84.00
1955	122.00
1956	110.00
1957	58.00
1958	78.00
1959	75.00
1960	95.00
1961	93.00
1962	138.00
1963	53.00
1964	42.00
1965	38.00
1966	31.00
1967	28.00
1968	19.00

1969	21.00
1970	28.00
1971	15.00
1972	13.00
1973	12.50
1974	11.00
1975	12.00
1976	22.00
1977	13.00
1978	14.00
1979	39.00
1980	18.00
1981	18.00
1982	23.00
1983	24.00
1984	26.00
1971 Mother's Day, American Mother	18.00
1972 Mother's Day, Oriental Mother	6.00
1973 Mother's Day, Danish Mother ..	7.00
1974 Mother's Day, Greenland Mother	7.00
1975 Mother's Day, Bird in Nest	8.00
1976 Mother's Day, Mermaids	7.00
1977 Mother's Day, The Twins	9.00
1978 Mother's Day, Mother & Child	9.00
1979 Mother's Day, A Loving Mother	9.00
1980 Mother's Day, An Outing with Mother	11.00
1981 Mother's Day, Reunion	13.00
1982 Mother's Day, Children's Hour	14.00

SCHMID HUMMEL

1971 Christmas, Angel	25.00
1972 Christmas, Angel with Flute ...	23.00
1973 Christmas, The Nativity	100.00
1974 Christmas, The Guardian Angel	26.00
1975 Christmas, Christmas Child	25.00
1976 Christmas, Sacred Journey	22.00
1977 Christmas, Herald Angel	14.00
1978 Christmas, Heavenly Trio	21.00
1979 Christmas, Starlight Angel	26.00
1980 Christmas, Parade into Toyland	26.50
1981 Christmas, A Time to Remember	25.00
1982 Christmas, Angelic Procession	26.50
1983 Christmas, Angelic Messenger	26.00
1984 Christmas...................	29.00

SPODE

1970 Christmas, Partridge	43.00
1971 Christmas, Angels Singing	20.00
1972 Christmas, Three Ships A-Sailing	20.00
1973 Christmas, Three Kings of Orient	45.00

1974 Christmas, Deck the Halls	44.00
1975 Christmas, Christbaum	21.50
1976 Christmas, Good King Wenceslas	21.50
1977 Christmas, Holly & Ivy	25.00
1978 Christmas, While Shepherds Watched	21.50
1979 Christmas, Away in a Manger	28.50
1980 Christmas, Bringing in the Boar's Head	27.00
1981 Christmas, Make We Merry....	47.00

WEDGWOOD

1969 Christmas, Windsor Castle.....	183.00
1970 Christmas, Trafalger Square ...	22.00
1971 Christmas, Picadilly Circus.....	27.00
1972 Christmas, St. Paul's Cathedral	28.00
1973 Christmas, Tower of London ...	35.00
1974 Christmas, Houses of Parliament	28.00
1975 Christmas, Tower Bridge	34.00
1976 Christmas, Hampton Court	23.00
1977 Christmas, Westminster Abbey	25.00
1978 Christmas, Horse Guards......	34.00
1979 Christmas, Buckingham Palace	38.00
1980 Christmas, St. James Palace ...	29.00
1981 Christmas, Marble Arch	35.00
1982 Christmas, Lambeth Palace ...	49.00
1983 Christmas, All Souls, Langham Palace	45.00
1984 Christmas, Constitution Hall ...	42.00

(End of Commemorative Plate Section)

COOKBOOKS

Cape Cod Cookbook

Cookbook collectors are usually good cooks and will buy important new cookbooks as well as seek out notable older ones. Many early cookbooks were published and given away as advertising premiums for various products used extensively in cooking. While some rare, scarce first edition cookbooks can be very expensive, most collectible cookbooks are reasonably priced.

Advertising, "All Doors Open to
Jell-O," 1917 . . . . $15.00
Advertising, "Arm & Hammer Valua-
ble Recipes," 1921 . . . . 4.50
Advertising, "Baker's Best Chocolate
Recipes," 1932, LaBelle
Chocolatiere on cover, 60 pp. 9.00
Advertising, "Crisco Cook Book,"
hardbound, ca. 1915, w/mailing
envelope 15.00
Advertising, "Fleischmann's Yeast
Cookbook," 1910 . . . . 12.00
Advertising, "Granite Iron Ware
Cookbook," 1887, "The Little
Housewife" on cover 80.00
Advertising, "Hood's Apothecaries
Company Cookbook," 1879 . . . . . . 14.50
Advertising, "Jewel Tea Cookbook,"
by Mary Dunbar, 1927 . . . . 16.00
Advertising, "KC Baking Powder,
The Cooks' Book," 1911 . . . . 15.00
Advertising, "Knox Gelatin Dainty
Desserts for Dainty People," 1924,
children & cow on cover 4.00
Advertising, "Larkin Company Cook-
book," 1908 . . . . 11.00
Advertising, "Pillsbury's Best Bake-
Off Cookbook," No. 10, 14 or 16,
each 10.00
Advertising, "Ralston Recipes," 1920,
old woman in shoe w/children on
cover 8.00
Advertising, "Red Wing Home Can-
ning Cookbook" 100.00
Advertising, "Sleepy Eye Milling Co.
Cook Book," portrait of Old
Sleepy Eye on cover, bread
shape 150.00
Advertising, "Watkins Salad Cook-
book," 1946 . . . . 14.00
"Amana Recipes," 1948, w/dust
jacket 11.00
"Chef Ford Naylor - Recipes &
Menus," 1940, w/illustrations from
various world-famous locations . . . 50.00
"Cupid's Cookbook," 1933, hard
cover 14.00
"Everyday Cookbook (The)," by Miss
E. Neil, 1892 . . . . 30.00
"Good Housekeeping Institute
Recipes, Menus," 1930, 256 pp. . . . 10.00
"Household Discoveries & Mrs. Cur-
tis's Cook Book," 1908, leather
bound 22.50

"Joy of Cooking," 1946, hardbound,
820 pp. 9.00
"Let's Cook It Right," by Davis, 1947,
625 pp. 8.50
"Luchow's German Cookbook,"
1952 . . . . 10.00
"Miss Parloa's Cookbook," 1881 . . . . 15.00
"Mrs. Lincoln's Boston Cookbook,"
1892, 527 pp. 35.00
"New American Cookbook," by Lily
Wallace, 1941, w/dust jacket 14.00
"Pennsylvania Dutch," 1936, Sunbon-
net Girl cover, illustrated 10.00
"Peter Hunt's Cape Cod Cookbook,"
1962, 181 pp., w/dust jacket
(ILLUS.) 8.00
"Washington Herald Recipe Book,"
1940's 10.00
"White House Cookbook," 1890 . . . . . 44.00

COOKIE CUTTERS

Standing Bird Cutter

Recently there has been an accelerated interest in old tin cookie cutters. For the most part, these were made by tinsmiths who shaped primitive designs of tin strips and then soldered them to a backplate, pierced to allow air to enter and prevent a suction from holding the rolled cookie dough in the form. Sometimes an additional handle was soldered to the back. Cookie cutters were also manufactured in great quantities in an outline form that could depict animals, birds, star and other forms, including the plain round that sometimes carried embossed advertising for flour or other products on the handle. Aluminum cookie cutters were made after 1920. Only tin cutters are listed below.

Bird in standing position, flat backplate pierced w/single hole,
4½" l., 2¾" h. (ILLUS.) $25.00
Chick, flat backplate pierced w/sin-
gle hole, w/strap handle, 4" h. 18.00
Cornucopia, flat backplate, w/strap
handle, 3½" l. 45.00
Deer, flat backplate pierced w/two
holes, 4¾" l. 20.00
Dog w/large raised ears, flat back-
plate pierced w/single hole, 4" l.
(minor rust) 55.00

Duck Cutter

Duck w/raised wings, flat backplate
  pierced w/two holes (ILLUS.) 55.00
Eagle in flight, flat backplate
  pierced w/two holes, 5¼" l. 22.50
Elephant, flat backplate pierced
  w/single hole, 5" l. 37.50
Fish w/sharply detailed fins & tail,
  flat backplate pierced w/two
  holes, 5¼" l. (handle missing)....   75.00
Giraffe, flat backplate pierced
  w/five holes, 5¾" h. (handle
  missing) 105.00
Guitar, flat backplate pierced w/sin-
  gle large hole, 4½" h...........   85.00
Hand, flat backplate, 4¾" l. 25.00
Heart w/crimped edge, flat backplate pierced w/two holes,
  w/beaded strap handle, 3 x 3" ...   35.00
Hen, flat backplate, 5" h. 10.00
Horse trotting, flat backplate
  pierced w/single hole, 6" l.
  (minor rust)....................   75.00
Horse & rider, flat backplate pierced
  w/eight holes, 6¾" l. (handle
  missing) 175.00
Kitten, flat backplate pierced w/star
  design, 4" h....................   20.00
Leaf outline, 2½" d...............   20.00
Lion, flat backplate pierced w/two
  holes, 3½" l. 9.00
Man & woman standing, flat backplate pierced w/single hole, 4¾"
  & 5" h., pr. 36.00
Pig, flat backplate pierced w/single
  hole, 6" l. 65.00
Pistol, flat backplate pierced w/sin-
  gle hole, 3¼" l.................   65.00
Rabbit w/short legs & fat body, flat
  backplate pierced w/two holes,
  5¾" l. 65.00
Squirrel, flat backplate pierced
  w/star design, 4" h.............   20.00
Stag, flat backplate pierced w/three
  holes, 6" l. 85.00
Star, 5-pointed, flat backplate,
  w/strap handle, 4¾" w. 35.00

Woman wearing cap & standing
  w/arm outstretched, flat backplate pierced w/single hole,
  5½" h....................... 105.00
Woman w/long arms, flat backplate
  pierced w/two holes, 5¾" h......   75.00

CORONATION ITEMS

Edward VII & Alexandra

*Items commemorating the coronation of
English monarchs have been produced for
many years. The spectacular 1981 Royal Wedding, uniting Charles, the Prince of Wales,
and Lady Diana Spencer in matrimony, has
created new interest in English Royalty. Listed in chronological order according to reign,
the following items have been sold, or offered
for sale, in recent months.*

Edward VII (1901-10) beaker, china,
  portraits of Edward & Alexandra
  front, coat of arms & "Coronation
  1902" reverse, Burslem, 4" h. $70.00
Edward VII bowl, china, portrait of
  Edward & Alexandra, Longston,
  10" d. 25.00
Edward VII cup & saucer, china, portrait of Edward & Alexandra 55.00
Edward VII mug, china, dated 1902,
  Royal Doulton.................   70.00
Edward VII mug, china, lithophane
  portrait of Edward in base 90.00
Edward VII picture, woven silk, Edward & Alexandra w/Scottish thistles, English roses & Royal seal,
  original frame, 9½ x 15½"
  (ILLUS.)...................... 315.00
Edward VII pitcher, china, portraits
  of Edward & Alexandra 65.00

Edward VII plate, china, portrait of
Edward & Alexandra center,
6" d. 28.00

Edward VII straight razor, engraved
bust portrait of Edward on
blade 25.00

Edward VII tape measure, silver,
portrait of Edward in relief 65.00

Edward VII teapot, china, relief-
molded florals & fan decor w/oval
portrait of Edward on dark brown
ground 90.00

Edward VII tumbler, glass,
enameled portrait of Edward,
4" h. 80.00

George V (1910-36) baby plate,
china, Shelley 175.00

George V beaker, china, portraits of
George & Mary of Teck w/crown
& sceptor & "1911 - June 22nd,"
4" h. 60.00

George V cup & saucer, demitasse,
china 37.50

George V cup & saucer, china, portraits of George & Mary of Teck . . 50.00

George V handkerchief, cotton, 10
vignettes of The British Empire . . . 17.50

George V mug, china, dated 1911,
Moorcroft 195.00

George V pitcher, stoneware, portrait of George & Mary, dated
1911, Royal Doulton, 4½" h. 125.00

George V pitcher, stoneware, portrait of George & Mary, dated
1911, Royal Doulton, 6" h. 165.00

George V plate, china, reticulated
rim, portraits of George & Mary,
9" d. 52.00

George V playing cards, portrait of
George, 1911, in original box 38.00

George V teapot, cov., china, por-
trait of George 52.00

George V tumbler, glass, sepia-tone
portrait of George, 1911, 4" h. . . . 60.00

Edward VIII (January 1936-December
1936) ashtray, china, portrait of
Edward, Shelley, 5" 20.00

Edward VIII beaker, china,
Wedgwood 60.00

Edward VIII box, scalloped rim, embossed bust of Edward w/crown
suspended above on wreath, base
w/embossed wreath, blue & white
Wedgwood Creamware, 5¼" d.,
2¼" h. 50.00

Edward VIII creamer, portrait of Edward, blue & white Wedgwood
Creamware 35.00

Edward VIII cup & saucer, china,
Tuscan 17.50

Edward VIII goblet, glass, engraved
w/coronation date, quadruple air
bubble stem, signed Stuart 65.00

Edward VIII handkerchief, lace 25.00

Edward VIII medallion, relief portrait
of Edward, Wedgwood Basaltes . . 125.00

Edward VIII mug, china, Royal Doul-
ton, small 75.00

Edward VIII mug, china, designed by
Dame Laura Knight 40.00

Edward VIII plate, china, portrait of
Edward, 6" d. 15.00

Edward VIII plate, china, portrait of
Edward, 8½" d. 22.00

Edward VIII teapot, cov., china, portrait of Edward 85.00

Edward VIII tumbler, china,
Minton 50.00

COUNTRY STORE COLLECTIBLES

*Country store museums have opened across
the country in an effort to recreate those
slower-paced days of the late 19th and early
20th centuries when the general store served
as the local meeting place for much of rural
America. Here one not only purchased necessary supplies for upcoming weeks, but caught
up on important news events and local gossip. With strong interest in colorful tin cans
during the early 1960's, came the realization
that these stores and neighborhood groceries
were fast disappearing, replaced by the so-
called supermarkets, and collectors began
buying all items associated with these early
stores. Also see ADVERTISING ITEMS,
CANS & CONTAINERS, CASH REGIS-
TERS and SIGNS & SIGNBOARDS.*

Account register, metal,
"McCaskey," last patent date of
1907, holds 100 individual
accounts $65.00

Bin, tin, barrel-shaped, 20 x 14" 39.00

Buggy whip holder, cast iron 50.00

Catalogue holder, metal, "Sears" . . . 27.00

Cheese cutter, wire w/turned wood
handle & 29 x 18" cutting board . . 185.00

Cocoa bin, hinged lid w/brass
knobs, tin, "Bensdorp's," gold lettering on red ground, 11" d.,
14" h. 35.00

Coffee bin, lift-lid, tin, "Parton &
Gallagher Gas Roasted Coffee,
Omaha, Nebraska" 135.00

Counter, mahogany & oak, paneled
on 3 sides, 5' l. 225.00

Meat hanging rack, wrought iron,
crown-shaped w/eight hooks
around band & center ring for
hanging, 12½" d. 175.00

Needle display case, tin, "New
Simplicity" 28.00

Pocket knife display case, oak

w/glass lift-lid, "Winchester-
Simmons," 12 x 8", 3" h......... 395.00
Rack on wheels, 4-shelf, "National
Biscuit Company" on top & ends,
47" w., 6' h. 300.00
Scoop, brass, 9" l................. 40.00
Scoop, copper, 10" l. 20.00
Shoe fitting stool, twisted wire legs,
bentwood seat 24.00
Tobacco bin, slant lid, printed tin,
"Sweet Cuba," portrait of a lady
on green ground 80.00

COW CREAMERS

Whieldon-type Cow Creamer

*These silver and earthenware cream jugs
were modeled in the form of that beautiful bo-
vine animal, the original source of their intended contents. The most desirable versions
are the early silver and Dutch Delft faience
creations turned out in the 18th century, as
well as those produced in the Staffordshire
potteries before the mid-19th century. However, traditional style cow creamers, made in
the late 19th or in the 20th centuries, are also
deemed collectible. The following group of
cow creamers were offered for sale, or sold at
auction, within recent months.*

Pottery, Delft-type faience, cow in
recumbent position, blue & white,
impressed "Germany" on base ... $65.00
Pottery, Jackfield-type, cow standing on embossed base, w/lid,
black glaze, 7" l., 5" h. 110.00
Pottery, Staffordshire, cow standing
on base, Blue Willow patt. transfer on white, ca. 1840, 7½" l. 175.00
Pottery, Staffordshire, cow standing
on base, sponged in brown &
white, ca. 1850 .... 150.00
Pottery, Staffordshire, cow standing,

white w/painted brown spots, ca.
1875 .... 85.00
Pottery, Staffordshire, cow standing,
white w/painted black spots, ca.
1860 .... 115.00
Pottery, Whieldon-type, cow standing
w/tail curled up to form handle &
mouth forming spout, w/calf at
side, splashed in grey & ochre, on
oblong base w/cut corners enriched
in green, repairs to horns, foot
chip, ca. 1765, 6" l., pr. (ILLUS.
of one) 1,650.00
Pottery, Yorkshire-type, cow standing w/tail curled up to form handle & mouth forming spout &
sponged in brown & ochre,
w/seated figure of milkmaid
w/bucket by her feet covered in
green glaze, on shaped oblong
base enriched in green, ca. 1760,
6" l. 715.00
Sterling silver, cow w/long horns
standing, insect chased on lid,
4½" l., 2¾" h.................. 210.00
Sterling silver, cow standing, insect
chased on lid, detailed hair, 6" l.,
3½" h. 275.00

CURRIER & IVES

Arguing the Point

*This lithographic firm was founded in 1835
by Nathanial Currier with James M. Ives becoming a partner in 1857. Current events of
the day were portrayed in the early days and
the prints were hand-colored. Landscapes,
vessels, sport, and hunting scenes of the west
all became popular subjects. The firm was in
existence until 1906. All prints listed are
hand-colored unless otherwise noted.*

American Farm Scenes, No. 1
(Spring), after F. F. Palmer, large
folio, N. Currier, 1853, framed ..$3,850.00
American Field Sports - "A Change

for Both Barrels," large folio,
1857, framed 2,100.00

American Jockey Club Races, Jerome
Park, large folio 1,980.00

Among the Pines - "A First Settle-
ment," small folio 295.00

Arguing the Point, after A.F. Tait,
large folio, N. Currier, 1855,
framed (ILLUS.) 2,750.00

Battle of Antietam, Md. (The), small
folio 160.00

Battle of Gettysburg, Pa. (The),
small folio, 1863 . . . . 180.00

Birthplace of Washington (The),
small folio. 285.00

Bombardment and Capture of Fort
Henry, Tenn., small folio 195.00

"Bridal Veil" Fall, Yo-Semite Valley,
Calif., small folio 250.00

Bride (The), small folio, N. Currier,
1847 . . . . 50.00

Brook Trout - Just Caught, medium
folio, 1858 . . . . 375.00

Burning of Chicago (The), small fo-
lio, 1871 . . . . 265.00

California Scenery - "Seal Rocks-
Points Lobos," small folio 195.00

Camping in the Woods - "Laying
Off," after A.F. Tait, large folio,
1863, framed 4,180.00

Capture of Andre 1780, small folio,
N. Currier, 1845 . . . . 295.00

Clipper Ship "Dreadnought" - Off
Tuskar Light, large folio, N. Cur-
rier, 1856 . . . . .2,200.00

Death Shot (The), small folio 235.00

Declaration (The), small folio, N.
Currier, 1846. . . . . 40.00

"Edward" and "Swiveller," small
folio, 1882 . . . . 225.00

Enoch Arden - The Lonely Isle, large
folio, 1869 . . . . 600.00

Fast Team Taking a Smash (A),
small folio 125.00

First Flight Between Iron Clad Ships
of War (The), small folio, 1862 . . . 270.00

First Trot of the Season, large folio,
1870. . . . . .1,950.00

Four Seasons of Life (The) - Middle
Age, large folio, 1868 . . . . 800.00

Fox-Hunting - The Death, medium
folio 875.00

Fruits of Temperance (The), small
folio, N. Currier, 1848 . . . . 135.00

General Meagher at the Battle of
Fair Oaks, Va., small folio, 1862. . 125.00

General Tom Thumb & Wife, Com.
Nutt & Minnie Warren - "The
Greatest Wonders in the World,"
small folio, 1863 . . . . 125.00

Great Pole Mares, "Belle Hamlin" &
"Justina," small folio 225.00

Harbor for the Night (A), small
folio 225.00

Home in the Country (A), medium
folio 495.00

Hunter's Shanty (The) - In the
Adirondacks, large folio, 1861,
framed 990.00

Indian Lake - Sunset, large folio,
1860, framed, overall 27¾ x 20".. 425.00

Ingleside Winter (The), small folio .. 375.00

John Quincy Adams - 6th President,
small folio, N. Currier 95.00

Landing of the American Forces under General Scott at Vera Cruz,
small folio, N. Currier, 1847 . . . . . 125.00

Midnight Race on the Mississippi
(A) - "Natchez" & "Eclipse," after
F. F. Palmer, large folio, 1860,
framed. . . . . .4,950.00 to 7,700.00

Mink Trapping - "Prime," after A. F.
Tait, large folio, 1862 . . . . .10,175.00

Moosehead Lake, small folio 185.00

Mount Washington and the White
Mountains, From the Valley of
Conway, after F. F. Palmer, large
folio, 1860 . . . . .1,650.00

My Little White Kittens Learning
their ABC's, small folio 75.00

Narrows, New York Bay, from Stat-
en Island (The), small folio,
framed, overall 19 x 15¼" 85.00

Naval Heroes of the United States,
No. 2, (Battle of Lake Champlain
center), small folio, N. Currier,
1846 . . . . 275.00

Old Farm House (The), winter
scene, small folio, 1872,
framed 375.00

Old Oaken Bucket (The), small folio,
1872 . . . . 220.00

Pioneer's Home (The) - On the Western Frontier, after F. F. Palmer,
large folio, 1867 . . . . .2,420.00

Playful Family (The), cat & kittens
small folio, N. Currier 55.00

Prairie Hunter (The) - "One rubbed
out," after A. F. Tait, large folio,
N. Currier, 1852 . . . . .4,400.00

Puritan and Genesta on the Home-
stretch (The), large folio, 1885,
framed 990.00

Return from the Woods (The), after
F. F. Palmer, medium folio,
framed 310.00

Rising Family (A), after A. F. Tait,
large folio, 1857 . . . . .2,420.00

Rubber (The) - "Put to his Trumps,"
medium folio, N. Currier,
framed 1,100.00

Sale of the Pet Lamb (The), small
folio, old molded frame 120.00

Sleigh Race (The), small folio, N.
Currier, 1848, framed 240.00

Snipe Shooting, after F. F. Palmer,
large folio, N. Currier, 1852,
framed (ILLUS.) 3,850.00

Snipe Shooting

Splendid Naval Triumph on the Mississippi, April 24th, 1862 (The), large folio, 1862 . . . . .3,630.00

Spring (group of 7 beneath trees), small folio, N. Currier, 1849 . . . . . . 145.00

Summer Fruits, medium folio, old giltwood frame, overall 22¼" w., 17¾" h. (margins trimmed) 195.00

Trotting Queen Maud S., Record 2:08¾, small folio, 1881 . . . . 110.00

Two Pets (The), small folio, N. Currier, 1848 . . . . 45.00

U.S. Military Academy, West Point, From the opposite shore, after F. F. Palmer, medium folio, 1862 . . . . .2,090.00

View of Harper's Ferry, Va., From the Potomac Side, large folio 1,540.00

View of New York From Brooklyn Heights, after F. F. Palmer, medium folio, N. Currier, 1849, framed (margins trimmed) 1,430.00

View on Long Island, N.Y.

View on Long Island, N.Y., after F. F. Palmer, large folio, 1857, framed (ILLUS.) . . . . . .1,540.00 to 2,310.00

Vigilant and Valkyrie in a "Thrash to Windward" In their International Race for "The America's Cup" Oct. 7th, 9th & 13th, 1893, Won by the Vigilant, large folio, 1893 . . . . 770.00

Washington at Mount Vernon 1789 - "Agriculture is the most healthy, the most useful, and the most noble employment of man," small folio, N. Currier, 1852, framed . . . 380.00

Western Farmer's Home (The), small folio, 1871, beveled mahogany

veneer frame, overall 16½ x 12½" 175.00

Western River Scenery, medium folio, 1866, framed 1,430.00

Whale Fishery (The), The sperm whale in a flurry, large folio 4,950.00

Woodcock (1 w/bill in sand), small folio, 1871, framed 180.00

Yacht "Dauntless," of New York (The), large folio, 1869, framed . . . 660.00

Yosemite Falls, California, small folio 100.00

DECOYS

Mallard Drake and Hen

Decoys have been utilized for years to lure flying water fowl into target range. They have been made of carved and turned wood, papier mache, canvas and metal, and some are in the category of outstanding folk art and command high prices.

Black-Bellied Plover, carved wood, by George Boyd, Seabrook, New Hampshire $3,080.00

Black Duck, carved wood, by the Ward Brothers, Crisfield, Maryland 4,400.00

Black Duck Hen, carved wood, hollow construction, glass eyes, by Ken Anger, Dunnville, Ontario, Canada, ca. 1940, 16" l. (paint & bill expertly restored) 85.00

Bluebill Drake, carved wood, old worn black & white paint, 13" l. (repairs to neck) 95.00

Bluebill Drake, Mason Standard Grade, old worn repaint, glass eyes, 13¼" l. 60.00

Blue Wing Teal Hen, carved wood, original paint, glass eyes, 12" l. (age cracks) 150.00

Brant Goose, flat sheet iron stick-up type w/attached wings, worn paint, 30¼" h. on wooden base . . 40.00

Brant Goose, weathered original paint, inletted lead weight & original leather thong, bottom impressed "J.M." 165.00

Canada Goose, Herter's Decoy Co., balsa wood body w/wooden head, glass eyes, 20½" l.............. 110.00

Canada Goose, canvas covered wire & wood frame, carved wooden head, bottom initialed "C.B.," 24½" l. 75.00

Canada Goose, carved wood, original paint, by Charles Perdew, Henry, Illinois 9,900.00

Canada Goose, carved wood, by George Warin, Toronto, Canada 7,150.00

Canvasback Drake, Mason Challenge Grade, repainted & varnished, glass eyes, 15" l. 135.00

Canvasback Drake, carved wood, tack eyes, 16" l. 100.00

Coot, carved wood, glass eyes, by Tony Collins, Monroe, Michigan (1915-77), 11¼" l. 265.00

Crow, composition, worn black paint, glass eyes & nail feet, 15½" l. 45.00

Dove silhouette, wooden, 10" h. on base 30.00

Dowitcher, carved wood, by John Dilley, Quogue, Long Island, New York 11,000.00

Fish, carved wood w/copper fins & tail, old worn repaint, 6" l. 135.00

Fish, carved mahogany w/brass fins, marked No. 5 & initialed "K.C.," 8¼" l. 195.00

Fish, carved wood w/metal fins, brown & white paint, 8½" l. 50.00

Fish, carved wood w/metal fins & curved wooden tail, shiner w/worn silver paint, 9¼" l. 55.00

Fish, "Trout," carved wood w/metal fins & tack eyes, old paint, 12¾" l. 235.00

Fish, carved wood w/metal fins, painted brown & yellow w/polka dots, by Miles Smith, Marine City, Michigan, 14" l. 95.00

Fish, carved wood w/metal fins, rainbow paint, by Miles Smith, Marine City, Michigan, 14½" l. 200.00

Goldeneye Drake, carved wood, hollow body, old worn working repaint, glass eyes, by Fred Croft, Alexandria Bay, New York, 13¾" l. 125.00

Goldeneye Drake, Stevens Factory, hollow body, glass eyes, 15" l. 150.00

Goldeneye Drake, carved wood, by Orel Le Boeuf, St. Anicet, Quebec 1,320.00

Goose, carved wood, by Capt. Harry Jobes 145.00

Great Horned Owl w/dead crow at base, Herter's................. 850.00

Mallard Drake w/slightly turned head, carved wood, hollow construction, worn old working repaint w/original paint showing through, glass eyes, by Stephen Tyler, Dallas City, Illinois (1880-1950), 15½" l. (split in neck) 175.00

Mallard Drake, carved wood, by Ward Brothers, Crisfield, Maryland, ca. 1936 (ILLUS. top) 10,450.00

Mallard Hen, Mason Detroit Grade......................... 125.00

Mallard Hen, carved wood, by Ward Brothers, Crisfield, Maryland, ca. 1936 (ILLUS. bottom) 9,350.00

Pintail Drake w/turned head, carved wood, hollow construction, original paint, glass eyes, branded "L. T. Ward, Maker" (possibly Torri Ward, Manitoba, Canada), 20" l. (small chip on bill) 295.00

Pintail Drake, carved wood, by Robert Elliston, Bureau, Illinois...1,870.00

Pintail Drake, Mason Premier Grade......................... 450.00

Pintail Hen & Drake, carved wood, by Charles Perdew, Henry, Illinois, pr. 4,675.00

Redhead Drake, Mason Challenge Grade, old working repaint, original glass eyes, 14¾" l. (age cracks & shot scars) 95.00

Redhead Drake w/head high, carved wood, old working repaint, glass eyes, Canada, 14¾" l. (age cracks in neck & bill) 85.00

Redhead Drake, carved wood, by Edward Gage, 1947 (shot scar) ... 90.00

Shorebird, carved wood, inserted wooden beak, worn original paint, stamped "Mackey Collection," 11¼" h. on contemporary stand 375.00

Swan, carved wood, by Capt. Harry Jobes, 28 x 19" 425.00

Wood Duck Drake

Wood Duck Drake, carved wood, by Elmer Crowell, East Hartwich, Massachusetts (ILLUS.) 25,000.00

Yellowlegs, carved wood, by Ira Hudson, Chincoteague, Virginia ..1,870.00

DISNEY COLLECTIBLES

Davy Crockett Lamp

Scores of objects ranging from watches to dolls have been created in imitation of Walt Disney's copyrighted animated cartoon characters, and an increasing number of collectors are now seeking these, made primarily by licensed manufacturers. Also see BIG LITTLE BOOKS, COMIC BOOKS and CHRISTMAS TREE LIGHTS.

Alice in Wonderland cookie jar, ceramic	$80.00
Alice in Wonderland salt & pepper shakers, pr.	48.00
Bambi animated clock, Bayard, France	185.00
Bambi baby's glider, iron frame w/wooden seat & sides, original painted decor, 32 x 16 x 16"	75.00
Bambi jigsaw puzzle, Jaymar	10.00
Big Bad Wolf sheet music, "Who's Afraid," 1932	12.50
Big Bad Wolf & Three Little Pigs alarm clock, animated, Ingersoll	175.00
Big Bad Wolf & Three Little Pigs pocket watch, die-debossed back "May the Big Bad Wolf Never Come to Your Door - Walt Disney," leather strap w/fob, 1934	325.00
Cinderella costume	30.00
Cinderella figure, chalkware	18.00
Davy Crockett billfold	14.50
Davy Crockett cookie jar	125.00
Davy Crockett hat, coonskin	18.00
Davy Crockett lamp, ceramic base w/figure of Davy & bear by tree, glossy green & brown-toned glaze, Premco Mfg. Co., Chicago, 1955, 8" h. (ILLUS.)	50.00
Davy Crockett mug, Brush pottery	20.00
Davy Crockett pinback button, w/ribbon & miniature gun	10.00
Davy Crockett ring	12.50
Disney characters blocks, wooden, 1940's	50.00

Disney characters book, "Disney's Silly Symphonies," 1930's	18.50
Disney characters book, "Surprise Package," 1948	15.00
Disney characters drum, tin, w/original drumsticks	25.00
Disney characters game, "Remember," 1950's	15.00
Disney characters kaleidoscope, tin & cardboard	30.00
Disney characters pillow, Mickey, Minnie, Donald & Pluto action portraits	22.00
Disney characters tool chest	15.00
Donald Duck "Auto-Magic" projector	65.00
Donald Duck ball, rubber, Sun Rubber Co.	35.00
Donald Duck bank, composition, w/life preserver, Crown Toy Co., ca. 1938, 6" h.	140.00
Donald Duck bank, tin, "First National," semi-mechanical, Chein	95.00
Donald Duck bank, tin, "Second National," semi-mechanical, Chein	75.00
Donald Duck bank, dime register, tin	85.00
Donald Duck book, "Walt Disney Story of Donald Duck," 1938	35.00
Donald Duck bowl, Beetleware, yellow w/raised ABC's	15.00
Donald Duck candy container, papier mache, West Germany	30.00
Donald Duck card game, 1949	18.00
Donald Duck clothes hanger, 1950's	25.00
Donald Duck costume & mask, 1930	200.00
Donald Duck doll, cloth w/composition feet, Knickerbocker Toy Co., original tag, 13"	275.00
Donald Duck feeding dish, 3-compartment, Patriot China, blue, ca. 1940, 8" d.	52.50
Donald Duck figure, bisque, long-billed Donald, 1930's, 1¾" h.	27.50

Donald Duck Handkerchief

Donald Duck handkerchief, cotton,
printed scene of Donald center,
blue border, 8¼" sq. (ILLUS.)..... 12.00
Donald Duck lapel pin, gold-plated
metal & enamel, on original card,
England, 1950's, 2" 20.00
Donald Duck mug, ceramic, Walt
Disney Productions, 1940's 35.00
Donald Duck nodding figure, plastic,
Louis Marx & Co................ 15.00
Donald Duck paint box, Transogram,
1938 .... 30.00
Donald Duck paint box, Walt Disney
Enterprises, 1946 .... 15.00
Donald Duck perfume bottle, glass,
figural, 4" h.................... 40.00
Donald Duck planter, ceramic,
Donald fishing, Walt Disney
Productions, 1930's 30.00
Donald Duck soap figure, Castile
bar marked "Copyright Walt Dis-
ney Enterprises" 55.00
Donald Duck soda straws, "Sun-
shine," in original box 13.50
Donald Duck sprinkling can, tin,
Ohio Art, 1938, 6" h. 45.00
Donald Duck tambourine, tin &
paper, Noble, Cooley 65.00
Donald Duck tape measure,
celluloid...................... 100.00
Donald Duck tea set, tin, Ohio Art,
29 pcs........................ 115.00
Donald Duck toy, pull-type, Donald
w/drum, lithographed paper on
wood, Fisher-Price 22.50
Donald Duck toy, windup tin "Dipsy
Car," Louis Marx & Co. 310.00
Donald Duck toy, windup tin skier .. 175.00
Donald Duck toy, windup "Donald
Duck on Trapeze," celluloid fig-
ure, Line Mar 350.00
Donald Duck & Minnie Mouse carpet
sweeper, tin, red, 1940, 27"...... 87.50
Dumbo the Elephant bank, china,
marked "W. Disney U.S.A.,"
1940's 35.00
Dumbo the Elephant pitcher, ceram-
ic, 6" h. 55.00
Dumbo the Elephant song book,
1941 .... 10.50
Dwarf Bashful doll, composition
head, cloth body, Knickerbocker
Toy Co. 100.00
Dwarf Bashful figure, ceramic, Evan
Shaw, 6¼" h................... 75.00
Dwarf Doc party mask 12.00
Dwarf Dopey bank, painted papier
mache, 7" h................... 40.00
Dwarf Dopey doll, composition
head, cloth body, Knickerbocker
Toy Co., 9" 100.00
Dwarf Dopey lamp, figural Dopey
base, marked "Walt Disney," 1938
(no shade).................... 125.00

Dwarf Grumpy Figure

Dwarf Grumpy figure, rubber
squeezable-type, 8" h. (ILLUS.) ... 18.00
Dwarf Happy figure, hard rubber,
Seiberling 32.50
Dwarf Happy soap figure, copyright
1938, 3" h. 17.50
Dwarf Sleepy figure, bisque, 5" h. .. 32.50
Dwarf Sleepy figure, hard rubber,
Seiberling 35.00
Ferdinand the Bull figure, composi-
tion, marked Knickerbocker 75.00
Ferdinand the Bull figure, composi-
tion, jointed, signed Walt Disney
Enterprises & Ideal .....110.00 to 175.00
Ferdinand the Bull toy, windup tin
Ferdinand & the Matador, Louis
Marx & Co., 1938 .... 100.00
Figaro toy, windup tin, Louis Marx &
Co. 125.00
Goofy doll, stuffed cloth, 11" h. 65.00
Goofy tea tile, ceramic, Goofy the
Gardener scene, 4 x 4".......... 6.00
Goofy wrist watch, Helbros......... 185.00
Goofy & Pluto handkerchief, printed
cotton 15.00
Horace Horsecollar tumbler, clear
glass w/scene of Horace bending
over for coin, 1930's, 3½" h. 20.00
Lady & the Tramp modeling clay 20.00
Lady & the Tramp sheets & pillow
case, boxed set 75.00
Mickey Mouse action figure, "hin-
gie," cardboard, 1940's, original
envelope 25.00
Mickey Mouse ash tray, china,
lustre-glazed finish 45.00
Mickey Mouse baby's rattle, celluloid, 1932 .... 100.00
Mickey Mouse bank, composition,
Mickey w/movable head standing
beside chest, Crown Toy Co.,
1940's, 6¼" h. 135.00

Mickey Mouse bicycle bell, chrome, 1930's 25.00

Mickey Mouse "birthday cake" candle holders, original package 50.00

Mickey Mouse book, "The Adventures of Mickey Mouse Book No. 1," published by David McKay Co., Philadelphia, ca. 1931 .... 100.00

Mickey Mouse book, "Mickey Mouse ABC Story," 1936, published by Whitman Publishing Co. & Walt Disney Enterprises............... 80.00

Mickey Mouse book, "Mickey Mouse Goes Christmas Shopping," Little Golden Book, 1940-50's, 8 x 6" ... 3.75

Mickey Mouse book, "Mickey Mouse the Miracle Maker," 1948 .... 18.00

Mickey Mouse book, "Mickey Never Fails," hardbound, Heath, 1939 ... 40.00

Mickey Mouse book, "Mickey Mouse in Pygmy Land," 1936, Walt Disney Enterprises, 7 1/8 x 9½", 70 pp......................... 65.00

Mickey Mouse book, "Mickey Wins the Race," 1934, Whitman 30.00

Mickey Mouse book, "Silly Symphony Babes in the Woods," pop-up type 75.00

Mickey Mouse bowl, Beetleware, yellow 20.00

Mickey Mouse certificate of merit, "Good Teeth Brigade" 15.00

Mickey Mouse cookie jar, w/birthday cake 55.00

Mickey Mouse crayons w/labels, in original box, 1949 .... 24.00

Mickey Mouse doll, plastic & hard rubber, swivel head, movable arms & legs, Knickerbocker, 3¾" h...................... 29.00

Mickey Mouse doll, stuffed, Steiff, early 1930's, 11½" h............. 400.00

Mickey Mouse drum set, 1950's 90.00

Mickey Mouse feeding dish, Patriot china, 7" d.................... 50.00

Mickey Mouse figure, bisque, marked Walt Disney & Japan, 3" h......................... 48.00

Mickey Mouse figure, rubber, Seiberling, 3" h................ 50.00

Mickey Mouse game, "Coming Home," ca. 1930 .... 28.00

Mickey Mouse game, "Ludo," 1930's 135.00

Mickey Mouse game, "Slugaroo," die-cut cardboard, 6½" h. Mickey batter, 18" of fence, ca. 1950..... 45.00

Mickey Mouse game, "Target," heavy cardboard, Marks Bros., Boston, 10½" d. 95.00

Mickey Mouse gumball machine, by Hamilton Enterprises of Kansas City, Mo., ca. 1938 .... 775.00

Mickey Mouse hair brush, 1930's 30.00

Mickey Mouse Halloween costume, 1934 .... 200.00

Mickey Mouse hand puppet, 1931 ... 125.00

Mickey Mouse handkerchief, printed cotton, 1930's 26.00

Mickey Mouse Headscarf

Mickey Mouse headscarf, printed cotton, colorful figures of Mickey on white, green border, 22" sq. (ILLUS.)....................... 17.50

Mickey Mouse lamp, painted plaster, 7" h. Mickey figure 500.00

Mickey Mouse lapel pin, enameled metal 65.00

Mickey Mouse "Magic Slate," ca. 1939 .... 22.00

Mickey Mouse Movie Projector

Mickey Mouse movie projector, Keystone Mfg. Co., 1930's (ILLUS.).... 250.00

Mickey Mouse mug, silverplate 95.00

Mickey Mouse night light, Walt Disney Enterprises, dated 1939 ...... 110.00

Mickey Mouse paint box, tin, late 1930's 40.00

Mickey Mouse pencil sharpener, celluloid figure of Mickey, 1930's .... 50.00 to 95.00

Mickey Mouse pinback button, advertising Emerson Radios, through special permission of Walt Disney Enterprises, 1930's, 1¼" d. 50.00

Mickey Mouse playing card, marked

Walt Disney Enterprises, 2½ x
1¾" 25.00
Mickey Mouse porringer, silver-
plate ....85.00 to 125.00
Mickey Mouse postcard, early
1930's 20.00
Mickey Mouse recipe book, color
illustrations, 1930's 47.50
Mickey Mouse sand pail, tin, Ohio
Art Co., 1938 ....45.00 to 70.00
Mickey Mouse sheet music, "Mickey
Mouse's Birthday Party," 1936 .... 22.00
Mickey Mouse snow shovel, printed
tin, Walt Disney Enterprises,
28" l. 50.00
Mickey Mouse soap figure,
"Castile," 1932, 5" h. 65.00
Mickey Mouse soda straws, original
box 9.00
Mickey Mouse tambourine, 7" d. ... 15.00
Mickey Mouse tea set: teapot,
creamer, cov. sugar bowl & 3 c/s;
china, tan w/blue lustre trim,
Japan, 9 pcs. 90.00
Mickey Mouse teaspoon, silverplate,
Branford 12.50
Mickey Mouse toy, Mickey on trac-
tor, Sun Rubber Co. 35.00
Mickey Mouse toy "sparkler," hand-
pull spring action, Borgfeldt,
1932 .... 225.00
Mickey Mouse toy wash tub &
board, metal, 1930's 120.00
Mickey Mouse toy, windup tin ferris
wheel w/Disney characters in
seats, Chein, 1950,
17" h. ....175.00 to 250.00
Mickey Mouse toy, windup tin road-
ster, w/original plastic figures of
Mickey, Minnie, Donald & Huey,
Louis Marx & Co. 135.00
Mickey Mouse umbrella, red rayon,
1930's ....45.00 to 75.00
Mickey Mouse vase, figural Mickey
seated on chair, Crown Devon
China, 1930's, 6" h. 200.00
Mickey Mouse viewmaster & film, in
original treasure chest box 115.00
Mickey Mouse wallet, plastic 12.00
Mickey Mouse Club footstool 22.00
Mickey Mouse Club lunch pail &
thermos bottle 16.00
Mickey Mouse Club mug, 1955 ...... 7.00
Mickey Mouse Club pinback button,
3½" 8.00
Mickey Mouse Club ring, 1950's 8.00
Mickey Mouse Club TV tray, "Fun
Tray," 1960's, 20½ x 15" 30.00
Mickey & Minnie Mouse cookie jar,
"turnabout" ....50.00 to 75.00
Mickey & Minnie Mouse toothbrush
holder, bisque, names impressed
on back, 1930's, 1¾ x 3½ x
4½" 150.00

Mickey, Minnie & Donald Hooked Rug

Mickey, Minnie & Donald hooked
rug, 1930's, 36 x 22" (ILLUS.) 300.00
Mickey Mouse & Pluto mug, Patriot
china 45.00
Minnie Mouse cookie cutter, tin 16.00
Minnie Mouse figure, bisque, Minnie
carrying purse & umbrella, 4" h. .. 65.00
Minnie Mouse fork & spoon, sterling
silver, pie-eyed, cut-out handles,
International Sterling,
pr. ....85.00 to 125.00
Minnie Mouse handkerchief, printed
cotton, Minnie serving tea,
8½" sq. 8.00
Minnie Mouse lapel pin, enameled
metal, 1930's 18.00
Minnie Mouse pencil sharpener 25.00
Minnie Mouse plate, Bavarian china,
Minnie playing coronet & chased
by 2 cars decor, 1930's, 6" d. 50.00
Minnie Mouse toy nurse kit 25.00
Peter Pan belt, on original card 35.00
Peter Pan game, Walt Disney
Productions, 1953 .... 15.00

Pinocchio Metal Bank

Pinocchio bank, electroplated pot
metal, 6" h. (ILLUS.) 35.00
Pinocchio book, "Pinocchio's Christmas Party," 1939, premium for
Bloomingdale's Toy Department .. 18.00
Pinocchio celluloid, w/donkey ears
underwater surrounded by sea-
horses, applied to airbrushed
background, 1939, 7¾" d.
(ILLUS.) 2,970.00

Pinocchio Movie Cel

Pinocchio doll, jointed, original
  clothes, by Knickerbocker, 8½" ..   45.00
Pinocchio figure, wood, Multi-Wood
  Products, 1940's, 5" h. 40.00
Pinocchio harmonica..............   6.50
Pinocchio paint book, Whitman
  No. 573, Walt Disney Productions,
  1939, 11 x 15" 55.00
Pinocchio pencil sharpener, green
  celluloid w/decal, 1½" h.........   22.00
Pinocchio salt & pepper shakers,
  5" h., pr. 75.00
Pinocchio toy, wind-up tin "Pinocchio
  the Acrobat," Louis Marx & Co.,
  1939 .... 155.00
Pluto bank, plastic, w/beanie cap,
  1950's 10.00
Pluto book, "Pluto the Pup," Walt
  Disney Enterprises, 1937 ....   28.00
Pluto cookie jar, "turnabout" 49.00
Pluto figure, rubber, 3" h. 18.00
Pluto puppet, Walt Disney
  Productions 15.00
Pluto "push-tail" scooter, Louis Marx
  & Co. 110.00
Pluto toy, friction-type, Line Mar,
  marked "W.D.P." 20.00
Pluto toy, string operated, Fisher
  Price 50.00
Pluto toy, wooden stand-up type on
  paddle 35.00
Pollyanna doll, original dress, 29" ..   70.00
Silly Symphonies book, pop-up type,
  1933 .... 125.00
Snow White animated alarm clock,
  Bayard, France................. 105.00
Snow White bank, ceramic 20.00
Snow White billfold, 1937 ....   20.00
Snow White book, linen, 1938,
  12 pp.........................   21.00
Snow White brush & mirror, boxed
  set...........................   50.00
Snow White candy container, glitter
  covered papier-mache, Walt Dis-
  ney Productions 28.00

Snow White celluloid, Snow White
  w/two sleeping deer, applied to
  airbrushed ground, Walt Disney
  Enterprises, 1937, 6½ x 8¾" 1,430.00
Snow White Christmas tree lights,
  Noma, boxed set...............   95.00
Snow White coloring book, original
  box, 1938, 40 pp. 32.00
Snow White "Dairy Recipes," 1955 ..   7.00

Snow White Cut-Out Figure

Snow White cut-out figure, paper,
  Walt Disney Enterprises, 1938
  (ILLUS.).......................   8.00
Snow White doll, composition, mold-
  ed hair w/blue ribbon, Knickerbocker Toy, 12" 190.00
Snow White doll, cloth body, white
  mask face, 7 Dwarfs on skirt,
  16" 125.00
Snow White doll, composition shoul-
  der plate head, cloth body, com-
  position arms & legs, Ideal, 19" .. 100.00
Snow White drum 37.00
Snow White figure, bisque,
  3½" h. 30.00
Snow White figure, ceramic, Ameri-
  can Pottery, 9" h. 165.00
Snow White figure, composition,
  dressed, 13" h. 150.00
Snow White handkerchief 8.00
Snow White ironing board,
  lithographed tin, Wolverine 30.00
Snow White jigsaw puzzle, 1938 ....   35.00
Snow White kitchen appliances:
  refrigerator, sink & stove; Wolver-
  ine, original box, 3 pcs. 100.00
Snow White lamp, Modeware, Walt
  Disney Enterprises...............   82.00
Snow White lunch pail w/thermos ..   52.00
Snow White paper doll, 1938,
  w/box, cut 80.00
Snow White pencil sharpener, cel-
  luloid, Snow White playing
  mandolin 34.00
Snow White playing cards, minia-
  ture, w/box 95.00

Snow White rug, 1930's, 40 x 22" ... 20.00
Snow White sand pail 35.00
Snow White soap figure, Lightfoot
   Schultz Co., 1938 .... 125.00
Snow White sprinkling can, Ohio
   Art, Walt Disney Enterprises,
   1938 .... 45.00
Snow White teapot, pottery, musi-
   cal, plays "Hi Ho, Hi Ho," Walt
   Disney Productions, late 1930's ... 185.00
Snow White toothbrush holder,
   6" h. 69.00
Snow White top, Chein 43.00
Snow White valentine, pull-tab, Walt
   Disney Enterprises, 1938 .... 15.00
Snow White wrist watch, 1st model
   w/Snow White curtsying 225.00
Snow White wrist watch, 1950's 30.00
Snow White & the Seven Dwarfs
   bake set, w/original box 45.00
Snow White & the Seven Dwarfs
   book, "Snow White & the 7
   Dwarfs," Whitman, 1938 .... 22.00
Snow White & the Seven Dwarfs but-
   tons, 3½" d., set of 8 .... 50.00
Snow White & the Seven Dwarfs
   desk set: 12½ x 19½" desk pad,
   calendar, ink blotter, letter opener & inkwell; Staco, original box,
   1938 .... 600.00

Snow White & the Seven Dwarfs Figures

Snow White & the Seven Dwarfs
   figures, metal, Britains set
   No. 1654, set of 8 (ILLUS.) 1,320.00
Snow White & the Seven Dwarfs
   figures, rubber, Sieberling, set of
   8 .... 243.00
Snow White & the Seven Dwarfs
   game, board-type, Walt Disney
   Enterprises, 1937 .... 120.00
Snow White & the Seven Dwarfs
   poster, cardboard, advertising Armour & Company ham, full color,
   1937, 36 x 30" 95.00
Snow White & the Seven Dwarfs radio, cream colored cottage
   w/molded figures of Snow White
   & the Seven Dwarfs, Emerson,
   7¼" w., 7½" h. 750.00
Snow White & the Seven Dwarfs
   sheet music, "Some Day My
   Prince Will Come" 20.00
Snow White & the Seven Dwarfs
   souvenir album, songs by Irving

Berlin, 14 full page illustrations,
   1937, 9 x 12" 40.00
Snow White & the Seven Dwarfs
   stamp set, w/box, 1937 .... 40.00
Snow White & the Seven Dwarfs
   tumbler, glass, 1938 .... 20.00
Three Caballeros book, "The 3
   Caballeros," 1944 .... 38.00
Three Little Pigs alarm clock,
   Ingersoll 350.00
Three Little Pigs bank, tin, Chein,
   3" h. 35.00
Three Little Pigs cup, Patriot
   China 20.00
Three Little Pigs vase, bud,
   silverplate 55.00
Thumper (from Bambi) cookie jar,
   ceramic 70.00
Zorro wrist watch, original band,
   Walt Disney Productions 17.50

DOLL FURNITURE & ACCESSORIES

Brass Coal Bucket

Bassinet, wicker, 8 x 6½" $35.00
Bed, cast iron, 14" l. 55.00
Bed, walnut, turned posts, elaborate
   headboard, "alligatored" varnish
   finish, w/bedding, 12¾ x 7¾",
   13½" h. 370.00
Bed, wooden, Mission-style, w/mat-
   tress, pillows, linens & crocheted
   coverlet 80.00
Buggy, metal, red paint, "Gendron,"
   24 x 22" 45.00
Buggy, tin, pink & blue w/bears
   decor, Ohio Art 40.00
Cake pan, graniteware, blue &
   white marbleized 35.00
Candlesticks, pressed glass, Patrician patt., clear, Heisey, pr. 75.00
Candlesticks, pressed glass, Tom
   Thumb patt., clear, Heisey, pr. ... 95.00
Canister set & cake box, printed tin,
   Dutch scenes around sides, Wol-
   verine, 5 pcs. 50.00

Carriage, wicker, woven open latticework sides, wooden spoke
wheels w/metal rims, 28″ l....... 225.00
Chair, wicker, 8″ h. 35.00
Chamber pot, yellowware w/white
band decor 47.00
Chest of drawers, walnut & cherrywood, oblong top above 2 short &
2 long drawers, scalloped apron
continuing to bracket feet, turned
wood pulls, 17¾″ w., 13 3/8″
deep, 16½″ h. (refinished) 250.00
Chest of drawers w/mirror, Victorian, Eastlake substyle, oak, tall
mirror plate flanked by candle
shelves over chest w/three long
drawers, ca. 1870, 21″ h. 185.00
Coal bucket, brass, ca. 1890, 3″ l.
(ILLUS.)........................ 12.00
Coffee pot w/tin lid, granitware,
grey mottled................... 37.50
Cooking set: 3 blue & white mixing
bowls (1 impressed "Weller") & 5
utensils w/blue & white handles;
in original box labeled "Mother's
Little Helper," dated 1923,
8 pcs. 145.00
Cradle, low country-style on rockers, pine & poplar, heart-shaped
headboard, tombstone-type footboard, shaped canted sides,
shaped rockers, square nail construction, old blue paint,
26″ l. 175.00
Cradle, low country-style on rockers, wooden, rounded head &
footboards, shaped canted sides,
oak-grained painted finish w/red
& black striping 195.00
Crib, folding-type, oak, spindle
sides........................... 50.00
Cupboard, pine, porcelain knobs,
old dark finish w/red on sides &
top, 13¾ x 7″, 18¼″ h.......... 135.00

Pine Cupboard

Cupboard, pine, open top w/one
shelf above board-and-batten cupboard door in base, cut-out feet,
17¾ x 7″, 36½″ h. (ILLUS.)...... 200.00
Doll house, wooden, Schoenhut,
2-story, 4 rooms & attic, painted
yellow w/red shingled roof,
covered porch & green-shuttered
windows, front opening, original
decal on base, 19 x 12″,
18″ h.......................... 440.00

Colonial-style Doll House

Doll house, 7-room Colonial-style
w/clapboard siding, double-hung
latticed windows, columned portico, side sunroom & porch, hall-
ways, central staircase & some
built-in furnishings, front & back
opening, white w/green trim,
1930's, 48 x 22″, 28″ h. (ILLUS.) ..1,650.00
Doll house, lithographed tin, 7
rooms & patio, 36″ l. 40.00
Doll house, Mattel, "Barbie's Dream
House," 1962 .... 32.50
Doll house, Tudor-style, plaster
w/wood paneling, glassine windows, fitted stairway, mantel &
bookcases, 1920's 275.00
Doll house bathtub, metal, pink,
Renwal......................... 8.00
Doll house crib, metal, Renwal 10.00
Doll house living room furniture:
couch, 4 chairs, table w/checker-
board game top & upright piano;
Bliss-type, 7 pcs. 245.00
Doll house playpen, metal,
Renwal......................... 9.00
Doll house radio, console model,
diecast metal & tin, 3″ h. 25.00
Doll house telephone, metal, pink,
Renwal......................... 8.00
Egg beater, "A&J," 1923 .... 18.00
Egg beater, tin w/wooden
handle ....14.00 to 20.00
Fainting couch, gold velvet uphol-
stery, 30½ x 13″ 200.00
Fairy lamp, green satin glass shade
w/enameled florals, clear glass
base, 1½″ h. 110.00
Food chopper, "Rollman No. 21".... 45.00
Highchair, Victorian, Eastlake sub-
style, fruitwood, bamboo-turned,
cane seat (ILLUS.) 200.00

Victorian Highchair

Highchair, wicker 45.00
Ice cream parlor set, table & 4 bent
iron wire chairs, ca. 1890,
5 pcs. 250.00
Ironing board, lithographed tin,
Snow White & 7 Dwarfs decor 20.00
Kitchen cabinet, tin, "Wolverine,"
w/fifteen cardboard food product
boxes, 14" w., 13½" h. 65.00
Kitchen set: sink, stove & refrigerator; tin, "Wolverine," 12" h.,
3 pcs. 17.00
Living room suite: sofa, table & 3
chairs; upholstered, Victorian,
5 pcs. 125.00
Meat grinder, cast iron, "Pony" 40.00
Parlor (or porch) suite: settee & pr.
armchairs; woven wicker & China
seagrass, 8" h. chairs, late
19th c., 3 pcs. 175.00
Potato masher, wooden, 3" l. 6.00
Purse, metal mesh, w/chain handle,
3 x 2" 18.00
Quilt, pierced Log Cabin patt., 4
rows of 4 radiating square & diamond motifs in blue, black, brown
& printed patches within embroidered turkey stitch borders, red
piping, late 19th c., 13 5/8" sq.... 110.00
Refrigerator, tin, "Wizard" 30.00
Roaster, aluminum, oval 9.00
Rolling pin, china, Blue Onion patt.
transfer, wooden handles 180.00
Sad iron, "Dover No. 602" 39.00
Sad iron w/bentwood handle & triv-
et, "Williams," 4", 2 pcs. 45.00
Salt box, hanging-type, blue
graniteware 60.00
Table, drop-leaf, walnut 85.00
Tea kettle w/swing lid & porcelain
knob, cast iron, "Griswold" 95.00
Tea kettle, cov., copper 10.00
Tray, wooden, 2-handled, painted
red, 6½ x 3½" 15.00
Trunk, wooden, dome-top, w/inside
tray, 12" l. 85.00
Tumblers, clear glass, 1½" h., set of
4 .... 20.00
Waffle iron, cast iron, "Arcade" 55.00

Waffle iron, cast iron, "Stover Jr." .. 150.00
Wash basin, graniteware, turquoise
blue, 5" d...................... 65.00
Wash board, glass, "Crystal" 15.00
Wash board, pine w/corrugated
scrub surface one side, "Little
Darling No. 818," 7" w., 15" h. 16.00

DOLLS

Madame Alexander's Little Women

*Also see DISNEY COLLECTIBLES,
KEWPIE COLLECTIBLES, PAPER
DOLLS and PIN CUSHION DOLLS.*

A.B.G. (Alt, Beck & Gottschalk)
bisque socket head character girl
marked "1361," blue glass sleep
eyes, pierced nostrils, dark brown
h.h. (human hair) wig in braids,
composition toddler body,
dressed, 27" $690.00
Alexander (Madame) Dionne Quintuplets, all composition, brown
sleep eyes, molded & painted
brown hair, 7½", set of 5 in original crib 950.00
Alexander (Madame) Little Women,
Meg, Jo, Marme, Beth & Amy,
hard plastic, ca. 1950, dressed,
14", set of 5 (ILLUS.)............ 750.00
Alexander (Madame) Little Genius,
composition head, brown sleep
eyes, molded & painted hair, cloth
body w/composition arms & legs,
1937, dressed, 18".............. 65.00
Alexander (Madame) Alice in Won-
derland, cloth, early construction
w/mask-type face & oil-painted
features on head jointed to turn,
pink cotton body w/limbs sewn
on, blonde wig, ca. 1930, dressed,
20" 650.00

Alexander (Madame) Jane Withers,
all composition, blue sleep eyes,
closed mouth, 1937, dressed,
21" 900.00

Alexander (Madame) Melanie, hard
plastic, sleep eyes, ash blonde
wig, 1971, dressed in original
ivory ball gown w/layers of ruf-
fles, 21" 1,100.00

Alexander (Madame) Cissy, hard
plastic body w/vinyl over plastic
limbs, blue sleep eyes, brown
h.h. wig, 1952, dressed 165.00

Bisque Head Babies

"Googlies"

A.M. (Armand Marseille) bisque
socket head "googlie" boy, painted "googlie" eyes, molded &
painted hair, watermelon smile,
ball-jointed composition body,
dressed, 7½" (ILLUS. right) 300.00

A.M. bisque solid dome socket head
baby marked "A.M. Kiddie Joy,"
blue glass sleep eyes, "pouty"
baby mouth, molded & painted
hair, cloth body, composition legs
& arms, celluloid hands, dressed,
13" 250.00

A.M. bisque socket head baby
marked "341," called "My Dream
Baby" (copyrighted by Arranbee
Doll Co. in the United States in
1925), blue glass sleep eyes,
closed mouth, molded hair, jointed composition body, composition
hands, dressed, 16" 395.00

A.M. bisque socket head girl
marked "390," blue glass stationary eyes, open mouth w/teeth,
mohair wig, jointed composition
body, dressed, 16" 225.00

A.M. bisque socket head character
baby marked "A.M. 518 10K,"
blue glass sleep eyes, open

mouth w/teeth, molded hair, ball-
jointed composition body w/bent
limbs, dressed, 18" head circumference (ILLUS. rear)............ 700.00

A.M. bisque socket head girl
marked "985," blue glass sleep
eyes, open mouth w/two teeth &
dimples, ball-jointed composition
body w/bent limbs, dressed,
18" 265.00

A.M. bisque socket head "breather"
baby marked "996," blue glass
sleep eyes, open-closed mouth
w/two teeth, double chin, ball-
jointed composition body,
dressed, 21" 600.00

A.M. bisque solid dome socket head
girl marked "351," blue glass
sleep eyes, open mouth
w/tongue, composition chest &
arms, remainder of body is cloth,
dressed, 26" 595.00

A.M. bisque socket head girl
marked "390 D.R.G.M. 246/1 Germany," blue glass sleep eyes,
blonde h.h. wig, ball-jointed composition body, dressed, 28" 475.00

A.M. bisque socket head girl
marked "Germany 390 A 12 M,"
brown glass stationary eyes, long
brown h.h. wig, ball-jointed composition body, dressed, 30" 825.00

A.M. bisque socket head character
baby marked "990," blue glass
sleep eyes, open mouth, chubby
ball-jointed composition body
w/bent limbs, dressed, 30" 1,200.00

Amberg (Louis & Son) composition
head boy, painted eyes, smiling
mouth, molded blonde hair, original cloth body, dated 1912,
dressed 225.00

American Character "Sweet Sue,"
hard plastic, 1955, dressed, 21"... 125.00

Amosandra, all rubber, molded features, painted hair & eyes, hole in

mouth for bottle, movable arms & legs, squeaker in stomach, Sun Rubber Company, designed by Ruth E. Newton, Barberton, Ohio, ca. 1949, w/birth certificate, dressed, 10" 100.00

Arranbee "Little Angel," hard plastic head, blue sleep eyes w/lashes, closed mouth, molded & painted hair, stuffed pink cotton body w/soft vinyl arms & legs, 1947-52, dressed, 21" 70.00

Baby Phyllis (Armand Marseille) bisque head w/flanged neck, blue glass sleep eyes, closed mouth, molded & painted hair, cloth body, dressed, 13" (ILLUS. front) 275.00

Barbie No. 4, blonde bubble cut hairstyle, No. 850, 1962...90.00 to 150.00

Barbie "Fashion Queen," No. 870, 1963, w/only one extra wig, wearing Roman Holiday outfit No. 968 .... 55.00

Bed doll, composition head, red mohair wig, original dress & bonnet, 25" 50.00

Belton-Type Girl

Belton-type bisque head girl, brown glass stationary paperweight eyes, closed mouth, pierced ears, blonde h.h. wig, gusseted kid body, dressed, 10½" (ILLUS.) 850.00

Belton-type bisque head girl, blue glass bulgy paperweight stationary eyes, closed mouth, brown h.h. curly wig, original ball-jointed composition body, straight wrists, dressed but no shoes, 12½" 850.00

Belton-type bisque head girl, blue threaded glass paperweight eyes, outlined closed mouth, pierced ears, gusseted kid body, dressed, 20" 770.00

Biedermeier-type china head lady, painted blue eyes, red eyelines, bald head w/mohair wig, leather body w/china limbs, dressed, 15½" 750.00

Bisque head girl marked "E.D." (E. Denamur), blue glass stationary eyes, open mouth w/upper row of teeth, brown h.h. wig, jointed composition body, straight wrists, dressed, 11½" 550.00

Bisque head 3-face girl marked "C.B." (Carl Bergner), sleeping face, crying face w/brown glass stationary eyes, molded tears & open-closed mouth, smiling face w/brown glass stationary eyes, original cloth-covered body, jointed composition arms & legs, 12" 1,250.00

Bisque head two-faced girl (probably Fritz Bartenstein), one face w/blue paperweight glass eyes & open mouth w/inset teeth, other face crying & w/blue paperweight eyes & open mouth w/molded tongue, cloth body, w/crying voicebox, dressed, 19" 825.00

Bisque head boy marked "L.A.S." (Louis Amberg & Son - American doll importing firm), intaglio blue eyes, open-closed smiling mouth, molded blonde hair, cloth body, celluloid forearms, dressed, 20" .. 195.00

Bisque head clown marked "K. & W. 155/13" (Koenig & Wernicke, Germany, 1912-57), white bisque head w/red & blue markings, blue glass eyes, 5-piece toddler body, dressed, 21" 850.00

French Bisque Doll

Bisque swivel head girl marked
"A.T." (A. Thuillier), blue paperweight glass eyes, closed mouth,
pierced ears, mohair wig, dress-
ed, ca. 1875 (ILLUS.) 16,000.00
Bisque head girl marked "IB's RD
(Rabery & Delphieu), blue paperweight glass eyes, outlined closed
mouth, pierced ears, ball-jointed
composition body, dressed,
21½" 1,430.00
Bisque head girl marked "F.G."
(F. Gaultier) in scroll, blue paperweight stationary glass eyes,
closed mouth, pierced ears, brown
h.h. wig, ball-jointed composition
body, jointed wrists, dressed,
23½" 2,800.00
Bisque head girl marked "M.B. Japan" (Morimura Brothers, Japan),
blue glass sleep eyes, open
mouth, original h.h. wig, jointed
composition body, dressed,
23½" 300.00

Bru Negro Girl

seted & jointed kid body, bisque
forearms, dressed (ILLUS.) 23,000.00
Buddy Lee, trademark doll for H.D.
Lee Co., composition, dressed in
railroad engineer overalls, w/cap,
14" .... 135.00 to 165.00
Bye-lo Baby twins, bisque heads
marked "Grace S. Putnam," blue-
grey glass sleep eyes, cloth body,
celluloid hands, dressed, 10" head
circumference, pr. 1,200.00
Bye-lo Baby, bisque head marked
"Grace S. Putnam," blue glass
eyes, cloth body, celluloid hands,
dressed, 15" head circum-
ference .... 700.00 to 950.00

Mulatto Girl

Bisque head mulatto girl marked
"DEP 247 Germany," rich brown
complexion tones, brown glass
sleep eyes, original wig, dressed,
24" (ILLUS.) 525.00
Bru bisque swivel head girl marked
"Bru Jne-5," blue paperweight
glass eyes, open-closed mouth,
pierced ears, kid body w/wooden
legs & bisque forearms, dressed,
17½" 9,350.00
Bru bisque swivel head Negro girl,
dark rich complexion, amber
paperweight glass eyes, open-
closed mouth, pierced ears, gus-

Rag-Stuffed Campbell Kid

Campbell Kid, cloth, rag-stuffed
body, printed features, yellow
yarn hair, dressed, 16" (ILLUS.) ... 25.00
Campbell Kid, composition head, tin
sleep eyes, cloth body, composition arms & legs, dressed,
13½" 275.00

"Peanut" Doll

Celluloid "peanut-sized" doll in celluloid peanut, overall 4½" l.
(ILLUS.)..................20.00 to 40.00
Celluloid head girl, molded hair
w/red head band, cloth body,
dressed as Norwegian skier w/ski
poles & leather boots, 11" 50.00
Celluloid head baby, blue glass
eyes, cloth body, dressed, 11"
head circumference 225.00

Chad Valley Royal Family

Chad Valley (Johnson Bros. Ltd., Birmingham, England - before 1923)
Royal Family, pressed felt faces,
plush velvet bodies, mohair wigs,
authentically copied garments:
Princess Elizabeth (ILLUS. rear
left), 1,200.00; Princess Margaret
Rose (ILLUS. rear right), 1,150.00;
Duchess & Duke of Kent, each
(ILLUS. front)................... 800.00
Charlie McCarthy, composition head,
excelsior-stuffed cloth body,
dressed 85.00
Chase (Martha) stockinette baby,
molded head & face w/h.p. features & brown eyes, pink sateen
cloth body, dressed, 16" 675.00
Chase (Martha) stockinette boy,
molded & h.p. head & features,
sateen cloth body, dressed, 28" .. 785.00
China head lady, pink lustre, molded & painted covered wagon hairstyle & painted brown eyes & red
eyelines, wooden body, china
limbs, dressed, 6".............. 695.00
China head lady, molded & painted
black common hairstyle w/name
"Mabel" molded in china shoul-
derplate, cloth body w/china
limbs, dressed, 11"............. 155.00
China head lady, molded black hair
w/center part & short vertical
curls, (new) cloth body & china
limbs, dressed, 18½"........... 175.00

China Head "Marion"

China head lady, molded & painted
black common hairstyle w/name
"Marion" molded in china shoul-
derplate, painted blue eyes & red
eyelines, cloth body w/china
limbs, dressed, 21½" (ILLUS.) 200.00
China head lady, molded & painted

black "flat-top" hair style, painted brown eyes, red eyelines & blushed "apple" cheeks, original leather body & leather hands, 1860's, dressed, 22" 485.00

Composition Negro girl, painted features w/eyes to the right, molded hair, jointed arms, dressed in coveralls, 11" 47.00

Composition head Negro Mammy, brown cloth body, composition hands & feet, attributed to Tony Sarg, original clothes, 18" 735.00

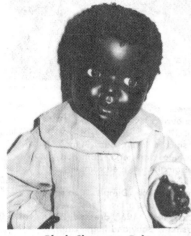

Black Character Baby

Composition head Negro character baby, dressed, 24" (ILLUS.) 475.00

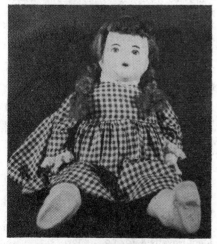

Composition Doll

Composition girl, grey glass sleep eyes, strawberry blonde h.h. wig, cloth body w/composition arms & legs, dressed, 24" (ILLUS.) 85.00

Denny Dimwit (from Winnie Winkle) "swing & sway" type, composition,

3-section head, body & legs hinged on inside, by Wondercraft Co., 11" 55.00

Effanbee "Candy Kid" (girl), composition, 1946, dressed, 12½" 155.00

Effanbee "Baby Grumpy," composition head, cloth body, dressed, 16" 165.00

Effanbee "Ann Shirley," composition, dressed as drum majorette w/baton, 18" 175.00

Effanbee "Bubbles," composition, straight leg, dressed, 28" 295.00

Florodora (Armand Marseille) bisque shoulder head girl marked "A 8/0 Made in Germany," sleep eyes, kid body, riveted joints, dressed, 13" 145.00

Foxy Grandpa, printed & stuffed cloth, 2-sided printed doll w/eyeglasses, bow tie, vest, suit & spats, 11¼" 45.00

French Fashion, bisque head, pale blue stationary glass eyes, smiling mouth, pierced ears, blonde mohair wig, kid body, articulated wooden arms, dressed, 13" 1,210.00

French Fashion, bisque shoulder head attributed to A. Dehors, "brevete" signed unique body style w/patent date of 1866, dressed, 14" 3,800.00

French Fashion, china shoulder head signed Rohmer, blue stationary glass eyes, leather body, dressed, 1857-80, 16" 4,500.00

Frozen Charlie, grey-tinted molded boy's hair-style, painted blue eyes & blushed cheeks, 11" 285.00

Fulper Pottery bisque socket head girl, blue glass sleep eyes, balljointed composition body, original clothes, 18" 450.00

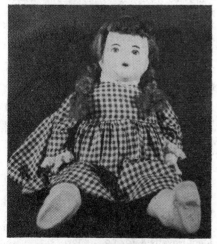

"Bonnie Babe"

Georgene Averill bisque head "Bonnie Babe," flange neck, brown glass sleep eyes, open mouth

w/two lower teeth, molded &
painted hair, cloth body jointed at
shoulders & hips, rubber arms &
legs, ca. 1920, dressed, 15" head
circumference (ILLUS.) 975.00
G.I. Joe, all plastic w/vinyl head,
painted features, ball & pin jointed at neck, shoulders, mid biceps,
elbow, wrist, waist, hip, knees &
ankles, marked "GI Joe TM, Copyright 1964, Hasbro, Patent Pend-
ing, Made In USA," dressed,
11½" 48.00

Grace Corry Rockwell Boy

Grace Corry Rockwell signed composition head boy, dressed
(ILLUS.)...................... 450.00
Handwerck (Max) bisque socket
head girl marked "2½," brown
glass eyes, pierced ears, brown
h.h. wig, dressed, 19" 315.00
Handwerck (Max) bisque shoulder
head girl marked "139," brown
glass eyes, new cloth body,
dressed, 28" 300.00
Heubach (Ernst) - Koppelsdorf
bisque socket head baby girl
marked "300," brown glass sleep
eyes, open mouth w/two upper
teeth, brown h.h. wig, curved
limb composition body, dressed,
10" 275.00
Heubach (Gebruder) bisque socket
head "googlie" girl, "googlie"
sleep eyes, watermelon smile,
mohair wig in braids, papier
mache body & limbs w/molded
shoes, dressed, 9" (ILLUS. w/A.M.
"Googlie" at left) 650.00
Heubach (Gebruder) bisque shoulder
head character girl, blue sleep

Heubach Girl

eyes, "pouty" mouth, original
auburn h.h. wig, dressed, 19"
(ILLUS.) 1,950.00
Horsman colored "Baby Bumps,"
composition head, cloth body,
original checkered romper suit,
12" 150.00
Horsman "Baby Dimples," composition head & arms, sleep eyes,
cloth body, 1927, dressed, 22" 175.00
Horsman "Babyland Rag," cloth,
lithographed face, blonde wavy
hair, brown eyes, closed mouth,
body jointed at shoulders & hips,
dressed, 14½" 495.00
Horsman "Campbell Kid," jointed
composition body, dressed, 12" ... 180.00
Horsman "Ella Cinders," composition
head, arms & legs, molded black
hair, painted blue eyes & freckles,
cloth body, dressed, 18" 295.00
Horsman "HeBee-SheBee" (doll
based on illustrations by Charles
Twelvetrees), composition, 11" ... 275.00
Horsman "Poor Pitiful Pearl," vinyl
head, plastic body, dressed 58.00
Horsman "Rosebud," composition
head, blue tin eyes, original h.h.
wig, cloth body, composition arms
& legs, dressed, 19" 175.00
Howdy Doody, composition head,
stuffed cloth body 145.00
Hummel boy & girl, rubber, original
clothes except shoes, pr. 300.00
Ideal Novelty & Toy Co., "Baby
Snooks," composition head &
hands, wooden torso, wire limbs,
dressed, 12" 160.00
Ideal Novelty & Toy Co. "Deanna
Durbin," composition, painted
eyes, original wig, original dress,
21" 275.00

Ideal Novelty & Toy Co. "Dorothy" from the Wizard of Oz, composition, dressed, 16" 850.00

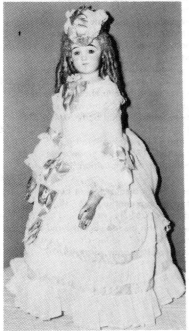

Jumeau Bisque Head Girl

Jumeau bisque head girl, blue paperweight eyes, outlined closed mouth, applied pierced ears, blonde h.h. wig, dressed (ILLUS.) 5,000.00

Jumeau bisque head girl marked "9," brown paperweight eyes, outlined closed mouth, applied pierced ears, brown h.h. wig, ball-jointed wood & composition body, dressed, 20" 4,675.00

Jutta Shoulder Head Girl

Jutta bisque shoulder head girl (produced by Cuno & Otto Dressel using Simon & Halbig or Ernst Heubach heads), ball-jointed composition body, dressed, 34" (ILLUS.) 975.00

K (star) R (Kammer & Reinhardt) bisque head character girl known as "Marie" marked "101," painted blue eyes, closed mouth, blonde mohair wig, jointed composition body, dressed, 7½" 825.00

K (star) R bisque head character known as "Hilda" marked "117," glass sleep, closed mouth, jointed composition body, jointed wrists, dressed, 17" 2,970.00

"Moritz"

K (star) R bisque socket head character known as "Moritz" marked "124," brown "flirty" eyes, closed "watermelon" mouth, w/dimples, ball-jointed wood & composition body, straight wrists, dressed, 17" (ILLUS.) 8,500.00

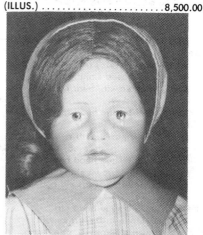

"Gretchen"

K (star) R bisque head girl known as "Gretchen" marked "114," painted intaglio eyes, closed mouth, h.h. wig, ball-jointed composition body, dressed, 19" (ILLUS.) 3,700.00

K (star) R bisque socket head girl known as "Mein Liebling" marked "117," blue sleep eyes, closed "pouty" mouth, original h.h. wig, dressed, 20"..............4,500.00

K (star) R bisque socket head baby known as "Kaiser Baby" marked "100," blue-painted intaglio eyes, open-closed mouth, molded & painted hair, 5-piece composition body, dressed, 20".....660.00 to 1,000.00

K (star) R - Simon & Halbig bisque socket head baby marked "126," blue glass "flirty" eyes, open mouth w/two upper teeth, h.h. wig, composition toddler body, dressed, 30" 2,700.00

Kamkins girl, cloth, painted deep blue eyes w/dot pupils & arched eyebrows, closed red mouth w/full lower lip, pug nose, brown curly h.h. wig w/center part & red ribbons, body w/seams down legs & arms, flexible limbs, stitched fingers, Louise Kampes, Atlantic City, New Jersey, 1919-25, dressed, 18" 700.00

Kathe Kruse girl (Schlenkerchen Model II), molded muslin, painted brown eyes, open-closed smiling mouth, painted brown hair, early 1920's, dressed, 13"............1,980.00

Kathe Kruse girl, molded muslin, painted brown eyes, open-closed smiling mouth, painted brown hair, dressed, 20" ....950.00 to 1,200.00

Ken, No. 1 (750 stock number), hard plastic, blue eyes, brunette flocked crew-cut hair, hollow torso marked "Ken T.M. Pats. Pend. MCMLX by Mattel, Inc.," 1961, dressed, 12" ....35.00 to 70.00

Kestner (J.D.) bisque head character baby marked "152," grey sleep eyes, open-closed smiling mouth, blonde mohair wig, bent limb body, dressed, 9½" 165.00

Kestner (J.D.) bisque head toddler marked "21/JDK Sammy," blue sleep eyes, open mouth w/wobbly tongue, h.h. wig, dressed, 13" ... 495.00

Kestner (J.D.) bisque head boy marked "148," brown stationary eyes, original h.h. wig, kid body, dressed, 16" 375.00

Kestner (J.D.) bisque head girl marked "Made in D Germany 8 162," brown sleep eyes, open mouth w/teeth, ball-jointed wood

& composition body, dressed, 17" 715.00

Kestner (J.D.) bisque head baby marked "211," blue "flirty" sleep eyes, open-closed mouth, original blonde mohair wig, bent limb body, dressed, 19" 825.00

Kestner (J.D.) bisque head girl marked "1070 Hilda," blue eyes, molded hair, dressed, 22" 3,200.00

Kestner (J.D.) bisque shoulder head girl marked "154," brown sleep eyes, gusseted kid body, dressed, 25" 395.00

Kestner (J.D.) bisque head girl marked "171," blue sleep eyes, ball-jointed composition body, dressed, 27" 700.00

Kley & Hahn bisque socket head toddler boy marked "167 15," dressed, 26" 700.00

Kley & Hahn bisque socket head girl marked "167," open-closed mouth, composition body, dressed, 28" ... 800.00

Lenci Felt Dolls

Lenci girl (Model 110/57), felt, hair in braided coils at the ears, ca. 1930, dressed & holding a doll, 17" (ILLUS. left) 990.00

Lenci girl, felt, brown "flirty" glass eyes, blonde hair, ca. 1930, dressed & w/matching pocketbook, 20"........................2,750.00

Lenci girl (Model 109), felt, hair in braided coils at the ears, ca. 1925, dressed, 22" (ILLUS. right) .. 825.00

Lenci girl (Model 187), felt, hair in long braids, ca. 1925, dressed in Russian costume, 39" 1,045.00

Liberty of London cloth "Speaker of the House of Commons," w/wrist tag, 1930's, original clothes, 9½" 30.00

Minerva tin head girl, blue glass
eyes, closed mouth, molded hair,
kid leather body, arms & legs,
original clothes, 11" 225.00

Pierrot Musical Automaton

Musical automaton of a Pierrot playing a violin, turning & nodding his
head (eye mechanism inoperative),
bow arm moving across the violin,
wearing original red, cream &
green silk outfit w/lace collar,
w/original 2-air tune sheet,
Leonard Lambert, France, late
19th c., 25" (ILLUS.) 3,575.00
Nancy & Sluggo, cloth, 1930's, 13",
pr............................... 475.00
Nancy Ann Storybook "Beauty"
(from "Beauty & the Beast"),
bisque, mohair wig, dressed,
5½" 30.00
Nancy Ann Storybook "January" -
"A January Maid for New Year,"
bisque, jointed head & arms,
dressed, 6" 60.00
Nippon (all) bisque boy, painted
features, molded blond hair,
moveable arms, molded swim-
ming trunks, 5" h............... 50.00
Papier mache head girl, braided
mohair wig, cloth body, arms &
legs, Polish costume, 11½" 30.00
Parian head girl, painted eyes,
molded blonde hair w/lustre ribbon tassel & snood, kid leather &
cloth body, dressed, 19" 850.00
Parian head girl, pink cloth body,
dressed, 25" 225.00
Queen Louise (Armand Marseille)
bisque head girl, blue glass sleep
eyes, ball-jointed composition
body, dressed, 24" 395.00
Queen Louise (Armand Marseille)

bisque socket head girl marked
"15," sleep eyes, open mouth,
h.h. wig, ball-jointed composition
body, dressed, 33" 600.00
Rag-stuffed black woman, bead
eyes, dressed, 11½" 300.00
Rag-stuffed black Mammy, embroidered highlights to eyes & mouth,
original clothes, 21½" (1 hand
damaged) 302.50
Rag-stuffed (Rollinson) girl, painted
features, ca. 1916, dressed, 22"
(has 2 left feet) 975.00
Schmidt (Franz & Co.) bisque socket
head toddler marked "1295," blue
sleep eyes, open mouth w/teeth,
pierced nostrils, brown h.h. wig,
jointed composition chunky body,
original clothes, 16½" head circumference 1,250.00
Schoenau & Hoffmeister bisque
socket head girl marked "914,"
blue glass sleep eyes, h.h. wig,
ball-jointed composition body,
dressed, 28" 475.00
Schoenhut girl, wooden, intaglio
eyes, "pouty" expression, molded
hair, original paint, dressed,
15".........................1,250.00
Scootles, vinyl, sleep eyes, 1960's,
original clothes, 19" 495.00
S.F.B.J. (Societe Francaise de Fabri-
cation de Bebes et Jouets) bisque
head girl marked "60," brown stationary eyes, open mouth
w/molded upper row of teeth,
brown h.h. wig, ball-jointed composition body, jointed wrists,
dressed, 15" 575.00

S.F.B.J. Bisque Head Boy

S.F.B.J. bisque socket head character boy marked "235," brown stationary glass eyes, open-closed mouth, flocked hair, ball-jointed composition body, jointed wrists, dressed, 15" (ILLUS.) 1,395.00

S.F.B.J. bisque socket head girl marked "60," original brown paperweight stationary eyes, open mouth w/molded upper row of teeth, black h.h. wig, ball-jointed composition adult body, jointed wrists, dressed, 20" 895.00

S.F.B.J. bisque socket head character toddler marked "236," blue glass sleep eyes, open-closed mouth, original brown h.h. wig, dressed, 23" 1,650.00

Shirley Temple, vinyl, 1957, dressed, 12" 95.00

Shirley Temple, composition, dressed, 13" 350.00

Shirley Temple, rag-stuffed, mask-type face, brown mohair wig, Wacker Mfg. Co., Chicago, 17" ... 85.00

Simon & Halbig bisque socket head girl marked "1078," blue paperweight eyes, cloth body, bisque lower arms, dressed, 12" 350.00

Simon & Halbig bisque socket head girl marked "939," brown stationary glass eyes, closed mouth, pierced ears, dark brown h.h. wig, original jointed composition body, straight wrists, dressed, 17" 1,800.00

Simon & Halbig bisque socket head girl marked "1079," blue sleep eyes, brown h.h. wig in long curls, dressed, 19" 440.00

Simon & Halbig brown bisque socket head girl marked "939," brown glass eyes, open mouth w/teeth, dark brown h.h. wig, dressed, 28" (ILLUS.) 2,900.00

Simon & Halbig bisque head child marked "1079 DEP 14," blue glass eyes, open mouth w/four inset teeth above a dimpled chin, pierced ears, ball-jointed wood & composition body, dressed, 29" ... 675.00

Springfield, Vermont (D.M. Smith & Co.) composition over wood head lady, wooden body, arms & legs, metal hands & feet, dressed 400.00

Steiner (Jules) bisque head "Phenix Bebe" marked "82," blue paperweight stationary eyes, closed mouth, pierced ears, dark brown h.h. wig, jointed composition body, straight wrists, dressed, 11½" ...1,595.00

Steiner (Jules) bisque head girl, vivid blue eyes, blushed eyelids, closed mouth, pierced ears, original h.h. wig, composition body, original clothes, 20½" 4,125.00

Steiner (Jules) bisque head girl marked "A. 19" & "Le Parisien," blue stationary paperweight eyes, closed mouth, applied pierced ears, original brown h.h. wig, jointed composition body, jointed wrists, dressed, 28½" 4,500.00

UNIS (Union Nationale Inter Syndicale) bisque head character boy marked "251," blue sleep eyes, open mouth w/tongue & 2 upper teeth, original brown h.h. wig, ball-jointed composition body, jointed wrists, dressed, 27" 1,700.00

Wax head girl marked "J," blue stationary glass eyes, closed mouth, original blonde h.h. wig, cloth body, dressed, 15½" 550.00

Wooden "peddlar" lady, hair pulled up into a "tuck" comb, basket filled w/kitchenware, dressed, 15" 1,750.00

Yellow Kid, composition, jointed, dressed & w/original button, 7" .. 395.00

(End of Doll Section)

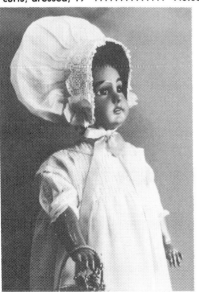

Simon & Halbig Bisque Head Girl

DOOR KNOCKERS

Brass, American eagle, 8" h. $75.00

Brass, domed circular backplate w/scrolling S-shaped striker, late 18th-early 19th c., 9" d. 275.00

Brass, Mission San Gabriel 20.00
Bronze, lion's head w/open snarling
    mouth, wishbone-shaped striker .. 165.00
Cast iron, basket of flowers,
    marked "Hubley, No. 13" 60.00
Cast iron, bust of Minerva w/brass
    plate engraved "1833," marked
    "Wilson's Patent," old worn black
    paint, 8½" h. 85.00
Cast iron, cherub's head 40.00
Cast iron, gargoyle animal head
    w/striker ring through its mouth,
    19th c., 9½" h. 247.50
Cast iron, Grecian lady w/basket of
    grapes on her head, dark mustard
    yellow paint, 8" h. 75.00
Cast iron, parrot on a leafy branch,
    colorful repaint, indoor
    model .... 20.00 to 30.00

DOOR STOPS

Charleston Dancers Door Stop

*All door stops listed are flat-back cast iron
unless otherwise noted.*

Apple blossoms in basket, Hubley,
    7 5/8" h. $50.00
Aunt Jemima, full figure, old poly-
    chrome repaint, Hubley,
    12" h. .... 165.00 to 220.00
Bennington Monument, 7¾" h. 55.00
Boy w/fruit basket, old repaint,
    9¼" h. 100.00
Boy in Tuxedo, original paint, wood-
    en wedge, 7¼" h. 225.00
Cape Cod cottage, original poly-
    chrome paint, Eastern Speciality
    Mfg. Co., 5¾" h. 75.00
Cat, Fireside, Angora in reclining
    position, full figure, worn original
    grey & white paint w/pink trim,
    marked "Hubley," 10¾" l. 165.00
Cat, Hunchback, w/raised tail, full
    figure, original black paint
    w/green eyes & red mouth,
    Hubley, 10¾" h. 85.00

Cat, Persian, in seated position
    w/head turned, full figure, origi-
    nal worn white paint w/pink &
    green accents, marked "Hubley,"
    8½" h. .... 125.00 to 155.00
Cat, sleeping, full figure, original
    paint, National Foundry,
    9 5/8" l. 195.00
Charleston Dancers, worn original
    polychrome paint, marked "Copy-
    right Fish" & "Hubley," 8 7/8" h.
    (ILLUS.) 1,025.00
Clipper ship, original polychrome
    paint, 11¼ x 10½" .... 45.00 to 70.00
Colonial Dame, wearing bonnet &
    carrying bouquet of flowers,
    Hubley, 8" h. 95.00
Colonial Lawyer, original paint, WS
    in triangle mark, 9 5/8" h. 275.00
Cottage, w/roses around door,
    Hubley or National Foundry,
    5¾" h. 70.00
Cow standing on oblong grassy
    base, worn original gilt & green
    paint, "New Holland Machine Co.,
    Compliments of A.M. Zimmer-
    man," 9 5/8" l., 7¼" h. 155.00
Deco girl, standing w/arms out-
    stretched & grasping the hem of
    her skirt, old repaint, 9" h. 170.00
Dog, Boxer in standing position on
    oval base, traces of old paint,
    Hubley, 8½" h. 95.00
Dog, Dachshund, standing on oval
    base, Taylor Cook, 1930, 5½" h... 165.00
Dog, French Bulldog, full figure,
    original paint, Hubley, National
    Foundry & others, 7 5/8 x 6¾" ... 75.00
Dog, "Mutt & his Bone," original
    paint, 8¼ x 5½" 200.00
Dog, Pekingese w/glass eyes, full
    figure, 14½" l. 250.00
Dog, Setter in hunting stance, full
    figure, original black & white
    paint, Hubley, 15 7/8" l.,
    8¾" h. .... 100.00 to 125.00
Dolly Dingle, Hubley, 9½" h. 285.00
Ducks (2), Hubley, 8¼ x 6¼" 185.00
Dutch girl w/shoulder yoke & buck-
    ets, original polychrome paint, pa-
    per label "Littco Products, Howe &
    Fory Co.," 13" h. .... 185.00 to 225.00
Elephant by palm tree, wedge-type,
    13¾" h. 200.00
Fawn, copyright 1930 Taylor Cook,
    10" h. 125.00
Flower basket, National or Albany
    Foundry, 15 7/8" h. 150.00
Flower basket, poppies & cornflow-
    ers, Hubley, 7¼" h. 40.00
Frog, yellow & black eyes, original
    green paint, 5¼" l., 3" h. 50.00
Fruit bowl, melon-ribbed footed
    bowl filled w/grapes, oranges,

plums & foliage, worn original
polychrome paint, Hubley, 7" h. . .   85.00
Geese (3), Hubley, 8 x 8" 380.00
Gladiolus, Hubley, 10 x 8" 75.00
Gnome w/lantern & keys, 10" h. . . .   250.00
Heron, original polychrome paint,
Albany Foundry, 7½" h. 100.00
Horse, full figure, original paint,
10" h. 145.00
Humpty Dumpty, full figure,
4½ x 3½" 245.00
Iris, worn original polychrome paint,
Hubley, 10 5/8" h. 205.00
Lafayette, standing w/sword drawn,
11 5/8" h.   350.00
Lil Bo Peep w/hand raised shading
her eyes, on semi-circular stepped
base, old polychrome paint over
silver, 6¾" h. 130.00
Little Heiskell Soldier, original color-
ful polychrome paint, marked "Little Heiskell, Hagerstown, Md.
1769," 10½" h. 225.00

Maid & Penguin Door Stops

Maid curtsying, dark uniform
w/white ruffled apron & cap,
9" h. (ILLUS. left) . . . . . . .225.00 to 300.00
Major Domo, red suit, 8 3/8" h. . . .   185.00
"Old Salt," full figure, man wearing
yellow slicker & black rain hat,
original polychrome paint,
11" h. 150.00
Owl, sitting on 2 books, original
paint, Eastern Specialty Mfg. Co.,
9¼" h. 125.00
Pansy bowl, original paint, Hubley,
7" h. 70.00
Parrot on stump, old worn colorful
paint, 12½" h. 70.00
Peacock, worn old colorful repaint,
6¼" h. 90.00
Penguin with top hat, full figure,
original paint, 10¼" h. (ILLUS.
right) . . . . .250.00 to 300.00
Rabbit by fence, original paint, Al-
bany Foundry, 6 7/8 x 8 1/8" 245.00
Rooster crowing, on floral base,
original polychrome paint,
10" h. 125.00
Sailor, original paint, 11 3/8" h. . . .   575.00
Scottish Highlander, holding spear,
original black paint, 15½ x 13" . . .   195.00

Sheep (ram) standing on mound
base, old black repaint,
7¼" h. . . . . .110.00 to 145.00
Spanish girl w/fan, Hubley, 9" h. . . .   165.00
Squirrel on log, old multicolored
repaint, 11" h. 250.00
Tiger lilies (3) & foliage, original
paint, Hubley, 10½" h. 135.00
Tropical woman carrying basket of
fruit on her head, 12" h. 140.00
Tulips, old repaint, 12¾" h. 75.00
Turkey, strutting on grassy mound
base, polychrome repaint,
13" h. 375.00
Woman w/muff, solid full figure,
9¼" h. 100.00
Yawning child, full figure,
9" h. . . . . .100.00 to 155.00

ENAMELS

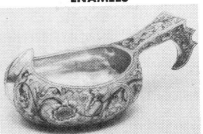

Russian Enamel Kovsh

Enamels have been used to decorate a variety of substances, particularly metals. The best-known small enameled wares such as patch and other small boxes and napkin rings are the Battersea Enamels made by the Battersea Enamel Works in the last half of the 18th century. However, the term is often loosely applied to other English enamels. Russian enamels, usually on a silver or gold base, are famous and expensive. Early 20th century French enamel on copper wares and those items produced in China at the turn of the century in imitation of the early Russian style, are also drawing dealer and collector attention. Also see CLOISONNE and FABERGE.

Battersea bonbonniere in the form
of a bear's head, enameled in
tones of brown & red, hinged lid
w/interior scene of recumbent lion,
ca. 1775, 2¼" l. (repair to
enamel) $1,430.00
Bonbonniere in the form of a Pug
dog reclining on a grassy mound,
hinged cover w/interior scene of
a dog standing near a classical
ruin, Bilston, ca. 1770, 2" d. 2,970.00

Cigarette box, cov., trunk form
w/swing handles & latch hook,
silver-gilt, enameled multicolor
stylized florals, foliage & geometric
forms on olive green, purple & sea
green ground, 4 bracket feet, Russian, The Sixth Artel, Moscow, ca.
1910, 3 3/8" l. 2,840.00
Creamer & sugar basket w/tongs,
silver-gilt, enameled each side
w/stylized flowers on white & turquoise blue ground, surrounds
w/multicolor stylized foliage, tongs
enameled similarly, Russian, Vasili
Agafonov, Moscow, ca. 1900, 4¼"
to 4¾" l., 3 pcs. 3,080.00
Kovsh, silver, enameled w/colorful
scrolling foliage & fantastic ser-
pents, white bead borders, Vasili
Agafonov, Moscow, ca. 1900,
overall 10¾" l. (ILLUS.) 4,675.00
Magnifying glass, circular container
w/molded silver mounts, one side
enameled w/a gentleman examining
a globe through a magnifying
glass, the other w/a gentleman
peering out to sea through a spy
glass, South Staffordshire, ca.
1765, 2 3/8" d. 1,100.00
Vase, bud, silver-gilt, lower half
enameled in the Art Nouveau style
w/multicolor stylized butterflies
on a dense foliate ground rising to
a creamy white tapered stem enhanced w/violet & rose floral
sprays, beaded rim, Russian, The
Twentieth Artel, Moscow, 1908-17,
5" h. 4,400.00

Faure Limoges Enamel Vase

Vase, ovoid w/waisted neck, enameled light blue diamonds enclosing
stylized white flowers bordered by
black, white, silver & blue geometric pattern, signed C. Faure
Limoges, 11½" h. (ILLUS.) 2,200.00

EPERGNES

Cranberry Glass Epergne

*Epergnes were popular as centerpieces on
tables of last century. Many have receptacles
of colored glass for holding sweetmeats or
other edible items or for flowers or fruits.
Early epergnes were made entirely of metal
including silver.*

Amethyst glass, single lily, ruffled
lily in bowl w/ruffled edge,
10" d., 14½" h. $120.00
Blue frosted glass, single lily w/cen-
ter fluted bowl & 3 smaller bowls,
air trap dot pattern, enameled
white dots, florals & red berries
w/gold branches decor, silverplated brass mountings, 17¼" d.,
22¼" h. 450.00
Blue opalescent glass, 3-lily, ruffled
edge lilies, 14" bowl 250.00
Chartreuse opalescent glass, 3-lily,
flower-shaped top lilies w/clear
spiral trim, ruffled chartreuse
opalescent base, 9½" d.,
19½" h. 295.00
Cranberry glass, 3-lily, applied clear
spiral trim, in ruffled cranberry
bowl-base, 10 1/8" d., 22¼" h.
(ILLUS.) 335.00
Cranberry glass, 5-bowl, large base
bowl w/three smaller bowls on
clear stems & center top bowl on
clear stem, applied clear leaves
around top, 10¼" d., 16" h. 650.00
White opaline glass, single lily,
fluted rim w/ruby red trim, in 9"
white opaline bowl, 10½" h. 80.00
White glass, 3-lily, blue ruffled
edges, 12" w., 17" h. 265.00

EYE CUPS

Paneled Eye Cup

The eye cup was an early means of treating an injured or infected eye. The oval cup, filled with a medicated solution, was held over the open eye. With the advent of eye droppers and plastic dropper bottles, the eye cup became obsolete.

Blue, "Wyeth"	$5.00
Blue, set of 3 (including "John Bull")	45.00
Clear, w/eyes in relief	47.00
Clear, "John Bull," 1917	13.50
Clear, dated 1937	17.50
Clear, paneled (ILLUS.)	8.00
Cobalt blue, "John Bull," dated 1917	30.00
Cobalt blue	18.00 to 23.00
Custard	16.00
Emerald green, pedestal style	22.00
Emerald green, "John Bull"	31.00
Green, "John Bull"	56.00
Green, set of 3	60.00
Milk white	17.50

FABERGE

Carl Faberge (1846-1920) was goldsmith and jeweler to the Russian Imperial Court, and his creations are recognized as the finest of their kind. He made a number of enamel fantasies, including Easter eggs, for the Imperial family and utilized precious metals and jewels in other work.

Box, silver-gilt & shaded enamel, oblong, cover enameled "en plein" w/a shaped reserve depicting Ivan & the Grey Wolf, within a border of green foliage, sides enameled w/colorful florals, Fyodor Ruckert, Moscow, ca. 1910, 2¾" l. $7,150.00

Buttons, silver, enamel & diamond, enameled translucent lilac & decorated w/diamond-set swirls, workmaster Henrik Wigstrom, St. Petersburg, ca. 1900, set of 6 in original fitted holly wood case 5,500.00

Cigarette case, gold, silver & translucent enamel, oblong, enameled translucent apricot over a "guilloche" ground, cover applied w/gold leafy scrolls set w/diamonds, molded gold mount, diamond thumbpiece, signed in Cyrillic, workmaster Michael Perchin, St. Petersburg, ca. 1890, 4" l. 15,400.00

Cuff links, translucent enamel & gold double link of elliptical shape w/pink translucent enamel within rose-cut diamond borders, mounted in gold, workmaster Michael Perchin, St. Petersburg, ca. 1900, pr. 4,620.00

Faberge Desk Clock

Desk clock, gold, silver & translucent enamel, oblong, enameled translucent oyster white over a sun-ray ground, green-gold border chased w/berried leafage & edged in polished red-gold, the dial bordered w/pearls w/an outer perimeter of translucent royal blue enamel, workmaster Henrik Wigstrom, St. Petersburg, ca. 1910, 2¾" h. (ILLUS.) 17,600.00

Egg replica, miniature, enameled translucent white over a "guilloche" ground, gold suspension ring, ca. 1900 ....2,090.00

Ice tongs, silver, in the form of eagle's talons rising from acanthus leafage, inner side gilded, Moscow, ca. 1900, 8¾" l. 1,760.00

Letter opener, dagger-shaped, slightly tapering nephrite handle set

w/small cabochon rubies, fitted
w/silver-gilt guard & blade, in
fitted case, Moscow, 1899-1908,
8" l. 1,870.00
Locket, silver-gilt & enamel, heart-
shaped, enameled translucent rose-
pink over a sunburst ground, center set w/a faceted colored stone,
ca. 1900, 1¾" h. 1,100.00

Faberge Match Case

Match case, gold, silver & enamel,
oblong w/rounded corners, enameled in a green, black & white
striped pattern, hinged cover
w/gold border chased w/acanthus
leaves, cabochon ruby thumbpiece,
w/pendant loop on side, base
w/striker, signed in Cyrillic,
workmaster Fyodor Afanassiev,
St. Petersburg, ca. 1900, 1¾" h.
(ILLUS.) 4,400.00
Model of a Persian cat, coral, carved
in an attentive seated position
w/paws together, eyes set w/cab-
ochon red stones, original fitted
holly wood case, St. Petersburg,
1905-10, 1 7/8" h. 22,000.00
Vodka beakers, silver, plain tapering
cylinder w/band of leaf-tips, gilt
interior, signed in Cyrillic w/Imper-
ial warrant, Moscow, ca. 1900,
1¾" h., set of 6 . . . . .5,500.00
Whistle, gold & translucent enamel,
cylindrical, enameled translucent
royal blue over a "guilloche"
ground, signed in Cyrillic w/initials
K.F., St. Petersburg, ca. 1900,
2¼" l. 6,600.00

FAIRY LAMPS

*These are candle burning night lights of the
Victorian era. Best known are the Clarke
Fairy Lamps made in England, but they were
also made by other firms. They were produced*

*in two sizes, each with a base and a shade.
The Fairy Pyramid Lamps listed below all
have a clear glass base and are approximately 2 7/8" d. and 3¼" h. The Fairy Lamps are
usually at least 4" d. and 5" h. when assembled and these may or may not have an additional saucer or bottom holder to match the
shade in addition to the clear base.*

FAIRY PYRAMID LAMPS

Burmese Glass Fairy Pyramid Lamp

Amber "overshot" glass shade, Swirl
patt., marked Clarke clear glass
base, 2 7/8" d., 3½" h. $115.00
American Beauty Rose mother-of-
pearl satin glass shade w/white
lining, Diamond Quilted patt.,
marked Clarke clear glass base,
2 7/8" d., 3 3/8" h. 145.00
Blue opalescent glass shade w/em-
bossed ribs, marked Clarke clear
glass base, 2 7/8" d., 3¾" h. 90.00
Burmese glass shade, salmon pink
shaded to yellow, acid finish,
marked Clarke clear glass base,
2 7/8" d., 3 5/8" h.
(ILLUS.) . . . . .210.00 to 300.00
Pink "overshot" glass shade, Swirl
patt., marked Clarke clear glass
base, 2 7/8" d., 3 5/8" h. 110.00
Pink satin glass shade w/white lin-
ing, marked Clarke clear glass
base, 2 7/8" d., 3 5/8" h. 118.00
Rose mother-of-pearl satin glass
shade w/white lining, Diamond
Quilted patt., marked Clarke clear
glass base, 2 7/8" d., 3½" h. 150.00
Vaseline crackle glass shade w/em-
bossed fans, marked Clarke clear
glass base, 2 7/8" d., 4 1/8" h. . . . 110.00
Yellow "overshot" cased glass
shade, Swirl patt., marked Clarke
clear glass base, 2 7/8" d.,
3½" h. 120.00

FAIRY LAMPS
American Beauty Rose mother-of-

pearl satin glass shade w/white lining, Diamond Quilted patt., marked Clarke clear glass base, 4" d., 4½" h. 195.00

Burmese glass shade, salmon pink shaded to yellow w/enameled red berries & green leaves decor, acid finish, on cream-colored Tunnecliffe pottery base w/pink bands, garlands of pink roses & green leaves, marked Clarke clear glass candle cup, 4" d., 4¼" h. 458.00

Burmese glass shade, salmon pink shaded to yellow, acid finish, Webb, on cream-colored Tunnecliffe pottery base w/aqua bands, blue florals & gold trim, marked Clarke clear glass candle cup, 5¾" d., 4¾" h. 365.00

Burmese glass shade & matching bowl-shaped footed base w/crimped rim, salmon pink shaded to yellow w/enameled prunus decor, Thomas Webb & Sons, marked Clarke pressed Burmese glass insert & clear glass candle cup, 4½" d., 6 5/8" h. 1,500.00

Green overlay glass shade w/white lining, marked Clarke clear glass candle cup, on brass & clear glass column w/green swirl & brass foot, 4" d., 13" h. 275.00

Green & opaque white striped acid finish glass shade, Stevens & Williams, marked Clarke clear glass base, 3 7/8" d., 4½" h. 175.00

Lemon yellow satin glass shade w/white lining & enameled bird & floral decor, on cream-colored Tunnecliffe pottery base w/floral decor, 4" d., 4 1/8" h. 325.00

Spatter glass shade w/embossed ribs, peach, pink & cream spatter, white lining, marked Clarke clear glass base, 4" d., 4¾" h. 145.00

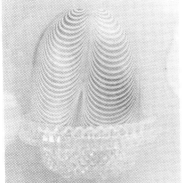

Verre Moire Fairy Lamp

Verre Moire (Nailsea) glass shade, frosted cranberry w/white opaque

loopings, marked Clarke clear glass base, 4" d., 4 1/8" h. (ILLUS.)........................ 151.00

Verre Moire (Nailsea) glass shade & matching bowl base, frosted chartreuse w/white opaque loopings, marked Clarke clear glass candle cup, 5 3/8" d., 4 5/8" h. 425.00

Verre Moire (Nailsea) glass shade & matching fluted base, frosted heavenly blue w/white opaque loopings, marked Clarke clear glass candle cup, 8" d., 5" h. 425.00

Yellow mother-of-pearl satin glass shade & matching base w/pleated rim & 2 rows of applied clear yellow rigaree, Diamond Quilted patt., marked Clarke clear glass candle cup, large 425.00

FIGURAL FAIRY LAMPS

Bisque, dog's head, brown glass eyes, shaded brown & tan coat, black collar, 3½" d., 4" h. 145.00

Glass, double owl head, frosted cranberry, marked Clarke clear glass base, 3½" d., 4¾" h. 195.00

Glass, flower, 5 rows of clear petals applied to clear glass shade, marked Clarke clear glass base, etched "Clarke's Fairy" on shade, 4½" d., 5 1/8" h. 245.00

Porcelain, cottage, Art Deco style, orange roof w/pierced windows & door, green saucer base, English, 4¾" d. base, 3¼" h. 115.00

Porcelain, 3-face, owl, cat & dog ... 150.00

FANS

Circular Folding Fan

Also see ADVERTISING ITEMS and COCA-COLA ITEMS.

Ivory "brise," folding-type, carved w/figures in a landscape scene, China, ca. 1830 (ribbon missing) ..$300.00

Oil cloth, circular-type folding into handle, stenciled floral decor (ILLUS.)........................ 20.00

Ostrich feather, celluloid handle, silk ribbon, 1900's 35.00

Ostrich feather, white, tortoise shell sticks, 13" l. 75.00

Painted & embroidered lawn w/rust lace edging, carved teakwood sticks, Victorian, 13" l., opening to 23" 40.00

Painted gauze, center w/scene of 2 cherubs on black ground surrounded by white bobbin applique on black net, slender mother-of-pearl sticks w/foil floral decor, artist-signed, Europe, late 19th c., 13½" l., in gilded double-sided frame carved w/ribbon & roses decor 220.00

Painted gauze & silk, Venus & cherubs on white silk & black gauze surrounded by feather motif, orchid dyed mother-of-pearl sticks, France, late 19th c., 12¾" l. (damage & staining) 132.00

Painted lace, scene of lady & gentleman in a garden setting w/elaborate florals, trees & doves, artist-signed, tortoise shell sticks, opening to 18" 145.00

Painted net, orange & yellow florals on white, bone sticks, 13" l., opening to 30" 75.00

Painted paper, "gouache" painting to Louis XVI style scene of an al fresco lover's tryst, pierced & carved mother-of-pearl sticks applied w/love trophies, Europe, ca. 1870, 11" l., gilded & painted Italian case 137.50

18th Century Painted Fan

Painted paper, ink & color scene of lady reclining on couch while female attendant plays stringed instrument, signed Chen Lang Shining gonghui & dated 1757, reverse w/ink calligraphy on gold paper, signed Chen Dong Gao jingshu & dated 1746, 6 5/8" l., opening to 20" (ILLUS.) 2,970.00

Painted paper, silver foliage on purple ground, wooden sticks, 12" l., opening to 22" 25.00

Painted vellum, folding-type, watercolor painting of 2 lovers in a landscape center w/similar scenes at either side, slender pierced & carved ivory sticks w/foil accents, Europe, ca. 1770, 11" l. (repairs to 2 sticks) 125.00

Paper, folding-type, lithographed & h.p. scene of an 18th century style musical gathering in a garden setting, backed w/central reserve of lady & gentleman, pierced & carved mother-of-pearl sticks, ca. 1860, 10½" l. 82.50

Peacock feather, h.p. pierced ivory sticks, China, ca. 1825 .... 125.00

Printed fabric w/red velvet handles, Victorian 28.00

Woven grasses, Osage Indian, geometric design 50.00

FARM COLLECTIBLES

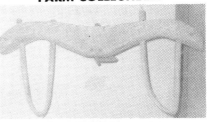

Ox Yoke

Also see BASKETS, BELLS and SCALES.

Barn door strap hinges, wrought iron, 18th c., 27" l. $60.00

Blueberry rake, wooden, long handle, 19th c. 95.00

Corn dryer, wooden 20.00

Corn dryer, wrought iron, 10-prong 9.50

Corn planter, "Acme" 15.00

Dehorning clipper for cattle 65.00

Egg carrier, tin, w/advertising "Kennedy the Shoe Dealer," 1800's 125.00

Egg crate, wooden slat construction, "Gardner," 2-dozen size ...45.00 to 50.00

Egg crate, slat-type, maple, early 1900's, 12-dozen size ......30.00 to 50.00

Egg gathering basket, collapsible folding-type, iron wire, small..... 15.00

Grain flail, wooden & leather 50.00

Grain measure, wooden, carved initials & dated "1854," 12½" d., 9" h. 75.00

Grain shovel, hewn from single piece of wood, open "D" handle, ca. 1810 .... 200.00

Hay fork, wooden, 3-tine	85.00
Hay knife, 2 wooden handles, serrated blade	14.00
Hen's nest eggs, blown milk white glass, set of 12	70.00
Hen's nest egg, wooden, machine-carved	6.50
Hog ringer, cast iron, "Hill's," dated 1872	15.00
Milking stool, wooden, 3-legged, round top w/mortised & wedged stretcher base, mustard paint, 9" d., 11" h.	95.00
Milk pail, tin, hooded lip & pouring spout w/screen insert, 12-qt.	25.00
Ox yoke, double, wooden (ILLUS.) . .	127.50
Pig snout trimmer, dated 1882	22.00
Scythe w/mortised wood grain cradle, varnished, 48½" l.	55.00
Tractor seat, cast iron, "Deere Co., Moline, Ill."	40.00

FIREARMS

1860 Colt Army Revolver

Carbine pistol, U.S. Springfield Military w/Maynard tape primer	$700.00
Revolver, Colt 1849 pocket model, .31 caliber, 6" barrel . . . . 180.00 to 235.00	
Revolver, Colt 1860 Army model, Richards Conversion-type, inscribed w/New York address, marked "US" on left side, traces of original blueing, cylinder engraved w/naval engagement scene, walnut grips slightly chipped, serial numbers mixed, 1873-78, 7 7/8" barrel (ILLUS.)	1,980.00
Revolver, Colt 1862 Pocket Navy model, silver trigger guard & strap, Colt black powder series, new in box, .36 caliber	450.00
Revolver, Colt 1862 Police model, good Colt markings, fine grips, .36 caliber	425.00
Revolver, Manhattan Firearms Company, Newark, New Jersey, pocket model, 1858-62, .31 caliber, (rusted)	75.00
Rifle, Colt Lightning, .22 caliber . . .	325.00
Rifle, Kentucky full stock, cherry-wood stock, brass patch box, blacksmith-made, ca. 1835	395.00

Rifle, Kentucky full stock, curly maple stock, flintlock-type, signed "J. Dickert"	950.00
Rifle, Kentucky full stock, walnut stock, brass trim, 45" l. barrel, overall 60" l.	325.00
Rifle, Kentucky half-stock, curly maple stock, percussion-type, fancy brass trigger guard, butt plate & fittings, 47½" l.	250.00
Rifle, Kentucky half-stock, curly walnut stock, percussion lock marked "T. Neave & Sons, Cincinnati," barrel marked "J. M. Zink," 33" l. barrel, overall 49" l.	375.00
Rifle, Kentucky half-stock, curly maple stock w/engraved brass patch box, percussion-type, barrel marked "S. Small," 41¼" l. barrel, overall 56" l.	450.00
Rifle, Kentucky half-stock, striped maple stock, signed "Joseph Golcher," ca. 1835	595.00
Rifle, Winchester, Model 90, pump action, octagonal barrel, dated 1911, .22 caliber	225.00
Rifle, Winchester, Model 1886, .48 caliber	395.00
Rifle, Winchester, Model 1886, .60 caliber	450.00
Rifle, Winchester, Model 1894, fine condition	225.00
Shotgun, Parker, 12 gauge, 30" l. . . .	800.00
Shotgun, Parker, 12 gauge, 32" l. . . .	850.00
Shotgun-rifle, "over-and-under" model, curly maple stock w/brass patch box, percussion locks, top barrel signed "W. P DeWitt, Elmira, N.Y.," 30" l. barrels overall 46¾" l.	775.00

FIRE FIGHTING COLLECTIBLES

Fireman's Leather Helmet

Alarm box, cast iron, "Gamewell," complete w/key, ca. 1924	$92.00
Alarm box, cast iron stand, clock drive, Chicago Fire, ca. 1920	275.00

Ax, w/35" hickory handle 40.00
Ax, parade-type, Viking-style, ca.
   1880 . . . . 160.00
Badge, "Bridgeport Fire Dept.,
   Badge No. 44, Bridgeport, Conn.,"
   brass, shield-shaped 40.00
Badge, "Honorary Kensington" 20.00
Badge, "President, Norwood Vol.
   Fire Co., No. 1," brass, fire truck
   pictured 25.00
Banner, cloth, tan w/red & blue
   printing of fire helmet, axes,
   picks, trumpet, hook & ladder &
   lantern, "Welcome Firemen" &
   "Loyal To Our Duty," 2' x 4' 95.00
Bell, fire engine, nickel-plated
   bronze, no hanger 125.00
Belt, parade-type, "Active Hose,"
   leather w/original red & white
   paint, 1890 . . . . 85.00
Belt buckles, 2 w/trucks pictured,
   set of 3 . . . . 30.00
Book, "The Conquest of Fire,"
   1914 . . . . 28.00
Book, "Fighting A Fire," by Charles
   Hill, illustrated by Charles Hill,
   1897, hard cover 48.00
Book, "Fire Dept., Haverhill, Mas-
   sachusetts," 1897-98, twelve 8 x
   10 photographs, hard cover, 8 x
   10½", 148 pp. 85.00
Book, "History of St. Louis Fire
   Department," 1914, illustrated,
   299 pp. 55.00
Book, "Sheyboygan Fire Dept. 1901
   Regulations," gilt-edged leather
   bound 50.00
Booklet, 25th Anniversary souvenir,
   West New York, New Jersey Em-
   pire No. 2, Hickory Engine No. 1,
   1914, illustrated, 86 pp. 27.50
Bucket, leather, old black paint
   w/white lettering "B.O. Vis,
   No. 5," 11" h. 95.00
Bucket, leather, painted w/reserve
   scene of American ship burning in
   harbor, lettered "Alert Eagle Fire
   Society Instituted 1799" 2,250.00
Bucket, leather, inscribed "Richard
   Ayers" in banner over oval
   medallion reserve lettered
   "C.F.S. - 1813" 300.00
Buttons, uniform, Chicago Fire
   Dept., set of 12 . . . . 15.00
Cap, black, 2 buttons, "F.D." on
   front 39.50
Catalogue, "American-LaFrance,"
   1947, 132 pp. 25.00
Engine plate from a steamer, nickel-
   plated cast brass, "No. 30,"
   6¾" d. 85.00
Fire mark, cast iron, "Fire Associa-
   tion of Philadelphia, B U No. 88,"
   1863 issue, 7 7/16 x 11½" 150.00

Helmet, company initials on front,
   2½" h. brass hook & ladder,
   trumpet & pick crossed on back . . 45.00
Helmet, fire chief, aluminum, eagle,
   marked "Chief E.C.F.C.," H.A.K.
   Pat. 1897 . . . . 65.00
Helmet, leather, w/bugler bracket &
   high shield 350.00
Helmet, leather, w/eagle head tor-
   rent marked "C.F.F.D.," manufactured by Cairns & Bros., New York
   (ILLUS.). 195.00
Helmet, leather, w/embossed de-
   sign, brass eagle head 130.00
Helmet, miniature, "Volunteer Fire-
   men's Assoc.," fire fighting tools
   engraved on brim 20.00
Hose nozzle, brass, 10" l. 19.50
Lantern, "Dietz Fire King," brass 172.50
Lantern, "Dietz," copper bottom,
   steel top 117.50
Lantern, "Dietz," brass, "King, the
   Seagrave Co., Columbus, Ohio" . . 287.50
Lantern, red over clear, etched brass
   presentation frame, 1881 . . . . .1,100.00
Photograph, cabinet-size, fireman
   wearing high eagle helmet, badge
   & parade belt, ca. 1880, East
   Providence, R.I. 18.00
Pumper, horse drawn, w/six rolls of
   leather hoses & brass connections
   & ladders 7,500.00
Ribbon, "Rescue Engine and Hose
   Co. 1, Attica, N.Y.," silk print,
   equipment pictured, 1885 . . . . 35.00

Fireman's Convention Ribbon

Ribbon, convention, "Spring St.,
   Hose Co. No. 5, Galena, Ill.,"
   crossed flags above medallion picturing mustached fireman in a fire
   helmet blowing on a fire horn
   (ILLUS.). 60.00

Ticket, "Fireman's Ball, Athol,
Mass.," ornate, 1853 . . . .   25.00
Trumpet horn, silverplate presenta-
tion piece, inscribed "To Our
Chief from the Protectives,"
w/working fireman's speaking
trumpet, 2 pcs. 600.00
Trumpet horn, silverplate, conical
form w/fluted bell w/engraved
floral design, Meriden Silver Co.,
Meriden, Connecticut, late 19th c.,
21½" l., w/two badges from
Marlboro, 3 pcs. 660.00
Uniform, coat & vest w/crossed
speaking trumpets on lapels
w/original badge, pill-shaped hat
w/crossed trumpet badge, 1890,
3 pcs. 325.00

FIREPLACE & HEARTH ITEMS

Cast Iron Figural Andirons

Andirons, brass, Federal, ring-
turned acorn finial, ring-turned
standard, spurred arch supports,
ball feet, early 19th c., 19½" h.,
pr. $300.00
Andirons, brass & wrought iron, urn-
form finial, molded rectangular
base w/applied winged female &
lyre, spurred arch supports, claw-
and-ball feet, early 19th c., 19" h.,
pr. 3,850.00
Andirons, cast iron, modeled as a
dolphin, impressed "Pat App for"
& "B & H/9512," probably New
York, 1825-44, 14" h., pr.
(ILLUS.) 275.00
Andirons, cast iron, figural George
Washington standing w/hat in one
hand & scroll in other, leaning on
sculptured column, American,
21" h., pr. 850.00
Bellows, painted & decorated wood,
gilt-stenciled leaf & shell design
w/black striping on green ground,

professionally releathered sides,
brass nozzle, 16½" l. 115.00
Bellows, painted & decorated pine,
stenciled & free-hand decoration
in red, green, black & gold on
yellow ground, worn leather
sides, brass nozzle, overall
17¼" l. 180.00
Bellows, painted & decorated wood,
stenciled & free-hand florals in
gilt, red, green & yellow on
brown ground, releathered sides,
brass nozzle, 18¼" l. 250.00
Bellows, painted & decorated wood,
turtle-back style, stenciled compote of fruit & foliage on original
yellow smoke-grained ground,
brass nozzle, 18¼" l. 145.00
Chestnut roasting pan, copper, reticulated lid w/opening lever on ferrule, turned walnut handle,
46" l. 115.00
Ember shovel, cast iron, short open
heart-shaped handle, 18th c. 65.00
Ember tongs, wrought iron, accordi-
on scissors-type, 18th c., 16" l. . . .   350.00
Fireboard, pine, oblong panel paint-
ed w/border of trees in green,
blue & white set in circles &
squares effecting a tile border,
interior of red bricks & white vase
of red, blue & white flowers, minor
surface abrasions, probably Massachusetts, early 19th c., 38 x
27 5/8" 10,450.00

Fireboard with Painted Scene

Fireboard, pine w/oil painting, scene
of white farmhouse under a large
tree in an open landscape, Massachusetts, ca. 1800, 47¼ x 26¼"
(ILLUS.) 5,500.00
Fireplace fender, brass, Federal,
D-shaped, molded rim above
pierced foliate band, molded
base, paw feet, early 19th c.,
47" w., 8½" h. 495.00
Hearth apple roaster, tin, footed,
open half cylinder, strap handle
extended to form back foot 395.00
Hearth broiler, rotary-type, wrought
iron, alternating wavy & straight
bars within circular rim, curled
feet, tooled handle w/initials &
stars, 18th c. 385.00

Hearth broiler, stationary-type, wrought iron, scrolled bars, easel back, 16½" h. 110.00

Hearth brush, turned wood handle, original black paint w/red & gold striping & foliage decor, 22" l. 130.00

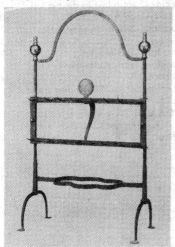

Hearth Game Roaster

Hearth game roaster, wrought iron & brass, brass ball finials centering an arched carrying handle above 2 adjustable pronged braces over shaped brace on arched legs ending in penny feet, signed "Bainbridge" on circular medallion, reverse dated "June 22, 1833," American or English (ILLUS.). 660.00

Hearth skewer, wrought iron, wide twisted shaft, rattail handle, 17" l. 75.00

Hearth toaster, rotary-type, wrought iron w/twisted wire arches, well-shaped handle, 18th c. 375.00

Hearth toaster, stationary-type, wrought iron, rack of arched bars w/stylized hearts design, footed, 13 x 10½" (pitted) 1,800.00

Oven peel, wrought iron, ram's horn handle end, 18th c., 26½" l. 130.00

Reflector oven (for toasting meat before open fire), tin, w/hinged door opening to spit, 2 handles on top, ca. 1830, 12 x 10" 385.00

Trammel, wrought iron, sawtooth-type, adjusts up from 9" 410.00

Trammel, wrought iron, sawtooth-type, good detail, adjusts up from 36" l. 200.00

Trammel chain, wrought iron. . . . . 85.00 to 130.00

FISHER (Harrison) GIRLS

A Typical Harrison Fisher Girl

The Fisher Girl, that chic American girl whose face and figure illustrated numerous magazine covers and books at the turn of the century, was created by Harrison Fisher. A professional artist who had studied in England and was trained by his artist father, he was able to capture an element of refined, cultured elegance in his drawings of beautiful women. They epitomized all that every American girl longed to be and catapulted their creator into the ranks of success. Harrison Fisher, who was born in 1877, worked as a commerical artist full time until his death in 1934. Today collectors seek out magazine covers, prints, books and postcards illustrated with Fisher Girls.

Book, "A Dream of Fair Women," 20 illustrations by Harrison Fisher, 1907, first edition $175.00

Book, "A Dream of Fair Women," 1909 . . . . 90.00

Book, "American Beauties," illustrations by Harrison Fisher, 1909 . . . . 142.00

Book, "American Girls in Miniature," 1912 . . . . 195.00

Book, "Hiawatha," by Henry Wadsworth Longfellow, illustrations by Harrison Fisher, 1906 . . . . 75.00

Book, "Song of Hiawatha," illustrations by Harrison Fisher 150.00

Book, "Their Hearts Desire," by Francis Foster Perry, illustrations by Harrison Fisher. 22.50

Plates, "American Girls," miniature, 1912, set of 32 . . . . 115.00

Postcards, "The Greatest Moments of a Girl's Life" series, set of 6, original black oak frame, 25½ x 8½" 85.00

Postcards, "Senses" series, set of 6 . . . . 57.00

Print, "Final Instructions," framed... 40.00
Print, "How Pleasant To Have Mon-
ey," Colliers Publishing Co., 1908,
10 x 15"........................ 15.00
Print, "Ready For Spin," 1908, Colliers Publishing Co., 10 x 15"...... 15.00
Prints, "Stages of a Girl's Life" series, set of 6................... 195.00

FLUE COVERS

*These decorative, round disks were used to
cover the stove pipe holes left in walls when
wood or coal-burning heating stoves were tak-
en down and stored during warm weather
months. Most were stamped tin or heavy
cardboard with stamped metal rims.*

Boys climbing fence & dogs grabbing
pant leg...................... $22.00
English cottage & flower garden
scene, marked England, 10" d.,
pr.......................... 25.00
Girl w/flowers.................. 22.00
Sheep, w/chain handles 35.00
Victorian boy & girl in holiday attire,
gathering holly, 9½" d.......... 50.00
Victorian girl in center, brass rim
w/chain, 7½" d. 38.00
Victorian girl, German............ 22.00
Victorian lady, round, large 22.50
Winged cherub, 7½" d............ 36.00

FOOD, CANDY & MISC. MOLDS

Cast Iron Cake Mold

Also see BUTTER MOLDS & STAMPS.

Cake, hen, cast iron, 2-part $110.00
Cake, lamb, cast iron,
Griswold .... 55.00 to 95.00

Cake rabbit, cast iron, marked
"Griswold," 2-part, 11" h.
(ILLUS.) ....150.00 to 175.00
Cake, Santa Claus, "Hello Kiddies,"
cast iron, marked
"Griswold"...........235.00 to 300.00
Candle, 12 tin tubes in dovetailed
cherrywood frame, 10¼" l. 900.00
Chocolate, American shield, tin,
2-part......................... 35.00
Chocolate, cats (5), tin............ 75.00
Chocolate, early automobile, tin,
3-part, 7½" l.................. 40.00
Chocolate, elves (2) standing beside
Easter eggs, tin, hinged, marked
"D.R.G.M.," German, 4 1/8"h.... 55.00
Chocolate, Father Christmas, tin,
2-part, 7½" h. 95.00

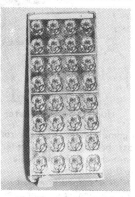

Tin Chocolate Mold

Chocolate, florals w/candy maker's
monogram (32), tin, 19½ x 8"
(ILLUS.)........................ 125.00
Chocolate, flower, tin, 4" sq........ 17.50
Chocolate, lions (6), copper 50.00
Chocolate, rabbit in seated position,
tin, hinged 55.00
Chocolate, rabbits (3), tin,
12" l. 65.00
Chocolate, rabbits (4), tin,
8" l. 60.00
Chocolate, rabbit in Easter egg,
tin 55.00
Chocolate, Santa Clauses (2),
marked "Anton Reiche 1900 Dres-
den," 5 x 7¾"................. 95.00
Chocolate, Santa Clauses (4), tin,
10 x 6"........................ 52.50
Chocolate, Santa Clauses (6), tin,
marked "Anton Reiche 1900 Dresden," 7 x 4".................. 75.00
Chocolate, Torahs (40) w/Hebrew in-
scriptions, 11½ x 11"........... 30.00
Food, cauliflower, ironstone,
Alcock 50.00
Food, deeply fluted sides, flat bottom, stoneware, Albany slip
glaze, 8" d. 45.00

Food, ear of corn, graniteware,
grey 70.00
Food, ear of corn, yellowware 58.00
Food, fish, ironstone, Copeland,
large 65.00
Food, fish, redware, dark greenish
glaze, 10¼" l. (minor rim chips) . . 75.00
Food, fish, tin, w/original ring for
hanging, ca. 1870, 13" l. 48.00
Food, flower center, footed, stone-
ware, tan glaze, oval 60.00
Food, fluted, graniteware, grey 35.00
Food, fluted, graniteware, white . . . 52.00
Food, fruit center, tin, 5¾" d. 40.00
Food, grape cluster center, iron-
stone, medium 45.00
Food, lilies & leaves, ironstone 75.00
Food, melon-ribbed, graniteware,
cobalt blue 38.00
Food, pineapple, copper, tinned in-
terior, 2 1/8 x 4 5/8 x 6¼" 45.00
Food, pinwheel, yellowware,
miniature 125.00

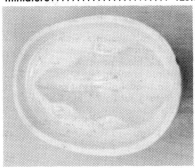

Ironstone Rabbit Food Mold

Food, rabbit, ironstone, 5½ x 4½",
3½" deep (ILLUS.) 45.00
Food, rose center, copper w/tin lin-
ing, 6 x 4¼" oval 90.00
Food, seafood, ironstone 40.00
Food, turk's turban, redware
w/brown sponge-daubed designs,
clear glaze, 10" d. (small edge
chips) 30.00
Food, turkey in seated position,
earthenware, white glazed,
pierced to hang, Villeroy & Boch,
9¼" l., 3¼" h. 75.00
Ice cream, American eagle w/can-
nons & shield, pewter, 5" l. 35.00
Ice cream, baked potato, pewter . . . 42.50
Ice cream, banana, pewter 35.00
Ice cream, battleship, pewter 35.00
Ice cream, boy on bike, pewter 60.00
Ice cream, Brownie, pewter 60.00
Ice cream, calla lily, pewter,
3-part 50.00
Ice cream, cherub, pewter 50.00
Ice cream, Chinese girl, pewter 40.00
Ice cream, dog in shoe, pewter 50.00

Ice cream, donkey, pewter, 3-part . . 40.00
Ice cream, eagle, large, pewter 50.00
Ice cream, grapes, pewter 22.00
Ice cream, lady's shoe, pewter 50.00
Ice cream, liberty bell, pewter 35.00

Pewter Lily Ice Cream Mold

Ice cream, lily, pewter, 3-part
(ILLUS.) 50.00
Ice cream, lovebirds, pewter, pr. . . . 75.00
Ice cream, Masonic emblem, pew-
ter, marked "E. & Co." 33.00
Ice cream, pear, pewter, marked "E.
& Co N.Y.," 4½" d. 25.00
Ice cream, pineapple, pewter,
marked "E. & Co., N.Y.,"
3¾" h. 34.00
Ice cream, pumpkin, pewter 30.00
Ice cream, Santa standing, pewter . . 65.00
Ice cream, strawberry, pewter,
marked "Long" & "Brevete,"
2 5/8" h. 22.50
Ice cream, turkey, pewter 36.00
Ice cream, witch riding broomstick,
pewter, 5 5/8" l. 55.00
Jelly, geometric, white ironstone . . . 35.00
Jelly, roasted pig, white ironstone . . 95.00
Maple sugar, floral, hand-carved
wood, 10" 60.00
Maple sugar, 4 squares, wooden,
12" 50.00
Maple sugar, dark pine, w/handle,
4 x 17" 95.00
Maple sugar candy, 3-D houses (8),
wooden, 2½ x 2½ x 1½" 325.00
Pudding, tin, w/lid, marked
"Kreamer" 25.00
Pudding, melon-ribbed, tin, pull-
apart handles, 2-part, 8 x 6" 15.00
Pudding, star, tin 12.50

FOOT & BED WARMERS

Bed warmer, brass pan w/hinged lid
chased w/running stag & stamped
date "1623," twisted wrought iron
handle, 33" l. $357.50
Bed warmer, brass pan w/engraved

floral design on lid, turned wood
handle, 42" l. 160.00

Bed warmer, brass pan w/pierced &
chased stylized floral decor on lid
above a conforming base, black-
painted baluster-turned handle,
43" l. 220.00

Bed warmer, brass pan w/stamped
floral decor, turned wood handle
w/splotches of dark green paint &
varnished, 19th c., 10" d.,
43" l. 308.00

Bed warmer, brass pan w/perforat-
ed cover w/stylized florals, turned
wooden handle w/putty grained
decor, American, early 19th c.,
43" l. (cover ring missing) 220.00

Bed warmer, brass pan w/chased
floral decor on lid, turned wood
handle, English, 19th c., 44" l.
(top repaired) 209.00

Bed warmer, brass pan w/perforat-
ed fitted cover w/stylized floral &
insect designs, turned maple handle w/old natural finish, early
19th c., 45" l. 357.50

Bed warmer, brass & copper,
pierced circular lid w/chased floral decor, turned wood handle,
late 18th-early 19th c., 45" l. 182.00

Bed warmer, copper pan w/simple
pierced design on lid, dovetail
construction, wrought iron hinged,
ring-turned wood handle, 42" l. . . 625.00

Bed warmer, copper pan w/pierced
& chased foliate design on brass
lid, turned fruitwood handle, 19th
c., 43½" l. 209.00

Bed warmer, copper pan w/pierced
& engraved standing peacock
flanked by florals on lid above
conforming base, turned wooden
handle, 47" l. 286.00

Foot warmer, cherrywood, pierced,
18th c., square 260.00

Foot warmer, Fresian carved wood,
6 sides chip-carved w/pinwheels,
stars, fans & various other geometric motifs, small brass feet,
brass wire handle, 8" h. 600.00

Pierced Tin Foot Warmer

Foot warmer, pierced tin box in
wooden frame, metal ember pan,
8" sq., 6" h. (ILLUS.) 90.00

Foot warmer, pierced tin box
w/soapstone insert in top, original whale oil burner, ca. 1830,
4½ x 6 x 9½" 120.00

Foot warmer, pierced tin box, in
mortised wooden frame w/turned
corner posts, 8¾" l. 110.00

Foot warmer, stoneware pottery,
cylindrical, mottled brown Rock-
ingham glaze, 14" l. 60.00

Foot warmer, stoneware pottery,
marked "Henderson Foot Warmer," incised "Dorchester Pottery
Works, Boston, Ma." & dated
11/1/1921 . . . . 100.00

FOOT SCRAPERS

Cast iron, cat silhouette, walking
animal w/tail erect, on oblong
base, old black paint, 9½" h.
(repaired break in leg) $125.00

Cast iron, model of horse mounted
on rectangular board, black, 11½
x 12½" 190.00

Cast iron, model of Dachshund dog,
15¾" l. 45.00

Cast iron, model of Dachshund dog,
21½" l. 65.00

Cast iron, model of Scottie dog,
5½ x 12" 65.00

Wrought iron, exaggerated ramhorn
scrolls, set in a stone block,
12 x 8" 225.00

FRACTURS

*Fractur paintings are decorative birth and
marriage certificates of the 18th and 19th centuries and also include family registers and
similar documents. Illuminated family documents, birth and baptismal certificates, religious texts and rewards of merit, in a
particular style, are known as "fractur" because of the similarity to the 16th century
type-face of that name. Gay watercolor borders, frequently incorporating stylized birds,
angels, animals or flowers surrounded the
hand-lettered documents, which were executed by local ministers, school masters or itiner-
ant penmen. Most are of Pennsylvania Dutch
origin.*

Fractur Reward of Merit

Birth record for John Taut, pen & ink & watercolor, vital statistics in ornamental calligraphy on lined paper w/stylized florals, corner fans & blue border, Strasburg, Lancaster County, Pennsylvania, dated May 22, 1861, in grain-painted frame, 9¾ x 12"........$275.00

Birth record for Lecha County, Pennsylvania infant, pen & ink & watercolor, vital statistics recording birth in 1814 in center, w/painting of an eagle & border of stylized florals executed in red, black & yellow, signed Martin Brechall, contemporary frame, 11 5/8 x 16 5/8" 800.00

Birth record for Northampton County, Pennsylvania infant in 1801, pen & ink & watercolor, vital statistics in ornamental German calligraphy surrounded by colorful birds, stylized florals & angels executed in shades of red, yellow, olive green & black, attributed to the "Flying Angel," framed, 20½ x 17½" 3,450.00

Birth & Baptismal record for Georg Miller, vital statistics in ornamental German calligraphy & strapwork lettering within heart-shaped reserve surrounded by open blossoms, vines & paired hearts sprouting luxuriant tulip buds & blossoms, borders enclosing vines & buds, recording birth March 16, 1786, Shenandoah County, Virginia, 12 1/8 x 14¼" 1,925.00

Bookplate for Esther Weber, pen & ink & watercolor, red & black lettering within a blue inner design all within a border of red & green florals on yellow, dated 1815, in ornate chip-carved frame hewn from single piece of wood 1,850.00

Reward of Merit, pen & ink & watercolor, presented to Johann Adam Eyer, Montgomery County, Pennsylvania, stylized tulip decorated w/a cross-hatched checkerboard motif emanating from a heart inscribed in ornamental German calligraphy w/a virtuous precept & dated 1761, executed in bright tones of red, yellow, green & blue, 2¾ x 6½", together w/a tiny bookmark dated 1754, 2 pcs. (ILLUS. of Reward of Merit) 1,650.00

FRAMES

Victorian Frame

Bird's eye maple, plain, 22 x 17" ... $75.00
Brass, model of a sailboat w/cherub in stern, opening for picture in sail, Victorian, 13¼ x 9½" 75.00
Bronze, easel-type, ½" w. framework cast w/tulip blossoms & foliage, 5" w., 7" h. 55.00
Bronze, ornately cast filigree framework set w/two shell cameos, 9¼" w., 11½" h. 275.00
Bronze-finish cast iron, rococo-style cast w/pierced leaf scrolls & crest, 8½" w., 12" h. (ILLUS.) 65.00
Giltwood & gesso, central circular aperature within a leaf-molded border, matted corners applied w/cherub's heads within a deeply cavetto outer border centered by shells, corners carved & pierced w/foliage, 48½" w., 58" h. 3,300.00
Oak, plain, 19½ x 17½" 49.00
Painted pine, 2" w. beveled framework, original orangish red flame graining, 13¾" w., 18" h. 145.00
Painted poplar, 1¾" w. framework,

original yellow & dark brown combed graining, 17 x 13″ 155.00

Pine, plain, 13 x 11″, pr. 75.00

Silverplate, Art Nouveau style floral border, 5 x 7″ oval 28.00

Sterling silver, central circular medallion w/hammered border & ornate repousse floral design, impressed "HM," w/English hallmarks for 1903 & 1906, 5¾″ & 6¼″ h., pr. 1,760.00

Sterling silver, textured border w/sinuous repousse floral design, J. Zimmerman, Birmingham, 1902, 8¼″ d. 440.00

Sterling silver, textured surface, scalloped border w/beaded scroll-work design, Walker & Hall, Sheffield, 1906, 8½″ h. 330.00

Sterling silver, rectangular center in convex border w/rounded corners, impressed "WJM & Co.," English hallmark for 1906, 10″ h. 550.00

Tin, filigree framework, Victorian, 7 x 5″ 38.00

Walnut, cross-bar, applied leaves at corners, 16 x 14″ 30.00

Walnut, w/gilt inner liner, Victorian, ca. 1860, 35″ h. oval 198.00

FRATERNAL ORDER COLLECTIBLES

B.P.O.E. Match Safe

B.P.O.E. (Benevolent & Protective Order of Elks) badge, metal alligator above large bronze elk head, New Orleans Reunion 1898 .... $20.00

B.P.O.E. lap robe, 51″ w., 71″ l. 150.00

B.P.O.E. match safe, sterling silver w/elk head decor (ILLUS.) 85.00

B.P.O.E. mug, elk, clock on purple ground, Burnt Art Ware 35.00

B.P.O.E. stein, "Detroit, Mich. Elk's Temple Court House," beige & dark green 60.00

F.O.E. (Fraternal Order of Eagles) medal, enameled bronze w/embossed eagle, 1904 .... 10.00

I.O.O.F. (Independent Order of Odd Fellows) banner, silk, on rod, 5 colorful symbols, heart in hand, etc., 19th c., 19″ wide, 31″ l. 75.00

I.O.O.F. sign, brass, 9 x 5½″ 15.00

Knights of Pythias goblet, green glass, 1900, Rochester 45.00

Knights Templar loving cup, 1898, Philadelphia, American China, Toronto, Ohio.................. 75.00

Masonic apron, blue velvet w/silver metallic thread embroidery & fringe, painted eye emblem, in old gilt frame, overall 21¾ x 19½″ 50.00

Masonic bookends, cast iron, emblem, tools & 13 steps decor, pr.......................... 90.00

Masonic door knocker, brass 65.00

Masonic pin w/fob, gold,"St. Paul 1908," Kansas City Ararat 25.00

Masonic teaspoon, sterling silver, openwork, "AAONMS"........... 26.00

O.E.S. (Order of Eastern Star) badge, celluloid, ear of corn, 1908, Mitchell, S.D. 15.00

Redmen Council badge, celluloid, colorful Indian maiden & warrior, 1916, Brookings, S.D. 15.00

Shrine 1894 whiskey glass, "Syrian Temple," Denver 85.00

Shrine 1900 goblet, clear glass, "Rochester, New York" 80.00

Shrine 1902 cocktail tumbler, clear glass, "Pittsburgh" & "San Francisco," pedestal, sword, etc., 5″ h. . . 75.00

Shrine 1903 mug, clear glass, "Pittsburgh," head of Chief Saratoga, scimitar handle 85.00

Shrine 1905 3-handled mug, clear glass, "Niagara Falls" 57.00

Shrine 1908 champagne, clear glass, "Louisville" 67.00

Shrine 1908 goblet, "Pittsburgh" & "St. Paul"..................... 52.00

Shrine 1909 bowl, iridescent glass w/gold & amber tobacco leaves base, "Louisville"............... 57.00

Shrine 1910 champagne, clear glass, "Pittsburgh," alligators.......... 55.00

Shrine 1911 loving cup, double-handled, "Rochester" 75.00

Shrine 1917 tumbler, 3-sided, "Minneapolis".................. 60.00

Shrine paperweight, spelter, figural

Shriner wearing fez, tie & coat,
advertising roofing, "Made by
American Art Works, Coshocton,
Ohio," 2¼ x 2½ x 4½".......... 32.00
Shrine plate, Shriner w/fez, camel
border, 10½" d. 32.00
Shrine water set: tankard pitcher &
3 mugs; fez & sword insignia, "Alhambra," 4 pcs................. 350.00

FRUIT JARS

Swayzee's Improved Mason

Agnew & Co. or John Agnew & Son
on bottom, wax sealer, aqua,
qt. $75.00
Atlas E-Z Seal, aqua, pt. 2.00
Ball (The), Pat. Apl'd. For, green,
qt. 165.00
Ball Perfect Mason, blue, qt. 1.50
Ball Perfect Mason, olive amber,
qt. 38.00
Ball Standard, dark green, ½ gal. .. 8.00
Beaver, dark green, midget 78.00
"The Best" Fruitkeeper, aqua, qt.
(no glass lid) 25.00
Cohansey, aqua, ½ pt. 90.00
Decker's Victor, Mason City, Iowa,
clear, qt. (no glass lid) 8.00
D G Co., w/monogram, aqua, qt.... 45.00
Fahnstock Fortune & Co., wax seal-
er, aqua, ½ gal. 38.00
Flaccus (E.C.) Co., w/steers head,
clear, pt. ....50.00 to 75.00
Flaccus (E.C.) Co., w/steers head,
milk white, pt. 225.00
Fruit-Keeper, aqua, qt. 35.00
Glassboro Trade Mark Improved,
aqua, ½ gal. 15.00
Globe, amber, ½ gal. 55.00

Golden-State Trade (S in triangle)
Mark Mason, Pat'd. Dec. 20, 1910,
Other Patents Pen., clear, qt. 10.00
Hero (The), green, qt. (no glass
lid) 17.00
J & B Fruit Jar, Patd. June 14, 1898,
aqua, qt. 55.00
Kerr Glass Top Mason, clear, pt. ... 1.00
Kerr Self Sealing Trade Mark Reg
Mason, clear, ½ gal. 150.00
Kline (A.R.), Pat. Oct. 27, 1863 on
glass stopper, blue, pt. 42.50
Leader (The), aqua, ½ gal. 45.00
Lightning, aqua, ½ pt............. 12.00
Lightning, amber, qt. 30.00
Lightning Trade Mark, light olive
yellow, qt...................... 105.00
Lindell Glass Co. on bottom, wax
sealer, amber, qt................ 17.50
Lyon & Bossard's Jar, East Strouds-
burg, Pa., aqua, qt. 325.00
Macomb, Ill. on bottom, stoneware,
gal............................ 28.50
Mason Fruit Jar, Patent Nov. 30th,
1858 below keystone, aqua, qt.... 12.00
Mason Improved, amber, ½ gal. ... 35.00
Mason's Patent Nov. 30th, 1858,
w/Hero cross, aqua, midget...... 12.50
Mason's Patent Nov. 30th, 1858,
w/CFJ monogram, amber,
½ gal. 550.00
Mason's Patent Nov. 30th, 1858,
w/moon, star & sunburst, aqua,
½ gal. 110.00
Millville Atmospheric Fruit Jar,
clear, qt. (no glass lid) 19.00
Millville, Pat. June 18, 1861, green,
½ gal. 45.00
Peoria Inspected Pottery on base,
stoneware, wax sealer, qt. 22.50
Perfect Seal, Made in Canada, Wide
Mouth Adjustable, dark seven-up
green, pt. 125.00
Pettit (H.W.), Westville, N.J. on
base, aqua, pt. 12.00
Queen (The), w/CFJ Co. monogram,
aqua, qt. 35.00
Royal of 1876, green, qt............ 145.00
Safety, amber, pt................. 250.00
Schram Automatic Sealer, clear,
½ gal. 7.00
Simplex, amethyst, pt............. 25.00
Standard, W. McC. & Co., wax seal-
er, aqua, qt. 12.50
Swayzee's Improved Mason, aqua,
½ gal. (ILLUS.) 5.50
Veteran, w/bust & stars, clear,
qt. 5.00
Weir (The), Patented March 1st,
1892, stoneware, ½ gal. 24.00
Western Stoneware, pottery, qt..... 20.00

FURNITURE FOR CHILDREN

by Connie Morningstar

Special Focus!

Certain furniture items designed especially for children have been around since ancient times. One of the oldest examples extant is a slat-sided rocking crib found in the ruins of Herculaneum, an Italian city destroyed by the Vesuvius eruption in A.D. 79.

But it wasn't until the mid-19th century, and more especially the early 20th, that children were considered important enough to have a significant variety of furniture designed for their particular proportions. By 1920, a number of furniture manufacturers were producing a line of juvenile pieces. A writer for the *Grand Rapids Furniture Record* noted in the March issue of that year, "This is the younger generation. Not only should parents be interested in the project of buying furniture for their children, but the youngsters themselves should be urged to buy furniture for their children–the dolls." He reasoned that a child who had bought doll furniture at a store that also supplied her bedroom or nursery outfittings would think kindly of that place when the time came to furnish her own home.

"Far greater attention is being paid to children's furniture now than in the past," he wrote. "In former years, a child's wants were supposed to be provided amply if she had a little red chair, or a miniature rocker–but now complete bedroom suites are hers, as well as dining room and drawing room furniture that may be set up in the nursery."

Also in 1920, the John M. Smyth Company of Chicago used a full-page ad in the local papers to tell about its juvenile line: "There are breakfast room sets that are patterned identically after those we sell to grown-ups; there are little Windsor chairs, juvenile Morris chairs, and an assortment of chairs, rockers, tables, etc."

Lord & Taylor, New York City, carried out the idea of a child's room in an alcove off its large furniture department. The furniture, blue with touches of gold, consisted of a child-size dressing table, chiffonier, several rocking chairs, and a table. Abraham & Strauss, Brooklyn, was the first store to establish an entire house to display children's furnishings. There, a two-story, 12-foot house, complete with broad veranda with hammock and porch swing, was presided over by a "little miss dressed as a little old woman" who escorted visitors through the display pointing out features of the various pieces, naming their prices, and directing the prospective buyer to the proper department to complete the sale.

Cradles and cribs. As noted above, cradles have been around since earliest times. (See *Antique Trader Price Guide* special focus, "Cradles," Summer 1983). In fact, the oldest extant furniture piece made in America is Peregrin White's wicker cradle, now in the Pilgrim Hall collection at Plymouth, Mass. Early cradles were solid-sided, hooded affairs that effectively shut out air along with the drafts they were intended to discourage. Holes or knobs along the upper edges of the side rails were for the purpose of anchoring mosquito netting and/or to lace in the already swaddled infant. Clearly, he was meant to breathe little and move less. Once the baby graduated from the cradle, he invariably moved into an adult bed with one or more others.

New philosophies began to develop about the middle of the 19th century and the closed cradle gradually gave way to a variety of airy, spindle-sided forms, followed by patented cribs that rocked or swung on a platform; and, by the 1920's, sanitary, enameled steel or wood-spindled cribs with a foot-latch controlled drop side.

In 1927, Sears offered just such a crib in white enamel, without mattress, for $6.75. New also at that time was the youth bed designed to serve the average child of twelve. Side rails were low and fixed; springs were link steel fabric; and its hardwood frame had a washable ivory enamel finish. Price was $12.85 with $5.50 additional for the 34x64-inch felt mattress.

The "Kar-O-Kid," patented in 1917, was touted by its maker, Union Furniture &

Novelty Company, Warren, Pa., as the most complete and modern baby tender. Light, durable, and screen sided, it was mounted on large rubber-tired wheels and had a "sanitary" mattress over woven-wire adjustable springs. The manufacturer claimed it was the best combination of bassinet, playpen, baby-walker, and sleeping car for outside and indoor use. At any rate, it was somewhat less a cage than its completely screened successor. The latter had a lift top and a drop side hinged at its mid-section.

Highchairs. Researchers have noted that the child's highchair was known in 16th-century England but was a rare luxury in America more than a hundred years later. Dating here from the late 18th century, highchairs were essentially scaled-down dining chairs without footrest, tray, and often, arms. By the middle of the 19th century, the footrest had been added as well as arms through which a rod might be placed in order, hopefully, to restrain the child.

The all-important tray (called "table" or "shelf" in old catalogs) seems to have appeared on the child's highchair, attachable to the arms or hinged to the rear stiles, by the 1880's. Other highchairs were a bit wider, lower, and lacked a tray. Identified variously as a youth chair, table chair, or misses' highchair, these pieces were intended for the older child who might be trusted to take his meals at the family dining table.

Children's highchairs advertised in Montgomery Ward's 1895 catalog ranged from a plain spindleback model with wood seat and a tray that attached across the arms for $1 to a reed version with tray that raised over the back for $2.45. Eight models were offered at the time, and cane seats were available on each for twenty cents additional. None had safety straps. In fact, straps apparently were not used until the 1920's and evidence of one today could be an aid in dating the piece from that time. Even then, they appeared only on the more expensive models, i.e., $4.75 to $5.25 for Sears' top-of-the-line highchairs in 1927.

Most intriguing were the combination pieces that could be adjusted to become a highchair, rocker, child's chair, or stroller (carriage). They were manufactured by various firms at least from the early 1880's into the 1920's. Hale & Kilburn Manufacturing Company, Philadelphia, in 1883 offered a child's "Chariot" chair that combined a "High Chair on Wheels, a Low Chair on Wheels, a Rocking Chair, a Parlor Chariot (carriage), a Chariot with Propellers, a Chariot with Shafts." The rockers were used as handles for pushing the chair and also as shafts for pulling the piece.

J. S. Ford & Johnson, Chicago, offered highchair/carriage models in 1901 from $24 to $39 per dozen, wholesale; and the high-chair/rocker/carriage models from $39 to $48. All were made of oak or birch, golden oak finish, with double pressed and spindle backs or cane backs and cane seats. In 1922, Heywood-Wakefield Company, Buffalo, N.Y. (warehouse), advertised nine models of combination chairs–five of which could be adjusted to four positions: table (high) chair, youth's diner, carriage, and rocker. Available in oak with a golden or fumed finish or gum finished in mahogany, walnut, or white enamel, they retailed from $14 to $18 each. Four other models had two positions–highchair/rocker or highchair/carriage. Prices ranged from $9.50 to $12.

Chairs and rockers. At least since the late 1700's, chairs, rockers, and a few rare settees and sofas have been made for children. But they were likely to be found only in the parlors of the affluent before the late 19th century. They came in all styles–Chippendale, Queen Anne, Louis XV, Gothic, Shaker, Hitchcock, and Mission and more–scaled-down versions of parlor pieces of the times. There were folding carpet rockers, bentwood pieces, wicker pieces, deck chairs, and frames made of horn. Seats were rarely less than nine inches or more than fourteen inches in height.

An 1877 ad by bentwood manufacturers Thonet Brothers of Vienna noted "children's furniture a specialty." In 1895, a child's version of the popular "bamboo" folding rocker was priced at eighty-five cents in Montgomery Ward's catalog. A child's large oak rocker with cane seat and pressed back brought $1.70 at the same time. Heywood Brothers & Wakefield Company showed twenty-one models of children's wicker rockers and two armchair models in its 1898 catalog. Sears' 1908 catalog listed a child's wicker rocker at $2.50.

In 1922, the Larkin catalog offered a child's varnished reed rocker for $10, cash or coupons, and a Mission style, solid oak piece for $5. Sears listed a Mission rocker in bright pink enamel for $1.48 ($1.50 in blue) in 1927.

Tables, desks, and bureaus. Fine late 18th and early 19th-century pieces in this category were made–highboys, lowboys, chests, drop-leaf tables, and slant-top bureau desks–but they are rare and more likely found in a museum than an antiques shop. For while the average Victorian child could expect to have a crib and rocking chair, only a privileged few were likely to have a little parlor table or bureau.

The A. H. Andrews & Company, Chicago, received the highest award at the Philadelphia Centennial in 1876 for its patented school desk (the one with the desk attached to the seat in front), a style used well into this century. Thonet offered child-size bentwood tables, washstands, and a unique one-piece bench (attached table and chair) in 1904. Union Furniture & Novelty Company advertised juvenile furniture in "grown up" patterns in 1919. Pieces included desks, chairs, secretaries, rolltops, tea tables, and blackboards.

In the late 1920's, Phoenix Chair Company, Sheboygan, Wis., produced children's tables in Windsor style to match the firm's popular Windsor chairs, rockers, and highchairs. Stock colors were plain ivory enamel, mahogany, and combination ivory and blue. At the same time, Urbana Furniture Company, Urbana, Ohio, advertised "one hundred exclusive designs" in its Happi-Tyme Nursery line. And York Furniture Manufacturing Company, York, Pa., turned out a juvenile line finished in ivory or grey enamel with a choice of handpainted decoration. Items included a chifforobe, chest of drawers, dresser, bed, chair, rocker, costumer (clothes tree), night table, and nursery chair.

Nursery chairs and other things. Next to cribs and rockers, nursery or cabinet (potty) chairs are most numerous. Montgomery Ward noted in 1895 that sales of its willow cabinet chair with attaching shelf and lifting seat were so great that it was almost impossible to supply the demand. The piece cost seventy-five cents. M-W's bow-back nursery chair with wood seat and no tray was priced at sixty-five cents at the same time. Heywood Brothers & Wakefield showed four models of the wicker cabinet chair, all with supported tray, in the 1898 catalog. An overhead swing tray appeared on the 1922 version available from Larkin Company for $7. A Mission style hardwood chair, ivory enameled and decorated with a transfer print, cost $3.55 from Sears in 1927. This piece had a safety strap, shaped seat, and came complete with chamber pot for $3.55.

Walkers descended from 17th-century walking or standing stools--spindled circular frames that effectively kept the infant from creeping, a development stage that was regarded as animalistic and to be avoided as much as possible. There was no seat. Out of popular use for nearly half a century, walkers re-appeared in the 1890's with casters, and, usually, a suspended seat. Two models were marketed by Montgomery Ward in 1895. One was a willow frame on casters, without seat, at $1.75; the other, a four-leg, castered piece with seat, tray, and fringed skirt, was priced at $2.40.

About the turn of the century, variations of the swing and jumper became popular items. Often a chair hung from a doorway sufficed, but there were more elaborate combination models such as Glascock Brothers Manufacturing Company's 1902 piece that was suspended from a frame by springs and

could be used as a jumper, highchair, crib, or rocking chair. Although swings and jumpers are still being made, they lost popularity to the playpen about 1920.

Today, prices of children's furniture, antique and nearly so, vary widely from the pitifully low at the average estate sale to the inflated tag prices at prestigious shows and the spectacular amounts received at auction for highly desirable authenticated pieces.

A number of museums have collections of children's furniture, among them the Essex Institute in Salem, Mass., and the Strong Museum in Rochester, N.Y. The latter features a continuing exhibit, "A Century of Childhood 1820-1920." An excellent 142-page illustrated catalog accompanies the exhibit and covers aspects of social and material culture, including furniture, of American childhood in that era. The book is available for $9.95 plus $2 postage and handling from the Museum Shop, The Strong Museum, One Manhattan Square, Rochester, NY 14607.

(Editor's Note: *Connie Morningstar, author of several books on furniture, including* Early Utah Furniture, *has also written numerous articles for various periodicals and is a regular columnist for* THE ANTIQUE TRADER WEEKLY *newspaper. Delving into the records of early cabinet makers, furniture shops and factories, she has become respected for her thorough research which enables her to write with accuracy, clarity and authority about American furniture styles and trends.)*

All furniture included in this listing was designed for children and is "child-sized."

CRADLES, CRIBS & YOUTH BEDS

Hooded Cradle

Cradle, hooded-type on rockers, birch, arched hood, canted & shaped sides, warm brownish finish, 41" l. (ILLUS.) $500.00

Cradle, hooded-type on rockers,
painted pine, arched hood, canted
sides, original worn red & black
grain-painted finish w/white striping & gilt-stenciled fruit baskets
decor, 39" l. (glued repairs &
replaced rockers) 175.00
Cradle, low country-style on rockers, birch, scalloped headboard
w/turned rail at crest, canted
sides, turned corner posts w/elon-
gated finials, 37½" l. (refinished
& w/repair to headboard)....... 275.00
Cradle, low country-style on rockers, cherrywood, canted sides,
pierced w/heart-shaped handgrips
in ends, refinished, 39" l. 185.00
Cradle, low country-style on rockers, painted pine, shaped head &
footboards, canted shaped sides,
shaped rockers pierced w/heart
design, original red & black
flame-painted graining, 38" l. 250.00
Cradle, low country-style on rockers, painted pine, shaped canted
sides, cut-out handgrip in footboard only, w/remnants of original red-painted finish 225.00
Cradle, low country-style on rockers, pine, square nail construction, canted sides, mitered joints,
refinished, 36" l. 275.00
Cradle, low country-style on rockers, walnut, dovetail construction,
rounded head & footboards,
shaped canted sides, 40" l........ 275.00

Platform Crib

Cradle, platform-type, Victorian
Renaissance Revival substyle, walnut w/burl walnut trim (ILLUS.) ... 575.00
Cradle, field or slave cradle, suspended-type, bentwood slats in

Field or Slave Cradle

frame w/sleigh-like runners &
cast iron wheels, Ford-Johnson
Co., Chicago (ILLUS.) 550.00

Bentwood Cradle by Thonet

Cradle, suspended-type, bentwood
by Thonet, Spanish Wall patt.
around sides, bentwood framework w/arched mosquito net rod
rising at one end, ca. 1890, unsigned, 57" l., 76" to top of rod
(ILLUS.) 1,100.00
Crib on rockers, spindle-sided,
birch, bowed head & footrails continuing to form legs on rockers,
narrow spindles all sides,
ca. 1915 .... 110.00
Crib on rockers, spindle-sided, maple, ring- and baluster-turned

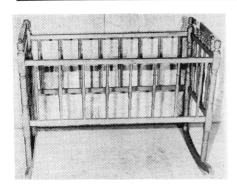

Spindle-sided Crib on Rockers

spindles & conforming corner
posts, 19th-20th c. (ILLUS.) 225.00

Brass Crib with Canopy

Crib, brass, tubular rods on all
  sides, corner posts w/finials
  supporting canopy frame
  (ILLUS.) . . . . .850.00 to 1,500.00
Crib, cast iron, rod spindles on
  sides, layers of peeling paint 85.00

Cast Iron Crib

Crib, cast iron, bent iron rod sides
  cast w/scrolls at juncture w/top &
  bottom rails, corner posts w/brass
  ball finials, one fold-down side,
  traces of original white paint,
  53 x 28", 37" h. (ILLUS.) 250.00

Wicker Crib

Crib, wicker, Victorian, natural rattan
  & reed, ornate
  (ILLUS.) . . . . .1,000.00 to 1,200.00
Crib, walnut, Victorian cottage-style,
  spool-turned, tall corner posts 595.00
Trundle bed, painted hardwood,
  shaped head & footboards flanked
  by short cannonball posts, original
  rope pegs, wooden wheels, worn
  yellow repaint 300.00
Trundle bed, painted hardwood,
  shaped headboard, block- and
  ring-turned posts & legs on wood-
  en wheels, rope-type, blue paint,
  42" w., 52" l., 15½" h. posts 462.50

Youth's Bed

Youth's bed, Victorian, walnut,
shaped headboard above baluster-turned spindles flanked by
turned posts w/shaped finials,
lower conforming footboard,
31" w., 38" h. (ILLUS.) 425.00

Youth's bed, American Empire
country-style, painted maple,
bulbous-turned head & footrails
on spindles, worn old red finish,
ca. 1845, 55" l., 24" h. posts 275.00

Youth's bed, American Empire
country-style, walnut, shaped
head & footboards flanked by
blocked & turned short posts, on
casters 650.00

Youth's bed, brass, tubular, single
size 200.00

HIGHCHAIRS

"Ladderback" Highchair

Highchair, American Colonial/Early
Federal "ladderback" model, 3
arched slats flanked by stiles
w/turned finials, turned arms on
shaped supports, refinished & replaced paper rush seat (ILLUS.) ..1,450.00

Highchair, Federal country-style,
painted, plain crestrail above 3-
spindle back flanked by "thumb-
back" uprights, plank seat,
splayed tapering turned legs
w/stretchers, old black repaint,
first half 19th c................ 235.00

Highchair, Turn-of-the-Century, oak,
pressed pattern in crestrail above
5-spindle back, plank seat, turned
legs w/footrest, w/"overhead"
tray, ca. 1900 .... 195.00

Highchair, Turn-of-the-Century, oak,
pressed pattern in crestrail above
4-spindle back, cane seat, ring-

Turn-of-the-Century Highchair

turned legs w/stretchers & footrest, w/"overhead" tray,
ca. 1900 (ILLUS.) 195.00

Spindle-back Highchair

Highchair, 20th century, spindle-
back, painted hardwood, w/"overhead" tray, factory-made, ca. 1920
(ILLUS.)........................ 75.00

Highchair, Victorian cottage-style,
painted finish, plain crestrail
above 3-spindle back flanked by
turned uprights, arms on single
turned support, plank seat, turned
slightly splayed legs w/stretchers
& footrest, late 19th c., now painted black....................... 115.00

Highchair, Windsor, plain crestrail above 4-spindle back flanked by bamboo-turned stiles, saddle seat, splayed legs w/turned stretchers, worn black paint w/remnants of yellow pin striping, New England, ca. 1780 . . . . 715.00

Highchair, Windsor, painted & decorated, "step-down" crestrail above 5-spindle back & shaped stiles, shaped seat, splayed bamboo-turned legs w/stretchers, old brown paint w/free-hand green foliage at crest, New England, ca. 1810 . . . . 495.00

Highchair, Windsor (late) lowback, bamboo-turned, U-shaped backrail above turned spindles, 36½" h. (footrest old replacement) 150.00

Windsor-style Highchair

Highchair, Windsor-style, bowed crestrail above beaker-form splat w/decal & 2 turned spindles, plank seat, turned legs w/stretchers & footrest, varnish finish, ca. 1930 (ILLUS.) 45.00

Highchair-Rocker

Highchair-rocker combination, Turn-of-the-Century, oak w/cane seat & cane back (ILLUS. in rocking chair position) 350.00

Highchair-Stroller

Highchair-stroller combination, Turn-of-the-Century, oak, pressed pattern back, shaped arms on spindle-turned supports, seat w/perforated plywood inset, X-form legs on cast iron wheels, ca. 1890 (ILLUS.) 240.00

Highchair-Stroller

Highchair-stroller combination, early 20th Century, birch, plain crestrail above beaker-form splat, "overhead" tray, arms on turned spindles, folding legs on small cast iron wheels, ca. 1920, refinished (ILLUS.) 295.00

ROCKERS

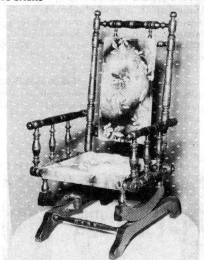

Platform Rocker

Platform rocker w/arms, Victorian
Eastlake substyle, spindle-
galleried crestrail & uprights
w/typical incised rings, ebonized
finish, replaced green velvet floral
upholstery, ca. 1890, 10" h. seat,
29" h. back (ILLUS.) 325.00

Early Sewing Rocker

Sewing rocker, Early American "ladderback" style, maple, 3-slat
back, woven rush seat, "carpet-
cutter" rockers, New England, ca.
1830, refinished, 13½" h. seat,
31" h. back (ILLUS.) 500.00

Sewing rocker, Shaker No. 0 size,
3-slat back, uprights w/turned
finials, (worn) tape seat, early
20th c. 195.00
Rocker w/arms, Adirondack (bent
twig construction), back w/five
vertical slats attached to bowed
twigs looped & continuing to
double-twist scrolling arms, slat
seat w/plain apron 340.00
Rocker w/arms, bentwood w/cane
seat, w/Thonet (Austria) label,
19th c. 475.00
Rocker w/arms, "Boston" type,
painted & decorated ..... 105.00 to 195.00

Garden or Lawn Rocker

Rocker w/arms, garden or lawn furniture, slat construction, varnish
finish, 20th c., 10" h. seat, 25" h.
back (ILLUS.) 95.00

Mission Oak Rocker

Rocker w/arms, Mission-style (Arts & Crafts movement), oak, plain crestrail above vertical splat, plain seat, flattened arms on squared supports, ca. 1915 (ILLUS.) 60.00

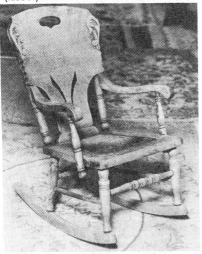

Turn-of-the-Century Rocker

Rocker w/arms, Turn-of-the-Century, back w/quarter-sawn veneer pierced w/handgrip & V-shape designs & die-stamped scrolls at ears, shaped arms on turned supports, leather-inset seat, now stripped of finish (ILLUS.) 125.00

Turn-of-the-Century Rocker

Rocker w/arms, Turn-of-the-Century, oak, pressed pattern crestrail

over 5-spindle back flanked by turned stiles, original fibreboard inset seat, shaped arms on turned support, 12" h. seat, 30" h. back (ILLUS.) 225.00

Rocker w/arms, Victorian, "Grecian" style, walnut w/caned seat & caned back .... 195.00 to 225.00

Rocker w/arms, Windsor-style, plain crestrail above 5 bamboo-turned spindles, turned arms on spindle support, shaped seat, bamboo-turned legs w/stretchers on rockers, refinished & w/light brown stain 135.00

Wicker Rocker

Rocker w/arms, wicker, painted white, early 1900's, 26" h. (ILLUS.) 135.00

Upholstered Wicker Rocker

Rocker w/arms, wicker, woven rattan & reed, upholstered back & seat w/loose cushion, reed-wrapped crestrail & legs, w/woven sides & apron, early 1900's (ILLUS.). 125.00

Wicker Rocker

Rocker w/arms, wicker, loom-woven fibre, w/loose cushion, 1920's (ILLUS.). 70.00

ARMCHAIRS & SIDECHAIRS

Corner Armchair

Armchair, corner-type, William & Mary, horseshoe-shaped back w/cushion-molded crest on turned supports, rush seat, New England, ca. 1750 (ILLUS.). 2,640.00

Armchair, Early American "ladderback" style, chestnut, maple & other hardwoods, 3 shaped back slats between turned uprights w/shaped finials, arms on vase-

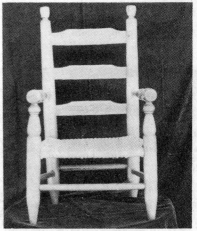

"Ladderback" Armchair

turned supports, (replaced) woven splint seat, pegged construction throughout, ca. 1800 (ILLUS.) 425.00

Armchair, English Regency, mahogany w/caned back & seat, tub-shaped backrest continuing to form arms, slightly bowed seat w/loose cushion, turned legs w/cross-scretchers, England, ca. 1820 . . . . 550.00

Federal Armchair

Armchair, Federal country-style "fancy," painted & decorated 2-slat back, downswept arms, upholstered seat, square tapering legs w/H-stretcher, worn stenciling & pinstriping on painted ground, 11" h. at seat, 23" h. back (ILLUS.). 695.00

Armchair, Mission-style (Arts & Crafts movement), oak, 3-slat

back between squared uprights,
red leather-covered seat flanked
by flattened arms, square legs
w/stretchers, ca. 1915, 11½" h.
at seat, 25½" h. back 125.00

Windsor "Lowback" Armchair

Armchair, Windsor "lowback" (so-
called "Firehouse" Windsor), U-
shaped backrail w/cushion-
molded crest above turned spindles in back, plank seat, splayed
tapering legs, ca. 1830 (ILLUS.) ... 350.00

Windsor-type Armchair

Armchair, Windsor-type, 1920's copy
of early "bowback" style, mahogany finish, 10" h. at seat,
24½" h. back (ILLUS.) 150.00
Deck chair, folding-type, oak, slat
construction 39.00
Desk chair, swivel-seat model, oak,
pressed pattern crestrail above
spindle back, upholstered inset on
adjustable seat, ca. 1900, 30" h.
back (ILLUS.).................. 125.00

Swiveling Desk Chair

Ice cream parlor chair, bent iron
wire frame, oak seat ...... 25.00 to 40.00

Nursery Chair

Nursery (or potty) chair, wicker,
woven willow back & skirt, wood-
en seat w/lift lid to chamber pot,
painted white, 19" h. back
(ILLUS.).................. 40.00 to 70.00

Adirondack Chair

Side chair, Adirondack, bent rustic branches (ILLUS.) 35.00

Side chair, Sheraton-style, curly maple, original rush seat, turned legs, old worn yellow paint, 24" h. back 215.00

Side chair, Mission-style, oak, 2-slat back, plank seat, square legs 25.00

Child's Shaker "Tilting" Chair

Side chair, Shaker "tilting" type, maple, 3-slat back, turned uprights w/shaped finials, woven reed seat, Enfield, Connecticut, ca. 1840 (ILLUS.) 1,320.00

Turn-of-the-Century Side Chair

Side chair, Turn-of-the-Century, ash, pressed pattern crestrail above 4-spindle back, 1900-15 (ILLUS.) 110.00

Side chair, Victorian (late), oak, plain crestrail w/incised leaf carvings over 4-spindle back, reinforced between spindles & stiles

w/twisted wire, plank seat, turned legs w/twisted wire cross-stretcher, 10" h. at seat, 22" h. back 115.00

Windsor Birdcage

Side chair, Windsor "birdcage," 6-spindle back, bamboo-turned throughout (ILLUS.) 575.00

Windsor Rodback

Side chair, Windsor "rodback," plain crestrail above 5-spindle back flanked by uprights, bamboo-turned throughout, shaped seat, splayed legs w/stretchers (ILLUS.) 265.00

Youth's chair, Turn-of-the-Century, oak, pressed pattern crestrail above 5 ball-turned spindles, cane seat, turned legs w/stretchers, ca. 1900, 21" h. at seat, 41" h. back . . 225.00

CHESTS & CUPBOARDS

Blanket chest, Federal country-style, painted walnut, oblong top lifting to well in case, paneled sides & cut-out feet, 19th c. 495.00

William & Mary Child's Blanket Chest

Blanket chest, William & Mary period, painted pine, New England, ca. 1740, 28 x 14" (ILLUS.) 6,050.00

Child's American Empire Chest

Chest of drawers, American Empire, cherrywood & tiger stripe maple, 30" h. (ILLUS.) 3,800.00

Chest of drawers, American Empire, mahogany & curly maple, oblong top set w/three recessed drawers above case w/deep upper drawer over 3 slightly recessed drawers flanked by ogee-molded stiles, cut-out scroll feet, refinished & w/some veneer damage 550.00

Chest of drawers, American Empire, painted & decorated, oblong top above case w/deep upper drawers over 3 slightly recessed graduated long drawers flanked by

Child's American Empire Decorated Chest

turned columns, curved apron, bulbous-turned feet, gilt-stenciled turned columns & apron on dark ground, (replaced) brass pulls, New England, ca. 1820 (ILLUS.). . .1,045.00

Cupboard, Hutch-type, painted finish, 1-piece construction, superstructure w/plain shelf above single open shelf & work surface above pr. cupboard doors w/picture frame molding, paneled sides 595.00

Stepback Cupboard

Cupboard, stepback-type, pine, 1-piece construction, crest w/molded cornice above pr. single-pane glazed cupboard doors opening to shelves above pr. short drawers & pr. paneled cupboard doors, 23" w., 39" h. (ILLUS.) 395.00

Primitive Cupboard

Cupboard, stepback-type, primitive pine, 1-piece construction, plain top above pr. single-pane glazed cupboard doors above open pie shelf over pr. short drawers & (replaced plywood) cupboard doors, original hinges & white porcelain pulls, 1930's, 27" w., 43½" h. (ILLUS.) 189.00

DESKS

Cylinder-front Desk

Cylinder-front (simulated tambour) desk, oak, shaped crest above shelf over shallow drawer, interior pigeonholes w/shelf below, trestle base, ca. 1885, 22" w., 12½" deep, 32" h. (ILLUS.) 450.00

Folding Lift-top Desk

Folding lift-top desk, oak, hinged top lifting to open compartment, folding X-base, ca. 1920, 20 x 12½" top, 21½" h. (ILLUS.) 115.00

Lift-top desk, schoolmaster's type w/superstructure case filled w/small drawers, hinged lid opening to compartment, square tapering legs, dovetail construction, ca. 1840 . . . . 1,100.00

Lift-top Desk

Lift-top desk, oak, w/inner blackboard beneath upper lift-top, diepressed pattern on crest, trestle base, 24 x 17¾" slant-top, 32½" h. at crest (ILLUS.) 175.00

Roll-top desk, painted finish, C-roll opening to pigeonholes, single pedestal to one side w/two drawers, painted red, 24" w., 15" deep, 34" h. 145.00

Roll-top Desk with Single Pedestal

Roll-top desk, oak, C-roll opening to pigeonholes, single pedestal to side w/two short drawers, square legs, 29" w., 35" h. (ILLUS.) 350.00

Slant-top desk, Tramp Art, chip-carved layers, slanting hinged writing surface opening to compartment over base w/drawer & w/cupboard door to one side, light red-painted finish, original white porcelain pulls, 1890's, 25" h. 265.00

LOUNGES, SETTEES, ETC.

Lounge-Toy Chest

Lounge, reupholstered, hinged padded top lifts to reveal toy box, ca. 1900, 42" l., 16" w., 16" h. (ILLUS.) 250.00

Mammy's bench, painted finish, plain crestrail above 11-spindle back, shaped arms on turned supports, plank seat w/baby guard, turned legs w/flattened frontal stretcher on rockers, original painted finish 950.00

Schoolhouse bench, Amish, painted pine, plank seat w/diagonal braces to sides that form cut-out feet 125.00

Settle bench, painted finish, double-back, painted black w/gold striping & free-hand acorns & tulip decor, Lancaster, Pennsylvania 1,550.00

TABLES

Dining Table

Dining table, golden oak, round top, pedestal base, ca. 1920, 25½" d., 24" h. (ILLUS.) 395.00

Dining table, oak veneer, round top, pedestal base 265.00

Ice Cream Parlor Table

Ice cream parlor table, round oak top w/metal frame, bent iron wire legs w/cross-stretcher support, 18½" d., 19" h. (ILLUS.)..... 150.00

Parlor table, golden oak, 14" square top, shaped apron, vase- and ring-turned splayed legs joined by shaped medial stretcher-shelf ball feet, ca. 1900, 19" h. 195.00

Playtime table, graniteware top w/Jumbo elephant & ABC's center & nursery rhyme characters at corners on white ground, painted birch apron, square legs 125.00

Work table, Amish, walnut, oblong top w/low rim on 3 sides, plain apron w/single drawer, turned legs, Pennsylvania origin 800.00

(End of Special Focus)

FURNITURE

Furniture made in the United States during the 18th and 19th centuries is coveted by collectors. American antique furniture has a European background, primarily English, since the influence of the Continent usually found its way to America by way of England. If the style did not originate in England, it came to America by way of England. For this reason, some American furniture styles carry the name of an English monarch or an English designer. However, we must realize that, until recently, little research has been conducted and even less published on the Spanish and French influences in the areas of the California missions and New Orleans.

After the American Revolution, cabinetmakers in the United States shunned the prevailing styles in England and chose to bring the French styles of Napoleon's Empire to the United States and we have the uniquely named "American Empire" style of furniture in a country that never had an emperor.

During the Victorian period, quality furniture began to be mass-produced in this country with its rapidly growing population. So much walnut furniture was manufactured, the vast supply of walnut was virtually depleted and it was of necessity that oak furniture became fashionable as the 19th century drew to a close.

For our purposes, the general guidelines for dating furniture will be:

Pilgrim Century - 1620-85
William & Mary - 1685-1720
Queen Anne - 1720-50
Chippendale - 1750-85
Federal - 1785-1820
  Hepplewhite - 1785-1800
  Sheraton - 1800-20
American Empire - 1815-40
Victorian - 1840-1900
  Early Victorian - 1840-50
  Gothic Revival - 1840-90
  Louis XV (rococo) - 1845-70
  Louis XVI - 1865-75
  Eastlake - 1870-95
  Renaissance - 1860-85
  Jacobean & Turkish Revival -
    1870-90
Art Nouveau - 1890-1918
Turn-of-the-Century - 1895-1910
Mission (Arts & Crafts movement) -
  1900-15
Art Deco - 1925-40

All furniture included in this listing is American unless otherwise noted. Also see MINIATURES (Replicas).

ARMOIRES & WARDROBES

Armoire, Art Nouveau, fruitwood, pierce-carved crest w/delicate spring blossoms above center section & flanking section, each set w/mirrored doors opening to drawers at center & open shelves at sides, signed Majorelle, France, ca. 1900, overall 80½" w., 81" h. $5,500.00

Armoire, Art Nouveau, walnut & fruitwood, berry-carved projecting cornice above mirrored door carved w/sinuous vines & opening to shelves above & below 5 short drawers inlaid w/wisteria & w/floriform brass keyhole escutcheons, base w/burlwood drawers set w/mistletoe handles, 4 lug feet, attributed to Majorelle, France, ca. 1900, 55½" w., 88" h. 12,650.00

Art Nouveau Armoire

Armoire, Art Nouveau, walnut w/inlaid kingwood panels at sides, crest carved w/foliate vines & undulating tendrils above pr. mirror-inset cupboard doors, by Louis Majorelle, France, ca. 1900 (ILLUS.) 4,620.00

Schrank (Pennsylvania-German version of a massive wardrobe), walnut, 2 part construction: upper section w/crown-molded cornice above plain frieze over raised double-panel cupboard doors opening to shelves; lower section w/arrangement of 3 shallow drawers over pr. deeper drawers, cut-out ogee bracket feet, 51" w. (59½" w. at cornice), 79¾" h. (refinished & w/replaced hardware & replaced drawers in base) 3,400.00

Schrank, walnut, 3-part construction: removable molded cornice over wide overhang; center section w/pr. 6-panel cupboard doors flanked by applied turned half-round columns; base w/pr. short drawers w/conforming applied columns & ogee-molded bracket feet, Chester County, Pennsylvania 11,500.00

American Empire "Classical" Wardrobe

Wardrobe, American Empire in the "classical" taste, mahogany, 3-part construction: removable projecting cornice; middle section w/pr. cross-banded cupboard doors opening to fitted compartment flanked by free-standing columns; base raised on carved animal paw feet; New York, ca. 1825, 60" w., 86" h. (ILLUS.) 4,400.00

Wardrobe, Federal, mahogany, 2-part construction: removable projecting cornice; case w/pr. paneled cupboard doors opening to adjustable shelves & small drawers, ring-turned legs on brass ball feet, 64" w., 93" h. 3,300.00

Victorian Gothic Wardrobe

Wardrobes, Victorian Gothic sub-style, mahogany, crest w/central Gothic spire w/"fleur-de-lis" finial above case w/pr. paneled cupboard doors applied w/cartouche-shaped molding panels, molded base, elaborate feet, probably Philadelphia, ca. 1845, pr. (ILLUS. of one) 2,530.00

Wardrobe, Victorian country-style, butternut, beveled cornice above single double-paneled door w/cast iron lock & porcelain knob opening to interior shelf above wooden hooks, cut-out bracket feet, 47¾" w., 79½" h. 400.00

Wardrobe, Victorian country-style, poplar, coved beveled cornice above pr. 4-panel cupboard doors opening to shelf over hooks, scalloped base, bracket feet, layers of old blue paint over original grain-painted finish, 49½" w., 79" h. 400.00

Wardrobe, Victorian country-style, walnut, beveled cornice above pr. paneled cupboard doors w/original cast iron lock, bracket feet, 80¼" h. 500.00

BEDS

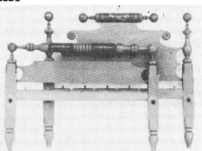

American Empire Masonic Bed

American Empire low poster bed w/Masonic decoration, maple, headboard w/"rolling pin" crest-rail painted black & gilt-stenciled w/basket of fruit above grain-painted headboard w/scrolling ears painted black & gilt-stenciled w/Masonic devices, flanked by vigorously turned & blocked low posts w/"cannonball" finials, foot-board w/turned blanket rail decorated in conforming taste, New York, ca. 1830 (ILLUS.) 660.00

American Empire tall poster bed, cherrywood & maple, shaped headboard & footrail flanked by ring- and baluster-turned posts, ca. 1830, refinished & w/replaced siderails, 52" w., 59" h. posts 525.00

American Empire "tester" bed, birch, shaped headboard w/turned crest-rail ending in bell-shaped ends & flanked by rope-ring- and baluster-turned posts, original rope-pegged siderails & arched tester, stained finish, 66¾" h. posts (double size).......................... 1,300.00

American Empire country-style low poster bed, poplar w/red-stained finish, solid shaped headboard flanked by heavy baluster-turned posts w/flattened ball finials, conforming lower footboard & original rope-peg siderails (single size) 275.00

Art Nouveau bed, bird's eye walnut & oak marquetry, high headboard w/curving crest centering circular keystone flanked by inlaid design of thorny flowers, matching lower footboard, France, ca. 1900, 56" w., 63" h. headboard 1,320.00

Art Nouveau bed, fruitwood, shaped headboard pierce-carved in medium relief w/spring blossoms & undulating vines, matching lower footboard, attributed to Louis Majorelle, France, ca. 1900, 65" w., 46" h............................ 1,980.00

Art Nouveau bed, mahogany, carved entwined openwork crest w/clematis blossoms, vines & leaves above paneled headboard, w/matching lower vine-carved paneled footboard, attributed to Louis Majorelle, France, early 20th c. (queen size)......................... 4,400.00

Brass bed, tubular, plain, burnished (double size).................... 895.00

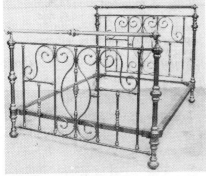

Brass Bed

Brass bed, tubular, ornate S-scrolls, burnished, early 20th c., double size (ILLUS.) 1,375.00

Cast iron bed, head & footboard w/iron rods within framework, complete w/wire mesh spring, three-quarter size (needs painting) 65.00

Cast Iron Bed with Brass Trim

Cast iron bed w/brass trim, folding-type, painted white w/burnished brass trim, complete w/flat spring, patented Jan. 26, 1904 (ILLUS.)....................... 750.00

Federal tall poster bed, mahogany, shaped headboard flanked by turned tapering posts & plain footrail flanked by fluted, turned tapering posts, square legs, spade feet, Pennsylvania, ca. 1780, 56½" w., 92½" h. posts 9,900.00

Federal Tall Poster Bed

Federal tall poster bed, mahogany, shaped headboard flanked by reeded- and acanthus-carved tapering headposts & conforming footposts on tapering legs ending in brass caps, probably New York, ca. 1810, tops of posts restored & lacking casters, 59½" w., 78" l. (ILLUS.) 4,675.00

Federal tester bed, mahogany, shaped headboard flanked by baluster- and ring-turned posts & w/con-

forming footposts w/waterleaf carvings above reeded urns, circular
spade feet, Massachusetts, 1800-15,
w/replaced tester, 56" w., 74½" l.,
92" h. 5,500.00

Pair Tester Beds

Federal tester beds, mahogany,
shaped headboard w/foliate-carved
crest & scrolling ears & plain footrail flanked by pineapple- and foliate-carved tapering posts on reeded legs & turned spade feet, pr.
(ILLUS.) 3,200.00
Federal country-style low poster
bed, maple, paneled head & footboards flanked by elaborate
baluster-turned posts w/shaped
finials, New England, 1810-30,
original finish, 49" w., 75" l.,
43½" h. posts 440.00
Federal country-style low poster
bed, maple, solid headboard &
footboard w/blanket roll added at
later date, flanked by baluster-
turned posts w/acorn finials,
48" h. posts (three-quarter
size) 850.00

Federal Country-Style Low Poster Bed

Federal country-style low poster
bed, pine & maple, shaped pine
headboard w/scrolling ears

flanked by curly maple ring- and
baluster-turned posts w/"cannonball" finials, shaped footboard &
turned footrail flanked by conforming posts, original rope-peg
siderails, 41½" w., 67¾" l.,
49" h. posts (ILLUS.) 275.00
Federal country-style tall poster bed,
maple, shaped headboard flanked
by baluster-turned curly maple
posts w/shaped finials, original
rope-peg footrail flanked by conforming posts, 72 x 55" w., 72" l.,
82" h. posts (replaced siderails &
headboard) 1,100.00
Federal country-style tall poster bed,
tiger stripe maple, shaped headboard flanked by baluster- and
ring-turned posts w/acorn finials,
turned legs & feet, rope-peg side-
rails, 1840-50 (double size) 2,500.00
Hired man's rope-type bed, pine &
hardwoods, square posts w/taper-
ing legs & turned flattened finials,
raking headboard, old red finish,
76 x 32¼" 350.00
Mission-style (Arts & Crafts move-
ment) bed, stained oak, plain
(single size) 350.00
Victorian bed, Eastlake substyle,
walnut, typical machine carvings
& incised lines, original finish
(double size) 475.00
Victorian bed, Renaissance Revival
substyle, walnut & burl walnut,
high back w/arched crest applied
w/oval medallions & burl inset
panels, lower conforming foot-
board, 1870-80 (double size) 800.00
Victorian "half-tester" bed, Early
Victorian, rosewood, shaped headboard flanked by tapering turned
posts supporting cove-molded
canopy frame, attributed to Pru-
dent Mallard, New Orleans, third
quarter 19th c. (double size) 7,700.00

BENCHES

Child's Bench in Mission-Style

Child's bench, Mission-style (Arts &
Crafts movement), oak, back w/two
horizontal slats above plank seat,
slab sides joined by stretcher ending in exposed tenons w/key, red
decal mark of Gustav Stickley,
Model No. 215, ca. 1904, 38" l.
(ILLUS.) 1,980.00
Church pew, oak, solid-board back,
plank seat, carved ends, 126" l. .. 400.00
Mammy's bench, painted & decorated, plain crestrail above 3 vase-
form splats & turned spindles flanked by stiles, shaped arms supported on turned spindles, oblong seat
w/baby-guard rail, turned legs
w/flattened frontal stretcher on
rockers, gilt-stenciled swan decor
on black-over-red painted graining
w/sponge-decorated seat 1,800.00

Aesthetic Style Piano Bench by Stickley

Piano bench, Art Nouveau aesthetic
style, oak, w/red decal mark of
Gustav Stickley, Model No. 160,
ca. 1901, 38 5/8 x 15½" seat,
19¾" h. (ILLUS.) 11,000.00
Watch maker's bench, oak, roll-top,
43" w., 26½" deep, 51" h. 650.00
Water bucket bench, walnut, 2-tier,
top shelf enclosed by low solid
board gallery on all sides, lower
shelf w/apron joined to 1-board
sides w/cut-out feet, old blue-
green paint, 40" w. 495.00
Water bucket bench, painted poplar,
2-tier, upper shelf w/three-
quarter gallery partially formed
by sides that continue to form cut-
out feet, partially cleaned down
to old green finish, 42" w., 11½"
deep, 32½" h. 150.00
Water bucket bench, primitive pine,
3-tier, 2 full shelves & half-width
shelf at top, 1-board sides tapering in at top, old warm brown
varnish finish w/traces of old blue
paint beneath, 45¾" w., 13"
deep, 42½" h. 525.00
Federal bench, mahogany w/reverse-
serpentine upholstered seat,
square tapering legs inlaid w/bell-

flowers & stringing, New England,
early 19th c., 41½ x 19" seat,
19¾" h. 1,980.00
Federal country-style bench, painted
& decorated, 3-chairback style
w/triple "angel wing" cresting
above bold bootjack splats, plank
seat flanked by scrolling arms on
turned supports, turned legs
w/stretchers, early repaint
w/free-hand colorful morning
glories & other flowers & foliage
at crest & yellow & white pinstriping on brown ground,
76" l. 950.00
Primitive pine bench, 1-board top,
plain apron, sides w/cut-out feet,
square nail construction, 28 x 8¾"
top, 22" h..................... 85.00
Primitive pine bench, 1-board plank
top w/rounded ends, plain apron,
square legs mortised through top,
worn old brown finish, 68 x 7¾"
top, 16½" h.................... 175.00
Primitive poplar bench, 1-board
plank top, 2-slat back w/edge
beading, thick 1-board ends
w/cut-out arms & feet, square
nail construction & w/wrought
iron bolt-braces, old brown finish,
123" l. 250.00
Turn-of-the-Century hall bench,
quarter-sawn golden oak, back
w/slightly arched crestrail w/ap-
plied carvings, straight sides continuing to high roll-over arms,
plank seat w/lift-lid to storage
compartment below, molded
base, machine-carved animal paw
feet.......................... 825.00

BOOKCASES

Victorian Bookcase

American Empire Revival style bookcase, mahogany, oblong top

above pr. glazed cupboard doors
opening to shelves flanked by
brass-capped columns over pr.
split drawers (w/brass laurel-leaf
bail handles) in base, ball feet,
early 20th c. 330.00
Mission-style (Arts & Crafts movement) bookcase, oak, oblong top
w/three-quarter gallery w/keyed
tenons above pr. 6-pane glazed &
mullioned cupboard doors opening
to shelves, red decal mark of
Gustav Stickley, ca. 1907, 36" w.,
45" h. 1,320.00
Mission-style (Arts & Crafts movement) bookcase, oak, 5-shelf
model w/three-quarter gallery
top, vertical slat sides & open
back, early 20th c., 46" w., 9"
deep, 46½" h. 330.00
Mission-style (Arts & Crafts movement) bookcase, oak, oblong top
w/three-quarter gallery above pr.
glazed & mullioned 12-pane cupboard doors opening to shelves,
hammered copper hinges & keyhole
escutcheons, L. & J.G. Stickley,
ca. 1910, 49" w., 12" deep,
54" h. 2,310.00
Mission-style (Arts & Crafts movement) bookcase, oak, oblong top
w/low three-quarter gallery above
case w/pr. 4-pane glazed cupboard
doors, red decal mark of Gustav
Stickley, No. 171, ca. 1907,
48" w., 13" deep, 56" h. 1,870.00
Turn-of-the-Century bookcase, mahogany, 3-stack type w/glass-
fronted doors lifting to shelves,
pr. short drawers below, 34" w.,
51" h. 385.00
Turn-of-the-Century bookcase, gold-
en oak, 6-stack type w/glass-
fronted doors lifting to shelves,
"Globe Wernicke" label, original
finish 695.00
Victorian bookcase, Renaissance Revival substyle, walnut, projecting
cornice above pr. glazed doors
flanked by stiles w/incised & burl
panel decoration, pr. drawers
w/carved pulls in base, mid-
19th c., 53" w., 60" h. 522.50
Victorian bookcase, Eastlake substyle, oblong top w/low three-
quarter gallery, frieze w/typical
incised machine carvings over pr.
glazed doors opening to shelves
above pr. burl-fronted drawers at
base, 62" h. (ILLUS.) 1,095.00
Victorian bookcase, rococo substyle, rosewood, 2-part construction: upper part w/molded cornice,
bead-molded frieze & pr. glazed

Victorian Rococo Bookcase

doors w/pierce-carved fretwork;
base w/pr. side-by-side drawers
w/applied scroll-carved moldings,
shaped apron, bracket feet, ca.
1865, 96" h. (ILLUS.) 2,200.00
Victorian bookcase, Renaissance
Revival substyle, walnut & burl
walnut, 3-part "breakfront":
center section w/shaped cornice
above single glazed cupboard door
opening to shelves & flanking
side sections w/flat top over
glazed cupboard door; each section
w/drawer in molded plinth base,
101" h. 4,400.00

BOXES

Decorated Storage Box

Bible box, carved & black-painted
wood, rectangular w/chamfered
sliding lid, top & sides carved
w/stylized sunburst & fan decor,
19th c., 11" l. 187.00
Bible box w/hinged lid, American
Colonial, oak, incised compass-
type designs on front & sides,
plain lid, early 18th c. 275.00
Blanket box, painted & decorated,

hinged top opening to well, red & black painted graining in imitation of rosewood, early 19th c., 43 x 19½", 23" h. 187.50

Bonnet box, large bentwood form w/fitted lid, decorated in the manner of a dower chest w/large central stellate device in tones of red, yellow, black & white flanked by two large sprouting leaf forms w/dark green feathers either side, back w/further leafage, lid w/leafage & vines, all on a green ground, Pennsylvania, late 18th c., 21" oval, 11¾" h. 5,775.00

Candle box w/sliding lid, table model, dry red pine, dovetailed construction, ca. 1880, 4 x 7 x 10" . . . 120.00

Candle box w/sliding lid, old red paint, ca. 1820, 6 x 7 x 13" 265.00

Knife boxes, Federal, mahogany & mahogany veneer, sloping lids w/wide inlaid border bands & ovolo corners above conforming case w/light & dark inlay simulating fluting, American or English, ca. 1790, some restoration, 14½" h. 1,045.00

Knife boxes, George III, mahogany, serpentine sloping hinged lid, centrally inlaid w/stylized floral medallion, edges w/satinwood & mahogany chevron pattern & enclosing a fitted interior, sides w/brass bail handles, late 18th c., 14½" h., pr. 2,420.00

Storage box, painted & decorated beechwood, domed lid w/original wire staple hinges & wrought iron lock, original free-hand red, blue, green & white florals & birds & white striping on yellow ground, 14½" l. 825.00

Storage box, w/hinged domed lid, painted & decorated, vigorous & loose circles of dark green w/concentric stripings of red & other green squiggled brushwork, New England, ca. 1830, 24 x 14", 13" h. (ILLUS.) 6,600.00

Storage box, w/hinged domed lid, painted & decorated beechwood, wire staple hinges (one broken) & wrought iron lock (hasp damaged), nailed construction, original free-hand florals w/swags, birds & baskets in white, blue, red & olive yellow on yellow ground, interior lined w/wallpaper, 25½" l. 825.00

Storage box, w/hinged lid, painted & decorated, pine, opening to a deep well, boldly executed "columns" of red & yellow vinegar

graining, top w/script initials "M.H.," " Capt. GF Kitts, Rochester, NY, by RR" on bottom, probably New York, ca. 1830, 30¼ x 14", 13¼" h. 2,200.00

Table-top box w/slant-front lift lid, painted pine, original brown paint w/white striping, 12" l. 85.00

Table-top box, American Empire, cherrywood w/mahogany facade, oblong top above veneered chamfered drawer w/turned pulls, carved paw feet, 14¼ x 10¼" top, 7¾" h. 125.00

Wood (or kindling) box, Art Nouveau, inlaid fruitwood, hinged shaped oblong top lifting to storage compartment, top inlaid w/sheep & wool-dying pot, front w/woman weaving & the sides w/musical hunting trophies, signed "Galle" in marquetry, early 20th c., 24" w., 17" deep, 25½" h. 3,300.00

BUREAUS PLAT

Louis XV style bureau plat, kingwood & tulipwood w/ormolu mounts, shaped oblong leather-lined writing surface w/ormolu rim, above pr. frieze drawers flanking a false drawer, cabriole legs w/ormolu pierced "chutes" & "sabots," 19th c., 47 x 26½" top, 29½" h. .6,875.00

Louis XVI bureau plat, ormolu-mounted mahogany, oblong top inset w/black leather writing surface within brass-molded mahogany borders, frieze w/three working drawers & three false drawers opposite, all w/applied brass molding & lockplates & w/ormolu ribbon-tied bellflowers mounted at the corners, stop-fluted circular legs w/beaded ormolu capitals & ormolu "toupie" feet, France, late 18th c., 52" w., 29" h. 9,900.00

Louis XVI bureau plat, mahogany w/brass mounts, oblong leather-inset top w/brass border, apron w/two drawers, circular tapering legs w/brass "sabots," France, late 18th c., 45 x 23¼" top, 29¼" h. .4,400.00

Louis XVI bureau plat, kingwood & tulipwood w/ormolu mounts, oblong leather-inset top w/ormolu rim, apron w/three working drawers one side & three false drawers opposite, square tapering legs, ormolu wreath form handles, rosette corner mounts & "toupie sabots," 76¼" l., 37¾" h. 16,500.00

CABINETS

Oak China Cabinet

Cane display cabinet, oak, glass-
fronted door & glass sides 395.00
China cabinet, Turn-of-the-Century,
golden oak, plain top above pr.
glazed cupboard doors flanked by
shaped stiles, glass sides, turn-
under C-scroll toes, mirrored
back, ca. 1910, 42½" w., 58" h.
(ILLUS.) 210.00
China cabinet, Turn-of-the-Century,
golden oak, flat bow-fronted top
above egg-and-dart frieze over
glazed bow-fronted cupboard door
flanked by rope-twist carved columns & bent glass side panels,
molded base, bulbous-turned feet
on casters, large size 1,155.00

China Cabinet with Bent Glass Sides

China cabinet, Turn-of-the-Century,
golden oak, oval beveled glass
mirror plate in crest flanked by
lion-head motifs above flat shelf
over glazed cupboard door
flanked by curved glass sides, applied carvings at door frame, animal paw feet, ca. 1900, 42" w.,
75" h. (ILLUS.) 950.00
Dental cabinet, light mahogany,
20-drawer, amethyst glass knobs,
opaque "slag" glass on pr.
recessed cupboard doors above
marble slab work shelf top 475.00

Dental Cabinet

Dental cabinet, golden oak,
21-drawer, superstructure w/bev-
eled glass mirror plate above
work shelf over case w/arrange-
ment of 21 various-sized drawers
& single cupboard door, early
20th c. (ILLUS.) 650.00
Filing cabinet, walnut, horizontal
model, 72-drawer, marked "Amberg's Patent - Sept. 24, 1878,"
72 x 42", 12" deep 650.00

Kitchen Cabinet

Kitchen cabinet, Turn-of-the-Century, maple, plain top above "flour bin" cupboard & pr. short cupboard doors over tambour slide opening to canister storage, white granite-ware work surface over arrangement of drawers & cupboard door, square legs on casters (ILLUS.) ... 650.00

Optician's lens cabinet, oak, 2-drawer 75.00

Vitrine cabinet, Art Nouveau, inlaid mahogany, shaped oblong top w/molded edge above pr. small glazed cupboard doors over 3 open shelves flanked by free-standing columns, back of shelves inlaid w/large fruitwood leaves, demi-cabriole legs, attributed to Emile Galle', France, early 20th c., 62½" h. 11,000.00

Vitrine cabinet, Art Nouveau, carved fruitwood w/inlaid marquetry, oblong top above open shelf inlaid w/waterfall landscape above enclosed cupboard w/glass-fronted panel over inlaid scenic panel door centering open shelves supported on sinuously carved uprights, short demi-cabriole legs, signed "L. Majorelle, Nancy," France, 1890's, 31" w., 67¼" h. ...9,350.00

Vitrine cabinet, Art Nouveau, mahogany, oblong top w/molded cornice above frieze w/lily & chrysanthemum carvings over central cupboard door w/arched & glazed upper panel applied w/pierce-carved Nouveau tree-form, flanked by shaped shelves & free-standing squared & rope-twist columns, floral-carved skirt flanked by flaring feet, Louis Majorelle, France, 1900-25, 35" w., 16½" deep, 74½" h. 7,700.00

Watchmaker's cabinet, oak, 20-drawer, original porcelain pulls 225.00

CANDLESTANDS

Chippendale tilt-top candlestand, cherrywood, square top w/serpentine sides, tapering turned standard, downswept cabriole tripod, pad feet, Massachusetts, 1780-1800, 19" sq. top, 28" h. 1,760.00

Chippendale tilt-top candlestand, walnut, round top w/dished edge tilting & revolving on birdcage support, vase- and ring-turned standard, downswept cabriole tripod, pad feet, Middle Atlantic Colonies, 1760-80, 19½" top d., 28½" h. (reglued top) 5,500.00

Chippendale candlestand, cherry-wood, shaped top w/rounded outset corners & serpentine sides, turned & suppressed ball standard, downswept cabriole tripod, snake feet, 18½" top d., 27½" h. (old repair to standard) 14,850.00

Federal tilt-top candlestand, mahogany, octagonal top w/cross-banded edge tilting above ring- and baluster-turned standard, downswept square-legged tripod, New England, 1790-1810, 26" w. top, 28¾" h. 825.00

Federal tilt-top candlestand, mahogany w/satinwood inlay, oval top w/satinwood oval reserve tilting above rib-carved & turned standard, downswept cabriole tripod, snake feet, probably New York, ca. 1795, 24 x 18" top, 27½" h. (repair to one leg) 4,125.00

Federal Candlestand

Federal candlestand, birch, square top w/serpentine sides, vase- and ring-turned standard, downswept cabriole tripod, pad feet, original red-stained finish, New England, ca. 1790, 17 x 16¾" top, 26¾" h. (ILLUS.) 2,090.00

Federal candlestand, cherrywood, square top w/serpentine sides, ring- and baluster-turned standard, downswept cabriole tripod, snake feet, attributed to the Deerfield, Connecticut area, 16 x 15¾" top, 28" h. 5,900.00

Federal country-style tilt-top candlestand, exotic wood, square top w/serpentine sides tilting above vase- and ring-turned standard, downswept cabriole tripod w/notch-carved shoulders, pad feet, possibly Connecticut, ca. 1810, 19¾ x 18" top, 27 5/8" h. .. 990.00

Tiger Stripe Maple Candlestand

Federal country-style tilt-top candlestand, tiger stripe maple, oblong top w/notched ovolo corners tilting above baluster-turned standard, downswept square-legged tripod, ca. 1820, 22¼" l. top, 28¼" h. (ILLUS.) 900.00

Federal country-style candlestand, cherrywood, octagonal top w/beveled edge, ring- and baluster-turned standard, downswept cabriole tripod, snake feet, traces of old red stain, 19½ x 15¼" top, 26½" h. 1,000.00

Federal country-style candlestand, painted finish, octagonal top, ring- and baluster-turned standard, downswept square-legged tripod, old red paint, New England, ca. 1800, 19¼ x 16½" top, 27" h. 2,310.00

Checkerboard Candlestand

Federal country-style candlestand w/checkerboard top, painted & decorated, hexagonal top painted w/black & yellow checkerboard & w/red zig-zag border, baluster-

turned standard, downswept square-legged tripod, New England, ca. 1820, one leg restored & some paint restoration, 21 x 16½" top, 25" h. (ILLUS.) 1,320.00

Federal country-style candlestand, tiger stripe maple, oblong top w/rounded corners & inlaid central mahogany oval reserve, vase- and ring-turned standard, downswept square-legged tripod, New England, ca. 1800, 18 x 14" top, 27½" h. (some inlay loss) 605.00

Queen Anne candlestand, curly maple, round top, baluster-turned standard, downswept cabriole tripod, snake feet, 15" top d., 25½" h. (refinished & w/replaced top) 1,400.00

Queen Anne country-style candlestand, painted maple, square top w/invected corners, turned & hexagonal standard w/acorn-shaped terminal, downswept cabriole tripod, pad feet, original red paint, New Hampshire, ca. 1780, 15 x 14½" top, 26" h. 990.00

Victorian tilt-top candlestand, papier mache, elaborate gilt scrolls & scene of Westminster Abbey & Royal Barge on top of black ground, England, ca. 1850 .... 1,500.00

CHAIRS

Chairs in the Style of Robert Adam

Adam-style armchairs, cane-back centered w/painted oval medallion & cane seat, painted & decorated overall, England, early 19th c., pr. (ILLUS.) 1,600.00

Adirondack (bent rustic twigs & branches) rocker w/arms, interwoven latticework back & downswept arms, round seat w/curlicue skirt, early 20th c. .... 165.00 to 245.00

American Colonial "ladder-back" armchair, 3-slat back w/shaped slats between turned uprights w/turned finials, arms w/shaped handgrips on baluster-turned supports, turned legs w/stretchers, green paint over original finish, 1710-40 (now on "carpet-cutter" rockers) 1,450.00

American Colonial "ladder-back" armchairs, curly maple, 5-slat back w/arched slats between turned uprights w/ball finials, shaped arms, splint seat, turned legs w/turned stretchers, Delaware River Valley, ca. 1775, pr. (one chair w/replaced arms) 4,125.00

American "Classical" Armchair

American Empire armchair in the "classical" taste, mahogany, gondola-form w/shaped backrail above upholstered back & seat, downswept arms ending in bold C-scrolls above palmette-carved plinth, sabre legs, Boston, ca. 1830 (ILLUS.) ...2,200.00

"Cane-Seat" Chair

American Empire "cane-seat" dining chair, curly maple, roll-over "angel-wing" crestrail above vase-form splat, cane seat, sabre legs w/flattened concave frontal stretcher, ca. 1845 (ILLUS.) ....145.00 to 175.00

American Empire "slip-seat" side chair, curly maple, plain crestrail over medial stayrail, needlepoint-covered slip seat, sabre legs w/concave frontal stretcher 185.00

Art Deco Chair by Donald Deskey

Art Deco upholstered armchair, tub-shaped, U-shaped back, arms & loose cushion upholstered in black fabric, silvered-metal feet, by Donald Deskey for the Seligman house, ca. 1929 (ILLUS.) 2,420.00

Biedermeier side chairs, tiger stripe maple, shaped crestrail w/scrolling ears above lyre-form back, over-upholstered seat, square tapering legs, Sweden, ca. 1820, pr. 3,000.00

Centennial (1876) Chippendale-style "ribbon-back" dining chairs, mahogany, 1 arm & 5 side chairs, refinished, set of 6 ....1,200.00

Chippendale corner armchair, maple, horseshoe-shaped backrail w/cushion-molded crest above 2 pierced beaker-form splats & 3 turned uprights, slip seat, shaped seatrail, square legs, New England, 1760-80 (beaker-form splats restored) 880.00

Chippendale open armchair, walnut, cupid's bow crestrail w/scrolling ears centering carved shell above pierce-carved splat, shaped arms, slip seat (concealing potty seat baffle), molded square legs w/inside chamfer joined by H-stretcher, original finish & some early repairs, Philadelphia area (ILLUS.) 2,900.00

Chippendale Open Armchair

Chippendale open armchair, walnut, cupid's bow crestrail centering fan-carved device above pierce-carved vase-form splat, shaped arms w/scrolled handholds, damask up-holstered slip seat, plain seatrail, molded square legs w/box stretch-ers, attributed to Lancaster, Pennsylvania 6,250.00

Chippendale Wing Armchair

Chippendale wing armchair, mahog-any, upholstered back w/arched crest & ogival wings, scrolled arms, seat w/loose cushion, mold-ed square legs w/H-stretcher, Massachusetts, ca. 1780 (ILLUS.) 7,425.00

Chippendale wing armchair, mahog-any, upholstered back w/serpen-tine crest & shaped wings, roll-over arms, seat w/loose cushion,

acanthus-carved & cross-hatched cabriole legs, claw-and-ball feet, New York, ca. 1780 (repair to one foot) 12,100.00

Chippendale side chair, walnut, rope-and swag-carved cupid's bow crest-rail centering a convex-carved shell & volutes above pierce-carved beaker-form splat flanked by fluted stiles, slip seat, molded seatrail centering convex-carved shell, acanthus-carved cabriole legs, claw-and-ball feet, Philadelphia, ca. 1780 . . . . .20,900.00

Chippendale side chairs, mahogany, cupid's bow crestrail centering ribbed shell above pierce-carved vase-form splat, slip seat, square tapering legs w/H-stretchers, Rhode Island, 1780-1800, pr. (repair to one leg) 4,400.00

Chippendale side chairs, cherrywood, plain crestrail above 4 vertical slats flanked by molded uprights, plain seatrail, slip seat, square chamfered legs w/H-stretchers, Long Island, New York, 1780-1800, set of 4 . . . . .4,950.00

Chippendale country-style corner armchair, maple, horseshoe-shaped backrail w/cushion-molded crest above 2 vase-shaped splats & 3 turned uprights, rush seat, turned legs w/box stretcher, ball feet, New England, ca. 1780 . . . . 465.00

Chippendale country-style "ribbon-back" side chair, birch, blue damask upholstered slip seat, square legs w/H-stretcher 600.00

English Regency "begeres" (arm-chairs w/upholstered inward-cur-ing arms), painted to simulate rosewood w/parcel-gilding, molded curving arched back pierced w/flanking double arches, over-upholstered seat, sabre legs w/parcel-gilt flutes & brass casters, England, early 19th c., pr. 5,500.00

Federal (Martha Washington) "lol-ling" open armchair, inlaid mahog-any, upholstered back w/serpen-tine crest, shaped arms w/line-inlaid design, upholstered seat, line-inlaid square tapering legs w/H-stretcher, Massachusetts, ca. 1795 . . . . .10,450.00

Federal "rush-seat" armchair, painted & decorated, shaped crest center-ing painted musical trophies above pierced splat, rush seat flanked by downswept arms, turned tapering legs w/stretchers, painted red

w/gilt highlights & stenciling, Baltimore, ca. 1815 . . . . .1,540.00
Federal wing armchair, mahogany, upholstered back w/serpentine crest flanked by shaped wings & roll-over arms, seat w/loose cushion, ring-turned reeded legs, New England, ca. 1810 . . . . .3,080.00
Federal dining chairs, mahogany, square molded crestrail above pierce-carved "Prince of Wales" plumes & swag-molded tassel splat, over-upholstered seat, square reeded tapering legs, spade feet, New York, ca. 1805, 2 armchairs & 4 side chairs, set of 6 . . . . . . .22,000.00

Federal "Arrow-back" Side Chairs

Federal "arrow-back" side chairs, painted & decorated, ornate crestrail w/scrolling earred top above step-down rail over 3 arrow-form spindles, saddle seat, bamboo-turned legs w/stretchers, freehand grapevine motif at crestrail & spindles on yellow ground highlighted w/black striping (cracked crestrail on one), Essex, Massachusetts, ca. 1815, set of 4 (ILLUS. of part) 2,090.00
Federal "lyre-back" side chair, mahogany, plain crestrail above pierced lyre-form splat, reeded stiles, slip seat, acanthus-carved legs, hairy paw feet, legs painted gold & black, attributed to Duncan Phyfe, New York, ca. 1805 . . . . . .3,575.00
Federal "rush-seat" side chairs, curly maple, rope-twist & ring-turned bowed crestrail above acanthus- and scroll-carved stayrail, balloon-shaped rush seat, plain seatrail, baluster-turned & rope-twist carved flaring legs, New York State, ca. 1825, set of 10 . . . . .19,800.00
Federal country-style "balloon-back" side chairs, painted & decorated, rounded crestrail above vase-form

splat, plank seat, turned legs w/stretchers, gilt-stenciled urn of fruit at crest on brown ground w/white & yellow striping, pr.. . . . 470.00
Federal country-style "fancy" side chairs, painted & decorated, angel-wing crestrail above half-spindles below stayrail, plank seat, turned legs w/stretchers, free-hand decoration at crest, green ground, set of 4 . . . . 795.00

French Empire Dining Chairs

French Empire dining chairs, mahogany, curving crestrail w/roll-over top rail above plain splat flanked by shaped stiles, over-upholstered seat, plain seatrail, square tapering splayed legs, France, early 19th c., set of 6 (ILLUS. of pr.) . .11,550.00

Signed Hitchcock Chair

Hitchcock signed side chair, painted & decorated, original stenciled fruit basket on black ground, signed "Hitchcock, Alford & Co., Hitchcocksville Warranted" on back of seatrail, 1832-45, set of 4 (ILLUS. of one) 1,000.00
Invalid's wheel chair, cane seat & back, on wheels, late 19th/early 20th c. 150.00

Louis XV "bergeres" (armchairs w/up-
holstered inward-curving arms),
beechwood, upholstered back &
sides w/serpentine beechwood
toprail carved w/flowerheads,
loose cushion, cabriole legs
w/flowerhead-carved knees,
France, ca. 1750, pr...........14,300.00

Louis XV "fauteuils" (open armchairs),
beechwood, cartouche-shaped backrest within finely carved frame
w/flowerhead & acanthus scrolls,
padded armrests on voluted
supports, serpentine-fronted upholstered seat, cabriole legs w/flower-
head-carved knees, signed
"I. Lebas," France, mid-18th c.,
pr..........................11,550.00

Chair attributed to Gustav Stickley

Mission-style (Arts & Crafts movement) "Morris" armchair, oak, adjustable back w/horizontal slats &
seat w/loose cushion flanked by
flattened "bent" arms above 5
vertical slats, attributed to Gustav
Stickley, Style No. 369, ca. 1907
(ILLUS.)......................2,090.00

Mission-style (Arts & Crafts movement) armchair, oak, oblong crestrail above oblong slat flanked by
square stiles, leather cushion seat
flanked by angled straight arms,
square legs, incised "Roycroft"
across front seatrail, Roycroft
Shops, East Aurora, New York,
ca. 1905......................1,320.00

Mission-style (Arts & Crafts movement) "spindle-back" dining chair,
oak, plain crestrail above 9-spindle
back, original soft leather slip seat,
square legs w/conforming spindles
joining seatrail to stretchers at
sides, unsigned but w/paper label
of Gustav Stickley under seat,
ca. 1905......................4,180.00

Mission-style (Arts & Crafts movement) sewing rocker, oak, plain
crestrail above 9 vertical spindles
flanked by squared stiles, seat
w/leather upholstery, red decal
mark of Gustav Stickley, Model
No. 359, ca. 1905.............. 660.00

Victorian armchair, Gothic Revival
substyle, walnut, elaborate crest
over back pierced w/Gothic Arch
designs & centering a pierced com-
passwheel below crest design
flanked by rope-twist uprights,
padded arms & over-upholstered
seat, rope-twist & ring-turned
legs on casters, attributed to John
& Joseph Meeks, New York City,
ca. 1855.....................5,225.00

Victorian parlor armchair, Renaissance Revival substyle, walnut
w/bronze medallion of Roman
warrior, possibly by Alexandre
Roux (& Company), New York,
1847-81, original finish.......... 365.00

Victorian parlor armchair, Louis XV
(rococo) substyle, walnut, finger-
molded frame, demi-cabriole legs,
padded open arms (needs new
upholstery).................... 360.00

Belter Armchair

Victorian parlor armchair, rococo
substyle, pierce-carved laminated
rosewood, by John Henry Belter,
New York, New York, ca. 1855
(ILLUS.)......................8,500.00

Victorian parlor armchairs, in the
rococo taste, Bombay-carved black-
wood, overall pierce-carved foliate
framework w/demi-cabriole legs,
upholstered cushion seat, India,
19th c., pr....................2,310.00

Victorian parlor armchair, steer's
horn frame w/high back, sloping
arms & splayed legs incorporating
long Texas steer's horns, original
black velvet upholstery......... 200.00

Renaissance Revival Dining Chair

Victorian dining chairs, Renaissance Revival substyle, walnut, shaped back w/incised carving at crest above inset leather panel, shaped arms, round seat w/upholstery, turned legs w/stretchers, ca. 1870, set of 12 (ILLUS. of one)..............1,045.00

Victorian dining chairs, rococo substyle, walnut, shaped leaf-carved crestrail pierced w/hand-hold at center above medial arched stayrail, cane seat, sabre legs w/flattened concave frontal stretcher, 1860-80, set of 6 .... 700.00

Victorian "Grecian" rocker w/arms, walnut, caned back & seat, scrollcut arms, turned legs on rockers, ca. 1860, refinished & recaned.... 350.00

Victorian "balloon-back" side chair, early cottage-style, painted finish, balloon-shaped back w/rounded crestrail over vase-form splat, plank seat, turned legs w/stretchers, ca. 1850 (worn paint)........ 150.00

Victorian parlor side chair, Louis XV substyle, papier mache, balloonshaped back w/central cartouche painted w/landscape scene, upholstered seat, serpentine seatrail, demi-cabriole legs, giltstenciled scrolls on black ground, England, 19th c................. 225.00

Victorian parlor side chair, rococo substyle, pierce-carved laminated rosewood frame in the manner of John & Joseph Meeks, upholstered cartouche-shaped back & serpentine-fronted over-upholstered seat, demi-cabriole legs..............1,300.00

Victorian parlor side chairs, rococo substyle, Rosalie patt., carved laminated rosewood, by John Henry Belter, New York, New York, ca. 1855, pr..............3,300.00

Wallace Nutting signed "Windsor brace-back continuous" armchair, early 20th c., w/repair 900.00

Wallace Nutting signed "Windsor brace-back" side chair, early 20th c. 545.00

Wallace Nutting signed "Windsor fan-back" side chairs, early 20th c., pr. 850.00

Wicker armchair, woven rolled crest & armrails above C-scroll & woven latticework back & seat, wrapped legs enhanced w/wickerwork joined by X-stretcher, w/label of Wakefield Reed Co., Leominster, Massachusetts, late 19th c....... 305.00

Wicker armchair, woven reed, shaped scalloped back & roll-over arms interspersed w/continuous openwork band of woven latticework alternating w/reed-entwined spherules, round seat w/shaped seatrail over conforming latticework band, wrapped balusterturned legs, Heywood Brothers & Company, Gardner, Massachusetts.................1,430.00

Wicker "photographer's studio prop" chair, ornate back w/curlicue details, reed-wrapped legs w/curlicue trim at X-stretchers.......... 650.00

Wicker rocker w/arms, woven reed, ornate curlicue designs & padded seat w/springs, ca. 1890 .... 275.00

1920's Wicker Rocker

Wicker rocker w/arms, loom-woven fibre, padded back flanked by flattened downswept arms, seat w/loose cushion, turned & fibrewrapped legs on rockers, painted white (ILLUS.) 145.00

CHESTS & CHESTS OF DRAWERS

Painted Pine Blanket Chest

Herb Chest

Apothecary chest, 13-drawer, poplar, 12 short drawers over single long drawer, all w/turned wood pulls, 21" w., 8¼" deep, 21" h.... 470.00

Apothecary chest, 44-drawer, painted finish, arrangement of 6 rows of 6 drawers each over 2 rows of 4 drawers each, original turned wood pulls, green paint, 19th c....................4,800.00

Blanket chest, painted pine, oblong top w/molded edge lifting to deep well w/till in dovetailed case, molded base, cut-out bracket feet, painted free-hand red & yellow flowers, flower pots & foliate surrounds in arched reserves on blue ground, Pennsylvania, late 18th c., 33¼ x 16½", 18" h. (ILLUS.) 3,850.00

Blanket chest, painted pine, oblong top w/molded edge lifting to deep well w/till, sides continuing to form cut-out feet, red-brown painted graining over earlier green, 34¾ x 16½", 27" h. 525.00

Blanket chest, pine, oblong top w/molded edge lifting to deep well w/till in dovetailed case, applied molding at base, ball-turned feet, worn old red finish, 42½ x 19", 24" h..................... 225.00

Blanket chest, walnut, oblong top w/molded edge on wrought iron strap hinges, lifting to deep well w/till in dovetailed case, original iron bear trap lock, molded base, cut-out bracket feet, 46 x 17½", 22½" h...................... 600.00

Blanket chest, painted & decorated poplar, oblong top w/applied molded edge lifting to deep well w/till in case applied w/molding at base, cleaned down to original red paint w/unusual geometric design in blue, white & red & w/central heart dated "1776," 50½ x 22½", 22" h............. 800.00

Herb chest, grain-painted finish, 30-drawer, 5 graduated rows of 6

drawers each, one drawer signed "Aaron Page" in pencil & another signed "Sarah Page Tourald," 48¼" w., 8¼" deep, 20½" h. (ILLUS.) 1,650.00

Mule chest (box chest w/one or more drawers below storage compartment---forerunner of chest of drawers), poplar, 6-board construction w/sides continuing to form bootjack feet, hinged lid opening to deep well in case w/drawer below, applied molding at base w/sides continuing below, replaced brasses & refinished, 37 3/8" w., 38½" h............. 725.00

Mule Chest

Mule chest, painted pine & oak, oblong top w/molded edge on pintel-hinged cleats opening to deep well in case w/two false drawers over 2 working drawers, all w/cast & engraved brass teardrop pulls, molded base, large flattened ball-shaped feet, ca. 1720 with early 19th c. grain-painted finish over original painted surface, 39½" w., 36" h. (ILLUS.) 7,150.00

American Empire "butler's" chest, mahogany & cherrywood, oblong top above case w/false deep upper drawer folding out to form writing surface & reveal numerous pigeonholes & small drawers over 4 long drawers, w/turned wood pulls, flanked by applied half-round columns, C-scroll feet, 48" h......................... 798.00

American Empire "bow-front" chest of drawers, mahogany & mahogany veneer, oblong top w/scrolling backsplash set w/three recessed short drawers over case w/four bow-fronted drawers flanked by ring- and rope-carved columns continuing to baluster-turned legs, original brass drop-ring handles, 41" w., 51 7/8" h. (old finish & minor veneer damage) 1,250.00

American Empire chest of drawers, cherrywood & tiger stripe maple, oblong cherrywood top w/tiger maple raking backsplash w/pillar ends above case w/pr. shallow short drawers over deep long drawer above 3 slightly recessed graduated long drawers flanked by pineapple & acanthus-carved pilasters, vigorously carved animal paw feet, signed on drawer rail "Made by D. Ferguson, No. 2, Feb., 1830, Nichols," 47½" w., 58¼" h. (replaced gilt brass drop-ring handles) 900.00

American Empire Chest of Drawers

American Empire chest of drawers, cherrywood & tiger stripe maple, oblong top above deep upper drawer over 3 slightly recessed long graduated drawers (w/replaced wood-composition pulls) flanked by turned pilasters, turned feet (ILLUS.) 475.00

American Empire country-style chest of drawers, painted poplar, oblong top above 3 short drawers over long drawer above 3 slightly recessed & graduated drawers flanked by black-painted turned columns, original red-painted graining on yellow ground w/sponging, compass designs & other motifs, 44½" w., 51½" h. (minor damage to beading on drawers) 3,000.00

Art Nouveau Dresser

Art Nouveau dresser & chiffonier, mahogany, ca. 1900, matching pr. (ILLUS. of dresser only) 1,265.00

Chippendale "bonnet-top" chest-on-chest, cherrywood, 2-part construction: upper part w/swan's neck cresting ending in foliate-carved punchwork-decorated terminals centering a wine-glass form finial & flanking flame finials above punchwork-decorated typhanum (recessed panel) over 3 short drawers & 4 long graduated drawers flanked by fluted quarter columns; lower section w/four long graduated drawers flanked by conforming columns, scroll-cut ogee bracket feet, Colchester area of Connecticut, ca. 1780, 41" w., 83½" h. (minor repairs to drawer lips) 42,900.00

Chippendale chest-on-chest, painted cherrywood & maple, 2-part construction: upper part w/molded projecting cornice above 5 graduated long drawers; lower section w/three long drawers, cut-out bracket feet, original brass bat's wing handles & keyhole escutcheons, painted red, attributed to Nathan King, Newport, Rhode Island, 39½" w., 75" h. 9,000.00

Chippendale tall chest of drawers, tiger stripe maple & plain maple, projecting oblong top w/applied molding below above case w/six graduated thumb-molded long drawers, cut-out bracket feet, New England, ca. 1775, 39½" w., 56¼" h. 5,500.00

Chippendale tall chest of drawers, walnut, projecting oblong top w/applied molding below above case w/three short drawers over 4 graduated long thumb-molded drawers, (replaced) ogee bracket feet, 37" w., 51¼" h. 1,450.00

Chippendale "Bombe" Chest of Drawers

Chippendale "bombe" chest of drawers, mahogany, oblong top w/molded edge above case w/swollen "bombe" sides & 4 graduated long drawers within cockbeaded surrounds, molded base w/shaped pendant, ogee bracket feet, Boston, Massachusetts, ca. 1765, 35½" w., 33½" h. (ILLUS.). 38,500.00

Chippendale "serpentine-front" chest of drawers, mahogany, oblong top w/molded edge & serpentine front above case of conforming outline w/four graduated drawers within cockbeaded surrounds, cut-out bracket feet, New England, ca. 1775, 42" w., 31½" h. (one rear foot restored) 9,900.00

Chippendale chest of drawers, cherrywood, oblong top w/molded edge above case w/four graduated thumb-molded drawers flanked by molded quarter columns, ogee-molded bracket feet, Connecticut, 1760-80, 39½" w., 41½" h. 1,320.00

Chippendale chest of drawers, walnut, oblong top w/molded edge above case w/two short drawers over 3 long graduated drawers, ogee-molded bracket feet, Pennsylvania, ca. 1775, 36" w., 36" h. (minor repair to feet) 4,950.00

Chippendale country-style tall chest of drawers, cherrywood, oblong top w/molded edge above 7 graduated thumb-molded drawers, shaped bracket feet, 36¼" w., 63" h. 3,750.00

Federal tall chest of drawers, Hepplewhite-style, inlaid cherrywood, oblong top w/wide over-

hang & applied molding below above case w/three short drawers over 4 graduated long line-inlaid drawers flanked by cross-banded inlaid stiles, flaring French feet, refinished & w/replaced oval brass drop ring handles, early 19th c., 42" w., 52½" h. 2,600.00

Federal "bow-front" chest of drawers, cherrywood, oblong top w/bowed front & pattern-inlaid edge above case w/four cross-banded & cockbeaded drawers of conforming outline, inlaid apron, flaring bracket feet, New England, ca. 1800, 38½" w., 39½" h. 6,875.00

Federal Cherrywood & Maple Chest

Federal "bow-front" chest of drawers, cherrywood w/tiger stripe maple facade, oblong top w/bowed front & canted corners above case w/four cockbeaded & graduated drawers of conforming outlined flanked by horizontally-reeded stiles continuing to turned legs, possibly Pennsylvania, ca. 1815, 41½" w., 40" h. (ILLUS.) 990.00

Federal Maple & Birch Chest

Federal chest of drawers, bird's eye maple & birch, oblong top w/inlaid edge above case w/four cockbeaded & graduated long drawers w/inlaid stringing, skirt w/cross-banded inlaid panel, turned legs, New Hampshire, ca. 1820, refinished, 37¾" w., 38" h. (ILLUS.) 1,760.00

Federal Classical - American Empire transitional, mahogany w/white marble slab top & gilt metal mounts, oblong slab top resting on case w/long upper drawer over 2 slightly recessed long drawers flanked by flat pilasters w/brass foliate-cast capitals, bulbous-turned feet, stamped "H. Lannuier New York" (Charles Honore Lannuier) in 4 places, ca. 1815, 49" w., 40" h. 11,550.00

Federal country-style chest of drawers, birch, oblong top above 4 graduated thumb-molded drawers w/turned wood pulls, scalloped apron, cut-out bracket feet, 41½" w., 42" h................. 950.00

Mission-style (Arts & Crafts movement) chest of drawers w/attached mirror, oblong top supporting superstructure w/framed mirror swiveling on squared uprights above case w/pr. short drawers over pr. long drawers, square legs, designed by Harvey Ellis & produced by Gustav Stickley, Model No. 911, ca. 1904, 48" w., 34½" h. 3,520.00

Queen Anne Chest on Frame

Queen Anne chest-on-frame, curly maple, 2-part construction: upper part w/oblong top & molded edge above case w/four long graduated drawers; frame w/heart-pierced skirt, incised pinwheel carvings & scalloped edge, angular cabriole legs, pad feet, Northeastern New England, 1770-90, w/inscription "C.T. Collins Sh ----field Me."

in black paint on backboard, 38¼" w., 36¾" h. (ILLUS.) 6,600.00

Queen Anne chest-on-frame, maple & walnut, 2-part construction: upper part w/cove-molded cornice above pr. short drawers over 3 long graduated drawers; frame w/scalloped apron centering a shaped pendant, turned legs w/shod pad feet, New York State, 1740-80, 38¼" w., 56½" h. 8,250.00

Queen Anne-Chippendale transitional tall chest of drawers, pine, oblong top w/molded cornice above 5 graduated long drawers w/replaced brass bat's wing handles & keyhole escutcheons, bracket feet, 39" w., 44¾" h. 1,100.00

Shaker Chest of Drawers

Shaker chest of drawers, birch, oblong top above case w/four graduated cockbeaded drawers w/turned pulls, cut-out feet, traces of red-orange stain, New England, ca. 1840, 38½" w., 35¾" h. (ILLUS.) 440.00

Turn-of-the-Century chest of drawers w/attached mirror, golden oak, shaped oblong top w/mirror swiveling between uprights recessed at rear of oblong top over case w/three long drawers, square legs, original brass hardware & finish 250.00

Turn-of-the-Century chest of drawers w/attached mirror, golden oak veneer, oblong top w/framed mirror swiveling between uprights recessed at rear of oblong top over case w/two short drawers over 2 long drawers, original turned wood pulls, S-scroll frontal feet, white porcelain casters (ILLUS.)........................ 155.00

Oak Dresser

Victorian chest of drawers, Early
Victorian style, walnut, oblong top
above 4 graduated long drawers
w/turned wood pulls flanked by
rounded & slightly canted corners
applied w/spool-turned pendant
drops 495.00

Victorian Walnut Chest of Drawers

Victorian chest of drawers, rococo
substyle, walnut, oblong top
above case w/pr. short drawers
over 3 long drawers, cut-out
bracket feet (ILLUS.) 450.00

Victorian chest of drawers, cottage-
style, painted & decorated, oblong
top w/shaped backsplash above
case w/three drawers, scalloped
apron continuing to bracket feet,
original painted graining finish &
colorful line borders, small commode size, 30" w. 450.00

Victorian chest of drawers, Renaissance Revival substyle, walnut &
burl walnut, oblong top w/shaped

three-quarter gallery above case
w/five drawers w/burl walnut
panels, molded base, ca. 1870,
36" w., 51½" h. (replaced
handles)....................... 715.00

Victorian Marble-Top Chest with Mirror

Victorian chest of drawers w/mirror,
rococo substyle, walnut, superstructure w/pierce-carved C-scroll
& S-scroll cresting above arch-top
mirror flanked by candle shelves
over handkerchief boxes on oblong white marble slab top above
case w/three long drawers
w/carved grape cluster pulls
flanked by rounded corners, plinth
base, on casters (ILLUS.) 522.50

COMMODES

French Provincial Commode

Art Deco commode, amboyna wood &
ivory, top w/single step to ivory
band above case w/two drawers,
w/ivory keyhole escutcheons &
ivory loop handles held by silk
cord to backplate, flanked by

square tapering legs inlaid
w/ivory stringing, branded "J.
Ruhlmann" & w/"atelier" mark,
50½" w., 37" h. 24,200.00
Louis XV Provincial, oak, oblong top
w/"ox-bow" front above case of
conforming outline w/three drawers w/ormolu handles & keyhole
escutcheons, rounded corners,
shaped skirt continuing to scrolling feet, France, 18th c.
(ILLUS.) 4,510.00
Louis XV-XVI transitional commode,
tulipwood marquetry w/ormolu
mounts, oblong "breche d'Alep"
marble top w/cut corners above
case w/single drawer above pr.
cupboard doors, chamfered corners, cabriole legs, veneered
overall w/floral sprays on
tulipwood ground & w/ormolu keyhole escutcheons, handles, apron
mount, "chutes" & "sabots,"
France, third quarter 18th c.,
28" w., 29" h. 10,450.00
Turn-of-the-Century commode, oak,
lyre-shaped towel rack raised
above shaped backsplash,
serpentine-fronted top w/molded
edge above case w/single drawer
over pr. cupboard doors, square
legs, ca. 1900, refinished 295.00

Victorian Demi-Commode

Victorian demi-commode, Renaissance Revival substyle, walnut
w/white marble slab top above
case w/single drawer over cupboard door w/applied carvings
flanked by canted corners w/or-
nate applied carvings, plinth base
on casters, ca. 1860, 20" w., 17"
deep, 31½" h. (ILLUS.) 825.00
Victorian commode, Eastlake sub-
style, walnut w/white marble top
& backsplash above case w/single

drawer over pr. cupboard
doors . . . . 460.00 to 525.00
Victorian commode, rococo substyle,
walnut w/white marble top above
case w/single drawer w/fruit-
carved pulls & pr. cupboard doors,
darkened & "alligatored" varnish
finish 310.00
Victorian "lift-top" commode, paint-
ed pine, hinged lid w/molded
edge raising to deep well
w/drawer at one side over single
cupboard door, stripped of
finish 275.00

CUPBOARDS

Butternut Corner Cupboard

Chimney cupboard, painted pine,
flat-molded cornice above cabinet
w/two raised panel (over & under)
cupboard doors within cockbeaded
surrounds, the top door opening to
3 shelves & lower door to compartment, original red paint w/right
side never painted, written "From
old Pickard House torn down in
1881" in chalk inside door, 25" w.,
15½" deep, 78" h. 6,270.00
Chimney cupboard, painted pine,
cove-molded cornice w/wide overhang above cabinet w/two 1-board
(over & under) cupboard doors
w/wooden turn latches, worn red
painted finish 3,150.00
Corner cupboard, Federal, butternut,
molded cornice above reeded
frieze over pr. double-paneled cupboard doors over pr. single panel
cupboard doors, all within cockbeaded surrounds, canted corners,
cut-out bracket feet, old refinishing, 44" w., 90½" h. (ILLUS.) . . 1,900.00
Corner cupboard, Federal, cherrywood, 1-piece construction, reeded

& cove-molded cornice above pr. 6-pane glazed cupboard doors opening to shelves flanked by reeded pilasters above reeded mid-section banding over arrangement of 3 short drawers over pr. paneled cupboard doors, all within cockbeaded surrounds, bracket feet, refinished & w/replaced hinges, ca. 1830, 56¼" w., 90" h...........1,250.00

Corner cupboard, Federal country-style, painted & decorated, 1-piece construction, molded cornice above 12-pane glazed door above pr. paneled cupboard doors, canted corners, cut-out bracket feet, original red-brown painted graining in imitation of mahogany, light grey interior, Pennsylvania, ca. 1820, 44" w., 84" h............3,575.00

Corner cupboard, Federal country-style, walnut, 1-piece construction, molded cornice above pr. 8-pane glazed cupboard doors within cockbeaded surrounds over pr. short drawers & pr. double-paneled cupboard doors within conforming cockbeading, bracket feet, original finish, 52" w., 84½" h..........2,000.00

Corner cupboard, Pennsylvania painted & decorated, 1-piece construction, coved cornice above 12-pane glazed door above pr. paneled cupboard doors, canted sides, cut-out bracket feet, orange sponge-daubed decoration, Centre County, Pennsylvania....18,000.00

Miniature Decorated Corner Cupboard

Hanging corner cupboard, painted & decorated pine & poplar, scalloped top & base, paneled door opening to single shelf, original salmon pink w/red & yellow pin striping &

free-hand urn & leaf on door & vining berries on stiles, 8½" w., 13¾" h. (ILLUS.)...............1,650.00

Hanging corner cupboard, painted & decorated, scalloped top & base, pr. narrow cupboard doors w/h.p. yellow, blue & red tulips & green stems full-length of each door, brown ground, ca. 1850, 12" w., 9" deep, 19" h. 350.00

Hanging Corner Cupboard

Hanging corner cupboard, Chippendale, pine, cove-molded cornice above double-paneled thumb-molded cupboard door opening to 3 shelves, molded base, Pennsylvania, 1760-85, 26½" w., 46" h. (ILLUS.)......................1,430.00

Hanging cupboard, Shaker, painted pine, plain top above case w/plain 2-board cupboard door opening to shelves, painted red, Tyringham, Massachusetts, ca. 1820, 18½" w., 8½" deep, 21½" h. 880.00

Hanging cupboard, primitive pine, plain top above case w/plain 1-board cupboard door on original wrought iron butterfly hinges, molded strip below door, worn old green paint, 19¼" w., 30¼" h. 900.00

Hanging cupboard, walnut, molded cornice above openwork frieze over pr. double-paneled cupboard doors w/white porcelain pulls, molded base, refinished, 27" w., 39" h. 550.00

Jelly cupboard, pine, oblong top w/projecting molded cornice above pr. paneled cupboard doors opening to shelves, scalloped base, worn old paint w/added green wash, worn white repaint interior, 39" w.......................1,100.00

Jelly cupboard, painted pine, oblong top above pr. paneled cupboard

doors opening to shelves, 1-board
sides, cut-out bracket feet,
cleaned down to old blue repaint,
42½" w., 48½" h.............. 435.00
Jelly cupboard, painted pine & poplar, oblong top w/three-quarter
cut-out gallery above case w/sin-
gle long drawer over pr. paneled
cupboard doors, cut-out bracket
feet, old worn grey paint expos-
ing red beneath, 41" w., 54" h.... 500.00
Jelly cupboard, primitive pine,
oblong top w/applied coved molding below overhang above case
w/pr. short drawers w/turned
wood pulls & pr. raised panel
cupboard doors opening to 4
shelves, cut-out bracket feet,
Amish origins, refinished........1,200.00
Linen press, Federal, mahogany,
2-part construction: upper part
w/cove-molded cornice above plain
frieze & pr. cross-banded cupboard doors w/cockbeaded edges;
lower section w/molded & cross-
banded cupboard doors opening to
pull-out writing shelf & other
shelves, short reeded baluster-
turned legs, brass ball feet, New
York, 1800-15, 46¼" w.,
85½" h. 4,400.00
Pewter cupboard, pine, 1-piece construction, molded cornice above 3
open shelves over pr. single-
board cupboard doors, scalloped
base, dark reddish brown repaint,
45¾" w., 74¾" h. (chewed hole
in bottom corner of one door &
one end of cornice replaced) 675.00
Pewter cupboard, primitive pine,
1-piece construction, molded cornice above 3 open shelves
w/molded front edges flanked by
scalloped sides over single board-
and-batten cupboard door, old
darkened finish, 55" w.,
74½" h. 2,500.00
Pie safe, hanging-type, plain top
w/hanging hooks atop corner
posts, single cupboard door
w/punched tin panels of compass
& quarter circle design & sides
w/panels of compass-stars,
stripped of all finish 685.00
Pie safe, painted finish, oblong top
above pr. cupboard doors w/two
punched tin panels of circle
designs & w/conforming panels
in sides, square legs & feet, original red-painted finish 1,400.00
Pie safe, poplar, oblong top w/ap-
plied molding over pr. cupboard
doors w/four punched tin
starflower & circle design panels

Poplar Pie Safe

& w/conforming panels in sides,
scalloped apron, square legs,
Kentucky origins, doors have been
rehinged & divided to make four
doors from original two, some
edge damage, 50½" w., 19¾"
deep, 78¼" h. (ILLUS.)..........., 800.00
Pie safe, walnut, 1-board oblong top
above case w/long drawer over
pr. cupboard doors w/three
pierced tin stylized floral
panels in each & w/conforming
panels in sides, turned legs, old
green & yellow painted finish,
41" w., 18¾" deep, 53¾" h......1,050.00
Step-back wall cupboard, painted
finish, 1-piece, molded cornice
above scalloped frieze over 2
open shelves & oblong top over
single paneled cupboard door
flanked by 2 small panels, molded
base, painted blue & highlighted
w/polychrome details, late
19th c., 46" w., 76" h. (paint
restored) 990.00
Step-back wall cupboard, Chippendale, walnut, 2-part construction:
upper part w/cove-molded projecting cornice above dentil-carved
frieze & pr. paneled cupboard
doors flanked by reeded pilasters
over open pie shelf; lower section
w/three short drawers w/original
brass drop handles above pr.
paneled cupboard doors flanked
by conforming pilasters, cut-out
bracket feet, Pennsylvania, ca.
1775, 62¾" w., 85¾" h........23,100.00
Step-back wall cupboard, grain-
painted poplar, 2-part construction:
upper part w/simple cornice above
pr. 6-panel glazed cupboard doors
over open pie shelf; lower section
w/three overlapping beveled short

Two Piece Wall Cupboard

drawers w/turned wood pulls above pr. paneled cupboard doors, scalloped base, cut-out feet, original worn red-painted flame graining, 60" w., 95¼" h. (ILLUS.)........1,850.00

One Piece Pine Cupboard

Wall cupboard, painted pine, 1-piece, coved cornice w/dentil molding below above pr. 6-pane glazed cupboard doors over pr. paneled cupboard doors, all within reeded & zig-zag "picture frame" molding, short cut-out feet, black repaint w/some wear, 49¼" w., 72" h. (ILLUS.)......................4,800.00

Wall cupboard, Federal country-style, cherrywood, 1-piece, coved cornice w/fluted details above pr. 6-pane glazed cupboard doors over raised panel cupboard doors, all flanked by turned & rope-twist quarter columns, scalloped apron, cut-out bracket feet, 42" w., 86" h......4,700.00

Wall cupboard, Federal country-

style, poplar, 2-part construction: upper part w/molded cornice above pr. paneled cupboard doors opening to shelves; lower section w/pr. paneled cupboard doors, cut-out bracket feet, 47¾" w., 71½" h........................ 750.00

Wall cupboard, Turn-of-the-Century, golden oak, 2-part construction: upper part w/raking cornice applied w/split medallions at center & flanking corners above pr. single-pane glazed cupboard doors opening to shelves above open pie shelf; base w/oblong top over 3 short drawers w/original brass pulls over pr. paneled cupboard doors w/brass handles, square tapering feet, ca. 1910, refinished....................1,350.00

Wall cupboard, Victorian, cherry-wood, 1-piece, molded cornice w/wide overhang above pr. 8-pane glazed cupboard doors over pr. short drawers w/white porcelain pulls & pr. paneled cupboard doors, shaped apron, cut-out bracket feet, original brass latches, ca. 1850, 46½" w., 88 7/8" h. (cornice damage one side) 1,400.00

DESKS

Gustav Stickley Fall-Front Desk

Art Deco lady's writing desk, rosewood & burled walnut, rounded rectangular top inset w/conforming leather writing surface above deep scalloped burl apron set w/one long drawer w/angular bronze handle, raised on 4 faceted & tapering cabriole legs, attributed to Louis Sue & Andre Mare, ca. 1925, 43" l., 28¾" h........... 7,150.00

Art Deco lady's desk, mahogany,

rectangular top w/silvered-bronze surround above skirt w/one long & 2 short drawers above 2 cupboard doors, raised on tapering legs w/scrolling terminals & silvered-bronze sabots, branded "Ruhlmann," w/chair w/square upholstered back & oblong seat on square legs, desk 39" l., 30¼" h., 2 pcs. 16,500.00

Art Nouveau lady's writing desk, mahogany, 2-part construction: upper section surmounted by arched top cabinet w/open shelf carved w/blossoms & leafage one side & adjoining open lower shelf-cabinet w/exaggerated corners; oblong desk top w/exaggerated flaring corners, apron w/two short drawers w/gilt-bronze foliate handles, raised on thumb-molded tapering legs w/pad feet, front legs conjoined to desk top w/undulating foliate devices, by Louis Majorelle, France, ca. 1900, 47½" w., overall 56" h. 8,800.00

Chippendale slant-front desk, tiger stripe maple, oblong hinged lid opening to small drawers, valanced pigeonholes & central document door flanked by pilasters, above case w/four graduated long drawers within cockbeaded surrounds, ogee bracket feet, probably original brass bail handles, possibly Maine, ca. 1790, 40" w., 38¾" h. 2,530.00

Chippendale slant-front desk, maple, hinged lid opening to fitted interior w/central fan-carved drawer flanked by 8 valanced pigeonholes over 5 small drawers over 2 short drawers above case w/three graduated overlapping drawers, bracket feet, old brown finish, pine & chestnut secondary wood, 35¾" w., 42 3/8" h. (pigeonhole valances replaced, replaced brasses) 5,500.00

Federal "butler's" desk, Hepplewhite style, inlaid mahogany, oblong top over deep drawer inlaid w/ovals of figured mahogany edged w/banding & hinged at front to open & form writing surface, fitted w/pigeonholes, 6 small line-inlaid drawers & central drawer opening to 2 drawers, above case w/three cockbeaded & graduated long drawers, scrolled skirt w/inlaid edge banding, original oval brass drop ring handles embossed w/eagles, 47" w., 42¼" h. 1,000.00

Federal lady's writing desk, inlaid mahogany, 2-part construction:

upper part w/two short drawers above pr. cupboard doors opening to small drawers over pigeonholes; lower section w/hinged baize-lined writing flap above 3 long drawers flanked by inlaid dies, inlaid double-tapering legs, New England, ca. 1810, 41½" w., 52" h. 5,225.00

Federal slant-front desk, Hepplewhite country-style, curly maple, hinged lid opening to cherrywood & maple fitted interior w/shallow drawers over shaped pigeonholes centering a document drawer door above case w/four drawers, scalloped apron continuing to French feet, 38½" w., 44½" h. (repairs & separation in slant front) 2,050.00

Federal slant-front desk, Hepplewhite-style, cherrywood w/figuring in lid, hinged lid opening to fitted interior w/valanced pigeonholes over 4 short drawers & centering pull-out compartment w/three secret drawers over case w/four graduated overlapping drawers, bracket feet, 35¾" w., 40½" h. . . . . ,. . .4,300.00

Mission-style (Arts & Crafts movement) so-called "chalet" desk, tall, slender frame w/drop front writing surface below gallery w/L-shaped piercings, tapered sides joined w/three exposed tenons w/keys, wide shoe feet, Model No. 505, by Gustav Stickley, ca. 1900, 23½" w., 46" h. 880.00

Mission-style (Arts & Crafts movement) fall-front desk, oak, rectangular top over square fall w/brass hardware on sloped square sides joined by undershelf, opening to reveal pigeonholed interior, Model No. 706, by Gustav Stickley, ca. 1900, 13" w., 44" h. (ILLUS.) 1,650.00

Plantation desk, Victorian, tiger maple, 2-part construction: upper case w/flat cove-molded crest above 4 shallow round-front drawers over wide drop-front opening to numerous pigeonholes & other compartments; lower case w/rectangular top over 4 long drawers; ring- and baluster-turned legs, Baltimore, ca. 1850 . . . . .6,500.00

Queen Anne slant-front desk on frame, cherrywood, 2-part construction: upper part w/molded hinged lid opening to fitted interior w/four short drawers below pigeonholes; frame w/single thumb-molded drawer, shaped skirt, cabriole legs, pad feet, 36½" w., 36½" h. 5,775.00

Queen Anne slant-front desk on

frame, cherrywood, hinged lid opening to valanced pigeonholes & short drawers above case w/four graduated thumb-molded long drawers; on molded base w/shaped apron continuing to cabriole legs, slipper feet, Connecticut, ca. 1750, 34" w., overall 42" h. (one drawer bottom replaced) 18,700.00

Queen Anne country-style slant-front desk, curly maple, hinged lid opening to interior w/valanced pigeonholes over 5 short drawers above 2 pull-out letter drawers above case w/four overlapping graduated drawers, scalloped base, short cabriole legs, trifid feet, 38"w ., 43" h. 5,300.00

School desk, pine, single unit w/seat in front, square slighly tapered & splayed legs, mortised & pinned construction, hinged slanttop lid, worn grey paint 175.00

Schoolmaster's desk, Hepplewhite country-style, primitive pine, hinged slant lid opening to interior w/three pigeonholes, plain apron, square tapering legs, 31" w., 20½" deep, 34" h. (worn painted finish & repair to one leg) 295.00

Schoolmaster's desk, Hepplewhite country-style, painted pine, slant lid lifting to well w/fitted interior of 4 pigeonholes & small drawers, apron w/dovetailed drawer, square tapering legs, brownish-yellow comb-painted graining over early red, 31" w., 21" deep, 43¾" h. 300.00

Schoolmaster's desk, pine & tiger stripe maple, pegged construction, low gallery partly around hinged slant lid opening to storage compartment, turned legs, tapering feet, ca. 1825 . . . . 675.00

Schoolmaster's desk, pine, hinged lid w/backsplash & applied molding at edges lifting to well above case w/three graduated drawers w/turned wood pulls, square legs, mellowed good patina 1,000.00

Shaker sewing desk, butternut, superstructure w/oblong top above arrangement of central cupboard door flanked by 3 short drawers above counter-top over 3 short drawers to left & pr. deeper, large drawers to right, Enfield, Connecticut 22,000.00

Turn-of-the-Century roll-top desk, golden oak, S-roll opening to numerous small drawers & pigeonholes, kneehole flanked by banks

of drawers, paneled sides & back, molded base, 50" w. 1,400.00

Turn-of-the-Century roll-top desk, golden oak, S-roll opening to 19 pigeonholes, drawers & locked compartments, all w/brass pulls; center drawer above kneehole flanked by 4-drawer pedestal to left & 2 drawer & double ledge file drawer to right, paneled sides, 50" w. 4,200.00

Turn-of-the-Century roll-top desk, golden oak, S-roll opening to numerous compartments & drawers & w/inner-roll covering 12 open compartments, kneehole flanked by 4 graduated drawers, molded base, by American Case & Register Co., Alliance, Ohio, ca. 1900, refinished, 60" w., 58" h. 7,500.00

Turn-of-the-Century roll-top desk, cherrywood, S-roll opening to numerous pigeonholes & drawers above kneehole flanked by drawers 1,900.00

Oak S-Roll Top Desk

Turn-of-the-Century roll-top desk, golden oak, S-roll opening to center section of pigeonholes flanked by 3 small drawers over single long drawer above writing surface, kneehole flanked by 4 graduated drawers to left & 1 drawer over paneled door to right, paneled sides (ILLUS.) 1,495.00

Victorian "Davenport" desk, rococo substyle, rosewood, cushion-molded crest above sloping writing surface lifting to well raised on cabriole legs w/foliate-carved knees & scrolling feet, w/drawers at side, ca. 1850, 23" w., 38" h. . . 522.00

Victorian lady's writing desk, Eastlake substyle, walnut, 1-piece construction, upper part w/mirrored cupboard door opening to narrow shelves & flanked by open shelves

Eastlake Lady's Writing Desk

forming three-quarter gallery over
hinged slant-front opening to form
writing surface & reveal cubby-
holes & small drawers above case
w/single drawer w/brass pulls, on
turned & squared legs joined by
medial shelf w/three-quarter fretwork gallery, signed "Lejambre"
(A. & H. Lejambre), Philadelphia,
Pennsylvania, 1878-85, 28 3/8" w.,
49" h. (ILLUS.) 2,860.00

Wooton Standard Grade Desk

Victorian "patent" desk, Wooton
Standard Grade, walnut & bird's
eye maple, hinged doors opening
to cubbyhole sections & drop-front
writing surface (ILLUS.) 6,000.00

Victorian desk, walnut w/inset
leather writing surface on top,
low three-quarter gallery, long
drawer w/line incised decor
above kneehole flanked by 4
graduated drawers w/line incised
decor to the left & single drawer
w/line incised decor over paneled
door w/line incised decor to the
right, drawers w/turned wood
pulls, paneled sides, bracket feet
(ILLUS.) 895.00

Victorian Walnut Desk

GARDEN & LAWN FURNITURE (Cast Iron)

Ornate Cast Iron Settee

Armchairs, Branch patt., cast
w/arched crest above openwork
back formed of interconnecting
branches, conforming seat flanked
by arched armrests on curving
supports, curving legs w/branch-
form brackets, 19th c., pr.......1,430.00

Benches, cast w/swans's head finials at back, slate seats, painted
grey-green, 23½ x 17", pr........ 210.00

Benches, Vintage patt., cast w/lacy
openwork grapevines & clusters,
33" l., pr. 150.00

Benches, 2-chairback style, Gothic
design, cast w/gothic arches in
overall outline & w/wooden slat
seats fitted in framework, England,
19th c., pr.....................3,300.00

Settee, Victorian rococo style, cast
w/ornate C-scrolls, full relief roses
& other florals & latticework in
back & w/lattice medallion serpentine-fronted seat, C-scroll apron

continuing to demi-cabriole legs,
ca. 1850 (ILLUS.) 3,300.00

Fern Pattern Settee

Settee, Fern patt., cast fern design
in back & downswept arms, openwork scroll design seat, 19th c.,
56" l. (ILLUS.) . . . . 1,000.00 to 1,320.00
Suite: love seat & side table; Vin-
tage patt., cast w/lacy openwork
grapevines & clusters in love seat
& w/palmette & grapevine design
in table, 19th c., repainted white,
2 pcs. 312.50
Table, cast w/intricate geometric
designs in perforated top, tripod
base w/leafy supports, New York,
1850-60, 30½" d., 29¼" h. 1,320.00
Table, cast w/pierced top & scalloped rim, 4 scroll-molded &
pierced cabriole legs joined by
medial shelf, 19th c., now painted
light green, 38½" d., 26½" h. 385.00

HALL RACKS & TREES

American Gothic Hall Tree

Hall tree, American Gothic, oak, ornate arched opencut upper frame
w/hooks at side above white marble-slab shelf above ornate opencut base flanked by umbrella
racks, ca. 1855 (ILLUS.) 10,000.00

Hall tree, Victorian, Renaissance Revival substyle, walnut, pierce-
carved cresting above shaped mirror within molded framework
above white marble-slab shelf
above single small drawer flanked
by umbrella racks w/original
brass pans, ca. 1875 . . . . 600.00

Victorian Renaissance Hall Tree

Hall tree, Victorian, Renaissance
Revival substyle, walnut, ornate
carved cresting above shaped mirror within molded framework
w/drop columns at each side &
candle sockets & candle shelves
& sockets at lower sides, above
white marble-slab shelf over single
small drawer flanked by umbrella
racks, ca. 1870 (ILLUS.) 1,430.00
Hat rack, mahogany, slender circu-
lar shaft w/four hanging hooks
rising from quadruple base, 58" h. 165.00
Hat rack, Victorian, walnut,
expandable-type w/turned pegs
fitted w/brass rosettes & white
porcelain buttons 50.00
Umbrella rack, Mission-style (Arts &
Crafts movement), golden oak,
11 x 11" sq., 27" h. 45.00

HIGHBOYS

Chippendale "bonnet-top" highboy,
mahogany, 2-part construction:
upper part w/swan's neck cresting
centering 3 corkscrew finials above
arrangement of fan-carved central
drawer flanked by short drawers
over 4 graduated long drawers;
lower section w/long drawer over
fan-carved central drawer flanked
by short drawers, cabriole legs
w/acanthus-carved knees, claw-
and-ball feet, Massachusetts,
1760-80, 42" w., 86¼" h. 30,800.00

Queen Anne "bonnet-top" highboy, cherrywood, 2-part construction: upper part w/swan's neck cresting centering 3 urn finials above case w/pr. short & 4 graduated long thumb-molded drawers; lower section w/single thumb-molded long drawer over central short & flanking deeper drawers, ogival-arched skirt centering pr. turned pendant drops, cabriole legs, shod pad feet, Connecticut or New York, 1740-70, 39" w., 83½" h. (restored bonnet) 8,800.00

Queen Anne "bonnet top" highboy, cherrywood, 2-part construction: upper part w/molded swans' neck cresting centering 3 spirally-carved finials above 3 short & 4 long graduated drawers; lower section w/single long drawer over central fan-carved short drawer & flanking deeper drawers, shaped skirt, cabriole legs, pad feet, New England, ca. 1765, 40½" w., 88" h. (restoration to one foot) 10,450.00

Queen Anne Highboy

Queen Anne "flat-top" highboy, walnut & maple, 2-part construction: upper part w/flat-molded cornice above pr. short & 3 graduated long thumb-molded drawers; lower section w/long shallow drawer over short central drawer flanked by deeper drawers, valanced skirt, cabriole legs, pad feet, possibly original brasses throughout, New England, ca. 1770, 38" w., 67" h. (ILLUS.) 14,300.00

Queen Anne "flat-top" highboy, maple & pine, 2-part construction:

upper part w/flat-molded cornice above 4 thumb-molded graduated drawers; lower section w/long drawer above shallow central drawer flanked by deeper short drawers, shaped skirt, cabriole legs, pad feet, New Hampshire, 1760, replaced brass bat's wing handles, 37½" w., 69¼" h. 7,975.00

William & Mary "flat-top" highboy, walnut, 2-part construction: upper part w/molded cornice above arrangement of 3 short & 3 long graduated drawers; lower section w/applied molding at top edge above shallow central drawer flanked by deeper drawers, shaped skirt, trumpet-turned legs joined by shaped stretcher, large bun feet, w/brass teardrop handles & keyhole escutcheons, England, ca. 1700, 42" w., 68" h. 5,500.00

William & Mary Highboy

William & Mary "flat-top" highboy, maple, 2-part construction: upper part w/molded cornice above pr. short drawers over 3 long drawers; lower section w/applied molding above arrangement of 3 short drawers, shaped skirt, elaborately turned legs joined by shaped stretcher, large ball feet, probably New York, ca. 1820, minor repairs to base & replaced brasses, 76¾" h. (ILLUS.) 9,350.00

LOVE SEATS, SOFAS & SETTEES

Chaise longue, bentwood, canted rectangular back & seat w/rounded corners set between elaborate bentwood scrolls forming looped armrests & scrolling supports, Vienna, ca. 1900, 67" l. 4,125.00

Chaise (or double) longue, Victorian, Eastlake substyle, oak, typical

Victorian Chaise Longue

incised carvings, green velvet floral pattern upholstery (ILLUS.) 150.00
Couch (so-called Mormon couch), walnut, spindle-turned frame w/alternating slats in seat that slide-out to make double bed, no cushion, 73¾" l. 550.00
Day bed, American Empire, mahogany, shaped ends w/roll-over crests & paneled sides, upholstered cushion, ca. 1830 ....1,100.00
Day bed, American Empire, maple, shaped crestrail & baluster-turned armrest above turned spindles on 3 sides, seat w/loose cushion, ring- and baluster-turned legs, ca. 1850, 70" l. 525.00
Day bed, Sheraton-style, mahogany, paneled ends w/curving crests & reeded detailing on ears, ring- and baluster-turned reeded legs, brass feet, seat w/loose cushion, 78" l. 450.00

William & Mary Day Bed

Day bed, William & Mary, green-painted maple & cherrywood, adjustable back w/arch-molded crest above vertical spindles flanked by vase- and ring-turned stiles, rush seat, baluster- and ring-turned legs, bulbous-turned stretchers, 18th c., 76½" l. (ILLUS.) 4,950.00
Love seat, Art Nouveau, walnut, tri-lobed back w/pierce-carved splayed center apple blossom & trellis form section above floral-upholstered back & seat, outward

Art Nouveau Love Seat

flaring tapering legs, by Louis Majorelle, France, ca. 1900, 46½" l. (ILLUS.) 3,575.00
Love seat, Victorian, rococo substyle, walnut, serpentine finger-molded crestrail w/floral & foliate-carved cresting above upholstered back & serpentine-fronted seat, conformingly carved seatrail, demi-cabriole legs, original finish & upholstery, ca. 1865 .... 535.00

Victorian Rococo "Meridienne"

"Meridiennes," Victorian rococo substyle, rosewood, fruit & floral carved crest at top of crestrail which continues down to form scrolled sides, tufted upholstered back & upholstered seat, demi-cabriole legs, ca. 1855, pr. (ILLUS. of one) 9,000.00
Recamier, American Empire, mahogany, upholstered scrolled back & seat, plain seatrail, winged animal-paw feet, 75" l. (needs upholstery) 605.00
Settee, bentwood, interlaced scrolled back above inward-scrolled arms & a shaped oval

seat, raised on flared cylindrical
legs, original paper label for
"Jacob & Josef Kohn, Vienna,"
4' 6" l. 880.00

Chinese Rosewood Settee

Settee, carved rosewood, ornately
scroll-carved crestrail continuing to
form back frame encircling panel
inlaid w/mother-of-pearl scenes of
flowers & birds & Chinese characters, scrolled arms, rectangular
wood seat, open-carved front
apron continuing to cabriole legs,
w/a pair of rosewood occasional
tables, China, 3 pcs. (ILLUS. of
settee) 6,000.00
Settee, Federal, mahogany, arched &
upholstered crestrail continuing to
form the arms, molded arm supports continuing to form tapering
square legs, Massachusetts, ca.
1790, 6' 8" l. 2,750.00
Settee, Federal country-style, painted & decorated, 3-chairback style
w/shaped crestrail w/"angel
wings" above half-spindle back,
scrolled arms, plank seat, turned
legs w/flattened stretchers, old
green repaint w/polychrome stenciled birds & flowers & yellow &
black striping, 76½" l. 495.00
Settee, Mission-style (Arts & Crafts
movement), oak, plain crestrail,
arms w/two vertical slats, upholstered leather seat, Model No. 229,
by L. & J.G. Stickley, ca. 1910,
72" l., 35" h. 1,980.00
Settee, Queen Anne, mahogany,
triple chairback style w/shell-
carved crests, slip seats, cabriole
legs w/carved knees joined by serpentine stretcher base, paw feet,
England, ca. 1760 ....5,500.00
Settee, Sheraton-style, mahogany,
upholstered back & sides continuing to baluster-turned reeded arm
supports, upholstered seat, reeded seatrail, ring-turned & reeded
baluster-shaped legs on casters,
late 19th c., 49" w. 250.00

Turn-of-the-Century Oak Settee

Settee, Turn-of-the-Century, quarter-
sawn oak, scrolled crestrail above
3 vase-shaped splats, slightly
scrolled arms w/curved front supports continuing down to form
front legs, upholstered spring
seat, ca. 1890 (ILLUS.) 165.00
Settee, Victorian, rococo substyle,
carved laminated rosewood, triple-
arched crestrail elaborately carved
w/flowers & fruit leading to voluted armrests, serpentine seat
above flower-carved apron,
"Rosalie" pattern, John Henry
Belter, New York, New York, ca.
1855, 4' 9" l. 4,400.00
Settee, Victorian, rococo substyle,
pierce-carved laminated rosewood,
serpentine back w/rose- and floral-
carved crest above molded
C-scrolls over pierce-carved floral
vine & tufted (worn) upholstery,
down-swept molded arms, serpentine-fronted seat w/carved central
floral spray, demi-cabriole legs,
attributed to John Henry Belter,
New York, New York, ca. 1855,
66" w. 8,800.00
Sofa, American Empire, mahogany,
roll-over crestrail flanked by
carved eagle's heads above upholstered back & S-scrolled arms on
carved fruit & water-leaf supports,
upholstered seat w/rounded apron,
carved paw feet w/water-leaf
brackets, ca. 1840, 71½" w. 1,100.00
Sofa, American Empire, mahogany,
shaped crestrail w/carved rosette
flowerheads continuing to scrolling
arms, seat w/loose cushion,
eagle's wing & animal paw carved
feet, attributed to Samuel Field
McIntire, Salem, Massachusetts,
ca. 1825 (repair to left front &
rear feet), 87" l. (ILLUS.) 7,150.00

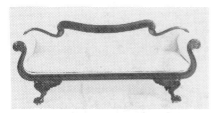

American Empire Sofa

Sofa, Chippendale "camel-back," mahogany, upholstered serpentine back continuing to scrolled arms, serpentine-fronted seat, molded square legs w/stretchers, signed "John Harris," Newburyport, Massachusetts, ca. 1770, 88" l. 39,600.00

Sofa, Federal, mahogany, molded crestrail centering swag-and-tassel carved motif flanked by panels of bowknots & thunderbolts above upholstered back & downswept arms on reeded baluster-turned supports, reeded seatrail & reeded tapering legs on casters, attributed to the school of Duncan Phyfe, New York, ca. 1810, 80" l. (one leg reduced) 8,250.00

Victorian Rococo Sofa

Sofa, Victorian, rococo substyle, laminated rosewood, triple-arched pierce-carved crestrail ornately decorated w/wide band of leafscrolls between center crest of carved blossoms in urn & end crests of carved blossoms & scrolls, ornate twist-scroll arms continuing to short cabriole legs, wide scroll-carved front apron, upholstered, attributed to John Henry Belter, New York, New York, ca. 1860 (ILLUS.) 24,000.00

Sofa, wicker, loom-woven fibre, solid back continuing to arms, 3 loose cushions w/upholstery at seat, painted white, w/matching armchair on rockers, 2 pcs. 525.00

LOWBOYS

Chippendale lowboy, walnut, oblong top w/thumb-molded edge & notch-ed corners above case w/single long drawer over 3 short drawers, shaped skirt, cabriole legs, claw-and-ball feet, Pennsylvania, ca. 1770, 36" w., 29¾" h. 26,400.00

Queen Anne lowboy, cherrywood, oblong top w/molded edge above case w/single long drawer over central half-pinwheel carved short drawer flanked by deeper short drawers, deeply scalloped skirt, cabriole legs, pad feet, Eastern Connecticut, 1740-60, 37¾" w., 30½" h. (reset top) 14,300.00

Queen Anne lowboy, cherrywood, oblong top w/molded edge above case w/long drawer over central shell-carved drawer flanked by deeper short drawers, scroll-carved skirt, cabriole legs, duck feet, 34" w., 31½" h. (replaced brass bat's wing handles) 9,500.00

Queen Anne lowboy, walnut, oblong top w/molded edge above case w/single long drawer (faced to resemble 3 short drawers) over two short drawers, shaped skirt, shell-carved cabriole legs, stockinged trifid feet, Pennsylvania, ca. 1760, 37½" w., 29¾" h. 30,800.00

William & Mary lowboy, maple w/some curl, oblong 2-board top w/thumb-molded edge above shallow central drawer & flanking deeper drawers w/brass teardrop pulls & engraved brass keyhole escutcheons, ball- and vase-turned legs w/shaped X-stretcher centering a turned urn finial, ball feet, 30¾" w., 27¾" h. (old repair to section of stretcher & top w/glued break in one corner) 15,500.00

MIRRORS

Adam wall mirror, giltwood, oblong mirror plate within upright frame w/vase & leaf finial & w/openwork scroll & leaf decoration at edges, England, ca. 1780, 28" w., 64" h. 880.00

American Empire wall mirror, giltwood, overhanging cornice w/gilt-gesso panel above 2-part mirror plate flanked by heavy baluster-and ring-turned applied half columns & w/corner blocks 165.00

Chippendale wall mirror, walnut, giltwood & gesso, scrolling high crest w/scrolling ears centered w/gilt gesso phoenix bird, oblong mirror plate within giltwood liner, conforming pendant below, 15¾" w., 29½" h. (old repairs & replacements) 475.00

Federal "convex" wall mirror, carved giltwood, convex mirror plate within molded framework hung w/gilt spherules & surmounted by spread-winged American eagle flanked by acanthus foliage & w/chain of spherules hung from beak, pomegranate pendant below, 1825-50, 31" w., overall 54" h. 4,675.00

Federal wall mirror, inlaid mahogany & giltwood, swan's neck cresting ending in gilt flowerheads & centering urn w/spray of wheat, framework centering mirror w/giltwood liner & w/gilt fillets over shaped pendant, ca. 1795, 23" w., 55½" h. 5,500.00

Queen Anne pier mirror, parcel-gilt & "verre eglomise," triple glass plates w/shaped upper section within border of gilt arabesque work incorporating two figures on a green ground, 27½" w., 64" h. 4,400.00

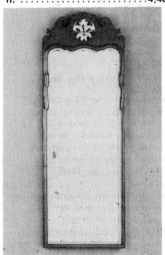

Queen Anne Mirror

Queen Anne wall mirror, mahogany & giltwood, 2-plate, shaped cresting pierced & centered w/giltwood pierced shell above shaped mirror plates within framework, w/label of John Elliot, Philadelphia, ca. 1765, 18¼" w., 51" h. (ILLUS.) . .12,650.00

Queen Anne country-style wall mirror, pine, molded & scrolled crest w/traces of "chinoiserie" decoration, original (discolored) mirror plate, 13½" w., 24½" h. 725.00

Turn-of-the-Century "haberdashery" floor-standing 3-way mirror, oak frame w/carved lion's head at crest & 3 beveled glass mirror plates 750.00

Victorian "Cheval" Mirror

Victorian "cheval" mirror, bird's eye maple frame in the "bamboo" taste, ca. 1890, 33" w., 71" h. (ILLUS.) 1,320.00

Victorian wall mirror, Eastlake substyle, walnut, typical incised carvings, 25¼" w., 56½" h. 450.00

PARLOR SUITES

Steer Horn Parlor Furniture

Art Nouveau: settee, pr. armchairs & pr. side chairs; fruitwood frames carved w/delicate spring blossoms at crest & vine-carved scrolling legs, upholstered in pink brocade, Majorelle, France, ca. 1900, 5 pcs. 6,600.00

Steer's horn eclectic style: settee, pr. armchairs, 1 side chair & a stool; each w/shaped horn back & arms above upholstered seat, raised on outswept horn legs, ca. 1890, 5 pcs. (ILLUS. of part) . .6,050.00

Victorian, Eastlake substyle: settee, armchair & side chair; cherry-stained maple w/floral tapestry up-

holstery, typical machine-carved
details in crests, turned legs,
1880's, 3 pcs. .1,475.00

Eastlake Parlor Suite

Victorian, Eastlake substyle: sofa &
pr. side chairs; walnut w/gilt-
incised details, flat crestrails
w/pierce-carved bands above upholstered backs set in machine-
carved square panels, upholstered
seat above gilt-incised apron,
round turned legs w/line incised
decor on porcelain casters, ca.
1880, 3 pcs. (ILLUS. of part) 1,540.00
Victorian, Renaissance Revival sub-
style: sofa & 2 gentleman's armchairs; triple-back sofa w/three
separate shield-shaped sections upholstered in tufted material, center
section topped w/open-carved
crest w/carved lady's face in center, open padded arms w/lady's
face carved at front of each arm,
short turned legs on casters, attributed to John Jelliff, 3 pcs. 4,700.00
Victorian, Renaissance Revival sub-
style: sofa, pr. armchairs & 4 side
chairs; walnut medallion-carved
crests w/urn finials, oval back
w/tufted upholstery, trumpet-
turned legs, ca. 1860, 7 pcs. 2,530.00

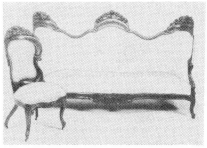

Victorian Rococo Parlor Suite

Victorian, Rococo substyle: settee &
pr. side chairs; carved laminated
rosewood, molded frames w/carv-
ed floral & fruit cresting enhanced
w/C-scrolls, serpentine upholstered
back & seat on sofa w/C-scroll &
floral carved seatrail, demi-cabriole legs, attributed to John Henry
Belter, New York, New York, ca.
1855, 3 pcs. (ILLUS. of part) 4,225.00

Wicker: sofa & armchair, loom-
woven fiber, original finish
w/painted diamond designs in
back & apron, label of Heywood-
Wakefield, 1920's, pr. 895.00

SCREENS

Victorian Fire Screen

Fire screen, Victorian, Eastlake substyle, ebonized wood frame
w/gilt-highlighted incised line decor typical of Eastlake form,
w/turned spindles in openwork
cresting, centering fabric panel,
on trestle base, ca. 1870
(ILLUS.) 650.00
Fire screen, Victorian, rococo sub-
style, walnut frame w/carved
C-scroll & S-scroll details,
cartouche-shaped crest centering
cross-stitch embroidered panel on
trestle base, ca. 1865, 28" w.,
51" h. 450.00
Fire screen, rococo substyle, carved
laminated rosewood frame incorporating C-scroll & S-scroll details
centering needlework panel & continuing to scrolling toes, attributed to John Henry Belter, New
York, New York, ca.1855 . . . . .2,500.00
Folding screen, 3-fold, Turn-of-the-
Century, golden oak frame
w/openwork spindle-turned details above shirred fabric insert,
original finish & worn fabric 175.00
Folding screen, 4-fold, tooled leather
w/continuous frieze of stylized
chrysanthemums, stars & butterflies in shaded brown to deep
brown, Continental, ca. 1910, each
panel 23½ x 70" 1,210.00

Folding screen, 4-fold, brass & mirrored peach-colored glass, each double-hinged oblong panel set w/peach-colored glass, black-painted tin reverse, attributed to Jacques Adnet, ca. 1930, each panel 11 7/8" w., 41¾" h........1,100.00

Folding screen, 6-fold, Coromandel lacquer, carved & painted continuous scene of Immortals on their mythical animal mounts supported on clouds in river landscape in subtle colors within wide-band blossoming floral borders on dark brown ground, each panel 18¾" w., 103" h. (old restoration)........8,800.00

Folding screen, 12-fold, Coromandel lacquer, gilt ground carved in crisp relief w/processions of Daoist Immortals visiting "Shoulao" in mountainous landscape within dragon border sides & mythical bird & animal borders at top & sides, undecorated black reverse, late 18th c., each panel, 17" w., 93" h. 17,600.00

SECRETARIES

Chippendale Secretary-Bookcase

Chippendale secretary-bookcase, walnut, 2-part construction: upper part w/molded cornice above pr. arch-molded cupboard doors opening to an arrangement of shelves & short drawers, flanked by fluted quarter columns; lower section w/hinged slant-front lid opening to fitted interior w/eight valanced pigeonholes & short drawers centering 2 columnar document drawers & shell-carved & blocked prospect door opening to an additional removable compartment w/short drawers

& secret drawers, above case w/four thumb-molded graduated drawers flanked by fluted quarter columns, ogee bracket feet, Pennsylvania, ca. 1770, 42" w., 89" h. (ILLUS.) 26,400.00

Federal secretary-bookcase, mahogany, 2-part construction: upper part w/shaped pediment above pr. double Gothic arch glazed cupboard doors above tambour slide opening to central line-inlaid prospect door flanked by small drawers & pigeonholes; lower section w/folding writing flap above 3 line-inlaid & graduated long drawers, shaped skirt w/inlaid contrasting oval center, flaring French feet, Massachusetts, 1800-20, 36" w., 77" h. 4,620.00

Federal secretary-bookcase, mahogany, 2-part construction: upper part w/molded freize centering 3 brass urn finials above pr. glazed mullioned cupboard doors opening to shelves; lower section w/hinged folding writing flap above 4 graduated cockbeaded long drawers w/line inlay continuing to bracket feet, Massachusetts, ca. 1805 (losses to veneer) 4,180.00

Federal secretary-bookcase, mahogany w/maple veneer, 3-part construction: upper-most section w/glass paneled "temple" pediment highlighted by gilt "eglomise" borders; middle section w/glazed Gothic-arch cupboard doors flanked by Ionic columns, opening to shelves above pr. shallow drawers; lower section w/hinged writing flap opening to reveal small utensil compartments above case w/two graduated maple-veneered long drawers, reeded & baluster-turned legs joined by medial shelf, on casters, New York, 1800-10, 37" w., overall 66" h. 28,600.00

Federal secretary-bookcase, Hepplewhite style, mahogany & mahogany veneer, 2-part construction: upper part w/shaped cornice centering 3 (replaced) brass ball finials above pr. geometrically glazed cupboard doors opening to shelves; lower section w/upper oval-veneered drop-front drawer opening to fitted interior w/pigeonholes & 3 dovetailed drawers above 3 long drawers within cockbeaded surrounds, shaped apron, French feet, Boston, early 19th c., 40½" w., 82" h. 5,000.00

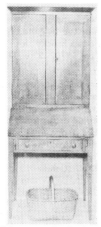

Federal Country-Style Secretary

Federal country-style secretary table-desk, curly maple, 2-part construction: period upper section w/flat cornice w/angled molding above pr. paneled cupboard doors opening to shelves; on hand-made reproduction slant-front desk on square tapering legs, 30¾" w., 75½" h. (ILLUS.) ....1,350.00 to 1,500.00

Country Hepplewhite Secretary

Federal secretary, Hepplewhite country-style, 2-part construction: upper section w/scroll-cut crest (recut) above 2 reeded, paneled cupboard doors opening to pigeonholes & 2 dovetailed drawers above 2 reeded, paneled doors; lower section w/fold-out writing surface top above 3 graduated drawers w/brass pulls, cut-out feet, some drawers stamped "Curtis Cady, Madison, July 21 ----" (refinished, small repairs & replaced brasses), 42" w., 81" h. (ILLUS.) 1,950.00

Louis XV-XVI "secretaire a' abattant," kingwood w/ormolu mounts, slightly bow-fronted veined brown & grey marble slab top above fall-front enclosing leather-lined writing surface & arrangement of drawers & shelves w/pr. cupboard doors below enclosing shelves, short cabriole legs, fitted w/pierced acanthus & bellflower ormolu corner mounts, keyhole escutcheons, scrolled "sabots" & apron mount incorporating mask of Diana, France, third quarter 18th c., 39" w., 51" h. 8,250.00

Louis XVI "secretaire a' abattant," mahogany w/ormolu mounts, 2-part construction: oblong black marble top above single frieze drawer & fall-front opening to form writing surface & reveal fitted interior; lower section w/pr. cupboard doors opening to shelves, "toupie" feet, the whole veneered w/mahogany & outlined w/brass & fitted w/ormolu handles & thimble "sabots," signed "Delorme," France, late 18th c., 38½" w., 57¼" h. 4,400.00

Queen Anne child's secretary-desk, maple, 2-part construction: upper part w/molded swan's neck pediment above 2 glazed cupboard doors; lower part w/thumb-molded slant-lid opening to fitted interior w/seven pigeonholes over 4 short drawers, the case w/four thumb-molded long drawers above shaped skirt, cabriole legs w/pad feet, 18th c., 26½" w., 67" h.....1,210.00

"Side-by-Side" Secretary-Bookcase

Turn-of-the-Century "side-by-side" secretary-bookcase, golden oak, wide, flat crest w/central shelf w/rounded crest & scroll-carved support above frieze of machine-carved scrolls over oblong low mirror to the left & shelf over beveled mirror to the right, curved-glass cupboard door to the left of secretary unit comprised of single narrow drawer above hinged drop-front lid w/machine-carved scroll design above narrow round-front drawer over 3 plain drawers, claw feet, ca. 1900, 38" w., 73" h. (ILLUS.) 650.00

Turn-of-the-Century "side-by-side" secretary-bookcase, golden oak, drop-front desk w/mirror-backed compartment beneath short cupboard w/ornate crest above 3 short drawers below beside glazed bow-fronted "curio" (or bookcase) cabinet, demi-cabriole legs, paw feet, original brass hardware 875.00

Turn-of-the-Century "side-by-side" secretary-bookcase, oak, drop-front desk w/compartmented interior above 3 drawers & surmounted by shaped mirror beside glazed "curio" (or bookcase) cabinet, applied machine carving details, brass handles, ca. 1915 . . . . . 525.00

Early Victorian Secretary-Bookcase

Victorian secretary-bookcase, carved rosewood, 2-part construction: upper section w/flat cove-molded crest above 2 glazed cupboard doors w/glass framed by carved scroll bands opening to interior shelves; lower section w/hinged fold-down writing surface opening to 7 small drawers surrounding pigeonholes above two paneled cupboard doors trimmed w/carved scrolls, scrolled apron w/bracket feet, 1840-50 (ILLUS.) 3,500.00

Victorian "Butler's" Secretary-Bookcase

Victorian "butler's" secretary-bookcase, Renaissance Revival substyle, walnut, 2-part construction: shaped crest w/pierce-carved scrolling cartouche over pr. arch-top glazed cupboard doors opening to shelves; base w/single pull-out writing surface faced to resemble 2 drawers over pr. cupboard doors w/applied moldings & carved fruit medallions, plinth base, ca. 1860, 40¾" w., 97" h. (ILLUS.) 2,090.00

Victorian cylinder-roll secretary-bookcase, Renaissance Revival substyle, walnut & burl walnut, 2-part construction: upper part w/architectural cornice above pr. glazed cupboard doors opening to shelves; lower section w/cylinder roll opening to small drawers & pigeonholes above case w/long graduated drawers w/handles, 8' 7" h. 4,500.00

Cylinder-Roll Victorian Secretary

Victorian cylinder-roll secretary-bookcase, Renaissance Revival substyle, walnut & burl walnut, 2-part construction: upper part w/molded cornice above pr. glazed cupboard doors opening to shelves; lower section w/cylinder rolling back to fitted interior above case w/long drawer w/burl panels above 2 paneled cupboard doors w/burl trim, plinth base, 1870-80 (ILLUS.) 990.00

SIDEBOARDS

Federal Inlaid Mahogany Sideboard

Federal sideboard, inlaid mahogany, oblong top w/bowed front above conformingly-shaped case w/three drawers above pr. of cupboard doors flanked by pr. of convex doors centering inlaid dies on tapering reeded legs ending in tapering vase-form feet, Northeastern Massachusetts, ca. 1810, 60" w., 41¼" h. (ILLUS.) 11,000.00

Federal sideboard, mahogany w/inlaid satinwood stringing, superstructure centering inlaid oval reserve at bow-fronted center drawer w/flanking drawers over bow-fronted oblong top above central drawer & pr. cupboard doors of conforming outline flanked by plain cupboard doors, square tapering legs w/cross-banded cuffs, New York, ca. 1795, 65½" w., 44" h. 4,400.00

Philadelphia Federal Sideboard

Federal sideboard, mahogany, serpentine-fronted oblong top surmounted by brass gallery above conformingly-shaped case w/two convex drawers centering central serpentine drawer above pr. of serpentine cupboard doors flanked by pr. of convex cupboard doors, on square tapering legs ending in cross-banded cuffs, Philadelphia, ca. 1800, 72¾" w., 43" h. (ILLUS.) 37,400.00

Federal country-style hunt board, pine, oblong top above 3 short drawers, square legs joined by medial shelf, ca. 1840, 70 x 22" top, 32" h. 528.00

Federal country-style hunt board, pine, oblong top, apron w/long shallow drawer, block- and ring-turned legs w/double box stretcher, 1840's, 65½ x 27½" top, 30½" h. 715.00

Mission-style (Arts & Crafts movement) sideboard, oak, backboard banded to form plate rack at rear of oblong top above 3 central small drawers flanked by 2 cupboard doors over long drawer, Model No. 734, L. & J.G. Stickley, 48" w., 39¾" h. 352.00

Mission-style (Arts & Crafts movement) sideboard, oak, oblong top w/open plate rack to rear above case w/long drawer over 3 central drawers flanked by cupboard doors, square legs, Gustav Stickley red decal mark, Model No. 814, ca. 1907, 48" w., 45" h. 5,720.00

Mission-style (Arts & Crafts movement) sideboard, oak, rectangular top w/long shaped frame w/mirror at rear above 3 short drawers over 1 long drawer, each w/brass bail pulls, square legs, Model No. 819, branded mark of Gustav Stickley, ca. 1913, 52" w., 50" h. 1,430.00

Mission-style (Arts & Crafts movement) sideboard, oak, oblong top w/plate rail to rear, case w/arrangement of pr. short drawers over 2 short drawers flanked by pr. cupboard doors w/long drawer below all, square legs, original copper strap hinges & hardware, Model No. 735, L. & J.G. Stickley, unsigned 1,870.00

Turn-of-the-Century sideboard-china cabinet, oak, scroll-carved crest on upper left above curved-glass cupboard door opening to shelves beside scalloped scroll-carved crest on upper right above large beveled mirror w/half-shelf half

Turn-of-the-Century Sideboard

way down side of frame above
serving area above round-front
long drawer over single drawer
above 2 cabinet doors w/scroll-
carved trim, simple cabriole front
legs, ca. 1900, 47" w., 68½" h.
(ILLUS.) 825.00

Victorian Eastlake Sideboard

Victorian sideboard, Eastlake eclectic
substyle, oak, superstructure w/ob-
long framed mirror flanked by
spindle-galleried 2-tier shelf arrangement; base w/oblong top
above 2 central drawers over
openwork bin w/spindled front rail
flanked by arrangement of short
drawers over paneled cupboard
doors, square feet, w/label of
Herter Bros., New York, New
York, ca. 1870 (ILLUS.) 1,650.00
Victorian sideboard, Renaissance Revival substyle, walnut & burl walnut, superstructure w/fruit & car-

Renaissance Revival Sideboard

touche-carved crest above 2
mirror-backed shelves flanked by
S-scrolls over Italian marble
D-shaped top w/molded edge &
conforming case w/two short
drawers over pr. cupboard doors
w/shaped panel insets hung w/ap-
plied carved fruit clusters, molded
plinth base, ca. 1860, 56" w.,
87½" h. (ILLUS.) 1,320.00

Victorian Rococo Sideboard

Victorian sideboard, rococo substyle,
rosewood, superstructure composed
of pyramidal arrangement of 4
graduated shaped shelves backed
by a mirror & framed by ornate
pierce-carved C-scrolls & florals
& w/scrolled shelf supports above
serpentine white marble top on
conformingly shaped base w/two
central cupboard doors w/ornate
pierce-carved panels & 2 sides
w/matching carved panels, open-

cut florals swags & central swag
drop along apron, 4 long S-scroll
legs w/acanthus leaf carving at
the knees, 1850-60, 52" w.
(ILLUS.) 5,390.00

STANDS

Brass & Marble Fern Stand

Basin stand, corner-type, Federal,
mahogany & curly maple, shaped
top pierced for basin & other vessels w/three-quarter gallery,
shaped apron, square legs joined
by medial shelf w/drawer below,
splayed feet joined by shaped
stretcher, the apron & drawer front
faced in curly maple, New England,
ca. 1810, 22¼" w., 38¼" h. 2,750.00

Basin stand, Federal, mahogany,
oblong top pierced for basin &
other small vessels w/high three-
quarter gallery & fitted w/corner
shelves, scalloped apron, reeded
baluster- and ring-turned tapering
legs joined by medial shelf
w/drawer below, turned feet,
Salem, Massachusetts, ca. 1810,
20" w., 16" deep, 40" h.........4,675.00

Basin stand, Federal country-style,
painted & decorated, oblong top
pierced for basin w/three-quarter
shaped gallery, ring-turned bulbous legs joined by stretcher-shelf
w/drawer below, turned feet,
original paint w/pin-striping,
signed "A. Van Doorn, Brattle-
boro, Vermont" 950.00

Bedside stand, Mission-style (Arts &
Crafts movement), oak, oblong top
above 2 short drawers over single
drawer, all w/copper handles, red
decal & paper label of Gustav
Stickley, No. 842, ca. 1907,
22 x 16" top, 29½" h...........1,210.00

Crock stand, painted pine, semi-

circular 3-tier step-back style, old
worn red grain-painted finish,
36" w., 18¼" deep, 27" h. 350.00

Crock stand, painted finish, semi-
circular 4-tier step-back style,
Gothic arched supports w/square
end posts, turned feet w/por-
celain casters, weathered red
repaint, 48½" w., 39" h......... 225.00

Fern stand, Victorian (late), brass &
marble, square marble slab top in
cast brass openwork scrolling
frame w/cabriole legs joined by
openwork shelf centered w/ala-
baster urn form w/brass finial,
33" h. (ILLUS.) 375.00

Plant stand, Mission-style (Arts &
Crafts movement), oak, square
top w/three-slat sides joined by
horizontal cross-members, attributed to Stickley Bros.,
14" w. 418.00

Plant stand, Adirondack (twig) construction, square top, 3-legged
base w/bent twig heart forms attached to one side & w/box
stretcher at base 95.00

Shoeshine stand, double chair style,
oak w/marble slab top supporting
brass footrests, ca. 1910 ....1,500.00

Wash stand, American Empire
country-style, maple, square top
w/shaped & scrolling splashboard
above convex-molded drawer,
ring-turned legs joined by medial
shelf w/shaped skirt, ball-turned
feet, 1835, 20" w., 30" h. 285.00

Shaker Wash Stand

Wash stand, Shaker, pine, tiger
stripe maple & butternut, oblong
top w/dovetailed three-quarter
gallery above case w/three small
drawers above recessed panel
at front & w/single peg above
recessed panel over 2 (small &

larger) cupboard doors w/turned pulls at side, square tapering legs, attributed to the Hancock or New Lebanon area, 20¼"w., 18" deep, 36½" h. (ILLUS.) 11,000.00

Pine Wash Stand of 1890's

Wash stand, Victorian cottage-style (late), pine, oblong top w/shaped backsplash flanked by towel bars above apron w/single drawer, ring- and baluster-turned legs joined by shaped stretcher-shelf, turned feet, 1890's, 25 x 18" top, 33" h. (ILLUS.) 325.00

American Empire 1-drawer stand, tiger stripe & curly cherrywood drawer front, 1-board square top, apron w/single drawer, baluster-turned & blocked legs, turnip feet, refinished, 21" w. top, 30¼" h.... 350.00

American Empire 2-drawer stand, mahogany, 2-board oblong top above case w/two drawers faced w/flame grained veneer & flanked by turned columns w/biscuit corners, acanthus-carved turned standard on quadrupled platform, brass paw feet w/castors, 21½ x 17½" top, 29¼" h. 700.00

Federal country-style basin stand, painted & decorated pine, oblong top w/three-quarter gallery fitted w/shelf & pierced for basin, plain apron, square tapering legs joined by medial shelf w/drawer below, original red & black graining & green & yellow striping, 19¼" w., 15 5/8" deep, overall 37¾" h..... 375.00

Federal 1-drawer stand, bird's-eye & tiger stripe maple, oblong top above apron w/single drawer, turned legs, New England, ca. 1825, refinished, 18½ x 17½" top, 27½" h. 550.00

Federal 1-drawer stand, curly maple, square top over single cockbeaded drawer, turned splayed legs w/ball feet, New England, 1800-20, 19" w. top, 29¾" h. 1,100.00

Federal (late) 1-drawer stand, maple & curly maple, square top, plain apron w/single drawer w/turned wood pull, bold ring- and vase-turned legs, tapering feet, 19¼ x 18½" top, 28" h. (age cracks in top) 275.00

Federal 1-drawer country-style stand, cherrywood, square top, apron w/single drawers, ring- and baluster-turned legs, Massachusetts, 1810-30, 19 x 17" top, 29" h. 352.00

Federal 1-drawer country-style stand, tiger stripe maple, 1-board square top, single drawer w/replaced walnut turned pull, 23¼ x 22½" top 425.00

Federal 2-drawer country-style stand w/drop leaf, cherrywood w/bird's-eye maple drawer fronts, oblong top flanked by oblong drop leaves, maple drawers w/turned pulls, ring-turned tapering legs, flattened ball feet, ca. 1845, original finish 535.00

Federal 2-drawer country-style stand, cherrywood, square top above apron w/two drawers w/original turned mushroom-shaped pulls, heavy turned legs, flattened ball feet, ca. 1840 ...... 375.00

Federal, Hepplewhite-style 1-drawer stand, cherrywood, oblong top w/rounded corners, apron w/single drawer w/original brass pull & (replaced) lock within cockbeaded surround, square tapering legs, 20½ x 17¾", 27½" h. 800.00

Federal, Hepplewhite country-style stand, painted & decorated maple, oblong top w/wide overhang, plain frieze, square tapering legs, painted overall w/vinegar graining tin shades of reddish brown & yellow, New England or Midwest, ca. 1830, 22 x 20½" top, 30¾" h. ...8,800.00

Federal, Sheraton country-style 1-drawer stand, cherrywood, square top, apron w/single drawer w/turned pull & band of yellow painted reeding at base, slender turned legs (top old replacement; repairs to reeding), 17¼ x 16¾" top, 28½" h................... 325.00

Federal, Sheraton country-style 1-drawer stand, painted & decorated, oblong top above single drawer, turned legs, original

Country Sheraton Stand

black on red grain-painted finish,
New England, ca. 1825, 18" w.,
29" h. (ILLUS.) 550.00
Federal, Sheraton country-style
1-drawer stand, tiger stripe maple, square (reset) top, single
drawer w/original pressed lacy
opalescent glass pull, bold ring-
and baluster-turned legs, ball
feet, refinished, 18½" w.,
28½" h........................ 325.00
Federal, Sheraton country-style
1-drawer stand, cherrywood w/ti-
ger stripe maple drawer front,
(replaced) cherrywood square top,
plain apron w/single maple-
fronted drawer, ring- and
baluster-turned tapering legs, ball
feet, 20 x 20" top, 28" h. 275.00
Federal, Sheraton country-style
1-drawer stand, curly maple,
1-board oblong top, apron w/sin-
gle cockbeaded drawer, turned
legs, refinished, 22½ x 19½",
27½" h........................ 425.00
Federal, Sheraton country-style
1-drawer stand, curly maple &
cherrywood, square top, apron
w/single drawer, turned legs, button feet 500.00
Federal, Sheraton country-style
2-drawer stand, cherrywood &
maple, oblong top, apron w/pr.
bird's-eye maple veneer-fronted
drawers w/clear lacy glass pulls,
turned curly maple legs, 20¾ x
19¾" top, 29" h. 525.00
Federal, Sheraton country-style
washstand, painted pine & other
wood, oblong top w/low three-
quarter gallery above apron
w/single drawer, turned legs
joined by medial shelf w/apron
all around below, continuing to

tapering legs w/turned feet, original red paint w/worn gold stenciling, 18½" sq. top, 31" h. 310.00
Mission-style (Arts & Crafts movement) magazine stand, oak, oblong top over 2 straight sides, 3
open shelves, Stickley Bros.,
16 x 12½", 47" h. 308.00
Shaker 1-drawer stand, painted pine
& hardwood, oblong 2-board top,
apron w/single rounded front
drawer w/replaced brass pull,
turned tapering legs, original red
paint, attributed to Watervliet
Community, 23 x 17¾",
28½" h........................ 600.00
Victorian cottage-style 1-drawer
stand, painted pine, square top,
apron w/single drawer, ring- and
baluster-turned legs, turned feet,
dark brown painted flame graining, 18" w., 28¼" h. 135.00

Victorian Renaissance Plant Stand

Victorian, Renaissance Revival substyle plant stand, walnut, round
top w/inlaid design, ca. 1870,
17" d., 29" h. (ILLUS.)........... 275.00
Victorian country-style wash-
stand/commode, poplar, oblong
top w/low backsplash flanked by
towel bars over long drawer
above pr. paneled cupboard
doors, old red finish, 36½" w.
plus towel bars, 29½" h. 400.00
Victorian washstand, walnut, oblong
top w/three-quarter gallery above
single drawer, turned legs joined
by medial shelf, ca. 1860,
refinished 500.00

STOOLS

Foot stool, Federal country-style,
painted & decorated, oval top,
splayed turned legs w/turned

H-stretcher, old worn blue paint over earlier colors, 16 x 9¼", 6 3/8" h. 205.00

Foot stool, Victorian, brass, cast w/openwork rim, upholstered top, screw-in legs, 14" d., 12½" h..... 145.00

Foot stool, Victorian, cast iron frame & legs, upholstered top 95.00

Foot stool, Victorian, caned top, carved paw feet, 12 x 9¼" top, 5¾" h. 45.00

Organ stool, ebonized oak, round seat w/spindle back swiveling on column w/four adjacent legs ....95.00 to 175.00

Piano stool, oak, round seat swiveling on column w/four adjacent legs on cast iron claw & glass ball feet 110.00

Charles X stools, mahogany, oblong upholstered seat, curule base w/X-shaped supports joined by baluster-turned stretcher, France, 1825-50, pr. 11,550.00

Directoire stool, mahogany w/parcel-gilt mounts, slightly concave oblong upholstered seat on curule base w/X-shaped supports & parcel-gilt mounts, joined by baluster-turned stretcher, France, late 18th/early 19th c., 10½" w. seat, 19¼" h. 5,500.00

Queen Anne stool, burr walnut, contemporary needlework-covered slip seat in frame raised on square legs w/box stretchers, England, early 18th c., 20½" w. 11,000.00

Louis XV stool, giltwood, upholstered seat, serpentine seatrail carved at front & back w/stylized heart-shaped cartouche enclosing flowerheads & w/floral sprays at sides, cabriole legs w/flowerhead-carved knees, France, mid-18th c., 23" w., 17¾" h. 12,100.00

Victorian Renaissance Revival Stool

Victorian stool, Renaissance Revival substyle, parcel-gilt walnut, floral needlepoint upholstered seat, cabriole legs headed by classical female masks, ca. 1870, together w/similar chair, 2 pcs. (ILLUS. of stool) 525.00

TABLES

American Empire Table

American Empire (Classical Revival) card table, hinged oblong top w/canted corners, conforming frieze, spirally-turned, reeded & ring-turned colonettes above shaped plinth on acanthus-carved paw feet w/casters, 36¼ x 17½" folded top, 29" h...............1,760.00

American Empire center table, rosewood w/white marble round top, veneered apron, on 3 columnar supports w/gilt capitals raised above shaped triangular plinth base on disc feet, New York, 1825-35, 36" top d., 29¾" h.....4,400.00

American Empire drop-leaf dining table, cherrywood & bird's eye maple, oblong cherrywood top w/deep drop leaves, bird's eye maple apron, 8 turned legs (w/four swinging as gate supports), New England, ca. 1825, 48½" w. opening to 74" l., 30½" h........1,320.00

American Empire occasional table, mahogany, round top w/gadrooned edge, plain apron, acanthus-carved standard on shaped plinth raised on carved paw feet (ILLUS.) 700.00

American Empire pier table, marble & gilt-stenciled ebonized wood, oblong white-veined marble top & plain frieze w/gilt-stenciled decor supported on marble columns w/mirror plate to rear, plinth base w/gilt-stenciled grapevine motif, acanthus-carved animal paw feet, New York, ca. 1825, 42" l., 36" h. 5,225.00

American Empire sewing table, mahogany & mahogany veneer, oblong top above convex drawer over deeper drawer w/brass drop ring handles flanked by turned corner columns, bulbous-turned standard on shaped plinth base raised on C-scroll feet, probably New York, ca. 1835 . . . . 850.00

Art Deco Two-Tier Table

Art Deco 2-tier table, lacquered wood & chromed metal, graduated wood tiers supported on metal U-forms, by Donald Deskey, ca. 1929, 20 x 12" shelves, 18" h. (ILLUS.) 1,430.00

Art Nouveau Two-Tier Table

Art Nouveau 2-tier table, fruitwood marquetry, oblong top w/notched

corners & molded edge inlaid w/strutting penguins in Arctic landscape, 4 scrolling legs centering medial shelf, signed "Galle" in marquetry, France, ca. 1900, 27¼" w., 29" h. (ILLUS.). 2,970.00

Art Nouveau low table, inlaid marquetry, oblong top w/inlaid vignette of elephants passing beneath palm trees, signed "Galle," 18½ x 16½" top, 16½" h. 2,090.00

Bentwood center table, white marble shaped oblong top, minimal frieze, elaborate bentwood cruciform base w/interlocking & overlapping scrolls centering a turned wood standard, Austria, ca. 1900, 45½" w., 28½" h. 165.00

Bentwood Table by Thonet

Bentwood center table, shaped oval top supported on 4 curved legs joined at center & continuing into scrolling legs, attributed to Thonet, Austria, stamped "XIII," 32½ x 23" top, 30" h. (ILLUS.) 660.00

Biedermeier Center Table

Biedermeier center table, fruitwood
w/ebonized details, oblong top,
apron w/single drawer, lyre-form
trestle base w/ebonized stretcher,
Germany, early 19th c., 23½" w.,
29½" h. (ILLUS.) 1,760.00

Biedermeier center table, walnut,
figured walnut round top, square
baluster-shaped pedestal on
stepped incurvate square plinth,
flattened bun feet, Germany or
Austria, early 19th c. 2,640.00

Walnut & Cast Iron Billiards Table

Billiards (or pool) table, inlaid walnut & cast iron, oblong top w/geo-
metrically inlaid edge & frieze,
cast iron base in the form of conjoined lions forming x-stretcher,
by B.A. Stevens, Co., Toledo, Ohio,
1850-75, 110" l., together w/pr.
game counters, 12 cue sticks, 16
balls, pr. triangles & cue rack
(ILLUS.) 7,975.00

Butcher's "block" table, solid maple
oblong block w/canted corners
raised on blocked & turned heavy
legs, late 19th c., 48½ x 24" top,
34" h. 650.00

Chinese Export center tables, gilt-
decorated black lacquer, oblong
top w/oriental landscape vignettes,
apron w/pierced fretwork & legs
w/gilt-toned & red chinoiserie
florals on black ground, 40½ x
16" top, 33" h., pr. 7,700.00

Chippendale card table, mahogany,
hinged oblong top, apron w/single
long drawer over gadroon-carved
lower edge w/pierced brackets to
square chamfered legs ending in
blocked feet, ca. 1780, 35¾ x
16½" folded top, 29½" h. 4,950.00

Chippendale drop-leaf dining table,
mahogany, oblong top flanked by
oblong drop leaves, shaped skirt,
cabriole legs, claw-and-ball feet,
Philadelphia, ca. 1765, top opening
to 53 x 48", 28" h. (repair to one
leg) 5,500.00

Chippendale Pembroke table, mahogany, oblong top flanked by oblong
drop leaves, apron w/single draw-

er w/pierced brackets below,
square legs joined by pierced
X-stretcher, New England, ca.
1780, 36¼ x 29½" extended top,
27½" h. 7,975.00

Chippendale tilt-top tea table, mahogany, round dished 1-board top
tilting & revolving on birdcage
support, ring- and baluster-turned
standard, cabriole legs, claw-and-
ball feet, Pennsylvania, ca. 1780,
33½" d., 29" h. 9,350.00

Chippendale tea table, mahogany,
round top, tapering spirally-turned
urn-standard, downswept cabriole
tripod, claw-and-ball feet, New
England, 1765-85, 20½" d., 29" h.
(old crack to pedestal) 2,090.00

Federal 2-part banquet table, cherrywood, each section w/shaped
D-form top w/deep oblong drop
leaf at one side, plain apron,
reeded turned legs, tapering turned
feet, New England, ca. 1810, top
opening to 84" l., 28¾" h........4,125.00

Federal card table, inlaid cherrywood, hinged D-shaped top w/round-
ed corners & cross-banded edge
above conforming apron w/banded
edge & center oblong reserve
flanked by inlaid floral sprays
& diamond-inlaid dies, square
tapering legs inlaid w/pendant
bellflowers & stringing, Eastern
Connecticut, 1800-10, 35¾" w.,
30" h. 9,350.00

Federal card table, inlaid mahogany,
hinged serpentine-fronted top
above conforming apron inlaid
w/figured maple & rosewood panel,
reeded legs, vase-form feet, Massachusetts, ca. 1810...............5,500.00

Federal dressing table, mahogany,
oblong top w/outset rounded
"cookie" corners affixed w/super-
structure supporting framed oblong
mirror that swivels between turned
& blocked posts, case w/arrange-
ment of 2 short & single long
drawer flanked by ring-turned dies
continuing to ring- and baluster-
turned legs joined by medial shelf
on brass ball feet, New York, ca.
1810, 36¼" w., 60½" to top of
mirror 2,200.00

Federal drop-leaf dining table, tiger
stripe maple, oblong top w/shaped
oblong drop leaves, plain apron
w/single drawer one end, ring-
and baluster-turned legs on brass
casters, New England, ca. 1820,
49½ x 42" extended top,
28½" h. 2,090.00

Federal Pembroke table, inlaid ma-

hogany, oblong top w/rounded
ends flanked by D-shaped drop
leaves, line-inlaid apron, bellflower & line-inlaid square tapering
legs, spade feet, Annapolis or Baltimore, Maryland, ca. 1795, top
opening to 40¾ x 32½",
28¾" h. .8,250.00
Federal serving table, mahogany,
oblong top w/reeded edge above
case w/two short drawers & single
long drawer flanked by reeded
dies continuing to ring-turned &
reeded tapering legs joined by
medial shelf, on brass ball feet,
New York, ca. 1805, 36" w., 36" h.
(some restoration to drawer inter-
iors & shelf). 4,400.00
Federal sewing table, mahogany,
astragal-shaped flame-grained
mahogany top w/reeded edge
opening to fitted interior w/stor-
age compartments & felt-covered
writing board above tambour-sided
case w/one working & 3 false
drawers, ring- and urn-turned
standard on 4 reeded sabre legs
w/brass animal paw feet & brass
casters, attributed to the shop of
Duncan Phyfe, New York, ca. 1810,
26½ x 14" top, 30¼" h. 24,200.00
Federal work table, maple & wal-
nut, oblong top, apron w/single
tiger stripe maple-fronted drawer,
baluster-turned & reeded legs,
ball feet, New England, 1815-25,
20" w., 28" h. 990.00
Federal country-style drop-leaf din-
ing table, cherrywood, oblong top
w/oblong drop leaves, plain
apron, square tapering legs,
44½ x 38¾" extended top 400.00
Federal country-style work table,
Hepplewhite style, pine, 2-board
top, plain apron, square tapering
splayed legs, worn brown paint
on base & scrubbed finish on top,
71 x 34½" top 850.00

Georgian Rent Table

George III "rent" table, inlaid mahogany, round leather-inset top w/cen-

tral well above 12 frieze drawers
inlaid w/letters of the alphabet,
rotating above square base w/pan-
eled door at either end, plinth
base, England, late 18th c., 48" w.,
29" h. (ILLUS.) 33,000.00
Georgian tilt-top tea table, mahog-
any, oval top tilting above ring-
and baluster-turned standard,
downswept tripod on casters,
England, ca. 1810, 38 x 29" oval
top, 26¼" h. 1,175.00
Harvest table, Hepplewhite country-
style, poplar, birch & pine,
oblong top flanked by short drop
leaves, plain apron, square tapering legs, 71 x 18½" top w/10"
drop leaves, 29" h. 2,150.00
Harvest table, Sheraton country-style,
birch, oblong top flanked by oblong drop leaves, turned legs,
85" l. 2,900.00
Hutch (or chair) table, Queen Anne
country-style, birch & pine, round
top tilting above box-form seat
w/drawer below, old red-painted
finish 3,100.00

Hutch Table

Hutch table, William & Mary, cherrywood & maple, oval top tilting on
hinged base w/cut-out & pinned
ends on trestle feet, w/drawer
beneath seat, probably Hudson
River Valley, 18th c., 46 x 36" oval
top, 26½" h. (ILLUS.). 5,500.00
Hutch table, pine, 3-board oblong top
w/rounded corners pinned to chair
base w/lift-lid seat & sides continuing to form shoe feet, old red
stain, 53 x 44¾" top, 26½" h.
repairs to feet & seat lid
replaced) .1,500.00
Hutch table, pine & poplar, 3-board
round top tilting above trestle
base w/single drawer between
scalloped 1-board ends, shoe feet,
Pennsylvania, 37½" d.,
26¼" h. 1,000.00
Mission-style (Arts & Craft move-
ment) dining table, oak, round

extension-type top, 5 block legs, by L. & J.G. Stickley, Model 720, 54" top d., 30" h., w/two extension leaves 1,430.00

Mission-style (Arts & Crafts movement) dining table, oak, square top, plain apron, square pedestal w/four downswept supports, w/label of L. & J.G. Stickley, 50" sq. top (extending to 124" l.), 30" h., w/six extension leaves ...2,860.00

Mission-Style Oblong Library Table

Mission-style (Arts & Crafts movement) library table, oak, oblong top, apron w/two short drawers w/hammered copper pulls, square legs joined by medial shelf, branded mark of Gustav Stickley, ca. 1910, 42" l., 30¾" h. (ILLUS.) 1,870.00

Mission-Style Round Library Table

Mission-style (Arts & Crafts movement) library table, oak, round top w/wide overhang, arched apron, flat splayed legs w/arched cross-stretchers, red decal mark of Gustav Stickley, No. 633, ca. 1904, 48" d., 29" h. (ILLUS.) 1,870.00

Mission-style (Arts & Crafts movement) occasional table, oak, round top, plain apron, arched square legs w/cross-stretchers, attributed to L. & J.G. Stickley,

Fayetteville, New York, ca. 1912, 24¼" d., 28¼" h. 302.50

Mission-style (Arts & Crafts movement) occasional table, oak, round top, shallow apron, 4 square legs w/medial round shelf above cross-stretchers, possibly Stickley Bros., ca. 1910, 40" d., 29½" h. 440.00

Mission-style (Arts & Crafts movement) oval-top table, oak, shaped skirt, cut-out sides, square legs, branded Limbert, No. 146, ca. 1910, 45 x 30¼" oval top, 29" h. 660.00

Mission-style (Arts & Crafts movement) serving table, oak, oblong top w/oblong backsplash, apron w/three short drawers, square legs joined by oblong stretcher-shelf, original brass drop handles, w/label of Gustav Stickley, No. 818, ca. 1910, 48 x 19½" top, 39" h. 1,045.00

Mission-style (Arts & Crafts movement) tea table, oak, round top, square legs w/round medial shelf at cross-stretchers, red decal label of Gustav Stickley, No. 608, ca. 1907, 24" d., 26" h. 365.00

Mission-style (Arts & Crafts movement) tilt-top table, oak, square top w/tilting mechanism on square pedestal base, attributed to L. & J.G. Stickley, ca. 1912, 27¾" sq. top, 27½" h. 660.00

Queen Anne "concertina-action" card table, walnut, hinged oblong top w/rounded outset corners opening to baize-lined playing surface fitted w/candle supports & wells for counting, conforming apron w/short drawer, cabriole legs, pad feet, w/rear legs fitted w/accordion mechanism, Boston, Massachusetts, 33½" w., 26¾" h. (repair to one rear leg) 29,700.00

Queen Anne drop-leaf dining table, cherrywood, oblong top flanked by oblong drop leaves, arched apron, cabriole legs, trifid feet, Pennsylvania, ca. 1765, top opening to 51 x 46", 28" h. 4,950.00

Queen Anne drop-leaf dining table, curly maple, oblong top flanked by oblong drop leaves, syma-shaped skirt, cabriole legs, pad feet, Massachusetts, ca. 1765, top opening to 47½ x 43", 28" h. 13,750.00

Queen Anne drop-leaf tea table, mahogany, oblong top flanked by half-round drop leaves, shaped apron, cabriole legs, pad feet,

probably Massachusetts, ca. 1770,
35 x 29½" extended top, 25½" h.
(one pad foot w/small patch) 8,250.00
Queen Anne tilt-top tea table,
mahogany, circular dished top tilting & revolving above birdcage
support, turned standard w/sup-
pressed ball, cabriole tripod, snake
feet, Philadelphia, ca. 1770,
31¾" d., 29" h. (repair to
base) 8,800.00
"Sawbuck" table, pine, mortised &
pinned construction, 2-board top
w/breadboard ends, X-bar base
w/stretchers, traces of old red &
green paint, 38½ x 24¾" top,
26¼" h. 850.00
"Sawbuck" table, pine, 1-board top
on sawbuck X-bar base w/stretch-
er boards, New England, 19th c.,
59 x 24" top, 28" h. 660.00
Tavern table, Chippendale, pine &
maple, oblong pine top w/bread-
board ends, maple base w/plain
apron w/single drawer & square
legs w/box stretcher, New
England, ca. 1780, 48 x 29½" top,
27½" h. 2,420.00
Tavern table, curly maple & pine,
oblong top w/breadboard ends,
apron w/single drawer, turned
legs w/H-stretcher, New England,
1740-70, 43 x 24" top, 27¾" h. . . . 3,300.00
Tavern table, grain-painted finish,
square top, molded frieze, turned
tapering legs w/"turnip" feet,
overall ochre grained finish, early
19th c., 23½" sq. top, 26" h. 1,100.00
Tavern table, Hepplewhite country-
style, pine, oblong top w/bread-
board ends, apron w/beaded
edge & single drawer, square tapered legs, scrubbed top, old blue
paint on base, 34¼ x 22½",
27" h. 750.00

Tavern table, Queen Anne, curly
maple, oval top over 1 drawer
frieze, on ring-turned tapering
legs ending in button feet, Massachusetts, ca. 1730, 30" w., 26½" h.
(ILLUS.) 15,400.00

Tavern Table

Tavern table, walnut, oblong top,
apron w/two thumb-molded drawers,
baluster-turned legs w/box stretcher, ball feet, Pennsylvania, ca.
1750, 54 x 31½" top, 30" h.
(ILLUS.) 2,970.00
Tavern table, William & Mary, red-
painted finish, oblong top, plain
apron w/molded lower edge &
single drawer, baluster- and ring-
turned legs w/box stretchers,
turned feet, New England,
1730-70, 40¼ x 25¾" top,
26½" h. (top of different
origin) 990.00
Turn-of-the-Century conference table,
golden oak, 10' oval top supported
on twin pedestals 3,950.00
Turn-of-the-Century dining table,
oak, extension-type, round top,
plain pedestal, plinth base,
C-scroll feet, refinished, 45" d.
top, w/four extension leaves 800.00
Turn-of-the-Century dining table,
mahogany, extension-type, round
top, gadroon-carved apron, acanthus-carved pedestal w/carved lion
mask & hairy paw feet, 66" d.,
28½" h., w/three extension
leaves 2,650.00

Queen Anne Tavern Table

Oak Extension Dining Table

Turn-of-the-Century dining table, oak, extension-type, square top above ridged frieze, bulbous ring-turned & fluted legs on casters, refinished, w/three extension leaves (ILLUS.) 595.00

Turn-of-the-Century oval-top parlor table, golden oak, oval top above plain apron w/gadrooned edge, winged griffin carved legs joined by shaped stretcher & raised on flattened ball feet, original finish 1,600.00

Victorian tilt-top breakfast table, walnut, oval top tilting above ring-turned bulbous pedestal raised on carved shaped quadruple supports, mid-19th c., 52" l., 28" h. 935.00

Victorian console table, rococo substyle, carved rosewood w/white marble top, shaped rectangular top above pierce-carved frieze of berry vines intertwined w/scrolls, on scrolled legs topped by clusters of berries, joined by shaped stretcher centered by berries & leafage, ca. 1850, 6' 6" w., 34½" h. 4,125.00

Victorian library table, oak, eclectic style, oblong top w/molded & leaf-carved edge, apron w/two short drawers, carved square legs joined by medial stretcher shelf, late 19th c., 51 x 21" top, 31" h... 165.00

Victorian library table, Renaissance Revival substyle, walnut, oblong top w/rounded corners & molded edge, apron w/two working burl-inlaid drawers & two false drawers, ring-turned & fluted legs joined by medial shelf w/low ball-turned gallery, continuing to ring-turned tapering legs, on casters, ca. 1860 ....2,090.00

Renaissance Revival Library Table

Victorian library table, Renaissance Revival substyle, walnut & burled walnut, molded rectangular top w/canted corners & a cloth writing surface above molded & paneled

skirt w/two drawers, on baluster-turned legs joined by baluster-turned stretchers, on casters, label of Alexander Roux, New York, New York, ca. 1860, 48" w., 30" h. (ILLUS.) 2,090.00

Victorian parlor center table, Renaissance Revival substyle, inlaid & ebonized walnut, oval top w/finger-molded edge above ornate pedestal w/four outswept supports ending in flattened hoof feet, Berkey & Gay, 50" oval top . 775.00

Victorian parlor center table, rococo substyle, rosewood, turtle-shaped top, conforming apron w/applied carvings, shaped cabriole legs w/vigorous C-scroll carvings w/cross-stretcher centering turned urn, 48 x 42" top 2,000.00

Victorian parlor center table, rococo substyle, walnut w/white marble turtle-shaped top, apron w/ornate foliate, rose & bird medallion carvings, semi-cabriole legs joined by cross-stretchers w/center urn, worn dark finish, 41 x 34¼" top, 29" h. 2,550.00

Victorian parlor center table, rococo substyle, walnut w/white marble oval slab top, finger-molded apron, shaped legs w/center column, on white porcelain casters, original finish, medium size 550.00

Victorian parlor lamp table, Renaissance Revival substyle, walnut, round top w/molded edge, apron w/light carving & applied burl walnut roundels, center standard joining 4 baluster uprights ending in quadruped base, on casters, old finish 225.00

Wallace Nutting table, marked "William & Mary Trestle Base," oblong top, turned supports w/stretcher, branded signature, Framingham, Massachusetts, early 20th c., 60 x 30¼" top, 30" h. 880.00

William & Mary Drop-Leaf Table

William & Mary gate-leg drop-leaf dining table, bowed top w/oval drop leaves above single long drawer, on block & baluster ring-turned legs w/similar turned stretchers & baluster-turned feet (top not original to base), 44 x 53½" top (open), 27" h. (ILLUS.) 3,960.00

William & Mary gate-leg drop-leaf dining table, walnut & maple, oblong top w/rounded ends flanked by half-round drop leaves, apron w/single frieze drawer, vase- and ring-turned legs w/stretchers, half-ball feet, New England, 1720-60, 50 x 41" top (open), 27" h. (slight repair to top) 4,620.00

Zoar (Ohio) work table, walnut, 2-board removable scrubbed top, apron w/drawer, boldly turned legs............................ 800.00

WHATNOTS & ETAGERES

Victorian Rococo Rosewood Etagere

Etagere, corner-type, rosewood, pierced-carved superstructure supporting two shelves above quarter-round white-veined marble-slab top over case w/pr. cupboard doors of conforming outline applied w/pendant game carving, w/label "Manufactured by Wm. McCracken, New Orleans".......3,300.00

Etagere, Victorian, Eastlake substyle, cherrywood, molded coved cornice w/incised carving above 4 tiers of shelves & mirrored back, w/pr. cupboard doors enhanced w/carved front panels at first & third tiers & pr. short drawers

above 2nd tier, all raised on tapering spiral-carved spindles, bun feet, ca. 1875 ....2,995.00

Etagere, Victorian, Rococo substyle, walnut & rosewood, elaborately carved & w/mirrored back.......1,600.00

Etagere, Victorian, Renaissance Revival substyle, walnut, superstructure w/ornately carved & paneled crest above tall round-top mirror flanked by mirrored side panels w/three shelves on each side, above base w/serpentine white marble slab over conformingly shaped drawered base, ca. 1870 ....2,450.00

Etagere, Victorian, Rococo substyle, rosewood, ornately floral-carved top in pyramidal form topped by pierce-carved crest above two graduated shelves above 4-segment section divided by ornately carved S-scrolls w/two small mirrored doors in front center, above curved base section w/open shelves at each side & paneled door in center, supported on short scroll legs, 1850-60, New York, 51¼" w., 84" h. (ILLUS.).........15,400.00

Victorian Rococo Walnut Etagere

Etagere, Victorian, Rococo substyle, walnut, pierce-carved top crest above round-top mirror flanked by pierce-carved framing w/two shelves on each side, above 3-tier base w/serpentine front, four scrolled legs support base shelves, ca. 1865, 39½" w. (ILLUS.)........................ 825.00

(End of Furniture Section)

AMERICAN GAMES

by Bruce Whitehill

Though boardgames have been manufactured in this country for over 140 years, games have traditionally been seen by the public as a subclass of toys. Now they have come into their own as collectibles, and just in the last year or two we have seen a number of major game exhibits (no toys!), the formation of a national association for game collectors, the publication of the country's first game book and price guide, and a monthly feature on antique games and game collecting in a major national toy magazine; even the advertising for toy and collectible shows has specifically listed "games" with increasing frequency. Game prices have jumped drastically in a year, and many antiques investors are looking at games as the hottest new collectible.

The term "game" has come to mean many things in this culture. In the nineteenth century, "game" usually referred to a sport or a parlor pastime which required no implements, except for maybe a pencil and paper. When we talk about an antique or collectible game, we define it as a specific device or object with which players compete with one another (or with one's self to better one's performance) in accordance with a specific set of rules; it is this latter "rules" component that distinguishes games from toys. Many early 1900's boxed "playthings" with "game" written on the cover (such as Milton Bradley's *Toy Town Conductors Game* or Parker Brothers' *Post Office Game*) were really activity sets or "role-playing games" rather than games per se, as they encouraged open-ended play rather than stipulating a set of rules by which one player could best another; such playthings (as well as puzzles and blocks) are not discussed here since they are not games by definition, but they *are* collected by many game collectors because they were manufactured by game companies and have the box cover lithography collectors look for.

Playing cards were probably first used in this country by the settlers at Jamestown, but, under Puritan rule, were banned in New England for a long time. Large table games like bagatelle (an early form of pinball game) were brought over from Europe and then manufactured here; skittles (a game using tops to knock down small "bowling" pins in a compartmentalized box) was also a popular pastime (and is still made today). Early Americans carved sometimes intricate wooden gameboards upon which such classic games as chess, checkers, backgammon, and Parcheesi variants were played; these early boards, now very high-priced, are collected primarily as folk art, rather than as games. In the early 1800's, the first American-manufactured games were produced as "secondary pursuits" by lithographers and other businesses specializing in paper goods; these early games were "published" rather than "manufactured". Most of these early games, which are extremely difficult to locate, were card games similar to the European *Quartet* or *Authors,* or were games of conundrums (question and answer riddle games) or fill-in-the-blank story games.

The first boardgame to be made in America was published by W. & S.B. Ives in 1843. Called *The Mansion of Happiness,* it was based on a European game of the same name. Ives produced mainly card games, and then sold out to George S. Parker, one of the four major game makers in this country before the turn of the century. Parker began his business in 1883 with his first game, *Game of Banking.* Five years later his brother joined the firm, thus creating Parker Brothers, a company which, though no longer family-owned, still produces games today.

When George Parker first started out, Milton Bradley had already been in business 23 years; Bradley started in 1860 with his *Checkered Game of Life* (a game reissued 100 years later by the same Milton Bradley Company as *The Game of Life*). Bradley first made games for soldiers during the Civil War. A prolific inventor, he produced and adapted many things until his death in 1911; besides being famous for children's games and kindergarten supplies, Bradley made his own color wheel and watercolors, manufactured jigsaw puzzles, patented a paper cutter and his own hoop toss games, and developed the *Zoetrope* or *Wheel of Life* (a moving picture toy). After his death, the company continued to prosper. Milton Bradley Co. and Parker Brothers were the two companies that had the greatest impact on the American game industry.

While Bradley was working in Springfield, Massachusetts, and long before George Parker began work in Salem, Massachusetts, E.G. Selchow began producing games in downtown New York City. He obtained the rights to a toy and game business in 1867, changed the name to E.G. Selchow & Co., and, three years later, brought in the manager of the old firm, John Righter, as his partner. In 1880, he changed the name of the company to Selchow & Righter Co., and by then was prospering, especially with the help of the revenue from a game he had been marketing from the beginning, *Parcheesi.* This is America's oldest famous game, and its 1874 trademark is one of the oldest trademarks in the country. But Selchow & Righter were selling other company's games (they were called "jobbers"), and they did not abandon this practice in favor of manufacturing their own games until 1927. The company produced many interesting games up until it bought the rights to the game for which it would become famous, *Scrabble.* After Milton Bradley Co. was bought by Hasbro in 1984, Selchow & Righter was the last of the family-owned giants to sell out; it was purchased by Coleco Industries this year, just a short time after its success with one of the largest-selling games in the history of this country, *Trivial Pursuit.*

The most prolific pre-1900 game company was McLoughlin Brothers, and it's the McLoughlin games that seem to generate the most excitement among collectors. John McLoughlin took over his father's book publishing concern and changed the name to his own in 1850. His brother joined the firm in 1858 at which time the company became known as McLoughlin Brothers. The company was famous for its incredible lithography -- the intricate design and beautiful color used on the game boxes, gameboards, and cards. Only R. Bliss in Pawtucket, Rhode Island, produced games to match McLoughlin games in quality. McLoughlin produced many card games, puzzles, blocks, oversized games, and folded wooden gameboards which, when closed, resembled two books as they would appear on a shelf. The early John McLoughlin games have value for their antiquity, rarity, and hand-coloring, but the later McLoughlin games are even more highly valued for their design and style. McLoughlin Brothers was bought by Milton Bradley

Co. in 1920, and few McLoughlin name games can be found after that date; Milton Bradley Co. did, however, reproduce certain McLoughlin games, such as *Transatlantic Flight,* exactly the same, only with the Bradley name and logo. McLoughlin games, in general, bring the highest price of any American games.

Other major companies to look for which produced quality games in the late 1800's are Bliss, Chaffee & Selchow, Clark & Sowden, E.I. Horsman, J. Ottmann, W.S. Reed, and J.H. Singer. Most collectors who are interested in the early games value the games primarily for their lithography, and, because of changes in art, style, and manufacturing, limit their collection to games prior to 1920. Later games are often collected because of their theme or contents, or because the game represents a particular character. Many games have value as a "cross-collectible": a game which depicts an activity of interest to a non-game collector. For example, collectors of baseball cards will pay more than twice what a game collector would pay for an early baseball game with illustrations of named baseball players.

The factors which affect the value of a game are: company, age, condition, graphics, theme, components or implements, and, to a lesser degree, rarity. Older games are worth more *if* the graphics are interesting; some later games have high values because of the character depicted on the cover or gameboard and a Beatles game or 1950's television character game may be worth more than an early turn-of-the-century game.

Condition of a game, as with any antique, is of paramount concern; any tears, stains, missing lithography, or other imperfections can reduce the value to half (or make the game worthless if the damage is great enough). The graphics on the box and gameboard is the most important element in determining the value of a game.

Theme is of major importance, since a game with a specific "motif" will secure a higher price than a general game; games showing modes of transportation, black characters, old radios, combat, cartoon characters, and so forth, demand higher prices than other games and unusual playing pieces can also increase the value of a game.

(Editor's Note: *Bruce Whitehill, known as "The Big Game Hunter," is the country's foremost historian on antique American games. He has one of the largest and most diversified collections of games in the country and exhibits games throughout the United States and often lectures on American games and leisure and is the founder of the American Game Collectors Assocation and editor of the organization's magazine.)*

PRICING GAMES

It is still possible to find interesting games from before World War II for under $25, but most items are selling for $30 to $60. Turn-of-the-Century board games can be up to $100, and pre-1900 McLoughlin Brothers games are often well over $100; early classic board games (1870-80's) can be as high as $250, and games with special themes or illustrations or historical value are worth even more (see main text).

The common games, sometimes priced as high as their less common counterparts, should still be available for between $5 and $20. Exceptions are very early (pre-1890) versions of these games, the ones with extraordinary lithography, or the games with cards depicting black characters (as often found in *Dr. Busby, Old Maid* and *Snap*). At antique shows you may see games which you will never see again at any price, but if you find a high-priced common game like *Anagrams, Authors, Bingo, Dr. Busby, Fish Pond, Flinch, Lotto, Monopoly, Old Maid, Parcheesi*

(and its variants of *Home, India*, etc.), *Peter Coddle, Pit, Rook, Snap, Tiddley* (also *"Tiddledy"*) *Winks* or *Touring*, pass it up---you'll come across it again.

Generally, board games are worth more than card games, and games with wooden or metal boards are more valuable than standard cardboard games. Metal implements, toy-like devices (such as moving figures in race and skill-and-action games), hand-colored lithography, and names and pictures of well-known personalities or events (especially for baseball games) can greatly increase the value of a game.

Prices listed are for complete games in excellent condition. Missing implements, marred or a worn box or board can reduce the value of a game by as much as 50 percent. Prices fluctuate from region to region but the cost of games is rapidly increasing (as much as 100 to 200 percent in the past two years), and this trend is expected to continue.

Games illustrated below are from the collection of Bruce Whitehill and have been valued by him. Other games in the listing are from the on-going compilation of game prices in The Antique Trader Price Guide *files.*

Aerial Catapult, Milton Bradley,
original box, 1932 . . . . $25.00

Air Mail Game

Air Mail board game, box bottom is gameboard, Milton Bradley, 1920's (ILLUS. of box detail) 26.00

Aeroplane Race Game

Aeroplane Race board game, metal board & 4 metal planes, Wolverine, early 1920's (ILLUS.) 55.00

Airplane Express Game

Airplane Express board game, 6 pressed cardboard planes, Milton Bradley, 1930's (ILLUS. of box cover detail) 35.00

Anagrams & Other Letter Games, chromolithographed cover w/Mary & Lamb, McLoughlin Brothers, 1890's 10.00

Annette's Secret Passage Game

Annette's Secret Passage board game, Annette Funicello from Mickey Mouse Club, Parker Bros., 1956 (ILLUS.) 35.00

Authors card game, common-type, various companies, each 5.00

Baby Barn Yard Game

Baby Barn Yard board game, monochromatic children's game, octagonal board, wooden spinner, B.L. Fry Prod., 1943 (ILLUS.) 28.00

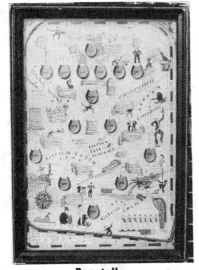

Bagatelle

Bagatelle, Cocktail Tray, Sheraton Crafts, ca. 1930 (ILLUS.) 120.00

Bagatelle, Poosh-Em-Up, common-type 22.00

Ballyhoo board game, spoof of 1930's products, Saml. Gabriel Sons & Co., 1931 .... 25.00

Barney Google & Spark Plug board game, original box, Milton Bradley, 1923 .... 65.00

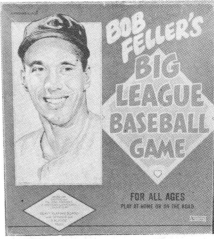

1890's Bicycle Game

Bicycle board game, large wooden box w/drawer for parts, Parker Bros., 1894 (ILLUS.) ..... 175.00 to 225.00

Billy Whiskers board game, w/spinner, pieces & original box, Saalfield Publishing Co., Akron, Ohio, 1923-26 .... 35.00

Bionic Woman (The) board game, boxed 9.00

Black Cat Fortune Telling card game, chromolithographed black cat on box, Parker Bros., 1897 copyright .... 45.00 to 65.00

Bob Feller's Big League Baseball

Bob Feller's Big League Baseball board game, 1-piece board, w/photo of Feller on box cover, Saalfield Publishing Co., 1950 (ILLUS.) 40.00

Bomb The Navy Game

Bomb the Navy marble roll target
game, J. Pressman, early 1940's
(ILLUS.) 32.00

Bomber Ball Game

Bomber Ball, marbles dropped from
   plane onto boat below for points,
   Game Makers Inc., 1940's
   (ILLUS.) 27.00
Buster Brown Necktie Party game,
   Selchow & Righter 225.00
Can the Kaiser game, World War I
   era, round box 45.00
Canasta cards, tray, cards & leather
   case, Moore-McCormack Lines 20.00
Champion Road Race board game,
   advertising for Champion Spark
   Plugs 35.00

The Great Charlie Chan

Charlie Chan (The Great) Detective
   Mystery board game, w/large
   board, cards w/"wise" sayings,
   Milton Bradley, 1937
   (ILLUS.) . . . . .65.00 to 85.00

Charlie McCarthy's Flying Hats

Charlie McCarthy's (Edgar Bergen's
   and) Flying Hats game, wooden
   hats sprung into canister container, Whitman Publishing, ca. 1938
   (ILLUS.) 45.00
Charlie McCarthy Radio Party Game,
   1938 . . . .   30.00
Checkerboard, wooden, original
   black & red-painted squares,
   19th c. (no pieces) 125.00

Library of Games

Children's Library of Games, 6
   games originally published by
   Noble & Noble, Stoll & Edwards,
   1922, set (ILLUS.) . . . . .65.00 to 75.00
Chiromagica mechanical game,
   McLoughlin Bros., 1870's 200.00
Chutes and Ladders board game,
   adapted from English game of
   "Snakes & Ladders," Milton Brad-

Chutes and Ladders

ley, 1943 (ILLUS. of original version) 45.00

1940's Conflict Game

Conflict board game, 48 metal
pieces (battleships, airplanes,
cannons, etc.), Parker Bros., 1940
(ILLUS.)...................45.00 to 60.00
Conflict board game, complete
w/pieces, 1960 version ....25.00 to 45.00
Contack domino-type game, Parker
Bros., 1939 .... 8.50

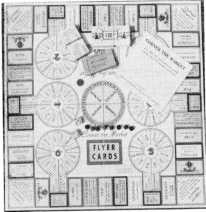

Corner the Market

Corner the Market board game,
Monopoly-type game, Whitman,
1938 (ILLUS.)..............35.00 to 48.00
Count Down board game, spaceship
theme w/rocket-shaped playing
pieces & astronaut cards, 1967 ... 20.00

Davy Crockett Rescue Race board
game, 1955 .... 10.00
Dick Tracy Playing Card game, Whitman Publishing Co., 1937 .... 24.00
Dissected Map of the United States
puzzle game, chromolithographed
interlocking puzzle pieces,
McLoughlin Bros., 1890 .... 85.00
Dollar A Second board game, Jan
Murray T.V. personality on box
cover, 1954-57 .... 18.00
Dr. Busby (Game of) card game, 20
h.p. cards, W. & S.B. Ives, 1846... 65.00

Game of the Dudes

Dudes (Game of the) board game,
folding board, box w/metal reinforced corners, Bliss, 1890
(ILLUS.) ....120.00 to 165.00
Ed Wynn - The Fire Chief board
game, w/dice, dice cups, counters
& playing pieces, Selchow &
Righter, 1934 .... 40.00
Eddie Cantor's "Tell It To The Judge"
board game, w/dice, cards, counters, etc., Parker Bros., 1936 ..... 47.50
Fairies (The) Cauldron Tiddledy
Winks game, w/hanging black
wooden bucket on 3-legged tripod, "winks" & pieces, Parker
Bros., 1925 .... 20.00
Fast Mail (Train) board game, chromolithographed train on box &
board, Milton Bradley, ca. 1900... 150.00
Fibber McGee Party board game,
Milton Bradley, 1936-40 .... 17.50
Fish Pond (The Game of) board
game, w/fishing poles, numbered
fish & board, chromolithographed
leprechaun on cover, Milton Bradley, 1890's 65.00

Fish Pond (The Improved Game of)
game of skill, w/fishing poles,
numbered fish & playing board
resembling pond, McLoughlin
Bros., 1890 . . . . 45.00
Flinch card game, Flinch Card Co.,
Kalamazoo, Michigan, 1902 . . . . . . 25.00
Flinch card game, Parker Bros.,
1938 .7.50 to 10.00

Flying Aces

Flying Aces board game, folding
board & 12 large metal planes,
Selchow & Righter, 1940's
(ILLUS.). 45.00
Flying United States Airmail board
game, w/pieces, dice cup, dice &
cards & w/United States map on
board, Parker Bros., 1929 . . . . 85.00
Foolish Questions card game illustrated by Rube Goldberg, Wallie
Dorr Co., 1924 . . . . 32.00 to 40.00
Fortune Teller game, chro-
molithographed fortune teller
w/wand on easel & revolving
wheel of cards, Milton Bradley,
1907 . . . . 65.00

Foxy Grandpa Hat Party

Foxy Grandpa Hat Party game of
skill (variant of Pin the Tail on the
Donkey), cardboard envelope
w/large cloth figure of Grandpa
plus hats to cut out, Selchow &
Righter, 1905 (ILLUS.) . . . . . .75.00 to 95.00
Halma board game, E.I. Horsman,
1887 . . . . 70.00
Hokum card game, Parker Bros.,
1927 . . . . 12.00
How Silas Popped the Question card
game, Parker Bros., 1915 . . . . 25.00
India (Game of) board game (vari-
ant of Parcheesi), board, counters, spinner & playing pieces,
multicolored box, McLoughlin
Bros., 1920's 35.00
Jack Straws, balsa wood pieces,
ca. 1900 . . . . 15.00

Jan-Ken-Po Game

Jan-Ken-Po card game, w/Japanese
illustrations & instructions in
English & Japanese for this
"paper-rock-scissors" game, Par-
ker Bros., 1906 (ILLUS.) . . . .35.00 to 48.00

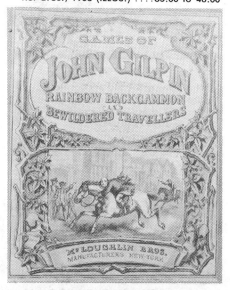

Games of John Gilpin

John Gilpin (Games of) Rainbow Backgammon and Bewildered Travellers, wood "bookshelf" game, w/block spinner & story booklet, McLoughlin Bros., 1875 (ILLUS. of slipcover case detail) ....175.00 to 225.00

Kentucky Derby Racing Game, Whitman Publishing Co., 1960 .... 12.00

Kindergarten Lotto

Kindergarten Lotto (variant of Bingo wherein pieces form puzzle pictures), exceptional European-style chromolithographs, Strauss Mfg., 1904 (ILLUS.)...........80.00 to 110.00

Knapp Electric Questioner Game, lithographed cards, wooden box, P. R. Mallory & Co., 1940 .... 30.00

Double Gameboard

Lincoln Highway & Checkers double gameboard, track board game one side & checkers reverse, Parker Bros., 1920's (ILLUS.) 35.00

Little Orphan Annie Travel Game

Little Orphan Annie Travel Game, board game w/box bottom as playing board, Milton Bradley, 1920's (ILLUS.) ....48.00 to 68.00

Little Orphan Annie Treasure Hunt

Little Orphan Annie Treasure Hunt board game, folding board w/cardboard sheet of sailboats to cut out, w/mailing envelope, Ovaltine advertising premium, Wonder Co., 1933 (ILLUS.)........ 42.00

Logomachy card game, 60 chromolithographed cards of children wearing Victorian costumes, McLoughlin Bros., 1874 .... 75.00

Lo Lo Game

Lo Lo (table-top Tiddley Winks), table-top game played on felt mat set up as croquet field, Lawrence, 1891 (ILLUS.) 70.00

Lone Ranger game, spinner card, pieces, 4 equestrian figures, Parker Bros., 1938................. 37.50

The Long Green

Long Green (The) horse race board
game, metal die-cut standup
horses & metal die, Milton Brad-
ley, 1936 (ILLUS.) 42.00

Game of Lotto

Game of Lotto

Lotto (Game of), form of Bingo, eye-
catching box cover, J.H. Singer,
1890's (ILLUS.) 22.00

Magic Miles

Magic Miles track board game, Has-
senfeld (Hasbro), 1950's (ILLUS.) . . 25.00
Mail Express (Game of) board
game, 45 pieces, 2 dice cups, dice
& 35 cards, chromolithographed
map of United States on playing
board & railroad engine on box
cover, McLoughlin Bros., 1895 . . . . 125.00

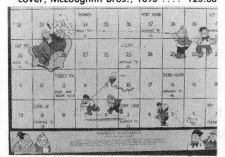

Mama's Darlings Game

Mama's Darlings board game, based
on Rudolph Dirk's "Captain & the
Kids" (Katzenjammer Kids) comic
strip, 1916-18 & revived in the
1930's, unknown maker
(ILLUS.) . . . . 45.00 to 65.00
Mansion of Happiness board game,
chromolithographed box & board,
Ives, 1843, 300.00 to 450.00; Parker Bros., 1894, 125.00 to 175.00;
McLoughlin Bros., 1895 . . 150.00 to 200.00

Mary and John

Mary and John board game, created
by the originator of the "Uncle
Wiggily" game (Howard R. Garis),
bride & groom on cover, Milton
Bradley, ca. 1940 (ILLUS.) 40.00
Mayflower (The) card game, Cincin-
nati Game Co., 1897 . . . . 24.00

Mill Game

Mill board game, large 1-piece
board w/wooden frame (reversing
to Chinese Checkers) w/scene of
classic mill center, Straits Mfg.
Co., 1938 (ILLUS.) 55.00

Original Monopoly Board

Monopoly board game, original version did not come w/playing
pieces, by Charles Darrow (before
being sold to Parker Bros.),
1933-34 (ILLUS.) . . . . 300.00 to 600.00

Movie Land Keeno card game, 24
cards depicting movie stars as Lon
Chaney, Gary Cooper, etc., Wilder
Mfg. Co., 1930's 70.00

Mumbly Peg

Mumbly Peg (tiddley winks variation) game of skill, Toy Airship
Co., 1940 (ILLUS.) 20.00

My Mother Sent Me to the Grocery
Store card game, original colorful
box, Parker Bros., 1902-15 . . . . 15.00

Mystery Shooter game of skill
w/board & marbles, tin,
Wolverine 28.00

Nancy Drew Mystery board game,
Parker Bros., 1957 . . . . 25.00

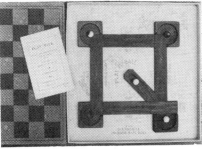

National In-Door Baseball

National In-Door Baseball game of
skill, marble roll dexterity game,
in plain checkerboard box, Harrison Game Co., 1930's
(ILLUS.) . . . . 38.00 to 48.00

Old Maid card game, cartoon
representations of popular actors,
actresses & characters of the day,
Milton Bradley, 1915 . . . . . . 25.00 to 45.00

Opportunity Hour for Amateurs
party game, in original envelope,

Opportunity Hour for Amateurs

American Toy Works, 1937
(ILLUS.) 22.00

Educational Game

Our Bird Friends card game, 52
cards featuring different black &
white drawings of birds, played
like the game "Authors," Sarah H.
Dudley, ca. 1910 (ILLUS.) . . . 28.00 to 45.00

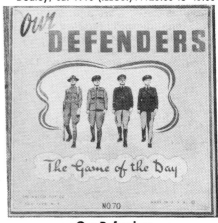

Our Defenders

Our Defenders puzzle game of luck,
Master Toy Co., 1940's
(ILLUS.)................25.00 to 40.00
Par Golf card game, 90 cards, score
cards & instructions, invented by
comedian Bert (Wheeler) Moore-
man, National Golf Service Co.,
1926 .... 35.00

Parkers' Board Games

Parkers' Board Games, parts box &
playing board for various children's classic games (Ludo, Checkers, Race Games, Backgammon,
etc.), Parker Bros., 1928 (ILLUS.) .. 22.00
Pegity board game, Parker Bros.,
1925 .... 25.00
Peter Coddle Tells of His Trip to
Chicago card game, Parker Bros.,
ca. 1890...................... 25.00
Peter Coddle's Trip to New York
card game, Parker Bros.,
1920's.................12.00 to 20.00

Sgt. Bilko of Television

Phil Silver's "You'll Never Get Rich"
board game, based on CBS TV
game show, dice in see-through
cup, 4 plastic military men, Gardener, ca. 1955 (ILLUS.)....38.00 to 45.00

Pieces of Eight Party Game

Pieces of Eight party game ("for the
harrassed hostess"), Parker Bros.,
1940's (ILLUS.)................. 18.00
Pin the Tail on the Donkey game of
skill, printed cloth donkey w/six
tails, Saalfield Publishing Co., ca.
1910 ....35.00 to 60.00
Pit card game, 64 cards, Parker
Bros., 1919 .... 12.00

Post Toasties Advertising Premium

Play Horseshoes with Mickey Mouse
ring toss game, cut-out & assembled from back of cereal box,
Post Toasties advertising premium, 1935 (ILLUS.).........15.00 to 20.00

Play Safe Game

Play Safe board game, folding
board, 12 metal cars & pedestri-
ans, game cards & play money,
Milton Bradley, 1936 (ILLUS.) 48.00

Pollyanna Game

Pollyanna board game, Parcheesi-
style game, Parker Bros., 1915
(ILLUS. of box) 62.00
Prince Valiant Game of Valor board
game, by Harold Foster 42.50

Radio Amateur Hour Game

Radio Amateur Hour board game,
w/built-up spinner on board,
1940's (ILLUS.) 28.00

Rainbow Game

Rainbow board game, complete,
Milton Bradley, 1940's (ILLUS.) 22.00

Rainy Day Golf

Rainy Day Golf board game, w/four
metal golf balls as playing pieces,
Selchow & Righter, ca. 1920
(ILLUS.) . . . . .48.00 to 68.00
Ring the Pin game of skill, target on
wooden supports w/base, rings &
squares, original box, Parker
Bros., 1910 . . . .   18.00
Scoop (The Game of), newspaper
reporter game w/six small playing boards, 54 story cards & card-

The Game of Scoop

board phone dial, Parker Bros.,
1956 (ILLUS.) 42.00

Skyscraper Game

Skyscraper game "for adults," 67
wooden pieces used to build small
village on individual cards in
game format, Parker Bros., 1937
(ILLUS.) . . . . .47.00 to 60.00
Snake Eyes dice & card game, 120
cards, dice, dice cups & chips,
black characters theme, Selchow
& Righter 38.00
Soldier Ten Pins game of skill, box
cover by Maxfield Parrish, Parker
Bros., 1921 . . . . .200.00 to 400.00

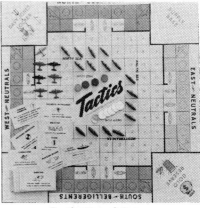

Tactics Board Game

Tactics board game, folding playing
board, metal planes & ships,
Northwestern Products, 1940
(ILLUS.)................35.00 to 45.00

Tactics II

Tactics II board game, 2-fold playing
board, simulated war strategy,
Avalon Hill, 1961 (ILLUS.) 20.00

Take It or Leave It

Take It or Leave It board game,
based on radio's $64 Question
(forerunner of TV's $64,000 Ques-
tion), 8 categories of trivia including radio program sponsors,
Zondine Game Co., 1942
(ILLUS.)........................ 36.00

Taxi Game of the 1940's

Taxi path-type game, Selchow &
Righter, 1940's (ILLUS. of detail on
box) 45.00
Telegrams (Game of), party game
for 2 to 8 players, Whitman Publishing, 1941 .... 34.00
Telegraph Boy & District Messenger
Boy board games, boards of same
pattern w/different graphics, thick

Telegraph Boy & District Messenger Games

wooden box & metal delivery
boys, McLoughlin 1886 & 1888,
each (ILLUS.) ....165.00 to 185.00
Tell Bell card game, chromolithographed cards, wooden
box, Knapp Electric Inc., 1926 .... 50.00
Test Driver Game at the Chrysler
Corp. Proving Grounds path-type
board game, Milton Bradley,
1950's 50.00

Three Musketeers

Three Musketeers - Game of Strategy, fox & geese type game that
pits 3 black pawns against 50
white, Milton Bradley, 1930's
(ILLUS.)........................ 38.00
Thunderball 007 board game, Milton
Bradley, 1965 .... 22.00
Tip Top Fish Pond game of skill,
w/fishing poles, 6 fish, gameboard & instructions, little boy in
boat on box cover, Milton Bradley, 1930's 18.00

To the North Pole by Air-Ship

To the North Pole by Air-Ship board
game, box bottom is playing
board, exceptional chromolithograph on lid w/early blimp,
McLoughlin Bros., ca. 1900
(ILLUS.) ....165.00 to 185.00

Treasure Hunt

Treasure Hunt parlor game, letter
cards to spell words suggested by
subject cards, Cadaco-Ellis,
1940-50 (ILLUS.) . . . . .18.00 to 24.00

Trilby

Trilby (The Game of) board game,
superbly illustrated game based
on du Maurier novel of Svengali's
obsession w/female pupil Trilby,
outstanding chromolithograph on
gameboard back
(ILLUS.) . . . . .80.00 to 130.00

Who's Afraid of the Big Bad Wolf

Who's Afraid of the Big Bad Wolf
board game, black-and-white wolf
silhouette on gameboard
w/"patented" color scheme, Par-
ker Bros., 1933 (ILLUS.) 64.00
Who's Who (The Game of) card
game, 36 comical illustrations of
characters & professions,
McLoughlin Bros., 1900's . . .45.00 to 55.00

(End of Special Focus)

GIBSON (Charles Dana) ARTWORK

Postcard by Charles Dana Gibson

*Charles Dana Gibson (1867-1944) displayed
artistic talent at an early age, selling his first
drawing at 19. At age 23, filled with a deep
admiration for American women, he began
creating his "ideal woman" – wholesome,
charming, self-reliant and filled with a spirit
of adventure. For two decades the elegant
Gibson Girl was the envy of women and the
dream of men and her image appeared on
everything from silk handkerchiefs to broom
holders. During World War I, Gibson and a
number of his contemporaries donated artwork for various government posters to
stimulate recruitment, Liberty Bond sales
and Red Cross support. In his later years,
Gibson devoted his time to impressionist-
style oil painting. Also see GIBSON GIRL
PLATES.*

Book, "A Widow & Her Friends," 84
large black & white illustrations,
1900 . . . .$65.00 to 85.00
Book, "Americans," 84 large black &
white illustrations, 1900 . . . .   80.00
Book, "Drawings by C.D. Gibson,"
1896 . . . .   95.00
Book, "The Education of Mr. Pipp,"
1899 . . . .   95.00
Book, "The Gibson Book," Vols. 1 &
2, 1906 . . . .   200.00
Book, "London," 1897,
17 x 11" . . . . .50.00 to 100.00
Book, "Pictures of People," 81 illus-
trations, 1896 . . . .   100.00
Book, "Sketches & Cartoons," 1898,
84 pp. 95.00
Book, "The Social Ladder,"
ca. 1902 . . . .   75.00
Portfolio, "Series A: Gibson Girl
Proofs," published by Collier's,
1909, set of 12 . . . .   120.00
Postcard, "Has She A Heart?"
(ILLUS.) . . . . .7.00 to 10.00
Prints, "The Seven Ages of Women,"
set of 7 . . . .   30.00
Print, "Two Strikes & Bases Full,"
1904, framed, 8 x 10" 20.00

GLASS

AGATA

Green Opaque Agata Bowl

Agata was patented by Joseph Locke of the New England Glass Co., in 1887. The application of a mineral stain left a mottled effect on the surface of the article. It was applied chiefly to the Wild Rose (Peach Blow) line but sometimes was applied as a border on pale opaque green. In production for a short time, it is scarce. Items listed below are of the Wild Rose line unless otherwise noted.

Bowl, 9½" d., 3½" h., green
  opaque (ILLUS.)...............$1,250.00
Celery vase, 6¼" h. 1,000.00
Cruet w/original stopper, green
  opaque, 5¾" h................. 795.00
Finger bowl, 5½" d.,
  2½" h.................685.00 to 950.00
Mustard pot w/silverplate top,
  green opaque, 3" h......450.00 to 525.00
Mustard pot w/silverplate top 1,295.00
Punch cup, green opaque 300.00
Toothpick holder, 2 3/8" h......... 500.00
Tumbler 550.00
Tumbler, green opaque 450.00
Vase, 6¾" h., lily-form ....450.00 to 850.00

AKRO AGATE

This marbled ware was made by the Akro Agate Company in Clarksburg, West Va., between 1932 and 1951 and most articles bear on the reverse side the likeness of a crow flying through a capital letter A. The majority of these pieces were small.

Ash tray, shell-shaped, marbleized
  orange swirls in white $10.00
Cup, child's playtime item, Concentric Ring patt., green transparent 10.00
Cup, child's playtime item, Octagonal patt., orange opaque 10.00
Cup & saucer, child's playtime item,
  Concentric Ring patt., pumpkin
  cup, green saucer 14.00

Cup & saucer, child's playtime item,
  Interior Panel patt., marbleized
  blue swirls in white opaque 10.00
Cup & saucer, demitasse, marbleized orange swirls in white
  opaque..................12.50 to 15.00
Flower pot, green opaque, 2¾" h... 7.00

Mexicali Jar

Jar, Mexicali patt., marbleized
  orange swirls in white
  (ILLUS.)..................35.00 to 50.00
Match holder, urn-shaped, mar-
  bleized orange swirls in white
  opaque........................ 19.00
Planter, Concentric Ring patt.,
  orange opaque, 6" oval 15.00
Plate, child's playtime item, Concentric Ring patt., yellow transparent 4.00
Plate, child's playtime item,
  Octagonal patt., white opaque ... 4.00
Powder jar, Colonial lady cover,
  blue opaque, 6" h. ....45.00 to 60.00
Powder jar, Colonial lady cover,
  pink opaque 40.00
Powder jar, Scottie dog cover, powder blue opaque 65.00
Tea set, child's playtime item: cov.
  teapot, creamer, sugar bowl & 4
  c/s; Chiquita patt., green transparent, 11 pcs.................. 75.00
Tea set, child's playtime item: cov.
  teapot, cov. sugar bowl, creamer,
  4 c/s & 4 plates; Octagonal patt.,
  multicolored, 15 pcs. 125.00
Tea set, child's playtime item, Stippled Band patt., green transparent, 17 pcs.................... 60.00

ALBERTINE

Albertine is an opal glass decorated by painting and enameling produced by the Mount Washington Glass Company in the late 19th century. The same company's Crown Milano ware appears to be identical. Pieces listed below were offered as Albertine and pieces listed under Crown Milano were offered as that ware.

Albertine Vase

Bowl, cov., 4" h., melon-ribbed shell, enameled raised gold chrysanthemums on shaded pink to white ground, silverplate lid & handle $450.00

Card tray, shell-molded w/two folded-in sides, painted pink to rose carnations highlighted w/raised gold & w/gold-edged rim, 6¼ x 6¼" 245.00

Cookie jar, raised gold florals on pink shaded to white ground, silverplate rim, cover & bail handle, 7¼" h. 775.00

Cookie jar, painted pastel florals & pink & lavender leaves outlined in gold, silverplate rim, cover & bail handle 495.00

Syrup pitcher w/silverplate collar & lid, melon-ribbed, raised gold oak leaves & acorns decor on pink to lemon yellow ground 985.00

Vase, 8 7/8" h., bulbous base, fluted trumpet-shaped neck, enameled scattered daisies on peach to pale tan ground, late 19th c. (ILLUS.) 357.50

ALEXANDRITE

This glass, shading from a yellowish color to rose to blue, was produced by Thomas Webb & Sons and Stevens & Williams of England. A somewhat similar ware was made by Moser of Carlsbad.

Compote, 6¾" d., 2 3/8" h., fluted, amber stem & foot, Honeycomb patt. $1,475.00

Goblet, blue twisted knarled tree trunk stem, 4 textured leaves applied to the stem where it joins the bowl, amber tulip-shaped bowl w/twelve ribs, 8½" h. 1,750.00

Spooner, cylindrical, piecrust crimped collar, Expanded Diamond patt. interior, 3" d., 4¼" h. 545.00

Toothpick holder, bulbous base, square top, 2¼" w., 2 7/8" h. 695.00

Vase, 2¾" h., 6-petal top, 11 optic panels 495.00

Vase, 3 1/8" h., 2½" d., bulbous w/star-shaped top.............. 550.00

AMBERINA

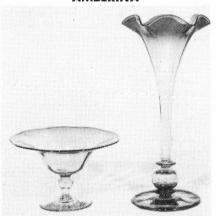

Amberina Compote & Vase

Amberina was devised by the New England Glass Company, and pressed Amberina was made by Hobbs, Brockunier & Company (under a license from the former) and by other glass factories. A similar ware called Rose Amber was made by Mt. Washington Glass Works. The glass shades from amber to red. Cut and plated Amberina also were made. About the turn of this century and again in the 1920's, the Libbey Glass Co. made some Amberina.

Bowl, 5½" d., 3 7/8" h., ruffled rim, Swirl patt.........................$125.00

Bowl, 8½ x 6¼", 7 1/8" h., applied amber feet & ruffle at rim, enameled gold & blue florals, gold birds & bug decor 350.00

Bowl, master berry, 9" sq., pressed Daisy & Button (101) patt., Hobbs, Brockunier & Co........200.00 to 350.00

Bowl, 9" d., 9 3/8" h., applied wishbone handles & feet & pulled amber fan-shaped points around rim, applied large amber salamander & enameled pink & white florals w/green & gold branches at front & blue & white florals reverse 695.00

Celery vase, Inverted Thumbprint patt., 3¾" d., 6½" h. 510.00

Compote, 5" d., 5" h., signed Libbey 250.00

Compote, 7" d., 5½" h. (ILLUS. left) 500.00

Creamer, bulbous w/squared top, applied amber reeded handle, Inverted Thumbprint patt., 3½" h. ....165.00 to 195.00

Creamer, Plated Amberina, New England Glass Co. 600.00

Cruet w/original facet-cut amber stopper, applied amber handle, Inverted Thumbprint patt., New England Glass Co. 250.00

Cuspidor, lady's, Optic Rib interior patt., Mt. Washington Glass Works, 2½" h. 250.00

Dish, shallow, pressed Daisy & Button (101) patt., Hobbs, Brockunier & Co., 7" d. ....250.00 to 375.00

Finger bowl, 10 folded-in pleats at rim, New England Glass Co., 5 3/8" d., 2½" h. 185.00

Flower holder, mushroom-shaped, signed Libbey & w/original paper label, 5" top d., 6" h. 575.00

Ice cream dish, square w/invected corners, Daisy & Button (101) patt., Hobbs, Brockunier & Co., 5¾" w. 95.00

Lamp shade, pressed Daisy & Button (101) patt., Hobbs, Brockunier & Co., 8½" widest d., 4 3/8" at fitter opening 200.00

Lemonade set: 7½" h. pitcher w/square neck & applied reeded handle & 6 pear-shaped cups w/loop handles; Reverse Thumbprint patt., 7 pcs. 750.00

Mug, applied amber handle, enameled pink, white & blue florals & leaves decor, 2¾" d., 3¾" h. 75.00

Mug, barrel-shaped, applied amber handle, 3" d., 4¼" h............. 60.00

Perfume bottle w/bulbous stopper w/long tester, paneled swelling ovoid w/ruffled lip & circular foot, Libbey, ca. 1917, 8½" h. 660.00

Pickle castor, baluster-shaped, Inverted Coin Spot patt., enameled floral decor, silverplate lid & frame, late 19th c., 9 3/8" h. 275.00

Pitcher, 4½" h., applied clear handle, Baby Thumbprint patt. 125.00

Pitcher, 5" h., squared melon-ribbed body, applied amber smooth handle, Herringbone patt. 225.00

Pitcher, tankard, 5" h., applied reeded handle, paneled, Mt. Washington Glass Co. 300.00

Pitcher, 5 7/8" h., 4½" d., squared dimpled bulbous shape w/round mouth, applied amber handle, Inverted Thumbprint patt.......... 165.00

Pitcher, 6" h., bulbous, applied handle, melon-ribbed, Thumbprint patt. 135.00

Pitcher, milk, tankard, 7" h., 4 1/8" d., round mouth, applied amber handle, Diamond Quilted patt., New England Glass Co. 300.00

Pitcher, water, 7½" h., 5½" d., bulbous w/square mouth, applied amber reeded handle, Inverted Thumbprint patt., ground pontil, New England Glass Co. 375.00

Pitcher, water, 8 5/8" h., square top, applied reeded shell handle, Coin Spot patt................. 375.00

Punch bowl, Inverted Thumbprint patt., 12" d. 375.00

Punch cup, applied amber reeded handle, Expanded Diamond patt. 75.00

Punch cup, applied amber reeded handle, Inverted Thumbprint patt. 85.00

Rose bowl, ruffled top, Venetian Diamond patt., New England Glass Co...................... 350.00

Salt shaker w/original top, tubular, Inverted Thumbprint patt., 3 5/8" h. 100.00

Sauce dish, pressed Daisy & Button patt., 5" sq. (ILLUS. right) 85.00

Sugar bowl, 2-handled, Inverted Thumbprint patt., Boston & Sandwich Glass Co., 6" h. 350.00

Sugar shaker w/original pewter lid & collar, Inverted Thumbprint patt. w/enameled daisies & foliage decor 295.00

Tazza, Honeycomb patt., Webb, 4 7/8" w., 1 5/8" h. 425.00

Toothpick holder, pressed Daisy & Button patt...................... 173.00

Amberina Toothpick and Sauce Dish

Toothpick holder, cylindrical w/flaring tricornered top, Libbey, 2 1/8" h. (ILLUS. left) 200.00

Tumbler, Plated Amberina, ribbed, New Bedford Glass Co., ca. 1886, 2½" d., 3¾" h. 1,145.00

Tumbler, wheel etched floral band, New England Glass Co., ca. 1883, 3¾" h. 247.50

Tumbler, Diamond Quilted patt., New England Glass Co., 2½" d., 3¾" h. 104.00

Vase, 6 1/8" h., 5½" d., "crackle," applied clear ruffled top, loop feet & 3 leaves 395.00

Vase, 7" h., lily-shaped, ribbed, Mt. Washington Glass Co. 350.00

Vase, 8¼" h., 6 3/8" w., fan-shaped amber wishbone feet, amber top edging, Swirl patt. 135.00

Vase, 9½" h., Reverse Amberina, Swirl patt. w/gold florals & vines, satin finish 1,315.00

Vases, 10" h., 5 1/8" d., cylindrical, Swirl patt., enameled pink & white florals w/green leaves & gold designs around top, pr. 335.00

Vase, 11" h., 4¼" d., jack-in-pulpit type, paneled, amber edging around top edge 140.00

Vase, 12" h., jack-in-pulpit type, in ornate Sheffield holder 185.00

Vase, 12" h., trumpet-shaped, ruffled rim, Libbey Glass Co. (ILLUS. left)............................. 650.00

Vases, 12¾" h., 5½" d., fluted top, applied amber feet, encrusted dull Roman gold lilies & leaves decor, pr............................. 425.00

Vase, 14¼" h., 5" d., cylindrical, footed, Swirl patt., dull Roman gold chrysanthemums decor, applied amber serpentine trim around bottom 265.00

Vase, 16" h., cornucopia swirled form, applied serpent entwined around lower third 350.00

Wine decanter w/clear facet-cut stopper, applied clear handle, enameled gold florals, branches & leaves decor, 4¼" d., 9" h. 225.00

Wine decanter w/amber "bubble" stopper, applied amber handle, Swirl patt., 4¼" d., 9 7/8" h...... 175.00

ANIMALS

Americans evidently like to collect glass animals and for the past fifty years, American glass manufacturers have turned out a wide variety of animals to please the buying public. Some were produced for long periods and some were later reproduced by other companies, while others were made for only a short period of time and are rare. We have not included late reproductions in our listings and have attempted to date the productions where possible. Evelyn Zemel's book, "American Glass Animals A to Z," will be helpful to the novice collector.

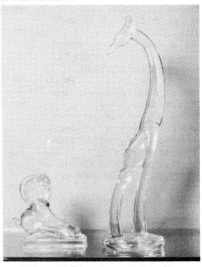

Heisey Balking Pony & Giraffe

Angel Fish bookend, clear, American Glass Co., 8¼" h. (single) ... $40.00

Angel Fish bookends, clear, A.H. Heisey & Co., 3½ x 2¼" wave base, 7" h., pr. ....135.00 to 225.00

Baby Bear, clear, New Martinsville Glass Mfg. Co., 4¼" l., 3½" h. ....40.00 to 50.00

Bull, clear, A.H. Heisey & Co., 1948-52, 4" h........1,100.00 to 1,125.00

Bunny, transparent blue, Paden City Glass Mfg. Co., 5" h. 50.00

Chinese Pheasant, clear, Paden City Glass Mfg. Co., 13¾" l., 5¾" h... 55.00

Clydesdale Horses, clear, A.H. Heisey & Co., 1942-48, 8" l., 8" h., pr............................. 450.00

Colt sitting, clear, Fostoria Glass Co., 1938-44, 3 x 1" base, 2¾" w., 2¼" h...........22.50 to 35.00

Colt standing, clear, Fostoria Glass Co., 1938-44, 2¼ x 1" base, 2½" w., 4" h.................... 30.00

Deer sitting, clear, Fostoria Glass Co., 2 x 1" base, 2¼" h......... 35.00

Deer standing, clear, Fostoria Glass Co., 2 x 1" base, 4½" h......... 27.50

Duck, chocolate (caramel slag), Imperial Glass Co., Heisey mold 25.00

Eagle bookend, clear, Fostoria Glass Co., 1938-44, 4½ x 3" base, 7¼" h. (single) 95.00

Elephant w/long trunk extended, clear, A.H. Heisey & Co., 1944-53, medium 175.00

Elephant w/trunk up, clear, A.H. Heisey & Co., 1944-53, large, 6½" l., 4¼" h. ....240.00 to 285.00

Elephant bookends, clear, New Martinsville Glass Mfg. Co., 3¼ x 5¼" base, 6¼" l., 5¼" h., pr....................95.00 to 140.00

Elephant covered dish, clear, Co-Operative Flint Glass Co., 1927-30, 7½" l., 4¾" h. 40.00

Fish candle holder, clear, A.H. Heisey & Co., 7" h. (single) 79.00

Gazelle, clear, A.H. Heisey & Co., 1927-49, 11" h. 1,100.00

Gazelle bookend, clear, New Martinsville Glass Mfg. Co., 8½" h. (single) 75.00

Giraffe w/head turned, clear, A.H. Heisey & Co., 1942-52, 11" h. (ILLUS. right).................... 165.00

Giraffe w/head straight, clear, A.H. Heisey & Co., 1942-52, 11¼" h. ....120.00 to 135.00

Goose (Mallard) w/wings down, clear, A.H. Heisey & Co., 1942-53, 5¾" h. 225.00

Goose (Mallard) w/wings up, clear, A.H. Heisey & Co., 1942-53, 6½" h. ....65.00 to 90.00

Heron standing, clear, Duncan & Miller Glass Co., 2¾" base d., 7¼" h. 78.00

Horse Head bookends, clear, A.H. Heisey & Co., 1937-55, 7¼" h., pr............................ 185.00

Horse rearing bookends, clear, Fostoria Glass Co., 6" l., 7½" h., pr.......................48.00 to 75.00

Horse rearing bookends, amber, L.E. Smith, 1940's, 5¾" l., 8" h., pr............................ 45.00

King Fish aquarium, green, L.E. Smith, 1920's, 15" l., 10" h. 250.00

Mama Bear, clear, New Martinsville Glass Mfg. Co., 6" l., 4½" h.................145.00 to 175.00

Mama Pig, clear, New Martinsville Glass Mfg. Co., 6½" l., 3¾" h.... 350.00

Papa Bear, clear, New Martinsville Glass Mfg. Co., 6½" l., 4¾" h.... 225.00

Pelican, clear, Fostoria Glass Co., 1938-44, 3" sq. base, 4½" w., 4½" h. 65.00

Penguin decanter w/stopper, clear, A.H. Heisey & Co., 8½" h. 200.00

Pheasant w/turned head, light blue, Paden City Glass Mfg. Co., 2½ x 2¾" base, 12" l., 7" h. 90.00

Plug Horse Sparky, amber, A.H. Heisey & Co., 1941-46, 3½" l., 4¼" h. 550.00

Plug Horse Sparky, clear, A.H. Heisey & Co., 1941-46, 3½" l., 4¼" h. 85.00

Polar Bear, clear, Fostoria Glass Co., 1936-44, 3 x 3" base, 4¾" h....................50.00 to 75.00

Pony balking, clear, A.H. Heisey & Co., 1941-45, 3 1/8 x 1½" base, 4" h. (ILLUS. left)............... 135.00

Pony kicking, clear, A.H. Heisey & Co., 1941-45, 2¼ x 1½" base, 3" l., 4" h...................... 130.00

Pony standing, clear, A.H. Heisey & Co., 1940-52, 2¼ x 1½" base, 3" l., 5" h...................60.00 to 80.00

Pony standing, clear, Paden City Glass Mfg. Co., 5½ x 3" base, 12" h.......................... 48.00

Pouter Pigeon, clear, A.H. Heisey & Co., 1947-49, 6½" h. 450.00

Rabbit paperweight, clear, A.H. Heisey & Co., 3¾ x 1¾" base, 2¼" h. 90.00

Ringneck Pheasant, clear, A.H. Heisey & Co., 1942-53, 11" l., 4¾" h...............135.00 to 155.00

Ringneck Pheasants, clear, K.R. Haley, 1947, 11½" l., pr.......... 40.00

Rooster, clear, A.H. Heisey & Co., 1948-49, 5 3/8" h. 418.00

Rooster (Chanticleer), clear, Paden City Glass Mfg. Co., 9¼" h....... 50.00

Rooster fighting, clear, A.H. Heisey & Co., 1940-46, 8½" h. 130.00

Scottie Dog bookends, clear, A.H. Heisey & Co., 1941-46, 3¾" l. base, 5" h., pr. 175.00

Scottie Dog bookends, clear, Cambridge Glass Co., 6½" h., pr. 120.00

Sea Horse, clear, unknown maker, 2½ x 3¾" shell base, 8½" h. 50.00

Sea Horse bookends, clear, Fostoria Glass Co., 1938-44, 8" h., pr...... 98.00

Sparrow, clear, A.H. Heisey & Co., 1942-45, 4" l., 2¼" h............ 65.00

Squirrel Bookend

Squirrel bookend, clear, New Martinsville Glass Mfg. Co., 6¼ x 2¼" base, 5¼" h. (ILLUS.) 40.00

Starfish bookends, clear, New Martinsville Glass Mfg. Co., 6¼ x · 2¾" base, 7¾" h., pr. 85.00

Tropical Fish centerpiece, large & small angel fish w/coral, clear, A.H. Heisey & Co., 12" h. 1,000.00

Wolfhound (Russian) bookend, clear, New Martinsville Glass Mfg. Co., 1920's, 9" l., 7¼" h. (single) 58.00

Wood Duck, clear, A.H. Heisey & Co., 7" l., 5½" h. 500.00

Wood Duck, clear, Imperial Glass Co., 1964-67 (Heisey mold) 105.00

APPLIQUED

Stevens & Williams Bowl

Simply stated, this is an art glass form with applied decoration. Sometimes master glass craftsmen applied stems or branches to an art glass object and then added molded glass flowers or fruit specimens to these branches or stems. At other times, a button of molten glass was daubed on the object and a tool pressed over it to form a prunt in the form of a raspberry, rosette or other shape. Always the work of a skilled glassmaker, applied decoration can be found on both cased (2-layer) and single layer glass. The English firm of Stevens and Williams is renowned for the appliqued glass they produced.

Basket, applied vaseline twisted handle, blue opalescent body shading to vaseline at base w/applied pink flower & vaseline branch & leaf, 4" d., 7¼" h. $135.00

Basket, rose bowl shape, applied amber twisted handle, cream opaque body w/applied pink florals w/amber centers, amber leaves & branches, 4¾" d., 8 1/8" h. 195.00

Basket, piecrust edge, pedestal foot, applied green twisted thorn handle, green opalescent body w/two

applied pink & white florals, green leaves & branch, 6 x 7½", 9" h. 195.00

Bowl, 6¼" d., 3¼" h., 8-crimp top, cranberry w/applied clear leaves & branches 245.00

Bowl, 5¼" h., cream opaque cased in clear, applied amber branch & leaves continuing to form feet & applied trumpet flowers & fruit on sides, Stevens & Williams (ILLUS.) 400.00

Perfume bottle w/matching "bubble" stopper, cranberry w/applied clear serpentine trim around neck, 2½" d., 7¼" h. 125.00

Vase, 5" h., 4" d., tricornered top, cranberry, applied clear wafer foot & 3 applied clear florals w/leaves each side 165.00

Vase, 7¼" h., 5 7/8" d., 4 applied clear ball feet, turned & curled top, cased, cream exterior w/two applied clear ruffled leaves, pink lining, Stevens & Williams 345.00

ART GLASS BASKETS

Basketweave Pattern Basket

Popular in the late Victorian era, these ornate hand-crafted glass baskets were often given as gifts. Sometimes made with unusually tall handles and applied feet, these fragile ornaments usually command a good price when they survive intact. Also see other listings in the Glass section.

Amber, applied clear rosette feet, clear rosette scalloped top edge, applied clear handle, 5" d., 8¼" h. $165.00

Cased, lavender-pink exterior w/embossed Basketweave patt., ruffled rim, applied clear twisted handle, 5 x 3 5/8", 5¾" h. (ILLUS.) 100.00

Cased, opaque white exterior, deep rose interior, square folded inward shape, applied clear feet & handle, 5 5/8" d., 5¾" h. 135.00

Cased, light pink shaded to deep rose mother-of-pearl satin Herringbone patt. exterior, white interior, quatrefoil rim, applied

frosted edge & handle, 5¼ x 5",
9½" h. 350.00
Cased, red & white striped exterior,
white interior, applied clear thorn
handle, 9¾" w., 6" h. 285.00
Cased, wide maroon swirling stripes
alternating w/thin white stripes
exterior, white interior, tricornered w/ruffled edge, 5¾" d.,
6¾" h. 165.00
Clear w/cranberry threading pulled
up at 8 points to form a draped
effect, applied clear florals &
leaves both sides, applied clear
feet & clear over cranberry center
handle, 8½" w., 11¾" h. 660.00
Cranberry, applied clear feet, border of leaves around top edge &
reeded handle, 4½" d., 7¼" h. ... 175.00
Green shading to creamy opalescent
to salmon pink, swirled body,
footed, ruffled rim, applied clear
rope-twisted handle, 6½" d.,
6½" h. 138.00
Green opalescent, applied clear
scalloped feet, edging at rim &
twisted thorn handle, 5" d.,
8" h. 260.00
Lemon yellow opaque, embossed
hobnail exterior, clear edging
around ruffed rim, applied clear
thorn handle, 7 3/8 x 5¾",
7¼" h. 175.00
Lime green, paneled body, applied
clear petal edge & handle,
4¾" d., 6½" h. 100.00
Pink opalescent w/white stripes,
embossed hobnail effect at ruffled
rim, applied pink twisted thorn
handle, 7¾ x 6¼", 7½" h. 195.00
Purple & white, overall arboresque
design, applied clear twisted handle, 10" h. 265.00
Rubina Crystal, embossed hobnail
exterior, enameled white daisies,
blue forget-me-nots & green
leaves interior, applied clear
twisted reeded handle, 9¼ x 8",
8" h. 210.00
Shaded pink overlay, clear edging
around ruffle, applied clear handle, 6½ x 8 1/8", 6¾" h. 115.00
Vaseline, embossed drape design,
applied pink opalescent band
around closely crimped top, applied vaseline thorn handle,
7½ x 5½", 7" h. 250.00
Vaseline, blue opaque threading
around crimped star-shaped top,
applied clear handle, 7½" d.,
7½" h. 175.00
Yellow opaque, embossed hobnail
exterior, applied clear edging &
thorn handle, 5" d., 6¾" h. 175.00

BACCARAT

Baccarat Rose Tiente Swirl Pattern

Baccarat glass has been made by Cristalleries de Baccarat, France, since 1765. The firm has produced various glasswares of excellent quality and paperweights. Baccarat's Rose Tiente is often referred to as Baccarat's Amberina. Also see PAPERWEIGHTS.

Candlesticks, Eiffel Tower patt.,
Rose Tiente, 10¾" h., pr. $225.00
Carafe, Rose Tiente Swirl patt. (no
stopper) 135.00
Cologne bottle w/original stopper,
Rose Tiente Shell patt., 5½" h. ... 65.00
Cologne bottle, Rose Tiente Swirl
patt., no stopper, 5¾" h.
(ILLUS.) 45.00
Cologne bottle w/matching stopper,
Rose Tiente Swirl patt., 2 3/8" d.,
6" h. 65.00
Cologne bottle w/matching stopper,
Rose Tiente Swirl patt., 2½" d.,
6¾" h. 68.00
Cologne bottle w/original stopper,
square form, Rose Tiente, 8" h. .. 98.00
Compote, 4½" d., 3¾" h., Rose
Tiente Swirl patt. 58.00
Condiment set, 5-bottle, Rose
Tiente, silverplate frame 175.00
Decanter w/hollow stopper, plain
bulbous base w/elongated neck,
clear w/gilt trim, signed 85.00
Finger bowl, Rose Tiente Swirl patt.,
5" d. 110.00
Goblets, cone-shaped amber bowls
etched w/vintage grape design,
cut stem & base, set of 5 .... 75.00
Jar, cov., Rose Tiente Swirl patt.,
3" d., 5" h. 75.00
Jewelry box w/hinged lid, Button &
Bow patt., sapphire blue, brass
fittings, 4" d., 2¾" h. 120.00
Match holder, Rose Tiente Swirl
patt., 2¼" d., 3¼" h. 85.00
Perfume bottle w/matching stopper,
Rose Tiente Swirl patt., 1½" d.,
4" h. 50.00

Perfume bottle, made for "Guer-
lain," clear, large ....35.00 to 50.00
Perfume bottle, made for
"Houbigant" 35.00

Baccarat Helical Twist Pattern

Pitcher, 9¼" h., Helical Twist patt.,
Rose Tiente (ILLUS.) 275.00
Tumbler, Rose Tiente Swirl patt.,
2½" d., 3½" h. 50.00
Tumble-up (carafe w/tumbler) on
plate, Rose Tiente Swirl patt...... 198.00
Vase, 8¼" h., bamboo stalk form
w/relief-molded leaf sprig at side
& w/snake coiled around circular
mound base, enameled colorful &
gilt insect at rim & naturalistic
base, early 20th c., signed 495.00
Wines, cobalt blue bowl, clear cylindrical stem, 7¾" h., set of 8 ..... 495.00

BLOWN THREE MOLD

Blown Three Mold Hat Shape

This type of glass was entirely or partially
blown in a mold from about 1820 in the
United States. The object was formed and the
decoration impressed upon it by blowing the
glass into a metal mold, usually of three but
sometimes more sections, hinged together.

*Mold-blown glass actually dates back to an-
cient times. Recent research reveals that certain geometric patterns were reproduced in
the 1920's and collectors are urged to read all
recent information available. McKearin reference numbers are to George L. and Helen
McKearin's book, "American Glass."*

Bottle (no stopper), 8-sided, geomet-
ric, aquamarine, 7¾" h.
(GI-18)......................$1,550.00
Carafe, flanged mouth, rayed base,
geometric, deep green, qt.
(GI-29)........................1,800.00
Decanter (no stopper), geometric,
olive green, 7" h. (GIII-16) 325.00
Decanter w/mismatched stopper, 3
applied rings, geometric, clear,
9" h. plus stopper (GII-34)....... 225.00
Decanter w/original stopper, rayed
base, geometric, clear, qt.
(GIII-15) 110.00
Dish, geometric, purple-blue,
4½" d. (GIII-23) 3,900.00
Dish, folded rim, rayed base, geo-
metric, clear, 6" d., 1 3/8" h.
(GIII-24) 80.00
Flip glass, geometric, clear, 5½" h.
(GII-18)....................... 150.00
Hat shape, folded rim, geometric,
clear, 2¼" h., GIII-3 (ILLUS.) 110.00
Inkwell, geometric, dark olive am-
ber, open pontil, 2 5/8" d.,
1 7/8" h. (GII-18F).............. 125.00
Inkwell, geometric, olive amber,
open pontil, 2 1/8" d., 2" h.
(GII-2)........................ 95.00
Salt dip, ringed base, purple-blue,
pontil, 2 7/8" d., 2" h. (GIII-25)... 425.00
Salt dip (from hat mold), rayed
base, geometric, clear, pontil,
2½" d., 2 1/8" h. (GII-21) 250.00
Salt dip, galleried rim, geometric,
clear, 2½" h. (GIII-25) 195.00
Toilet bottle, flanged mouth, rayed
base, geometric, amethyst, pontil
(GI-7) 400.00
Toilet bottle w/original solid "Tam-
o-Shanter" stopper, flanged
mouth, rayed base, geometric,
purple-blue, pontil (GI-7)........ 210.00

BOHEMIAN

*Numerous types of glass were made in the
once-independent country of Bohemia and
fine colored, cut and engraved glass was
turned out. Flashed and other inexpensive
wares also were made and many of these, including ruby-shaded glass and etched ruby
glass, were exported to the United States last*

*century and in the present one. One favorite
pattern in the late 19th and early 20th centuries was Deer and Castle. Another was Deer
and Pine Tree.*

Box w/domed lid, Vintage patt., engraved grape clusters & vines,
   ruby, frosted & clear, gilt brass
   fittings, 3½" l.................$120.00
Box w/domed hinged lid, engraved
   buildings & scrolling foliate bands,
   ruby, frosted & clear, brass fittings, 3¾" l..................... 82.50
Candy jar, cov., ruby to clear deep
   cut florals, small 85.00
Compote, 9½" d., 6½" h., Deer &
   Castle patt., engraved animals,
   castle & trees, amber, frosted &
   clear........................ 145.00
Cruet w/stopper, Deer & Castle
   patt., ruby, frosted & clear 67.50

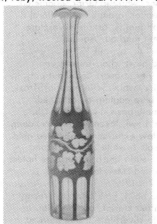

Bohemian Decanter

Decanter, Vintage patt., etched
   grape clusters & vines, ruby,
   frosted w/panels cut to clear,
   13" h. (ILLUS.) 100.00
Liqueur mug, engraved dog, grass &
   trees, ruby, frosted & clear,
   1 3/8" d., 2¼" h. 40.00
Stein, engraved dog & deer in forest
   on sides & "Souvenir de Luchon"
   on front, ruby, frosted & clear,
   pewter mounts, 2¾" d., 4½" h. ... 225.00
Stein, engraved cathedral panel
   flanked by leaves & scrolls, ruby,
   frosted & clear, pewter mounts
   w/ruby-inset lid, 3" d., 6½" h. ... 295.00
Teapot, cov., cranberry cut to clear
   w/panels of florals, gilt spout &
   handle, 11" across handle........ 185.00
Vase, 10" h., 7" rim d., Deer & Castle patt., ruby, frosted & clear 190.00
Vase, 15" h., etched birds & florals
   highlighted in gilt, ruby, frosted &
   clear (ILLUS.) 90.00

Bohemian Glass Vase

Whiskey set: decanter w/stopper &
   4 whiskey shot glasses; green cut
   to clear, 5 pcs.................. 125.00
Wine set: decanter w/stopper & 2
   wine goblets; Deer & Castle patt.,
   ruby, frosted & clear, 3 pcs....... 195.00
Wine set: decanter & 4 wine
   goblets; Vintage patt., overall
   etched grape clusters & vines,
   ruby, frosted & clear, 5 pcs....... 195.00

BREAD PLATES & TRAYS

Railroad Train Platter

*Scores of special bread plates were
produced last century and early in this one,
of pattern glass and as commemorative
pieces. Also see CUT, HISTORICAL &
COMMEMORATIVE and PATTERN
GLASS.*

"A Good Mother Makes A Happy
   Home" plate, w/star rosettes,
   clear........................... $29.00
Bible tray, open Bible center, clear,
   10½ x 7"....................... 60.00
Carpenter's Hall (Washington Centennial patt.) platter, clear 82.50

Columbia tray, shield-shaped,
Columbia superimposed against
13 vertical bars, blue,
11½ x 9½" 125.00
Egyptian patt. tray, Cleopatra center, inscribed w/daily bread mot-
to, clear, 13¼ x 8½" 55.00
Flower Pot patt. tray, clear w/"In
God We Trust" in stippled letter-
ing along sides, 12 x 8" 45.00
Garden of Eden tray, clear 25.00
George Washington platter, bear
paw handles, clear 75.00
Maltese Cross patt. platter, clear ... 45.00
Mitchell (John) tray, gilded portrait
of Mitchell center, "Leader, Coun-
sellor, Friend, President United
Mine Workers of America," clear,
10¾ x 6¾" 185.00
Railroad train platter, Union Pacific
Engine No. 350, clear, 12 x 9"
(ILLUS.) 90.00
Rock of Ages tray, clear 60.00
Rock of Ages tray, clear w/opaque
white inlaid center 170.00
Sheaf of Wheat plate, "Give Us This
Day," clear 36.00
Sheaf of Wheat tray, "Give Us This
Day," clear 47.50

BRIDE'S BASKETS

Custard Glass Bride's Basket

These are berry or fruit bowls, once popu-
lar as wedding gifts; hence the name.

Apricot bowl w/enameled blue
florals & gold leaves, ruffled,
ornate silverplate frame,
10¾" deep $250.00
Blue opalescent bowl, ruffled rim,
ornate silverplate frame 100.00
Cased bowl, deep pink interior
w/enameled grey & white bird
center amidst florals & foliage,
white exterior, folded over ruffled

rim w/amber edging, ormolu
frame w/applied foliage & bow at
top, 8¾ x 7", 10½" h........... 275.00
Cased bowl, white interior, cobalt
blue exterior w/enameled gold
florals & leaves, ruffled rim, tall
silverplate stand w/embossed
leaves, 10" d., overall 14¼" h.... 395.00
Cased bowl, deep pink to cream interior, white exterior, scalloped
edge, silverplate basket frame,
11" d., 13" h. 235.00
Cased bowl, white Satin interior,
shaded pink mother-of-pearl Diamond Quilted patt. exterior, ruffled rim w/frosted edging, silverplate frame w/applied leaves
at sides, marked "Manhattan,"
11½ x 7", 10½" h. 795.00
Cased bowl, shaded blue Satin interior, white exterior, enameled
lavender, orange & blue floral &
scroll motifs, ornate silverplate
frame marked "Adelphi,"
11¾" d., overall 13" h. 600.00
Cased bowl, chartreuse green
mother-of-pearl Coin Spot patt. interior, white Satin exterior, frosted blue edging, on attached
ormolu base, 14 x 9", 8½" h. 750.00
Cased bowl, lavender interior, deep
yellow exterior w/enameled gold
florals & white vines, crimped
rim, satin finish, silverplate holder
marked "Meriden," overall
14½ x 12½" 850.00
Cased bowl, pink interior, creamy
white exterior, crimped rim, ornate silverplate frame marked
"Manhattan Silver Plate Co.,"
overall 12½" h. 350.00
Cased bowl, shaded rose interior,
white exterior, gold enameling,
signed Webb, in original silverplate holder marked "Pairpoint" .. 275.00
Cranberry-pink bowl w/applied topaz frilly rim, ornate footed silverplate holder 225.00
Custard melon-ribbed bowl
w/enameled daisies, applied Rubina Crystal rim, 4-footed heavily
embossed silverplate frame
w/twisted & beaded handle
marked "Wilcox," 10" sq.
(ILLUS.)....................... 425.00
Deep rose shading to pink then to
white bowl, enameled blue & gold
decor, ornate silverplate holder,
11" d 285.00
Emerald green Satin (shaded light to
dark) bowl, enameled decor, ornate footed silverplate frame,
11¼" d. 265.00
Mother-of-pearl salmon pink Satin

bowl, Diamond Quilted patt.,
frosted edging around ruffle, white
enameled florals, gold leaves &
crescent moon, exterior w/three
gold birds sitting on gold branch
& enameled dainty lavender &
white florals w/gold leaves,
9¼ x 16¼" oval, 9 3/8" h. 1,450.00
Pink Satin bowl, enameled floral decor, ornate silverplate holder 150.00
Rubina Crystal (ruby shaded to
clear) fluted shell-shaped bowl,
enameled white, blue & aqua
florals & gold leaves decor, silverplate cupid compote stand,
11 1/8" h. 295.00
Spatter bowl, yellow & pink spatter,
applied piecrust rim, footed silverplate frame w/leaves, marked
"Rogers" 195.00

BRISTOL

Bristol Cologne Bottle

*While glass was made in several glass-
houses in Bristol, England, the generic name
Bristol glass is applied today by collectors to
a variety of semi-opaque glasses, frequently
decorated by enameling, and made both
abroad and in United States glasshouses in
the 19th and 20th centuries.*

Candlesticks, soft green w/gold
band, 7" h., pr. $56.00
Castor set, 3-bottle, cream opaque
w/enameled leaves & fruit decor,
silverplate frame & tops 110.00
Cologne bottle w/matching ball-
shaped stopper, green opaque
w/pink roses, blue & white
florals, white scrolls & gold trim,
2 1/8" d., 5¼" h. 70.00
Cologne bottle w/matching stopper,

deep blue opaque w/enameled
white floral decor, gold trim,
10½" h. (ILLUS.) 75.00
Cookie jar, pink w/enameled yellow
& blue florals w/green leaves, silverplate rim, lid & bail handle,
5" d., 6½" h. 165.00
Cookie jar, green opaque
w/enameled pink florals, green &
yellow leaves & white, pink & tan
heron, brass base, rim, cover
w/strawberry finial & bail handle,
5" d., 7½" h. 150.00
Decanter w/stopper, blue, late
19th c., 8" h. 75.00
Dresser set: pr. cologne bottles
w/clear stoppers & cov. powder
jar; white w/gilt butterflies decor,
3 pcs. 45.00
Mug, blue w/white enameled floral
decor & lettered "Remember Me"
in worn gilding, applied handle,
4" h. 25.00
Sweetmeat jar, cov., green opaque
w/enameled garlands of pink,
white, yellow, blue & green
florals & 4 butterflies, silverplate
rim, cover & bail handle, 5¾" d.,
4½" h. 118.00
Sweemeat jar, soft grey opaque
w/red cherries & tan branches of
green & tan leaves decor, silverplate rim, cover & bail handle,
3¼" d., 5" h. 75.00
Sweetmeat jar, deep pink
w/enameled flying duck, leaves &
blue floral decor, white lining, silverplate rim, cover & bail handle,
3" d., 5½" h. 105.00
Vases, 13½" h., 4¾" d., pedestal
bases, blue shaded to creamy
white opaque w/winter scenes of
mountains, trees & houses, pr. ... 195.00
Vase, 15" h., 5" d., scallop-cut top,
pink w/enameled blue & white
florals & white heron in marsh
scene reserved in panel outlined
in enameled blue dots, gold
trim............................ 195.00

BURMESE

*Burmese is an homogeneous glass that
shades from pink to pale yellow and was
patented by Frederick S. Shirley and made
by the Mt. Washington Glass Co. A license
to produce the glass in England was granted to Thomas Webb & Sons, which called its
articles Queen's Burmese. Gunderson Burmese was made briefly about the middle of
this century. Also see FAIRY LAMPS.*

Mount Washington Perfume

Basket, pedestal base, tall overhead
handle w/button terminals, Gun-
derson era $925.00
Bowl, 3¾" d., 2 3/8" h., scalloped &
ruffled rim, glossy, Thomas Webb
& Sons 325.00
Bowl, 3¾" w., 2½" h., footed, re-
fired yellow rim, glossy, Mt.
Washington Glass Co. 225.00
Bowl, 3¾" d., 2¾" h., fluted rim,
acid finish, attributed to Thomas
Webb & Sons 185.00
Bowl, 5" d., enameled birds &
branches decor, signed "Queen's
Burmese Patent Thos. Webb &
Comp." 400.00
Candlestick, decorated, signed
Webb, 6" h. (single) 975.00
Cologne bottle w/hallmarked
English silver screw-on lid,
enameled prunus blossoms decor,
Thomas Webb & Sons, 3¾"
widest d., 5" h. 585.00
Condiment set: cruet w/original
stopper, salt (w/metal agitator) &
pepper shakers; Mt. Washington
Glass Co., in original silverplate
castor frame marked
"Pairpoint" 750.00
Cookie jar, oak leaves & acorns de-
cor, Mt. Washington Glass Co.,
silverplate rim, cover & bail
handle 595.00
Creamer, ball-shaped w/collared
neck & ruffled rim, applied lemon
yellow handle, h.p. prunus blossoms decor, Thomas Webb &
Sons, 2½" h. 535.00
Creamer, acid finish, h.p. berries &
vines decor, Mt. Washington
Glass Co., 2¾" h. 375.00
Creamer & open sugar bowl, acid
finish, Mt. Washington Glass Co.,
pr. 425.00

Creamer & open sugar bowl, ball-
shaped w/shaped rims, h.p. pine-
cones, brown buds & green pine
needles decor, Thomas Webb &
Sons, pr. 925.00
Cruet w/original stopper, narrow-
ribbed body, acid finish, applied
lemon yellow handle, Mt.
Washington Glass Co., 3¾" d.,
7" h. .... 795.00 to 850.00
Finger bowl, 9-crimp top, acid finish, Mt. Washington Glass Co.,
4½" d., 2 1/8" h. .... 195.00 to 245.00
Mustard jar w/silverplate domed lid,
narrow-ribbed body, glossy,
2" h. 250.00
Perfume bottle w/original lemon
yellow stopper, narrow-ribbed
body, acid finish, original "Mt.
W.G. Co. Burmese Pat. Applied
For" paper label, overall 5½" h.
(ILLUS.) 500.00
Pitcher, water, 6 7/8" h., 6" d., applied angular yellow handle, acid
finish, signed "Thos. Webb & Sons
Queen's Burmese Ware" 675.00
Pitcher, 12" h., tall ewer form
duck's bill spout, pedestal stem
& wafer base, applied angular
handle, acid finish, Mt. Washington Glass. Co. .... 985.00 to 1,500.00

Burmese Pitcher

Pitcher, squat form, acid etched, Mt.
Washington Glass Co., 2-qt.
(ILLUS.) 585.00
Plate, 6" d., plain rim, acid finish,
ca. 1890 .... 165.00
Plate, 7½" d., ruffled edge, h.p.
florals & leaves decor, Thomas
Webb & Sons 465.00
Vase, 10" h., stick-type w/bulbous
base & narrow neck w/shaped
rim, enameled black dragon & flo-
ral decor, Mt. Washington Glass
Co. 835.00
Vase, 10¾" h., h.p. spray of
daisies, butterfly & verse by James
Montgomery .... 1,950.00 to 2,300.00

CAMBRIDGE

Rubina Compote in Honeycomb Pattern

The Cambridge Glass Company was founded in Ohio in 1901. Numerous pieces are now sought, especially those designed by Arthur J. Bennett, including Crown Tuscan. Other productions included crystal animals, "Black Amethyst," "blanc opaque," and other types of colored glass. The firm was finally closed in 1954, and should not be confused with the New England Glass Co., Cambridge, Mass.

Ash tray, 3-footed, Moonlight (delicate pastel blue) or Pistachio (delicate pastel green), each $10.00

Bowl, 9½" d., 2-handled, etched Rose Point patt., crystal 55.00

Bowl, 11" oval, 2-handled, 4-footed, pressed Caprice patt., blue 50.00

Bowl, 11" d., Jade (blue-green opaque) 65.00

Bowl, 11" d., Ram's Head handles, 4-toed, Gadroon patt., amber 185.00

Bowl, 12¼ x 9½", 4-toed, crimped, etched Diane patt., crystal 40.00

Brandy, Carmen (clear brilliant ruby red) bowl, clear Nude Lady stem 85.00

Butter dish, cov., etched Diane patt., crystal 100.00

Cake plate, 2-handled, etched Rose Point patt., crystal, 13½" d. 50.00

Candlesticks, Everglade patt., crystal, 5½" h., pr. 65.00

Candlesticks, Doric Column, Heliotrope (purple opaque), 9½" h., pr. 160.00

Candlesticks, 3-light, pressed Caprice patt., blue, 10" h., pr. 80.00

Candlesticks, 3-light, pressed Caprice patt., crystal, 10" h., pr. 57.50

Candy dish, cov., footed, Heliotrope 80.00

Champagne, etched Elaine patt., crystal 25.00

Cigarette box, cov., etched Rose Point patt., crystal 75.00

Claret, etched Rose Point patt., crystal, 4½ oz. 50.00

Claret, Carmen bowl, clear Nude Lady stem, 7 5/8" h 68.00

Coaster, pressed Caprice patt., blue 25.00

Cocktail, crystal bowl & base, Ebony (black opaque) Nude Lady stem . . 75.00

Cocktail, etched Rose Point patt., crystal 30.00

Cocktail shaker, etched Wildflower patt., crystal 95.00

Comport, amethyst w/Farberware chrome lady holder, 7½" h. 55.00

Compote, 6¾" d., 5" h., pressed Caprice patt., blue 45.00

Compote, 8½" d., 4" h., Honeycomb patt., Rubina, ruby top blending to blue, then to green (ILLUS.) 150.00

Compote, 10½" d., 7½" h., Heliotrope 75.00

Console set: Ram's Head bowl & pr. Doric Column candlesticks; Azure Blue (dark opaque blue), 3 pcs. . . 275.00

Console set: console bowl, stand & pr. tall candlesticks; Tomato (yellow-green at top, blending into red & yellow-green at the bottom), 4 pcs. 275.00

Creamer & sugar bowl, etched Chantilly patt., crystal, sterling silver bases, pr. 36.00

Crown Tuscan candlestick, Nude Lady stem (single) 125.00

Crown Tuscan candlesticks, 2-light, dolphin stem, 5" h., pr. 80.00

Crown Tuscan compote, 8", Seashell patt., Charleton decor 70.00

Crown Tuscan Seashell Flower Center

Crown Tuscan flower center, Seashell patt., 8" (ILLUS.) 80.00

Crown Tuscan flower or fruit center, Seashell patt. w/Flying Nude Lady, enameled roses decor, gold trim, 10" l. 325.00

Crown Tuscan swan, 3½" 35.00

Crown Tuscan vase, 4½" h., 5" d., gold-encrusted etched Portia patt. 55.00

Crown Tuscan vase, 8" h., footed, Seashell patt. 80.00

Cup & saucer, etched Diane patt., crystal 35.00

Figure flower holder, "Bashful Charlotte," crystal, 13" h. . . . . . 95.00 to 150.00

Figure flower holder, "Bashful Char-
lotte," pink, 13"h. 220.00

Figure flower holder, "Bashful Charlotte," pink frosted, 13" h. 200.00

Figure flower holder, "Draped
Lady," apple green,
8½" h. . . . . .95.00 to 135.00

Figure flower holder, "Draped
Lady," Mandarin Gold (very light
golden yellow), 8½" h. 225.00

Figure flower holder, "Draped
Lady," blue, 8½" h. 325.00

Figure flower holder, "Draped
Lady," crystal, 8½" h. 90.00

Figure flower holder, "Draped
Lady," dark pink, 8½" h. 90.00

Figure flower holder, "Draped
Lady," light pink, 13" h. 250.00

Figure flower holder, "Rose Lady,"
amber, 9½" h. 210.00

Heron Flower Holder

Flower holder, Heron, crystal, 12" h.
(ILLUS.) 145.00

Goblet, pressed Caprice patt., La
Rosa (delicate pastel pink) 30.00

Ice bucket, etched Candlelight patt.,
crystal 88.00

Ice bucket, etched Cleo patt., pink . . 35.00

Ice bucket, etched Diane patt.,
crystal 55.00

Ice bucket, etched Rose Point patt.,
crystal 135.00

Ivy ball, keyhole stem, amber, 8" . . . 30.00

Jug, pressed Caprice patt., blue,
32 oz. 195.00

Lemon dish, cov., etched Rose Point
patt., crystal 185.00

Luncheon set: creamer, sugar bowl,
4 c/s, 4 plates & handled sand-
wich/cake plate; Heartherbloom
(delicate orchid), 15 pcs. 175.00

Martini pitcher, etched Rose Point
patt., crystal 125.00

Mayonnaise bowl & underplate,
gold-decorated Magnolia patt.,
crystal, 2 pcs. 37.00

Mayonnaise set: bowl, underplate &
ladle; etched Rose Point patt.,
crystal, 3 pcs. 60.00

Mug, Tally Ho patt., clear 20.00

Nut cup, pedestal base, Peach-Blo,
3" 12.00

Nut cup, 4-footed, etched Rose Point
patt., crystal 24.00

Pitcher, pressed Caprice patt., blue,
80 oz. 205.00

Pitcher, water, 7" h., etched Rose
Point patt., crystal 130.00

Plate, 6½" d., pressed Caprice
patt., blue 17.50

Plate, 7½" d., pressed Caprice
patt., blue 22.50

Plate, salad, 7½" d., etched Rose
Point patt., crystal 12.50

Plate, 8½" d., Cascade patt.,
crystal 5.50

Plate, 9" d., etched Cleo patt.,
pink 11.00

Plate, dinner, 9½" d., Decagon
patt., Moonlight 25.00

Plate, 9½" d., etched Diane patt.,
crystal 36.00

Plate, 10½" d., etched Rose Point
patt., crystal 105.00

Plate, 16" d., Everglade patt.,
Ebony 50.00

Plate w/center handle, etched Appleblossom patt., yellow 25.00

Plate w/center handle, Azure Blue . . 35.00

Platter, 18", etched Diane patt.,
crystal 125.00

Platter, 20" l., pressed Caprice
patt., crystal 109.00

Puff box, etched Appleblossom
patt., crystal, 3½" 45.00

Punch bowl & tray, etched Rose
Point patt., crystal, sterling silver
rims, 2 pcs. 450.00

Relish dish, 3-part, etched Appleblossom patt., amber 35.00

Relish dish, 5-part, etched Rose
Point patt., crystal, 12" 60.00

Rose bowl, pressed Caprice patt.,
crystal, 8" 100.00

Sherbet, etched Elaine patt., crystal,
tall 15.00

Sherbet, etched Rose Point patt.,
crystal 20.00

Swan, crystal, 3½" 20.00

Swan, Ebony, 3½" 55.00

Swan, pink, 3½" 32.50

Swan, Ebony, 10" . . . . 275.00 to 350.00

Tumbler, footed, pressed Caprice
patt., blue 35.00

Vase, 5½" h., hat-shaped, etched
Blossomtime patt., crystal 165.00

Vase, 8" h., Ebony w/silver deposit
decor 95.00

Vase, bud, 10" h., etched Rose Point
patt., crystal 47.50

CARNIVAL GLASS

Earlier called Taffeta glass, the Carnival glass now being collected was introduced early in this century. Its producers gave it an iridescence that attempted to imitate that of some Tiffany glass. Collectors will find available books by leading authorities Donald E. Moore, Sherman Hand, Marion T. Hartung and Rose M. Presznick.

ACANTHUS (Imperial)

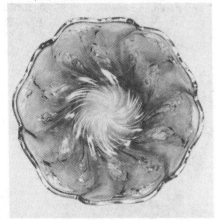

Acanthus Bowl

Bowl, 7" d., green	$20.00
Bowl, 8" to 9" d., green	75.00
Bowl, 8" to 9" d., marigold (ILLUS.)	52.50
Bowl, 8" to 9" d., purple	55.00
Bowl, 8" to 9" d., smoky	60.00
Plate, 9" to 10" d., marigold	150.00
Plate, 9" to 10" d., smoky	200.00

ACORN (Fenton)

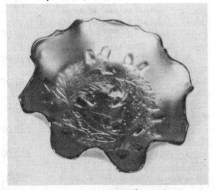

Acorn Bowl

Bowl, 5" d., ribbon candy rim, blue	60.00
Bowl, 7" d., ruffled, amber	110.00

Bowl, 7" d., aqua opalescent	85.00
Bowl, 7" d., blue	55.00
Bowl, 7" d., green	65.00
Bowl, 7" d., ice blue	150.00
Bowl, 7" d., marigold	40.00
Bowl, 7" d., marigold over milk white	155.00
Bowl, 7" d., purple	47.50
Bowl, 7" d., red	425.00 to 495.00
Bowl, 7" d., ruffled, vaseline	100.00
Bowl, 8" to 9" d., blue	60.00
Bowl, 8" to 9" d., marigold w/opalescent rim	300.00
Bowl, 8" to 9" d., ribbon candy rim, purple	55.00
Bowl, 8" to 9" d., ruffled, red (ILLUS.)	525.00
Compote, vaseline (Millersburg)	1,250.00 to 2,000.00

ACORN BURRS (Northwood)

Acorn Burrs Water Set

Berry set: master bowl & 4 sauce dishes; green, 5 pcs.	260.00
Berry set: master bowl & 6 sauce dishes; marigold, 7 pcs.	225.00
Bowl, master berry, 10" d., marigold	70.00
Bowl, master berry, 10" d., purple	130.00
Butter dish, cov., green	150.00 to 185.00
Butter dish, cov., purple	225.00
Creamer, marigold	80.00
Creamer, purple	125.00
Pitcher, water, marigold	315.00
Pitcher, water, purple	450.00
Punch bowl, marigold	400.00
Punch bowl base, ice blue	175.00
Punch bowl base, ice green	100.00
Punch bowl & base, ice green, 2 pcs.	1,800.00
Punch bowl & base, purple, 2 pcs.	450.00
Punch cup, green	30.00
Punch cup, ice blue	65.00
Punch cup, ice green	55.00
Punch cup, marigold	25.00
Punch cup, purple	32.50
Punch cup, white	65.00 to 80.00
Punch set: bowl, base & 6 cups; green, 8 pcs.	975.00

Punch set: bowl, base & 6 cups; ice
    blue, 8 pcs. .3,750.00
Punch set: bowl, base & 6 cups;
    marigold, 8 pcs. . . . . .500.00 to 575.00
Punch set: bowl, base & 6 cups; pur-
    ple, 8 pcs. 775.00
Punch set: bowl, base & 6 cups;
    white, 8 pcs. 3,500.00
Sauce dish, green 42.50
Sauce dish, marigold 20.00
Sauce dish, purple 58.00
Spooner, green 80.00
Spooner, marigold. 67.50
Spooner, purple. 85.00
Sugar bowl, cov., marigold. 95.00
Sugar bowl, open, purple 125.00
Table set: cov. sugar bowl, creamer,
    spooner & cov. butter dish; pur-
    ple, 4 pcs. 675.00
Tumbler, green 60.00
Tumbler, marigold. 45.00
Tumbler, purple. 55.00
Water set: pitcher & 6 tumblers;
    green, 7 pcs. 900.00
Water set: pitcher & 6 tumblers;
    purple, 7 pcs. (ILLUS. of part) 700.00

ADVERTISING & SOUVENIR ITEMS

Cleveland Memorial Ash Tray

Ash tray, souvenir, "Cleveland
    Memorial," purple, Millersburg
    (ILLUS.) 1,400.00
Basket, "John H. Brand Furniture
    Co., Wilmington, Del.,"
    marigold 48.00
Basket, "Miller's Furniture,"
    marigold 85.00
Bell, souvenir, BPOE Elks, "Parkers-
    burg, 1914," blue 1,250.00
Bowl, 6¼" d., "Isaac Benesch," pur-
    ple (Millersburg) . . . . .150.00 to 185.00
Bowl, "Burnheimer," blue 500.00
Bowl, "Horlacher," Butterfly patt.,
    purple 125.00
Bowl, "Horlacher," Peacock Tail
    patt., purple. 60.00

Bowl, "Horlacher," Thistle patt., pur-
    ple .80.00 to 95.00
Bowl, "Sterling Furniture," purple . . . 190.00
Bowl, souvenir, BPOE Elks, "Atlantic
    City, 1911," blue, 1-eyed
    Elk . . . . .325.00 to 410.00
Bowl, souvenir, BPOE Elks, "Detroit,
    1910," green, 1-eyed Elk 475.00
Bowl, souvenir, BPOE Elks, "Detroit,
    1910," purple, 1-eyed Elk 450.00
Bowl, souvenir, "Brooklyn Bridge,"
    marigold . . . . .270.00 to 400.00
Bowl, souvenir, "Brooklyn Bridge,"
    unlettered, marigold. 550.00

"Millersburg Courthouse" Bowl

Bowl, souvenir, "Millersburg Court-
    house," purple (ILLUS.) 475.00
Card tray, "Isaac Benesch," Holly
    Whirl patt., marigold 65.00
Hat, "John Brand Furniture," open
    edge, marigold 50.00
Hat, "Horlacher," Peacock Tail patt.,
    green 100.00
Hat, "Miller's Furniture - Harris-
    burg," basketweave, marigold. . . .   78.00
Plate, "Cambell & Beasley," w/hand-
    grip, purple. 420.00
Plate, "Eagle Furniture Co.,"
    purple . . . . .180.00 to 225.00
Plate, "Fern Brand Chocolates,"
    6" d., purple . . . . .180.00 to 220.00
Plate, "Jockey Club," w/handgrip,
    6" d., purple . . . . .220.00 to 350.00
Plate, "Old Rose Distillery,"
    green . . . . .175.00 to 265.00
Plate, souvenir, BPOE Elks, "Atlantic
    City, 1911," blue 670.00
Plate, souvenir, BPOE Elks, "Par-
    kersburg, 1914," 7½" d., blue 785.00

AGE HERALD
Bowl, 8" to 9" d., collared base,
    straight edge, purple 775.00
Plate, 9½" d., purple 1,200.00

APPLE BLOSSOMS

Bowl, 7" d., collared base,
marigold 30.00
Bowl, 7" d., collared base, peach
opalescent ....75.00 to 110.00
Bowl, 7" d., collared base, purple .. 60.00
Bowl, 7" d., ribbon candy rim,
white 125.00
Rose bowl, marigold.............. 35.00

APPLE BLOSSOM TWIGS

Banana boat, ruffled, peach
opalescent...................... 175.00
Bowl, 8" to 9" d., peach
opalescent ....80.00 to 125.00
Bowl, 8" to 9" d., purple 110.00
Bowl, 8" to 9" d., white............ 70.00
Bowl, 10" d., purple 250.00
Plate, 9" d., blue................. 175.00
Plate, 9" d., marigold 85.00
Plate, 9" d., peach opalescent 175.00
Plate, 9" d., purple............... 250.00
Plate, 9" d., ruffled, smoky 350.00
Plate, 9" d., ruffled, white 100.00

APPLE TREE

Pitcher, water, marigold 150.00
Pitcher, water, white 475.00
Tumbler, amber................... 55.00
Tumbler, blue.................... 48.00
Tumbler, marigold................ 32.50
Tumbler, white ....125.00 to 150.00
Water set: pitcher & 3 tumblers;
blue, 3 pcs...................... 600.00
Water set: pitcher & 6 tumblers;
marigold, 7 pcs................. 275.00

AUSTRALIAN

Bowl, 9" to 10" d., Kangaroo,
purple 125.00
Bowl, 9" to 10" d., Kingfisher,
purple 110.00
Bowl, 9" to 10" d., Kookaburra,
purple 100.00
Bowl, 9" to 10" d., Swan, purple.... 100.00
Bowl, 9" to 10" d., Thunderbird,
purple 110.00
Compote, Butterfly & Bush, purple .. 110.00
Sauce dish, Emu, marigold 75.00
Sauce dish, Kangaroo, purple 52.50
Sauce dish, Kingfisher, purple 45.00
Sauce dish, Kookaburra, marigold .. 30.00
Sauce dish, Kookaburra, purple 45.00
Sauce dish, Thunderbird, purple 45.00

AUTUMN ACORNS (Fenton)

Bowl, 7" d., blue................. 40.00
Bowl, 8" to 9" d., amber.......... 65.00
Bowl, 8" to 9" d., blue............ 60.00
Bowl, 8" to 9" d., green 37.50
Bowl, 8" to 9" d., marigold........ 50.00
Bowl, 8" to 9" d., purple 45.00
Plate, green 825.00

BASKET (Northwood)

Ice Green Basket

Aqua opalescent, 4½" d., 4¾" h. .. 335.00
Cobalt blue 135.00
Green........................... 235.00
Ice green (ILLUS.) 235.00
Lavender 95.00
Marigold 62.50
Purple 110.00
Smoky 250.00
White 185.00

BASKETWEAVE CANDY DISH (Fenton's Hat)

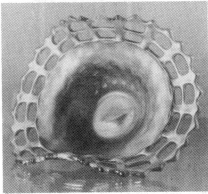

Basketweave Variant Dish

Amber 65.00
Aqua 65.00
Blue 30.00
Green........................... 55.00
Ice green 70.00
Marigold (ILLUS.) 45.00
Red 220.00

BEADED CABLE (Northwood)

Bowl, 7" d., 3-footed, ruffled,
marigold 30.00
Candy dish, green................ 65.00
Candy dish, marigold 32.50
Candy dish, purple 55.00
Rose bowl, aqua 345.00
Rose bowl, aqua opalescent....... 275.00
Rose bowl, blue.................. 70.00
Rose bowl, green 75.00

Rose bowl, ice blue 1,000.00
Rose bowl, marigold.............. 72.50

Beaded Cable Rose Bowl

Rose bowl, purple (ILLUS.) 85.00
Rose bowl, white .... 475.00 to 600.00

BEADED SHELL (Dugan or Diamond Glass Co.)

Beaded Shell Mug

Berry set: master bowl & 3 footed
    sauce dishes; purple, 4 pcs. 185.00
Butter dish, cov., purple 160.00
Creamer, marigold 60.00
Creamer, purple .... 45.00 to 70.00
Mug, blue 97.50
Mug, marigold 140.00
Mug, purple (ILLUS.) 80.00
Mug, white .... 800.00 to 1,000.00
Pitcher, water, purple 530.00
Rose bowl, green 40.00
Sauce dish, marigold 20.00
Spooner, footed, marigold 40.00
Sugar bowl, open, marigold 45.00
Table set, marigold, 4 pcs. 245.00
Table set, purple, 4 pcs. 525.00
Tumbler, blue 42.50
Tumbler, marigold................. 55.00
Tumbler, purple 52.50
Water set: pitcher & 6 tumblers;
    marigold, 7 pcs.................. 700.00

BEADS & BELLS
Bowl, 7" d., peach opalescent 50.00
Bowl, 7" d., purple 40.00

BEAUTY BUD VASE
Marigold, 8" h. .... 25.00 to 35.00
Purple, 8" h..................... 36.00
Marigold, 9½" h. 22.00

BIG FISH BOWL (Millersburg)
Green.......................... 325.00
Marigold 250.00
Marigold, ruffled 425.00
Marigold, square 435.00
Purple, ice cream shape 535.00
Vaseline w/marigold, tricornered .. 2,250.00

BIRDS & CHERRIES

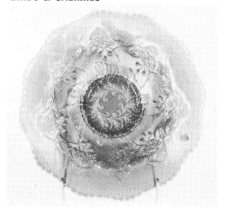

Birds & Cherries Chop Plate

Bon bon, blue.................... 60.00
Bon bon, green 65.00
Bon bon, marigold 38.00
Bon bon, purple.................. 70.00
Bowl, 8" to 9" d., blue............ 400.00
Bowl, 10" d., blue 450.00
Compote, blue 65.00
Compote, green.................. 65.00
Compote, marigold 55.00
Compote, purple 55.00
Plate, chop, blue 1,000.00
Plate, chop, marigold (ILLUS.) 385.00

BIRD WITH GRAPES
Wall vase, marigold, 8" h.,
    7½" w. 75.00

BLACKBERRY (Fenton)

Miniature Compotes

Basket, blue 40.00
Basket, red 240.00
Bowl, 8" to 9" d., ruffled, green 85.00
Bowl, 8" to 9" d., ruffled, purple ... 55.00
Compote, miniature, blue 90.00
Compote, miniature, green 45.00
Compote, miniature, marigold
 (ILLUS.)........................ 50.00
Compote, miniature, purple
 (ILLUS.)........................ 55.00
Compote, miniature, white 425.00
Plate, openwork rim, white 400.00

BLACKBERRY BLOCK (Fenton)

Blackberry Block Pitcher

Pitcher, water, green 1,000.00
Pitcher, water, marigold 465.00
Pitcher, water, purple (ILLUS.) 1,000.00
Pitcher, water, vaseline 5,000.00
Tumbler, blue..................... 55.00
Tumbler, green 175.00
Tumbler, marigold................. 57.50
Tumbler, purple 85.00
Water set: pitcher & 4 tumblers;
 purple, 5 pcs. 1,300.00

BLACKBERRY BRAMBLE
Compote, ruffled, green 40.00
Compote, ruffled, marigold 47.50
Compote, ruffled, purple 45.00

BLACKBERRY SPRAY
Compote, 5½" d., green 42.00
Compote, 5½" d., purple 45.00
Hat shape, amber 45.00
Hat shape, Amberina 235.00
Hat shape, amethyst opalescent 295.00
Hat shape, aqua 60.00
Hat shape, aqua opalescent 145.00
Hat shape, blue 30.00
Hat shape, ice green opalescent 300.00
Hat shape, milk white w/marigold
 overlay....................... 145.00

Hat shape, marigold.........40.00 to 80.00
Hat shape, red................... 270.00
Hat shape, red slag ....375.00 to 425.00
Hat shape, vaseline w/marigold
 overlay....................... 50.00

BLACKBERRY WREATH (Millersburg)
Bowl, 5" d., green 55.00
Bowl, 5" d., marigold............. 30.00
Bowl, 5" d., purple 65.00
Bowl, 7" d., blue 350.00
Bowl, 7" d., green 45.00
Bowl, 7" d., marigold............. 32.50
Bowl, 7" d., purple 42.50
Bowl, 7" w., tricornered, purple 80.00
Bowl, 8" to 9" d., green 65.00
Bowl, 8" to 9" d., marigold........ 42.50
Bowl, 8" to 9" d., purple 65.00
Bowl, 10" d., green 65.00
Bowl, 10" d., marigold............ 67.50
Bowl, 10" d., purple 155.00
Bowl, ice cream, large, marigold ... 110.00

BLOSSOM TIME COMPOTE
Compote, purple 125.00

BLUEBERRY (Fenton)
Pitcher, water, blue 625.00
Tumbler, blue.................... 70.00
Tumbler, marigold................ 40.00
Tumbler, white................... 200.00
Water set: pitcher & 5 tumblers;
 blue, 5 pcs.................... 900.00
Water set: pitcher & 6 tumblers;
 marigold, 7 pcs................ 375.00

BO PEEP
Mug, marigold 125.00
Plate, marigold 300.00

BOUQUET
Pitcher, water, blue ....385.00 to 425.00
Pitcher, water, marigold 179.00
Tumbler, blue.................... 40.00
Tumbler, marigold................ 25.00
Water set: pitcher & 4 tumblers;
 blue, 5 pcs.................... 675.00

BROKEN ARCHES (Imperial)

Broken Arches Punch Set

Punch bowl & base, marigold,
12" d., 2 pcs. 200.00
Punch cup, marigold 22.00
Punch cup, purple 25.00
Punch set: bowl, base & 6 cups;
marigold, 8 pcs. (ILLUS.) 335.00
Punch set: bowl, base & 6 cups;
purple, 8 pcs. 550.00

BUTTERFLIES

Butterflies Bon Bon

Bon bon, blue 50.00
Bon bon, green 55.00
Bon bon, marigold 35.00
Bon bon, purple (ILLUS.) 55.00
Bon bon, smoky 85.00

BUTTERFLY & BERRY (Fenton)

Butterfly & Berry Pitcher

Berry set: master bowl & 6 sauce
dishes; blue, 7 pcs. 400.00
Berry set: master bowl & 6 sauce
dishes; marigold, 7 pcs. 200.00
Bowl, 8" to 9" d., footed, blue 70.00
Bowl, 8" to 9" d., footed,
marigold 60.00
Bowl, 8" to 9" d., footed, purple 95.00
Bowl, master berry or fruit,
4-footed, blue 128.00
Bowl, master berry or fruit,
4-footed, green 125.00

Bowl, master berry or fruit,
4-footed, marigold 50.00
Bowl, master berry or fruit,
4-footed, purple 130.00
Bowl, master berry or fruit,
4-footed, white 200.00
Butter dish, cov., blue 160.00
Butter dish, cov., marigold 95.00
Creamer, green 110.00
Creamer, marigold 60.00
Creamer, purple 110.00
Hatpin holder, blue 700.00
Nut bowl, blue 725.00
Nut bowl, purple 185.00
Pitcher, water, blue 375.00
Pitcher, water, marigold (ILLUS.).... 190.00
Sauce dish, blue 32.50
Sauce dish, green 45.00
Sauce dish, marigold 25.00
Spooner, blue 95.00
Spooner, green 70.00
Spooner, marigold 45.00
Sugar bowl, cov., green 95.00
Sugar bowl, cov., marigold 65.00
Table set: cov. butter dish, cov.
sugar bowl & creamer; blue,
3 pcs. 450.00
Table set, marigold, 4 pcs. 300.00
Tumbler, blue 40.00
Tumbler, green 50.00
Tumbler, marigold 22.50
Tumbler, purple 125.00
Vase, 6" h., blue 55.00
Vase, 8" h., marigold 30.00
Vase, 9" h., blue 55.00
Water set: pitcher & 6 tumblers;
marigold, 7 pcs. ....300.00 to 425.00

BUTTERFLY & FERN (Fenton)
Pitcher, water, blue ....300.00 to 450.00
Pitcher, water, green 450.00
Pitcher, water, marigold 325.00
Tumbler, amber 45.00
Tumbler, blue 45.00
Tumbler, green 45.00
Tumbler, marigold 32.50
Tumbler, purple 47.50
Water set: pitcher & 6 tumblers;
blue, 7 pcs. 600.00
Water set: pitcher & 6 tumblers;
marigold, 7 pcs. 500.00
Water set: pitcher & 6 tumblers;
purple 7 pcs. 650.00

BUTTERFLY & TULIP
Bowl, 9" w., 5½" h., footed,
marigold 240.00
Bowl, 9" w., footed, purple 700.00
Bowl, 10½" square flat shape,
footed, marigold 310.00
Bowl, 10½" square flat shape,
footed, purple
(ILLUS.) ....1,000.00 to to 2,000.00

Butterfly & Tulip Bowl

CAPTIVE ROSE

Bon bon, 2-handled, blue, 7½" d. ..	55.00
Bon bon, 2-handled, marigold, 7½" d.	45.00
Bon bon, 2-handled, purple, 7½" d.	55.00
Bowl, 8" to 9" d., amber	65.00
Bowl, 8" to 9" d., blue	45.00
Bowl, 8" to 9" d., green	52.50
Bowl, 8" to 9" d., ruffled rim, marigold	42.50

Captive Rose Bowl

Bowl, 8" to 9" d., ribbon candy rim, purple (ILLUS.)	40.00
Compote, green	50.00
Compote, purple	45.00
Plate, 9" d., blue	140.00 to 215.00
Plate, 9" d., green	175.00 to 225.00
Plate, 9" d., marigold	95.00
Plate, 9" d., purple	160.00

CAROLINA DOGWOOD

Bowl, 8½" d., blue opalescent	275.00
Bowl, 8½" d., marigold on milk white	265.00
Bowl, 8½" d., peach opalescent	95.00 to 125.00
Plate, 8½" d., peach opalescent	300.00

CAROLINE

Basket w/applied handle, peach opalescent	250.00 to 290.00

Bowl, 8" to 9" d., peach opalescent	50.00
Bowl, 8" to 9" w., tricornered, peach opalescent	80.00
Plate, w/handgrip, peach opalescent	80.00 to 110.00

CHATELAINE

Pitcher, purple	2,000.00
Tumbler, purple	290.00

CHECKERBOARD

Checkerboard Pattern

Goblet, marigold	310.00
Goblet, purple	165.00
Pitcher, water, purple (ILLUS.)	1,750.00
Tumbler, purple (ILLUS.)	370.00

CHERRY

Bowl, 7" d., 3-footed, crimped rim, peach opalescent	60.00 to 75.00
Bowl, 8" to 9" d., 3-footed, marigold	45.00
Bowl, 8" to 9" d., 3-footed, peach opalescent	90.00
Bowl, 8" to 9" d., 3-footed, purple ..	85.00
Plate, ruffled, purple	115.00
Sauce dish, peach opalescent	52.50

CHERRY or CHERRY CIRCLES (Fenton)

Bon bon, 2-handled, aqua	160.00
Bon bon, 2-handled, blue	55.00
Bon bon, 2-handled, marigold	45.00
Bon bon, 2-handled, purple	50.00
Bon bon, 2-handled, red	1,700.00
Bowl, 5" d., fluted, blue	18.00
Bowl, 7" d., 3-footed, peach opalescent w/plain interior	77.50
Bowl, 8" to 9" d., marigold	30.00
Bowl, 8" to 9" d., white	70.00
Plate, 6" d., marigold	40.00

CHERRY or HANGING CHERRIES (Millersburg)

Banana compote (whimsey), purple	1,300.00

Bowl, 5" d., ruffled, blue satin 600.00
Bowl, 5" d., ruffled, marigold 55.00
Bowl, 5" d., piecrust rim, purple.... 35.00
Bowl, 7" d., green 70.00
Bowl, 7" d., marigold 60.00
Bowl, 7" d., purple 100.00
Bowl, 8" to 9" d., dome-footed,
    marigold 65.00
Bowl, 8" to 9" d., purple .....60.00 to 85.00
Bowl, ice cream, 10" d.,
    green ....75.00 to 90.00
Bowl, ice cream, 10" d.,
    marigold ....75.00 to 110.00
Bowl, ice cream, 10" d.,
    purple 140.00
Bowl, ice cream, 10" d., teal
    blue 850.00
Butter dish, cov., green 300.00
Butter dish, cov., marigold 150.00
Butter dish, cov., purple 175.00
Creamer, green 62.50
Creamer, marigold 55.00
Creamer, purple 77.50
Pitcher, milk, marigold 650.00
Pitcher, milk, purple............. 560.00
Pitcher, water, green 700.00

Millersburg Cherries Pattern

Pitcher, water, purple (ILLUS.) 545.00
Plate, 6" d., purple 165.00
Plate, 7" d., purple 250.00
Plate, 8" d., green 475.00
Spooner, green 75.00
Spooner, marigold................ 65.00
Spooner, purple................. 75.00
Sugar bowl, cov., green 85.00
Sugar bowl, cov., marigold........ 92.50
Sugar bowl, cov., purple 125.00
Tumbler, green ....150.00 to 200.00
Tumbler, marigold................ 310.00
Tumbler, purple (ILLUS.) 320.00

CHERRY CHAIN (Fenton)
Bon bon, 2-handled, marigold 42.50

Bowl, 5" d., blue 40.00
Bowl, 5" d., Orange Tree exterior,
    marigold 27.50
Bowl, 8" to 9" d., white........... 90.00
Bowl, ice cream, 10" d.,
    vaseline.................190.00 to 225.00
Bowl, 10" d., Orange Tree exterior,
    blue ....60.00 to 75.00
Bowl, 10" d., Orange Tree exterior,
    white 120.00
Plate, 6" to 7" d., blue .....95.00 to 135.00
Plate, 6" to 7" d., marigold 40.00

CHRISTMAS COMPOTE

Christmas Compote

Marigold ....1,500.00 to 2,100.00
Purple (ILLUS.) ....2,100.00 to 2,750.00

CHRYSANTHEMUM or WINDMILL & MUMS
Bowl, 8" to 9" d., 3-footed, blue 100.00
Bowl, 8" to 9" d., 3-footed, green... 80.00
Bowl, 8" to 9" d., 3-footed,
    marigold 40.00
Bowl, 10" d., 3-footed, blue 165.00
Bowl, 10" d., 3-footed, marigold 55.00
Bowl, 10" d., 3-footed, purple 65.00
Bowl, 10" d., collared base, red 950.00

CIRCLED SCROLL (Dugan or Diamond Glass Co.)

Circled Scroll Tumbler

Creamer, marigold 45.00
Pitcher, water, marigold 950.00
Spooner, marigold................. 125.00
Tumbler, marigold (ILLUS.) 250.00
Tumbler, purple 1,050.00
Vase, 7½" h., purple 52.50
Vase, 9" h., marigold............. 75.00
Vase, hat-shaped, purple 85.00

COBBLESTONES BOWL (Imperial)
Green, 9" d...................... 37.50
Purple, 9" d..................... 55.00

COIN DOT (Northwood)

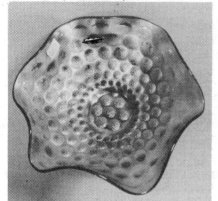

Coin Dot Bowl

Bowl, 7" d., blue 35.00
Bowl, 7" d., ribbon candy rim,
   green 37.50
Bowl, 7" d., marigold (ILLUS.) 36.00
Bowl, 7" d., purple 28.00
Bowl, 7" d., red..........675.00 to 750.00
Bowl, 8" to 9" d., blue 40.00
Bowl, 8" to 9" d., green 37.50
Bowl, 8" to 9" d., marigold......... 25.00
Bowl, 8" to 9" d., purple 40.00
Bowl, 8" to 9" d., ruffled,
   vaseline 55.00
Pitcher, water, marigold 150.00
Plate, purple..................... 55.00
Rose bowl, green 55.00
Rose bowl, marigold............... 50.00
Tumbler, marigold................. 50.00
Water set: pitcher & 6 tumblers;
   marigold, 7 pcs.................. 425.00

COIN SPOT (Dugan)
Compote, 4½" d., peach
   opalescent..................... 60.00
Compote, 7" d., blue 125.00
Compote, 7" d., fluted, peach
   opalescent.................... 50.00
Plate, 9" d., aqua 295.00
Plate, 9" d., purple 35.00

COMET or RIBBON TIE (Fenton)
Bowl, 8" to 9" d., blue............. 50.00

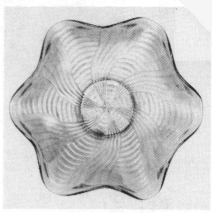

Comet Bowl

Bowl, 8" to 9" d., marigold
   (ILLUS.)....................... 40.00
Bowl, 8" to 9" d., purple 50.00
Plate, 9" d., ruffled, blue 145.00
Plate, 9" d., ruffled, marigold 225.00
Plate, 9" d., ruffled, purple 115.00

CONSTELLATION (Dugan)
Compote, marigold 48.00
Compote, white 110.00

CORAL (Fenton)
Bowl, 8" to 9" d., collared base,
   green 120.00
Bowl, 8" to 9" d., collared base,
   marigold 70.00
Plate, 9" d., marigold 400.00

CORN BOTTLE

Smoky Corn Bottle

Marigold 200.00
Smoky (ILLUS.) 210.00

CORN VASE (Northwood)
Green........................... 375.00
Ice blue 1,250.00
Ice green....................... 265.00

Marigold Corn Vase

Marigold (ILLUS.) 550.00
Purple 415.00
White 250.00

CORNUCOPIA
Candlestick, white (single) 85.00
Candlesticks, ice blue, pr. 115.00
Vase, 5" h., marigold 30.00

COSMOS
Bowl, 9" d., green 60.00
Bowl, 9" d., marigold 40.00
Bowl, 10" d., marigold 45.00
Plate, 9" d., green 62.50

COSMOS & CANE

Cosmos & Cane Butter Dish

Bowl, 8" to 9" d., marigold 50.00
Bowl, 8" to 9" sq., white 100.00
Bowl, 10" d., white 130.00
Butter dish, cov., marigold 245.00
Butter dish, cov., white (ILLUS.) 300.00
Compote, white 150.00
Pitcher, white 1,200.00
Sauce dish, green 40.00
Sauce dish, marigold 35.00
Sauce dish, white 60.00
Tumbler, amber 95.00

Tumbler, marigold 55.00
Tumbler, white 175.00

COUNTRY KITCHEN (Millersburg)
Bowl, 5" d., ruffled, marigold 97.50
Butter dish, purple 325.00
Spooner, marigold 100.00

CRAB CLAW (Imperial)

Crab Claw Water Set

Bowl, 8" to 9" d., marigold 35.00
Bowl, 8" to 9" d., fluted, smoky 45.00
Tumbler, marigold 45.00
Water set: pitcher & 6 tumblers;
    marigold, 7 pcs. (ILLUS.) 300.00

CRACKLE
Automobile vase w/bracket,
    marigold 25.00
Plate, 9½" d., purple 40.00
Tumbler, dome-footed, marigold 15.00
Water set: cov. pitcher & 5 tum-
    blers; marigold, 6 pcs. 90.00

CRUCIFIX
Candlesticks, marigold,
    pr. ....295.00 to 375.00

CUT ARCS
Bowl, 9" d., marigold 16.50

DAHLIA (Dugan or Diamond Glass Co.)
Berry set: master bowl & 4 sauce
    dishes; white, 5 pcs. 635.00
Berry set: master bowl & 5 sauce
    dishes; purple, 6 pcs. 275.00
Bowl, master berry, 10" d., footed,
    white 170.00
Butter dish, cov., marigold 140.00
Butter dish, cov., white 350.00
Creamer, marigold 60.00
Creamer, purple 125.00
Creamer, white 125.00
Creamer & cov. sugar bowl, white,
    pr. 275.00
Pitcher, water, purple 685.00
Pitcher, water, white 575.00

Sauce dish, marigold 40.00
Sauce dish, purple 45.00
Sauce dish, white 40.00
Spooner, marigold................. 60.00
Spooner, purple 75.00
Sugar bowl, cov., purple 100.00
Table set: cov. sugar bowl, cov. but-
   ter dish & spooner; marigold,
   3 pcs. 200.00
Table set, purple, 4 pcs. ...825.00 to 850.00
Table set, white, 4 pcs. 695.00
Tumbler, marigold ....95.00 to 125.00
Tumbler, purple 92.50
Tumbler, white.................... 165.00
Water set: pitcher & 1 tumbler;
   white, 2 pcs.................... 700.00
Water set: pitcher & 6 tumblers;
   marigold, 7 pcs. 1,025.00

DAISIES & DRAPE VASE (Northwood)

Daisies & Drape Vase

Aqua opalescent 375.00
Blue (ILLUS.) 300.00
Marigold 145.00
Purple 310.00
White 175.00

DAISY & LATTICE BAND

Pitcher, tankard, marigold ..90.00 to 125.00
Tumbler, blue..................... 50.00
Tumbler, marigold................. 35.00
Water set: pitcher & 4 tumblers;
   marigold, 5 pcs................. 215.00

DAISY & PLUME

Candy dish, footed, green 48.00
Candy dish, footed, marigold....... 40.00
Candy dish, footed, peach
   opalescent..................... 60.00
Candy dish, footed, purple 80.00
Compote, green.................... 50.00
Compote, marigold 32.50
Compote, purple 45.00
Rose bowl, 3-footed, green
   (ILLUS.)....................... 65.00

Daisy & Plume Rose Bowl

Rose bowl, 3-footed, ice blue....... 800.00
Rose bowl, 3-footed, ice green 675.00
Rose bowl, 3-footed, marigold...... 45.00
Rose bowl, 3-footed, purple 98.00

DAISY BASKET
Marigold 45.00

DAISY BLOCK ROWBOAT
Marigold, 12" l., 4" w.,
   3¼" h.................150.00 to 175.00
Purple 300.00

DAISY CUT BELL
Marigold ....350.00 to 425.00

DAISY SQUARES
Compote, amber 325.00
Goblet, green.................... 275.00

DAISY WREATH (Westmoreland)
Bowl, 8" to 9" d., blue
   opalescent..................... 365.00
Bowl, 8" to 9" d., milk glass w/mar-
   igold overlay ....150.00 to 200.00
Bowl, 8" to 9" d., peach
   opalescent..................... 70.00
Plate, 9" d., ruffled, aqua.......... 350.00

DANDELION (Northwood)
Mug, aqua opalescent 550.00
Mug, blue 375.00
Mug, green...................... 695.00
Mug, marigold 285.00
Mug, purple 245.00
Mug, Knight's Templar, ice blue 935.00
Mug, Knight's Templar, ice green ... 895.00
Mug, Knight's Templar, marigold ... 495.00
Pitcher, water, tankard, green 750.00
Pitcher, water, tankard, marigold... 375.00
Pitcher, water, tankard,
   purple ....450.00 to 590.00
Pitcher, water, tankard, white
   (ILLUS.) 2,000.00
Tumbler, green 90.00
Tumbler, ice blue 165.00
Tumbler, lavender................ 225.00
Tumbler, marigold................ 42.50

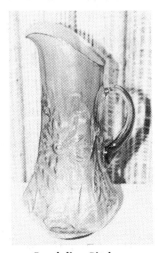

Dandelion Pitcher

Tumbler, purple 45.00
Tumbler, white.................... 105.00
Water set: pitcher & 6 tumblers;
  marigold, 7 pcs................. 600.00
Water set: pitcher & 6 tumblers;
  purple, 7 pcs............850.00 to 975.00

DANDELION, PANELED (Fenton)
Pitcher, water, blue ....325.00 to 375.00
Pitcher, water, green 325.00
Pitcher, water, marigold 265.00
Pitcher, water, purple 500.00
Tumbler, blue.................... 45.00
Tumbler, green 45.00
Tumbler, marigold................ 37.50
Tumbler, purple.................. 35.00
Water set: pitcher & 4 tumblers;
  marigold, 5 pcs................ 375.00
Water set: pitcher & 6 tumblers;
  blue, 7 pcs..................... 850.00
Water set: pitcher & 6 tumblers;
  purple, 7 pcs.................. 650.00

DIAMOND & RIB VASE
Vase, 10" h., green 30.00
Vase, 11" h., ice green 65.00
Vase, 19" h., purple 450.00
Vase, 20"h., marigold 300.00

DIAMOND & SUNBURST
Decanter w/stopper, marigold...... 60.00
Wine, marigold 25.00
Wine, purple..................... 55.00
Wine set: decanter w/stopper & 6
  wines; marigold, 7 pcs. 275.00
Wine set: decanter w/stopper & 6
  wines; purple, 7 pcs. 495.00

DIAMOND CONCAVE
Pitcher w/cover, vaseline 550.00
Tumbler, ice blue 25.00
Tumbler, vaseline 185.00

Tumble-up (water carafe w/tumbler
  top), ice blue 325.00

DIAMOND LACE (Imperial)

Diamond Lace Pitcher & Tumbler

Bowl, 5" d., marigold............. 15.00
Bowl, 5" d., purple 22.00
Bowl, 8" to 9" d., marigold........ 30.00
Bowl, 8" to 9" d., purple 50.00
Bowl, 10" d., purple 65.00
Pitcher, water, purple (ILLUS.)...... 215.00
Tumbler, purple (ILLUS.) 45.00
Water set: pitcher & 6 tumblers;
  purple, 7 pcs................... 400.00

DIAMOND POINT COLUMNS
Bowl, 5" d., 2½" h., marigold 22.00
Creamer, marigold 35.00
Vase, 6" h., marigold............. 12.00
Vase, 8" h., green 40.00
Vase, 10" h., white............... 65.00
Vase, 16" h., blue................ 365.00

DIAMOND RING (Imperial)

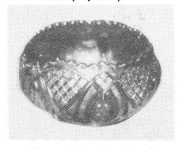

Diamond Ring Rose Bowl

Bowl, 8" to 9" d., marigold........ 30.00
Bowl, 8" to 9" d., smoky 27.50
Rose bowl, marigold (ILLUS.) 300.00

DIAMONDS (Millersburg)
Pitcher, water, green 180.00
Pitcher, water, marigold 140.00
Pitcher, water, purple 175.00
Punch bowl & base, marigold,
  2 pcs. 1,600.00

Punch bowl & base, purple,
2 pcs. 900.00
Tumbler, amber 42.50
Tumbler, green . . . . .40.00 to 50.00
Tumbler, marigold 40.00
Tumbler, purple 45.00
Water set: pitcher & 4 tumblers;
marigold, 5 pcs. 350.00
Water set: pitcher & 5 tumblers;
green, 6 pcs. 400.00
Water set: pitcher & 6 tumblers;
purple, 7 pcs. 475.00

DIVING DOLPHINS FOOTED BOWL (Sowerby)

Diving Dolphins Bowl

Marigold, embossed scroll interior . . 120.00
Marigold 160.00
Purple (ILLUS.) 215.00

DOGWOOD SPRAYS

Bowl, 8" to 9" d., dome-footed,
peach opalescent . . . . . . .95.00 to 125.00
Bowl, 8" to 9" d., dome-footed,
purple 65.00

DOLPHINS COMPOTE (Millersburg)

Blue, Rosalind interior 2,500.00
Purple, Rosalind interior . . .675.00 to 800.00

DOUBLE DUTCH BOWL

Marigold, 7" d. 20.00
Purple, 7" d. 42.00
Green, 8" to 9" d., footed 55.00
Marigold, 8" to 9" d., footed 47.50
Purple, 8" to 9" d., footed 80.00

DOUBLE STAR or BUZZ SAW (Cambridge)

Cruet w/stopper, green, small,
4" 425.00
Cruet w/stopper, green, large,
6" 435.00
Cruet w/stopper, marigold, large,
6" . . . . .200.00 to 300.00
Pitcher, water, marigold . . .425.00 to 500.00
Tumbler, green 45.00
Water set: pitcher & 1 tumbler;
green, 2 pcs. 425.00

DOUBLE STEM ROSE

Bowl, 8" to 9" d., dome-footed,
blue 325.00
Bowl, 8" to 9" d., dome-footed,
marigold 35.00
Bowl, 8" to 9" d., dome-footed,
peach opalescent 85.00
Bowl, 8" to 9" d., dome-footed,
purple 55.00
Bowl, 8" to 9" d., dome-footed,
white 95.00
Plate, dome-footed, white 150.00

DRAGON & LOTUS (Fenton)

Dragon & Lotus Bowl

Bowl, 7" d., 3-footed, blue 55.00
Bowl, 7" d., 3-footed, green 47.50
Bowl, 7" d., 3-footed, purple 47.50
Bowl, 8" to 9" d., collared base,
amber . . . . .130.00 to 175.00
Bowl, 8" to 9" d., collared base,
aqua opalescent 650.00
Bowl, 8" to 9" d., collared base,
lime green opalescent 575.00
Bowl, 8" to 9" d., collared base, ruf-
fled, peach opalescent 475.00
Bowl, 8" to 9" d., 3-footed, blue
(ILLUS.) 50.00
Bowl, 8" to 9" d., 3-footed,
green 85.00
Bowl, 8" to 9" d., 3-footed,
marigold . . . . .35.00 to 48.00
Bowl, 8" to 9" d., 3-footed, peach
opalescent . . . . .365.00 to 450.00
Bowl, 8" to 9" d., red . . . . .625.00 to 900.00
Bowl, ice cream shape, 9" d., col-
lared base, blue 60.00
Bowl, ice cream shape, 9" d., col-
lared base, green 55.00
Bowl, ice cream shape, 9" d., col-
lared base, marigold 40.00
Plate, collared base, blue 635.00
Plate, collared base, ruffled,
marigold 350.00
Plate, spatula footed, marigold 650.00

DRAGON & STRAWBERRY BOWL (Fenton)
Bowl, 9" d., blue . . . . 400.00 to 450.00
Bowl, 9" d., green . . . . 400.00 to 475.00
Bowl, 9" d., marigold . . . . . 210.00 to 300.00

DRAPERY (Northwood)
Candy dish, tricornered, aqua
  opalescent 150.00
Candy dish, tricornered, ice blue . . . 115.00
Candy dish, tricornered, ice green . . 110.00
Candy dish, tricornered, purple 120.00
Candy dish, tricornered, white 120.00
Rose bowl, aqua opalescent 260.00
Rose bowl, blue 250.00
Rose bowl, ice blue 550.00
Rose bowl, marigold 335.00
Rose bowl, purple 125.00
Rose bowl, white 360.00
Vase, 7" h., aqua opalescent 150.00
Vase, 7" h., ice green 69.00
Vase, 7" h., marigold 40.00
Vase, 8" h., white 52.50

EMBROIDERED MUMS (Northwood)

Embroidered Mums Bowl

Bowl, 8" to 9" d., ruffled, aqua
  opalescent 1,250.00
Bowl, 8" to 9" d., blue 150.00
Bowl, 8" to 9" d., ice blue 435.00
Bowl, 8" to 9" d., ice green 265.00
Bowl, 8" to 9" d., mari-
  gold . . . . 55.00 to 85.00
Bowl, 8" to 9" d., purple
  (ILLUS.) 135.00
Plate, ice green . . . . 775.00 to 875.00

ESTATE (Westmoreland)
Creamer, marigold opalescent 45.00
Creamer, peach opalescent 75.00
Mug, marigold 72.50

FAN (Dugan)
Sauceboat, purple 65.00
Sauceboat, peach opalescent 80.00

FANCIFUL (Dugan)
Bowl, 8" to 9" d., blue 82.50
Bowl, 8" to 9" d., peach
  opalescent 150.00

Fanciful Ruffled Bowl

Bowl, 8" to 9" d., ruffled, purple
  (ILLUS.) 110.00
Bowl, 8" to 9" d., ruffled, white 120.00
Plate, 9" d., blue 200.00
Plate, 9" d., marigold 90.00
Plate, 9" d., peach opalescent 300.00
Plate, 9" d., purple . . . . 175.00 to 225.00
Plate, 9" d., white 175.00

FANTAIL
Bowl, 9" d., footed, blue 72.50
Bowl, 9" d., shallow, footed, w/But-
  terfly & Berry exterior, blue 95.00
Bowl, 9" d., footed, green 80.00
Bowl, 9" d., footed, marigold 100.00

FARMYARD (Dugan)

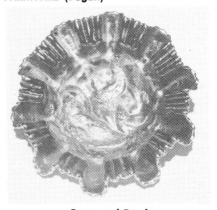

Farmyard Bowl

Bowl, ribbon candy rim, purple
  (ILLUS.) . . . . 2,250.00 to 2,600.00
Plate, 10" d., purple 8,125.00

FASHION (Imperial)
Bowl, 9" d., clambroth 30.00
Bowl, 9" d., marigold 20.00
Bowl, 9" d., ruffled, smoky 45.00
Bowl, 10" d., marigold 45.00
Creamer, marigold 22.50

Fashion Tumbler & Pitcher

Pitcher, water, marigold
  (ILLUS.) ....100.00 to 130.00
Pitcher, water, purple 900.00
Pitcher, water, smoky 335.00
Punch bowl & base, marigold,
  12" d., 2 pcs. 90.00
Punch cup, marigold.............. 13.50
Punch cup, smoky 30.00
Punch set: 12" d. bowl, base & 6
  cups; marigold, 8 pcs. ....165.00 to 210.00
Rose bowl, marigold, 7" d......... 65.00
Sugar bowl, marigold............. 20.00
Sugar bowl, smoky 90.00
Tumbler, marigold (ILLUS.) 25.00
Tumbler, smoky 60.00
Water set: pitcher & 6 tumblers;
  marigold, 7 pcs................. 275.00
Water set: pitcher & 6 tumblers;
  smoky, 7 pcs. 400.00

FEATHER & HEART

Feather & Heart Tumbler

Pitcher, water, green 550.00
Pitcher, water, marigold 375.00
Pitcher, water, purple 475.00
Tumbler, green 150.00
Tumbler, marigold................ 50.00
Tumbler, purple (ILLUS.) 92.50
Water set: pitcher & 1 tumbler;
  green, 2 pcs. 500.00
Water set: pitcher & 5 tumblers;
  marigold, 6 pcs. ....550.00 to 700.00

FEATHERED SERPENT

Berry set: master bowl & 6 sauce
  dishes; marigold, 7 pcs. 195.00
Berry set: master bowl & 6 sauce
  dishes; purple, 7 pcs............. 160.00
Bowl, 8" to 9" d., green 70.00
Bowl, 8" to 9" d., marigold........ 40.00
Bowl, 8" to 9" d., purple 60.00
Bowl, 10" d., fluted, green 48.00
Bowl, 10" d., marigold............ 45.00
Bowl, 10" d., flared, purple 62.50
Sauce dish, blue 20.00
Sauce dish, green 27.50
Sauce dish, marigold 16.50

FEATHER STITCH BOWL

Blue 65.00
Marigold 45.00
Purple 55.00

FENTONIA

Fentonia Water Set

Berry set: master bowl & 4 sauce
  dishes; marigold, 5 pcs. 195.00
Bowl, master berry, blue 95.00
Butter dish, cov., footed, blue 150.00
Butter dish, cov., footed, marigold .. 120.00
Creamer, blue 50.00
Creamer, marigold 65.00
Pitcher, water, blue 700.00
Pitcher, water, marigold 230.00
Spooner, marigold................ 60.00
Table set: creamer, cov. sugar bowl
  & spooner; blue, 3 pcs. 350.00
Table set, marigold, 4 pcs. 350.00
Tumbler, blue.................... 48.00
Tumbler, marigold................ 35.00
Water set: pitcher & 6 tumblers;
  blue, 7 pcs. (ILLUS.) 800.00

FENTON'S (OPEN EDGE) BASKET

Aqua ....60.00 to 75.00
Aqua, 2 sides turned up 80.00
Black 365.00
Blue 50.00
Green........................... 45.00
Ice blue, w/three rows of lace 90.00
Ice green................125.00 to 150.00
Lavender 75.00

Marigold 25.00
Purple 50.00
Red 235.00
Vaseline .... 45.00 to 75.00
White, square.................... 75.00

FENTON'S FLOWERS
Rose bowl, blue............. 60.00 to 80.00
Rose bowl, clambroth.............. 88.00
Rose bowl, green 56.50
Rose bowl, ice green opalescent.... 650.00
Rose bowl, marigold .... 45.00 to 60.00
Rose bowl, purple................. 110.00
Rose bowl, white................. 275.00

FERN

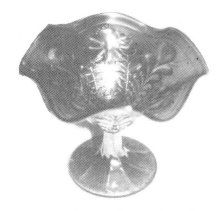

Fern Compote by Northwood

Compote, w/Daisy & Plume exterior,
green, Northwood (ILLUS.) 45.00
Compote, w/Daisy & Plume exterior,
marigold (Northwood) 75.00
Compote, w/Daisy & Plume exterior,
purple (Northwood) 60.00
Dish, hat-shaped, red (Fenton) 375.00

FIELD FLOWER (Imperial)
Pitcher, water, amber 250.00
Pitcher, water, green...... 175.00 to 295.00
Pitcher, water, marigold 115.00
Pitcher, water, purple 400.00
Pitcher, water, teal blue 285.00
Tumbler, green 70.00
Tumbler, marigold .... 20.00 to 35.00
Tumbler, purple.................. 70.00
Water set: pitcher & 1 tumbler;
green, 2 pcs. 350.00
Water set: pitcher & 6 tumblers;
marigold, 7 pcs. .... 250.00 to 300.00

FIELD THISTLE (English)
Bowl, 10" d., marigold............ 50.00
Butter dish, cov., marigold 75.00
Pitcher, water, marigold 250.00
Plate, 6" d., marigold 110.00
Plate, 9" d., marigold 395.00
Spooner, marigold................ 55.00

Table set: cov. butter dish, creamer
& spooner; marigold, 3 pcs. 175.00
Tumbler, marigold................. 45.00
Vase, 7" h., marigold.............. 45.00

FILE & FAN
Compote, blue opalescent......... 495.00
Compote, peach opalescent 85.00

FINECUT & ROSES (Northwood)
Candy dish, 3-footed, amber 55.00
Candy dish, 3-footed, aqua
opalescent..................... 425.00
Candy dish, 3-footed, green 65.00
Candy dish, 3-footed, ice blue 175.00
Candy dish, 3-footed, marigold 32.50
Candy dish, 3-footed,
purple .... 35.00 to 55.00
Candy dish, 3-footed, white 120.00
Rose bowl, aqua opalescent 700.00
Rose bowl, green .... 125.00 to 165.00
Rose bowl, ice blue ...... 225.00 to 275.00
Rose bowl, marigold.............. 75.00
Rose bowl, purple 75.00
Rose bowl, white................. 250.00

FINE RIB (Northwood & Fenton)

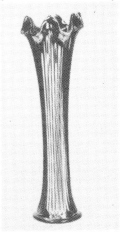

Fine Rib Vase

Vase, 6½" h., 5" d., marigold 32.00
Vase, 7" h., green 40.00
Vase, 9" h., fluted rim, ice green ... 40.00
Vase, 10" h., amber (Fenton)....... 27.00
Vase, 10" h., aqua
(Northwood) .... 70.00 to 85.00
Vase, 10" h., red (Fenton) 250.00
Vase, 11" h., blue (ILLUS.) 37.50
Vase, 11" h., ice green
(Northwood) 65.00
Vase, 11" h., red (Fenton) 200.00
Vase, 12" h., blue................ 30.00
Vase, 14" h., marigold............ 38.00
Vase, 15" h., blue................ 50.00
Vase, 15" h., purple 65.00
Vase, 16" h., red (Fenton) 350.00

FISHERMAN'S MUG

Fisherman's Mug

Marigold 215.00
Peach opalescent 1,250.00
Purple (ILLUS.) . . . . .75.00 to 90.00

FISHSCALE & BEADS

Banana boat, peach opalescent,
   7" l. 35.00
Bon bon, marigold, 6" 35.00
Bon bon, peach opalescent, 6" 52.00
Plate, 7" d., marigold 60.00
Plate, 7" d., ruffled rim, peach
   opalescent 125.00
Plate, 7" d., purple 300.00
Plate, 7" d., white 80.00

FLEUR DE LIS (Millersburg)

Fleur de Lis Bowl

Bowl, 10" d., green 200.00
Bowl, 10" d., marigold (ILLUS.) 145.00
Bowl, 10" d., purple . . . . . . .175.00 to 250.00

FLORAL & GRAPE (Dugan or Diamond Glass Co.)

Pitcher, water, blue 215.00
Pitcher, water, green 325.00
Pitcher, water, marigold . . .100.00 to 125.00
Pitcher, water, purple 165.00
Pitcher, water, white 260.00
Tumbler, blue. 32.50

Tumbler, green 65.00
Tumbler, marigold. 20.00
Tumbler, purple 27.50
Tumbler, white. 60.00
Water set: pitcher & 4 tumblers;
   marigold, 5 pcs. 185.00
Water set: pitcher & 4 tumblers;
   white, 5 pcs. 675.00
Water set: pitcher & 5 tumblers;
   purple, 6 pcs. 325.00
Water set: pitcher & 6 tumblers;
   marigold, 7 pcs. . . . . .175.00 to 245.00

FLORAL & WHEAT COMPOTE (Dugan)

Blue 50.00
Clambroth 35.00
Marigold 25.00
Peach opalescent. 75.00
White 70.00

FLOWERS & BEADS

Card tray, tricornered, purple,
   7" w. 65.00
Plate, 7½" w., 6-sided, peach
   opalescent . . . . .95.00 to 145.00

FLOWERS & FRAMES

Flowers & Frames Bowl

Bowl, 7" d., dome-footed, purple . . . 100.00
Bowl, 9" d., dome-footed, peach
   opalescent. 67.50
Bowl, 9" d. , dome-footed, fluted,
   purple (ILLUS.) 90.00

FLUTE (Imperial)

Berry set: master bowl & 6 sauce
   dishes; purple, 7 pcs. 200.00
Bowl, 8" to 9" d., purple 70.00
Creamer, marigold 29.00
Pitcher, water, marigold 300.00
Punch cup, green 12.50
Punch cup, marigold 30.00
Punch cup, purple 28.00
Punch set: bowl, base & 5 cups;
   purple, 7 pcs. (ILLUS.) 535.00
Sauce dish, green 35.00
Sugar bowl, cov., green 35.00

Flute Punch Set

Table set: creamer, sugar bowl &
   toothpick holder; purple, 3 pcs.... 200.00
Toothpick holder, green 50.00
Toothpick holder, marigold........ 47.50
Toothpick holder, purple 67.50
Tumbler, marigold................. 40.00
Tumbler, purple 80.00

FLUTE & CANE
Goblet, marigold................. 65.00
Pitcher, milk, marigold ....100.00 to 125.00
Pitcher, tankard, marigold 365.00

FOUR FLOWERS - See Pods & Posies Pattern

FOUR SEVENTY FOUR (Imperial)

Four Seventy Four Pitcher & Tumbler

Goblet, water, marigold ....70.00 to 125.00
Pitcher, milk, green 200.00
Pitcher, milk, marigold 195.00
Pitcher, milk, purple.............. 200.00
Pitcher, water, green......225.00 to 400.00
Pitcher, water, marigold ...125.00 to 190.00
Pitcher, water, purple .....425.00 to 600.00
Punch bowl & base, green, 2 pcs.... 390.00
Punch bowl & base, purple, 2 pcs. .. 900.00
Punch cup, green 25.00
Punch cup, marigold.............. 18.00
Punch cup, purple 47.50

Punch set: bowl, base & 4 cups;
   marigold, 6 pcs................. 175.00
Tumbler, green (ILLUS.) 125.00
Tumbler, marigold................. 25.00
Tumbler, purple..........125.00 to 150.00
Vase, 16" h., green 1,925.00
Vase, 16" h., marigold............ 525.00
Water set: pitcher & 4 tumblers;
   marigold, 5 pcs................. 325.00
Water set: pitcher & 6 tumblers;
   purple, 7 pcs. (ILLUS. of part) 1,800.00
Wine, marigold 165.00

FROLICKING BEARS (U.S. Glass)
Pitcher, green ....5,000.00 to 7,000.00

FROSTED BLOCK
Bowl, 8" to 9" d., scalloped & fluted,
   clambroth 26.50
Compote, clambroth 65.00
Plate, 9" d., clambroth 32.50
Plate, 9" d., marigold 50.00
Rose bowl, clambroth ....50.00 to 70.00
Rose bowl, marigold.............. 35.00
Rose bowl, white................. 45.00
Sugar bowl, clambroth............ 20.00

FRUIT SALAD
Punch bowl & base, purple, 2 pcs. .. 650.00
Punch cup, marigold.............. 15.00
Punch cup, peach opalescent 100.00

FRUITS & FLOWERS (Northwood)
Berry set: master bowl & 6 sauce
   dishes; purple, 7 pcs............. 230.00
Bon bon, stemmed, 2-handled, aqua
   opalescent..................... 415.00
Bon bon, stemmed, 2-handled,
   blue ....95.00 to 145.00
Bon bon, stemmed, 2-handled,
   green ....65.00 to 80.00
Bon bon, stemmed, 2-handled, ice
   blue 450.00
Bon bon, stemmed, 2-handled,
   lavender 195.00
Bon bon, stemmed, 2-handled,
   marigold 45.00
Bon bon, stemmed, 2-handled,
   purple 65.00
Bon bon, stemmed, 2-handled,
   white 245.00
Bowl, 7" d., purple 85.00
Bowl, 7" d., ruffled, ice green 300.00
Bowl, master berry, 10" d.,
   green ....65.00 to 110.00
Bowl, master berry, 10" d., ice
   green 750.00
Bowl, master berry, 10" d.,
   marigold 35.00
Bowl, master berry, 10" d.,
   purple 90.00
Card tray, green 100.00
Plate, 7" d., blue................ 320.00
Plate, 7" d., green 130.00

Plate, 7" d., marigold ....80.00 to 95.00
Plate, 7" d., purple............... 135.00
Plate, 7½" d., hand-grip, pastel
  marigold 185.00
Plate, 7½" d., hand-grip, purple.... 200.00
Sauce dish, marigold 29.00
Sauce dish, purple 37.50

GARDEN PATH

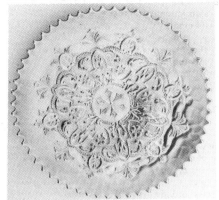

Garden Path Chop Plate

Berry set: master bowl & 6 sauce
  dishes; white, 7 pcs. 350.00
Bowl, 8" to 9" d., marigold........ 55.00
Bowl, 10" d., ruffled,
  white ....200.00 to 235.00
Plate, 7" d., peach opalescent...... 500.00
Plate, chop, 11" d., purple
  (ILLUS.) 1,750.00
Sauce dish, peach opalescent 115.00
Sauce dish, purple 75.00

GARLAND ROSE BOWL (Fenton)

Blue ....65.00 to 75.00
Marigold ....40.00 to 60.00

GAY NINETIES (Millersburg)

Pitcher, amethyst.................7,500.00
Pitcher, green ....5,500.00 to 8,000.00
Tumbler, purple ....600.00 to 1,000.00

GOD & HOME

God & Home Tumbler & Pitcher

Pitcher, blue (ILLUS.
  right) ....1,200.00 to 1,400.00
Tumbler, blue (ILLUS. left) 150.00
Water set: pitcher & 6 tumblers;
  blue, 7 pcs. 2,400.00

GODDESS OF HARVEST (Fenton)

Bowl, blue 3,100.00
Bowl, marigold 4,200.00

GOLDEN HARVEST (U.S. Glass)

Decanter w/stopper, marigold...... 95.00
Decanter w/stopper,
  purple..............150.00 to 175.00
Wine, marigold 18.00
Wine, purple.................... 30.00
Wine set: decanter & 6 wines;
  marigold, 7 pcs.................. 250.00
Wine set: decanter & 6 wines; pur-
  ple, 7 pcs..................... 450.00

GOOD LUCK (Fenton & Northwood)

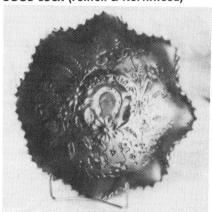

Good Luck Bowl

Bowl, 7" d., ruffled, blue 240.00
Bowl, 7" d., ruffled, purple......... 165.00
Bowl, 8" to 9" d., fluted, aqua
  opalescent.........625.00 to 700.00
Bowl, 8" to 9" d., fluted, blue
  (ILLUS.) ....150.00 to 250.00
Bowl, 8" to 9" d., fluted,
  green ....180.00 to 245.00
Bowl, 8" to 9" d., fluted, marigold .. 100.00
Bowl, 8" to 9" d., fluted, purple 145.00
Bowl, 8" to 9" d., fluted, teal blue
  (Northwood) 500.00
Plate, 9" d., blue................... 450.00
Plate, 9" d., green 375.00
Plate, 9" d., marigold 195.00
Plate, 9" d., purple............... 325.00
Plate, 9" d., white 1,600.00

GRAPE & CABLE

Banana boat, blue ....225.00 to 400.00
Banana boat, green ....185.00 to 260.00
Banana boat, stippled, green....... 400.00

Banana boat, ice blue 495.00
Banana boat, ice green 545.00
Banana boat, marigold . . . .140.00 to 175.00
Banana boat, purple 165.00
Banana boat, white 775.00
Berry set: master bowl & 6 sauce
    dishes; green, 7 pcs. 210.00
Berry set: master bowl & 6 sauce
    dishes; marigold, 7 pcs. 250.00
Berry set: master bowl & 6 sauce
    dishes; purple, 7 pcs. 225.00
Bon bon, 2-handled, blue . . . .60.00 to 85.00
Bon bon, 2-handled, green 50.00
Bon bon, 2-handled, purple 50.00
Bowl, 5" d., blue (Fenton) 25.00
Bowl, 5" d., marigold 32.50
Bowl, 5" d., purple 55.00
Bowl, 6" d., red (Fenton) 350.00
Bowl, 7½" d., ball-footed, amber
    (Fenton) 100.00
Bowl, 7½" d., ball-footed, aqua
    (Fenton) 85.00
Bowl, 7½" d., ball-footed, green
    (Fenton) 40.00
Bowl, 7½" d., ball-footed, marigold
    (Fenton) 25.00
Bowl, 7½" d., ball-footed, purple
    (Fenton) 68.00
Bowl, 7½" d., ball-footed, vaseline
    (Fenton) 80.00
Bowl, 7½" d., ruffled, ice blue 500.00
Bowl, 7½" d., spatula-footed,
    marigold (Northwood) 28.00
Bowl, 7½" d., spatula-footed, purple
    (Northwood) 60.00
Bowl, 8" to 9" d., aqua opalescent
    (Northwood) 750.00
Bowl, 8" to 9" d., ball-footed, blue
    (Fenton) 58.00
Bowl, 8" to 9" d., ball-footed,
    celeste blue (Fenton) 500.00
Bowl, 8" to 9" d., ball-footed, green
    (Fenton) 52.50
Bowl, 8" to 9" d., ball-footed, purple
    (Fenton) 55.00
Bowl, 8" to 9" d., ball-footed, red
    (Fenton) 1,200.00
Bowl, 8" to 9" d., spatula-footed,
    blue (Northwood) 30.00
Bowl, 8" to 9" d., spatula-footed,
    green (Northwood) . . . . .55.00 to 85.00
Bowl, 8" to 9" d., spatula-footed,
    marigold (Northwood) 65.00
Bowl, 8" to 9" d., spatula-footed,
    ruffled, purple (Northwood) 55.00
**Bowl, 8" to 9" d., stippled, blue
    (Northwood)** 75.00
**Bowl, 8" to 9" d., stippled, green
    (Northwood)** 95.00
**Bowl, 8" to 9" d., stippled, ice blue
    (Northwood)** 650.00
Bowl, berry or fruit, 9" d., blue 175.00
Bowl, berry or fruit, 9" d.,
    green . . . . .60.00 to 85.00

Bowl, berry or fruit, 9" d.,
    ice green 650.00
Bowl, berry or fruit, 9" d.,
    marigold 115.00
Bowl, berry or fruit, 9" d.,
    purple 85.00
Bowl, berry or fruit, 9" d.,
    teal blue 125.00
Bowl, orange, 10½" d., footed, Per-
    sian Medallion interior, blue
    (Fenton) . . . . .180.00 to 250.00
Bowl, orange, 10½" d., footed, Per-
    sian Medallion interior, green
    (Fenton) 235.00
Bowl, orange, 10½" d., footed, Per-
    sian Medallion interior, marigold
    (Fenton) . . . . .80.00 to 100.00
Bowl, orange, 10½" d., footed, Per-
    sian Medallion interior, purple
    (Fenton) 155.00
Bowl, orange, 10½" d., footed,
    blue 225.00
Bowl, orange, 10½" d., footed, ice
    blue 1,100.00
Bowl, orange, 10½" d., footed,
    marigold 120.00
Bowl, orange, 10½" d., footed,
    purple . . . . .190.00 to 285.00
Bowl, orange, 10½" d., footed,
    white . . . . .575.00 to 750.00
Bowl, 10½" d., ruffled, Basket-
    weave exterior, green 110.00
Bowl, 10½" d., ruffled, Basket-
    weave exterior, purple 120.00
Bowl, ice cream, 11" d., green 115.00
Bowl, ice cream, 11" d., marigold . . 90.00
Bowl, ice cream, 11" d.,
    white . . . . .225.00 to 375.00
Breakfast set: individual size cream-
    er & sugar bowl; green, pr. 135.00
Breakfast set: individual size cream-
    er & sugar bowl; marigold, pr. . . . 140.00
Breakfast set: individual size cream-
    er & sugar bowl; purple,
    pr. . . . . .125.00 to 200.00
Butter dish, cov., green . . . .150.00 to 210.00
Butter dish, cov., marigold 150.00
Butter dish, cov., purple . . .160.00 to 225.00
Candle lamp, green 585.00
Candle lamp, marigold . . . .395.00 to 550.00
Candle lamp, purple 385.00
Candle lamp shade, marigold 210.00
Candle lamp shade, purple 235.00
Candlestick, green (single) 80.00
Candlestick, marigold (single) 75.00
Candlestick, purple (single) 125.00
Candlesticks, marigold, pr. 155.00
Candlesticks, purple, pr. 235.00
Centerpiece bowl, blue 625.00
Centerpiece bowl, green . . .225.00 to 400.00
Centerpiece bowl, ice blue 850.00
Centerpiece bowl, ice green 625.00
Centerpiece bowl,
    marigold . . . . .165.00 to 200.00

Centerpiece bowl, purple 350.00
Centerpiece bowl, white 450.00
Cologne bottle w/stopper, green ... 200.00
Cologne bottle w/stopper,
   marigold ....110.00 to 135.00
Cologne bottle w/stopper,
   purple ....175.00 to 250.00
Cologne bottles w/stoppers,
   marigold, pr. 450.00
Compote, cov., marigold, large 1,250.00
Compote, cov., purple, small 175.00
Compote, cov., purple,
   large ....390.00 to 475.00
Compote, open, green, large 400.00
Compote, open, purple, small 300.00
Compote, open, purple, large 400.00
Cookie jar, cov., marigold 275.00
Cookie jar, cov., purple............ 235.00
Cookie jar, cov., white ...975.00 to 1,250.00
Creamer, green 100.00
Creamer, purple 110.00
Creamer, individual size,
   green ....50.00 to 65.00
Creamer, individual size, marigold .. 75.00
Creamer, individual size, purple 67.50
Creamer & cov. sugar bowl, purple,
   pr....................225.00 to 400.00
Cup & saucer, marigold 265.00
Cuspidor, purple ....4,000.00 to 7,000.00
Decanter w/stopper, whiskey,
   marigold 550.00
Decanter w/stopper, whiskey, pur-
   ple ....600.00 to 1,000.00
Dresser set, purple, 6 pcs..........1,500.00
Dresser tray, green 265.00
Dresser tray, marigold ....100.00 to 125.00

Grape & Cable Dresser Tray

Dresser tray, purple
   (ILLUS.) ....175.00 to 225.00
Fernery, marigold 1,250.00
Fernery, white ....700.00 to 1,000.00
Hatpin holder, green ......195.00 to 250.00
Hatpin holder, marigold 150.00
Hatpin holder, purple .....155.00 to 195.00
Hat shape, green 75.00
Hat shape, marigold............... 35.00
Hat shape, purple 50.00
Humidor (or tobacco jar), cov.,
   blue 950.00
Humidor, cov., marigold 215.00

Humidor, cov., purple 375.00
Ice cream dish, ice green 625.00
Nappy, single handle, green 72.50
Nappy, single handle, marigold 42.50
Nappy, single handle, purple 90.00
Perfume bottle w/stopper,
   marigold ....350.00 to 450.00
Perfume bottle w/stopper, purple .. 550.00
Pin tray, green.................... 125.00
Pin tray, marigold.........100.00 to 150.00
Pin tray, purple 225.00
Pitcher, water, 8¼" h., green 350.00
Pitcher, water, 8¼" h., marigold ... 160.00
Pitcher, water, 8¼" h., purple 225.00
Pitcher, tankard, 9¾" h., ice
   green 2,400.00
Pitcher, tankard, 9¾" h.,
   marigold ....415.00 to 500.00
Pitcher, tankard, 9¾" h.,
   purple ....575.00 to 700.00
Plate, 5" to 6" d., purple
   (Northwood) 110.00
Plate, 7½" d., turned-up hand grip,
   green 85.00
Plate, 7½" d., turned-up hand grip,
   marigold 50.00
Plate, 7½" d., turned-up hand grip,
   purple 85.00
Plate, 8" d., footed, green
   (Fenton)................65.00 to 110.00
Plate, 8" d., footed,
   purple ....60.00 to 85.00
Plate, 9" d., green 110.00
Plate, 9" d., spatula-footed, green .. 80.00
Plate, 9" d., marigold 65.00
Plate, 9" d., spatula-footed,
   marigold 55.00
Plate, 9" d., purple.........75.00 to 125.00
Plate, 9" d., spatula-footed,
   purple 65.00
Plate, 9" d., Basketweave exterior,
   green 85.00
Plate, 9" d., Basketweave exterior,
   marigold 70.00
Plate, 9" d., Basketweave exterior,
   purple 72.50
Plate, 9" d., stippled, blue 340.00
Plate, 9" d., stippled, green 250.00
Plate, 9" d., stippled, ice blue 1,700.00
Plate, 9" d., stippled, marigold 70.00
Plate, 9" d., stippled,
   purple ....170.00 to 195.00
Powder jar, cov., green............ 95.00
Powder jar, cov., marigold ...50.00 to 80.00
Powder jar, cov., purple ....85.00 to 110.00
Punch bowl & base, blue, 11" d.,
   2 pcs......................... 395.00
Punch bowl & base, purple, 11" d.,
   2 pcs.................300.00 to 450.00
Punch bowl & base, purple, 14" d.,
   2 pcs. 550.00
Punch cup, aqua opalescent 260.00
Punch cup, blue ....35.00 to 50.00
Punch cup, stippled, blue ....50.00 to 70.00

Punch cup, green 32.00
Punch cup, stippled, green 45.00
Punch cup, ice blue 70.00
Punch cup, ice green ....55.00 to 75.00
Punch cup, marigold.............. 18.50
Punch cup, purple 22.50
Punch cup, white.................. 55.00
Punch set: 11" bowl, base & 6 cups;
  marigold, 8 pcs................. 360.00
Punch set: 11" bowl, base & 6 cups;
  white, 8 pcs. 1,600.00
Punch set: 17" bowl, base & 6 cups;
  marigold, 8 pcs................. 895.00
Punch set: 17" bowl, base & 8 cups;
  purple, 10 pcs. 1,350.00
Sauce dish, green 30.00
Sauce dish, marigold 32.50
Sauce dish, purple 40.00
Sauce dish, white 350.00
Sherbet or individual ice cream dish,
  purple 50.00
Spooner, green 90.00
Spooner, ice green 200.00
Spooner, marigold................. 50.00
Spooner, purple.................. 100.00
Sugar bowl, cov., green 125.00
Sugar bowl, cov., marigold 75.00
Sugar bowl, cov., purple ...95.00 to 125.00
Sugar bowl, individual size, green .. 50.00
Sugar bowl, individual size,
  marigold 40.00
Sugar bowl, individual size, purple.. 50.00
Sweetmeat jar, cov., marigold...... 750.00
Sweetmeat jar, cov., purple 225.00
Table set, green, 4 pcs............ 500.00
Table set, marigold, 4 pcs......... 450.00
Table set, purple, 4 pcs. 450.00
Tumbler, green 45.00
Tumbler, marigold................. 27.50
Tumbler, purple.................. 32.50
Tumbler, smoky 30.00
Tumbler, stippled, marigold 49.00
Tumbler, stippled, purple 75.00
Tumbler, tankard, green 200.00
Tumbler, tankard, marigold 80.00
Tumbler, tankard, purple 55.00
Water set: pitcher & 6 tumblers;
  green, 7 pcs. 525.00
Water set: pitcher & 6 tumblers; ice
  green, 7 pcs...................2,400.00

Grape & Cable Water Set

Water set: pitcher & 6 tumblers;
  purple, 7 pcs. (ILLUS.) ...350.00 to 425.00
Water set: tankard pitcher & 6 tumblers; marigold, 7 pcs............ 825.00
Water set: tankard pitcher & 6 tum-
  blers; purple, 7 pcs............. 850.00
Whimsey compote (sweetmeat
  base), green................... 175.00
Whimsey compote (sweetmeat
  base), purple 245.00
Whimsey teacup, purple 100.00
Whiskey set: whiskey decanter
  w/stopper & 1 shot glass;
  marigold, 2 pcs................ 750.00
Whiskey shot glass, marigold 170.00
Whiskey shot glass,
  purple ....120.00 to 170.00
Wine, marigold 35.00

GRAPE & GOTHIC ARCHES (Northwood)

Grape & Gothic Arches Table Set

Berry set: master bowl & 4 sauce
  dishes; blue, 5 pcs............. 150.00
Berry set: master bowl & 6 sauce
  dishes; blue, 7 pcs............. 185.00
Butter dish, cov., green 225.00
Creamer, blue 60.00
Creamer & spooner, blue, 2 pcs..... 90.00
Pitcher, water, blue ....250.00 to 300.00
Pitcher, water, green 235.00
Sauce dish, aqua 25.00
Sauce dish, marigold 18.00
Spooner, blue.................... 60.00
Spooner, marigold................. 28.00
Sugar bowl, cov., green 67.50
Sugar bowl, cov., marigold........ 45.00
Table set: creamer, cov. sugar bowl
  & spooner; blue, 3 pcs. 315.00
Table set, blue, 4 pcs. (ILLUS.)...... 450.00
Table set, marigold,
  4 pcs....................175.00 to 195.00
Tumbler, amber 35.00
Tumbler, blue.................... 45.00
Tumbler, green 38.50
Tumbler, marigold................. 22.50
Water set: pitcher & 6 tumblers;
  blue, 7 pcs..................... 500.00
Water set: pitcher & 6 tumblers;
  marigold, 7 pcs................. 375.00

GRAPE & LATTICE
Tumbler, blue.................... 36.00

Tumbler, marigold 20.00
Water set: pitcher & 6 tumblers;
　marigold, 7 pcs. 300.00

GRAPE ARBOR (Northwood)

Grape Arbor Pitcher

Bowl, 10" d., footed,
　marigold . . . . 90.00 to 135.00
Hat shape, blue 95.00
Hat shape, ice green 375.00
Pitcher, water, ice green
　(ILLUS.) 3,250.00
Pitcher, water, marigold . . .225.00 to 350.00
Pitcher, water, purple 495.00
Pitcher, water, white 550.00
Tumbler, blue . . . . 100.00 to 175.00
Tumbler, ice blue 140.00
Tumbler, ice green 600.00
Tumbler, marigold 30.00
Tumbler, purple 52.50
Tumbler, white . . . . 85.00 to 100.00
Water set: pitcher & 4 tumblers;
　purple, 5 pcs. 800.00
Water set: pitcher & 6 tumblers;
　white, 7 pcs. 975.00

GRAPE DELIGHT

Grape Delight Rose Bowl

Nut bowl, 6-footed, blue . . . .85.00 to 115.00
Nut bowl, 6-footed, marigold 75.00
Nut bowl, 6-footed, purple 70.00
Nut bowl, 6-footed, white 95.00
Rose bowl, 6-footed, blue 90.00
Rose bowl, 6-footed, marigold 45.00
Rose bowl, 6-footed, purple . .60.00 to 85.00
Rose bowl, 6-footed, white
　(ILLUS.) . . . . .80.00 to 125.00
Wine, purple 23.00

GRAPEVINE LATTICE

Bowl, 7" d., ruffled, marigold 28.00
Bowl, 7" d., ruffled, white 42.50
Hat shape, white 65.00
Pitcher, water, blue . . . . . . .225.00 to 410.00
Pitcher, water, marigold . . .160.00 to 230.00
Pitcher, water, white 850.00
Plate, 6" to 7" d., blue 80.00
Plate, 6" to 7" d., marigold 55.00
Plate, 6" to 7" d., peach
　opalescent 140.00
Plate, 6" to 7" d., purple 65.00
Plate, 6" to 7" d., white 67.50
Tumbler, marigold 40.00
Tumbler, purple 45.00
Tumbler, white 85.00
Water set: pitcher & 6 tumblers;
　marigold, 7 pcs. 525.00

GREEK KEY (Northwood)

Greek Key Plate

Bowl, 8" to 9" d., fluted, blue 200.00
Bowl, 8" to 9" d., fluted,
　green .70.00 to 90.00
Bowl, 8" to 9" d., fluted, marigold . . 60.00
Bowl, 8" to 9" d., purple 65.00
Pitcher, water, green 700.00
Pitcher, water, marigold 700.00
Pitcher, water, purple 875.00
Plate, 9" d., marigold . . . . .275.00 to 375.00
Plate, 9" d., green (ILLUS.) 450.00
Tumbler, green 80.00
Tumbler, marigold 65.00
Tumbler, purple 85.00

HAMMERED BELL
Chandelier shade, white 80.00

HANGING CHERRIES - See Cherry, Millersburg Pattern

HARVEST FLOWER (Dugan or Diamond Glass)

Harvest Flower Tankard Pitcher

Pitcher, tankard, marigold
(ILLUS.) 1,600.00
Tumbler, marigold . . . . 90.00 to 125.00

HATTIE (Imperial)

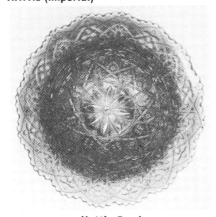

Hattie Bowl

Bowl, 8" to 9" d., marigold. 35.00
Bowl, 8" to 9" d., purple 65.00
Bowl, 8" to 9" d., smoky (ILLUS.) . . . 62.50
Plate, chop, 10½" d., amber. 1,000.00
Plate, chop, green 300.00
Plate, chop, marigold. 200.00
Rose bowl, marigold. 110.00

HEADDRESS BOWL (Imperial)
Blue 55.00
Marigold 37.50

HEART & VINE (Fenton)

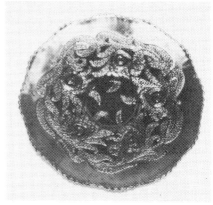

Heart & Vine Plate

Bowl, 8" to 9" d., ribbon candy rim,
blue 50.00
Bowl, 8" to 9" d., green 57.50
Bowl, 8" to 9" d., marigold. 48.00
Bowl, 8" to 9" d., purple 50.00
Plate, 9" d., blue (ILLUS.) 325.00
Plate, 9" d., purple 175.00

HEARTS & FLOWERS (Northwood)

Hearts & Flowers Compote

Bowl, 8" to 9" d., ribbon candy rim,
green . . . . .585.00 to 700.00
Bowl, 8" to 9" d., ruffled, blue 90.00
Bowl, 8" to 9" d., ruffled, ice
blue .200.00 to 325.00
Bowl, 8" to 9" d., ruffled, ice
green 495.00
Bowl, 8" to 9" d., ruffled, purple . . . 90.00
Bowl, 8" to 9" d., ruffled, white 200.00
Compote, 6¾" h., aqua opalescent
(ILLUS.) . . . . .375.00 to 495.00
Compote, 6¾" h., blue 150.00
Compote, 6¾" h., green 550.00
Compote, 6¾" h., ice green. 575.00
Compote, 6¾" h., marigold 70.00
Compote, 6¾" h., purple 125.00
Plate, green 515.00
Plate, ice green 1,000.00
Plate, marigold . . . . .200.00 to 275.00
Plate, purple. 225.00
Plate, white 695.00

HEAVY GRAPE (Dugan or Diamond Glass - formerly attributed to Millersburg)

Bowl, master berry, 10" d., peach
  opalescent...................... 650.00
Bowl, master berry, 10" d., purple .. 175.00
Bowl, ice cream, purple 600.00

HEAVY GRAPE (Imperial)

Bowl, 5" d., 2" h., marigold 30.00
Bowl, 5" d., 2" h., purple 32.50
Bowl, 7" d., fluted, green 30.00
Bowl, 7" d., purple 42.50
Bowl, 8" to 9" d., green 55.00
Bowl, 8" to 9" d., marigold........ 38.00
Bowl, 10" d., purple 50.00
Plate, 7" to 8" d., amber.......... 75.00
Plate, 7" to 8" d., blue 65.00
Plate, 7" to 8" d., green .....55.00 to 75.00
Plate, 7" to 8" d., marigold 50.00
Plate, 7" to 8" d., purple.......... 80.00
Plate, chop, 11" d., amber....... 165.00
Plate, chop, 11" d., marigold 175.00
Plate, chop, 11" d., purple 275.00

HEAVY IRIS (Dugan or Diamond Glass)

Heavy Iris Water Set

Pitcher, water, marigold (ILLUS.).... 375.00
Pitcher, water, peach opalescent ... 900.00
Pitcher, water, white 1,250.00
Tumbler, marigold (ILLUS.) 60.00
Tumbler, purple................... 50.00
Tumbler, white................... 175.00
Water set: pitcher & 5 tumblers;
  marigold, 6 pcs. ....500.00 to 635.00
Water set: pitcher & 6 tumblers;
  purple, 7 pcs. 1,800.00

HERON MUG (Dugan)

Marigold 75.00
Purple 225.00

HOBNAIL (Millersburg)

Butter dish, cov., marigold 350.00
Butter dish, cov., purple (ILLUS.).... 625.00
Cuspidor, marigold 475.00
Cuspidor, purple ....460.00 to 600.00
Pitcher, water, blue..............1,100.00

Millersburg Hobnail Butter Dish

Pitcher, water, marigold 1,500.00
Pitcher, water, purple.............1,500.00
Rose bowl, marigold............... 175.00
Rose bowl, purple 315.00
Sugar bowl, cov., marigold........ 300.00
Tumbler, blue 1,000.00
Tumbler, marigold................ 750.00
Tumbler, purple................... 600.00
Whimsey, jardiniere, purple........ 600.00

HOBSTAR (Imperial)

Hobstar Pickle Castor

Butter dish, cov., marigold 62.50
Compote, marigold 45.00
Cookie jar, cov., marigold 150.00
Creamer, marigold 42.50
Pickle castor, cov., marigold, com-
  plete w/silverplate frame
  (ILLUS.)........................ 450.00
Spooner, marigold................ 45.00
Spooner, purple.................. 85.00
Sugar bowl, cov., marigold........ 40.00
Table set, marigold, 4 pcs. 110.00

HOBSTAR & FEATHER (Millersburg)

Punch cup, green 28.50
Punch cup, marigold........20.00 to 45.00
Punch cup, purple..........65.00 to 80.00

Punch set: bowl, base & 12 cups;
  marigold, 14 pcs. 1,525.00
Rose bowl, green, 7½" top d.,
  13" h. 1,600.00

Hobstar & Feather Vase

Vase, 13" h., purple (ILLUS.) 4,500.00

HOBSTAR BAND

Celery vase, 2-handled, marigold . . .   75.00
Pitcher, marigold. 140.00
Tumbler, marigold . . . . .45.00 to   60.00
Water set: pitcher & 6 tumblers;
  marigold, 7 pcs. 395.00

HOLLY, HOLLY BERRIES & CARNIVAL HOLLY

(Slightly varied patterns)

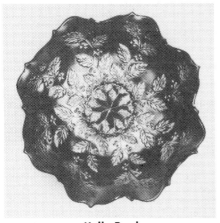

Holly Bowl

Bon bon, 2-handled, blue 65.00
Bon bon, 2-handled, purple 60.00
Bowl, 5" d., marigold. 25.00
Bowl, 7" d., fluted, peach opales-
  cent (Dugan). 45.00

Bowl, 8" to 9" d., blue. . . . . . .40.00 to   60.00
Bowl, 8" to 9" d., green 55.00
Bowl, 8" to 9" d., marigold. . .30.00 to 45.00
Bowl, 8" to 9" d., purple
  (ILLUS.). . . . . .40.00 to 55.00
Bowl, 8" to 9" d., red
  (Fenton). . . . . .565.00 to 750.00
Bowl, 8" to 9" d., vaseline 80.00
Bowl, 8" to 9" d., white. 70.00
Bowl, 10" d., aqua 195.00
Bowl, 10" d., fluted, green 65.00
Bowl, 10" d., fluted, marigold 90.00
Bowl, 10" d., 10-sided, peach
  opalescent. 62.50
Bowl, 10" d., ribbon candy rim,
  vaseline (Fenton) 175.00
Compote, small, aqua w/marigold
  overlay. 45.00
Compote, small, blue 35.00
Compote, small, green 32.00
Compote, small, marigold. 25.00
Compote, small, red (Fenton) 400.00
Dish, hat-shaped, amber, 5¾" 30.00
Dish, hat-shaped, aqua, 5¾" 50.00
Dish, hat-shaped, blue, 5¾" 30.00
Dish, hat-shaped, green, 5¾" 32.50
Dish, hat-shaped, marigold, 5¾" . . .   22.00
Dish, hat-shaped, milk white
  w/marigold overlay 60.00
Dish, hat-shaped, red, 5¾" 260.00
Dish, hat-shaped, vaseline, 5¾" 40.00
Goblet, marigold 27.50
Goblet, red (Fenton). 315.00
Plate, 9" to 10" d., blue . . .135.00 to 200.00
Plate, 9" to 10" d., clambroth 65.00
Plate, 9" to 10" d., green 375.00
Plate, 9" to 10" d.,
  marigold . . . . .60.00 to 100.00
Plate, 9" to 10" d., purple 250.00
Plate, 9" to 10" d., white 130.00
Sauceboat, handled, peach opales-
  cent (Dugan). 80.00
Sauceboat, handled, purple 48.00
Sherbet, red (Fenton) 380.00

HOLLY STAR PANELED or HOLLY STAR (Northwood)

Bon bon, green 50.00
Bon bon, marigold 20.00

HOLLY WHIRL or HOLLY SPRIG (Millersburg, Fenton & Dugan)

Bowl, 8" to 9" d., ruffled, blue 55.00
Bowl, 8" to 9" d., green . . . .60.00 to   75.00
Bowl, 8" to 9" d., marigold. 40.00
Bowl, 8" to 9" d., purple 55.00
Nappy, single handle, peach opales-
  cent (Dugan). 48.00
Nappy, single handle, purple
  (Dugan) 35.00
Nappy, tricornered, green (Dugan) . .   80.00
Nappy, tricornered, purple
  (Dugan) 85.00

Holly Whirl 2-Handled Nappy

Nappy, 2-handled, amethyst,
   Millersburg (ILLUS.)........65.00 to 80.00
Nappy, 2-handled, green........... 78.00
Nut dish, 2-handled, green........ 60.00
Nut dish, 2-handled, purple 65.00
Sauceboat, peach opalescent
   (Dugan) 50.00
Sauce dish, purple, 5½" d. (Millers-
   burg) 150.00
Sauce dish, green, 6½" d. (Millers-
   burg) 165.00

HOMESTEAD (Imperial)
Plate, amber..................... 575.00
Plate, blue 1,125.00
Plate, green ....725.00 to 950.00
Plate, marigold 425.00
Plate, purple ....400.00 to 500.00
Plate, white 600.00

HONEYCOMB
Rose bowl, marigold.............. 110.00
Rose bowl, peach opalescent 200.00

**HORSE HEADS or HORSE MEDALLION
(Fenton)**

Horse Heads Bowl

Bowl, 5" d., footed, marigold....... 55.00
Bowl, 7" to 8" d., blue 115.00
Bowl, 7" to 8" d., green (ILLUS.) 130.00
Bowl, 7" to 8" d., marigold........ 65.00
Bowl, 7" to 8" d., red............ 800.00

Bowl, jack-in-the-pulpit shaped,
   blue 120.00
Bowl, jack-in-the-pulpit shaped,
   marigold 85.00
Bowl, jack-in-the-pulpit shaped,
   vaseline 125.00
Nut bowl, 3-footed, blue ...130.00 to 175.00
Nut bowl, 3-footed, red ..950.00 to 1,200.00
Nut bowl, 3-footed, vaseline 110.00
Plate, 7" to 8" d., blue 275.00
Plate, 7" to 8" d., marigold 135.00
Rose bowl, blue................... 250.00
Rose bowl, marigold.............. 110.00

HORSESHOE CURVE - See Twins Pattern

ILLINOIS SOLDIER'S & SAILOR'S PLATE
Blue 600.00
Marigold 550.00

ILLUSION (Fenton)

Illusion Bon Bon

Bon bon, 2-handled, blue (ILLUS.) ... 60.00
Bon bon, 2-handled, marigold 75.00

IMPERIAL GRAPE (Imperial)
Basket, marigold 60.00
Berry set: master bowl & 6 sauce
   dishes; green, 7 pcs. 200.00
Berry set: master bowl & 6 sauce
   dishes; marigold,
   7 pcs. ....150.00 to 200.00
Bowl, 7" d., 2½" h., green........ 40.00
Bowl, 7" d., 2½" h., marigold 22.50
Bowl, 7" d., 2½" h., ruffled,
   purple 35.00
Bowl, 8" to 9" d., aqua 50.00
Bowl, 8" to 9" d., green 40.00
Bowl, 8" to 9" d., marigold........ 20.00
Bowl, 8" to 9" d., purple 45.00
Bowl, 8" to 9" d., white 55.00
Bowl, 10" d., clambroth 40.00
Bowl, 10" d., marigold............ 32.50
Bowl, 10" d., purple 57.50
Bowl, 11" d., ruffled, purple........ 165.00
Compote, marigold 55.00
Cup & saucer, green.............. 75.00
Cup & saucer, marigold 65.00
Decanter w/stopper,
   green ....95.00 to 120.00

Decanter w/stopper,
   marigold . . . . .60.00 to 75.00
Decanter w/stopper,
   purple . . . . .120.00 to 150.00
Goblet, clambroth 45.00
Goblet, green 50.00
Goblet, marigold . . . . .30.00 to 45.00
Goblet, purple 55.00
Pitcher, water, green 250.00
Pitcher, water, marigold 97.00
Pitcher, water, purple 200.00
Pitcher, smoky 300.00
Plate, 6" d., amber 160.00
Plate, 6" d., green 50.00
Plate, 6" d., marigold 50.00
Plate, 6" d., purple 70.00
Plate, 8" d., green 75.00
Plate, 8" d., marigold 45.00
Plate, 9" d., ruffled,
   clambroth . . . . .50.00 to 85.00
Plate, 9" d., ruffled, green 105.00
Plate, 9" d., flat, marigold 100.00
Plate, 9" d., ruffled, marigold 35.00
Plate, 9" d., ruffled, purple 65.00
Plate, 9" d., purple 310.00
Plate, 9" d., ruffled, white 50.00
Platter, 11 x 7½", green 65.00
Punch bowl, green 225.00
Punch bowl & base, marigold,
   2 pcs. 250.00
Punch bowl & base, purple,
   2 pcs. 285.00
Punch cup, green 20.00
Punch cup, marigold 15.00
Punch cup, purple 30.00
Punch set: bowl, base & 5 cups;
   marigold, 7 pcs. 250.00
Punch set: bowl, base & 5 cups;
   purple, 7 pcs. 450.00
Punch set: bowl, base & 6 cups;
   green, 8 pcs. 250.00
Rose bowl, amber 175.00
Sauce dish, green 20.00
Sauce dish, ruffled, marigold 14.00
Tumbler, green 20.00
Tumbler, marigold 15.00
Tumbler, purple 45.00
Water bottle, green 100.00
Water bottle, marigold 85.00
Water bottle, purple 125.00
Water set: pitcher & 6 tumblers;
   green, 7 pcs. 340.00
Water set: pitcher & 6 tumblers;
   marigold, 7 pcs. 185.00
Water set: pitcher & 6 tumblers;
   purple, 7 pcs. . . . . .400.00 to 550.00
Wine, green . . . . .20.00 to 30.00
Wine, marigold 30.00
Wine, purple 30.00
Wine, vaseline 40.00
Wine set: decanter w/stopper & 6
   wines; green, 7 pcs. 200.00
Wine set: decanter w/stopper & 6
   wines; marigold, 7 pcs. . . .175.00 to 210.00

Imperial Grape Wine Set

Wine set: decanter w/stopper & 6
   wines; purple, 7 pcs. (ILLUS. of
   part) 325.00

INVERTED FEATHER (Cambridge)
Cookie jar, cov., green 250.00
Cookie jar, cov., purple 750.00
Parfait, marigold 65.00
Pitcher, milk, marigold 750.00
Pitcher, water, tankard, marigold . .4,000.00
Tumbler, green . . . . .450.00 to 500.00
Tumbler, marigold . . . . .450.00 to 500.00

INVERTED STRAWBERRY (Cambridge)
Berry set: master bowl & 6 sauce
   dishes; purple, 7 pcs. 320.00
Bowl, 7" d., green 75.00
Bowl, master berry, 10" d., purple . . 155.00
Candlestick, green (single) 125.00
Candlesticks, marigold, 7" h., pr. . . . 380.00
Compote, open, giant, marigold 200.00
Compote, open, giant, purple 400.00
Creamer & sugar bowl, purple, pr. . . 325.00
Cuspidor, green 600.00
Cuspidor, marigold 600.00
Decanter, green, marked
   Near-Cut 3,550.00
Pitcher, milk, purple 1,300.00
Pitcher, tankard, green . . .850.00 to 1,200.00
Pitcher, tankard, marigold 775.00
Pitcher, tankard, purple 800.00
Powder jar, cov., green 160.00
Powder jar, cov., marigold 90.00
Spooner, green 75.00
Sugar bowl, cov., green 100.00
Table set: creamer, sugar bowl &
   spooner; marigold, 3 pcs. 550.00
Tumbler, marigold 250.00
Tumbler purple 180.00

IRIS
Compote, 6¾" d., blue 190.00
Compote, 6¾" d., green 65.00

Compote, 6¾″ d., marigold	48.00
Compote, 6¾″ d., purple	60.00
Compote, 6¾″ d., white	285.00
Goblet, buttermilk, green	80.00
Goblet, buttermilk, marigold	48.00
Goblet, buttermilk, marigold,	
souvenir.	69.00
Goblet, buttermilk, purple	55.00

IRIS, HEAVY - See Heavy Iris Pattern

JARDINIERE (THE)
Marigold	325.00
Purple	600.00

JEWELED HEART (Dugan or Diamond Glass)

Jeweled Heart Water Pitcher

Dish, 2 turned-up sides, peach	
opalescent.	25.00
Pitcher, marigold (ILLUS.) . .650.00 to	850.00
Plate, 7″ d., ruffled, peach	
opalescent.	38.00
Plate, 7″ d., ruffled, purple	16.00
Sauce dish, peach	
opalescent. . . . . .22.50 to	30.00
Sauce dish, purple	42.00
Tumbler, marigold . . . . .50.00 to	65.00

KITTENS (Fenton)

Kittens Cup & Saucer

Bowl, cereal, blue.	265.00
Bowl, cereal, marigold . . . . .90.00 to	125.00
Bowl, 4-sided, blue	240.00
Bowl, 4-sided, ruffled,	
marigold . . . . .85.00 to	140.00
Bowl, 6-sided, ruffled,	
marigold . . . . .100.00 to	135.00

Cup, marigold	100.00
Cup & saucer, blue	675.00
Cup & saucer, marigold	
(ILLUS.) . . . . .165.00 to	300.00
Dish, turned-up sides, blue.	225.00
Dish, turned-up sides, marigold	100.00
Plate, 4½″ d., marigold	150.00
Saucer, marigold	125.00
Spooner, blue.	250.00
Spooner, marigold.	150.00
Toothpick holder, blue	300.00
Toothpick holder, marigold	135.00
Vase, blue.	210.00
Vase, marigold	125.00

LATTICE & GRAPE (Fenton)
Pitcher, water, blue	250.00
Pitcher, water, marigold	115.00
Tumbler, blue.	40.00
Tumbler, marigold.	20.00
Water set: pitcher & 1 tumbler;	
white, 2 pcs.	850.00
Water set: tankard pitcher & 6 tum-	
blers; blue, 7 pcs.	645.00
Water set: tankard pitcher & 6 tum-	
blers; marigold, 7 pcs.	275.00

LATTICE & POINSETTIA (Northwood)

Lattice & Poinsettia Bowl

Bowl, cobalt blue (ILLUS.)	325.00
Bowl, marigold.	175.00
Bowl, purple. . . . . .185.00 to	210.00

LEAF & BEADS (Northwood)

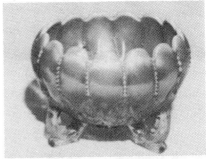

Leaf & Beads Rose Bowl

Candy bowl, footed, aqua
opalescent 550.00
Nut bowl, handled, green 45.00
Nut bowl, handled, marigold 32.00
Nut bowl, handled, purple 65.00
Rose bowl, aqua 300.00
Rose bowl, aqua opalescent
(ILLUS.) 265.00
Rose bowl, blue . . . . 100.00 to 135.00
Rose bowl, green 65.00
Rose bowl, ice blue 1,200.00
Rose bowl, ice green
opalescent 1,600.00
Rose bowl, lavender 500.00
Rose bowl, marigold 70.00
Rose bowl, purple 75.00
Rose bowl, interior pattern, teal
blue 1,000.00
Rose bowl, white 1,000.00

LEAF & FLOWERS or LEAF & LITTLE FLOWERS (Millersburg)

Compote, green, miniature 285.00
Compote, marigold, miniature 300.00
Compote, purple, miniature 250.00

LEAF CHAIN (Fenton)

Bowl, 7" d., aqua 105.00
Bowl, 7" d., marigold . . . . 30.00 to 50.00
Bowl, 7" d., red 500.00
Bowl, 7" d., vaseline w/marigold
overlay 60.00
Bowl, 7" d., white 72.50
Bowl, 8" to 9" d., aqua 165.00
Bowl, 8" to 9" d., blue 45.00
Bowl, 8" to 9" d., clambroth 45.00
Bowl, 8" to 9" d., green 45.00
Bowl, 8" to 9" d., marigold 35.00
Bowl, 8" to 9" d., white 80.00
Plate, 7" to 8" d., blue 85.00
Plate, 7" to 8" d., marigold 52.50
Plate, 9" d., clambroth 80.00
Plate, 9" d., green 95.00
Plate, 9" d., marigold . . . . . . 75.00 to 100.00
Plate, 9" d., white 125.00

LEAF RAYS NAPPY

Leaf Rays Nappy

Marigold 18.00
Peach opalescent 35.00
Purple (ILLUS.) 35.00
White 38.00

LEAF TIERS

Berry set: 9" d. master bowl & 4
sauce dishes; marigold, 5 pcs. 75.00
Butter dish, cov., marigold 135.00
Creamer, marigold 42.50
Pitcher, footed, marigold 300.00
Sauce dish, footed, marigold 21.50
Tumbler, marigold 75.00

LILY OF THE VALLEY (Fenton)

Pitcher, water, blue . . . . 3,900.00 to 4,500.00
Tumbler, blue 325.00
Tumbler, marigold 400.00

LION (Fenton)

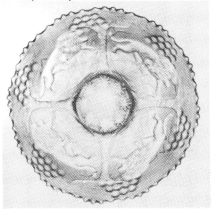

Lion Bowl

Bowl, 5" d., marigold 130.00
Bowl, 7" d., blue 275.00
Bowl, 7" d., marigold (ILLUS.) 110.00
Plate, 6" d., marigold 500.00

LITTLE BARREL PERFUME

Little Barrel Perfume

Green (ILLUS.) 80.00
Marigold 60.00
Smoky . . . . 85.00 to 120.00

LITTLE FISHES (Fenton)

Little Fishes Bowl

Bowl, 6" d., 3-footed, marigold 47.50
Bowl, 6" d., 3-footed,
  purple . . . . .70.00 to 110.00
Bowl, 8" to 9" d., 3-footed, blue 160.00
Bowl, 8" to 9" d., 3-footed,
  marigold 135.00
Bowl, 10" d., 3-footed, blue
  (ILLUS.) 165.00
Bowl, 10" d., 3-footed, marigold 135.00

LITTLE FLOWERS (Fenton)

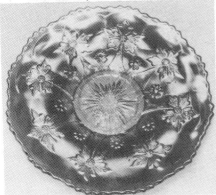

Little Flowers Chop Plate

Berry set: master bowl & 3 sauce
  dishes; blue, 4 pcs. . . . . . .75.00 to 100.00
Berry set: master bowl & 6 sauce
  dishes; green, 7 pcs. 235.00
Bowl, 5" d., aqua 100.00
Bowl, 5" d., blue 28.00
Bowl, 5" d., green 25.00
Bowl, 5" d., marigold 23.00
Bowl, 8" to 9" d., blue 82.50
Bowl, 8" to 9" d., green 50.00
Bowl, 8" to 9" d., purple 75.00
Bowl, 10" d., purple 70.00
Bowl, 10" d., spatula-footed, red . . . 850.00
Nut bowl, blue 75.00
Nut bowl, marigold 65.00
Plate, 6" d., marigold . . . . .150.00 to 180.00
Plate, chop, marigold
  (ILLUS.) . . . . .350.00 to 600.00

LITTLE STARS BOWL (Millersburg)
Bowl, 7" d., green . . . . .90.00 to 140.00

Bowl, 7" d., fluted, marigold 70.00
Bowl, 7" d., purple 80.00
Bowl, 8" d., ruffled, marigold 90.00
Bowl, 8" d., ruffled, purple 125.00
Bowl, ice cream, 9" d., marigold . . . 475.00

LOGANBERRY VASE (Imperial)
Amber 350.00
Green 195.00
Purple 360.00

LONG THUMBPRINTS
Creamer, marigold 20.00
Creamer & sugar bowl, marigold,
  pr. 40.00
Sugar bowl, marigold 20.00
Vase, 7" h., green 32.00

LOTUS & GRAPE (Fenton)

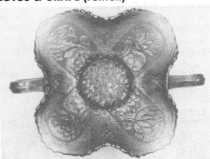

Lotus & Grape Bon Bon

Bon bon, 2-handled, blue 25.00
Bon bon, 2-handled, celeste blue
  (ILLUS.) 185.00
Bon bon, 2-handled, marigold 32.50
Bon bon, 2-handled, purple 50.00
Bowl, 5" d., footed, blue 40.00
Bowl, 5" d., footed, green 70.00
Bowl, 5" d., footed, marigold 45.00
Bowl, 8" to 9" d., green 125.00
Plate, 9" d., blue . . . . .375.00 to 500.00
Plate, 9" d., green . . . . . . .475.00 to 625.00

LOUISA

Louisa Rose Bowl

Bowl, 8" to 9" d., 3-footed, green... 45.00
Bowl, 8" to 9" d., 3-footed, peach
  opalescent...................... 500.00
Bowl, 8" to 9" d., 3-footed, purple .. 45.00
Bowl, 8" to 9" d., 3-footed, teal
  blue 40.00
Nut bowl, footed, green 40.00
Nut bowl, footed, marigold 28.00
Nut bowl, footed, purple .. 35.00
Plate, 9½" d., footed, marigold .. 137.50
Plate, 9½" d., footed, teal blue 98.00
Rose bowl, footed, green (ILLUS.)... 65.00
Rose bowl, footed, lavender 75.00
Rose bowl, footed, marigold 60.00
Rose bowl, footed, purple......... 60.00
Salt & pepper shakers, marigold,
  pr........................... 22.50

LUSTRE FLUTE (Northwood)
Creamer, green 19.00
Hat shape, fluted, green, 5" d. 35.00
Hat shape, fluted, marigold, 5" d. .. 25.00
Nappy, green 35.00
Nappy, marigold 20.00
Punch cup, green 16.00
Sugar bowl, green 20.00
Sugar bowl, marigold............. 15.00

LUSTRE ROSE (Imperial)

Lustre Rose Pitcher

Bowl, 8" to 9" d., 3-footed, amber .. 70.00
Bowl, 8" to 9" d., 3-footed, blue 65.00
Bowl, 8" to 9" d., 3-footed,
  clambroth 30.00
Bowl, 8" to 9" d., 3-footed, green... 50.00
Bowl, 8" to 9" d., 3-footed,
  marigold 40.00
Bowl, 8" to 9" d., 3-footed, purple .. 65.00
Bowl, 10½" d., 3-footed, marigold .. 35.00
Bowl, 10½" d., 3-footed, smoky 75.00
Butter dish, cov., marigold 50.00
Creamer, marigold ....30.00 to 40.00
Fernery, amber 75.00
Fernery, blue 80.00
Fernery, marigold 35.00

Fernery, purple 95.00
Fernery, smoky 70.00
Pitcher, water, clambroth (ILLUS.)... 80.00
Pitcher, water, 8" h., marigold 52.50
Plate, 9" d., amber 85.00
Plate, 9" d., marigold ....45.00 to 60.00
Rose bowl, green 45.00
Sauce dish, green 24.00
Spooner, marigold................ 35.00
Sugar bowl, cov., marigold........ 45.00
Table set, marigold, 4 pcs. 160.00
Tumbler, green 35.00
Tumbler, marigold................ 15.00
Tumbler, purple................. 32.50
Water set: pitcher & 2 tumblers;
  purple, 3 pcs.................. 495.00
Water set: pitcher & 6 tumblers;
  marigold, 7 pcs................ 225.00
Water set: pitcher & 6 tumblers;
  purple, 7 pcs.................. 595.00

MANY FRUITS (Dugan)

Many Fruits Punch Bowl

Punch bowl, 9¾" d., marigold...... 180.00
Punch bowl, 9¾" d., purple 245.00
Punch bowl & base, purple, 2 pcs.
  (ILLUS.)...................... 475.00
Punch cup, marigold.............. 22.50
Punch cup, purple 38.00
Punch cup, white 65.00
Punch set: bowl, base & 6 cups;
  blue, 8 pcs................... 500.00
Punch set: bowl, base & 6 cups;
  marigold, 8 pcs................ 375.00
Punch set: bowl, base & 10 cups;
  white, 12 pcs. 1,600.00

MANY STARS (Millersburg)
Bowl, 10" d., ruffled, purple........ 435.00
Bowl, ice cream, 10" d., green 420.00
Bowl, ice cream, 10" d., marigold .. 350.00

MAPLE LEAF (Dugan)
Berry set: master bowl & 5 small
  berry bowls; marigold, 6 pcs. 75.00

Berry set: master bowl & 6 small
   berry bowls; pedestaled, purple,
   7 pcs. 225.00
Bowl, 6" d., small berry, marigold . .   14.00
Bowl, 6" d., small berry, purple 22.50
Bowl, master berry or fruit,
   marigold 100.00
Bowl, master berry or fruit,
   purple . . . . .70.00 to 95.00
Butter dish, cov., blue 85.00
Creamer, purple 60.00

Maple Leaf Pitcher

Pitcher, water, purple (ILLUS.) 165.00
Spooner, marigold. 50.00
Spooner, purple 55.00
Sugar bowl, cov., purple 95.00
Table set: cov. sugar bowl, creamer
   & spooner; purple, 3 pcs. 235.00
Table set, marigold, 4 pcs. 200.00
Tumbler, blue.   50.00
Tumbler, marigold. 20.00
Tumbler, purple 35.00
Water set: pitcher & 6 tumblers;
   marigold, 7 pcs. 175.00
Water set: pitcher & 6 tumblers;
   purple, 7 pcs. 725.00

MARILYN (Millersburg)
Pitcher, water, green 675.00
Pitcher, water, purple 750.00
Tumbler, green 210.00
Tumbler, purple. . . . . .100.00 to 120.00
Water set: pitcher & 5 tumblers;
   marigold, 6 pcs. 700.00
Water set: pitcher & 6 tumblers;
   purple, 7 pcs. 1,500.00

MARY ANN VASE (Dugan)
Marigold 45.00
Purple 105.00
Vaseline 350.00

MAYAN (Millersburg)
Bowl, 8" to 9" d., green 60.00
Bowl, 8" to 9" d., purple 65.00

MEMPHIS (Northwood)

Memphis Punch Bowl

Punch bowl, 11½" d., marigold. 62.50
Punch bowl, 11½" d., purple 190.00
Punch bowl & base, green, 2 pcs. . . .   175.00
Punch bowl & base, ice green,
   2 pcs. 2,950.00
Punch bowl & base, purple, 2 pcs.
   (ILLUS.). 340.00
Punch cup, green 35.00
Punch cup, ice blue 60.00
Punch cup, ice green 60.00
Punch cup, marigold. 20.00
Punch cup, purple 32.50
Punch cup, white. 55.00
Punch set: bowl, base & 4 cups;
   ice blue, 6 pcs. 2,000.00
Punch set: bowl, base & 6 cups;
   marigold, 8 pcs. . . . . .315.00 to 400.00
Punch set: bowl, base & 6 cups;
   purple, 8 pcs. . . . . .425.00 to 495.00

MIKADO (Fenton)
Compote, 10" d., blue 250.00
Compote, 10" d., marigold 120.00

MILADY (Fenton)

Milady Pitcher & Tumbler

Pitcher, water, blue (ILLUS.) 650.00
Pitcher, water, marigold 475.00
Tumbler, blue (ILLUS.) 75.00
Tumbler, marigold................ 72.50

MILLERSBURG PIPE HUMIDOR - See Pipe Humidor Pattern

MILLERSBURG TROUT & FLY - See Trout & Fly Pattern

MIRRORED LOTUS
Bon bon, blue.................... 55.00
Bowl, 7" d., blue 65.00
Bowl, 7" d., ice green 250.00
Bowl, 7" d., marigold............. 55.00
Rose bowl, white................. 525.00

MITERED OVALS (Millersburg)
Vase, green.....................1,700.00
Vase, marigold 2,450.00

MORNING GLORY (Millersburg)
Pitcher, tankard, green 9,000.00
Pitcher, tankard, marigold........5,350.00
Tumbler, green...................1,150.00
Tumbler, purple 1,000.00

MULTIFRUITS & FLOWERS (Millersburg)

Multifruits & Flowers Pitcher

Pitcher, water, green...5,250.00 to 7,500.00
Pitcher, water, marigold 4,400.00
Pitcher, water, purple
    (ILLUS.) 3,000.00
Punch bowl & base, purple, 2 pcs. .. 850.00
Punch cup, green 60.00
Punch set: bowl, base & 3 cups; purple, 5 pcs....................... 950.00
Punch set: bowl, base & 4 cups;
    marigold, 6 pcs................. 700.00

NAUTILUS (Dugan)
Creamer, peach
    opalescent ....170.00 to 300.00
Creamer, purple 175.00

Creamer & sugar bowl, peach
    opalescent, pr.................. 375.00
Sugar bowl, open, peach
    opalescent.................... 250.00
Sugar bowl, open, purple ..165.00 to 245.00
Vase, peach opalescent........... 195.00

NESTING SWAN (Millersburg)
Bowl, 10" d., amber 225.00
Bowl, 10" d., green 225.00
Bowl, 10" d., marigold............ 175.00
Bowl, 10" d., purple 225.00

NIGHT STARS (Millersburg)
Bon bon, green 285.00
Card tray, purple................ 300.00

NIPPON (Northwood)
Bowl, 8" to 9" d., 2¼" h., ice blue.. 175.00
Bowl, 8" to 9" d., marigold........ 50.00
Bowl, 8" to 9" d., purple 100.00
Bowl, 8" to 9" d., teal blue........ 140.00
Bowl, 8" to 9" d., fluted, white 180.00
Plate, 9" d., marigold 350.00
Plate, 9" d., white 600.00

NU-ART
Plate, Chrysanthemum, green 350.00
Plate, Chrysanthemum, marigold ... 450.00
Plate, Chrysanthemum,
    purple ....800.00 to 1,100.00
Plate, Chrysanthemum, smoky...... 530.00

OCTAGON (Imperial)

Octagon Decanter

Bowl, 11½" d., marigold.......... 45.00
Bowl, 10" sq., green.............. 49.00
Butter dish, cov., marigold 110.00
Compote, jelly, green 75.00
Compote, jelly, marigold.......... 50.00
Creamer, marigold 30.00
Decanter w/stopper, marigold
    (ILLUS.)...................... 80.00
Goblet, water, marigold 35.00
Pitcher, water, 8" h., marigold 80.00

Pitcher, water, 8" h., purple 400.00
Pitcher, water, tankard, 9¾" h.,
   marigold 100.00
Pitcher, water, tankard, 9¾" h.,
   purple ....300.00 to 400.00
Spooner, marigold................. 45.00
Sugar bowl, cov., marigold........ 50.00
Table set, marigold, 4 pcs......... 225.00
Toothpick holder, marigold........ 170.00
Tumbler, green 80.00
Tumbler, marigold................ 30.00
Tumbler, purple 75.00
Vase, 8" h., marigold............. 55.00
Water set: pitcher & 1 tumbler; pur-
   ple, 2 pcs...................... 425.00
Water set: pitcher & 6 tumblers;
   marigold, 7 pcs................ 170.00
Wine, marigold 25.00
Wine, purple 50.00
Wine set: decanter & 1 wine; mari-
   gold, 2 pcs. ....90.00 to 125.00

OHIO STAR (Millersburg)
Vase, marigold 300.00
Vase, purple..................... 725.00

OPEN ROSE (Imperial)
Berry set: master bowl & 6 sauce
   dishes; marigold, 7 pcs. 85.00
Bowl, 5" d., marigold............. 16.00
Bowl, 7" d., footed, green 65.00
Bowl, 7" d., footed, purple 40.00
Bowl, 8" to 9" d., amber.......... 67.50
Bowl, 8" to 9" d., aqua 52.00
Bowl, 8" to 9" d., green 40.00
Bowl, 8" to 9" d., marigold........ 30.00
Bowl, 8" to 9" d., purple 65.00
Bowl, 8" to 9" d., smoky 55.00
Bowl, 10" d., marigold............ 50.00
Plate, 9" d., amber............... 175.00
Plate, 9" d., green 70.00
Plate, 9" d., marigold 58.00
Plate, 9" d., purple 110.00
Plate, chop, purple 375.00
Rose bowl, amber 58.00
Rose bowl, green 60.00
Spooner, marigold................ 29.00
Tumbler, marigold................ 20.00
Water set: pitcher & 6 tumblers;
   marigold, 7 pcs................ 200.00
Water set: pitcher & 6 tumblers;
   purple, 7 pcs.................. 375.00

ORANGE TREE (Fenton)
Berry set: master bowl & 4 sauce
   dishes; white, 5 pcs. 165.00
Berry set: master bowl & 6 sauce
   dishes; marigold, 7 pcs. 220.00
Bowl, 7" d., white................ 80.00
Bowl, 8" to 9" d., amber.......... 60.00
Bowl, 8" to 9" d., blue........... 55.00
Bowl, 8" to 9" d., clambroth........ 45.00
Bowl, 8" to 9" d., green (ILLUS.) 65.00

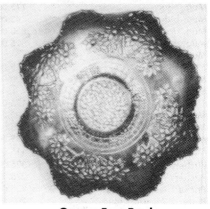

Orange Tree Bowl

Bowl, 8" to 9" d., marigold........ 35.00
Bowl, 8" to 9" d., purple 75.00
Bowl, 8" to 9" d., red ..1,400.00 to 1,900.00
Bowl, 8" to 9" d., white 85.00
Bowl, 10" d., 3-footed, blue 100.00
Bowl, 10" d., 3-footed,
   marigold ....55.00 to 85.00
Bowl, milk glass w/marigold
   overlay 1,400.00
Breakfast set: individual size cream-
   er & cov. sugar bowl; blue,
   pr.....................90.00 to 120.00
Breakfast set: individual size cream-
   er & cov. sugar bowl; marigold,
   pr........................... 70.00
Breakfast set: individual size cream-
   er & cov. sugar bowl; purple,
   pr........................... 95.00
Compote, 5" d., blue 65.00
Compote, 5" d., green 85.00
Compote, 5" d., marigold 25.00
Creamer, footed, blue 50.00
Creamer, footed, marigold 35.00
Creamer, footed, white 50.00
Creamer, individual size, blue 52.50
Creamer, individual size, marigold .. 37.50
Creamer, individual size, purple 42.50
Creamer & sugar bowl, footed, blue,
   pr........................... 115.00
Dish, ice cream, footed, blue....... 45.00
Dish, ice cream, footed, marigold... 20.00
Goblet, blue 55.00
Goblet, green.................... 75.00
Goblet, marigold................. 25.00
Goblet, marigold, w/advertising 60.00
Hatpin holder, blue ....140.00 to 200.00
Hatpin holder, green 335.00
Hatpin holder, marigold 145.00
Hatpin holder, purple............. 165.00
Loving cup, blue ....195.00 to 225.00
Loving cup, green 200.00
Loving cup, marigold 135.00
Loving cup, purple 200.00
Loving cup, white 200.00
Mug, amber 125.00
Mug, Amberina 300.00

Mug, aqua......................... 175.00
Mug, blue 45.00
Mug, green...............225.00 to 850.00
Mug, marigold 25.00
Mug, marigold w/blue
  base ....95.00 to 125.00
Mug, marigold w/green base 120.00
Mug, marigold w/vaseline
  base ....140.00 to 175.00
Mug, purple 92.50
Mug, red 405.00
Mug, teal blue 275.00
Mug, vaseline.................... 115.00
Pitcher, water, blue 325.00
Pitcher, water, marigold 275.00
Pitcher, water, white ......300.00 to 425.00
Plate, 9" d., flat, blue 200.00
Plate, 9" d., flat,
  clambroth ....85.00 to 120.00
Plate, 9" d., flat, green 275.00
Plate, 9" d., flat, marigold 95.00
Plate, 9" d., flat, white 125.00
Powder jar, cov., blue 70.00
Powder jar, cov., green........... 350.00
Powder jar, cov., marigold 60.00
Punch bowl & base, blue,
  2 pcs..................225.00 to 275.00
Punch bowl & base, marigold,
  2 pcs..................110.00 to 135.00
Punch bowl & base, white, 2 pcs.... 325.00
Rose bowl, purple 125.00
Rose bowl, red.................... 575.00
Rose bowl, white.................. 250.00
Sauce dish, footed, blue 30.00
Sauce dish, footed, marigold 12.00
Shaving mug, amber 125.00
Shaving mug, blue 65.00
Shaving mug, marigold 30.00
Shaving mug, purple ......110.00 to 200.00
Shaving mug, red 450.00
Spooner, blue.................... 75.00
Sugar bowl, blue 65.00
Sugar bowl, purple 52.50
Sugar bowl, white................ 50.00
Sugar bowl, open, breakfast size,
  marigold 20.00
Sugar bowl, open, breakfast size,
  white 50.00
Tumbler, blue.................... 45.00

Tumbler, marigold (ILLUS.) 40.00
Tumbler, white................... 75.00
Water set: pitcher & 6 tumblers;
  blue, 7 pcs.................... 395.00
Wine, blue 42.50
Wine, green 175.00
Wine, marigold 26.00

ORANGE TREE ORCHARD (Fenton)
Pitcher, marigold................. 165.00
Pitcher, white.................... 525.00
Tumbler, blue.................... 45.00
Tumbler, white................... 165.00
Water set: pitcher & 4 tumblers;
  white, 5 pcs...................1,025.00
Water set: pitcher & 6 tumblers;
  blue, 7 pcs.................... 750.00

ORANGE TREE SCROLL

Orange Tree Scroll Tumbler

Pitcher, marigold................. 130.00
Pitcher, white.................... 325.00
Tumbler, blue.................... 87.50
Tumbler, marigold (ILLUS.) 65.00
Water set: pitcher & 6 tumblers;
  blue, 7 pcs.................... 900.00

ORIENTAL POPPY (Northwood)

Orange Tree Tumbler   **Oriental Poppy Pitcher**

Pitcher, water, green 750.00
Pitcher, water, marigold . . .195.00 to 400.00
Pitcher, water, purple (ILLUS.) 500.00
Pitcher, water, white . . . . .895.00 to 1,200.00
Tumbler, green 50.00
Tumbler, ice blue 175.00
Tumbler, marigold 35.00
Tumbler, purple 45.00
Tumbler, white 100.00
Water set: pitcher & 6 tumblers; ice
    green, 7 pcs. 4,000.00
Water set: pitcher & 6 tumblers;
    marigold, 7 pcs. 525.00
Water set: pitcher & 6 tumblers;
    purple 7 pcs. 650.00

PALM BEACH (United States Glass Co.)

Palm Beach Rose Bowl

Bowl, 5" d., 4 turned-in sides,
    marigold 90.00
Butter dish, cov., white 195.00
Creamer, marigold 70.00
Creamer, white 80.00
Pitcher, water, marigold 450.00
Pitcher, water, white 725.00
Rose bowl, amber (ILLUS.) 125.00
Sauce dish, white 30.00
Spooner, marigold 85.00
Spooner, white 85.00
Tumbler, amber 80.00
Tumbler, marigold 210.00
Tumbler, white 155.00
Whimsey banana boat, marigold,
    6" . . . . .75.00 to 90.00
Whimsey banana boat, purple, 6" . . . 115.00
Whimsey vase, white 250.00

PANELED DANDELION - See Dandelion, Paneled Pattern

PANSY and PANSY SPRAY

Bowl, 8" to 9" d., amber 20.00
Bowl, 8" to 9" d., green 45.00
Bowl, 8" to 9" d., marigold 27.00
Bowl, 9" d., fluted, purple (ILLUS.) . . 45.00
Creamer, amber 35.00
Creamer, marigold 18.50
Creamer, purple 30.00
Creamer & sugar bowl, green, pr. . . . 39.00
Creamer & sugar bowl, marigold,
    pr. 37.50

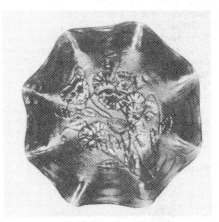

Pansy Bowl by Imperial

Dresser tray, green 55.00
Dresser tray, marigold 45.00
Nappy, amber 38.00
Nappy, green 18.00
Nappy, lavender 25.00
Nappy, marigold 20.00
Pickle (or relish) dish, amber,
    9 x 6" 47.50
Pickle (or relish) dish, blue,
    9 x 6" 25.00
Pickle (or relish) dish, clambroth,
    9 x 6" 20.00
Pickle (or relish) dish, green,
    9 x 6" 28.00
Pickle (or relish) dish, marigold,
    9 x 6" 25.00
Pickle (or relish) dish, purple,
    9 x 6" 35.00
Pickle (or relish) dish, smoky,
    9 x 6" 48.00
Plate, 9" d., ruffled, smoky 65.00
Sugar bowl, amber 35.00
Sugar bowl, marigold 25.00
Sugar bowl, purple 50.00
Sugar bowl, smoky 35.00

PANTHER (Fenton)

Panther Centerpiece Bowl

Berry set: master bowl & 6 sauce
dishes; blue, 7 pcs.............. 700.00
Berry set: master bowl & 6 sauce
dishes; marigold, 7 pcs. 375.00
Bowl, 5" d., footed, aqua 325.00
Bowl, 5" d., footed, blue 75.00
Bowl, 5" d., footed, marigold....... 37.00
Bowl, 5" d., footed, red ...400.00 to 650.00
Bowl, 9" d., claw-footed, marigold.. 135.00
Bowl, 9" d., claw-footed, purple 150.00
Bowl, 9" d., claw-footed, white..... 625.00
Centerpiece bowl, blue (ILLUS.)..... 900.00

PEACH (Northwood)

Peach Water Pitcher

Berry set: master bowl & 6 sauce
dishes; white, 7 pcs. ....395.00 to 425.00
Bowl, 9" d., white................. 175.00
Butter dish, cov., white 300.00
Pitcher, water, blue (ILLUS.) 1,250.00
Pitcher, water, white 450.00
Sauce dish, white 50.00
Spooner, white ....80.00 to 110.00
Sugar bowl, cov., white ....90.00 to 125.00
Table set, white, 4 pcs.....550.00 to 650.00
Tumbler, blue.................... 65.00
Tumbler, marigold 2,100.00
Tumbler, white................... 125.00
Water set: pitcher & 6 tumblers;
blue, 7 pcs. ....900.00 to 1,200.00
Water set: pitcher & 6 tumblers;
white, 7 pcs.................... 875.00

PEACH & PEAR OVAL FRUIT BOWL
Marigold ....40.00 to 60.00
Purple 80.00

PEACOCK, FLUFFY (Fenton)
Pitcher, water, blue 650.00
Pitcher, water, green............. 585.00
Pitcher, water, marigold 325.00
Pitcher, water, purple 500.00
Tumbler, blue.................... 57.50

Tumbler, green 55.00
Tumbler, marigold................. 45.00
Tumbler, purple.................. 65.00

Fluffy Peacock Water Set

Water set: pitcher & 6 tumblers;
purple, 7 pcs. (ILLUS. of part) 925.00

PEACOCK & DAHLIA (Fenton)
Bowl, 7" d., ruffled, aqua opales-
cent ....125.00 to 175.00
Bowl, 7" d., ruffled, blue 95.00
Bowl, 7" d., marigold.............. 50.00
Bowl, 8" d., footed, green 49.00
Plate, 8½" d., marigold 225.00

PEACOCK & GRAPE (Fenton)
Bowl, 7" d., marigold.............. 10.00
Bowl, 7" d., red.................. 975.00
Bowl, 8" to 9" d., 3-footed, amber .. 100.00
Bowl, 8" to 9" d., 3-footed, blue 45.00
Bowl, 8" to 9" d., 3-footed, green... 60.00
Bowl, 8" to 9" d., 3-footed, ice
green opalescent............... 595.00
Bowl, 8" to 9" d., flat, ribbon candy
rim, lavender 75.00
Bowl, 8" to 9" d., 3-footed,
lavender 125.00
Bowl, 8" to 9" d., 3-footed,
marigold 45.00
Bowl, 8" to 9" d., 3-footed, purple .. 50.00
Bowl, 8" to 9" d., 3-footed, red 535.00
Bowl, 8" to 9" d., 3-footed,
vaseline 60.00
Bowl, 8" to 9" d., 3-footed, vaseline
opalescent.................... 400.00
Bowl, 8" to 9" d., collared base,
blue 55.00
Bowl, 8" to 9" d., collared base,
marigold 35.00
Bowl, 8" to 9" d., collared base,
peach opalescent ....550.00 to 575.00
Bowl, 8" to 9" d., collared base,
purple 50.00
Bowl, 8" to 9" d., collared base, ruf-
fled, red 800.00
Bowl, 8" to 9" d., collared base,
smoky ....575.00 to 650.00
Plate, 9" d., collared base, blue 325.00
Plate, 9" d., collared base,
marigold 270.00

Plate, 9" d., 3-footed, green 110.00
Plate, 9" d., 3-footed,
marigold ....160.00 to 225.00
Plate, 9" d., 3-footed, purple 270.00

PEACOCK & URN

Peacock & Urn Bowl

Berry set: master bowl & 4 sauce
dishes; marigold, 5 pcs. 225.00
Berry set: master bowl & 6 sauce
dishes; purple, 7 pcs............ 675.00
Bowl, 7" d., ruffled, green (Millers-
burg) ....225.00 to 270.00
Bowl, 7" d., ruffled, marigold
(Millersburg).................... 375.00
Bowl, 7" d., ruffled, purple (Millers-
burg) 265.00
Bowl, 8" to 9" d., blue
(Fenton)................75.00 to 125.00
Bowl, 8" to 9" d., green
(Fenton)...............140.00 to 165.00
Bowl, 8" to 9" d., green (Millers-
burg) ....295.00 to 425.00
Bowl, 8" to 9" d., marigold
(Fenton)................50.00 to 75.00
Bowl, 8" to 9" d., marigold (Millers-
burg) 145.00
Bowl, 8" to 9" d., purple, Fenton
(ILLUS.)........................ 150.00
Bowl, 8" to 9" d., purple (Millers-
burg) ....265.00 to 350.00
Bowl, 8" to 9" d., white (Fenton) ... 150.00
Bowl, 10" d., fluted, green (Millers-
burg) ....190.00 to 225.00
Bowl, 10" d., marigold
(Millersburg).................... 90.00
Bowl, ice cream, 10" d., blue
(Northwood) 300.00
Bowl, ice cream, 10" d., green
(Northwood) 950.00
Bowl, ice cream, 10" d., ice blue
(Northwood)...........650.00 to 750.00
Bowl, ice cream, 10" d., ice green
(Northwood) 800.00

Bowl, ice cream, 10" d., marigold
(Millersburg).................... 335.00
Bowl, ice cream, 10" d., marigold
(Northwood) 160.00
Bowl, ice cream, 10" d., purple
(Northwood) 425.00
Bowl, ice cream, 10" d., white
(Northwood) 385.00
Bowl, 10½" d., ruffled, blue
(Millersburg) 1,325.00
Bowl, 10½" d., ruffled, green
(Millersburg)...........225.00 to 300.00
Bowl, 10½" d., ruffled, marigold
(Millersburg) 225.00
Bowl, 10½" d., ruffled,
purple ....150.00 to 225.00
Bowl, 10½" d., ruffled, vaseline
(Millersburg) 1,900.00
Compote, 5½" d., 5" h., aqua
(Fenton)....................... 325.00
Compote, 5½" d., 5" h., blue
(Fenton)....................... 105.00
Compote, 5½" d., 5" h., marigold
(Fenton)....................... 45.00
Compote, 5½" d., 5" h., purple
(Fenton)....................... 55.00
Compote, 5½" d., 5" h., red
(Fenton) ....695.00 to 1,000.00
Compote, 5½" d., 5" h., vaseline
(Fenton)....................... 160.00
Compote, 5½" d., 5" h., white
(Fenton)....................... 300.00
Compote, blue (Millersburg
Giant)......................... 475.00
Compote, green (Millersburg
Giant) 1,250.00
Compote, marigold (Millersburg
Giant)......................... 500.00
Compote, purple (Millersburg
Giant)......................... 845.00
Ice cream dish, aqua opalescent,
small (Northwood) .....700.00 to 1,100.00
Ice cream dish, blue, small (North-
wood)......................... 85.00
Ice cream dish, green, small 145.00
Ice cream dish, ice blue, small 225.00
Ice cream dish, marigold, small 60.00
Ice cream dish, purple, small....... 50.00
Ice cream dish, white, small 110.00
Ice cream set: large bowl & 4 small
dishes; ice blue, 5 pcs. 950.00
Ice cream set: large bowl & 4 small
dishes; marigold, 5 pcs. 375.00
Ice cream set: large bowl & 6 small
dishes; purple, 7 pcs............ 650.00
Ice cream set: large bowl & 6 small
dishes; purple, 7 pcs. (North-
wood).................500.00 to 645.00
Ice cream set: large bowl & 6 small
dishes; white, 7 pcs. 1,250.00
Plate, 6½" d., purple............. 235.00
Plate, 9" d., blue................. 215.00
Plate, 9" d., marigold 165.00
Plate, 9" d., white 250.00

Plate, chop, 11" d., marigold (North-
wood).......................... 350.00
Plate, chop, 11" d., purple (Millers-
burg) 725.00
Plate, chop, 11" d., purple (North-
wood).......................... 325.00
Sauce dish, blue (North-
wood)....................60.00 to 95.00
Sauce dish, ice green, 6" d. (North-
wood)................170.00 to 200.00
Sauce dish, marigold (Millersburg) .. 65.00
Sauce dish, marigold (Northwood) .. 40.00
Sauce dish, purple (Millers-
burg) ....150.00 to 195.00
Sauce dish, purple (Northwood) 55.00
Sauce dish, white (Northwood) 125.00
Whimsey sauce dish, 5¼" d.,
purple 135.00

PEACOCK AT FOUNTAIN (Northwood)

Peacock at Fountain Spooner

Berry set: master bowl & 6 sauce
dishes; marigold, 7 pcs. 200.00
Berry set: master bowl & 6 sauce
dishes; purple, 7 pcs............. 215.00
Bowl, master berry, ice blue 100.00
Bowl, master berry, marigold 125.00
Bowl, master berry, purple........ 145.00
Bowl, master berry, white 275.00
Bowl, orange, 3-footed, aqua
opalescent 2,000.00
Bowl, orange, 3-footed, blue 280.00
Bowl, orange, 3-footed, green 525.00
Bowl, orange, 3-footed, lavender ... 325.00
Bowl, orange, 3-footed,
marigold ....135.00 to 175.00
Bowl, orange, 3-footed,
purple ....240.00 to 285.00
Butter dish, cov., marigold 135.00
Butter dish, cov., purple ...220.00 to 285.00
Butter dish, cov., white 380.00
Compote, aqua opalescent 2,650.00
Compote, blue 475.00
Compote, ice blue ....795.00 to 1,250.00
Compote, ice green 650.00
Compote, marigold 390.00
Compote, purple 750.00
Compote, white 950.00

Creamer, marigold 62.50
Creamer, purple 95.00
Pitcher, water, blue 365.00
Pitcher, water, green...1,500.00 to 1,750.00
Pitcher, water, ice blue 1,600.00
Pitcher, water, purple 345.00
Pitcher, water, white ......450.00 to 650.00
Punch bowl, marigold 125.00
Punch bowl, purple............... 375.00
Punch bowl & base, ice blue,
2 pcs. 2,350.00
Punch bowl & base, marigold,
2 pcs. 350.00
Punch cup, blue 25.00
Punch cup, ice blue 90.00
Punch cup, marigold 32.50
Punch cup, purple 30.00
Punch cup, white................. 60.00
Punch set: bowl, base & 1 cup;
green, 3 pcs.................2,250.00
Punch set: bowl, base & 6 cups; ice
blue, 8 pcs.................2,650.00
Punch set: bowl, base & 6 cups;
marigold, 8 pcs................. 365.00
Punch set: bowl, base & 6 cups; pur-
ple, 8 pcs..................... 650.00
Punch set: bowl, base & 6 cups;
white, 8 pcs.................2,100.00
Sauce dish, blue 35.00
Sauce dish, ice blue 70.00
Sauce dish, marigold 16.00
Sauce dish, purple 35.00
Sauce dish, teal blue 110.00
Sauce dish, white 65.00
Spooner, blue 125.00
Spooner, marigold................ 55.00
Spooner, purple (ILLUS.) .....75.00 to 85.00
Spooner, white ....90.00 to 135.00
Sugar bowl, cov., marigold........ 75.00
Sugar bowl, cov., purple 85.00
Sugar bowl, cov., white........... 180.00
Table set, marigold, 4 pcs. 395.00
Table set, purple, 4 pcs. 565.00
Tumbler, blue.................... 45.00
Tumbler, green 350.00
Tumbler, ice blue 200.00
Tumbler, marigold ....30.00 to 45.00
Tumbler, purple.................. 50.00
Tumbler, white.................. 185.00
Water set: pitcher & 1 tumbler; ice
blue, 2 pcs....................1,800.00
Water set: pitcher & 5 tumblers;
marigold, 6 pcs.................. 410.00
Water set: pitcher & 6 tumblers;
blue, 7 pcs.................... 500.00
Water set: pitcher & 6 tumblers;
marigold, 7 pcs................. 375.00

PEACOCKS ON FENCE (Northwood Peacocks)

Bowl, 8" to 9" d., aqua
opalescent ....575.00 to 750.00
Bowl, 8" to 9" d., piecrust rim,
blue 425.00

Bowl, 8" to 9" d., piecrust rim,
   green 900.00
Bowl, 8" to 9" d., piecrust rim, ice
   blue 375.00
Bowl, 8" to 9" d., piecrust rim, ice
   green 900.00
Bowl, 8" to 9" d., piecrust rim,
   marigold .... 125.00 to 225.00
Bowl, 8" to 9" d., piecrust rim,
   purple 350.00
Bowl, 8" to 9" d., piecrust rim,
   white .... 275.00 to 375.00

Peacocks on Fence Bowl

Bowl, 8" to 9" d., ruffled rim, blue
   (ILLUS.) 360.00
Bowl, 8" to 9" d., ruffled rim,
   marigold 165.00
Plate, 8" d., blue 420.00
Plate, 9" d., green 550.00
Plate, 9" d., ice blue 785.00
Plate, 9" d., ice green 365.00
Plate, 9" d., lavender 395.00
Plate, 9" d., marigold .... 200.00 to 265.00
Plate, 9" d., purple 425.00
Plate, 9" d., white .... 285.00 to 425.00

PEACOCK STRUTTING (Westmoreland)

Breakfast set: individual size
   creamer & open sugar bowl;
   purple, pr. 90.00
Creamer, cov., individual size,
   purple 40.00
Sugar bowl, cov., individual size,
   purple 50.00

PEACOCK TAIL (Fenton)

Bon bon, 2-handled, blue .... 18.00 to 35.00
Bon bon, 2-handled, green 30.00
Bon bon, 2-handled, marigold 30.00
Bon bon, tricornered, green 70.00
Bon bon, tricornered, marigold 27.00
Bon bon, tricornered, purple 38.00
Bowl, 5" d., ruffled, marigold 22.50
Bowl, 5" d., ruffled, purple 30.00
Bowl, 7" d., purple 33.00

Bowl, 7" d., red 575.00
Bowl, 9" d., blue 47.50
Bowl, 9" d., green 50.00
Bowl, 9" d., crimped, marigold 30.00
Bowl, 9" d., ribbon candy rim,
   purple 55.00
Bowl, ice cream, red 600.00
Compote, 6" d., 5" h., green 60.00
Compote, 6" d., 5" h., marigold 55.00
Compote, 6" d., 5" h., purple 70.00

Peacock Tail Plate

Plate, 6" d., marigold (ILLUS.) 28.00
Plate, 9" d., marigold 350.00

PERFECTION (Millersburg)

Perfection Water Pitcher

Pitcher, water, marigold 2,700.00
Pitcher, water, purple
   (ILLUS.) .... 2,000.00 to 3,000.00
Tumbler, green 500.00
Tumbler, purple 350.00

PERSIAN GARDEN (Dugan)

Berry set: 11" d. fruit bowl &
   4 sauce dishes; peach opalescent,
   5 pcs. 700.00

Berry set: master bowl & 6 sauce
dishes; peach opalescent, 7 pcs. . . 400.00
Bowl, 5" d., white 50.00

Persian Garden Ice Cream Bowl

Bowl, ice cream, 11" d., peach
opalescent (ILLUS.) 900.00
Bowl, ice cream, 11" d., purple 625.00
Bowl, ice cream, 11" d.,
white . . . . 175.00 to 225.00
Fruit bowl (no base), marigold,
11½" d. . . . . .70.00 to 85.00
Fruit bowl (no base), peach opales-
cent, 11½" d. 195.00
Fruit bowl (no base), purple,
11½" d. 135.00
Fruit bowl (no base), white,
11½" d. 225.00
Fruit bowl & base, peach opales-
cent, 2 pcs. 385.00
Fruit bowl & base, purple, 2 pcs. . . . 300.00
Ice cream dish, white, small 55.00
Ice cream set: 11" d. master ice
cream bowl & 4 small dishes;
white, 5 pcs. 550.00
Plate, 6" to 7" d., blue 80.00
Plate, 6" to 7" d., marigold 55.00
Plate, 6" to 7" d., purple . .175.00 to 200.00
Plate, 6" to 7" d., white . . . .85.00 to 125.00
Plate, chop, 11" d.,
purple . . . . .1,400.00 to 2,000.00
Plate, chop, 11" d., white 900.00

PERSIAN MEDALLION (Fenton)
Bon bon, 2-handled, amber 60.00
Bon bon, 2-handled, aqua 100.00
Bon bon, 2-handled, blue 47.50
Bon bon, 2-handled, marigold 40.00
Bon bon, 2-handled, purple 35.00
Bon bon, 2-handled, red 450.00
Bon bon, 2-handled, vaseline 60.00
Bowl, 5" d., green 30.00
Bowl, 5" d., purple 22.50
Bowl, 7" d., green 60.00
Bowl, 7" d., marigold 55.00
Bowl, 8" to 9" d., fluted,
blue . . . . .45.00 to 65.00
Bowl, 8" to 9" d., ribbon candy rim,
green 55.00

Bowl, 8" to 9" d., marigold 45.00
Bowl, 8" to 9" d., ribbon candy rim,
purple 65.00
Bowl, 8" to 9" d., ruffled rim,
red . . . . .900.00 to 1,175.00
Bowl, 10½" d., fluted, blue 70.00
Compote, 6½" d., 6½" h., blue 75.00
Compote, 6½" d., 6½" h., green . . . 45.00
Compote, 6½" d., 6½" h.,
marigold 37.50
Compote, 6½" d., 6½" h., purple . . 110.00
Compote, 6½" d., 6½" h., white . . . 400.00
Hair receiver, blue 70.00
Hair receiver, marigold 50.00
Hair receiver, white 97.00
Plate, 6½" d., blue 65.00
Plate, 6½" d., marigold 45.00
Plate, 6½" d., purple 90.00
Plate, 6½" d., white 75.00
Plate, 9" d., blue 110.00
Plate, 9" d., marigold 125.00
Plate, 9" d., white 395.00
Plate, chop, 10½" d., white 225.00
Rose bowl, blue 65.00
Rose bowl, marigold 50.00
Rose bowl, white 120.00

PETAL & FAN (Dugan)
Berry set: master bowl & 4 sauce
dishes; peach opalescent, 5 pcs. . . 270.00
Bowl, 5" d., peach opalescent 38.00
Bowl, 5" d., purple 30.00
Bowl, 11" d., peach opalescent 110.00
Bowl, 11" d., ruffled, purple 125.00
Plate, 6" d., ribbon candy edge,
purple 225.00

PETALS (Northwood or Dugan)

Petals Compote

Compote, green (ILLUS.) 60.00
Compote, purple 80.00
Plate, 7" d., purple 25.00

PETER RABBIT (Fenton)
Bowl, 8" d., marigold 750.00
Plate, blue 2,000.00
Plate, green .3,000.00
Plate, marigold 1,200.00

PILLOW & SUNBURST (Westmoreland)
Bowl, marigold................... 25.00
Bowl, purple...............30.00 to 48.00
Plate, 8" d., aqua 38.00
Wine, marigold 25.00
Wine, purple.................... 50.00

PINEAPPLE (Sowerby, England)
Bowl, 5" d., marigold............. 30.00
Bowl, 8" d., marigold............. 38.00
Compote, purple 45.00
Creamer, marigold, 4½" h. 28.00
Creamer, purple 38.00
Plate, 8" d., purple.............. 135.00
Rose bowl, marigold............. 45.00
Sugar bowl, aqua 215.00

PINE CONE (Fenton)

Pine Cone Bowl

Bowl, 5" d., blue................. 40.00
Bowl, 5" d., marigold............. 25.00
Bowl, 5" d., purple 35.00
Bowl, 7" d., ruffled, blue (ILLUS.) ... 60.00
Bowl, 7" d., ruffled, green 35.00
Bowl, 7" d., marigold 30.00
Bowl, 7" d., ruffled, purple........ 40.00
Plate, 6½" d., blue............... 55.00
Plate, 6½" d., green ......100.00 to 135.00
Plate, 6½" d., marigold .....40.00 to 60.00
Plate, 6½" d., purple............. 92.50
Plate, 7½" d., blue............... 150.00
Plate, 7½" d., marigold 75.00

PIPE HUMIDOR (Millersburg)
Green 3,375.00
Marigold.....................3,200.00

PLAID (Fenton)
Bowl, 9" d., marigold............. 75.00
Bowl, ice cream, 10" d., blue....... 150.00
Bowl, ice cream, 10" d., green 92.50

PLUME PANELS VASE (Fenton)
Blue 35.00
Marigold 30.00

PODS & POSIES or FOUR FLOWERS (Dugan)
Bowl, 6" d., peach opalescent 37.50
Bowl, 6" d., purple 48.00
Bowl, 8" to 9" d., marigold........ 40.00
Bowl, 8" to 9" d., purple 50.00
Bowl, 10" d., peach opalescent 72.50
Plate, 6" d., green 250.00
Plate, 6" d., purple.............. 145.00
Plate, 6" to 7" d., Basketweave ex-
    terior, peach opalescent 108.00
Plate, 9" d., purple.............. 400.00
Plate, chop, 11" d., peach
    opalescent.................... 425.00
Plate, chop, 11" d., purple 750.00

POINSETTIA (Imperial)
Pitcher, milk, amber.............. 59.00
Pitcher, milk, green 250.00
Pitcher, milk, marigold 65.00
Pitcher, milk, smoky.............. 105.00

POINSETTIA & LATTICE
Bowl, 8" to 9" d., footed, stippled,
    marigold 130.00
Bowl, amethyst 220.00
Bowl, aqua opalescent 3,250.00
Bowl, cobalt blue 250.00
Bowl, marigold................... 71.00

POND LILY
Bon bon, blue.................... 62.50
Bon bon, green 75.00
Bon bon, marigold 60.00

PONY
Bowl, 8" to 9" d., aqua 400.00
Bowl, 8" to 9" d., ice green 250.00
Bowl, 8" to 9" d., marigold........ 57.00
Bowl, 8" to 9" d., purple.......... 140.00
Bowl, 8" to 9" d., vaseline 70.00
Plate, marigold 475.00

POPPY (Millersburg)
Compote, green.................. 525.00
Compote, marigold 350.00
Compote, purple 466.00

POPPY (Northwood)

Poppy Pickle Dish
Pickle dish, blue (ILLUS.) 59.00

Pickle dish, green 45.00
Pickle dish, ice blue 150.00
Pickle dish, marigold 42.50

POPPY SHOW (Northwood)
Bowl, 8" to 9" d., blue 280.00
Bowl, 8" to 9" d., clambroth 190.00
Bowl, 8" to 9" d., ice blue 525.00
Bowl, 8" to 9" d., ice green 600.00
Bowl, 8" to 9" d., marigold 168.00
Bowl, 8" to 9" d., purple 295.00
Bowl, 8" to 9" d., white 238.00
Plate, green 1,200.00
Plate, ice blue 705.00
Plate, ice green 340.00
Plate, marigold 358.00
Plate, white 406.00

POPPY SHOW VASE (Imperial)
Green 495.00
Marigold 304.00
Purple 783.00

PRIMROSE BOWL (Millersburg)
Green 103.00
Marigold 76.00
Purple 88.00

PRINCESS LAMP
Purple, complete 1,000.00
Purple, base only 225.00

PRISMS
Compote, 7¼" d., 2½" h.,
　2-handled, marigold 50.00
Compote, 7¼" d., 2½" h.,
　2-handled, purple 55.00

PULLED LOOP
Vase, 5½" h., marigold 28.00
Vase, 9½" h., peach opalescent 37.00

QUESTION MARKS
Bon bon, footed, marigold, 6" d.,
　3¾" h. 29.00
Bon bon, footed, pastel marigold,
　6" d., 3¾" h. 35.00
Bon bon, footed, peach opalescent,
　6" d., 3¾" h. 62.00
Bon bon, footed, purple, 6" d.,
　3¾" h. 34.00
Bonbon, footed, white, 6" d.,
　3¾" h. 120.00
Plate, dome-footed, Georgia Peach
　exterior, purple 100.00

QUILL (Dugan or Diamond Glass Co.)
Pitcher, water, marigold 2,500.00
Tumbler, marigold 275.00
Tumbler, purple 400.00

RAINDROPS (Dugan)
Bowl, 9" d., dome-footed, peach
　opalescent 63.00
Bowl, 9" d., dome-footed, purple . . . 58.00

RAMBLER ROSE (Dugan)
Pitcher, water, marigold 135.00
Pitcher, water, purple 325.00
Tumbler, blue 34.00
Tumbler, marigold 25.00
Water set: pitcher & 6 tumblers;
　marigold, 7 pcs. 295.00
Water set: pitcher & 6 tumblers;
　purple, 7 pcs. 525.00
Water set: pitcher & 8 tumblers;
　marigold, 9 pcs. 350.00

RANGER
Pitcher, milk, marigold 145.00
Tumbler, marigold 105.00
Whiskey shot glass, marigold 95.00

RASPBERRY (Northwood)

Raspberry Sauceboat

Pitcher, milk, green 195.00
Pitcher, milk, marigold 117.00
Pitcher, milk, purple 169.00
Pitcher, water, green 250.00
Pitcher, water, ice green 2,275.00
Pitcher, water, purple 210.00
Sauceboat, green (ILLUS.) 155.00
Sauceboat, marigold 65.00
Sauceboat, purple 75.00
Tumbler, green 45.00
Tumbler, ice blue 223.00
Tumbler, ice green 875.00
Tumbler, marigold 31.00
Tumbler, purple 41.00
Water set: pitcher & 2 tumblers;
　green, 3 pcs. 290.00
Water set: pitcher & 3 tumblers;
　purple, 4 pcs. 375.00
Water set: pitcher & 4 tumblers;
　green, 5 pcs. 360.00
Water set: pitcher & 6 tumblers;
　marigold, 7 pcs. 350.00

RAYS & RIBBONS (Millersburg)
Banana boat, green 850.00
Bowl, 8" to 9" d., green 56.00
Bowl, 8" to 9" d., purple 75.00
Bowl, 10" d., green 46.00
Bowl, 10" sq., green . . . . . . 250.00 to 275.00
Bowl, 10", ice cream shape, turned-
　down rim, green 135.00

Bowl, 10" d., marigold 54.00
Bowl, 10" d., purple 65.00

RIBBON TIE - See Comet Pattern

RIPPLE
Vase, 9½" h., marigold 20.00
Vase, 11½" h., amber 55.00
Vase, 18¾" h., green 125.00
Vase, 20" h., marigold 75.00
Vase, purple 32.00

RISING SUN
Pitcher, water, pedestal base,
   marigold 675.00
Tumbler, marigold 363.00
Water set: pitcher & 4 tumblers;
   marigold, 5 pcs. 2,950.00

ROBIN (Imperial)
Mug, marigold 51.00
Mug, smoky 65.00
Water set: pitcher & 4 tumblers;
   marigold, 5 pcs. 300.00

ROCOCO VASE
Bowl, 6" d., dome-footed,
   marigold 20.00
Vase, clambroth 40.00
Vase, marigold 43.00
Vase, smoky 62.50

ROSALIND (Millersburg)
Bowl, 8¾" d., ice cream shape,
   green 425.00
Bowl, 10" d., marigold 132.00
Bowl, 10" d., purple 118.00
Compote, 6" d., small, ruffled,
   purple 485.00
Compote, 6" d., tall, ruffled,
   marigold 650.00
Plate, 9" d., green 575.00

ROSE COLUMNS VASE
Amethyst 1,500.00
Amethyst, experimental, factory-
   painted roses decoration 3,250.00
Green 1,156.00
Marigold 1,200.00

ROSE SHOW
Bowl, 9" d., aqua opalescent 517.00
Bowl, 9" d., blue 340.00
Bowl, 9" d., ice blue 363.00
Bowl, 9" d., ice green 500.00
Bowl, 9" d., marigold 132.00
Bowl, 9" d., purple 215.00
Bowl, 9" d., white 258.00
Plate, 9" d., blue (ILLUS.) 458.00
Plate, 9" d., ice blue 1,000.00
Plate, 9" d., ice green 750.00
Plate, 9" d., marigold 369.00
Plate, 9" d., white 400.00

Rose Show Plate

ROUND UP (Dugan)
Bowl, 9" d., low, fluted, blue 70.00
Bowl, 9" d., marigold 50.00
Bowl, 9" d., purple 90.00
Bowl, ice cream shape, peach
   opalescent 165.00
Bowl, ice cream shape, white 165.00
Plate, 9" d., blue 257.00
Plate, 9" d., ruffled, marigold 120.00
Plate, 9" d., white 270.00

RUSTIC VASE
Blue, 9" h. 40.00
Blue, 16" h. 63.00
Blue, 19" h. 165.00
Blue, 21" h. 237.00
Blue, 23½" h.   270.00
Green, 14" h.   43.00
Green, 16" h.   55.00
Marigold, 11" h. 30.00
Marigold, 16¾" h. 45.00
Marigold, 20" h. 188.00
Purple, 9" h. 40.00
Purple, 16" h.   100.00
White, 7" h. 150.00
White, 18" h.   225.00
White, 20" h.   418.00

SAILBOAT (Fenton)

Sailboat Bowl

Bowl, 5" d., aqua 83.00
Bowl, 5" d., ruffled, blue 55.00
Bowl, 5" d., clambroth 40.00
Bowl, 5" d., purple 70.00
Bowl, 5" d., ruffled, red 475.00
Bowl, 6" d., ruffled, green
   (ILLUS.)...................... 95.00
Compote, blue 100.00
Compote, marigold 45.00
Goblet, water, green 225.00
Goblet, water, marigold 185.00
Goblet, water, purple 350.00
Plate, 6" d., blue 350.00
Plate, 6" d., marigold 217.00
Wine, aqua ....195.00 to 225.00
Wine, marigold 30.00
Wine, vaseline 125.00

SCALE BAND
Pitcher, marigold.................. 85.00
Plate, 6" d., flat, marigold 22.00
Water set: pitcher & 6 tumblers;
   marigold, 7 pcs.................. 175.00

SCALES
Bowl, 5" d., purple 25.00
Bowl, 7" d., marigold 22.50
Bowl, 7" d., peach opalescent 45.00
Bowl, 7" w., tricornered, peach
   opalescent.................... 155.00
Bowl, 7" d., purple 40.00
Bowl, 8" to 9" d., aqua opalescent .. 275.00
Bowl, 8" to 9" d., peach
   opalescent 110.00
Plate, 6½" d., marigold 40.00
Plate, 6½" d., peach opalescent 31.00
Plate, 6½" d., purple 40.00

SCOTCH THISTLE COMPOTE
Blue 57.00
Green......................... 57.00
Marigold 55.00
Purple 45.00

SCROLL EMBOSSED
Bowl, 7" d., purple 25.00
Bowl, 8" to 9" d., aqua 60.00
Bowl, 8" to 9" d., marigold........ 35.00
Bowl, 8" to 9" d., purple 38.00
Compote, marigold 28.00
Compote, purple 82.00
Plate, 9" d., green ....55.00 to 75.00
Plate, 9" d., marigold 85.00
Plate, 9" d., purple.............. 142.00

SEACOAST PIN TRAY (Millersburg)
Green......................... 325.00
Marigold 290.00
Purple 330.00

SEAWEED (Millersburg)
Bowl, 6" d., purple 475.00
Bowl, 10" d., ruffled,
   green.................175.00 to 200.00

Bowl, 10" d., ruffled, marigold 210.00
Bowl, 10" d., ruffled,
   purple ....195.00 to 250.00
Plate, 9" d., green 550.00
Plate, 9" d., marigold 500.00

SHELL (Imperial)
Bowl, footed, purple.............. 35.00
Plate, smoky..................... 165.00

SHELL & JEWEL
Creamer, cov., marigold 25.00
Creamer & cov. sugar bowl, green,
   pr............................ 57.00
Sugar bowl, cov., green 28.00
Sugar bowl, cov., marigold........ 20.00

SHELL & SAND
Bowl, 7" d., marigold 30.00
Bowl, 7" d., purple 48.00
Bowl, 8" to 9" d., ruffled, purple ... 57.00
Mug, purple 75.00
Plate, green 80.00

SINGING BIRDS (Northwood)

Singing Birds Water Set

Berry set: master bowl & 6 sauce
   dishes; green, 7 pcs. 335.00
Berry set: master bowl & 6 sauce
   dishes; purple, 7 pcs............. 270.00
Bowl, master berry, purple........ 90.00
Butter dish, cov., marigold 151.00
Butter dish, cov., purple 214.00
Creamer, marigold 49.00
Creamer, purple 77.50
Mug, aqua opalescent 957.00
Mug, blue 114.00
Mug, green.................... 118.00
Mug, ice blue 850.00
Mug, lavender 125.00
Mug, marigold 55.00
Mug, stippled, marigold 123.00
Mug, purple 61.00
Mug, purple, w/advertising, "Hotel
   Verdome" 133.00
Pitcher, green 275.00
Pitcher, marigold................. 220.00

Pitcher, purple 275.00
Sauce dish, blue 35.00
Sauce dish, marigold 32.00
Sauce dish, purple 35.00
Spooner, marigold 50.00
Spooner, purple 85.00
Sugar bowl, cov., green 185.00
Sugar bowl, cov., marigold 80.00
Table set, marigold, 4 pcs. 375.00
Table set, purple, 4 pcs. 900.00
Tumbler, green 40.00
Tumbler, marigold 25.00
Water set: pitcher & 3 tumblers;
   green, 4 pcs. 410.00
Water set: pitcher & 4 tumblers;
   marigold, 5 pcs. 375.00
Water set: pitcher & 5 tumblers;
   marigold, 6 pcs. 375.00
Water set: pitcher & 5 tumblers;
   purple, 6 pcs. 708.00
Water set: pitcher & 6 tumblers;
   green, 7 pcs. 590.00
Water set: pitcher & 6 tumblers;
   purple, 7 pcs. (ILLUS.) 728.00

SINGLE FLOWER

Bowl, 9" d., peach opalescent 40.00
Plate, crimped rim, peach
   opalescent 80.00

SIX PETALS (Dugan)

Bowl, 5" d., marigold 20.00
Bowl, 7" w., tricornered, peach
   opalescent 60.00
Bowl, 8" d., purple 63.00
Bowl, 8" d., white 62.50

SKI STAR (Dugan)

Banana bowl, peach opalescent 102.00
Banana bowl, purple 95.00
Basket, peach opalescent 395.00
Berry set: master bowl & 4 sauce
   dishes; peach opalescent, 5 pcs. . . . 210.00
Bowl, 5" d., peach opalescent 35.00
Bowl, 5" d., fluted, peach
   opalescent 65.00
Bowl, 5" d., ruffled, purple 55.00
Bowl, 7" d., ruffled, purple 75.00
Bowl, 8" to 9" d., dome-footed,
   peach opalescent 80.00
Bowl, 8" to 9" d., dome-footed,
   purple 70.00
Bowl, 10" d., peach opalescent 124.00
Bowl, 11" d., peach opalescent 79.00
Bowl, 11" d., purple 190.00
Bowl, tricornered, dome base,
   peach opalescent 105.00
Plate, 8½" d., dome-footed,
   w/handgrip, peach opalescent 181.00
Plate, 8½" d., dome-footed,
   w/handgrip, purple 240.00

SODA GOLD (Imperial)

Basket, marigold, small 22.00

Bowl, 9" d., marigold 48.00
Candlesticks, marigold, 7½" h.,
   pr. 37.00
Candlesticks, smoky, 7½" h., pr. 50.00
Console set: bowl & pr. candle-
   sticks; marigold, 3 pcs. 45.00
Cuspidor, marigold . . . . 45.00 to 60.00
Pitcher, milk, marigold 195.00
Pitcher, water, marigold . . . 125.00 to 160.00
Pitcher, water, smoky 375.00
Tumbler, marigold . . . . 25.00 to 40.00
Tumbler, smoky 62.00
Water set: pitcher & 6 tumblers;
   marigold, 7 pcs. 250.00
Water set: pitcher & 6 tumblers;
   smoky, 7 pcs. 650.00

SOUTACHE (Dugan)

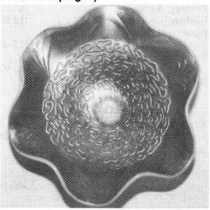

Soutache Bowl

Bowl, 8" d., dome footed, ruffled,
   peach opalescent (ILLUS.) 85.00
Plate, 9½" d., dome-footed, peach
   opalescent 300.00

SPRINGTIME (Northwood)

Springtime Butter Dish

Berry set: master bowl & 6 sauce
   dishes; green, 7 pcs. 280.00

Bowl, 5" d., green	45.00
Bowl, 5" d., marigold	25.00
Bowl, 5" d., purple	34.00
Bowl, master berry, green	150.00
Bowl, master berry, marigold	75.00
Butter dish, cov., green	400.00
Butter dish, cov., marigold (ILLUS.)	195.00
Creamer, marigold	85.00
Creamer, purple	103.00
Pitcher, green	495.00
Pitcher, marigold	438.00
Pitcher, purple	625.00
Spooner, green	150.00
Spooner, marigold	90.00
Spooner, purple	92.00
Sugar bowl, cov., purple	120.00
Table set, marigold, 4 pcs.	500.00 to 535.00
Tumbler, marigold	68.00
Tumbler, purple	110.00
Water set: pitcher & 3 tumblers; green, 4 pcs.	525.00
Water set: pitcher & 4 tumblers; purple, 5 pcs.	865.00
Water set: pitcher & 6 tumblers; marigold, 7 pcs.	690.00

STAG & HOLLY (Fenton)

Bowl, 7" d., spatula-footed, blue	107.00
Bowl, 7" d., spatula-footed, marigold	49.00
Bowl, 7" d., spatula-footed, red	1,250.00
Bowl, 8" to 9" d., spatula-footed, blue	125.00
Bowl, 8" to 9" d., spatula-footed, marigold	69.00
Bowl, 8" to 9" d., spatula-footed, purple	119.00
Bowl, 10" to 11" d., 3-footed, aqua	480.00
Bowl, 10" to 11" d., 3-footed, blue	205.00
Bowl, 10" to 11" d., 3-footed, green	375.00
Bowl, 10" to 11" d., 3-footed, marigold	101.00
Bowl, 10" to 11" d., 3-footed, amberina	838.00
Bowl, 10" to 11" d., 3-footed, vaseline	170.00
Bowl, 11" d., flat, marigold	125.00
Plate, 9" d., marigold	415.00
Plate, chop, 12" d., 3-footed, marigold	555.00
Rose bowl, blue, large	595.00
Rose bowl, marigold, large	185.00

STAR & FILE (Imperial)

Bowl, 5" d., marigold	25.00
Bowl, 7" d., marigold	16.00
Bowl, 8" to 9" d., marigold	35.00
Card tray, 2 turned-up sides, marigold, 6¼" d.	22.50

Celery vase, 2-handled, marigold	27.50
Compote, jelly, clambroth	50.00
Compote, jelly, marigold	55.00
Creamer, marigold	23.00
Creamer & sugar bowl, marigold, pr.	47.50
Pitcher, milk, smoky	40.00
Pitcher, water, marigold	120.00
Plate, 6" d., marigold	36.00
Punch cup, marigold	35.00
Relish tray, 2-handled, marigold	45.00
Rose bowl, marigold	51.00
Sugar bowl, marigold	15.00
Tumbler, marigold	48.00
Water set: pitcher & 6 tumblers; marigold, 7 pcs.	255.00
Wine, marigold	35.00
Wine set: decanter w/stopper & 2 wines; marigold, 3 pcs.	195.00

STAR FISH

Star Fish Compote

Compote, peach opalescent (ILLUS.)	65.00
Compote, purple	45.00

STAR MEDALLION

Bowl, 5" sq., marigold	25.00
Bowl, 7" d., smoky	22.50
Bowl, 8" d., marigold	30.00
Celery vase, footed, clambroth	38.00
Goblet, marigold	35.00
Goblet, smoky	25.00
Pitcher, milk, clambroth	35.00
Pitcher, milk, marigold	37.00
Pitcher, milk, smoky	67.00
Plate, 9" to 10" d., marigold	35.00
Punch cup, marigold	15.00
Rose bowl, marigold	35.00
Sherbet, stemmed, marigold	25.00
Tumbler, marigold	30.00
Tumbler, tall, tankard form, marigold	35.00

STAR OF DAVID (Imperial)

Bowl, 8" to 9" d., collared base, green	55.00
Bowl, 8" to 9" d., collared base, marigold	50.00

Bowl, 8" to 9" d., collared base,
  purple 59.00
Bowl, 9" d., flat, ruffled, purple 88.00

STAR OF DAVID & BOWS (Northwood)

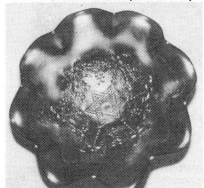

Star of David & Bows Bowl

Bowl, 7" d., dome-footed, marigold
  (ILLUS.)......................... 60.00
Bowl, 7" d., dome-footed, purple ... 51.00
Bowl, 8" to 9" d., dome-footed,
  fluted, purple 63.00

STIPPLED PETALS

Bowl, peach opalescent 95.00
Bowl, white...................... 60.00

STIPPLED RAYS

Stippled Rays Bon Bon

Berry set: master bowl & 4 sauce
  dishes; green, 5 pcs. 150.00
Bon bon, 2-handled, green (ILLUS.).. 34.00
Bon bon, 2-handled, ice green 80.00
Bon bon, 2-handled, purple 25.00
Bon bon, 2-handled, red 260.00
Bowl, 5" d., blue 40.00
Bowl, 5" d., green 30.00
Bowl, 5" d., purple 37.50
Bowl, 5" d., red.................. 221.00
Bowl, 6" d., Amberina 100.00
Bowl, 7" d., blue................. 35.00
Bowl, 7" d., dome-footed, green.... 25.00

Bowl, 7" d., marigold............. 25.00
Bowl, 8" to 9" d., amber 97.50
Bowl, 8" to 9" d., green 50.00
Bowl, 8" to 9" d., ribbon candy rim,
  green 57.50
Bowl, 8" to 9" d., marigold........ 36.00
Bowl, 8" to 9" d., ribbon candy rim,
  marigold 33.00
Bowl, 8" to 9" d., purple 40.00
Bowl, 8" to 9" d., ribbon candy rim,
  purple 42.50
Bowl, 8" to 9" d., teal blue........ 20.00
Bowl, 10" d., green 60.00
Bowl, 10" d., ruffled, marigold 47.50
Bowl, 10" d., purple 55.00
Bowl, 10" d., red slag 450.00
Bowl, 10" d., white........275.00 to 300.00
Bowl, ruffled, red 350.00
Creamer & sugar bowl, marigold,
  pr............................. 38.00
Plate, 6" to 7" d., blue 40.00
Plate, 6" to 7" d., marigold 23.00
Plate, 6" to 7" d., red 375.00
Sugar bowl, open, blue 27.50
Sugar bowl, open, marigold 15.00
Sugar bowl, open, red 320.00

STORK & RUSHES (Dugan or Diamond Glass Works)

Basket, handled, marigold 90.00
Bowl, master berry or fruit,
  marigold 40.00
Creamer, marigold 70.00
Hat shape, marigold 25.00
Mug, aqua base w/marigold
  overlay........................ 450.00
Mug, marigold 25.00
Mug, purple 149.00
Pitcher, water, blue 375.00
Pitcher, water, purple 365.00
Punch bowl & base, marigold,
  2 pcs. 200.00
Punch cup, marigold.............. 14.00
Punch cup, purple 19.00
Punch set: bowl, base & 6 cups;
  marigold, 8 pcs................. 273.00
Sauce dish, marigold 20.00
Sauce dish, purple 27.50
Spooner, marigold................ 63.00
Tumbler, aqua 210.00
Tumbler w/lattice band, blue....... 55.00
Tumbler, marigold................ 17.00
Tumbler, marigold w/pale blue
  base 128.00
Tumbler, purple 35.00
Vase, marigold 22.00
Water set: pitcher & 1 tumbler;
  blue, 2 pcs.................... 500.00
Water set: pitcher & 6 tumblers;
  marigold, 7 pcs................. 400.00

STRAWBERRY (Fenton)

Bon bon, 2-handled, blue 50.00
Bon bon, 2-handled, green 42.50

Bon bon, 2-handled, ice green
　　opalescent 450.00
Bon bon, 2-handled, red 285.00
Bon bon, 2-handled, vaseline
　　w/marigold iridescence 133.00

STRAWBERRY (Millersburg)

Bowl, 5" d., green 55.00
Bowl, 5" d., marigold 20.00
Bowl, 7" d., green 80.00
Bowl, 8" to 9" d., purple 150.00
Bowl, 8" to 9" d., vaseline 450.00
Compote, amber 45.00
Compote, green 175.00
Compote, marigold 120.00
Compote, vaseline 640.00

STRAWBERRY (Northwood)

Strawberry Plate

Berry set: master bowl & 4 sauce
　　dishes; marigold, 5 pcs. 165.00
Bowl, 5" d., marigold 27.50
Bowl, 7" d., green 56.00
Bowl, 7" d., marigold 48.50
Bowl, 8" to 9" d., stippled, blue 185.00
Bowl, 8" to 9" d., stippled, ribbon
　　candy rim, green 150.00
Bowl, 8" to 9" d., marigold 43.00
Bowl, 8" to 9" d., purple 63.00
Plate, 9" d., green 113.00
Plate, 9" d., lavender 135.00
Plate, 9" d., marigold 87.00
Plate, 9" d., purple (ILLUS.) 110.00

STRAWBERRY SCROLL (Fenton)

Pitcher, water, blue 1,965.00
Pitcher, water, marigold 1,300.00
Tumbler, blue 200.00
Tumbler, marigold 168.00

SUNFLOWER BOWL (Northwood)

Bowl, 8" d., footed, blue (ILLUS.) . . . 250.00
Bowl, 8" d., footed, clambroth 75.00
Bowl, 8" d., footed, marigold 34.00
Bowl, 8" d., footed, purple 48.00

Sunflower Bowl

SUNFLOWER PIN TRAY (Millersburg)

Clambroth 195.00
Green 210.00
Marigold 350.00
Purple 233.00

SWAN PASTEL NOVELTIES (Dugan)

Salt dip, ice blue 29.00
Salt dip, ice green 29.00
Salt dip, marigold 112.00
Salt dip, peach opalescent 205.00
Salt dip, pink 30.00
Salt dip, purple 140.00
Salt dip, vaseline 58.00

SWIRL HOBNAIL (Millersburg)

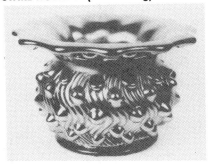

Swirl Hobnail Cuspidor

Cuspidor, marigold 538.00
Cuspidor, purple (ILLUS.) 472.00
Rose bowl, marigold 255.00
Rose bowl, purple 285.00
Vase, green 135.00
Vase, marigold . . . . 220.00 to 250.00
Vase, purple 200.00

SWIRL RIB

Pitcher, tankard, marigold 150.00
Tumbler, marigold . . . . 20.00 to 25.00
Vase, 5½" h., peach opalescent 46.00
Vase, 9½" h., peach opalescent 37.00
Vase, 14½" h., peach opalescent . . . 48.00
Vase, marigold 35.00

TARGET VASE (Fenton)

Vase, 6" h., white 50.00
Vase, 11½" h., peach opalescent . . . 52.00

TEN MUMS (Fenton)

Ten Mums Pitcher

Bowl, 8" to 9" d., ribbon candy
　edge, blue 80.00
Bowl, 8" to 9" d., ribbon candy
　edge, green 120.00
Bowl, 10" d., ruffled, blue 135.00
Bowl, 10" d., footed, green 78.00
Bowl, 10" d., footed, marigold 210.00
Bowl, 10" d., ribbon candy edge,
　purple 104.00
Pitcher, water, marigold 375.00
Pitcher, water, white 1,200.00
Tumbler, blue 75.00
Tumbler, marigold 30.00
Tumbler, white 210.00
Water set: pitcher & 5 tumblers;
　blue, 6 pcs. (ILLUS. of pitcher
　only) 2,900.00
Water set: pitcher & 6 tumblers;
　marigold, 7 pcs 850.00

THIN RIB VASE

6" h., bud, green 45.00
7½" h., ice green (Northwood) 80.00
8" h., aqua 60.00
9" h., aqua opalescent 90.00
9" h., blue 45.00
9" h., green 25.00
9½" h., aqua 30.00
9½" h., aqua opalescent 28.00
11" h., aqua opalescent 110.00
11" h., red 155.00
12" h., aqua 50.00
12" h., white 110.00
13" h., ice blue 125.00

THISTLE

Banana boat, amber 170.00
Banana boat, blue (ILLUS.) 162.00
Banana boat, green 185.00

Thistle Banana Boat

Banana boat, marigold . . . . 100.00 to 150.00
Banana boat, purple . . . . . . 165.00 to 200.00
Bowl, 8" to 9" d., ribbon candy
　edge, blue 50.00
Bowl, 8" to 9" d., flared, green 45.00
Bowl, 8" to 9" d., ribbon candy
　edge, green 40.00
Bowl, 8" to 9" d., ribbon candy
　edge, marigold 37.00
Bowl, 8" to 9" d., ribbon candy
　edge, purple 39.00
Plate, 9" d., green . . . . 800.00 to 1,000.00
Plate, 9" d., purple 1,167.00
Plate, marigold 1,600.00

THISTLE & THORN (Sowerby's, England)

Bowl, 5" to 6" d., footed,
　marigold 52.00
Bowl, 9" d., footed, marigold 35.00
Creamer, marigold 29.00
Creamer & open sugar bowl, mari-
　gold, pr. 60.00
Plate, 9" d., 4-footed, ruffled, scal-
　loped rim, marigold 42.00
Plate, 3-footed, marigold 90.00
Sugar bowl, footed, marigold,
　5¼" h. 29.00

THREE FRUITS (Northwood)

Three Fruits Plate

Bowl, 8½" d., piecrust rim,
　purple 84.00

Bowl, 9" d., dome-footed, basketweave & grapevine exterior,
green 75.00
Bowl, 9" d., dome-footed, basketweave & grapevine exterior, ice
green 750.00
Bowl, 9" d., dome-footed, basketweave & grapevine exterior,
marigold 75.00
Bowl, 9" d., dome-footed, basketweave & grapevine exterior,
purple 200.00
Bowl, 9" d., dome-footed, basketweave & grapevine exterior,
white 230.00
Bowl, 9" d., spatula-footed, aqua
opalescent...................... 484.00
Bowl, 9" d., spatula-footed, blue ... 110.00
Bowl, 9" d., spatula-footed, ruffled,
green 68.00
Bowl, 9" d., spatula-footed, ice
green 385.00
Bowl, 9" d., spatula-footed,
marigold 49.00
Bowl, 9" d., spatula-footed, pastel
marigold .... 40.00 to 60.00
Bowl, 9" d., spatula-footed, purple.. 65.00
Bowl, 9" d., spatula-footed, white .. 250.00
Plate, 9" d., aqua opalescent 1,300.00
Plate, 9" d., stippled, aqua
opalescent 1,000.00
Plate, 9" d., stippled, blue
(ILLUS.)........................ 260.00
Plate, 9" d., green 114.00
Plate, 9" d., stippled, lavender 250.00
Plate, 9" d., marigold 96.00
Plate, 9" d., stippled, marigold 104.00
Plate, 9" d., purple............... 105.00
Plate, 9" d., stippled, purple 170.00
Plate, 9½" w., 12-sided, clambroth
(Fenton) 60.00
Plate, 9½" w., 12-sided, blue
(Fenton)....................... 105.00
Plate, 9½" w., 12-sided, green
(Fenton) 100.00
Plate, 9½" w., 12-sided, marigold
(Fenton) 102.00
Plate, 9½" w., 12-sided, purple
(Fenton) 105.00
Plate, stippled, teal blue 900.00

TIGER LILY (Imperial)

Pitcher, water, green 155.00
Pitcher, water, marigold 100.00
Tumbler, aqua 204.00
Tumbler, blue.................... 87.50
Tumbler, green 35.00
Tumbler, marigold................. 23.00
Tumbler, purple.................. 50.00
Water set: pitcher & 4 tumblers;
marigold, 5 pcs.................. 225.00
Water set: pitcher & 5 tumblers;
green, 6 pcs. (ILLUS. of three
pieces) 325.00

Tiger Lily Pitcher & Tumblers

Water set: pitcher & 6 tumblers;
clambroth, 7 pcs................. 395.00
Water set: pitcher & 6 tumblers;
purple, 7 pcs. 900.00

TORNADO VASE (Northwood)

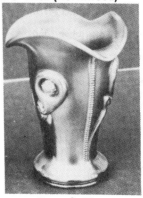

Tornado Vase

Green............................ 184.00
Marigold (ILLUS.).................. 150.00
Purple 194.00

TOWN PUMP NOVELTY (Northwood)

Northwood Town Pump

Marigold . . . . .1,000.00 to 1,300.00
Purple (ILLUS.) 635.00

TREE TRUNK VASE (Northwood)
7" h., ice green 145.00
8" h., green 31.00
9" h., aqua 95.00
9" h., aqua opalescent. 275.00
9" h., green 60.00
9" h., purple. 35.00
9" h., white 110.00
10" h., aqua 125.00
10" h., aqua opalescent. 300.00
10" h., ice blue 168.00
10" h., ice green 170.00
10" h., marigold 24.00
10" h., purple. 35.00
11½" h., green 100.00
12" h., green 35.00
12" h., ice blue 175.00
12" h., 5" d., ice green 350.00
13½" h., blue. 85.00
13½" h., green 50.00
15" h., purple, w/elephant
    foot. . . . . .325.00 to 375.00
18" h., green 550.00
18" h., purple . . . . .350.00 to 385.00

TROUT & FLY (Millersburg)

Trout & Fly Bowl

Bowl, ice cream, green 382.00
Bowl, ice cream, lavender 950.00
Bowl, ice cream, marigold 250.00
Bowl, ice cream, purple 463.00
Bowl, ruffled, green 380.00
Bowl, ruffled, lavender 750.00
Bowl, ruffled, marigold 345.00
Bowl, ruffled, marigold, satin
    finish . . . . .175.00 to 250.00
Bowl, ruffled, purple (ILLUS.) 406.00
Bowl, square, marigold 550.00
Bowl, square, purple 467.00

TWINS or HORSESHOE CURVE (Imperial)
Bowl, 6" d., green 16.00
Bowl, 6" d., marigold. 17.50
Fruit bowl, marigold. 50.00

Fruit bowl & base, marigold,
    2 pcs. 68.00

TWO FLOWERS (Fenton)

Two Flowers Bowl

Bon bon, stemmed, blue 87.00
Bowl, 6" d., footed, aqua 155.00
Bowl, 6" d., footed, marigold. 27.50
Bowl, 6" d., footed, vaseline 140.00
Bowl, 7" to 8" d., footed, blue. 55.00
Bowl, 7" to 8" d., footed,
    marigold 34.00
Bowl, 7" to 8" d., footed, fluted,
    purple 45.00
Bowl, 7" to 8" d., footed, red
    (ILLUS.) 2,700.00
Bowl, 10" d., footed, scalloped rim,
    blue 61.00
Bowl, 10" d., footed, scalloped rim,
    green 67.00
Bowl, 10" d., footed, scalloped rim,
    marigold 39.00
Bowl, 10" d., footed, scalloped rim,
    purple 72.50
Bowl, 10" d., footed, aqua 237.00
Bowl, 10" d., footed, vaseline 200.00
Bowl, 11½" d., footed, blue. 125.00
Plate, 9" d., footed, marigold 340.00
Plate, chop, 11½" d., 3-footed,
    marigold 350.00
Plate, chop, 13" d., 3-footed,
    marigold 475.00
Rose bowl, 3-footed, blue 129.00
Rose bowl, 3-footed, marigold. 98.00
Rose bowl, 3-footed, purple 263.00

TWO FRUITS
Bon bon, divided, blue. 85.00
Bon bon, divided, green 135.00
Bon bon, divided, marigold 45.00

VICTORIAN
Bowl, 11" d., purple 220.00

VINEYARD
Pitcher, water, marigold 102.00
Tumbler, marigold. 18.00

Tumbler, purple................... 45.00
Water set: pitcher & 4 tumblers;
purple, 5 pcs.................... 405.00
Water set: pitcher & 6 tumblers;
marigold, 7 pcs................ 246.00

VINTAGE

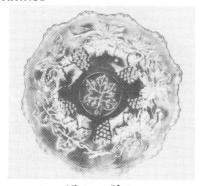

Vintage Plate

Berry set: master bowl & 5 sauce
dishes; green, 6 pcs. (Fenton) 110.00
Bon bon, 2-handled, blue (Fenton) .. 60.00
Bon bon, 2-handled, green
(Fenton)...................... 38.00
Bon bon, 2-handled, purple
(Fenton)...................... 27.00
Bowl, 6" d., blue (Fenton).......... 32.50
Bowl, 6" d., green (Fenton) 35.00
Bowl, 6" d., purple (Fenton)........ 40.00
Bowl, 7" d., fluted, green (Fenton).. 32.50
Bowl, 7" d., fluted, purple
(Fenton)...................... 30.00
Bowl, 7" d., purple (Millersburg).... 60.00
Bowl, 8" to 9" d., footed, blue
(Fenton)...................... 41.00
Bowl, 8" to 9" d., green (Fenton) ... 54.00
Bowl, 8" to 9" d., marigold
(Fenton)...................... 34.00
Bowl, 8" to 9" d., footed, purple
(Fenton)...................... 40.00
Bowl, 9" d., red (Fenton)........... 850.00
Bowl, 10" d., Hobnail exterior, mari-
gold (Millersburg) 375.00
Bowl, 10" d., ruffled, purple........ 50.00
Bowl, ice cream, 10" d., red
(Fenton)...................... 688.00
Bowl, ice cream, 11" d., blue
(Fenton)...................... 190.00
Bowl, ice cream, 11" d., peach
opalescent.................... 650.00
Compote, 7" d., blue (Fenton) 45.00
Compote, 7" d., fluted, green
(Fenton)...................... 38.50
Compote, 7" d., marigold (Fenton) .. 37.00
Compote, 7" d., purple (Fenton) 44.00
Epergne, blue (Fenton) 118.00
Epergne, green (Fenton) 142.00
Epergne, purple, small............ 40.00
Epergne, purple (Fenton).......... 130.00
Fernery, footed, blue (Fenton)...... 49.00

Fernery, footed, green (Fenton) 52.00
Fernery, footed, marigold (Fenton).. 44.00
Fernery, footed, purple (Fenton).... 60.00
Fernery, footed, red
(Fenton)...............275.00 to 350.00
Nut dish, footed, blue, 6" d.
(Fenton)...................... 49.00
Nut dish, footed, green, 6" d.
(Fenton)...................... 47.00
Nut dish, footed, marigold, 6" d.
(Fenton)...................... 48.00
Nut dish, footed, purple, 6" d.
(Fenton)...................... 60.00
Nut dish, footed, red 430.00
Nut dish, footed, white 95.00
Plate, 5" d., blue................. 73.00
Plate, 6" d., green 90.00
Plate, 6" d., purple 50.00
Plate, 7" d., blue, Fenton (ILLUS.)... 75.00
Plate, 7" d., green (Fenton) 98.00
Plate, 7" d., marigold (Fenton) 87.50
Plate, 7" d., purple (Fenton)........ 110.00
Plate, 8" d., blue................. 110.00
Powder jar, cov., marigold
(Fenton)...................... 57.00
Powder jar, cov., purple (Fenton) ... 110.00
Sandwich tray, handled, marigold .. 23.00
Sandwich tray, handled, purple..... 30.00
Sauce dish, marigold (Fenton) 20.00
Wine, marigold (Fenton) 18.00
Wine, purple (Fenton) 30.00

VINTAGE BAND

Mug, marigold 23.00
Pitcher, water, marigold 170.00
Tumbler, marigold................ 500.00

WAFFLE BLOCK

Basket w/tall handle, clambroth,
10" h....................40.00 to 65.00
Basket w/tall handle, marigold,
10" h......................... 33.00
Basket w/tall handle, turquoise,
10" h......................... 100.00
Compote, clambroth 135.00
Creamer, clambroth 28.00
Pitcher, water, marigold 125.00
Punch bowl & base, clambroth...... 165.00
Punch cup, marigold.............. 16.00
Punch set: bowl, base & 5 cups;
marigold, 7 pcs................ 115.00
Punch set: bowl, base & 6 cups;
marigold, 8 pcs................ 125.00
Sugar bowl, clambroth 25.00
Sugar bowl, marigold............. 30.00
Tumbler, marigold................ 150.00

WATERLILY (Fenton)

Bon bon, blue, 7½" d............. 75.00
Bon bon, marigold, 7½" d......... 25.00
Bowl, 6" d., aqua 130.00
Bowl, 6" d., ruffled, aqua 85.00
Bowl, 6" d., blue 27.00
Bowl, 6" d., green 58.00

Bowl, 6" d., footed, marigold....... 20.00
Bowl, 6" d., footed, red............ 500.00
Bowl, 6" d., vaseline w/marigold
  overlay........................ 84.00
Bowl, 10" d., footed, fluted, blue ... 100.00
Bowl, 10" d., footed, marigold..... 42.00
Tumbler, marigold................ 45.00

WATERLILY & CATTAILS

Waterlily & Cattails Pitcher

Banana boat, blue ....150.00 to 185.00
Banana boat, marigold 140.00
Bon bon, 2-handled, marigold,
  large............................ 43.00
Bowl, 5" d., marigold.............. 32.00
Dish, 3 turned up sides, marigold,
  6" d. 29.00
Pitcher, water, marigold (ILLUS.).... 543.00
Plate, 6" d., marigold............. 70.00
Sauce dish, marigold 17.50
Sauce dish, footed, vaseline w/mari-
  gold overlay 75.00
Spooner, marigold................. 50.00
Tumbler, marigold................. 23.00
Water set: pitcher & 6 tumblers;
  marigold, 7 pcs................. 725.00
Whimsey, marigold 45.00

WHIRLING LEAVES BOWL (Millersburg)

Green, 9" d...................... 75.00
Marigold, 9" d. 63.00
Purple, 9" d...................... 78.00
Green, 9½" w., tricornered 145.00
Marigold, 9½" w., tricornered...... 132.00
Purple, 9½" w., tricornered 175.00
Vaseline, 9½" w., tricornered 650.00
Green, 10" d..................... 88.00
Purple, 10" d.................... 76.00

WHITE OAK TUMBLERS

Tumbler, marigold................. 153.00

WIDE PANEL

Bowl, 8" to 9" d., marigold........ 19.00
Bowl, 12" d., marigold............. 45.00
Epergne, 4-lily, green............. 592.00
Epergne, 4-lily, marigold 550.00

Goblet, red...................... 100.00
Plate, 8" d., marigold 30.00
Plate, chop, 14" d., marigold 60.00
Rose bowl, clambroth............. 12.00
Salt dip, marigold 40.00
Vase, 9½" h., red................ 140.00
Vase, 13" h., ice blue 45.00
Vase, 18½" h., green 125.00

WILD ROSE

Wild Rose Syrup Pitcher

Bowl, 7" d., 3-footed, open heart
  rim, green (Northwood).......... 44.00
Bowl, 7" d., 3-footed, open heart
  rim, marigold (Northwood) 34.00
Bowl, 7" d., 3-footed, open heart
  rim, purple (Northwood) 58.00
Bowl, 8" to 9" d., marigold
  (Northwood) 35.00
Candy dish, open edge, blue,
  5¾" d. 70.00
Lamp, w/original burner & etched
  chimney shade, marigold, small
  (Millersburg) 1,250.00
Lamp, w/original burner & etched
  chimney shade, purple (Millers-
  burg) 500.00
Syrup pitcher, marigold (ILLUS.) 550.00

WILD STRAWBERRY (Northwood)

Bowl, 6" d., green 55.00
Bowl, 6" d., purple 40.00
Bowl, 10" d., ice green............1,325.00
Bowl, 10" d., marigold............. 87.00
Bowl, 10" d., purple 100.00
Plate, 6" to 7" d., w/handgrip,
  green 135.00
Plate, 6" to 7" d., w/handgrip,
  marigold 76.00
Plate, 6" to 7" d., w/handgrip,
  purple 102.00

WINDFLOWER

Bowl, 8" to 9" d., blue............. 42.00
Bowl, 8" to 9" d., marigold........ 26.00

Bowl, 8" to 9" d., purple 39.00
Plate, 9" d., blue 132.00
Plate, 9" d., marigold 54.00
Sauceboat, marigold 36.00
Tumbler, marigold 220.00

WINDMILL or WINDMILL MEDALLION (Imperial)

Windmill Tumbler

Bowl, 7" d., green 45.00
Bowl, 7" d., marigold 37.50
Bowl, 7" d., purple 43.00
Bowl, 8" to 9" d., rufffled,
  marigold 95.00
Bowl, 8" to 9" d., ruffled, purple . . . 42.50
Bowl, 8" to 9" d., ruffled, vaseline . . 70.00
Bowl, 9" d., ribbon candy edge, milk
  white w/marigold overlay 145.00
Dresser tray, oval, marigold 40.00
Dresser tray, oval, purple 47.50
Pickle dish, green 22.50
Pickle dish, marigold 32.00
Pickle dish, purple 45.00
Pitcher, milk, purple 275.00
Pitcher, milk, smoky 132.00
Pitcher, water, marigold 90.00
Plate, 8" d., marigold 20.00
Sauce dish, clambroth 30.00
Sauce dish, purple 24.00
Tumbler, green 38.00
Tumbler, marigold (ILLUS.) 25.00
Tumbler, purple 90.00
Water set: pitcher & 1 tumbler;
  green, 2 pcs. 150.00
Water set: pitcher & 2 tumblers;
  purple, 3 pcs. 1,200.00
Water set: pitcher & 6 tumblers;
  marigold, 7 pcs. 225.00

WINDMILL & MUMS - See Chrysanthemum Pattern

WINE & ROSES

Pitcher, water, marigold . . . 285.00 to 425.00
Water set: pitcher & 6 tumblers;
  marigold, 7 pcs. 362.00
Wine, blue 55.00
Wine, marigold 32.00

Wine set: decanter & 6 wines; mari-
  gold, 7 pcs. . . . . 325.00 to 390.00

WISHBONE (Northwood)

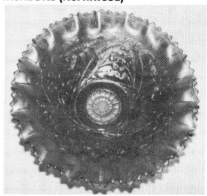

Wishbone Bowl

Bowl, 8" to 9" d., footed,
  blue . . . . 75.00 to 85.00
Bowl, 8" to 9" d., footed, green 85.00
Bowl, 8" to 9" d., footed, ice blue . . 950.00
Bowl, 8" to 9" d., footed,
  ice green 875.00
Bowl, 8" to 9" d., footed, lavender . . 185.00
Bowl, 8" to 9" d., footed, lime
  green 80.00
Bowl, 8" to 9" d., footed,
  marigold 68.00
Bowl, 8" to 9" d., footed, purple 80.00
Bowl, 8" to 9" d., footed, white 510.00
Bowl, 10" d., footed, blue 550.00
Bowl, 10" d., piecrust rim, green . . . 100.00
Bowl, 10" d., piecrust rim, marigold
  (ILLUS.) 75.00
Bowl, 10" d., piecrust rim, purple . . . 148.00
Bowl, 10" d., footed, ruffled,
  purple 124.00
Bowl, 10" d., footed, ruffled,
  white 650.00
Bowl, ice cream shape, footed, ruf-
  fled, green 1,850.00
Epergne, green 265.00
Epergne, marigold 225.00
Epergne, purple 383.00
Epergne, white 950.00
Pitcher, water, purple 1,098.00
Plate, 8½" d., footed, marigold 225.00
Plate, 8½" d., footed, purple 282.00
Plate, 8½" d., footed, tricornered,
  purple 375.00
Plate, chop, 11" d., marigold 552.00
Plate, chop, 11" d., purple 600.00
Tumbler, green 135.00
Tumbler, marigold 100.00
Tumbler, purple 180.00
Water set: pitcher & 2 tumblers;
  purple, 3 pcs. 1,300.00
Water set: pitcher & 6 tumblers;
  green, 7 pcs. 1,600.00

Water set: pitcher & 6 tumblers;
  marigold, 7 pcs. 1,500.00

WISHBONE & SPADES
Banana bowl, ruffled, peach opalescent, 10" l. 175.00
Bowl, 6" d., ruffled, peach
  opalescent...................... 55.00
Bowl, ice cream shape, 9" d., peach
  opalescent...................... 175.00
Plate, 6½" d., purple............. 140.00
Plate, chop, 11" d., purple 750.00
Sauce dish, peach opalescent 75.00
Sauce dish, purple 53.00

WREATH OF ROSES
Bon bon, 2-handled, blue, 8" d. 45.00
Bon bon, 2-handled, green, 8" d. ... 53.00
Bon bon, 2-handled, marigold,
  8" d.......................... 32.00
Bon bon, 2-handled, purple, 8" d.... 90.00
Compote, 6" d., blue 45.00
Compote, 6" d., fluted, green 42.00
Compote, 6" d., marigold 25.00
Compote, 6" d., fluted, purple...... 45.00
Punch bowl, Persian Medallion interior, blue 200.00
Punch bowl, Grape interior,
  purple 145.00
Punch bowl & base, Persian Medallion interior, marigold, 2 pcs. 175.00
Punch bowl & base, purple, 2 pcs. .. 255.00
Punch cup, blue.................. 24.00
Punch cup, Persian Medallion interior, amber 25.00
Punch cup, Persian Medallion interior, blue 35.00
Punch cup, Vintage interior, blue ... 25.00
Punch cup, green 27.50
Punch cup, Persian Medallion interior, green...................... 30.00
Punch cup, marigold............... 12.00
Punch cup, Persian Medallion interior, marigold 16.00
Punch cup, Vintage interior,
  marigold 40.00
Punch cup, purple ....15.00 to 25.00
Punch set: bowl, base & 2 cups;
  green, 4 pcs. 395.00
Punch set: bowl, base & 4 cups; purple, 6 pcs...................... 495.00
Punch set: bowl, base & 5 cups; Persian Medallion interior, marigold,
  7 pcs........................ 285.00
Punch set: bowl, base & 6 cups;
  blue, 8 pcs..................... 695.00
Punch set: bowl, base & 6 cups;
  green, 8 pcs. 468.00
Punch set: bowl, base & 6 cups; Vintage interior, purple, 8 pcs. 400.00
Rose bowl, marigold................ 37.50
Rose bowl, purple 50.00
Whimsey, tricornered, marigold 36.00

WREATHED CHERRY (Dugan)
Berry set: master bowl & 4 sauce
  dishes; marigold, 5 pcs. 153.00
Berry set: master bowl & 6 sauce
  dishes; white, 7 pcs. 345.00
Bowl, 8" d., 3-footed, marigold 35.00
Bowl, berry, 12 x 9" oval,
  marigold 81.00
Bowl, berry, 12 x 9" oval, peach
  opalescent.................... 275.00
Bowl, berry, 12 x 9" oval, purple ... 114.00
Bowl, berry, 12 x 9" oval, white 215.00
Creamer, marigold 55.00
Creamer, purple 65.00
Pitcher, water, purple 275.00
Pitcher, water, white w/red
  cherries 350.00
Sauce dish, oval, marigold 33.00
Sauce dish, oval, peach
  opalescent.................... 60.00
Sauce dish, oval, purple 46.00
Sauce dish, oval, white 47.50
Spooner, marigold................ 55.00
Spooner, purple 60.00
Spooner, white.................. 100.00
Tumbler, marigold 45.00
Tumbler, purple 70.00
Tumbler, white.................. 120.00
Water set: pitcher & 4 tumblers;
  marigold, 5 pcs................. 375.00

ZIG ZAG (Millersburg)
Bowl, 9½" d., marigold........... 130.00
Bowl, 9½" d., green 375.00
Bowl, 10" d., marigold 163.00
Bowl, 10" w., tricornered,
  marigold 275.00
Bowl, 10" w., tricornered, purple ... 443.00
Bowl, ribbon candy edge, purple ... 185.00

ZIPPERED HEART
Berry set: master bowl & 5 sauce
  dishes; purple, 6 pcs............ 225.00
Rose bowl, green 450.00
Sauce dish, purple, 5" d........... 25.00
Vase, 9" h., green...............1,975.00

ZIPPERED LOOP LAMP (Imperial)
Lamp, hand, marigold, 4½" h. 650.00
Lamp, sewing, marigold, medium ... 375.00
Lamp, sewing, smoky, medium 650.00

(End of Carnival Glass Section)

CHOCOLATE

This glass is often called Caramel Slag. It was made by the Indiana Tumbler and Goblet Company of Greentown, Ind., and other glasshouses, beginning at the turn of this century. Various patterns were produced, high-

ly popular among them being Cactus and Leaf Bracket.

Dewey Pattern Mug

Animal covered dish, Dolphin, smooth rim, Greentown, 9" l., 4" h. . . . .$275.00 to 325.00

Barber (or cologne) bottle w/original stopper, Venetian patt., McKee & Brothers 300.00

Berry set: master bowl & 6 sauce dishes; Leaf Bracket patt., Greentown, 7 pcs. 265.00

Bowl, 8¼ x 5¼" oval, Geneva patt., McKee & Brothers 125.00

Bowl, 8¼" d., Cactus patt., Greentown 85.00

Bowl, master berry, 9½" d., Cactus patt., Greentown. 135.00

Butter dish, cov., flat base, Cactus patt., Greentown. 175.00

Butter dish, cov., Dewey patt., Greentown, 4" d. 125.00

Celery tray, Leaf Bracket patt., Greentown, 11" l. . . . . 65.00 to 85.00

Celery vase, Chrysanthemum Leaf patt., 6" h. 675.00

Compote, jelly, 5¼" d., 5" h., Cactus patt., Greentown 135.00

Creamer, Austrian patt., Greentown, large 110.00

Creamer, Chrysanthemum Leaf patt. 395.00

Creamer, cov., Cupid patt., Greentown (professional repair to spout) 295.00

Creamer & cov. sugar bowl, Cactus patt., Greentown, pr. 250.00

Cruet w/original stopper, Cactus patt., Greentown . . . . 155.00 to 175.00

Cruet w/original stopper, Leaf Bracket patt., Greentown 160.00

Lamp, Wild Rose with Festoon patt., McKee 625.00

Mug, Dewey patt., Greentown (ILLUS.) 380.00

Mug, Indoor Drinking Scene, Greentown, 5" h. 150.00

Mug, Swirl patt., attributed to McKee, 4" h. 650.00

Nappy, triangular, Leaf Bracket patt., Greentown. 48.00

Nappy, triangular, Masonic patt., McKee 110.00

Pitcher, water, Cactus patt. 325.00

Pitcher, water, Heron patt., Greentown 395.00

Pitcher, water, Squirrel patt., Greentown 310.00

Plate, 7½" d., Cactus patt., Greentown 70.00

Powder jar, cov., Orange Tree patt., Fenton 385.00

Relish tray, Leaf Bracket patt., Greentown, 7¼ x 4½" oval 50.00

Salt shaker w/original top, Leaf Bracket patt., Greentown (single) 95.00

Salt & pepper shakers w/original tops, Geneva patt., McKee, pr. 150.00

Sauce dish, Dewey patt., Greentown 40.00

Spooner, Chrysanthemum Leaf patt. 395.00

Spooner, 2-handled, Fleur-de-lis patt., Greentown 125.00

Sugar bowl, cov., Leaf Bracket patt., Greentown 75.00

Syrup pitcher w/original top, Chrysanthemum Leaf patt. 950.00

Syrup pitcher w/original top, Cord Drapery patt., Greentown, 6 5/8" h. 175.00

Table set: cov. butter dish, cov. sugar bowl, creamer & spooner; Cactus patt., Greentown, 4 pcs. 380.00

Table set: cov. butter dish, cov. sugar bowl, creamer & spooner; Leaf Bracket patt., Greentown, 4 pcs. 400.00

Toothpick holder, Cactus patt., Greentown 70.00

Toothpick holder, Leaf Bracket patt., Greentown 240.00

Tray, Venetian patt., McKee & Brothers, 6 x 5" 275.00

Tray, Wild Rose with Bowknot patt., McKee, 10½ x 8" 295.00

Tumbler, Cattail & Waterlily patt., Fenton 175.00

Tumbler, Cord Drapery patt., Greentown 215.00

Tumbler, Early Diamond (Icicle) patt., Greentown. 125.00

Tumbler, Sawtooth patt., Greentown 80.00

Tumbler, Wild Rose with Bowknot patt., McKee. 125.00

Vase, 6" h., Scalloped Flange patt., Greentown 60.00

Vase, 6¼" h., Beaded Triangle patt. 180.00

Cactus Pattern Water Pitcher

Water set: pitcher & 6 tumblers;
   Cactus patt., Greentown, 7 pcs.
   (ILLUS. of pitcher) 750.00

CHRYSANTHEMUM SPRIG, BLUE

Blue Chrysanthemum Sprig Creamer

Some collectors of off-white to near yellow Custard Glass have referred to this blue opaque glass in the Chrysanthemum Sprig pattern as "blue custard." This misnomer is being replaced and this scarce glassware, produced by the Northwood Glass Company at the turn of the century, deserves a classification of its own. Also see CUSTARD GLASS.

Berry set, master berry or fruit bowl
   & 6 sauce dishes,
   7 pcs. .... $1,200.00 to 1,400.00
Bowl, master berry or
   fruit .... 375.00 to 415.00
Butter dish, cov. 950.00
Celery vase..................... 950.00
Compote, jelly 390.00
Creamer (ILLUS.) .... 300.00 to 385.00
Cruet w/original stopper ..600.00 to 700.00
Pitcher, water 750.00
Salt shaker w/original top (single) .. 185.00
Sauce dish .... 110.00 to 150.00

Spooner 215.00
Sugar bowl, cov. 325.00
Table set, cov. sugar bowl, creamer
   & spooner, 3 pcs. 1,300.00
Table set, cov. butter dish, cov.
   sugar bowl, creamer & spooner,
   4 pcs. 1,750.00
Toothpick holder 325.00
Tumbler 175.00
Water set, pitcher & 6 tumblers,
   7 pcs. ....1,200.00 to 1,400.00

CORALENE

Coralene Tumbler

Coralene is a method of decorating glass, usually Satin glass, with the use of a beaded-type decoration customarily applied to the glass with the use of enamels, which were melted. Coralene decoration has been faked with the use of glue.

Tumbler, yellow coralene seaweed
   on shaded blue satin, white lining, 2¾" d., 3¾" h. (ILLUS.) $265.00
Vase, 5 1/8" h., 4" d., yellow coralene stars at diamond intersections on shaded blue mother-
   of-pearl Diamond Quilted patt.
   satin 450.00
Vase, 5¼" h., coralene seaweed on
   cranberry, gold trim 225.00

Coralene Vase

Vase, 5½" h., coralene florals &
leaves on yellow mother-of-pearl
Diamond Quilted patt. satin,
white lining (ILLUS.) 365.00

Vase, 6" h., stick-type, yellow coralene seaweed on shaded aqua
satin, signed Thomas Webb 345.00

Vase, 6 1/8" h., 5" w., flattened
oval, yellow coralene wheat on
shaded pink satin, creamy white
lining 435.00

Vase, 6¼" h., 3 1/8" d., yellow
coralene on shaded white to gold-
en yellow mother-of-pearl Snowflake patt. satin, gold trim, white
lining 425.00

Vase, 6½" h., blue coralene florals
on pink shaded to yellow satin ... 145.00

Vase, 6¾" h., 3½ x 5½" flattened
oval, coralene wheat on shaded
deep pink to white satin, white
lining 495.00

Vase, 8" h., 5" d., yellow coralene
seaweed on pink, white & green
rainbow Stripe patt. satin, off-
white lining.................... 495.00

Vase, 8" h., footed, ribbed, multicolored coralene florals & leaves
on translucent purple 165.00

Vase, 11" h., coralene seaweed on
cased lime green glossy finish.... 275.00

Condiment set, salt & pepper shakers & mustard on original glass
stand 475.00

Creamer, pink band decor 160.00

Creamer & cov. sugar bowl, pink
band decor, pr. 250.00

Pickle castor, w/original silverplate
footed frame & cover 295.00

Pitcher, water, 8½" h., 7" d., pink
band decor (ILLUS.) .....200.00 to 295.00

Salt & pepper shakers w/original
tops, pink band decor,
pr....................135.00 to 195.00

Spooner, pink band decor 150.00

Sugar bowl, cov., pink band
decor 185.00

Syrup pitcher w/original top, pink
band decor ....195.00 to 245.00

Table set: cov. butter dish, cov.
sugar bowl, creamer & spooner;
pink band decor, 4 pcs...495.00 to 625.00

Tumbler, blue band decor 47.50

Water set: pitcher & 6 tumblers;
pink band decor, 7 pcs........... 550.00

CRACKLE

Crackle Rose Bowl

*Sometimes called Iced Glass and also
known by a trade name Craquelle, this type
of ware has been made for centuries by sub-
mersing hot glass in cold water, reheating it
and then blowing it to produce a crackled or
frosted effect on the outside of the articles,
or by other methods. The interior of the articles remains smooth. Also see FRY GLASS.*

Basket, vaseline opalescent, hobnail
effect at rim, applied twisted
vaseline handle, 9¼ x 8",
6½" h. $195.00

Ice cream set: tray & 9 dishes; clear
w/gold trim, Sandwich, 10 pcs. ... 185.00

Pitcher, tankard, 7¼" h., 3¾" d.,
cranberry w/applied clear reeded
handle 135.00

Pitcher, water, 7¾" h., 6" d., bulbous, medium blue w/applied
pink handle.................... 165.00

COSMOS

Cosmos Water Pitcher

*A pattern of Cosmos flowers applied to
milk-white glass gives this ware its name. The
flowers are stained with various colors.*

Butter dish, cov., pink band
decor $200.00

Cologne bottle w/original stopper,
pink band decor 95.00

Rose bowl, 8-crimp top, Rubina
Crystal (ruby shaded to clear),
5½" d., 4¾" h. (ILLUS.) 105.00
Rose bowl, iridescent champagne
beige w/enameled fish & coral
overall, 6" d., 5" h. 125.00
Water set: pitcher & 6 tumblers; am-
ber shaded to clear, inscribed,
"Sophia Ohge World's Fair 1893,"
7 pcs. 575.00

CRANBERRY

Cranberry Sugar & Creamer

*Gold was added to glass batches to give
this glass its color on reheating. It has been
made by numerous glasshouses for years and
is currently being reproduced. Both blown
and molded articles were produced. A less expensive type of cranberry was made with the
substitution of copper for gold. Also see
JACK-IN-PULPIT VASES and OPALES-
CENT GLASS.*

Basket, applied clear handle & feet,
ruffled, 5 3/8" d., 5 3/8" h. $150.00
Basket, applied clear twisted thorn
handle, fluted edge, 5 3/8" d.,
6¼" h. 150.00
Bowl, 4¾" d., 5" h., 3 applied clear
reeded scroll feet, applied clear
rigaree garlands & 6 large berry
prunts around top 325.00
Bowl, 5" d., 8¼" h., "arboresque,"
rose bowl shape, 4-crimp top,
fastened in ormolu holder 245.00
Box w/hinged lid, enameled black &
white silhouette-type Colonial girl
carrying basket of flowers,
4 3/8" d., 2 5/8" h. 145.00
Box w/hinged lid, enameled white
geometric designs, 4½" d.,
3½" h. 110.00
Box w/hinged lid, ormolu feet, rings
at sides, large spray of white
florals w/yellow centers & small
blue florals on lid, white florals
around base, 5" d., 5" h. 325.00
Celery vase, scalloped rim,
enameled birds & flowers decor,
in silverplate holder 165.00
Cookie jar, ribbed, 4 applied ruffled
clear panels & ruffled vaseline

collar, silverplate rim, lid & bail
handle, 8" h. to top of handle 540.00
Creamer, applied clear handle &
feet, "sanded" gold leaves outlined in white, small white
enameled florals, "sanded" gold
band around top of mouth, 3" d.,
3¾" h. 118.00
Creamer & open sugar bowl, lightly
ribbed, fluted top, applied shell
feet, pr. (ILLUS.) 160.00
Cruet w/original clear cut faceted
stopper, applied clear handle, bulbous, lacy engraved gold geomet-
ric band, 3¾" d., 7 1/8" h. 125.00
Cruet w/clear ball stopper, applied
clear handle, slightly paneled effect, enameled white daisies
w/blue centers & small blue
forget-me-nots w/green leaves
decor, 3¼" d., 8" h. 145.00
Cruet w/original clear flattened
stopper, applied clear collared
foot & handle, engraved lacy
grasses & leaves, 3½" d.,
10½" h. 135.00
Cup & saucer, demitasse, clear han-
dle, gilt near-Eastern decor 75.00
Decanter w/clear faceted stopper,
applied clear handle, melon-
ribbed interior, 7¾" h. 195.00
Dresser set: ring tree, 2 cov. boxes,
pin dish & tray; lacy gold decor &
gold trim, 5 pcs. 295.00
Finger bowl, Inverted Thumbprint
patt., 4¾" d., 2½" h. 85.00
Finger bowl, blown, Hobnail
patt. 85.00
Jar, cov., 4 applied clear berry
prunts & ball finial on lid, 3¾" d.,
5¼" h. 110.00
Lemonade set: pitcher & 4 tumblers;
applied reeded handles, 5 pcs. . . . 285.00
Liqueur mug, applied clear handle,
enameled blue & white florals &
blue & green leaves decor,
1 3/8" d., 1¾" h. 28.00
Liqueur set: decanter w/clear ball
stopper, 6 mugs & 8½" d. tray;
applied clear handles, enameled
blue & white florals & scrolls &
blue forget-me-nots on cruet &
mugs, plain tray, 8 pcs. (3 mugs
w/hairlines) 225.00
Pin dish, enameled white daisies
w/yellow centers & other small
white florals, in footed ormolu
holder, 3¾" d., 3" h. 85.00
Pitcher, 10" h., bulbous w/long
neck, applied amber handle,
enameled floral & leaves decor . . . 310.00
Rose bowl, melon-ribbed interior,
3½" h. 125.00
Rose bowl, egg-shaped, applied

clear swags of berries & scroll feet, berry pontil, 4¾" h. 255.00

Salt dip, applied row vaseline shell trim, in footed silverplate holder, 2¾" d., 1½" h. 90.00

Salt dip, in silverplate holder w/lion's mask & claw feet, 3½" d., 1½" h. 75.00

Salt dip, ribbed, applied clear petal rigaree below rim, in silverplate holder, 3¼" d., 2" h. 85.00

Sugar shaker w/original top, Venetian Diamond patt. . . . . . . 90.00 to 140.00

Sweetmeat dish, fluted, applied clear shell trim, in silverplate basket holder, 5" d., 5¾" h. 110.00

Sweetmeat dish, scalloped rim, threaded body, in silverplate basket holder, 5 5/8" d., 6¼" h. 88.00

Cranberry Toothpick Holder

Toothpick holder, applied clear base, Inverted Thumbprint patt., 3½" h. (ILLUS.) 50.00

Tumbler, Inverted Thumbprint patt. w/enameled white daisies, blue forget-me-nots & white lily-of-the-valley decor, 2¼" d., 4" h. 35.00

Cranberry Tumbler

Tumbler, plain (ILLUS.) 28.00

Vases, 2¼" h., 2 5/8" d., ball-shaped w/collared top, sanded gold florals w/enameled blue centers outlined in white & dainty white florals decor, pr. 110.00

Vase, 4½" h., 4 5/8" d., bulbous rose bowl shape w/waisted neck

& flaring scalloped rim, applied clear neckband w/three pendant tassels, enameled florals & green leaves decor, gold trim 175.00

Vase, 6¾" h., bulbous w/long neck & square top, Inverted Thumbprint patt. 170.00

Vase, 8½" h., 4 5/8" d., applied clear ruffle around top & clear wafer foot 158.00

Vases, 9 3/8" h., 3¾" d., enameled white daisies & leaves decor, pr. 225.00

Cranberry Vase

Vase, 12" h., footed, interior ribs, enameled florals & foliage decor (ILLUS.) 160.00

Vase, 12 1/8" h., 4 5/8" d., trumpet-shaped w/applied clear foot & top edging, Swirl patt. 145.00

Water set: pitcher & 4 tumblers; enameled decor, 5 pcs. 195.00

CROWN MILANO

This glass, produced by Mt. Washington Glass Company late last century, is opal glass decorated by painting and enameling. It appears identical to a ware termed Albertine, also made by Mt. Washington.

Bowl, 9" d., melon-ribbed, h.p. roses on patterned white, ornate silverplate rim, signed $450.00

Box, cov., brick-red scrolls & florals on off-white shiny finish, signed, 6" d., 2¾" h. 810.00

Cookie jar, lush pink & creamy ivory roses w/leaves outlined in raised gold on pale greenish ground, silverplate rim, cover signed "M.W." & bail handle, 7" widest d., 6" h. 885.00

Cookie jar, raised gold thistles decor on ivory patterned ground, gold-washed silverplate rim, cover & bail handle, 6" h. . . . . . .800.00 to 1,100.00

Cookie jar, melon-ribbed, 18 randomly placed sprays of roses, tulips, daisies, etc. & gold embelishments on shiny white ground w/hint of pink at creases of ribs, silverplate rim, cover signed "M.W." & bail handle, 7" d., 8½" h. 875.00

Cookie jar, autumn-colored oak branch, leaves & acorns on Burmese-colored ground, original paper label, silverplate rim, cover & bail handle, overall 9" h. 885.00

Cookie jar, melon-ribbed, h.p. blackberry branch w/autumn leaves, branches & white blossoms & colorful berries on pale pinkish mauve, silverplate rim, cover & bail handle, unsigned 735.00

Creamer, squat body w/angled ribbed handle, elongated flaring spout, yellow & gilt scrolls on off-white ground w/shadow flowers, signed, 4¼" h. 495.00

Creamer & cov. sugar bowl, squat form w/molded feet, burnished h.p. blossoms & leaves on shiny white ground, rim w/burnished gold finish signed "M.W. Pat. Appld. For" in lid of sugar bowl, pr. 750.00

Pitcher, 8½" h., jug-type w/applied rope-twist handle, gold spider mums decor on white ground, signed & numbered. 700.00

Powder jar, cov., squat bulbous form w/ribbed base, enameled gilt ribboned bouquets & random blossoms on shiny ivory, 3" h. 485.00

Sweetmeat jar, alternating diagonal panels of salmon & creamy ivory w/raised gold florals, signed "M.W." in lid, 4" h. 495.00

Sweetmeat jar w/ornate hinged silverplate lid, pastel roses, shasta daisies & other florals & heavy gold decor, signed "M.W." in lid . . 550.00

Syrup jug w/original ornate collar & lid, melon-ribbed, bouquets of full-blown roses, buds & green leaves & rust & blue daisies, all outlined in heavy gold on overall tan shadow flower ground, signed . . . . .950.00 to 1,250.00

Vase, 7" h., stick-type w/bulbous base, maidenhair fern decor on creamy ivory ground, gold trim, signed 400.00

Vase, 10" h., thorn handles, multicolored pansies & raised gold

scrolls on creamy ground, signed 750.00

Vase, 10½" h., applied handles, thorny branches laden w/full-blown roses & 6 raised gold roses on creamy shadow flower ground 745.00

Vase, 13" h., stick-type w/bulbous base, 3 cherubs frolicking on white tableau 2,000.00

Vase with Guba Ducks

Vase, stick-type w/bulbous base, ducks (by Frank Guba) & gilt stars & sunrays decor (ILLUS.) 2,800.00

CRUETS

Blown Blue Cruets

We list here a random sampling of the many cruets advertised for sale within the past year. Also see CUSTARD, CUT, OPALESCENT and PATTERN GLASS.

Amber, blown, enameled fuchsia blossoms & leaves decor, applied

amber reeded & twisted handle,
amber ball stopper, 3" d.,
6¾" h. $110.00
Amber & white arabesque designs,
blown, applied amber handle &
pedestal foot, round mouth, original flattened amber stopper,
Stevens & Williams, 3½" d.,
9½" h. 150.00
Blue, blown, enameled florals &
gold leaves decor, original stopper, pr. (ILLUS.) 190.00
Blue opalescent, mold-blown, Herringbone patt., trefoil lip, applied
clear handle, original clear ball
stopper, 3½" d., 7 5/6" h. 110.00
Blue, pressed, Log & Star patt.,
original stopper, large . . . . . 50.00 to 65.00
Canary yellow, pressed, Daisy &
Cube patt., original stopper 78.00
Clear, blown, enameled floral decor, twisted handle, original
stopper 65.00
Cranberry, pressed, Hobnail patt.,
applied clear handle, clear facet-cut stopper, 6½" h. 35.00
Cranberry, mold-blown, Venecia
patt., original stopper 195.00
Emerald green, pressed, Empress
patt., original stopper 295.00
Emerald green, pressed, Shoshone
patt., original stopper 85.00
Green, mold-blown, Ivy Scroll patt.,
w/gold, original clear stopper 95.00
Milk white, mold-blown, Alba patt.,
enameled pink floral decor, original patterned stopper 155.00
Milk white, pressed, Forget-Me-Not
patt., original stopper . . . . . 45.00 to 65.00
Sapphire blue, blown, engraved lacy
designs, gold trim, applied amber
handle, original amber stopper,
6 5/8" h. 135.00
Sapphire blue, blown, squared
slightly bulbous shape w/round
mouth, enameled white lily-of-the-valley decor, applied amber
handle & amber "bubble" stopper,
3 1/8" d., 7¾" h. 110.00
Vaseline, pressed, Optic patt., original stopper 60.00
Vaseline, pressed, Swag with Brackets patt., original stopper 155.00

CUP PLATES

*Produced in numerous patterns for almost
150 years, these little plates were designed to
hold a cup while the tea or coffee was allowed
to cool in a saucer. Cup plates were also made
of ceramics. Where numbers are listed below,*
*they refer to numbers assigned these plates
in the book "American Glass Cup Plates," by
Ruth Webb Lee and James H. Rose. Plates
are of clear glass unless otherwide noted. A
number of cup plates have been reproduced.
Also see CUP PLATES under Ceramics.*

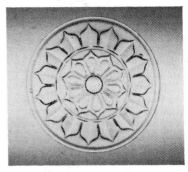

Geometric Cup Plate

L & R No. 24 (minor flakes)	$18.00
L & R No. 65	25.00
L & R No. 89, opalescent opaque . . .	125.00
L & R No. 106-B	35.00
L & R No. 127	125.00
L & R No. 225-A	20.00
L & R No. 269-A	20.00
L & R No. 271	20.00
L & R No. 272	10.00
L & R No. 272, opalescent opaque . .	195.00
L & R No. 273	28.00
L & R No. 280	20.00
L & R No. 312	12.00
L & R No. 324, amethyst	110.00
L & R No. 324	15.00
L & R No. 331	28.00
L & R No. 339	12.00
L & R No. 351	45.00
L & R No. 364	18.00
L & R No. 369 (ILLUS.)	20.00
L & R No. 377	28.00
L & R No. 439-A, deep emerald green	650.00
L & R No. 440-B, blue	55.00
L & R No. 440-B	18.00
L & R No. 445	85.00
L & R No. 457-B	15.00
L & R No. 467-A	35.00
L & R No. 477	9.50
L & R No. 531, yellow-green	85.00
L & R No. 568	54.00
L & R No. 590	25.00
L & R No. 596 . . . . 25.00 to 50.00
L & R No. 610-A, blue	210.00
L & R No. 610-A . . . . 20.00 to 35.00
L & R No. 610-A, opalescent	300.00
L & R No. 612-A . . . . 80.00 to 155.00
L & R No. 617	36.00
L & R No. 640	25.00
L & R No. 641-A	12.00
L & R No. 645-A, opalescent	145.00

L & R No. 662 . . . . .35.00 to 50.00
L & R No. 662, opalescent 110.00
L & R No. 666-A 50.00
L & R No. 670-A 15.00
L & R No. 675-A 20.00
L & R No. 677-A, blue 375.00
L & R No. 680, blue 375.00
L & R No. 828 . . . . .45.00 to 65.00
L & R No. 830 . . . . 80.00

CUSTARD GLASS

This ware takes its name from its color and is a variant of milk-white glass. It was produced largely between 1890 and 1915 by the Northwood Glass Co., Heisey Glass Company, Fenton Art Glass Co., Jefferson Glass Co., and a few others. There are 21 major patterns and a number of minor ones. The prime patterns are considered Argonaut Shell, Chrysanthemum Sprig, Inverted Fan and Feather, Louis XV and Winged Scroll. Most custard glass patterns are enhanced with gold and some have additional enameled decoration or stained highlights. Unless otherwise noted, items in this listing are fully decorated.

ARGONAUT SHELL (Northwood)

Salt & Pepper Shakers & Toothpick Holder

Berry set, master bowl & 6 sauce
   dishes, 7 pcs. $500.00
Bowl, master berry or fruit, 10½" l.,
   5" h. . . . . .150.00 to 195.00
Butter dish, cov. . . . . .170.00 to 245.00
Compote, jelly, 5" d., 5" h. 125.00
Creamer 115.00
Cruet w/original stopper 445.00
Pitcher, water 295.00
Salt & pepper shakers w/original
   tops, pr. (ILLUS. left) 350.00
Sauce dish 55.00
Spooner . . . . .95.00 to 150.00
Sugar bowl, cov. 155.00
Table set, cov. butter dish, cov.
   sugar bowl, creamer & spooner,
   4 pcs. 650.00
Toothpick holder (ILLUS.
   right) . . . . .200.00 to 315.00
Tumbler 60.00
Water set, pitcher & 5 tumblers,
   6 pcs. 725.00

BEADED CIRCLE (Northwood)

Beaded Circle Water Pitcher

Berry set, master berry bowl & 5
   sauce dishes, 6 pcs. 495.00
Bowl, master berry or fruit 185.00
Butter dish, cov. 235.00
Compote, jelly 350.00
Creamer 170.00
Cruet w/original stopper 650.00
Pitcher, water (ILLUS.) 460.00
Salt & pepper shakers w/original
   tops, pr. 255.00
Sauce dish 55.00
Spooner . . . . .80.00 to 95.00
Sugar bowl, cov. 165.00
Tumbler 75.00
Water set, pitcher & 4 tumblers,
   5 pcs. 850.00

BEADED SWAG (Heisey)

Beaded Swag Goblet & Wine

Goblet 52.50
Goblet, souvenir (ILLUS. left) 80.00
Pickle dish (or tray) 250.00
Sauce dish, souvenir 35.00
Wine, w/advertising (ILLUS. right) . . 75.00
Wine, souvenir 60.00

CARNELIAN - See Everglades Pattern

CHERRY & SCALE or FENTONIA (Fenton)

Cherry & Scale Spooner & Sugar Bowl

Berry set, master bowl & 6 sauce
  dishes, 7 pcs. 325.00
Butter dish, cov. 225.00
Creamer 110.00
Pitcher, water 325.00
Spooner (ILLUS. left) 90.00
Sugar bowl, cov. (ILLUS. right) 125.00
Tumbler 48.00
Water set, pitcher & 6 tumblers,
  7 pcs. 600.00

CHRYSANTHEMUM SPRIG (Northwood)

Chrysanthemum Sprig Berry Set

Berry set, master bowl & 6 sauce
  dishes, 7 pcs. (ILLUS.) 550.00
Bowl, master berry or fruit,
  10½" oval 160.00
Bowl, master berry or fruit,
  10½" oval (undecorated) 135.00
Butter dish, cov. . . . . 195.00 to 250.00
Celery vase . . . . 525.00 to 650.00
Compote, jelly . . . . 90.00 to 110.00
Compote, jelly (undecorated) 40.00
Condiment set, tray, cruet w/origi-
  nal stopper & salt & pepper shak-
  ers w/original tops, 4 pcs. 900.00
Condiment tray 575.00
Creamer 100.00
Cruet w/original stopper . . 300.00 to 385.00
Pin tray 20.00
Pitcher, water 360.00
Salt & pepper shakers w/original
  tops, pr. 230.00
Sauce dish 50.00
Spooner 95.00
Sugar bowl, cov. 200.00
Sugar bowl, cov. (undecorated) 110.00
Table set, cov. sugar bowl, creamer
  & spooner, 3 pcs. 375.00
Table set, 4 pcs. . . . . 500.00 to 675.00

Toothpick holder 235.00
Tumbler 50.00
Water set, pitcher & 4 tumblers,
  5 pcs. 565.00

DIAMOND WITH PEG (Jefferson)

Diamond with Peg Berry Set

Berry set, master bowl & 6 sauce
  dishes, 7 pcs. (ILLUS. of part) 600.00
Bowl, master berry or fruit 225.00
Butter dish, cov. 200.00
Creamer 75.00
Creamer, souvenir 40.00
Mug, souvenir 45.00
Napkin ring, souvenir 145.00
Pitcher, tankard, 7½" h. 125.00
Pitcher, water, tankard 375.00
Punch cup 60.00
Salt & pepper shakers w/original
  tops, souvenir, pr. 90.00
Sauce dish 35.00
Sauce dish, souvenir 32.00
Spooner 95.00
Sugar bowl, cov. 165.00
Sugar bowl, cov., souvenir 105.00
Sugar bowl, open 95.00
Toothpick holder 95.00
Tumbler 42.50
Tumbler, souvenir 38.00
Vase, 6" h., souvenir 50.00
Vase, 8" h. 85.00
Water set, pitcher & 6 tumblers,
  7 pcs. 480.00
Whiskey shot glass, souvenir 45.00
Wine 47.50

EVERGLADES or CARNELIAN (Northwood)

Everglades Tumbler

Berry set, master bowl & 6 sauce
  dishes, 7 pcs. 585.00
Bowl, master berry or fruit, footed
  compote 195.00
Butter dish, cov. 370.00
Compote, jelly 350.00
Creamer 135.00
Cruet w/original stopper 750.00

Pitcher, water 650.00
Salt shaker w/original top (single) .. 150.00
Salt & pepper shakers w/original
  tops, pr........................ 450.00
Sauce dish........................ 65.00
Spooner 135.00
Sugar bowl, cov. 150.00
Tumbler (ILLUS.)................. 105.00

FAN or NORTHWOOD FAN

Northwood Fan Water Set

Berry set, master bowl & 6 sauce
  dishes, 7 pcs................... 450.00
Bowl, master berry or fruit........ 180.00
Butter dish, cov. 215.00
Creamer 95.00
Ice cream set, master bowl & 6 in-
  dividual ice cream dishes,
  7 pcs.......................... 500.00
Pitcher, water ....255.00 to 285.00
Sauce dish........................ 55.00
Spooner 60.00
Sugar bowl, cov. 95.00
Table set, cov. butter dish, cov.
  sugar bowl & spooner,
  3 pcs..................350.00 to 450.00
Table set, 4 pcs. ....550.00 to 700.00
Tumbler 50.00
Water set, pitcher & 6 tumblers,
  7 pcs. (ILLUS. of part)........... 650.00

FENTONIA - See Cherry & Scale Pattern

FLUTED SCROLLS
Bowl, master berry or fruit,
  footed 145.00
Creamer 50.00
Cruet w/original stopper........... 185.00
Cruet w/replaced stopper 125.00
Pitcher, water, footed 250.00
Salt & pepper shakers w/original
  tops, pr........................ 95.00
Sauce dish........................ 42.50
Sugar bowl, cov. 135.00
Spooner 50.00
Tumbler 37.50
Water set, pitcher & 6 tumblers,
  7 pcs. 475.00

**FLUTED SCROLLS WITH FLOWER BAND - See
Jackson Pattern**

GENEVA (Northwood)

Geneva Cruet

Banana boat, 4-footed, 11" oval 140.00
Berry set, oval master bowl & 6
  sauce dishes, 7 pcs............. 335.00
Bowl, master berry or fruit, 8½"
  oval, 4-footed ....85.00 to 125.00
Bowl, master berry or fruit, 8½" d.,
  3-footed.................90.00 to 120.00
Butter dish, cov. 120.00
Compote, jelly 92.50
Creamer 75.00
Cruet w/original stopper (ILLUS.) .. 250.00
Pitcher, water 200.00
Salt & pepper shakers w/original
  tops, pr........................ 135.00
Sauce dish, oval 32.50
Sauce dish, round 35.00
Spooner 70.00
Sugar bowl, cov. 125.00
Syrup pitcher w/original top 250.00
Table set, 4 pcs. 395.00
Toothpick holder ....135.00 to 175.00
Tumbler 45.00

GEORGIA GEM or LITTLE GEM (Tarentum)

Georgia Gem Butter Dish

Berry set, master bowl & 6 sauce
  dishes, 7 pcs................... 275.00
Bowl, master berry or fruit........ 87.50
Bowl, master berry or fruit (undecorated) 70.00

Butter dish, cov. (ILLUS.)	175.00
Butter dish, cov. (undecorated)	100.00
Celery vase	160.00
Creamer	40.00
Creamer & open sugar bowl, breakfast size, pr.	125.00
Creamer & open sugar bowl, breakfast size (undecorated), pr.	72.00
Cruet w/original stopper	250.00
Hair receiver, souvenir	55.00
Pitcher, water	310.00
Pitcher, water (undecorated)	200.00
Powder jar, cov.	45.00
Salt & pepper shakers w/original tops, pr.	75.00
Sauce dish	35.00
Spooner	55.00
Spooner, souvenir	60.00
Sugar bowl, cov.	80.00
Sugar bowl, open, breakfast size, souvenir	42.50
Table set, 4 pcs.	375.00
Toothpick holder	65.00
Toothpick holder, souvenir	40.00
Tumbler	48.00
Water set, pitcher & 4 tumblers, 5 pcs.	435.00

GRAPE & CABLE - See Northwood Grape Pattern

GRAPE & GOTHIC ARCHES (Northwood)

Grape & Gothic Arches Master Berry Bowl

Berry set, master bowl & 6 sauce dishes, 7 pcs.	475.00
Bowl, master berry or fruit (ILLUS.)	175.00
Butter dish, cov.	200.00
Creamer	90.00
Goblet	50.00
Pitcher, water	285.00
Sauce dish	37.50
Spooner	70.00 to 85.00
Sugar bowl, cov.	110.00
Tumbler	50.00 to 65.00
Vase, 10" h. ("favor" vase made from goblet mold)	60.00
Vase, ruffled hat shape	60.00 to 85.00
Water set, pitcher & 6 tumblers, 7 pcs.	695.00

GRAPE & THUMBPRINT - See Northwood Grape Pattern

INTAGLIO (Northwood)

Intaglio Fruit Compote

Berry set, 9" d. footed compote & 6 sauce dishes, 7 pcs.	495.00
Bowl, fruit, 7½" d., footed compote	210.00
Bowl, fruit, 9" d., footed compote (ILLUS.)	375.00
Butter dish, cov.	225.00
Compote, jelly	100.00
Creamer	85.00 to 110.00
Cruet w/original stopper	300.00 to 340.00
Pitcher, water	325.00
Salt & pepper shakers w/original tops, pr.	235.00
Sauce dish	55.00
Spooner	65.00
Sugar bowl, cov.	105.00
Table set, 4 pcs.	550.00
Tumbler	45.00
Water set, pitcher & 4 tumblers, 5 pcs.	550.00

INVERTED FAN & FEATHER (Northwood)

Inverted Fan & Feather Pattern

Berry set, master bowl & 6 sauce dishes, 7 pcs.	565.00
Bowl, master berry or fruit, 10" d., 5½" h., 4-footed	210.00
Butter dish, cov.	275.00 to 365.00
Compote, jelly	350.00
Creamer	125.00
Cruet w/original stopper	630.00
Pitcher, water	435.00
Punch cup	210.00
Salt & pepper shakers w/original tops, pr.	485.00
Sauce dish	45.00 to 65.00
Spooner (ILLUS. right)	110.00

Sugar bowl, cov. (ILLUS. left) 175.00
Table set, cov. butter dish, creamer
    & spooner, 3 pcs. 695.00
Toothpick holder . . . . .500.00 to 550.00
Tumbler 75.00
Water set, pitcher & 6 tumblers,
    7 pcs. 750.00

IVORINA VERDE - See Winged Scroll Pattern

JACKSON or FLUTED SCROLLS WITH FLOWER BAND (Northwood)

Jackson Water Set

Salt shaker w/original top, undeco-
    rated (single) 45.00
Salt & pepper shakers w/original
    tops, pr. 150.00
Tumbler 35.00
Water set, 5 pcs. (ILLUS. of part) . . . 435.00

LITTLE GEM - See Georgia Gem Pattern

LOUIS XV (Northwood)

Louis XV Salt & Pepper Shakers & Cruet

Berry set, master bowl & 5 sauce
    dishes, 6 pcs. . . . . .280.00 to 395.00
Bowl, berry or fruit, 10 x 7¾"
    oval 145.00
Butter dish, cov. . . . . .145.00 to 175.00
Creamer 90.00
Cruet w/original stopper (ILLUS.
    right) 275.00
Cruet (no stopper) 140.00
Pitcher, water . . . . .150.00 to 225.00
Salt & pepper shakers w/original
    tops, pr. (ILLUS. left) 215.00

Sauce dish, footed, 5" oval 40.00
Spooner 75.00
Sugar bowl, cov. . . . . .85.00 to 110.00
Table set, 4 pcs. 525.00
Tumbler 42.50
Water set, pitcher & 6 tumblers,
    7 pcs. 550.00

MAPLE LEAF (Northwood)

Maple Leaf Sugar Bowl & Creamer

Banana bowl 195.00
Berry set, master bowl & 6 sauce
    dishes, 7 pcs. 800.00
Bowl, master berry or fruit 325.00
Butter dish, cov. 230.00
Compote, jelly 400.00
Creamer (ILLUS. right) 80.00
Cruet w/original stopper 1,100.00
Pitcher, water 350.00
Salt & pepper shakers w/original
    tops, pr. 500.00
Sauce dish 85.00
Spooner 72.50
Sugar bowl, cov. (ILLUS. left) 185.00
Table set, 4 pcs. . . . . .500.00 to 650.00
Toothpick holder 475.00
Tumbler . . . . .70.00 to 95.00
Water set, pitcher & 6 tumblers,
    7 pcs. . . . . .750.00 to 1,200.00

NORTHWOOD FAN - See Fan Pattern

NORTHWOOD GRAPE, GRAPE & CABLE or GRAPE & THUMBPRINT (Northwood)

Grape & Cable Breakfast Set

Banana boat 375.00
Berry set, master bowl & 6 sauce
    dishes, 7 pcs. 300.00
Bowl, 7½" d., ruffled rim . . . .50.00 to 70.00
Bowl, master berry or fruit, 11" d.,
    flat rim, footed 270.00
Butter dish, cov. 225.00
Cologne bottle w/original stopper . . 500.00

Cookie jar, cov., 2-handled 500.00
Creamer 100.00
Creamer & open sugar bowl, break-
   fast size, pr. (ILLUS.) 115.00
Dresser tray ....195.00 to 275.00
Fernery, footed, 7½" d., 4½" h..... 150.00
Hatpin holder.................... 450.00
Humidor, cov.................... 550.00
Nappy, 2-handled 47.50
Pin dish 145.00
Pitcher, water 385.00
Plate, 7" d. 47.00
Plate, 8" w., 6-sided............. 70.00
Plate, 8" d..................... 55.00
Punch bowl & base, 2 pcs. 800.00
Punch cup 40.00
Sauce dish, flat 40.00
Sauce dish, footed 55.00
Spooner........................ 95.00
Sugar bowl, cov................. 125.00
Table set, cov. butter dish, cov.
   sugar bowl & creamer, 3 pcs. 475.00
Tumbler....................... 70.00
Vase, 3½" h. 46.00
Water set, pitcher & 5 tumblers,
   6 pcs......................... 700.00

Creamer, individual size, souvenir .. 45.00
Mug, souvenir 55.00
Salt & pepper shakers w/original
   tops, souvenir, pr. 80.00
Toothpick holder, souvenir 65.00
Tumbler, floral decor, souvenir
   (ILLUS.)...................... 46.50
Vase, 5½" h., souvenir 75.00
Wine, souvenir.................. 50.00

RIBBED DRAPE (Jefferson)

Ribbed Drape Cruet

Butter dish, cov. 265.00
Compote, jelly 180.00
Creamer 110.00
Cruet w/original stopper (ILLUS.) ... 250.00
Salt & pepper shakers w/original
   tops, pr....................... 175.00
Sauce dish...................... 40.00
Spooner........................ 75.00
Sugar bowl, cov. 145.00
Toothpick holder 95.00
Tumbler 75.00

PRAYER RUG

Prayer Rug Nappy

Nappy, 2-handled, ruffled, 6" d.
   (ILLUS.)....................... 55.00
Plate, 7½" d. 12.50
Tumbler 80.00
Vase 50.00

PUNTY BAND (Heisey)

Punty Band Tumbler

RING BAND (Heisey)

Ring Band Celery Vase & Toothpick Holder

Berry set, master bowl & 6 sauce
   dishes, 7 pcs. 275.00
Bowl, master berry or fruit........ 115.00
Butter dish, cov. 170.00
Celery vase (ILLUS. left) 300.00
Compote, jelly ....155.00 to 200.00

Condiment set, condiment tray, jelly
   compote, toothpick holder & salt
   & pepper shakers, 5 pcs.......... 429.00
Condiment tray ....70.00 to 110.00
Creamer ....65.00 to 85.00
Cruet w/original stopper........... 300.00
Mug, souvenir 45.00
Nappy 40.00
Pitcher, water 230.00
Punch cup 60.00
Punch cup, souvenir 26.00
Salt shaker w/original top, undeco-
   rated (single) 38.00
Salt & pepper shakers w/original
   tops, souvenir, pr. 115.00
Sauce dish...................... 42.50
Spooner 100.00
Sugar bowl, cov...........120.00 to 180.00
Syrup pitcher w/original
   top ....200.00 to 300.00
Table set, 4 pcs. 410.00
Toothpick holder, 2½" h. (ILLUS.
   right) ....85.00 to 110.00
Toothpick holder, souvenir 50.00
Tumbler 55.00
Tumbler, souvenir 35.00
Water set, pitcher & 6 tumblers,
   7 pcs......................... 495.00
Whimsey, hat shape (from tumbler
   mold) 295.00

VICTORIA (Tarentum)

Victoria Master Berry Bowl

Berry set, master bowl & 5 sauce
   dishes, 6 pcs.................... 575.00
Bowl, master berry or fruit
   (ILLUS.)........................ 165.00
Butter dish, cov. 285.00
Celery vase..................... 225.00
Creamer 85.00
Pitcher, water 350.00
Sauce dish...................... 50.00
Spooner 85.00
Spooner (undecorated)............. 45.00
Sugar bowl, cov. 165.00
Tumbler 60.00

WINGED SCROLL or IVORINA VERDE (Heisey)

Berry set, master bowl & 4 sauce
   dishes, 5 pcs. (undecorated)...... 200.00

Berry set, master bowl & 6 sauce
   dishes, 7 pcs. 365.00
Bowl, fruit, 8½" d. 170.00
Bowl, master berry, 11" l., boat-
   shaped 100.00
Butter dish, cov. 150.00
Cake stand 325.00
Celery vase..................... 275.00
Cigarette jar.............135.00 to 175.00
Cologne bottle w/original stopper .. 245.00
Creamer 85.00
Creamer (undecorated) 55.00
Cruet w/original stopper........... 225.00
Custard cup..................... 45.00
Dresser tray 150.00
Hair receiver 125.00
Nappy, folded side handle, 6" 58.00
Pitcher, water, 9" h., bulbous 235.00
Pitcher, water, tankard 225.00
Pitcher, water, tankard (undeco-
   rated)........................ 140.00
Powder jar, cov. 80.00
Powder jar, cov., souvenir 55.00

Winged Scroll Pattern

Salt & pepper shakers w/original
   tops, pr. (ILLUS. at sides) 175.00
Sauce dish, 4½" d................. 35.00
Spooner 80.00
Sugar bowl, cov. 185.00
Sugar bowl, cov. (undecorated)..... 95.00
Syrup pitcher w/original top (ILLUS.
   center) 290.00
Table set, cov. butter dish, creamer
   & spooner, 3 pcs. 375.00
Table set, 4 pcs. 500.00
Toothpick holder 95.00
Tumbler 75.00
Vase, bud, 10" h. 95.00
Water set, tankard pitcher & 6 tum-
   blers, 7 pcs. 600.00

(End of Custard Glass Section)

CUT GLASS

Cut glass most eagerly sought by collectors is American glass produced during the so-called Brilliant Period from 1880 to about 1915. Pieces listed below are by type of article in alphabetical order.

BASKETS

Brilliant Period cutting, 8 x 6" ob-
long, overall 8¼" h. $185.00
Fry signed, hobstars & floral cutting,
double-twisted handle, low 350.00
Hobstars, expanding stars &
intaglio-cut florals, double-twisted
handle, 6½" d., 4½" h. 70.00
Hobstars, strawberry diamond, fan
& other cutting, footed, flaring
rim, notched handle, overall
14" h. 1,500.00
Hobstars, strawberry diamond & flo-
ral cutting, notched handle, over-
all 14" h. 375.00
Hunt signed, intaglio-cut sprays of
daisies & leaves above wide band
of St. Louis diamond, 10 x 5",
overall 14" h. 495.00

BOTTLES

Smelling salts, Brilliant Period cutting, ornate sterling silver top,
5½" h. 65.00
Water, Hawkes signed, Brilliant
Period cutting, 7"h. 120.00
Water, Libbey signed, Brilliant Peri-
od cutting, 8½" h. 160.00
Whiskey, intaglio-cut thistle blos-
soms & foliage, sterling silver
stopper 250.00

BOWLS

Harvard Pattern Bowl

Bishop's hat shape, pedestal base,
flat stars, cane, strawberry diamond & other cutting, 12-point
hobstar base, 12" d., 8½" h. 1,750.00
Bishop's hat shape, Tuthill signed,
intaglio-cut Vintage patt. 500.00
Fruit, 2-part, square bowl w/round-
ed corners, Harvard patt. & finecut florals, step-cut stem, matching base, 9½" w., 7¾" h. 375.00
Orange, cane, fan & other cutting,
scalloped & serrated rim, hobstar
base, 9" d., 3¾" h. 140.00
Orange, Libbey signed, Delphos
patt., 11½ x 8¼", 4¾" h. 1,000.00
Ambassador patt. (Russian patt.
w/strawberry diamond button) al-

ternating w/hobstars, base
w/strawberry diamond vesicas &
small hobstars, scalloped & ser-
rated rim, 8" d., 4" h. 300.00
Cetus patt., panels of small cane alternating w/panels of hobstars,
large hobstar base, scalloped
edges w/serrations at hobstar
panels, 9" d., 4" h. 850.00
Clark signed, Prima Donna (Triple
Square) patt., octagonal, dentil
rim, 9¼" w. 395.00
Clusters of (3) hobstars, hobnail &
strawberry diamond separated by
hobstars, hobnail & star, hobstar
center, 9" d., 4 1/8" h. 225.00
Egginton signed, Arabian patt., clus-
ter of hobstars around hexagon
center, scalloped & serrated rim,
9" d., 4" h. 950.00
Fry signed, chain of hobstars & fan,
rayed base, 9" d. 190.00
Harvard patt., 9" d. (ILLUS.) 325.00
Harvard patt. surrounding central
motif of vesicas (4) w/pyramidal
star, large hobstar base, 11¾" d.,
6½" h. 300.00
Hawkes signed, Lace patt.,
7" d. 375.00
Hawkes signed, rosettes, cross-
hatching & hobstar, serrated rim,
8" d. 360.00
Hawkes signed, intaglio-cut straw-
berries, low, 9" d. 250.00
Hawkes signed, comet-type design
w/hobstars, triple mitre cane &
other cutting, scalloped & serrated
rim, 10" d., 4" h. 1,500.00
Hoare signed, fan, hobnail, hobstar,
star & strawberry diamond,
8" d. 250.00
Hoare signed, Newport patt., low,
10" d. 270.00
Hobstars, feathered fan & cross-
hatching, scalloped & serrated
rim, 7¼" d., 3½" h. 225.00
Hobstars (4), crossed bars of cane,
beading & strawberry diamond,
8¾" sq., 2¾" h. 250.00
Hobstars, hobnail, cane, strawberry
diamond & zipper, hobstar center,
11 x 7" oval, 4 7/8" h. 295.00
Hunt signed, Royal patt., low,
9" d. 245.00
Intaglio-cut asters & scrolling, Art
Nouveau sterling silver rim, 24-
point hobstar base 225.00
Libbey signed, panels of engraved
leaf design between vertical
bands of deep ribbing, 8" d. 245.00
Libbey's Stratford patt., cluster of
hobstars around hexagon center,
scalloped & serrated rim, 9" d.,
4" h. 850.00

Maple City Glass Company signed,
hobstars, nailhead diamond, star,
strawberry diamond & fan, 9"
hexagon, 3½" h. 210.00
Meriden's Alhambra (Greek Key)
patt., hobstars & cane, wide Greek
Key border, straight sides, dentil
rim, 8" d., 4" h. 1,000.00
Pairpoint's Silsbee patt., intaglio-cut
florals, 9" d., 4" h. 200.00
Persian patt. (Russian patt. w/hob-
star buttons), 8½" sq. 645.00
Sinclaire signed, Pattern No. 4 and
Engraved, w/Marie border, chain
of hobstars above engraved floral
panels, 24-point hobstar center,
11 7/8" octagon, 2¾" h. 375.00

BOXES

Libbey's Florence Pattern Box

Dresser, Brilliant Period cutting,
hinged lid, 5 x 3¼" oval,
3½" h. 110.00
Dresser, Russian patt. & hobstars on
hinged lid, hobstars, diamond &
stars on sides, 5" sq., 4" h. 295.00
Dresser, strawberry diamond & fan
sides, sterling silver lid w/em-
bossed & engraved cherubs riding
a dolphin, 5½" d., 3½" h. 250.00
Dresser, Pairpoint's Silsbee patt.,
hinged lid, 6" d. 395.00
Dresser, hobstars, pinwheel &
intaglio-cut florals, 7" d., 4" h. . . . 295.00
Dresser, central large Florence hobstar on hinged lid, notched prism
sides, 7½" d. 450.00
Dresser, large hobstar & notched
prism on hinged lid, sides cut
w/hobstars, vertical notched
prism & fan, 8" d., 4¾" h. 700.00
Dresser, kidney-shaped, hobstars,
strawberry diamond & other cut-
ting, 9" l., 4½" w. 225.00
Powder, Art Deco style florals &
leaves, star-cut base, sterling sil-

ver lid engraved w/flowers &
scrolls marked "Alvin," 4½" d.,
2 3/8" h. 125.00
Powder, Libbey's Florence patt.,
hinged lid, 5" d. (ILLUS.) 370.00
Powder, Clark signed, Brilliant Peri-
od cutting on hinged lid & sides,
silverplate fittings, 5¼" d. 235.00
Powder, large hobstar on hinged
lid, Brilliant Period cutting on
sides, 7½" d. 475.00

BUTTER DISHES & TUBS

Cut Glass Butter Dish

Covered dish, Harvard patt. &
florals, dome lid & underplate
(ILLUS.) 375.00
Covered dish, hobstars & other cut-
ting, dome lid & underplate 285.00
Covered dish, Libbey signed, Brilliant Period cutting, dome lid &
8" d. underplate 350.00
Covered dish, Russian patt., dome
lid & underplate 295.00
Tub, hobstars & other cutting,
matching underplate 175.00

BUTTER PATS

Cross-cut Diamond & Fan

Brilliant Period cutting, set
of 8 . . . . 100.00
Cross-cut diamond & fan (ILLUS.) 28.00
Flute-cut sides, 8-point hobstar center w/rayed fans at points,
2½" d., set of 12 in original
box 550.00

Hawkes signed, Brilliant Period
  cutting 35.00
Hobstars, strawberry diamond &
  fan, set of 6 .... 195.00
Nailhead diamond & fans, star center, set of 4 .... 100.00
Russian patt..................... 35.00

CANDLESTICKS & CANDLE HOLDERS

Hobstars & other cutting, teardrop
  stem, 5¾" h., pr. 160.00
Hobstar & cross-cut diamond base,
  notched prism stem, 7½" h., pr... 390.00
Rayed base w/fan cutting between
  points, hobstars, single stars &
  vesica of strawberry diamond,
  teardrop stem, flute-cut candle
  cup, 7½" h., pr. 625.00
Rayed base, faceted knob, cylindrical stem w/teardrop above & below band of hobstars, 9" h., pr. .. 395.00
Hexagonal base, notch-cut stem
  w/large teardrop above faceted
  knob, 9¼" h. (single)........... 110.00
Brilliant Period cutting, teardrop
  stem, 10" h., pr. 210.00
Eight-petal flower & foliage on base,
  tubular stem w/teardrop & 2 large
  8-petal flowers w/hobstar centers,
  nozzle cut in bull's eyes, 4¼"
  base d., 10" h., pr.............. 325.00
Notched flute w/lapidary-cut knob
  at base & top, large teardrop in
  stem, 10" h., pr. 550.00
Pairpoint signed, polished florals &
  foliage, silverplate mounts engraved w/matching decor, 7"
  base d., 11¾" h. (single) 135.00
Pairpoint, hollow stem w/bull's eye
  & mitre cutting, 12" h., pr....... 215.00
Hawkes signed, hollow stem
  w/intaglio-cut florals, 12¼" h.,
  pr............................ 260.00
Pairpoint signed, tapering hollow
  stem w/split ovals motif, in embossed bronze base, 16" h., pr. .. 450.00

CARAFES

Button & Star patt., 8" h. 115.00
Dorflinger signed, Brilliant Period
  cutting 125.00
Elmira Glass Co.'s Pattern No. 33,
  ovoid 175.00
Hawkes signed, Centauri patt., hobstars, strawberry diamond & fan,
  honeycomb neck, star-cut base,
  mushroom-shaped, 6½" d.,
  7" h......................... 195.00
Hawkes signed, Chrysanthemum
  patt......................... 275.00
Hobstars, strawberry diamond &
  prism, mushroom-shaped, 6½" d.,
  7 1/8" h., pr. 250.00
Hobstars, fan, crosshatching & other

cutting, notched prism neck, hobstar base, bulbous, 6" d.,
  8" h.......................... 115.00
Hobstars (3 large & 9 smaller), hobnail, strawberry diamond & fan,
  notched panel- & step-cut neck,
  24-point hobstar base, 6" d.,
  8¼" h........................ 125.00

Brilliant Period Carafe

Pinwheel, hobstars, strawberry diamond & other cutting, flute-cut
  neck, scalloped & serrated rim
  (ILLUS.)...................... 270.00
Pinwheel & star, 7" h. 75.00

CELERY TRAYS & VASES

Tray, Brilliant Period cutting,
  11½ x 5¾".................... 95.00
Tray, Clark signed, Brilliant Period
  cutting, 12 x 4½" 110.00
Tray, Hawkes signed, hobstars &
  other cutting, 10½" l. 140.00
Tray, Hawkes' Centauri patt. 190.00
Tray, Hoare signed, Harvard patt.,
  11¼" l. 135.00
Tray, 2 large 16-point hobstars, 2
  triangles of Russian patt.
  w/starred buttons, beading,
  strawberry diamond & fan,
  10 7/8" l...................... 85.00
Tray, hobstars & other Brilliant Period cutting, 11" l. 165.00
Tray, large central hobstar surrounded by cane, serrated rim,
  11 x 5"....................... 50.00
Tray, hobstars & prism, rolled sides,
  12" l. 125.00
Tray, Libbey's Harvard patt., 11" l.... 110.00
Tray, Libbey's Lovebirds (Wisteria)
  patt.......................... 995.00
Vase, Brilliant Period cutting, pedestal base 165.00
Vase, hobstars, diamond & fan,
  6½" h........................ 185.00
Vase, hobstars & other cutting, scalloped & serrated rim, rayed
  base 250.00

CHAMPAGNES, CORDIALS & WINES

Vaseline Cut to Clear Wine

Champagne, Brilliant Period cutting,
double teardrop stem 35.00
Champagne, Hoare's Monarch patt.,
set of 12 . . . . .1,200.00
Champagne, overall hobnail cutting,
set of 6 . . . . 300.00
Champagne, Libbey signed, hollow
stem 85.00
Champagne, Russian patt. w/starred
buttons, knobbed teardrop stem . . 120.00
Champagne, step-cut bowl, panel-
cut teardrop stem, set of 12 . . . . . . 300.00
Cordial, comet motif, knobbed teardrop stem, 4" h., set of 8 . . . . 275.00
Cordial, Hawkes signed, Adam patt.
variant, set of 6 . . . . 450.00
Cordial, overall hobstars, faceted
knob at center of stem 65.00
Cordial, hobstars & other cutting,
set of 6 . . . . 225.00
Wine, brilliant blue cut to clear,
intaglio-cut roses, clear teardrop
stem w/knob, 8" h. 110.00
Wine, celery green cut to clear, Lib-
bey signed, teardrop stem 150.00
Wine, cranberry cut to clear, fan,
stars & other cutting, clear stem,
6½" h. 55.00
Wine, Dorflinger's Old Colony
patt. 60.00
Wine, green cut to clear, Strawberry
Diamond patt., fluted stem,
4¾" h. 125.00
Wine, Hawkes signed, Brilliant Peri-
od cutting 21.00
Wine, Hoare's Monarch patt. 60.00
Wine, Russian patt. 45.00
Wine, vaseline cut to clear, cane,
star & fan, clear notched stem,
star-cut base, 8½" h. (ILLUS.) 90.00
Wine, Rhine-type, cranberry cut to
clear, block cutting, rayed base,
2¾" d., 6¾" h. 65.00

Wine, Rhine-type, green cut to
clear, Hawkes signed, Hobnail
patt., 6½" h. 150.00

CHEESE DISHES

Russian Pattern Cheese Dish

Brilliant Period cutting & intaglio-cut
florals, dome lid & underplate 375.00
Cluster pattern, 7" h. dome lid &
9½" d. underplate 595.00
Comet motif, hobstar & zipper, 7" d.
dome lid w/faceted ball finial &
9" d. underplate 475.00
Hobstars overall, dome lid & under-
plate, large 295.00
Hobstars, cane, flashed star & fan,
dome lid & underplate 350.00
Hobstars, crosshatching & stars,
7" h. dome lid w/faceted knob &
9" d. underplate 180.00
Hobstars, diamond & fan, dome lid
& underplate 350.00
Hobstars, pinwheel, fan & diamond,
dome lid & underplate 375.00
Pairpoint's Strawberry Diamond
patt., 7½" d. dome lid w/match-
ing finial & 9½" d. underplate 375.00
Russian patt., dome lid w/faceted
knob & underplate w/scalloped &
serrated rim (ILLUS.) 525.00
Russian patt. variant, hobstars &
diamond, dome lid & matching
underplate 325.00

COMPOTES

Brilliant Period cutting, teardrop in
stem, cut base, 6" d., 9¼" h. 265.00
Cane, hobstars & strawberry dia-
mond cutting on bowl & base,
hobstar base, faceted knob in
stem, 7½" d., 5" h. 140.00
Chain of hobstars & strawberry dia-
mond, serrated rim, hobstar base,
8" d., 3½" h. 187.00
Clark signed, Cornflower (Wild
Rose) patt., flashed star base,
7¼" d., 3" h. 245.00
Elmira Glass Company's Pattern
No. 100, chalice form, 8" h. 375.00
Florence stars, fan, strawberry dia-

mond & deep mitre cutting on
bowl & cover, 16-point hobstar
base, notched prism stem, faceted
finial, 6" d., 11" h. 950.00
Hawkes signed, Josephine patt.,
7" d., 7" h. 110.00
Hoare signed, Brilliant Period cut-
ting, step-cut flaring open base,
5" d., 6" h. 195.00
Hobstars & pinwheel, teardrop in
stem, 8¼" d., 2" deep bowl,
7½" h. 250.00
Hobstars & strawberry diamond ves-
icas, teardrop in stem, hobstar
base, 6½" d., 7½" h. 195.00
Hobstars separated by cross-cut vesicas & fan, step-cut stem, 20-point
star-cut base, 9" d., 5" h. 235.00
Hobstars separated by panels of
crosshatching, horizontal step-cut
stem, star-cut base, turned in serrated rim, 9½" d., 6½" h. 600.00
Libbey signed, Lovebirds (Wisteria)
patt., 7" d., 4½" h. 495.00
Pairpoint's Colias patt., intaglio-cut
butterfly in web & florals, 6½" d.,
6" h. 58.00
Prism & chain of hobstars w/bull's
eyes, serrated base, 9¼" h. 215.00
Sinclaire signed, Adam No. 2 (Silver
Thread) patt., engraved floral
panels, 12" d., 2" h. 700.00

CREAMERS & SUGAR BOWLS
Brilliant Period cutting, pedestal
base, pr. 400.00
Florals, birds & other intaglio-cut
motifs, pedestal base, pr. 125.00
Harvard patt. & florals, notched
handles, pr. 75.00
Hawkes signed, Harvard patt.,
large, pr. 145.00
Hoare signed, Brilliant Period cut-
ting, pr. 160.00
Hoare signed, hobstars, strawberry
diamond & fan, pedestal base,
pr. 325.00
Hobstar in diamond field, cane &
other cutting, pedestal base, St.
Louis Diamond handles, scalloped
& serrated rim, pr. 275.00
Intaglio-cut florals & diamond hob-
nail, pedestal base, notched handles, scalloped & serrated rim,
pr. 175.00
Libbey signed, Brilliant Period cut-
ting, large, pr. 165.00
Single stars & hobnail, low pedestal
base, notched handles, pr. 110.00
Star motif overall, notched handles,
small, pr. 75.00

CRUETS
Arcadia patt., triple-notched handle,
faceted stopper, 7" h., pr. 225.00

Brilliant Period cutting, bell-shaped,
flat stopper w/teardrop 135.00
Bull's eye & zipper, original
stopper 60.00
Clark signed, Brilliant Period cut-
ting, faceted stopper, 5½" h. 65.00
Hawkes signed, hobstars & intaglio-
cut strawberries w/vining leaves,
rayed base, original tall faceted
stopper 125.00
Hobstars, pinwheel & other cutting,
lighthouse shape, double-notched
handle, notched neck, original tall
lapidary-cut stopper, 9½" h. 68.00
Hobstars (7) & vesicas around sides,
Harvard patt. & crosshatching at
base, triple-notched handle, tri-
pour lip, original stopper 225.00

Brilliant Period Cruet

Hobstars & strawberry diamond,
triple-notched handle, hobstar
base, tri-pour lip, original stop-
per (ILLUS.) 120.00
Libbey signed, Brilliant Period cut-
ting, faceted stopper, 6½" h.,
pr. 165.00
Libbey signed, chain of hobstars,
original stopper 60.00
Strawberry diamond, fan & cross-
hatching, tri-pour lip, original
stopper, 7" h. 65.00

DECANTERS
Captain's, hobstars overall, stopper
w/teardrop, 5½" d., 7" h. 325.00
Whiskey, Harvard patt. & vesicas of
hobstars & strawberry diamond,
horizontal step-cut neck, step-cut
controlled bubble stopper,
15" h. 275.00
Wine, cross-cut diamond & fan 175.00

Wine, Hawkes signed, Brilliant
Period cutting, 10" h. 135.00
Chain of ovals above & below
columns of beading, step- and
panel-cut notched neck, star-cut
base, hinged Gorham sterling silver top w/swirl design & chain
that hooks into small glass loop
on body, 5¼" d., 9¼" h., pr. 650.00
Cranberry cut to vaseline, cane, fan
& crosshatching, 16" h. 4,200.00
Dorflinger's Parisian patt., bulbous,
long slender neck, original ball
stopper, 13½" h. 225.00
Elite Cut Glass Company's Expand-
ing Star patt., fan, hobstar, star &
strawberry diamond, w/music box
(bottom w/hollowed out base for
insertion of music box that plays
when decanter is raised & tilted),
9¼" h. plus matching ball
stopper 950.00
Green cut to clear, chain of large
cross cuts w/horizontal bands
above & below, panel-cut neck,
matching green cut to clear stopper w/large teardrop, 4½" d.,
11" h. 150.00
Harvard patt., pyramid shape, step-
cut neck, original steeple stopper,
17" h. 275.00
Hoare's Wheat patt., notched han-
dle, original lapidary-cut stopper,
5½" d., 11½" h. 950.00
Hobstars, fan, strawberry diamond,
star & clear tusks, panel-cut neck,
triple honeycomb handle, hobstar
base, original lapidary-cut stop-
per, 6 x 4 3/8" oval, 10" h. 375.00
Libbey signed, Brilliant Period cut-
ting, 8¼" h. 170.00
Straus' Drape patt., hobstars, bead-
ing, strawberry diamond & other
cutting, notched panel-cut neck,
star-cut bottom, lapidary-cut stop-
per, 5" d., 9½" h. 250.00
Tuthill signed, Primrose patt., exaggerated lip, faceted stopper 450.00

DISHES, MISCELLANEOUS

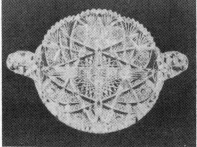

Four-Compartment Candy Dish

Candy, 2-handled, 4-compartment,
hobstars, vesicas & prism,
9¼" l. 135.00
Candy, 2-handled, 4-compartment,
hobstar-centered flower w/mitre-
cut petals in each section,
notched handles w/bull's eye
thumbrests, 12" l. across
handles 165.00
Candy, 2-handled, 4-compartment,
hobstars, splits & other cutting,
12" l. across handles (ILLUS.) 325.00
Elmira Cut Glass Company's Pattern
No. 17, hobstars, cane, strawberry diamond & star, 18-point hob-
star center, 7" d., 1 5/8" h. 125.00
Hawkes signed, Queen's patt.,
6" d. 150.00
Heart-shaped, Harvard patt. overall,
5 7/8 x 5¾", 1½" h. 125.00
Honey, Hawkes signed, chain of
hobstars above strawberry diamond, hobstar center, 3¼" widest
d., 1 5/8" h. 75.00
Ice cream, Brazilian patt. 85.00
Leaf-shaped, Russian patt. w/hob-
star buttons (Persian), 7¼ x 5¼",
1" h. 225.00
Leaf-shaped, hobstars, cane, fan &
other cutting, serrated rim,
13½ x 12" 500.00
Libbey signed, bands of miter cuts
radiating from hobstar center,
double-cut 6-point stars separated
by deep step cuts between bands,
scalloped rim, 6" d., 1½" h. 95.00
Libbey's Prism patt., 6¾" d. 130.00
Nut, Fruit patt., intaglio-cut
peaches, stems & leaves, 4" d.,
1¼" h., set of 6 . . . . 195.00
Nut, Hawkes signed, Brilliant Period
cutting, 7 x 6" 65.00
Relish, Brilliant Period cutting, ped-
estal base, 7" l., 4½" h. 185.00
Relish, Hoare signed, Brilliant Period
cutting, 8 x 5½" 95.00
Relish, Hunt's Royal patt., hobstars
& other cutting around sides, Russian patt. w/hobstar button (Persian) center, 7½ x 3½",
1 3/8" h. 95.00
Relish, Pitkin & Brooks signed, Bril-
liant Period cutting, 11" l. 125.00
Square, Pitkin & Brooks' Rajah patt.,
hobstars, strawberry diamond &
fan, 6 5/8" sq., 1¼" h. 95.00
Three-lobed, hobstars, strawberry
diamond, split zipper & fan, 6" d.,
1 5/8" h. 125.00

FERNERIES

Chain of elongated 8-point hobstars
w/fans between, star-cut bottom,
3-footed, 7½" d., 3 7/8" h. 85.00

Geometric & floral cutting, footed,
7½" d., 4¼" h. 55.00
Harvard patt. overall, 3-footed,
8" d. . . . . .125.00 to 155.00
Harvard patt. on side panels, hob-
stars, strawberry diamond & fan
base, 7 7/8" octagon, 3 7/8" h. 175.00

Triangular Fernery

Intaglio-cut florals & polished
leaves, triangular, 3-footed
(ILLUS.) 120.00
Libbey signed, Brilliant Period cut-
ting, footed, 8" d. 125.00
Pinwheel & other cutting, 3-footed . . 145.00

GOBLETS

Brunswick patt. variant, hobstars &
clear flutes w/horizontal line cutting between, 24-point rayed
base, 6" h. 100.00
Dorflinger's Kalana Lily patt. 60.00
Double Lozenge patt., fan, hobstar
& strawberry diamond 125.00
Hawkes signed, Adam patt. variant,
set of 6 . . . . 450.00
Hawkes signed, Brilliant Period cut-
ting, notched stem, star-cut base,
3" d., 6" h. 35.00
Hoare signed, Pluto patt., chain of
hobstars, beading, fan & straw-
berry diamond, set of 12 . . . . 895.00
Hoare's Croesus patt., 6" h. 325.00
Pinwheel & other cutting, set of 8 . . 600.00
Strawberry diamond & fan, notched
prism stem 75.00

ICE BUCKETS & TUBS

Harvard Pattern Ice Tub

Bucket, Brilliant Period cutting,
large tab handles 325.00
Bucket, checkerboard motif, squares
of hobstars alternating w/squares
of cane separated by deep ribbon
cutting continuing to base & 3
handles, 8" w. across handles,
6" h. 495.00
Bucket, Harvard patt., 8-point hob-
star w/strawberry diamond points
& fans on base, 5 1/8" d., 4½" h.
including 1" tab handles 175.00
Tub, Harvard patt. on sides & base,
tab handles, overall 5½" h.
(ILLUS.) 595.00
Tub, Hawkes signed, fields of small
hobstars & notched prism, 20-
point hobstar base, cut handles,
scalloped & serrated rim, 9½" d.,
6" h., w/matching underplate 600.00
Tub, Straus' Imperial patt., chain of
hobstars & strawberry diamond,
tab handles 245.00

JARS & JARDINIERES

Caviar, Florence Star patt., St. Louis
Diamond stopper 145.00
Cookie, Hawkes signed, Brilliant
Period cutting on cover & base,
9½" h. 175.00
Cookie, Honeycomb patt., sterling
silver cover, 5" d., 6" h. 175.00
Horseradish, Brilliant Period cutting,
matching hollow stopper, 5" h. . . . 45.00
Mustard, Brilliant Period cutting
overall, cover w/lapidary-cut
knob, 2½" d., 4" h. 55.00
Mustard, hobstars & fan, cover
w/hobstar & lapidary-cut knob,
3½" d., 3½" h. 60.00
Mustard, Pineapple & Fan patt.,
hinged silverplate lid & handle . . . 58.00
Mustard, strawberry diamond & fan,
ball-shaped, hinged silverplate lid
& handle 60.00
Pill, feathered pinwheel & cane,
fluted notch-cut neck, rayed base,
hollow stopper w/rayed top &
bull's eye band, 4½" h. 100.00
Powder, Brilliant Period cutting, silverplate cover w/Art Nouveau floral design & monogram, 3½" d.,
3" h. 95.00
Powder, Brilliant Period cutting,
sterling silver cover w/"repousse"
Art Nouveau design, 4" d.,
3" h. 90.00
Powder, Brilliant Period cutting,
sterling silver cover w/"repousse"
florals & foliage, 5½" d.,
3½" h. 175.00
Powder, Brilliant Period cutting,
Alvin sterling silver cover
w/monogram 75.00

Powder, bull's eyes & cross-hatched
vesicas, rayed base, sterling silver
"repousse" cover 115.00
Powder, intaglio-cut butterfly &
florals on hinged cover, bull's eye
sides, 8½" d., 4" h. 335.00
Powder, overall hobstars, sterling
silver cover w/Art Nouveau
design 125.00
Tobacco, chain of hobstars, fan &
bull's eye above step cutting &
strawberry diamond, sterling silver rim & cover, 5½" d.,
7¼" h. 650.00

LAMPS

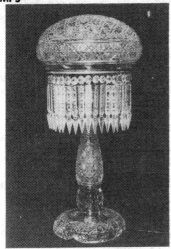

Harvard Pattern Table Lamp

Boudoir, mushroom-shaped shade,
overall florals & foliage, conformingly cut trumpet-shaped base, silver ring w/notch-cut spear prisms,
12" h. 350.00
Boudoir, mushroom-shaped shade,
Thistle patt., silverplate ring
w/prisms, 15" h. 895.00
Table, mushroom-shaped shade,
32-point hobstar center, columns
of large 32-point hobstar rosettes
& 3 small hobstars alternating
w/vesicas of 24-point hobstar
rosettes w/stars above & below,
hobstars in stem & base, silverplate ring w/prisms, 10" d. shade,
17½" h. 2,000.00
Table, mushroom-shaped shade,
Brilliant Period cutting, 2-light,
12" d. shade, 21½" h. 1,500.00
Table, mushroom-shaped shade,
Harvard patt., conforming baluster-shaped stem w/band of
St. Louis Diamond cutting above
scalloped base, silverplate ring
w/notch-cut spear prisms, 24" h.
(ILLUS.) 6,000.00

Table, strawberry-shaped shade,
Harvard patt. & hobstars,
27" h. 2,700.00
Table, strawberry-shaped shade,
Brilliant Period cutting, flared
base, silverplate ring w/notch-cut
spear prisms, 30" h. 1,500.00

MISCELLANEOUS

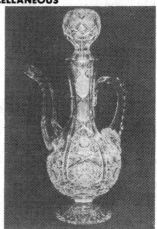

Hawkes Signed Champagne Decanter

Bon bon basket, Brilliant Period cutting, applied twisted handle, over-
all 6½" h. 175.00
Cake plate, Pairpoint signed, Arbu-
tus patt. 175.00
Cake stand, Allen Cut Glass Com-
pany's Lotus patt., 1" h. gallery
cut in chain of strawberry diamond diamonds, honeycomb stem
w/teardrop, leaf-cut foot, 8" d.,
7½" h. 750.00
Cake stand, hobstars, cane & straw-
berry diamond, scalloped & serrated rim, on 32-point hobstar base
w/bulbous notched-prism stem,
12½" d., 9" h., 2 pcs. 3,500.00
Canoe, Harvard patt., 12" l.,
3" h. . . . . .150.00 to 175.00
Canoe, hobstars, fine cut & other
cutting, 12" l. 225.00
Canoe, Pitkin & Brooks' Plaza patt.,
11½" l. 245.00
Centerpiece bowl, Hawkes signed,
panel-cut base w/engraved bands
radiating up & out, oval cartouches (4) w/intaglio-cut scenes
of a bird on a branch, flared rim,
10" d. 250.00
Centerpiece bowl, Hawkes signed,
"gravic" florals & geometric cut-
ting, 12" d. 185.00
Centerpiece bowl, Hawkes signed,
Sheraton patt. 750.00
Centerpiece bowl, Tuthill signed, re-
lief diamond & cross-cut vesicas,

rolled rim w/garlands of intaglio-
cut florals & foliage, large
intaglio-cut flower in center,
12½" d., 6" h. 600.00
Champagne decanter w/original stopper, Hawkes signed, beading, fan,
hobstar & strawberry diamond,
24-point hobstar in base, 15" h.
(ILLUS.) 3,750.00
Cheese & cracker server, hobstar
center surrounded by strawberry
diamond & fan, 10" d. 275.00
Chocolate tankard, hobstars & other
cutting, rayed base, notched handle, 11¾" h..................... 275.00
Coffee pot, cov., Sherwood patt.
variant, 9" wide from spout to
handle, 11" h. 3,500.00
Cube sugar holder, Hawkes signed
Brilliant Period cutting 135.00
Cup & saucer, demitasse, Hawkes
signed, Adam patt. variant....... 300.00
Dresser set: tray, cov. powder box,
cov. hair receiver, cologne bottle
& ring box; Tuthill signed, Wild
Rose patt., 5 pcs. 795.00
Finger bowl, Clark's Baker's Gothic
patt., scalloped rim 85.00
Finger bowl, Hoare's Croesus patt.,
scalloped rim 150.00
Finger bowl & underplate, Star of
David patt., 5" d. bowl &
7 3/8" d. underplate, pr.......... 175.00
Flask, lady's, irregular notched
prism, sterling silver "repousse"
screw-on cap, 2½" w., 4" h. 135.00
Flask, lady's, hobstar & other cutting
within circle of beading, sterling
silver screw-on cap, 2½" w.,
4 1/8" h. 125.00
Flask, lady's, overall Brilliant Period
cutting, sterling silver top
w/beading, 2¼" w., 4¼" h. 150.00
Flask, lady's, lay-down type,
almond-shaped w/bulbous vertical
ribs lower section & block cutting
w/stars at shoulder, sterling silver
"repousse" screw-on cap, 2½" w.,
4¼" h. 110.00
Flask, lady's, serrated ribbing, diamond point & prism, sterling silver "repousse" screw-on cap 135.00
Flask, beading & diamonds, sterling
silver screw-on cap w/applied
beading, monogrammed, 3" w.,
6 1/8" h. 150.00
Flower center, Hoare's Monarch
patt., step-cut neck, scalloped
rim, 3½ x 3" 260.00
Flower center, rayed stars, fan &
single stars, fluted top, 5½" d.,
4¼" h. 225.00
Flower center, hobstars topped
w/rayed stars, 10" d., 8" h. 400.00

Cut Glass Flower Center

Flower center, daisies, butterflies &
mitre-cut foliage, rolled rim,
9 1/8" h. (ILLUS.)............... 880.00
Flower center, fields of cane & crosshatching alternating w/sixteen-
point hobstars, narrow step-cut
neck w/flaring mouth, matching
flared base, 10" d., 15" h........1,600.00
Hair receiver, bull's eye & intaglio-
cut florals w/trailing vines, star-
cut base, sterling silver top w/en-
graved design 100.00
Hair receiver, flute-cutting
w/intaglio-cut florals & vining
leaves on sides, star-cut base, engraved sterling silver cover 95.00
Humidor, hobstars, cross-cut diamond & vertical notched prism,
cover w/large hobstar, 10" h. 475.00
Ice cream set: 13½ x 8½" tray & six
6" d. plates; crossed ellipticals &
hobstars, 7 pcs................. 750.00
Ice cream set: 15 x 10½" tray &
nine 6 1/8" d. dishes; Dorflinger's
Windsor patt., 10 pcs...........1,800.00
Jug, Hawkes signed, Brilliant Period
cutting, 2-pt.................... 365.00
Liqueur set: decanter & 6 long-
stemmed cordials; cranbery cut to
clear, floral & vintage design,
7 pcs. 300.00
Mayonnaise bowl & underplate, hobstars, strawberry diamond, pinwheels & cane, 5¼ x 4" bowl &
7½ x 6½" underplate,
pr.....................90.00 to 150.00
Mayonnaise bowl & underplate,
Maple City Glass Co. signed,
Brilliant Period cutting,
pedestal base, pr............... 290.00
Mug, cobalt blue cut to clear, overall diamond cutting, 4" h......... 150.00
Picture frames, floral-cut panels, 2½
x 4½" opening, overall 4¾ x
6¾", pr. 250.00

Punch ladle, notched prism handle,
silverplate bowl & stem,
11½" l. 145.00
Punch ladle, Brilliant Period cutting,
Pairpoint silverplate bowl,
14" l. 280.00
Rum jug, Pitkin & Brooks' Heart
patt., triple-notched strap
handle 600.00
Sherbet, Egginton signed, Brilliant
Period cutting.................. 32.00
Sherbet, Libbey signed, Pineapple &
Fan patt., 4½" h. 22.00
Sherbet & underplate, Dorflinger's
Kalana Lily patt. 280.00
Sugar shaker, pear-shaped, irregu-
lar notched vertical prism alternating w/star & thumbprint
panels, silverplate top w/beaded
trim.......................... 70.00
Sugar shaker, varied overall notch-
cutting, beaded sterling silver
top 130.00
Tantalus set, Hawkes signed, one
bottle engraved w/full smiling
moon & owl in tree, the other
w/two hens & trees, in silverplate
holder 600.00
Teapot, Sinclaire signed, Brilliant
Period cutting.................. 600.00
Tumble-up (water carafe w/tumbler
lid), green cut to clear, Flutes &
Vines patt., rayed bases, 2 pcs. .. 225.00
Whiskey jug, Tuthill signed, intaglio-
cut thistles 350.00

NAPPIES

Libbey Signed Nappy

Geometric star within a star, cane
cutting in points w/intaglio-cut
florals & foliage between, scalloped & serrated rim 95.00
Hobstars, cane, strawberry diamond
& fan, 2-handled, 11½" across
handles 145.00
Libbey signed, band of relief diamond, star-cut center, single handle, 6" d., 2½" h. 65.00
Libbey signed, Brilliant Period cutting, 7¾" d. (ILLUS.)........... 125.00

Maple City Glass Co. signed ovals
(3) radiating from central 16-point
hobstar on strawberry diamond
field, nailpoint diamond, strawberry diamond & fan, flashed
stars between ovals, 6 1/8" d.,
1" h.......................... 65.00
Pinwheel, hobnail & fan, salesman's
sample, triangular, 2½" w. 75.00
Pinwheels (4) surrounding small central hobstar, serrated rim,
square 55.00
Russian patt. w/cut buttons 85.00
Star of Bethlehem patt., large 65.00

PERFUME & COLOGNE BOTTLES

Colognes, double mitered buttons
separated by raised clear vesicas,
original stopper, 5" h., pr. 285.00
Cologne, Harvard patt., Meriden
sterling silver stopper, 6" h....... 145.00
Colognes, hobstars, vesicas of cane
& other cutting, sterling silver
"repousse" stoppers w/florals &
foliage, 6 3/8" h., pr............ 220.00
Cologne, Maple City Glass Co.
signed, bulbous, checkerboard
motif, original facet-cut stopper .. 195.00
Cologne, Russian patt., original
facet-cut stopper 500.00
Perfume, block & horizontal line cutting, engraved sterling silver
hinged lid w/stopper, 3½" h. 58.00
Perfume, Brilliant Period cutting,
sterling silver hinged lid w/inside
glass stopper, 8" h. 200.00
Perfume, hexagonal, alternating
panels of Harvard patt. & intaglio-
cut florals, faceted stopper, rayed
base, 5¾" h. 130.00
Perfume, double-ended purse-type,
green cut to clear, overall thumbprint cutting, sterling silver
"repousse" lids, w/inside glass
stoppers, 7" l., w/original case ... 275.00
Perfume, lay-down type, diagonal
panel cutting, horizontal ribbing &
cross-cut diamond, lapidary-cut
stopper, 6¼" l. 70.00
Perfume, lay-down type, Russian
patt., sterling silver lid, 10" l. 165.00
Perfume, lay-down type, Russian
patt. overall, Gorham sterling silver screw-on lid w/ornate monogram, 10¾" l. 195.00

PITCHERS

Champagne, Mt. Washington Glass
Co.'s Wheeler patt., cross-cut diamond, fan, star & strawberry diamond, 11¼" h. 395.00
Champagne, Brilliant Period cutting,
Gorham sterling silver rim,
12" h......................... 200.00

Cut Glass Champagne Pitcher

Champagne, hobstars in diamond
fields, beaded vesicas of hobstars
& cane, strawberry diamond &
other cutting, notched handle,
13" h. (ILLUS.) 1,450.00
Cider, Hoare signed, Brilliant Period
cutting, 7½"h 165.00
Cream, tankard, Almy & Thomas
signed, hobstars, fan & checker-
ing, 4½" h..................... 115.00
Milk, chain of hobstars & cane
w/fans between, hobstar base,
applied horizontal step-cut handle, flute-, notch- and ring-cut
neck, 5½" h. 300.00
Milk, hobstars & vertical flute, rayed
base, applied double-notched handle, flute- and notch-cut lip, scalloped & serrated rim, 6" h. 275.00
Tankard, Libbey signed, hobstars,
fan, fields of diamond point &
other cutting, notched handle,
serrated rim, 7½" h. 275.00
Tankard, Bumble Bee patt., 2 groups
of flowers & leaves w/bumble bee
between, blaze border around
base, 24-point hobstar bottom, triple honeycomb handle, 5" d.,
9¼" h. 450.00
Tankard, 16-point hobstars, hobnail,
strawberry diamond & fans, 24-
point hobstar base, triple-notched
handle, 5¼" d., 9 3/8" h...... 275.00
Tankard, Hawkes signed, Harvard
patt., rayed base, double thumbprint handle, 11" h. 315.00
Tankard, Harvard patt., applied
thumbprint handle, 11½" h....... 450.00
Tankard, Russian & Swirl patt.,
notched handle, band of notch
cutting at rim, 4" d., 11½" h.....1,800.00
Tankard, intaglio-cut roses & hob-

stars within bands of cane, cane
pedestal base, applied double-
notched handle, step-cut lip, scalloped & serrated rim, 7" d.,
13" h......................... 800.00
Tankard, Clarks' Winola patt., half-
gal........................... 275.00
Water, Straus' Ducal patt., squatty
w/narrow neck, 6½" base d.,
7¼" h. 350.00
Water, Libbey signed, large sunburst
w/notched rays either side, hobstars & other cutting, rayed base,
double thumbprint handle, 8" h. ... 275.00
Water, Hawkes' Grecian patt., vesica, fan & Russian patt., honeycomb handle, 6" d., 8¾" h. 650.00
Water, hobstars w/bull's eye, strawberry diamond & elongated fan,
9" h.......................... 400.00
Water, Russian patt. w/cut buttons,
9½" h........................ 700.00
Water, Fry signed, Brilliant Period
cutting, 10" h. 185.00
Water, Keystone Cut Glass Co.'s
Rose patt., 10" h. 150.00
Water, pinwheels & other cutting,
notched handle, 10" h. 375.00
Water, Libbey's Senora patt.,
notched handle, 11½" h. 300.00

PLATES

Hawkes "Gravic" Carnation Pattern

6" d., Egginton signed, hobstars &
strawberry diamond, hobstar
center......................... 60.00
6" d., Hawkes' "gravic" Carnation
(ILLUS.)...................... 85.00
6" d., Tuthill signed, Primrose patt.,
intaglio-cut blossoms, buds & foliage, paperweight base 110.00
6½" d., Hawkes signed, Brilliant
Period cutting................. 50.00
7" d., Bergen's Elegance patt., scalloped & serrated rim 90.00
7" d., Hawkes signed, Brilliant Period cutting 85.00

7" d., Hawkes signed, strawberry
diamond & fan border, rayed
base 40.00

7" d., Hoare signed, Hindoo patt.,
chain of hobstars, beading &
fan 125.00

7" d., Libbey signed, Aztec patt.,
cross-cut vesicas, cane & other
cutting 360.00

7" d., Star of David patt. variant,
scalloped & serrated rim 90.00

7 1/8" d., Hawkes signed, chain of
diamonds alternating w/cross-cut
diamond & strawberry diamond
w/fans above & split squares below, star-cut center 55.00

10" d., floral sprays & butterflies ... 125.00

10" hexagon, central hobstar
w/points of strawberry diamond
forming stars 80.00

10¾" d., Hawkes signed, Adam
patt. variant 300.00

12" d., Libbey signed, Brilliant Period cutting 400.00

PUNCH BOWLS

Libbey Signed Punch Bowl

Brilliant Period cutting overall,
matching base, 9" d., 9" h.,
2 pcs. 395.00

Clark signed, Brilliant Period cutting, 10" d. 550.00

Cranberry cut to clear, Hawkes' Brazilian patt., fan, star & strawberry
diamond, matching base, 14" d.,
12½" h., 2 pcs................. 1,800.00

Hawkes signed, chain of hobstars,
strawberry diamond vesicas &
other cutting, hobstar base,
14" d., 7" h. 1,400.00

Hobstars & other cutting, matching
base, 10" d., 11½" h., 2 pcs...... 900.00

Hobstars & geometric motifs, matching flared base, 14" d., 14" h.,
2 pcs. 2,500.00

Libbey signed, chain of hobstars,
strawberry diamond, fan & other
cutting, scalloped & serrated rim
& foot (ILLUS.).................. 1,430.00

Maple City Glass Company's Temple
patt., serrated rim, matching flared
base, 14" d., 2 pcs. 1,600.00

Meriden's Old Irish patt., fan, prism
& relief diamond, matching base,
2 pcs. 3,000.00

Pitkin & Brooks signed, chain of
hobstars, strawberry diamond,
notched prism & fan motifs, scalloped & serrated rim, matching
base, 13¾" d., 16½" h., 2 pcs. ..2,500.00

PUNCH CUPS

Brilliant Period cutting, set of 6..... 135.00

Hoare's Monarch patt., hobstars,
cross-cut split vesicas & fan, set
of 10......................... 300.00

Hobstars & fan, set of 4 .... 60.00

Hobstars & other cutting, hobstar
base 20.00

Pineapple & Fan patt. variant 15.00

PUNCH SETS

Harvard patt., 12" d., 14" h. bowl
w/step-cut base, 10 cups & ladle,
13 pcs. 1,550.00

Libbey signed, Brilliant Period
cutting, bowl, low base & 8 cups,
10 pcs. 3,750.00

Sinclaire signed, Snowflakes & Holly
patt., faceted checkerboard motif
w/intaglio-cut holly berries &
leaves, 12½" d., 12" h. bowl &
eight 3¾" h. cups, 9 pcs.........8.500.00

Tuthill signed, geometric cutting,
12" d., 10½" h. bowl, base & 9
cups, 11 pcs. 1,650.00

ROSE BOWLS

Sunburst Motif Rose Bowl

Hoare's Monarch patt., hobstars,
cross-cut split vesicas & fan 185.00

Hobstars & other cutting, 6" d. 125.00

Russian patt. w/strawberry diamond
button, 7½" d., 7" h. 175.00

Sunburst motif, beading & other cutting, large (ILLUS.) 485.00

SALT & PEPPER SHAKERS
Brilliant Period cutting, sterling silver top, 2" h., pr. 30.00
Hawkes signed, Venetian patt.,
chain of hobstars, fan, star &
strawberry diamond split vesicas,
sterling silver top, pr. 190.00
Hobstars & strawberry diamond,
sterling silver top, 3" h., pr. 45.00
Stars & other cutting, bulbous, sterling silver beaded top, pr. 38.00
Vertical irregular notched prism,
flared base, sterling silver top,
3 7/8" h., pr. 35.00

SALT DIPS

Cut Glass Salt Dip

Brilliant Period cutting, serrated rim,
individual size 25.00
Brilliant Period cutting, heart-
shaped, set of 6 .... 75.00
Electric blue, beveled rim & base,
star-cut base, hexagonal, set
of 4 .... 45.00
Hawkes signed, floral clusters &
foliage 30.00
Hobstars, canoe-shaped w/fan ends,
serrated rim, 3½" l., 1½" w. 55.00
Libbey signed, Brilliant Period cutting, footed 30.00
Relief diamond, strawberry diamond
& fan, star-cut base, tapering
sides, 1¾" sq. (ILLUS.).......... 25.00
Zipper patt., set of 6 .... 60.00

SPOONERS
Cane & other cutting, undulating
scalloped & serrated rim,
4½" h....................... 205.00
Cane, blazed stars & fan, 5" h. 95.00
Drape patt., hobstars & other
cutting 175.00
Floral cutting overall, 2-handled 135.00
Hoare signed, Brilliant Period cutting, 2-handled................. 120.00
Hobstars, strawberry diamond, fan
& other cutting, hobstar base,
scalloped & serrated rim,
4¾" h....................... 200.00

Hobstars & other cutting, serrated
rim 125.00

SYRUP PITCHERS & JUGS
Hobstars & other cutting, bulbous
body, silverplate hinged lid &
handle 135.00
Vertical irregular band of notched
prism, silverplate hinged lid &
handle, 3¾" h. 70.00
Vertical notched prism, sterling silver hinged lid.................. 115.00
Zipper patt., double-notched handle,
sterling silver lid 185.00

TOOTHPICK HOLDERS
Brilliant Period cutting, pedestal
base, scalloped & serrated rim,
3¼" h........................ 90.00
Brilliant Period cutting, barrel-
shaped 40.00
Fluted diamond 38.00
Fry signed, hobstars & Russian patt.
w/strawberry diamond button,
3¾ x 2" oblong, 1 5/8" h. 85.00
Hoare signed, Brilliant Period cutting, pedestal base 65.00
Hobstars overall, pedestal base 75.00

TRAYS

Tuthill Signed Ice Cream Tray

Bread, Clark signed, Strawberry
patt., intaglio-cut berries & foliage, 11½ x 8" 195.00
Bread, Floral patt., blazed star &
other cutting, 12 5/8 x 5 7/8" 135.00
Bread, chain of hobstars, cane &
strawberry diamond, 13½ x 6" ... 165.00
Bread, Hawkes signed, large central
hobstar surrounded by 12 smaller
hobstars, 13½ x 8¼"............ 235.00
Bread, Libbey signed, Brilliant Period cutting, 13½" l. 170.00
Cake, hobstars & hobnail in cross-
cut vesicas, serrated & scalloped
rim, 12¼" d. 375.00
Dresser, Brilliant Period cutting
overall, 15½ x 7" 275.00
Game, Sinclaire's Pheasant patt.,
2" w. sterling silver rim 3,500.00
Ice cream, Tuthill signed, intaglio-
cut grape cluster & vining leaves

center, chain of hobstars border,
serrated rim, open handles,
13½ x 8½" (ILLUS.) 1,500.00
Ice cream, Brilliant Period cutting,
16" l. 350.00
Ice cream, hobstars & fan, scalloped
& serrated rim, 17" l., 10½" w. . . . 975.00
Ice cream, Libbey signed, Rosella
patt., 17½ x 10½" shaped oval . . 950.00
Ice cream, large & small 8-point
hobstars w/engraved fans between strawberry diamond & star-
filled points, flashed fans & zipper
cutting centering a large 24-point
hobstar, 17½ x 10 1/8",
2 3/8" h. 500.00
Ice cream, overall hobstars, 18" l. . . 395.00
Ice cream, overall fern motif,
19 x 16" 275.00
Sugar cube, Cane patt., 9" l. 75.00
Chain of hobstars alternating
w/strawberry diamond border,
32-point hobstar center surrounded
by notched prism radiants,
14" d. 1,800.00
Clark signed, Prima Donna (Triple
Square) patt., 12 x 8 3/8" oval . . . 650.00
Hawkes signed, hobstars center &
border, 14 x 8" 950.00
Hawkes' Brunswick patt., chain of
hobstars, zipper & flute, 10" d. . . . 675.00
Hobstars (4), strawberry diamond
blocks & kites, large 24-point hobstar center, 11 5/8 x 8¼" oval,
2 5/8" h. 235.00
Hobstar center, fine-cut flowers, cut
leaves & 4 oval Parisian-cut
panels, turned up borders cut in
Harvard patt., crenellated top,
13¼ x 8¼", 1¾" h. 250.00
Hobstars overall, 15" oval 325.00
Overlapping large vesicas (4), large
32-point hobstar rosettes (4) &
small hobstars, lobed cane & fan
border alternating w/serrations,
16¼" d. 3,500.00
Strawberry diamond centering large
hobstar, leaf-shaped, leaf-form
handle, 14" l. 250.00

TUMBLERS

Juice, cranberry cut to clear, Bril-
liant Period cutting 110.00
Juice, Hoare signed, Brilliant Period
cutting, set of 6 . . . . 275.00
Juice, hobstars & other cutting 25.00
Juice, pinwheel cutting, set of 9 . . . . 225.00
Juice, strawberry diamond 25.00
Water, Brilliant Period cutting 32.00
Water, Hawkes signed, triple-mitre
cane cutting, set of 10 . . . . 575.00
Water, Hawkes' Queens patt. 58.00
Water, hobstars 25.00

Water, hobstars & other cutting, set
of 6 . . . . 300.00
Water, Libbey signed, Pineapple &
Fan patt., 5½" h. 25.00

VASES

Libbey Signed Wisteria Pattern Vase

Beading, bull's eye, hobstar &
strawberry diamond, slender
w/flaring base, 18" h. 1,400.00
Brilliant Period cutting w/elaborate
sunburst motif, bulbous, serrated
rim, 12" h. 160.00
Brilliant Period cutting, pedestal
base w/teardrop in stem, 14" h. . . 225.00
Chartreuse cut to clear, Libbey's
Harvard patt., cross-cut diamond,
fan & strawberry diamond,
12" h. 875.00
Egginton signed, band of hobstars at
base & top, St. Louis Diamond
neck, 9½" h. 240.00
Harvard patt., scalloped rim, sun-
burst base, 18" h. 1,500.00
Hawkes signed, intaglio-cut florals,
3½" h. 40.00
Hawkes signed, Brilliant Period cut-
ting, bulbous base w/slender flar-
ing neck, 9½" h. 550.00
Hawkes signed, intaglio-cut butter-
flies & flowers, sterling silver rim,
14" h. 245.00
Herringbone patt. w/hobstars at
rim, bull's eye within diamond
base, 15" h. 375.00
Hobstar & diamond, fan-shaped,
hobstar foot, 9" w., 9" h. 325.00
Hobstars & fan alternating w/panels
of bull's eye & prism, low pedes-
tal foot, 12" h. 160.00
Hobstars & strawberry diamond,
16" h. 190.00
Hobstars, strawberry diamond &
stars, corset-shaped, hobstar
base, 6" d., 18" h. 850.00

Libbey signed, Wisteria (Lovebirds) patt., corset-shaped, 7½" h. (ILLUS.)......................... 425.00

Libbey signed, intaglio-cut florals, ruffled rim, 8" h................ 225.00

Libbey signed, Russian patt. w/elongated flower front & back, corset-shaped, 5" d., 12" h. 450.00

Libbey's Drape (Morello) patt., 5½" d., 9¾" h. 2,000.00

Pinwheels and other Brilliant Period cutting, corset-shaped, serrated rim, 8" h. 95.00

Pinwheels, fans, beading & flute, bulbous, rayed pedestal base, scalloped rim, 10" widest d., 16" h. 600.00

Sinclaire signed, intaglio-cut daisy-type florals, trumpet-shaped, 4½" h., pr. 165.00

Sinclaire's Diamonds and Silver Threads patt., 12" h. 525.00

Stars, hobstars & flute w/alternate panels of zipper columns & stars, 24-point star-cut base, 4½" base d., 10" h. 125.00

Thistle patt., 6 flowers cut in blazed star above a strawberry diamond oval, polished leaves, star-cut base, 5¼" d., 11 7/8" h......... 110.00

Tuthill's Primrose & Hobstars patt., 10" h. 395.00

Unger Brothers' Leola patt., 10" h. ... 325.00

Zipper cutting w/large hobstar at rim, bull's eye base, 15" h. 375.00

WATER SETS

Brilliant Period Water Set

Pitcher & 3 tumblers, Butterfly & Daisy patt., 4 pcs............... 265.00

Pitcher & 5 tumblers, butterflies & other cutting, 6 pcs. 265.00

Pitcher & 6 tumblers, Hawkes' Queens patt., chain of hobstars & bull's eye, 7 pcs. 2,000.00

Pitcher & 6 tumblers, Meriden's Thalia patt., blazed florals & polished leaves, 7 pcs................... 280.00

Pitcher & 8 tumblers, Daisy patt., 9 pcs........................ 180.00

Pitcher & 10 tumblers, pinwheel & other cutting, 11 pcs. (ILLUS. of part) 575.00

Pitcher & 12 tumblers, Straus' Drape patt., 8¾" h. bulbous pitcher w/scalloped rim, hobstars in bottom of pitcher & tumblers, 13 pcs. 1,800.00

(End of Cut Glass Section)

CUT VELVET

Cut Velvet Pitcher

Several glasshouses, including Mt. Washington, produced this two-layered glass with its velvety or acid finish and raised pattern. The inner casing is frequently white, and the pattern was developed by blowing into a mold.

Pitcher, 3 3/8" h., 2¾" d., bulbous w/squared mouth, applied opaque white satin handle, Diamond Quilted patt., rose $195.00

Pitcher, 3½" h., 2 7/8" d., bulbous w/round mouth, Diamond Quilted patt., rich green, white lining 225.00

Pitcher, 6" h., applied frosted reeded handle, deep rose (ILLUS.) 285.00

Pitcher, 8" h., Honeycomb patt., blue, attributed to Webb (small ash fleck between layers)........ 295.00

Rose bowl, 6-crimp top, Diamond Quilted patt., rose, white lining, 3 3/8" d., 3 5/8" h. 165.00

Rose bowl, 4-crimp top, Diamond Quilted patt., heavenly blue, white lining, 3½" d., 3 1/8" h. 145.00

Rose bowl, 6-crimp top, Diamond Quilted patt., American Beauty rose, white lining, 3½" d., 3½" h. 195.00

Vase, 6¼" h., 3½" d., stick-type, ribbed, apple green 118.00

Vase, 7¾" h., 3" w., squared shape, ribbed, rose, white lining 145.00

CZECHOSLOVAKIAN

Iridescent Blue Czechoslovakian Vase

At the close of World War I, Czechoslovakia was declared an independent republic and immediately developed a large export industry. Czechoslovakian glass factories produced a wide variety of colored and hand-painted glasswares from about 1918 until 1939, when the country was occupied by Germany at the outset of World War II. Between the wars, fine quality blown glasswares were produced along with a deluge of cheaper, vividly colored spatterwares for the American market. Subsequent production was primarily limited to cut crystal or Bohemian-type etched wares for the American market. Although it was marked, much Czechoslovakian glass is mistaken for the work of Tiffany, Loetz, or other glass artisans it imitates. It is often misrepresented and overpriced.

Basket, applied handle, rippled
  edge, multicolored spatter,
  7½" h. $85.00
Candy jar & cover w/clear knob, applied black feet, mottled pink &
  white striped exterior, white
  lining 55.00
Finger bowl, vaseline w/threaded
  exterior 25.00
Perfume atomizer, footed, vaseline
  w/enameled decor (no bulb) 35.00
Perfume bottle w/clear ball-shaped
  faceted stopper, 6-sided, purple
  w/frosted highlights, 2½" w.,
  4" h. 65.00
Perfume bottle w/stopper, cylindrical, blue frosted w/center band of
  enameled yellow roses, black
  trim, 2½" d., 6" h. 35.00
Perfume bottle w/stopper, yellow
  w/cut criss-cross design 65.00
Perfume bottles, Art Deco style,
  clear w/black stoppers, signed,
  pr. 95.00
Perfume bottles w/cut stoppers, red
  & citron, pr. 250.00

Pitcher, 8½" h., multicolored millefiori canes in vaseline 65.00
Vase, 7½" h., bulbous base, applied
  handles, Loetz-type, iridescent
  blue (ILLUS.) 120.00
Vase, 9" h., fan-shaped, pink
  w/blue threading 40.00
Vase, 9½" h., ruffled rim, pumpkin
  orange w/applied black band at
  waist & rim 65.00
Vase, 10" h., 6" widest d., clear
  w/enameled blue & yellow iris
  decor, signed 125.00

D'ARGENTAL

D'Argental Cameo Vase

Glass known by this name is so-called after its producer, who fashioned fine cameo pieces in France late last century.

Cameo bowl-vase, carved navy blue
  to soft yellow shore scene w/row-
  boat moored at bank & woman
  washing clothes & w/hills & trees
  in background against soft pink
  translucent ground, signed,
  3½" d., 3½" h. $550.00
Cameo vase, 4 1/8" h., 2 3/8" d.,
  carved brown florals against frosted gold ground, signed 245.00
Cameo vase, 5 5/8" h., 3" d.,
  carved purple Venetian scene
  w/man in gondola in foreground
  & city in background against frosted translucent white ground,
  signed 650.00
Cameo vase, 6¾" h., 4 1/8" d.,
  carved brown to rust scene
  w/house & trees in foreground &
  distant castle towers on hill
  against frosted translucent white
  ground, signed 595.00

Cameo vase, 7¾" h., carved orange-brown to brown pendant cherry clusters & foliage against tan ground, signed (ILLUS.) 625.00

Cameo vase, 8½" h., 4½" d., carved navy blue to yellow forest & lake scene w/two small deer standing by water in foreground & flying ducks forming band around top against soft pink frosted translucent ground, signed 975.00

Cameo vase, 11¾" h., carved brown-orange harbor scene of men in sailboats & smaller boats in foreground & city in distance against creamy yellow ground, signed . . . 1,650.00

Cameo vase, 12¼" h., 4 3/8" d., carved shaded brown landscape scene w/chateau on distant hill against frosted gold ground, signed 950.00

Cameo vase, 12¾" h., 4 3/8" d., carved purple to lavender Mediterranean Riviera scene w/palm trees, mountains & villas against frosted translucent white ground, signed 1,150.00

Cameo vase, 14 1/8" h., 6 3/8" d., carved maroon to rose landscape scene w/boat anchored in cove against green to frosted clear to green ground, signed 1,800.00

khaki green, deep violet & berry red poppy blossoms, pods & leaves against clear mottled w/violet & sea green ground, ca. 1910, signed, 5¼" w. 1,045.00

Cameo cruet w/flattened stopper, carved & enameled shaded green, gold & white leaves & berries decor, signed, 5½" h. 850.00

Cameo rose bowl, 3-petal top, carved & enameled brown tree landscape along a river against mottled gold satin ground, 3¼" d., 3" h. 595.00

Cameo salt dip, oval, carved red crocus & large green leaves, signed 375.00

Cameo toothpick holder, carved pink florals against frosted ground, signed 195.00

Cameo toothpick holder, carved & enameled barren forest scene w/snow-laden trees & snow-covered ground, signed (ILLUS. left) 275.00

Cameo tumbler, carved & enameled slender summer tree landscape against mottled white frosted ground, signed, 2 3/8" d., 4¾" h. 550.00

Cameo vase, 4 1/8" h., carved & enameled brown & white barren forest scene w/snow-laden trees & snow-covered ground against mottled orange & yellow ground, signed (ILLUS. right) 396.00

DAUM NANCY

Daum Nancy Cameo Glass

This fine glass, much of it cameo, was made by Auguste and Antonin Daum, who founded a factory in 1875 in Nancy, France. Most of their cameo and enameled glass was made from the final decade of last century.

Cameo bowl, 8¼" w., quatrefoil, carved & enameled shaded inky blue & green wood hyacinths against mottled ice blue to azure blue & green ground, base w/strapwork edged in gilding, ca. 1900, signed $825.00

Cameo box, cov., octagonal, carved

1930's Daum Nancy Vase

Cameo vase, 11" h., ovoid, carved angular geometric designs on orange-brown transparent ground, ca. 1930, signed (ILLUS.) 1,540.00

Cameo vase, 11¾" h., baluster-shaped, carved salmon & forest green daisies & leafage against grey "martele" ground splashed w/apricot, partially fire-polished, ca. 1900, signed 2,200.00

DEPRESSION GLASS

The phrase "Depression Glass" is used by collectors to denote a specific kind of transparent glass produced primarily as tablewares, in crystal, amber, blue, green, pink, milky-white, etc., during the late 1920's and 1930's when this country was in the midst of a financial depression. Made to sell inexpensively, it was turned out by such producers as Jeannette, Hocking, Westmoreland, Indiana and other glass companies. We list all the major Depression Glass patterns.

ADAM (Process-etched)

Adam Creamer

Ash tray, clear, 4½" d.	$9.00
Ash tray, green, 4½" d.	14.50
Ash tray, pink, 4½" d.	19.00
Bowl, nappy, 4¾" sq., green	8.50
Bowl, nappy, 4¾" sq., pink	9.00
Bowl, nappy, 5¾" sq., green or pink	20.00
Bowl, nappy, 7¾" sq., green or pink	13.00
Bowl, cov. vegetable, 9" sq., green	55.00
Bowl, cov. vegetable, 9" sq., pink	35.00
Bowl, 9" sq., green	25.00
Bowl, 9" sq., pink	16.00
Bowl, 10" oval vegetable, green	16.00
Bowl, 10" oval vegetable, pink	14.00
Butter dish, cov., green	205.00
Butter dish, cov., pink	66.00
Cake plate, green, 10" sq.	14.00
Cake plate, pink, 10" sq.	12.00
Candlesticks, green, 4" h., pr.	74.00
Candlesticks, pink, 4" h., pr.	55.00
Candy jar, cov., green	72.00
Candy jar, cov., pink	47.50
Coaster, clear	10.00
Coaster, green	11.50
Coaster, pink	15.00
Creamer, green	12.00
Creamer, pink (ILLUS.)	12.00
Cup & saucer, green	18.50
Cup & saucer, pink	22.00

Pitcher, 8" h., 32 oz., cone-shaped, clear	33.00
Pitcher, 8" h., 32 oz., cone-shaped, green	31.00
Pitcher, 8" h., 32 oz., cone-shaped, pink	23.00
Plate, sherbet, 6" sq., green or pink	3.50
Plate, salad, 7¾" sq., green or pink	7.00
Plate, dinner, 9" sq., green	13.50
Plate, dinner, 9" sq., pink	15.00
Plate, grill, 9" sq., green or pink	11.50
Platter, 12" l., green	13.00
Platter, 12" l., pink	9.50
Relish, 2-part, green or pink, 8" oblong	10.50
Salt & pepper shakers, footed, green, 4" h., pr.	67.50
Salt & pepper shakers, footed, pink, 4" h., pr.	45.00
Sherbet, green	23.00
Sherbet, pink	14.50
Sugar bowl, cov., green	35.00
Sugar bowl, cov., pink	23.00
Sugar bowl, open, green	9.50
Sugar bowl, open, pink	8.00
Tumbler, cone-shaped, green, 4½" h., 7 oz.	13.50
Tumbler, cone-shaped, pink, 4½" h., 7 oz.	15.00
Tumbler, cone-shaped, green, 5½" h., 9 oz.	28.00
Tumbler, cone-shaped, pink, 5½" h., 9 oz.	40.00
Vase, 7½" h., green	33.00
Vase, 7½" h., pink	175.00
Water set: pitcher & 4 tumblers; green, 5 pcs.	79.50

AMERICAN SWEETHEART (Process-etched)

American Sweetheart Cup & Saucer

Berry set: 9" bowl & 6 sauce dishes; Cremax, 7 pcs.	50.00
Bowl, berry, 3½" d., pink	24.00
Bowl, cream soup, 4½" d., Monax	44.00
Bowl, cream soup, 4½" d., pink	26.50
Bowl, cereal, 6" d., Cremax	7.00
Bowl, cereal, 6" d., Monax	9.50
Bowl, cereal, 6" d., Monax "smoke" w/black edge	25.00
Bowl, cereal, 6" d., pink	8.00

Bowl, 9" d., Cremax	29.00
Bowl, 9" d., Monax	32.50
Bowl, 9" d., pink	18.50
Bowl, 10" oval vegetable, Monax	40.00
Bowl, 10" oval vegetable, pink	29.00
Bowl, soup w/flange rim, 10" d., Monax	37.00
Bowl, soup w/flange rim, 10" d., pink	25.00
Console bowl, Monax, 18" d.	265.00
Console bowl, ritz blue, 18" d.	800.00
Creamer & cov. sugar bowl, Monax, pr.	200.00
Creamer & open sugar bowl, Monax, pr.	11.00
Creamer & open sugar bowl, pink, pr.	14.00
Creamer & open sugar bowl, ritz blue, pr.	172.00
Creamer & open sugar bowl, ruby red, pr.	175.00
Cup & saucer, Monax	10.00
Cup & saucer, pink	11.00
Cup & saucer, ritz blue	121.00
Cup & saucer, ruby red (ILLUS.)	113.00
Lamp shade, Monax	370.00
Lamp shade & base, Monax	565.00
Lazy Susan, Monax, 15½" plate on metal stand	220.00
Pitcher, 7½" h., 60 oz., jug-type, pink	355.00
Pitcher, 8" h., 80 oz., pink	325.00
Plate, bread & butter, 6" d., Monax	3.00
Plate, bread & butter, 6" d., pink	2.50
Plate, salad, 8" d., Monax	5.50
Plate, salad, 8" d., pink	6.00
Plate, salad, 8" d., ruby red	61.00
Plate, luncheon, 9" d., Monax	7.00
Plate, luncheon, 9" d., pink	8.50
Plate, luncheon, 9" d., ruby red	60.00
Plate, dinner, 10" d., Monax	13.50
Plate, dinner, 10" d., pink	14.50
Plate, chop, 11" d., Monax	10.00
Plate, chop, 11" d., pink	11.00
Plate, salver, 12" d., Monax or pink	10.00
Plate, salver, 12" d., ritz blue	159.00
Plate, salver, 12" d., ruby red	155.00
Plate, 15" d., w/center handle, Monax	163.00
Plate, 15" d., w/center handle, ruby red	250.00
Plate, 15½" d., Monax	162.50
Plate, 15½" d., ruby red	252.00
Platter, 13" oval, Monax	34.00
Platter, 13" oval, pink	19.00
Platter, 13" oval, ritz blue	17.00
Salt & pepper shakers, Monax, pr.	217.00
Salt & pepper shakers, pink, pr.	259.00
Sherbet, footed, Monax, 4" h.	12.00
Sherbet, footed, pink, 4" h.	10.50
Sherbet, low foot, Monax, 4¼" h.	12.50
Sherbet, low foot, pink, 4¼" h.	8.50

Sherbet, ice cream in metal holder, clear	3.00
Sherbet, ice cream in metal holder, Monax or pink	6.00
Tid bit server, 2-tier, Monax	43.00
Tid bit server, 2-tier, pink	58.00
Tid bit server, 3-tier, Monax	175.00
Tid bit server, 3-tier, ruby red	545.00
Tumbler, pink, 3½" h., 5 oz.	37.00
Tumbler, pink, 4" h., 9 oz.	37.50
Tumbler, pink, 4½" h., 10 oz.	46.00

BLOCK or Block Optic (Press-mold)

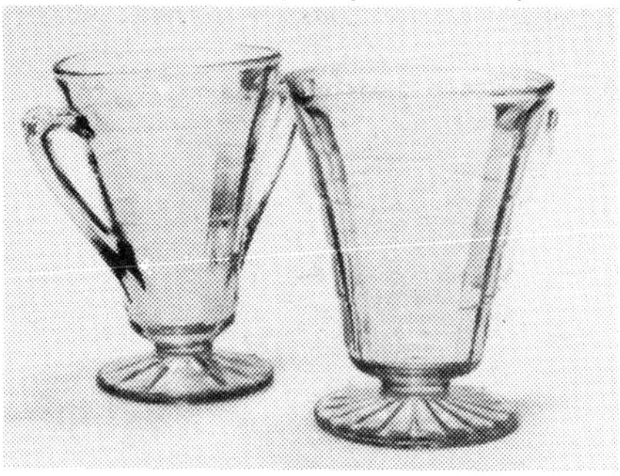

Block Creamer & Sugar Bowl

Bowl, nappy, 4¼" d., green	4.00
Bowl, nappy, 5¼" d., green	7.00
Bowl, nappy, 5¼" d., pink	4.25
Bowl, nappy, 7" d., green or pink	11.00
Bowl, nappy, 8½" d., green	13.00
Butter dish, cov., oblong, green	34.50
Butter dish, cov., round, green	32.00
Candlesticks, green, pr.	50.00
Candlesticks, pink, pr.	31.50
Candlesticks, yellow, pr.	30.00
Candy jar, cov., green or pink, 2¼" h.	28.50
Candy jar, cov., yellow, 2¼" h.	37.50
Candy jar, cov., clear, 6¼" h.	17.50
Candy jar, cov., green, 6¼" h.	33.00
Candy jar, cov., pink, 6¼" h.	46.50
Candy jar, cov., yellow, 6¼" h.	36.00
Compote, 4" d., cone-shaped, green	17.00
Creamer, round, footed, green	8.00
Creamer, round, footed, yellow	9.00
Creamer, straight sides, green or yellow	5.00
Creamer & open sugar bowl, green or pink, pr.	15.00
Creamer & open sugar bowl, yellow, pr.	16.00
Creamer & open sugar bowl, cone-shaped, green, pr. (ILLUS.)	17.00
Creamer & open sugar bowl, cone-shaped, pink, pr.	16.50
Creamer & open sugar bowl, cone-shaped, yellow, pr.	20.00
Cup & saucer, clear	4.00
Cup & saucer, green	9.50
Cup & saucer, pink or yellow	7.00

Goblet, wine, clear, 4" h., 2 oz.	8.00	Sugar bowl, round, green, pink or	
Goblet, wine, green, 4" h., 2 oz. . . .	17.50	yellow	6.50
Goblet, wine, pink, 4" h., 2 oz.	20.50	Sugar bowl, straight sides, green . . .	7.50
Goblet, clear, 6" h.	6.00	Tumbler, whiskey, clear, 2½" h.	5.50
Goblet, green, 6" h.	15.50	Tumbler, whiskey, green, 2½" h. . . .	21.50
Goblet, pink or yellow, 6" h.	11.00	Tumbler, whiskey, pink, 2½" h.	26.00
Goblet, clear, 7¼" h.	6.00	Tumbler, juice, green, 3" h., 5 oz. . .	10.50
Goblet, green, 7¼" h.	14.00	Tumbler, juice, pink, 3" h., 5 oz. . . .	9.50
Goblet, pink, 7¼" h.	10.00	Tumbler, juice, footed, green,	
Goblet, yellow, 7¼" h.	17.00	3¼" h., 5 oz.	12.50
Ice tub, clear	14.00	Tumbler, juice, footed, pink,	
Ice tub, green	25.00	3¼" h., 5 oz.	9.00
Ice tub, pink	50.00	Tumbler, clear, 9 oz.	3.50
Mug (or cup), green	26.00	Tumbler, green, 9 oz.	10.00
Nite set: 3" tumbler bottle & 6" tum-		Tumbler, pink, 9 oz.	7.50
bler; green, set	43.00	Tumbler, footed, clear, 9 oz.	6.50
Nite set bottle, green, 3"	11.00	Tumbler, footed, green, 9 oz.	12.50
Pitcher, 7 5/8" h., 68 oz., green	44.50	Tumbler, footed, pink, 9 oz.	9.50
Pitcher, 8" h., 80 oz., clear	11.00	Tumbler, footed, yellow, 9 oz., ...	12.00
Pitcher, 8" h., 80 oz., green	38.00	Tumbler, iced tea, clear, 10 oz.	5.50
Pitcher, 8" h., 80 oz., pink	37.00	Tumbler, iced tea, green, 10 oz.	11.00
Pitcher, 8½" h., 54 oz., clear	20.00	Tumbler, iced tea, pink, 10 oz.	8.50
Pitcher, 8½" h., 54 oz., green	32.00	Tumbler, iced tea, footed, green,	
Pitcher, 8½" h., 54 oz., pink	29.50	6" h., 10 oz.	15.00
Plate, 6" d., clear or pink	1.00	Tumbler, iced tea, footed, pink,	
Plate, 6" d., green	1.50	6" h., 10 oz.	14.00
Plate, 6" d., yellow	2.00	Tumbler, iced tea, footed, yellow,	
Plate, luncheon, 8" d., green or		6" h., 10 oz.	12.50
pink	2.50	Tumbler, green, 14 oz.	17.00
Plate, luncheon, 8" d., yellow	3.50	Tumbler, pink, 14 oz.	13.00
Plate, dinner, 9" d., clear	4.00	Water set: pitcher & 6 footed	
Plate, dinner, 9" d., green	12.00	tumblers; green, 7 pcs.	125.00
Plate, dinner, 9" d., yellow	20.00		
Plate, grill, 9" d., clear	4.00	**BUBBLE (Press-mold)**	
Plate, grill, 9" d., green	10.00		
Plate, sandwich, 10" d., clear	6.50		
Plate, sandwich, 10" d., green	12.50		
Plate, sandwich, 10" d., pink	11.00		
Salt & pepper shakers, squat, green,			
pr.	33.50		
Salt & pepper shakers, squat, pink,			
pr.	50.00		
Salt & pepper shakers, squat, yel-			
low, pr.	62.50		
Salt & pepper shakers, footed,			
clear, pr.	25.00		
Salt & pepper shakers, footed,			
green, pr.	22.50		
Salt & pepper shakers, footed, pink,			
pr.	46.00		
Sandwich server w/center handle,			
green	30.00		
Sandwich server w/center handle,			
pink	26.00	**Bubble Pitcher**	
Sherbet, round or V shaped, clear . .	2.50	Berry set: master bowl & 6 sauce	
Sherbet, round or V shaped, green		dishes; milk white, 7 pcs.	12.50
or pink	4.00	Berry set: master bowl & 8 sauce	
Sherbet, round or V shaped,		dishes; clear, 9 pcs.	17.50
yellow	5.50	Bowl, 4" d., blue	9.00
Sherbet, stemmed, clear, 5" h.	5.00	Bowl, 4" d., clear	1.75
Sherbet, stemmed, green or pink,		Bowl, 4" d., pink	15.00
5" h.	9.50	Bowl, fruit, 4½" d., blue	5.50
Sherbet, stemmed, yellow, 5" h.	10.50	Bowl, fruit, 4½" d., clear	1.75
Sugar bowl, round, clear	3.00		

Bowl, fruit, 4½" d., green	4.50
Bowl, fruit, 4½" d., milk white	2.00
Bowl, fruit, 4½" d., ruby red	3.50
Bowl, cereal, 5¼" d., blue	5.75
Bowl, cereal, 5¼" d., clear	3.00
Bowl, cereal, 5¼" d., green	5.00
Bowl, soup, 7¾" d., blue	7.00
Bowl, soup, 7¾" d., clear	3.75
Bowl, soup, 7¾" d., ruby red	5.75
Bowl, 8 3/8" d., blue or ruby red	8.00
Bowl, 8 3/8" d., clear	5.50
Bowl, 8 3/8" d., green	10.00
Bowl, 8 3/8" d., milk white	3.50
Bowl, 8 3/8" d., pink	4.75
Bowl, 9" d., flanged, milk white	30.00
Candlesticks, clear, pr.	10.00
Creamer & open sugar bowl, blue, pr.	33.00
Creamer & open sugar bowl, clear or green, pr.	13.50
Creamer & open sugar bowl, milk white, pr.	5.50
Cup & saucer, blue or pink	3.75
Cup & saucer, clear	2.50
Cup & saucer, green	4.75
Cup & saucer, ruby red	6.50
Dinner service for 6, w/serving pieces, blue, 56 pcs.	250.00
Lamp, clear	35.00
Lamps, clear (electric), pr.	75.00
Pitcher w/ice lip, 64 oz., clear	41.00
Pitcher w/ice lip, 64 oz., ruby red (ILLUS.)	33.00
Plate, bread & butter, 6¾" d., blue or clear	1.50
Plate, bread & butter, 6¾" d., green	2.25
Plate, dinner, 9¼" d., blue	4.00
Plate, dinner, 9¼" d., clear	2.50
Plate, dinner, 9¼" d., green	4.75
Plate, dinner, 9¼" d., ruby red	6.00
Plate, grill, 9¼" d., blue	8.00
Plate, grill, 9¼" d., clear	4.00
Platter, 12" oval, blue or green	8.00
Platter, 12" oval, clear	7.00
Salt & pepper shakers, blue, small, pr.	10.00
Salt & pepper shakers, green, small, pr.	45.00
Tid bit server, blue	29.00
Tid bit server, ruby red	27.00
Tumbler, juice, clear, 6 oz.	6.50
Tumbler, juice, green, 6 oz.	17.50
Tumbler, juice, ruby red, 6 oz.	5.00
Tumbler, old fashioned, clear or ruby red, 9 oz.	5.00
Tumbler, old fashioned, green, 9 oz.	4.50
Tumbler, clear, 12 oz.	5.50
Tumbler, ruby red, 12 oz.	6.50
Tumbler, iced tea, clear or ruby red, 16 oz.	11.00
Tumbler, footed, clear, 7" h.	9.50
Tumbler, footed, green, 7" h.	6.00

CAMEO (Process-etched)

Cameo Tumblers

Bowl, cream soup, 4¾" d., green	48.00
Bowl, nappy, 5½" d., clear	4.50
Bowl, nappy, 5½" d., green	18.50
Bowl, nappy, 5½" d., yellow	20.00
Bowl, nappy, 7" d., green	28.00
Bowl, nappy, 8¼" d., green	22.00
Bowl, nappy, 8¼" d., yellow	21.00
Bowl, soup w/flange rim, 9" d., green	27.50
Bowl, 10" oval vegetable, green	19.50
Bowl, 10" oval vegetable, yellow	35.00
Butter dish, cov., green	133.00
Cake plate, footed, clear, 10" d.	12.00
Cake plate, footed, green, 10" d.	14.00
Candlesticks, green, 4" h., pr.	75.00
Candy dish, cov., low, green	40.00
Candy dish, cov., low, yellow	55.00
Candy jar, cov., green, 6½" h.	79.00
Compote, 4" h., cone-shaped, green	19.50
Console bowl, 3-footed, green, 11" d.	47.50
Console bowl, 3-footed, pink, 11" d.	16.00
Console bowl, 3-footed, yellow, 11" d.	52.50
Cookie jar, cov., green	34.00
Creamer, green, 4" h.	16.00
Creamer, pink, 4" h.	62.50
Creamer, yellow, 4" h.	17.00
Creamer & open sugar bowl, green, 3" h., pr.	24.50
Creamer & open sugar bowl, yellow, 3" h., pr.	23.00
Cup & saucer, green	12.00
Cup & saucer, pink or yellow	7.50
Dinner service for 6, w/serving pieces, green, 46 pcs.	400.00
Domino tray, green, 7" d.	87.00
Goblet, wine, green, 4" h.	46.00
Goblet, green, 6" h.	37.00
Goblet, pink, 6" h.	150.00
Ice bowl, green, 3½" h.	112.50
Ice bowl, pink, 3½" h.	425.00
Jar, cov., closed handles, green, 2"	102.00
Juice set: pitcher & 6 tumblers; green, 7 pcs.	162.50

Mayonnaise bowl w/ladle, green,
2 pcs. 24.00
Mayonnaise bowl w/underplate,
green, 2 pcs. 24.50
Mayonnaise set: bowl, underplate &
ladle; green, 3 pcs. 35.00
Pitcher, syrup or milk, 5¾" h.,
20 oz., green 133.50
Pitcher, juice, 6" h., 36 oz., green . . 41.50
Pitcher, 8½" h., 56 oz., jug-type,
green 38.50
Plate, sherbet, 6" d., green or
yellow 2.00
Plate, 7" d., clear w/platinum rim . . 2.75
Plate, luncheon, 8" d., green 6.50
Plate, luncheon, 8" d., pink 20.00
Plate, luncheon, 8" d., yellow 5.50
Plate, salad, 8" sq., green 23.00
Plate, salad, 8" sq., yellow 7.00
Plate, dinner, 9½" d., green 12.00
Plate, dinner, 9½" d., yellow 5.50
Plate, sandwich, 10" d., green 11.00
Plate, sandwich, 10" d., pink 28.50
Plate, dinner, 10½" d., closed han-
dles, green 10.00
Plate, dinner, 10½" d., closed han-
dles, yellow 11.50
Plate, grill, 10½" d., closed han-
dles, green 39.50
Plate, grill, 10½" d., closed han-
dles, yellow 5.50
Plate, grill, 10½" d., green 6.00
Plate, grill, 10½" d., yellow 5.50
Plate, 11½" d., closed handles,
green 10.50
Plate, 11½" d., closed handles,
pink 25.00
Platter, 10½" oval, green 12.50
Platter, 10½" oval, pink 5.00
Platter, 10½" oval, yellow 31.00
Platter, 12", closed handles, green . . 13.50
Platter, 12", closed handles,
yellow 25.00
Salt & pepper shakers, green, pr. . . . 54.00
Sherbet, green, 3" 10.00
Sherbet, pink, 3" 26.00
Sherbet, yellow, 3" 22.00
Sherbet, thin, high stem, green 21.00
Sherbet, thin, high stem, yellow 25.00
Sugar bowl, open, pink, 3" h. 65.00
Sugar bowl, open, green, 4" h. 14.00
Sugar bowl, open, yellow, 4" h. 12.50
Tumbler, juice, footed, green,
3 oz. 38.00
Tumbler, juice, green, 3" h., 5 oz. . . 18.50
Tumbler, juice, footed, green,
5 oz. 39.50
Tumbler, juice, footed, pink, 5 oz. . . 45.00
Tumbler, clear, 4" h., 9 oz. 7.50
Tumbler, green or yellow, 4" h.,
9 oz. 16.00
Tumbler, pink, 4" h., 9 oz. 55.00
Tumbler, footed, green, 5" h.,
9 oz. 19.00

Tumbler, footed, pink, 5" h., 9 oz. . . 45.00
Tumbler, footed, yellow, 5" h., 9 oz.
(ILLUS.) 12.00
Tumbler, green or yellow, 4¾" h.,
10 oz. 20.00
Tumbler, green, 5" h., 11 oz. 17.50
Tumbler, yellow, 5" h., 11 oz. 40.00
Tumbler, footed, green, 6" h.,
11 oz. 39.00
Tumbler, footed, yellow, 6" h.,
11 oz. 12.00
Tumbler, green, 5¼" h., 14 oz. 34.00
Vase, 5¾" h., clear 85.00
Vase, 5¾" h., green 107.00
Vase, 8½" h., green 17.00
Water bottle w/stopper, green 89.00
Water bottle, green frosted,
8½" h. 29.00
Water bottle, dark green "White
House Vinegar" base, 8½" h. 16.00
Water set: pitcher & 6 tumblers;
green, 7 pcs. 200.00

CHERRY BLOSSOM (Process-etched)

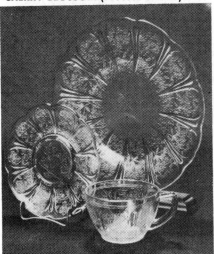

Cherry Blossom Pattern

Berry set: master bowl & 6 sauce
dishes; Delfite, 7 pcs. 90.00
Berry set: master bowl & 7 sauce
dishes; green, 8 pcs. 75.00
Bowl, nappy, 4¾" d., Delfite or
green 10.00
Bowl, nappy, 4¾" d., pink 8.00
Bowl, nappy, 5¾" d., Delfite 12.50
Bowl, nappy, 5¾" d., green or
pink 22.00
Bowl, soup, 7¾" d., green 37.00
Bowl, soup, 7¾" d., pink 33.50
Bowl, nappy, 8½" d., Delfite 36.50
Bowl, nappy, 8½" d., green 16.50
Bowl, nappy, 8½" d., pink 14.00
Bowl, 9" d., handled, clear 15.50
Bowl, 9" d., handled, Delfite 13.50

Bowl, 9" d., handled, green	18.50
Bowl, 9" d., handled, pink	16.00
Bowl, 9" oval vegetable, green	18.50
Bowl, 9" oval vegetable, pink	20.50
Bowl, fruit, 10½" d., 3-footed, green	41.00
Bowl, fruit, 10½" d., 3-footed, pink	38.50
Butter dish, cov., green	65.00
Butter dish, cov., pink	53.00
Cake plate, green or pink, 10¼" d.	16.00
Coaster, green	9.00
Coaster, pink	10.50
Creamer, clear	9.50
Creamer, Delfite	14.00
Creamer, green or pink	11.00
Cup & saucer, Delfite	15.50
Cup & saucer, green	17.50
Cup & saucer, pink (ILLUS.)	15.00
Mug, green, 8 oz.	166.00
Mug, pink, 8 oz.	140.00
Pitcher, 6½" h., 36 oz., jug-type, overall patt., Delfite	85.00
Pitcher, 6½" h., 36 oz., jug-type, overall patt., green	33.00
Pitcher, 6½" h., 36 oz., jug-type, overall patt., pink	30.00
Pitcher, 8" h., 36 oz., cone-shaped, patt. top, Delfite	67.00
Pitcher, 8" h., 36 oz., cone-shaped, patt. top, green	34.50
Pitcher, 8" h., 36 oz., cone-shaped, patt. top, pink	38.00
Pitcher, 8" h., 42 oz., straight side, patt. top, Delfite	89.00
Pitcher, 8" h., 42 oz., straight side, patt. top, green	37.00
Pitcher, 8" h., 42 oz., straight side, patt. top, pink	30.00
Plate, sherbet, 6" d., Delfite	7.00
Plate, sherbet, 6" d., green or pink	4.50
Plate, salad, 7" d., clear	12.00
Plate, salad, 7" d., green	13.00
Plate, salad, 7" d., pink	12.50
Plate, dinner, 9" d., Delfite	13.00
Plate, dinner, 9" d., green	14.00
Plate, dinner, 9" d., pink (ILLUS.)	11.50
Plate, grill, 9" d., green	16.00
Plate, grill, 9" d., pink	14.50
Platter, 11" oval, clear	12.00
Platter, 11" oval, Delfite	34.00
Platter, 11" oval, green	27.50
Platter, 11" oval, pink	17.50
Platter, 13" oval, Delfite	36.00
Platter, 13" oval, green	33.50
Platter, 13" oval, pink	31.00
Platter, 13" oval, divided, green	33.50
Salt & pepper shakers, green, pr.	845.00
Sandwich tray, handled, Delfite or green, 10½" d.	15.00
Sandwich tray, handled, pink, 10½" d.	12.50

Sherbet, Delfite	11.00
Sherbet, green	12.00
Sherbet, pink	10.50
Sugar bowl, cov., clear	17.00
Sugar bowl, cov., green	19.00
Sugar bowl, cov., pink	18.00
Sugar bowl, open, Delfite	14.50
Sugar bowl, open, green	9.00
Sugar bowl, open, pink	7.50
Tumbler, juice, footed, Delfite, 3½" h., 4 oz.	12.50
Tumbler, juice, footed, green, 3½" h., 4 oz.	14.00
Tumbler, juice, footed, pink, 3¼" h., 4 oz.	10.00
Tumbler, patt. top, green, 3½" h., 5 oz.	13.50
Tumbler, patt. top, pink, 3½" h., 5 oz.	11.50
Tumbler, patt. top, clear, 4" h., 9 oz.	8.50
Tumbler, patt. top, Delfite, 4" h., 9 oz.	21.50
Tumbler, patt. top, green, 4" h., 9 oz.	14.50
Tumbler, patt. top, pink, 4" h., 9 oz.	12.50
Tumbler, footed, Delfite, 4½" h., 9 oz.	15.50
Tumbler, footed, green, 4½" h., 9 oz.	26.00
Tumbler, footed, pink, 4½" h., 9 oz.	21.50
Tumbler, patt. top, clear, 5" h., 12 oz.	17.00
Tumbler, patt. top, Delfite, 5" h., 12 oz.	15.00
Tumbler, patt. top, green, 5" h., 12 oz.	43.00
Tumbler, patt. top, pink, 5" h., 12 oz.	34.00
Water set: pitcher & 6 tumblers; Delfite, 7 pcs.	165.00
Water set: pitcher & 7 tumblers; green, 8 pcs.	120.00

JUNIOR SET:

Creamer & sugar bowl, Delfite, pr.	42.00
Creamer & sugar bowl, pink, pr.	49.00
Cup, Delfite	22.00
Cup, pink	25.00
Cup & saucer, Delfite	24.00
Cup & saucer, pink	26.00
Plate, 6" d., Delfite or pink	6.50
Saucer, Delfite or pink	4.00
10 pc. set, pink	150.00
12 pc. set, Delfite	142.50
20 pc. set, Delfite	265.00

CLOVERLEAF (Process-etched)

Ash tray, black, 4" d.	50.00
Ash tray, black, 5¾" d.	66.50
Bowl, dessert, 4" d., green	13.00

Bowl, dessert, 4" d., pink	8.50
Bowl, dessert, 4" d., yellow	16.00
Bowl, nappy, 5" d., green	15.50
Bowl, nappy, 5" d., yellow	21.00
Bowl, 7" d., green	26.00
Bowl, 7" d., yellow	35.50
Bowl, 8" d. , green	41.00
Candy dish, cov., green	31.50
Candy dish, cov., yellow	84.00
Creamer & open sugar bowl, black, pr.	20.00
Creamer & open sugar bowl, green, pr.	12.00
Creamer & open sugar bowl, yellow, pr.	23.50
Cup & saucer, black	11.50
Cup & saucer, clear or pink	5.50
Cup & saucer, green	6.50
Cup & saucer, yellow	13.00
Plate, sherbet, 6" d., black	23.50
Plate, sherbet, 6" d., green	3.50
Plate, sherbet, 6" d., yellow	4.50
Plate, salad, 8" d., black	10.50
Plate, salad, 8" d., clear or green ..	3.75
Plate, salad, 8" d., pink	4.75
Plate, salad, 8" d., yellow	8.00
Plate, grill, 10" d., green	15.00
Plate, grill, 10" d., yellow	10.00
Salt & pepper shakers, black, pr.	65.00
Salt & pepper shakers, green, pr. ...	22.50
Salt & pepper shakers, yellow, pr. ..	75.00
Sherbet, black	12.00
Sherbet, clear, green or pink	4.50
Sherbet, yellow	7.50
Sugar bowl, open, black	10.50
Sugar bowl, open, green	6.50
Sugar bowl, open, yellow	10.00
Tumbler, green, 4" h., 9 oz.	21.00
Tumbler, pink, 4" h., 9 oz.	13.00
Tumbler, green, 3¾" h., 10 oz.	28.00
Tumbler, pink, 3¾" h., 10 oz.	17.00
Tumbler, footed, green, 5¾" h., 10 oz.	15.50
Tumbler, footed, yellow, 5¾" h., 10 oz.	20.00
Tumbler, footed, green, 6½" h., 13 oz.	19.00
Tumbler, footed, yellow, 6½" h., 13 oz.	21.00

COLONIAL or Knife & Fork (Press-mold)

Bowl, berry, 4" d., clear	4.00
Bowl, berry, 4" d., green	8.00
Bowl, berry, 4" d., pink	19.50
Bowl, cream soup, 4½" d., green ...	33.00
Bowl, cream soup, 4½" d., pink	28.00
Bowl, nappy, 4½" d., clear	5.50
Bowl, nappy, 4½" d., green	7.50
Bowl, nappy, 4½" d., pink	6.00
Bowl, nappy, 5½" d., green	7.50
Bowl, nappy, 5½" d., pink	31.00
Bowl, soup, 7" d., clear	13.50
Bowl, soup, 7" d., green	40.00
Bowl, soup, 7" d., pink	28.50

Bowl, 9" d., clear .... 7.00 to	9.50
Bowl, 9" d., green	16.50
Bowl, 9" d., pink	13.50
Bowl, 10" oval vegetable, clear	12.00
Bowl, 10" oval vegetable, green	19.00
Bowl, 10" oval vegetable, pink	15.00
Butter dish, cov., clear	26.00
Butter dish, cov., green	44.00
Butter dish, cov., pink	250.00
Celery or spooner, clear	36.00
Celery or spooner, green	98.00
Celery or spooner, pink	93.00
Cheese dish, wooden base w/clear dome cover	65.00
Creamer & cov. sugar bowl, clear, pr.	19.00

Colonial Creamer & Sugar Bowl

Creamer & cov. sugar bowl, green, pr. (ILLUS.)	35.50
Creamer & cov. sugar bowl, pink, pr.	65.00
Creamer & open sugar bowl, clear, pr.	12.00
Creamer & open sugar bowl, green, pr.	20.00
Cup & saucer, clear	6.00
Cup & saucer, green	10.50
Cup & saucer, milk white	12.00
Cup & saucer, pink	9.50
Goblet, cordial, clear, 3¾" h., 1 oz.	10.00
Goblet, cordial, green, 3¾" h., 1 oz.	22.00
Goblet, cordial, pink, 3¾" h., 1 oz.	15.50
Goblet, wine, clear, 4½" h., 2½ oz.	6.50
Goblet, wine, green, 4½" h., 2½ oz.	20.00
Goblet, cocktail, clear, 4" h., 3 oz.	6.50
Goblet, cocktail, green, 4" h., 3 oz.	17.50
Goblet, cocktail, pink, 4" h., 3 oz.	13.00
Goblet, claret, clear, 5" h., 4 oz.	8.50
Goblet, claret, green, 5" h., 4 oz.	16.00
Goblet, clear, 5¾" h., 8½ oz.	9.00
Goblet, green, 5¾" h., 8½ oz.	20.00
Goblet, pink, 5¾" h., 8½ oz.	18.00

Pitcher, 7" h., 54 oz., clear.......... 17.00
Pitcher, 7" h., 54 oz., green or
  pink 32.50
Pitcher, 7½" h., 67 oz., clear....... 23.00
Pitcher, 7½" h., 67 oz., green 41.50
Pitcher, 7½" h., 67 oz., pink 43.00
Plate, sherbet, 6½" d., clear 1.75
Plate, sherbet, 6½" d., green or
  pink 3.00
Plate, luncheon, 8½" d., clear...... 3.00
Plate, luncheon, 8½" d., green 6.00
Plate, luncheon, 8½" d., pink 5.00
Plate, dinner, 10" d., clear 12.00
Plate, dinner, 10" d., green 43.00
Plate, dinner, 10" d., milk white.... 10.50
Plate, dinner, 10" d., pink 24.50
Plate, grill, 10" d., clear 9.00
Plate, grill, 10" d., green 19.00
Plate, grill, 10" d., pink........... 14.50
Platter, 12" oval, clear............. 9.00
Platter, 12" oval, green............ 14.00
Platter, 12" oval, pink 21.00
Salt & pepper shakers, clear, pr. ... 42.00
Salt & pepper shakers, green, pr.... 107.50
Salt & pepper shakers, pink, pr. 105.00
Sherbet, clear.................... 3.50

Colonial Sherbet

Sherbet, green (ILLUS.) 9.00
Sherbet, pink 5.50
Tumbler, whiskey, clear, 2½" h.,
  1½ oz........................ 3.75
Tumbler, whiskey, green, 2½" h.,
  1½ oz........................ 8.50
Tumbler, whiskey, pink, 2½" h.,
  1½ oz........................ 6.00
Tumbler, cordial, footed, clear,
  3¼" h., 3 oz. 8.50
Tumbler, cordial, footed, green,
  3¼" h., 3 oz. 13.00
Tumbler, cordial, footed, pink,
  3¼" h., 3 oz. 10.50
Tumbler, juice, clear, 3" h., 5 oz. ... 4.00
Tumbler, juice, green, 3" h., 5 oz. ... 17.00
Tumbler, juice, pink, 3" h., 5 oz. ... 9.00
Tumbler, claret, footed, clear, 4" h.,
  5 oz. 7.00
Tumbler, claret, footed, green,
  4" h., 5 oz. 19.00

Tumbler, claret, footed, pink, 4" h.,
  5 oz. 11.50
Tumbler, clear, 4" h., 9 oz. 6.00
Tumbler, green, 4" h., 9 oz. 17.50
Tumbler, pink, 4" h., 9 oz. 8.50
Tumbler, cordial, footed, clear,
  5¼" h., 10 oz. 8.50
Tumbler, cordial, footed, green,
  5¼" h., 10 oz. 35.00
Tumbler, cordial, footed, pink,
  5¼" h., 10 oz. 16.00
Tumbler, clear, 10 oz. 12.00
Tumbler, green, 10 oz. 29.00
Tumbler, pink, 10 oz. 19.00
Tumbler, iced tea, green, 12 oz. 33.50
Tumbler, iced tea, pink, 12 oz. 28.00
Tumbler, lemonade, clear, 15 oz. ... 10.50
Tumbler, lemonade, green, 15 oz. .. 70.00
Tumbler, lemonade, pink, 15 oz..... 40.00

COLUMBIA (Press-mold)
Bowl, cereal, 5" d., clear 10.00
Bowl, soup, 8" d., clear............ 11.50
Bowl, salad, 8½" d., clear 11.50
Bowl, salad, 8½" d., pink 12.00
Bowl, 10½" d., ruffled rim, clear ... 13.50
Bowl, 10½" d., ruffled rim, pink 12.50
Butter dish, cov., clear 12.50
Butter dish w/metal lid, clear 20.00
Cup & saucer, clear 5.00
Plate, bread & butter, 6" d., clear .. 1.50
Plate, luncheon, 9½" d., clear...... 3.50
Plate, luncheon, 9½" d., pink 9.50
Plate, chop, 11¾" d., clear 6.00
Plate, chop, 11¾" d., pink 8.50

CUBE or Cubist (Press-mold)

Cube Creamer

Bowl, dessert, 4½" d., clear 1.00
Bowl, dessert, 4½" d., green....... 3.00
Bowl, dessert, 4½" d., pink 4.00
Bowl, 4½" d., deep, clear 3.00
Bowl, 4½" d., deep, green or
  pink 4.00
Bowl, salad, 6½" d., clear 4.00
Bowl, salad, 6½" d., green 9.00
Bowl, salad, 6½" d., pink.......... 5.50
Bowl, 7 3/8" d., scalloped rim,
  clear........................ 9.00
Bowl, 7 3/8" d., scalloped rim,
  green 15.50

Bowl, 7 3/8" d., scalloped rim,
pink 11.50
Butter dish, cov., green 46.00
Butter dish, cov., pink 38.50
Candy jar, cov., green, 7½" h. 21.00
Candy jar, cov., pink, 7½" h. 16.00
Coaster, clear, 3¼" d. 18.00
Coaster, green, 3¼" d. 3.50
Coaster, pink, 3¼" d. 4.00
Creamer, clear, 2" h. 3.50
Creamer, green, 2" h. 5.50
Creamer, pink, 2" h. (ILLUS.) 2.50
Creamer & cov. sugar bowl, green,
3" h., pr. 19.00
Creamer & cov. sugar bowl, pink,
3" h., pr. 14.00
Creamer, open sugar bowl & tray,
clear, 3 pcs. 6.50
Cup & saucer, green 7.00
Cup & saucer, pink 5.00
Pitcher, 8¾" h., 45 oz., green 160.00
Pitcher, 8¾" h., 45 oz., pink 130.00
Plate, sherbet, 6" d., clear 1.00
Plate, sherbet, 6" d., green or
pink 1.75
Plate, luncheon, 8" d., green 4.00
Plate, luncheon, 8" d., pink 3.50
Powder jar, cov., 3-footed, clear 8.00
Powder jar, cov., 3-footed, green ... 12.50
Powder jar, cov., 3-footed, pink 11.00
Salt & pepper shakers, clear, pr. ... 16.00
Salt & pepper shakers, green, pr. ... 22.00
Salt & pepper shakers, pink, pr. 23.00
Sherbet, clear 2.00
Sherbet, green 5.50
Sherbet, pink 4.50
Sugar bowl, open, clear, 2" h. 1.50
Sugar bowl, open, green, 2" h. 11.00
Sugar bowl, open, pink, 2" h. 2.00
Sugar bowl, open, green, 3" h. 5.00
Sugar bowl, open, pink, 3" h. 3.50
Tumbler, green, 4" h., 9 oz. 33.50
Tumbler, pink, 4" h., 9 oz. 25.50
Water set: pitcher & 4 tumblers;
pink, 5 pcs. 200.00

DAISY or Number 620 (Press-mold)
Bowl, berry, 4½" d., amber 5.50
Bowl, berry, 4½" d., clear 3.50
Bowl, cream soup, 4½" d., amber .. 5.00
Bowl, cream soup, 4½" d., clear ... 3.50
Bowl, cereal, 6" d., amber 18.00
Bowl, cereal, 6" d., clear 9.50
Bowl, berry, 7 3/8" d., amber 17.50
Bowl, berry, 7 3/8" d., clear 3.00
Bowl, berry, 9 3/8" d., amber 17.50
Bowl, berry, 9 3/8" d., clear 11.00
Bowl, 10" oval vegetable, clear 5.00
Creamer, footed, amber 4.50
Creamer, footed, clear 3.50
Creamer & open sugar bowl, footed,
amber, pr. 10.50
Creamer & open sugar bowl, footed,
clear, pr. 7.00

Cup & saucer, amber or clear 4.50
Plate, sherbet, 6" d., amber 1.50
Plate, sherbet, 6" d., clear 2.00
Plate, salad, 7 3/8" d., amber 5.00
Plate, salad, 7 3/8" d., clear 1.50
Plate, luncheon, 8 3/8" d., amber .. 4.50
Plate, luncheon, 8 3/8" d., clear ... 3.50
Plate, dinner, 9 3/8" d., amber or
clear 5.00
Plate, grill, 10 3/8" d., amber 8.00
Plate, grill, 10 3/8" d., clear 3.00
Plate, 11½" d., amber 7.50
Plate, 11½" d., clear 4.50
Platter, 10¾", amber 9.00
Platter, 10¾", clear 8.00
Relish, 3-part, amber, 8 3/8" 14.00
Relish, 3-part, clear, 8 3/8" 7.00
Sherbet, amber 5.50
Sherbet, clear 4.50
Sugar bowl, open, footed, amber ... 6.00
Sugar bowl, open, footed, clear ... 3.50
Tumbler, footed, amber, 9 oz. 13.00
Tumbler, footed, clear, 9 oz. 7.50
Tumbler, footed, amber, 12 oz. 25.00
Tumbler, footed, clear, 12 oz. 13.50

**DIAMOND QUILTED or Flat Diamond
(Press-mold)**
Bowl, cream soup, 4¾" d., blue 14.00
Bowl, cream soup, 4¾" d., green ... 8.00
Bowl, cream soup, 4¾" d., pink 7.00
Bowl, cereal, 5" d., pink 5.00
Bowl, 5½" d., single handle,
black 10.50
Bowl, 5½" d., single handle,
green 5.00
Bowl, 5½" d., single handle, pink .. 6.00
Bowl, 7" d., black 16.50
Bowl, 7" d., blue 13.50
Bowl, 7" d., green 6.50
Bowl, 7" d., pink 7.50
Candlesticks, black, pr. 18.00
Candlesticks, blue, pr. 22.00
Candlesticks, green, pr. 12.50
Candlesticks, pink, pr. 10.00
Candy jar, cov., footed, pink 60.00
Coaster, pink, 3" d. 4.00
Console bowl, rolled edge, pink 28.00
Creamer & open sugar bowl, black,
pr. 20.00
Creamer & open sugar bowl, blue,
pr. 17.50
Creamer & open sugar bowl, green,
pr. 13.00
Creamer & open sugar bowl, pink,
pr. 11.50
Cup & saucer, black 11.50
Cup & saucer, green 3.00
Cup & saucer, pink 8.00
Goblet, champagne, pink, 6" h.,
9 oz. 8.50
Ice bucket, blue 47.50
Mayonnaise dish & underplate,
3-footed, green, 2 pcs. 32.50

Mayonnaise set: 3-footed dish, plate
  & ladle; pink, 3 pcs. 45.00
Plate, sherbet, 6" d., black 5.00
Plate, sherbet, 6" d., blue 3.50
Plate, sherbet, 6" d., green 2.50
Plate, sherbet, 6" d., pink 3.00
Plate, salad, 7" d., black or green . . 5.00
Plate, salad, 7" d., blue 5.50
Plate, salad, 7" d., pink 2.50
Plate, luncheon, 8" d., black 9.50
Plate, luncheon, 8" d., blue 9.00
Plate, luncheon, 8" d., green or
  pink 4.00
Plate, 14" d., green 21.00
Punch bowl w/stand, green,
  2 pcs. 275.00
Sherbet, black 8.00
Sherbet, blue 9.00
Sherbet, green 4.00
Sherbet, pink 4.50
Tumbler, whiskey, green, 1½ oz. . . . 6.50
Tumbler, footed, pink, 6 oz. 6.00

DIANA (Press-mold)

Bowl, cereal, 5" d., amber 5.00
Bowl, cereal, 5" d., clear 2.50
Bowl, cereal, 5" d., pink 3.50
Bowl, cream soup, 5½" d., amber . . 8.00
Bowl, cream soup, 5½" d., clear . . . 4.50
Bowl, cream soup, 5½" d., pink 3.00
Bowl, salad, 9" d., amber 7.50
Bowl, salad, 9" d., clear 7.00
Bowl, salad, 9" d., pink 9.00
Bowl, 12" d., scalloped rim,
  amber 7.00
Bowl, 12" d., scalloped rim, clear . . . 6.50
Bowl, 12" d., scalloped rim, pink . . . 9.50
Candy jar, cov., round, amber 26.50
Candy jar, cov., round, clear 15.50
Candy jar, cov., round, pink 21.50
Coaster-ash tray, amber or clear,
  3½" d. 6.50
Coaster-ash tray, pink, 3½" d. 3.50
Console bowl, amber, 11" d. 9.50
Console bowl, clear, 11" d. 5.00
Console bowl, pink, 11" d. 7.00
Creamer & open sugar bowl, oval,
  amber, pr. 10.50
Creamer & open sugar bowl, oval,
  clear, pr. 7.50
Creamer & open sugar bowl, oval,
  pink, pr. 12.00
Cup & saucer, demitasse, amber 7.50
Cup & saucer, demitasse, clear 4.00
Cup & saucer, demitasse, pink 15.00
Cup & saucer, amber 8.00
Cup & saucer, clear 5.00
Cup & saucer, pink 7.50
Plate, bread & butter, 6" d.,
  amber 2.50
Plate, bread & butter, 6" d., clear . . 1.00
Plate, bread & butter, 6" d., pink . . . 2.00
Plate, dinner, 9½" d., amber 6.00
Plate, dinner, 9½" d., clear 4.00

Plate, dinner, 9½" d., pink 7.00
Plate, 11¾" d., amber 7.00
Plate, 11¾" d., clear 3.50
Plate, 11¾" d., pink 5.50
Platter, 12" oval, amber 9.00
Platter, 12" oval, clear or pink 6.00
Salt & pepper shakers, amber, pr. . . . 71.00
Salt & pepper shakers, clear, pr. . . . 20.00
Salt & pepper shakers, pink, pr. 36.00
Sherbet, amber 7.50
Sherbet, pink 9.50
Tumbler, amber or pink, 4 1/8" h.,
  9 oz. 15.00
Tumbler, clear, 4 1/8" h., 9 oz. 13.00
Water set: pitcher & 6 tumblers;
  green, 7 pcs. 125.00
Junior set: 6 cups, saucers & plates
  w/round rack; clear, set 43.00

DOGWOOD or Apple Blossom or Wild Rose (Process-etched)

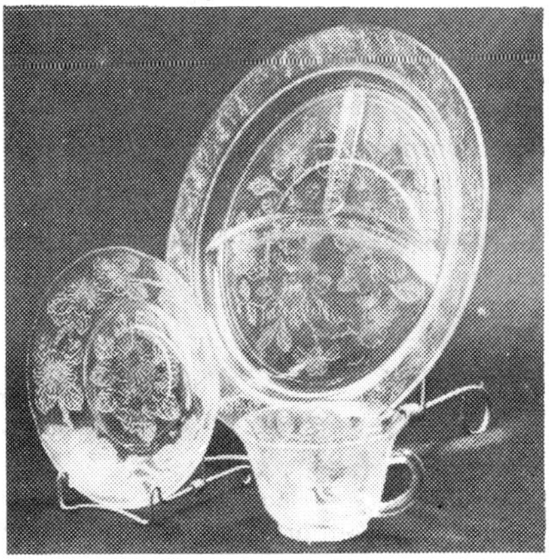

Dogwood Pattern

Bowl, cereal or dessert, 5½" d.,
  clear 6.00
Bowl, cereal or dessert, 5½" d.,
  Cremax 7.50
Bowl, cereal or dessert, 5½" d.,
  green 15.00
Bowl, cereal or dessert, 5½" d.,
  pink 14.00
Bowl, nappy, 8½" d., Cremax 35.00
Bowl, nappy, 8½" d., green 56.00
Bowl, nappy, 8½" d., pink 32.00
Bowl, fruit, 10¼" d., Cremax 60.00
Bowl, fruit, 10¼" d., green 100.00
Bowl, fruit, 10¼" d., pink 197.50
Cake plate, green, 13" d. 55.00
Cake plate, pink, 13" d. 66.00
Creamer & open sugar bowl, thin,
  green, 2¾" h., pr. 74.00
Creamer & open sugar bowl, thin,
  pink, 2¾" h., pr. 18.00
Creamer & open sugar bowl, thick,
  green, 3¼" h., pr. 56.00
Creamer & open sugar bowl, thick,
  pink, 3¼" h., pr. 20.00

Cup & saucer, Cremax 32.00
Cup & saucer, green 16.50
Cup & saucer, pink (ILLUS.) 11.50
Dinner service for 6, pink, 46 pcs. . . 450.00
Pitcher, 8" h., jug-type, green 42.50
Pitcher, 8" h., jug-type,
   pink .30.00 to 45.00
Pitcher, 8" h., jug-type, hand-
   decorated, clear 170.00
Pitcher, 8" h., jug-type, hand-
   decorated, green 375.00
Pitcher, 8" h., jug-type, hand-
   decorated, pink 110.00
Plate, bread & butter, 6" d., green . . 3.50
Plate, bread & butter, 6" d., pink . . . 4.00
Plate, luncheon, 8" d., clear 3.00
Plate, luncheon, 8" d., green 4.50
Plate, luncheon, 8" d., pink 4.00
Plate, dinner, 9¼" d., pink 16.00
Plate, grill, 10½" d., overall patt.,
   green 18.00
Plate, grill, 10½" d., overall patt.,
   pink (ILLUS.) 11.50
Plate, grill, 10½" d., border patt.,
   green 9.50
Plate, grill, 10½" d., border patt.,
   pink 11.00
Plate, salver, 12" d., Monax 17.50
Plate, salver, 12" d., pink 19.50
Platter, 12" oval, pink 290.00
Sherbet, low foot, pink 16.00
Tid bit server, 2-tier, pink 43.00
Tumbler, plain, pink, 3½" h.,
   5 oz. 4.00
Tumbler, decorated, green, 4" h.,
   10 oz. 67.50
Tumbler, decorated, pink, 4" h.,
   10 oz. 20.00
Tumbler, plain, green, 4" h.,
   10 oz. 4.00
Tumbler, plain, pink, 4" h.,
   10 oz. 4.50
Tumbler, decorated, green, 4¾" h.,
   11 oz. 105.00
Tumbler, decorated, pink, 4¾" h.,
   11 oz. 30.00
Tumbler, plain, green, 4¾" h.,
   11 oz. 10.00
Tumbler, plain, pink, 4¾" h.,
   11 oz. 4.50
Tumbler, decorated, pink, 5" h.,
   12 oz. 34.00
Tumbler, plain, pink, 5" h.,
   12 oz. 9.00
Water set: decorated pitcher & 6
   decorated tumblers; pink, 7 pcs. . . . 275.00
Water set: plain pitcher & 6 plain
   tumblers; pink, 7 pcs. 175.00
Water set: plain pitcher & 6 plain
   tumblers; green, 7 pcs. 80.00

DORIC (Press-mold)

Bowl, nappy, 4½" d., Delfite 6.00
Bowl, nappy, 4½" d., green 4.50

Doric Bowl

Bowl, nappy, 4½" d., pink (ILLUS.) . . 4.50
Bowl, cereal, 5½" d., green 41.00
Bowl, cereal, 5½" d., pink 19.00
Bowl, 9" d., handled, green 12.00
Bowl, 9" d., handled, pink 11.00
Bowl, 9" oval vegetable, green 12.00
Bowl, 9" oval vegetable, pink 11.50
Butter dish, cov., green 66.00
Butter dish, cov., pink 55.00
Cake plate, green, 10" d. 12.50
Cake plate, pink, 10" d. 11.50
Candy dish, 3-section, Delfite or
   pink, 6" 4.00
Candy dish, 3-section, green, 6" 6.00
Candy jar, cov., green or pink,
   8" h. 26.00
Coaster, green, 3" d. 12.00
Coaster, pink, 3" d. 9.00
Creamer & cov. sugar bowl, green,
   pr. 31.00
Creamer & cov. sugar bowl, pink,
   pr. 24.00
Creamer & open sugar bowl, green,
   pr. 14.00
Creamer & open sugar bowl, pink,
   pr. 18.00
Cup & saucer, green 9.00
Cup & saucer, pink 7.50
Pitcher, 5" or 6" h., 36 oz., jug-type,
   green 31.50
Pitcher, 5" or 6" h., 36 oz., jug-type,
   pink 25.00
Pitcher, 7" h., 47 oz., pink 200.00
Plate, sherbet, 6" d., green or
   pink 2.00
Plate, salad, 7" d., green 11.50
Plate, salad, 7" d., pink 10.00

Doric Plate

Plate, dinner, 9" d., pink
(ILLUS.) 7.50
Plate, grill, 9" d., green 10.50
Plate, grill, 9" d., pink 7.00
Platter, 12" oval, green 12.50
Platter, 12" oval, pink 13.00
Relish, clear, 4 x 4" 7.50
Relish, green, 4 x 4" 7.00
Relish, pink, 4 x 4" 5.50
Relish, green, 4 x 8" 10.00
Relish, pink, 4 x 8" 6.50
Relish, green, 8 x 8" 12.50
Relish, pink, 8 x 8" 11.00
Relish, square inserts in metal
holder, green 37.00
Relish, square inserts in metal
holder, pink 34.00
Relish, 4-part, handled, green 30.00
Relish, 4 part, handled, pink 33.00
Salt & pepper shakers, clear, pr. 22.00
Salt & pepper shakers, green, pr. 29.50
Salt & pepper shakers, pink, pr. 23.00
Sandwich tray, handled, green,
10" d. 10.00
Sandwich tray, handled, pink,
10" d. 12.50
Sherbet, Delfite 4.50
Sherbet, green 8.50
Sherbet, pink 7.00
Tumbler, green, 4½" h., 9 oz. 57.00
Tumbler, pink, 4½" h., 9 oz. 28.50
Tumbler, footed, green, 4" h.,
10 oz. 47.00
Tumbler, footed, pink, 4" h.,
10 oz. 22.50
Tumbler, footed, green, 5" h.,
13 oz. 51.50
Tumbler, footed, pink, 5" h.,
13 oz. 35.50

DORIC & PANSY (Press-mold)

Bowl, 4½" d., clear, green
or pink 6.50
Bowl, 4½" d., ultramarine 9.50
Bowl, 8" d., clear 16.00
Bowl, 8" d., pink 17.50
Bowl, 8" d., ultramarine 60.00
Bowl, 9" d., handled, clear 16.50
Bowl, 9" d., handled, green 20.00
Bowl, 9" d., handled, ultramarine . . . 21.00
Butter dish, cov., ultramarine 505.00
Creamer & open sugar bowl,
ultramarine, pr. 300.00
Cup & saucer, clear 13.00
Cup & saucer, ultramarine 15.00
Plate, sherbet, 6" d., green 8.00
Plate, sherbet, 6" d., pink 6.50
Plate, sherbet, 6" d., ultramarine . . . 7.00
Plate, salad, 7" d., ultramarine 23.50
Plate, dinner, 9" d., green 19.00
Plate, dinner, 9" d., ultramarine 21.50
Salt & pepper shakers, ultramarine,
pr. 425.00
Tray, handled, clear, 10" 15.00

Tray, handled, green, 10" 9.00
Tray, handled, ultramarine, 10" 17.50
Tumbler, green, 4½" h., 9 oz. 31.00
Tumbler, ultramarine, 4½" h.,
9 oz. 32.50

PRETTY POLLY PARTY DISHES

Creamer, pink 25.00
Creamer, ultramarine 30.00
Creamer & sugar bowl, pink, pr. . . . 40.00
Creamer & sugar bowl, ultramarine,
pr. . . . . 55.00 to 70.00
Cup & saucer, pink 21.50
Cup & saucer, ultramarine 29.00
Plate, pink 6.00
Plate, ultramarine 8.00
Sugar bowl, pink 23.00
Sugar bowl, ultramarine 26.00
14 piece set, pink 167.50
14 piece set, ultramarine 210.00

ENGLISH HOBNAIL (Handmade - not true Depression)

English Hobnail Nut Cup

Ash tray, clear, 4½" d. 20.00
Ash tray, pink, 4½" d. 26.00
Bowl, nappy, 4½" d., amber 8.00
Bowl, nappy, 4½" d., clear 4.00
Bowl, nappy, 4½" d., green 7.00
Bowl, nappy, 4½" d., pink 10.00
Bowl, nappy, 4½" sq., pink 14.00
Bowl, cream soup, 4¾" d., clear . . . 8.50
Bowl, cream soup, 4¾" d., pink 11.00
Bowl, mayonnaise, 6" d., clear 11.50
Bowl, mayonnaise, 6" d., green 10.00
Bowl, nappy, 6½" d., clear 6.00
Bowl, nappy, 6½" d., green 9.00
Bowl, nappy, 6½" d., pink 8.00
Bowl, 6¾" d., turquoise 22.50
Bowl, fruit, 8" d., 2-handled, footed,
amber 35.00
Bowl, fruit, 8" d., 2-handled, footed,
clear 17.50
Bowl, fruit, 8" d., 2-handled, footed,
green 25.50
Bowl, fruit, 8" d., 2-handled, footed,
pink 28.00
Bowl, fruit, 8" d., 2-handled, footed,
turquoise 34.00
Bowl, nappy, 8" d., green 26.00
Bowl, 12" d., canted (bell) sides,
clear 35.00

Bowl, 12" d., canted (bell) sides,
   turquoise 77.00
Bowl, 12" d., flared, blue 50.00
Bowl, 12" d., flared, green 23.00
Bowl, 12" d., flared, turquoise 30.00
Candlesticks, amber or clear,
   3½" h., pr. 19.50
Candlesticks, green, 3½" h., pr. 28.00
Candlesticks, pink, 3½" h., pr. 30.00
Candlesticks, turquoise, 3½" h.,
   pr. 67.50
Candlesticks, amber or green,
   8½" h., pr. 75.00
Candlesticks, clear, 8½" h., pr. 27.50
Candlesticks, pink, 8½" h., pr. 39.00
Candlesticks, turquoise, 8½" h.,
   pr. 42.50
Candy dish, cov., amber 35.00
Candy dish, cov., clear 25.00
Candy dish, cov., cobalt blue 275.00
Candy dish, cov., green 40.00
Candy dish, cov., pink 46.00
Celery tray, clear, 9" l. 12.00
Celery tray, clear, 12" l. 8.00
Cigarette jar, cov., clear 14.00
Cigarette jar, cov., pink 23.50
Coaster, clear, 5½" d. 4.00
Cologne bottle, blue 30.00
Cologne bottle, clear 22.50
Cologne bottle, green 28.00
Cologne bottle, pink 27.00
Cologne bottle, turquoise 31.00
Cologne bottles w/stoppers, cobalt
   blue, pr. 100.00
Cologne bottles w/stoppers, tur-
   quoise, pr. 125.00
Compote, 5" d., rounded sides,
   clear 12.00
Creamer, clear 6.50
Creamer, pink 17.00
Creamer, turquoise 33.75
Cruet, oil, clear, 2 oz. 40.00
Cruet, oil, clear, 6 oz. 21.00
Cruet, oil, pink, 6 oz. 25.00
Cup & saucer, clear 8.50
Cup & saucer, green or pink 35.00
Dish, cov., 3-footed, blue 14.00
Dish, cov., 3-footed, clear 35.00
Dish, cov., 3-footed, green 37.00
Dish, cov., 3-footed, pink 47.50
Dresser set: cov. puff box & 2 co-
   logne bottles; turquoise, 3 pcs. 120.00
Egg cup, clear 14.50
Finger bowl, clear, 4½" d. 4.50
Finger bowl, pink, 4½" d. 9.00
Flip jar, cov., amber 225.00
Goblet, cordial, clear, 1 oz. 11.00
Goblet, wine, clear, 2 oz. 8.00
Goblet, cocktail, clear, 3 oz. 8.00
Goblet, cocktail, green or pink,
   3 oz. 15.00
Goblet, claret, clear, 5 oz. 6.00
Goblet, claret, green, 5 oz. 20.00
Goblet, claret, pink, 5 oz. 12.50

Goblet, clear, 6¼" h., 8 oz. 6.50
Goblet, green, 6¼" h., 8 oz. 22.50
Goblet, pink, 6¼" h., 8 oz. 19.50
Goblet, topaz, 6¼" h., 8 oz. 12.00
Goblet, turquoise, 6¼" h., 8 oz. 44.00
Ivy ball, clear 10.00
Lamp, clear, 6¼" h. 41.00
Lamp, green, 6¼" h. 70.00
Lamp, pink, 6¼" h. 66.00
Lamp, amber, 9¼" h. 97.50
Lamp, clear, 9¼" h. 24.00
Lamp, green, 9¼" h. 74.00
Lamp, pink, 9¼" h. 85.00
Lamp, turquoise, 9¼" h. 120.00
Marmalade jar, cov., clear 13.50
Marmalade jar, cov., pink 24.50
Nut cup, individual size, footed,
   amber or clear 5.50
Nut cup, individual size, footed,
   blue 14.00
Nut cup, individual size, footed,
   green 11.00
Nut cup, individual size, footed,
   pink (ILLUS.) 12.50
Nut cup, individual size, footed,
   turquoise 25.00
Pickle dish, clear, 8" oblong 5.00
Pitcher, 38 oz., clear 38.00
Pitcher, 38 oz., pink 250.00
Pitcher, ½ gal., straight sides,
   amber 125.00
Plate, sherbet, 6" d., clear or
   pink 3.00
Plate, sherbet, 6" d., green 4.00
Plate, luncheon, 8" d., clear 3.50
Plate, luncheon, 8" d., green or
   pink 6.50
Plate, luncheon, 8" d., turquoise 15.00
Plate, luncheon, 8" sq., clear 4.50
Plate, luncheon, 8" sq., green 8.00
Plate, luncheon, 8" sq., turquoise ... 16.00
Plate, dinner, 10" d., clear 7.50
Plate, dinner, 10" d., green 16.50
Plate, dinner, 10" d., pink 18.50
Plate, 10" d., clear 17.50
Puff box, cov., blue 38.00
Puff box, cov., clear 35.00
Puff box, cov., green 26.50
Puff box, cov., pink 28.00
Puff box, cov., turquoise 44.50
Relish, 3-part, clear, 8" d. 18.00
Relish, 5-part, clear, 10" d. 26.00
Rose bowl, clear, 4" 15.00
Rose bowl, clear, 6" 16.00
Salt & pepper shakers, amber, pr. ... 54.00
Salt & pepper shakers, clear, pr. 19.00
Salt & pepper shakers, green, pr.... 45.00
Salt & pepper shakers, pink, pr. 56.00
Salt & pepper shakers, turquoise,
   pr. 138.00
Sherbet, low foot, clear 4.50
Sherbet, low foot, pink 11.50
Sherbet, high foot, clear 6.50
Sugar bowl, open, clear 5.00

Sugar bowl, open, green 8.00
Sugar bowl, open, footed, clear 7.00
Sugar bowl, open, footed, pink 12.50
Sugar bowl, open, footed,
  turquoise 25.00
Tid bit server, 2-tier, clear 18.50
Tumbler, whiskey, clear, 3 oz 5.50
Tumbler, clear, 3¾" h., 5 oz. 5.50
Tumbler, footed, clear, 7 oz. 6.00
Tumbler, amber, 3¾" h., 8 oz. 6.00
Tumbler, clear, green or pink,
  3¾" h., 8 oz. 8.00
Tumbler, footed, clear, 9 oz. 7.50
Tumbler, footed, green, 9 oz. 15.00
Tumbler, clear, 4" h., 10 oz. 6.00
Tumbler, clear, 5" h., 12 oz. 6.00
Tumbler, pink, 5" h., 12 oz. 12.00
Tumbler, footed, clear, 12½ oz. 8.00
Tumbler, footed, green, 12½ oz. . . . 11.00
Vase, 5¾" h., clear 20.00
Vase, 7¼" h., green 29.50

FLORAL or Poinsettia (Process-etched)

Floral Sugar Bowl

Bowl, berry, 4" d., green 11.50
Bowl, berry, 4" d., pink 9.50
Bowl, nappy, 7½" d., green 12.00
Bowl, nappy, 7½" d., pink 13.00
Bowl, cov. vegetable, 8" d., green . . 28.00
Bowl, cov. vegetable, 8" d., pink . . . 22.50
Bowl, 9" oval vegetable, green 12.00
Bowl, 9" oval vegetable, pink 10.00
Butter dish, cov., green 66.00
Butter dish, cov., pink 64.00
Candlesticks, green, pr. 62.00
Candlesticks, pink, pr. 49.00
Candy jar, cov., green 27.00
Candy jar, cov., pink 25.50
Coaster, green, 3¼" d. 6.75
Coaster, pink, 3¼" d. 6.00
Creamer, green or pink 8.50
Cup & saucer, green 13.50
Cup & saucer, pink 12.00
Ice tub, oval, pink, 3½" h. 495.00
Pitcher, 5½" h., 24 oz., green 370.00
Pitcher, 8" h., 32 oz., cone-shaped,
  green 22.50
Pitcher, 8" h., 32 oz., cone-shaped,
  pink 20.00
Pitcher, lemonade, 10¼" h., 48 oz.,
  jug-type, green 225.00

Pitcher, lemonade, 10¼" h., 48 oz.,
  jug-type, pink 180.00
Plate, sherbet, 6" d., green 3.50
Plate, sherbet, 6" d., pink 3.00
Plate, salad, 8" d., green 6.50
Plate, salad, 8" d., pink 6.00
Plate, dinner, 9" d., green 11.50
Plate, dinner, 9" d., pink 9.50
Platter, 10¾" oval, green 11.00
Platter, 10¾" oval, pink 10.00
Powder jar, cov., green 197.50
Refrigerator dish, cov., green 46.00
Refrigerator dish, cov., Jadite 15.00
Refrigerator dish, cov., pink 8.50
Relish, 2-part, green 10.50
Relish, 2-part, pink 9.50
Rose bowl, footed, green 385.00
Salt & pepper shakers, footed,
  green, 4" h., pr. 33.00
Salt & pepper shakers, footed, pink,
  4" h., pr. 28.00
Salt & pepper shakers, green, 6" h.,
  pr. 34.00
Salt & pepper shakers, pink, 6" h.,
  pr. 30.00
Sherbet, green 9.00
Sherbet, pink 8.00
Sugar bowl, cov., green 19.00
Sugar bowl, cov., pink 17.00
Sugar bowl, open, green 7.00
Sugar bowl, open, pink (ILLUS.) 7.75
Tray, handled, green, 6" sq. 14.00
Tray, handled, pink, 6" sq. 12.00
Tumbler, footed, green, 4" h.,
  5 oz. 14.00
Tumbler, footed, pink, 4" h., 5 oz. . . 11.50
Tumbler, footed, green, 4¾" h.,
  7 oz. 13.00
Tumbler, footed, pink, 4¾" h.,
  7 oz. 10.50
Tumbler, green, 4½" h., 9 oz. 155.00
Tumbler, footed, green, 5¼" h.,
  9 oz. 31.00
Tumbler, footed, pink, 5¼" h.,
  9 oz. 30.00
Vase, 6 7/8" h., octagonal, green . . 405.00
Water set: cone-shaped pitcher & 6
  footed tumblers; pink, 7 pcs. 80.00

(OLD) FLORENTINE or Poppy No. 1 (Process-etched)

Bowl, berry, 5" d., clear 5.50
Bowl, berry, 5" d., cobalt blue 17.00
Bowl, berry, 5" d., green 9.00
Bowl, berry, 5" d, pink 8.50
Bowl, berry, 5" d., yellow 9.50
Bowl, nappy, 6" d., green 29.00
Bowl, nappy, 6" d., pink 14.00
Bowl, 8½" d., green 23.00
Bowl, 8½" d., pink 32.00
Bowl, 8½" d., yellow 21.00
Bowl, cov. vegetable, 9½" oval,
  clear 27.50

Bowl, cov. vegetable, 9½" oval, green 29.00
Bowl, cov. vegetable, 9½" oval, pink 44.50
Bowl, 9½" oval vegetable, green or yellow 19.00
Bowl, 9½" oval vegetable, pink 18.00
Butter dish, cov., clear 115.00
Butter dish, cov., green 117.50
Butter dish, cov., pink 130.00
Butter dish, cov., yellow 107.00
Candy dish, cov., clear 75.00
Coaster-ash tray, green 20.00
Coaster-ash tray, pink 31.50
Coaster-ash tray, yellow 35.00
Creamer, plain rim, clear 6.50
Creamer, plain rim, green 7.50
Creamer, plain rim, pink 8.50
Creamer, plain rim, yellow 8.00
Creamer, ruffled rim, clear 13.75
Creamer, ruffled rim, cobalt blue ... 41.50
Creamer, ruffled rim, green 22.00
Creamer, ruffled rim, pink 20.00
Cup & saucer, clear 6.50
Cup & saucer, green or yellow 8.00
Cup & saucer, pink 10.00
Nut dish, ruffled rim, green 50.00
Pitcher, 6½" h., 36 oz., jug-type, clear 30.00
Pitcher, 6½" h., 36 oz., jug-type, green 32.50
Pitcher, 6½" h., 36 oz., jug-type, pink 38.00
Pitcher, 6½" h., 36 oz., jug-type, yellow 37.00

Florentine Pitcher & Tumblers

Pitcher, 7½" h., 54 oz., clear (ILLUS.)........................ 41.50
Pitcher, 7½" h., 54 oz., green 68.50
Pitcher, 7½" h., 54 oz., pink 98.00
Pitcher, 7½" h., 54 oz., yellow 137.50
Plate, sherbet, 6" d., clear 2.50
Plate, sherbet, 6" d., green or pink 3.75
Plate, sherbet, 6" d., yellow 3.00
Plate, luncheon, 8" d., clear 4.50
Plate, luncheon, 8" d., green 6.00

Plate, luncheon, 8" d., pink 8.00
Plate, luncheon, 8" d., yellow 6.50
Plate, dinner, 9¾" d., clear 6.50
Plate, dinner, 9¾" d., green 10.00
Plate, dinner, 9¾" d., pink 15.00
Plate, dinner, 9¾" d., yellow 11.50
Plate, grill, 9¾" d., clear or green.. 6.50
Plate, grill, 9¾" d., pink........... 10.50
Plate, grill, 9¾" d., yellow 9.50
Platter, 11½" oval, clear 8.50
Platter, 11½" oval, green 14.00
Platter, 11½" oval, pink 11.50
Platter, 11½" oval, yellow 12.00
Salt & pepper shakers, clear, pr. ... 24.00
Salt & pepper shakers, green, pr.... 27.50
Salt & pepper shakers, pink, pr. 45.00
Salt & pepper shakers, yellow, pr. ... 38.00
Sherbet, clear.................... 4.00
Sherbet, green, pink or yellow 7.50
Sugar bowl, cov., clear 18.50
Sugar bowl, cov., green 23.00
Sugar bowl, cov., pink 26.00
Sugar bowl, cov., yellow 24.50
Sugar bowl, open, clear 5.00
Sugar bowl, open, cobalt blue 35.50
Sugar bowl, open, green 6.50
Sugar bowl, open, pink 12.50
Sugar bowl, open, yellow 8.50
Tumbler, juice, footed, clear, 3¼" h., 5 oz................... 7.50
Tumbler, juice, footed, green, 3¼" h., 5 oz................... 12.00
Tumbler, juice, footed, pink, 3¼" h., 5 oz................... 10.50
Tumbler, juice, footed, yellow, 3¼" h., 5 oz................... 13.50
Tumbler, water, footed, clear, 4" h., 9 oz. (ILLUS.) 6.75
Tumbler, water, footed, green, 4" h., 9 oz................... 8.75
Tumbler, water, footed, pink, 4" h., 9 oz................... 17.50
Tumbler, water, footed, yellow, 4" h., 9 oz................... 14.00
Tumbler, iced tea, footed, clear, 5" h., 12 oz................. 8.50
Tumbler, iced tea, footed, green, 5" h., 12 oz................. 13.50
Tumbler, iced tea, footed, pink, 5" h., 12 oz................. 20.50
Tumbler, iced tea, footed, yellow, 5" h., 12 oz................. 17.00

FLORENTINE or Poppy No. 2 (Process-etched)

Ash tray, clear, 2½" d. 8.00
Ash tray, green, 2½" d. 13.50
Ash tray, yellow, 2½" d. 18.50
Bowl, berry, 4½" d., clear 7.50
Bowl, berry, 4½" d., green 8.00
Bowl, berry, 4½" d., pink......... 6.00
Bowl, berry, 4½" d., yellow....... 12.00
Bowl, cream soup w/plain rim, 4¾" d., clear 6.00

Bowl, cream soup w/plain rim, 4¾" d., green	8.00
Bowl, cream soup w/plain rim, 4¾" d., pink	7.50
Bowl, cream soup w/plain rim, 4¾" d., yellow	12.50
Bowl, 5½" d., yellow	27.50
Bowl, cereal, 6" d., clear	14.50
Bowl, cereal, 6" d., green	15.50
Bowl, cereal, 6" d., pink	10.00
Bowl, cereal, 6" d., yellow	28.00
Bowl, nappy, 8" d., green	13.50
Bowl, nappy, 8" d., pink	16.50
Bowl, nappy, 8" d., yellow	21.00
Bowl, cov. vegetable, 9" oval, clear	29.50
Bowl, cov. vegetable, 9" oval, green	34.00
Bowl, cov. vegetable, 9" oval, yellow	40.00
Bowl, 9" oval vegetable, clear	16.00
Bowl, 9" oval vegetable, green	21.00
Bowl, 9" oval vegetable, yellow	18.50
Butter dish, cov., clear	87.50
Butter dish, cov., green	102.50
Butter dish, cov., pink	80.00
Butter dish, cov., yellow	100.00
Candlesticks, clear, 3" h., pr.	45.00
Candlesticks, green, 3" h., pr.	50.00
Candlesticks, yellow, 3" h., pr.	40.00
Candy dish, cov., clear	64.00
Candy dish, cov., green	91.00
Candy dish, cov., pink	90.00
Candy dish, cov., yellow	136.00
Celery, oval, clear	22.00
Celery, oval, green	14.50
Coaster, clear, 3¼" d.	7.50
Coaster, green, 3¼" d.	10.00
Coaster, yellow, 3¼" d.	14.50
Coaster-ash tray, clear, 3¾" d.	13.00
Coaster-ash tray, green, 3¾" d.	14.00
Coaster-ash tray, yellow, 3¾" d.	16.00
Coaster-ash tray, green, 5½" d.	19.00
Compote, 3½" d., blue	42.50
Compote, 3½" d., clear or pink	11.00
Compote, 3½" d., green	22.50
Condiment set: creamer, sugar bowl, salt & pepper shakers & 8½" d. tray; yellow, 5 pcs	115.00
Creamer & cov. sugar bowl, green, pr.	35.00
Creamer & cov. sugar bowl, yellow, pr.	28.00
Creamer & open sugar bowl, clear, pr.	10.00
Creamer & open sugar bowl, green, pr.	14.00
Creamer & open sugar bowl, pink, pr.	50.00
Creamer & open sugar bowl, yellow, pr.	15.50
Cup & saucer, clear	6.00
Cup & saucer, green, pink or yellow	9.00
Custard cup, clear	25.00
Custard cup, green	75.00
Custard cup, yellow	59.00
Custard cup w/underplate, yellow, 2 pcs.	105.00
Gravy boat, yellow	32.00
Gravy boat w/platter, pink, 11½" oval	75.00
Gravy boat w/platter, yellow, 11½" oval	65.00
Nut dish, handled, ruffled rim, blue	32.50
Nut dish, handled, ruffled rim, clear	16.50
Nut dish, handled, ruffled rim, green	50.00
Nut dish, handled, ruffled rim, pink	8.00
Nut dish, handled, ruffled rim, yellow	19.00
Pitcher, 6" h., 24 oz., cone-shaped, yellow	96.00
Pitcher, 7¼" h., 30 oz., cone-shaped, clear or yellow	17.00
Pitcher, 7¼" h., 30 oz., cone-shaped, green	20.50
Pitcher, 7½" h., 36 oz., footed, cone-shaped, clear	17.50
Pitcher, 7½" h., 36 oz., footed, cone-shaped, green	29.00
Pitcher, 7½" h., 36 oz., footed, cone-shaped, yellow	21.00
Pitcher, 7½" h., 54 oz., straight sides, clear or green	39.00
Pitcher, 7½" h., 54 oz., straight sides, pink	96.00
Pitcher, 7½" h., 54 oz., straight sides, yellow	107.00
Pitcher, 8" h., 76 oz., jug-type, clear	77.50
Pitcher, 8" h., 76 oz., jug-type, green	67.50
Pitcher, 8" h., 76 oz., jug-type, pink	225.00
Pitcher, 8" h., 76 oz., jug-type, yellow	18.00
Pitcher, 80 oz., bulbous, clear	44.00
Pitcher, 80 oz., bulbous, pink	190.00
Plate, sherbet, 6" d., clear	2.00
Plate, sherbet, 6" d., green	2.50
Plate, sherbet, 6" d., pink	4.00
Plate, sherbet, 6" d., yellow	3.00
Plate, 6¼" d., w/indentation, clear	7.00
Plate, 6¼" d., w/indentation, green	3.00
Plate, 6¼" d., w/indentation, pink	4.00
Plate, 6¼" d., w/indentation, yellow	20.00
Plate, luncheon, 8½" d., clear	4.00
Plate, luncheon, 8½" d., green	5.00
Plate, luncheon, 8½" d., yellow	5.50
Plate, dinner, 10" d., clear	6.50

Plate, dinner, 10" d., green	8.50
Plate, dinner, 10" d., yellow	10.00
Plate, grill, 10½" d., clear	5.75
Plate, grill, 10½" d., green	10.50
Plate, grill, 10½" d., yellow	8.00
Platter, 11" oval, clear	8.75
Platter, 11" oval, green	13.00
Platter, 11" oval, yellow	11.00
Relish, clear, 10"	10.00
Relish, green, 10"	15.00
Relish, yellow, 10"	16.00
Relish, 3-part, clear	12.00
Relish, 3-part, green	13.00
Relish, 3-part, pink	14.50
Relish, 3-part, yellow	15.50
Salt & pepper shakers, clear, pr. ...	24.00
Salt & pepper shakers, green, pr....	30.00
Salt & pepper shakers, pink, pr.	28.00
Salt & pepper shakers, yellow, pr. ..	36.00
Sherbet, green or pink	5.75
Sherbet, yellow	7.00
Tray, yellow, 8½" d.	66.00
Tumbler, clear, 3½" h., 5 oz.	5.75
Tumbler, green, 3½" h., 5 oz.......	8.50
Tumbler, pink, 3½" h., 5 oz.	8.00
Tumbler, yellow, 3½" h., 5 oz.	10.50
Tumbler, footed, clear, 3½" h., 5 oz.	6.00
Tumbler, footed, green or pink, 3½" h., 5 oz.	8.50
Tumbler, footed, yellow, 3½" h., 5 oz.	9.00
Tumbler, blue, 4" h., 9 oz.	47.00
Tumbler, clear, 4" h., 9 oz.	7.00
Tumbler, green, 4" h., 9 oz.	9.00
Tumbler, pink, 4" h., 9 oz.	9.50
Tumbler, yellow, 4" h., 9 oz.	12.50
Tumbler, footed, clear, 4½" h., 9 oz.	8.00
Tumbler, footed, green, 4½" h., 9 oz.	14.50
Tumbler, footed, pink, 4½" h., 9 oz.	9.25
Tumbler, footed, yellow, 4½" h., 9 oz.	15.50
Tumbler, iced tea, clear, 5" h., 12 oz.	17.50
Tumbler, iced tea, green, 5" h., 12 oz.	27.50
Tumbler, iced tea, pink, 5" h., 12 oz.	25.00
Tumbler, iced tea, yellow, 5" h., 12 oz.	35.00
Tumbler, footed, clear, 5" h., 12 oz.	15.00
Tumbler, footed, green, 5" h., 12 oz.	17.00
Tumbler, footed, yellow, 5" h., 12 oz. (ILLUS.)	19.00
Vase (or parfait), 6" h., clear	17.50
Vase (or parfait), 6" h., green	38.00
Vase (or parfait), 6" h., yellow	47.00
Water set: cone-shaped pitcher & 6 tumblers; yellow, 7 pcs.	80.00

Florentine Footed Tumbler

GEORGIAN or Lovebirds (Process-etched)

(All items in green only.)

Bowl, berry, 4½" d.	4.50
Bowl, cereal, 5¾" d.	12.00
Bowl, 6½" d.	37.50
Bowl, berry, 7½" d.	43.50
Bowl, 9" oval vegetable	43.00
Butter dish, cov.	60.00
Creamer, footed, 3" h.	6.50
Creamer, footed, 4" h.	10.00
Cup & saucer	9.00
Hot plate, center design, 5" d.	34.50
Plate, sherbet, 6" d.	2.75
Plate, luncheon, 8" d.	6.00
Plate, dinner, 9¼" d.	15.50
Plate, 9¼" d., center design only ...	13.00
Platter, 11" oval	41.50
Sherbet	8.25
Sugar bowl, cov., footed, 3" h.	32.00
Sugar bowl, cov., footed, 4" h.	8.00
Sugar bowl, open, footed, 3" h.	7.50
Sugar bowl, open, footed, 4" h.	7.50
Tumbler, 4" h., 9 oz.	37.50
Tumbler, iced tea, 5¼" h., 12 oz....	66.00

HOBNAIL (Press-mold)

Bowl, nappy, 5½" d., clear	5.50
Bowl, nappy, 7" d., clear	3.00
Creamer & sugar bowl, clear, pr. ...	5.00
Cup & saucer, clear	3.75
Cup & saucer, pink	4.75
Decanter w/stopper, clear, 32 oz. ..	13.00
Goblet, clear, 10 oz.	5.00
Goblet, pink, 10 oz.	35.00
Pitcher, milk, 18 oz., clear	13.50
Pitcher, 8" h., 55 oz., clear or pink	16.00
Pitcher, 67 oz., jug-type, clear or pink	15.00
Plate, sherbet, 6" d., clear or pink ..	1.50
Plate, luncheon, 8½" d., clear......	2.50
Plate, luncheon, 8½" d., pink	3.75

Sherbet, clear	2.00
Sherbet, pink	3.50
Tumbler, whiskey, clear, 1½ oz.	3.25
Tumbler, wine, footed, clear, 3 oz.	4.25
Tumbler, wine, footed, pink, 3 oz.	30.00
Tumbler, clear, 5 oz.	3.50
Tumbler, footed, clear, 5 oz.	3.50
Tumbler, clear, 9 oz.	3.75
Tumbler, pink, 9 oz.	5.00
Tumbler, clear, 10 oz.	6.25
Tumbler, clear, 15 oz.	5.50

HOLIDAY (Press-mold)

Holiday Tumbler

(All items in pink only. Later iridescent pieces not included.)

Bowl, berry, 5 1/8" d.	6.50
Bowl, cereal or flat soup, 7¾" d.	29.00
Bowl, fruit, 8½" d.	14.50
Bowl, 9½" oval vegetable	11.00
Butter dish, cov.	31.50
Cake plate, footed, 10½" d.	56.00
Candlesticks, 3" h., pr.	51.50
Creamer & cov. sugar bowl, pr.	17.00
Cup & saucer, plain base	7.50
Cup & saucer, rayed base	7.00
Pitcher, milk, 4½" h., 16 oz.	42.50
Pitcher, 6¾" h., 52 oz.	22.50
Plate, sherbet, 6" d.	2.75
Plate, dinner, 9" d.	8.50
Plate, chop, 13 5/8" d.	64.00
Platter, 11 3/8 x 8"	10.00
Sandwich tray, 10½" d.	8.50
Sherbet	4.50
Sugar bowl, open	5.75
Tumbler, footed, 4" h., 5 oz.	24.00
Tumbler, footed, 6" h., 9 oz. (ILLUS.)	69.00
Tumbler, 4" h., 10 oz.	14.00
Water set, pitcher & 6 tumblers, 7 pcs.	125.00

HOMESPUN or Fine Rib (Press-mold)

Bowl, 4½" d., closed handles, pink	4.25

Bowl, cereal, 5" d., clear	5.00
Bowl, cereal, 5" d., pink	6.50
Bowl, berry, 8¼" d., pink	8.00
Butter dish, cov., clear	25.50
Butter dish, cov., pink	36.00
Coaster-ash tray, pink	4.50
Creamer, footed, clear	7.00
Creamer, footed, pink	5.00
Cup & saucer, pink	6.00
Pitcher, 96 oz., ball tilt type, pink	61.00
Plate, sherbet, 6" d., pink	2.00
Plate, dinner, 9¼" d., pink	8.50
Platter, 13", closed handles, pink	10.50
Sherbet, clear	4.00
Sherbet, pink	6.00
Sugar bowl, footed, pink	5.25
Tumbler, juice, footed, clear, 4" h., 5 oz.	4.00
Tumbler, juice, footed, pink, 4" h., 5 oz.	4.50
Tumbler, water, pink, 4" h., 9 oz.	8.50
Tumbler, footed, pink, 6¼" h., 9 oz.	9.00
Tumbler, iced tea, clear, 5¼" h., 13 oz.	7.00
Tumbler, iced tea, pink, 5¼" h., 13 oz.	15.00
Tumbler, footed, clear, 6½" h., 15 oz.	13.50
Tumbler, footed, pink, 6½" h., 15 oz.	19.50

CHILD'S TEA SET:

Cup & saucer, clear	20.00
Cup & saucer, pink	28.00
Plate, clear	4.50
Plate, pink	5.50
Teapot, pink	69.00
14 piece set, pink	197.50

IRIS or Iris & Herringbone (Press-mold)

Iris Tumbler

Berry set: 11" d. flared fruit bowl & 6 sauce dishes; clear, 7 pcs.	25.00
Bowl, fruit, 4½" d., amber iridescent	6.50
Bowl, fruit, 4½" d., clear	27.50

Bowl, nappy, 5" d., amber
iridescent 6.00
Bowl, nappy, 5" d., clear 4.75
Bowl, nappy, 6" d., amber
iridescent 10.00
Bowl, nappy, 6" d., clear 36.00
Bowl, soup, 7½" d., amber
iridescent 23.50
Bowl, soup, 7½" d., clear 72.00
Bowl, fruit, 8" d., beaded rim,
amber iridescent 13.00
Bowl, fruit, 8" d., beaded rim,
clear 53.50
Bowl, fruit, 8" d., ruffled rim, amber
iridescent 7.75
Bowl, fruit, 8" d., ruffled rim,
clear 11.50
Bowl, nappy, 9½" d., amber irides-
cent or clear 8.00
Bowl, 11" d., amber iridescent 5.50
Bowl, 11" d., clear 31.00
Bowl, fruit, 11" d., flared, amber
iridescent 6.75
Bowl, fruit, 11" d., flared, clear 8.00
Butter dish, cov., amber iridescent .. 30.00
Butter dish, cov., clear 26.00
Candlesticks, 2-branch, amber
iridescent, pr................... 22.50
Candlesticks, 2-branch, clear, pr. ... 16.00
Candy jar, cov., clear.............. 105.00
Coaster, clear..................... 33.00
Creamer, amber iridescent 7.50
Creamer, clear.................... 6.00
Cup & saucer, demitasse, amber
iridescent 112.50
Cup & saucer, demitasse, clear 58.00
Cup & saucer, demitasse, ruby 100.00
Cup & saucer, amber iridescent..... 10.50
Cup & saucer, clear 13.00
Goblet, wine, amber iridescent,
4" h., 3 oz. 14.00
Goblet, wine, clear, 4" h., 3 oz. 11.00
Goblet, wine, amber iridescent,
4½" h., 3 oz. 12.50
Goblet, wine, clear, 4½" h., 3 oz. .. 11.00
Goblet, amber iridescent, 5¾" h.,
4 oz........................... 14.50
Goblet, clear, 5¾" h., 4 oz........ 14.00
Goblet, clear, 5¾" h., 8 oz........ 13.50
Goblet, amber iridescent, 7" h...... 22.50
Goblet, clear, 7" h. 11.50
Lamp, shade, blue or pink, 11½" .. 35.00
Lamp shade, clear, 11½" 22.50
Nut bowl w/metal insert, frosted
w/pink roses, 11½" 49.50
Nut set: bowl w/metal holder,
cracker & picks; clear, set 43.00
Pitcher, 9½" h., jug-type, amber
iridescent 23.50
Pitcher, 9½" h., jug-type, clear..... 18.00
Plate, sherbet, 5½" d., amber
iridescent 5.50
Plate, sherbet, 5½" d., clear 7.00
Plate, luncheon, 8" d., clear........ 32.00

Plate, dinner, 9" d., amber
iridescent 18.00
Plate, dinner, 9" d., clear 29.50
Plate, sandwich, 11¾" d., amber
iridescent 10.50
Plate, sandwich, 11¾" d., clear 12.00
Sherbet, amber iridescent, 2½" h... 7.50
Sherbet, clear, 2½" h.............. 14.00
Sherbet, amber iridescent, 4" h..... 8.50
Sherbet, clear, 4" h................ 10.00
Sugar bowl, cov., amber
iridescent 11.50
Sugar bowl, cov., clear 12.00
Sugar bowl, open, amber iridescent
or clear 5.00
Tumbler, clear, 4" h. 44.00
Tumbler, footed, amber iridescent,
6" h........................... 9.50
Tumbler, footed, clear, 6" h. 10.00
Tumbler, footed, clear, 7" h.
(ILLUS.)....................... 12.00
Vase, 9" h., amber iridescent 10.00
Vase, 9" h., clear 13.00
Vase, 9" h., pink 48.00
Water set: pitcher & 6 tumblers;
amber iridescent, 7 pcs. 79.00
Water set: pitcher & 6 tumblers;
clear, 7 pcs. 93.00

LACE EDGE or Open Lace (Press-mold)

Lace Edge Compote

Bowl, cereal, 6½" d., clear 6.00
Bowl, cereal, 6½" d., pink 12.00
Bowl, nappy, 7¾" d., plain or
ribbed, pink 23.00
Bowl, 9½" d., plain or ribbed,
clear.......................... 11.50
Bowl, 9½" d., plain or ribbed,
pink 12.50
Butter dish (bon bon or preserve),
cov., pink 43.50
Candlesticks, pink, pr............. 134.00
Candlesticks, pink frosted, pr....... 42.00
Candy jar, cov., ribbed, clear or
pink, 4" h..................... 31.00
Candy jar, cov., ribbed, pink
frosted, 4" h. 27.50
Compote, cov., 7" d., pink 34.00
Compote, open, 7" d., clear 11.50
Compote, open, 7" d., pink
(ILLUS.)....................... 14.00

Console bowl, 3-footed, pink,
10½" d. 121.00
Console bowl, 3-footed, pink
frosted, 10½" d. 54.00
Cookie jar, cov., clear, 5" h. 32.50
Cookie jar, cov., pink, 5" h. 45.00
Creamer, pink 15.00
Cup & saucer, clear 17.50
Cup & saucer, pink 22.50
Fish bowl, clear, ½ gal. 14.00
Fish bowl, pink, ½ gal. 20.00
Flower bowl w/crystal block,
pink 19.00
Flower bowl w-o/crystal block,
pink 13.50
Plate, bread & butter, 7¼" d.,
pink 12.00
Plate, salad, 8½" d., clear 3.50
Plate, salad, 8½" d., pink 11.50
Plate, dinner, 10½" d., clear 16.00
Plate, dinner, 10½" d., pink 17.50
Plate, grill, 10½" d., pink 12.00
Platter, 12¾" oval, clear 10.00
Platter, 12¾" oval, pink 17.00
Platter, 12¾" oval, 5-part, clear 17.50
Platter, 12¾" oval, 5-part, pink 15.00
Relish, pink, 7½" d. 46.50
Relish, 3-part, clear, 10½" d. 12.00
Relish, 3-part, pink, 10½" d. 12.50
Relish, 4-part, pink, 13" d. 28.50
Sherbet, pink 47.00
Sugar bowl, open, clear 9.50
Sugar bowl, open, pink 13.00
Tumbler, pink, 4½" h., 9 oz. 8.50
Tumbler, footed, pink, 5" h.,
10½ oz. 45.00
Vase, 7" h., pink 262.50
Vase, 7" h., pink frosted 55.00

Cake plate, yellow, 11½" d. 30.00
Creamer, footed, clear 11.00
Creamer, footed, green 10.50
Creamer, footed, yellow 16.00
Cup & saucer, clear 9.50
Cup & saucer, green 12.00
Cup & saucer, yellow (ILLUS.) 15.50
Plate, sherbet, 5½" d., clear 4.00
Plate, sherbet, 5½" d., green 3.00
Plate, sherbet, 5½" d., yellow 5.50
Plate, salad, 7¾" d., clear 6.00
Plate, salad, 7¾" d., green 6.75
Plate, salad, 7¾" d., yellow 9.75
Plate, luncheon, 8 3/8" d., green ... 11.00
Plate, luncheon, 8 3/8" d., yellow .. 18.00
Plate, dinner, 9 3/8" d., yellow 37.00
Plate, dinner, 10¼" d., clear 20.00
Plate, dinner, 10¼" d., green 29.50
Plate, dinner, 10¼" d., yellow 39.50
Platter, 11½", clear 8.75
Platter, 11½", green 20.00
Platter, 11½", yellow 29.00
Relish, 4-part, clear, 8" 8.00
Relish, 4-part, green, 8" 13.00
Relish, 4-part, yellow, 8" 25.00
Sherbet, clear................... 10.00
Sherbet, green 13.50
Sherbet, yellow 25.50
Sugar bowl, open, footed, clear 9.50
Sugar bowl, open, footed, green ... 10.50
Sugar bowl, open, footed, yellow ... 15.00
Tumbler, footed, clear or green,
4¾" h., 9 oz. 14.50
Tumbler, footed, yellow, 4¾" h.,
9 oz. 18.50
Tumbler, footed, green, 5 1/8" h.,
12 oz. 17.50
Tumbler, footed, yellow, 5 1/8" h.,
12 oz. 23.50

LORAIN or Basket or Number 615 (Process-etched)

Lorain Cup & Saucer

Bowl, cereal, 6" d., clear 15.00
Bowl, cereal, 6" d., green.......... 37.00
Bowl, cereal, 6" d., yellow 38.50
Bowl, salad, 7¼" d., green 30.00
Bowl, salad, 7¼" d., yellow........ 41.50
Bowl, berry, 8" d., green 63.50
Bowl, berry, 8" d., yellow.......... 127.00
Bowl, 9¾" oval vegetable, green ... 28.00
Bowl, 9¾" oval vegetable, yellow .. 39.50

MADRID (Process-etched)

Madrid Salt & Pepper Shakers

Ash tray, amber, 6" sq............. 177.00
Ash tray, green, 6" sq. 73.50
Bowl, cream soup, 4¾" d., amber
or blue........................ 8.50
Bowl, cream soup, 4¾" d., clear ... 7.00
Bowl, cream soup, 4¾" d., green... 11.00
Bowl, nappy, 5" d., amber 4.00
Bowl, nappy, 5" d., clear 3.00

Bowl, nappy, 5" d., green or pink ..	5.00
Bowl, soup, 7" d., amber or blue ...	8.50
Bowl, soup, 7" d., clear	7.00
Bowl, soup, 7" d., green	9.50
Bowl, 8" d., amber	12.50
Bowl, 8" d., blue	55.00
Bowl, 8" d., clear	9.25
Bowl, 8" d., green	19.00
Bowl, 8" d., pink	15.00
Bowl, fruit, 9 3/8" d., amber	15.5C
Bowl, fruit, 9 3/8" d., green	19.00
Bowl, fruit, 9 3/8" d., pink	10.00
Bowl, salad, 9½" d., amber or green	19.50
Bowl, salad, 9½" d., blue	67.00
Bowl, salad, 9½" d., pink	17.00
Bowl, 10" oval vegetable, amber ...	11.00
Bowl, 10" oval vegetable, blue	26.00
Bowl, 10" oval vegetable, clear	7.00
Bowl, 10" oval vegetable, green ...	13.50
Bowl, 11¾" d., blue	40.00
Bowl, 11¾" d., green	13.00
Bowl, 11¾" d., pink	20.00
Butter dish, cov., amber	54.50
Butter dish, cov., clear	135.00
Butter dish, cov., green	65.00
Cake plate, amber, 11½" d.	9.50
Cake plate, clear, 11½" d.	14.50
Cake plate, pink, 11½" d.	8.50
Candlesticks, amber or carnival, 2" h., pr.	13.50
Candlesticks, clear, 2" h., pr.	12.00
Candlesticks, pink, 2" h., pr.	14.50
Console bowl, flared, amber, 11" d.	11.50
Console bowl, flared, carnival or pink, 11" d.	10.00
Console bowl, flared, clear, 11" d. ...	15.00
Console set: bowl & pr. candlesticks; carnival, 3 pcs.	18.00
Console set: bowl & pr. candlesicks; pink, 3 pcs.	23.00
Cookie jar, cov., amber	33.50
Cookie jar, cov., clear	24.00
Cookie jar, cov., pink	26.50
Creamer & cov. sugar bowl, amber, pr.	30.00
Creamer & cov. sugar bowl, clear, pr.	31.00
Creamer & cov. sugar bowl, green, pr.	35.50
Creamer & open sugar bowl, amber, pr.	9.00
Creamer & open sugar bowl, blue, pr.	26.50
Creamer & open sugar bowl, clear, pr.	12.00
Creamer & open sugar bowl, green, pr.	14.50
Cup & saucer, amber or pink	6.50
Cup & saucer, blue	18.50
Cup & saucer, green	8.50
Gravy boat & platter, amber ....895.00 to 1,000.00	

Hot dish coaster, amber, 5" d.	23.00
Hot dish coaster, clear, 5" d.	21.00
Hot dish coaster, green, 5" d.	30.00
Hot dish coaster w/ring, amber	31.50
Hot dish coaster w/ring, clear	20.00
Hot dish coaster w/ring, green	32.50
Jam dish, amber, 7" d.	13.50
Jam dish, blue, 7" d.	26.50
Jam dish, clear, 7" d.	8.50
Jam dish, green, 7" d.	14.50
Jello mold, amber or blue, 2" h.	7.00
Pitcher, juice, 5" h., 36 oz., amber ..	27.50
Pitcher, juice, 5" h., 36 oz., pink ..	31.00
Pitcher, 8" h., 60 oz., square, amber or pink	31.00
Pitcher, 8" h., 60 oz., square, blue ..	125.00
Pitcher, 8" h., 60 oz., square, clear	21.75
Pitcher, 8" h., 60 oz., square, green	105.00
Pitcher, 8½" h., 80 oz., jug-type, amber	44.50
Pitcher, 8½" h., 80 oz., jug-type, green	170.00
Pitcher w/ice lip, 8½" h., 80 oz., amber	43.00
Plate, bread & butter, 6" d., amber	2.25
Plate, bread & butter, 6" d., blue ...	7.50
Plate, bread & butter, 6" d., clear .	3.75
Plate, bread & butter, 6" d., green ..	3.00
Plate, salad, 7½" d., amber	6.50
Plate, salad, 7½" d., blue	18.50
Plate, salad, 7½" d., clear	5.50
Plate, salad, 7½" d., green	7.50
Plate, luncheon, 9" d., amber or clear	4.50
Plate, luncheon, 9" d., blue	15.00
Plate, luncheon, 9" d., green	7.00
Plate, dinner, 10½" d., amber, clear or pink	25.00
Plate, dinner, 10½" d., blue	53.00
Plate, dinner, 10½" d., green	28.00
Plate, grill, 10½" d., amber or pink	8.00
Plate, grill, 10½" d., clear	6.75
Plate, grill, 10½" d., green	12.00
Platter, 11½" oval, amber or pink ..	10.00
Platter, 11½" oval, blue	24.50
Platter, 11½" oval, green	13.00
Relish, amber, 10½" d.	9.00
Relish, pink, 10½" d.	10.50
Salt & pepper shakers, amber, 3½" h., pr.	33.00
Salt & pepper shakers, blue, 3½" h., pr.	120.00
Salt & pepper shakers, clear or pink, 3½" h., pr.	40.50
Salt & pepper shakers, green, 3½" h., pr. (ILLUS.)	55.00
Salt & pepper shakers, footed, amber, 3½" h., pr.	51.00
Salt & pepper shakers, footed, blue, 3½" h., pr.	115.00

Salt & pepper shakers, footed,
  clear, 3½" h., pr. 39.50
Salt & pepper shakers, footed,
  green, 3½" h., pr. 67.00
Sherbet, amber or clear 4.50
Sherbet, blue 10.00
Sherbet, green 5.50
Sherbet, pink 7.00
Tumbler, juice, amber, 3 7/8" h.,
  5 oz. 11.00
Tumbler, juice, blue, 3 7/8" h.,
  5 oz. 20.50
Tumbler, juice, green, 3 7/8" h.,
  5 oz. 49.00
Tumbler, footed, amber, 4" h.,
  5 oz. 15.00
Tumbler, footed, green, 4" h.,
  5 oz. 44.00
Tumbler, amber, clear or pink,
  4½" h., 9 oz. 10.50
Tumbler, blue, 4½" h., 9 oz. 21.00
Tumbler, green, 4½" h., 9 oz. 19.00
Tumbler, footed, amber, 5¼" h.,
  10 oz. 18.00
Tumbler, footed, blue, 5¼" h.,
  10 oz. 21.00
Tumbler, footed, green, 5¼" h.,
  10 oz. 25.50
Tumbler, amber, 5½" h., 12 oz. 14.00
Tumbler, blue, 5½" h., 12 oz. 31.50
Tumbler, clear, 5½" h., 12 oz. 17.50
Tumbler, green, 5½" h., 12 oz. 25.00
Water set: pitcher & 6 tumblers;
  amber, 7 pcs. 135.00

MANHATTAN or Ribbed Horizontal (Press-mold)

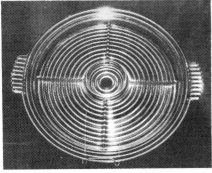

Manhattan Relish

Ash tray, clear 6.50
Bowl, dessert, 4½" d., clear 4.00
Bowl, fruit, 5 3/8" d., handled,
  clear 7.00
Bowl, fruit, 5 3/8" d., handled,
  pink 11.00
Bowl, 7½" d., clear 8.50
Bowl, 7½" d., pink 5.50
Bowl, 8" d., 2-handled, clear 9.50
Bowl, 9" d., clear or pink 12.00
Bowl, fruit, 9½" d., clear or pink ... 18.00

Candlesticks, double, square, clear,
  4¼" h., pr. 8.50
Candlesticks, double, square, pink,
  4¼" h., pr. 23.00
Candy dish, cov., clear 19.00
Candy dish, cov., pink 5.25
Candy dish, open, 3-legged, clear .. 19.00
Candy dish, open, 3-legged, pink ... 5.50
Coaster, clear, 3½" d. 5.00
Coaster, pink, 3½" d. 3.75
Compote, 5¾" h., clear or pink 15.00
Cookie jar, cov., clear 31.00
Creamer, clear 4.50
Creamer, pink 6.00
Cup & saucer, clear 11.50
Pitcher, juice, 42 oz., clear 14.50
Pitcher w/ice lip, 80 oz., ball tilt
  type, clear 22.00
Pitcher w/ice lip, 80 oz., ball tilt
  type, pink 34.00
Plate, sherbet, 6" d., clear 2.50
Plate, salad, 8½" d., clear 7.00
Plate, dinner, 10½" d., clear 9.50
Plate, 14" d., clear 11.50
Relish, 4-part, clear, 14" (ILLUS.) .. 11.00
Relish, 4-part, pink, 14" 37.50
Relish, 5-part, clear, 14" 23.50
Relish, 5-part, clear w/pink inserts,
  14" 32.50
Relish, 5-part, clear w/ruby inserts,
  14" 36.00
Relish tray insert, clear 3.00
Relish tray insert, pink or ruby 4.00
Salt & pepper shakers, clear, 2" h.,
  pr. 15.00
Salt & pepper shakers, pink, 2" h.,
  pr. 29.00
Sherbet, clear 4.50
Sherbet, pink 5.25
Sugar bowl, open, clear 4.50
Sugar bowl, open, pink 6.50
Tumbler, footed, clear, 10 oz. 8.50
Tumbler, footed, green or pink,
  10 oz. 10.00
Vase, 8" h., clear 8.50
Vase, 8" h., pink 15.00
Water bottle, cov., clear 13.50
Wine, clear, 3½" 5.00

MAYFAIR or Open Rose (Process-etched)

Mayfair Covered Vegetable Bowl

Bowl, cream soup, 5" d., pink 29.00
Bowl, cream soup, 5" d., pink
  frosted 23.50

Bowl, fruit, 5½" d., blue 32.00
Bowl, fruit, 5½" d., pink 13.50
Bowl, nappy, 7" d., blue 29.00
Bowl, nappy, 7" d., pink 15.50
Bowl, 9½" oval vegetable, blue 40.00
Bowl, 9½" oval vegetable, pink 18.00
Bowl, cov. vegetable, 10" d., blue . . 75.00
Bowl, cov. vegetable, 10" d., pink
(ILLUS.) 65.00
Bowl, 10" d., blue 38.50
Bowl, 10" d., pink 13.50
Bowl, 10" d., handled, blue 35.00
Bowl, 10" d., handled, pink 13.50
Bowl, 10" d., handled, pink
frosted 12.00
Bowl, 11¾" d., blue 43.00
Bowl, 11¾" d., green 19.00
Bowl, 11¾" d., pink 35.00
Bowl, fruit, 12" d., flared, blue 45.00
Bowl, fruit, 12" d., flared, green 22.00
Bowl, fruit, 12" d., flared, pink 33.50
Butter dish, cov., blue 210.00
Butter dish, cov., pink 43.00
Cake plate, footed, blue, 10" d. 40.00
Cake plate, footed, green, 10" d. . . . 18.00
Cake plate, footed, pink, 10" d. 16.00
Cake plate, handled, blue, 12" d. . . . 37.50
Cake plate, handled, pink, 12" d. . . . 32.00
Cake plate, handled, pink frosted,
12" d. 23.00
Candy jar, cov., blue 140.00
Candy jar, cov., pink or pink
frosted 32.50
Celery dish, blue, 10" d. 25.00
Celery dish, pink, 10" d. 24.00
Celery dish, 2-part, blue, 10" d. 28.00
Celery dish, 2-part, pink, 10" d. 117.50
Cookie jar, cov., blue 145.00
Cookie jar, cov., green 625.00
Cookie jar, cov., pink 28.00
Cookie jar, cov., pink frosted 30.00
Creamer & open sugar bowl, blue,
pr. 92.00
Creamer & open sugar bowl, pink,
pr. 28.50
Cup, blue 29.00
Cup, pink 11.00
Cup & saucer, blue 43.00
Cup & saucer, pink 22.50
Decanter w/stopper, pink, 10" h. . . . 100.00
Goblet, pink, 4" h., 2½ oz. 62.00
Goblet, wine, green, 4½" h.,
3 oz. 300.00
Goblet, wine, pink, 4½" h., 3 oz. . . . 59.00
Goblet, cocktail, pink, 4" h.,
3½ oz. 56.50
Goblet, champagne, blue, 5¼" h.,
4½ oz. 65.00
Goblet, water, pink, 5¾" h., 9 oz. . . 43.00
Goblet, water, thin, blue, 7¼" h.,
9 oz. 100.00
Goblet, water, thin, pink, 7¼" h.,
9 oz. 125.00
Pitcher, juice, 6" h., 37 oz., blue 89.00

Pitcher, juice, 6" h., 37 oz., clear . . . 10.00
Pitcher, juice, 6" h., 37 oz., pink 29.00
Pitcher, 8" h., 60 oz., jug-type,
blue 98.00
Pitcher, 8" h., 60 oz., jug-type,
pink 36.00
Pitcher, 8½" h., 80 oz., jug-type,
blue 120.00
Pitcher, 8½" h., 80 oz., jug-type,
pink 54.50
Plate, bread & butter, 6" w., blue . . 11.00
Plate, bread & butter, 6" w., pink . . 8.00
Plate, sherbet, 6½" d., blue 9.50
Plate, sherbet, 6½" d., green 45.00
Plate, sherbet, 6½" d., pink 7.50
Plate, sherbet, 6½" d., off-center
indentation, blue 18.50
Plate, sherbet, 6½" d., off-center
indentation, pink 19.50
Plate, luncheon, 8½" d., blue 23.00
Plate, luncheon, 8½" d., pink 14.50
Plate, dinner, 9½" d., blue 45.00
Plate, dinner, 9½" d., pink 35.50
Plate, grill, 9½" d., blue or pink . . . 22.00
Plate, 12" d., 2-handled, blue 40.50
Plate, 12" d., 2-handled, pink 32.50
Plate, 12" d., 2-handled, pink
frosted . . . . '. 20.00
Platter, 12" oval, pierced handles,
blue 33.50
Platter, 12" oval, pierced handles,
clear 15.50
Platter, 12" oval, pierced handles,
pink 16.50
Relish, 2-part, blue 41.00
Relish, 2-part, clear 11.00
Relish, 4-part, blue 30.00
Relish, 4-part, pink 23.00
Relish, 4-part, pink frosted 13.50
Salt & pepper shakers, blue, pr. 185.00
Salt & pepper shakers, pink, pr. 41.00
Salt & pepper shakers, pink frosted,
pr. 29.00
Salt & pepper shakers, footed, blue,
pr. 155.00
Sandwich server w/center handle,
blue, 12" 45.00
Sandwich server w/center handle,
green, 12" 17.50
Sandwich server w/center handle,
pink, 12" 26.00
Sandwich server w/center handle,
pink frosted, 12" 23.50
Sherbet, blue, 2¼" h. 52.00
Sherbet, pink, 2¼" h. 107.50
Sherbet, pink, 3¼" h. 11.00
Sherbet, footed, blue, 4¾" h. 50.00
Sherbet, footed, pink, 4¾" h. 43.00
Sherbet w/underplate, blue, 2¼" h.
sherbet 73.00
Tumbler, whiskey, green, 2¼" h.,
1½ oz. 40.00
Tumbler, whiskey, pink, 2¼" h.,
1½ oz. 56.00

Tumbler, juice, footed, pink,
3¼" h., 3 oz. 53.00
Tumbler, juice, blue, 3½" h.,
5 oz. 67.00
Tumbler, juice, pink, 3½" h.,
5 oz. 30.00
Tumbler, water, blue, 4¼" h.,
9 oz. 76.00
Tumbler, water, pink, 4¼" h.,
9 oz. 22.00
Tumbler, footed, blue, 5¼" h.,
10 oz. 86.00
Tumbler, footed, pink, 5¼" h.,
10 oz. 24.00
Tumbler, blue, 4¾" h., 11 oz. 85.00
Tumbler, pink, 4¾" h., 11 oz. 98.00
Tumbler, water, footed, pink,
4¾" h., 11 oz. 78.00
Tumbler, iced tea, blue, 5¼" h.,
13½ oz. 100.00
Tumbler, iced tea, pink, 5¼" h.,
13½ oz. 31.00
Tumbler, iced tea, footed, blue,
6½" h., 15 oz. 102.50
Tumbler, iced tea, footed, pink,
6½" h., 15 oz. 26.00
Vase, 5½ x 8½", sweetpea, hat-
shaped, blue. 63.00
Vase, 5½ x 8½", sweetpea, hat-
shaped, pink. 98.00
Water set: pitcher & 6 tumblers;
pink, 7 pcs. 150.00

MISS AMERICA (Press-mold)

Miss America Creamer & Sugar Bowl

Bowl, nappy, 4½" d., green 6.50
Bowl, nappy, 4½" d., pink 12.50
Bowl, cereal, 6¼" d., clear 5.00
Bowl, cereal, 6¼" d., green 8.00
Bowl, cereal, 6¼" d., pink 11.00
Bowl, fruit, 8" d., curved top,
clear 26.00
Bowl, fruit, 8" d., curved top,
pink 42.00
Bowl, fruit, 8" d., curved top, ruby. . 125.00
Bowl, fruit, 8¾" d., deep, clear 24.00
Bowl, fruit, 8¾" d., deep, pink 38.00
Bowl, 10" oval vegetable, clear 9.50
Bowl, 10" oval vegetable, pink 15.50
Butter dish, cov., clear 160.00
Butter dish, cov., pink 320.00
Cake plate, footed, clear, 12" d. 15.50
Cake plate, footed, pink, 12" d. 27.50

Candy dish w/metal lid, clear,
6¼" d. 20.00
Candy jar, cov., clear. 44.00
Candy jar, cov., pink 93.00
Celery tray, clear, 10½" oblong 7.50
Celery tray, pink, 10½" oblong 14.00
Coaster, clear, 5¾" d. 10.50
Coaster, green, 5¾" d. 6.00
Coaster, pink, 5¾" d. 16.00
Compote, 5" d., clear. 10.00
Compote, 5" d., pink 14.00
Creamer & open sugar bowl, clear,
pr. (ILLUS.) 11.50
Creamer & open sugar bowl, pink,
pr. 21.50
Cup & saucer, clear 8.50
Cup & saucer, pink 17.00
Goblet, wine, clear, 3¾" h., 3 oz. . . 13.00
Goblet, wine, pink, 3¾" h., 3 oz. . . . 41.00
Goblet, wine, ruby, 3¾" h., 3 oz. . . 175.00
Goblet, juice, clear, 4¾" h., 5 oz. . . 15.00
Goblet, juice, pink, 4¾" h., 5 oz. . . . 47.00
Goblet, water, clear, 5½" h.,
10 oz. 14.50
Goblet, water, pink, 5½" h.,
10 oz. 33.50
Goblet, water, ruby, 5½" h.,
10 oz. 150.00
Pitcher, 8½" h., 65 oz., clear. 45.50
Pitcher, 8½" h., 65 oz., pink 70.00
Pitcher w/ice lip, 8½" h., 65 oz.,
clear 46.50
Pitcher w/ice lip, 8½" h., 65 oz.,
pink 92.00
Plate, sherbet, 5¾" d., clear 2.75
Plate, sherbet, 5¾" d., pink 4.00
Plate, bread & butter, 6¾" d.,
clear 2.00
Plate, bread & butter, 6¾" d.,
green 7.00
Plate, bread & butter, 6¾" d.,
pink 5.00
Plate, salad, 8½" d., clear 4.50
Plate, salad, 8½" d., pink 12.00
Plate, dinner, 10¼" d., clear 9.00
Plate, dinner, 10¼" d., pink 16.50
Plate, grill, 10¼" d., clear 6.50
Plate, grill, 10¼" d., pink. 11.50
Platter, 12" oval, clear. 9.00
Platter, 12" oval, pink 15.00
Relish, 4-part, clear, 8½" d. 7.00
Relish, 4-part, pink, 8½" d. 11.50
Relish, divided, clear, 12" d. 15.00
Relish, divided, pink, 12" d. 13.50
Salt & pepper shakers, clear, pr. . . . 21.00
Salt & pepper shakers, green, pr.. . . 187.50
Salt & pepper shakers, pink, pr.. . . . 40.00
Sherbet, clear. 6.00
Sherbet, pink 10.50
Tid bit server, 2-tier, clear 15.00
Tumbler, clear, 4" h., 5 oz. 10.00
Tumbler, pink, 4" h., 5 oz. 34.00
Tumbler, clear, 4½" h., 10 oz. 13.00
Tumbler, green, 4½" h., 10 oz. 11.00

Tumbler, pink, 4½" h., 10 oz.	22.00
Tumbler, clear, 6¾" h., 14 oz.	19.00
Tumbler, pink, 6¾" h., 14 oz.	42.50
Tumbler, ruby, 6¾" h., 14 oz.	41.00

MODERNTONE (Press-mold)

Ash tray, blue, 5½" d.	18.50
Ash tray w/match holder, blue, 7¾" d.	130.00
Bowl, cream soup, 4¾" d., amethyst	8.00
Bowl, cream soup, 4¾" d., blue	10.50
Bowl, berry, 5" d., blue	14.00
Bowl, cream soup w/ruffled rim, 5" d., amethyst	9.00
Bowl, cream soup w/ruffled rim, 5" d., blue	17.00
Bowl, nappy, 6½" d., blue	27.50
Bowl, soup, 7½" d., blue	75.00
Bowl, nappy, 8¾" d., amethyst	15.50
Bowl, nappy, 8¾" d., blue	26.00
Butter dish w/metal lid, blue	61.00
Creamer, amethyst	5.50
Creamer, blue	7.00
Cup & saucer, amethyst	6.50
Cup & saucer, blue	8.50
Custard or jello cup, amethyst or blue	9.50
Plate, sherbet, 5¾" d., amethyst or blue	2.75
Plate, salad, 6¾" d., amethyst	4.25
Plate, salad, 6¾" d., blue	5.50
Plate, luncheon, 7¾" d., amethyst or blue	5.00
Plate, dinner, 8 7/8" d., amethyst	6.50
Plate, dinner, 8 7/8" d., blue	8.00
Plate, 10½" d., amethyst	12.50
Plate, 10½" d., blue	20.50
Platter, 11" oval, amethyst	17.50
Platter, 11" oval, blue	23.50
Platter, 12" oval, amethyst	19.50
Platter, 12" oval, blue	23.50
Punch set: punch bowl in metal holder, 8 cups & ladle; amethyst, 11 pcs.	125.00
Salt & pepper shakers, amethyst, pr.	31.50
Salt & pepper shakers, blue, pr.	23.00
Sherbet, amethyst	6.00
Sherbet, blue	7.00
Sugar bowl, open, amethyst	5.50
Sugar bowl, open, blue	6.25
Sugar bowl w/metal lid, blue	25.00
Tea set, "Little Hostess," 16 pcs.	70.00
Tumbler, whiskey, blue, 1½ oz.	16.50
Tumbler, amethyst, 5 oz.	28.00
Tumbler, blue, 5 oz.	23.00
Tumbler, amethyst, 4" h., 9 oz.	16.50
Tumbler, blue, 4" h., 9 oz.	15.00
Tumbler, amethyst, 12 oz.	43.00

MOONSTONE (Press-mold)

(All items clear to opalescent only. Also see Hobnail pattern.)

Moonstone Tumblers

Berry set, master bowl & 6 sauce dishes, 7 pcs.	38.00
Bon bon, heart-shaped, 6½" w.	7.00
Bowl, dessert, 5½" d., crimped	5.50
Bowl, 5½" d., straight	7.50
Bowl, 6½" d., handled, crimped	8.00
Bowl, 7¾" d.	7.50
Bowl, 9½" d., crimped	11.00
Candle holder, 4¼" h. (single)	6.00
Candy jar, cov.	16.00
Cigarette box, cov.	13.00
Creamer & sugar bowl, pr.	11.00
Cup & saucer	7.00
Dish, cloverleaf-shaped, 6" w.	7.00
Goblet, 10 oz.	13.50
Perfume bottle w/stopper, 5¼" h.	10.00
Plate, sherbet, 6¼" d.	2.50
Plate, luncheon, 8" d.	7.50
Plate, 10" d., crimped	18.00
Plate, 11" d.	15.00
Puff box, cov.	14.00
Relish, divided	7.00
Salt & pepper shakers, pr.	37.50
Sherbet	5.75
Tumbler, 3½" h., 4 oz.	6.50
Tumbler, footed, 5½" h., each (ILLUS.)	14.00
Vase, 3½" h.	10.50
Vase, 5" h.	8.00

MOROCCAN AMETHYST (Early 1960's - not true Depression)

Ash tray, 6 7/8" triangle	9.00
Basket	28.00
Bowl, fruit, 4¾" d.	3.50
Bowl, cereal, 5¾" d.	5.50
Candy jar, cov.	18.00
Cocktail shaker w/chrome lid	16.00
Creamer	8.00
Cup & saucer	4.50
Plate, 6" w.	3.25
Plate, salad, 7¼" w.	3.25
Plate, dinner, 9 3/8" w.	5.00
Punch cup	4.00

Relish, 8".......................... 7.50
Tid bit server, 2-tier 16.50
Tid bit, server, 3-tier 19.50
Tumbler, juice, 2½" h., 4 oz........ 3.50
Tumbler, old fashion, 3¼" h.,
  8 oz............................. 4.00
Tumbler, water, 4½" h., 11 oz...... 4.00
Tumbler, ice tea, 16 oz............. 9.50

NORMANDIE (Process-etched)
Bowl, nappy, 5" d., amber or
  carnival 3.75
Bowl, nappy, 5" d., pink 4.50
Bowl, 6½" d., amber 7.00
Bowl, 6½" d., carnival............. 5.50
Bowl, 6½" d., pink 16.50
Bowl, nappy, 8½" d., amber 11.00
Bowl, nappy, 8½" d., carnival 10.00
Bowl, nappy, 8½" d., pink 13.50
Bowl, 9½" oval vegetable, amber .. 9.50
Bowl, 9½" oval vegetable,
  carnival 11.50
Bowl, 9½" oval vegetable, pink 21.00
Creamer & cov. sugar bowl, amber,
  pr............................... 66.50
Creamer & open sugar bowl, amber
  or carnival, pr................... 10.00
Cup & saucer, amber, carnival or
  pink 6.50
Pitcher, 8" h., 80 oz., amber 46.00
Pitcher, 8" h., 80 oz., pink 72.00
Plate, bread & butter, 6" d.,
  amber 3.00
Plate, bread & butter, 6" d., carnival
  or pink........................... 2.00
Plate, salad, 8" d., amber.......... 5.50
Plate, salad, 8" d., pink 7.00
Plate, luncheon, 9¼" d., amber 5.00
Plate, luncheon, 9¼" d., carnival ... 8.00
Plate, luncheon, 9¼" d., pink 6.75
Plate, dinner, 10½" d., amber...... 20.00
Plate, dinner, 10½" d., carnival 11.50
Plate, dinner, 10½" d., pink 41.00
Plate, grill, 10½" d., amber........ 7.00
Plate, grill, 10½" d., carnival 5.50
Plate, grill, 10½" d., pink.......... 16.00
Platter, 12" oval, amber or
  carnival 9.50
Platter, 12" oval, pink 14.00
Salt & pepper shakers, amber, pr. .. 30.50
Salt & pepper shakers, pink, pr..... 53.00
Sherbet, amber or pink 5.00
Sherbet, carnival 4.00
Sherbet, clear..................... 2.00
Tumbler, amber, 4" h., 5 oz. 8.50
Tumbler, pink, 4" h., 5 oz.......... 28.50
Tumbler, amber, 4½" h., 9 oz. 9.00
Tumbler, pink, 4½" h., 9 oz. 24.50
Tumbler, amber, 5" h., 12 oz....... 17.50
Tumbler, pink, 5" h., 12 oz. 34.50

NUMBER 612 or Horseshoe (Process-etched)
Bowl, berry, 4½" d., green 19.00
Bowl, berry, 4½" d., yellow........ 16.00

Bowl, cereal, 6½" d., green or
  yellow 16.00
Bowl, salad, 7½" d., green 15.50
Bowl, salad, 7½" d., yellow........ 14.00
Bowl, berry, 9" d., green 21.50
Bowl, berry, 9" d., yellow......... 25.00
Bowl, 10½" oval vegetable, green .. 15.00
Bowl, 10½" oval vegetable,
  yellow 22.50
Butter dish, cov., green............ 625.00
Candy in metal holder, motif on lid,
  pink 89.00
Creamer & open sugar bowl, footed,
  green or yellow, pr.............. 22.00
Cup & saucer, green............... 8.50
Cup & saucer, yellow 10.50
Pitcher, 8½" h., 64 oz., green 165.00
Pitcher, 8½" h., 64 oz., yellow 235.00
Plate, sherbet, 6" d., green 2.75
Plate, sherbet, 6" d., yellow 4.00
Plate, salad, 8 3/8" d., green or
  yellow 5.50
Plate, luncheon, 9 3/8" d., green ... 13.50
Plate, luncheon, 9 3/8" d., yellow .. 7.50
Plate, dinner, 10 3/8" d., green or
  yellow 11.00
Plate, grill, 10 3/8" d., green....... 22.50
Plate, 11¼" d., green 10.50
Plate, 11¼" d., yellow............. 11.50
Platter, 10¾" oval, green 14.00
Platter, 10¾" oval, yellow 15.00
Relish, 3-part, footed, green 17.50
Relish, 3-part, footed, yellow 25.00
Sherbet, green 9.00

Number 612 Sherbet

Sherbet, yellow (ILLUS.)............ 10.00
Tumbler, footed, green or yellow,
  9 oz............................. 15.00
Tumbler, footed, green, 12 oz. 75.00
Tumbler, footed, yellow, 12 oz...... 100.00

OLD CAFE (Press-mold)
Ash tray, ruby 4.00
Bowl, nappy, 3¾" d., clear or
  pink 2.50
Bowl, nappy, 3¾" d., ruby 2.00
Bowl, nappy, 5" d., handled, clear
  or pink.......................... 3.50
Bowl, nappy, 5½" d., clear w/ruby
  cover 9.00
Bowl, nappy, 5½" d., pink 13.00

Bowl, 9" d., handled, clear......... 7.00
Bowl, 9" d., handled, pink or ruby .. 8.00
Candy dish, cov., clear 3.00
Candy dish, cov., pink 5.00
Candy dish, cov., ruby 8.00
Cookie jar, cov., pink 32.50
Cup & saucer, pink 6.00

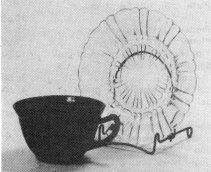

Old Cafe Cup & Saucer

Cup & saucer, ruby cup, clear saucer
  (ILLUS.)....................... 6.50
Mint tray, low, flared, clear, 8" 4.50
Mint tray, low, flared, pink, 8" 5.00
Mint tray, low, flared, ruby, 8" 8.00
Olive dish, clear or pink, 6"
  oblong 4.00
Pitcher, 8" h., 80 oz., pink 67.50
Plate, sherbet, 6" d., clear 3.00
Plate, sherbet, 6" d., pink 6.50
Plate, dinner, 10" d., pink 14.50
Sherbet, clear.................... 3.00
Sherbet, pink.................... 4.50
Tumbler, juice, clear, 3" h......... 4.00
Tumbler, juice, pink, 3" h. 5.00
Tumbler, clear, 4" h. 4.00
Tumbler, pink, 4" h................ 8.00
Tumbler, ruby, 4" h............... 10.00
Vase, 7¼" h., clear 7.00

OYSTER & PEARL (Press-mold)
Bowl, 5¼" heart shape, clear 5.00
Bowl, 5¼" heart shape, pink 5.50
Bowl, 5¼" heart shape, ruby....... 12.00
Bowl, 5¼" heart shape, white
  w/green or white w/pink 5.00
Bowl, 5¼" d., handled, clear 4.00
Bowl, 5¼" d., handled, pink 4.50
Bowl, 5¼" d., handled, ruby 8.00
Bowl, 5¼" d., handled, white 3.50
Bowl, 6½" d., handled, clear....... 4.00
Bowl, 6½" d., handled, pink 7.00
Bowl, 6½" d., handled, ruby 13.50
Candlesticks, clear, pink or white
  w/pink, pr.................... 15.00
Candlesticks, green, pr............ 8.00
Candlesticks, ruby, pr............. 26.50
Candlesticks, white, pr........... 10.00
Candlesticks, white w/green, pr. ... 11.50
Console bowl, clear or pink,
  10½" d...................... 14.50

Console bowl, ruby, 10½" d. 29.00
Console bowl, white or white
  w/green, 10½" d............... 10.50
Console bowl, white w/pink,
  10½" d...................... 15.00
Plate, 13½" d., clear 9.00
Plate, 13½" d., pink.............. 12.00
Plate, 13½" d., ruby 20.00
Relish, divided, clear, 10¼" oval ... 5.00
Relish, divided, pink, 10¼" oval 5.50
Vase, jadite 8.50
Vase, white 14.50
Vase, white w/green or white
  w/pink...................... 13.00

PARROT or Sylvan (Process-etched)
Bowl, berry, 5" d., amber......... 13.50
Bowl, berry, 5" d., green 14.00
Bowl, soup, 7" d., amber or green .. 25.00
Bowl, berry, 8" d., green 46.00
Bowl, 8¼" sq., green............. 68.00
Bowl, 10" oval vegetable, amber ... 37.50
Bowl, 10" oval vegetable, green 35.00
Butter dish, cov., green........... 227.50
Creamer, footed, green........... 18.00
Cup & saucer, amber 29.00
Cup & saucer, green.............. 31.00
Jam dish, amber 24.00
Plate, sherbet, 5¾" d., amber...... 7.50
Plate, sherbet, 5¾" d., green 12.50
Plate, salad, 7½" d., amber....... 22.50
Plate, salad, 7½" d., green 14.00
Plate, dinner, 9" d., amber or
  green 25.00
Plate, grill, 10½" d., amber 14.00
Plate, grill, 10½" d., green 21.00
Platter, 11¼" oblong, amber 33.00
Platter, 11¼" oblong, green 24.50
Salt & pepper shakers, green, pr.... 185.00
Sherbet, cone-shaped, amber 13.00
Sherbet, cone-shaped, green 14.00
Sherbet, amber, 4¼" h............ 11.50
Sherbet, green, 4¼" h. 14.00
Sugar bowl, cov., green 100.00
Sugar bowl, open, amber 10.00
Sugar bowl, open, green.......... 19.50
Tumbler, green, 4¼" h., 10 oz...... 86.00
Tumbler, amber, 5½" h., 12 oz. 117.50
Tumbler, green, 5½" h., 12 oz...... 100.00
Tumbler, footed, cone-shaped,
  amber, 5¾" h.................. 93.00
Tumbler, footed, cone-shaped,
  green, 5¾" h. 102.50

PATRICIAN or Spoke (Process-etched)
Bowl, cream soup, 4¾" d., amber .. 8.50
Bowl, cream soup, 4¾" d., clear ... 5.50
Bowl, cream soup, 4¾" d., green or
  pink 14.50
Bowl, nappy, 5" d., amber or
  green 7.00
Bowl, nappy, 5" d., clear 5.00
Bolw, nappy, 5" d., pink 8.50
Bowl, cereal, 6" d., amber 13.50

Bowl, cereal, 6" d., clear	10.50
Bowl, cereal, 6" d., green	15.50
Bowl, cereal, 6" d., pink	16.00
Bowl, nappy, 8½" d., amber	26.00
Bowl, nappy, 8½" d., clear	16.00
Bowl, nappy, 8½" d., green	18.00
Bowl, nappy, 8½" d., pink	16.50
Bowl, 10" oval vegetable, amber	16.50
Bowl, 10" oval vegetable, clear or green	14.00
Bowl, 10" oval vegetable, pink	16.00
Butter dish, cov., amber or clear	61.00
Butter dish, cov., green	77.00
Butter dish, cov., pink	142.50
Cookie jar, cov., amber	48.00
Cookie jar, cov., clear	56.00
Cookie jar, cov., green	220.00
Creamer, amber	6.00
Creamer, clear	5.50
Creamer, green or pink	8.00
Cup & saucer, amber or green	11.00
Cup & saucer, clear	8.00
Cup & saucer, pink	12.00
Jam dish, amber, 6"	16.00
Jam dish, green, 6"	21.00
Jam dish, pink, 6"	17.00
Pitcher, 8" h., 60 oz., amber	70.00
Pitcher, 8" h., 60 oz., clear	68.00
Pitcher, 8" h., 60 oz., green	76.50
Pitcher, 8" h., 60 oz., pink	135.00
Pitcher, 8½" h., 80 oz., jug-type, amber	87.00
Pitcher, 8½" h., 80 oz., jug-type, clear	71.00
Pitcher, 8½" h., 80 oz., jug-type, green	85.00
Pitcher, 8½" h., 80 oz., jug-type, pink	65.00
Plate, bread & butter, 6" d., amber	6.00
Plate, bread & butter, 6" d., clear, green or pink	4.00
Plate, salad, 7½" d., amber or green	8.00
Plate, salad, 7½" d., clear	6.50
Plate, salad, 7½" d., pink	10.00
Plate, luncheon, 9" d., amber or green	6.00

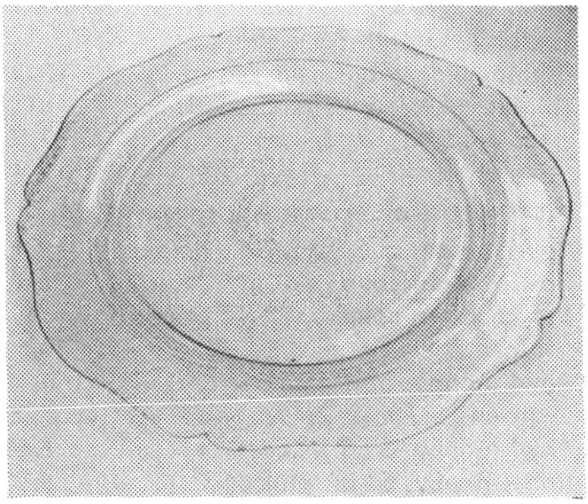

Patrician Dinner Plate

Plate, dinner, 10½" d., amber (ILLUS.)	4.50
Plate, dinner, 10½" d., clear	4.00
Plate, dinner, 10½" d., green	27.50
Plate, dinner, 10½" d., pink	15.50
Plate, grill, 10½" d., amber	6.00
Plate, grill, 10½" d., clear	4.50
Plate, grill, 10½" d., green or pink	10.50
Platter, 11½" oval, amber	15.00
Platter, 11½" oval, clear	9.00
Platter, 11½" oval, green or pink	13.00
Salt & pepper shakers, amber or clear, pr.	36.50
Salt & pepper shakers, green, pr.	41.50
Salt & pepper shakers, pink, pr.	63.00
Sherbet, amber	6.00
Sherbet, clear	5.50
Sherbet, green or pink	7.50
Sugar bowl, cov., amber	52.50
Sugar bowl, cov., green	41.50
Sugar bowl, cov., pink	46.00
Sugar bowl, open, amber	5.00
Sugar bowl, open, clear	4.00
Sugar bowl, open, green	6.00
Sugar bowl, open, pink	7.00
Tumbler, amber, 4" h., 5 oz.	19.00
Tumbler, green, 4" h., 5 oz.	22.00
Tumbler, footed, amber, 5¼" h., 8 oz.	28.00
Tumbler, footed, clear, 5¼" h., 8 oz.	32.50
Tumbler, footed, green, 5¼" h., 8 oz.	45.00
Tumbler, amber, 4½" h., 9 oz.	16.50
Tumbler, clear or green, 4½" h., 9 oz.	19.00
Tumbler, pink, 4½" h., 9 oz.	17.50
Tumbler, iced tea, amber or green, 5" h., 12 oz.	26.50
Tumbler, iced tea, clear, 5" h., 12 oz.	15.00
Tumbler, iced tea, amber or green, 5 3/8" h., 14 oz.	27.00
Tumbler, iced tea, clear, 5 3/8" h., 14 oz.	21.50
Tumbler, iced tea, pink, 5 3/8" h., 14 oz.	32.50
Water set: pitcher & five 4½" h. tumblers; amber, 6 pcs.	145.00

PETALWARE (Press-mold)

Bowl, cream soup, 4½" d., clear or Monax	5.50
Bowl, cream soup, 4½" d., Cremax	6.50
Bowl, cream soup, 4½" d., pink	6.00
Bowl, cereal, 5¾" d., clear	3.50
Bowl, cereal, 5¾" d., Cremax or Monax	5.00
Bowl, cereal, 5¾" d., pink	4.50
Bowl, 8¾" d., clear	10.00
Bowl, 8¾" d., Cremax, Monax or pink	11.50

Bowl, 9¼" oval vegetable, Cremax	9.00
Bowl, 9¼" oval vegetable, Monax	16.50
Bowl, 9¼" oval vegetable, pink	12.50
Creamer & open sugar bowl, Cremax, pr.	8.00
Creamer & open sugar bowl, Monax or pink, pr.	9.00
Cup & saucer, clear	3.00
Cup & saucer, Cremax or Monax	5.50
Cup & saucer, pink	4.50
Lamp, clear	92.50
Lamp shade, Monax, 6" h.	7.00
Lamp shade, pink, 10" h.	8.00
Mustard jar w/metal cover, blue	10.50
Plate, bread & butter, 6" d., clear	1.00
Plate, bread & butter, 6" d., Cremax or Monax	2.00
Plate, bread & butter, 6" d., pink	1.50
Plate, salad, 8" d., clear	2.00
Plate, salad, 8" d., Cremax or Monax	3.50
Plate, salad, 8" d., pink	3.00
Plate, dinner, 9" d., clear	3.50
Plate, dinner, 9" d., Cremax or Monax	4.50
Plate, dinner, 9" d., pink	5.00
Plate, salver, 11" d., clear	4.50
Plate, salver, 11" d., Cremax	5.00
Plate, salver, 11" d., Monax	6.00
Plate, salver, 11" d., pink	8.50
Plate, salver, 12" d., Cremax or Monax	6.50
Platter, 13" oval, clear	7.50
Platter, 13" oval, Cremax	8.50
Platter, 13" oval, Monax	11.00
Platter, 13" oval, pink	9.50
Sherbet, Cremax or Monax	6.00
Sherbet, pink	4.50
Tid bit server, clear	12.00
Tid bit server, Monax	21.50

Bowl, berry, 4½" d., clear	31.00
Bowl, cream soup, 4 5/8" d., amber	15.00
Bowl, cream soup, 4 5/8" d., clear	17.00
Bowl, cereal, 6" d., clear	16.00
Bowl, salad, 7" d., clear	3.00
Bowl, 10" oval vegetable, amber	13.00
Bowl, 10" oval vegetable, clear	17.00
Compote, diamond-shaped, amber	7.50
Compote, diamond-shaped, clear	2.00
Creamer, diamond-shaped, amber	7.00
Creamer, diamond-shaped, clear	6.00
Cup & saucer, amber or clear	9.00
Plate, sherbet, 6" d., amber (ILLUS.)	4.00
Plate, sherbet, 6" d., clear	3.00
Plate, salad, 8 3/8" d., amber	6.00
Plate, salad, 8 3/8" d., clear	5.00
Plate, dinner, 9 3/8" d., amber	11.00
Plate, dinner, 9 3/8" d., clear	8.50
Plate, grill, 10½" d., clear	12.50
Plate, 11½" d., amber or clear	10.50
Plate, 11½" d., w/indentation, clear	17.50
Platter, 11", closed handles, amber	11.50
Platter, 11", closed handles, clear	9.50
Relish, divided, clear, 11½"	12.00
Sherbert, amber	9.00
Sherbet, clear	12.50
Sugar bowl, open, diamond-shaped, amber or clear	5.50
Tumbler, clear, 4¼" h., 8 oz.	19.00
Tumbler, iced tea, clear, 5" h., 12 oz.	39.00
Vase, 12½" h., cone-shaped, clear	24.00

PINEAPPLE & FLORAL or Number 618 or Wildflower (Press-mold)

Pineapple & Floral Plate

Ash tray, clear, 4½"	11.50
Bowl, berry, 4½" d., amber	14.50

PRINCESS (Process-etched)

Princess Candy Jar

Ash tray, green, 4"	48.00
Bowl, nappy, 4½" d., green	16.00
Bowl, nappy, 4½" d., pink	11.00
Bowl, 5½" d., amber or green	18.00

Bowl, 5½" d., pink	13.00
Bowl, 5½" d., pink frosted	7.00
Bowl, 5½" d., yellow	20.00
Bowl, salad, 9" octagon, green or pink	23.00
Bowl, salad, 9" octagon, yellow	71.50
Bowl, 9½" hat shape, green	22.50
Bowl, 9½" hat shape, green frosted	10.00
Bowl, 9½" hat shape, pink	26.00
Bowl, 9½" hat shape, pink frosted	12.50
Bowl, 10" oval vegetable, green	15.00
Bowl, 10" oval vegetable, pink	13.00
Bowl, 10" oval vegetable, yellow	40.00
Butter dish, cov., green or pink	67.00
Cake stand, footed, green, 10" d.	13.50
Cake stand, footed, pink, 10" d.	12.00
Candy jar, cov., green	31.50
Candy jar, cov., pink (ILLUS.)	35.00
Coaster, green, 4"	21.00
Cookie jar, cov., green	31.00
Cookie jar, cov., green frosted	21.00
Cookie jar, cov., pink	33.00
Creamer, amber	6.00
Creamer, green, pink or yellow	8.00
Cup & saucer, amber, pink or yellow	8.50
Cup & saucer, green	10.50
Dinner service for 6 w/serving pieces, green, 46 pcs.	500.00
Pitcher, 6" h., 37 oz., jug-type, green	31.50
Pitcher, 6" h., 37 oz., jug-type, pink	26.00
Pitcher, 8" h., 60 oz., jug-type, amber	49.00
Pitcher, 8" h., 60 oz., jug-type, green	31.50
Pitcher, 8" h., 60 oz., jug-type, pink	30.00
Pitcher, 8" h., 60 oz., jug-type, yellow	55.00
Plate, sherbet, 6" d., amber or green	4.50
Plate, sherbet, 6" d., pink or yellow	3.50
Plate, salad, 8" d., amber	6.00
Plate, salad, 8" d., green	8.00
Plate, salad, 8" d., pink or yellow	6.50
Plate, dinner, 9½" d., amber	7.50
Plate, dinner, 9½" d., green	16.50
Plate, dinner, 9½" d., pink	10.00
Plate, dinner, 9½" d., yellow	9.00
Plate, grill, 9½" d., amber or yellow	5.00
Plate, grill, 9½" d., green	8.00
Plate, grill, 9½" d., pink	7.50
Plate, grill, 11½" d., handled, amber or pink	6.00
Plate, grill, 11½" d., handled, green	8.00
Plate, grill, 11½" d., handled, yellow	5.50

Plate, 11½" d., handled, green	13.00
Plate, 11½" d., handled, pink	11.00
Platter, 12" oval, green or pink	13.00
Platter, 12" oval, yellow	51.00
Relish, green, 7"	60.00
Relish, divided, green	15.50
Relish, divided, pink	13.00
Salt & pepper shakers, green, 4½" h., pr.	35.50
Salt & pepper shakers, pink, 4½" h., pr.	40.00
Salt & pepper shakers, yellow, 4½" h., pr.	67.00
Salt & pepper (or spice) shakers, green, 5½" h., pr.	29.50
Salt & pepper (or spice) shakers, yellow, 5½" h., pr.	48.00
Sherbet, green	12.00
Sherbet, pink	10.50
Sherbet, yellow	21.50
Sugar bowl, cov., amber or green	19.00
Sugar bowl, cov., pink	21.50
Sugar bowl, cov., yellow	20.00
Sugar bowl, open, amber	7.00
Sugar bowl, open, green or yellow	8.50
Sugar bowl, open, pink	6.50
Sugar bowl, open, pink frosted	4.50
Tumbler, green or yellow, 3½" h., 5 oz.	19.00
Tumbler, pink, 3½" h., 5 oz.	13.50
Tumbler, green, 4" h., 9 oz.	19.00
Tumbler, pink, 4" h., 9 oz.	14.50
Tumbler, yellow, 4" h., 9 oz.	13.50
Tumbler, footed, green, 5¼" h., 10 oz.	19.50
Tumbler, footed, pink or yellow, 5¼" h., 10 oz.	14.50
Tumbler, footed, green, 6½" h., 12 oz.	51.50
Tumbler, footed, pink, 6½" h., 12 oz.	28.50
Tumbler, footed, yellow, 6½" h., 12 oz.	19.50
Tumbler, green, 5¼" h., 13 oz.	24.50
Tumbler, pink, 5¼" h., 13 oz.	14.50
Tumbler, yellow, 5¼" h., 13 oz.	17.00
Vase, 8" h., green	18.50
Vase, 8" h., pink	19.50
Vase, 8" h., pink frosted	12.00
Water set: pitcher & 4 tumblers; green, 5 pcs.	112.50

QUEEN MARY or Ribbed Vertical (Press-mold)

Ash tray, oval, clear	2.00
Ash tray, square, clear	4.00
Bowl, nappy, 4" d., clear or pink	2.50
Bowl, nappy, 4" d., handled, clear	2.50
Bowl, nappy, 4" d., handled, pink	3.00
Bowl, dessert, 4½" d., clear	2.00
Bowl, dessert, 4½" d., pink	3.00
Bowl, 5½" d., 2-handled, clear	2.50
Bowl, 5½" d., 2-handled, pink	3.50

Bowl, 6" d., clear or pink 4.00
Bowl, nappy, 7" d., clear 5.00
Bowl, nappy, 7" d., pink 6.50
Bowl, 8¾" d., clear 6.50
Bowl, 8¾" d., pink 11.00
Butter (or jam) dish, cov., clear 19.00
Butter (or jam) dish, cov., pink 76.00
Candlesticks, clear, 4½" h., pr. 10.50
Candy jar, cov., clear............. 12.50
Candy jar, cov., pink 21.50
Celery dish, oval, clear 4.00
Celery dish, oval, pink 17.00
Cigarette jar, clear, 2 x 3" oval.... 4.50
Coaster, clear or pink, 3½" d. 2.00
Coaster-ash tray, clear, 4¼" d...... 2.00
Coaster-ash tray, pink, 4¼" d. 9.00
Coaster-ash tray, ruby, 4¼" d. 4.00
Compote, 5¾" d., clear........... 6.00
Creamer & open sugar bowl, clear,
  pr........................... 6.00
Creamer & open sugar bowl, pink,
  pr........................... 8.00
Cup & saucer, clear 5.00

Queen Mary Cup & Saucer

Cup & saucer, pink (ILLUS.)........ 7.00
Pickle dish, clear.................. 5.00
Plate, sherbet, 6" d., clear or pink .. 2.00
Plate, 6¾" d., clear 2.00
Plate, 6¾" d., pink 3.50
Plate, salad, 8½" d., clear 3.50
Plate, salad, 8½" d., pink 6.00
Plate, dinner, 10" d., clear 10.50
Plate, dinner, 10" d., pink 20.00
Plate, 12" d., clear 6.00
Plate, 12" d., pink.............. 12.00
Plate, 14" d., pink.............. 15.00
Punch cup, pink.................. 4.00
Punch set: punch bowl, 4 cups &
  ladle; clear, 6 pcs. 55.00
Relish, 3-part, clear, 12" d......... 7.50
Relish, 4-part, clear, 14" d......... 8.00
Salt & pepper shakers, clear, pr. ... 13.50
Salt & pepper shakers, clear w/ruby
  tops, pr...................... 20.00
Sherbet, clear.................... 3.50

Sherbet, pink 4.00
Sugar bowl, open, clear or pink 4.00
Tumbler, juice, clear, 3½" h.,
  5 oz........................ 2.50
Tumbler, juice, pink, 3½" h.,
  5 oz........................ 5.00
Tumbler, water, clear, 4" h., 9 oz. .. 4.50
Tumbler, water, pink, 4" h., 9 oz. .. 5.00
Tumbler, footed, clear, 5" h.,
  10 oz....................... 10.00
Tumbler, footed, pink, 5" h.,
  10 oz....................... 21.00

RAINDROPS or Optic Design (Press-mold)

(All items listed are green.)

Bowl, berry, 4½" d. 4.00
Bowl, cereal, 6" d. 5.75
Creamer 5.50
Cup & saucer 4.50
Plate, sherbet, 6" d. 2.00
Plate, luncheon, 8" d. 3.50
Sherbet 3.50
Sugar bowl, cov. 15.00
Tumbler, whiskey, 1 7/8" h........ 3.50
Tumbler, 3" h., 4 oz. 3.50
Tumbler, 4 1/8" h., 9½ oz......... 7.50
Tumbler, 11 oz. 8.50

RIBBON (Press-mold)

(While pattern was also made in black, all items listed are green.)

Bowl, 4" d. 7.50
Bowl, 8" d. 8.50
Candy dish, cov. 23.00
Creamer, footed 6.00
Cup & saucer 5.00
Plate, sherbet, 6¼" d. 1.50
Plate, luncheon, 8" d. 3.00
Salt & pepper shakers, pr. 14.00
Sherbet 3.50
Sugar bowl, open, footed 5.50
Tumbler, 5½" h., 10 oz. 10.50
Tumbler, 6½" h., 13 oz. 14.00

RING or Banded Rings (Press-mold)

Bowl, 5" d., clear or green 4.00
Bowl, 8" d., green 7.00
Butter tub or ice bucket, clear 8.00
Butter tub or ice bucket, green 17.00
Cocktail shaker, clear 9.00
Cocktail shaker, green............ 12.00
Creamer, footed, clear or green 4.50
Cup & saucer, clear or green 4.50
Decanter w/stopper, clear 13.00
Decanter w/stopper, green 18.50
Goblet, clear, 7" h., 9 oz.......... 5.00
Goblet, green, 7" h., 9 oz. 8.00
Ice tub, clear 10.00
Pitcher, 8" h., 60 oz., clear....... 8.50
Pitcher, 8" h., 60 oz., green....... 10.00
Pitcher, 8½" h., 80 oz., clear...... 10.00
Pitcher, 8½" h., 80 oz., green 17.00

Plate, sherbet, 6¼" d., clear 1.50
Plate, sherbet, 6¼" d., green 2.00
Plate, 6½" d., off-center ring,
   clear 1.50
Plate, 6½" d., off-center ring,
   green 2.50
Plate, luncheon, 8" d., clear 4.50
Plate, luncheon, 8" d., green 3.00
Salt & pepper shakers, clear, 3" h.,
   pr 19.00
Sandwich server w/center handle,
   clear 8.50
Sandwich server w/center handle,
   green 15.00
Sherbet, low, clear 3.50
Sherbet, low, green 6.00
Sherbet, footed, clear, 4¾" 3.50
Sherbet, footed, green, 4¾" 5.00
Sugar bowl, open, footed, clear 4.00
Sugar bowl, open, footed, green . . .   5.50
Tumbler, whiskey, clear, 2" h.,
   1½ oz. 3.00
Tumbler, clear, 3½" h., 5 oz. 2.50
Tumbler, green, 3½" h., 5 oz. 3.50
Tumbler, clear, 4¼" h., 9 oz. 3.00
Tumbler, green, 4¼" h., 9 oz. 4.00
Tumbler, clear, 5 1/8" h., 12 oz. 4.00
Tumbler, green, 5 1/8" h., 12 oz. . . .   5.00
Tumbler, cocktail, footed, clear,
   3½" h. 3.50
Tumbler, water, footed, clear,
   5½" h. 3.50
Tumbler, water, footed, green,
   5½" h. 7.50
Tumbler, iced tea, footed, clear or
   green, 6½" h. 4.00

ROULETTE or Many Windows (Press-mold)

Bowl, fruit, 9" d., green 10.00
Cup & saucer, green 4.50
Pitcher, 8" h., 64 oz., green 35.50
Pitcher, 8" h., 64 oz., pink 22.50
Plate, sherbet, 6" d., green 2.00
Plate, luncheon, 8½" d., clear 3.00
Plate, luncheon, 8½" d., green 3.50
Plate, 12" d., green 8.50
Sherbet, green 4.00
Sherbet, pink 2.50
Tumbler, whiskey, green, 2½" h.,
   1½ oz. 7.00
Tumbler, whiskey, pink, 2½" h.,
   1½ oz. 6.00
Tumbler, juice, pink, 3¼" h.,
   5 oz. 5.00
Tumbler, old fashioned, green,
   3¼" h., 8 oz. 3.00
Tumbler, water, green or pink,
   4 1/8" h., 9 oz. 10.50
Tumbler, footed, green, 5½" h.,
   10 oz. 12.00
Tumbler, iced tea, green, 5 1/8" h.,
   12 oz. 12.00
Tumbler, iced tea, pink, 5 1/8" h.,
   12 oz. 8.50

ROYAL LACE (Process-etched)

Royal Lace Cup & Saucer

Bowl, cream soup, 5" d., blue 22.00
Bowl, cream soup, 5" d., clear 7.50
Bowl, cream soup, 5" d., green 20.00
Bowl, cream soup, 5" d., pink 11.50
Bowl, nappy, 5" d., blue 23.00
Bowl, nappy, 5" d., clear 9.50
Bowl, nappy, 5" d., green 16.50
Bowl, nappy, 5" d., pink 15.00
Bowl, nappy, 10" d., blue 37.00
Bowl, nappy, 10" d., clear 12.00
Bowl, nappy, 10" d., green 20.00
Bowl, nappy, 10" d., pink 16.00
Bowl, 10" d., 3-footed, rolled edge,
   blue 42.00
Bowl, 10" d., 3-footed, rolled edge,
   pink 31.50
Bowl, 10" d., 3-footed, ruffled edge,
   blue 185.00
Bowl, 10" d., 3-footed, ruffled edge,
   clear 18.00
Bowl, 10" d., 3-footed, ruffled edge,
   green 32.00
Bowl, 10" d., 3-footed, ruffled edge,
   pink 23.50
Bowl, 10" d., 3-footed, straight
   edge, blue 44.00
Bowl, 10" d., 3-footed, straight
   edge, clear 12.00
Bowl, 10" d., 3-footed, straight
   edge, pink 17.50
Bowl, 11" oval vegetable, clear 13.50
Bowl, 11" oval vegetable, green 18.50
Bowl, 11" oval vegetable, pink 16.00
Butter dish, cov., blue 375.00
Butter dish, cov., clear 48.00
Butter dish, cov., green 205.00
Butter dish, cov., pink 102.50
Candlesticks, rolled edge, blue,
   pr. 90.00
Candlesticks, rolled edge, clear or
   pink, pr. 35.00
Candlesticks, rolled edge, green,
   pr. 56.00
Candlesticks, ruffled edge, blue,
   pr. 95.00
Candlesticks, ruffled edge, clear or
   pink, pr. 35.00
Candlesticks, ruffled edge, green,
   pr. 42.50
Candlesticks, straight edge, blue,
   pr. 90.00

Candlesticks, straight edge, clear, pr. 25.00
Candlesticks, straight edge, green, pr. 56.00
Candlesticks, straight edge, pink, pr. 31.00
Cookie jar, cov., blue 215.00
Cookie jar, cov., clear 29.00
Cookie jar, cov., green 55.00
Cookie jar, cov., pink 34.00
Creamer, blue 28.00
Creamer, clear.................... 7.00
Creamer, green 15.50
Creamer, pink 10.50
Cup & saucer, blue (ILLUS.)......... 28.00
Cup & saucer, clear 7.50
Cup & saucer, green............... 16.50
Cup & saucer, pink 12.50
Nut dish, green, 5" d. 130.00
Nut dish, pink, 5" d. 105.00
Pitcher, 48 oz., straight sides, blue 85.00
Pitcher, 48 oz., straight sides, clear 34.00
Pitcher, 48 oz., straight sides, green 69.00
Pitcher, 48 oz., straight sides, pink 56.00
Pitcher, 8" h., 68 oz., blue 107.50
Pitcher, 8" h., 68 oz., clear......... 36.00
Pitcher, 8" h., 68 oz., green 73.00
Pitcher, 8" h., 68 oz., pink 46.50
Pitcher, 8" h., 80 oz., blue 102.50
Pitcher, 8" h., 80 oz., clear......... 38.50
Pitcher, 8" h., 80 oz., green 76.00
Pitcher, 8" h., 80 oz., pink 52.50
Pitcher, 8½" h., 96 oz., blue 145.00
Pitcher, 8½" h., 96 oz., clear....... 42.00
Pitcher, 8½" h., 96 oz., green 100.00
Pitcher, 8½" h., 96 oz., pink 64.00
Plate, sherbet, 6" d., blue 8.00
Plate, sherbet, 6" d., clear or pink.. 3.00
Plate, sherbet, 6" d., green 5.50
Plate, luncheon, 8½" d., blue 24.00
Plate, luncheon, 8½" d., clear...... 4.50
Plate, luncheon, 8½" d., green 17.50
Plate, luncheon, 8½" d., pink 12.00
Plate, dinner, 10" d., blue 29.00
Plate, dinner, 10" d., clear 8.00
Plate, dinner, 10" d., green 17.00
Plate, dinner, 10" d., pink 12.00
Plate, grill, 10" d., blue........... 20.00
Plate, grill, 10" d., clear 10.00
Plate, grill, 10" d., green or pink ... 12.50
Platter, 13" oval, blue 40.00
Platter, 13" oval, clear 11.50
Platter, 13" oval, green 22.00
Platter, 13" oval, pink 15.00
Salt & pepper shakers, blue, pr. 200.00
Salt & pepper shakers, clear, pr. ... 35.00
Salt & pepper shakers, green, pr.... 90.00
Salt & pepper shakers, pink, pr. 40.00
Sherbet, blue 24.00
Sherbet, clear.................... 6.50

Sherbet, green 15.50
Sherbet, pink 9.00
Sherbet in metal holder, blue 16.50
Sherber in metal holder, clear...... 7.00
Sugar bowl, cov., blue............. 127.00
Sugar bowl, cov., clear............ 24.50
Sugar bowl, cov., green 44.00
Sugar bowl, cov., pink............. 31.50
Sugar bowl, open, blue 21.50
Sugar bowl, open, clear or pink 7.00
Sugar bowl, open, green........... 12.50
Toddy set: cov. cookie jar w/metal lid & 6 roly poly tumblers; blue, 7 pcs. 125.00
Tumbler, blue, 3" h., 5 oz. 26.00
Tumbler, clear, 3" h., 5 oz. 9.00
Tumbler, green, 3" h., 5 oz. 18.00
Tumbler, pink, 3" h., 5 oz. 13.50
Tumbler, blue, 4" h., 9 oz. 23.50
Tumbler, clear, 4" h., 9 oz. 8.00
Tumbler, green, 4" h., 9 oz. 19.50
Tumbler, pink, 4" h., 9 oz. 10.00
Tumbler, blue, 4 7/8" h., 10 oz. 46.50
Tumbler, clear, 4 7/8" h., 10 oz. ... 12.00
Tumbler, green, 4 7/8" h., 10 oz. ... 40.50
Tumbler, pink, 4 7/8" h., 10 oz. 20.00
Tumbler, blue, 5 3/8" h., 12 oz. 45.00
Tumbler, clear, 5 3/8" h., 12 oz. ... 31.50
Tumbler, green, 5 3/8" h., 12 oz. ... 39.00
Tumbler, pink, 5 3/8" h., 12 oz. 33.00

ROYAL RUBY (Press-mold)

(All items in ruby red.)

Ash tray, 4½" sq. 3.50
Bowl, berry, 4¼" d. 3.50
Bowl, 5¼" d. 6.50
Bowl, soup, 7½" d. 8.50
Bowl, 8" oval vegetable 18.50
Bowl, berry, 8½" d. 15.00
Bowl, salad, 11½" d. 20.00
Creamer, flat or footed 6.00
Cup & saucer 4.50
Goblet, ball stem 7.00
Lamp 14.50
Pitcher, 22 oz., tilted or upright 21.00
Pitcher, 42 oz., tilted or upright 20.50
Pitcher, 3-qt., tilted or upright...... 27.50
Plate, sherbet, 6½" d. 2.50
Plate, salad, 7" d. 3.00
Plate, luncheon, 7¾" d. 4.00
Plate, dinner, 9" d. 6.50
Plate, 13¾" d. 25.00
Playing card box, divided clear base 30.00
Punch bowl 27.00
Punch bowl & base 41.00
Punch cup 2.00
Punch set, punch bowl, base & 12 cups, 14 pcs. 77.00
Salt & pepper shakers, pr. 59.00
Sherbet 5.00
Sugar bowl, flat or footed......... 6.00
Sugar bowl w/slotted lid, footed.... 14.00

Tumbler, cocktail, 3½ oz.	5.00
Tumbler, juice, 5 oz.	4.00
Tumbler, water, 9 oz.	4.00
Tumbler, water, 10 oz.	4.50
Tumbler, iced tea, 13 oz.	7.50
Vase, 4″ h., ball-shaped	3.50
Vase, bud, 5½″ h., ruffled top	5.50
Vase, 6½″ h., bulbous	6.00
Wine, 2½ oz.	7.00

SANDWICH (Press-mold)

Sandwich Punch Set

Berry set: master bowl & 8 sauce dishes; clear, 9 pcs.	30.00
Bowl, dessert, 4 7/8″ d., amber or desert gold	2.50
Bowl, dessert, 4 7/8″ d., clear	3.00
Bowl, dessert, 4 7/8″ d., green	1.50
Bowl, dessert, 4 7/8″ d., pink	3.50
Bowl, 5¼″ d., ruby	13.00
Bowl, 6″ d., amber	6.50
Bowl, 6″ d., clear	7.00
Bowl, 6″ d., desert gold	8.50
Bowl, 6″ d., green	15.00
Bowl, salad, 6½″ d., amber	6.00
Bowl, salad, 6½″ d., clear	4.00
Bowl, salad, 6½″ d., desert gold	7.00
Bowl, salad, 6½″ d., green	22.00
Bowl, 6½″ d., scalloped, ruby	10.00
Bowl, nappy, 7″ d., clear	5.50
Bowl, nappy, 7″ d., green	29.50
Bowl, 8″ d., clear	7.00
Bowl, 8″ d., desert gold	5.00
Bowl, 8″ d., green	39.50
Bowl, 8″ d., pink	7.50
Bowl, 8½″ d., ruby	24.00
Bowl, 8½″ oval vegetable, clear	4.00
Bowl, 8½″ oval vegetable, green	40.00
Bowl, 9″ d., clear	12.00
Butter dish, cov., amber	37.50
Butter dish, cov., clear	25.00
Cookie jar, cov., amber	26.00
Cookie jar, cov., clear	22.00
Cookie jar, cov., desert gold	24.50
Cookie jar, cov., green	13.50
Creamer, clear	3.00
Creamer, green	12.00
Cup & saucer, amber or desert gold	4.00

Cup & saucer, clear	3.00
Cup & saucer, green	17.50
Custard cup, clear	3.00
Custard cup, green	2.00
Pitcher, juice, 6″ h., 36 oz., clear	54.00
Pitcher, juice, 6″ h., 36 oz., green	86.50
Pitcher w/ice lip, 2-qt., clear	39.00
Pitcher w/ice lip, 2-qt., green	160.00
Plate, 4½″ d., amber or green	1.50
Plate, 4½″ d., clear	7.50
Plate, dessert, 7″ d., amber	3.50
Plate, dessert, 7″ d., clear	4.50
Plate, dessert, 7″ d., desert gold	2.50
Plate, 8″ d., clear	3.00
Plate, dinner, 9″ d., amber or desert gold	4.50
Plate, dinner, 9″ d., clear	8.50
Plate, dinner, 9″ d., green	40.00
Plate, snack, 9″ d., clear	5.00
Plate, 10″ d., clear	25.00
Plate, serving, 12″ d., amber	6.00
Plate, serving, 12″ d., clear	18.00
Punch bowl, clear (no base)	12.00
Punch bowl & base, clear	27.00
Punch cup, clear	1.50
Punch set: punch bowl, base & 8 cups; clear, 10 pcs. (ILLUS. of part)	40.00
Punch set: punch bowl & 13 cups; white, 14 pcs.	27.50
Sherbet, clear	4.00
Sugar bowl, cov., clear	11.00
Sugar bowl, cov., green	16.50
Sugar bowl, open, clear	3.50
Sugar bowl, open, green	12.00
Tumbler, clear, 5 oz.	4.00
Tumbler, green, 5 oz.	2.50
Tumbler, water, clear, 9 oz.	5.00
Tumbler, water, green, 9 oz.	2.50
Tumbler, footed, clear, 9½ oz.	11.50

SHARON or Cabbage Rose (Chip-mold)

Sharon Tumblers

Bowl, cream soup, 5″ d., amber	15.00
Bowl, cream soup, 5″ d., green	29.00

Bowl, cream soup, 5" d., pink 24.00
Bowl, nappy, 5" d., amber 5.00
Bowl, nappy, 5" d., green 7.50
Bowl, nappy, 5" d., pink 6.00
Bowl, cereal, 6" d., amber 9.00
Bowl, cereal, 6" d., green 16.50
Bowl, cereal, 6" d., pink 12.50
Bowl, soup, 7½" d., amber
  or pink 23.50
Bowl, soup, 7½" d., green 26.50
Bowl, nappy, 8½" d., amber 3.50
Bowl, nappy, 8½" d., green 18.50
Bowl, nappy, 8½" d., pink 14.00
Bowl, 9½" oval vegetable, amber .. 9.50
Bowl, 9½" oval vegetable, green ... 15.50
Bowl, 9½" oval vegetable, pink 13.00
Bowl, fruit, 10½" d., amber 13.50
Bowl, fruit, 10½" d., green 20.00
Bowl, fruit, 10½" d., pink 18.50
Butter dish, cov., amber 34.00
Butter dish, cov., green 66.00
Butter dish, cov., pink 30.00
Cake plate, footed, amber,
  11½" d. 15.00
Cake plate, footed, clear, 11½" d... 8.50
Cake plate, footed, green,
  11½" d. 49.00
Cake plate, footed, pink, 11½" d. .. 20.00
Candy jar, cov., amber 29.50
Candy jar, cov., green 123.00
Candy jar, cov., pink 31.00
Cheese dish, cov., amber 124.00
Cheese dish, cov., pink 580.00
Creamer, green 12.00
Creamer & cov. sugar bowl, amber,
  pr. 23.00
Creamer & cov. sugar bowl, pink,
  pr. 31.00
Creamer & open sugar bowl, amber,
  pr. 13.00
Creamer & open sugar bowl, pink,
  pr. 19.00
Cup & saucer, amber 9.00
Cup & saucer, green 16.00
Cup & saucer, pink 12.00
Jam dish, amber, 7½" 21.50
Jam dish, green, 7½" 29.50
Jam dish, pink, 7½" 80.00
Pitcher, 9" h., 80 oz., amber
  or pink 87.00
Pitcher, 9" h., 80 oz., green 500.00
Pitcher w/ice lip, 9" h., 80 oz.,
  amber 90.00
Pitcher w/ice lip, 9" h., 80 oz.,
  clear 45.00
Pitcher w/ice lip, 9" h., 80 oz.,
  green 325.00
Pitcher w/ice lip, 9" h., 80 oz.,
  pink 96.50
Plate, bread & butter, 6" d.,
  amber 2.50
Plate, bread & butter, 6" d., green.. 4.00
Plate, bread & butter, 6" d., pink ... 3.00
Plate, salad, 7½" d., amber 9.00

Plate, salad, 7½" d., green 11.50
Plate, salad, 7½" d., pink 15.00
Plate, dinner, 9¼" d., amber 7.50
Plate, dinner, 9¼" d., green 11.00
Plate, dinner, 9¼" d., pink 9.50
Platter, 12¼" oval, amber 9.50
Platter, 12¼" oval, green 13.50
Platter, 12¼" oval, pink 12.00
Salt & pepper shakers, amber, pr. .. 30.00
Salt & pepper shakers, green, pr.... 49.00
Salt & pepper shakers, pink, pr. ... 32.50
Sherbet, amber 7.50
Sherbet, green 22.50
Sherbet, pink 8.50
Sugar bowl, cov., green 33.00
Sugar bowl, open, green 8.50
Tumbler, amber, 4" h., 9 oz. 18.50
Tumbler, green, 4" h., 9 oz. 44.50
Tumbler, pink, 4" h., 9 oz. 19.50
Tumbler, amber, 5¼" h., 12 oz.
  (ILLUS. left) 23.50
Tumbler, green, 5¼" h., 12 oz. 69.00
Tumbler, pink, 5¼" h., 12 oz. 29.00
Tumbler, footed, amber, 6½" h.,
  15 oz. (ILLUS. right) 50.00
Tumbler, footed, clear, 6½" h.,
  15 oz. 17.00
Tumbler, footed, green, 6½" h.,
  15 oz. 85.00
Tumbler, footed, pink, 6½" h.,
  15 oz. 31.00
Water set: ice lip pitcher & 8 tumb-
  lers; amber, 9 pcs. 245.00

SIERRA or Pinwheel (Press-mold)
Bowl, berry, 4" d., green or pink ... 5.50
Bowl, cereal, 5½" d., green or
  pink 6.50
Bowl, berry, 8½" d., green 17.50
Bowl, berry, 8½" d., pink 11.00
Bowl, 9½" oval vegetable, green ... 39.50
Bowl, 9½" oval vegetable, pink 22.50
Butter dish, cov., green 42.50
Butter dish, cov., pink 41.50
Creamer, green 10.50
Creamer, pink 9.00
Cup & saucer, green 11.00
Cup & saucer, pink 10.00
Pitcher, 6½" h., 32 oz., green 64.50
Pitcher, 6½" h., 32 oz., pink 47.00
Plate, dinner, 9" d., green 12.00
Plate, dinner, 9" d., pink 9.00
Platter, 11" oval, green 24.50
Platter, 11" oval, pink 19.50
Salt & pepper shakers, green, pr.... 34.00
Salt & pepper shakers, pink, pr. 27.00
Serving tray, 2-handled, green or
  pink 9.00
Sugar bowl, cov., green 20.00
Sugar bowl, cov., pink 23.00
Tumbler, footed, green, 4½" h.,
  9 oz. 40.00
Tumbler, footed, pink, 4½" h.,
  9 oz. 22.00

SPIRAL (Press-mold)

(All items in green only.)

Bowl, berry, 4¾" d.	4.00
Bowl, mixing, 7" d.	16.50
Bowl, berry, 8" d.	11.00
Candlesticks, low, pr.	15.00
Candy dish, cov.	15.50
Creamer & sugar bowl, flat, pr.	15.00
Creamer & sugar bowl, footed, pr.	16.50
Cup & saucer	5.00
Ice or butter tub	12.00
Pitcher, 7 5/8" h., 58 oz.	27.50
Plate, sherbet, 6" d.	1.50
Plate, luncheon, 8" d.	2.50
Preserve, cov.	15.00
Salt & pepper shakers, pr.	21.50
Sandwich server w/center handle	16.00
Sherbet	3.50
Tumbler, water, 5" h., 9 oz.	7.50
Tumbler, iced tea, 5¼" h., 12 oz.	11.50

SWIRL (Press-mold)

Swirl Salt & Pepper Shakers

Ash tray, ultramarine, 5 3/8"	10.00
Berry set: master bowl & 6 sauce dishes; Delfite, 7 pcs.	35.00
Bowl, nappy, 5¼" d., Delfite or pink	5.50
Bowl, nappy, 5¼" d., ultramarine	6.50
Bowl, nappy, 9" d., Delfite	11.50
Bowl, nappy, 9" d., pink	10.00
Bowl, nappy, 9" d., ultramarine	13.00
Bowl, fruit, 10" d., handled, footed, ultramarine	18.50
Butter dish, cov., pink	95.00
Butter dish, cov., ultramarine	170.00
Candlesticks, double, pink or ultramarine, pr.	23.50
Candy dish, cov., pink	46.50
Candy dish, cov., ultramarine	62.50
Candy dish, open, 3-footed, pink, 5½" d.	5.00
Candy dish, open, 3-footed, ultramarine, 5½" d.	8.00
Coaster, pink, 1 x 3¼"	5.00
Coaster, ultramarine, 1 x 3¼"	10.00
Coaster, pink (Goodyear Tire)	15.00
Console bowl, footed, ultramarine, 10½" d.	21.00

Creamer, Delfite or pink	7.00
Creamer, ultramarine	8.00
Cup & saucer, Delfite	13.00
Cup & saucer, pink	5.50
Cup & saucer, ultramarine	8.00
Plate, sherbet, 6½" d., Delfite	4.00
Plate, sherbet, 6½" d., pink	1.50
Plate, sherbet, 6½" d., ultramarine	3.00
Plate, salad, 7¼" d., ultramarine	7.00
Plate, 8" d., pink	4.50
Plate, 8" d., ultramarine	8.50
Plate, dinner, 9½" d., Delfite or ultramarine	8.00
Plate, dinner, 9½" d., pink	5.00
Plate, 12½" d., pink	8.50
Plate, 12½" d., ultramarine	10.50
Platter, 12" oval, Delfite	17.00
Salt & pepper shakers, ultramarine, pr. (ILLUS.)	23.50
Sherbet, pink	5.00
Sherbet, ultramarine	9.00
Soup bowl w/lug handles, pink	9.50
Soup bowl w/lug handles, ultramarine	14.50
Sugar bowl, open, Delfite or ultramarine	7.50
Sugar bowl, open, pink	4.50
Tumbler, pink, 4" h., 9 oz.	9.00
Tumbler, ultramarine, 4" h., 9 oz.	14.00
Tumbler, footed, pink, 9 oz.	9.00
Tumbler, footed, ultramarine, 9 oz.	18.00
Tumbler, pink, 4¾" h., 12 oz.	12.00
Tumbler, ultramarine, 4¾" h., 12 oz.	29.00
Vase, 6½" h., pink	6.50
Vase, 6½" h., ultramarine	15.00
Vase, 8½" h., ultramarine	14.50
Water set: pitcher & 6 tumblers; pink, 7 pcs.	64.00

TEA ROOM (Press-mold)

Tea Room Creamer & Sugar on Tray

Banana split dish, clear, 7½"	42.00
Banana split dish, green, 7½"	73.00
Banana split dish, pink, 7½"	110.00
Bowl, salad, 8¾" d., green	72.50
Bowl, salad, 8¾" d., pink	48.00

Bowl, 9½" oval vegetable, green ... 46.00
Bowl, 9½" oval vegetable, pink 38.00
Candlesticks, green, pr. 47.00
Candlesticks, pink, pr. 39.00
Celery or pickle dish, clear, 8½" . .. 11.50
Celery or pickle dish, green, 8½" .. 22.00
Creamer, clear or pink 10.50
Creamer, green 11.50
Creamer & open sugar bowl on tray,
 green 48.00
Creamer & open sugar bowl on tray,
 pink (ILLUS.) 50.00
Cup & saucer, green 34.50
Cup & saucer, pink 42.00
Goblet, clear, 9 oz. 33.00
Goblet, green, 9 oz. 64.00
Goblet, pink, 9 oz. 55.00
Ice bucket, clear 50.00
Ice bucket, green 54.00
Ice bucket, pink 57.00
Lamp, electric, green, 9" 46.00
Lamp, electric, pink, 9" 50.00
Marmalade w/notched lid, clear 110.00
Mustard, cov., clear 48.50
Mustard, cov., pink 120.00
Parfait, green 52.00
Parfait, pink 29.00
Pitcher, 64 oz., green 98.00
Pitcher, 64 oz., pink 89.00
Plate, sherbet, 6½" d., green or
 pink 17.00
Plate, luncheon, 8¼" d., green 32.50
Plate, luncheon, 8¼" d., pink 31.00
Relish, divided, clear 11.00
Relish, divided, green or pink 15.50
Salt & pepper shakers, clear, pr. ... 43.50
Salt & pepper shakers, green, pr.... 52.50
Salt & pepper shakers, pink, pr. 38.50
Sandwich server w/center handle,
 green or pink 110.00
Sherbet, low footed, green 25.00
Sherbet, low footed, pink 22.00
Sherbet, low flared edge, clear or
 green 17.50
Sherbet, low flared edge, pink 16.50
Sherbet, tall footed, clear 21.50
Sherbet, tall footed, green 31.50
Sherbet, tall footed, pink 26.00
Sugar bowl, cov., green, 4" h....... 11.50
Sugar bowl, cov., pink, 4" h. 8.00
Sugar bowl, cov., footed, amber,
 4½" h......................... 47.50
Sugar bowl, cov., footed, clear,
 4½" h......................... 14.00
Sugar bowl, cov., footed, green,
 4½" h......................... 10.50
Sugar bowl, cov., footed, pink,
 4½" h......................... 9.50
Tumbler, footed, clear, 6 oz. 28.00
Tumbler, footed, green, 6 oz. 19.00
Tumbler, footed, pink, 6 oz........ 23.00
Tumbler, green or pink, 8½ oz. 17.50
Tumbler, footed, clear, 9 oz. 17.50
Tumbler, footed, green, 9 oz. 24.00

Tumbler, footed, pink, 9 oz......
Tumbler, green, 11 oz. ....
Tumbler, pink, 11 oz. ....
Tumbler, clear, 12 oz. 14.5
Tumbler, green or pink, 12 oz. 35.00
Vase, 6" h., ruffled rim, green 70.00
Vase, 6" h., ruffled rim, pink 52.00
Vase, 9" h., ruffled rim, clear 19.50
Vase, 9" h., ruffled rim, green 51.50
Vase, 11" h., ruffled rim, green 92.50
Vase, 11" h., straight, green 65.00
Vase, 11" h., straight, pink 60.00
Water set: pitcher & 6 tumblers;
 pink, 7 pcs. 180.00

TWISTED OPTIC (Press-mold)
Bowl, cream soup, 4¾" d., pink 6.50
Bowl, cereal, 5" d., green or pink .. 7.00
Bowl, 9" d., pink 17.00
Candlesticks, amber, green or pink,
 3", pr. 11.00
Candy jar, cov., green 14.00
Candy jar, cov., pink 28.00
Console bowl, rolled edge, pink,
 12" d. 12.00
Creamer, green 6.00
Creamer, pink 5.00
Creamer, yellow 8.50
Cup & saucer, amber or pink 5.00
Plate, sherbet, 6" d., amber or
 green 1.50
Plate, luncheon, 8" d., amber, clear,
 green or pink 3.00
Plate, luncheon, 8" d., yellow 5.00
Preserve jar w/slotted lid, green ...   13.00
Preserve jar w/slotted lid, pink.....   12.00
Sandwich server w/center handle,
 amber or green 13.50
Sandwich server w/center handle,
 yellow 27.50
Sherbet, amber 3.50
Sherbet, green 4.50
Sherbet, pink 4.00
Sherbet, yellow 6.00
Sugar bowl, open, amber or
 green 4.00
Sugar bowl, open, pink 4.50
Tumbler, pink, 4½" h., 9 oz. 7.00
Tumbler, pink, 5¼" h., 12 oz. 8.00

WATERFORD or Waffle (Press-mold)
Ash tray, pink, 4" 27.50
Bowl, dessert, 4¾" d., clear 3.50
Bowl, dessert, 4¾" d., pink 6.50
Bowl, nappy, 5½" d., clear 7.00
Bowl, nappy, 5½" d., pink 18.00
Bowl, nappy, 8¼" d., clear 6.00
Bowl, nappy, 8¼" d., pink 10.00
Butter dish, cov., clear 16.50
Butter dish, cov., pink 165.00
Cake plate, handled, clear,
 10¼" d. 4.50
Cake plate, handled, pink,
 10¼" d. 7.50

. . . . 1.50
. . . . 2.50
bowl, clear,
. . . . 8.00
bowl, pink,
. . . . 33.00
ar bowl, clear,
pr. 5.50
Creamer & open sugar bowl, pink,
pr. 12.00
Cup & saucer, clear 5.50
Cup & saucer, pink 12.00
Goblet, clear, 5¼" h. 11.50
Goblet, clear, 6" h. 11.00
Goblet, pink, 6" h. 40.00
Lamp, clear, 4" h. 28.00
Pitcher, 42 oz., jug-type, clear 14.00
Pitcher w/ice lip, 80 oz., clear. 22.00
Pitcher w/ice lip, 80 oz., pink 100.00
Plate, sherbet, 6" d., clear 1.50
Plate, sherbet, 6" d., pink 4.00

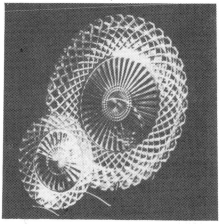

Waterford Plates

Plate, salad, 7½" d., clear (ILLUS.
left). 2.50
Plate, salad, 7½" d., pink 6.00
Plate, dinner, 9 5/8" d., clear 4.50
Plate, dinner, 9 5/8" d., pink 10.50
Plate, 13¾" d., clear (ILLUS. right). . 7.00
Plate, 13¾" d., pink. 16.00
Relish, 5-section, clear w/ruby
inserts, 13¾" d. 15.50
Relish, 5-section, green w/ivory
inserts, 13¾" d. 31.00
Salt & pepper shakers, clear, short,
pr. 5.50
Salt & pepper shakers, clear, tall,
pr. 5.50
Salt & pepper shakers, pink, tall,
pr. 16.00
Sherbet, clear. 2.50
Sherbet, pink 6.00
Tumbler, footed, clear, 3½" h.,
5 oz. 5.50
Tumbler, footed, pink, 3½" h.,
5 oz. 11.50

Tumbler, footed, clear, 5" h.,
10 oz. 8.00
Tumbler, footed, pink, 5" h.,
10 oz. 9.00

WINDSOR DIAMOND or Windsor (Press-mold)

Windsor Diamond Bowl

Ash tray, Delfite, 5¾" d. 39.00
Ash tray, green, 5¾" d. 45.50
Ash tray, pink, 5¾" d. 28.50
Bowl, nappy, 4¾" d., clear 3.50
Bowl, nappy, 4¾" d., green 5.00
Bowl, nappy, 4¾" d., pink (ILLUS.). . 6.00
Bowl, cream soup, 5" d., green 15.50
Bowl, cream soup, 5" d., pink 18.50
Bowl, cereal, 5 1/8" d., green 15.00
Bowl, cereal, 5 1/8" d., pink 13.00
Bowl, 5 3/8" d., pink 11.50
Bowl, 7" d., footed, clear 5.00
Bowl, 7" d., footed, pink 15.00
Bowl, 8" d., pink 23.00
Bowl, 8" d., 2-handled, pink. 10.50
Bowl, nappy, 8½" d., clear
or green 11.00
Bowl, nappy, 8½" d., pink 9.00
Bowl, 9½" d., handled, green 16.00
Bowl, 9½" d., handled, pink 10.00
Bowl, 9½" oval vegetable, clear. . . . 7.00
Bowl, 9½" oval vegetable, green . . . 13.00
Bowl, 9½" oval vegetable, pink 9.50
Bowl, fruit, 10½" d., clear 11.00
Bowl, fruit, 10½" d., pink. 105.00
Bowl, 11¾ x 7" boat shape, clear . . 10.00
Bowl, 11¾ x 7" boat shape, green. . 18.00
Bowl, 11¾ x 7" boat shape, pink . . 19.50
Bowl, 12½" d., pink 66.00
Butter dish, cov., clear 17.00
Butter dish, cov., green 64.50
Butter dish, cov., pink 34.50
Cake plate, footed, green,
10¾" d. 13.50
Cake plate, footed, pink, 10¾" d. . . 10.00
Cake plate, green, 13½" d. 14.50
Candlesticks, clear, 3" h., pr. 10.50
Candlesticks, green, 3" h., pr. 21.00
Candlesticks, pink, 3" h., pr. 64.50
Candy jar, cov., clear. 9.00
Coaster, green, 3" d. 11.00

Coaster, pink, 3" d.	6.00
Creamer, footed, clear	2.50
Creamer, footed, green	9.50
Creamer, footed, pink	7.50
Creamer & cov. sugar bowl, flat, clear, pr.	10.00
Creamer & cov. sugar bowl, flat, green or pink, pr.	22.50
Cup & saucer, clear	3.50
Cup & saucer, green or pink	8.50
Pitcher, milk, 4½" h., 16½ oz., clear	12.00
Pitcher, milk, 4½" h., 16½ oz., pink	107.00
Pitcher, juice, 5" h., 20 oz., clear ...	7.00
Pitcher, juice, 5" h., 20 oz., pink....	16.00
Pitcher, 6¾" h., 52 oz., clear.......	8.50
Pitcher, 6¾" h., 52 oz., green	37.50
Pitcher, 6¾" h., 52 oz., pink	17.00
Plate, sherbet, 6" d., green or pink......................	3.00
Plate, salad, 7" d., green or pink	10.50
Plate, dinner, 9" d., clear	3.50
Plate, dinner, 9" d., green	10.50
Plate, dinner, 9" d., pink	9.00
Plate, chop, 13 5/8" d., clear	6.00
Plate, chop, 13 5/8" d., green	16.50
Plate, chop, 13 5/8" d., pink	17.00
Platter, 11½" oval, clear...........	4.50
Platter, 11½" oval, green	11.50
Platter, 11½" oval, pink	10.50
Powder jar, cov., clear	7.00
Relish, divided, clear, 11½"	5.50
Salt & pepper shakers, clear, pr. ...	13.00
Salt & pepper shakers, green, pr....	35.00
Salt & pepper shakers, pink, pr.	25.00
Sandwich tray, handled, clear, 10¼" d.	5.00
Sandwich tray, handled, green or pink, 10¼" d...................	9.00
Sherbet, green	7.00
Sherbet, pink	6.00
Sugar bowl, cov., footed, clear	3.50
Sugar bowl, cov., footed, green	20.00
Sugar bowl, cov., footed, pink......	13.50
Sugar bowl, open, clear	2.50
Sugar bowl, open, green or pink ...	7.00
Tray, pink, 4" sq.	24.00
Tray, pink, 8" sq.	67.50
Tray, clear, 9 x 4 1/8"	4.00
Tray, green, 9 x 4 1/8"	15.50
Tray, pink, 9 x 4 1/8"	25.00
Tray, pink, 9¾ x 8½"	34.00
Tray, handled, green or pink, 9¾ x 8½"	26.00
Tray, green, 13½"	16.50
Tray, pink, 13½"	11.00
Tray, pink, 15½"	12.00
Tumbler, clear, 3¼" h., 5 oz.	3.50
Tumbler, green, 3¼" h., 5 oz.......	23.50
Tumbler, pink, 3¼" h., 5 oz.	8.50
Tumbler, clear, 4" h., 9 oz.	3.50
Tumbler, green, 4" h., 9 oz.	16.00

Tumbler, pink, 4" h., 9 oz.	8.50
Tumbler, footed, clear, 4" h., 9 oz...........................	6.00
Tumbler, clear, 5" h., 12 oz.	5.00
Tumbler, green, 5" h., 12 oz........	28.50
Tumbler, pink, 5" h., 12 oz.	13.50
Tumbler, footed, clear, 7¼" h.	7.50
Water set: pitcher & 6 tumblers; pink, 7 pcs.....................	54.00
Water set: pitcher, 13½" tray & 6 tumblers; pink, 8 pcs.	66.00

(End of Depression Glass Section)

DE VEZ & DEGUE

Cristallerie de Pantin Cameo Vase

Cameo glass with the name De Vez was made in Pantin, France, by Saint-Hilaire, Touvier De Varreaux and Company. Some pieces made by this firm were signed "Degue," after one of the firm's glassmakers. The official company name was "Cristallerie de Pantin."

Cameo vase, 3½" h., carved navy blue florals & leaves against frosted ground, signed Degue $375.00

Cameo vase, 5" h., gourd-shaped, carved deep aqua & fuchsia leaves against iridescent ground, gold highlights, signed Pantin 360.00

Cameo vase, 5¼" h., 2¼" d., carved navy blue to creamy yellow tree landscape along a river w/mountainous background against soft pink translucent frosted ground, signed DeVez 495.00

Cameo vase, 5½" h., carved scene w/sailboats, trees & water against orange mottled ground, signed Degue 625.00

Cameo vase, 6" h., 2 7/8" d., carved navy blue to yellow scene w/mountains, bay w/island & branches framing top of scene

against translucent frosted pink
ground, signed DeVez 495.00

Cameo vase, 7½" h., 3" d., carved
navy blue to rose scene of water
w/boat & village against yellow
translucent satin ground, leafy
branches & florals frame top of
scene, signed DeVez 550.00

Cameo vase, 7 5/8" h., 4" d., carved
navy blue scene w/two bearded
men carrying box in foreground,
large sailboat full of men in background, clouds in sky & roses &
leaves framing top of scene
against soft yellow satin translucent ground w/touch of pale
pink at top, signed DeVez 1,650.00

Cameo vase, 8 1/8" h., 3" d.,
carved navy blue to yellow scene
w/sailboat on water, house on island, mountains in background &
tree branches framing top of
scene against soft translucent
pink ground, signed DeVez 695.00

Cameo vase, 8½" h., carved red
poppies against lime green
ground, signed DeVez 750.00

Cameo vase, 8¾" h., 3 3/8" d.,
carved navy blue to soft yellow
scene w/island in water, trees &
mountains in background against
shell pink frosted translucent
ground, signed DeVez 650.00

Cameo vase, 9¼" h., 2½" d.,
carved purple scene of sailboats
in harbor & village in background
against soft aqua to white
ground, signed DeVez 695.00

Cameo vase, 10" h., 2½" d., carved
brown to yellow scene of men in
boat anchored near shore w/other
boat & house on far shore against
creamy translucent satin ground,
vine branches & florals framing
top of scene, signed DeVez 625.00

Cameo vase, 11" h., carved blue
leaves & vines against frosted
ground, signed Pantin 500.00

Cameo vase, 11¾" h., 4¾" d.,
carved navy blue Venetian scene
w/man in gondola foreground &
other boats in background,
w/pillars entwined w/wisteria
framing the scene in panels
against frosted gold ground,
signed DeVez 1,295.00

Cameo vase, 15½" h., cylindrical,
carved pink butterflies flitting
amidst flowers against acid-cut
frosted ground, signed DeVez ...1,430.00

Cameo vase, 15 7/8" h., pyriform,
carved cherry red boughs of pendant honeysuckle against grey to
lemon yellow & cherry red ground

w/internal spiralling, ca. 1900,
signed Pantin (ILLUS.)........... 880.00

Cameo vase, 19 3/8" h., 5½" d.,
carved brown squirrel on branch
w/acorns & oak leaves & mountains in background against pale
frosted translucent green ground,
signed DeVez 1,895.00

Vase by Degue

Vase, 16½" h., baluster-shaped,
brilliant orange streaked w/black
drip designs from shoulder,
signed Degue (ILLUS.) 440.00

DUNCAN & MILLER

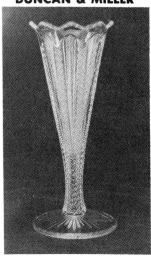

Mardi Gras Pattern Vase

*Duncan & Miller Glass Company, a succes-
sor firm to George A. Duncan & Sons Company, was operated by George A. Duncan &
Edwin C. Miller in Washington, Pa., from the
late 19th century and produced many types
of pressed wares and novelty pieces, many of*

which are now eagerly sought by collectors. George A. Duncan was a pioneer glass manufacturer, associated earlier with several firms.

Bowl, 6½" d., Canterbury patt.,
  pink opalescent $25.00
Cake plate, Mardi Gras patt.,
  clear 69.00
Champagne, Hobnail patt., clear ... 10.00
Champagne, Teardrop patt., clear .. 6.00
Cocktail shaker, Chanticleer patt.,
  ruby 215.00
Cordial, Mardi Gras patt., clear
  w/gold........................ 45.00
Goblet, First Love patt., clear 20.00
Goblet, Hobnail patt., pink
  opalescent.................... 27.50
Ice bucket, Teardrop patt., clear.... 65.00
Pitcher, tankard, Mardi Gras patt.,
  clear.......................... 69.00
Plate, 9" d., Sanibel patt., pink
  opalescent.................... 16.00
Punch set: bowl, base & 18 cups;
  Mardi Gras patt., clear, 20 pcs. .. 350.00
Rose bowl, Hobnail patt., pink 65.00
Salt & pepper shakers w/metal tops,
  Mardi Gras patt., clear, pr. 40.00
Swan, yellow opalescent, 5½" l..... 45.00
Swan, ruby w/clear neck, 7" l. 35.00
Swan, avocado green w/clear neck,
  10" l. 45.00
Swan, pink opalescent,
  13" l. ....135.00 to 150.00
Toothpick holder, Mardi Gras patt.,
  clear 40.00
Toothpick holder, Quartered Block
  patt., clear w/gold 26.00
Tray, shell-shaped, Sanibel patt.,
  yellow opalescent, 13 x 9" 68.00
Tumbler, Chanticleer patt., frosted
  green 25.00
Vase, 5" h., Canterbury patt., pink
  opalescent.................... 30.00
Vase, 6" h., trumpet-shaped, Mardi
  Gras patt., clear (ILLUS.) 35.00
Water set: pitcher & 6 tumblers;
  Mardi Gras patt., clear w/gold,
  7 pcs. 170.00

DURAND

Fine decorative glass similar to that made by Tiffany and other outstanding glasshouses of its day was made by the Vineland Flint Glass Works Co. in Vineland, N.J., first headed by Victor Durand, Sr., and subsequently by his son Victor Durand, Jr., in the 1920's.

Cup & saucer, iridescent gold $350.00
Dish, almond-shaped, iridescent
  gold, signed, 6" l............... 275.00

Durand Covered Jar

Jar, cov., green & gold swirling design on orange ground, domical cover w/applied node, early 20th c., unsigned, 10¾" h. (ILLUS.)....................... 880.00
Goblet, rose w/pulled white feathering, yellow stem & foot ... 150.00
Perfume atomizer, iridescent orange lustre, marked DeVilbiss, 7½" h...................... 225.00
Plate, 8" d., ruby w/white pulled feathering 195.00
Rose bowl, iridescent blue w/random streaks, 4" h. 375.00
Vase, 5¾" h., shouldered ovoid w/short cylindrical rim, iridescent rose-amber w/gilt webbing, ca. 1925, signed 330.00
Vase, 6" h., 5¾" d., stepped beehive shape, iridescent peacock blue w/purple, green & gold highlights, signed & numbered 765.00
Vase, 6½" h., iridescent gold w/blue lily pad decor, signed & numbered 350.00
Vase, 6½" h., bulbous, narrow neck flaring to furled rim, iridescent gold w/random green heart-shaped leaves & vines 400.00

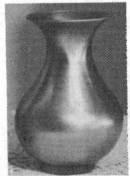

Durand Iridescent Gold Vase

Vase, 7½" h., iridescent gold, signed & numbered (ILLUS.) 425.00

Vase, 8¾" h., 7½" d., deep iridescent blue & purple w/silver
threading, signed 1,150.00
Vases, 10¼" h., baluster form, foot-
ed, iridescent green w/silver King
Tut patt., pr. 1,050.00
Vase, 12" h., 10½" widest d., bul-
bous w/flared top, iridescent
blue, signed & numbered 790.00
Vase, 15" h., trumpet-shaped, flat
circular base, iridescent gold,
signed 875.00
Vase, 16" h., iridescent blue, origi-
nal paper label 925.00
Wine, emerald green w/white &
green pulled feathers, opalescent
stem & foot, 4¼" h. 225.00

FENTON

Dancing Ladies Vase

*Fenton Art Glass Company began produc-
ing glass at Williamstown, West Virginia, in
January 1907. Organized by Frank L. and
John W. Fenton, the company began operations in a newly built glass factory with an
experienced master glass craftsman, Jacob
Rosenthal, as their factory manager. Fenton
has produced a wide variety of collectible
glassware through the years, including Carnival (which see). Still in production today,
their current productions may be found at
finer gift shops across the country.*

Basket, Diamond Optic patt., mul-
berry, 7" $110.00
Bon bon, ruffled hat shape, Flower-
ing Dill patt., blue opalescent 45.00
Bon bon, Lotus & Grape patt.,
pink 35.00
Bowl, 6" d., cupped rim, lilac 65.00
Bowl, 10" d., Mandarin red
(opaque), w/original black glass
stand, 2 pcs. 40.00
Candy jar, cov., pedestal foot, Man-
darin red 65.00

Console bowl, footed, flared rim,
pink opalescent, 11" d. 35.00
Creamer, Coin Dot patt., cranberry
opalescent, 4" h. 37.00
Decanter, Hobnail patt., blue
opalescent 85.00
Epergne, 4-lily, Burmese-type
coloring 350.00
Flower frog, "September Morn
Nymph," opaque red 135.00
Ice bucket, cov., Jade green 60.00
Mug, Rose patt., custard w/gold 50.00
Plate, 6" d., Hobnail patt., blue
opalescent 12.00
Powder jar, cov., cranberry
opalescent 17.00
Salt & pepper shakers, Hobnail
patt., cranberry opalescent, pr. 35.00
Sandwich tray, center dolphin-form
handle, Diamond Optic patt.,
green, 10" d. 25.00
Vase, 7¾" h., Hobnail patt., vase-
line opalescent 55.00
Vase, 9" h., Dancing Ladies patt.,
periwinkle blue (ILLUS.) 168.00
Water set: pitcher & 6 tumblers;
Coin Dot patt., blue opalescent,
7 pcs. 185.00
Whimsey, hat shape, Optic patt.,
lime green, 10" 160.00

FINDLAY ONYX & FLORADINE

Findlay Onyx Toothpick Holder

*These wares were introduced by Dalzell,
Gilmore & Leighton Co., of Findlay, Ohio, in
January, 1889. Onyx ware is a white-lined
glass and was produced primarily in onyx
(creamy yellowish-white) but also bronze and
ruby, which are sometimes described as cinnamon, rose or raspberry. The raised flowers
and leaves are silver colored or, less often,
bronze. The Floradine line was made in ruby
and autumn leaf (gold) with opalescent flowers and leaves and is not lined.*

Bowl, 8" d., ruby w/opalescent $200.00
Celery vase, creamy white w/silver,
6½" h. 350.00
Salt shaker w/nickel-plated top,
creamy white w/silver, 5½" h. 250.00

Salt & pepper shakers w/silverplate
tops, creamy white w/silver, pr... 600.00
Sauce dish, creamy white w/silver .. 185.00
Spooner, creamy white w/silver 230.00
Spooner, ruby w/opalescent,
4¼" h. 495.00
Sugar bowl, ruby w/opalescent,
4¼" d., 3¾" h. (no lid) 570.00
Sugar shaker w/original top, creamy
white w/silver 375.00
Toothpick holder, creamy white
w/silver (ILLUS.) 315.00

FOSTORIA

Fostoria's Chintz Pattern

*Fostoria Glass Company, founded in 1887,
is still in operation today in Moundsville,
West Va. It has produced numerous types of
fine wares through the years, many of which
are now being collected. Also see ANIMALS
under Glass.*

Bowl, 9" oval, Fairfax patt.,
topaz $20.00
Bowl, 12" d., rolled edge, Versailles
patt., Azure blue............... 30.00
Centerpiece bowl, Trojan patt.,
topaz, 12" d................... 33.50
Centerpiece bowl, Vernon patt.,
orchid, 13" oval 68.00
Cocktail, Corsage patt., clear 22.50
Cordial, Chintz patt., clear,
3 7/8" h. 38.00
Creamer & sugar bowl, individual
size, Minuet patt., green, pr...... 25.00
Cruet w/original stopper, Chintz
patt., clear 59.00
Cup & saucer, demitasse, Minuet
patt., green 25.00
Cup & saucer, Baroque patt., Azure
blue 32.00
Cup & saucer, June patt., topaz 25.00
Goblet, Bouquet patt., clear........ 17.50
Goblet, Chintz patt., clear (ILLUS.
right) 18.00

Goblet, Corsage patt., clear........ 20.00
Goblet, June patt., topaz, 8¼" h. .. 30.00
Goblet, Romance patt., clear 17.00
Ice bucket, Versailles patt., Azure
blue 90.00
Pitcher (or water jug), 9¾" h., foot-
ed, June patt., Azure blue 420.00
Pitcher (or water jug), 9¾" h.,
Navarre patt., clear 195.00
Pitcher (or water jug), Trojan patt.,
topaz ....175.00 to 225.00
Pitcher (or water jug), Versailles
patt., Dawn (rose or pink) 300.00
Pitcher (or water jug), Versailles
patt., topaz............240.00 to 260.00
Plate, 7" sq., Minuet patt., green ... 18.00
Plate, 7½" d., Versailles patt.,
Azure blue 8.75
Plate, 9" sq., Minuet patt., green ... 20.00
Plate, 9½" d., Versailles patt.,
Azure blue 20.00
Punch cup, Baroque patt., Azure
blue 38.00
Salt & pepper shakers w/glass tops,
Navarre patt., clear, pr. 95.00
Salt & pepper shakers w/original
tops, footed, Trojan patt., topaz,
pr............................. 75.00
Salt & pepper shakers w/original
tops, Versailles patt., Azure blue
or Dawn pink, each pr. 115.00
Sherbet, Chintz patt., clear, 4¼" h.
(ILLUS. left) 15.00
Sherbet, Minuet patt., green, tall ... 20.00
Tumbler, footed, Colony patt.,
clear 11.00
Tumbler, footed, Minuet patt.,
green, 10 oz. 20.00
Vase, 8" h., flared, Seville patt.,
green 72.00
Whipped cream pail w/nickel-plated
silver bail handle, Versailles patt.,
Azure blue ....115.00 to 150.00

FRANCES WARE

Creamer & Covered Sugar Bowl

This was made by Hobbs, Brockunier & Co., Wheeling, West Va., in the 1880's. It is frosted or clear glass with stained amber tops or rims and was both mold-blown and pressed. It usually has a pattern of hobnails or swirled ribs.

Berry set: master bowl & 10 sauce dishes; frosted swirl w/amber rim, 11 pcs. $225.00
Bowl, berry, 7½" sq., frosted hobnail w/amber rim . . . . 60.00 to 80.00
Celery tray, frosted hobnail w/amber rim, 12 x 7" 85.00
Celery vase, frosted hobnail w/amber rim 110.00
Creamer, clear hobnail w/amber rim 70.00
Finger bowl, frosted swirl w/amber rim 25.00
Ice cream tray, frosted hobnail w/amber rim, 14 x 9½" 225.00
Lemonade set: pitcher & 4 tumblers; frosted hobnail w/amber rim, 5 pcs. 465.00
Pitcher, milk, 5" h., clear hobnail w/amber rim 165.00
Pitcher, milk, 5½" h., frosted hobnail w/amber rim 185.00
Pitcher, water, 8" h., bulbous, clear hobnail w/amber rim . . . . 165.00 to 180.00
Salt shaker w/original top, frosted swirl w/amber rim 75.00
Sauce dish, clear hobnail w/amber rim, 4" sq. 28.00
Sauce dish, frosted hobnail w/amber rim, 4" sq. . . . . 25.00 to 32.00
Spooner, clear hobnail w/amber rim 50.00
Spooner, frosted hobnail w/amber rim 35.00
Sugar bowl, cov., frosted swirl w/amber rim . . . . 85.00 to 110.00
Sugar bowl, open, frosted hobnail w/amber rim 55.00
Syrup pitcher w/original top, frosted hobnail w/amber rim 195.00
Table set: cov. butter dish, cov. sugar bowl, creamer & spooner; frosted hobnail w/amber rim, 4 pcs. (ILLUS. of part) . . . 325.00 to 360.00
Toothpick holder, frosted hobnail w/amber rim 42.50
Toothpick holder, frosted swirl w/amber rim . . . . 55.00 to 65.00
Tray, cloverleaf-shaped, frosted hobnail w/amber rim 125.00
Tumbler, clear hobnail w/amber rim 35.00
Tumbler, frosted hobnail w/amber rim 45.00
Water set: pitcher & 4 tumblers; clear hobnail w/amber rim, 5 pcs. 295.00

FRY

Fry "Crackle" Lemonade Pitcher

Numerous types of glass were made by the H.C. Fry Company, Rochester, Pa. One type of its art line was called Foval (and also Pearl Art Glass) and was blown in the mid-1920's. Cheaper was its silky-opalescent ovenware made for utilitarian purposes but also now being collected. The company also made fine cut glass.

Candlestick, Foval, white opaline w/Delft blue spiral threading & blue wafers, 8¾" h. (single) $85.00
Casserole dish, cov., ovenware, 1½ qt. oval 32.50
Cheese dish, cov., Foval, opaline, 8½" d. plate, 4½" h. dome 125.00
Custard cup, ovenware 7.50
Bread pan, ovenware 20.00
Creamer, Foval, opaline w/applied Delft blue handle 30.00
Lemonade mug, opaline w/applied Jade green handle, 5" h. 60.00
Lemonade pitcher, cov., clear "crackle" w/applied Delft blue handle & finial on lid (ILLUS.) 125.00
Lemonade pitcher, cov., Foval, opaline w/applied Delft blue handle & finial 160.00
Measuring cup, ovenware, 3-spout, signed 28.00
Pie plate, ovenware . . . . 10.00 to 22.00
Smoke bell, Foval, opaline w/Delft blue trim, 4½" h. 90.00
Smoke bell, clear w/etched design, Delft blue trim, 7" h. 85.00
Tea set: cov. teapot & 4 c/s; Foval, opaline, 9 pcs. 450.00

GALLE'

Galle' glass was made in Nancy, France, by Emile Galle', a founder of the Nancy School and a leader in the Art Nouveau movement *in France. Much of his glass, both enameled and cameo, is decorated with naturalistic motifs. The finest pieces were made in the last two decades of the 19th century and the opening years of the present one. Pieces marked with a star preceding the name were made between 1904, the year of Galle's death, and 1914.*

Galle' Cameo Vase

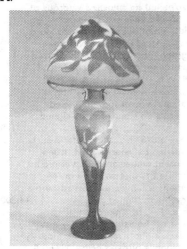

Galle' Cameo Lamp

Cameo bowl, 11¼" d., carved blue morning glory vines against translucent pale blue-green ground on body & w/band of stylized morning glory blossoms at foot, ca. 1900, signed $1,540.00

Cameo box, cov., carved amethyst florals & leaves against light amethyst & blue ground, signed, 7" d. 850.00

Cameo lamp, umbrella-shaped shade, carved green butterflies against frosted yellow ground, black metal tripod base, signed, 2½" d. shade, 4½" h. 525.00

Cameo lamp, domed shade, spherical base, mold-blown & cameo-carved orange, burgundy & pink rhododendron blossoms against matte yellow ground, pink flowers heightened w/orange, bronze mounts, signed, 19" h. 55,000.00

Cameo lamp, conical shade, trumpet-shaped base, carved red, violet & brown magnolia blossoms & leafy branches against translucent yellow ground, signed, 26½" h. (ILLUS.) 22,000.00

Cameo vase, 3 5/8" h., slightly flattened sphere w/short cylindrical neck, carved purple floral spray & leafage against yellow ground, ca. 1900, signed (ILLUS.) 357.50

Cameo vase, 6 5/8" h., flattened ovoid w/slender tapering neck, carved mahogany flowering prunus branches against lemon yellow ground, ca. 1900, signed 990.00

Cameo vase, 7" h., ovoid, carved deep purple & green butterfly bush against opaque smoky white ground, ca. 1900, signed . . . . . . ,. . . 715.00

Cameo vase, 7¼" h., conical, carved purple & blue florals & reeds against creamy blue opaque ground, signed 605.00

Cameo vase, 7¾" h., bottle-shaped, carved brown river scene w/trees & shrubbery reflected in the water against pale green to yellow & peach ground, signed 750.00

Cameo vase, 8" h., flattened bulbous base w/slender neck, carved pink leaves & berries against opaque ground tinged w/yellow, signed w/star (1904-14) 550.00

Cameo vase, 8¼" h., flattened triangle w/flared lip, carved sky blue & deep purple landscape view of mountains, trees & a stream against opaque golden ground, ca. 1900, signed 1,980.00

Cameo vase, 8 3/8" h., elongated pear shape, carved brown forest flowers against matte white ground 440.00

Cameo vase, 9 1/8" h., expanding cylinder, internally decorated w/deep ochre wheat sheaves, wheel-carved blue-grey dragon-flies in flight w/bodies set w/applied opal cabochons against ochre matte ground, ca. 1895, signed 5,830.00

Cameo vase, 9 5/8" h., baluster form w/straight cylindrical neck, 2 applied ribbed C-scroll handles, carved & enameled violet, mauve, yellow & ochre poppy blossoms

& leafage heightened w/gilding
against frosted pale mint green
etched ground, ca. 1900, signed . .1,870.00
Cameo vase, 10¾" h., pilgrim flask
form, mold-blown & cameo-carved
purple & chestnut brown grape
clusters amongst dense foliage
against matte yellow ground,
signed 3,300.00

Cameo Vase

Cameo vase, 11½" h., ovoid, mold-
blown & cameo-carved pumpkin,
violet & avocado leafy vines &
berries against frosted golden
ground, ca. 1900, signed 4,400.00
Cameo vase, 12" h., 4½" w., carved
orchid sweet peas w/trailing foliage against frosted pink & white
ground, signed 1,675.00
Cameo vase, 12" h., elongated ovoid,
mold-blown & cameo-carved dark
pink & maroon flowering hyacinths
against matte dusty yellow ground,
signed 3,960.00
Cameo vase, 13" h., bulbous ovoid,
mold-blown & cameo-carved
Chinese red & burnt sienna pendant fruiting plum branches against
lemon yellow & orange ground, ca.
1900, signed 11,550.00
Cameo vase, 14 1/16" h., ovoid,
carved opaque white & creamy
white marine panorama of sea-
gulls above foamy cresting waves
against translucent ice blue ground,
signed 20,900.00
Cameo vase, 17" h., baluster-shaped,
carved pink & burgundy magnolia
sprays against yellow-tinted matte
white ground, signed 3,300.00
Cameo vase, 20" h., baluster-
shaped, carved turbulent swirls of
amber & firey orange w/depiction
of Notre Dame above inscription
1914 one side, reverse carved
w/jagged ruins & inscription,

marigold yellow ground, ca. 1920,
signed 4,675.00
Cameo vase, 24 1/8" h., baluster-
shaped, carved claret, orange &
green poppy sprays above green
foliage against matte yellow
ground, signed 12,100.00
Chalice, pale yellow domical bowl
w/pulled lip splashed w/drops of
mustard yellow & streaked w/vio-
let, violet baluster form standard
w/mustard yellow, olive green,
green, grey-green & oxblood red
spiraling, ca. 1900, signed,
9¼" h. 7,150.00
Toothpick holder, banded barrel
shape w/oval top, enameled
florals on clear ground, signed,
2" h. 175.00
Vase, 6 3/8" h., "marqueterie-sur-
verre," baluster-shaped, transparent amber ground overlaid in
white & violet w/inlaid green
stems & leaves & 2 carved purple
gentians, signed 14,300.00
Vase, 7¼" h., "marqueterie-sur-
verre," baluster-shaped w/swelling
neck & short conical foot, sides
w/bands of deep ochre, clear &
deep purple w/lime green & silver
foil inclusions & internal air bubbles, inlaid w/pendant fuchsias
in lavender, lime green & amber,
blossoms & leafage heightened
w/further wheel carving, ca. 1900,
signed 6,050.00

Galle' Vase

Vase, 7 7/8" h., flaring cylinder,
etched orange & red dahlias w/ap-
plied crimson centers on yellow &
white ground, signed (ILLUS.) 3,080.00
Vase, 8½" h., "marqueterie-sur-
verre," flattened tapering cylinder
on short rolled foot, pale grey
sides internally decorated
w/amber & lavender stringing &

controlled air bubbles , stringing
shading at foot to grey-green,
deep amber & violet, sides inlaid
w/lavender, amber & yellow meadow saffron blossoms heightened
w/further wheel carving, ca. 1895,
signed 7,700.00
Vase, 12½" h., "marqueterie-sur-
verre," bulbous w/waisted cylindrical neck & split lip, 2 applied
scrolling handles terminating in
long, sinuous tendrils wrapped
about the body, inlaid & carved
w/two moths, 1 bright ochre, the
other violet, caramel brown lower
body, ca. 1900, signed 22,000.00
Vase, 17½" h., cylindrical w/cushion
base, etched & enameled rose, green
& brown trailing branch of bleeding hearts on translucent green-
tinted ground, signed 1,430.00

GOOFUS

Goofus Vase

This is a name collectors have given a pressed glass whose colors were sprayed on and then fired. Most pieces have intaglio or convex designs and were produced by the Northwood Glass Co.

Bowl, 7" d., relief-molded red carnations on gold $18.00
Bowl, 9" d., relief-molded red cherries on gold 12.00
Bowl, 9" d., relief-molded red poppies on gold 15.00
Bowl, 9" d., footed, relief-molded
red roses on gold 27.50
Bowl, 10" d., relief-molded red
strawberries on gold 15.00
Bowl, master berry, relief-molded
red dogwood blossoms on gold ... 45.00
Bowl, master berry, relief-molded

red morning glory blossoms on
gold 42.50
Bread tray, "The Lord's Supper," red
& gold, w/clear grapes 50.00
Cake plate, relief-molded red dogwood blossoms on gold 45.00
Compote, 10" d., 2½" h., relief-
molded red poppies on gold...... 55.00
Compote, 10½" d., 8¾" h., relief-
molded red strawberries on
gold 55.00
Dresser jar, relief-molded red roses
on gold 23.50
Plate, 8" d., relief-molded red apples on gold 15.00
Plate, 8" d., relief-molded red
waterlilies on gold 10.00
Plate, 10½" d., footed, relief-
molded red roses on gold........ 25.00
Powder box, cov., relief-molded red
roses on gold 30.00
Sauce dish, boat-shaped, relief-
molded red roses on gold........ 35.00
Vase, 6" h., relief-molded red roses
on gold (ILLUS.) 21.00
Vase, 7" h., relief-molded red cabbage roses on gold............. 15.00
Vase, 7" h., relief-molded red
grapes on gold................. 15.00

GREENTOWN

Austrian Pattern Goblet

Greentown glass was made in Greentown, Ind., by the Indiana Tumbler & Goblet Co. from 1894 until 1903. In addition to its famed Chocolate and Holly Amber glass, which see, it produced other types of clear and colored glass. Miscellaneous pieces are listed here. Also see CHOCOLATE, HOLLY AMBER and PATTERN GLASS.

Animal covered dish, Cat on Tall
Hamper, amber $195.00

Animal covered dish, Hen on Nest,
amber 135.00
Animal covered dish, Rabbit,
amber 135.00
Berry set: master bowl & 6 sauce
dishes; Cord Drapery patt., clear,
7 pcs. 50.00
Bowl, 7¼ x 5" rectangle, Austrian
patt., clear 50.00
Bowl, 8¼ x 5¼" oval, footed,
Geneva patt., clear 30.00
Bowl, master berry, Pattern No. 11,
clear 20.00
Bowl, "Mitted Hand," clear 35.00
Butter dish, cov., Cord Drapery
patt., clear, small 65.00
Butter dish, cov., Squirrel patt.,
clear 210.00
Cake plate, Pattern No. 11,
clear 20.00
Cake stand, Herringbone Buttress
patt., clear 185.00
Celery vase, Pattern No. 11,
clear 25.00
Compote, open, 5¼" d., 5 1/8" h.,
Teardrop & Tassel patt., clear 30.00
Creamer, individual size, Austrian
patt., clear 25.00
Creamer, individual size, Brickwork
patt., clear 12.00
Creamer, Austrian patt.,
clear ....25.00 to 40.00
Creamer, Overall Lattice patt.,
clear 15.00
Creamer, Teardrop & Tassel patt.,
clear 30.00
Creamer, cov. & cov. sugar bowl,
Greentown Daisy patt., milk
white, 2 pcs.................... 30.00
Cruet w/original stopper, Cord
Drapery patt., amber 345.00
Dish, Cord Drapery patt., blue,
5" 40.00
Goblet, Austrian patt., clear
(ILLUS.)........................ 42.50
Goblet, Beehive patt., clear 65.00
Goblet, Brazen Shield patt., clear ... 37.50

Dewey Pattern Mug

Mug, Dewey patt., amber
(ILLUS.)........................ 60.00

Mug, Dewey patt., Nile green 275.00
Mug, Herringbone Buttress patt.,
clear 95.00
Mug, Shuttle patt., clear 15.00
Nappy, open, Austrian patt., clear .. 45.00
Pickle dish, Aurora patt., clear 10.00
Pickle dish, Cord Drapery patt.,
clear 25.00
Pickle dish, Cord Drapery patt., co-
balt blue 100.00
Pitcher, water, Cord Drapery patt.,
amber 168.00
Pitcher, water, Early Diamond patt.,
clear 53.00
Pitcher, water, Heron patt., clear ... 285.00
Pitcher, water, Teardrop & Tassel
patt., clear 50.00
Punch cup, Austrian patt., clear 15.00
Punch cup, footed, Cord Drapery
patt., clear 12.00
Punch cup, Herringbone Buttress
patt., clear 45.00
Punch cup, Overall Lattice patt.,
clear 25.00
Relish, Cord Drapery patt., clear,
9¼" 22.50
Relish, serpentine-shaped, Dewey
patt., green 43.00
Relish, Holly patt., clear, oblong.... 85.00
Rose bowl, Austrian patt., clear,
4" h............................ 40.00
Salt shaker w/original top, Cord
Drapery patt., clear 45.00
Salt shaker w/original top, Dewey
patt., green 55.00
Sauce dish, Brazen Shield patt.,
blue 25.00
Sauce dish, Dewey patt., amber or
green, each 20.00
Sauce dish, Leaf Bracket patt.,
clear 20.00
Spooner, Austrian patt., clear 22.00
Spooner, Pattern No. 11, clear
w/amber 35.00
Stein, Indoor Drinking Scene, Nile
green 90.00
Sugar bowl, cov., Dewey patt.,
green 50.00
Table set: cov. butter dish, cov.
sugar bowl, creamer & spooner;
Herringbone Buttress patt., green
w/gold, 4 pcs. 650.00
Toothpick holder, picture frame
shape, amber 145.00
Tray, serpentine-shaped, Dewey
patt., amber 65.00
Tumbler, Cord Drapery patt., blue .. 125.00
Tumbler, Cord Drapery patt., clear.. 40.00
Tumbler, Dewey patt., amber 50.00
Tumbler, Dewey patt., green 46.00
Vase, 6" h., Herringbone Buttress
patt., emerald green 175.00
Vase, 6" h., Pattern No. 11, emerald
green 32.00

Water set: pitcher & 4 tumblers;
  Brazen Shield patt., blue, 5 pcs. . . 345.00
Water set: pitcher & 6 tumblers;
  Dewey patt., yellow,
  7 pcs. . . . . 225.00 to 300.00
Whimsey, hairbrush, clear 47.00
Wine, Austrian patt., clear 30.00
Wine, Pattern No. 11, clear 14.00

ar bowl, creamer & spooner;
  white w/gold trim, 4 pcs. 350.00
Toothpick holder, green 60.00
Toothpick holder, turquoise blue
  satin 110.00
Water set: pitcher & 6 tumblers;
  white w/gold, 7 pcs. 250.00

GUTTATE

Guttate Syrup Pitcher

Guttate is a mold-blown glassware made by the Consolidated Lamp & Glass Company at Fostoria, Ohio, during the late 1890's. A beautifully designed pattern, it was made primarily in opaque pastel colors, sometimes cased in clear to form a glossy finish and sometimes in a satin finish with a white lining. It is also found in transparent cranberry. Because of its appealing design, it is popular and somewhat scarce. Cased cranberry items available today are new pieces currently being reproduced along with a variety of tumblers. Collectors should exercise caution.

Butter dish, cov., white w/gold
  trim $65.00
Creamer, cranberry 125.00
Pitcher, water, 8½" h., clear han-
  dle, pink cased in clear 317.50
Pitcher, water, pink satin 195.00
Salt shaker w/original top, green . . . 26.00
Salt shaker w/original top, pink
  satin 65.00
Salt & pepper shakers w/original
  tops, pink cased in clear, pr. 65.00
Sugar bowl, cov., pink satin 45.00
Sugar shaker, pink satin 135.00
Syrup pitcher w/original top, squat-
  ty, cranberry 275.00
Syrup pitcher w/original top, pink
  cased in clear (ILLUS.) 175.00
Table set: cov. butter dish, cov. sug-

HEISEY

Heisey Basket

Numerous types of fine glass were made by the A.H. Heisey Glass Co., Newark, O., from 1895. The company's trademark — an H enclosed within a diamond — has become known to most glass collectors. The company's name and molds were acquired by Imperial Glass Co., Bellaire, O., in 1958, and some pieces have been reissued. The glass listed below consists of miscellaneous pieces and types. Also see ANIMALS under Glass and PATTERN GLASS.

Basket, 6-sided, clear w/wheel-
  engraved daisy-like flowers &
  leaves, w/vertical line cuts at bottom, 22-point rayed base, signed,
  8¼ x 5", overall 11" h. (ILLUS.) . . . $165.00
Basket, Rib & Panel patt., clear,
  10" 175.00
Bowl, 6½" d., seahorse handles,
  Waverly patt., clear 45.00
Bowl, 7" d., dolphin-footed, Empress
  patt., Sahara (yellow) 50.00
Butter dish, cov., Waverly blank,
  rose etching, clear 150.00
Butter pat, Old Sandwich patt.,
  cobalt blue 29.00
Candlesticks, Trident patt., Tanger-
  ine (orange), pr. 1,800.00
Celery tray, Greek Key patt., clear,
  signed, 12" l. 65.00
Cigarette box, Crystolite patt.,
  clear 30.00

Cigarette set: cigarette box & 4 ash trays; Ridgeleigh patt., clear, signed, 5 pcs. 59.50

Cigarette set: cigarette box & 4 ash trays; Wampum patt., clear, original labels, 5 pcs. 195.00

Compote, jelly, 5", Rib & Panel patt., Moongleam (green) 37.00

Creamer, Pineapple & Fan patt., emerald green 80.00

Creamer, Prince of Wales - Plumes patt., ruby-stained 55.00

Creamer & sugar bowl, dolphin footed, Flamingo (pink), pr. 69.00

Cruet w/original stopper, Diamond Optic patt., Moongleam 59.00

Cruet w/original stopper, Winged Scroll patt., emerald green, gold trim 265.00

Epergne, single lily, Plantation patt. w/etching, clear, 5" 50.00

Goblet, footed, Colonial patt., clear 12.50

Goblet, Duquesne stem, Tangerine 150.00

Goblet, Narrow Flute patt., clear . . . 22.50

Goblet, Sussex patt., Stiegel (cobalt blue) 95.00

Ice bucket, Crystolite patt., clear, chrome handle & tongs 110.00

Ice bucket, dolphin footed, etched Lafayette patt., Flamingo 67.00

Lamp, figural "Chanticleer" rooster, clear, original oval silverplate base, 4 small ball feet, original cloth cord, unsigned, overall 9½" h. 235.00

Lemon dish, cov., dolphin handles, Empress patt., clear, 6½" 56.00

Marmalade jar, cov., Crystolite patt., clear 40.00

Mustard jar, cov., Empress patt., green 80.00

Pitcher (water jug), Empress patt., Sahara, signed, 3-pt. 150.00

Pitcher (water jug), Rib & Panel patt., clear, half-gal. 125.00

Plate, 6" sq., Empress patt., Sahara 12.00

Plate, 8" d., Ribbed Octagon patt., Moongleam 22.00

Plate, 8½" d., Coarse Rib patt., Moongleam 13.00

Plates, 8½" d., Waverly patt., rose etching, clear, set of 8 . . . . 160.00

Punch bowl & base, Colonial patt., clear, signed, 2 pcs. . . . . . . 125.00 to 185.00

Punch cup, Colonial patt., clear . . . . 5.00 to 8.50

Punch cups, Flute patt., clear, signed, set of 6 . . . . 48.00

Punch set: bowl, 11 cups, ladle & tray; Crystolite patt., clear, 14 pcs. 315.00

Relish, 3-section, Lariat patt., clear 45.00

Rose bowl, Diamond Optic patt., Moongleam 45.00

Salt dip, Puritan patt., clear 8.00

Salt dip & underplate, Diamond Point patt., clear, pr. 25.00

Sauce dish, Prince of Wales - Plumes patt., clear, 5" d. 15.00

Sugar shaker, Plantation patt., clear 110.00

Syrup pitcher w/original top, Beaded Swag patt., white opaque 105.00

Table set: cov. butter dish, creamer, sugar bowl & spooner; Beaded Swag patt., white opaque, 4 pcs. 375.00

Heisey Toothpick Holder

Toothpick holder, Prince of Wales - Plumes patt., clear w/gold (ILLUS.) . . . . 125.00 to 150.00

Toothpick holder, Priscilla patt., clear 65.00

Torte plate, Queen Ann patt., clear, 11" d. 95.00

Tumbler, iced tea, footed, Minuet patt., clear 30.00

Tumbler, Pied Piper patt., clear 12.00

Tumbler, Pineapple & Fan patt., emerald green w/gold 60.00

Tumbler, Prison Stripe patt., clear . . 75.00

Vase, 8" h., Ridgeleigh patt., Zircon (blue-green) 140.00

Wine, Locket on Chain patt., clear 100.00

Wine, Old Dominion patt., Alexandrite (orchid) 105.00

HISTORICAL & COMMEMORATIVE

Reference numbers are to Bessie M. Lindsey's book, "American Historical Glass." Also see BREAD PLATES & TRAYS, MILK WHITE and PATTERN GLASS.

Admiral Dewey plate, bust portrait of Dewey, clear, 5½" d., No. 392 . . . . $25.00

Admiral Dewey Pitchers

Admiral Dewey water pitcher, bust portrait of Dewey & flagship Olympia reverse, w/mounted cannons, crossed rifles, U.S. & Cuban flags & stacks of cannon balls toward base, clear, No. 400 (ILLUS. right) 62.50

Admiral Dewey water pitcher, portrait of Dewey within laurel leaves, "Gridley You May Fire When Ready," eagle, w/shield, etc., 9¼" h., No. 401 (ILLUS. left) .... 85.00 to 125.00

American Hen covered dish, American Eagle hatching eggs of "Porto Rico," "Cuba" & "Philippines," inscribed "The American Hen" each side, milk white, 6¼ x 3 5/8", 4" h., No. 476 .... 70.00

Bates (General John Coulter) plate, portrait center, dewdrop & vine border, clear, 8" d., No. 375 ..... 60.00

Blaine - Logan tray, frosted bust portraits center, stippled ivy border, 11½ x 8½", No. 315 .... 195.00 to 225.00

Bryan (William J.) covered cup, bust portrait of Bryan, "The People's Money" above, clear, No. 336 .... 47.50

Bunker Hill platter, "Prescott 1776 Stark - Warren 1876 Putnam," clear, 13½ x 9", No. 44 .... 65.00

Civil War tumbler, one side w/large 13-star flag & large 5-star shield, separated by rifle & flagstaff, 10-sided scalloped base, No. 148 variant 195.00

Columbus mug, bust portraits of Columbus & George Washington, inscribed on base, "World's Columbian Exposition, 1893," clear, 2½" d., No. 2 .... 72.50

Columbus plate, bust portrait of Columbus center w/dates "1492-1892," pilot wheel border, clear, 9" d., No. 4 .... 42.50

Eden pitcher, overall fig leaf design, log handle, clear, 8½" h., No. 208 .... 75.00

Faith, Hope & Charity plate, maidens posed as Three Graces center, w/1875 patent date, clear, 10" d., No. 230 .... 78.00

Garfield "ABC" plate, clear w/frosted bust of Garfield center, 6" d., No. 301 .... 55.00 to 110.00

Garfield cup plate, flaring rim, clear, 3" d., No. 297 .... 95.00

Garfield Star plate, frosted bust of Garfield center, star border, clear, 6" d., No. 299 .... 32.50

Garfield plate, frosted bust of Garfield center, one-o-one border, clear, 9" d., No. 300 .... 37.50

Garfield Memorial plate, Garfield center, laurel wreath against stippled ground border, clear, 10" d., No. 302 .... 46.50

Garfield shaving mug, milk white, 2¾" h., No. 307 .... 185.00

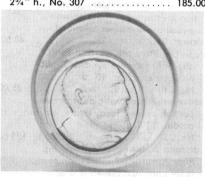

Garfield Tumbler

Garfield tumbler, w/portrait in base, clear, 3 7/8" h., No. 296 (ILLUS.)........................ 35.00

Gladstone (William Ewart) plate, "In Memory of England's Statesman," clear, 5 1/8" d., No. 442 .... 40.00

Golden Rule plate, "Do Unto Others, etc.," clear, 11" d., No. 221 ...... 35.00

Grant Memorial plate, bust portrait of Grant center, laurel wreath on stippled border, amber, 10" d., No. 288 .... 65.00

Grant Memorial plate, portrait of Grant center, laurel wreath on stippled border, clear, 10" d., No. 288 .... 50.00

Grant Peace plate, bust portrait of Grant center, maple leaf border, apple green, 10½" d., No. 289 ... 60.00

Grant Peace plate, bust portrait of Grant center, maple leaf border, clear, 10½" d., No. 289 .... 40.00

Independence Hall platter, "The Nation's Birthplace," w/bear paw handles, clear, No. 29 .... 85.00

Industry bowl, log cabin & cider barrel center, border w/man plow-

ing, sailing ship & factory against
stippled ground, clear, 6¼" d.,
No. 267 .... 210.00
I.O.O.F. goblet, Horseshoe patt.
w/I.O.O.F. insignia, 3 links
superimposed on stippled panel,
clear, 6¼" h. 37.50
Lincoln's Tribute tumbler, clear,
3¾" h., No. 282 .... 30.00
Martyr's mug, Lincoln & Garfield
bust portraits & inscription, clear,
2 5/8" h., No. 272 .... 65.00
McKinley tumbler, portrait in base,
clear, 3 7/8" h., No. 337 .... 32.50
McKinley & Spanish American War
tumbler, center oval w/frosted
bust of McKinley & 4 ovals around
w/frosted busts of Dewey, Miles,
Sampson & Schley, No. 337
variant 75.00
McKinley-Hobart tumbler, "Protection & Prosperity," bust portrait
medallions w/names inscribed,
clear, 2½" h., No. 338 .... 48.50
Pope Leo XIII plate, portrait center,
alternating chruch symbols & hobnail border, clear, 10" d.,
No. 240 .... 35.00
Roosevelt (Theodore) platter, frosted
portrait center, teddy bears, etc.
border, 10¼ x 7¾",
No. 357 ....100.00 to 130.00
Sampson pattern pitcher, honoring
Rear Admiral William T. Sampson,
leafy garlands, tassels & drops,
clear w/partly stippled background, No. 402................ 80.00
Shakespeare statuette, frosted bust
of Shakespeare, marked "Gillinder & Sons, Centennial Exhibition," 5" h., No. 405.....140.00 to 175.00
Sir Moses Montefiore plate, portrait
of Jewish philanthropist center,
ornate inscribed border, clear,
10½" d., No. 239 ......100.00 to 135.00

Tecumseh mustard jar, log cabin
shape, inscribed "Tecumseh"
above door, clear, 2" sq., 3¾" h.,
No. 11 (ILLUS.) 95.00
Tennessee mug, Cherokee rose &
clematis blossoms within shield
one side & American 16-star flag
reverse, camphor, 3½" h.,
No. 102 ....45.00 to 65.00
Three Presidents platter, bust portraits of Garfield, Washington &
Lincoln, inscribed "In Remem-
brance," clear, 12½ x 10",
No. 249 ....45.00 to 60.00
Three Presidents platter, bust portraits of Garfield, Washington &
Lincoln, inscribed "In Remem-
brance," clear w/frosted center,
12½ x 10", No. 249 ......65.00 to 95.00
Three Shields covered dish, shield-
shaped, clear, 5½" w., 8½" l.,
No. 60 .... 95.00
Washington Monument paperweight,
milk white, 2¾" sq. base, 5½" h.,
No. 255 ....100.00 to 150.00

HOLLY AMBER

Holly Amber Plate

*Holly Amber was produced by the Indiana
Tumbler and Goblet Co. A molded glass, it
is characterized by a glossy finish, shadings
that range from opalescent to brownish amber, and holly leaf patterns. It is also called
Golden Agate. It is scarce and therefore expensive. Collectors are alerted to the fact that
the St. Clair Glass Company has reproduced
some Holly Amber pieces.*

Bowl, master berry,
 8½" d................$450.00 to 750.00
Butter dish, cov. 950.00
Cake stand, pedestal base 1,800.00
Compote, cov., 6½" d. ...750.00 to 1,000.00
Compote, cov., 8¼" d............1,200.00

Tecumseh Mustard Jar

Cruet w/original
   stopper ....1,260.00 to 2,000.00
Mug 425.00
Parfait 550.00
Plate, 7½" d. 500.00
Sauce dish, 4¼" d........195.00 to 280.00
Tumbler w/beads on top rim 425.00
Vase, 6" h. 425.00

IMPERIAL

Free Hand Ware Vase

Imperial Glass Company, Bellaire, Ohio, was organized in 1901 and was in continuous production, except for very brief periods, until its closing in June, 1984. It had been a major producer of Carnival Glass (which see) earlier in this century and also produced other types of glass, including an Art Glass line called "Free Hand Ware" during the 1920's and its "Jewels" about 1916. The company acquired a number of molds of other earlier factories, including the Cambridge and A.H. Heisey companies, and had reissued numerous items through the years.

Free Hand Ware hat shape, ruffled
   rim, cobalt blue w/imbedded
   iridescent white vines & leaves,
   9" widest d. $95.00
Free Hand Ware vase, 7" h., cobalt
   blue w/imbedded iridescent white
   vines & heart-shaped leaves 200.00
Free Hand Ware vase, 8¼" h., deep
   iridescent blue w/white King Tut
   style drag loops (ILLUS.) 310.00
Free Hand Ware vase, 8¾" h.,
   pearly white lustre w/yellow drag
   loops, iridescent orange interior .. 110.00
Free Hand Ware vase, 9" h., deep
   iridescent blue w/white drag
   loops 200.00
Free Hand Ware vase, 9" h., iridescent emerald green w/imbedded

white opal heart-shaped leaves &
   vines, orange lustre throat
   interior....................... 175.00
Free Hand Ware vase, 10" h., gold
   lustre w/white drag loops 148.00
Free Hand Ware vase, 10¼" h.,
   green lustre w/iridescent orange
   lining 110.00
Free Hand Ware vase, 11" h., iridescent bronze exterior, blue-grey
   interior...................... 80.00
Jewels bowl, rose lustre 159.00
Jewels vase, 6" h., iridescent pearl
   green & purple lustre........... 135.00
Jewels vase, 7½" h., bulbous melon
   shape w/wide flared mouth,
   iridescent reddish lustre 80.00

JACK-IN-PULPIT VASES

Jack-in-Pulpit Hobnail Vase

Glass vases in varying sizes and resembling in appearance the flower of this name have been popular with collectors since the 19th century. They were produced in various solid colors and in shaded wares.

Blue opalescent, 3 7/8" widest d.,
   6½" h........................ $69.00
Blue to vaseline opalescent, 7" h. .. 75.00
Blue to vaseline opalescent,
   5½" widest d., 9 1/8" h.......... 88.00
Cased, clear exterior, white interior,
   deep green top & throat, 8" h. ... 85.00
Cased, creamy opaque exterior
   w/white & yellow florals w/green
   leaves & gold, deep rose pink interior w/amber edging, ormolu
   leaf feet, 4" widest d., 7¼" h. ... 118.00
Cased, heavenly blue exterior,
   white interior, applied clear foot
   & shell trim, 7" widest d.,
   15¾" h........................ 175.00
Cased, white exterior, shaded
   maroon interior, ruffled, 6½"
   widest d., 6½" h. 110.00
Cased, white exterior, shaded cran-

berry interior, satin finish,
3-dimpled, 7" h., pr.............. 225.00
Cased, white exterior, shaded blue
hobnail effect interior, 6¾"
widest d., 7¼" h. (ILLUS.)........ 110.00
Cranberry, Diamond Quilted patt.,
ruffled, clear wishbone feet, 4¼"
widest d., 6 3/8" h. 125.00
Cranberry, applied clear foot &
spiral trim, 4½" widest d.,
9 3/8" h. 118.00
Cranberry w/clear rigaree spirals,
clear pedestal foot, 4¼"
widest d., 9½" h. 118.00
Cranberry, 6¼" widest d.,
12¾" h. 135.00
Cranberry opalescent, clear rigaree
trim, 7" h...................... 85.00
Green opalescent stripes, applied
green leaf & pink flower, 9" h. ... 125.00
Light green to amber, 6¾" h. 95.00
Maroon edge shading to apple
green opaque, ruffled, hobnailed
edge, 7 1/8" widest d., 7½" h. ... 114.00
Spatter, mustard, white & pigeon
blood on sapphire blue, Tiny
Diamond Quilted patt., 6¾"
widest d., 7" h. 90.00
Spatter, maroon & white, applied
vaseline opalescent 5-point top,
5¾" widest d., 11 1/8" h........ 95.00
Vaseline w/opalescent edge, cranberry & vaseline spatter border,
Tiny Diamond Quilted patt., 7" h.. 95.00
Vaseline opalescent, applied ruffled
transparent pink spiral trim, 4¼"
widest d., 7¾" h. 86.00
Verre Moire, frosted chartreuse
green w/white loopings, applied
frosted feet, 3¾" widest d.,
7½" h. 135.00
White opalescent shaded to green,
green coil stem, clear petal feet,
5" widest d., 8" h. 88.00

KELVA

*Kelva was made early in this century by
the C.F. Monroe Co., Meriden, Conn., and was
a type of decorated opal glass very like the
same company's Wave Crest and Nakara
wares. This type of glass was produced until
about the time of the first World War. Also
see NAKARA and WAVE CREST.*

Box w/hinged lid, 6-sided, blown-
mold & h.p. rose in full relief on
lid, mottled blue ground, signed,
3" d. $285.00
Box w/hinged lid, mottled grey
w/h.p. pink & white florals,
signed, 4½" d.................. 365.00

Jewelry box w/hinged lid, mottled
blue w/h.p. pink florals, original
lining, signed, 6" d. 495.00
Planter, footed, deep mottled pink
w/large h.p. blue & white florals,
7¾ x 6¼"..................... 550.00
Vase, 10" h., ornate ormolu handles
& footed base, mottled green
w/pink floral decor, signed 495.00

Kelva Vase

Vase, 13½" h., mottled green
w/h.p. petaled florals & foliage,
signed (ILLUS.) 600.00
Vase, 18" to top of ornate silverplate handles, mottled green
w/pink floral decor, silverplate
footed base 1,700.00

KEW BLAS

Kew Blas Vases

*Glass of this name was made by the Un-
ion Glass Works, Somerville, Mass. These*

iridescent wares were similar to those produced by other art glass firms during the same period in the 1890's.

Compote, 7" h., twisted stem, ribbed bowl, iridescent gold w/pink highlights $375.00

Tumbler, pinched sides, iridescent gold, signed, 4" h. 185.00

Vase, 5" h., spherical w/rolled gold rim, green & gold pulled feathering on white, early 20th c., signed 467.50

Vase, 5" h., baluster form, yellow pulled feathering on white, signed 385.00

Vase, 6" h., dark blue w/light blue pulled loops, signed 810.00

Vase, 6" h., iridescent ivory w/green & gold pulled feathering 650.00

Vase, 6¼" h., swollen cylinder w/rolled rim, gold & green swag design on pale orange, early 20th c., signed & w/original paper label (ILLUS. right) 605.00

Vase, 7 7/8" h., baluster form, narrow neck w/flaring mouth, iridescent orange w/metallic looping... 150.00

Vase, 8" h., floriform, iridescent gold, ca. 1910.................. 165.00

Vase, 8¼" h., swollen cylinder w/flared rim, green & gold pulled design, early 20th c., signed & w/original paper label (ILLUS. left)....................... 385.00

Vase, 8¼" h., baluster form w/flared rim, gold & yellow pulled feathering on white, gold interior, early 20th c., signed & w/original paper label........... 495.00

LALIQUE

Fine glass, including numerous extraordinary molded articles, has been made by the glass house established by Rene' Lalique early in this century in France. The firm was carried on by his son, Marc, until his death in 1977 and is now headed by Marc's daughter, Marie-Claude. All Lalique glass is marked, usually on, or near, the bottom with either an engraved or molded signature. Unless otherwise noted we list only those pieces marked "R. Lalique" produced before the death of Rene' Lalique in 1945. Also see COMMEMORATIVE PLATES.

Ash tray, central pillar molded w/two nude women, amber, 4½" d. $330.00

Bookends, "Hirondelles," molded frosted swallows in flight, pr. 375.00

Lalique Bottle & Stopper

Bottle w/stopper, 12 figurines "avec Bouchon," molded medium relief pairs of frolicking couples on body & stopper w/full figure kneeling nude female, frosted, ca. 1925, 11½" h. (ILLUS.) 2,200.00

Bowl, 8" d., "Gui No. 2," hemispherical, mistletoe berries & leafage molded in low relief, brown-stained.......................... 275.00

Bowl, 10" d., "Nemours", hemispherical, molded radiating columns of flowers, brown-stained w/black-enameled flower centers....................... 600.00

Box, cov., "Roger," cover molded w/stylized birds amidst grapevines & clusters, frosted amber, 5¼" d. 660.00

Carafe w/original stopper, "Sirenes," molded columns of nude women below elongated frogs, frosted & brown-stained, 15¼" h. 2,420.00

Lalique Centerpiece

Centerpiece, "Anvers," broad rim molded w/fish amdist seaweed, frosted blue, 15 3/8" d. (ILLUS.) . .3,850.00

Clock, table model, circular face w/frosted Arabic numerals, in a thick arched frame molded w/two standing women holding a garland of roses, clear & frosted, raised on an electrified nickel-plated metal base, 15" h. 4,950.00

Cocktail shaker, cylindrical, molded grapevines & clusters, frosted, w/fitted strainer & cover, 9¼" h. 660.00

Cologne bottle, "Marguerite," flat-sided round form, molded w/flowerheads heightened w/sienna enamel, frosted & clear, 7" h. 385.00

Decanter w/tapered ribbed stopper, "Sirenes," expanding neck of square section above gourd form body w/four frog's heads issuing streams of water forming panels alternating w/sirens molded in low relief, whole washed in charcoal grey stain, ca. 1910, 15½" h. 3,575.00

Figure of "Grande Nue," standing nude female, her left arm covering her eyes, frosted, original wooden base, 16" h. 5,280.00

Figure of "Source De La Fontaine," woman standing, holding water-lilies & lily pads, frosted, mounted on wooden base, 26¾" h. 3,300.00

Figure of "Tete Penchee"

Figure of "Tete Penchee," frosted maiden clad in diaphanous drapery, standing on top of lappet domed base, within clear arched stele surrounded w/frosted florette garlands, traces of grey enamel in recesses, 14½" h. (ILLUS.) 2,090.00

Figure of "Thais," molded nude female w/head bent to dexter, her

outstretched arms supporting flowing drapery, frosted, 8½" h. 1,210.00

Frame, "Muguets," lilies-of-the-valley, frosted & clear, 4" sq. 455.00

Hood ornament, "Coq Nain," model of a fighting cock, frosted purple, 8" h. 10,450.00

Hood ornament, "Hirondelle," model of a swallow, clear & frosted, 5¾" h. 2,640.00

Hood ornament, "Levrier," model of a greyhound, clear & frosted, 7¾" oval .4,950.00

Hood ornament, "Sanglier," model of a boar, clear & frosted, 3 5/8" l. 1,540.00

Ink stand, "Sirenes," 4 molded mermaids, frosted, 6 1/8" d. 1,870.00

Luminaire, "Suzanne," standing nude female w/robe draped over her outstretched arms, frosted yellow, original electrified patinated bronze (unsigned) base, 9" h. figure 8,250.00

Perfume bottle, "Couer Joie," heart-shaped, made for Nina Ricci, 5½" h. 450.00

Perfume bottle, "Dans La Nuit," round, blue w/enameled stars, Worth, 8 oz. 295.00

Perfume bottle, "Volnais," square, molded w/thorny branches, frosted & clear, 3½" h. 418.00

Plates, 6¾" d., "Assiette Figurine et Fleurs," molded central nude woman surrounded by flowers, brown-stained, pr. 660.00

Powder box, "Agnes," frosted w/aqua wash, 3" 595.00

Tumbler, "Cerises," molded frosted cherries in high relief, 4½" h. 150.00

Tumbler, large raised overlapping feathers, deep honey color, 4¾" h. 125.00

Vase, 5¼" h., "Dahlias," ovoid, molded frosted dahlias w/black-enameled centers 770.00

Vase, 6" h., "Lievres," overall scrolling leafy branches, blue-tinted stain in center w/molded frieze of running rabbits 950.00

Vase, 8¼" h., "Escargot," flattened disc, molded spirals simulating a snail shell, red, ca. 1925 . . . . . . .3,850.00

Vase, 9¼" h., "Poissons," bulbous w/waisted neck & cylindrical base, molded in low relief w/swimming fish, frosted ruby red, ca. 1925 . .1,540.00

Vase, 10½" h., "Sauterelles," ovoid, molded grasshoppers perched on tall arching grasses in medium relief, brilliant emerald green, ca. 1925 . . . . .6,050.00

LEAF MOLD

Though the maker of this attractive glass pattern remains elusive, the Leaf Mold pattern becomes more popular with collectors each year. Thought to have been made in the 1890's, there are several colors and color combinations available and it was made in both satin and shiny finish as well as in a cased version.

Bowl, master berry, cranberry spatter, shiny finish $62.00
Cruet w/original stopper, cased cranberry spatter 445.00
Cruet w/original stopper, cased cranberry & white spatter 295.00
Cruet w/original stopper, cased cranberry & white spatter w/mica flecks 225.00
Pitcher, water, vaseline w/cranberry spatter, satin finish 155.00
Rose bowl, vaseline w/cranberry spatter 90.00
Salt & pepper shakers w/original tops, vaseline spatter, satin finish, pr. 110.00
Sugar shaker w/original top, cased cranberry & white spatter w/gold mica flecks 149.00
Sugar shaker w/original top, cranberry spatter 195.00
Sugar shaker w/original tops, vaseline spatter, satin finish 95.00
Toothpick holder, vaseline spatter . . 125.00
Tumbler, cranberry spatter 65.00

LEAF UMBRELLA

This attractive pattern is attributed to the Northwood Company and dates from 1889. A complete table service was made in cranberry glass and cased glass in shades of blue, pink and yellow. Some cased cranberry and white spatter glass is also found and sometimes the wares were given a satin finish. A somewhat brittle glassware that readily flakes, items offered for sale have sometimes had the rims polished or smoothed.

Bowl, master berry, cased cranberry & white spatter $95.00
Butter dish, cov., cased cranberry & white spatter 225.00
Celery vase, cranberry, 5¼" h. 59.00
Cruet w/clear stopper, cased cranberry spatter 350.00
Pitcher, water, cased blue, satin finish 375.00
Pitcher, water, cased cranberry & white spatter 295.00

Salt & pepper shakers w/original tops, cased pink-mauve, pr. 110.00
Sauce dish, cranberry . . . . 25.00 to 40.00
Sugar shaker w/original top, cased blue 150.00
Sugar shaker w/original top, cased cranberry spatter 165.00
Syrup pitcher w/original top, cranberry 325.00
Toothpick holder, cased blue 120.00
Toothpick holder, cased cranberry spatter 115.00
Toothpick holder, cranberry 110.00
Tumbler, cased pink-mauve 100.00
Tumbler, cased yellow 32.00
Tumbler, cranberry 45.00

LE GRAS

Le Gras Enameled Bowl

Cameo and enameled glass somewhat similar to that made by Galle', Daum Nancy and other factories of the period was made at the Le Gras works in Saint Denis, France, late last century and until the outbreak of World War I.

Bowl, 8" w., 4½" h., enameled clusters of red cherries w/dark brown branches & brownish green leaves on light green ground, signed (ILLUS.) $350.00
Cameo bowl, 4¼ x 3¼", carved scene of ships, lake & mountains against orange ground, signed . . . 275.00
Cameo vase, 5" h., quatrefoil lip, carved brown leaves against cream ground, signed 250.00
Cameo vase, 5" h., 4¾" d., carved green leaves & berries against orange to lemon yellow ground, signed 350.00
Cameo vase, 6" h., carved yellow, red, green & blue house & trees scene, signed 550.00
Cameo vase, 7¾" h., carved & enameled scene of shepherdess & her flock w/trees & mountains in the background, signed 360.00
Cameo vase, 8" h., 15" d., compressed & inverted bell form,

carved shaded green & gold florals
& foliage 1,100.00
Cameo vase, 8¾" h., carved &
enameled brown florals against
cream & orange ground, signed . . 425.00
Cameo vase, 15¾" h., swelling cylinder, carved magenta maple
leaves against frosted ground, ca.
1925, signed 715.00

LE VERRE FRANCAIS

Le Verre Francais Cameo Vase

*This glass was made in France by Charles
Schneider and fairly large quantities of the
cameo ware were exported to the United
States in the early part of this century. Much
of it was sold by Ovingtons, New York City.
See SCHNEIDER for further details on this
company.*

Cameo bowl, 9" d., 5¾" h., pedestal foot, carved Art Deco designs,
signed $325.00
Cameo bowl-vase, carved bright
blue & orange stylized florals
against yellow mottled ground,
signed, 6½" d. 375.00
Cameo vase, 5" h., 7¼" widest d.,
carved brown geese (12) in flight
over rushes w/splotches of dark
blue against mottled brown & yel-
low ground 700.00
Cameo vase, 7" h., carved deep or-
ange stylized florals against mottled ground, signed Charder 650.00
Cameo vase, 7½" h., carved orange
& yellow stylized roses & thorns,
signed 275.00
Cameo vase, 8¾" h., cylindrical,
carved tango red & emerald green
fish swimming amidst feathering
seaplants against clear acid-etched
to sea blue ground enclosing controlled air bubbles, ca. 1925,
signed (ILLUS.) 1,540.00

Cameo vase, 9" h., 9½" widest d.,
narrow neck, carved dark blue to
red w/blue flecks stylized fuchsia
blossoms against acid-etched
clear ground splashed w/cream &
blue 600.00
Cameo vase, 13" h., baluster form,
footed, carved pale blue vertical
bands of foliage against lapis blue
ground shading to dark blue &
black at the foot, signed
Charder 660.00

LIBBEY

Maize Celery Vase & Tumbler

*In 1878, William L. Libbey obtained a lease
on the New England Glass Company of Cambridge, Mass., changing the name to the New
England Glass Works, W.L. Libbey and Son,
Proprietors. After his death in 1883, his son,
Edward D. Libbey, continued to operate the
company in Cambridge until 1888 when the
factory was closed. Edward Libbey moved to
Toledo, Ohio, and set up the company subsequently known as Libbey Glass Co. During
the 1880's, the firm's master technician,
Joseph Locke, developed the now much
desired colored art glass lines of Agata,
Amberina, Peach Blow and Pomona. Re-
nowned for its Cut Glass of the Brilliant
Period, the company continues in operation
today as Libbey Glassware, a division of
Owens-Illinois, Inc.*

Candlestick, Lightware, engraved
base & candle cup, twisted stem,
signed (single) $105.00
Candlesticks, opalescent silhouette
of camel in stem, signed, 5½" h.,
pr. 495.00
Champagne, clear bowl, opalescent
silhouette of squirrel in stem 135.00
Cocktail, clear bowl, opalescent silhouette of kangaroo in stem 145.00
Cordial, clear bowl, opalescent silhouette of Greyhound in stem 95.00
Goblet, clear bowl, opalescent silhouette of cat in stem 115.00

Maize butter dish, cov., pale green
w/gold-edged green husks,
7¼" d. 425.00
Maize celery vase, creamy opaque
w/gold-edged yellow husks,
4¼" d., 6½" h. (ILLUS. left) 155.00
Maize cruet w/original stopper, applied handle w/pattern-molded
turned-up end, clear w/pale
amber opalescence & pale blue
husks, 7" h. 945.00
Maize pitcher, water, 8¾" h.,
5½" d., applied strap handle,
white w/green husks 335.00
Maize sugar shaker, custard color
w/green husks.................. 175.00
Maize syrup pitcher w/original pewter top, white opaque w/green
husks, 7½" h. 385.00
Maize tumbler, creamy opaque
w/gold-edged blue husks,
4 1/8" h. (ILLUS. right) 185.00
Pitcher, 8½" h., slightly bulbous,
applied strap handle, clear
w/blue Nailsea-type decor, ca.
1930 .... 155.00
Toothpick holder, Little Lobe patt.,
pink to white w/enameled blue
florals, green leaves & name in
gold 110.00

LOETZ

Loetz Vase

*Iridescent glass, some of it somewhat
resembling that of Tiffany and other contemporary glasshouses, was produced by the Bohemian firm of J. Loetz Witwe of Klostermule
and is referred to as Loetz. Some cameo pieces
were also made. Not all pieces are marked.*

Bowl, 4¼" d., iridescent green,
signed $275.00
Bowl, 9¼" d., scalloped rim, irides-

cent green "crinkle" finish,
signed 175.00
Bowl, oval, deep amethyst, in brass
Art deco style basket-frame...... 265.00
Box w/hinged lid, enameled bloom-
ing thistles on oil-stained ground,
5½" d. 260.00
Candlestick, iridescent gold, signed,
17½" h. (single) 225.00
Compote, 9" d., scalloped, iridescent green, metal base, signed ... 210.00
Cookie jar, slightly swirled narrow
vertical ribs, iridescent green
w/applied intertwined criss-cross
threading, silverplate rim, cover &
bail handle, 5½" d., 6" h. 175.00
Flower bowl, egg-shaped, iridescent
gold & blue, bronze undulating
cloverleaf form base, 5½" d.,
9¾" h. 300.00
Inkwell w/brass cover, squatty,
iridescent blue, green & purple,
5¼" d., 2" h. 325.00
Rose bowl, scalloped rim, iridescent
green, signed, 6" h. 175.00
Spooner, iridescent cranberry
w/threading, signed, 5½" 160.00
Sweetmeat dish, iridescent blue
w/darker blue random threading,
in holder, 5½" d., 5½" h. 110.00
Sweetmeat jar, swirled narrow ribs,
iridescent green w/random
threading, silverplate lid, rim &
bail handle, unsigned, 6" 195.00
Vase, 4½" h., 5¼ x 3½", diamond-
shaped, iridescent blue & gold,
signed 650.00
Vase, 4½" h., peacock blue w/gold
iridescence, twisted into gentle
folds, signed................... 250.00
Vase, 6" h., iridescent green "lava-
textured" exterior, purple interi-
or, signed 125.00
Vase, 6½" h., cylindrical w/pinched
neck & ruffled lip, iridescent amber w/rows of wavy lines in salmon & deep amber iridescence, ca.
1900, signed (ILLUS.)............ 935.00
Vase, 6½" h., ribbed body, scalloped rim, dark green, signed 110.00
Vase, 7" h., 5¼" d., dimpled sides,
green w/iridescent blue-green &
silver highlights, unsigned 610.00
Vase, 8¼" h., bulbous base, deep
ruby red at top w/silvery blue
iridescence blending to a lime yellow, overall angled elongated
thumbprints, signed 240.00
Vase, 9" h., indented square, iridescent green, signed 220.00
Vase, 10" h., clear w/iridescent
green oil splotches 150.00
Vase, 10½" h., 8½" d., applied

iridescent gold handles, iridescent
blue & gold 425.00
Vase, 10 5/8" h., top folded back to
form graceful handles, iridescent
blue w/iridescent gold stripes,
ovals & circles, signed 850.00
Vase, 11¼" h., slender cylindrical
neck w/ruffled outward flaring lip,
deep red w/silvery blue & cobalt
blue pulled, scrolling loopings &
trailings, ca. 1900, unsigned 1,210.00
Vase, 12" h., bulbous w/slender
knopped neck, iridescent amber
w/silvery amber-blue iridescent
interconnecting lappets, ca. 1900,
unsigned......................1,540.00
Vase, 12½" h., twisted Art Nouveau
style, green, cranberry & rainbow
iridescence 300.00
Vase, 13¾" h., swollen cylinder,
waisted neck, iridescent peacock
green & blue on iridescent deep
purple ground, unsigned 1,430.00

LUTZ AND LUTZ TYPE

Lutz Decanter

*This refers to filigree or other glass made
in the Venetian manner by numerous glasshouses. It takes its name from the work of
Nicholas Lutz, a specialist in this type of
ware, who worked for several factories,
among them the Boston & Sandwich Glass
Works. Attribution of specific pieces to Lutz,
however, is difficult.*

Bowl, clear w/multicolored threading forming a spiraling pinwheel
design $125.00
Decanter w/original hollow blown
stopper, clear w/pink & white
threading, 11½" h. (ILLUS.) 400.00
Finger bowl & underplate, clear

w/pink threading, 4¼" d. bowl,
7" d. plate...................... 115.00
Perfume bottle, clear w/white
latticino 175.00
Plate, 7" w., 1 side slightly folded,
clear w/green & white
threading...................... 95.00
Tumbler, alternating white & blue-
green ribbons w/goldstone
threading, applied prunts, red
threading around rim, 3¼" h. 70.00
Whimsey, hat shape, Diamond Quilted patt., blue w/threading 175.00
Whiskey tumbler, white latticino alternating w/pink & gold ribbons .. 58.00

MARBLE

Pink Marble Jelly Compote

*Slag and Agate glass are other names ap-
plied to this variegated glass ware made from
the middle until the close of the last century
and now being reproduced. It is characterized
by variegated streaks of color. Pink slag was
made only in the Inverted Fan & Feather Pattern and is rare.*

Berry set: master bowl & 6 sauce
dishes; Inverted Fan & Feather
patt., pink, 7 pcs. . . . .$2,200.00 to 3,500.00
Butter dish, cov., Flower & Panel
patt., purple 62.50
Candlesticks, 3 entwined dolphins
around base, purple, English,
3¾" d., 7" h., pr. 118.00
Celery vase, Jewel patt., purple 125.00
Compote, jelly, 5" h., Inverted Fan &
Feather patt., pink (ILLUS.)....... 545.00
Compote, Jenny Lind patt., purple .. 145.00
Creamer, Scroll with Acanthus patt.,
purple 60.00
Creamer, Sunflower patt., purple ... 68.00
Creamer, ribbed body, lace edge
rim, green..................... 45.00
Creamer & spooner, Flower & Panel
patt., purple, pr. 75.00

Creamer & open sugar bowl, scalloped top, footed, purple, 4½" h. creamer, 5½" h. sugar bowl, pr. 95.00

Cruet w/original stopper, Inverted Fan & Feather patt., pink 1,500.00

Nut bowl, footed, Beaded Cable patt., purple 65.00

Pitcher, 6½" h., 3 3/8" d., stippled ribbed body w/central band of molded roses, purple 70.00

Sauce dish, footed, Inverted Fan & Feather patt., pink 200.00

Spooner, Flower & Panel patt., purple . . . . .65.00 to 80.00

Spooner, Flute patt., purple 75.00

Sugar bowl, open, Swan patt., butterscotch (brown) 60.00

Toothpick holder, square w/molded ring handles, purple 25.00

Tumbler, Inverted Fan & Feather patt., pink, 2¾" d., 4" h. .275.00 to 385.00

Vase, Beads & Bark patt., purple . . . 45.00

MARY GREGORY

Mary Gregory Mug

Glass enameled in white with silhouette-type figures, primarily children, is now termed "Mary Gregory" and attributed to the Boston and Sandwich Glass Company. However, recent research has proven conclusively that this ware was not decorated by Mary Gregory nor was it made at the Sandwich factory. Miss Gregory was employed by the Boston and Sandwich Glass Company as a decorator, however, records show her assignment was the painting of naturalistic landscape scenes on larger items such as lamps and shades but never the charming children for which her name has become synonymous. Further, in the inspection of fragments from the factory site, no paintings of children were found. It now believed that the original "Mary Gregory" glass came from England, Germany and Bohemia by way of an English import wholesale house. For further information see The Glass Industry in Sandwich, Volume 4, by Raymond E. Barlow and Joan E. Kaiser.

Box w/hinged lid, cranberry, white enameled girl w/hat standing amidst foliage on lid, gold trim, 3" d., 3 3/8" h. $235.00

Box w/hinged lid, amethyst, white enameled girl blowing bubbles w/pipe on lid, white dot trim around sides, 3½" d., 3¾" h. 245.00

Box w/hinged lid, brass feet, sapphire blue, white enameled girl carrying basket of flowers on lid, white sprays around sides, brass rings on sides, 5 3/8" d., 4¾" h. 395.00

Box w/lift-off lid, cranberry, white enameled boy standing by fence on lid, white sprays around sides, 2 7/8" d., 2" h. 145.00

Box w/lift-off lid, sapphire blue, white enameled girl on lid, garlands of flowers & leaves around base, 4¼" d., 3¼" h. 175.00

Cake plate, cranberry, white enameled girl, 9½" d 395.00

Cologne bottle w/original "bubble" stopper, sapphire blue, white enameled girl, 3 1/8" d., 9" h. 165.00

Cordials, pedestal base, turquoise blue ribbed top, clear bottom, white enameled girl on one & boy on other, 4" h., pr 275.00

Dresser tray, chartreuse green, white enameled girl feeding birds & boy w/bird on his hand, 10 3/8 x 7 3/8" oval 245.00

Goblet, cranberry w/clear foot, white enameled boy holding food for birds, 3" d., 5¾" h. 110.00

Jewelry box w/hinged lid, ormolu feet & rim, amber, white enameled girl amidst foliage on lid & floral garlands on sides, brass rings at sides, 4 x 2¾", 4¼" h. 425.00

Liqueur mug, applied clear handle, amethyst, white enameled boy w/hat, 1 3/8" d., 1 5/8" h. 50.00

Mug, amethyst w/applied handle, white enameled boy, 1½" h. 78.00

Mug, applied clear handle, slightly ribbed, cranberry, white enameled boy, 2 3/8" d., 3 5/8" h. 75.00

Mug, cranberry w/applied clear handle, Baby Thumbprint patt., white enameled girl w/basket in one handle & flower in other amidst ferns, gold rim, 4" h. (ILLUS.) 90.00

Perfume atomizer, sapphire blue, white enameled girl, 2½" d., 6½" h. (no atomizer bulb) 135.00

Perfume bottle w/original bubble stopper, cranberry, white

enameled boy jumping rope,
3" d., 6" h. 195.00

Pin dish, amethyst, white enameled
boy carrying flag, brass figured
rim, 3¾" d., 1 1/8" h. 95.00

Pitcher, 5" h, ruffled rim, applied
handle, electric blue, white
enameled boy in garden 150.00

Pitcher, 9½" h., ruffled rim, clear,
white enameled girl chasing
butterfly 175.00

Pitcher, lemonade, 10 5/8" h., applied amber handle, amber, white
enameled girl fishing,
w/inscription 185.00

Pitcher, water, tankard, 11 1/8" h.,
4½" d., applied amber handle,
olive amber, white enameled
girl 230.00

Rose bowl, 7-crimp top, cranberry,
white enameled boy w/sailboat,
3¼" d., 2¾" h. 225.00

Toothpick holder, clear, white
enameled boy, 2½" h........... 65.00

Trinket box w/hinged lid, black
amethyst, white enameled girl
w/locket on chain holding a
branch, ring of flowers around
base, 2½" d., 2¾" h. 165.00

Tumbler, green, white enameled
boy holding flower, 4½" h. 75.00

Tumble-up (water carafe w/tumbler
lid), sapphire blue, white
enameled boy on carafe & girl on
tumbler, 3¼" d., 8¼" h......... 225.00

Urn, cov., cranberry, white
enameled girl, 22" h. 625.00

Vases, 2 7/8" h., 2 5/8" d., ball-
shaped, amber, white enameled
boy on one & girl on other, pr. 175.00

Vase, 6 3/8" h., 4" d., bulbous
w/flared top, amber, white
enameled girl carrying floral
bouquet 150.00

Mary Gregory Vase

Vases, 8" h., black amethyst, white
enameled boy on one & girl on
other, pr. (ILLUS. of one)........ 325.00

Vases, 10" h., 4¼" d., cobalt blue,
white enameled girl w/basket of
flowers on one & boy w/hat &
cane on other, tinted features,
pr............................. 225.00

Vase, 11 5/8" h., 5" d., pedestal
foot, applied reeded snail handles
w/gold trim, lime green, white
enameled girl sitting on shore
waving handkerchief, small sailboat in background............. 275.00

Vase, 16¾" h., 10" w. across handles, ornate ormolu footed base,
rim & handles, light blue, white
enameled boy & girl examining
bird nest in tree................1,100.00

Wine decanter w/original bubble
stopper, cranberry, white
enameled girl standing by fence,
5" d., 12" h. 395.00

MC KEE

"Danse de Lumiere"

The McKee name has been associated with
glass production since 1834, first producing
window glass and later bottles. In the 1850's
a new factory was established in Pittsburgh,
Pa., for production of flint and pressed glass.
The plant was relocated at Jeannette, Pa. in
1888, and operated there as an independent
company, almost continuously until 1951
when it sold out to Thatcher Glass Manufacturing Company. Many types of collectible

glass were produced by McKee through the years including Depression, Pattern, Milk White and a variety of utility kitchen wares. Also see CHOCOLATE GLASS.

Butter dish, cov., Rock Crystal,
  clear $195.00
Candlesticks, Ray patt., clear,
  1910-30, 8" h., pr. 50.00
Champagne, Rock Crystal, ruby-
  flashed 27.50
Compote, 8" d., Rock Crystal,
  clear 40.00
Creamer, Comet patt., clear 39.00
Creamer & cov. sugar bowl, Rock
  Crystal, ruby-flashed, pr. 180.00
Cruet w/original stopper, Rock Crys-
  tal, clear 35.00
Cup & saucer, Laurel patt., blue 9.00
Juice reamer, Jade green opaque,
  5" 27.00
Lamp, "Danse de Lumiere," canary
  yellow, satin finish (ILLUS.) 475.00
Pitcher, straight sided, Rock Crystal,
  clear 55.00
Plate, salad, 7½" d., Rock Crystal,
  clear 6.00
Punch cup, Rock Crystal, clear 5.00
Salt & pepper shakers, Roman patt.,
  custard color, pr. 20.00
Sugar bowl, cov., Comet patt.,
  clear 50.00
Toothpick holder, Stars & Stripes
  patt., clear 25.00
Tumbler, Rock Crystal, clear 10.00
Vase, 8½" h., Art Deco flapper,
  green 65.00
Vase, 8½" h., triangular, 3 nudes
  w/flowing hair, green 28.00

MERCURY

Mercury Glass Compote

This glass has a silvery appearance due to a coating of silver nitrate in double-walled objects. A gold effect was obtained by placing the silver nitrate in amber glass. The hole

through which the solution was injected was subsequently sealed. It was made in this country and England from the middle of the 19th century.

Candlesticks, 4" h., pr. $45.00
Candlesticks, 9½" h., pr. 200.00
Compote, 7" h., enameled green
  band w/pink roses decor
  (ILLUS.) 130.00
Creamer, applied clear handle,
  6 3/8" h. 65.00
Curtain tiebacks, etched vintage de-
  sign, 4" & 4½" d., set of 7 .... 65.00
Goblet, etched vintage design, New
  England Glass Co., 1866-70,
  5 5/8" h. 35.00
Salt dip, master size, etched
  design 30.00
Sugar bowl, open, 5¼" h. 65.00
Vase, 6" h., cylindrical 45.00
Vase, 8" h., enameled red & yellow
  floral decor 50.00
Vase, bud, 9" h. 25.00
Vase, 10½" h., pedestal base,
  etched floral design 32.00

MILK WHITE

Milk White Glass Dishes

This is opaque white glass that resembles the color of and was used as a substitute for white porcelain. Opacity was obtained by adding oxide of tin to a batch of clear glass. It has been made in numerous forms and shapes in this country and abroad from about the first quarter of last century. It is still being produced, and there are many reproductions of earlier pieces. Also see COSMOS, CRUETS and PATTERN GLASS.

Animal covered dish, Camel resting,
  6¼" l. $95.00
Animal covered dish, Cat on Drum,
  Porteaux 45.00
Animal covered dish, Cat on lacy
  edge base .... 95.00 to 145.00
Animal covered dish, Chick & Eggs

on lacy edge pedestal base, Atterbury, 1880's 120.00

Animal covered dish, Crawfish on 2-handled oblong base, overall 7½" l. ....100.00 to 125.00

Animal covered dish, Dog on ribbed base (ILLUS. rear) 50.00

Animal covered dish, Hen w/red glass eyes on lacy edge base, Atterbury (ILLUS. rear) 95.00

Animal covered dish, Pintail Duck, 5¼" l., 4¼" h. 30.00

Animal covered dish, Quail on scroll-embossed oval base w/scalloped top, 6½" l., 4½" h. 50.00

Animal covered dish, Turtle on 2-handled oblong base, overall 7½" l. 195.00

Bottle, Statue of Liberty base w/metal lid, 10" h. 175.00

Bowl, 8" d., openwork Arch Border, Atterbury 30.00

Bowl, 8¾" d., 3½" h., openwork Crinkled Lacy Edge patt. 37.50

Breakfast set: Hen covered dish, 6 egg cups, cov. salt basket & tray; signed Vallerystahl, set 475.00

Butter dish, cov., Tree of Life patt. 97.50

Compote, cov., 7¼" d., Blackberry patt. 75.00

Covered dish, Battleship "Maine," 7½" l. 52.50

Covered dish, Cruiser ship, 6" l. (ILLUS. center front) 47.50

Covered dish, Uncle Sam on Battleship, 6½" l. (ILLUS. right) 60.00

California Pattern Creamer

Creamer, lacy, California patt., flint, ca. 1850 (ILLUS.) 400.00

Creamer, Owl, miniature, 3½" h.... 33.00

Creamer, Paneled Wheat patt. 35.00

Cruet w/original stopper, Tree of Life patt. 75.00

Cup, footed, Swan & Cat Tails patt. 35.00

Egg cup, double, Blackberry patt., 4 1/8" h. 70.00

Goblet, Blackberry patt. 18.00

Goblet, Strawberry patt. 14.00

Jar, cov., figural Owl, Atterbury, 7" h. .... 100.00 to 135.00

Match holder, model of a pipe 27.00

Mustard jar, Bull's Head, w/ladle ... 130.00

Plaque, Lincoln bust portrait in relief center, interwoven slat border, 8 x 10½" 190.00

Plate, 5½" d., Woof Woof 35.00

Plate, 6¼" d., Emerging Chick, heart-shaped lacy border 40.00

Plate, 6½" d., The Serenade 30.00

Plate, 7" d., ABC border, beaded rim 40.00

Plate, 7" d., Ancient Castle 25.00

Plate, 7" d., Bryan center, eagle, flag & star border 70.00

Plate, 7" d., Contrary Mule, w/gilt paint 24.00

Plate, 7" d., Owl Lovers 32.00

Plate, 7" d., Three Kittens 28.00

Plate, 7¼" d., Anchor & Yacht 20.00

Plate, 7¼" d., Chick & Eggs 34.00

Plate, 7½" d., Cupid & Psyche...... 16.00

Plate, 8¼" d., Washington bust portrait in relief, 13-star border 60.00

Relish dish, figural fish, inscribed "Pat. June 4, 1872," 11 x 4½" 37.50

Salt & pepper shakers w/original tops, Scroll patt., pr. 45.00

Salt dip, figural swan, 5" l. (ILLUS. front left) 65.00

Spooner, Cameo patt. 20.00

Spooner, Princess Feather patt...... 55.00

Sugar bowl, cov., Twin Horn patt. .. 30.00

Sugar bowl, open, Strawberry patt. 41.00

Sugar shaker w/original top, Netted Oak patt...................... 50.00

Toothpick holder, Swan & Cat Tails patt. 22.00

Tray, Child in Shell, 8¾ x 6¼" 90.00

Tray, Monkey Face, 11 x 6¾" 43.00

Fleur de Lis Tumbler

Tumbler, Fleur de Lis patt. (ILLUS.)........................ 9.00

MILLEFIORI

Millefiori Pitcher

Millefiori glass is decorated or patterned, with tiny slices of thin multicolored glass canes and is familiar in paperweights, often filled with closely packed canes. These flower pattern canes have also been used in the production of other objects for many years and the technique is ancient. This type of glass is still being made in Murano, Italy, and elsewhere. Also see PAPERWEIGHTS.

Bowl, 4" d., applied handles,
  predominantly blue & white
  canes $80.00
Coffee pot, applied blue handle &
  spout, white canes w/yellow
  centers in cobalt blue, satin finish, 3" d., 5¾" h. 225.00
Creamer, white canes w/yellow
  centers in cobalt blue, satin finish, 3" d., 4¼" h. 100.00
Cruet w/matching stopper, bulbous,
  applied camphor handle, multicolored canes.................. 97.50
Cruet w/matching stopper, applied
  reeded camphor handle, blown,
  ribbed body 89.50
Cup & saucer, white canes w/yellow
  centers in cobalt blue, satin
  finish 85.00
Dish, swan-shaped, applied eyes,
  multicolored canes & gold flecks,
  5" l. body 65.00
Pitcher, 6½" h., applied candy cane
  handle, multicolored canes
  (ILLUS.)....................... 165.00
Punch cup, applied opaque blue
  handle, multicolored canes
  throughout, ca. 1910............ 150.00
Sugar bowl, cov., white canes
  w/yellow centers in cobalt blue,
  satin finish, 4" d., 3½" h........ 110.00
Tumbler, multicolored canes,
  3½" h. 85.00
Vase, 4" h., applied double handles,
  multicolored canes 95.00

MONT JOYE

Cameo and enameled glass bearing this mark was made in Pantin, France, by the same works that produced pieces signed De Vez.

Bowl-vase, enameled florals on
  acid-etched ground, gold trim,
  signed, 8¾ x 3¾", 4" h.........$250.00
Cameo rose bowl, crimped rim,
  carved & enameled florals against
  light green ground, 3½" d. 250.00

Mont Joye Cameo Vase

Cameo vase, 6½" h., carved &
  enameled violets w/gold stems &
  leaves against soft green ground,
  border of gold violets at rim,
  signed (ILLUS.) 335.00
Cameo vase, 8½" h., carved cab-
  bage roses against yellow ground,
  signed 355.00
Cameo vase, 9½" h., carved red &
  green florals against "chipped ice"
  ground, signed.................. 425.00
Cameo vase, 12" h., carved amber
  flower & buds outlined in gold
  against textured goldish bronze
  ground, top & base border also
  carved, unsigned............... 375.00
Vase, 5" h., indented sides,
  enameled gold florals on acid-
  etched ground 195.00
Vase, 10" h., Rubina Crystal
  w/enameled swallows decor 175.00
Vase, 14" h., amethyst w/enameled
  horse chestnuts, blossoms & foliage, signed.................... 850.00

MOSER

High-quality Art Nouveau glass was produced from around the turn of the centu-

ry by Moser, Ludwig & Sohne in Carlsbad and Mierhofen. Much of the base glass was amethyst in color, but this expert craftsman turned out various types of glass, some with exquisite enameling.

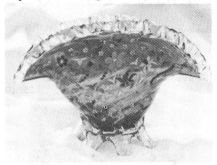

Moser Vase

Bowl, 5" d., 4½" h., 2-handled, amber w/enameled multicolored oak leaves & applied black acorns, signed $560.00

Box w/lift-off lid, green w/enameled multicolored leaves & applied pink berries on lid, sides w/gold leaves & branches & pink berries, 3 3/8" d., 2 1/8" h. 245.00

Cameo vase, 5" h., 5½" d., carved gold lions & palm trees against amber ground, signed 210.00

Cologne bottle w/original tall stopper, elongated pear shape, clear w/overall lacy gold scrollwork & applied w/central porcelain portrait medallion of a child flanked by floral medallion, 9¾" h. 295.00

Creamer, applied amber handle, round mouth, blue opalescent w/enameled multicolored leaves & bug, applied berries, unsigned, 2" d., 3" h. 450.00

Cup & saucer, pale blue w/enameled gold & yellow florals & scrollwork 165.00

Decanter w/original stopper, applied handle w/gold trim, decorated pedestal foot, cobalt blue w/enameled multicolored grape leaves, gold tendrils & clusters of green, red & clear grapes w/gold trim, 3 7/8" d., 17" h. ...1,295.00

Ewer, slender, yellow spatter w/applied gold acorns, 9" h. 375.00

Finger bowl & underplate, Amberina, enameled decor on borders, signed, pr. 485.00

Measuring mug, enameled bird & florals, "Franzensbad" in gold, milliliter measures on side 175.00

Vase, bud, 3¾" h., green cut to clear 145.00

Vase, 4 1/8" h., 2¼" d., shaded apricot opalescent w/enameled multicolored oak leaves & applied lustred acorns, signed 245.00

Vase, 5¼" h., dimpled sides, sapphire blue w/overall enameled multicolored florals, birds & insects 185.00

Vase, 6" h., grey w/applied salamander wrapped around body, signed 525.00

Vase, 7½" h., 11½" w., applied clear ruffled rim & feet, electric blue w/enameled multicolored florals (ILLUS.) 500.00

MOUNT WASHINGTON

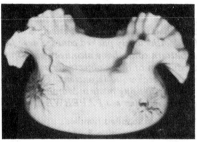

Mt. Washington Bowl

A wide diversity of glass was made by the Mt. Washington Glass Company, of New Bedford, Mass., between 1869 and 1900. It was succeeded in 1900 by the Pairpont Corporation. Miscellaneous types are listed below, but also see AMBERINA, BURMESE, CROWN MILANO, CUT VELVET, NAPOLI, PEACH BLOW, ROYAL FLEMISH and SMITH BROTHERS.

Bowl, squared top w/crimped rim, white satin finish shaded to yellow, enameled deep pink spider mums decor (ILLUS.) $325.00

Cologne bottle w/original pewter shaker to, egg-shaped, lustreless white, enameled clusters of maroon berries, white flowers & green foliage 495.00

Compote, 9" h., scalloped rim, light sandy brown, enameled pink florals, in ornate silverplate stand 275.00

Cookie jar, melon-ribbed, satin finish, enameled pastel blossoms & foliage, ornate silverplate cover .. 235.00

Cookie jar, melon-ribbed, light melon green, enameled gold florals & stems decor, silverplate rim, cover & bail handle 400.00

Creamer, melon-ribbed, lustreless white, enameled gold florals &

leaves decor, silverplate collar,
rim & handle, 3" h.............. 225.00
Ferner, pale lemon yellow,
enameled pink florals, 9 x 5" 195.00
Flower frog, mushroom-shaped,
lustreless white, enameled
floral decor, 5" d.,
2¾" h.................135.00 to 190.00
Mustard pot, fig mold, pink,
enameled leaves decor, silverplate pagoda-shaped cover....... 165.00
Salt shaker w/original top, egg-
shaped, multicolored rooster
decor (single) 245.00
Salt shaker w/original top, egg-
shaped, white shaded to cobalt
blue, enameled floral decor
(single)........................ 45.00
Salt shaker w/original top, fig mold,
lustreless white, enameled lavender & blue florals (single) 135.00
Salt shaker w/original top, flat-
sided egg shape, pale blue,
"Columbian Exhibition 1893"
enameled in raised gold
lettering (single) 125.00
Salt shaker, model of a chick w/sil-
verplate head, glossy "orange
peel" textured white, sprays of
roses decor (single) 335.00

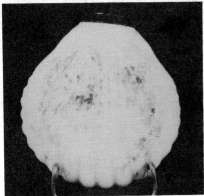

Cockle Shell Salt Shaker

Salt & pepper shakers w/original
tops, cockle shell mold, seaweed
decor, pr. (ILLUS. of one) 600.00
Salt & pepper shakers w/original
tops, egg-in-cup mold, satin finish, enameled floral decor, pr. ... 195.00
Salt & pepper shakers w/original
tops, Ribbed Pillar mold, lustreless white, pr., in silverplate handled frame 260.00
Salt & pepper shakers, model of a
chick w/silverplate head, matte
finish "orange peel" textured
pink, one w/yellow-centered blue
florals & green leaves, the other
w/yellow-centered mauve

chrysanthemum-like blossoms &
green shaded to mustard yellow
leaves, pr....................... 675.00
Sugar shaker w/original top, egg-
shaped, satin finish, enameled
blue & white forget-me-nots
w/yellow centers............... 235.00
Sugar shaker w/original top, egg-
shaped, lustreless white,
enameled blue florals 185.00
Sugar shaker w/original top, egg-
shaped, lustreless white,
enameled ferns decor 275.00

Egg Form Sugar Shaker

Sugar shaker w/original top, egg-
shaped, lustreless white, multicolored pansies, green leaves &
buds decor (ILLUS.) 235.00
Sugar shaker w/original silverplate
blossom-embossed lid, melon-
ribbed, yellow, autumn foliage &
raised blueberries decor, 4" d.,
3" h. 485.00
Syrup pitcher w/ornate silverplate
lid & handle, melon-ribbed, lustreless white, floral decor, 7¼" h. .. 315.00
Toothpick holder, fig mold, lustreless white, blue floral decor...... 245.00
Vase, 6" h., "lava," black w/inlaid
pastel blue, coral pink, light &
dark grey, pale green & white
chips, some of which are highlighted w/gold touches 885.00
Vase, 9" h., gourd form, lustreless
white, enameled pastel florals &
foliage 395.00
Vases, 10" h., square, blue, white
enameled pelicans in marsh scene
decor, in metal frames w/tall
legs, pr........................ 475.00
Vase, 13" h., lustreless white w/ice
green coralene.................. 695.00
Vase, 14" h., 6½" base d., narrow
neck flaring to scalloped petal-
form mouth w/gold trim, "Vero-
na," clear w/pale lavender shaded to white florals outlined in
gold 340.00

MULLER FRERES

The Muller Brothers made acid-etched cameo and other fine glass at Luneville, France, starting in 1910 and until the outbreak of World War II in Europe. Also see SHADES under Glass.

Cameo bowl, 6" h., double conical
form w/waisted neck & flaring lip,
carved & enameled pumpkin, rust,
ochre & cinnamon Millet-type harvest scene w/workers in the fields
beside a cottage against rust
ground, ca. 1900, signed $3,575.00

Cameo vase, 5½" h., 2½ x 5" flattened oval, carved brown to gold
lake scene w/boat by shore
against translucent yellow & gold
satin ground w/tree framing top
of vase, signed 595.00

Cameo vase, 7" h., carved orange &
black scrolling vine w/leaves &
fruit against mottled yellow &
blue ground, ca. 1900, signed 1,045.00

Cameo vase, 9½" h., 6¾" d., carved
black to blue to rust mountain &
waterfall scene against frosted
mottled ground w/gold & blue,
signed 2,650.00

Cameo vase, 9 7/8" h., 4½" d.,
carved deep maroon to rose scene
of 2 large dragonflies in flight
along a river bank within a framework of willow tree branches
against frosted ground, signed ...1,975.00

Muller Freres Scenic Cameo Vase

Cameo vase, 10½" h., globular
w/everted lip, carved blue-grey,
slate blue & deep midnight blue
mountain scene w/conifers against
milky grey ground, ca. 1910,
signed (ILLUS.) 4,675.00

Cameo vase, bud, 12¼" h., slender
elongated neck on squat bulbous
base, carved amethyst honeysuckle vine, ca. 1920, signed 330.00

Muller Freres Cameo Vase

Cameo vase, 11¾" h., baluster form,
carved ochre, Chinese red & white
pendant berry-laden leafy branches
& a moth against grey ground splashed w/lime green, salmon pink,
white, Chinese red & ochre, ca.
1920, signed (ILLUS.) 2,970.00

Cameo vase, 13¼" h., 4 7/8" oval
top, carved deep brown scene of
windmill & cottages by shore
against deep golden yellow satin
translucent ground, signed 1,195.00

NAILSEA

Nailsea Vase

Glass was made at Nailsea, near Bristol, England, from 1788 to 1873. Although the bulk of the products were similar to Bristol wares, collectors today visualize Nailsea primarily as a glass characterized by swirls and loopings, usually white, on a colored ground. Much glass attributed to Nailsea was made in glasshouses elsewhere.

Cruet w/original stopper, green
w/white & maroon loopings $85.00

Flask, clear w/opalescent loopings,
7 5/8" l. 50.00

Flask, clear w/red, white & blue
loopings, 8¼" l. 125.00

Perfume flask, pink w/opaque white
loopings, 5¾" l. 215.00
Perfume flask, cobalt blue w/pink &
opaque white loopings, 8" l. 245.00
Rose bowl, egg-shaped, 8-crimp top,
frosted cranberry w/opaque white
loopings, 3 5/8" d., 4¾" h. 175.00
Sweetmeat jar, white w/pink & yellow loopings, embossed silverplate cover, rim & ornate handle,
4" d., 5" h. 485.00
Vase, 4" h., 6½" widest d., sapphire blue w/opaque white loopings (ILLUS.) 235.00
Vase, 9½" h., applied black foot &
handles, clear w/red & white
loopings...................... 275.00
Whimsey, crochet hook, pink
w/white swirled loopings 60.00
Wine decanter w/matching bubble
stopper, clear w/opaque white &
cranberry loopings, 4 5/8" d.,
12¼" h....................... 350.00

NAKARA

Cigar Humidor with Indian Portrait

*Like Kelva (which see), Nakara ware was
made early in this century by C.F. Monroe
Company. For details see WAVE CREST.*

Box w/hinged lid, Crown mold, red
& white roses on shocking pink
ground w/enameled blue & white
beading, signed, 6" d. $395.00
Box w/hinged lid, reserve scene of
cupids on lid on pink to moss
green ground w/areas of pale
blue enhanced w/enameled white
beading, signed, 6" d., 3½" h. ... 475.00
Box w/hinged lid, plain round mold,
enameled floral decor on pink to
cream ground, signed, 8" d....... 350.00
Box w/hinged lid, Spindrift mold,
pink, blue & white floral decor,
signed, 8" d., 5" h. 1,295.00

Box w/hinged lid, reserve scene of
2 women in garden w/flowers &
birds on soft olive green ground,
signed, 8½" d.................. 650.00
"Cigars" humidor, h.p. Indian chief
in war bonnet on brown ground
(ILLUS.)....................... 650.00
"Collars and Cuffs" box w/hinged
lid, blue florals & leaves & white
beading on rose ground, signed,
8½" d., 5½" h. 275.00
Jewelry box w/hinged lid, reserve
scene of h.p. cupids on lid, red
ground, pink satin lining, 3¾" d.,
2½" h........................ 375.00
Jewelry box w/hinged lid, octagonal, h.p. iris on apricot
ground, original lining, signed,
6" w. 625.00
Letter rack, footed, h.p. Indian portrait decor, 5 x 4½"............ 465.00
Ring box w/hinged lid, Bishop's Hat
mold, white enameled beading on
leaf design on lavender to purple,
original pink lining, signed,
2½" d. 315.00
Ring box w/hinged lid, h.p. portrait,
signed, 2½" d.................. 596.00
Vase, 8¾" h., white florals & white
enameled beaded scrolls on pink
to steel blue ground, ormolu footed base ....400.00 to 475.00

NAPOLI

*This clear glass, decorated inside & outside,
is a Mount Washington production patented in 1894 by Albert Steffin. Interior designs
are sometimes outlined in gold on the exteri-
or while at other times a gold linear fishnet
design is laid over the outside surface. Sometimes signed "Napoli" on the base, the combination of interior and exterior decoration
serve to identify this scarce ware.*

Punch cup, Palmer Brownies decor,
signed $950.00
Rose bowl, 12-ribbed, yellow florals
interior, enameled gold outlining
exterior, unsigned, 5½" h........ 545.00
Sweetmeat jar, 4 deep depressions
at widest section & 6 shallow
depressions around base, interior
w/three Brownies & 2 rabbits between depressions w/scenes outlined in gold exterior, silverplate
rim, cover & bail handle,
5¾" h. 1,085.00
Vase, 3½" h., 4½" d., semi-jack-in-
pulpit rim, blue chrysanthemums
interior, gold outlining exterior,
signed 1,000.00

NASH

Nash Chintz Pattern Goblet

This glass was made by A. Douglas Nash Corp., which purchased the Corona Works from L.C. Tiffany in December, 1928. Nash, who formerly worked for Tiffany, produced outstanding glass for a brief period of time since the manufacture ceased prior to March of 1931, when A. Douglas Nash became associated with Libbey Glass in Toledo, Ohio. This fine quality ware is scarce.

Bowl, 7¾" d., 2¼" h., Jewel patt.,
　gold phantom lustre $275.00
Bowl, 8¾" d., 2" h., Chintz patt.,
　light green, signed 165.00
Bowl, 12" d., 3½" h., iridescent
　blue, signed & numbered 735.00
Candlesticks, ball stem, Chintz patt.,
　blood red w/silver, signed, 4" h.,
　pr. 450.00
Centerpiece bowl, Chintz patt.,
　blood red w/silver, signed,
　10" d. 425.00
Goblet, Chintz patt., blue w/silver,
　signed, 5" h. (ILLUS.) 110.00
Vase, 6¼" h., square top, iridescent
　gold, signed 275.00

OPALESCENT

Presently, this is one of the most popular areas of glass collecting. The opalescent effect was attained by adding bone ash chemical to areas of an item while still hot and refiring this object at tremendous heat. Both pressed and mold-blown patterns are available to collectors and we distinguish the types in our listing below. Opalescent Glass From A to Z by William Heacock, is the definite reference book for collectors. Also see CARNIVAL GLASS, JACK-IN-PULPIT VASES and PATTERN GLASS.

MOLD-BLOWN OPALESCENT PATTERNS

ARABIAN NIGHTS
Pitcher, water, cranberry $325.00
Tumbler, blue 55.00
Water set: pitcher & 6 tumblers;
　blue, 7 pcs. 395.00
Water set: pitcher & 6 tumblers;
　white, 7 pcs. 290.00

BLOWN DRAPES
Pitcher, water, blue 195.00

BUBBLE LATTICE
Pitcher, water, cranberry 175.00
Sugar bowl, cov., cranberry 125.00
Sugar shaker w/original top, blue . . 135.00
Sugar shaker w/original top,
　cranberry 145.00
Syrup pitcher w/original top, blue . . 140.00
Syrup pitcher w/original top, canary
　yellow 145.00

BULL'S EYE
Water bottle, blue 110.00
Water bottle, cranberry 150.00

BUTTONS & BRAIDS
Pitcher, water, blue 135.00
Pitcher, water, cranberry 235.00
Pitcher, water, green 125.00
Tumbler, blue 35.00
Water set: pitcher & 5 tumblers;
　blue, 6 pcs. 265.00

COIN SPOT & SWIRL
Syrup pitcher w/original top,
　blue . . . . 95.00 to 125.00
Syrup pitcher w/original top,
　white 67.50

CONSOLIDATED CRISS-CROSS
Bowl, master berry, 8" d.,
　cranberry 145.00
Celery vase, Rubina, satin finish 245.00
Salt shaker w/original top, cran-
　berry, satin finish 85.00
Spooner, cranberry or Rubina,
　each 125.00
Tumbler, cranberry 83.00
Tumbler, white 49.00

DAFFODILS
Celery vase, blue 75.00
Pitcher, water, blue 195.00
Pitcher, water, green 180.00
Pitcher, water, white 145.00
Tumbler, blue 50.00
Tumbler, white 42.50
Water set: water pitcher & 5 tum-
　blers; blue, 6 pcs. 650.00

DAISY IN CRISS-CROSS
Pitcher, water, blue . . . . 225.00 to 265.00
Pitcher, water, white 85.00

Syrup pitcher w/original top, blue .. 250.00
Syrup pitcher w/original top,
   cranberry...................... 350.00
Tumbler, blue.................... 47.50

HERRINGBONE
Cruet w/original clear teardrop form
   stopper, blue 110.00
Cruet w/original clear teardrop form
   stopper, cranberry 190.00
Tumbler, cranberry 75.00

POINSETTIA
Pitcher, water, tankard, 13" h.,
   blue ....180.00 to 225.00
Pitcher, water, tankard, 13" h.,
   green 135.00
Syrup pitcher w/original top, blue .. 450.00
Tumbler, blue.................... 45.00
Tumbler, green 35.00
Water set: bulbous pitcher
   w/crimped rim & 7 tumblers;
   blue, 8 pcs.................... 500.00

POLKA DOT
Barber bottle, blue ....95.00 to 125.00
Barber bottle, cranberry 125.00
Cruet w/original stopper,
   cranberry..................... 120.00
Pitcher, water, cranberry 185.00
Syrup pitcher w/original top,
   blue 175.00
Syrup pitcher w/original top,
   cranberry..................... 220.00
Toothpick holder, cranberry 75.00
Tumbler, blue.................... 50.00

REVERSE SWIRL

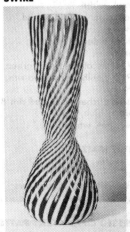

Reverse Swirl Vase

Bowl, berry, 9" d., canary yellow ... 125.00
Carafe, blue 135.00
Carafe, canary yellow 125.00
Celery vase, blue 68.00
Celery vase, canary yellow........ 50.00

Cruet w/original stopper, canary
   yellow 150.00
Cruet w/original stopper,
   cranberry..................... 235.00
Mustard jar, canary yellow 35.00
Pitcher, water, bulbous, blue 145.00
Pitcher, water, bulbous, canary
   yellow 100.00
Pitcher, water, tankard, cranberry .. 295.00
Pitcher, water, tankard, white...... 105.00
Salt & pepper shakers w/original
   tops, white, pr. 48.00
Sauce dish, blue 20.00
Spooner, blue.................... 55.00
Sugar bowl, cov., blue............ 115.00
Sugar shaker w/original top, blue .. 120.00
Sugar shaker w/original top, canary
   yellow 90.00
Sugar shaker w/original top,
   cranberry..................... 125.00
Syrup pitcher w/original top,
   cranberry..................... 220.00
Toothpick holder, blue 85.00
Toothpick holder, canary yellow 65.00
Toothpick holder, white........... 40.00
Tumbler, juice, white 45.00
Tumbler, canary yellow 38.00
Tumbler, cranberry 65.00
Tumbler, white................... 45.00
Vase, 8" h., cranberry 48.00
Vase, 12" h., twisted form, cran-
   berry (ILLUS.) 200.00
Whiskey shot glass, white 45.00

RIBBED LATTICE

Ribbed Lattice Pattern

Celery vase, cranberry............ 85.00
Creamer, blue (ILLUS. right) 95.00
Cruet w/original stopper,
   cranberry..................... 165.00
Pitcher, water, white 130.00
Pitcher, water, tankard, cranberry .. 275.00
Salt shaker w/original top,
   cranberry..................... 45.00
Sugar shaker w/original top,
   cranberry..................... 100.00
Sugar shaker w/original top,
   white 67.50
Syrup pitcher w/original top, blue
   (ILLUS. left) 175.00
Syrup pitcher w/original top,
   cranberry..................... 265.00

Syrup pitcher w/original top,
white 95.00
Toothpick holder, blue 65.00
Toothpick holder, cranberry 72.50
Toothpick holder, white 30.00
Tumbler, cranberry 65.00

SPANISH LACE

Spanish Lace Sugar Shaker

Bowl, 7" d., ruffled rim, blue 80.00
Carafe, blue 125.00
Celery vase, canary yellow 55.00
Finger bowl, canary yellow,
4 5/8" d. 40.00
Pitcher, 5½" h., blue 48.00
Pitcher, water, 9" h., canary
yellow 145.00
Pitcher, water, tankard, 11½" h.,
cranberry 385.00
Pitcher, water, white 95.00
Rose bowl, blue 65.00
Rose bowl, white 50.00
Sugar shaker w/original top, blue .. 130.00
Sugar shaker w/original top, cran-
berry (ILLUS.) 145.00
Syrup pitcher w/original top, canary
yellow 145.00
Syrup pitcher w/original top,
cranberry 165.00
Tumbler, cranberry 60.00
Vase, 6" h., crimped & folded-over
rim, blue 50.00
Water set: pitcher & 6 tumblers;
blue, 7 pcs. 345.00

STRIPE

Barber bottle, cranberry 95.00
Cruet w/original stopper,
cranberry 125.00
Cruet w/original stopper, white 135.00
Pitcher, water, blue (ILLUS.) 250.00
Rose bowl, cranberry, enameled
forget-me-nots 65.00
Sugar shaker w/original top, bowl-
ing pin shape, cranberry 75.00
Syrup pitcher w/original top, blue .. 185.00
Syrup pitcher w/original top, canary
yellow 125.00

Stripe Pitcher

Syrup pitcher w/original top,
cranberry 250.00

SWIRL

Barber bottle w/original stopper,
blue 110.00
Barber bottle w/original stopper,
cranberry 85.00
Cruet w/original stopper,
cranberry 150.00
Pitcher, 4¼" h., bulbous, blue 48.00
Pitcher, 6¼" h., bulbous, blue 75.00
Pitcher, water, 8½" h., blue 110.00
Pitcher, water, 8½" h., white 75.00
Pitcher, water, 9¼" h., square ruf-
fled top, cranberry ......150.00 to 180.00
Rose bowl, blue 52.50
Rose bowl, white 37.50
Strawholder jar w/original lid,
cranberry 275.00
Toothpick holder, blue 42.50
Tumbler, blue 28.50
Vase, 7" h., scalloped rim, green ... 39.50
Vase, 9" h., bulbous, ruffled rim,
cranberry 130.00
Water set: pitcher w/ruffled rim & 4
tumblers; blue, 5 pcs. 190.00
Whimsey, hat, white 50.00

SWIRLING MAIZE

Pitcher, water, blue 135.00
Tumbler, cranberry 75.00
Water set: pitcher & 6 tumblers;
blue, 7 pcs. 435.00

PRESSED OPALESCENT PATTERNS

BEADED DRAPES

Bowl, 9" d., fluted rim, footed,
canary yellow 27.00
Candy dish, white 23.00
Dish, ruffled, white 25.00
Rose bowl, canary yellow 31.00
Rose bowl, green 32.50

DOUBLE GREEK KEY
Celery vase, blue 115.00
Sauce dish, blue 32.50
Tumbler, blue..................... 95.00
Vase, 6" h., 4" w., blue 130.00

FLORA
Bowl, master berry, canary yellow .. 95.00
Butter dish, cov., canary yellow 175.00
Butter dish, cov., canary yellow
w/gold trim 225.00
Celery vase, blue ....95.00 to 125.00
Compote, jelly, blue 125.00
Cruet w/original stopper, canary
yellow 500.00
Sauce dish, blue 35.00
Spooner, blue...............60.00 to 75.00
Spooner, canary yellow w/gold
trim.......................... 85.00
Sugar bowl, cov., canary yellow
w/gold trim 125.00

FLUTED SCROLLS

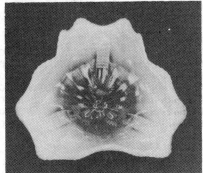

Fluted Scrolls Card Tray

Berry set: master bowl & 6 sauce
dishes; vaseline w/enameled
florals, 7 pcs. 245.00
Bowl, master berry, blue 60.00
Butter dish, cov., blue .....145.00 to 175.00
Butter dish, cov., vaseline
w/enameled florals 195.00
Card tray, white, 7" w. (ILLUS.)..... 35.00
Creamer, blue 45.00
Creamer, blue w/enameled florals.. 55.00
Creamer, vaseline...........40.00 to 55.00
Creamer, white 35.00
Cruet w/original stopper, vasline ... 150.00
Epergne, blue.................... 120.00
Pitcher, water, blue 230.00
Pitcher, water, vaseline ...145.00 to 195.00
Puff jar, cov., blue 55.00
Puff jar, cov., vaseline.......40.00 to 50.00
Puff jar, cov., white 30.00
Rose bowl, white................. 45.00
Salt & pepper shakers w/original
tops, blue, pr. 75.00
Sauce dish, blue 16.00
Sauce dish, vaseline.............. 25.00
Spooner, blue.................... 55.00

Spooner, vaseline w/enameled
florals........................ 95.00
Sugar bowl, cov., blue............ 80.00
Sugar bowl, cov., vaseline 125.00
Table set: cov. butter dish, cov.
sugar bowl, creamer & spooner;
vaseline, 4 pcs.........350.00 to 395.00
Tumbler, blue w/enameled florals .. 65.00
Tumbler, vaseline 45.00
Water set: pitcher & 6 tumblers;
blue, 7 pcs..................... 425.00

GONTERMAN SWIRL

Gonterman Swirl Spooner

Bowl, master berry, 10" d.,
blue top 135.00
Celery vase, amber top.....85.00 to 150.00
Compote, jelly, amber top 110.00
Lamp shade, amber rim 110.00
Pitcher, water, amber top.......... 200.00
Spooner amber top (ILLUS.) 85.00
Sugar bowl, cov., blue top......... 160.00
Syrup pitcher w/original lid, amber
top 250.00
Syrup pitcher w/original lid, blue
top 240.00
Toothpick holder, amber top 120.00
Toothpick holder, blue top 105.00

HOBNAIL & PANELED THUMBPRINT

Hobnail & Paneled Thumbprint Pattern

Berry set: master bowl & 6 sauce
dishes; canary yellow, 7 pcs. 140.00

Bowl, master berry, blue 25.00
Butter dish, cov., blue 145.00
Creamer, blue 45.00
Sauce dish, blue 20.00
Spooner, canary yellow (ILLUS.
  right) 60.00
Sugar bowl, cov., canary yellow
  (ILLUS. left) 95.00
Table set: cov. butter dish, cov.
  sugar bowl & spooner; blue,
  3 pcs. 275.00
Table set, canary yellow,
  4 pcs. .... 255.00 to 335.00

INTAGLIO
Bowl, master berry, blue 150.00
Compote, jelly, canary
  yellow .... 40.00 to 55.00
Compote, jelly, white 30.00
Creamer, blue , ... 48.00
Creamer, white .... 20.00 to 25.00
Cruet w/original stopper,
  blue .... 120.00 to 155.00
Pitcher, water, blue 250.00
Sauce dish, blue 38.00
Spooner, blue 80.00
Sugar bowl, cov., blue .... 140.00 to 175.00
Tumbler, blue 75.00
Tumbler, white 30.00

IRIS WITH MEANDER
Berry set: master bowl & 5 sauce
  dishes; canary yellow, 6 pcs. 225.00
Butter dish, cov., blue .... 200.00 to 300.00
Butter dish, cov., canary yellow 195.00
Compote, jelly, blue .... 75.00 to 100.00
Compote, jelly, canary
  yellow .... 65.00 to 75.00
Pitcher, water, canary
  yellow .... 250.00 to 300.00
Salt & pepper shakers w/original
  tops, canary yellow,
  pr. .... 120.00 to 145.00
Spooner, canary yellow ...... 50.00 to 75.00
Table set: cov. butter dish, cov.
  sugar bowl & spooner; blue,
  3 pcs. 550.00
Toothpick holder, blue 65.00
Toothpick holder, canary yellow 100.00
Toothpick holder, green ..... 35.00 to 45.00
Toothpick holder, green w/gold 50.00
Tumbler, canary yellow 40.00

JEWEL & FLOWER
Berry set: master bowl & 6 sauce
  dishes; canary yellow, 7 pcs. 260.00
Butter dish, cov., canary yellow 175.00
Butter dish, cov., white 95.00
Creamer, white 35.00
Cruet w/clear stopper, white 135.00
Pitcher, water, blue (ILLUS.) 395.00
Salt shaker w/original top, blue
  (single) 50.00
Sauce dish, canary yellow 35.00

Jewel & Flower Water Pitcher

Sauce dish, white 25.00
Spooner, canary yellow 90.00
Spooner, white 35.00
Table set, blue, 4 pcs. 380.00
Water set: pitcher & 5 tumblers;
  canary yellow, 6 pcs. 850.00

OVER-ALL HOB
Celery blue 85.00
Creamer, white 45.00
Pitcher, footed, white 225.00
Toothpick holder, blue ...... 35.00 to 45.00
Toothpick holder, canary yellow 55.00
Toothpick holder, white 30.00
Tumbler, blue 35.00

PALM BEACH
Berry set: master bowl & 6 sauce
  dishes; canary yellow, 7 pcs. 295.00
Creamer & cov. sugar bowl, blue,
  pr. 105.00
Nappy, blue 65.00
Sauce dish, blue 28.00
Sauce dish, canary yellow 18.00
Spooner, blue 47.00
Tumbler, canary yellow 85.00

PANELED HOLLY

Paneled Holly Butter Dish

Butter dish, cov., white (ILLUS.) 145.00
Spooner, blue 50.00

Table set: cov. butter dish, cov. sugar bowl, creamer & spooner;
white, 4 pcs. 295.00
Water set: pitcher & 4 tumblers;
white, 5 pcs. 650.00
Water set: pitcher & 6 tumblers;
blue w/gold, 7 pcs. 375.00

REGAL
Butter dish, cov., blue 195.00
Butter dish, cov., green w/gold. 145.00
Butter dish, cov., white 105.00
Celery vase, blue . . . . 115.00 to 125.00
Compote, jelly, blue 75.00
Creamer, blue 95.00
Pitcher, water, blue 245.00
Salt & pepper shakers w/replaced
tops, blue, pr. 75.00
Spooner, blue. 65.00
Spooner, green 60.00
Sugar bowl, cov., green 65.00
Tumbler, blue. 50.00

RIBBED SPIRAL
Bowl, 8" d., ruffled, canary yellow. . 40.00
Compote, jelly, blue 47.00
Salt shaker w/original top, blue
(single). 39.00
Spooner, blue. 55.00
Toothpick holder, blue 75.00
Toothpick holder, canary
yellow . . . . 58.00 to 65.00
Toothpick holder, white 55.00

SCROLL WITH ACANTHUS

Scroll with Acanthus Compote

Compote, jelly, blue (ILLUS.) 35.00
Compote, jelly, white 28.00
Creamer, blue 45.00
Cruet w/clear stopper, blue 185.00
Pitcher, water, blue 140.00
Spooner, blue. 55.00
Spooner, canary yellow 70.00
Tumbler, blue. 45.00

SHELL
Bowl, master berry, green 80.00
Sauce dish, footed, blue, 4" 24.00
Sauce dishes, white, set of 6 . . . . 100.00

SWAG WITH BRACKETS

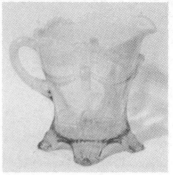

Swag with Brackets Creamer

Butter dish, cov., canary yellow 155.00
Compote, jelly, blue 38.00
Compote, jelly, vaseline 38.00
Creamer, green (ILLUS.) 35.00
Spooner, blue. 60.00
Sugar bowl, cov., green 55.00
Table set: cov. butter dish, cov.
sugar bowl, creamer & spooner;
blue, 4 pcs. 314.00
Table set: cov. butter dish, cov.
sugar bowl, creamer & spooner;
canary yellow, 4 pcs. 355.00
Toothpick holder, white 50.00
Tumbler, blue. 40.00
Tumbler, canary yellow 40.00
Tumbler, green 15.00
Water set: pitcher & 6 tumblers; ca-
nary yellow, 7 pcs. 389.00

TOKYO

Tokyo Jelly Compote

Bowl, fruit, 9" d., 4" h., scalloped,
blue 60.00
Bowl, master berry, green 50.00
Compote, jelly, green (ILLUS.) 25.00
Pitcher, water, green 125.00
Toothpick holder, white 45.00
Tumbler, blue. 27.50

WILD BOUQUET

Wild Bouquet Spooner

Compote, jelly, white	24.00
Cruet w/original stopper, blue	175.00
Pitcher, water, blue	250.00
Spooner, blue (ILLUS.)	85.00
Sugar bowl, cov., white	55.00
Sugar bowl, open, white	45.00
Tumbler, green	55.00

WREATH & SHELL

Wreath & Shell Cuspidor & Rose Bowl

Berry set: master bowl & 6 sauce dishes; blue or vaseline, 7 pcs., each set	250.00
Butter dish, cov., vaseline w/enameled decor	195.00
Cuspidor, lady's, vaseline (ILLUS. left)	125.00
Rose bowl, blue (ILLUS. right)	125.00
Sauce dish, canary yellow	20.00

Wreath & Shell Spooner

Spooner, blue (ILLUS.)	70.00
Tumbler, blue	52.00
Tumbler, vaseline	50.00

OPALINE

French Opaline Vase

Also called opal glass (once a name applied to milk white glass), opaline is a fairly opaque glass with a color resembling the opal; however, pieces in such colors as blue, pink, green and others, also are referred to now as opaline glass. Many of the objects were decorated.

Bowl w/cover & stand, inverted pyriform raised on short pedestal & circular foot, circular stand w/scalloped border, white w/gilt line borders & finial, 2nd half 19th c., 12¼" d., overall 13½" h.	$220.00
Box w/lift-off lid, French blue w/overall gold enameling & white beading, 3¾"h	50.00
Compote, attached to powder blue dolphin base	750.00
Decanter w/stopper, baluster form, everted rim, fluted shoulder, green, gilt outlining, 12" h.	330.00
Perfume bottle w/original stopper, French blue w/gold florals & leaves decor, 2¾" h.	40.00
Perfume bottle w/matching stopper, French blue w/gold, white & yellow decor, 4" h.	65.00
Perfume bottle w/matching stopper, white w/gold & cream satin leaves & scrolls decor, 3" d., 6¼" h.	110.00
Perfume bottle w/clear stopper, pink w/enameled decor & gold trim, 7" h.	85.00
Perfume bottle w/matching deco-	

rated stopper, pink w/cream &
gold fleur-de-lis decor, 3¼" d.,
8½" h. 165.00

Vase, 1 3/8" h., ball-form, French
blue w/gold blossoms & leaves
decor 28.00

Vase, 4" h., footed, French blue
w/gold florals & leaves decor 48.00

Vase, 5 3/8" h., French blue w/gold
& yellow trim 48.00

Vases, 6" h., pink w/blue & gold
enameled decor, pr............. 150.00

Vases, 7" h., flattened oval, h.p.
floral decor, gold on crenulated
rim, pr. 135.00

Vases, 10" h., creamy ivory
w/florals & gold decor, pr....... 125.00

Vase, 10½" h., footed, French blue
w/gold, yellow & white decor 140.00

Vase, 46" h., white baluster form
w/gilt bronze mounts on lip, collar & top of base & raised on gilt-
bronze base w/molded feet,
French, 2nd half 19th c.
(ILLUS.) ....1,800.00 to 2,00.00

Water set: pitcher & 2 tumblers; yellow, 3 pcs. 275.00

ORREFORS

Orrefors Vase by Simon Gate

*This Swedish glasshouse, founded in 1898
for production of tablewares, has made
decorative wares as well since 1915. By 1925,
Orrefors had achieved an international reputation for its Graal glass, an engraved art
glass developed by master glass blower Knut
Bergqvist and artist-designers Simon Gate
and Edward Hald. Ariel glass, recognized by
a design of controlled air traps, and the heavy
Ravenna glass, usually tinted, were both developed in the 1930's. While all Orrefors glass
is collectible, pieces signed by early designers and artists are now bringing high prices.*

Ash tray, red, 1950's, artist-signed,
6 x 3"......................... $75.00

Vase, 5" h., paperweight-type,
bullet-shaped, clear, internally
decorated w/green swimming
fish, artist-signed & numbered.... 325.00

Vase, 5 3/8" h., flaring cylinder, engraved w/four stylized nymphs
posed on leaf-embellished
pedestals within lozenge & scroll
bordered panels, designed by
Simon Gate, mid-20th c. 467.50

Vase, 5½" h., Graal, paperweight-
type, internally decorated w/un-
derwater scene of fish & sea
plants, signed Edward Hald 275.00

Vase, 6" h., 4¾ x 3¾" oblong,
clear, engraved w/children carrying basket of flowers, by Sven
Palmquist 375.00

Vase, 6¼" h., Ariel, blue, lady's
head decor 535.00

Vase, 6½" h., Graal, clear, internally decorated w/green fish & seaweed decor, designed by Edward
Hald 325.00

Vase, 7" h., Ariel, square, heavy
chased clear glass vessel enclosing
a blue air-trapped design of a
female profile & a panel of a dove
in flight within a stylized geometric
& floral border, designed by Edvin
Ohrstrom, ca. 1939 ....2,200.00

Vase, 8" h., clear, swirled body,
artist-signed 175.00

Vase, 8" h., clear, engraved
w/scene of child w/bird & goose,
paper label 150.00

Vase, 9½" h., tapering cylinder,
clear smoky body engraved
w/nude figures of a man & a
woman seated together on a rock
at water's edge, signed Simon
Gate w/inscription, dated 1935
(ILLUS.) 1,320.00

PAIRPOINT

*Originally organized in New Bedford, Mas-
sachusetts, in 1880, as the Pairpoint Manufacturing Company, on land adjacent to the
famed Mount Washington Glass Works, this
company first manufactured silver and plated wares. In 1894, the two famous factories
merged as the Pairpoint Corporation and en-
joyed renowned success for more than forty
years. The company was sold in 1939, to a
group of local businessmen and eventually
bought out by one of the group who turned
the management over to Robert M. Gunderson. Subsequently, it operated as the Gunder-*

son *Glass Works until 1952 when, after Gunderson's death, the name was changed to Gunderson-Pairpoint. This factory closed in 1956. Subsequently, Robert Bryden took charge of this glass works, at first producing glass for Pairpoint abroad and eventually, in 1970, began glass production in Sagamore, Massachusetts. Bryden's Pairpoint company continues in operation today manufacturing fine quality blown and pressed glass. Also see CUT and PEACH BLOW GLASS and PAIRPOINT-LIMOGES under Ceramics.*

Bowl, 8½" d., "peppermint stick," clear satin finish w/overlay rose rim cut to clear stripes, w/engraved design $125.00
Box w/hinged lid, biscuit colored w/enameled gold & silver iris & leaves, signed, 7¼ x 6"...............425.00 to 455.00
Candlesticks, amethyst w/clear "controlled bubble" ball connector in stem, 4" h., pr............... 125.00
Candlesticks, mushroom-shaped top, green w/clear "controlled bubble" ball in stem, 4½" h., pr......... 95.00
Candlesticks, light green w/clear "controlled bubble" paperweight base, 11" h., pr. 185.00
Candy dish & cover w/clear "controlled bubble" ball finial, Auroria (reddish amber), engraved Vintage (grape clusters & vine) patt., 6" h. 160.00
Card holder, engraved floral decor, clear w/"controlled bubble" ball connector to saucer base, 5" d.... 125.00
Collars & cuffs box w/hinged lid, lavender florals & gold trim on white satin ground, signed, 5½" h. 235.00
Compote, 5" d., low, ruby w/clear "controlled bubble" paperweight base 125.00
Compote, 12½" d., 6½" h., wheel-etched floral swags, Auroria (reddish amber) w/clear "controlled bubble" ball connector in stem ... 137.50
Console set: bowl & pr. candlesticks; green w/clear "controlled bubble" connector in stem, 3 pcs. 250.00
Cornucopia-vase, ruby w/clear "controlled bubble" paperweight base, 9" h............................ 125.00
Perfume bottle w/original stoper, clear w/"controlled bubble" base & stopper, 5½" h.............. 110.00
Punch cup, handleless, cylindrical w/flaring rim & low foot, Canaria (vaseline) - engraved Vintage patt. 27.50
Rose bowl, egg-shaped, "Pairpoint

Delft," enameled blue windmill scene on white opaline, 1890-1920, 6½" h. 575.00
Vase, bud, 5½" h., amethyst w/clear "controlled bubble" ball connector in stem, original label.. 90.00
Vase, 7¾" h., jack-in-pulpit type, ruby w/enameled bird on pine bough decor 155.00
Vase, 9" h., "Ambero," textured finish, interior-painted w/scene of couple strolling down country lane 745.00
Vase, 12" h., "Pairpoint Delft," enameled blue village scene w/castle in the distance on white opaline, 1890-1920.............. 285.00
Vases, 12½" h., 6" top d., cobalt blue w/light swirls & clear "controlled bubble" ball connector, pr............................ 325.00

Pairpoint Vase

Vase, clear w/engraved floral decor, "controlled bubble" ball connector, rayed foot (ILLUS.) 150.00
Wines, Morey patt., Flambeau (tomato red opaque) w/black stem, set of 6.................. 265.00

PATE DE VERRE

Pate de Verre, or "paste of glass," was molded by very few glass artisans. In the pate de verre technique, powdered glass is mixed with a liquid to make a paste which is then placed in a mold and baked at a high temperature. These articles have a finely-pitted or matte finish and are easily distinguished from blown glass. Duplicate pieces are possible with this technique.

Ash tray, trapezoidal, pale blue translucent shading to darker hue beneath blue & green moth at back, signed A. Walter Nancy & Berge Sc, 6 3/8" l. $2,860.00

Bowl, 3½" h., wide mouth, pale grey molded in low relief w/band of white bunnies above wavy bands in brown, salmon & ochre, ca. 1925, signed G. Agry-Rousseau . .8,800.00

Bowl, 11" oblong, 2 central brown & black stag beetles on a knotted tree root, streaked tan & chestnut brown shading to pale brown on one side, signed Berge Sc & A. Walter Nancy 6,600.00

Box, cov., cornflower blossoms on grey ground w/some purple, signed G. Argy-Rousseau, 3" h. 350.00

Pate de Verre Box

Box, cov., base w/purple ivy leaves framed by arches & stars, cover w/central Bacchanalian mask in dark red ringed by mauve ivy leaves & scalloped border w/stars, frosted ground mottled w/mauve, signed G. Argy-Rousseau, 6" d. (ILLUS.) 5,280.00

Dish, circular, w/school of half-submerged chestnut brown fish in translucent pale green water, signed Berge Sc. & A. Walter Nancy, 6" d. 3,850.00

Dish, canoe-shaped, modeled in full relief one end w/chameleon on berry-laden branches, matte translucent canary yellow shading to green, signed Daum Nancy, 10 5/8" l. 2,860.00

Figure of a nude woman kneeling, draped in a garland, deep lime green & dusty rose, ca. 1920,

signed A. Walter Nancy & Lavalley. Sc, 8½" h. 3,300.00

Model of a pheasant, lime green head shading to emerald green in the body & tail, on streaked dark green ground, signed A. Houillon & A. Walter Nancy, 7½" l. 1,045.00

Paperweight, model of a frog on a turtle's back, matte pale green frog, brown turtle w/traces of green & incised detailing, signed A. Walter Nancy, 2 7/8" h. 2,640.00

Pendant, beetle on aqua ground, signed A.W. 495.00

Tray, 6-sided, green & opalescent ground molded w/ochre & dark blue florals at the corners & large central green & dark blue dragonfly, signed A. Walter Berge, 7" l. 4,620.00

Vase, 3½" h., waisted flaring body, band of berried & leafy branches, amber, green & cinnamon on frosted ground, lightly mottled w/yellow, signed G. Argy-Rousseau France 2,640.00

Vase, 3¾" h., wide mouth, molded in low to high relief w/brilliant magenta stars shading to inky blue on grey ground streaked w/magenta, ca. 1925, signed G. Argy-Rousseau 3,575.00

Vase, 6" h., expanding circle w/swollen shoulder, grey streaked w/purple & molded w/red blossoms w/violet & green centers on gnarled black vines, ca. 1925, signed G. Argy-Rousseau 3,080.00

Pate de Verre Vase

Vase, 8" h., ovoid, molded mauve berried sea grass & green seaweed on matte blue-mottled yellow ground above 3 yellow triton shells at the foot, signed A. Walter Nancy H. Berge (ILLUS.) 1,980.00

PATTERN GLASS

Though it has never been ascertained whether glass was first pressed in the United States or abroad, the development of the glass pressing machine revolutionized the glass industry in the United States and this country receives the credit for improving the method to make this process feasible. The first wares pressed were probably small flat plates of the type now referred to as "lacy" Sandwich, the intricacy of the design concealing flaws.

In 1827, both the New England Glass Co., Cambridge, Massachusetts and Bakewell & Co., Pittsburgh, took out patents for pressing glass furniture knobs and soon other pieces followed. This early pressed glass contained red lead which made it clear and resonant when tapped (flint). Made primarily in clear, it is rarer in blue, amethyst, olive green and yellow.

By the 1840's, early simple patterns such as Ashburton, Argus and Excelsior appeared. Ribbed Bellflower seems to have been one of the earliest patterns to have had complete sets. By the 1860's, a wide range of patterns were available.

In 1864, William Leighton of Hobbs, Brockunier & Co., Wheeling, West Virginia, developed a formula for "soda lime" glass which did not require the expensive red lead for clarity. Although "soda lime" glass did not have the brilliance of the earlier flint glass, the formula came into widespread use because glass could be produced cheaply.

By 1900, patterns had become ornate in imitation of the expensive brilliant cut glass.

ACTRESS

Actress Cheese Dish

Bowl, 6" d., footed $40.00
Bowl, 8" d., Adelaide Neilson 85.00
Bread tray, Miss Neilson,
  12½" l. ....75.00 to 90.00
Butter dish, cov., Fanny Davenport &
  Miss Neilson.................. 85.00

Cake stand, Maude Granger &
  Annie Pixley, 10" d.,
  7" h....................125.00 to 165.00
Celery vase, Pinafore scene 160.00
Cheese dish, cov., "Lone Fisherman"
  on cover, "The Two Dromios" on
  underplate (ILLUS.) ......245.00 to 295.00
Cologne bottle w/original stopper,
  11" h.......................... 48.50
Compote, cov., 6" d.,
  10" h...................100.00 to 125.00
Compote, cov., 8" d., 12" h......... 165.00
Compote, cov., 10" d., 14½" h.,
  Fanny Davenport & Maggie
  Mitchell 150.00
Compote, open, 6" d., 11" h........ 95.00
Creamer, Miss Neilson & Fanny
  Davenport 85.00
Goblet, Lotta Crabtree & Kate
  Claxton 85.00
Marmalade jar, cov., Maude
  Granger & Annie Pixley 70.00
Mug, Pinafore scene.............. 47.50
Pickle dish, Kate Claxton, "Love's
  Request is Pickles," 9¼ x 5¼" ... 52.50
Pitcher, water, 9" h., Miss Neilson &
  Maggie Mitchell................ 250.00
Platter, 11½ x 7", Pinafore scene... 110.00
Relish, Miss Neilson, 8 x 5" 32.50
Salt shaker w/original pewter top
  (single)........................ 45.00
Sauce dish, Maggie Mitchell &
  Fanny Davenport, 4½" d.,
  2½" h...................17.50 to 30.00
Spooner, Mary Anderson & Maude
  Granger....................... 70.00
Sugar bowl, cov., Lotta Crabtree &
  Kate Claxton................... 135.00

ADONIS (Pleat & Tuck or Washboard)
Bowl, master berry, canary yellow .. 12.00
Creamer, blue 35.00
Creamer 15.00
Sauce dish, canary yellow......... 12.00

ALABAMA (Beaded Bull's Eye with Drape)
Butter dish, cov., ruby-stained...... 80.00
Butter dish, cov. 55.00
Castor set, 4-bottle, original silver-
  plate stand 135.00
Celery tray 25.00
Compote, cov., 5" d. 65.00
Creamer 36.00
Creamer, individual size 13.00
Cruet w/original stopper 55.00
Honey dish, cov. 47.50
Mustard pot & cover w/slot for
  spoon 55.00
Pitcher, water 95.00
Relish, 8 1/8 x 5" 18.00
Sauce dish 15.00
Spooner 35.00
Sugar bowl, cov. 45.00

Syrup pitcher w/original top 110.00
Toothpick holder 50.00
Tray, water, 10½" 42.50
Tumbler 22.00

ALASKA (Lion's Leg)

Alaska Pattern

Banana boat, blue opalescent 255.00
Berry set: master bowl & 6 sauce
  dishes; blue opalescent, 7 pcs. ... 325.00
Berry set: master bowl & 6 sauce
  dishes; vaseline opalescent,
  7 pcs. .... 250.00 to 275.00
Bowl, 8" sq., blue
  opalescent .... 75.00 to 95.00
Bowl, 8" sq., clear w/enameled
  florals 65.00
Bowl, 8" sq., green w/enameled
  florals 65.00
Bowl, 8" sq., vaseline opalescent ... 92.00
Butter dish, cov., blue opalescent ... 225.00
Butter dish, cov., green w/enameled
  florals 155.00
Butter dish, cov., vaseline
  opalescent 250.00
Card tray, blue opalescent 28.50
Card tray, vaseline opalescent 30.00
Celery (or jewel) tray, blue
  opalescent 170.00
Celery tray, blue opalescent
  w/enameled florals 200.00
Celery tray, vaseline opalescent 140.00
Celery tray, vaseline opalescent
  w/enameled florals 175.00
Creamer, blue opalescent .... 65.00 to 85.00
Creamer, clear to opalescent 45.00
Creamer, green w/enameled
  florals 70.00
Creamer, vaseline
  opalescent .... 55.00 to 75.00
Creamer & cov. sugar bowl, blue
  opalescent, pr. 225.00
Cruet w/original stopper, blue
  opalescent (ILLUS.) 250.00
Cruet w/original stopper, vaseline
  opalescent 255.00
Pitcher, water, blue
  opalescent .... 285.00 to 325.00

Pitcher, water, vaseline
  opalescent .... 325.00 to 385.00
Salt shaker w/original top, clear to
  opalescent (single) 25.00
Salt & pepper shakers w/original
  tops, blue opalescent, pr.
  (ILLUS.) 125.00
Salt & pepper shakers w/original
  tops, vaseline opalescent, pr. 125.00
Sauce dish, blue opalescent 50.00
Sauce dish, clear to opalescent 25.00
Sauce dish, vaseline opalescent 35.00
Spooner, blue opalescent 50.00
Spooner, clear to opalescent 30.00
Spooner, green 36.50
Spooner, green w/enameled
  florals 65.00
Spooner, vaseline opalescent 60.00
Spooner, vaseline opalescent
  w/enameled florals 95.00
Sugar bowl, cov., blue opalescent .. 150.00
Sugar bowl, cov., blue opalescent
  w/enameled florals 135.00
Sugar bowl, cov., green
  w/enameled florals 95.00
Sugar bowl, cov., vaseline opales-
  cent .... 125.00 to 150.00
Table set: creamer, cov. sugar bowl,
  spooner & cov. butter dish; blue
  opalescent, 4 pcs. .... 625.00 to 750.00
Table set: creamer, cov. sugar bowl,
  spooner & cov. butter dish; vase-
  line opalescent, 4 pcs. 615.00
Tumbler, blue opalescent 70.00
Tumbler, green 45.00
Tumbler, vaseline opalescent 65.00
Water set: pitcher & 4 tumblers;
  blue opalescent, 5 pcs. 485.00
Water set: pitcher & 6 tumblers;
  vaseline opalescent, 7 pcs. 725.00

ALEXIS - See Priscilla Pattern

ALMOND THUMBPRINT (Pointed Thumbprint)

Master Salt

Bowl, 4½" d., 4 7/8" h., footed,
  non-flint 20.00
Butter dish, cov., ruby-stained, non-
  flint 105.00

Champagne, flint.................. 67.50
Champagne, non-flint.............. 25.00
Egg cup, flint 25.00
Salt dip, master size, flint (ILLUS.) .. 20.00
Spooner, fluted, non-flint 20.00
Sugar bowl, cov., non-flint 35.00
Wine, flint...................... 30.00

AMAZON (Sawtooth Band)

(Items may be plain or with etched designs)

Banana stand 65.00
Bowl, 6" d. 25.00
Bowl, 9" d. 20.00
Butter dish, cov. 50.00
Cake stand, 8" to 9½" d. ....37.50 to 47.50
Celery vase...................... 35.00
Champagne...................... 28.50
Compote, cov., 7" d., 11½" h....... 62.50
Compote, open, jelly, 4½" d. 20.00
Compote, open, 6" d., high stand ... 32.50
Compote, open, 8¾" d., 7¼" h..... 42.50
Cordial 32.50
Creamer ....26.00 to 35.00
Creamer, child's miniature 27.50
Creamer & cov. sugar bowl, pr. 65.00
Cruet w/bar in hand stopper,
 amethyst 250.00
Cruet w/bar in hand stopper 42.50
Egg cup 14.00
Goblet ....22.50 to 30.00
Pitcher, water 60.00
Salt dip, master size.........12.50 to 18.00
Sauce dish, flat or footed .....4.00 to 11.50
Spooner ....25.00 to 30.00
Spooner, child's miniature.......... 25.00
Sugar bowl, cov. 40.00
Sugar bowl, child's miniature....... 30.00
Syrup pitcher w/original top 42.50
Table set: cov. butter dish, creamer,
 cov. sugar bowl & spooner; child's
 miniature, 4 pcs................. 150.00
Tumbler ....15.00 to 25.00
Wine.....................25.00 to 30.00

AMBERETTE (English Hobnail Cross or Klondike)

Amberette Butter Dish

Berry set: master bowl & 4 sauce
dishes; frosted w/amber cross,
5 pcs. 385.00

Berry set: 8" sq. master bowl & 6
 sauce dishes; clear w/amber
 cross, 7 pcs. 175.00
Bowl, master berry or fruit, 8" sq.,
 clear w/amber cross 75.00
Bowl, master berry or fruit, 8" sq.,
 frosted w/amber cross.......... 250.00
Bowl, 11" sq., flared, clear w/amber
 cross.......................... 130.00
Butter dish, cov., clear w/amber
 cross.......................... 250.00
Butter dish, cov., frosted w/amber
 cross (ILLUS.) ....350.00 to 450.00
Celery tray, frosted w/amber cross,
 10 7/8 x 4½", 2 7/8" h.......... 185.00
Celery vase, clear w/amber cross .. 142.50
Celery vase, frosted w/amber
 cross.......................... 200.00
Creamer, clear w/amber cross 75.00
Creamer, frosted w/amber cross ... 210.00
Goblet, clear w/amber cross 125.00
Goblet, frosted w/amber cross 250.00
Pitcher, water, clear w/amber
 cross.......................... 285.00
Pitcher, water, frosted w/amber
 cross..................600.00 to 900.00
Punch cup, clear w/amber cross 60.00
Punch cup, frosted w/amber cross .. 110.00
Relish, clear w/amber cross, boat-
 shaped, 9 x 4" 118.00
Salt shaker w/original top, clear
 w/amber cross (single) 69.00
Salt & pepper shakers w/original
 tops, frosted w/amber cross,
 pr............................. 200.00
Sauce dish, flat or footed, clear
 w/amber cross................. 20.00
Sauce dish, flat or footed, frosted
 w/amber cross ....85.00 to 145.00
Spooner, clear w/amber cross...... 50.00
Spooner, frosted w/amber cross 200.00
Sugar bowl, cov., clear w/amber
 cross, 6¾" h. 185.00
Sugar bowl, cov., frosted w/amber
 cross, 4" d., 6¾" h. 250.00
Syrup pitcher w/original top, frosted
 w/amber cross ....550.00 to 850.00
Table set, frosted w/amber cross,
 4 pcs. 1,100.00
Toothpick holder, clear w/amber
 cross.......................... 145.00
Toothpick holder, frosted w/amber
 cross.......................... 275.00
Tumbler, clear w/amber cross...... 135.00
Tumbler, frosted w/amber
 cross..................150.00 to 185.00
Vase, 8" h., trumpet-shaped, clear
 w/amber cross................. 85.00

APOLLO

(Items may be plain or with etched designs)

Bowl, 8" d. 22.50
Butter dish, cov. 50.00

Cake stand, 9" to 10½" d. 45.00
Celery tray 22.50
Celery vase. . . . . .37.50 to 45.00
Compote, cov., 6" d. 55.00
Compote, open, 7" d., low stand . . . 25.00
Creamer . . . . .30.00 to 40.00
Cruet w/original stopper. 45.00
Goblet 29.00
Lamp, kerosene-type, canary yel-
   low, 9" h. 165.00
Lamp, kerosene-type, 10" h. 48.00
Lamp, kerosene-type, frosted,
   12" h. 65.00
Pitcher, water, bulbous 65.00
Plate, 9½" sq. 26.50
Salt dip, master size. 25.00
Sauce dish, flat or footed . . . . .6.00 to 10.50
Spooner 32.50
Sugar bowl, cov. 45.00
Sugar shaker w/original top 45.00
Tray, water. 45.00
Tumbler 20.00

ARGUS (McKee & Brother, Pittsburgh)

Ale glass, footed, flint, 5½" h. 70.00
Butter dish, footed, flint, 8" d. 85.00
Celery vase, flint. 50.00
Champagne, flint. 50.00
Champagne (Hotel Argus), non-
   flint. 18.50
Compote, open, 6" d., 4½" h.,
   flint. 50.00
Creamer, applied handle, flint. 110.00
Egg cup, flint 22.50
Egg cup, handled, flint. 70.00
Goblet, flint 48.00
Goblet (Barrel Argus), flint. 45.00
Goblet (Hotel Argus), non-
   flint. . . . . .25.00 to 30.00
Goblet, master size, flint 45.00
Honey dish, flint 20.00
Mug, applied handle, flint 60.00
Pitcher, water, 8¼" h., applied han-
   dle, flint. 200.00
Punch bowl, pedestal base, scal-
   loped rim, 11½" d., 9½" h. 160.00
Salt dip, master size, flint. 27.50
Spillholder, flint. 45.00
Spooner, flint 48.50
Sugar bowl, cov., flint 65.00
Tumbler (Barrel Argus), flint 60.00
Tumbler, bar-type, flint 60.00
Tumbler, footed, flint, 4" h. 40.00
Tumbler, footed, flint, 5" h. 60.00
Tumbler, whiskey, handled. 57.50
Wine, flint, 4" h. 45.00
Wine (Barrel Argus) 35.00
Wine (Hotel Argus), non-
   flint. .15.00 to 22.00

ART (Job's Tears)

Banana stand 150.00
Bowl, 7" d., flared rim, footed 27.00

Bowl, 8½" d. 38.00
Butter dish, cov. 52.50
Butter dish, cov., ruby-stained 65.00
Cake stand, 9" to 10½" d. . . .45.00 to 55.00
Celery vase 35.00
Compote, cov., 6" d., 10" h. 55.00
Compote, open, 8" d., high stand. . . 35.00
Compote, open, 9" d., 7¼" h. 45.00
Compote, open, 10" d., 9" h. 65.00
Creamer 37.50
Cruet w/original stopper 65.00
Goblet . . . . .25.00 to 32.50
Pitcher, milk, ruby-stained . .95.00 to 150.00
Pitcher, water, bulbous 85.00
Plate, 10" d. 55.00
Relish, 7¾ x 4¼" 22.00
Relish, ruby-stained 65.00
Sauce dish, flat or footed . . . .10.00 to 20.00
Spooner 25.00
Sugar bowl, cov. 40.00
Tumbler 20.00

ASHBURTON

Ale glass, flint, 5" h. 87.50
Ale glass, flint, 6½" h. 65.00
Bowl, 6½" d., low, footed, flint 72.50
Carafe, flint 175.00
Celery vase, scalloped rim, canary
   yellow, flint 400.00
Celery vase, plain rim, flint 70.00
Celery vase, scalloped rim, flint 95.00
Champagne, flint. 55.00
Champagne, creased ovals, flint 60.00
Champagne, cut ovals, flint 75.00
Claret, flint, 5¼" h. . . . . .40.00 to 55.00
Cordial, flint, 4¼" h. 70.00
Cordial, non-flint 42.50
Cordial, vaseline, flint 140.00
Creamer, applied handle, flint. 180.00
Decanter w/original stopper, canary
   yellow, flint . . . . .850.00 to 1,000.00
Decanter w/original stopper, flint,
   qt. 67.50
Egg cup, clambroth, flint 125.00
Egg cup, flint . . . . .22.50 to 32.50
Egg cup, non-flint 16.50
Egg cup, double, flint 95.00
Flip glass, handled, flint, 7" h. 150.00
Goblet, barrel-shaped, flint 55.00
Goblet, flared, flint 52.50
Goblet, non-flint 28.00
Goblet, disconnected ovals 35.00
Goblet, "giant," straight stem,
   flint. 55.00
Honey dish, 3½" d. 8.50
Pitcher, water, applied hollow han-
   dle, flint. 450.00
Plate, 6 5/8" d., flint 60.00
Sauce dish, flint. 7.50
Sugar bowl, cov., flint 140.00
Sugar bowl, open, non-flint 32.50
Toddy jar, cov. 110.00
Tumbler, bar, flint. 60.00
Tumbler, water, flint 55.00

Tumbler, water, footed 67.50
Tumbler, whiskey, applied handle,
  flint........................... 125.00
Vase, 10½" h., flint 80.00
Wine, barrel-shaped, flint 41.50
Wine, flint 30.00
Wine, cut ovals 65.00
Wine, non-flint.................. 22.50
Wine, emerald green, flint 425.00
Wine, peacock green, flint 525.00

ATLANTA - See Lion Pattern

ATLAS (Crystall Ball or Cannon Ball)

Atlas Toothpick

Bowl, cov., large, flat 35.00
Bowl, open, 9" d. 20.00
Butter dish, cov. 45.00
Cake stand, 8" to 10" d. .....25.00 to 45.00
Cake stand, ruby-stained, 8" to
  10" d. 95.00
Celery vase 25.00
Champagne, 5½" h. 22.50
Compote, cov., 8" d., 8" h. 55.00
Compote, open, 8" d., 8" h. 89.00
Cordial 35.00
Creamer, flat or pedestal base 22.50
Goblet 27.50
Pitcher, milk, tankard, applied
  handle 42.50
Pitcher, water, tankard, applied
  handle 55.00
Salt dip, individual size 8.00
Salt dip, master size.............. 18.00
Sauce dish, flat or footed .....7.50 to 12.50
Sauce dish, flat or footed, ruby-
  stained........................ 20.00
Spooner 26.00
Spooner, ruby-stained, gold trim.... 35.00
Sugar bowl, cov. 38.00
Toothpick holder (ILLUS.).......... 20.00
Tumbler 27.50
Wine............................ 22.50

AURORA (Diamond Horseshoe)

(Items may be plain or with etched designs)

Celery vase...................... 32.50
Creamer, applied handle.......... 38.00
Decanter w/original stopper 30.00
Decanter w/original stopper, ruby-
  stained....................... 145.00
Goblet 27.50
Pitcher, water, tankard, 9½" h. 40.00
Pitcher, water, tankard, 12" h. 45.00
Salt & pepper shakers w/original
  tops, pr....................... 30.00
Tray, wine, 10" d............20.00 to 30.00
Tray, wine, ruby-stained, 10" d. 45.00
Wine 20.00
Wine, ruby-stained 40.00

AZTEC

Aztec Creamer

Bon bon, footed, 7" d., 4½" h. 13.50
Bowl, 8½" d., sapphire blue 45.00
Butter dish, cov. 40.00
Carafe, water.................... 37.50
Champagne...................... 15.00
Cordial 17.00
Creamer 26.50
Creamer, individual size (ILLUS.).... 16.00
Cruet w/original stopper 35.00
Dresser bottle w/original stopper ... 37.50
Goblet 28.00
Punch cup 5.00
Salt & pepper shakers w/original
  tops, pr....................... 35.00
Sugar bowl, cov. 35.00
Tumbler 20.00
Wine........................... 17.50

BABY FACE

Baby Face Compote

Butter dish, cov., 5¼" d............ 150.00
Compote, cov., 5¼" d., 6½" h...... 140.00
Compote, cov., 8" d., 13" h., scal-
  loped rim..................... 250.00
Compote, open, 8" d., 4¾" h.
  (ILLUS.)....................... 85.00
Compote, open, 8" d., 8" h........ 95.00
Creamer 110.00
Goblet ....85.00 to 150.00
Pitcher, water 175.00
Spooner....................... 95.00

BABY THUMBPRINT - See Dakota Pattern

BALDER (Kamoni or Pennsylvania - Late)

Balder Sauce Dish

Bowl, berry or fruit, 8½" d., gold
  trim.......................... 27.50
Butter dish, cov. 47.50
Carafe 45.00
Celery tray, 11 x 4½" 25.00
Cheese dish, cov. 62.50
Creamer, gold trim, small, 3" h..... 18.00
Creamer, green w/gold trim, small,
  3" h.......................... 70.00
Creamer, large, 4" h.............. 32.50
Creamer & open sugar bowl, in-
  dividual size, gold trim, pr. 40.00
Cruet w/original stopper........... 47.50
Decanter w/original stopper,
  10¾" h........................ 75.00
Goblet 20.00
Mustard jar w/pewter lid 40.00
Pitcher, water 45.00
Plate, 8" d. 29.50
Punch cup 12.50
Relish 10.00
Salt & pepper shakers w/original
  tops, pr...................... 32.50
Sauce dish, boat-shaped (ILLUS.).... 22.00
Sauce dish, round or
  square ....8.00 to 15.00
Spooner........................ 22.50
Sugar bowl, cov., child's, gold
  trim.......................... 38.50
Sugar bowl, cov. 45.00
Sugar bowl, cov., ruby-stained 102.00
Sugar bowl, open 25.00
Syrup pitcher w/original top 37.50
Table set, 4 pcs. 140.00
Toothpick holder 25.00
Tumbler, juice 10.50
Tumbler, water, blue, souvenir 42.00

Tumbler, water 20.00
Tumbler, water, gold trim.......... 25.00
Tumbler, water, ruby-stained....... 50.00
Tumbler, whiskey 12.50
Vase, 5¾" h., gold trim 17.50
Whiskey shot glass 61.50
Wine........................... 17.50
Wine, green w/gold trim 40.00

BALTIMORE PEAR

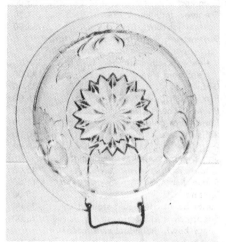

Baltimore Pear Bowl

Bowl, 6" d. (ILLUS.)............... 29.00
Bowl, berry or fruit, 9" d., footed... 40.00
Bread plate, 12½" l. 60.00
Butter dish, cov. 70.00
Cake plate, side handles, 10"
  octagon 31.50
Cake stand, high pedestal 55.00
Celery vase..................... 50.00
Compote, cov., 7" d., high stand ... 75.00
Creamer 32.50
Creamer & open sugar bowl, pr..... 50.00
Goblet 32.00
Pitcher, water ....75.00 to 95.00
Plate, 9" d...................... 35.00
Relish, 8¼" l 25.00
Sauce dish, flat or footed ....15.00 to 23.00
Spooner........................ 35.00
Sugar bowl, cov. 45.00

BAMBOO - See Broken Column Pattern

BANDED BEADED GRAPE MEDALLION
Creamer 50.00
Goblet 30.00
Spooner........................ 28.50
Sugar bowl, open 25.00

BANDED BUCKLE
Spooner........................ 26.50
Tumbler, bar.................... 55.00

BANDED PORTLAND (Portland w/Diamond Point Band)

Butter pat	18.00
Candlesticks, pr.	75.00
Carafe, water	82.50
Celery tray, gold-stained, 12 x 5"	25.00
Celery vase	25.00
Cologne bottle w/original stopper	48.00
Compote, cov., jelly	35.00
Compote, open, 10" d., high stand	50.00
Creamer	35.00
Creamer, individual size	37.50
Dresser jar, cov., 3½" d.	35.00
Dresser set: large tray, pin tray, pr. cov. pomade jars, pr. cologne bottles w/original stoppers & ring tree; gold trim, 7 pcs.	195.00
Goblet	32.50
Pickle dish, 6 x 4"	15.00
Pitcher, water	65.00
Punch cup, gold trim	17.00
Relish, 8½ x 4" oval	10.00
Ring tree, gold-stained	40.00
Salt & pepper shakers w/original tops, pr.	45.00
Sauce dish	11.50
Spooner	35.00
Sugar bowl, cov., gold-stained	36.00
Sugar bowl, individual size	25.00
Sugar bowl, individual size, green-stained	25.00
Sugar shaker w/original top	40.00
Syrup jug w/original top	50.00
Toothpick holder	20.00
Tumbler	25.00
Vase, 6" h., flared	16.50
Vase, 9" h.	18.50
Wine	25.00
Wine, gold-stained	35.00
Wine set, tray & 6 wines, 7 pcs.	145.00

BANDED PORTLAND W/COLOR - See Portland Maiden Blush Pattern

BAR & DIAMOND - See Kokomo Pattern

BARBERRY

Barberry Footed Sauce Dish

Bowl, 8" oval	20.00
Bread plate	23.00

Butter dish, cov., shell finial	55.00
Cake stand, 9½" d.	35.00
Celery vase	37.50
Compote, cov., 6" d., high stand, shell finial	45.00
Compote, cov., 8" d., low stand, shell finial	48.50
Compote, open, 8½" d., 7" h.	25.00
Creamer	32.50
Cup plate	35.00
Egg cup	20.00
Goblet	25.00
Pitcher, water, 9½" h., applied handle	75.00 to 97.50
Plate, 6" d.	15.00
Salt dip, master size	18.00
Sauce dish, flat	8.00
Sauce dish, footed (ILLUS.)	18.00
Spooner, footed	38.00
Sugar bowl, cov., shell finial	45.00
Sugar bowl, open	27.50
Syrup jug w/original top	85.00 to 110.00
Tumbler, footed	22.50
Wine	22.50

BARLEY

Barley Goblet

Bowl, 10" oval	18.50
Bread platter, plain rim, 11½ x 9½"	22.00
Bread platter, scalloped rim, 11½ x 9½"	32.50
Butter dish, cov.	32.50
Cake stand, 8" to 10½" d.	25.00 to 37.50
Celery vase	32.50
Compote, cov., 7" d., high stand	60.00
Compote, open, 6" d., high stand	30.00
Compote, open, 8½" d., 8" h.	35.00
Compote, open, 8¾" d., 6½" h., scalloped rim	35.00
Creamer	26.00
Egg cup	17.50
Goblet (ILLUS.)	22.50 to 30.00
Pickle castor w/frame & tongs	82.50
Pitcher, milk	30.00
Pitcher, water	47.50

Platter, 13 x 8" 25.00
Relish, 8 x 6" 15.00
Relish, handled, 9½ x 5¼" 18.00
Salt shaker w/original top (single) .. 23.50
Sauce dish, flat or footed .....7.00 to 12.00
Spooner 21.50
Sugar bowl, cov. 27.00
Table set, creamer, open sugar
　　bowl & cov. butter dish, 3 pcs. ... 110.00
Wheelbarrow sugar cube dish
　　w/metal wheels ....65.00 to 75.00
Wine, 3¾" h. 30.00

BARRED HOBSTAR - See Checkerboard Pattern

BARRED STAR - See Spartan Pattern

BASKETWEAVE

Cup & saucer, amber 32.00
Goblet, amber 25.00
Goblet 17.00
Goblet, vaseline 30.00
Mug, 3" h. 12.00
Pitcher, water, vaseline.......... 60.00
Plate, 8¾" d., handled, blue 19.50
Plate, 8¾" d., handled 11.00
Tray, water, scenic center, vaseline,
　　12" 45.00

BEADED BAND

Creamer 18.00
Goblet 26.50
Relish, 8½ x 5¼" 9.50
Sauce dish, flat, 4¼" d. 5.00
Sugar bowl, cov. 40.00

BEADED BULL'S EYE WITH DRAPE - See Alabama Pattern

BEADED DEWDROP - See Wisconsin Pattern

BEADED GRAPE (California)

Beaded Grape Creamer

Bowl, 5½" sq. 16.50
Bowl, 5½" sq., green............ 19.50
Bowl, 8" sq. 25.00
Bowl, 8" sq., green............ 35.00
Bowl, 8½ x 6¼" rectangle, green .. 30.00
Butter dish, cov., sq. 60.00

Butter dish, cov., sq., green....... 85.00
Cake stand, 9" sq., 6" h........... 55.00
Cake stand, green, 9" sq., 6" h. 90.00
Celery tray 35.00
Celery tray, green 45.00
Compote, open, 6" sq., green 75.00
Compote, open, 7" sq., high
　　stand 38.00
Compote, open, 8½" sq., high
　　stand 75.00
Creamer (ILLUS.) 35.00
Creamer, green 47.50
Cruet w/original stopper........... 65.00
Cruet w/original stopper,
　　green ....95.00 to 125.00
Dish, 8¼" sq..................... 30.00
Egg cup 16.00
Goblet 35.00
Goblet, green 45.00
Pitcher, water, round, green 85.00
Pitcher, water, square,
　　green ....95.00 to 120.00
Plate, 8" sq. 26.00
Plate, 8" sq., green 40.00
Relish, 7 x 4" 20.00
Salt & pepper shakers w/original
　　tops, pr...................... 45.00
Sauce dish 12.00
Sauce dish, green 16.50
Spooner 40.00
Spooner, green ....35.00 to 45.00
Sugar bowl, cov. 47.50
Sugar bowl, cov., green 60.00
Sugar bowl, open 20.00
Sugar bowl, open, green......... 28.00
Toothpick holder 27.50
Toothpick holder, green 48.50
Tumbler 25.00
Tumbler, green 40.00
Vase, 7" h., green 32.50
Wine........................... 35.00
Wine, green 65.00

BEADED GRAPE MEDALLION

Bowl, 7" oval 24.50
Butter dish, cov. 38.50
Celery vase.................... 55.00
Compote, cov., 8¼" d., low stand .. 75.00
Creamer, applied handle........... 40.00
Egg cup 20.00
Goblet 25.00
Goblet, buttermilk 40.00
Goblet, lady's................. 27.50
Pitcher, water, applied handle 80.00
Relish, oblong 15.00
Salt dip, master size, footed, oval .. 40.00
Salt dip, flat 15.00
Sauce dish..................... 8.00
Spooner 32.50
Sugar bowl, cov. 45.00
Sugar bowl, open 27.50
Vegetable dish, cov., footed, dated
　　"1869" 75.00
Wine.......................... 50.00

BEADED LOOP (Oregon)

Berry set, master bowl & 5 sauce dishes, 6 pcs.	50.00
Bowl, berry, 9¼ x 6¾" oval, ruby-stained	35.00
Bread platter	26.50
Butter dish, cov.	50.00
Cake stand, 9" to 10½" d. ...28.00 to	45.00
Celery vase, 7" h.	27.50
Compote, open, jelly	37.50
Compote, open, 7½" d., low stand	20.00
Compote, open, 9" d., 7¼" h.	50.00
Creamer	21.50
Cruet w/faceted stopper	67.50
Cruet, no stopper	47.50
Goblet	30.00
Honey dish	8.00
Mug, ruby-stained	25.00
Pickle dish, boat-shaped, 9" l.	15.00
Pitcher, milk, 8½" h.	40.00
Pitcher, water, tankard	50.00
Relish	12.00
Relish, w/advertising in base for "Denver Furniture & Carpet Company"	45.00
Salt shaker w/original top (single)	15.00
Salt & pepper shakers w/original tops, pr.	32.50
Sauce dish, flat or footed ....8.00 to	13.00
Spooner, ruby-stained	55.00
Sugar bowl, cov., ruby-stained	42.50
Sugar bowl, open	18.00
Syrup pitcher w/original top	65.00
Toothpick holder	32.50
Tumbler	42.50
Tumbler, ruby-stained	35.00
Wine	32.50

BEADED MEDALLION - See Beaded Mirror Pattern

BEADED MIRROR (Beaded Medallion)

Butter dish, cov.	40.00
Castor bottle (mustard)	15.00
Castor bottle w/original stopper, "Oil"	25.00
Celery vase	36.50
Egg cup	18.50
Goblet	20.00
Goblet, buttermilk	22.00
Salt dip	18.00
Sauce dish, flat	8.00
Spooner	22.50
Sugar bowl, cov.	45.00
Sugar bowl, open	23.50

BEADED TULIP

Goblet	40.00
Pitcher, water	67.50
Wine	25.00

BEARDED HEAD - See Viking Pattern

BEARDED MAN (Old Man of the Woods or Neptune)

Butter dish, cov.	52.50
Celery vase	35.00
Compote, cov., 9" h.	60.00
Creamer	40.00
Pitcher, water, 2-qt.	58.00
Spooner	40.00
Sugar bowl, open	50.00

BELLFLOWER

Bellflower Creamer

Bowl, 6" d., 1¾" h., single vine	75.00
Bowl, 8" d., 4½" h., scalloped rim	70.00
Bowl, 9 x 6" oval, rayed base	125.00
Butter dish, cov.	80.00
Castor bottle w/original stopper	28.00
Celery vase, fine rib, single vine	80.00
Celery vase, w/cut bellflowers	175.00
Champagne, barrel-shaped, fine rib, knob stem, plain base	95.00
Champagne, barrel-shaped, fine rib, single vine, knob stem, rayed base	95.00
Compote, open, 4½" d., low stand, scalloped rim	100.00
Compote, open, 7" d., 5" h., fine rib, double vine	125.00
Compote, open, 8" d., 5" h., scalloped rim, single vine ....55.00 to	75.00
Compote, open, 8" d., 8" h., single vine	245.00
Compote, open, 8¼" d., 7" h., scalloped base, w/cut bellflowers	130.00
Compote, open, 9½" d., 8½" h., scalloped rim, single vine ...100.00 to	125.00
Cordial, fine rib, single vine	165.00
Creamer, fine rib, double vine, applied handle (ILLUS.)	190.00
Decanter w/bar lip, fine rib, single vine, pt.	185.00
Decanter w/bar lip, double vine, pt.	225.00
Decanter w/bar lip, single vine, qt.	140.00

Decanter w/bar lip, patent stopper,
   double vine, qt. 250.00
Egg cup, coarse rib 20.00
Egg cup, fine rib, single vine 36.50
Goblet, barrel-shaped, fine rib, sin-
   gle vine ....35.00 to 50.00
Goblet, coarse rib 35.00
Goblet, double vine 65.00
Goblet, single vine, rayed base 37.50
Goblet, fine rib, double vine, w/cut
   bellflowers 300.00
Goblet, buttermilk 55.00
Honey dish, cov., single vine 115.00
Lamp, kerosene-type, 7½" h. 275.00
Lamp, kerosene-type, clear font,
   milk white base, flint, 9½" h. 165.00
Lamp, whale oil, brass stem, marble
   base ....95.00 to 125.00
Pitcher, water, 8¾" h., coarse rib,
   double vine................... 325.00
Pitcher, water, single vine 250.00
Plate, 6" d., fine rib, single
   vine 85.00
Salt dip, cov., master size, footed,
   beaded rim, fine rib, single vine.. 75.00
Salt dip, open, master size, footed,
   scalloped rim, single vine 35.00
Sauce dish, double vine 20.00
Sauce dish, single vine 20.00
Spooner, low foot, double vine 47.50
Spooner, scalloped rim, single
   vine 40.00
Sugar bowl, cov., single vine 95.00
Sugar bowl, open, double vine 42.50
Syrup pitcher w/original top,
   applied handle, fine rib, single
   vine 750.00
Table set: cov. butter dish, creamer,
   open sugar bowl & spooner; fine
   rib, single vine, 4 pcs. 325.00
Tumbler, bar..................... 77.50
Tumbler, coarse rib, double vine ... 95.00
Tumbler, fine rib, single vine 82.50
Tumbler, whiskey 135.00
Wine, barrel-shaped, knob stem,
   fine rib, single vine, rayed base .. 85.00
Wine, straight sides, plain stem,
   rayed base 52.50

BIGLER

Bowl, 10" d. 75.00
Celery vase..................... 75.00
Champagne..................... 95.00
Cordial 60.00
Decanter w/bar lip, pt. 50.00
Goblet, 6" h. 34.50
Lamp, whale oil, 7" h. 125.00
Plate, toddy, 4" d. 11.00
Plate, 6" d., amethyst 225.00
Plate, 6" d., canary yellow 195.00
Sauce dish, canary yellow.......... 95.00
Tumbler ....50.00 to 60.00
Whiskey, handled 100.00
Wine........................... 70.00

BIRD & FERN - See Hummingbird Pattern

BIRD & STRAWBERRY (Bluebird)

Bird & Strawberry Tumbler

Bowl, 5½" d. 22.50
Bowl, 7½" d., footed 65.00
Bowl, 7½" d., footed, w/color...... 72.50
Bowl, 9½ x 6" oval, footed 48.00
Bowl, 10" d., flat............... 45.00
Bowl, 10" d., flat, w/color & gold
   trim........................... 90.00
Butter dish, cov. ....85.00 to 110.00
Butter dish, cov., w/color 255.00
Cake stand, 9" to 9½" d. 45.00
Celery tray, 10" l. 35.00
Celery vase, pedestal base,
   7½" h........................ 65.00
Compote, cov., 6" d., low stand 50.00
Compote, cov., 7" d., high
   stand 125.00
Compote, cov., 8" d., low
   stand 65.00
Compote, open, 4½" d.,
   5" h......................... 55.00
Compote, open, 6" d., ruffled
   rim 18.00
Compote, open, 8" d., 6" h., scal-
   loped & ruffled rim, w/color 110.00
Creamer 50.00
Creamer, w/color 135.00
Dish, heart-shaped 50.00
Goblet 40.00
Pitcher, water 190.00
Pitcher, water, w/color 275.00
Plate, 12" d. 70.00
Punch cup 20.00
Relish, 8¼" oval 22.00
Sauce dish, flat or footed ....18.00 to 26.50
Spooner 45.00
Spooner, w/color................ 125.00
Sugar bowl, cov. 55.00
Table set, creamer, cov. butter dish
   & spooner, 3 pcs. 350.00
Table set, w/color, 4 pcs. 450.00
Tumbler 45.00

Tumbler, w/color (ILLUS.) 50.00
Water set, pitcher & 5 tumblers,
   6 pcs. 198.00
Wine 40.00

BIRD IN RING (Butterfly & Fan)
Bread tray 39.00
Spooner 25.50

BLEEDING HEART

Bleeding Heart Spooner

Bowl, cov., 9½" d. 55.00
Bowl, 7¼" oval 27.50
Bowl, 8" 35.00
Bowl, 9¼" oval 30.00
Butter dish, cov. 46.50
Cake stand, 9½" to 11" d. . . .70.00 to 80.00
Compote, cov., 7" d., w/Bleeding
   Heart finial 65.00
Compote, cov., 9" d., 12" h.,
   w/Bleeding Heart finial 110.00
Compote, open, 7" d., 6" h. 25.00
Compote, open, 8½" d., high
   stand 30.00
Creamer 42.50
Egg cup 40.00
Goblet, buttermilk 25.00
Goblet, knob stem 30.00
Mug, 3" h. 38.50
Pitcher, water 100.00
Relish, 5 1/8 x 3 5/8" oval 30.00
Salt dip, master size, footed 42.50
Sauce dish, flat 10.00
Spooner (ILLUS.) 32.50
Sugar bowl, cov. 52.50
Sugar bowl, open 25.00
Tumbler, flat. 75.00
Wine, plain stem 42.50

BLOCK

(Also see Red Block)

Carafe 25.00
Celery 15.00
Creamer, large 8.00

Cruet w/original stopper 20.00
Pitcher, water 65.00
Punch cup, applied handle 8.00
Sauce dish, flat 5.00
Tumbler 40.00
Water set, pitcher & 6 tumblers,
   gold trim, 7 pcs. 110.00
Wine 14.50

BLOCK & FAN

Block & Fan Rose Bowl

Bowl, berry, 8" d., footed 22.50
Bowl, 9¾" d. 32.50
Bowl, 10 x 6" rectangle 50.00
Butter dish, cov. 45.00
Cake stand, 9" to 10" d. 35.00
Carafe, water 47.50
Celery tray 30.00
Celery vase 30.00
Compote, open, 8" d., high stand . . . 50.00
Cookie jar, cov. 65.00
Creamer 38.00
Creamer, individual size, ruby-
   stained 32.50
Cruet w/original stopper, large 29.50
Finger bowl. 29.50
Goblet 57.50
Goblet, ruby-stained 95.00
Ice bucket 42.50
Pitcher, milk 35.00
Pitcher, water 45.00
Plate, 6" d. 21.50
Plate, 10" d. 19.50
Rose bowl (ILLUS.) 25.00
Salt shaker w/original top (single) . . 15.00
Salt & pepper shakers w/original
   tops, pr. 40.00
Sauce dish, flat or footed . . . . .6.50 to 12.50
Sauce dish, flat or footed, ruby-
   stained 25.00
Spooner 25.00
Spooner, ruby-stained 30.00
Sugar bowl, cov. 40.00
Sugar bowl, open 18.00
Sugar shaker w/original top 35.00
Syrup pitcher w/original top, 7" h. . . 75.00
Tumbler 30.00
Wine. 45.00

**BLOCK & STAR - See Valencia Waffle
Pattern**

BLUEBIRD - See Bird & Strawberry Pattern

BOW TIE
Bowl, berry, 8" d. 27.50
Bowl, 10" d., 5" h. 65.00
Butter dish, cov. . . . . .55.00 to 65.00
Cake stand, 9" d. 55.00
Compote, open, 5½" d., 10½" h. . . . 60.00
Compote, open, 8" d., low stand . . . 40.00
Compote, open, 9¼" d., high
    stand 50.00
Compote, open, 10½" d., 10½" h. . . 70.00
Creamer 42.50
Goblet 42.50
Marmalade jar w/cover 45.00
Marmalade jar (no cover) 32.50
Pitcher, milk 65.00
Pitcher, water 70.00
Relish, rectangular 20.00
Salt dip, master size 35.00
Salt shaker w/original top (single) . . 35.00
Spooner 36.50
Sugar bowl, cov. 55.00

BRAZILIAN

Brazilian Sugar Bowl

Celery vase 30.00
Olive dish, ring handle 15.00
Spooner, emerald green 40.00
Sugar bowl, cov. (ILLUS.) 35.00

BROKEN COLUMN (Irish Column, Notched Rib or Bamboo)
Banana stand 100.00
Basket, applied handle, 15" l.,
    12" h. 150.00
Bowl, 7¼" d. 45.00
Bowl, 8" d. 35.00
Bowl, 9" d. 37.50
Bowl, cov., vegetable 95.00
Butter dish, cov. 60.00
Cake stand, 9" to 10" d. . . . . .58.00 to 80.00
Carafe, water 72.50
Celery vase 42.50
Celery vase, w/red notches 155.00
Champagne 65.00

Claret 45.00
Compote, cov., 4¾" d. 56.00
Compote, cov., 5¼" d.,
    10½" h. 52.50
Compote, cov., 5¼" d., 10½" h.,
    w/red notches 225.00
Compote, cov., 7" d.,
    12" h. . . . . .100.00 to 120.00

Broken Column Compote

Compote, cov., 8" d., high
    stand (ILLUS.) 150.00
Compote, open, jelly, w/red
    notches 110.00
Compote, open, 5" d., 6" h. 35.00
Compote, open, 6" d., low stand,
    flared rim 50.00
Compote, open, 6" d., low stand,
    w/red notches 135.00
Compote, open, 7" d., low
    stand 36.00
Compote, open, 10" d., low
    stand 110.00
Cookie jar, cov. 70.00
Creamer, w/red notches 110.00
Creamer & open sugar bowl,
    w/red notches, pr. 150.00
Cruet w/original stopper 65.00
Decanter w/original stopper,
    10½" h. 85.00
Goblet 37.50
Marmalade jar w/original
    cover 62.50
Pickle castor, w/frame & tongs 95.00
Pitcher, water 85.00
Pitcher, water, w/red notches 210.00
Plate, 7" d. 32.50
Plate, 8" d. 35.00
Powder jar, cov. 25.00
Punch cup 15.00
Relish, 9 x 5" 30.00
Relish, w/red notches,
    9 x 5" 110.00

Salt shaker w/original top,
  (single) 30.00
Sauce dish 13.50
Sauce dish, w/red notches 37.50
Spooner 20.00
Sugar bowl, cov. 55.00
Syrup pitcher w/metal top 135.00
Tumbler 30.00
Tumbler, w/red notches 55.00

BRYCE - See Ribbon Candy Pattern

BUCKLE

Bowl, 10" d., rolled edge 75.00
Butter dish, cov. 68.00
Cake stand, 9¾" d., 5¼" h. 30.00
Champagne, flint 60.00
Compote, cov., 6" d., 8½" h. 80.00
Creamer, applied handle, flint 110.00
Creamer, small size, non-flint 25.00
Egg cup, flint 38.00
Egg cup, non-flint 25.00
Goblet, flint 40.00
Goblet, non-flint 23.50
Goblet, buttermilk, non-flint 24.00
Lamp, kerosene-type, brass & iron
  base 165.00
Lamp, kerosene-type, clear font,
  clambroth base 125.00
Pitcher, water, bulbous, applied
  handle, flint 525.00
Pitcher, water, bulbous, applied
  handle, non-flint 85.00
Salt dip, master size, footed,
  flint 35.00
Salt dip, master size, flat, oval,
  flint 30.00
Sauce dish, flint .... 10.00 to 15.00
Sauce dish, non-flint 7.00
Spooner, flint 37.50
Spooner, non-flint 22.50
Sugar bowl, cov., w/acorn finial,
  flint 65.00
Sugar bowl, open, non-flint 25.00
Tumbler, bar, flint 55.00
Tumbler, non-flint 30.00
Wine, flint 77.50
Wine, non-flint 27.50

BUCKLE WITH STAR

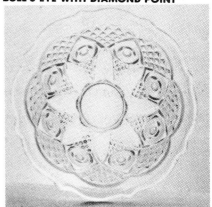

Buckle with Star Relish

Bowl, 8" oval 15.00
Butter dish, cov. 35.00

Cake stand, 9" d. 25.00
Celery vase 35.00
Compote, cov., 7" d. 60.00
Compote, open, 7" d., 5½" h. 19.50
Compote, open, 10" d., 7" h. 30.00
Creamer 35.00
Goblet 32.50
Pitcher, water, applied handle 80.00
Relish, 7¼ x 5 1/8" oval 10.00
Salt dip 25.00
Sauce dish, flat or footed .....5.00 to 12.00
Spillholder 50.00
Spooner 20.00
Sugar bowl, cov. 42.50
Sugar bowl, open 25.00
Tumbler, bar 55.00
Wine 25.00

BULL'S EYE

Celery vase, flint 72.50
Cordial, flint 45.00
Creamer, applied handle, flint 110.00
Decanter w/bar lip, flint, qt. 120.00
Egg cup, flint 45.00
Egg cup, opaque blue 575.00
Goblet, flint 75.00
Salt dip, individual size,
  rectangular 32.50
Salt dip, master size, footed, flint .. 32.50
Spillholder, flint 32.50
Spooner, flint 95.00
Sugar bowl, cov., flint 135.00
Tumbler, bar, flint 85.00
Tumbler, flat, flint 75.00
Wine, knob stem, flint 45.00

BULL'S EYE VARIANT - See Texas Bull's Eye Pattern

BULL'S EYE WITH DIAMOND POINT

Bull's Eye with Diamond Point Honey Dish

Celery vase 140.00
Cologne bottle 85.00
Creamer, applied handle 175.00
Goblet 115.00
Honey dish (ILLUS.) 30.00

Lamp, kerosene-type, applied handle	150.00
Salt dip, master size	45.00
Salt dip, basket-shaped	85.00
Sauce dish	25.00
Spillholder	75.00
Spooner	135.00
Tumbler, bar	110.00
Tumbler, water	150.00
Wine	120.00

BULL'S EYE WITH FLEUR DE LIS

Bull's Eye with Fleur de Lis Pitcher

Celery vase, 11" h.	85.00
Creamer	65.00
Goblet	75.00
Lamp, kerosene-type, pear-shaped font w/brass standard on marble base	150.00
Pitcher, water, 9½" h. (ILLUS.)	485.00
Salt dip, master size	52.50
Sugar bowl, cov.	135.00

BUTTERFLY & FAN - See Bird in Ring Pattern

BUTTON ARCHES

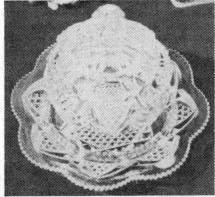

Button Arches Butter Dish

Basket, ruby-stained handle	25.00
Berry set: 8" d. master bowl & 6 sauce dishes; ruby-stained, 7 pcs.	135.00
Bowl, 8" d., ruby-stained, souvenir	45.00
Butter dish, cov. (ILLUS.)	48.00
Butter dish, cov., ruby-stained, souvenir	65.00
Compote, open, jelly, 4½" h., ruby-stained	45.00
Creamer	18.50
Creamer, ruby-stained	45.00
Creamer, individual size, ruby-stained	18.50 to 25.00
Cruet w/original stopper, ruby-stained	160.00
Goblet, clambroth	28.50
Goblet	20.00
Goblet, ruby-stained	37.50
Mug, ruby-stained, souvenir, 3½" h.	35.00
Pitcher, 7" h., ruby-stained, souvenir	60.00
Pitcher, tankard, 8¾" h.	100.00
Pitcher, water, tankard, 12" h.	85.00
Pitcher, water, tankard, 12" h., ruby-stained	115.00
Punch cup	10.00
Punch cup, ruby-stained, souvenir	18.00
Salt shaker w/original top, ruby-stained (single)	22.50
Sauce dish, ruby-stained	35.00
Spooner	27.50
Spooner, ruby-stained & etched	40.00
Sugar bowl, cov.	30.00
Sugar bowl, cov., ruby-stained & etched	65.00 to 80.00
Syrup pitcher w/original top, ruby-stained	125.00
Table set, ruby-stained, 4 pcs.	235.00
Toothpick holder	14.50
Toothpick holder, ruby-stained, souvenir	30.00
Tumbler, clambroth, souvenir	19.00
Tumbler	17.50
Tumbler, ruby-stained	25.00
Water set: pitcher & 5 tumblers; w/frosted band & gold, 6 pcs.	225.00
Whiskey shot glass, ruby-stained	14.50
Wine, clambroth	25.00
Wine	15.00
Wine, ruby-stained, souvenir	32.50

CABBAGE LEAF

Butter dish, cov., frosted	500.00
Celery vase, clear & frosted	85.00
Custard cup, frosted, marked Libbey Glass Co., "Columbian Expo" on base	80.00
Pitcher, water, frosted	135.00
Rose bowl, amber	175.00
Sauce dish, frosted, w/rabbit center	45.00

CABBAGE ROSE

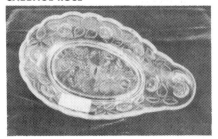

Cabbage Rose Relish

Bitters bottle, 6½" h.	100.00
Bowl, master berry, 9" oval	40.00
Butter dish, cov.	62.50
Cake stand, 9½" to 12½" d.	40.00 to 70.00
Celery vase	50.00
Champagne	42.50
Compote, cov., 6" d., low stand	95.00
Compote, cov., 7½" d., high stand	110.00
Compote, cov., 8½" d., 7" h.	120.00
Compote, open, 7½" d., high stand	75.00
Compote, open, 9½" d., low stand	90.00
Compote, open, 9½" h., high stand	100.00
Cordial	50.00
Creamer, applied handle	55.00
Dish, 7" d.	25.00 to 32.50
Egg cup	33.00
Goblet	37.50
Mug, child's	65.00
Pickle or relish, 7½" to 8½" l. (ILLUS.)	18.50 to 32.50
Pitcher, water, qt.	125.00
Pitcher, 3-pint	165.00
Salt dip, master size	20.00
Sauce dish	20.00
Spooner	32.50
Sugar bowl, cov.	55.00
Sugar bowl, open	40.00
Tumbler	40.00
Wine	42.50

CABLE

Bowl, 9" d.	70.00
Butter dish, cov.	110.00
Celery vase	75.00
Champagne	275.00
Compote, open, 7" d., 5" h.	55.00
Compote, open, 8" d., 4¾" h.	65.00
Compote, open, 9" d., 4½" h.	55.00
Creamer	365.00 to 500.00
Decanter w/bar lip, qt.	95.00 to 125.00
Decanter w/stopper, qt.	295.00
Egg cup, cov., blue opaque, 5¼" h.	2,200.00
Egg cup, clambroth, flint	550.00
Egg cup	45.00
Goblet	60.00
Goblet, lady's	65.00
Honey dish, 3½" d., 1" h.	14.00
Lamp, whale oil, 11" h.	125.00
Plate, 6" d.	85.00
Salt dip, individual size	20.00
Salt dip, master size	40.00
Sauce dish	28.00
Spooner, clambroth	185.00
Spooner	35.00
Sugar bowl, cov.	95.00
Wine	77.50

CABLE WITH RING

Lamp, kerosene-type, w/ring handle, flint	175.00
Lamp, whale oil, clambroth font, flint, reeded brass stem, marble base	325.00
Sugar bowl, cov., flint	78.00

CALIFORNIA - See Beaded Grape Pattern

CAMEO - See Classic Medallion Pattern

CANADIAN

Canadian Footed Sauce Dish

Bowl, berry, 7" d., 4½" h., footed	75.00
Bread plate, handled, 10" d.	59.00
Butter dish, cov.	85.00
Cake stand, 9¾" d., 5" h.	32.50 to 50.00
Celery vase	55.00
Compote, cov., 6" d., 9" h.	98.00
Compote, cov., 7" d., 11" h.	85.00
Compote, open, 6" d., footed	40.00
Compote, open, 8" d., 5" h.	45.00
Creamer	42.50
Goblet	55.00
Pitcher, milk, 8" h.	140.00
Pitcher, water	95.00
Plate, 6" d., handled	25.00
Plate, 8" d., handled	35.00
Sauce dish, flat	12.50
Sauce dish, footed (ILLUS.)	28.00
Spooner	45.00
Sugar bowl, cov.	70.00
Wine	42.50

CANE

Bread platter, amber	25.00
Candlestick (single)	15.00
Creamer, amber	30.00

Creamer, blue	35.00
Creamer	25.00
Goblet, amber	27.50
Goblet, apple green	35.00
Goblet, blue	35.00
Goblet	16.00
Goblet, vaseline	37.50
Match holder, model of a cauldron, amber	18.00
Match holder, model of a cauldron, blue	16.00
Mustard jar, cov., amber	37.00
Pitcher, water, amber or blue, each	62.50
Pitcher, water, apple green	47.00
Pitcher, water	40.00
Relish, 8 x 5¼" oval	12.50
Sauce dish, flat, apple green	9.50
Sauce dish, footed	10.50
Spooner, amber	42.00
Spooner, apple green	35.00
Sugar bowl, cov., amber	55.00
Sugar bowl, cov.	40.00
Toddy plate, amber, 4½" d.	12.00
Toddy plate, apple green, 4½" d.	12.00
Toddy plate, blue, 4½" d.	16.50
Toddy plate, 4½" d.	14.00
Tumbler, apple green	28.50
Tumbler, blue	25.00
Tumbler	16.50
Waste bowl, amber or apple green, each	30.00

CANNON BALL - See Atlas Pattern

CAPE COD

Bowl, 6" d., handled	20.00
Bowl, 8" d.	32.00
Bread platter	55.00
Compote, cov., 8" d., 12" h.	135.00
Compote, open, 7" d., 6" h.	37.00
Compote, open, 8" d., 5½" h.	36.00
Cruet w/original stopper	25.00
Goblet	35.00
Pitcher, water	65.00
Plate, 8" d., open handles	55.00
Sauce dish, flat or footed	14.00 to 18.50
Spooner	35.00

CARDINAL BIRD

Butter dish, cov.	65.00
Butter dish, cov., 3 identified birds	100.00
Creamer	30.00
Goblet	32.00
Honey dish, cov., 3½"h.	35.00
Honey dish, open	18.50
Sauce dish, flat or footed	12.50 to 20.00
Spooner	36.50
Sugar bowl, cov.	60.00
Sugar bowl, open	30.00

CATHEDRAL

Cathedral Compote

Bowl, 6" d., crimped rim, vaseline	35.00
Bowl, berry, 8" d., amber	48.00
Bowl, berry, 8" d., amethyst	60.00
Butter dish, cov.	50.00
Cake stand, blue, 10" d., 4½" h.	55.00
Cake stand, vaseline	68.00
Compote, cov., 7¼" d., 10½" h.	75.00
Compote, open, 7" d., fluted rim, amber	36.00
Compote, open, 7½" d., high stand, fluted rim, amethyst	145.00
Compote, open, 9" d., 5½" h., amber	50.00
Compote, open, 9" d., 7" h., amethyst	75.00
Compote, open, 9" d., 5½" h., blue	65.00
Compote, open, 9" d., 7" h. (ILLUS.)	48.00
Compote, open, 10" d., 6" h., amethyst	65.00
Compote, open, 10½" d., 8" h., shaped rim	55.00
Creamer	22.50
Creamer, ruby-stained	50.00
Cruet w/original stopper, amber	70.00
Goblet, amber	37.50
Goblet, amethyst	70.00
Goblet	27.50
Goblet, vaseline	52.50
Pitcher, water	125.00
Pitcher, water, ruby-stained	145.00
Relish, fish-shaped, amber	35.00
Relish, fish-shaped, ruby-stained	55.00
Sauce dish, flat or footed, amethyst	35.00
Sauce dish, flat or footed, blue	22.00
Sauce dish, flat or footed	12.50
Sauce dish, flat or footed, ruby-stained	15.00 to 22.00
Sauce dish, flat or footed, vaseline	12.00 to 24.00
Spooner, amber	40.00
Spooner	27.50
Sugar bowl, cov.	48.50

Sugar bowl, cov., ruby-stained 70.00
Sugar bowl, open 22.50
Table set: creamer, sugar bowl &
   spooner; vaseline, 3 pcs. 75.00
Tumbler 25.00
Wine, amber...................... 38.50
Wine............................. 27.50
Wine, ruby-stained 45.00
Wine, vaseline 37.50

CERES (Goddess of Liberty)
Compote, open, 6" d., low
   stand 25.00
Creamer 22.50
Mug, amber 25.00
Mug, blue 22.50
Mug 17.50

CHAIN
Bread plate...................... 27.00
Butter dish, cov. 35.00
Compote, cov., 7½" d., 12" h...... 45.00
Creamer 18.50
Creamer & cov. sugar bowl, pr. 35.00
Goblet 18.00
Plate, 7" d. 14.50
Relish, 8" oval 11.00
Sauce dish, flat or footed 8.50
Spooner 22.50
Sugar bowl, cov. 30.00
Wine............................. 19.00

CHAIN & SHIELD
Creamer 30.00
Goblet 31.50
Pitcher, water 50.00
Platter, oval 25.00

CHAIN WITH STAR

Chain with Star Goblet

Bread plate, handled 27.50
Butter dish, cov. 32.50

Cake stand, 8¾" to 10" d. ...30.00 to 42.50
Compote, jelly 17.00
Compote, open, 8" d., 6½" h...... 20.00
Compote, open, 9½" d............. 29.00
Creamer 20.00
Goblet (ILLUS.) 20.00
Pitcher, water 55.00
Plate, 7" d. 16.50
Relish 15.00
Sauce dish....................... 12.50
Spooner 25.00
Sugar bowl, cov. 37.50
Syrup pitcher (no lid) 45.00
Wine............................. 27.50

CHANDELIER (Crown Jewel)

Chandelier Celery Vase

Bowl, 8" d., 3¼" h. 25.00
Butter dish, cov. 60.00
Cake stand, 10" d. 67.50
Celery vase (ILLUS.) 36.50
Compote, open, 8" d., high stand,
   etched 95.00
Creamer 36.00
Finger bowl...................... 16.00
Goblet 57.50
Inkwell.......................... 65.00
Pitcher, water 68.00
Salt dip, footed 30.00
Sauce dish, flat 14.50
Spooner 27.50
Sugar bowl, cov. 40.00
Sugar shaker w/original top 60.00
Tumbler 40.00
Wine............................. 32.00

CHECKERBOARD (Barred Hobstar)
Bowl, 9" d., flat................. 20.00
Butter dish, cov. 42.50
Celery tray 30.00
Compote, jelly 25.00
Creamer ....12.00 to 20.00
Goblet 20.00
Honey dish, cov., 5" w. 45.00
Pitcher, milk 35.00

Pitcher, water 30.00
Plate, 7" d. 21.50
Punch cup 4.50
Sauce dish, flat 14.50
Sauce dish, flat, ruby-stained, gilt
    trim, 4½" d. 14.50
Spooner 22.50
Sugar bowl, cov. 30.00
Tumbler 15.00
Water set: pitcher & 4 tumblers;
    ruby-stained, 5 pcs. 210.00
Wine 17.50

CHERRY THUMBPRINT - See Paneled Cherry with Thumbprints Pattern

CLASSIC
Berry set, master bowl & 4 sauce
    dishes, 5 pcs. 275.00
Bowl, cov., 7" hexagon, open log
    feet 145.00
Bowl, open, 8" hexagon, open log
    feet 100.00
Butter dish, cov., collared base 125.00
Butter dish, cov., open log feet 175.00
Celery vase, collared
    base .... 120.00 to 175.00
Celery vase, open log
    feet .... 180.00 to 225.00
Compote, cov., 6½" d., collared
    base 150.00
Compote, cov., 7½" d., 8" h., open
    log feet 200.00
Compote, cov., 10" d., open log
    feet 295.00
Compote, open, 7¾" d., open log
    feet 160.00
Creamer, collared base 95.00
Creamer, open log feet 150.00
Goblet .... 195.00 to 225.00
Pitcher, milk 8½" h., open log
    feet 435.00
Pitcher, water, collared base 250.00
Pitcher, water, 9½" h., open log
    feet 325.00
Plate, 10" d., "Blaine" or "Hendricks," signed Jacobus, each ... 185.00
Plate, 10" d., "Logan" ..... 165.00 to 225.00
Plate, 10" d., "Warrior," signed
    Jacobus 160.00
Sauce dish, collared base 30.00
Sauce dish, open log feet 38.00
Spooner, collared base 80.00
Spooner, open log feet ..... 95.00 to 125.00
Sugar bowl, cov., collared base 150.00
Sugar bowl, cov., open log feet 175.00

CLASSIC MEDALLION (Cameo)
Bowl, 6¾" d., 3½" h., footed 38.00
Bowl, 7½" d., footed 25.00
Celery vase 30.00
Compote, open, 7" d., 3¾" h. 22.50
Compote, open, 8" d., 4" h. 23.00
Creamer 27.50

Creamer & open sugar bowl, pr..... 75.00
Pitcher, water 52.50
Sauce dish, footed 10.00
Spooner 26.50
Sugar bowl, open 20.00

COLLINS - See Crystal Wedding Pattern

COLONIAL (Empire Colonial)
Celery vase, flint 75.00
Champagne, flint 55.00
Claret, 5½" h. 47.50
Goblet, flint 55.00
Plate, 6¼" d., canary yellow 225.00
Salt dip, master size 17.50
Spooner 40.00
Sugar bowl, cov. 95.00
Tumbler, footed, flint .... 25.00 to 45.00
Tumbler, amethyst, flint 135.00
Wine, flint 75.00

COLORADO (Lacy Medallion)

Colorado Spooner

Berry set: master bowl & 6 sauce
    dishes; green w/gold, 7 pcs. 137.50
Bowl, 5" d., ruffled rim, blue 33.50
Bowl, 5" d., flared edge 20.00
Bowl, 5" d., green w/gold 45.00
Bowl, 7" d., flat, green 23.00
Bowl, 7" d., footed, scalloped rim,
    blue 25.00
Bowl, 7" d., footed 20.00
Bowl, 7½" d., footed, turned-up
    sides, blue w/gold 55.00
Bowl, 7½" d., footed, turned-up
    sides, green 30.00
Bowl, 8½" d., footed, crimped
    edge, green 35.00
Bowl, 9" d., footed, 3-turned up
    sides 29.00
Bowl, 9" d., green w/gold 36.50
Bowl, 10" d., footed, fluted, green .. 39.00
Butter dish, cov., blue w/gold 200.00
Butter dish, cov. 52.50
Butter dish, cov., green .... 125.00 to 160.00
Cake stand 50.00
Candy dish, green, souvenir 20.00
Card tray, blue 40.00

Card tray 20.00
Card tray, green 32.50
Celery vase, green 48.00
Compote, open, 6" d., 4" h.,
   crimped rim 32.50
Compote, open, 8" d., 7" h., beaded
   rim, green 77.50
Compote, open, 9½" d., blue 95.00
Compote, open, 10½" d., high
   stand, blue 215.00
Creamer 35.00
Creamer, individual size 28.00
Creamer, ruby-stained, individual
   size 40.00
Creamer, green w/gold, individual
   size 30.00
Creamer, green w/gold, large 75.00
Custard cup, green, large 28.00
Match holder, green 35.00
Mug, souvenir 18.50
Mug, green, souvenir 22.00
Nappy, tricornered, blue w/gold 38.00
Nappy, tricornered 16.00
Nappy, tricornered, green w/gold . . 32.50
Pitcher, 6" h., green w/gold 42.00
Pitcher, water, green w/gold 200.00
Plate, 7" d., footed 17.50
Punch cup 13.50
Punch cup, green w/gold,
   souvenir . . . . 20.00 to 30.00
Salt & pepper shakers w/original
   tops, green, pr. 95.00
Sauce dish, blue w/gold . . . . . 22.00 to 38.00
Sauce dish 12.00
Sauce dish, green w/gold . . . . 20.00 to 32.50
Sauce dish, green, souvenir 35.00
Spooner 25.00
Spooner, green w/gold (ILLUS.) 55.00
Sugar bowl, cov., large 30.00
Sugar bowl, cov., individual size,
   green 35.00
Sugar bowl, cov., large, green 85.00
Sugar bowl, open, large 25.00
Sugar bowl, open, individual size,
   blue or green, each 27.50
Table set, green w/gold, 4 pcs. 325.00
Toothpick holder, blue w/gold 47.50
Toothpick holder, w/gold 25.00
Toothpick holder, green w/gold 30.00
Tumbler, green w/gold 28.00
Vase, 10½" h., blue 80.00
Vase, 12" h., trumpet-shaped, blue
   w/gold 100.00
Vase, 12" h., trumpet-shaped,
   green 65.00
Violet vase, blue 35.00
Wine 25.00
Wine, green w/gold 35.00

COLUMBIAN COIN
Butter dish, cov., frosted
   coins . . . . 125.00 to 175.00
Butter dish, cov., gilded coins 175.00
Celery vase, frosted coins 85.00

Celery vase, gilded coins 90.00
Claret, gilded coins 75.00
Compote, open, 8" d., clear coins . . 80.00
Creamer, frosted coins 235.00
Creamer, gilded coins 150.00
Goblet, frosted coins 80.00
Goblet, gilded coins 67.50
Lamp, kerosene-type, frosted coins,
   12" h. 160.00
Pitcher, milk, gilded coins 165.00
Pitcher, water, 10" h., gilded
   coins . . . . 125.00 to 145.00
Salt & pepper shakers w/original
   tops, frosted coins, pr. 100.00
Sauce dish, flat or footed, gilded
   coins 32.50
Spooner, frosted coins 42.50
Spooner, gilded coins 47.50
Sugar bowl, cov., frosted coins 135.00
Syrup pitcher w/original top, clear
   coins 125.00
Syrup pitcher w/original top, frosted
   coins 135.00
Toothpick holder, frosted coins 95.00
Toothpick holder, gilded coins 72.50
Tumbler, gilded coins 55.00
Wine, frosted coins . . . . 55.00 to 80.00
Wine, gilded coins 55.00

COMET (Early Comet)
Goblet 75.00
Pitcher, water, tankard 400.00
Spooner 95.00
Sugar bowl, cov. 175.00
Tumbler, bar 95.00
Tumbler, bar, canary yellow 750.00
Tumbler, water 110.00
Tumbler, whiskey, handled 250.00

COMPACT - See Snail Pattern

CORD & TASSEL

Cord & Tassel Goblet

Butter dish, cov. 48.00
Cake stand, 9½" d. 42.50
Castor bottle 32.00
Compote, cov., 8" d. 50.00
Compote, open, 8" d., low stand . . . 26.50
Creamer 27.50

Goblet (ILLUS.) 26.50
Lamp, kerosene-type, applied
  handle 85.00
Mug 25.00
Pitcher, water 95.00
Salt & pepper shakers w/original
  tops, pr. 55.00
Sauce dish, flat 7.50
Spooner 28.00
Sugar bowl, open 26.00
Table set, creamer, open sugar
  bowl & spooner, 3 pcs. 68.00
Wine 30.00

CORD DRAPERY

Cord & Drapery Spooner

Berry set, master bowl & 6 sauce
  dishes, 7 pcs. 70.00
Bowl, 7" d., flat 28.50
Bowl, 8½" oval 35.00
Bowl, 10" d., 3½" h. 45.00
Butter dish, cov. . . . . 50.00 to 65.00
Butter dish, cov., green 150.00
Cake stand 38.50
Compote, cov., jelly, blue 55.00
Compote, cov., jelly 45.00
Compote, open, jelly 30.00
Creamer 30.00
Cruet w/original stopper, amber . . . 265.00
Cruet w/original stopper 90.00
Goblet 55.00
Mug 40.00
Pickle castor, 9¼ x 5¼" oval 20.00
Pitcher, water, amber 185.00
Pitcher, water 67.50
Punch cup 13.50
Relish, 7 x 4" 16.50
Salt & pepper shakers w/original
  tops, pr. 85.00
Sauce dish, flat or footed,
  blue . . . . 30.00 to 40.00
Sauce dish, flat or
  footed . . . . .7.50 to 20.00
Spooner (ILLUS.) 42.50

Sugar bowl, cov. 37.50
Syrup pitcher w/original top,
  amber 265.00
Toothpick holder 75.00
Tumbler, blue 125.00
Tumbler 40.00
Wine 70.00

CORDOVA

Banana stand 90.00
Butter dish, cov. 50.00
Celery vase 45.00
Cologne bottle, 5" h. 20.00
Creamer 22.50
Creamer, individual size 35.00
Creamer & cov. sugar bowl, pr. 65.00
Inkwell 75.00
Mug 16.50
Pitcher, milk 30.00
Pitcher, water 52.50
Punch cup 6.50
Spooner 30.00
Sugar bowl, cov. . . . . 35.00 to 40.00
Sugar bowl, cov., individual size 40.00
Toothpick holder 20.00
Tumbler 15.00
Vase, bud 15.00
Water set, pitcher & 5 tumblers, 6
  pcs. 95.00

CORD ROSETTE

Goblet . . . . 30.00 to 40.00
Lamp, kerosene-type, pedestal
  base, original burner 70.00

CORONA - See Sunk Honeycomb Pattern

COTTAGE (Dinner Bell or Fine Cut Band)

Cottage Cruet

Bowl, berry, 7" d., green 16.00
Bowl, berry, 9¼ x 6½" oval 17.50
Butter dish, cov. 45.00
Butter dish, cov., green 78.00

Cake stand, amber	65.00
Cake stand	36.50
Celery vase	30.00
Champagne	52.50
Compote, cov., 7" d., high stand	30.00
Compote, open, jelly, 4½" d., 4" h., blue	28.50
Compote, open, jelly, 4½" d., 4" h.	19.00
Compote, open, jelly, 4½" d., 4" h., green	45.00
Creamer, amber	76.50
Creamer	22.50
Cruet w/original stopper (ILLUS.)	37.50
Cup & saucer	35.00
Finger bowl	15.00
Goblet, amber	45.00
Goblet	26.50
Pitcher, milk	35.00
Pitcher, water, 2-qt.	40.00
Plate, 5" d.	11.50
Plate, 6" d.	15.00
Plate, 7" d.	18.00
Plate, 9" d.	35.00
Salt shaker w/original top (single)	25.00
Sauce dish	7.50
Saucer, green, 6" d.	20.00
Spooner	20.00
Sugar bowl, cov.	47.00
Syrup pitcher w/original top	57.50
Tray, water	27.50
Tumbler	20.00
Waste bowl	38.00
Wine	18.00

CROESUS

Croesus Pattern

Berry set: master bowl & 6 sauce dishes; green, 7 pcs.	325.00
Berry set: master bowl & 6 sauce dishes; purple, 7 pcs.	425.00
Bowl, 6¾" d., 4" h., footed, green w/gold	65.00
Bowl, 6¾" d., 4" h., footed, purple w/gold	185.00
Bowl, 8" d., green	100.00
Bowl, 8" d., purple	175.00
Bowl, berry or fruit, 9" d., green	100.00 to 125.00
Butter dish, cov.	75.00
Butter dish, cov., green	95.00 to 145.00
Butter dish, cov., purple	170.00
Celery vase, green w/gold	135.00
Compote, open, jelly, purple	225.00

Condiment set: cruet, salt & pepper shakers & tray; green w/gold, 4 pcs.	365.00
Condiment tray	18.00
Condiment tray, green	42.50
Condiment tray, purple	85.00
Creamer, green	80.00
Creamer, purple	125.00
Creamer, individual size, purple, 3" h.	95.00
Creamer & cov. sugar bowl, green, pr.	225.00
Cruet w/original stopper	75.00
Cruet w/original stopper, green	175.00
Cruet w/original stopper, purple	350.00
Pitcher, water, green	225.00
Pitcher, water, purple	550.00
Plate, 8" d., scalloped rim, green w/gold	110.00
Salt & pepper shakers w/original tops, green, pr.	120.00 to 135.00
Sauce dish	13.50
Sauce dish, green w/gold	32.50
Sauce dish, purple w/gold	42.50
Spooner, green	75.00
Spooner, purple	100.00
Sugar bowl, cov., green	125.00
Sugar bowl, cov., purple	150.00
Sugar bowl, open, green	85.00
Table set, green, 4 pcs.	395.00 to 425.00
Table set, purple, 4 pcs. (ILLUS. of part)	525.00 to 650.00
Toothpick holder, green	87.50
Toothpick holder, purple	98.00
Tumbler, green	45.00
Tumbler, purple	75.00
Water set: pitcher & 6 tumblers; purple, 7 pcs.	850.00

CROWFOOT (Turkey Track)

Butter dish, cov.	55.00
Cake stand, 9" d.	48.00
Goblet	32.50
Sauce dish, flat	12.00
Spooner	25.00

CROWN JEWEL - See Chandelier Pattern

CRYSTAL BALL - See Atlas Pattern

CRYSTAL WEDDING (Collins)

(Items may be plain or with etched designs)

Banana stand, 10" h.	97.50
Berry set, 8" sq. bowl & 6 sauce dishes, 7 pcs.	125.00
Bowl, cov., 7" sq.	75.00
Butter dish, cov.	65.00
Butter dish, cov., amber-stained	100.00
Cake stand, 9" sq., 8" h.	57.50
Cake stand, 10" sq.	75.00
Celery vase	45.00
Compote, cov., 6" sq., 9½" h.	52.50
Compote, cov., 7" sq.	85.00
Compote, open, 4" sq., 6" h.	22.50

Compote, open, 5" sq. 42.50
Compote, open, 7" sq., 8¾" h. 75.00
Compote, open, 8" sq., low stand . . 36.00
Creamer . . . . .30.00 to 42.50
Creamer, ruby-stained 52.50
Creamer & cov. sugar bowl, amber-
  stained, pr. . . . . .180.00 to 195.00
Cruet w/original stopper, amber-
  stained. 175.00
Goblet 45.00
Goblet, ruby-stained. 62.50
Lamp base, kerosene-type, square
  font, 10" h. 375.00
Pitcher, milk. 125.00
Pitcher, water 155.00
Salt dip 35.00
Salt shaker w/original top, ruby-
  stained (single) 68.00
Sauce dish. 12.00
Spooner 25.00
Spooner, ruby-stained 55.00
Sugar bowl, cov. 50.00

Crystal Wedding Sugar Bowl

Sugar bowl, cov., ruby-stained
  (ILLUS.). 100.00
Sugar bowl, open, scalloped rim 30.00
Syrup pitcher w/original top, ruby-
  stained. 210.00
Tumbler 38.50
Wine. 68.00

CUPID & VENUS (Guardian Angel)
Bowl, cov., 8" d., footed 125.00
Bowl, 6½" d. 20.00
Bowl, 9" d., scalloped rim, footed . . 37.50
Bread plate, amber, 10½" d. 115.00
Bread plate, 10½" d. 37.50
Butter dish, cov. 55.00
Cake plate 40.00
Celery vase. 42.50
Champagne. 62.50
Compote, cov., 7" d., high stand . . . 125.00
Compote, cov., 9½" d., low stand . . 95.00
Compote, open, 6" d., low stand . . . 30.00
Compote, open, 8½" d., low stand,
  scalloped rim 35.00

Cordial 85.00
Creamer 35.00
Goblet 60.00
Goblet, buttermilk 50.00
Honey dish, 3½" d. 7.50
Marmalade jar, cov. 85.00
Mug, 2½" h. 30.00
Mug, 3½" h. 32.50
Pickle castor w/resilvered frame,
  cover & tongs 80.00
Pitcher, milk, amber. 190.00
Pitcher, milk. 68.00
Pitcher, water 60.00

Cupid & Venus Sauce Dish

Sauce dish, footed, 3½" to 4½" d.
  (ILLUS.). 10.00
Spooner 36.50
Sugar bowl, cov. 65.00
Wine. 90.00

CURRANT
Cake stand, 9¼" d., 4¼" h. 75.00
Cake stand, 11" d. 65.00
Celery vase. 40.00
Compote, cov., 8" d., high stand . . . 195.00
Creamer 35.00
Egg cup 20.00
Goblet 28.50
Goblet, buttermilk 40.00
Honey dish, 3½" d. 16.00
Pitcher, water 70.00
Relish, 8 x 5" 12.00
Spooner 26.00
Wine. 37.50

CURRIER & IVES
Bitters bottle. 38.00
Bowl, master berry or fruit, 10"
  oval, flat w/collared base 40.00
Bread plate, Balky Mule on Railroad
  Tracks, blue 85.00
Bread plate, Balky Mule on Railroad
  Tracks 50.00
Bread plate, children sawing felled
  log, frosted center 75.00
Compote, cov., 7½" d., high
  stand 95.00
Compote, open, 7½" d., 9" h., scal-
  loped rim. 45.00

Creamer 30.00
Cup 15.00
Cup, vaseline 35.00
Cup & saucer 35.00
Decanter w/original stopper 55.00
Goblet 25.00
Lamp, kerosene-type, 11" h. 70.00
Pitcher, milk 57.50
Pitcher, water, amber 125.00
Pitcher, water 56.50
Relish, 10" oval ....16.00 to 20.00
Salt shaker w/original top, amber
 (single)........................ 45.00
Salt shaker w/original top, blue
 (single)........................ 55.00
Salt shaker w/original top
 (single)........................ 19.00
Salt shaker w/original top, vaseline
 (single)........................ 52.50
Salt & pepper shakers w/original
 tops, blue, pr. 90.00
Salt & pepper shakers w/original
 tops, pr........................ 58.00
Sauce dish, flat or footed, amber ... 20.00
Sauce dish, flat or footed, blue 25.00
Sauce dish, flat or footed .....7.00 to 12.50
Spooner 25.00
Sugar bowl, cov. ....35.00 to 45.00
Syrup jug w/original top 82.50
Tray, wine, 9½" d..........47.50 to 55.00
Tray, water, Balky Mule on Railroad
 Tracks, blue, 12" d. 110.00

"Balky Mule" Water Tray

Tray, water, Balky Mule on Railroad
 Tracks, 12" d. (ILLUS.) 68.00
Tray, water, Balky Mule on Railroad
 Tracks, vaseline, 12" d...100.00 to 125.00
Waste bowl...................... 45.00
Wine........................... 17.50
Wine set, decanter w/original stop-
 per & 6 wines, 7 pcs. 180.00

CURTAIN

Bowl, cov., 8" d. 60.00

Bowl, 7½" d. 22.00
Butter dish, cov. 50.00
Cake stand, 9½" d. 36.50
Celery boat..................... 48.50
Celery vase.................... 32.50
Compote, open, 10" d., 8" h........ 42.50
Condiment set, pr. salt & pepper
 shakers & mustard jar, 3 pcs. 65.00
Creamer ....25.00 to 35.00
Goblet 35.00

Curtain Salt Shaker

Salt shaker w/original top (ILLUS.) .. 15.00
Salt & pepper shakers (no tops),
 pr.............................. 24.00
Sauce dish, flat or footed, 4¾" d. ... 8.00
Spooner 25.00
Sugar bowl, cov. 40.00
Tumbler 20.00

CURTAIN TIE BACK

Curtain Tieback Goblet

Bowl, 7½" sq., flat 18.00
Bread tray 37.00
Butter dish, cov. 38.00
Cake stand, 9" d., 6½" h. 25.00
Celery vase..................... 30.00

Compote, cov., 7½" d., low stand .. 28.00
Creamer 35.00
Goblet (ILLUS.)..................... 25.00
Pitcher, water 55.00
Relish 10.00
Sauce dish, flat or footed ....10.00 to 15.00
Spooner 28.00
Sugar bowl, cov. 30.00

CUT LOG

Cut Log Creamer

Bowl, master berry or fruit,
  10½" d., footed 40.00
Butter dish, cov. ....65.00 to 70.00
Cake stand, 9" d., 6" h. 56.00
Cake stand, 10" d. 65.00
Celery tray 15.00
Celery vase...................... 36.50
Compote, cov., 5½" d., 7½" h..... 47.50
Compote, cov., 7" d., 8½" h........ 60.00
Compote, cov., 7" d., 10" h........ 75.00
Compote, open, 5" d............. 25.00
Compote, open, 6" d., 4¾" h...... 40.00
Compote, open, 8" d., 6½" h...... 28.00
Compote, open, 9" d., 6¼" h...... 35.00
Compote, open, 10" d., 8½" h.,
  scalloped rim ....75.00 to 85.00
Creamer (ILLUS.) 38.50
Creamer, individual size 15.00
Cruet w/original stopper, small 37.50
Cruet w/original stopper, large..... 45.00
Goblet ....35.00 to 50.00
Mug 15.00
Nappy, handled, 5" d. 18.50
Olive dish 20.00
Pitcher, water, tankard 72.50
Relish, boat-shaped, 9¼" l. 30.00
Salt shaker w/original tin top
  (single)....................... 37.50
Sauce dish, flat or footed ....25.00 to 30.00
Spooner 27.50
Sugar bowl, cov................... 52.50
Sugar bowl, cov., individual size.... 32.50
Sugar bowl, open, individual size ... 20.00
Tumbler 45.00
Tumbler, juice 22.50
Vase, 16" h. 35.00
Wine............................. 22.50

DAHLIA

Dahlia Pitcher

Bowl, 9 x 6" oval................. 16.50
Bread platter, 12 x 8" 30.00
Butter dish, cov. 55.00
Cake stand, amber, 9" d. 60.00
Cake stand, 9" d. 22.50
Champagne...................... 55.00
Compote, cov., 7" d., high stand ... 50.00
Creamer 18.00
Goblet 32.50
Goblet, vaseline 65.00
Mug 30.00
Mug, yellow 45.00
Mug, child's, blue 40.00
Mug, child's 20.00
Pitcher, milk, applied handle 32.00
Pitcher, milk, yellow 58.00
Pitcher, water, amber 67.50
Pitcher, water, blue (ILLUS.)........ 95.00
Pitcher, water 50.00
Pitcher, water, vaseline .....75.00 to 95.00
Plate, 7" d., amber............... 42.50
Plate, 7" d....................... 20.00
Plate, 9" d., w/handles, amber 30.00
Plate, 9" d., w/handles, blue....... 50.00
Plate, 9" d., w/handles 17.50
Plate, 9" d., w/handles, vaseline ... 38.50
Relish, 9½ x 5" 13.00
Sauce dish, flat, amber 9.00
Sauce dish, flat, blue 15.00
Sauce dish, flat 8.50
Spooner, amber 45.00
Spooner, blue.................... 50.00
Spooner 25.00
Sugar bowl, cov. 28.00
Sugar bowl, open 20.00
Wine............................ 42.50

DAISY & BUTTON

Berry set: master bowl & 6 sauce
  dishes; blue, 7 pcs.............. 85.00
Berry set: octagonal master bowl &
  9 sauce dishes; amber, 10 pcs. ... 150.00

Bowl, 8" w., tricornered, vaseline .. 37.50
Bowl, berry or fruit, 8½" d......... 40.00
Bowl, 9" sq., Amberina 200.00
Bowl, 11 x 8" oval, 3" h., amber.... 65.00
Bowl, 11 x 10 x 7¾", flared,
  vaseline...................... 95.00
Bread tray, amber ....22.00 to 35.00
Butter chip, fan-shaped 9.50
Butter chip, round, amber......... 9.00
Butter chip, round 6.00
Butter chip, square, amber........ 15.00
Butter chip, square, blue.......... 17.50
Butter chip, square 7.50
Butter dish, cov., scalloped base,
  blue 65.00
Butter dish, cov., square 45.00
Butter dish, cov., model of Victorian
  stove, blue 52.50
Butter tub, cov., 2-handled,
  vaseline 55.00

Daisy & Button Canoe

Canoe, amber, 8" l. (ILLUS.)........ 45.00
Canoe, Amberina, 8" l............. 495.00
Canoe, apple green, 8" l........... 32.50
Canoe, 8" l..................... 25.00
Canoe, vaseline, 8" l............. 90.00
Castor set, 3-bottle, in glass frame
  w/toothpick holder at top 50.00
Castor set, 5-bottle, blue, in original
  frame 225.00
Castor shaker bottle w/original top,
  amber 16.50
Celery vase, triangular, amber 40.00
Celery vase, triangular, green 35.00
Cheese dish, cov. 52.00
Cologne bottle w/original stopper .. 22.50
Compote, cov., 8" d., 12" h......... 65.00
Creamer, amber 32.50
Creamer 23.00
Creamer, ruby-stained buttons 45.00
Creamer & cov. sugar bowl, amber,
  large, pr..................... 125.00
Cup & saucer, blue 65.00
Dish, amber, deep, 5" sq.......... 85.00
Goblet, amber 27.50
Goblet 22.50
Hat shape, canary yellow, 1¾" h. .. 22.50
Hat shape, amber, 2½" h. 30.00
Hat shape, apple green, 2½" h. 35.00
Hat shape, blue, 2½" h. 28.00
Hat shape, 2½" h. 20.00
Hat shape, vaseline, 2½" h. 37.50
Hat shape, blue, from tumbler mold,
  4¾" widest d. 47.50

Hat shape, canary yellow, from tum-
  bler mold, 5" widest d., 3¾" h. .. 48.00
Humidor, cov., amber 185.00
Ice cream dish, scalloped corners,
  Amberina, 5¾" d. ....95.00 to 125.00
Ice cream dish, cut corners, 6" sq. .. 9.00
Inkwell, amber.................. 145.00
Match holder, cauldron w/original
  bail handle, amber 29.50
Match holder, wall-hanging scuff,
  amber, 4½" l. 30.00
Match holder, wall-hanging scuff,
  blue ....60.00 to 75.00
Match holder, wall-hanging scuff ... 18.00
Pickle castor, amber insert, w/sil-
  verplate frame & tongs 120.00
Pickle castor, sapphire blue insert,
  w/silverplate frame & tongs...... 250.00
Pickle castor, vaseline insert, silver-
  plate frame & tongs 150.00
Pitcher, water, bulbous, applied
  handle 55.00
Pitcher, water, square 58.00
Plate, 5½" sq., Amberina.......... 85.00
Plate, 7" sq., amber 18.00
Plate, 7" sq., blue............... 20.00
Plate, 7" sq. 15.00
Plate, 10" d., scalloped rim,
  amber 28.00
Plate, 10" d., blue................ 35.00
Platter, 13 x 9" oval, open handles,
  amber 35.00
Platter, 13 x 9" oval, open handles,
  blue 40.00
Platter, 13 x 9" oval, open handles,
  yellow 40.00
Relish, "Sitz bathtub" 65.00
Salt dip, canoe-shaped, amber,
  4 x 2"....................... 19.50
Salt dip, canoe-shaped, 4 x 2"..... 14.50
Salt dip, master size, blue, 3½" d... 12.50
Salt dip, master size, vaseline,
  3½" d....................... 23.00
Salt shaker w/original top, corset-
  shaped, blue (single) 21.00
Salt & pepper shakers w/original
  tops, pr...................... 20.00
Salt & pepper shakers w/original
  tops, vaseline, pr.............. 30.00
Sauce dish, amber, 4" to 5" sq...... 17.00
Sauce dish, Amberina, 4" to
  5" sq...................85.00 to 100.00
Sauce dish, blue, 4" to
  5" sq..................13.50 to 25.00
Sauce dish, 4" to 5" sq........6.00 to 12.00
Sauce dish, cloverleaf-shaped,
  amber 14.50
Sauce dish, tricornered, blue 13.00
Sauce dish, tricornered 16.00
Sauce dish, tricornered, vaseline ... 15.00
Sauce dish, tricornered,
  yellow ....9.00 to 15.00
Slipper, "1886 patent," blue 40.00
Slipper, "1886 patent" 52.50

Slipper, ruby-stained buttons 79.00
Smoke bell, amber 65.00
Spooner, amber 37.50
Spooner, blue 40.00
Spooner 35.00
Spooner, hat-shaped, amber 32.00
Sugar bowl, cov., amber . . . . . 35.00 to 45.00
Sugar bowl, cov., barrel-shaped,
   blue 50.00
Sugar bowl, cov. 30.00
Sugar bowl, cov., triangular,
   vaseline 40.00
Sugar bowl, open, purple 55.00
Syrup pitcher w/original pewter top,
   blue 175.00
Toothpick holder (or salt dip),
   "Bandmaster's cap," vaseline 45.00
Toothpick holder, coal hod form,
   blue 20.00
Toothpick holder, 3-footed, amber . . 35.00
Toothpick holder, 3-footed,
   Amberina . . . . 145.00 to 185.00
Toothpick holder, 3-footed,
   vaseline 39.50
Toothpick holder, urn-shaped 28.00
Toothpick holder, amber w/brass
   rim & base 20.00
Tray, water, triangular, green 45.00
Tumbler, water, amber 17.00
Tumbler, water, blue 28.00
Tumbler, water 15.00
Tumbler, water, ruby-stained
   buttons 35.00
Tumbler, water, vaseline 22.50
Vase, 6" h., hand holding cornuco-
   pia, blue 50.00
Vase, 6" h., hand holding cornuco-
   pia, ruby-stained buttons 58.50
Whimsey, sleigh, amber,
   7¾ x 4½" 115.00
Whimsey, "whisk broom" dish,
   amber 37.50

DAISY & BUTTON WITH CROSSBARS (Mikado)

Daisy & Button with Crossbars

Berry set: master bowl & 4 sauce
   dishes; blue, 5 pcs. 85.00

Bowl, 9 x 6", canary yellow 30.00
Bread tray, apple green 32.50
Bread tray, blue 42.00
Bread tray 25.00
Bread tray, vaseline 60.00
Butter dish, cov. 45.00
Cake stand, blue 85.00
Cake stand 55.00
Celery vase, amber 39.00
Celery vase, blue 40.00
Celery vase 27.00
Celery vase, vaseline 50.00
Compote, open, 6" h., canary
   yellow 38.00
Compote, open, 7" d., 4" h.,
   amber 26.50
Compote, open, 8½" d., 7½" h.,
   amber 45.00
Compote, open, 8½" d., 7½" h.,
   blue 45.00
Compote, open, 8½" d., 7½" h. 32.50
Compote, open, 9½" d. 35.00
Compote, open, 10" d., amber 60.00
Creamer, amber . . . . 30.00 to 40.00
Creamer, blue 45.00
Creamer . . . . 25.00 to 35.00
Creamer, individual size, blue 30.00
Creamer, individual size 15.00
Creamer & open sugar bowl, amber,
   pr. 70.00
Cruet w/original stopper,
   amber . . . . 115.00 to 125.00
Cruet w/original stopper 35.00
Cruet w/original stopper,
   vaseline 125.00
Cruet w/original stopper, blue 70.00
Goblet, amber 35.00
Goblet, blue 38.00
Goblet 25.00
Goblet, vaseline 40.00
Mug, amber, 3" h. 18.00
Mug, canary yellow, 3" h. 22.50
Mug, 3" h. 12.00
Pitcher, milk, amber (ILLUS.) 45.00
Pitcher, milk, blue 55.00
Pitcher, milk 45.00
Pitcher, water, amber 75.00
Pitcher, water, blue 90.00
Pitcher, water 52.50
Pitcher, water, vaseline 62.50
Sauce dish, flat or footed,
   amber . . . . 12.50 to 15.00
Sauce dish, flat or footed, canary
   yellow 16.50
Sauce dish, flat or footed,
   vaseline 22.00
Spooner, amber 50.00
Spooner 23.50
Spooner, vaseline 30.00
Sugar bowl, cov., blue 55.00
Sugar bowl, cov. 25.00
Toothpick holder 28.00
Tumbler, amber 22.00
Tumbler, blue 30.00

Tumbler	15.00
Tumbler, vaseline	25.00
Vase, vaseline	45.00
Waste bowl, canary yellow	22.50
Water set: pitcher & 8 tumblers; amber, 9 pcs.	185.00
Wine	30.00

DAISY & BUTTON WITH NARCISSUS

Daisy & Button with Narcissus

Bowl, 9½ x 6″ oval, footed	45.00
Butter dish, cov.	50.00
Creamer	45.00
Decanter w/original stopper	65.00
Goblet	18.00 to 22.50
Nappy, leaf-shaped	65.00
Pitcher, water (ILLUS.)	70.00
Punch cup	12.00
Sauce dish, flat or 3-footed	8.00 to 15.00
Spooner	30.00
Sugar bowl, cov.	42.50
Tray, 10½″ d.	30.00
Tumbler	18.00
Wine	17.50

DAISY & BUTTON WITH THUMBPRINT PANELS

Bowl, berry, cov., 8″ d., 8″ h., amber panels	130.00
Bowl, 9″ oval, amber panels	50.00
Bowl, 11″ d., collared base, amber panels	51.50
Bride's basket, w/silverplate holder, amber panels	125.00
Butter dish, cov.	78.00
Cake basket, amber panels, 11 x 7″, 5½″ h.	125.00
Cake stand, 9½″ d.	48.00
Celery vase	30.00
Celery vase, amber panels (ILLUS.)	85.00
Champagne, amber panels	25.00
Compote, cov., 6¾″ d., 10½″ h.	62.50
Creamer, applied handle, amber panels	59.00
Cruet w/original stopper	28.00

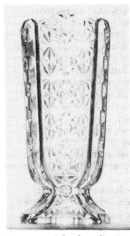

Daisy & Button with Thumbprint Panels

Dish, triangular, 5″ w., 2″ h.	20.00
Finger bowl	22.50
Goblet	27.50
Goblet, amber panels	55.00
Goblet, blue panels	42.50
Pitcher, water, applied handle, amber panels	135.00
Pitcher, water, applied handle, blue panels	85.00
Sauce dish, flat or footed, 5″ sq.	9.00 to 12.50
Sauce dish, flat or footed, amber panels, 5″ sq.	15.00 to 30.00
Sugar bowl, open, amber panels	32.50
Syrup jug w/original top, amber panels	125.00
Tumbler, amber	22.50
Tumbler, blue	25.00
Tumbler	20.00
Water set: pitcher & 5 tumblers; vaseline, 6 pcs.	295.00
Wine	15.00
Wine, amber panels	35.00
Wine, blue panels	40.00

DAISY & BUTTON WITH "V" ORNAMENT

Bowl, 9″ d., vaseline	50.00
Butter dish, cov., canary yellow	68.00
Butter dish, cov.	45.00
Celery vase, amber	40.00
Celery vase, canary yellow	65.00
Celery vase	25.00
Celery vase, vaseline	60.00
Creamer, amber	27.50
Creamer	30.00
Finger bowl, blue	45.00
Mug, blue	22.50
Mug	17.50
Mug, vaseline	25.00
Mug, miniature, vaseline	26.00
Pitcher, water, amber	90.00
Pitcher, water, blue	90.00
Pitcher, water	48.00

Sauce dish, amber		15.00
Sauce dish, blue		15.00
Sauce dish		10.00
Spooner, amber		37.50
Spooner, blue		35.00
Spooner		20.00
Sugar bowl, cov., blue		49.00
Toothpick holder, amber		25.00
Toothpick holder, blue		25.00
Toothpick holder		22.00
Toothpick holder, vaseline		35.00
Tumbler, amber		22.00
Tumbler		15.00
Waste bowl, amber		29.00
Waste bowl		22.50
Waste bowl, vaseline		28.00

DAISY IN PANEL - See Two Panel Pattern

DAKOTA (Baby Thumbprint)

Dakota Creamer

(Items may be plain or with etched designs)

Basket, 10" l., 2" h.	165.00
Butter dish, cov.	59.00
Cake stand, 8" to 10¼" d. . . .50.00 to 65.00
Celery vase, flat base	32.50
Celery vase, pedestal base	37.50
Compote, cov., jelly, 5" d., 5" h.	46.50
Compote, cov., 7" d., 11" h.	55.00
Compote, open, jelly, 5" d., 5" h.	32.50
Compote, open, 6" d.	27.50
Compote, open, 8" d., low stand	32.50
Compote, open, 8" d., 9" h. . .55.00 to 70.00
Compote, open, 10" d.	55.00
Creamer (ILLUS.) . . . . .40.00 to 60.00
Finger bowl	45.00
Goblet	27.50
Goblet, ruby-stained	40.00
Lamp, kerosene-type . . . . . .110.00 to 135.00
Mug, ruby-stained, 3½" h.	35.00
Pitcher, milk	78.50
Pitcher, water, 10" to 12" h.	70.00
Plate, 10" d.	75.00
Salt shaker w/original top (single)	42.50

Salt & pepper shakers w/original tops, pr.	90.00
Sauce dish, flat or footed . . . .12.00 to 18.00
Sauce dish, flat or footed, ruby-stained	22.50
Shaker bottle w/original top, hotel size, 6½" h.	58.00
Spooner	35.00
Sugar bowl, cov.	50.00
Sugar bowl, open, breakfast size	20.00
Tray, water, piecrust rim, 13" d.	65.00
Tray, wine	77.50
Tumbler	32.50
Tumbler, ruby-stained	47.50
Waste bowl	60.00
Wine	22.50
Wine, ruby-stained	42.50

DARBY - See Pleat & Panel Pattern

DART

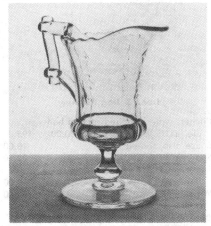

Dart Creamer

Butter dish, cov.	28.00
Compote, cov., 8½" d., high stand	35.00
Compote, open, jelly	17.00
Creamer (ILLUS.)	27.50
Goblet	24.00
Lamp, kerosene	45.00
Sauce dish, footed	10.00
Spooner	20.00
Sugar bowl, cov.	32.50
Table set, creamer, spooner & cov. sugar bowl, 3 pcs.	85.00

DEER & DOG

(Each piece etched w/scene of deer, dog & hunter)

Butter dish, cov., pedestal base & frosted dog finial	130.00
Celery vase, scalloped rim, signed "Gillinder"	95.00
Compote, cov., 8" oval, 8¾" h., frosted dog finial	135.00

Compote, cov., 8" d., 13" h., frosted
   dog finial........................ 250.00
Compote, open, 8" d............. 175.00
Cordial........................... 95.00
Creamer.......................... 75.00
Goblet, straight sides............. 55.00
Goblet, U-shaped 75.00
Goblet, V-shaped 50.00
Marmalade jar, cov............... 65.00
Pitcher, milk, 9" h. 165.00

Deer & Dog Pitcher

Pitcher, water, applied reeded han-
   dle (ILLUS.) ....180.00 to 195.00
Sauce dish, footed 18.00
Spooner.......................... 52.50
Sugar bowl, cov., frosted dog
   finial......................... 110.00
Wine......................60.00 to 85.00

DEER & PINE TREE

Deer & Pine Tree Butter Dish

Bowl, 8 x 5"...................... 22.00
Bread tray, amber, 13 x 8"........ 65.00
Bread tray, apple green, 13 x 8".... 78.00
Bread tray, blue, 13 x 8".......... 75.00
Bread tray, 13 x 8"............... 45.00
Bread tray, vaseline, 13 x 8" 80.00
Butter dish, cov. (ILLUS.) 65.00
Cake stand 77.50
Celery vase 72.50
Compote, cov., 8" sq., 6" h........ 68.00

Compote, cov., 8" sq., 12" h....... 130.00
Compote, open, 8" sq., high stand .. 48.00
Creamer 62.50
Finger bowl...................... 57.50
Goblet 47.50
Mug, child's, amber 45.00
Mug, child's, vaseline............. 55.00
Mug, large, apple green 65.00
Mug, large, blue 48.00
Mug, large 40.00
Pickle dish...................... 18.00
Pitcher, milk.................... 70.00
Pitcher, water ....85.00 to 95.00
Sauce dish, flat or footed, blue..... 25.00
Sauce dish, flat or footed ....12.00 to 22.00
Spooner......................... 35.00
Sugar bowl, cov. 62.50
Tray, water, handled, amber,
   15 x 9".................... 68.00
Tray, water, handled, 15 x 9" 55.00
Vegetable dish, 9 x 5¾"........... 50.00

DELAWARE (Four Petal Flower)

Delaware Banana Boat

Banana boat, amethyst w/gold,
   11¾" l. 125.00
Banana boat, w/gold, 11¾" l.
   (ILLUS.)....................... 50.00
Banana boat, green w/gold,
   11¾" l. 55.00
Banana boat, rose w/gold,
   11¾" l. 60.00
Berry set: master bowl & 4 sauce
   dishes; green w/gold, 5 pcs. 120.00
Berry set: master bowl & 4 sauce
   dishes; rose w/gold, 5 pcs. 155.00
Bowl, 8" d., amethyst w/gold 75.00
Bowl, 8" d., w/gold 30.00
Bowl, 8" d., green w/gold 45.00
Bowl, 8" d., rose w/gold.......... 57.50
Bowl, 9" d., w/gold 24.50
Bowl, 9" d., green w/gold 50.00
Bowl, 9" d., rose w/gold.......... 75.00
Bowl, 10" octagon, green w/gold ... 50.00
Bride's basket, boat-shaped open
   bowl, green w/gold, miniature ... 175.00
Butter dish, cov. 90.00
Butter dish, cov., green w/gold..... 105.00
Butter dish, cov., rose w/gold 120.00
Celery vase, green w/gold 68.00
Celery vase, rose w/gold 72.50
Claret jug, green w/gold 175.00
Creamer, w/gold.................. 37.50
Creamer, green w/gold 52.50

Creamer, individual size, w/gold ... 25.00
Creamer & sugar bowl, breakfast
  size, rose w/gold, pr. 125.00
Cruet w/original stopper 100.00
Dresser tray 30.00
Dresser tray, green w/gold 60.00
Dresser tray, rose w/gold 65.00
Finger bowl, w/gold 22.00
Marmalade dish w/silverplate
  holder, amethyst w/gold 45.00
Marmalade dish w/silverplate
  holder, green w/gold 38.50
Marmalade dish w/silverplate
  holder, rose w/gold 95.00
Pin tray, 7 x 3½" 14.50
Pin tray, 9 x 4¾" 17.50
Pitcher, milk, green w/gold ..60.00 to 85.00
Pitcher, tankard, w/cranberry &
  green florals & gold trim 125.00
Pitcher, tankard, green w/gold 90.00
Pitcher, tankard, rose w/gold 125.00
Pitcher, water, bulbous, rose
  w/gold 125.00
Pomade jar w/jeweled cover, rose
  w/gold 215.00
Powder jar, cov., green w/gold 135.00
Powder jar, cov., rose w/gold 145.00
Punch cup 15.00
Punch cup, green, souvenir 35.00
Punch cup, green w/gold 35.00
Punch cup, rose w/gold 38.50
Salt shaker w/original top, rose
  w/gold (single) 45.00
Sauce dish, boat-shaped 30.00
Sauce dish, boat-shaped, green
  w/gold 27.50
Sauce dish, boat-shaped, rose
  w/gold 40.00
Sauce dish, round, green w/gold ... 21.50
Sauce dish, round, rose w/gold 25.00
Spooner, w/gold 35.00
Spooner, green w/gold 45.00
Spooner, rose w/gold 57.50
Sugar bowl, cov. 65.00
Sugar bowl, cov., green w/gold 120.00
Sugar bowl, cov., rose w/gold 100.00
Sugar bowl, individual size, green .. 55.00
Table set, green w/gold,
  4 pcs. 395.00
Table set, rose w/gold, 4 pcs. 500.00
Toothpick holder 30.00
Toothpick holder, w/rose-stained
  florals & gold 65.00
Toothpick holder, green w/gold 90.00
Toothpick holder, rose w/gold 115.00
Tumbler 12.00
Tumbler, w/rose-stained florals 26.50
Tumbler, custard w/stained florals .. 65.00
Tumbler, green w/gold 42.50
Tumbler, rose w/gold 45.00
Vase, 6" h., green w/gold 40.00
Vase, 8" h., green w/gold 115.00
Vase, 9½" h., rose
  w/gold ....95.00 to 110.00

Water set: pitcher & 4 tumblers;
  green w/gold, 5 pcs. 250.00
Water set: pitcher & 6 tumblers;
  rose w/gold, 7 pcs. .....295.00 to 385.00

DEW & RAINDROP

Dew & Raindrop Wine

Bowl, 6½" d. 28.00
Bowl, berry, 8" d. 38.00
Butter dish, cov. 50.00
Compote, open, jelly 35.00
Cordial 20.00
Creamer 28.50
Goblet 30.00
Pitcher, water 40.00
Punch cup 7.50
Salt & pepper shakers w/original
  tops, pr. 40.00
Sauce dish, flat or footed ....10.00 to 12.00
Spooner 35.00
Sugar bowl, cov. 50.00
Tumbler ....15.00 to 22.00
Vase, bud, 6" h. 27.50
Wine (ILLUS.) 19.50

DEWDROP

Bread tray 25.00
Butter dish, cov. 30.00
Cake stand, 8½" d. 20.00
Cordial 40.00
Creamer 25.00
Egg cup, double 20.00
Goblet, amber 25.00
Goblet, blue 25.00
Goblet 20.00
Mug, applied handle 24.00
Relish 15.00
Salt shaker w/original top, footed
  (single) 22.00
Sauce dish 8.00
Spooner 25.00
Sugar bowl, open 40.00

Tumbler, blue	27.50
Tumbler	15.00
Wine	25.00

DEWDROP WITH STAR

Dewdrop With Star Sauce Dish

Bowl, 7" d.	14.00
Butter dish, cov.	45.00
Cake stand, 9" d.	42.50
Celery vase	40.00
Cheese dish, cov.	95.00
Compote, cov., 5" d.	60.00
Compote, open, 9" d., 9" h.	45.00
Creamer, applied handle	25.00
Pitcher, water, 8" h.	95.00
Plate, 5" d.	12.00
Plate, 9" d.	13.50
Plate, 11" d.	15.00
Relish, 9" l.	15.00
Sauce dish, flat (ILLUS.)	8.00 to 10.00
Sugar bowl, cov.	50.00

DEWEY (Flower Flange)

(Also see Chocolate Glass December 1986)

Bowl, 8" d., amber	30.00
Bowl, 8" d., green	45.00
Butter dish, cov., amber	65.00
Butter dish, cov.	55.00
Butter dish, cov., green	67.50
Butter dish, cov., yellow	95.00
Creamer, amber	35.00
Creamer	30.00
Creamer, green	42.50
Creamer & cov. sugar bowl, breakfast size, vaseline, pr.	95.00
Cruet w/original stopper, amber	130.00
Cruet w/original stopper	95.00
Cruet w/original stopper, green	140.00
Cruet w/original stopper, Nile green	750.00
Cruet w/original stopper, yellow	125.00 to 165.00
Mug, amber	65.00
Mug	35.00

Mug, green	36.50
Mug, Nile green	275.00
Parfait, green	35.00
Pitcher, water, amber	95.00
Pitcher, water	52.50 to 67.50
Plate, footed, amber	42.00
Plate, footed	15.00
Plate, footed, green	45.00
Plate, footed, yellow	55.00
Relish, serpentine shape, amber, small	35.00
Relish, serpentine shape, small	20.00
Relish, serpentine shape, green, small	38.50
Relish, serpentine shape, yellow, small	42.50
Relish, serpentine shape, amber, large	62.50
Relish, serpentine shape, Nile green, large	265.00
Salt shaker w/original top, green or amber (single)	55.00
Salt shaker w/original top, yellow (single)	45.00
Sauce dish, amber	20.00
Sauce dish, green	25.00
Sauce dish, yellow	25.00
Spooner, amber	60.00
Spooner, green	35.00

Dewey Spooner

Spooner, yellow (ILLUS.)	35.00
Sugar bowl, cov., green	50.00
Sugar bowl, open, amber	32.50
Tumbler, amber	60.00
Tumbler	52.50
Tumbler, green	45.00
Tumbler, canary yellow	50.00 to 65.00
Tumbler, vaseline	55.00
Water set, pitcher & 6 tumblers, 7 pcs.	250.00
Water set: pitcher & 6 tumblers; yellow, 7 pcs.	225.00 to 300.00

DIAGONAL BAND

Butter dish, cov.	35.00
Cake stand	30.00
Celery vase	22.50
Compote, cov., 7½" d., 9¼" h.	45.00

Compote, open, 7½" d., high
  stand 16.50
Creamer 30.00
Creamer & open sugar bowl, pr..... 50.00

Diagonal Band Goblet

Goblet (ILLUS.).................... 22.00
Marmalade jar w/original lid....... 22.00
Pitcher, milk..................... 32.00
Pitcher, water 39.00
Plate, 8" d. 10.50
Relish, 6 7/8" oval 7.50
Salt & pepper shakers w/original
  tops, pr...................... 30.00
Sauce dish, flat or footed .....7.00 to 10.00
Spooner 22.50
Sugar bowl, open 15.00
Wine........................... 22.50

DIAGONAL BAND & FAN

Butter dish, cov. 40.00
Champagne....................... 30.00
Compote, open 18.50
Goblet 19.00
Plate, 6" d. 11.50
Plate, 8" d. 12.50
Relish, 8" oval 15.00
Sauce dish, footed 13.50
Spooner 22.50
Wine........................... 20.00

DIAMOND & BULL'S EYE BAND - See Reverse Torpedo Pattern

DIAMOND & SUNBURST

Celery vase...................... 35.00
Compote, cov., 7" d., high stand ... 45.00
Compote, open, jelly 15.00
Goblet (ILLUS.).................. 20.00
Salt dip, master size............. 20.00
Spooner 18.00
Sugar bowl, open 25.00
Sugar shaker 22.00

Diamond & Sunburst Goblet

Syrup jug w/original top, applied
  handle 45.00
Tumbler 25.00
Wine........................... 20.00

DIAMOND BAR - See Lattice Pattern

DIAMOND HORSESHOE - See Aurora Pattern

DIAMOND MEDALLION (Finecut & Diamond or Grand)

Diamond Medallion Creamer

Bowl, 9 x 6¼" oval................ 12.50
Bread plate, 10" d. 21.50
Butter dish, cov. 35.00
Cake stand, 8" d. 20.00
Cake stand, 10" d. 30.00
Celery vase 28.00
Compote, cov., 7" d., high stand ... 36.00

Compote, open, 7" d., high stand ... 22.50
Compote, open, 8" d., 6" h. 19.50
Compote, open, 9" d., high stand ... 17.50
Creamer, footed (ILLUS.) 24.00
Goblet 20.00
Pitcher, water 45.00
Relish, 7½" oval 12.00
Salt & pepper shakers w/original
    tops, pr. 35.00
Sauce dish, flat or footed ..... 6.50 to 9.00
Spooner 20.00
Sugar bowl, cov. 35.00
Wine 35.00

DIAMOND POINT

Bar bottle, flint 55.00
Bowl, 8½" d., flint 95.00
Butter dish, cov., flint 85.00
Castor set, 4-bottle, flint, w/silver-
    plate frame 600.00
Celery vase, pedestal base w/knob
    stem, flint 65.00
Champagne, flint 75.00
Claret, flint 130.00
Compote, open, 6" d., high stand,
    flint .... 65.00 to 100.00
Creamer, applied handle,
    flint .... 100.00 to 130.00
Decanter w/original stopper, qt. 70.00
Decanter w/bar lip, qt. ...... 65.00 to 85.00
Egg cup, cov., clambroth, flint 550.00
Egg cup, canary yellow, flint 210.00
Egg cup, clambroth, flint 115.00
Egg cup, flint 37.50
Egg cup, chartreuse opaque, flint ... 425.00
Goblet, flint 50.00
Goblet, non-flint 20.00
Honey dish, flint 16.50
Honey dish, coarse points,
    non-flint 7.00
Pitcher, tankard, applied handle,
    flint, qt. 170.00
Pitcher, water, bulbous, flint 160.00
Plate, 6" d., non-flint 13.50
Salt dip, cov., master size 27.50
Sauce dish, non-flint, 3½" to
    5½" d. .... 6.00 to 12.50
Spillholder, flint 45.00
Spooner, flint 40.00
Spooner, non-flint 26.00
Sugar bowl, cov., flint 95.00
Sugar bowl, cov., non-flint 30.00
Tumbler, flint 47.50
Tumbler, bar, flint 65.00
Wine, flint 47.50
Wine, non-flint 10.00

DIAMOND POINT WITH PANELS - See Hino-to Pattern

DIAMOND QUILTED

Bowl, 6" d. 12.50
Bowl, 6" d., turquoise blue 12.50

Bowl, 7" d., amber 17.50
Bowl, 7" d., vaseline 22.00
Bowl, 8" d., amber 38.00
Bowl, 8" d., vaseline 30.00
Bowl, 9" d., amber 50.00
Butter dish, cov., amber ..... 42.00 to 50.00
Butter dish, cov., vaseline 75.00
Celery vase, amber 40.00
Celery vase, vaseline 40.00
Champagne 21.50
Champagne, turquoise blue 30.00
Compote, cov., 8" d., 13" h.,
    amber 95.00
Compote, cov., 8" d., 13" h. 75.00
Compote, open, 6" d., 6" h.,
    amber 25.00
Compote, open, 7" d., low stand,
    amber 17.50
Compote, open, 7" d., high stand,
    amber 18.50
Compote, open, 7" d., high stand,
    vaseline 38.00
Compote, open, 8" d., low stand,
    amber 19.50
Compote, open, 9" d., low stand,
    amber 22.00
Creamer, amber 38.00
Creamer & sugar bowl, amber, pr. ... 85.00
Goblet, amethyst 35.00
Goblet, blue 32.50
Goblet, vaseline 35.00
Mug, amber 20.00
Mug, amethyst 30.00

Diamond Quilted Mugs

Mug, each (ILLUS. of pr.) 15.00
Pitcher, water, amber 57.50
Pitcher, water, blue 80.00
Pitcher, water, vaseline 75.00
Relish, amber, 7½ x 4½" 10.00
Relish, leaf-shaped, amber,
    9 x 5½" 13.50
Relish, leaf-shaped, vaseline,
    9 x 5½" 22.00
Relish, leaf-shaped, vaseline,
    12 x 10" 28.00
Salt dip, vaseline 16.00
Salt shaker w/original top, blue
    (single) 35.00
Sauce dish, flat or footed, amber ... 7.00
Sauce dish, flat or footed,
    amethyst .... 12.00 to 18.00
Sauce dish, flat or footed, turquoise
    blue .... 8.00 to 15.00

Sauce dish, flat or footed,
  vaseline . . . . .12.00 to 18.00
Spooner, amber 30.00
Spooner, turquoise blue 40.00
Spooner, vaseline 32.00
Sugar bowl, cov., blue 43.50
Sugar bowl, cov., vaseline 60.00
Sugar bowl, open, turquoise blue . . . 30.00
Sugar bowl, open, vaseline 30.00
Tray, water, cloverleaf-shaped,
  amber, 12 x 10" . . . . .22.00 to 30.00
Tray, water, cloverleaf-shaped,
  vaseline, 12 x 10" 28.00
Tumbler, juice, amber 20.00
Tumbler, vaseline 25.00
Wine, amber 25.00
Wine, blue 38.00
Wine 12.50
Wine, vaseline 26.00

DIAMOND THUMBPRINT

Diamond Thumbprint Spooner

Butter dish, cov. 200.00
Carafe 115.00
Celery vase 325.00
Champagne 350.00
Compote, open, 7" d., 4½" h., ex-
  tended scalloped rim 60.00
Compote, open, 8" d., 6" h. 75.00
Compote, open, 10½" d., 7½" h. . . . 285.00
Creamer, applied handle . .165.00 to 200.00
Cup plate 50.00
Goblet 325.00
Lamp, whale oil, original burner,
  brass stem, marble base 265.00
Pitcher, water 575.00
Punch bowl, scalloped rim, pedestal
  base, 11½" d., 9 1/8" h. 425.00
Salt dip, master size 45.00
Sauce dish . . . . .11.00 to 20.00
Spillholder 40.00
Spillholder, vaseline 875.00
Spooner (ILLUS.) 90.00
Sugar bowl, cov. 125.00
Tumbler 95.00
Tumbler, whiskey, handled 300.00
Wine 245.00

DINNER BELL - See Cottage Pattern

DORIC - See Feather Pattern

DOUBLE LEAF & DART - See Leaf & Dart Pattern

DOUBLE LOOP - See Ribbon Candy Pattern

DOUBLE WEDDING RING (Wedding Ring)

Double Wedding Ring Footed Tumbler

Champagne 90.00
Goblet 65.00
Sauce dish 25.00
Tumbler, bar 90.00
Tumbler, footed (ILLUS.) 80.00
Wine 95.00

DRAPERY

Drapery Spooner

Butter dish, cov. 40.00
Cake plate, square, footed . . .40.00 to 45.00
Creamer, applied handle 37.50
Egg cup 21.00
Goblet 27.50
Goblet, buttermilk 28.00
Pitcher, water, applied handle 75.00
Plate, 6" d. 19.00
Sauce dish, flat 10.00
Spooner (ILLUS.) 29.00

Sugar bowl, cov.	40.00
Sugar bowl, open	25.00
Tumbler	27.00
Water set, pitcher & 6 tumblers, 7 pcs.	275.00 to 325.00

EGG IN SAND

Egg in Sand Pitcher

Bread tray, handled	32.50
Butter dish, cov.	48.00
Creamer	25.00
Goblet	25.00
Pitcher, milk (ILLUS.)	45.00
Pitcher, water, amber	70.00
Pitcher, water	50.00
Relish, 9 x 5½"	17.00
Sauce dish	12.00
Spooner, amber	47.50
Spooner	25.00
Sugar bowl, cov.	37.50
Tray, water, 12½" oblong	38.50
Tumbler	36.00

EGYPTIAN

Egyptian Spooner

Berry set, master bowl & 5 sauce dishes, 6 pcs.	150.00
Bowl, 8½" d.	48.00
Bread platter, Cleopatra center, 12 x 9"	45.00 to 57.50
Bread platter, Salt Lake Temple center	295.00
Butter dish, cov.	67.50
Celery vase	77.50
Compote, cov., 8" d., high stand, sphinx base	200.00
Compote, open, 6" d., low stand	50.00
Compote, open, 7½" d., sphinx base	65.00
Creamer	43.00
Goblet	43.50
Pickle dish	20.00
Pitcher, water	145.00 to 175.00
Plate, 10" d.	46.50
Plate, 12" d.	75.00
Relish, 8½ x 5½"	22.50
Sauce dish, flat or footed	14.00 to 27.50
Spooner (ILLUS.)	35.00
Sugar bowl, cov.	67.50
Sugar bowl, open	35.00
Table set, 4 pcs.	195.00

EMERALD GREEN HERRINGBONE - See Paneled Herringbone Pattern

EMPIRE COLONIAL - See Colonial Pattern

ENGLISH HOBNAIL CROSS - See Amberette Pattern

ESTHER

Esther Sauce Dish

(Items may be plain or with etched designs)

Butter dish, cov.	70.00
Butter dish, cov., amber-stained	110.00
Butter dish, cov., green	135.00
Celery vase	70.00
Celery vase, green	135.00
Compote, open, 5" d., 6½" h., green	57.50
Cookie jar, cov., amber-stained	225.00
Creamer	70.00
Creamer, green	135.00
Creamer & cov. sugar bowl, in-dividual size, pr.	95.00
Cruet w/ball-shaped stopper, green	245.00
Cruet w/original stopper, miniature	28.00
Cruet w/original stopper, green, miniature	95.00

Goblet	50.00
Goblet, green	90.00
Goblet, ruby-stained, souvenir	55.00
Pitcher, water, green	150.00
Plate, 10¼" d.	27.50
Relish, 8 x 4½"	21.00
Relish, green, 8½ x 4½"	22.50
Relish, green, 11 x 5½"	45.00
Salt & pepper shakers w/original tops, green, pr.	98.00
Sauce dish (ILLUS.)	17.00
Spooner	40.00
Spooner, green	55.00 to 75.00
Sugar bowl, cov.	40.00
Sugar bowl, cov., green	60.00
Table set, green, 4 pcs.	475.00
Toothpick holder	40.00
Toothpick holder, green	70.00
Tray, ice cream, green	145.00
Tumbler	35.00
Tumbler, green	48.00
Water set: pitcher & 5 tumblers; green, 6 pcs.	310.00
Wine	32.50

EUREKA

Bowl, 9" oval	30.00
Bread tray	28.00
Compote, open, jelly	55.00
Compote, open, jelly, ruby-stained	75.00
Creamer	45.00
Creamer, ruby-stained	65.00
Egg cup	15.00
Goblet	28.00
Salt dip, master size	25.00
Salt & pepper shakers w/original tops, ruby-stained, pr.	48.00
Spooner	40.00
Sugar bowl, cov.	55.00
Sugar bowl, open	25.00
Toothpick holder	35.00
Toothpick holder, ruby-stained	85.00
Tumbler, footed	25.00
Wine	30.00

EXCELSIOR

Bar bottle, pt.	35.00 to 50.00
Bar bottle, flint, qt.	65.00
Butter dish, cov.	100.00
Cake stand, flint, 9¼" h.	150.00
Candlestick, flint (single)	96.00
Castor set, 4-bottle, non-flint, w/pewter frame	65.00
Celery vase, flint	80.00
Claret, non-flint	16.00
Cordial	35.00
Creamer	55.00
Egg cup	30.00
Egg cup, double	35.00
Egg cup, double, fiery opalescent, flint	225.00
Flip glass, 8" h.	200.00
Goblet, "Barrel"	40.00
Goblet, flint (ILLUS.)	50.00

Excelsior Goblet

Mug	25.00
Pickle jar, cov.	56.50
Pitcher, water, flint	325.00
Salt dip, master size	18.50
Spillholder, flint	75.00
Sugar bowl, cov.	75.00
Syrup pitcher, applied handle	110.00
Syrup pitcher w/original top, green	750.00
Tumbler, bar, flint, 3½" h.	52.50
Tumbler, footed, flint	47.50
Wine, flint	65.00 to 80.00

EYEWINKER

Eyewinker Salt Shaker

Banana boat, flat, 8½" l.	85.00
Bowl, master berry or fruit, 9" sq., 4½" h.	65.00 to 75.00
Butter dish, cov.	60.00 to 75.00
Cake stand, 8½" to 9½" d.	75.00
Celery vase, 6½" h.	55.00
Compote, cov., 6½" d., 11" h.	49.00
Compote, open, 4" d., 5" h., scalloped rim	31.50

Compote, open, 6½" sq., 8½" h. . . .	70.00
Compote, open, 7½" d., 4½" h.	37.50
Compote, open, 9½" d., 6½" h.	90.00
Cookie jar, cov.	125.00
Creamer	45.00
Creamer, miniature	50.00
Creamer & cov. sugar bowl, pr.	100.00
Lamp, kerosene-type, w/original burner, 9½" h.	125.00
Pitcher, water	85.00
Plate, 9" sq., 2" h., turned-up sides	32.50
Salt shaker w/original top (ILLUS.) . .	32.50
Sauce dish, square	12.00
Spooner	35.00
Sugar bowl, cov.	55.00
Syrup pitcher w/silverplate top	125.00
Tumbler	24.00

FEATHER (Doric, Indiana Swirl or Finecut & Feather)

Feather Cake Stand

Banana boat, footed	75.00
Berry set, master bowl & 6 sauce dishes, 7 pcs.	120.00
Bowl, 7" oval . . . . 15.00 to	25.00
Bowl, 8½" oval, flat	25.00
Butter dish, cov.	55.00
Butter dish, cov., green	125.00
Cake stand, 8½" d. (ILLUS.)	35.00
Cake stand, 9½" d.	50.00
Cake stand, green, 9½" d.	175.00
Cake stand, 11" d. . . . . 75.00 to	90.00
Celery vase	32.50
Compote, cov., 8½" d., high stand	125.00
Compote, open, jelly, 5" d., 4¾" h.	28.00
Compote, open, 8" d., low stand . . .	40.00
Cordial	70.00
Creamer	36.00
Cruet w/original stopper . . . . . 45.00 to	55.00
Cruet w/original stopper, green	185.00
Doughnut stand, 8" w., 4½" h.	38.00
Goblet	52.50
Goblet, amber-stained	150.00
Honey dish, 3½" d. . . . . 9.00 to	15.00
Pitcher, milk	42.50
Pitcher, water . . . . 45.00 to	60.00

Pitcher, water, green	190.00
Plate, 10" d. . . . . 35.00 to	45.00
Relish, 8¼" oval	18.00
Relish, amber-stained, 8¼" oval	45.00
Salt shaker w/original top (single) . .	25.00
Sauce dish, flat or footed . . . . . 8.50 to	12.00
Spooner	25.00
Spooner, green	60.00
Sugar bowl, cov.	38.00
Sugar bowl, open, large	22.00
Syrup pitcher w/original top	100.00
Table set, 4 pcs.	125.00
Toothpick holder . . . . 45.00 to	60.00
Toothpick holder, green	185.00
Tumbler	46.00
Wine	32.50

FESTOON

Festoon Cake Stand

Berry set, 9½" d. master bowl & 6 sauce dishes, 7 pcs.	70.00
Bowl, 7 x 4½" rectangle	22.50
Bowl, berry, 9 x 5½" rectangle	32.50
Butter dish, cov.	48.00
Cake stand, high pedestal, 9" d. (ILLUS.)	45.00
Cake stand, high pedestal, 10" d. . . .	42.50
Compote, open, 9" d., high stand . . .	58.00
Creamer . . . . 22.50 to	35.00
Finger bowl, 4½" d., 2" h.	30.00
Marmalade jar, cov.	37.50
Pickle castor, silverplate frame & cover w/bird finial	85.00
Pitcher, water	68.00
Plate, 8" d.	27.50
Plate, 9" d.	22.50
Relish, 7 x 4"	15.00
Sauce dish	6.00
Spooner	30.00
Sugar bowl, cov.	55.00
Table set, 4 pcs.	185.00
Tray, water, 10" d. . . . . 25.00 to	35.00
Tumbler	25.00
Waste bowl	45.00
Water set, pitcher, tray & 4 tumblers, 6 pcs. . . . . 195.00 to	250.00

FINECUT

Finecut Salt & Pepper Shakers

Bowl, master berry, w/silverplate stand & spoon	95.00
Bread tray, amber	40.00
Butter dish, cov.	45.00
Cake stand	30.00
Celery vase, vaseline, ornate square silverplate holder	115.00
Compote, cov., 9¼" d., 7" h., amber	135.00
Creamer, blue	37.50
Creamer	18.00
Cruet w/matching stopper, amber	165.00
Goblet, amber	45.00
Goblet, blue	55.00
Goblet	17.50
Pickle dish, 9 x 6"	12.00
Pitcher, water, amber	80.00
Pitcher, water	40.00
Plate, 6" d., blue	20.00
Plate, 6" d.	10.00
Plate, 6" d., vaseline	22.50
Plate, 7" d., amber	22.50
Plate, 7" d.	20.00
Plate, 10" d.	18.00
Salt & pepper shakers w/original tops, pr. (ILLUS.)	25.00
Sauce dish, vaseline	18.00
Spooner, amber	35.00
Spooner	17.00
Sugar bowl, cov.	35.00
Toothpick holder, hat shape on plate, amber	22.00
Toothpick holder, hat shape on plate, blue	28.50
Toothpick holder, hat shape on plate, vaseline	30.00
Tray, water	45.00
Tumbler	15.00
Tumbler, vaseline	28.00
Waste bowl, vaseline	32.50
Whimsey, shoe on skate, amber	30.00
Whimsey, slipper, blue, 4" l.	35.00
Wine	14.00

FINECUT & BLOCK

Butter dish, cov., 2-handled	75.00
Cake stand	35.00

Celery tray, blue, 11" l.	65.00
Celery tray, 11" l.	27.50
Celery tray, clear w/blue blocks, 11" l.	60.00
Celery tray, clear w/pink blocks, 11" l.	60.00

Finecut & Block Celery Tray

Celery tray, clear w/yellow blocks (ILLUS.)	65.00
Champagne, clear w/blue blocks	85.00
Compote, open, jelly, blue	50.00
Compote, open, jelly	18.00
Compote, open, jelly, clear w/amber blocks	75.00
Compote, open, jelly, clear w/blue blocks	50.00
Compote, open, 8" d., 6½" h.	32.50
Compote, open, 8" d., clear w/blue blocks	65.00
Compote, open, 8" d., 4¼" h., clear w/yellow blocks	45.00
Cordial	85.00
Creamer	33.00
Creamer, clear w/amber blocks	67.00
Creamer, clear w/blue blocks	70.00
Creamer, clear w/pink blocks	75.00
Creamer, clear w/yellow blocks	76.50
Egg cup, single	27.50
Egg cup, double	29.00
Goblet, amber	50.00
Goblet	32.50
Goblet, clear w/blue blocks	65.00
Goblet, clear w/pink blocks	50.00
Goblet, buttermilk	25.00
Goblet, buttermilk, clear w/pink blocks	80.00
Goblet, buttermilk, clear w/yellow blocks	60.00
Ice cream tray, clear w/amber blocks	85.00
Pitcher, water, amber	85.00
Pitcher, water	42.50
Pitcher, water, clear w/amber blocks	85.00
Pitcher, water, clear w/blue blocks	90.00
Pitcher, water, clear w/pink blocks	125.00
Pitcher, water, clear w/yellow blocks	85.00
Plate, 5¾" d.	23.50
Relish, handled, clear w/yellow blocks, 7½"	140.00
Salt dip, clear w/blue blocks	20.00
Salt dip, clear w/pink blocks	20.00
Sauce dish, blue	14.50

Sauce dish	8.50
Sauce dish, clear w/amber blocks	20.00
Spooner	30.00
Spooner, clear w/amber blocks	45.00
Spooner, clear w/blue blocks	55.00
Sugar bowl, cov., clear w/yellow blocks	125.00
Table set, clear w/yellow blocks, 4 pcs.	265.00
Tumbler, amber	22.50
Tumbler, blue	30.00
Tumbler	17.50
Tumbler, clear w/pink blocks	40.00
Tumbler, clear w/yellow blocks	50.00
Waste bowl, amber	45.00
Waste bowl, clear w/yellow blocks	95.00
Wine	25.00
Wine, clear w/blue blocks	55.00

FINECUT & DIAMOND - See Diamond Medallion Pattern

FINECUT & FEATHER - See Feather Pattern

FINECUT & PANEL (Paneled Finecut)

Finecut & Panel Plate

Bowl, 8" oval, amber	18.50
Bowl, 8" oval	18.00
Bread tray, amber, 13 x 9"...35.00 to	50.00
Bread tray, blue, 13 x 9"	45.00
Bread tray, 13 x 9"	30.00
Butter dish, cov., amber	65.00
Cake stand, vaseline	55.00
Compote, open, high stand, amber	47.50
Compote, open, high stand, blue	65.00
Compote, open, high stand	32.00
Creamer, amber	35.00
Goblet, amber	40.00
Goblet	20.00
Goblet, clear w/amber bars..35.00 to	50.00
Pitcher, water amber	85.00
Plate, 6" d., amber (ILLUS.)	25.00
Plate, 6" d., blue	30.00
Plate, 6" d.	14.00

Plate, 6" d., vaseline	25.00
Plate, 7" d.	11.00
Relish, 7 x 3½"	22.50
Salt shaker w/original top (single)	10.00
Sauce dish, amber	11.00
Sauce dish	8.00
Sauce dish, vaseline	13.50
Spooner, vaseline	30.00
Tray, water, blue	55.00
Tumbler	18.00
Tumbler, vaseline	38.00
Wine, amber	30.00
Wine, blue	35.00
Wine	15.00
Wine, vaseline	35.00
Wine set: decanter & 4 wines; vaseline, 5 pcs.	185.00

FINECUT BAND - See Cottage Pattern

FINE RIB

Butter dish, cov.	75.00
Castor set, complete w/frame	190.00
Celery vase, flint	42.00
Celery vase, cut ovals, flint	115.00
Champagne, flint	75.00
Champagne, cut ovals, flint	85.00
Compote, open, 10¼" d., 8¼" h., scalloped foot, flint	185.00
Cordial, flint	40.00
Creamer, flint, 6" h.	325.00
Decanter w/bar lip, qt.	95.00
Egg cup, single, flint	42.00
Egg cup, double, flint	35.00
Goblet, flint	75.00
Goblet, cut ovals, flint	195.00
Honey dish, flint, 3½" d.	14.00
Pitcher, water, bulbous, applied handle, flint	425.00
Salt dip, individual size, flint	14.00
Salt dip, master size, footed, scalloped rim, flint	30.00
Sauce dish, non-flint	7.50
Spoonholder, flint	52.50
Sugar bowl, cov., flint	95.00
Tumbler, flint	75.00
Tumbler, whiskey, handled, flint, 3" h.	85.00
Tumbler, whiskey, non-flint	32.50
Wine, flint	42.50

FISHSCALE

Fishscale Pickle Dish

Berry set, 8½" d. master bowl & 8
sauce dishes, 9 pcs. 85.00
Bowl, cov., 8½" d. 35.00
Bowl, cov., 9½" d. 40.00
Bowl, 8" d. 18.00
Bowl, 9½" d. 22.00
Bread platter 26.00
Butter dish, cov. 45.00
Cake stand, 8", 9" or 10" d. . .30.00 to 36.00
Celery vase 27.50
Compote, cov., 7½" d. 45.00
Compote, open, jelly . . . . .15.00 to 25.00
Compote, open, 9" d., high stand . . . 45.00
Condiment tray, rectangular 35.00
Creamer 27.50
Goblet 25.00
Lamp, kerosene, hand-type w/finger
grip 65.00
Mug 30.00
Pickle dish (ILLUS.) 18.50
Pitcher, milk 27.50
Pitcher, water 42.50
Plate, 7" d. 15.00
Plate, 8" d. 22.00
Plate, 9" sq. 26.00
Relish, 8½ x 5" 17.00
Salt shaker w/original top (single) . . 27.50
Sauce dish, flat or footed . . . . .7.50 to 12.00
Spooner 22.50
Sugar bowl, cov. 36.50
Tray, water, round 35.00
Tumbler 45.00

**FLORIDA - See Paneled Herringbone
Pattern**

FLORIDA PALM

Florida Palm Creamer

Cake stand, 9½" d. 25.00
Celery vase 18.00
Compote, cov., 7" d., high stand . . . 50.00
Compote, open, 9" d. 35.00
Creamer (ILLUS.) 18.50
Goblet 22.50
Plate, 9" d. 15.00

Relish 12.00
Spooner 20.00
Sugar bowl, cov. 35.00
Tumbler, footed 28.00
Wine 23.50

FLOWER FLANGE - See Dewey Pattern

FLOWER POT (Potted Plant)

Flower Pot Sugar Bowl

Bread tray 45.00
Butter dish, cov. 40.00
Cake stand, 10½" d. 45.00
Compote, open, 7¼" h. 18.00
Creamer 30.00
Creamer, vaseline 45.00
Goblet 40.00
Pitcher, milk 40.00
Pitcher, water 58.00
Salt shaker w/original top (single) . . 20.00
Sauce dish 9.00
Sugar bowl, cov. (ILLUS.) 37.50
Spooner 22.00
Spooner, vaseline 45.00

FLUTE

Flute Decanter

Ale glass	50.00
Bar bottle, qt.	70.00
Bar bottle, blue, flint, qt.	250.00
Celery vase	80.00
Compote, open, 8¼" d., 3" h.	35.00
Decanter w/bar lip & original pewter-rimmed glass stopper, amethyst, flint (ILLUS.)	600.00
Egg cup, single	20.00
Egg cup, single, handled	65.00
Egg cup, double	24.00
Goblet, Bessimer Flute	20.00
Goblet, Brooklyn Flute	35.00
Goblet, Connecticut or New England Flute	17.50
Goblet	22.50
Mug, applied handle	39.50
Tumbler, 6 panels, cobalt blue	100.00
Tumbler, jelly glass shape, 3½" h.	16.00
Tumbler, whiskey, handled	27.50
Whiskey shot glass, footed	25.00
Wine, New England Flute	20.00
Wine, Pittsburgh Flute	45.00

FLYING ROBIN - See Hummingbird Pattern

FOUR PETAL

Four Petal Sugar Bowl

Creamer & cov. sugar bowl, pr.	155.00
Sugar bowl, cov. (ILLUS.)	75.00
Sugar bowl, open	45.00

FOUR PETAL FLOWER - See Delaware Pattern

FROSTED CIRCLE

Bowl, 6" d.	28.00
Bowl, 8" d., 3¼" h.	25.00
Butter dish, cov.	45.00
Cake stand, 9½" d.	37.50
Celery tray	20.00
Compote, cov., 5" d., 9" h.	43.50
Compote, open, 7" d., 6" h.	25.00
Compote, open, 9" d., 6" h.	32.50

Frosted Circle Compote

Compote, open, 10" d., high stand, scalloped rim (ILLUS.)	57.50
Creamer	35.00
Cruet w/original stopper	40.00
Goblet	32.50
Pitcher, water, tankard	75.00
Plate, 9" d.	22.00
Punch cup	15.00
Relish, 8 x 4½"	20.00
Salt shaker w/original top (single)	35.00
Sauce dish	10.00
Spooner	25.00 to 35.00
Sugar bowl, cov.	47.50
Sugar shaker w/original top	48.00
Syrup pitcher w/original top	110.00
Table set, 4 pcs.	145.00
Tumbler	30.00
Wine	32.50

FROSTED LEAF

Celery vase	140.00
Creamer	395.00
Egg cup	90.00
Goblet	80.00
Salt dip	50.00
Sauce dish	22.50
Spooner	65.00
Tumbler, footed	95.00

FROSTED LION (Rampant Lion)

Frosted Lion Bread Plate

(Items may be plain or with etched designs)

Bowl, cov., 7 7/16 x 4 5/8" oblong,
collared base 110.00
Bowl, cov., 8 7/8 x 5½" oblong, col-
lared base...................... 125.00
Bowl, open, oval 73.00
Bread plate, rope edge, closed han-
dles, 10½" d. (ILLUS.) 85.00
Butter dish, cov., rampant lion
finial...................100.00 to 125.00
Celery vase..................... 75.00
Compote, cov., 5" d., 8½" h........ 150.00
Compote, cov., 6¾" oval, 7" h., collared base, rampant lion
finial..................165.00 to 245.00
Compote, cov., 7" d., 11" h., lion
head finial 165.00
Compote, cov., 7¾" oval, low col-
lared base, rampant lion
finial..................100.00 to 125.00
Compote, cov., 8" d., 13" h., ram-
pant lion finial.........145.00 to 195.00
Compote, cov., 8½ x 7¾" oval, low
collared base, rampant lion
finial....................85.00 to 120.00
Compote, cov., 8¾ x 5½" oval,
8¼" h., rampant lion finial....... 110.00
Compote, cov., 10" d., collared
base, rampant lion finial 95.00
Compote, open, 7" d., 6¼" h....... 45.00
Compote, open, 7¾" d., high
stand 60.00
Creamer 60.00
Egg cup 65.00
Goblet 60.00
Marmalade jar, cov., rampant lion
finial...................85.00 to 110.00
Paperweight, embossed "Gillinder &
Sons, Centennial" 110.00
Pickle dish..................... 60.00
Pitcher, water 285.00
Platter, 10½ x 9" oval, lion
handles 80.00
Salt dip, cov., master size, collared
base, rectangular 225.00
Sauce dish, 4" to 5" d........15.00 to 30.00
Spooner 55.00
Sugar bowl, cov., rampant lion
finial...................60.00 to 75.00
Syrup pitcher w/original top 300.00
Wine, 4 1/8" h...........125.00 to 150.00

FROSTED RIBBON
Bowl, low 22.00
Bread platter 32.50
Butter dish, cov. 45.00
Celery vase.................... 40.00
Champagne.................... 100.00
Cologne bottle w/stopper 45.00
Compote, cov., 8" d., 11" h....... 85.00
Compote, open, 10" d., high stand.. 40.00
Creamer 35.00
Goblet 22.50

Pitcher, water 65.00
Salt dip, individual size 5.00
Salt dip, master size.............. 8.50
Sauce dish..................... 9.50
Spooner 28.00
Sugar bowl, cov. 42.50
Tray, water.................... 95.00
Waste bowl, 4½" d., 3½" h........ 45.00

FROSTED ROMAN KEY (Roman Key With Flutes or Ribs)

Frosted Roman Key Creamer & Goblet

Bowl, 9¾" d., 3½" h. 42.50
Butter dish, cov. 55.00
Celery vase.................... 75.00
Champagne.................... 77.50
Compote, cov., 7" d. 75.00
Compote, open, 6½" d........... 78.00
Cordial 45.00
Creamer, applied handle (ILLUS.
left).......................... 56.00
Egg cup 45.00
Goblet (ILLUS. right)........38.00 to 45.00
Goblet, buttermilk 42.50
Salt dip, master size............ 32.00
Sauce dish..................... 14.00
Spooner 27.50
Sugar bowl, cov. 82.50
Tumbler, bar................... 85.00
Tumbler, footed................ 70.00
Wine....................55.00 to 65.00

FROSTED STORK
Bowl, 9" oval, 101 border 50.00
Bread plate, round 50.00
Butter dish, cov. 70.00
Creamer 62.50
Finger bowl.................... 90.00
Goblet 58.00
Pickle castor w/original frame 195.00
Platter, 12 x 8" oval 45.00
Platter, deer & doe border 75.00
Relish, 101 border 58.00
Sauce dish..................... 32.00
Spooner 55.00
Sugar bowl, cov., stork finial 95.00
Tray, water, 15½ x 11" 125.00
Waste bowl.................... 40.00

FROSTED WAFFLE - See Hidalgo Pattern

GALLOWAY (Mirror or Virginia)

Basket, twisted handle,
8½ x 5 x 10" 75.00
Berry set, master bowl & 4 sauce
dishes, 5 pcs. 48.50
Bowl, 5¼ x 3½" rectangle 10.00
Bowl, 6½" d. 17.50
Bowl, 7¼" d., 3½" h. 19.50
Bowl, 9¾" d., flat 35.00
Bowl, ice cream, 11" d., 3½" h. 45.00
Butter dish, cov. 57.50
Butter dish, cov., ruby-stained 110.00
Cake stand, 9¼" d., 6" h. ...50.00 to 70.00
Carafe 75.00
Celery vase..................... 27.50
Celery vase, ruby-stained 75.00
Champagne...................... 35.00
Compote, open, 4¼" d., 6" h....... 30.00
Compote, open, 10" d., 8" h., scal-
loped rim...................... 55.00
Creamer 20.00
Creamer, individual size 15.00
Creamer & cov. sugar bowl, etched,
pr.............................. 95.00
Cruet w/stopper 36.00
Cruet, no stopper 25.00
Finger bowl, 6" d................. 22.00
Goblet 85.00
Mug, 4½" d...................... 40.00
Olive dish, 6 x 4" ....16.50 to 25.00
Olive dish, ruby-stained, 6 x 4"..... 30.00
Pickle castor w/silverplate lid &
frame 125.00
Pitcher, lemonade, applied handle .. 70.00
Pitcher, milk 40.00
Pitcher, water, 9" h..........50.00 to 70.00
Pitcher, water, ruby-stained 125.00
Pitcher, child's 22.50
Pitcher, child's, ruby-stained 85.00
Plate, 6½" d. 20.00
Plate, 8" d. 20.00
Punch bowl, 14" d. 145.00
Punch cup ....6.50 to 10.00
Relish, 8¼" l.................... 15.00
Relish, ruby-stained 30.00
Salt dip, master size, scalloped rim,
2" d........................... 25.00
Salt & pepper shakers w/original
tops, gold trim, 3" h., pr. 35.00
Sauce dish, flat or footed .....8.50 to 20.00
Spooner 25.00
Spooner, amber-stained........... 35.00
Sugar bowl, cov. 42.50
Sugar shaker w/original top 37.50
Syrup pitcher w/metal spring top ... 57.50
Syrup pitcher w/metal spring top,
ruby-stained 135.00
Toothpick holder 25.00
Tumbler 22.50
Vase, 8" h. 25.00
Vase, 9½" h..................... 30.00
Vase, 12" h. 27.50
Vase, 14" h. 20.00
Waste bowl..................... 25.00

Water set, pitcher & 6 tumblers,
7 pcs.......................... 220.00
Water set, child's, pitcher & 4 tumblers, 5 pcs. 50.00
Wine........................... 42.50

GARFIELD DRAPE

Garfield Drape Goblet

Bread plate, "We Mourn Our Na-
tion's Loss," 11½" d. 50.00
Butter dish, cov. 59.00
Cake stand, 9½" d. 47.50
Celery vase, pedestal base........ 45.00
Compote, cov., 6" d., low stand 50.00
Compote, cov., 8" d., 12½" h....... 125.00
Creamer 35.00
Goblet (ILLUS.).............28.00 to 35.00
Lamp, kerosene-type, cobalt blue,
9" h........................... 150.00
Pitcher, milk 57.50
Pitcher, water 65.00
Plate, 10" d., star center.......... 60.00
Sauce dish, flat or footed .....7.50 to 10.00
Spooner 27.50
Sugar bowl, cov. 60.00
Tumbler 30.00

GEORGIA - See Peacock Feather Pattern

GIANT BULL'S EYE

Cheese dish, cov. 45.00
Goblet 60.00
Wine........................... 25.00

GOBLETS WITH BIRDS & ANIMALS

Bear climber, etched 95.00
Bird in Swamp 65.00
Deer & Doe w/lily-of-the-valley,
pressed ....95.00 to 110.00
Dog w/rabbit in mouth, etched 65.00
Ibex, etched 62.50
Ostrich Looking at Moon, pressed .. 75.00
Owl-Possum, pressed 80.00
Pigs in Corn, pressed 350.00
Squirrel, pressed 300.00
Stork & Flowers, etched 55.00

GODDESS OF LIBERTY - See Ceres Pattern

GOOD LUCK - See Horseshoe Pattern

GOOSEBERRY

Gooseberry Compote

Butter dish, cov. 50.00
Compote, cov., 7" d. (ILLUS.) 70.00
Creamer 28.00
Goblet 25.00
Mug 26.00
Sauce dish....................... 8.00
Spooner 18.00
Sugar bowl, open 40.00
Tumbler, bar..................... 30.00
Tumbler, water ....22.00 to 30.00

GOTHIC

Gothic Egg Cup

Bowl, master berry or fruit, flat 70.00
Butter dish, cov. 85.00
Castor bottle.................... 18.00
Castor set, 5-bottle, w/pewter
    frame 125.00

Celery vase...................... 90.00
Champagne....................... 165.00
Compote, open, 8" d., 4" h........ 65.00
Creamer, applied handle.......... 90.00
Egg cup (ILLUS.).................. 42.50
Goblet 60.00
Sauce dish....................... 14.00
Spooner 45.00
Sugar bowl, cov. 80.00
Tumbler 95.00
Wine, 3¾" h. 135.00

GRAND - See Diamond Medallion Pattern

GRAPE & FESTOON

Grape & Festoon Spooner

Butter dish, cov., stippled leaf...... 50.00
Celery vase, stippled leaf ....30.00 to 45.00
Compote, cov., 8" d., high stand,
    acorn finial, stippled leaf 115.00
Compote, open, 8" d., low stand ... 75.00
Creamer, stippled leaf 47.50
Egg cup, stippled leaf 30.00
Goblet, stippled leaf ....25.00 to 36.50
Goblet, buttermilk stippled leaf 33.00
Goblet, veined leaf................ 25.00
Pitcher, water, stippled leaf........ 97.50
Plate, 6" d., stippled leaf 17.50
Relish, stippled leaf 6.00
Salt dip, footed, stippled leaf....... 24.00
Sauce dish, flat, stippled leaf,
    4" d. 8.00
Sauce dish, flat, veined leaf........ 12.50
Spooner, stippled leaf (ILLUS.) 24.00
Spooner, veined leaf 22.50
Sugar bowl, cov., stippled leaf 50.00
Sugar bowl, open, stippled leaf..... 25.00

GRAPE & FESTOON WITH SHIELD

Compote, cov., 8" d., low stand 39.50
Creamer, applied handle.......... 35.00
Goblet, w/shield & grapes 26.00
Goblet, w/American shield 47.50
Mug, 1 7/8" h.................... 16.50
Mug, cobalt blue, 2½" h. 27.50
Mug, 3¼" h..................... 18.50

Pitcher, water, applied handle 65.00
Relish, 7 x 4¼" 16.50
Sauce dish, flat or footed .....6.00 to 12.00
Spooner 26.50

GRASSHOPPER (Locust)

(Items may be plain or with etched designs)

Berry set, footed master bowl & 11
   sauce dishes, 12 pcs. 127.00
Bowl, cov., 7" d. 27.50
Bowl, open, 7" d., footed 20.00
Butter dish, cov. 50.00
Butter dish, cov., w/insect 55.00
Celery vase, w/insect 62.50
Compote, cov., 8¼" d. 52.50
Creamer ....25.00 to 35.00
Goblet, w/insect, amber 85.00
Goblet, w/insect 32.50
Pitcher, water 72.50
Plate, 8½" d., footed 20.00
Sauce dish, footed 8.00
Sauce dish, footed, w/insect 15.00
Spooner 45.00
Spooner, w/insect ....40.00 to 50.00
Sugar bowl, cov., w/insect 55.00
Sugar bowl, open, w/insect 42.00

GREEK KEY (Heisey's Greek Key)
Butter dish, cov. 125.00
Celery tray, 9" l. 38.00
Compote, open, jelly, 5" d., low
   stand 28.00
Goblet ....70.00 to 90.00
Humidor, cov. 285.00
Ice tub, small 95.00
Lamp, kerosene-type, miniature 75.00
Nut dish, individual size 22.00
Pitcher, tankard, 1½ qt. 225.00
Punch bowl & pedestal base, 2 pcs. . 250.00
Punch cup 15.00
Punch set, bowl, base & 12 cups,
   14 pcs. 425.00
Salt dip, master size 20.00
Sauce dish 20.00
Sherbet 22.50
Soda fountain (straw-holder) jar 128.00
Tumbler 75.00

GUARDIAN ANGEL - See Cupid & Venus Pattern

HAIRPIN (Sandwich Loop)
Bowl, 5½" hexagon 100.00
Bowl, 6¼" d. 100.00
Bowl, 8¼" d., 1½" h. 300.00
Celery vase, emerald green,
   11" h. 450.00
Champagne 85.00
Compote, open, 8" d., 4¼" h. 85.00
Compote, open, 9½" d., 9" h., milk
   white 225.00
Egg cup 17.50

Egg cup, fiery opalescent 75.00
Goblet ....35.00 to 50.00
Pitcher, 8" h. 175.00
Plate, 6¼" d. 100.00
Plate, 7" d. 120.00
Salt dip, cov. 85.00
Salt dip, master size 20.00
Spooner 36.50
Spooner, fiery opalescent 175.00
Sugar bowl, cov. 95.00
Tumbler 45.00
Tumbler, whiskey, handled........ 45.00
Wine, flint 55.00

HALLEY'S COMET

Halley's Comet Goblet

Celery vase 32.50
Goblet (ILLUS.) 40.00
Jar, cov., 3-footed 49.00
Pitcher, water 98.00
Relish, 7 x 4½" 15.00
Spooner ....40.00 to 55.00
Tumbler 26.00
Wine ....15.00 to 25.00

HAMILTON

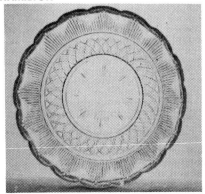

Hamilton Sauce Dish

Bar bottle, qt. 135.00
Butter dish, cov. 80.00
Cake stand 175.00
Compote, open, 7" d., low stand ... 46.00
Compote, open, 8" d., 8" h. 70.00
Creamer 65.00
Egg cup 32.50
Goblet 45.00
Pitcher, water ....225.00 to 335.00
Salt dip, footed 30.00
Sauce dish (ILLUS.) 12.00
Spooner 35.00
Sugar bowl, cov. 125.00
Tumbler, bar...................... 65.00
Tumbler, water 80.00
Tumbler, whiskey, applied handle .. 90.00
Wine 90.00

HAMILTON WITH LEAF
Butter dish, cov., frosted leaf 80.00
Compote, open, 6" d., 4½" h. 78.00
Creamer, frosted leaf............. 55.00
Egg cup, clear leaf 55.00
Egg cup, frosted leaf 65.00
Goblet, clear leaf 50.00
Goblet, frosted leaf 55.00
Lamp, kerosene-type, brass stem,
  marble base, blue, 9" h. 320.00
Spooner, clear leaf 30.00
Sugar bowl, cov., clear leaf 90.00
Sweetmeat dish, cov., clear leaf.... 90.00
Tumbler, clear leaf 55.00
Tumbler, frosted leaf 125.00
Tumbler, bar, frosted leaf......... 125.00
Tumbler, whiskey, handled, clear
  leaf 100.00
Wine 70.00

HAND (Pennsylvania, Early)
Bowl, 9" d. 36.50
Bread plate, 10½ x 8" oval 30.00
Butter dish, cov. 75.00
Cake stand 55.00
Celery vase...................... 40.00
Compote, cov., 8" d., high stand ... 92.50
Compote, open, 7¾" d., 6¾" h. ... 42.50
Compote, open, 9" d., low stand ... 27.50
Cordial 85.00
Creamer 37.50
Creamer, child's.................. 45.00
Goblet 40.00
Marmalade jar, cov................ 48.00
Mug 45.00
Pitcher, water 75.00
Sauce dish, 4½" d. 12.00
Sugar bowl, cov. 67.50
Wine 35.00

HARP
Goblet, flared sides 650.00
Goblet, straight sides............. 250.00
Lamp, kerosene, hand-type w/ap-
  plied finger grip 195.00
Spillholder (ILLUS.) 67.50

Harp Spillholder

HEART WITH THUMBPRINT
Banana boat, 7½ x 6½" 85.00
Banana boat, 11 x 6½" 75.00
Barber bottle w/original pewter
  stopper 125.00
Berry set, master bowl & 6 sauce
  dishes, 7 pcs................... 110.00
Bowl, 8" d., 2" h., flared rim 25.00

Heart with Thumbprint Bowl

Bowl, 10" d., scalloped rim
  (ILLUS.).................... 41.50
Butter dish, cov. 75.00
Carafe 55.00
Card tray 27.50
Card tray, green 45.00
Celery vase...................... 37.50
Creamer 30.00
Creamer, individual size 22.50
Creamer & open sugar bowl, in-
  dividual size, pr. 35.00
Creamer & open sugar bowl, in-
  dividual size, green w/gold, pr. .. 80.00
Cruet w/original stopper 65.00
Goblet 50.00
Ice bucket 57.50
Lamp, kerosene-type, 8" h. 112.00
Lamp, kerosene-type, green, 9" h... 117.00
Mustard jar w/silverplate cover 95.00
Nappy, heart-shaped 30.00
Olive dish, handled, green 42.50
Pitcher, water 50.00
Plate, 6" d. 22.50
Plate, 10" d. 35.00
Plate, 12" d. 45.00

Powder jar w/silverplate cover	45.00
Punch cup	17.50
Relish, w/gold	17.50
Rose bowl, 3¾" d.	22.50
Rose bowl, 5" d.	32.50
Salt shaker w/original top (single) . .	50.00
Salt & pepper shakers w/original tops, pr.	95.00
Sauce dish . . . . .10.00 to	17.00
Sauce dish, green	32.00
Spooner	40.00
Sugar bowl, cov., large	45.00
Sugar bowl, open	22.50
Sugar bowl, open, individual size, pewter rim	17.50
Sugar bowl, open, individual size, green w/gold	45.00
Syrup jug w/original pewter top	125.00
Tray, 8 1/8 x 4 1/8"	25.00
Tumbler, water	40.00
Tumbler, water, ruby-stained	115.00
Vase, 6" h., trumpet-shaped	26.50
Vase, 6" h., green	47.50
Vase, 7" h., green	55.00
Vase, 8" h.	35.00
Vase, 10" h., trumpet-shaped	45.00
Water set, carafe & 6 tumblers, 7 pcs.	265.00
Wine	45.00

HEARTS OF LOCH LAVEN - See Shuttle Pattern

HERCULES PILLAR (Pillar Variant)

Hercules Pillar Cordial

Butter dish, cov.	32.00
Celery vase	47.00
Cordial, 3¾" h. (ILLUS.)	38.00
Egg cup, double	27.50
Goblet	27.50
Syrup jug w/original top, blue	140.00
Tumbler	45.00
Whiskey taster	13.50
Wine	35.00

HERRINGBONE (Herringbone with Star & Shield Motif)

Celery vase	30.00
Creamer	22.00
Goblet	22.50
Salt dip, master size	14.00
Sauce dish	10.50
Spooner	20.00
Sugar bowl, cov.	24.00

HERRINGBONE BAND

Egg cup	18.50
Goblet	13.00
Sauce dish, 4" sq.	9.50
Spooner, pedestal base, scalloped rim	21.00
Sugar bowl, open	15.00
Wine	20.00

HICKMAN (Le Clede)

Hickman Relish

Banana stand	65.00
Bowl, 5" d., green w/gold	8.00
Bowl, 7" sq.	15.00
Bowl, 7 x 6", green w/gold	25.00
Bowl, 8" d.	18.00
Bowl, 10" d., green	16.00
Butter dish, cov.	37.50
Cake stand, 8½" to 9½" d. . .25.00 to	35.00
Celery dish, boat-shaped, green	25.00
Champagne	21.50
Compote, cov., 5" d.	36.00
Compote, cov., 7" d., high stand	55.00
Compote, open, jelly, green	16.00
Compote, open, 7½" d., 5½" h.	19.50
Compote, open, 8" d., 6½" h.	32.50
Compote, open, 9½" d., 8" h.	45.00
Condiment set: salt & pepper shakers & cruet w/original stopper on cloverleaf-shaped tray; miniature, 4 pcs.	100.00
Creamer, green	22.50
Creamer & open sugar bowl, individual size, oval, green, pr.	38.00
Cruet w/ball-shaped stopper	42.50
Doughnut stand, scalloped rim, 8" d.	45.00
Goblet	28.00

Goblet, green w/gold	35.00
Ice tub	47.50
Pickle dish, green	15.00
Pitcher, water	60.00
Punch cup	7.50
Punch cup, green	15.00
Punch set, punch bowl & 13 cups, 14 pcs.	125.00
Relish, 4" sq. (ILLUS.)	14.00
Relish, 5½" l.	15.00
Relish, green	15.00
Rose bowl	27.50
Salt shaker w/original top (single)	9.50
Sauce dish	7.00
Sauce dish, green	10.00
Spooner	22.50
Sugar bowl, cov.	38.00
Sugar bowl, cov., green	45.00
Sugar shaker w/original top	40.00
Table set, w/gold, 4 pcs.	175.00
Toothpick holder	55.00
Tumbler	25.00
Vase, 10" h.	38.50
Vase, 10½" h., purple	45.00
Vase, 12½" h.	26.00
Water set: pitcher & 6 tumblers; w/gold, 7 pcs.	225.00
Wine	25.00
Wine, green	30.00

HIDALGO (Frosted Waffle)

Hidalgo Compote

(Items may be plain or with etched deigns)

Bowl, salad, 11" sq.	22.00
Butter dish, cov.	45.00
Celery dish, boat-shaped, 13" l.	50.00
Celery vase	32.50
Compote, open, 7" d. (ILLUS.)	20.00
Creamer	27.50 to 40.00
Cruet w/original stopper	60.00
Egg cup	30.00
Goblet	13.00 to 18.00
Pitcher, water	50.00
Relish, shell-shaped	8.00 to 15.00

Sauce dish, handled	10.50
Spooner	33.50
Sugar bowl, cov.	35.00
Sugar shaker w/original top	45.00
Syrup pitcher w/original top	70.00
Tray, water	55.00
Tumbler	15.00

HINOTO (Diamond Point with Panels)

Hinoto Creamer

Butter dish, cov.	90.00
Celery vase	42.50
Champagne	75.00
Creamer, applied handle (ILLUS.)	75.00
Egg cup, handled	23.00
Goblet	45.00
Pitcher, tankard, 9" h., applied handle	110.00
Spooner	38.00
Sugar bowl, cov.	50.00
Tumbler, footed	40.00
Tumbler, whiskey, handled, footed	45.00
Wine	57.50

HOBNAIL

Hobnail Mug

(Also see Hobnail under OPALESCENT GLASS)

Barber bottle, applied rigaree at
    neck, blue 90.00
Bowl, 7½" d., ruffled rim, blue 35.00
Butter dish, cov., amber 35.00
Cake stand, pedestal base, square . . 85.00
Celery vase, footed,
    vaseline . . . . 70.00 to 95.00
Cologne bottle, 6½" h. 22.00
Compote, 6" h., fluted rim, blue 55.00
Creamer, fluted top, applied handle,
    amber, 3 x 2" 17.50
Creamer, 3-footed, blue 35.00
Creamer, scalloped & ornamented
    top, 6" h. 45.00
Cruet w/original stopper, 4½" h. . . . 45.00
Goblet, amber 27.50
Goblet, blue 26.00
Goblet 15.00
Hat shape, 10" d., 6" h. 49.00
Lamp, kerosene, hand-type w/finger
    grip 48.00
Lamp, kerosene, hand-type w/finger
    grip, opaque white w/amber foot
    & handle, 4¼" d., 6" h. 110.00
Mayonnaise dish, cov. 12.00
Mug, amber (ILLUS.) . . . . 22.50 to 35.00
Mug 15.00
Pitcher, 7½" h., amber 45.00
Pitcher, 8" h., flat base, blue 195.00
Pitcher, 8" h., square top 60.00
Punch cup 22.50
Rose bowl, 6" d., 5½" h. 85.00
Salt dip, master size, amber 16.00
Salt & pepper shakers w/original
    tops, sapphire blue, pr. 27.50
Sauce dish, square, ruby-stained . . . 45.00
Spooner, ruffled rim, amber 32.00
Spooner, ruffled rim, canary
    yellow 38.00
Spooner 26.50
Sugar shaker w/original top 42.50
Syrup pitcher w/original top 72.00
Toothpick holder, amber 30.00
Toothpick holder, blue 25.00
Toothpick holder, vaseline 32.50
Tray, water, blue, 11½" d. 50.00
Tumbler, amber 35.00
Tumbler, 10-row, blue 31.00
Tumbler, 10-row 25.00
Tumbler, 10-row, Rubina Frosted . . . 95.00
Tumbler, ruby-stained 45.00
Tumbler, vaseline 46.50
Vase, 3¾" h., 4¼" widest d., squat,
    cranberry 79.00
Wine, amber 20.00
Wine, blue 25.00
Wine 20.00

HOBNAIL WITH FAN

Bowl, 6" d. 20.00
Bowl, 7" d., blue (ILLUS.) 47.50
Celery vase 38.00
Creamer, blue 20.00
Goblet 30.00

Hobnail with Fan Bowl

Sauce dish 8.00
Spooner, blue 45.00

HOBNAIL WITH THUMBPRINT BASE

Butter dish, cov. 55.00
Butter dish, cov., child's, amber 95.00
Creamer, amber 37.50
Creamer, blue 45.00
Creamer, child's, blue 23.00
Finger bowl, scalloped rim, blue 45.00
Pitcher, 7" h. 24.00
Pitcher, 7" h., ruby-stained rim 57.50
Pitcher, 8" h., amber 90.00
Pitcher, 8" h., blue 72.50
Spooner, blue 45.00
Sugar bowl, cov. 35.00
Table set, vaseline, 4 pcs. 255.00
Waste bowl, amber 40.00

HONEYCOMB

Honeycomb Footed Tumbler

Ale glass 42.00
Barber bottle w/pewter top 45.00
Butter dish & cover w/knob finial,
    flint 60.00
Butter dish, cov., non-flint 40.00
Cake stand, 10½" d. 35.00
Candlesticks, cobalt blue, flint,
    9½" h., pr. 575.00
Celery vase, flint 32.50
Celery vase, Laredo Honeycomb,
    flint 35.00

Celery vase, New York Honeycomb,
non-flint 18.00
Celery vase, Vernon Honeycomb,
flint, 9" h. 65.00
Champagne, flint............38.00 to 50.00
Compote, cov., 6½" d., 8½" h.,
flint.......................... 80.00
Compote, cov., 9¼" d., 11½" h.,
flint.......................... 90.00
Compote, open, 7" d., 7" h., flint ... 55.00
Compote, open, 8¾" d., 7" h., non-
flint.......................... 45.00
Compote, open, 11" d., 8" h., flint .. 125.00
Cordial, flint, 3¼" h. 25.00
Creamer, applied handle, flint...... 30.00
Decanter w/bar lip, flint, 10½" h. .. 75.00
Decanter w/original stopper, flint,
13" h......................... 150.00
Egg cup 18.00
Finger bowl, flint.................. 45.00
Goblet, flint 22.50
Goblet, non-flint 13.00
Goblet, Banded Vernon
Honeycomb 22.00
Goblet, Barrel Honeycomb w/knob
stem 14.50
Mug 30.00
Pitcher, water, 8½" h., molded han-
dle, polished pontil, flint 100.00
Pitcher, water, 9" h., applied han-
dle, flint...................... 90.00
Pomade jar, cov., flint 48.00
Relish 30.00
Salt dip, pedestal base, flint 35.00
Sauce dish, flint.................. 11.00
Spillholder, flint.................. 22.00
Spooner, flint 33.50
Spooner, non-flint 20.00
Sugar bowl, cov., flint 75.00
Sugar bowl, open, scalloped rim 35.00
Syrup pitcher w/pewter top, flint ... 126.50
Tumbler, bar..................... 25.00
Tumbler, footed, flint (ILLUS.) 28.00
Tumbler, Vernon Honeycomb, flint .. 55.00
Tumbler, whiskey, footed, handled,
flint.......................... 45.00
Tumbler, whiskey, Vernon
Honeycomb 125.00
Vase, 7½" h., 4" d., Vernon Honey-
comb, flint.................... 45.00
Vases, 10¼" h., Vernon Honey-
comb, flint, pr.................. 150.00
Wine, flint 25.00
Wine, non-flint 12.50

HORN OF PLENTY

Bar bottle w/pewter pour spout,
8" 135.00
Bowl, 9 x 6¼" oval............... 145.00
Butter dish, cov. 145.00
Butter dish & cover w/Washington's
head finial 1,100.00
Celery vase...................... 150.00
Champagne...................... 160.00

Compote, cov., 6¼" d., 7½" h...... 175.00
Compote, cov., 8¼" oval, 5¾" h.... 350.00
Compote, open, 7" d., 3" h........ 125.00
Compote, open, 8" d., low stand ... 55.00

Horn of Plenty Compote

Compote, open, 8" d., 8" h.
(ILLUS.) 120.00
Compote, open, 9" d., 8½" h....... 200.00
Creamer, applied handle, 5½" h.... 235.00
Creamer, applied handle, 7" h...... 135.00
Decanter w/original stopper, pt..... 135.00
Decanter w/original stopper, qt..... 125.00
Dish, low foot, 7¼" d............. 85.00
Dish, low foot, 8" d............... 95.00
Egg cup, 3¾" h. 37.50
Goblet 80.00
Honey dish 17.50
Lamp, w/whale oil burner, 11" h.... 175.00
Peppersauce bottle w/stopper 170.00
Pitcher, water 575.00
Plate, 6" d. 65.00
Relish, 7 x 5" oval 65.00
Salt dip, master size, oval 125.00
Sauce dish.................12.50 to 20.00
Spillholder 65.00
Spooner 45.00
Sugar bowl, cov. ....85.00 to 130.00
Tumbler, bar..................... 70.00
Tumbler, water, 3 5/8" h. 95.00
Tumbler, whiskey, 3" h. 100.00
Tumbler, whiskey, handled........ 235.00
Wine............................ 135.00

HORSESHOE (Good Luck or Prayer Rug)

Horseshoe Bread Tray

Bowl, cov., 8 x 5" oval, flat, triple
   horseshoe finial 195.00
Bowl, open, 7" d., footed 29.00
Bowl, open, 8 x 5" oval, footed 37.50
Bread tray, single horseshoe han-
   dles (ILLUS.) 32.50
Bread tray, double horseshoe
   handles 45.00
Butter dish, cov. 50.00
Cake stand, 8", 9" or 10" d. . . 48.00 to 65.00
Celery vase . . . . 45.00 to 65.00
Cheese dish, cov., w/woman churn-
   ing butter in base 225.00
Compote, cov., 8" d., 9" h. 100.00
Compote, cov., 8" d., 11" h. 125.00
Compote, open, 4" h. 24.00
Compote, open, 8" d., 7¾" h. 35.00
Creamer 33.50
Creamer, individual size 38.50
Doughnut stand 57.50
Goblet, knob stem 36.00
Goblet, plain stem 28.50
Marmalade jar, cov. 97.50
Pitcher, milk 85.00
Pitcher, water . . . . 62.50 to 85.00
Plate, 7" d. 30.00
Plate 10" d. 50.00
Relish, 8 x 5" 12.50
Relish, 9 x 5½" 21.50
Salt dip, individual size 18.50
Salt dip, master size, horseshoe
   shape 90.00
Sauce dish, flat or footed . . . . . 8.50 to 18.00
Spooner 23.50
Sugar bowl, cov. 50.00
Sugar bowl, open 16.00
Sugar shaker w/original top 29.00
Waste bowl, 4" d., 2½" h. 55.00
Wine 145.00

HUBER

Huber Compote

(Items may be plain or with etched designs)

Celery vase 38.50
Champagne, barrel-shaped 25.00
Champagne, straight sides 40.00
Claret 27.00

Compote, open, 7" d. 55.00
Compote, open, 8" d. (ILLUS.) 75.00
Cordial . . . . 25.00 to 50.00
Creamer 80.00
Egg cup, single 16.50
Egg cup, double 30.00
Goblet 20.00
Goblet, barrel-shaped 12.50
Goblet, buttermilk 16.50
Mug 22.50
Salt dip, master size 17.50
Spooner 20.00
Sugar bowl, cov. 57.50
Tumbler, bar 22.50
Tumbler, water 20.00
Vase 18.50
Wine 18.00

HUMMINGBIRD (Flying Robin or Bird & Fern)

Butter dish, cov. 48.00
Celery vase, amber 72.50
Celery vase 35.00
Compote, open, 7" d. 48.00
Creamer, amber 52.50
Creamer, blue 50.00
Creamer 30.00
Goblet, amber 57.50
Goblet, blue 60.00
Goblet 30.00
Pitcher, milk, amber 65.00
Pitcher, milk, blue 120.00
Pitcher, milk 47.50
Pitcher, water, amber 125.00
Pitcher, water, blue 120.00
Pitcher, water 85.00
Sauce dish 12.00
Sugar bowl, cov. 55.00
Spooner, amber 40.00
Spooner, blue 50.00
Spooner 30.00
Tray, water, amber 175.00
Tray, water, blue 125.00
Tumbler, amber 55.00
Tumbler 32.50
Tumbler, bar, amber 45.00
Waste bowl 35.00
Water set: pitcher & 6 tumblers;
   amber, 7 pcs. 350.00

HUNDRED EYE

Compote, open, 5" d., low stand . . . 15.00
Creamer 18.50
Goblet 14.50
Mug, blue 25.00
Wine 9.00

ILLINOIS

Basket, applied reeded handle,
   11½ x 7" 140.00
Bowl, 5¼" sq. 25.00
Butter dish, cov., 7" sq. (ILLUS.) 60.00
Candlestick (single) 70.00
Celery tray 40.00

Illinois Butter Dish

Compote, open	145.00
Creamer, large	30.00
Cruet w/original stopper	40.00
Cruet w/replaced stopper	35.00
Marmalade jar in silverplate frame w/spoon, 3 pcs.	135.00
Pitcher, water, tankard	50.00 to 65.00
Pitcher, water, silverplate rim, green	80.00
Plate, 7" sq.	20.00
Relish, 8½ x 3"	11.50
Salt dip, individual size	12.50
Salt & pepper shakers w/original tops, pr.	35.00
Sauce dish	15.00
Soda fountain (straw-holder) jar, cov., 12½" h.	180.00
Soda fountain (straw-holder) jar, cov., green, 12½" h.	300.00
Spooner	27.50
Sugar bowl, cov.	50.00
Sugar bowl, open	35.00
Sugar bowl, cov., individual size	30.00
Syrup pitcher w/original pewter top	95.00
Toothpick holder	27.50
Vase, 5¾" h.	25.00
Vase, 9" h., 4" d.	40.00

INDIANA

Butter dish, cov.	75.00
Creamer	25.00
Sugar bowl, open	23.00

INDIANA SWIRL - See Feather Pattern

INVERTED FAN

Butter dish, cov.	57.50
Cake stand	475.00
Champagne	115.00
Compote, open, 8" d.	55.00
Creamer, applied handle	122.00
Egg cup	27.50
Goblet	36.50
Honey dish, 4" d.	18.00
Salt dip, master size, footed	38.00
Spooner	32.50

Inverted Fern Sugar Bowl

Sugar bowl, cov. (ILLUS.)	70.00
Tumbler	95.00
Wine	55.00

INVERTED LOOPS & FANS - See Maryland Pattern

IOWA (Paneled Zipper or Zippered Block)

Bowl, 9" d., 5½" h., ruby-stained	135.00
Carafe, water	35.00
Carafe, water, ruby-stained	60.00
Compote, 8½" d., high stand	95.00
Creamer, ruby-stained	65.00
Cruet w/original stopper	52.50
Nappy, handled	10.00
Olive dish	16.00
Punch cup	14.00
Salt & pepper shakers w/original tops, pr.	35.00
Salt & pepper shakers w/original tops, ruby-stained, pr.	55.00
Sauce dish, flat	7.50
Spooner	16.50
Sugar bowl, cov., ruby-stained	75.00
Sugar bowl, cov., small	20.00
Toothpick holder	20.00
Tumbler	20.00
Tumbler, ruby-stained	37.50
Vases, gold trim, pr.	18.00
Wine	27.50

IRISH COLUMN - See Broken Column Pattern

IVY IN THE SNOW

Butter dish, cov.	50.00
Cake stand, 8" to 10" d.	30.00 to 45.00
Cake stand, amber-stained ivy sprigs, 10" sq.	125.00

Celery vase, 8" h.	27.50
Compote, cov., 8" d., 13" h.	60.00
Compote, open, jelly	25.00
Creamer	17.50
Creamer, ruby-stained ivy sprigs	65.00
Goblet	25.00
Pitcher, water	47.50
Plate, 7" d.	17.50
Plate, 10" d.	22.50
Relish	20.00

Ivy in Snow Sauce Dish

Sauce dish, (flat or) footed (ILLUS.)	12.00
Spooner	30.00
Syrup jug w/original top	70.00
Tumbler	22.50
Wine	32.50

JACOB'S LADDER (Maltese)

Jacob's Ladder Compote

Bowl, 7¼" d., footed	30.00
Bowl, 8½ x 5½" oval, flat	18.00
Bowl, 10" d., flat	25.00
Butter dish, cov., Maltese Cross finial	60.00
Cake stand, 8" to 12" d.	30.00 to 52.50
Castor set, cruet w/original Maltese Cross stopper, salt & pepper shakers & mustard jar w/original tops & pewter frame, 5 pcs.	200.00
Celery vase	37.50
Cologne bottle w/original Maltese Cross stopper, footed	125.00

Compote, cov., 6½" d., 10¼" h. (ILLUS.)	60.00
Compote, cov., 9½" d., high stand	165.00
Compote, open, 7" d., low stand	30.00
Compote, open, 7" d., high stand	39.00
Compote, open, 9" d., low stand	38.00 to 50.00
Compote, open, 9½" d., high stand	45.00 to 68.00
Creamer	36.00
Cruet w/original stopper, footed	85.00 to 110.00
Goblet	62.50
Marmalade jar, cov.	85.00
Pickle castor, complete w/stand	135.00
Pickle dish, Maltese Cross handle, blue	65.00
Pickle dish, Maltese Cross handle	15.00
Pitcher, water, applied handle	155.00
Plate, 6" d.	26.00
Relish, Maltese Cross handles, 10 x 5½"	13.50
Salt dip, master size, footed	22.50
Sauce dish, flat or footed	7.50 to 10.00
Spooner	32.50
Sugar bowl, cov.	43.50
Sugar bowl, open	28.00
Syrup jug w/pewter top	85.00
Tumbler, bar	75.00
Wine	32.50

JEWEL & DEWDROP (Kansas)

Bowl, 8½" d.	37.50
Bread tray, "Our Daily Bread," 10½" oval	48.50
Butter dish, cov.	65.00
Cake stand, 8" to 10" d.	50.00 to 68.00
Cake tray, "Cake Plate," 10½" oval	60.00 to 75.00
Celery vase	38.00
Compote, cov., 6" d., high stand	67.50
Compote, open, 6" d.	23.50
Creamer	38.00
Dish, cov., 4½" d.	45.00
Goblet	47.50
Mug, child's, 3½" h.	17.00
Mug	14.00
Pitcher, milk	70.00
Pitcher, water	46.50
Plate, 7" sq.	15.00
Relish, 8½" oval	17.50
Salt shaker w/original top (single)	45.00
Sauce dish, 4" d.	12.00
Sugar bowl, cov.	65.00
Syrup jug w/original top	125.00
Toothpick holder	42.50
Tumbler, water, footed	55.00
Wine	50.00 to 65.00
Wine, ruby-stained w/gilt trim	70.00

JEWEL & FESTOON (Loop & Jewel)

Butter dish, cov.	35.00

Champagne	42.00
Creamer	24.00
Creamer, individual size	32.00
Dish, 5½" sq.	7.50
Goblet	16.50
Punch cup	18.00
Sauce dish	12.00
Spooner	29.00
Sugar bowl, cov.	32.50

Jewel & Festoon Sugar Bowl

Sugar bowl, open, individual size (ILLUS.)	25.00
Toothpick holder	30.00
Vase, 8¾" h.	40.00
Wine	30.00

JEWEL BAND (Scalloped Tape)

Jewel Band Creamer

Bowl, cov., 8" rectangle	35.00
Bread platter	35.00 to 45.00
Cake stand, 9½" d.	32.50
Celery vase, 8" h.	20.00
Compote, cov., 8¼" d., 12" h.	38.50
Creamer (ILLUS.)	30.00
Egg cup	20.00
Goblet	17.50
Pitcher, water, 9¼" h.	39.00
Relish, 7" l.	9.50
Sauce dish, flat or footed	8.00 to 10.00
Sugar bowl, cov.	30.00
Wine	18.00

JEWELED MOON & STAR (Moon & Star with Waffle)

Bowl, 6¾" d., flat	13.50
Cake stand, 8½" d.	29.50

Cake stand, w/amber & blue staining, 8½" d.	125.00
Carafe	42.50
Compote, open, 9" d., 8" h.	40.00
Creamer, w/amber & blue staining	47.50
Goblet	37.50
Pitcher, water, bulbous, applied handle	140.00
Salt shaker w/original top (single)	20.00
Salt shaker w/original top, w/amber & blue staining (single)	27.00
Sauce dish	8.50
Sauce dish, w/amber & blue staining	19.50
Spooner, w/amber & blue staining	48.00
Sugar bowl, cov., w/amber & blue staining	78.00 to 100.00
Tumbler	22.50
Wine	23.50

JOB'S TEARS - See Art Pattern

JUMBO and JUMBO & BARNUM

Jumbo Spoon Rack

Butter dish & cover w/frosted elephant finial, oblong	550.00
Butter dish & cover w/frosted elephant finial, round	450.00
Compote, cov., 12" h., frosted elephant finial	325.00 to 475.00
Creamer	125.00 to 195.00
Creamer, w/Barnum head at handle	250.00
Goblet	700.00
Match holder	40.00
Pitcher, water, w/elephant in base	695.00
Spoon rack (ILLUS.)	600.00 to 900.00
Sugar bowl w/Barnum head handles & cover w/frosted elephant finial	475.00
Toothpick holder, "Baby Mine"	70.00

KAMONI - See Balder Pattern

KANSAS - See Jewel & Dewdrop Pattern

KENTUCKY

Cake stand, 9½" d.	37.50
Cruet w/original stopper	35.00
Nappy, handled	10.00
Pitcher, water	55.00
Plate, 7" sq.	17.50
Punch cup, green	16.00
Sauce dish, footed, blue w/gold	16.00
Sauce dish, footed	6.50
Sauce dish, footed, green	12.50
Spooner	35.00
Sugar bowl, cov.	30.00
Toothpick holder	26.50
Toothpick holder, green	110.00
Tumbler, green	21.50
Wine	22.50
Wine, green	45.00

KING'S CROWN (Also see Ruby Thumbprint)

King's Crown Mustard

Banana stand	50.00
Bowl, 9¼" oval, scalloped rim, round base	40.00
Butter dish, cov.	37.50
Cake stand, 10" d.	45.00
Castor set, pepper, mustard & cruet w/stopper, w/handled frame	78.00
Celery vase	40.00
Compote, cov., 6" d., 6" h.	85.00
Compote, open, jelly	27.50
Compote, open, 7½" d., high stand	45.00
Compote, open, 8½" d., high stand	67.50
Compote, open, 9" d., low stand	38.50
Cordial	48.00
Creamer	40.00
Creamer, individual size	18.50
Creamer, green	75.00
Creamer, individual size, green	60.00
Cup & saucer	55.00
Goblet	27.50

Goblet, w/green thumbprints	21.50
Lamp, kerosene-type, stem base, 10" h.	135.00
Mustard jar, cov. (ILLUS.)	48.00
Pitcher, tankard, 8½" h.	75.00
Pitcher, tankard, 13" h.	95.00
Pitcher, bulbous	115.00
Plate, 7" d.	20.00
Punch bowl, footed	275.00
Punch cup	18.00
Salt dip, individual size	10.00
Salt dip, master size, footed	22.50
Salt & pepper shakers w/original tops, pr.	55.00
Sauce dish, boat-shaped	20.00
Sauce dish, round	7.50
Spooner	40.00 to 50.00
Toothpick holder	25.00
Tumbler, amber	38.00
Tumbler, blue	75.00
Tumbler	25.00
Water set, bulbous pitcher & 6 goblets, 7 pcs.	225.00
Wine	24.00

KLONDIKE - See Amberette Pattern

KOKOMO (Bar & Diamond)

Bowl, 8½" d., footed	22.50
Butter dish, cov., pedestal base	30.00
Cake stand	40.00
Celery vase	35.00
Compote, cov., 7½" d., low stand	28.00
Compote, open, 8½" d., low stand	15.00
Creamer, applied handle	40.00
Cruet w/stopper	22.50
Decanter	65.00
Goblet	25.00
Pitcher, water, bulbous, ruby-stained	95.00
Pitcher, water, tankard	40.00
Salt & pepper shakers w/original tops, pr.	45.00
Sauce dish, footed	7.50
Spooner	22.50
Sugar bowl, cov.	45.00
Syrup pitcher w/original top	55.00
Wine	26.00

LACY MEDALLION - See Colorado Pattern

LATTICE (Diamond Bar)

Bread plate, "Waste Not - Want Not," 10" d.	40.00
Cake stand, 8" d., 5" h.	38.00
Cake stand, 12½" d.	48.00
Compote, cov., 7½" d., high stand	50.00
Cordial	28.00
Creamer	35.00
Goblet	27.50
Pitcher, water	40.00
Plate, 6" d.	12.00

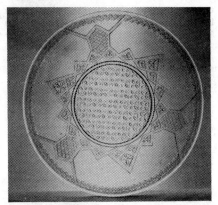

Lattice Plate

Plate, 7" d. (ILLUS.)	15.00
Spooner	25.00
Sugar bowl, cov.	30.00
Syrup pitcher w/original tin top	70.00
Wine	20.00

LEAF - See Maple Leaf Pattern

LEAF & DART (Double Leaf & Dart)

Leaf & Dart Tumbler

Bowl, 8¼" d., low foot	25.00
Butter dish, cov., pedestal base	85.00
Celery vase, pedestal base	35.00
Creamer, applied handle	35.00
Cruet w/original stopper	110.00
Egg cup	20.00
Goblet	30.00
Goblet, buttermilk	35.00
Lamp, kerosene-type, applied handle	75.00
Pitcher, milk	125.00
Pitcher, water, applied handle	95.00
Relish	18.00
Salt dip, cov., master size	68.00
Salt dip, open, master size	25.00
Sauce dish	8.50
Spooner	22.50

Sugar bowl, cov.	45.00
Sugar bowl, open	20.00
Tumbler, footed (ILLUS.)	26.00
Water set, pitcher & 5 footed tumblers, 6 pcs.	290.00
Wine	32.50

LE CLEDE - See Hickman Pattern

LIBERTY BELL

Liberty Bell Goblet

Bread platter, "John Hancock," shell handles, 11½ x 7 1/8"	150.00
Bread platter, shell handles, without John Hancock signature, 11½ x 7 1/8"	170.00
Bread platter, "John Hancock," shell handles, milk white, 11½ x 7 1/8"	295.00
Bread platter, "John Hancock," twig handles, milk white, 13½ x 9½"	235.00
Bread platter, "Signer's," twig handles	85.00 to 125.00
Butter dish, cov.	110.00 to 140.00
Butter dish, cov., miniature	150.00
Compote, open, 6" d.	95.00
Creamer, applied handle	80.00 to 125.00
Goblet (ILLUS.)	60.00
Mug, snake handle	375.00
Pickle dish, closed handles, 1776-1876, w/thirteen original states, 9¼ x 5½" oval	50.00
Pitcher, water	550.00 to 850.00
Plate, 6" d., closed handles, scalloped rim, w/thirteen original states	80.00
Plate, 6" d., no states, dated	60.00
Plate, 8" d., closed handles, scalloped rim, w/thirteen original states	75.00
Plate, 10" d., closed handles, scalloped rim, w/thirteen original states	95.00
Platter, 13 x 8¼", twig handles, w/thirteen original states	90.00

Relish, shell handles, 11¼ x 7".....	65.00
Salt dip	35.00
Sauce dish.....................	25.00
Spooner	80.00
Sugar bowl, cov...........95.00 to	125.00
Sugar bowl, open	50.00
Table set, 4 pcs.	450.00

LILY-OF-THE-VALLEY

Lily-of-the-Valley Sauce Dish

Butter dish, cov.	70.00
Celery vase....................	50.00
Compote, cov., 8½" d., high stand	85.00
Compote, open, 8½" d., 5" h.	42.50
Creamer, 3-footed, molded handle ..	80.00
Creamer, plain base, applied handle	60.00
Cruet w/original stopper	80.00
Egg cup	35.00
Goblet	48.00
Honey dish	12.00
Pickle dish......................	12.00
Pitcher, milk, applied handle	85.00
Pitcher, water, bulbous, applied handle ....85.00 to	125.00
Relish, 8 x 5½"	18.00
Salt dip, cov., master size, 3-footed	125.00
Salt dip, open, master size, 3-footed	27.50
Sauce dish (ILLUS.)	10.00
Spooner	35.00
Sugar bowl, cov., 3-footed	80.00
Sugar bowl, open, plain base	50.00
Tumbler, flat....................	9.50
Tumbler, footed	55.00
Wine	130.00

LINCOLN DRAPE & LINCOLN DRAPE WITH TASSEL

Celery vase.....................	90.00
Compote, open, 7½" d., 3½" h.	52.00
Compote, open, 8" d., medium stand	65.00
Creamer	200.00
Egg cup	42.50
Goblet	70.00

Goblet w/tassel..................	130.00
Lamp, kerosene-type, miniature	125.00
Salt dip, master size..............	35.00

Lincoln Drape Sauce Dish

Sauce dish, 4" d. (ILLUS.)	20.00
Spillholder......................	52.50
Spooner	52.50
Sugar bowl, cov.	92.50
Sugar bowl, open	85.00
Syrup pitcher w/original pewter top	120.00
Syrup pitcher w/original top, opaque white	650.00
Wine	55.00

LION (Square Lion's Head or Atlanta)

Bowl, 6½ x 4¼" oblong, flat	55.00
Bowl, 8 x 5" oblong, flat	60.00
Bread plate, "Give Us....," 12" sq. ....55.00 to	75.00
Butter dish, cov.	85.00
Butter dish, cov., miniature	110.00
Cake stand	75.00
Celery vase.....................	60.00
Cheese dish, cov...............	175.00
Compote, cov., 5" sq., 6" h........	85.00
Compote, cov., 7" sq., high stand...	150.00
Compote, open, 4¼" sq., 4" h.	45.00
Compote, open, 6" sq., 7½" h.	57.50
Compote, open, 8" sq., high stand ..	75.00
Creamer	40.00
Creamer, miniature	95.00
Cup & saucer, miniature	62.50
Dish, cov., oblong	85.00
Goblet	55.00
Pitcher, water	110.00
Platter, handled.................	80.00
Relish, boat-shaped	35.00
Salt shaker w/original top (single) ..	45.00
Sauce dish......................	23.00
Spooner	55.00
Sugar bowl, cov.	95.00
Sugar bowl, cov., miniature	78.00
Syrup pitcher w/original top	240.00
Toothpick holder	42.50
Tumbler	45.00

LION, FROSTED - See Frosted Lion Pattern

LION & BABOON
Sauce dish	30.00
Spooner	85.00

LION'S LEG - See Alaska Pattern

LOCUST - See Grasshopper Pattern

LOG CABIN

Log Cabin Pattern

Butter dish, cov. (ILLUS. front)	250.00
Compote, cov. (ILLUS. center	
rear)	295.00 to 400.00
Creamer, 4¼" h. (ILLUS. front)	130.00
Spooner	98.00 to 125.00
Sugar bowl, cov., 8" h. (ILLUS.	
rear)	250.00
Sugar bowl, cov., vaseline	675.00

LOOP (Seneca Loop)

Loop Goblet

Bowl, 9" d., flint	80.00
Butter dish, cov., flint	150.00
Celery vase, flint	57.50
Celery vase, non-flint	30.00
Compote, open, 8" d., 6" h., non-	
flint	30.00

Compote, open, 9" d., 7" h.,	
flint	125.00
Compote, open, 10" d., 8" h.,	
flint	85.00
Cordial, non-flint, 2¾" h.	18.50
Creamer, flint	50.00
Creamer, ruby-stained	30.00
Egg cup, flint	28.50
Egg cup, non-flint	12.00
Goblet, flint (ILLUS.)	30.00
Goblet, non-flint	15.00
Pitcher, water, applied handle,	
flint	145.00 to 170.00
Pitcher, water, non-flint	60.00
Salt dip, individual size, flint	18.00
Salt dip, master size, flint	22.50
Sauce dish, non-flint	6.50
Spooner, flint	22.50
Spooner, non-flint	16.00
Spooner, ruby-stained	30.00
Sugar bowl, cov., flint	115.00
Sugar bowl, cov., non-flint	29.50
Tumbler, flint	18.00
Tumbler, bar, non-flint	14.00
Wine, flint	30.00
Wine, non-flint	17.50

LOOP & DART

Loop & Dart Compote

Bowl, 9 x 6" oval, round	
ornaments	19.50
Butter dish, cov., diamond orna-	
ments, non-flint	35.00 to 45.00
Butter dish, cov., round ornaments,	
flint	80.00
Celery vase, round	
ornaments	30.00 to 45.00
Champagne, round ornaments,	
flint	65.00
Compote, cov., 8" d., 10" h., round	
ornaments (ILLUS.)	85.00
Compote, cov., 8" d., low stand,	
round ornaments	65.00

Compote, open, 8" d., 4½" h., round ornaments	42.50
Cordial, 3¾" h.	22.00
Creamer, applied handle, diamond ornaments	32.50
Creamer, applied handle, round ornaments	35.00
Egg cup, diamond ornaments	18.00
Egg cup, round ornaments	24.00
Goblet, diamond ornaments	22.50
Goblet, round ornaments	27.50
Goblet, buttermilk, round ornaments	39.00
Lamp, kerosene-type, round ornaments on font, milk white base	85.00
Pitcher, water, round ornaments	90.00
Plate, 6" d., round ornaments	35.00
Relish, diamond ornaments	15.00
Relish, round ornaments	25.00
Salt dip, master size, diamond ornaments	15.00
Salt dip, master size, round ornaments	28.50
Sauce dish, diamond ornaments	5.00
Sauce dish, round ornaments	6.50
Spooner, diamond ornaments	18.00
Spooner, round ornaments	35.00
Sugar bowl, cov., diamond ornaments	32.50
Sugar bowl, cov., round ornaments, flint	57.50
Sugar bowl, open, diamond ornaments	17.50
Sugar bowl, open, round ornaments	25.00
Tumbler, flat or footed, diamond ornaments	25.00
Tumbler, flat or footed, round ornaments	25.00
Wine, diamond ornaments	32.50
Wine, round ornaments	32.50

LOOP & JEWEL - See Jewel & Festoon Pattern

LOOP & PILLAR - See Michigan Pattern

LOOP WITH DEWDROPS

Bowl, 7" to 8" d.	17.50
Butter dish, cov.	27.50
Creamer	22.50
Goblet	25.00
Pitcher, water	65.00
Sugar bowl, cov.	25.00
Tumbler	17.00
Wine	25.00

LOOP WITH STIPPLED PANELS - See Texas Pattern

LOOPS & DROPS - See New Jersey Pattern

LOOPS & FANS - See Maryland Pattern

MAGNET & GRAPE

Butter dish, cov., frosted leaf, flint	185.00
Celery vase, frosted leaf, flint	150.00
Compote, cov., 4½" d., 9" h., frosted leaf, flint	125.00
Compote, open, 7½" d., high stand, stippled leaf, non-flint	68.00
Cordial, frosted leaf, flint, 4" h.	110.00 to 165.00
Creamer, frosted leaf, flint	160.00
Egg cup, clear leaf, non-flint	18.00
Egg cup, frosted leaf, flint	85.00
Goblet, clear leaf, non-flint	22.50
Goblet, frosted leaf, flint	65.00
Goblet, frosted leaf & American Shield, flint	300.00
Goblet, stippled leaf, non-flint	24.00
Salt dip, frosted leaf, flint	50.00
Sauce dish, frosted leaf, flint	18.00
Sauce dish, stippled leaf, non-flint	4.50
Spooner, frosted leaf, flint	77.50
Spooner, stippled leaf, non-flint	24.00
Sugar bowl, cov., frosted leaf, flint	95.00
Sugar bowl, frosted leaf & American Shield, flint	300.00
Sugar bowl, cov., stippled leaf, non-flint	50.00
Tumbler, frosted leaf, flint	85.00
Tumbler, stippled leaf, non-flint	24.00
Wine, frosted leaf, flint	135.00
Wine, stippled leaf, non-flint	40.00

MAINE (Stippled Flower Panels)

Maine Jelly Compote

Bowl, 6" d.	32.00
Bowl, master berry, 8½" d.	40.00
Bowl, master berry, 8½" d., green	32.50
Butter dish, cov.	45.00
Cake stand, green, 8½" d.	46.00
Compote, cov., small, green	65.00
Compote, open, jelly, 4¾" d. (ILLUS.)	26.00
Compote, open, 7" d.	35.00
Compote, open, 8" d.	38.00
Compote, open, 8" d., green	58.00

Creamer	28.50
Cruet w/original stopper	60.00
Pitcher, water	85.00
Pitcher, water, w/red & green stain	125.00
Platter, oval	38.00
Relish, 7¼" l.	15.00
Sauce dish	12.50
Spooner	30.00
Sugar bowl, cov., green	60.00
Syrup pitcher w/original top	75.00
Tumbler, w/red & green stain	45.00
Wine	45.00
Wine, green	75.00

MALTESE - See Jacob's Ladder Pattern

MANHATTAN

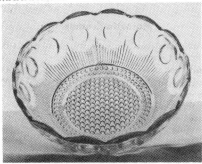

Manhattan Bowl

Basket, large	225.00
Berry set, master bowl & 3 flat sauce dishes, 4 pcs.	35.00
Bowl, 6" d.	27.00
Bowl, 8¼" d.	20.00
Bowl, 9" d. (ILLUS.)	25.00
Butter dish, cov.	55.00
Cake stand	47.50
Carafe, water	40.00
Carafe, water, pink-stained	75.00
Cookie jar, cov.	60.00
Cookie jar, cov., pink-stained	85.00
Creamer	20.00
Creamer, individual size	22.50
Creamer & open sugar bowl, pr.	35.00
Creamer & open sugar bowl, individual size, pr.	32.50
Cruet w/original stopper	47.50
Goblet	20.00
Pickle dish, 8 x 6" oval	25.00
Pitcher, water, w/silver rim	100.00
Plate, 5" d.	10.00
Plate, 5" d., pink-stained	25.00
Plate, 8" d.	16.00
Plate, 10¾" d.	22.50
Punch bowl, 14" d., 8" h.	110.00
Punch cup	15.00
Punch cup, pink-stained	23.00
Relish, 6" l.	10.00
Sauce dish, flat, amber or pink-stained	12.00

Sauce dish, flat	10.50
Sugar bowl, open	20.00
Toothpick holder	28.00
Toothpick holder, blue-stained	55.00
Vase, 7" h.	15.00
Violet bowl	20.00
Wine	30.00

MAPLE LEAF (Leaf)

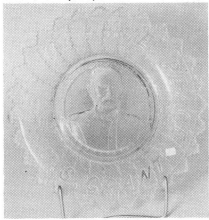

Grant "Let Us Have Peace" Plate

Berry set: oval master bowl, oval tray & 6 leaf-shaped sauce dishes; amber, 8 pcs.	95.00
Bowl, 5½" oval	25.00
Bowl, 5½" oval, vaseline	45.00
Bowl, 10 x 6" oval, footed, blue	60.00
Bowl, 10 x 6" oval, footed	35.00
Bowl, 10 x 6" oval, footed, green	55.00
Bowl, 10 x 6" oval, footed, vaseline	65.00
Bowl, 10" sq., crimped rim, blue	85.00
Bowl, 12 x 7½" oval, amber	70.00
Bowl, 12 x 7½" oval, blue	85.00
Bread plate, Grant, "Let Us Have Peace," amber, 9½" d.	65.00
Bread plate, Grant, "Let Us Have Peace," blue, 9½" d.	75.00
Bread plate, Grant, "Let Us Have Peace," 9½" d. (ILLUS.)	45.00
Bread plate, Grant, "Let Us Have Peace," vaseline, 9½" d.	55.00
Bread tray, 13¼ x 9¼"	35.00
Bread tray, vaseline, 13¼ x 9¼"	60.00
Butter dish, cov.	80.00
Celery vase	36.00
Compote, open, jelly, green	45.00
Creamer, blue	65.00
Creamer	52.50
Creamer, vaseline	50.00
Goblet, amber	85.00 to 110.00
Goblet, frosted tree trunk stem	150.00
Goblet, vaseline	90.00 to 110.00
Pitcher, water	67.50
Plate, 9" d., blue	35.00
Platter, 10½" oval, blue	45.00

Platter, 10½" oval	40.00
Platter, 10½" oval, vaseline	48.00
Sauce dish, leaf-shaped, 5½" l.	17.50
Spooner, blue....................	55.00
Spooner	40.00
Spooner, green	45.00
Spooner, vaseline	65.00
Sugar bowl, cov., blue	95.00
Sugar bowl, open	40.00
Tumbler	35.00

MARYLAND (Inverted Loops & Fans or Loops & Fans)

Maryland Tumbler

Banana bowl, flat, 11¼ x 5"	25.00
Bread platter	28.50
Butter dish, cov.	57.50
Cake stand, 8" d.	37.00
Celery tray, 12" l.	13.50
Celery vase......................	25.00
Compote, cov., 7" d., high stand ...	48.00
Compote, open, jelly	17.50
Compote, open, medium	30.00
Creamer	16.00
Goblet	25.00
Pickle dish......................	16.50
Pitcher, milk	39.00
Pitcher, water ....40.00 to	60.00
Plate, 7" d.	10.00
Relish	13.50
Salt & pepper shakers w/original tops, pr.......................	65.00
Sauce dish......................	10.00
Spooner	27.50
Table set, 4 pcs.	150.00
Toothpick holder	25.00
Tumbler (ILLUS.).................	24.00
Wine...........................	40.00

MASCOTTE

Butter dish, cov.	45.00
Butter dish, cov., horseshoe-shaped, "Maude S."	100.00
Butter pat	10.00
Cake basket w/handle.............	60.00
Cake stand	35.00
Celery vase.....................	32.00
Cheese dish, cov.	65.00
Compote, cov., 7" d.	45.00
Compote, cov., 9" d., high stand ..	175.00
Compote, open, jelly	25.00
Creamer (ILLUS.)	35.00

Mascotte Creamer

Goblet	28.00
Pitcher, water	65.00
Salt shaker w/original top (single) ..	9.00
Sauce dish, flat or footed .....8.50 to	18.00
Spooner	28.00
Sugar bowl, cov.	42.50
Tray, wine......................	20.00
Tumbler	18.00
Wine...........................	25.00

MASSACHUSETTS

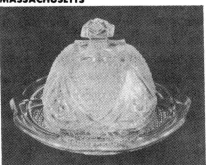

Massachusetts Butter Dish

Banana boat, 8½ x 6½"	55.00
Bar bottle, 11" h.	57.50
Basket w/applied handle, 4½ x 4½", 4¾" h.................	55.00
Bowl, 6" sq.	18.00
Bowl, master berry, 8½" sq.	25.00
Butter dish, cov. (ILLUS.)	52.50
Cologne bottle w/stopper	37.50
Cordial	57.50
Creamer	24.00
Creamer, breakfast size	15.00
Cruet w/original stopper..........	40.00
Cruet w/original stopper, miniature......................	55.00
Decanter w/stopper	90.00
Decanter (no stopper)	50.00

Goblet	45.00
Ice cream tray, 8"	16.50
Mug, 3½" h.	20.00
Olive dish, 5 x 3½"	8.50
Pitcher, water	75.00
Plate, 5" sq., serrated rim	19.00
Plate, 6" sq., w/advertising	16.50
Plate, 8" sq.	30.00
Punch cup	12.00
Relish, 8½" l.	12.50
Rum jug, 5" h.	85.00
Spooner	20.00
Sugar bowl, open, 2-handled	17.50
Sugar bowl, open, breakfast size	15.00
Table set, 4 pcs.	215.00
Toothpick holder	42.50
Tumbler, juice	13.50
Tumbler, water	35.00
Vase, 6½" h., trumpet-shaped	22.50
Vase, 6½" h., trumpet-shaped, cobalt blue w/gold	40.00 to 60.00
Vase, 9" h., trumpet-shaped, green	33.00
Vase, 10" h., trumpet-shaped, green	35.00
Whiskey shot glass	15.00
Whiskey set, bar bottle & 6 shot glasses, 7 pcs.	125.00
Wine	40.00

MELROSE

Butter dish, cov.	45.00
Cake stand, 8" to 10" d.	27.50
Celery vase	27.50
Compote, open, jelly, 5½" d.	14.00
Compote, open, 7" d., 7" h.	25.00
Compote, open, 7½" d., 5¾" h.	23.00
Compote, open, 9" d., high stand	35.00
Creamer	30.00
Goblet	18.00
Pitcher, water	40.00
Plate, 7" d.	16.00
Plate, 8" d.	10.00
Spooner	30.00
Sugar bowl, cov.	38.00
Tray, water, 11½" d.	45.00
Wine	23.50

MICHIGAN (Paneled Jewel or Loop & Pillar)

Berry set: master bowl & 4 sauce dishes; pink-stained, 5 pcs.	75.00
Bowl, cov., master berry or fruit	75.00
Bowl, 7½ x 5¼" oval	12.50
Bowl, 9" d., pink-stained	45.00
Bowl, 10" d.	35.00
Butter dish, cov.	45.00
Butter dish, cov., pink-stained	125.00
Butter dish, cov., yellow-stained, enameled florals	175.00
Carafe, water	150.00
Celery vase	27.00 to 35.00
Compote, open, jelly, 4½" d.	23.00
Compote, open, 9¼" d.	62.50
Creamer, 5" h.	25.00

Creamer, individual size	14.00
Creamer, individual size, yellow-stained, enameled florals	22.00
Cruet w/original stopper	57.00
Finger bowl	14.50

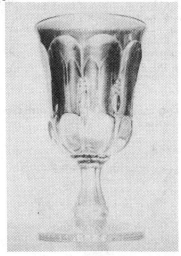

Michigan Goblet

Goblet (ILLUS.)	35.00
Honey dish, 3½" d.	8.00
Mug	22.50
Mug, pink-stained, gold trim	38.00
Pickle dish	12.00
Pitcher, water, 8" h.	45.00
Pitcher, water, 12" h.	60.00
Pitcher, water, 12" h., pink-stained	135.00
Platters, 12½ x 8½", 10¼ x 7¼" & 9½ x 6½", nested set of 3	125.00
Punch bowl, 8" d., 4½" h.	50.00
Punch cup, enameled decor	8.00
Relish	20.00
Salt shaker w/original top, enameled decor (single)	32.00
Salt shaker w/original top, yellow-stained, enameled florals (single)	45.00
Sauce dish	10.00
Sauce dish, pink-stained	20.00
Spooner	25.00
Spooner, miniature	25.00
Spooner, pink-stained	72.50
Sugar bowl, cov.	50.00
Sugar bowl, cov., pink-stained, gold trim	130.00
Sugar bowl, individual size	26.00
Syrup jug w/pewter top	95.00
Table set, pink-stained, 4 pcs.	375.00
Toddy mug, tall	45.00
Toothpick holder, blue-stained	75.00
Toothpick holder	35.00
Toothpick holder, enameled florals	45.00
Toothpick holder, yellow-stained	50.00

Toothpick holder, yellow-stained,
enameled florals 68.00
Tumbler 22.50
Tumbler, enameled decor 25.00
Tumbler, pink-stained, gold trim 50.00
Vase, 6" h. 10.00
Vase, 6" h., pink-stained, gold
trim............................ 17.50
Vase, 8" h., green-stained, white
enameled dots 35.00
Water set: pitcher & 6 tumblers;
pink-stained, 7 pcs. 325.00
Wine 28.00

MIKADO - See Daisy & Button with Cross-bars Pattern

MINERVA

Minerva Compote

Bread tray, 13" l. 60.00
Butter dish, cov. 75.00
Cake stand, 8" to 12" d. .... 82.50 to 150.00
Compote, cov., 7" d., 10¾" h....... 105.00
Compote, cov., 8" d., low stand 80.00
Compote, open, 8" d., 8½" h.
(ILLUS.) 85.00
Creamer 50.00
Creamer & open sugar bowl, pr..... 75.00
Goblet 85.00
Honey dish 17.50
Marmalade jar, cov............... 150.00
Pickle dish, "Love's Request is
Pickles," oval 30.00
Pitcher, milk, 7½" h. 72.50
Pitcher, water 175.00
Plate, 8" d., Bates (J.C.) portrait
center, scalloped rim 50.00
Salt dip, footed, master size 25.00
Sauce dish, flat or footed .... 10.00 to 17.50
Spooner 37.50
Sugar bowl, cov. 65.00
Tumbler 22.50
Waste bowl, 6" d. 55.00

MINNESOTA

Banana bowl, flat 50.00
Basket w/applied reeded handle ... 50.00

Berry set, 10" d. master bowl & 5
sauce dishes, 6 pcs. 55.00
Bowl, 8½" d. 30.00
Butter dish, cov. 50.00
Celery tray, 13" l. 25.00
Compote, open, 9" sq. 55.00
Creamer, 3½" h. 22.50
Creamer, individual size 16.50
Cruet w/original stopper 32.50
Flower frog, green, 2 pcs. 45.00
Goblet 22.50
Mug 18.00
Mustard jar w/silverplate lid,
handled 40.00
Nappy, 4½" d. 12.00
Olive dish, oval 12.50
Pickle dish...................... 10.00
Pitcher, water, tankard 75.00
Plate, 7 3/8" d., turned-up rim 12.50

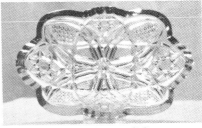

Minnesota Relish

Relish, 5 x 3" (ILLUS.) 9.00
Relish, 8¾ x 6½" oblong 15.00
Salt shaker w/original top, ruby-
stained (single) 50.00
Sauce dish....................... 12.00
Spooner 17.00
Sugar bowl, cov. 30.00
Table set, 4 pcs. 125.00
Toothpick holder, 3-handled 25.00
Tumbler 16.00
Water set: pitcher & 4 tumblers;
gold trim, 5 pcs. 125.00
Wine............................ 25.00

MIRROR - See Galloway Pattern

MIRROR, EARLY

Mirror Pomade Jar

Bar bottle	40.00
Bowl, 7" d.	17.50
Celery vase	75.00
Compote, open, 10" d., 7½" h.	120.00
Goblet	28.00
Goblet, bulb stem	65.00
Pomade jar w/ground stopper, 3½" h. (ILLUS.)	35.00
Spillholder	40.00
Spooner	22.00
Sugar bowl, cov.	60.00
Tumbler, bar	30.00
Tumbler, footed	45.00
Wine	37.50

MISSOURI (Palm & Scroll)

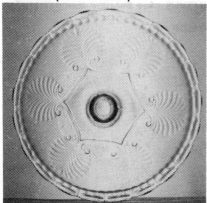

Missouri Doughnut Stand

Bowl, 8¾" d., green	30.00
Butter dish, cov.	55.00
Cake stand, 9" d., 4¾" h.	35.00
Celery vase	28.00
Compote, jelly	22.50
Creamer, green	40.00
Cruet w/original stopper, green	160.00
Doughnut stand, 6" d. (ILLUS.)	35.00
Goblet	45.00
Pitcher, milk	42.50
Pitcher, water, tankard, green	85.00
Relish	10.00
Relish, green	12.50
Salt & pepper shakers w/original tops, pr.	50.00
Sauce dish, green	12.50
Spooner	24.00
Spooner, green	40.00
Sugar bowl, cov.	50.00
Table set, green, 4 pcs.	325.00
Water set: pitcher & 6 tumblers; green, 7 pcs.	285.00
Wine	36.00
Wine, green	45.00

MONKEY

Butter dish, cov.	195.00
Dish, cov., milk white	99.00
Mug (ILLUS.)	90.00

Monkey Pattern

Pickle jar, cov., 7 3/8" h. (ILLUS.)	100.00
Spooner	50.00

MOON & STARS

Moon & Stars Compote

Berry set, master bowl & 6 sauce dishes, 7 pcs.	95.00
Bowl, cov., 7" d.	30.00
Bowl, 7" d., footed	25.00
Bowl, fruit, 9" d., footed	30.00
Bread tray, scalloped rim, 10¾ x 6½"	24.50
Butter dish, cov.	55.00
Cake stand, 9" to 12" d.	40.00 to 70.00
Celery vase	45.00
Compote, cov., 6" d., 10" h.	45.00
Compote, cov., 8" d., 12" h.	65.00
Compote, open, 8" d., 8" h. (ILLUS.)	45.00
Compote, open, 10" d., high stand	125.00
Creamer	50.00
Creamer & open sugar bowl, pr.	96.00
Cruet w/original stopper, applied handle	48.00
Goblet	35.00
Lamp, kerosene-type, table model, amber	190.00
Pickle dish, 8" l.	15.00 to 20.00
Pitcher, water, 9¼" h., applied rope handle	145.00
Relish, oblong	16.00

Salt dip, individual size, footed 15.00
Salt shaker w/original top (single) . . 20.00
Sauce dish, flat or footed . . . . 10.00 to 15.00
Spillholder 55.00
Spooner 45.00
Sugar bowl, cov. 70.00
Toothpick holder 15.00
Tumbler, flat. 45.00
Tumbler, footed, flint 67.50
Wine 35.00

MOON & STAR WITH WAFFLE - See Jeweled Moon & Star Pattern

MORNING GLORY

Compote, 9" d., 8" h., flint 165.00
Egg cup, flint 325.00
Honey dish, flint, 3½" 45.00
Sauce dish, flat, flint 45.00
Syrup pitcher w/original pewter top,
   opaque white 85.00

NAIL

(Items may be plain or with etched designs)

Bowl, 6" d., flat, ruby-stained 45.00
Butter dish, cov. 72.50
Cake stand 50.00
Celery vase 28.00
Celery vase, ruby-stained 55.00
Cordial 45.00
Decanter 40.00
Goblet, ruby-stained. 48.00
Pitcher, water 65.00
Sauce dish, flat or footed 10.00
Spooner, ruby-stained 65.00
Wine 68.00

NAILHEAD

Nailhead Compote

Bowl, 6" d. 16.00
Butter dish, cov. 46.50
Cake stand, 9" to 12" d. . . . . . 20.00 to 35.00
Celery vase. 50.00
Compote, cov., 6¼" d., 6¼" h. 40.00
Compote, cov., 6¼" d., 9½" h. 45.00
Compote, cov., 7" d., low stand 45.00
Compote, cov., 12" d. 65.00

Compote, open, 6½" d., 6¾" h.
  (ILLUS.) 25.00
Compote, open, 9" d., 6½" h. 35.00
Compote, open, 10" d., 7" h. 45.00
Creamer & open sugar bowl, pr. 30.00
Goblet 22.50
Pitcher, water . . . . 32.50 to 47.50
Plate, 6", 7" or 9" d. . . . . 14.00 to 18.00
Plate, 7" to 9" sq. . . . . 14.00 to 18.50
Relish, 8¾ x 5¼" 10.00
Sauce dish, 4" 7.00
Spooner 22.50
Sugar bowl, cov. 30.00
Tumbler 42.50
Wine 20.00

NEPTUNE - See Bearded Man Pattern

NESTOR

Nestor Butter Dish

Butter dish, cov., gold trim
  (ILLUS.) 65.00
Creamer, blue 40.00
Cruet w/original stopper, blue, gold
  trim 100.00
Cruet w/original stopper, green 70.00
Cruet w/original stopper, purple . . . 95.00
Sauce dish, purple, gold trim 25.00
Spooner, purple, gold trim 30.00
Table set, blue, 4 pcs. 525.00
Tumbler, blue, gold trim 75.00
Tumbler, purple, gold trim 28.00

NEW ENGLAND PINEAPPLE

Bowl, 8" d., footed, scalloped rim,
  flint 80.00
Cake stand, flint 115.00
Champagne, flint. 165.00
Compote, open, 7" d., 4" h., flint . . . 65.00
Compote, open, 8" d., 5" h., flint . . . 75.00
Cordial, flint, 4" h. 95.00
Creamer, applied handle, flint. 160.00
Decanter w/bar lip, flint, qt. 175.00
Decanter w/original stopper, flint,
  qt. 200.00
Egg cup, flint (ILLUS.) 32.50
Goblet, flint 60.00
Goblet, lady's, flint 70.00

New England Pineapple Egg Cup

Honey dish, flint	17.00
Plate, 6" d., flint	85.00
Salt dip, individual size, flint	25.00
Salt dip, master size, flint	40.00
Sauce dish, flint	10.00
Spillholder, flint	58.00
Spooner, flint	45.00
Sugar bowl, cov., flint	95.00
Sugar bowl, open, flint	60.00
Tumbler, bar, flint	95.00
Tumbler, water, flint	85.00
Wine, flint	135.00

NEW JERSEY (Loops & Drops)

Bowl, flat	20.00
Bread plate	30.00
Compote, open, jelly	20.00
Compote, open, 7" d., 3½" h.	12.50
Creamer	35.00
Cruet w/original stopper	45.00
Goblet	35.00
Olive dish	18.00
Pitcher, water	48.00
Plate, 8" d.	12.00
Plate, 8¾" d.	13.00
Plate, 11" d.	16.00
Relish	15.00
Sauce dish, flat	10.00
Sugar bowl, cov.	40.00
Toothpick holder	40.00
Tumbler	22.00
Tumbler, ruby-stained	50.00
Water set, pitcher & 6 tumblers, 7 pcs.	165.00
Wine	33.00

NORTHWOOD DRAPERY - See Opalescent Glass

NOTCHED RIB - See Broken Column Pattern

OAKEN BUCKET (Wooden Pail)

Butter dish, cov., blue	90.00
Butter dish, cov.	52.50
Creamer, amber	40.00
Creamer, amethyst	85.00
Creamer	36.50

Oaken Bucket Match Holder

Match holder w/original wire handle, amber, 2 5/8" d., 2 5/8" h. (ILLUS.)	20.00
Pitcher, water, amber	78.50
Pitcher, water, amethyst	120.00
Pitcher, water, blue	92.50
Pitcher, water	57.50
Spooner, amber	40.00
Spooner, blue	45.00
Spooner	17.50
Spooner, vaseline	55.00
Sugar bowl, cov., blue	45.00
Sugar bowl, cov.	35.00
Sugar bowl, cov., vaseline	55.00
Sugar bowl, open, blue	20.00
Sugar bowl, open, miniature, amethyst	22.50
Toothpick holder, blue	22.50
Toothpick holder, vaseline	27.50
Tumbler	15.00
Tumbler, bar, amethyst	35.00

OAK LEAF BAND

Oak Leaf Band Goblet

Bowl, 8 x 5½" oval	9.50
Butter dish, cov.	45.00
Goblet (ILLUS.)	32.50
Mug, applied handle, 3½" h.	37.50
Pitcher, 6" h.	36.00
Relish	10.00

OLD MAN OF THE MOUNTAIN - See Viking Pattern

OLD MAN OF THE WOODS - See Bearded Man Pattern

ONE-HUNDRED-ONE

One-Hundred-One Creamer

Bread plate, 10" d.	28.00
Creamer, 4¾" h. (ILLUS.)	25.00
Goblet	30.00
Pitcher, water	125.00
Sugar bowl, cov.	45.00

OPEN ROSE

Open Rose Tumbler

Compote, open, 7½" d.	32.50
Creamer	36.00
Egg cup	20.00
Goblet	24.00
Goblet, buttermilk	22.00
Goblet, lady's	28.00
Pitcher, water, applied handle	170.00
Relish, 8 x 5½"	13.50
Sauce dish	10.00
Spooner	26.00
Sugar bowl, cov.	52.50
Sugar bowl, open	25.00
Tumbler (ILLUS.)	40.00
Tumbler, applied handle	65.00

OREGON NO. 1 - See Beaded Loop Pattern

OREGON NO. 2 (Skilton)

Oregon No. 2 Celery Vase

Bowl, 7¾" d., 2½" h.	12.50
Butter dish, cov.	40.00
Cake stand, 9" d.	35.00
Celery vase (ILLUS.)	27.50
Compote, open, 5½" d., 4½" h.	22.50
Compote, open, 8½" d., low stand	35.00
Compote, open, 8½" d., low stand, ruby-stained	50.00
Decanter, whiskey	29.00
Pitcher, milk	25.00
Pitcher, water, tankard	40.00
Relish	15.00
Sauce dish	10.00
Spooner, ruby-stained	38.00
Syrup pitcher w/original top	65.00
Tumbler, ruby-stained	35.00
Wine	32.50

OWL IN FAN - See Parrot Pattern

PALM & SCROLL - See Missouri Pattern

PALMETTE

Bowl, 8" d., flat	25.00
Bread tray, handled, 9"	30.00
Butter dish, cov.	52.50
Butter pat	45.00
Cake stand	45.00
Castor set, 3-bottle, complete	75.00
Castor set, 5-bottle, complete	125.00
Celery vase	31.50
Champagne	68.00
Compote, cov., 8" d., high stand	85.00
Compote, open, 7" d., low stand	30.00
Compote, open, 8" d., low stand	27.50
Creamer, applied handle	50.00
Cup plate	45.00
Egg cup	22.00
Goblet (ILLUS.)	35.00
Lamp, kerosene-type, table model w/stem	75.00

Palmette Goblet

Lamp, kerosene-type, table model
  w/stem, milk white 135.00
Pickle dish, scoop-shaped 13.50
Pitcher, water, applied handle 125.00
Relish 16.00
Salt dip, master size, footed 20.00
Salt & pepper shakers w/original
  tops, 5½" h., pr................. 55.00
Sauce dish..................5.00 to 10.00
Spooner 30.00
Sugar bowl, cov. 42.50
Sugar bowl, open 20.00
Syrup pitcher w/original top, ap-
  plied handle 110.00
Tumbler, water, footed 47.50

PANELED CANE
Creamer & cov. sugar bowl, pr. 32.00
Goblet, amber 25.00
Goblet 20.00
Mug, 2¼" h...................... 9.50

**PANELED CHERRY WITH THUMBPRINTS
(Cherry Thumbprint)**

Paneled Cherry Table Set

*(All pieces in clear glass w/red-stained cher
ries & gilt cable trim)*

Berry set, master bowl & 6 sauce
  dishes, 7 pcs................... 135.00
Butter dish, cov. ....85.00 to 110.00

Celery dish 45.00
Creamer 45.00
Pitcher, water ....110.00 to 125.00
Punch cup, footed 26.00
Sauce dish.................12.00 to 15.00
Spooner 45.00
Sugar bowl, cov. 65.00
Table set, 4 pcs. (ILLUS.) 250.00
Tumbler 22.50
Water set, pitcher & 6 tumblers,
  7 pcs......................... 225.00

PANELED DAISY

Paneled Daisy Pickle Dish

Berry set, master bowl & 6 sauce
  dishes, 7 pcs.................... 80.00
Bowl, berry, 8¼ x 5¾" oval 20.00
Butter dish, cov. 40.00
Cake stand, high stand, 8" to
  11" d.......................... 45.00
Celery vase....................,.. 30.00
Compote, cov., 5" d., high stand ... 50.00
Compote, cov., 6" d., low stand 35.00
Compote, cov., large 47.50
Creamer 35.00
Goblet 25.00
Mug 30.00
Pickle dish, handled, 8½" l.
  (ILLUS.)....................... 15.00
Pitcher, water 45.00
Plate, 7½" to 9" sq.........15.00 to 22.50
Relish, 7 x 5" oval................ 12.00
Sauce dish, flat or footed 11.00
Spooner 22.50
Sugar shaker w/original top 35.00
Toothpick holder, footed, amber.... 25.00
Tray, water..................... 32.00

PANELED DEWDROP
Bowl, 8½" oval 24.00
Bread platter, 12½ x 9½" 52.50
Butter dish, cov. 65.00
Celery vase 35.00
Cordial, 3¼" h. 28.50
Creamer 20.00
Creamer, individual size 20.00
Goblet 26.50
Marmalade jar, cov............... 42.50
Mug, applied handle 35.00
Pitcher, milk 42.50
Plate, 7" to 10" d.........15.00 to 30.00
Relish, 7 x 4½" ....12.50 to 16.00
Sauce dish, flat or footed .....5.00 to 10.00
Spooner 35.00
Sugar bowl, cov. 38.00
Tumbler, applied handle 40.00
Wine 20.00

PANELED FINECUT - See Finecut & Panel Pattern

PANELED FORGET-ME-NOT

Paneled Forget-Me-Not Compote

Bread platter, 11 x 7" oval 30.00
Butter dish, cov. 35.00
Cake stand 38.50
Celery vase. 35.00
Compote, cov., 6" d., 9½" h. 45.00
Compote, cov., 8" d., high
   stand .48.00 to 75.00
Compote, open, 7¼" d., 7" h 35.00
Compote, open, 8½" d., 6½" h.
   (ILLUS.). 30.00
Compote, open, 8½" d., 12" h. 40.00
Creamer 28.00
Creamer, individual size 15.00
Goblet 35.00
Marmalade jar, cov. 30.00
Pitcher, milk 47.50
Pitcher, water 55.00
Relish, handled, 7¾ x 4½" 15.00
Relish, scoop-shaped, 9" l. 19.50
Salt & pepper shakers w/original
   tops, pr. 65.00
Sauce dish, flat or footed . . . . .9.00 to 15.00
Spooner 27.50
Sugar bowl, cov. 40.00
Wine. 38.50

PANELED GRAPE
Butter dish, cov. 68.00
Compote, open, 6½" h. 65.00
Creamer 25.00
Pitcher, water, 8¾" h. 65.00
Sauce dish 10.00
Sugar bowl, cov., small 25.00
Sugar bowl, open 25.00
Tumbler 18.00

PANELED HEATHER
Bowl, 7" d. 12.50
Bowl, 8¼" d., 3¾" h. 27.50
Butter dish, cov., ruby-stained 40.00

Cake stand 30.00
Compote, cov. 40.00

Paneled Heather Jelly Compote

Compote, open, jelly (ILLUS.) 20.00
Compote, open, 8" d. 27.50
Creamer 22.50
Cruet w/original stopper 30.00
Goblet 24.00
Pitcher, water 38.00
Plate, 12" d. 15.00
Sauce dish, flat or footed . . . . .7.00 to 10.00
Spooner 18.00
Sugar bowl, cov. 32.50
Tumbler 30.00
Water set, pitcher & 5 tumblers,
   6 pcs. 150.00
Wine 18.50

PANELED HERRINGBONE (Emerald Green Herringbone or Florida)

Paneled Herringbone Plate

Berry set: 9" d. master bowl & 6
   sauce dishes; green, 7 pcs. 110.00
Bowl, master berry, 9" sq., green . . 38.00
Bowl, oval vegetable, green,
   medium 17.50
Butter dish, cov., green 60.00
Cake stand 25.00
Cake stand, green 75.00

Creamer	20.00
Creamer, green	30.00
Cruet w/original stopper, green	90.00 to 125.00
Goblet	14.50
Goblet, green	35.00
Mustard pot, cov.	22.50
Nappy, green	19.00
Pickle dish, green	22.50
Pitcher, water	35.00
Pitcher, water, green	60.00
Plate, 5" to 7", green	22.00
Plate, 9" (ILLUS.)	28.00
Relish, green, 6" sq.	15.00
Relish, green, 8 x 4½" oval	13.50 to 20.00
Sauce dish, green	12.00
Spooner, green	24.00
Sugar bowl, cov., green	50.00
Syrup pitcher w/original top	175.00
Syrup pitcher w/original top, green	225.00
Tumbler, green	25.00
Water set: pitcher & 6 goblets; green, 7 pcs.	250.00
Water set: pitcher & 6 tumblers; green, 7 pcs.	195.00
Wine	22.50
Wine, green	50.00

PANELED HOBNAIL

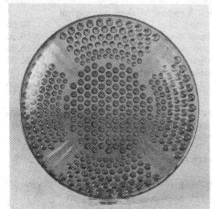

Paneled Hobnail Plate

Creamer, blue	65.00
Spooner, blue opaque	27.50
Plate, 7" d., sapphire blue (ILLUS.)	25.00
Toddy plate, 4½" d., blue	15.00

PANELED JEWEL - See Michigan Pattern

PANELED STAR & BUTTON - See Sedan Pattern

PANELED THISTLE (Thistle)

Basket w/applied handle, 7 x 4¾",
 2½" h. ... 35.00

Bowl, cov., 5½" d., 4" h., w/bee in base	48.00
Bowl, 6" d., 2½" h., footed	12.50
Bowl, 7" oval, 1¾" h.	15.00
Bowl, 9" d., deep, w/bee	35.00
Bowl, 10" d., flattened rim	27.50
Bread plate	40.00
Butter dish, cov., w/bee	55.00
Cake stand	40.00
Cake stand, w/bee	65.00
Candy dish, cov., footed, 5" sq., 6¼" h.	30.00
Celery tray	13.50
Celery vase	30.00
Champagne, flared, w/bee	37.00
Compote, open, 5" d., low stand	16.00
Compote, open, 5" d., high stand	25.00
Compote, open, 7½" d., 7" h.	35.00
Compote, open, 9" d., 6½" h.	35.00

Paneled Thistle Creamer

Creamer (ILLUS.)	30.00
Cruet w/stopper	40.00
Goblet	29.00
Honey dish, cov., square	50.00
Pitcher, water, w/bee	68.00
Plate, 7" sq., w/bee	20.00
Plate, 9½" d.	36.00
Punch cup	16.00
Relish, 8½ x 4"	16.50
Relish, w/bee, 9½ x 4"	24.00
Rose bowl, 5" d., 2¾" h.	20.00
Salt dip, master size	9.00
Sauce dish, flat or footed	10.00 to 20.00
Spooner, handled	18.50
Sugar bowl, cov.	30.00
Toothpick holder	29.00
Tumbler, ruby-stained	45.00
Vase, 8" h., trumpet-shaped	35.00
Wine	26.50

PANELED ZIPPER - See Iowa Pattern

PARROT (Owl in Fan)

Goblet	32.50
Pitcher, water	75.00
Spooner	25.00
Wine	50.00

PAVONIA (Pineapple Stem)

Pavonia Finger Bowl

(Items may be plain or with etched designs)

Butter dish, cov.	78.00
Butter dish, cov., ruby-stained	110.00
Cake stand, 10" d.	42.50
Celery vase......................	32.50
Compote, cov., 6" d., high stand ...	60.00
Compote, open, jelly	38.00
Compote, open, 7" d..............	50.00
Creamer	42.50
Creamer, ruby-stained	65.00
Creamer & cov. sugar bowl, ruby- stained.....................	125.00
Cup plate.......................	28.00
Finger bowl, 7" d. (ILLUS.)	36.00
Goblet	27.50
Mug, applied handle	15.00
Pitcher, water, tall tankard	65.00
Pitcher, water, tall tankard, ruby- stained........................	95.00
Salt dip, master size..............	18.50
Sauce dish, flat or footed	10.00
Spooner	35.00
Spooner, ruby-stained	45.00
Sugar bowl, cov.	55.00
Sugar bowl, cov., ruby-stained	75.00
Table set, ruby-stained, 4 pcs.................250.00 to	300.00
Tray, water	60.00
Tumbler	32.50
Tumbler, ruby-stained	42.50
Water set: pitcher & 6 tumblers; ruby-stained, 7 pcs.	350.00
Wine.......................24.00 to	35.00
Wine, ruby-stained	29.00

PEACOCK FEATHER (Georgia)

Bon bon dish, footed	25.00
Bowl, 8" d.	25.00
Butter dish, cov.	45.00
Cake stand, 8½" d., 5" h.	32.50
Cake stand, 10" d.	50.00
Celery tray, 11¾" l.	35.00
Compote, open, 6½" d., high stand	27.50
Compote, open, 8" d., high stand (ILLUS.)......................	42.50
Compote, open, 10" d., low stand ..	27.00
Creamer	28.00
Cruet w/original stopper..........	46.00

Peacock Feather Compote

Cup plate........................	25.00
Decanter, no stopper	30.00
Dish, tricornered	24.00
Lamp, kerosene-type, low hand-type w/handle, blue, 5¼" h.	135.00
Lamp, kerosene-type, low hand-type w/handle, 5¼" h...............	55.00
Lamp, kerosene-type, table model w/handle, blue, 9" h. ...225.00 to	255.00
Lamp, kerosene-type, table model w/handle, 9" h...........40.00 to	65.00
Lamp, kerosene-type, table model, amber, 12" h....................	350.00
Mug	20.00
Pitcher, water	52.50
Relish, 8" oval	15.00
Salt & pepper shakers w/original tops, pr.......................	50.00
Sauce dish.......................	9.00
Spooner	36.00
Sugar bowl, cov.	50.00
Table set, creamer, cov. sugar bowl & cov. butter dish, 3 pcs.	125.00

PENNSYLVANIA, EARLY - See Hand Pattern

PENNSYLVANIA, LATE - See Balder Pattern

PICKET

Picket Sauce Dish

Bread tray, 13 x 8"	67.50
Butter dish, cov. ....45.00 to	55.00
Celery vase......................	55.00
Compote, cov., 8" d., low stand	125.00
Creamer	42.50
Goblet	35.00
Lamp, kerosene-type, amber- stained........................	195.00
Pitcher, water ....70.00 to	80.00
Salt dip, master size..............	32.50
Sauce dish (ILLUS.) ....8.00 to	12.50

Spooner 30.00
Toothpick holder 30.00
Wine 50.00

PILLAR
Ale glass, 6½" h. 42.50
Claret 55.00
Compote, open, 8" d. 55.00
Creamer 70.00
Decanter w/bar lip, qt. 45.00
Goblet ....40.00 to 50.00
Saucer, footed, 8" d. 95.00
Wine 45.00

PILLAR & BULL'S EYE
Decanter w/bar lip, 10" h. 80.00
Goblet ....45.00 to 70.00
Pitcher, water, applied handle 325.00
Tumbler 65.00
Wine ....50.00 to 65.00

PILLAR VARIANT - See Hercules Pillar Pattern

PILLOW ENCIRCLED

(Called Ruby Rosette when ruby-stained)

Berry set: master bowl & 3 sauce
  dishes; Ruby Rosette, 4 pcs. 125.00
Bowl, 7" d., 3" h., Ruby Rosette 27.00
Bowl, 8" d. 28.00
Bowl, 8" d., Ruby Rosette 52.50
Butter dish, cov. 65.00
Butter dish, cov., Ruby Rosette 87.00
Celery vase 35.00
Celery vase, Ruby Rosette 50.00
Condiment set: 9½ x 5½" tray,
  cruet w/original stopper, salt &
  pepper shakers w/original tops;
  Ruby Rosette, 4 pcs. 210.00
Compote 40.00
Creamer 30.00
Creamer, Ruby Rosette 37.50
Creamer & cov. sugar bowl, pr. 75.00
Cruet w/original stopper, Ruby
  Rosette 135.00
Honey dish, cov., 2-handled, oval ... 10.00
Lamp, kerosene, finger-type, sap-
  phire blue 195.00
Pickle dish, 9" oval 10.50
Pitcher, milk, Ruby Rosette 85.00
Pitcher, water, tankard 33.00
Pitcher, water, tankard, Ruby
  Rosette 108.00
Sauce dish, footed 13.50
Sauce dish, footed, Ruby Rosette ... 20.00
Spooner ....25.00 to 30.00
Spooner, Ruby Rosette 50.00
Sugar bowl, cov. 32.50
Sugar bowl, cov., Ruby Rosette 41.00
Table set: cov. butter dish, sugar
  bowl & spooner; Ruby Rosette,
  3 pcs. 285.00
Tumbler 13.00

Tumbler, Ruby Rosette 28.00
Water set, pitcher & 5 tumblers,
  6 pcs. 120.00

PILLOW & SUNBURST
Creamer 20.00
Creamer & sugar bowl, pr. 32.50
Plate, 10¼" d. 30.00
Spooner 30.00

PINEAPPLE & FAN
Butter dish, cov. 35.00
Celery tray 25.00
Pickle castor in silverplate holder,
  w/tongs 65.00
Spooner 15.00
Sugar shaker 27.50
Tumbler, green w/gold 25.00

PINEAPPLE STEM - See Pavonia Pattern

PLEAT & PANEL (Darby)

Pleat & Panel Goblet

Box, cov., 8 x 5" 42.50
Bowl, 6" sq., flat 13.50
Bowl, 7" d., 4½" h., footed 22.50
Bread tray, closed handles,
  13 x 8½" 28.00
Bread tray, pierced handles 30.00
Butter dish, cov., footed 55.00
Cake stand, 8" sq. 31.00
Cake stand, 9" to 10" sq. 42.50
Compote, cov., 7" sq.,
  10½" h. ....45.00 to 65.00
Compote, cov., 8" d., 12" h. 43.00
Compote, open, 7" d., high stand ... 27.50
Creamer 26.00
Finger bowl 37.50
Goblet (ILLUS.) 20.00
Lamp, kerosene, stem 85.00
Marmalade jar, cov. & underplate .. 135.00
Pickle dish 20.00
Pitcher, milk 40.00
Plate, 5" sq. 24.00
Plate, 6" sq. 20.00
Plate, 7" sq., amber 32.50
Plate, 7" sq., canary yellow 25.00
Plate, 7" sq. 18.00

Plate, 8" sq. 22.50
Platter w/open handles 40.00
Relish, 7 x 4½" 12.00
Relish, 9½" l...................... 25.00
Salt dip, master size.............. 18.00
Salt & pepper shakers w/original
  tops, pr....................... 65.00
Sauce dish, flat, handled.......... 10.50
Sauce dish, footed 14.50
Spooner 31.00
Sugar bowl, cov. 43.50
Tray, water....................... 58.00
Waste bowl........................ 25.00
Wine 75.00

PLEAT & TUCK - See Adonis Pattern

PLUME

Plume Compote

Berry set, 8½" sq. master bowl &
  five 4½" sq. sauce dishes,
  6 pcs. 80.00
Berry set, pr. of 8½" sq. master
  bowls & eight 4½" sq. sauce dish-
  es, 10 pcs...................... 130.00
Bowl, 6" d. 22.50
Bowl, 8" d., shallow 28.00
Bowl, 8½" sq., master
  berry ....25.00 to 35.00
Butter dish, cov. 45.00
Butter dish, cov., ruby-stained...... 135.00
Cake stand, 9" d., 5¾" h. 47.50
Cake stand, 10¼" d. 55.00
Celery vase....................... 23.50
Celery vase, ruby-stained &
  etched 85.00
Compote, cov., 6½" d., 12" h....... 95.00
Compote, open, 7" d., 6¾" h.
  (ILLUS.)....................... 30.00
Compote, open, 8" d., 8" h........ 39.00
Compote, open, 9" d., 6½" h...... 48.00
Cookie jar w/original metal cover .. 75.00
Creamer, applied handle.......... 30.00
Creamer & cov. sugar bowl, pr. 65.00
Finger bowl....................... 45.00
Goblet 28.50
Goblet, ruby-stained & etched 55.00
Lamp, kerosene 60.00
Pitcher, water 82.50

Pitcher, water, ruby-stained 140.00
Relish 25.00
Sauce dish, flat or footed 10.00
Sauce dish, ruby-stained 20.00
Spooner 26.50
Spooner, ruby-stained 55.00
Sugar bowl, cov. 30.00
Sugar bowl, cov., ruby-stained 90.00
Sugar bowl, open 20.00
Sugar bowl, open, ruby-stained..... 37.50
Syrup pitcher w/original top, ap-
  plied handle 50.00
Tumbler 35.00
Waste bowl....................... 45.00
Water set, pitcher & 4 tumblers,
  5 pcs. 135.00

**POINTED THUMBPRINT - See Almond
Thumbprint Pattern**

POLAR BEAR

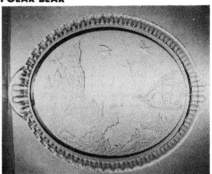

Polar Bear Water Tray

Bread tray, frosted 175.00
Claret............................ 120.00
Goblet 111.00
Goblet, clear & frosted 112.50
Pitcher, water, frosted ....250.00 to 350.00
Tray, water, 16" l. (ILLUS.) 95.00
Tray, water, frosted, 16" l......... 178.00
Tumbler 95.00
Waste bowl, frosted 110.00

POPCORN

Popcorn Cake Stand

Butter dish, cov.	49.00
Cake stand, 11" d. (ILLUS.)	72.00
Celery tray	17.50
Celery vase, 6½" h.	40.00
Cheese dish, cov., 11 x 8"	185.00
Creamer w/raised ears	47.50
Creamer & cov. sugar bowl, pr.	110.00
Goblet w/raised ears	42.50
Goblet	30.00
Pickle dish, oval	12.50
Pitcher, milk	75.00
Spooner w/raised ears	40.00
Spooner	35.00
Sugar bowl, cov.	47.50
Wine w/raised ears	58.00
Wine	31.00

PORTLAND

Portland Goblet

Basket w/high handle	125.00
Bowl, 4½" d., 3" h.	20.00
Bowl, 9" d.	25.00
Butter dish, cov.	49.00
Cake stand, 10½"	45.00
Candlestick (single)	50.00
Carafe	30.00
Celery tray	21.50
Celery vase	35.00
Compote, cov., 6½" d., high stand	115.00
Compote, open, 7½" d., 5½" h.	48.00
Cordial	30.00
Creamer	20.00
Creamer, individual size	14.00
Cruet w/original stopper	22.00
Dresser jar, cov., 5" d.	22.50
Goblet (ILLUS.)	22.00
Lamp, kerosene, 9" h.	65.00
Pitcher, water	60.00
Pitcher, water, miniature	20.00
Punch bowl, 5" d., 8½" h.	150.00
Punch cup	12.00
Relish, boat-shaped, 9" l.	12.50
Relish, boat-shaped, 12" l.	18.50
Salt shaker w/original top (single)	15.00

Sauce dish, 4½" d.	7.50
Spooner	32.50
Sugar bowl, cov.	36.50
Syrup pitcher w/original top	125.00
Toothpick holder	24.00
Tumbler	13.50
Vase, 6" h., scalloped rim	17.00
Vase, 9" h.	30.00
Water set, pitcher & 4 tumblers, 5 pcs.	100.00
Wine	23.50

PORTLAND MAIDEN BLUSH (Banded Portland with Color)

Bowl, 5½ x 3½" oval	35.00
Butter dish, cov.	165.00
Celery tray, 10" oval	65.00
Celery vase	67.50
Creamer	75.00
Creamer, breakfast size	26.00
Finger bowl, 4½" d., 2" h.	28.00
Goblet	50.00
Marmalade jar w/silverplate cover, frame & spoon, 3 pcs.	95.00
Olive dish	28.00
Pin tray, souvenir	12.50
Pitcher, tankard, 11" h.	167.50
Pitcher, water, child's	35.00
Powder jar, cov.	85.00
Punch cup	18.00 to 25.00
Relish, 6½ x 4"	25.00
Relish, boat-shaped, 8¾ x 4¼"	36.00
Salt shaker w/original top (single)	39.00
Sauce dish, boat-shaped, 4¾" l.	25.00
Sugar bowl, cov., large	115.00
Sugar shaker w/original top	120.00
Table set, 4 pcs.	285.00
Toothpick holder	54.00
Tumbler	27.00
Vase, 4" h.	25.00
Vase, 6" h.	27.50
Wine	55.00

PORTLAND WITH DIAMOND POINT BAND - See Banded Portland Pattern

POST (Square Panes)

(Items may be plain or with etched designs)

Bowl, cov., 6¾" d., footed	45.00
Bowl, 8" sq.	25.00
Butter dish, cov.	42.50
Cake stand, 9½" d.	60.00
Celery vase	42.50
Compote, cov., 5" sq., 10" h.	45.00
Compote, cov., 6" d., high stand	57.00
Creamer	40.00
Goblet	42.50
Pitcher, water	75.00
Relish, 7¼ x 4¾"	8.00
Salt dip, master size	7.00
Spooner	28.00
Table set, cov. sugar bowl, creamer & spooner, 3 pcs.	125.00

POTTED PLANT - See Flower Pot Pattern

POWDER & SHOT

Butter dish, cov.	80.00
Compote, open, 7 7/8" d., low stand	55.00
Creamer, applied handle, flint	95.00
Egg cup, flint	47.50
Goblet, flint	62.00
Goblet, buttermilk	37.50
Salt dip, master size	44.00
Sauce dish	20.00
Spooner	52.50
Sugar bowl, cov.	85.00
Table set, 4 pcs.	350.00

PRAYER RUG - See Horseshoe Pattern

PRESSED LEAF

Pressed Leaf Spooner

Bowl, 7" oval	40.00
Butter dish, cov.	50.00
Champagne	21.50
Compote, cov., acorn finial, low stand	47.50
Compote, cov., acorn finial, high stand	65.00
Cordial	18.00
Creamer, applied handle	35.00
Goblet	21.00
Goblet, buttermilk, non-flint	25.00
Pitcher, water, applied handle	84.50
Relish, 7 x 5"	12.50
Salt dip, master size	15.00
Sauce dish	9.00
Spooner (ILLUS.)	22.00
Sugar bowl, cov.	40.00
Wine	32.00

PRIMROSE

Bowl, 8" d., flat	25.00
Bread plate	30.00
Butter dish, cov.	40.00

Cake plate, 2-handled, amber, 9" d.	27.00
Card tray, amber w/wire frame, 4½" d.	32.00
Celery vase	18.50
Compote, cov., 5" d., milk white	28.00
Compote, open, low stand, large	25.00
Creamer	30.00
Goblet	40.00
Lamp, kerosene, clear to opalescent, complete, 8" h.	195.00
Pickle dish, amber	17.50
Pitcher, milk, blue	65.00
Pitcher, milk	26.00
Pitcher, water, amber	55.00
Pitcher, water	37.50
Plate, 4½" d., amber or blue	11.00
Plate, 6" d., amber	16.50
Plate, 6" d.	13.00
Plate, 7" d., amber	16.00
Platter, 12 x 8", amber	22.50
Relish, amber, 9¼ x 5"	18.00
Relish, blue	22.00
Sauce dish, flat, blue	9.00

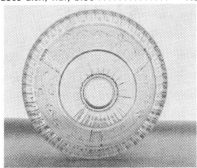

Primrose Sauce Dish

Sauce dish, flat or footed (ILLUS.)	10.00
Spooner	21.00
Sugar bowl, cov.	42.50
Tray, water, blue, 11" d.	58.00
Tray, water, 11" d.	27.50
Wine, amber	37.00
Wine	21.00
Wine, opaque turquoise	60.00

PRINCESS FEATHER (Rochelle)

Princess Feather Compote

Bowl, cov., 7½" d.	35.00
Butter dish, cov.	50.00
Celery vase	35.00
Compote, cov., 8" d., low stand	135.00
Compote, open, 8" d., low stand (ILLUS.)	32.50
Creamer	50.00
Egg cup	28.50
Egg cup, opalescent, 3¾" h.	180.00
Goblets, set of 8	225.00
Goblet, buttermilk	25.00
Honey dish	12.50
Lamp, kerosene, 12" h.	50.00
Lamp, kerosene, green, 9½" h.	175.00
Pitcher, water, bulbous, applied handle, flint	112.00
Plate, 6" d.	36.00
Plate, 7" d., amber, flint	165.00
Plate, 7" d.	28.00
Plate, 8" d.	29.50
Relish, 7 x 5" oval	17.50
Salt dip, master size	29.00
Sauce dish	10.00
Sauce dish, blue, flint	145.00
Spooner	24.00
Spooner, fiery opalescent milk white, flint, 5 1/8" h.	120.00
Sugar bowl, cov.	55.00
Sugar bowl, cov., milk white, flint	110.00

PRISCILLA (Alexis)

Priscilla Punch Cup

Banana stand	75.00
Basket	85.00
Bowl, 7" d., flat	28.00
Bowl, 8" d., 3½" h., straight sides, flat	38.00
Bowl, 8¾" d., 3 3/8" h., flared sides	55.00
Bowl, 9¼" d., 5" h.	37.50
Bowl, 9 7/8" d., 2" h.	35.00
Bowl, 10¾" d., shallow	31.00
Butter dish, cov.	145.00
Cake stand, 9" to 10" d., high stand	68.00
Compote, cov., jelly	50.00
Compote, cov., 6" d., 10" h.	55.00 to 65.00
Compote, open, 4¾" d., 4 7/8" h., flared sides	35.00
Compote, open, 6" d., 4" h., scalloped rim	60.00

Compote, open, 6 7/8" d., 7" h.	45.00
Compote, open, 8" d., 8" h.	55.00
Compote, open, 8¾" d., 9¾" h., flared rim	55.00
Compote, open, 9½" d., 9" h.	55.00
Cookie jar, cov.	175.00
Creamer	42.50
Creamer, individual size	32.50
Cruet w/original stopper	61.00
Doughnut stand, 5¾ x 4¼"	47.50
Egg cup	17.00
Goblet	49.00
Mug	15.00
Mustard jar, open	28.00
Nappy, handled	28.00
Pitcher, water	85.00 to 115.00
Plate, 10½" d., turned-up rim	26.00
Punch cup (ILLUS.)	15.00
Relish	20.00 to 28.00
Rose bowl, 3¾" h.	35.00
Rose bowl, miniature	45.00
Salt shaker w/original top (single)	35.00
Sauce dish, flat, 4½" to 5" d.	15.00
Spooner	31.00
Sugar bowl, cov.	32.50
Sugar bowl, cov., individual size	32.50
Syrup pitcher w/original pewter top	135.00
Table set, 4 pcs.	235.00
Toothpick holder	44.00
Tumbler	24.00
Wine	23.00

PRISM

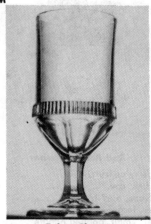

Prism Claret

Bowl, 7" d., flat	8.00
Celery vase	30.00
Champagne	45.00
Claret, 6" h. (ILLUS.)	22.00
Compote, open, 7" d., 5" h.	65.00
Creamer	55.00
Decanter, bar lip, qt.	125.00
Egg cup	25.00
Egg cup, double	27.00
Goblet	35.00
Honey dish	9.50

Pickle dish........................ 15.00
Pitcher, water 100.00
Plate, 7½" d. 25.00
Sauce dish........................ 16.00
Spooner 27.00
Sugar bowl, open 18.00
Tumbler, buttermilk 35.00
Wine............................. 38.00

PRISM WITH DIAMOND POINT
Goblet 45.00
Salt dip, master size.............. 17.50
Tumbler, bar...................... 65.00

PSYCHE & CUPID
Bread tray 35.00
Butter dish, cov. 65.00
Celery vase....................... 32.00
Compote, open, 5" d., 6¾" h....... 45.00
Creamer 45.00
Goblet 34.00
Pickle castor w/frame 195.00
Pitcher, water 78.00
Plate, 7" d., milk white 20.00
Relish, 9½ x 6½" 32.50
Sauce dish, footed 11.50
Spooner 38.00
Sugar bowl, cov. 42.50
Table set, 4 pcs. 210.00

PYGMY - See Torpedo Pattern

RED BLOCK

Red Block Spooner

Bowl, berry or fruit, 8" d.......... 65.00
Butter dish, cov. 72.50
Celery vase, 6½" h............... 84.00
Creamer, large 50.00
Creamer, small, applied handle .. 49.00
Decanter, whiskey, w/original stop-
  per, 12" h. 175.00
Goblet 35.00
Mug 27.00
Pansy bowl, 2¾" h. 65.00
Pitcher, 8" h., bulbous............ 115.00
Pitcher, tankard, 9 5/8" h. 120.00
Rose bowl 55.00
Salt dip, individual size, 2-handled.. 48.00
Salt shaker w/original top (single).. 49.00
Salt & pepper shakers w/original
  tops, pr........................ 80.00

Sauce dish, 4½" 24.00
Spooner (ILLUS.).................. 40.00
Sugar bowl, cov. 60.00
Sugar shaker w/original top 75.00
Table set, creamer, sugar bowl &
  spooner, 3 pcs. 150.00
Table set, 4 pcs. 222.00
Tumbler........................... 28.00
Water set, pitcher & 6 tumblers,
  7 pcs. 225.00
Wine............................. 32.00

REVERSE TORPEDO (Diamond & Bull's Eye Band)

Reverse Torpedo Bowl

Banana stand 115.00
Basket 65.00
Bowl, cov., 9" d. 75.00
Bowl, 5¾" d., piecrust rim 35.00
Bowl, 6¾" d. 35.00
Bowl, 7½" d., piecrust rim
  (ILLUS.)...................... 70.00
Bowl, 9" d., piecrust rim 65.00
Bowl, 10¼" d., piecrust rim 72.50
Bowl, 11¼" d., 7" h., footed 85.00
Butter dish, cov. 80.00
Cake stand 74.00
Celery vase...................... 70.00
Compote, cov., jelly 39.00
Compote, cov., 6" d., high stand ... 95.00
Compote, cov., 7" d., low stand 98.00
Compote, open, 7" d., piecrust
  rim 42.50
Compote, open, 7" d., 8" h........ 45.00
Compote, open, 8" d., piecrust
  rim 65.00
Compote, open, 9" d., 7" h., turned-
  over piecrust rim.............. 80.00
Compote, open, 10" d., 6½" h...... 70.00
Compote, open, 10 x 8½" oval,
  9¼" h., ruffled rim............. 145.00
Creamer 62.50
Dish, ruffled, 11¼" d., 2¾" h. 85.00
Goblet 75.00
Honey dish, cov., square.......... 145.00
Pitcher, water 165.00
Salt shaker w/original top (single).. 45.00
Sauce dish....................... 25.00
Spooner 55.00
Sugar bowl, cov. 70.00
Syrup pitcher w/original top 165.00
Tumbler 85.00

RIBBED GRAPE
Compote, open, 7½" d............. 42.00

Creamer, applied handle 130.00
Goblet 37.50
Goblet, buttermilk 50.00
Plate, 6" d. 32.50
Sauce dish, 4" d. 15.00
Spooner 37.00
Sugar bowl, cov. 95.00

RIBBED IVY

Berry set, master bowl & 4 sauce
   dishes, 5 pcs. 105.00
Bitters bottle w/original tulip-
   shaped stopper 175.00
Bowl, 8" d., 2" h. 67.50
Butter dish, cov. 95.00
Celery 225.00
Champagne. 145.00
Compote, cov., 6" d., high stand . . . 130.00
Compote, open, 7½" d., high stand,
   rope edge rim 92.50
Compote, open, 8" d., 5" h. 62.50
Creamer, applied handle. 110.00
Decanter w/original tulip-shaped
   stopper, ½ pt. 120.00
Egg cup 34.00
Goblet 39.00
Salt dip, cov., master size 115.00
Salt dip, open, master size, beaded
   rim 40.00
Sauce dish 12.00
Spooner 40.00
Sugar bowl, cov. 87.50
Sweetmeat, cov. 325.00
Tumbler, bar . . . . .105.00 to 125.00
Tumbler, water 80.00
Tumbler, whiskey 82.00
Wine. 97.00

RIBBED PALM

Ribbed Palm Egg Cup

Bowl, 8" d., footed 40.00
Butter dish, cov. 90.00
Celery vase. 65.00
Champagne. 113.00

Compote, open, 8" d. 85.00
Creamer . . . . .145.00 to 160.00
Egg cup (ILLUS.) 27.50
Goblet 32.00
Goblet, buttermilk 37.50
Honey dish 12.50
Pitcher, water, 9" h., applied
   handle 275.00
Plate, 6" d. 60.00
Relish, 8 x 5" 40.00
Salt dip, master size. 27.50
Sauce dish 9.00
Spillholder 45.00
Spooner 38.00
Sugar bowl, cov. 75.00
Tumbler, bar. 110.00
Wine. 48.00

RIBBON (Early Ribbon)

Ribbon Compote

Bowl, 3½" d., flat 8.50
Bowl, 8" d. 15.00
Bowl, 9 x 5" 20.00
Bread tray 28.00
Butter dish, cov. 69.00
Cake stand, 8½" d. 50.00
Cake stand, 9¼" d. 27.50
Celery vase 32.00
Cheese dish, cov. 145.00
Compote, open, 7" d., low stand . . . 30.00
Compote, open, 8" d., 8" h., frosted
   dolphin stem on dome base 250.00
Compote, open, 8½" d., 4½" h. 40.00
Compote, cov., 6" d. 32.00
Compote, cov., 8" d. (ILLUS.) 74.00
Creamer 32.00
Creamer & cov. sugar bowl, pr. 110.00
Goblet 28.00
Marmalade jar, cov. 45.00
Pitcher, water 75.00
Plate, 7" d. 35.00
Platter, 13 x 9" 62.50
Pomade jar, cov., squat 28.00

Sauce dish, flat or footed	12.00
Spooner	24.00
Sugar bowl, cov., 4¼" d., 7¾" h.	62.50
Table set, 4 pcs.	225.00
Tray, water, 15"	115.00
Wine	110.00

RIBBON CANDY (Bryce or Double Loop)

Ribbon Candy Plate

Bowl, cov., 6¼" d., footed	35.00
Bowl, 8" d., flat	20.00
Butter dish, cov.	45.00
Cake stand, child's, 6½" d., 3" h.	35.50
Cake stand, 8" to 10½" d.	33.00
Celery vase	28.00
Compote, cov., 5" d., 8½" h.	47.50
Compote, open, 8" d.	30.00
Creamer	20.00
Doughnut stand	35.00
Goblet	30.00
Mug	22.50
Pitcher, milk	47.50
Pitcher, water	70.00
Plate, 8½" d.	14.00
Plate, 9½" d.	17.00
Plate, 10½" d.	32.00
Plate, 12" d. (ILLUS.)	45.00
Relish, 8½" l.	11.00
Salt shaker w/original top (single)	25.00
Spooner	19.00
Sugar bowl, cov.	35.00
Syrup pitcher w/original top	85.00
Wine	27.50

RISING SUN

Berry set, master bowl & 6 sauce dishes, 7 pcs.	120.00
Bowl, 4½" d., handled, purple suns	9.00
Bowl, 6½" d., pink suns	8.00
Bowl, master berry, pink suns	30.00
Butter dish, cov.	68.00
Celery vase, gold suns	18.00
Celery vase, pink suns	32.50
Compote, open, jelly, purple suns	22.00
Compote, open, 7" d., 6" h.	18.50

Creamer	22.00
Cruet w/stopper	28.00
Goblet	24.00
Goblet, gold suns	17.50
Goblet, green suns	25.00
Goblet, pink suns	26.00
Goblet, purple suns	25.00
Pitcher, water	75.00
Pitcher, water, gold suns	35.00
Punch cup, green suns	20.00
Relish, red suns	7.50
Sauce dish, red suns	8.00
Spooner	40.00
Sugar bowl, open, scalloped rim, green suns	22.00
Table set, 4 pcs.	110.00
Toothpick holder, 3-handled	18.00
Toothpick holder, 3-handled, gold suns	25.00
Toothpick holder, 3-handled, green suns	30.00
Tumbler	15.00
Tumbler, gold suns	13.50
Tumbler, green suns	25.00
Tumbler, red suns	13.50
Tumbler, whiskey	8.50
Water set, pitcher & 4 tumblers, 5 pcs.	120.00
Wine	16.00
Wine, green suns	30.00
Wine, pink suns	30.00
Wine, purple suns	26.00

ROCHELLE - See Princess Feather Pattern

ROMAN KEY - See Frosted Roman Key Pattern

ROMAN ROSETTE

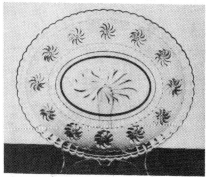

Roman Rosette Bread Platter

Berry set, 8" d. master bowl & six 5" d. sauce dishes; 7 pcs.	90.00
Bowl, 6" d.	19.50
Bowl, 7" d.	22.50
Bowl, 9½ x 6¼" oval	22.00
Bread platter, 11 x 9" (ILLUS.)	24.00
Butter dish, cov.	47.00
Butter dish, cov., ruby-stained	105.00
Cake stand, 9" to 10" d.	45.00 to 55.00

Castor set, salt & pepper shakers & cov. condiment jar, set	36.50
Celery vase.......................	20.00
Compote, cov., 5" d.	58.00
Compote, cov., 6" d., 10" h........	62.50
Compote, open, jelly, 5" d.	28.00
Cordial	42.50
Creamer	27.00
Creamer, ruby-stained	46.00
Goblet	44.00
Honey dish, cov. ....42.50 to	60.00
Marmalade dish, footed	38.00
Marmalade dish, footed, ruby-stained.....................	45.00
Mug, 3" h.........................	15.00
Pickle dish, oval	19.50
Pitcher, milk	40.00
Pitcher, water	70.00
Plate, 6" d., fiery opalescent, flint ..	140.00
Plate, 7" d.	18.00
Plate, 8" d., flint	45.00
Relish, 8½ x 3½"	10.00
Relish, 9 x 6"	20.00
Salt & pepper shakers w/original tops, pr.......................	32.00
Salt & pepper shakers w/original tops, ruby-stained, pr.	90.00
Sauce dish........................	10.00
Spooner	23.00
Spooner, ruby-stained	50.00
Sugar bowl, cov.	32.50
Toddy plate, 5½" d.	35.00
Toddy plate, purple, flint, 5½" d....	325.00
Tumbler	30.00
Tumbler, ruby-stained	38.50
Water set, pitcher & 6 tumblers, 7 pcs..........................	195.00
Wine.............................	35.00

ROSE IN SNOW

Rose In Snow Compote

Berry set, 8¼" sq. footed bowl & 4 footed sauce dishes, 5 pcs........	75.00
Bitters bottle w/original stopper	55.00
Bowl, 7" d., footed	32.00
Bowl, 10 x 7¼" oval..............	47.00
Butter dish, cov., round	46.00
Cake plate, handled, amber, 10" d........................	42.00
Cake plate, handled, 10" d.	28.00

Cake stand, 9" d.	73.00
Cologne bottle w/original stopper ..	90.00
Compote, cov., 6" d., 8" h.........	70.00
Compote, cov., 7" d., 8" h.........	85.00
Compote, cov., 8" d., 10" h........	80.00
Compote, cov., 8" d., 10" h., vaseline......................	110.00
Compote, open, 5" d., 5½" h.......	55.00
Compote, open, 5½" d., high stand	36.00
Compote, open, 5¾" d., vaseline ...	55.00
Compote, open, 6" d., 5" h., blue...	70.00
Compote, open, 6" d., low stand (ILLUS.)......................	24.00
Compote, open, 7" d., low stand ...	40.00
Compote, open, 7" d., 7" h.........	45.00
Creamer, round, amber............	45.00
Creamer, round, blue..............	55.00
Creamer, round	23.00
Creamer, square	34.00
Creamer, square, vaseline	60.00
Creamer & sugar bowl, square, pr.........................	95.00
Goblet, amber	42.50
Goblet	30.00
Goblet, vaseline	43.50
Mug, clear, 3½" h................	45.00
Mug, applied handle, "In Fond Remembrance"..................	32.00
Mug, applied handle, "In Fond Remembrance," yellow	45.00
Pitcher, water, applied handle, amber	112.50
Pitcher, water, applied handle, blue	225.00
Pitcher, water, applied handle	80.00
Plate, 5" d.	30.00
Plate, 7" d.	20.00
Plate, 8" d.	37.00
Powder jar, cov.	21.00
Relish, 8 x 5½" oval..............	15.00
Relish, 9¼ x 6¼"	19.00
Relish, double	80.00
Sauce dish, flat or footed	12.00
Spooner, round	28.50
Spooner, square	35.00
Sugar bowl, cov., round	37.50
Sugar bowl, cov., square	45.00
Table set, square, 4 pcs...........	170.00
Tumbler	38.00
Wine............................	20.00

ROSE SPRIG

Bowl, 8 x 7½", footed	32.00
Bowl, 9 x 6" rectangle, vaseline	27.50
Bread tray, 2-handled, blue	35.00
Bread tray, 2-handled, yellow	40.00
Cake stand, amber, 9" octagon, 6½" h..........................	60.00
Cake stand, blue, 9" octagon, 6½" h..........................	65.00
Cake stand, yellow, 9" octagon, 6½" h..........................	85.00
Celery vase, amber	45.00

Celery vase...................... 30.00
Celery vase, yellow 36.00
Compote, cov., high stand, large ... 75.00
Compote, open, 7" oval, amber 36.00
Compote, open, 7" d., 5" h.,
   yellow 37.00
Compote, open, 9" d., low stand ... 19.00
Compote, open, 9" d., high stand,
   amber 37.50
Creamer, amber 40.00
Creamer, yellow 40.00
Goblet, amber 30.00
Goblet, blue..................... 48.00
Goblet 24.00
Goblet, yellow 32.00
Honey dish, cov., amber, square ... 23.00
Nappy, handled, 6" sq. 18.00
Pitcher, milk, amber.............. 55.00
Pitcher, water, amber 65.00
Pitcher, water 43.00
Pitcher, water, yellow 70.00
Plate, 6" sq., amber 26.50

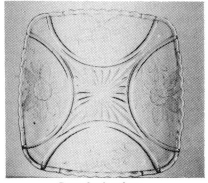

Rose Sprig Plate

Plate, 6" sq., blue (ILLUS.) 30.00
Plate, 6" sq. 20.00
Relish, handled, blue, 6 x 4" 32.50
Relish, handled, yellow, 6 x 4" 20.00
Relish, boat-shaped, amber, 8" l. ... 30.00
Relish, boat-shaped, blue, 8" l...... 36.00
Relish, boat-shaped, 8" l. 20.00
Relish, boat-shaped, yellow, 8" l. ... 32.00
Sauce dish, flat, amber 15.00
Sauce dish, flat 12.50
Sauce dish, footed, blue 17.50
Sauce dish, footed 8.00
Spooner 15.00
Tumbler, amber.................. 30.00
Tumbler w/applied handle 45.00
Wine, blue 50.00
Wine............................ 28.00
Whimsey, sleigh (salt dip), amber,
   4 x 6 x 4" 45.00

ROSETTE
Bowl, cov., 7¼" d., flat............ 30.00
Bowl, 7½" d. 20.00
Bread plate, handled, 11" d. 25.00
Butter dish, cov. 40.00

Cake stand, 8½" to 11" d. 32.00
Celery vase..................... 21.00
Compote, cov., 6" d., 9" h.......... 70.00

Rosette Compote

Compote, open, jelly, 4½" d., 5" h.
   (ILLUS.)....................... 15.00
Compote, open, 7¼" d., 6" h....... 22.00
Compote, open, 9" d., low stand ... 14.00
Creamer 28.50
Goblet 22.00
Pitcher, milk.................... 45.00
Pitcher, water, tankard 47.00
Plate, 7" d. 22.50
Plate, 9" d., 2-handled............ 20.00
Relish, fish-shaped 12.00
Salt shaker w/replaced top
   (single)....................... 23.00
Sauce dish...................... 8.00
Spooner 32.00
Sugar bowl, cov. 33.00
Tumbler, ruby-stained 29.00
Wine........................... 25.00

ROYAL IVY
Berry set: master bowl & 5 sauce
   dishes; rubina crystal, 6 pcs. 250.00
Berry set: master bowl & 5 sauce
   dishes; frosted rubina crystal,
   6 pcs. 295.00
Berry set: master bowl & 6 sauce
   dishes; clear & frosted, 7 pcs. 200.00
Berry set: master bowl & 8 sauce
   dishes; clear & frosted, 9 pcs. ... 250.00
Bowl, 8" d., rubina crystal 95.00
Bowl, 8" d., frosted rubina crystal .. 120.00
Bowl, fruit, 9" d., craquelle (cran-
   berry & vaseline spatter)........ 125.00
Bowl, fruit, 9" d., frosted
   craquelle 150.00
Butter dish, cov., clear & frosted ... 175.00
Butter dish, cov., frosted craquelle.. 137.50
Butter dish, cov., rubina crystal..... 162.00
Butter dish, cov., frosted rubina
   crystal 175.00
Creamer, clear & frosted.......... 50.00
Cruet w/original stopper, cased
   spatter (cranberry & vaseline) 395.00

Cruet w/original stopper, rubina crystal 275.00

Cruet w/original stopper, frosted rubina crystal 310.00

Dresser jar, clear & frosted 85.00

Lamp, kerosene, frosted rubina crystal, miniature 85.00

Marmalade jar, cov., clear & frosted 32.50

Marmalade jar, cov., rubina crystal 100.00

Pickle castor, rubina crystal insert, complete w/silverplate frame 260.00

Pickle castor, frosted rubina crystal insert, complete w/silverplate frame 275.00

Pickle castor, cased spatter (cranberry & vaseline) insert, complete w/silverplate frame & tongs 350.00

Pitcher, water, cased spatter (cranberry & vaseline)................ 225.00

Pitcher, water, clear & frosted...... 102.00

Pitcher, water, craquelle 450.00

Pitcher, water, frosted craquelle.... 400.00

Pitcher, water, rubina crystal ....165.00 to 225.00

Pitcher, water, frosted rubina crystal 268.00

Rose bowl, cased spatter (cranberry to vaseline)...................... 295.00

Rose bowl, clear & frosted 85.00

Rose bowl, rubina crystal 60.00

Rose bowl, frosted rubina crystal ... 80.00

Salt shaker w/original top, craquelle (single)......................... 52.00

Salt shaker w/original top, rubina crystal (single) 46.00

Salt & pepper shakers w/original tops, clear & frosted, pr.......... 69.00

Salt & pepper shakers w/original tops, rubina crystal, pr.......... 78.00

Salt & pepper shakers w/original tops, frosted rubina crystal, pr.... 100.00

Sauce dish, clear & frosted 37.50

Sauce dish, frosted rubina crystal ....35.00 to 40.00

Spooner, clear & frosted 40.00

Spooner, rubina crystal 79.00

Spooner, frosted rubina crystal 75.00

Sugar bowl, cov., clear & frosted ... 45.00

Sugar bowl, cov., rubina crystal 128.00

Sugar bowl, cov., frosted rubina crystal 130.00

Sugar shaker w/original top, cased spatter (cranberry to vaseline) ... 175.00

Sugar shaker w/original top, clear & frosted ....58.00 to 75.00

Sugar shaker w/original top, frosted craquelle 200.00

Sugar shaker w/original top, rubina crystal 110.00

Sweetmeat jar w/silverplate top, cased spatter (cranberry & vaseline), 4½" d., 3½" h............. 195.00

Syrup pitcher w/original top, cased spatter (cranberry & vaseline w/white lining) 500.00

Syrup pitcher w/original top, clear & frosted 155.00

Syrup pitcher w/original top, rubina crystal 250.00

Syrup pitcher w/original top, frosted rubina crystal 450.00

Table set: cov. butter dish, cov. sugar bowl & spooner, clear & frosted, 3 pcs. 200.00

Table set, cased spatter, 4 pcs..... 875.00

Table set, craquelle, 4 pcs......... 850.00

Table set, frosted rubina crystal, 4 pcs........................ 495.00

Toothpick holder, cased spatter (cranberry & vaseline) 75.00

Toothpick holder, clear & frosted ... 30.00

Toothpick holder, craquelle 125.00

Toothpick holder, rubina crystal 85.00

Toothpick holder, frosted rubina crystal 125.00

Tumbler, whiskey, handled, flint.... 95.00

Tumbler, clear & frosted 25.00

Tumbler, craquelle 78.00

Tumbler, frosted craquelle 125.00

Tumbler, rubina crystal 42.50

Tumbler, frosted rubina crystal 65.00

Water set: pitcher & 5 tumblers; cased spatter, 6 pcs. 850.00

Water set: pitcher & 5 tumblers; frosted rubina crystal, 6 pcs. 325.00

Water set: pitcher & 6 tumblers; rubina crystal, 7 pcs. ....400.00 to 500.00

ROYAL OAK

Royal Oak Sugar Shaker

Berry set: master bowl & 4 sauce dishes; rubina crystal, 5 pcs. 225.00

Bowl, berry, 7½" d., frosted crystal 65.00

Butter dish, cov., frosted crystal 65.00

Butter dish, cov., rubina crystal..... 135.00

Butter dish, cov., frosted rubina crystal 180.00

Creamer, frosted crystal 80.00

Creamer, rubina crystal	85.00
Creamer, frosted rubina crystal	245.00
Cruet w/original stopper, frosted crystal	95.00
Cruet w/original stopper, rubina crystal	425.00
Cruet w/original stopper, frosted rubina crystal	310.00
Dresser jar, cov., frosted crystal, 5" w., 5½" h.	150.00
Nappy, frosted crystal	30.00
Pickle castor, frosted rubina crystal insert, w/silverplate frame & cover	225.00
Pitcher, 8½" h., frosted crystal	100.00
Pitcher, water, rubina crystal	260.00
Pitcher, water, frosted rubina crystal	312.00
Salt shaker w/original top, frosted crystal (single)	60.00
Salt shaker w/original top, rubina crystal (single)	52.00
Salt shaker w/original top, frosted rubina crystal (single)	65.00
Salt & pepper shakers w/original tops, frosted crystal, pr.	135.00
Salt & pepper shakers w/original tops, frosted rubina crystal, pr.	150.00
Sauce cish, frosted crystal	12.50
Sauce dish, rubina crystal	40.00
Sauce dish, frosted rubina crystal	30.00
Spooner, frosted crystal	60.00
Spooner, rubina crystal	60.00
Spooner, frosted rubina crystal	100.00
Sugar bowl, cov., frosted crystal	55.00
Sugar bowl, cov., rubina crystal	140.00
Sugar bowl, cov., frosted rubina crystal	130.00
Sugar bowl, open, frosted rubina crystal	60.00
Sugar shaker w/original top, frosted crystal	65.00
Sugar shaker w/original top, rubina crystal	125.00
Sugar shaker w/original top, frosted rubina crystal (ILLUS.)	165.00
Syrup pitcher w/original (repaired) top, rubina crystal	275.00
Table set, frosted rubina crystal, 4 pcs.	600.00
Toothpick holder, frosted crystal	57.00
Toothpick holder, rubina crystal	89.00
Toothpick holder, frosted rubina crystal	125.00
Tumbler, frosted crystal	75.00
Tumbler, frosted rubina crystal	80.00
Water set: pitcher & 5 tumblers; frosted crystal, 6 pcs.	425.00

RUBY ROSETTE - See Pillow Encircled Pattern

RUBY THUMBPRINT

(Items may be plain or with etched designs)

Ruby Thumbprint Creamer

Berry set, boat-shaped master bowl & 5 boat-shaped sauce dishes, 6 pcs.	195.00
Berry set: master bowl & 6 sauce dishes; round, 7 pcs.	235.00
Berry set: master bowl & 8 sauce dishes; round, 9 pcs.	250.00
Bowl, 6½" d.	33.50
Bowl, 8½" d.	45.00
Bowl, master berry or fruit, 10" l., boat-shaped	125.00
Butter dish, cov.	105.00
Cake stand, 10" d.	125.00
Castor set, 5-bottle, w/frame	325.00 to 425.00
Celery vase	53.00
Champagne	35.00
Cheese dish, cov., 7" d.	55.00
Claret	46.50
Compote, open, jelly, 5¼" h.	43.00
Compote, open, 7" d.	90.00
Compote, open, 8½" d., 7½" h., scalloped rim	230.00
Cordial	28.00
Creamer	54.00
Creamer, souvenir, "Dear Mother" & date (ILLUS.)	60.00
Creamer, individual size	30.00
Creamer & sugar bowl, individual size, pr.	85.00
Dish, cov., 8" d., 7" h.	68.00
Goblet	38.00
Match holder	20.00
Mustard jar, cov.	58.00
Mustard jar, cov., etched "World's Fair, 1893"	127.50
Olive dish	125.00
Pitcher, milk, 7½" h., bulbous	120.00
Pitcher, milk, tankard, 8 3/8" h.	82.00
Pitcher, water, bulbous, large	250.00
Pitcher, water, tankard, 11" h.	136.00
Plate, 5" d.	22.00
Punch cup	18.00
Relish, 8" oblong	35.00
Salt dip, individual size	145.00

Salt & pepper shakers w/original
tops, pr. 62.50
Salt & pepper shakers w/original
tops, individual size, pr. 95.00
Sauce dish, boat-shaped 28.00
Sauce dish, round 20.00
Spooner 50.00
Sugar bowl, cov. 77.50
Sugar bowl, open 32.50
Sugar bowl, open, individual size,
2½" h. 26.00
Table set, 4 pcs. ....250.00 to 350.00
Toothpick holder 25.00
Tumbler 35.00
Tumbler, etched, "World's Fair,
1893" 29.00
Water set, bulbous pitcher & 5 tum-
blers, 6 pcs. 315.00
Water set, tankard pitcher & 5 tum-
blers, 6 pcs. 295.00
Water set, tankard pitcher & 7 tum-
blers, 8 pcs. 395.00
Wine............................ 34.00

SANDWICH LOOP - See Hairpin Pattern

SANDWICH STAR
Butter dish, cov. 195.00
Compote, open, 8½" d., low
stand 60.00
Compote, open, 12" d., 9½" h. 265.00
Decanter w/patented stopper, pt. ... 135.00
Decanter w/bar lip, pt. 70.00
Decanter w/bar lip, qt. 85.00
Decanter w/stopper, qt. 115.00
Lamp, whale oil, 6-sided font,
10½" h. 125.00
Lamps, whale oil, 10½" h., pr. 300.00
Spillholder 50.00
Spillholder, clambroth 440.00
Spillholder, electric blue ...565.00 to 750.00
Spooner 95.00
Spooner, clambroth................ 400.00

SAWTOOTH
Ale glass 35.00
Banana boat, non-flint 57.50
Bitters bottle w/stopper, flint 47.50
Butter dish, cov., flint 80.00
Butter dish, cov., non-flint 35.00
Cake stand, non-flint, 7½" d.,
6" h. 35.00
Cake stand, non-flint, 9½" d.,
4½" h.......................... 52.50
Carafe 45.00
Celery vases, knob stem, flint, pr. .. 105.00
Celery vase, knob stem, non-flint ... 38.00
Champagne, knob stem, flint 55.00
Champagne, non-flint.............. 32.50
Compote, cov., 6½" d., 9" h., milk
white, flint 105.00
Compote, cov., 7½" d., 8¼" h.,
flint........................... 65.00
Compote, cov., 7½" d., 11½" h.,
flint........................... 85.00

Compote, cov., 8" d., low stand,
flint........................... 125.00
Compote, cov., 8" d., high stand,
flint........................... 82.00
Compote, cov., 9¼" d., 4" h., non-
flint........................... 48.00
Compote, cov., 9½" d., 14" h.,
flint........................... 200.00
Compote, cov., 9½" d., 14" h., non-
flint........................... 62.50
Compote, open, 7½" d., 7½" h.,
flint........................... 47.00
Compote, open, 7¾" d., 6¼" h.,
flint........................... 72.00
Compote, open, 8" d., 6" h., non-
flint........................... 36.00
Compote, open, 10" d., 9" h., flint .. 60.00
Cordial, non-flint 20.00
Cordial, ruby-stained 38.00
Creamer, applied handle, flint...... 75.00
Creamer, applied handle, milk
white, flint, 5¼" h. .....160.00 to 300.00
Creamer, applied handle, non-flint.. 30.00
Creamer, miniature 14.00
Cruet w/original stopper, non-flint .. 22.50
Decanter w/acorn stopper, flint,
½ pt. 105.00
Egg cup, flint 43.00
Egg cup, cov., flint 65.00
Goblet, flattened sawtooth......... 47.00
Goblet, knob stem, flint 32.00
Goblet, knob stem, non-flint 20.00
Goblet, plain stem, non-flint 19.00
Honey dish, 3½" d. 28.00
Lamps, whale oil, w/marble bases,
pr.............................. 240.00
Pickle jar w/original cover 65.00
Pitcher, milk, non-flint 25.00
Pitcher, water, applied handle,
flint........................... 115.00
Pitcher, water, applied handle, milk
white, flint 345.00
Plate, 6" d., rayed center 17.00
Salt dip, cov., individual size, foot-
ed, flint 35.00
Salt dip, individual size, footed,
flint........................... 18.00
Salt dip, cov., master size, footed,
flint........................... 58.00
Salt dip, master size, flint 32.50
Salt dip, master size, non-flint...... 15.00
Salt dip, master size, fiery opales-
cent, flint 175.00
Salt dip, master size, milk white,
non-flint 19.50
Salt shaker w/original top, milk
white, non-flint (single) 19.50
Spillholder, flint.................. 66.00
Spillholder, non-flint.............. 22.50
Spooner, cobalt blue 70.00
Spooner, flint 45.00
Spooner, non-flint 22.00
Spooner, child's 30.00
Sugar bowl, cov., flint 75.00

Sugar bowl, cov., non-flint 28.50
Sugar bowl, cov., miniature 45.00
Sugar bowl, open, flint 48.00
Table set, 4 pcs. 125.00
Table set, milk white, 4 pcs. 310.00

Sawtooth Tumbler

Tumbler, bar, flint, 4½" h.
  (ILLUS.) 50.00
Tumbler, bar, non-flint 35.00
Tumbler, flat, flint 36.00
Tumbler, footed, flint 65.00
Tumble-up (carafe w/tumbler lid) . . . 175.00
Vase, 9 7/8" h. 25.00
Wine, flint 35.00
Wine, non-flint 27.50

SAWTOOTH BAND - See Amazon Pattern

SCALLOPED TAPE - See Jewel Band Pattern

SEDAN (Paneled Star & Button)
Butter dish, cov. 38.00
Compote, cov., 8" d., high stand . . . 26.00
Compote, open, high stand 20.00
Creamer 28.00
Goblet 22.00
Mug, miniature 12.50
Pitcher, water 45.00
Relish, 10" l. 10.00
Salt dip, master size 12.50
Sauce dish, flat, 4½" d. 6.00
Spooner 25.00
Sugar bowl, cov. 45.00
Sugar bowl, open 36.00
Wine 15.00

SENECA LOOP - See Loop Pattern

SHELL & JEWEL (Victor)
Berry set, master bowl & 4 sauce
  dishes, 5 pcs. 35.00
Bowl, 8" d. 20.00
Bowl, 10" d., amber 15.00
Butter dish, cov. 60.00

Cake stand, 10" d., 5" h. 40.00
Compote, cov., 8½" d., high
  stand 75.00
Compote, open, 7" d., 7½" h. 40.00
Creamer 40.00
Pitcher, milk, blue 75.00
Pitcher, milk 35.00
Pitcher, water, amber 100.00
Pitcher, water, blue or green 85.00
Pitcher, water 36.00
Relish, oblong 18.00
Sauce dish, amber 15.00
Sauce dish 8.50
Spooner 22.50
Sugar bowl, cov. 42.50
Tumbler, amber 35.00
Tumbler, blue 34.00

Shell & Jewel Tumbler

Tumbler (ILLUS.) 20.00
Tumbler, green 36.00
Water set, pitcher & 4 tumblers,
  5 pcs. 75.00
Water set: pitcher & 5 tumblers;
  blue, 6 pcs. 225.00
Water set: pitcher & 6 tumblers;
  amber, 7 pcs. 260.00
Water set, pitcher & 6 tumblers,
  7 pcs. 150.00
Water set: pitcher & 6 tumblers;
  green, 7 pcs. 225.00

SHELL & TASSEL
Berry set, 10" oval master bowl & 6
  square footed sauce dishes;
  7 pcs. 190.00
Bowl, 8 x 5" rectangle 24.00
Bowl, 9" oval, amber 50.00
Bowl, 9" oval 40.00
Bowl, 9" oval, vaseline 57.50
Bowl, 11½ x 6½" oval, amber 90.00
Bowl, 11½ x 6½" oval, blue 95.00
Bowl, 11½ x 6½" oval 49.00
Bowl, rectangular, amber 75.00
Bread tray, 13 x 9" 52.00

Bride's basket, 8" oval bowl in sil-
verplate frame 125.00
Bride's basket, 10 x 5" oval amber
bowl in silverplate frame 275.00
Butter dish, cov., round, dog finial . . 100.00
Cake stand, shell corners, 8" sq. . . . 45.00
Cake stand, shell corners, 9" sq. . . . 50.00
Cake stand, shell corners, 10" sq. . . 65.00
Cake stand, shell corners, 12" sq. . . 82.00
Celery vase, round, handled 47.50
Celery vase, square 48.00
Compote, cov., 4¼" sq., 8" h. 47.50
Compote, cov., 5¼" sq. 65.00
Compote, cov., 7" d., dog finial 155.00
Compote, cov., 7½" d., 8" h. 75.00
Compote, open, jelly 50.00
Compote, open, 4½" sq., high
stand 35.00
Compote, open, 5½" sq., 6" h. 29.50
Compote, open, 7½" sq., 7½" h. . . . 44.00
Compote, open, 8½" sq., 8" h. 60.00
Compote, open, 10" sq.,
8" h. 60.00 to 75.00
Creamer, round 32.00
Creamer, square 45.00
Creamer & cov. sugar bowl, square,
pr. 120.00
Dish, 10 x 7" 25.00
Doughnut stand, 8" sq. 55.00
Goblet, round, knob stem 40.00
Goblet, square, knob stem 24.50
Mug, miniature, blue 35.00
Oyster plate, 9½" d. 210.00
Pickle dish 22.00
Pitcher, water, round 60.00
Pitcher, water, square 68.00
Plate, shell-shaped w/three shell-
shaped feet, large 67.50
Platter, 11 x 8" oblong 50.00
Relish, blue, 8 x 5" 85.00
Relish, 8 x 5" 40.00
Salt dip, shell-shaped 20.00
Salt & pepper shakers w/original
tops, pr. 125.00
Sauce dish, flat or footed, 4" to
5" d. 10.00
Sauce dish, footed, w/shell
handle 13.50
Spooner, round 37.00
Spooner, square 29.00
Sugar bowl, cov., round, dog
finial 90.00
Sugar bowl, cov., square, shell
finial 75.00
Sugar bowl, open, round 52.00
Sugar bowl, open, square 25.00
Table set, 4 pcs. 295.00
Tray, ice cream 47.00
Tumbler 15.50
Vase 125.00

SHERATON

Bowl, 6 5/8 x 4 7/8", amber 23.00
Bowl, 10 x 8", 8-sided 18.50

Bread platter, amber, 10 x 8" 42.50
Bread platter, blue, 10 x 8" 33.00
Bread platter, 10 x 8" 23.00
Butter dish, cov., blue 50.00
Butter dish, cov. 40.00
Cake stand, amber, 10¼" d. 45.00
Cake stand, 10½" d. 32.00
Celery vase 24.00
Compote, cov., 8" d. 35.00
Compote, open, 7" d., 5" h.,
amber 28.00
Compote, open, 7" d., 5" h. 21.00
Compote, open, 8" d., 7¾" h 28.00
Compote, open, 8" d., low stand . . . 24.00
Compote, open, 10" d. 45.00
Creamer, amber 27.00
Creamer, blue 37.00
Creamer 23.00
Creamer & sugar bowl, amber, pr . . . 45.00
Goblet, blue 43.00

Sheraton Goblet

Goblet (ILLUS.) 26.00
Pickle dish, amber 16.00
Pickle dish 7.00
Pitcher, milk, amber 40.00
Pitcher, milk 24.00
Pitcher, water, amber 55.00
Pitcher, water 45.00
Plate, 7" sq., amber 20.00
Plate, 8½" sq. 8.50
Relish, handled, amber 16.50
Relish, handled, blue 31.00
Relish, handled 14.50
Sauce dish, blue, 4" d. 12.00
Sauce dish, 4" d. 9.00
Spooner, amber 30.00
Spooner, blue 32.50
Spooner 22.00
Sugar bowl, cov., amber 44.00
Sugar bowl, cov. 25.00
Tumbler 22.00
Wine 21.00

SHOSHONE

Bowl, 7" flat 11.00
Cake stand 23.50

Cake stand, green 55.00
Compote, jelly 17.50
Creamer, amber-stained 47.00
Plate, 11" d., reticulated rim, milk
  white 35.00
Relish, 7½" l..................... 11.00
Sauce dish, w/gold, 5" sq. 12.50

SHOVEL
Compote, open, jelly 18.00
Goblet 19.00
Syrup pitcher w/glass top 19.00
Tumbler 16.00
Wine............................. 18.00

SHRINE
Bowl, 6½" d., scalloped rim........ 20.00
Bowl, 8¼" d. 31.50
Butter dish, cov. 45.00
Champagne....................... 58.50
Compote, cov., high stand 75.00
Compote, open, jelly 22.50
Creamer 32.50
Goblet 37.50
Lamp, kerosene, w/fingergrip ped-
  estal base, 10" h. 145.00
Mug 38.50
Pickle dish....................... 19.00
Pitcher, cider, ½ gal............... 125.00
Pitcher, water 45.00
Plate, 6" d., scalloped rim 46.00
Salt shaker w/original top (single) .. 28.50
Salt & pepper shakers w/replaced
  tops, pr........................ 45.00
Sauce dish....................... 13.00
Spooner 26.50
Sugar bowl, cov. 47.50
Toothpick holder 85.00
Tumbler, 4" h. 37.50
Wine............................. 45.00

SHUTTLE (Hearts of Loch Laven)

Shuttle Creamer

Bowl, berry, large................. 30.00
Butter dish, cov. 50.00
Cake stand 57.50
Celery vase...................... 48.00
Champagne....................... 36.00
Cordial, small.................... 22.50
Creamer, tall tankard (ILLUS.) 35.00
Goblet 40.00
Mug, amber 50.00
Mug 28.00
Pitcher, water 70.00
Punch cup 12.00
Salt shaker w/original top (single) .. 42.50
Wine............................. 13.00

SKILTON - See Oregon Pattern

SMOCKING

Smocking Sugar Bowl

Bowl, 7" d., footed 38.50
Butter dish, cov. 90.00
Cake stand, purple, 8½" d. 750.00
Champagne, knob stem 85.00
Compote, 6" d., 4" h.............. 50.00
Compote, 7¾" d., low stand 52.00
Creamer, applied handle.......... 105.00
Creamer, individual size 125.00
Creamer w/applied handle & cov.
  sugar bowl, pr. 275.00
Goblet 45.00
Spillholder....................... 39.50
Spooner 37.50
Sugar bowl, cov. (ILLUS.)........... 67.00
Wine............................. 65.00

SNAIL (Compact)
Banana stand, 10" d., 7" h. 165.00
Bowl, 7" d., low 34.00
Bowl, berry, 8" d., 4" h. 32.50
Bowl, 9" d., 2" h. 30.00
Butter dish, cov. 82.00
Cake stand, 10" d. 87.50
Celery vase...................... 55.00

Compote, cov., 7" d., 11½" h...... 130.00
Compote, open, 8" d., 9" h........ 65.00
Cookie jar, cov., 8" d., 9" h....... 125.00
Creamer 48.00
Creamer, ruby-stained 75.00
Cruet w/original stopper.......... 93.00
Cruet w/original stopper, ruby-
   stained....................... 225.00
Goblet 65.00
Honey dish, cov................. 95.00
Pickle dish, 8 x 5½"............. 28.00
Pitcher, cider, bulbous.......... 150.00
Pitcher, milk, bulbous, applied han-
   dle, large 120.00
Pitcher, water, tankard 89.00
Pitcher, wine, tankard 155.00
Plate, 7" d..................... 27.50
Plate, 9" d..................... 34.00
Punch cup 27.00
Relish, 7" oval 25.00
Rose bowl, miniature, 3" h........ 23.00
Rose bowl, double, miniature 35.00
Rose bowl, large 50.00
Salt dip, individual size 20.00
Salt dip, master size, 3" d........ 50.00
Salt shaker w/original top, ruby-
   stained (single) 50.00
Salt & pepper shakers w/original
   tops, ruby-stained, pr........... 95.00
Sauce dish.................9.00 to 15.00

Snail Spooner

Spooner (ILLUS.).................. 32.00
Spooner, ruby-stained 85.00
Sugar bowl, cov. 60.00
Sugar shaker w/original top 100.00
Sugar shaker w/original top, ruby-
   stained....................... 193.00
Tumbler 46.00
Vase, 12½" h., scalloped rim 55.00
Vase, 17" h.................... 65.00

SNAKESKIN & DOT
Bread tray..................... 140.00
Celery vase.................... 35.00
Compote, cov. 60.00
Creamer 35.00
Goblet 30.00

Plate, 4½" d., amber.............. 9.00
Plate, 7" d., milk white........... 15.00
Plate, 9" d..................... 25.00
Sugar bowl, cov. 45.00

SPARTAN (Barred Star)
Cordial........................ 15.00
Goblet 22.50
Sauce dish, flat 10.00
Sugar bowl, cov. 60.00
Tumbler 17.50

SPIREA BAND
Bowl, 8" oval, flat, blue 39.00
Butter dish, cov., amber 50.00
Butter dish, cov., blue 57.50
Butter dish, cov................ 40.00
Cake stand, amber, 8½" d. 45.00
Celery vase, blue 35.00
Compote, cov., 7" d., high stand,
   blue 65.00
Compote, cov., 7" d., high stand ... 40.00
Compote, open, 7" d., low stand,
   amber 26.00
Compote, open, 8" d.............. 25.00
Creamer, amber 36.50
Creamer, blue 32.50
Creamer 20.00
Goblet, amber 22.50
Goblet, blue 36.00
Goblet 24.00
Pickle dish.................... 7.00
Pitcher, water, amber 42.50
Pitcher, water, blue 90.00
Pitcher, water 45.00
Platter, 10½ x 8½", amber 25.00
Platter, 10½ x 8½", blue 32.50
Platter, 10½ x 8½"............. 20.00
Platter, 10½ x 8½", vaseline....... 28.00
Relish, amber, 7 x 4½"........... 10.00
Relish, amber, 9 x 5½"........... 18.50
Salt shaker w/original top, blue
   (single)....................... 37.50
Salt & pepper shakers w/original
   tops, amber, pr. 30.00
Sauce dish, flat or footed,
   amber ....6.00 to 12.00
Sauce dish, flat or footed, blue 12.00
Spooner, amber................. 26.00
Spooner, blue.................. 33.00
Spooner 18.00
Spooner, vaseline 26.00
Sugar bowl, cov., blue........... 55.00
Sugar bowl, cov. 32.50
Sugar bowl, open, amber 22.00
Tumbler, blue.................. 50.00
Wine, amber................... 25.00
Wine, blue.................... 30.00
Wine......................... 18.50

SPRIG
Berry set, 8½" d. master bowl & 6
   sauce dishes, 7 pcs. 80.00
Bowl, 8" oval, footed 42.00
Bowl, 9" oval 40.00

Bread platter, 11" oval	32.00
Butter dish, cov.	47.50
Cake stand	42.50
Celery vase	36.50
Compote, cov., 6" d., high stand ...	50.00
Compote, cov., 8" d., low stand	45.00
Compote, open, 6" d.............	30.00
Compote, open, 6¾" d., 5½" h.....	17.50
Compote, open, 7" d., low stand ...	24.00
Compote, open, 8" d., high stand ...	24.00
Compote, open, 10" d., high stand..	42.50
Creamer	30.00
Goblet	32.00
Pickle castor, resilvered frame & tongs	85.00
Pitcher, water	50.00

Sprig Relish

Relish, 8¾" oval (ILLUS.)	22.00
Salt dip, master size...............	45.00
Sauce dish, flat or footed	8.00
Spooner	23.50
Sugar bowl, cov.	48.00
Sugar bowl, open	20.00
Wine...........................	38.00

SQUARE LION'S HEAD - See Lion Pattern

SQUARE PANES - See Post Pattern

STAR ROSETTED

Star Rosetted Goblet

Bowl, 7¼ x 5" oval...............	6.50
Butter dish, cov.	40.00
Cake (or bread) plate, "A Good Mother Makes A Happy Home"...	55.00
Creamer	30.00
Goblet (ILLUS.)....................	28.00
Relish, 3-handled, 9¾ x 5"	6.50

Sauce dish, flat or footed	4.50
Spooner	25.00
Sugar bowl, cov.	40.00

STATES (THE)

Bowl, 7" d., 3-handled	55.00
Bowl, 7½" d.	25.00
Bowl, 9" d.	60.00
Butter dish, cov.	58.00
Card tray, 7 3/8 x 5"	15.00
Celery	30.00
Cocktail, flared	24.00
Compote, open, 5½ x 5".........	27.00
Compote, open, 9¼" d., 9" h.......	80.00
Creamer	30.00
Creamer, individual size	29.00
Creamer & sugar bowl, individual size, pr......................	42.50
Goblet	32.00
Nappy, 2-handled	22.50
Olive dish	17.50
Pitcher, water	65.00
Punch cup	12.50
Salt shaker w/original top (single) ..	16.50
Salt & pepper shakers w/original tops, pr......................	54.00
Sauce dish......................	12.00
Spooner	26.50
Sugar bowl, cov.	48.00
Sugar bowl, open, individual size ...	17.50
Syrup jug	95.00
Toothpick holder	32.00
Tumbler	18.50
Water set, pitcher & 6 tumblers, 7 pcs.	125.00
Wine...........................	30.00

STEDMAN

Champagne......................	35.00
Compote, open, 7½" d., 7" h.......	45.00
Creamer	40.00
Egg cup	20.00
Goblet	27.50
Sauce dish, flat	14.00
Spooner	40.00
Syrup pitcher, applied handle, 4¼" d., 8¼" h.	100.00
Wine...........................	45.00

STIPPLED CHAIN

Creamer	30.00
Goblet	22.50
Relish, 8¼ x 6 1/8"	7.50
Salt dip, master size..............	19.50
Sauce dish......................	4.50
Spooner	22.50
Tumbler	20.00

STIPPLED CHERRY

Bowl, master berry, 8" d.	28.00
Bread platter	26.00
Butter dish, cov.	42.00
Creamer	22.50
Pitcher, water	52.00

Plate, 6" d.	20.00
Sauce dish, flat	6.50
Spooner	25.00
Tumbler	22.00

STIPPLED DOUBLE LOOP

Butter dish, cov.	40.00
Goblet	28.00
Spooner	22.00
Sugar bowl, cov.	35.00
Tumbler	15.00

STIPPLED FLOWER PANELS - See Maine Pattern

STIPPLED FORGET-ME-NOT

Stippled Forget-Me-Not Compote

Bread platter	37.00
Butter dish, cov.	48.00
Cake stand, 8" to 9" d.	42.50
Celery vase	32.00
Compote, cov., 8" d., high stand	55.00
Compote, open, 6" d., 6½" h. (ILLUS.)	32.50
Compote, open, 8" d.	45.00
Creamer	24.00
Goblet	35.00
Mug	20.00
Pitcher, milk	37.00
Pitcher, water	52.00
Plate, 7" d., w/kitten center	45.00
Salt dip, master size, oval	35.00
Salt shaker w/original top (single)	25.00
Syrup pitcher w/original top	80.00
Tray, water	75.00
Tumbler	30.00
Wine	42.50

STIPPLED GRAPE & FESTOON

Celery vase	28.00
Compote, 8" d., low stand	38.50
Creamer, w/clear leaf	38.50
Egg cup	25.00
Goblet	32.00
Pitcher, water	98.00
Spooner, w/clear leaf	26.00
Sugar bowl, open	21.00

STIPPLED IVY

Butter dish, cov.	45.00
Creamer, applied handle	35.00
Egg cup	28.00
Goblet	24.00
Salt dip, master size	23.00
Sauce dish, flat	8.00
Spooner	27.50
Sugar bowl, cov.	35.00
Sugar bowl, open	27.50
Tumbler, buttermilk	32.50

STIPPLED ROMAN KEY

Goblet	36.50
Tumbler	18.00

SUNK HONEYCOMB (Corona)

Sunk Honeycomb Cracker Jar

Cracker jar, cov., ruby-stained (ILLUS.)	485.00
Creamer, ruby-stained, 4½" h.	30.00
Cruet w/original stopper, ruby-stained, enameled floral decor	135.00
Mug, ruby-stained, 3" h.	16.00
Pitcher, 6½" h., ruby-stained, souvenir	20.00
Punch cup	6.50
Salt dip, master size, ruby-stained	65.00
Salt shaker w/original top (single)	6.50
Salt shaker w/original top, ruby-stained (single)	19.50
Syrup pitcher w/original top, ruby-stained	82.00
Toothpick holder, ruby-stained, souvenir	46.00
Tumbler, ruby-stained	32.00
Wine, etched	15.00
Wine, ruby-stained	32.50
Wine, ruby-stained, etched	40.00

SWAN

Butter dish, cov., swan finial	90.00
Celery vase	60.00
Compote, open, 8½" h.	45.00
Creamer (ILLUS. right)	42.00
Dish, cov.	55.00
Goblet, canary yellow	70.00
Goblet	50.00

Marmalade jar, cov. 57.50
Mug, footed 27.50
Mug, footed, ring handle, opaque
   blue 68.00
Mug, footed, ring handle, opaque
   purple 68.00
Mustard jar, cov., amber 75.00
Pitcher, water 140.00
Sauce dish, flat or footed 12.00

Swan Spooner & Creamer

Spooner (ILLUS. left) 55.00
Sugar bowl, open 40.00

TEARDROP & TASSEL

Teardrop & Tassel Salt Shaker

Berry set: master bowl & 5 sauce
   dishes; cobalt blue, 6 pcs. 145.00
Bowl, 7½" d.   40.00
Bowl, 7½" d., Nile green 35.00
Bowl, master berry or fruit, cobalt
   blue 45.00
Butter dish, cov. 55.00
Butter dish, cov., cobalt blue 135.00
Butter dish, cov., emerald green 130.00
Butter dish, cov., teal blue 160.00
Compote, open, 5" d. 29.00
Compote, open, 6" d. 32.50
Compote, open, Nile green 250.00
Creamer 25.00
Creamer, Nile green 80.00
Goblet 95.00
Pitcher, water 59.00
Pitcher, water, emerald green 195.00
Pitcher, water, teal blue 250.00

Relish 25.00
Relish, emerald green 45.00
Relish, Nile green 55.00
Salt shaker w/original top, single
   (ILLUS.) 65.00
Sauce dish 12.00
Sauce dish, cobalt blue 25.00
Sauce dish, emerald green 15.00
Spooner 30.00
Sugar bowl, cov. 45.00
Sugar bowl, cov., cobalt blue 135.00
Tumbler 26.00
Tumbler, cobalt blue 45.00
Tumbler, emerald green 40.00
Water set: pitcher & 6 tumblers;
   cobalt blue, 7 pcs. 550.00

TEASEL

Celery 20.00
Goblet 27.50
Plate, 7" to 9" d. . . . . .12.00 to 20.00
Sauce dish 5.50
Sugar bowl, open 30.00
Tumbler 10.00
Wine 12.00

TEXAS (Loop with Stippled Panels)

Texas Individual Creamer

Bowl, 8" oval 30.00
Butter dish, cov. 112.50
Cake stand, 9½" to 10¾" d. 75.00
Compote, cov., 6" d., 11" h. 90.00
Creamer 16.00
Creamer, individual size (ILLUS.) 16.00
Creamer & sugar bowl, individual
   size, pr. 29.00
Cruet w/original stopper 70.00
Cruet w/original stopper, ruby-
   stained 165.00
Goblet 45.00
Goblet, ruby-stained 95.00
Pitcher, water, 8½" h. 120.00
Plate, 8¾" d.   62.50
Relish, handled, 8½" l. 25.00
Salt dip, master size, footed, 3" d.,
   2¾" h. 22.50
Sauce dish, flat or footed 13.00
Spooner 52.50

Sugar bowl, cov. 60.00
Sugar bowl, open, individual size ... 16.00
Toothpick holder 29.00
Vase, bud, 8" h. 20.00
Vase, 9" h. 36.00
Vase, 10" h. 27.50
Wine............................... 78.00
Wine, ruby-stained 95.00

TEXAS BULL'S EYE (Bull's Eye Variant)

Celery vase........................ 32.00
Egg cup 15.00
Goblet 21.00
Lamp, kerosene-type, footed, hand-
   type w/finger grip 37.50
Sugar bowl, open 30.00
Tumbler 22.50
Wine.............................. 12.00

THISTLE - See Paneled Thistle Pattern

THOUSAND EYE

Thousand Eye Goblet

Bowl, 8" d., 4½" h., footed,
   amber 35.00
Bowl, 8" d., 4½" h., footed, blue
   opaque.......................... 55.00
Bowl, 11" rectangle, shallow,
   amber 38.00
Bowl, 11½" sq., 1¾" h., folded
   corners......................... 45.00
Bread tray, blue 37.50
Bread tray........................ 30.00
Butter dish, cov., amber 70.00
Butter dish, cov., apple green 80.00
Butter dish, cov., blue 82.50
Butter dish, cov. 37.50
Butter dish, cov., vaseline 70.00
Cake stand, amber, 8½" to
   10" d. ....47.50 to 60.00
Cake stand, apple green, 8½" to
   10" d. 67.50
Cake stand, 8½" to 10" d. 28.00
Celery vase, 3-knob stem, apple
   green 54.00
Celery vase, 3-knob stem 36.00

Celery vase, 3-knob stem, clear to
   opalescent w/purple tint 50.00
Celery vase, plain stem, amber..... 46.00
Celery vase, plain stem 35.00
Compote, cov., 12" h. 115.00
Compote, open, 6" d., low stand,
   amber 24.00
Compote, open, 6" d., low stand,
   apple green 31.00
Compote, open, 6" d., low stand,
   blue 37.00
Compote, open, 7½" d., 3-knob
   stem, amber 47.50
Compote, open, 7½" d., 3-knob
   stem, blue..................... 55.00
Compote, open, 7½" d., 5" h.,
   blue 48.00
Compote, open, 7½" d., 5" h. 25.00
Compote, open, 8" d., 3¾" h.,
   apple green 37.50
Compote, open, 8" d., 6" h., 3-knob
   stem, amber 35.00
Compote, open, 8" d., 6" h., 3-knob,
   apple green 45.00
Compote, open, 8" d., 6" h., 3-knob
   stem, blue..................... 41.00
Compote, open, 8" d., 6" h., 3-knob
   stem 40.00
Compote, open, 10" d., 6½" h.,
   apple green 45.00
Compote, open, 10" d., 6½" h.,
   3-knob stem, blue 75.00
Creamer, amber 37.00
Creamer 23.00
Creamer, vaseline................. 47.50
Creamer & cov. sugar bowl, amber,
   pr.............................. 80.00
Cruet w/original 3-knob stopper,
   amber 60.00
Cruet w/original 3-knob stopper,
   apple green 135.00
Cruet w/original 3-knob stopper,
   blue 75.00
Cruet w/original 3-knob stopper 40.00
Cruet w/original 3-knob stopper,
   vaseline 110.00
Cruet stand w/pr. cruets w/original
   stoppers, knob stem, amber,
   set............................ 210.00
Dish, apple green, 7 x 5" 25.00
Egg cup, blue 75.00
Egg cup 25.00
Egg cup, vaseline 65.00
Goblet, amber 27.00
Goblet, apple green 33.50
Goblet, blue 44.00
Goblet (ILLUS.) 25.00
Goblet, vaseline 34.00
Hat shape, small 12.00
Hat shape, vaseline, small 24.00
Honey dish, cov., apple green 125.00
Honey dish, cover w/knob finial,
   rectangular, vaseline 135.00
Inkwell, cov., 2" sq. 30.00

Lamp, kerosene-type, pedestal
base, amber, 14" h. to collar (22"
to chimney top) 165.00
Lamp, kerosene-type, pedestal
base, blue, 12" h. 165.00
Lamp, kerosene-type, flat base, ring
handle ....105.00 to 120.00
Lemonade set: tankard pitcher, lem-
on dish, 12" tray & 3 goblets; ap-
ple green, 6 pcs. 165.00
Mug, amber, 3½" h. 21.00
Mug, 3½" h. 12.50
Mug, vaseline, 3½" h. 27.50
Mug, miniature, amber 19.00
Mug, miniature, apple green 17.50
Mug, miniature, vaseline 25.00
Pitcher, milk, 3-knob stem 35.00
Pitcher, water, 3-knob stem,
amber 210.00
Pitcher, water, 3-knob stem, apple
green 85.00
Pitcher, water 57.50
Plate, 6" d., apple green.......... 18.00
Plate, 6" d., blue................ 25.00
Plate, 6" d. 12.00
Plate, 8" d., amber 22.00
Plate, 8" d., apple green.......... 25.00
Plate, 8" d., blue................ 30.00
Plate, 8" d. 18.00
Plate, 8" d., vaseline 26.00
Plate, 10" sq., w/folded corners,
blue 36.00
Plate, 10" sq., w/folded corners 23.00
Plate, 10" sq., w/folded corners,
vaseline 35.00
Platter, 11 x 8", blue 42.50
Platter, 11 x 8" 30.00
Salt dip, master size.............. 20.00
Salt shaker w/original top, amber
(single)........................ 21.00
Salt shaker w/original top, apple
green (single).................. 30.00
Salt shaker w/original top (single) .. 20.00
Salt shaker w/original top, vaseline
(single)........................ 30.00
Salt & pepper shakers w/brass tops,
blue, pr. 80.00
Sauce dish, flat or footed, amber ... 10.00
Sauce dish, flat or footed, apple
green ....10.00 to 14.00
Sauce dish, flat or footed,
blue ....12.00 to 25.00
Sauce dish, flat or footed .....7.00 to 9.50
Sauce dish, flat or footed,
vaseline.................15.00 to 27.00
Spooner, 3-knob stem, amber 29.00
Spooner, 3-knob stem, apple
green 35.00
Spooner, 3-knob stem, blue 35.00
Spooner, 3-knob stem 18.00
Sugar bowl, cov., 3-knob stem,
blue 55.00
Sugar bowl, cov. 37.50
Sugar bowl, open, 3-knob stem..... 42.50

Syrup pitcher w/original pewter top,
footed, apple green 113.00
Toothpick holder, amber 32.50
Toothpick holder, blue 32.50
Toothpick holder 21.00
Toothpick holder, vaseline 39.00
Tray, water, amber, 12½" d. 90.00
Tray, water, apple green, 12½" d... 80.00
Tray, water, 12½" d. 38.00
Tray, amber, 14" oval 60.00
Tray, apple green, 14" oval 85.00
Tray, 14" oval.................... 50.00
Tumbler, amber 24.00
Tumbler, blue.................... 35.00
Tumbler 18.50
Water set: oval tray, pitcher & 5
tumblers; apple green, 7 pcs. 240.00
Whimsey, model of a 4-wheeled
cart, amber.................... 115.00
Wine, amber..................... 25.00
Wine, blue 40.00
Wine........................... 22.50
Wine, vaseline 42.50

THREE FACE

Three Face "Mask Spout" Creamer

Bread plate...................... 78.00
Butter dish, cov. 112.00
Cake stand, 8" to 10½" d. 140.00
Celery vase..................... 100.00
Champagne...................... 127.50
Claret.......................... 105.00
Compote, cov., 4½" d., 6½" h...... 75.00
Compote, cov., 6" d. 125.00
Compote, cov., 8" d., 13" h........ 160.00
Compote, cov., 10" d. 145.00
Compote, open, 6" d., 7½" h...... 70.00
Compote, open, 8½" d., 8½" h..... 103.00
Compote, open, 9½" d., 9½" h..... 165.00
Creamer 85.00
Creamer w/mask spout (ILLUS.) 135.00
Creamer w/mask spout & cov. sugar
bowl, pr. 265.00
Goblet 80.00
Lamp, kerosene-type, pedestal
base, 8" h. 145.00

Pitcher, water 285.00
Salt dip 50.00
Salt shaker w/original top (single) .. 30.00
Salt & pepper shakers w/original
  tops, pr........................ 110.00
Sauce dish....................... 18.50
Spooner 90.00
Sugar bowl, cov. 115.00
Sugar bowl, open 75.00
Table set, creamer, cov. sugar bowl
  & spooner, 3 pcs. 285.00
Toothpick holder 50.00
Wine............................. 98.00

THREE PANEL

Three Panel Creamer

Berry set: 7" d. footed bowl & 4
  footed sauce dishes; blue,
  5 pcs. 75.00
Berry set, master bowl & 5 sauce
  dishes, 6 pcs. 57.50
Berry set, 9" d. master bowl & 6
  footed sauce dishes, 7 pcs........ 95.00
Berry set: master bowl & 8 sauce
  dishes; amber, 9 pcs. 150.00
Bowl, 7" d., footed, amber 25.00
Bowl, 7" d., footed, blue 35.00
Bowl, 7" d., footed 20.00
Bowl, 9" d., footed, amber 33.00
Bowl, 9" d., footed 20.00
Bowl, 9" d., footed, vaseline 45.00
Bowl, 10" d., amber 47.50
Bowl, 10" d., blue 52.00
Bowl, 10" d., vaseline 41.00
Butter dish, cov., amber 55.00
Butter dish, cov. 40.00
Celery vase, amber 40.00
Celery vase, blue 37.50
Celery vase...................... 35.00
Compote, open, 7" d., low stand,
  amber 25.00
Compote, open, 7" d., low stand,
  blue 32.50
Compote, open, 7" d., low stand ... 20.00
Compote, open, 8½" d., low stand,
  blue 43.00
Compote, open, 8½" d., low stand,
  vaseline....................... 32.50
Creamer, amber 36.00

Creamer, blue (ILLUS.)............ 42.00
Creamer 19.00
Creamer, vaseline................ 40.00
Goblet, amber 30.00
Goblet, blue 38.00
Goblet 24.00
Goblet, vaseline 40.00
Mug, amber 27.50
Mug, blue 37.50
Mug 22.00
Mug, vaseline................... 35.00
Pitcher, water, amber 85.00
Sauce dish, footed, amber 17.50
Sauce dish, footed, blue 14.00
Sauce dish, footed, vaseline....... 15.00
Spooner, amber.................. 40.00
Spooner, blue................... 40.00
Spooner 22.50
Spooner, vaseline 30.00
Sugar bowl, cov., amber 55.00
Sugar bowl, cov., blue............ 65.00
Sugar bowl, cov. 28.00
Sugar bowl, cov., vaseline 65.00
Sugar bowl, open, vaseline 25.00
Table set, creamer, sugar bowl &
  spooner, 3 pcs. 60.00
Table set, amber, 4 pcs. 195.00
Tumbler, amber.................. 35.00

THUMBPRINT, EARLY (Bakewell, Pears & Co.'s "Argus")

Early Thumbprint Water Pitcher

Ale glass, footed, 5" h. 31.00
Bowl, 5" d., 5" h., footed 32.00
Bowl, 8" d., flat................. 85.00
Butter dish, cov. 135.00
Cake stand, 8" to 9½" d. 85.00
Celery vase, plain base 90.00
Compote, cov., 6" d., 7½" h........ 225.00
Compote, cov., 7½" d., 11½" h..... 85.00
Compote, open, 5" d., 5½" h., scal-
  loped rim...................... 75.00
Compote, open, 8" d., low stand ... 36.00
Compote, open, 8½" d., high stand,
  scalloped rim 175.00
Compote, open, 12½" d., 11¼" h. .. 400.00

Creamer	70.00
Decanter, 11" h.	110.00
Egg cup	40.00
Goblet, baluster stem	55.00
Honey dish	16.00
Paperweight, panel-cut top	350.00
Pitcher, milk	95.00
Pitcher, water, 8¼" h. (ILLUS.)	275.00
Salt dip, individual size	15.00
Salt dip, master size, footed	27.50
Sauce dish	9.00
Spillholder	45.00
Spooner	53.00
Sugar bowl, cov.	55.00
Tumbler, bar	30.00
Tumbler, footed	48.50
Tumbler, whiskey, footed	32.50
Tumbler, whiskey, handled, footed	150.00
Wine, baluster stem	52.50

TONG

Celery vase	40.00
Spillholder	30.00
Sugar bowl, cov.	50.00

TORPEDO (Pygmy)

Torpedo Syrup Jug

Banana stand	55.00
Bowl, cov., master berry	80.00
Bowl, 7" d., flat	17.50
Bowl, 7" d., flat, ruby-stained	30.00
Bowl, 8" d.	18.50
Bowl, 8" d., ruby-stained	35.00
Bowl, 9" d.	32.50
Bowl, 9½" d.	45.00
Butter dish, cov.	75.00
Cake stand, 9" to 11" d.	55.00 to 82.50
Celery vase	40.00
Compote, cov., jelly	43.00
Compote, cov., 8" d., 14" h.	125.00
Compote, open, jelly, 5" d., 5" h.	43.00
Compote, open, 8" d., high stand, flared rim	50.00
Compote, open, 9" d., low stand	55.00
Creamer	43.00

Cruet w/original faceted stopper	49.00
Cup	25.00
Cup & saucer	60.00
Decanter w/original stopper	123.00
Goblet	45.00
Honey dish, cov.	20.00
Lamp, kerosene, hand-type w/finger grip, w/burner & chimney	67.50
Lamp, kerosene-type, pedestal base, 8½" h.	110.00
Pickle castor insert	28.00
Pitcher, milk, 7" h.	50.00
Pitcher, milk, 8½" h.	62.00
Pitcher, milk, 8½" h., ruby-stained	90.00
Pitcher, water, 10" h.	84.00
Pitcher, water, 10" h., ruby-stained	90.00
Pitcher, water, tankard, 12" h.	65.00
Salt dip, individual size, 1½" d.	32.50
Salt dip, master size	53.00
Salt shaker w/original top (single)	25.00
Sauce dish	15.00
Spooner	37.00
Sugar bowl, cov.	75.00
Sugar bowl, open	25.00
Syrup jug w/original top (ILLUS.)	60.00
Syrup jug w/original top, ruby-stained	186.00
Tray, 9¾" d.	70.00
Tumbler, ruby-stained	55.00
Waste bowl	60.00
Wine	58.00
Wine, ruby-stained, souvenir	45.00

TREE OF LIFE - Pittsburgh (Tree of Life with Hand)

Pittsburgh Tree of Life Creamer

Butter dish, cov.	55.00
Cake stand, 8¼" d.	75.00
Compote, cov., 6" d., 8" h., frosted hand & ball stem	65.00
Compote, open, 5½" d., 5½" h., clear hand & ball stem	37.00

Compote, open, 5½" d., 5½" h.,
  frosted hand & ball stem 47.50
Compote, open, 8" d., clear hand &
  ball stem 70.00
Compote, open, 8" d., 8½" h., frost-
  ed hand & ball stem 57.50
Compote, open, 9" d., frosted hand
  & ball stem 75.00
Compote, open, 10" d., 10" h., frost-
  ed hand & ball stem 95.00
Creamer, w/hand & ball handle
  (ILLUS.) 48.00
Creamer & sugar bowl, pr. 95.00
Pitcher, water, 9" h. 60.00
Relish, oval 29.00
Sauce dish, flat or footed ....12.00 to 20.00
Spooner 45.00
Sugar bowl, cov. 52.50
Sugar bowl, open 19.00
Tumbler 23.00
Waste bowl w/underplate 60.00
Wine 28.00

TREE OF LIFE - PORTLAND

Portland Tree of Life Compote

Berry set: master bowl & 4 sauce
  dishes; blue, 5 pcs. 325.00
Bowl, 5½" d., flat 12.00
Bowl, signed "Davis," green, in sil-
  verplate holder marked "Meriden
  Britannia Co." 235.00
Bread tray 40.00
Butter dish, cov. 55.00
Butter pat, blue 25.00
Butter pat 13.00
Butter pat, vaseline 25.00
Cake stand, signed "Davis," 9" to
  11½" d. ....45.00 to 60.00
Celery vase, in metal holder 75.00
Cologne bottle w/faceted stopper .. 48.00
Compote, cov., 5" d. 50.00
Compote, open, 6" d., 6" h. 35.00
Compote, open, 7¾" d., signed
  "P.G. Co." 75.00
Compote, open, 7¾" d., 11" h.,
  Infant Samuel stand, signed
  "Davis" 155.00
Compote, open, 10" d., 6" h., signed
  "Davis" (ILLUS.) 125.00
Creamer, signed "Davis" 65.00

Creamer, cranberry, in silverplate
  holder 85.00
Creamer & sugar bowl w/silverplate
  cover, in silverplate holder, pr.... 110.00
Cruet w/original stopper, blue 90.00
Dish, leaf handle, blue 40.00
Epergne, Infant Samuel stand,
  signed "Davis," 2 pcs. 125.00
Goblet 43.00
Goblet, signed "Davis" ......50.00 to 65.00
Ice cream set, tray & 5 leaf-shaped
  desserts, 6 pcs. 70.00
Mug, applied handle, 3½" h. 25.00
Pitcher, water, applied handle 75.00
Pitcher, water, applied handle,
  signed "Davis," amber...225.00 to 250.00
Plate, 6½" d. 18.00
Plate, 12" l., 3-footed, shell-
  shaped 85.00
Powder jar, red coiled serpent finial
  on cover 350.00
Salt dip, flat, 3" d. 10.00
Salt dip, footed, opaque green 95.00
Salt shaker w/original top (single) .. 25.00
Sauce dish, melon-ribbed, 4½" to
  5½" d. 18.00
Sauce dish, leaf-shaped, amber 11.50
Sauce dish, leaf-shaped 15.00
Spooner, handled silverplate holder
  w/two Griffin heads 57.50
Sugar bowl, cov. 55.00
Sugar bowl, silverplate holder 70.00
Toothpick holder, blue 75.00
Tray, ice cream, 14" rectangle 28.00
Tumbler, 4½" h. 22.50
Tumbler, footed, 6" h. 40.00
Waste bowl 14.00
Waste bowl, cranberry, flint 145.00
Wine 45.00

TULIP WITH SAWTOOTH

Celery vase, flint 70.00
Celery vase, non-flint 34.00
Champagne, non-flint 40.00
Compote, cov., 6" d., high stand,
  flint 120.00
Compote, open, 7" d., low stand,
  non-flint 69.00
Creamer, applied handle, flint 75.00
Decanter w/tulip-form stopper, flint,
  12" h., pt. 150.00
Decanter w/bar lip, flint, pt. 68.00
Goblet, flint 50.00
Goblet, non-flint 23.00
Marmalade jar, cov., non-flint 30.00
Pitcher, water, flint 175.00
Salt dip, master size, scalloped rim,
  flint 26.00
Sauce dish, flat, non-flint,
  3 7/8" d. 8.00
Spooner, flint 45.00
Spooner, non-flint 28.00
Sugar bowl, open, non-flint 32.50
Tumbler, bar, flint 85.00

Tumbler, bar, non-flint 27.50
Tumbler, flint 30.00
Tumbler, footed, flint 55.00
Wine, flint 60.00
Wine, non-flint 22.50

TURKEY TRACK - See Crowfoot Pattern

TWO PANEL (Daisy in Panel)

Two Panel Fruit Bowl

Bowl, cov., 7" oval, vaseline 55.00
Bowl, 7 x 5½" oval, amber 25.00
Bowl, 9 x 7½" oval, apple green . . . 37.50
Bowl, 10 x 8" oval, blue (ILLUS.) 65.00
Bowl, 10 x 8" oval, vaseline 50.00
Bread tray, apple green 39.00
Bread tray, blue 45.00
Bread tray 27.00
Butter dish, cov., amber 50.00
Butter dish, cov., blue 90.00
Butter dish, cov., vaseline 55.00
Celery vase, amber 30.00
Celery vase, blue 50.00
Compote, cov., 8 x 6½", 11" h.,
   vaseline 85.00
Compote, open, 9" oval, amber 37.00
Compote, open, 9" oval, blue 40.00
Creamer, apple green 40.00
Creamer, blue 35.00
Creamer 22.50
Creamer, vaseline 35.00
Goblet, amber 32.50
Goblet, apple green 31.00
Goblet, blue 35.00
Goblet 23.00
Goblet, vaseline 33.00
Lamp, kerosene-type, pedestal
   base, apple green, 9½" h. 90.00
Lamp, kerosene-type, pedestal
   base, vaseline, 7¾" h. 130.00
Marmalade jar, cov. 36.50
Marmalade jar, cov., vaseline 65.00
Pitcher, water, amber 50.00
Pitcher, water, apple green 55.00
Pitcher, water, blue 95.00
Pitcher, water 32.50
Pitcher, water, vaseline 65.00
Relish, amber 16.00
Relish, blue 22.50
Relish, vaseline 22.50
Salt dip, master size, amber 20.00
Salt dip, master size, apple green . . 18.50
Salt dip, master size, vaseline 22.00
Salt dip, individual size, apple
   green 14.00

Salt dip, individual size, blue 12.00
Sauce dish, flat or footed, amber . . . 11.00
Sauce dish, flat or footed, apple
   green .13.50 to 22.00
Sauce dish, flat or footed,
   blue .14.00 to 18.00
Sauce dish, flat or footed . . . . .7.50 to 15.00
Sauce dish, flat or footed,
   vaseline . . . . .15.00 to 19.00
Spooner, amber 35.00
Spooner, blue 35.00
Spooner 25.00
Spooner, vaseline 32.50
Sugar bowl, cov., amber 50.00
Sugar bowl, cov. 30.00
Tray, water, cloverleaf shape, vase-
   line, 10½ x 8¾" oval 55.00
Tray, water, amber, 15 x 10" oval . . 47.50
Tumbler, amber 25.00
Tumbler, vaseline 32.50
Waste bowl, blue 30.00
Water set: pitcher & 6 tumblers;
   blue, 7 pcs. 300.00
Wine, amber 35.00
Wine, apple green 35.00
Wine, blue 35.00
Wine 17.50
Wine, vaseline 35.00

U.S. COIN

U.S. Coin Handled Lamp

Bowl, 8" oval, frosted coins 315.00
Bread tray, dollars & half
   dollars . . . . .345.00 to 425.00
Butter dish, cov., dollars & half
   dollars 525.00
Cake plate, frosted coins, 7" d. 485.00
Cake stand, frosted dollars,
   10" d. 450.00
Candy dish, cov., 6" d. 275.00
Celery vase, frosted quarters 350.00
Champagne, frosted dimes 325.00
Compote, cov., 6 7/8" d., high
   stand, frosted coins 485.00
Compote, cov., 8" d., 11½" h.,
   frosted coins 535.00
Compote, cov., 9" d., frosted
   coins 500.00

Compote, open, 6½" d., 8" h., frost-
ed dimes & quarters 215.00
Compote, open, 7" d., 5¾" h., frost-
ed dimes & quarters 400.00
Compote, open, 8" d., 6½" h., frost-
ed coins 475.00
Compote, open, 9¼" d., 7" h., frost-
ed half dollars on bowl, quarters
on stem 375.00
Epergne, frosted dollars 1,100.00
Goblet, frosted dimes 325.00
Lamp, kerosene-type, round font,
frosted dollars in base 850.00
Lamp, kerosene-type, round font,
handled, clear quarters in base
(ILLUS.) 500.00
Mug, frosted coins 345.00
Pickle dish, clear coins, 7½ x 3¾".. 220.00
Pickle dish, frosted coins 180.00
Pitcher, water, frosted dollars 495.00
Relish, frosted coins 185.00
Salt shaker w/original top (single) .. 125.00
Sauce dish, frosted quarters, 4" d. .. 120.00
Spooner, clear quarters 215.00
Spooner, frosted quarters 375.00
Sugar bowl, cov., frosted coins 450.00
Syrup jug w/original dated pewter
top, frosted coins 500.00
Toothpick holder, frosted coins 190.00
Tumbler, frosted dollar in base 175.00
Wine, frosted half dimes 450.00

VALENCIA WAFFLE (Block & Star)

Valencia Waffle Master Salt

Bread platter 25.00
Butter dish, cov., amber 70.00
Butter dish, cov., apple green 60.00
Butter dish, cov. 42.50
Butter dish, cov., ruby-stained 110.00
Cake stand, amber 70.00
Cake stand, 10" d. 70.00
Celery vase, blue 39.00
Celery vase 32.00
Celery vase, yellow 35.00
Compote, cov., 6" d., 10" h........ 75.00
Compote, cov., 7" sq., low stand,
amber 64.00
Compote, cov., 7" sq., low stand,
apple green 75.00
Compote, cov., 7" sq., low stand,
blue 77.50
Compote, cov., 7" sq., low stand ... 55.00
Compote, cov., 8" d. 45.00

Compote, open, 6" d., low stand,
apple green 35.00
Compote, open, 6" sq., low stand,
blue 30.00
Compote, open, 8" d., low stand,
blue 29.50
Creamer 38.00
Goblet, amber 32.00
Goblet 24.00
Pitcher, water, 7½" h., amber 65.00
Pitcher, water, apple green 95.00
Pitcher, water 40.00
Relish, amber, 10¾ x 7½" 30.00
Relish, 10¾ x 7½" 10.00
Salt dip, master size, amber 22.50
Salt dip, master size (ILLUS.) 15.00
Salt dip, master size, yellow 26.00
Salt shaker w/original top (single) .. 20.00
Salt & pepper shakers w/original
tops, apple green, pr. 50.00
Sauce dish, footed, amber 13.50
Sauce dish, footed, blue 14.00
Sauce dish, footed 12.50
Spooner, amber 40.00
Spooner 18.00
Syrup jug w/original top, amber 100.00
Syrup jug w/original top, blue 75.00
Tray, water, amber, 13¼ x 9½",
amber ....37.50 to 45.00
Tray, water 26.00

VICTOR - See Shell & Jewel Pattern

VICTORIA

Victoria Compote

Compote, cov., 8" d., low stand
(ILLUS.)......................... 150.00
Compote, cov., 8" d., high stand ... 200.00
Compote, cov., 10½" d., 15¼" h.... 215.00

VIKING (Bearded Head or Old Man of the Mountain)

Bowl, cov., 8" oval 45.00
Bowl, 7" d., 4" h. 25.00
Bread tray, cupid hunt scene
center........................ 68.00

Butter dish, cov. 58.00
Cake stand, 10" d. 67.50
Celery vase...................... 52.00
Compote, cov., 7" d., low stand 45.00
Compote, cov., 8" d., low stand 70.00
Compote, cov., 9" d., low stand 89.00
Compote, open, 8" d., high stand... 62.50
Creamer 48.00
Creamer & cov. sugar bowl, pr. 79.00
Dish, cov., 8" oval 85.00
Egg cup 35.00
Goblet 95.00
Marmalade jar, footed, etched (no
    cover)........................ 27.50
Mug, applied handle 65.00
Pickle jar w/cover................ 95.00

Viking Water Pitcher

Pitcher, water, 8¾" h. (ILLUS.) 82.00
Salt dip, master size.............. 42.00
Sauce dish, footed 12.00
Shaving mug, milk white.......... 62.50
Spooner 33.00
Sugar bowl, cov. 55.00

VIRGINIA - See Galloway Pattern

WAFFLE
Celery vase, flint................. 56.00
Champagne...................... 135.00
Compote, open, 7" d., 5¼" h. 32.50
Compote, open, 9½" d., 8" h. 75.00
Creamer, applied handle.......... 135.00
Creamer, footed 45.00
Cruet 27.50
Egg cup 40.00
Goblet 58.00
Salt dip, master size.............. 27.50
Sugar bowl, cov. 55.00
Syrup pitcher, applied handle 85.00
Tumbler, footed 18.00
Tumbler, bar.................... 75.00
Waste bowl, ruffled top........... 75.00

WAFFLE AND THUMBPRINT
Bowl, 7¼" d., flint 35.00
Celery vase, flint ....85.00 to 100.00

Compote, open, 8" d., high stand... 80.00
Cordial, flint 85.00
Creamer, applied handle, flint...... 250.00
Decanter w/blown stopper & bar lip,
    pt............................ 135.00
Decanter w/original matching stop-
    per, canary yellow, qt. 275.00
Egg cup, flint 31.00
Goblet, flint 60.00
Lamp, w/original 2-tube burner,
    hand-type w/applied handle, flint,
    3" h.......................... 135.00
Lamp, w/original whale oil burner,
    flint, 11" h. ....135.00 to 170.00
Pitcher, water, flint 300.00
Salt dip, master size, flint......... 27.00

Waffle & Thumbprint Spillholder

Spillholder, flint (ILLUS.) 115.00
Sugar bowl, cov., flint 175.00
Tumbler, bar, flint................ 79.00
Tumbler, footed, flint............. 110.00
Tumbler, whiskey, flint 79.00
Wine, flint...................... 50.00

WASHBOARD - See Adonis Pattern

WASHINGTON (Early)
Claret, flint 135.00
Decanter w/original stopper, qt..... 225.00
Egg cup, flint 65.00
Goblet, flint ....60.00 to 80.00
Lamp, kerosene-type, cast iron
    base......................... 125.00
Pitcher, water, flint 225.00
Salt dip, individual size 12.50
Salt dip, master size, flat, round.... 27.50

WASHINGTON CENTENNIAL
Bowl, 8½" oval 22.50
Bread platter, Carpenter's Hall
    (ILLUS.)...................... 100.00
Bread platter, Carpenter's Hall,
    frosted 125.00
Bread platter, George Washington
    center....................... 84.00

"Carpenter's Hall" Platter

Bread platter, George Washington center, frosted	101.00
Bread platter, Independence Hall center	85.00
Butter dish, cov., footed	87.50
Cake stand, 8½" to 11½" d.	55.00
Celery vase	39.00
Champagne	42.50
Compote, cov., 8½" d., 12" h.	105.00
Compote, open, 8" d., 6½" h.	37.50
Compote, open, 8" d., high stand	36.50
Compote, open, 10½" d., high stand	70.00
Creamer, applied handle	80.00
Egg cup	42.50
Goblet	35.00
Pickle dish	25.00
Pitcher, milk	104.00
Pitcher, water	90.00
Relish, bear paw handles, dated 1876	56.00
Salt dip, master size	25.00
Sauce dish, flat or footed	9.00
Spooner	35.00
Sugar bowl, cov.	75.00
Sugar bowl, open	20.00
Syrup pitcher w/original metal top, applied handle, milk white	140.00
Toothpick holder	60.00
Tumbler, bar	65.00
Wine	40.00

WEDDING BELLS

Bowl, 8" d., flat, ruby-stained	32.50
Bowl, master berry, gold trim	28.00
Butter dish, cov.	38.00
Celery tray, pink-stained	27.50
Celery vase	27.50
Creamer, 4-footed	48.00
Goblet	50.00
Pitcher, water	50.00
Pitcher, water, alternate ruby-stained panels	85.00
Punch cup	15.00

Salt shaker w/original top (single)	20.00
Spooner	40.00
Sugar bowl, cov.	55.00
Toothpick holder, gold trim	55.00
Toothpick holder, pink-stained	80.00
Tumbler	18.00
Water set, pitcher & 4 tumblers, 5 pcs.	135.00
Wine	22.00
Wine, pink-stained	40.00

WEDDING RING - See Double Wedding Ring Pattern

WESTWARD HO

Westward Ho Covered Compote

Bread platter	92.50 to 110.00
Butter dish, cov.	150.00
Celery vase	125.00
Compote, cov., 5" d., 9" h.	98.00
Compote, cov., 6" d., low stand	120.00
Compote, cov., 6" d., 12" h.	155.00
Compote, cov., 6¾ x 4" oval	146.00
Compote, cov., 7¾ x 5" oval, 10" h.	160.00
Compote, cov., 8" d., low stand	263.00
Compote, cov., 8" d., 11½" h. (ILLUS.)	250.00
Compote, cov., 8 x 5½" oval, 12" h.	290.00
Compote, cov., 8" d., 14" h.	290.00
Compote, open, 6" d., high stand	127.00
Compote, open, 8 1/16" d., 8" h.	65.00
Creamer	113.00
Creamer & cov. sugar bowl, pr.	275.00
Creamer & open sugar bowl, pr.	175.00
Goblet	56.00
Pickle dish, oval	55.00
Pitcher, milk, 8" h.	250.00
Pitcher, water	250.00
Relish, deer handles	115.00
Sauce dish, footed	27.00
Spooner	82.50
Sugar bowl, cov.	150.00 to 165.00
Sugar bowl, open	35.00

WHEAT & BARLEY

Wheat & Barley Creamer

Bowl, cov., 8" d., flat	40.00
Bread plate, amber	25.00
Butter dish, cov., blue	75.00
Butter dish, cov.	35.00
Cake stand, amber, 8" to 10" d.	35.00
Cake stand, 8" to 10" d.	37.50
Compote, cov., 8½" d., high stand	55.00
Compote, open, jelly, blue	42.00
Compote, open, jelly	18.50
Compote, open, 8¼" d., amber	75.00
Compote, open, 8¾" d., 6¾" h.	37.00
Creamer, blue	45.00
Creamer (ILLUS.)	20.00
Doughnut stand, blue	58.00
Goblet, amber	37.50
Goblet, blue	34.00
Goblet	25.00
Mug, amber	32.50
Mug	20.00
Pitcher, milk, blue	65.00
Pitcher, milk	35.00
Pitcher, water, amber	85.00
Pitcher, water, blue	72.50
Pitcher, water	53.00
Plate, 7" d., blue	30.00
Plate, 7" d.	18.00
Plate, 9" d., closed handles, amber	35.00
Plate, 9" d., closed handles, blue	27.50
Plate, 9" d., closed handles	19.00
Salt shaker w/original top, blue (single)	44.00
Salt shaker w/original top (single)	14.50
Salt & pepper shakers w/original tops, pr.	30.00
Sauce dish, flat, handled, amber	12.00
Sauce dish, footed, amber	14.50
Sauce dish, footed	20.00
Spooner, amber	32.50
Spooner, blue	30.00
Spooner	19.00
Sugar bowl, cov.	30.00
Tumbler, amber	32.50
Tumbler, blue	30.00
Tumbler	21.00
Wine, amber	20.00

WILDFLOWER

Wildflower Goblet

Bowl, 5¾" sq.	15.00
Bowl, 6½" sq., blue	22.50
Bowl, 7" sq., footed, amber	29.00
Bowl, 7" sq.	14.50
Bowl, 8" sq., 5" h., footed, apple green	22.50
Bowl, 8" sq., 5" h., footed, blue	50.00
Butter dish, cov., amber	75.00
Butter dish, cov., flat	35.00
Butter dish, cov., collared base, vaseline	60.00
Cake stand, amber, 9½" to 11"	48.50 to 65.00
Cake stand, apple green, 9½" to 11"	60.00 to 95.00
Cake stand, blue, 9½" to 11"	50.00 to 85.00
Cake stand, 9½" to 11"	30.00 to 45.00
Cake stand, vaseline, 9½" to 11"	82.00
Celery vase, amber	57.50
Celery vase, blue	62.50
Celery vase	28.00
Compote, cov., 6" d., blue	70.00
Compote, cov., 6" d.	42.00
Compote, cov., 7" d., amber	50.00
Compote, cov., 8" d., amber	85.00
Compote, cov., 8" d.	29.00
Compote, cov., 9½" h., blue	70.00
Compote, cov., 10" d.	55.00
Compote, open, jelly	30.00
Compote, open, 7" d., low stand, apple green	23.50
Compote, open, 7" d., low stand, blue	38.00
Compote, open, 9½" d., amber	45.00
Compote, open, 10½" d., 8¼" h., amber	75.00
Creamer, amber	36.00
Creamer, apple green	40.00
Creamer, blue	42.00
Creamer	27.00
Creamer, vaseline	40.00
Creamer & sugar bowl, pr.	48.00
Goblet, amber	37.00

Goblet, apple green	35.00
Goblet, blue	25.00
Goblet (ILLUS.)	26.00
Goblet, vaseline	42.00
Pitcher, water, amber	52.50
Pitcher, water, apple green	75.00
Pitcher, water, blue	75.00
Pitcher, water	47.50
Pitcher, water, vaseline	58.00
Plate, 7" sq., apple green	24.50
Plate, 7" sq., blue	45.00
Plate, 10" sq., amber	35.00
Plate, 10" sq., apple green	32.50
Plate, 10" sq., blue	35.00
Plate, 10" sq.	27.00
Platter, 11 x 8", apple green	45.00 to 69.00
Platter, 11 x 8"	35.00
Relish, amber	17.50
Relish, apple green	19.50
Relish	22.50
Salt shaker w/original top, amber (single)	26.00
Salt shaker w/original top, vaseline (single)	45.00
Salt & pepper shakers w/original tops, apple green, pr.	57.50
Salt & pepper shakers w/original tops, blue, pr.	70.00
Salt & pepper shakers w/original tops, pr.	45.00
Sauce dish, flat or footed, amber	9.00 to 12.00
Sauce dish, flat or footed, apple green	13.50
Sauce dish, flat or footed, blue	10.00 to 30.00
Sauce dish, flat or footed	10.00
Sauce dish, flat or footed, vaseline	15.00
Spooner, amber	32.50
Spooner, apple green	35.00
Spooner	27.50
Sugar bowl, cov., blue	54.00
Sugar bowl, cov.	33.00
Sugar bowl, open, amber	20.00
Sugar bowl, open, apple green	35.00
Sugar bowl, open	19.00
Syrup pitcher w/original top, amber	180.00
Syrup pitcher w/original top, apple green	185.00
Syrup pitcher w/original top	115.00
Tray, dresser, amber, 9 x 4"	30.00
Tray, water, amber, 13 x 11"	44.00
Tray, water, apple green, 13 x 11"	55.00
Tray, water, 13 x 11"	39.00
Tray, water, vaseline, 13 x 11"	50.00
Tumbler, amber	36.00
Tumbler, apple green	28.00
Tumbler, blue	27.50
Tumbler	22.00
Tumbler, vaseline	30.00
Tumbler, yellow	27.50

Water set: pitcher, tray & 5 tumblers; apple green, 7 pcs.	318.00
Water set: pitcher, tray & 6 tumblers; apple green, 8 pcs.	325.00

WILLOW OAK

Willow Oak Water Pitcher

Bowl, cov., 7" d., flat	36.00
Bowl, 7" d., amber	20.00
Bowl, 7" d., blue	30.00
Bowl, 7" d.	14.50
Bowl, 8" d., 2½" h.	19.50
Bread plate, blue, 11" d.	27.00
Bread plate, 11" d.	22.00
Butter dish, cov., amber	65.00
Butter dish, cov.	60.00
Cake stand, amber, 8" to 10" d.	49.00
Cake stand, blue, 8" to 10" d.	60.00
Cake stand, 8" to 10" d.	36.00
Celery vase, amber	47.00
Celery vase	37.50
Compote, cov., 6½" d., 9" h.	47.50
Compote, open, 6" d., scalloped top	37.50
Compote, open, 7" d., high stand, amber	40.00
Compote, open, 7" d., high stand, blue	60.00
Compote, open, 7" d., high stand	28.00
Creamer, amber	37.50
Creamer, blue	42.50
Creamer	31.00
Goblet, amber	40.00
Goblet, blue	38.00
Goblet	32.00
Mug, amber	35.00
Mug, blue	42.50
Mug	27.00
Pitcher, milk, amber	55.00
Pitcher, milk	40.00
Pitcher, water, amber (ILLUS.)	85.00
Pitcher, water	46.00
Plate, 7" d., amber	35.00
Plate, 7" d.	23.00
Plate, 9" d., handled, amber	30.00

Plate, 9" d., handled, blue 45.00
Plate, 9" d., handled 20.00
Salt shaker w/original top, blue
  (single)...................... 68.00
Salt shaker w/original top (single) .. 25.00
Sauce dish, flat or footed ....10.00 to 18.00
Spooner, amber 40.00
Spooner, blue.................... 38.00
Spooner 22.00
Sugar bowl, cov., amber 62.50
Sugar bowl, cov. 38.00
Sugar bowl, open 20.00
Tray, water, blue, 10½" d......... 58.00
Tray, water, 10½" d. 30.00
Tumbler, amber 35.00
Tumbler, blue.................... 37.50
Tumbler 32.50
Waste bowl 29.00
Water set, pitcher, tray & 2 tum-
  blers, 4 pcs. 170.00
Water set: pitcher & 8 goblets;
  amber, 9 pcs. 325.00

WINDFLOWER
Bowl, 7 x 5" oval................. 27.50
Butter dish, cov. 55.00
Celery vase...................... 40.00
Compote, cov., 8½" d., low stand .. 45.00
Creamer 25.00
Egg cup 20.00
Goblet 40.00
Pitcher, water 65.00
Sauce dish...................... 10.00
Spooner 28.00
Sugar bowl, cov. 29.00
Sugar bowl, open 18.00
Tumbler, bar.................... 35.00
Tumbler, water 40.00
Wine........................... 29.00

WISCONSIN (Beaded Dewdrop)

Wisconsin Water Pitcher

Banana stand, turned-up sides,
  7½" w., 4" h................... 75.00
Bon bon, handled, 4" 27.50

Bowl, 6½" d. 37.00
Bowl, 8" d. 24.00
Bread tray...................... 45.00
Butter dish, cov. 90.00
Cake stand, 9¾" d. 42.00
Celery tray, flat, 10 x 5" 40.00
Celery vase..................... 47.50
Compote, cov., 10½" d. 65.00
Compote, open, 6½" d., 6½" h..... 22.00
Compote, open, 7½" d., 5½" h..... 40.00
Creamer, individual size 49.00
Cup & saucer 45.00
Dish, cov., oval 29.00
Goblet 49.00
Mug, 3½" h..................... 37.00
Nappy, handled, 4" d. 22.00
Olive dish, 2-handled 35.00
Pickle dish..................... 22.00
Pitcher, milk 48.00
Pitcher, water, 8" h. (ILLUS.) 47.00
Plate, 5" sq. 15.00
Plate, 6½" sq. 27.50
Punch cup 15.00
Relish, 8½ x 4" 22.50
Salt & pepper shakers w/original
  tops, pr...................... 45.00
Sauce dish..................... 10.00
Spooner 30.00
Sugar bowl, cov., 5" h. 37.50
Sugar shaker w/original top 65.00
Syrup pitcher w/original top,
  6½" h....................... 71.00
Toothpick holder 40.00
Tumbler 38.00
Wine........................... 55.00

WOODEN PAIL - See Oaken Bucket Pattern

ZIPPER
Bowl, 8" oval 18.00
Butter dish, cov. 40.00
Celery vase..................... 21.00
Cheese dish, cov. 50.00
Compote, cov., low stand 40.00
Creamer 20.00
Cruet w/original stopper.......... 38.00
Cruet w/original stopper, ruby-
  stained 145.00
Goblet 20.00
Humidor, cov.................... 45.00
Marmalade jar, cov. 35.00
Pitcher, water 35.00
Relish 15.00
Sauce dish, flat or footed .....6.00 to 8.00
Spooner 20.00
Sugar bowl, cov. 25.00
Sugar shaker w/silverplate top 28.00
Toothpick holder 15.00
Toothpick holder, ruby-stained 25.00
Wine........................... 16.00

ZIPPERED BLOCK - See Iowa Pattern

(End of Pattern Glass Section)

PEACH BLOW

Several types of glass lumped together by collectors as Peach Blow were produced by half a dozen glass houses. Hobbs, Brockunier & Co., Wheeling, West Va., made Peach Blow as a plated ware that shaded from red at the top to yellow at the bottom and is referred to as Wheeling Peach Blow. Mt. Washington Glass Works produced an homogeneous Peach Blow shading from a rose color at the top to pale blue in the lower portion. The New England Glass Works' Peach Blow, called Wild Rose, shaded from rose at the top to white. Gunderson—Pairpoint Co. also reproduced some of the Mt. Washington Peach Blow in the early 1950's, and some glass of a somewhat similar type was made by Steuben Glass Works, the Boston & Sandwich Factory and by Thomas Webb & Sons and Stevens & Williams of England. Sandwich Peach Blow is one-layered glass and the English is two-layered. A relative newcomer to the fold is called New Martinsville "Peach Blow." It is a single-layered glass.

GUNDERSON - PAIRPOINT

Gunderson - Pairpoint Peach Blow Creamer

Cornucopia-vase, single lily
  w/turned end & ruffled rim on
  base $245.00
Creamer, pedestal base (ILLUS.) 300.00
Cornucopia-vase, single lily
Cup & saucer, applied white
  handle 200.00
Toothpick holder 125.00

MOUNT WASHINGTON
Tumbler, acid finish,
  3¾" h...............1,000.00 to 1,210.00
Vase, 3¼" h., 2 7/8" d., petal rim,
  acid finish 850.00
Vase, 8" h., bulbous base 1,250.00
Vase, 12" h., baluster-shaped 995.00

NEW ENGLAND
Bowl, 4½" d., 2¾" h., glossy
  finish 265.00
Celery vase, square top w/scalloped

edge, acid finish,
  4¾" h.................350.00 to 450.00
Celery vase, square top w/scalloped
  edge, glossy finish, 4¾" h. 625.00
Creamer & open sugar bowl, applied white handles, pr 865.00
Darner, hooked handle end 125.00
Pear, w/stem intact 175.00
Pitcher, milk, 6¼" h., crimped rim,
  applied opaque white handle, acid
  finish 1,285.00
Punch cup, glossy finish 300.00
Rose bowl, 7-crimp rim, acid finish,
  3" d., 2½" h. 295.00
Toothpick holder, folded tricornered
  top, acid finish, 2¼" h. 485.00

Square Top Toothpick Holder

Toothpick holder, square top, acid
  finish (ILLUS.) 450.00
Tumbler, acid finish, 3¾" h. 450.00
Tumbler, glossy finish,
  3¾" h.................365.00 to 450.00
Vase, 6" h., gourd-shaped, glossy
  finish 425.00
Vase, 7" h., lily form, acid finish,
  original "Wild Rose" paper label
  on base & pencil notation "Aunt
  Alice 1888" 785.00

NEW MARTINSVILLE

New Martinsville Peach Blow

Bowl, 4 7/8" d., melon-ribbed, ruffled, "Sunburst" 165.00
Bowl, 7½" d., 3½" h., melon-
ribbed, ruffled, "Sunburst" 345.00
Bowl, 10¾" d., melon-ribbed, ruffled, "Sunburst" (ILLUS.) 395.00

SANDWICH

Bowl, ruffled rim w/"raindrop" air
traps, small.................... 235.00
Pitcher, ewer form, ruffled rim,
ribbed body, small 250.00
Pitcher, 7 1/8" h., bulbous w/irregu-
larly crimped rim, applied amber
thorn handle................... 357.50
Pitcher, water, applied reeded camphor handle, Pointed Hobnail
patt. 300.00

WEBB

Webb Peach Blow

Bowl, 9" d., glossy, creamy white
lining, silverplate rim 395.00
Celery vase, enameled floral decor,
in 2-handled silverplate pedestal
base, overall 8½" h. 220.00
Dish, shell-shaped, gold prunus
blossoms decor on glossy finish,
creamy white underside, 9 1/8 x
6¾", 2½" h. 295.00
Rose bowl, egg-shaped, applied
clear rigaree around 5-petal rim &
loop feet, glossy finish, creamy
white lining, 3¾" d.,
6½" h.................350.00 to 395.00
Scent bottle w/hinged silver lid,
small clear cut glass inside
dauber, gold leaves & vines decor
on acid finish, 1¼" d., 2 3/8" h... 295.00
Vase, 4½" h., enameled gold
acorns & oak leaves decor 375.00
Vase, 6½" h., enameled gold insects, pine & cherry branches,
creamy white lining 340.00
Vase, 7½" h., 4 3/8" d., gold-

encrusted florals, leaves, grasshopper & bandings on glossy finish, creamy white lining 850.00
Vase, 9" h., bottle-shaped, gold entwined branches on glossy finish,
creamy white lining (ILLUS.) 750.00

WHEELING

Wheeling Peach Blow

Claret pitcher, applied amber reeded handle & collar rigaree, 10" h.
(ILLUS. left) 1,735.00
Cruet w/original stopper, applied
reeded amber handle, glossy
finish.........................1,185.00
Lemonade pitcher, slightly
tapered.......................1,950.00
Morgan vase replica, 8" h., in original amber glass base (ILLUS.
right).........................1,500.00
Pitcher, 8" h., triangular, glossy
finish.........................1,695.00
Punch cup, applied amber ring handle, glossy finish, white lining,
2½" h. 325.00
Sugar bowl, open, glossy finish,
3½" h. 675.00
Syrup pitcher w/original pewter
top, applied amber handle 1,450.00
Tumbler, glossy, oyster white lining,
3¾" h.................275.00 to 350.00
Vase, 8½" h., stick-type w/bulbous
base, acid finish 950.00
Vase, 15½" h., bottle-shaped
w/elongated neck, glossy finish,
oyster white lining.............2,000.00

PEKING

*This is Chinese glass, some of it cameo-
carved, that has attracted collector interest.*

Peking Cameo Vases

Bowl, 6¼" d., cameo-carved green trees, peonies & butterfly against white ground $145.00

Bowl, 7" d., 3" h., cameo-carved butterfly, florals & leaves against white ground, on teakwood stand 245.00

Saki cup, cameo-carved leaves, jade green, in ornate footed handled holder 48.00

Vase, 2¾" h., octagonal cushion shape on 4 ruyi-head feet, cameo-carved monster masks between detached "C" borders outlined w/raised & knotted rope twists, yellow, Qianlong 7,150.00

Vase, 6¼" h., cameo-carved blue florals against white ground 185.00

Vases, 7" h., bulbous w/long neck, cameo-carved blossoming plum trees & peony blossoms, bright lemon yellow, ca. 1900, pr. (ILLUS.) 990.00

Vase, 8" h., cameo-carved green honeycomb against white ground 165.00

Vase, 8" h., globular w/tall cylindrical neck, cameo-carved reddish orange prunus & roses growing from rockwork against milky white ground, 19th c. 2,310.00

Vase, 12½" h., globular w/tall cylindrical neck, cameo-carved red figures in a walled compound against snowflake white ground, Qianlong 4,950.00

PELOTON

Made in Bohemia, Germany and England in the late 19th century, this glassware is characterized by threads or filaments of glass rolled into the glass body of the object in random patterns. Some of these wares were decorated.

Bowl, 3½" d., 2½" h., pinched in top, ribbed sides, clear w/white, blue, pink & olive green "coconut" threading, fiery opalescent pastel orchid lining (2 tiny inner lining skips in making) $185.00

Cookie jar, ribbed body, pale blue w/multicolored "coconut" threading, white lining, silverplate rim, cover & bail handle, 6¾" h. 500.00

Finger bowl, clear w/multicolor "coconut" threading 60.00

Rose bowl, 6-crimp top, opaque white w/pink, blue, yellow & white "coconut" threading, cased, 2½" d., 2¼" h. 245.00

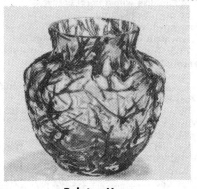

Peloton Vase

Vase, 2½" h., clear w/green "coconut" threading (ILLUS.) 100.00

Vase, 3" h., clear w/white "coconut" threading 125.00

Vase, 3¼" h., 3" d., ball-shaped w/flared ruffled top, orchid pink w/pink, blue, yellow & white "coconut" threading, cased 175.00

Vase, 3¾" h., applied w/clear rigaree around 4-point rim & 6 clear petal feet, white opaque w/rose, blue & yellow "coconut" threading 265.00

Vase, 4¼" h., 4¾" d., squat ribbed form w/tricornered folded-down rim, clear w/rose, yellow, blue & white "coconut" threading, white lining 295.00

Vase, 5" h., 4 3/8" d., ruffled fan-shaped top, orchid pink w/pink, blue, yellow & white "coconut" threading, cased 295.00

Vase, 6¾" h., 3" d., stick-type, yellow w/white, rose, blue & yellow "coconut" threading, white lining 225.00

PHOENIX

*This ware was made by the Phoenix Glass
Co. of Beaver County, Pa., which produced
various types of glass from the 1880's. One
special type that attracts collectors now is a
molded ware with a vague resemblance to
cameo in its "sculptured" decoration.*

Bowl, 8" d., sculptured white cherry
   clusters & branches on blue
   ground $65.00
Box, cov., sculptured purple florals
   & Bird of Paradise on white
   ground, 10½ x 6½" oval 235.00
Centerpiece bowl, boat-shaped,
   sculptured blue lovebirds & vines
   on pearly white ground, 8" w.,
   15" l. 295.00
Plate, 8¼" d., sculptured white Bird
   of Paradise within floral border
   on deep orchid ground 95.00
Rose bowl, sculptured white star-
   flowers & bands on green ground,
   7" d., 7" h 85.00
Vase, 6½" h., pear-shaped, sculp-
   tured white bluebells on chocolate
   ground 66.50
Vase, 7½" h., sculptured white
   Praying Mantis on blue ground . . . 105.00
Vase, 9¼" h., sculptured turquoise
   blue & red berries on white
   ground 125.00
Vase, 9½" h., 12" widest d., sculp-
   tured pink flying geese on white
   ground 210.00

Phoenix Vase with Flying Geese

Vase, 10" h., pillow-shaped, sculptured white flying geese on brilliant blue ground, original label
   (ILLUS.) 150.00
Vase, 10" h., sculptured pearly
   white wild roses on light green
   ground 95.00
Vase, 11" h., sculptured white danc-
   ing nudes on blue ground 350.00
Vase, 12¼" h., sculptured salmon to
   peach pink peonies & buds
   w/brown stems & greenish blue
   leaves on white ground 135.00

PIGEON BLOOD

Torquay Pattern

*This name refers to the color of the glass,
which was blood-red, and many wares have
been lumped into this category.*

Bowl, master berry, 9" d., Torquay
   patt., silverplate rim $110.00
Cookie jar, Torquay patt., silver-
   plate rim, cover & handles (ILLUS.
   without lid) 260.00
Pitcher, water, Torquay patt. 350.00
Salt & pepper shakers w/original
   tops, Bulging Loops patt.,
   pr. . . . . 85.00 to 115.00
Sugar shaker w/original top, Bulg-
   ing Loops patt. . . . . 130.00 to 195.00
Syrup pitcher w/original top,
   Torquay patt., glossy
   finish . . . . 350.00 to 425.00
Toothpick holder, Bulging Loops
   patt. 125.00
Tumbler 52.00
Water set: pitcher & 3 tumblers;
   pitcher w/applied clear handle,
   enameled floral decor, 4 pcs. 135.00

POMONA

First Grind Pomona Toothpick

*First produced by the New England Glass
Works in the 1880's, Pomona has a frosted*

ground on clear glass decorated with mineral stains, most frequently amber-yellow, sometimes pale blue. It may be recognized by its background of finely-etched lines crossing one another. Some pieces bore floral decorations. Two types were made. One called "first grind" was etched by acid that cut into the numerous etched lines made with a needle on glass that had been given an acid resistant coating. A cheaper method, "second grind," consisted of rolling the glass article in particles of acid-resisting material which were picked up by it. The glass was then etched by acid which attacked areas not protected by the resistant particles. A favorite design on Pomona was the cornflower.

Celery vase, Diamond Quilted patt., amber-stained, blueberry decor, 2nd grind, 6½" h. $150.00
Creamer, Inverted Thumbprint patt., amber-stained square top, 1st grind . . . . .125.00 to 165.00
Creamer & open sugar bowl, amber-stained rims, blue cornflower decor, 2nd grind, pr. 750.00
Finger bowl, Inverted Thumbprint patt., amber-stained rim, 2nd grind 75.00
Finger bowl, amber-stained rim, blue-stained cornflower decor, 2nd grind . . . . .95.00 to 125.00
Finger bowl, amber-stained rim, blue-stained blueberries decor, 2nd grind 125.00
Goblet, Diamond Optic patt., amber-stained rim, 2nd grind 85.00
Pitcher, 4" h., blue-stained cornflower decor, 2nd grind . . . . .185.00 to 250.00
Pitcher, 6¼" h., Inverted Thumbprint patt., amber-stained square top, 1st grind 300.00
Pitcher, tankard, 7" h., amber-tinted handle & amber-stained rim, Expanded Diamond patt., leafy stem centered w/amber & blue-stained pansy at front & w/amber & blue-stained butterfly wings reverse, 2nd grind 365.00
Pitcher, tankard, 12" h., Diamond Quilted patt., 2nd grind 325.00
Punch cup, 1st grind . . . . 50.00 to 90.00
Punch cup, amber-stained top, blue-stained cornflower decor, 1st grind . . . . .165.00 to 195.00
Sherbet, wide optic ribs, amber-stained top, 2nd grind 70.00
Toothpick holder, ovoid, applied clear rigaree at waisted neck flaring to amber-stained rim, 1st grind 265.00
Toothpick holder, tricornered, amber-stained rim, 1st grind (ILLUS.) 350.00
Toothpick holder, clear, 1st grind . . . 110.00

Tumbler, amber-stained rim, blue-stained cornflowers decor, 2nd grind 145.00
Tumbler, Inverted Thumbprint patt., 1st grind 90.00
Vase, 6" h., scalloped & crimped amber-stained rim, blue-stained cornflower decor, 2nd grind 465.00
Water carafe, blue-stained cornflower decor, 2nd grind 275.00
Water set: tankard pitcher & 6 tumblers; amber-stained rim & blue-stained cornflowers decor, 2nd grind, 7 pcs. 1,550.00

QUEZAL

Quezal Vase

These wares resembled those of Tiffany and other lustred "Art" glass houses of the late 19th and early 20th centuries and were made by the Quezal Art Glass and Decorating Co. of Brooklyn, N.Y., early in the century and until its closing in the mid-20's. Also see SHADES under Glass.

Bowl, 2½" d., iridescent rose, gold & green, signed $235.00
Candlestick, conical base, baluster stem, iridescent blue, signed, 7¾" h. (single) 150.00
Compote, 6¾" h., gold stem & foot, gold w/dark green swirls, signed 495.00
Cup & saucer, S-shaped handle, gold 475.00
Finger bowl, iridescent gold, 4" top d., 2½" h. 225.00
Salt dip, open, master size, gold, signed, 2¾" w. 175.00
Vase, 4½" h., baluster form w/four dimples, "Aurene" type iridescence, signed 265.00

Vase, 5 1/16" h., baluster form, random iridescent gold splashes on a striated green & white ground, applied w/blob-like prints, signed 880.00

Vase, 7" h., baluster form, band of gilt-edged striated green feathers on ivory, shoulder applied w/four trailing iridescent gold prunts, signed 1,320.00

Vase, 7" h., green & gold pulled feather decor, luster interior, signed 1,300.00

Vase, 8" h., baluster form, spiraling bands of iridescent dark green & silver peacock plumage within black lines, unsigned 462.00

Vase, 8" h., 6½" widest d., fluted, opal w/pulled green feather & gold lacing, stretched top w/pink highlights, gold lustre interior, signed & numbered 1,475.00

Vase, 8" h., jack-in-pulpit type, iridescent gold w/crackled decor, reverse w/band of gilt-edged striated green leaves on an elaborately scrolled green & white ground, signed 1,100.00

Vase, 10" h., onion form, iridescent blue, signed 475.00

Vase, 11¼" h., iridescent amber neck continuing to an opalescent body decorated about the shoulder w/iridescent green & amber scrolling lappets & about the body w/striated amber feathering, 1905-25, signed (ILLUS.) 1,045.00

Vases, bud, 12" h., gold, signed, pr............................ 800.00

ROSE BOWLS

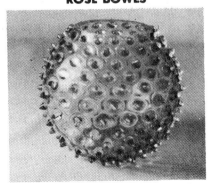

Hobnail Pattern Rose Bowl

Amber, Hobnail patt., 4" h.
(ILLUS.)...................... $80.00
Cameo, carved white to blue florals
& leaves against chartreuse green

satin ground, white band at top, white interior, 2 5/8" d., 2" h. ...1,000.00

Cased, pink exterior, w/gold prunus blossoms decor, white interior, 4-crimp top, clear wafer foot, marked Whitehouse Glass Works, Stourbridge, 3" d., 3" h. 302.00

Cased, light tan exterior w/mauve feathering, robin's egg blue interior, satin finish, closely crimped top, marked Patent, 4½" d., 3 1/8" h. 995.00

Cased, amethyst exterior w/applied white flower & clear foliate branch, white interior, 4" d., 3¾" h. 135.00

Cased, rose w/cream, tan & green morning glory blossoms, buds & trailing vines, white interior, satin finish, 4-crimp top, applied frosted petal feet, 4½" d., 5¼" h. 135.00

Cased, shaded rose to pink w/mauve & yellow pansies & foliage, white interior, egg-shaped, 4-crimp top, applied frosted petal feet, 3½" d., 5½" h. 140.00

Chartreuse green Satin, applied pink & frosted flowers w/frosted leaves, applied frosted petal feet, 3½" d., 4" h. 95.00

Cranberry, applied crystal branch, leaves & florals, clear wafer foot, 4" h. 215.00

Green, blown Optic patt., w/gold roses & scrollwork decor, 6" d., 5½" h. 95.00

Pink Satin, enameled white florals & maroon foliage, 5½" d., 5" h. 170.00

Spatter, pink shaded to raspberry w/white spatter upper portion, clear base w/white spatter, ruffled rim, 5" h. 95.00

Vaseline shaded to green, blown Swirl patt. w/elaborate enameling, 4½" h.................... 95.00

ROYAL FLEMISH

This ware, made by Mt. Washington Glass Co., is characterized by very heavy enameled gold lines dividing the surface into separate areas or sections. The body, with a matte finish, is variously decorated.

Cookie jar, gold line segments separating tan & beige panels & gold Roman coin medallions decor, silverplate rim, cover & bail handle, 9¾" h. $1,500.00

Cookie jar, ovoid, enameled w/irregular panels of mauve, rose & peach within raised gilt borders &

medallions enclosing a bust of
Nero, other classical figures & a
lion rampant, silverplate rim, cover & bail handle, ca. 1900,
10" h. 770.00

Cookie jar, cerise & sepia scrollwork
in circle designs outlined in gold
& w/gold leafy tendrils w/ruby red
jeweling, silverplate rim, cover
& bail handle.................1,750.00

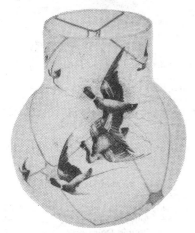

Royal Flemish Vase

Vase, 6 7/8" h., bulbous oval body
w/elongated neck, realistically
painted flying Mallard ducks
w/gold highlights, ca. 1885
(ILLUS.) 1,210.00

Vase, 8" h., 6¾" widest d., raised
gold mythical winged gargoyle
w/long scaly tail front & smaller
fish-like creature reverse, raised
gold florals & gold line segments
over tan & brown panels 2,450.00

Vase, 12¾" h., bulbous body w/slender tapering neck, body painted
w/peacock seated on a branch of
textured raised gold, his body in
shades of purple & set w/jeweled
eye & crest, fan-like tail heavily
enameled in shades of blue, set
w/jewels & heavily encrusted
w/gold, further decorated
w/raised gold florals, leaves &
scrolling devices on pale blue
shading to deep purple ground ..6,750.00

RUBINA CRYSTAL

*This glass, sometimes spelled "Rubena,"
is a flashed ware, shading from ruby to clear.
Some pieces are decorated, others are plain.*

Basket, applied clear thorn handle,
Honeycomb patt.................$225.00

Cruet w/original stopper, Inverted
Thumbprint patt. 165.00

Marmalade jar, cover w/clear
curved stem finial & underplate,
enameled gold florals & scrolls ... 65.00

Mug, applied clear handle, 8-panel,
enameled blue forget-me-nots, silver foliage & gold tracery,
2¼" d., 3¾" h. 55.00

Pitcher, 6" h., applied clear reeded
handle, Diamond Quilted patt. ... 75.00

Pitcher, water, 8" h., 5¾" d., Reverse Rubina Crystal, bulbous
w/square mouth, applied clear
braided spun rope handle, Inverted Thumbprint patt. 275.00

Rubina Crystal Tankard Pitcher

Pitcher, tankard, 8½" h., 5" d., applied clear handle, cut Diamond
patt. around top, notch-cut rim,
rayed base (ILLUS.) 200.00

Pitcher, water, 9" h., applied clear
handle, 8-panel, polished pontil .. 110.00

Salt dip, applied clear shell trim, in
silverplate stand, 3" d., 2" h...... 95.00

Sweetmeat dishes, applied vaseline
shell trim around center & ruffled
rim, double silverplate frame,
9¾ x 4¼", 6½" h. 175.00

Toothpick holder, 10-panel,
1¾" h. 75.00

Tumbler, Inverted Thumbprint patt.,
4" h. 40.00

Vase, 6" h., fluted body, rolled
rim 95.00

RUBINA VERDE

This glass shades from ruby or deep cranberry to green.

Rubina Verde Tumbler

Basket, applied vaseline thorn handle, applied white edging at scalloped rim, Diamond Quilted patt., 10½ x 8", 9" h. $265.00
Bowl, 9" d., 3½" h., footed, ruffled rim 135.00
Cruet w/original faceted stopper, Hobnail patt., 7¼" h. 565.00
Cruet w/original stopper, Inverted Thumbprint patt. . . . . 225.00 to 250.00
Pitcher, 8" h., triangular 295.00
Pitcher, water, Hobnail patt. 230.00
Pitcher, water, bulbous, Inverted Thumbprint patt. 300.00
Sauce dishes, square, Hobnail patt., set of 4 . . . . 150.00
Syrup pitcher w/original hinged pewter lid marked "Pat. Mar 20, 83," applied vaseline handle, Hobnail patt. 685.00
Tumbler, Hobnail patt. 190.00
Tumbler, Inverted Thumbprint patt. 130.00
Tumbler, 10-row Hobnail patt., 3" d., 4" h. (ILLUS.) 225.00
Vase, 9¼" h., trumpet-shaped, ruffled rim, enameled gold decor . . . 105.00
Vase, 9¾" h., 3¾" d., enameled gold fuchsias, leaves & branches outlined in white 100.00
Vase, 10" h., trumpet-shaped, fluted rim, applied rigaree around body 155.00

RUBY

This name derives from the color of the glass — a deep red. Much ruby glass was flashed or stained and was produced as souvenir items late last century and in the present one. Most items listed below are flashed glass. Also see PATTERN GLASS.

Ruby-Stained Patterns

Butter dish, cov., Fleur-de-Lis patt. $90.00
Butter dish, cov., Loop & Block patt. 75.00
Butter dish, cov., Prize patt. 135.00
Butter dish, cov., Punty Band patt. 115.00
Butter dish, cov., Tacoma patt. 90.00
Butter dish, cov., Triple Triangle patt. 65.00
Celery vase, Beaded Swirl & Lens patt. 55.00
Compote, jelly, Nail patt. 85.00
Compote, jelly, Prize patt. 45.00
Creamer, Double Daisy patt. 60.00
Creamer, Hexagon Block patt., w/etching 75.00
Creamer, Prize patt. 75.00
Creamer, Toltec patt. 39.00
Creamer, Truncated Cube patt. 35.00
Cruet w/original stopper, Block & Lattice patt. 100.00
Cruet w/original stopper, teakettle shape w/spout, Pioneer's Victoria patt. . . . . 225.00 to 350.00
Goblet, Beaded Dart Band patt. 35.00
Goblet, Loop & Block patt. 38.00
Goblet, Swag Block patt. 35.00
Mug, Crescent (or Fringed Drape) patt. 35.00
Mug, Heart Band patt., souvenir (ILLUS. right) 25.00
Pitcher, water, tankard, Double Daisy patt. 185.00
Pitcher, water, Gloria patt. 175.00
Pitcher, water, tankard, Hexagon Block patt. 135.00
Pitcher, water, Millard patt., w/etching 130.00
Pitcher, water, Nail patt. 135.00
Punch cup, Lace Band patt., souvenir 18.00
Punch cup, Late Block patt. 20.00
Punch cup, Prize patt. 25.00
Relish, Box-in-Box patt. 50.00
Salt shaker w/original top, O'Hara Star patt. 28.00
Salt shaker w/original top, Truncated Cube patt. (single) 25.00

Salt & pepper shakers w/original
tops, Box-in-Box patt., pr. 60.00
Salt & pepper shakers w/original
tops, Nail patt., pr. 80.00
Sauce dish, Block & Rosette patt. ... 14.00
Sauce dish, Cane with Scroll patt. .. 19.00
Sauce dish, Hero patt. 22.00
Sauce dish, Hexagon Block patt..... 12.00
Sauce dish, flat, Nail patt. 20.00
Spooner, Block & Lattice patt. 50.00
Spooner, Nail patt. 40.00
Spooner, O'Hara Diamond patt.
w/vintage etching 50.00
Spooner, York Herringbone patt. ... 48.00
Sugar bowl, cov., Double Daisy
patt. 75.00
Sugar bowl, cov., Helene patt. 75.00
Sugar bowl, open, Triple Triangle
patt. 45.00
Sugar shaker w/original top, Flower
& Pleat patt. 195.00
Syrup jug w/original spring lid,
Prize patt. 288.00
Syrup pitcher w/original top, Flower
& Pleat patt. 165.00
Syrup pitcher w/original top, Royal
Crystal patt., small 135.00
Syrup pitcher w/original top, Scal-
loped Yoke patt. 145.00
Table set: cov. butter dish, cov.
sugar bowl, creamer & spooner;
Loop & Block patt., 4 pcs. 225.00
Table set: cov. butter dish, cov.
sugar bowl, creamer & spooner;
Majestic patt., 4 pcs. 225.00
Table set: cov. butter dish, cov.
sugar bowl, creamer & spooner;
Triple Triangle patt., 4 pcs. 225.00
Toothpick holder, King's Royal patt.,
souvenir 25.00
Toothpick holder, Prize patt. 125.00
Toothpick holder, Shamrock patt.,
souvenir 30.00
Tumbler, Beaded Swirl patt. 30.00
Tumbler, Bracelet Band patt. 28.00
Tumbler, Button Arches patt., sou-
venir 1904 World Fair (ILLUS.
left) 32.50
Tumbler, Gloria patt. 45.00
Tumbler, Hero patt. 35.00
Tumbler, Hexagon Block patt. 30.00
Tumbler, O'Hara's Diamond patt. ... 45.00
Tumbler, Royal Crystal patt. 25.00
Tumbler, whiskey, O'Hara's No. 139
patt., souvenir 13.00
Water set: tankard pitcher & 2 tum-
blers; Box-in-Box patt., 3 pcs. 235.00
Water set: pitcher & 5 tumblers;
Tarentum's Bar & Diamond patt.,
6 pcs. 290.00
Water tray, Beveled Star patt. 65.00
Whimsey, model of a chamber pot,
souvenir (ILLUS. center) 15.00
Wine, Loop & Block patt. 30.00

Wine, Prize patt. 27.00
Wine, Royal Crystal patt. 35.00
Wine, Rustic Rose patt. 20.00
Wine, Zipper Slash patt., souvenir .. 30.00

SANDWICH

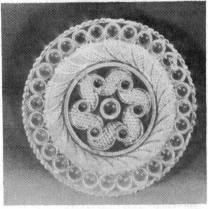

Lacy Peacock Eye Pattern

*Numerous types of glass were produced at
the Boston & Sandwich Glass Works, Cape
Cod, Mass., from 1826 to 1888. Those listed
here represent a sampling. Also see PAT-
TERN GLASS.*

Bowl, 6¼" d., shallow, Oak Leaf
patt., flint, clear $50.00
Bowl, 8¼" d., 1¾" h., lacy, Sun-
flower patt., flint, clear 450.00
Bowl, 8½" d., lady, Rayed Peacock
Eye patt., flint, clear 150.00
Bowl, 9" d., lacy, Peacock Eye patt.,
flint, clear 275.00
Bowl, 9¼" d., shallow, lacy, Oak
Leaf patt., flint, clear 375.00
Bowl, 9½" d., lacy, Dahlia patt.,
flint, clear 400.00
Bowl, 10" d., 2" h., lacy, Princess
Feather Medallion patt., plain ser-
rations, flint, clear 500.00
Candlestick, Crucifix, wafer-
connected tiered base, flint, ca-
nary yellow, 11¼" h. (single) 350.00
Candlestick, dolphin stem, square
base, petal top, vaseline, 10¼" h.
(single) 275.00
Candlesticks, dolphin stem, single
step base, canary yellow, pr...... 850.00
Candlesticks, dolphin stem, double
step base, vaseline, pr.......... 575.00
Candlesticks, Petal & Loop patt., canary yellow, pr................. 375.00
Cologne bottle, 36-rib, ground
mouth, pontil, brilliant sapphire
blue, 5½" h..................... 125.00

Compote, 10½" d., 6¼" h., lacy,
Peacock Eye patt., flint, clear 350.00
Compote, open, 10½" d., 8¾" h.,
lacy, Basket of Flowers patt.,
flint, clear 2,000.00
Compote, 11" w., 6" h., lacy, Peacock Eye patt., plain hexagonal
foot, flint, clear 1,100.00
Creamer, lacy, Gothic with Chain
patt., flint, clear, 4¼" h. 525.00
Curtain tie back w/original pewter
shank, Amberina, 3½" d.
(single) 68.00
Curtain tie backs w/original pewter
shanks, fiery opalescent,
4 5/8" d., set of 4 .... 95.00
Dish, lacy, Cadmus patt., flint,
clear, 6¼ x 4½" oval 800.00
Drawer knobs, clear, threaded,
"Patent" on base (June 11, 1829),
2½" d., pr. 80.00
Lamp base, onion-shaped, amber &
white opalescent, 8½" h. 195.00
Pitcher w/ice bladder, 11" h., applied reeded handle, clear
"overshot" 225.00
Plate, 7¼" d., lacy, Heart patt.,
flint, clear 160.00
Plate, 9" octagon, lacy, Beehive
patt., flint, clear 135.00
Pomade jar, figural bear, flint,
amethyst 425.00
Salt dip, footed, lacy, "H. Clay"
locomotive, flint, clear (minor
damage to feet) 1,100.00
Salt dip, Washington-Lafayette portraits, flint, clear 1,800.00
Salt shaker, "Christmas" salt w/agi-
tator & dated top, amber 85.00
Salt shakers, "Christmas" salt
w/agitator & dated top, amethyst,
pr. 170.00
Sugar bowl, cov., lacy, Shield patt.,
flint, clear, 5¼" h. 525.00
Toddy plate, lacy, Peacock Eye
patt., flint, clear, 5¼" d.
(ILLUS.) 50.00
Vases, 9¼" h., goffered rim, Block
& Punty patt., amethyst, pr. 1,200.00

SATIN

*Satin and Mother-of-Pearl wares were made
by numerous glasshouses over a large part
of the world. They continue in production
today. Also see BRIDE'S BASKETS.*

Basket, gilded thorn handle, blue
mother-of-pearl Raindrop patt.,
white lining, 10½" h............. $65.00
Bowl, 4 7/8" w., 4 5/8" h., tricornered, applied vaseline feet &

trim around top edge, pastel rainbow mother-of-pearl Diamond
Quilted patt., glossy cream
lining.......................... 1,100.00
Bowl, 9¼" d., 4" h., blue mother-of-
pearl Flower & Acorn patt. w/gold
florals, silver rim 1,010.00
Bowl-vase, applied frosted feet, ruffled top w/frosted edging, shaded
gold mother-of-pearl Ribbon patt.,
white lining, 6" d., 5¾" h. 245.00
**Box, cov., embossed design, light
blue w/enameled pink roses de-
cor, 5¾" d., 3¾" h.** 240.00
**Butter dish, cov., Beaded Drape
patt., red** 610.00
Cologne bottle w/knobby frosted
clear stopper, cylindrical, flared &
crimped collar, pink mother-of-
pearl Diamond Quilted patt.
w/enameled white butterfly
hovering among tall blossoms
highlighted w/gold 385.00
Cookie jar, shaded blue w/yellow
enameled decor, silverplate rim,
cover & bail handle, 7¾" h. 115.00
Creamer, applied frosted handle &
wafer foot, crimped top, heavenly
blue mother-of-pearl Swirl patt.,
white lining, 2½" d., 3½" h. 245.00

Mother-of-Pearl Satin Cruet

Cruet w/original stopper, salmon
shaded to pink mother-of-pearl
Herringbone patt. (ILLUS.)........ 395.00
Ewer, applied frosted handle, ruffled top, shaded heavenly blue
mother-of-pearl Herringbone
patt., white lining, 4" d., 8" h. ... 195.00
Finger bowl, 9-crimp top, peach
blow pink mother-of-pearl Diamond Quilted patt., off-white lining, 4¼" d., 2" h. 375.00
Pitcher, 6" h., 4½" widest d., bulbous w/oval top, applied frosted

handle, shaded heavenly blue
w/pink & yellow florals & green
foliage, white lining 220.00
Punch cup, applied frosted handle,
pink shaded to white mother-of-
pearl Herringbone patt. 95.00
Rose bowl, egg-shaped, 4-crimp top,
shaded rose mother-of-pearl Herringbone patt., white lining, 3" d.,
2½" h. 175.00
Rose bowl, egg-shaped, 8-crimp top,
applied frosted petal feet, shaded
heavenly blue w/cream florals &
dainty coralene-like foliage, white
lining, 3½" d., 6¼" h. 135.00
Rose bowl, 8-crimp top, frosted wa-
fer foot, chartreuse green mother-
of-pearl Ribbon patt. w/gold prunus & branches decor, white lin-
ing, 3 1/8" d., 2¼" h. 280.00
Rose bowl, 8-crimp top, heavenly
blue mother-of-pearl Ribbon patt.,
white lining, 4" d., 2 5/8" h. 216.00
Rose bowl, 8-crimp top, shaded
heavenly blue mother-of-pearl
Pinwheel patt., white lining,
6¼" d., 5¾" h. 225.00
Rose bowl, 9-crimp top, shaded
Amberina mother-of-pearl Diamond
Quilted patt., cream lining,
7½" d., 7¼" h. 1,200.00
Rose bowl, 12-crimp top, chartreuse
green mother-of-pearl Flower &
Acorn patt., white lining,
3 3/8" d., 2 7/8" h. 245.00
Scent bottle w/hallmarked silver
screw-on cap, rose mother-of-
pearl Ribbon patt., 2" d.,
2 3/8" h. 210.00
Sugar shaker w/original top,
heavenly blue mother-of-pearl
Diamond Quilted patt.
w/enameled white flowering
branch 215.00
Tumbler, shaded apricot mother-of-
pearl Herringbone patt., 2¾" d.,
3¼" h. 125.00
Tumbler, shaded rose mother-of-
pearl Coin Spot patt., 2 5/8" d.,
3¾" h. 110.00
Tumbler, pale to deep rose mother-
of-pearl Diamond Quilted patt. . . . 145.00
Vase, 7" h., 3½" d., shaded
heavenly blue mother-of-pearl
Herringbone patt. w/enameled
purple florals & gold leaves 225.00
Vase, 8½" h., 4 5/8" d., ruffled,
shaded peach mother-of-pearl
Coin Spot patt. w/enameled blue
flowers & gold leaves decor,
white lining. 550.00
Vase, 11½" h., baluster form, flared
rim, mother-of-pearl Federzeichnung patt., overall gilt pat-

Satin "Federzeichnung" Vase

tern & opaque scrolls, enameled
on base, patent 9159, ca. 1900
(ILLUS.) 1,045.00
Water set: pitcher & 6 tumblers;
deep apricot shaded to white
mother-of-pearl Diamond Quilted
patt., 7 pcs. 1,275.00

SCHNEIDER

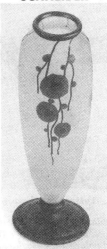

Schneider Cameo Vase

*This ware is made in France at Cristallerie
Schneider, established in 1913 near Paris by
Ernest and Charles Schneider. Some pieces
of cameo were marked "Le Verre Francais"
and others were signed "Charder." Also see
LE VERRE FRANCAIS.*

Bowl, 8¼" d., marbled charcoal &
orange, signed $175.00

Bowl, 10" d., webbed, amber,
signed 145.00
Candle holder, double, paperweight-
type, coral & pink clematis,
signed 145.00
Compote, cov., 9", orange w/black
base, signed 195.00
Compote, 6½" h., mottled orange,
iron stem w/glass balls 275.00
Compote, 6½" h., orange & yellow
mottling, wrought iron fence
w/glass berries, signed 375.00
Compote, 10" d., 12" h., amethyst
bowl, red stem, signed 650.00
Compote, black base, cobalt, pink &
white marbled top, signed 210.00
Pitchers, 6½" h., 4 1/8" d., applied
transparent amethyst handle,
mottled cream to mottled purple
opaque, ground pontil, unsigned,
pr............................. 210.00
Vase, 7¼" h., mottled rose & yellow
body, amethyst base, signed 375.00
Vase, cameo, 13" h., mottled aubergine circular foot, carved deep
aubergine trailing vines pendant
w/brilliant ruby red berries &
applied & wheel-carved ruby blossoms w/black centers against mottled grey ground, ca. 1925, signed
(ILLUS.) 1,045.00

SHADES

Lustre Art Shades

The popularity of collecting fine early Art Glass gas and electric shades has recently soared and values have escalated according-ly. Listed below, by manufacturer or type of glass, is a random sampling of shades offered for sale within the past six months.

Lustre Art, iridescent gold w/pulled
opal feathering, 4¾" h. $98.00
Lustre Art, opal w/blue short
hooked feathering bordered in
gold, gold lining 275.00
Lustre Art, opal w/band of gold
waves, 5" h., pr. (ILLUS.) 350.00

Lustre Art, opal w/iridescent gold
swirls upper body above green &
iridescent gold base, set of 5..... 675.00
Muller Freres, frosted w/overall cut
to clear design of birds & florals,
globular...................... 195.00
Muller Freres, satiny frosted white
top above cobalt blue touched
w/pale yellow, 6" h., set of 3 .... 225.00
NuArt, iridescent marigold Carnival
glass, pr...................... 125.00
Quezal, dark green w/platinum
feathering, gold lining, 5½".... 650.00
Quezal, iridescent gold, bell form,
5½" h. 150.00
Quezal, iridescent gold w/opal fishnet design 175.00
Quezal, iridescent gold w/opal
snakeskin, ribbed 175.00
Quezal, iridescent gold w/opal
snakeskin at top & iridescent gold
w/green snakeskin below, corset-
shaped, pr.................... 275.00
Quezal, iridescent gold w/white
King Tut patt., gold lining 160.00
Quezal, opal w/pulled gold feathering, gold lining, 2 3/8" d., 5" h. .. 165.00
Quezal, opal w/pulled green
feathering outlined in gold,
iridescent gold lining,
6½" h.................185.00 to 210.00
Quezal, opal w/iridescent gold trellis design, gold interior, ruffled
rim, 6 7/8" d. 765.00
Steuben, Calcite w/etched decor,
acorn-shaped 225.00
Steuben, iridescent blue Aurene
w/platinum leaf & vine motif 850.00
Steuben, iridescent brown Aurene
w/platinum applied border 425.00
Steuben, iridescent gold Aurene,
tulip-shaped, 4½" h. 175.00
Steuben, pale yellow w/lime green
feathering, gold lining, notched
rim, pr. 230.00
Tiffany, iridescent gold, ribbed,
5" h. 565.00
Tiffany, iridescent gold, lily form,
set of 3......................1,430.00
Tiffany, iridescent gold, bell-shaped,
5¼" h., set of 4 ....1,045.00
Tiffany, iridescent gold, 6-sided,
4 7/8" h., set of 6 ....1,500.00

SILVER OVERLAY & SILVER DEPOSIT

Silver Deposit and Silver Overlay have been made commercially since the last quar-ter of the 19th century. Silver is deposited on the glass by various means, the most widely adopted utilizing an electric current. The

glass was very popular during the first three decades of this century, and some pieces are still being produced. During the late 1970's, silver commanded exceptionally high prices and this was reflected in a surge of interest in silver overlay glass, especially in pieces marked "sterling" or "925" on the heavy silver overlay.

Perfume Bottle with Silver Overlay

Bowl, 4" h., green w/sterling silver overlay scrolling florals, marked "Alvin" $605.00

Card tray, footed, up-turned ruffled edge, black w/silver overlay, 9½" d. 55.00

Cordial set: decanter & 4 cordials; amethyst w/silver deposit, 5 pcs. 60.00

Creamer & sugar bowl, clear w/silver overlay geometric designs, pr. 95.00

Decanter w/matching stopper, globular, handled, clear w/silver overlay, 5" w., 10" h. 325.00

Dresser jar, cov., clear w/silver overlay, 2¾" w., 3¼" h. 65.00

Lemonade set: 9" h. pitcher & 6 tumblers; amethyst w/silver overlay, 7 pcs. 125.00

Loving cup, 3-handled, cranberry w/silver overlay, 3½" 495.00

Perfume bottle w/original stopper, clear w/sterling silver overlay Art Nouveau florals, 4" h. (ILLUS.) 125.00

Perfume bottle w/matching stopper, blue w/roses on front & bands of silver deposit, 1920's, 1¾" d., 6" h. 45.00

Pitcher, 9" h., cranberry w/silver overlay grapevines 895.00

Salt dips, cobalt blue w/silver overlay "S" designs, set of 6 .... 132.00

Vase, 4" h., green w/silver overlay florals 175.00

Vase, 7" h., green w/silver overlay oriental poppies & vines 138.00

Vase, 8" h., black satin w/silver overlay 150.00

Vase, 9" h., lobed oval shape, Diamond Optic patt., green w/wide silver overlay floral band, engraved garlands of florals & leaves 135.00

Vase, pedestal base, emerald green w/silver overlay overall swirls & center monogram, silver top & bottom borders 1,150.00

Whiskey decanter, amber w/silver overlay "Rye" 175.00

Whiskey shot glass, clear w/silver overlay, 2¼" h. 30.00

SINCLAIRE

Sinclaire Intaglio Glass Clock

H.P. Sinclaire & Co., Corning, New York, operated from 1904 until 1928, turning out fine quality cut and engraved glasswares on blanks supplied by Dorflinger, Pairpoint, Baccarat, Steuben and other glassworks. Its founder, H.P. Sinclaire, Jr., had been associated with T.G. Hawkes & Co., from 1883, and had risen to a high position with that firm. Sinclaire showed a preference for engraved glass over deeply cut glass and this was to be the specialty of the firm that carried his name. From 1920 on, most of the crystal and colored blanks were of the company's own manufacture and, after 1926, engraving gave way to acid-etched designs. Their trademark of an acid-stamped "S" within a laurel wreath interrupted by two shields was used on all perfect pieces but seconds were sold without the trademark from a special salesroom on the premises. Also see CUT GLASS.

Bowl, fruit, 14 x 8" oblong, clear, engraved apples, pears & grape clusters $395.00

Clock, peaked dome case w/intaglio

cuttings of baskets, flowers, cornu-
copiae & scrolls, silvered dial,
retailed by Tiffany & Co., ca. 1910,
12½" h. (ILLUS.) .....2,700.00 to 2,900.00
Console bowl, rolled rim, green,
etched flower garlands, bows &
medallions, signed, 10" d., 4" h... 150.00
Console set: compote & pr. candlesticks; deep amber, signed,
3 pcs. 145.00
Console set: compote & pr. candlesticks; deep amber w/etching,
signed, 3 pcs. 205.00
Console set: 12" d. bowl & pr. candle holders; topaz, signed,
3 pcs. 120.00
Cordials, clear w/engraving, signed,
set of 8 .... 175.00
Jar, cov., amber w/engraved
florals, 14½" h. 140.00
Vase, 11" h., clear w/engraved
florals overall................. 125.00
Vase, 12" h., clear w/engraved
florals, signed 150.00
Water set: pitcher & 5 tumblers; apple green pitcher w/applied amber handle & apple green
tumblers w/amber bases, etched
grapes & vines, 6 pcs. 400.00

SMITH BROTHERS

Smith Brothers Potpourri Vase

*This company first operated as a decorat-
ing department of the Mt. Washington Glass
Works in the 1870's and later on as an independent business in New Bedford, Mass.
The firm was noted for its outstanding
decorating work on glass and also carried on
a glass cutting trade.*

Bowl, 3½" widest d., 2¼" h.,
melon-ribbed, gold florals & foliage & enameled jeweling on
white ground, signed $215.00
Bowl, 4¼" d., melon-ribbed, yellow

daisies decor on creamy white
satin finish 235.00
Bowl, 9" d., large white florals &
green leaves outlined in gold on
cream ground, signed 350.00
Creamer, squatty, melon-ribbed,
leaves & blue berries on cream
ground, silverplate rim & handle,
ca. 1890, unsigned, 3 3/8" h...... 165.00
Mustard jar, ribbed, gold prunus
decor on white ground, 2" h..... 295.00
Mustard jar, narrow-ribbed body,
pink floral decor on white ground,
blue enameled dots around rim,
3" h. 155.00
Plate, 7½" d., h.p. "Santa Maria"
ship, blue & sepia,
signed ....265.00 to 325.00
Potpourri vase, enameled
chrysanthemums & leaves outlined
in gold on satin finish ground,
signed, 10" h. (ILLUS.) 950.00
Powder box, cov., melon-ribbed,
blue & gold florals on cream
ground, 5½" w., 3½" h......... 450.00
Rose bowl, beaded rim, pink & rose
pansies & green leaves on creamy
white ground, signed, 2½"
top d. 200.00
Salt dip, master size, melon-ribbed,
beaded rim, raised gold floral decor on creamy white 95.00
Salt shaker w/original pewter top,
melon-ribbed, ring neck, floral decor on white satin ground
(single)........................ 110.00

Smith Brothers Sugar Shaker

Sugar shaker w/original top,
narrow-ribbed body, pale pink
wild rose w/thorny stem & green
leaves on white ground (ILLUS.) .. 135.00
Toothpick holder, columned ribs,
pansies decor on white ground,
blue enameled dots around rim .. 115.00
Toothpick holder, melon-ribbed,
blue pansies on creamy ground,

blue rim w/white enameled beading, signed 195.00

Vase, 4½" h., scene of heron in rushes, signed 65.00

Vase, 5" h., 4" widest d., pinched tricorn shape, brown & gold, Shasta daisy decor, white enameled dots around rim, signed 225.00

Vase, 5¾" h., 3¼" widest d., Greenaway-type figures on glossy light green ground, unsigned 90.00

Vase, 8¾" h., pillow-shaped, leafy vine w/pink & blue clematis blossoms outlined in gold on front, single blue blossom reverse, unsigned 385.00

SPANGLED

Spangled Glass Ewer

Spangled glass incorporated particles of mica or metallic flakes and variegated colored glass particles imbedded in the transparent glass. Usually made of two layers, it might have either an opaque or transparent casing. The Vasa Murrhina Glass Company of Sandwich, Mass., first patented the process for producing Spangled glass in 1884 and this factory is known to have produced great quantities of this ware. It was, however, also produced by numerous other American and English glasshouses. This type, along with Spatter, which see below, is often erroneously called "End of Day."

Basket, applied clear handle & edging, heavenly blue w/mica flecks, 4 7/8 x 5 5/8", 4½" h...........$118.00

Basket, applied clear twisted thorn handle, pink w/mica flecks, white lining, 5" d., 5¾" h............. 105.00

Basket, applied clear rope twist handle, crimped ruffled top edged w/clear, shaded rose-red w/silver mica flecks, 7 x 8", 7" h. 235.00

Basket, rose bowl shape, 8-crimp top, applied clear thorn handle,

rose w/mica flecks, white lining, 4¼" d., 8¼" h. 175.00

Box w/hinged lid, rainbow spatter w/mica flecks, gilt brass fittings & ball feet, 4 5/8" oval 80.00

Bride's bowl, clear ruffled rim, deep butterscotch w/silver mica flecks, white lining, 11½" w. 135.00

Ewer, applied clear thorn handle, blue w/mica flecks, white lining, 8" h........................... 110.00

Ewer, applied clear handle, apricot w/mica flecks, 8 3/8" h. (ILLUS.).. 125.00

Ewer, applied clear handle & edging, cranberry w/gold mica flecks, 9¾" h.......................... 195.00

Finger bowl & underplate, ruffled, deep blue w/copper mica flecks, 2 pcs.......................... 45.00

Pitcher, 5½" h., 4¼" d., bulbous w/square mouth, applied clear reeded handle, rose w/silver mica flecks, white lining 195.00

Pitcher, 9¾" h., applied clear handle, yellow & pink w/mica flecks, white lining.................... 65.00

Rose bowl, 8-crimp top, beige w/brown & pink spatter & mica flecks in a swirl design, white lining, 3 7/8" d., 3¼" h. 95.00

Vase, 5½" h., 4 5/8" d., jack-in-pulpit type, green, white & maroon spatter w/mica flecks....... 55.00

Vase, 6" h., melon ribbed, emerald green w/silver mica flecks 45.00

Vase, 8¾" h., 4" d., ruffled fan top w/clear edging, pink w/mica flecks, white lining 85.00

Vase, 8 7/8" h., 3½" d., ruffled rim, pink w/mica flecks, white lining .. 105.00

SPATTER

Spatter Glass Bowl

This variegated-color ware is similar to Spangled glass but does not contain metallic flakes. The various colors are applied on an opaque white or colored body. Much of it was made in Europe and England. It is sometimes called "End of Day."

Basket, folded-in front, applied clear thorn handle, maroon, white, blue, yellow & green spatter, white lining, 4 x 7½", 5½" h. $165.00

Basket, applied clear twisted handle, star-shaped top, maroon, white, yellow, pink & green spatter w/white circular designs, white lining, 4 3/8" d., 6" h. 95.00

Basket, applied clear twisted thorn handle, embossed swirl & swirl rosette, opaque apple green & white spatter in clear, 4¾" d., 6¼" h. 95.00

Basket, applied clear thorn handle & clear fan-scalloped trim around top edge, pink w/maroon, green, yellow & blue spatter, white lining, 5½" d., 6½" h. 165.00

Basket, applied clear thorn handle, embossed swirls, pink & gold spatter, white lining, 5 5/8" d., 6½" h. 165.00

Bowl, 6" d., 1¾" h., green, yellow & white spatter cased in clear, white lining (ILLUS.) 45.00

Candlesticks, Swirl patt., multicolor cased spatter, 9½" h., pr. 118.00

Cruet w/replaced stopper, wide ribbed body, amber & white spatter, polished pontil 75.00

Pitcher, 2¾" h., white w/yellow spatter, orange trim 48.00

Pitcher, 7½" h., applied clear handle, pink & maroon spatter 80.00

Pitcher, 8" h., applied clear reeded handle, cranberry & white spatter in clear 165.00

Pitcher, 8½" h., bulbous w/ruffled top, applied clear handle, white & pink spatter 90.00

Pitcher, 9" h., swirl ribbed, red-brown, blue & white spatter 65.00

Pitcher, water, applied clear handle, fluted rim, yellow base, ruby spatter 365.00

Syrup pitcher w/original top, pink & white spatter 135.00

Tumbler, Inverted Thumbprint patt., cranberry spatter 35.00

Spatter Glass Tumbler

Tumbler, red, white & green spatter (ILLUS.) 42.00

Vase, 7" h., 6½" widest d., jack-in-pulpit type, Diamond Quilted patt. base, sapphire blue w/brown, white & maroon spatter 110.00

Vase, 12¼" h., maroon & blue spatter 65.00

Water set: pitcher & 6 tumblers; pitcher w/ribbed claw handle, triangular rim, red & white spatter, 7 pcs. 210.00

Whimsey, shoe, applied clear leaf across front & rigaree around top, green, tan & white spatter, white lining, 2 x 5¼", 3" h. 65.00

STEUBEN

The Steuben glass listed below was made at the Steuben Glass Works, now a division of Corning Glass, between 1903, when the factory was organized by T.G. Hawkes, Sr., the late Frederick Carder, and others, until about 1933. Mr. Carder devised many types of glass and revived many old techniques. Also see SHADES under Glass.

ACID CUT BACK
Plate, 8¾" d., Rosaline cut to Alabaster $275.00

Rose bowl, Rosaline cut to Alabaster Fircone patt., large 595.00

Vase, 6" h., classic shape, blue Aurene cut to Pomona green 2,750.00

Vase, 7" h., Rosaline cut to Alabaster Art Deco florals 1,000.00

Vase, 8" h., Jade green cut to Alabaster florals 700.00

ALABASTER
Flower block, Buddha figure in double-row base, pale celadon ... 250.00

Vase, 6" h., Alabaster w/black Jade handles & trim at top, signed 425.00

AURENE

Steuben Aurene Vase

Bowl, 8" d., blue Aurene, signed ... 440.00

Bowl, 8½" w., 3" h., 3-footed,

in-curved rim, blue Aurene,
signed 495.00
Bowl, 9¼" d., gold Aurene,
signed 440.00
Candlestick, twisted stem, blue
Aurene, 8" h. (single) ...295.00 to 325.00
Candlesticks, twisted stems, gold
Aurene, signed, 8" h., pr. 625.00
Champagne, gold Aurene w/reddish
highlights, signed & w/original
paper label, 3¾" h. 225.00
Compote, 8¼" h., blue Aurene &
Calcite, original paper label 425.00
Goblet, twisted stem, gold Aurene,
signed, 6" h. 275.00
Perfume atomizer, gold Aurene,
original bulb & fittings, signed,
7½" h. 300.00
Perfume bottle w/stopper, gold
Aurene, 4" h. 160.00
Perfume bottle w/stopper, blue
Aurene, 5 7/8" h. 725.00
Salt dip, pedestal base, gold
Aurene, 1½" h. 225.00
Salt dip, pedestal base, gold
Aurene & Calcite 175.00
Vase, 5½" h., floriform, ribbed
tapering body, flaring rim, blue
Aurene, signed 330.00
Vase, 6" h., 7" widest d., everted
rim, applied 3 scrolling handles at
shoulders, circular foot, gold
Aurene, ca. 1925, signed
(ILLUS.) 660.00
Vase, 10" h., stick-type, blue
Aurene 325.00

CALCITE

Calcite & Gold Aurene Vase

Bon bon, 6-scallop rim, Calcite exterior, blue Aurene lining, 6" d. ... 225.00
Bowl, 4" d., 2" h., turned-in rim,
Calcite exterior, gold Aurene
lining 95.00

Bowl, 11" d., 2" h., Calcite exterior,
gold Aurene lining 325.00
Bowl, 12 1/8" d., flared, low rounded foot, Calcite exterior, gold Aurene lining, ca. 1925, unsigned ... 357.50
Candlestick, baluster-shaped w/dou-
ble knop beneath bell-form nozzle, domical circular foot, Calcite
w/blue Aurene rim & footrim, ca.
1925, signed (single) 330.00
Sherbet & underplate, Calcite & blue
Aurene, pr. 165.00
Vase, 8" h., ruffled rim, Calcite
w/gold Aurene lining (ILLUS.) 295.00

CELESTE BLUE

Candlestick, ribbed stem w/amber
double ball connector, signed,
12¼" h. (single) 175.00
Tazza, clear stem, 6¾" d., 6¼" h. ... 95.00
Vase, 8¼" h., ribbed trumpet shape
on domed pedestal foot,
signed ....100.00 to 125.00

CINTRA

Cintra Champagne

Champagne, bowl & base w/blue &
rose striped effect, ribbed stem,
unsigned (ILLUS.) 225.00
Goblet, opal w/lavender Cintra
stem & border, signed,
7 1/8" h. 225.00

FRENCH BLUE

Goblet, threaded 85.00
Vases, 6¾" h., flaring slightly flattened undulating rim, spreading
lobed foot beneath a cushion
knop, ca. 1930, unsigned, pr. 357.50
Wines, flared bowl w/self reeding
on lower half, graceful stem,
signed, 7¼" h., set of 6 .... 210.00

GROTESQUE

Bowl, 6" h., pedestal base, shaded
emerald green to clear, signed ... 160.00

Bowl, 9" w., 5½" h., clear, signed . . 120.00
Bowl, Gold Ruby 155.00
Bowl, Ivrene 320.00
Vase, 6¼" h., 4-ribbed, emerald
   green to clear, signed 160.00

Steuben Grotesque Vase

Vase, 9¼" h., clear to emerald
   green, signed (ILLUS.) 275.00
Vase, 11¼" h., cranberry to clear . . 225.00
Vase, 12 x 6½ x 7", clear, signed . . 145.00
Vases, 20" h., pedestal foot, irregu-
   lar rim, Pomona Green, pr. 900.00

IVRENE

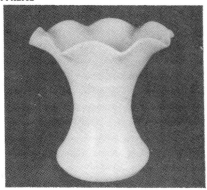

Ivrene Vase

Candlestick, foliate form, 4" d.,
   3" h. (single) 125.00
Compote, 7" d., black base,
   signed 250.00
Vase, 6" h., 4½" w., ruffled rim,
   signed (ILLUS.) 200.00
Vase, 6" h., ribbed & ruffled oval
   body on wafer stem & pedestal
   foot, signed 225.00
Vase, 10" h., ribbed, w/paper
   label 495.00
Vase, 12¼" h., lily, tall center jack-

in-the-pulpit form lily flanked by
two smaller lilies of the same
shape, all attached to round
base 1,295.00

JADE

Jade Tree Stump Vase

Bowl, 12" d., Alabaster base 100.00
Bowl, black Jade 260.00
Vase, 5½" h., 3-prong tree stump,
   green Jade, signed (ILLUS.) 260.00
Vase, 7" h., 4½" d., dark blue,
   signed 1,150.00
Vase, 7" h., swirled, green Jade,
   signed 125.00
Wine, green Jade w/twisted Alabas-
   ter stem, signed, 7¼" h. 95.00

MARINE BLUE

Candlesticks, clear inset w/Marine
   blue sections in the stem in 2
   places, round discs of hollow
   glass in the center artistically engraved, attached engraved
   bobeches, prunts on sides of
   discs, signed, 12" h., pr. 950.00
Plate, 8" d., etched design 55.00
Plate, 8¼" d., copper wheel en-
   graved rim, signed 85.00
Serving plate, copper wheel engrav-
   ing, 8" d. 65.00

POMONA GREEN

Ash tray, rounded body pulled into
   3 openings, applied handle,
   signed 120.00
Ash tray, rounded triangle, applied
   circular handle, signed 110.00
Bowl, Oriental Poppy w/Pomona
   Green foot, signed 750.00
Tazza, swirled, signed, 7" d.,
   7" h. 115.00
Vase, 10" h., diagonally ribbed body

w/hexagon top on amber foot,
signed 125.00
Vase, 10" h., footed, optic rib,
signed 100.00

ROSALINE

Rosaline Plate

Basket, white Alabaster handle,
polished pontil, 10" l., 8" h. 90.00
Bowl & underplate, Alabaster foot,
signed, pr. 125.00
Candlesticks, twisted Alabaster
stems, 10" h., pr. 425.00
Compote, 8½" w., 4" h., black top
border & ring on stand 475.00
Goblet, Alabaster base 45.00
Jar & cover w/Alabaster finial, Ala-
baster base, 4" d. 118.00
Plate, 8¼" d., signed (ILLUS.) 85.00
Vase, 6" h., signed 150.00
Vase, 18" h., carved Alabaster
handles 450.00

SELENIUM RUBY

Selenium Ruby Charger

Candlesticks, pr. 225.00
Centerpiece bowl, signed, 12" d. . . . 195.00

Centerpiece bowl, signed, 13" d.,
3½" h. 185.00
Charger, wide shallow bowl
w/rolled lip, signed, 17¾" d.
(ILLUS.) 3,520.00
Vase, 12" h., engraved grapes
around upper third 250.00

THREADED

Bowl, 12" d., Thumbprint patt., clear
w/blue threading, signed 135.00
Box, cov., clear w/black threading,
black faceted handle, signed,
6" d. 245.00
Compote, 7" d., 7" h., amber
threading on clear controlled
bubble 85.00
Nut dish, pedestal base, clear
w/applied green threads, signed,
3" d. 85.00
Vase, 12" h., diamond quilted,
green threading upper portion . . . 125.00
Wine tumbler, handled, clear
w/black threading 35.00

TOPAZ

Candlesticks, Topaz & apple green,
signed, 12" h., pr. 395.00
Centerpiece bowl, signed 325.00
Tumbler, Flemish Blue rim, signed,
5" h. 45.00
Vase, 6" h., fan-shaped, Topaz
w/Pomona Green stem & base,
signed 145.00
Vase, 8" h., Topaz diagonally ribbed
body pulled into hexagon rim, on
Pomona Green wafer & pedestal
foot, signed 125.00
Vase, 10" h., 8" d., diagonally
ribbed, flaring top, signed 125.00
Vase, 12" h., applied flaring base,
ribbed, signed 110.00

VERRE DE SOIE

Basket, unsigned, 10" w., 9" h. 175.00
Bowl, 6½" d., 3" h., blue edging . . . 65.00
Candlesticks, ribbed, domed foot,
double ball stem, signed, 12" h.,
pr. 250.00
Compote, 6¼", blue ball stem to
top & bottom edge trim 235.00
Compote, 8" d., 3¾" d., green
rim 110.00
Cruet w/engraved stopper, overall
wheel engraving, signed,
7½" h. 125.00
Goblet, pink trim on foot & rim,
5½" h. 175.00
Perfume bottle w/purple stopper,
4½" h. 175.00
Perfume bottle w/teardrop stopper,
7½" h. 125.00
Plate, luncheon, 8½" d., Celeste
Blue rim 32.00

Plate, dinner, 8½" d., signed
Carder 50.00
Salt dip, master size, white,
signed 125.00
Sherbet & underplate, signed....... 70.00
Tumblers, w/rainbow iridescence,
signed, 4¼" h., pr.............. 110.00
Tumbler, signed, 5" h.............. 45.00
Tumble-up, signed Carder, 7" h. 185.00
Vase, 3" h., 4" d., flared ruffled
top, signed 110.00
Vase, 14" h., ruffled edge 200.00

STEVENS & WILLIAMS

Stevens & Williams Pitcher

This long-established English glass house has turned out scores of types of glass through the years. The following represents a cross-section of its wares. Also see APPLIQUED GLASS.

Basket, applied amber ribbed handle, scissor-cut top edge, cream
opaque w/applied ruffled amber,
rose & green leaves w/stems
looping down to form feet, deep
rose pink lining, 6 x 7¾",
8¼" h. $595.00
Cameo sweetmeat jar, carved shaded green & white florals & leaves
against white opaque ground, silverplate rim, cover & bail handle,
unsigned, 4¼" d., 4¾" h. 375.00
Celery vase, panelled, cranberry
opalescent, 6½" h.............. 119.00
Chalice, deep cranberry bowl &
foot, clear stem w/interior threading, 5" opening, 12¾" h. 250.00
Finger bowl, tricornered, Diamond
Quilted patt., rose w/citron
threading..................... 140.00
Nappy, cranberry w/amber
threading..................... 145.00
Pitcher, 2 7/8" h., applied amber
handle, off-white opaque w/pink
lining, applied blue florette, green
leaves & amber stems 180.00

Pitcher, 4¾" h., applied frosted
handle, scissors-cut lip, swirl-
ribbed body, pink satin 175.00
Pitcher, 5¾" h., amber w/applied
blue teardrops on body & applied
blue handle (ILLUS.) 75.00
Pitcher, 9½" h., folded-over top,
opaque white w/applied pink &
gold florals, blue lining 310.00
Rose bowl, box-pleated top, Swirl
patt., blue satin opalescent,
4½" d., 3½" h. 195.00
Rose bowl, box-pleated top, heavenly blue to white mother-of-pearl
Diamond Quilted patt., white lining, 4 1/8" d., 3 7/8" h. 210.00
Rose bowl, 8-petal top, creamy
opaque w/three applied pink &
white flowers & pale green leaves
& stems, 5¾" d., 5" h. 158.00
Sweetmeat dish, fluted, blue &
white opaque swirled stripes, satin finish, in silverplate holder
w/spoon, 4 3/8" d., 6" h. 110.00
Sweetmeat jar, "Arboresque,"
crackled white on cranberry, silverplate rim, cover, bail handle &
spoon, 3" d., 5" h. 375.00
Vase, 5½" h., 4 7/8" d., 3-petal
shape rim w/pink lining & green
edging, cream w/applied vaseline
& green leaf w/cranberry center.. 145.00
Vase, 11" h., 4½" d., shaded orange mother-of-pearl Swirl patt.,
white lining.................... 265.00
Vase, 12" h., ruffled rim, candy
stripes on blue satin ground, coralene decor of colorful bird on
branch w/flowers & leaves 275.00

STIEGEL & STIEGEL-TYPE

Stiegel-type Flask

This glass was made at the American Flint Glass Works of "Baron" Henry W. Stiegel at Manheim, Pennsylvania, from 1765 until the 1770's. It is difficult to attribute pieces positively to Stiegel.

Flask, pocket-type, Daisy-Hexagon
    patt., amethyst $9,570.00
Flask, pocket-type, Diamond over
    Flute patt., amethyst 8,580.00
Flask, pocket-type, 12 dia-
    mond expanded ogival de-
    sign, purple-amethyst,
    5½" h. (ILLUS.) 3,200.00
Flip glasses, tapering cylinder,
    etched florals, clear, 6" to
    6½" h., set of 3................ 715.00
Flip glass, copper wheel engraved
    large stylized tulip, 1750-1800,
    7¾" h......................... 145.00

STRETCH

*Collectors have given this name to a
Carnival-type glass that is iridescent and
with a surface somewhat resembling the skin
of an onion. It was made in various glass factories and some is now being reproduced.*

Bowl, 7½" d., clear $11.00
Bowl, 8¼" d., 4-sided pedestal,
    blue 25.00
Bowl, 11" d., blue................ 38.00
Bowl, 11" d., vaseline w/black
    edge 65.00
Cake plate, pedestal base, blue 65.00
Cake plate, pedestal base,
    vaseline 65.00
Candle holders, vaseline, Fenton,
    pr........................... 75.00
Candlestick, white, 8¼" h.
    (single)...................... 35.00
Candlesticks, amethyst, 8" h., pr.... 85.00
Candlesticks, vaseline, 8½" h.,
    pr........................... 68.00
Compote, 10" d., vaseline......... 90.00
Console bowl, blue w/gold design
    on edge, Imperial, 13" d. 80.00
Console set: 10½" d., rolled edge
    bowl & pr. 12" h. sq. candlesticks;
    vaseline, 3 pcs................ 85.00
Plate, 6" octagon, vaseline........ 9.00
Plate, 8¾" d., lavender, Imperial ... 21.50
Plate, 10" d., vaseline 25.00
Plate, 12" d., gold................ 59.00
Plate, dessert, medium blue 15.00
Powder jar & cover w/elephant fini-
    al, pink, 6" d. 38.00
Sherbet, medium blue 15.00
Vase, 8" h., 5½" w., blue 40.00

TIFFANY

*This glassware, covering a wide diversity
of types, was produced in glasshouses operated by Louis Comfort Tiffany, America's
outstanding glass designer of the Art Nouveau period, from the last quarter of the 19th
century until the early 1930's. Tiffany revived
early techniques and devised many new ones.
Also see SHADES under Glass.*

Tiffany Compote

Bowl, 4½" w., 3" h., bulbous 4-
    footed base, indented sides, flar-
    ing & fluted rim, iridescent blue,
    signed L.C.T. Favrile &
    numbered $425.00
Bowl, 4 5/8" d., low, bulbous, deep
    iridescent green w/silver-blue lap-
    pets between borders of loop &
    zipper motifs at shoulders, ca.
    1899, signed L.C.T..............2,090.00
Bowl, 6½" d., iridescent blue,
    signed & numbered 235.00
Bowl, 7" d., peacock blue-black
    opaque, signed & numbered &
    original paper label 500.00
Bowl, 8¼" d., 3¼" h., pastel green
    w/opal herringbone & snowflake
    designs, signed 575.00
Bowl, 8½" d., 3" h., footed, scal-
    loped rim, iridescent gold w/radi-
    ating green jewel-like stripes,
    signed 525.00
Bowl, 10" d., fluted, iridescent blue
    & gold, signed L.C. Tiffany Favrile
    & w/original paper label 1,500.00
Bowl, 12" d., pastel green 625.00
Candlestick, swirled stem, iridescent
    blue, signed L.C.T., 8½" h.
    (single)....................... 550.00
Candy dish, peacock blue
    w/stretched edge, signed,
    8¼" d........................ 425.00
Centerpiece bowl w/matching flow-
    er frog, brilliant peacock blue
    w/radiating band of iridescent
    feathering, signed L.C. Tiffany,
    Favrile, 10½" d. 880.00
Chalice, "Cypriote," iridescent gold
    w/pitted & bubbled finish, gilt-
    metal mounts, signed L.C.T.
    Favrile 770.00
Compote, 4¼" h., clear & milky
    white bowl w/radiating feather
    bands, crackled iridescent blue in-
    terior, signed L.C.T. Favrile 605.00

Compote, 8" d., iridescent gold
w/imbedded green leaves & ten-
drils, signed (ILLUS.) 625.00

Favrile Cordial Set

Cordial set: decanter w/stopper & 6
cordial cups; dimpled sides on all
pieces, iridescent gold, signed
"L.C.T.," 11" h. decanter, 7 pcs.
(ILLUS. of part) 1,320.00

Cup & saucer, ornate handle on cup,
iridescent gold w/opal shell & zig-
zag design, signed 525.00

Finger bowl & underplate, ribbed
bowl w/undulating rim, iridescent
gold, signed L.C.T., 4¾" d. plate,
2 pcs. 308.00

Finger bowl & underplate, iridescent
amber, signed L.C.T., 2 pcs. 465.00

Goblet, gold, signed L.C.T. Favrile,
3¾" h. 325.00

Goblet, Vintage patt., gold, intaglio
cut bunches of grapes, signed,
7" h. 275.00

Liqueur, iridescent gold w/bronze,
blue & pink highlights, signed
L.C.T. Favrile, 4¾" h. 265.00

Liqueur set: decanter w/stopper &
12 liqueurs; pinched sides, iridescent gold, 1899-1920, signed
L.C.T., 13 pcs. 2,750.00

Model of a sword, iridescent gold,
ca. 1910 . . . . 600.00

Parfait, opalescent & iridescent
aqua, signed L.C.T. Favrile & num-
bered, 4½" h. 360.00

Perfume bottle w/stopper, squat,
green leaves & vines on gold,
signed, 3½" h. 550.00

Perfume vial w/gilt stopper, tapered,
tomato red w/amber & silvery blue
iridescent wavy trails, 1899-1920,
4" l. (ILLUS.) 1,210.00

Tiffany Perfume Vial

Plate, 11" d., pastel turquoise
w/white opalescent rays from
center, signed 250.00

Punch cup, applied reeded scroll
handle, opalescent swirl decor
around middle, signed & num-
bered, 3¼" d., 2 5/8" h. 325.00

Salt dip, Artichoke patt., gold,
signed L.C.T. Favrile, 2½" d. 350.00

Salt dip, ruffled, shiny white exteri-
or, gold interior, signed 185.00

Sherbet, clear to frosted green,
signed, 3½" h. 200.00

Toothpick holder, dimpled sides,
iridescent orange, signed & num-
bered, 2 1/8" h. 100.00

Tumbler, 4 dimples in lower half,
iridescent gold, signed, 3½" h. 140.00

Tumbler, pinched bottom, translucent gold, signed L.C.T. Favrile,
3¾" h. 185.00

Vase, 2½" h., baluster-form, green
lily pad leaves on trailing stems
on midnight blue to sky blue
ground, signed L.C. Tiffany-
Favrile 825.00

Vase, 3" h., "Cypriote," flattened
globular form, translucent brick
red, lightly pitted, w/iridescent
blue, green & rust coiling pulled
feather pattern, magenta highlights, ca. 1910, signed L.C.T. &
w/paper label 1,100.00

Vase, 3" h., free-form baluster
shape w/dimples, iridescent gold
w/pink & green highlights, signed
L.C.T. 308.00

Vase, 3¼" h., paneled, vivid bluish
gold lustre, signed L.C.T. 400.00

Vase, 3½" h., paperweight-type,
globular, brilliant yellow blossoms
& avocado green leaves & trailing

vines, interior washed in deep iridescent amber, ca. 1906, signed
L.C.T. 3,300.00

Vase, 3¾" h., fluted, ribbed, irides-
cent blue 625.00

Vase, 4" h., blue fish intermingled
w/swirls, signed 975.00

Vase, 4" h., opalescent Agate
w/pulled feathering toward ruffled top, gold stretched lining,
signed 350.00

Vase, 4½" h., "lava," globular w/tre-
foil lip, upper & lower sections
w/striated free-form band shading
from deep mustard to chocolate
brown & enclosing a deep brown-
black lava belt, 1900-20, original
paper label 9,900.00

Vase, 5 1/8" h., 4 1/8" d., iridescent
gold w/intaglio cut garlands &
leaves, signed L.C. Tiffany Favrile
& w/original foil label 1,100.00

Vase, 6" h., scalloped rim, ribbed,
iridescent gold, signed &
numbered 385.00

Vase, 6½" h., 5¾" d., bulbous,
iridescent gold w/green leaves &
vines decor, signed L.C. Tiffany
Favrile 1,100.00

Vase, 7" h., "Tel El Amarna," exaggerated baluster form, translucent
ruby red, applied green neck w/tur-
quoise highlights w/iridescent
amber striations superimposed
w/simple green zigzags, ca. 1916,
signed L.C. Tiffany Favrile 9,350.00

Vase, 7¼" h., pear-shaped, white
lustre w/frieze of gold pulls at top
& base, signed L.C.T. 660.00

Vase, bud, 8¼" h., cylindrical form
flaring towards base, elongated
green triangles on iridescent gold,
early 20th c., signed L.C. Tiffany-
Favrile 330.00

Vase, 9" h., urn-shaped w/cylin-
drical neck, intaglio cut free-form
leaves & vines, iridescent gold cut
to amber, signed Louis C. Tiffany,
Favrile & numbered 1,950.00

Vase, bud, 10½" h., bulbous body
raised to slender stem, clear
w/green & beige pulled feather
design, signed L.C.T. 495.00

Vase, 11½" h., floriform, light iridescent amber w/striated green
feathering & cased in creamy,
white, slender knopped stem,
raised on domed circular iridescent amber foot striped w/creamy
white, ca. 1905, signed 3,585.00

Vase, 12¼" h., floriform, short knob
stem on ribbed, domed foot, gold,
signed & numbered 750.00

Vase, 14" h., jack-in-pulpit type,

iridescent gold w/blue-pink lustre,
signed L.C.T. 1,876.00

Vase, 14¼" h., onion form bowl
w/ruffled lip, opalescent w/green
striated feather devices continuing
into the slender rod standard
w/medial knop, raised on iridescent amber circular domed foot,
iridescent amber interior, ca.
1908, signed L.C.T. 3,300.00

Tiffany Vase in Bronze Holder

Vase, 15" h., trumpet-shaped iridescent gold vase signed L.C.T.
Favrile, in gold "dore" bronze
base marked Tiffany Studios, N.Y.
& numbered, 12" h. vase, overall
15" h. (ILLUS.) 1,000.00

Vase, 16¾" h., wide ovoid, opaque
greyish mint green w/overall
striated deep green loops
& coils, ca. 1896, signed L.C.T. . . .3,520.00

Vase, 20" h., jack-in-pulpit type,
iridescent amber tinged w/gold,
silvery blue, aqua & rose, ca. 1905,
signed L.C. Tiffany - Favrile 7,975.00

Wine, iridescent gold, signed,
3¾" h. 155.00

TORTOISE SHELL

Tortoise Shell glass is primarily amber with
splotches of darker amber or brown and
resembles the actual tortoise shell, hence the
name. Some of this ware is attributed to
Sandwich, but it was also made in numerous
European glasshouses. Readily identified by
its peculiar coloring, it is admired by many
collectors.

Tortoise Shell Celery Vase

Captain's decanter, swirl-ribbed
   body, ground pontil $300.00
Celery vase, undulating rim, 7" h.
   (ILLUS.)........................ 165.00
Decanter, applied handle, attributed
   to Hobbs, Brockunier & Co. 125.00
Pitcher, water, applied amber han-
   dle, bulbous swirled body 195.00
Toothpick holder, bulging base 28.00
Tumbler 40.00
Vase, 8" h. 50.00
Vase, 9" h., ruffled rim, satin
   finish 100.00

VALLERYSTHAL

Vallerysthal Breakfast Set

Glass was made in Vallerysthal, France, for several centuries until 1939 when the factory there was demolished during the war. Most of its glass available to the collector today is of fairly recent vintage.

Animal covered dish, dog on patterned quilt top, raised flowers on
   base, milk white, signed $160.00
Breakfast set: hen covered dish, 6
   egg cups, cov. basket form master salt dip & tray; milk white,
   9 pcs. (ILLUS.)................. 450.00

Butter dish, cov., turtle w/snail finial, milk white.................. 100.00
Candlesticks, Baroque patt., amber,
   unsigned, pr. 75.00
Covered dish, figural lemon, milk
   white, signed ....50.00 to 75.00
Salt dip, cov., hen on nest, white
   opalescent..................... 35.00
Sugar bowl & cover w/salamander
   finial, Strawberry patt., milk
   white w/gold trim, 5" h. 70.00

VAL ST. LAMBERT

This Belgian glass works was founded in 1790. Items listed here represent a sampling of its numerous types of production.

Candy dish, cov., cobalt blue cut
   to clear, gold orange grape
   decor, signed $325.00
Cameo box, cov., carved blue river-
   bank landscape against soft gold
   frosted ground, signed, 4 3/8" d.,
   2 3/8" h. 550.00
Cameo rose bowl, carved florals
   against frosted white ground,
   signed, 8" d., 6" h. 285.00
Cameo toothpick holder, carved
   cranberry to frosted webbed
   design 225.00
Cameo vase, 11½" h., baluster-
   shaped, carved mottled aqua,
   spring green, ochre, oxblood
   & violet pendant wisteria blossoms on leafy vines against
   clear ground, ca. 1900,
   signed......................2,860.00
Compote, 8½" d., 6" h., clear,
   signed 40.00
Liqueur set: decanter & 12 jigger-
   shaped glasses; emerald green
   cut to clear diamond design,
   13 pcs. 795.00
Tumblers, blue cut to clear, band of
   gilt classical figures, 6" h., set of
   6 .... 350.00
Vase, 5" h., blue diamond shapes
   on clear, signed................ 175.00
Vase, 6½" h., swirled ribs, clear
   w/blue rim, signed 75.00
Vase, 8½" h., ruffled top, clear
   "crackle" w/Art Nouveau brass
   applique on front, signed 55.00
Vase, 10" h., 7½" widest d., diamond points & arrows, clear,
   signed 90.00
Vase, 11 3/16" h., oval, streaked
   brown free-form organic motif
   on cased pale blue ground,
   signed 550.00

VASELINE

This glass takes its name from its color, which is akin to that of petroleum jelly used for medicinal purposes. Pieces below are miscellaneous. Also see PATTERN GLASS.

Animal covered dish, canary bird on basketweave base, McKee	$175.00
Cake stand, Daisy & Button with Thumbprint patt., square	75.00
Candlestick, Imperial, 8½" (single)	95.00
Candlesticks, 3½" base, 7" h., pr.	35.00
Candlesticks, double, leaf & scroll design, 7 x 7", pr.	50.00
Centerpiece, blown, two "tree trunk w/thorns" vases attached to twig base & connected by twisted thorn branch, 6½" l., 4½" h.	85.00
Centerpiece bowl, scalloped panels w/opalescent edges, 11½" d., 5" h.	110.00
Compote, 2¾" h., everted rim, knob stem, square base	40.00
Compote, open, 8¼" d., 7" h., Lady Chippendale patt., opalescent	235.00
Compote, open, 10" d., pressed Diamond patt.	43.00
Cruet w/original stopper, Inverted Thumbprint patt.	100.00
Dish, boat-shaped, "War of Roses" patt., opalescent, 2¼ x 7 5/8", 3" h.	60.00
Finger bowl & underplate, threaded	95.00
Goblet, Medallion patt.	38.00
Gum stand, "Clark's Teaberry Gum"	52.50
Mug, Dahlia patt.	40.00
Pitcher, 6" h., Thumbprint patt.	95.00
Pitcher, water, applied handle, ruffled top, Coin Spot patt.	110.00
Pitcher, water, Riverside's Ransom patt., w/gold band	125.00
Salt dip, master size, footed, William & Mary patt., dated 1894	55.00
Salt shaker w/original top, Pleat Band patt.	45.00
Salt & pepper shakers, pressed Diamond patt., pr.	40.00
Table set: cov. butter dish, creamer & spooner; Wreathed Cherry patt., 3 pcs.	195.00
Table set: cov. butter dish, cov. sugar bowl, creamer & spooner; Petticoat patt., w/gold, 4 pcs.	500.00
Toothpick holder, Diamond Spearhead patt.	75.00
Vase, 11 7/8" h., 6¼" d., fluted top, applied ornate vaseline feet, Irises patt., opalescent	175.00

VENETIAN & VENETIAN-TYPE

Assorted Venetian Glass

Venetian glass has been made for six centuries on the island of Murano, where it continues to be produced. The skilled glass artisans developed numerous techniques, subsequently imitated elsewhere.

Box & cover w/pink & blue fruit finial, clear w/embedded gold, 5¼" w., 6" h.	$70.00
Candlesticks, green, ca. 1890, 13" h., pr.	500.00
Candlesticks, dolphin stem, aqua & clear w/gold flecks, pr.	125.00
Compote, 8¾", dolphin stem, red w/clear trim & gold mica flecks	180.00
Cruet w/original stopper, clear w/enameled swags & bows decor, 8" h.	95.00
Salt dip, green w/amethyst dolphins each side	60.00
Vase, 5" h., mauve & blue swirls	85.00
Vase, 10¼" h., goblet-shaped w/floral rigaree stem, quilted, pale sea green w/applied berries & gold	55.00

VERLYS

Verlys Alpine Thistle Vase

This glass is a relative newcomer for collectors and is not old enough to be antique, having been made for less than half a century in France and the United States, but fine pieces are collected. Blown and molded pieces have been produced.

Bowl, 6" d., Pinecone patt., French
blue $95.00
Bowl, 6" d., Pinecone patt.,
frosted 60.00
Bowl, 12" d., sculptured bluebirds &
dragonflies, frosted 135.00
Bowl, 12" d., Thistle patt., sapphire
blue 170.00
Bowl, 13¾" d., sculptured water
lilies & leaves, frosted & clear,
signed 130.00
Bowl, 14" d., Dragonfly patt.,
clear 150.00
Bowl, Mary & Her Lamb, signed &
dated 1940 .... 220.00
Candy dish, cov., sculptured florals
on lid, opalescent, 7" d. 375.00
Dish, 3-footed, Pinecone patt., clear,
signed 30.00
Vase, 4½" h., 6½" w., sculptured
lovebirds at base, frosted,
signed 75.00
Vase, 5 x 6", fan-shaped, sculptured
lovebirds, clear & frosted,
signed 120.00
Vase, 9" h., Alpine Thistle patt.,
amber, signed (ILLUS.) 275.00
Vase, 10" h., Thistle patt., frosted,
signed 250.00

WAVE CREST

Wave Crest Cookie Jar

Now much sought after, Wave Crest was produced by the C.F. Monroe Co., Meriden, Conn., in the late 19th and early 20th centuries from opaque white glass blown into molds. It was then hand-decorated in enamels and metal trims were often added. Boudoir accessories such as jewel boxes, hair receivers, etc., were predominant. Also see KELVA and NAKARA.

Bowl, 9¼" d., 2½" h., Helmschmied
Swirl mold, enameled pink &
white florals on robin's egg blue
ground, beaded ormolu rim &
openwork handles, signed $350.00
Box w/hinged lid, Helmschmied
Swirl mold, blue florals on shaded
pink ground, ormolu collar, unsigned, 3" sq., 2¾" h. 165.00
Box w/hinged lid, baroque shell
mold, enameled daisies on
heavenly blue satin ground,
signed, 3" d. 295.00
Box w/hinged lid, baroque shell
mold, enameled blue florals on
shaded pink ground, signed,
3¼" d., 3" h. 250.00
Box w/hinged lid, plain round mold,
h.p. lake scene w/trees & road on
creamy white ground, signed,
4" d. 225.00
Box w/hinged lid, Helmschmied
Swirl mold, blue florals on creamy
white ground, unsigned, 4" d. 210.00
Box w/hinged lid, embossed rococo
scroll mold, florals on robin's egg
blue ground, signed, 5¼ x 3½"
oval 285.00
Box w/hinged lid, embossed rococo
scroll mold, cupids & florals on
white ground, signed, 5¼" d.,
3" h. 540.00
Box w/hinged lid, baroque shell
mold, enameled florals on creamy
white ground, signed,
5½" d. .... 550.00 to 630.00
Box w/hinged lid, Helmschmied
Swirl mold, h.p. scene of 10
storks on lid, multicolored swirl
panels, gold trim, signed, 6½" d.,
4" h. 1,200.00
Box w/hinged lid, puffy egg crate
mold, pink florals & lavender trim
on cobalt blue matte finish
ground, ormolu rim & feet,
6¾" w., 7" h. 1,400.00
Box w/hinged lid, baroque shell
mold, undecorated creamy white,
signed, 7" d. .... 550.00 to 615.00
Box w/hinged lid, Helmschmied
Swirl mold, woodland scene &
enameled blue florals on creamy
white ground, unsigned, 7" d.,
4" h. .... 300.00 to 395.00
Box w/hinged lid, Helmschmied
Swirl mold, enameled holly berries & leaves on iridescent creamy
white satin ground, brass rims,
unsigned, 7" d., 4 1/8" h. 595.00
Card holder, embossed rococo mold,
pastel floral decor on white
ground, brass rim, unsigned,
4½" w., 2½" h. 140.00
Cigarette holder, scenic medallion

front & overall florals on creamy white, beaded ormolu rim & footed base, signed 255.00

Cookie jar, plain mold, green, pink & yellow florals on creamy white shiny finish, silverplate rim, cover & bail handle, signed in lid, 8" h. (ILLUS.) 400.00

Cookie jar, Helmschmied Swirl mold, florals outlined in white enameled dots on light blue ground, silverplate rim, cover & bail handle, 4¾" d., 10" h. 410.00

Jardiniere, embossed rococo scroll mold, yellow & pink florals on pink ground, plain ormolu rim & ormolu base w/cupid's masks at feet, 7¼" top d., 8½" h. 700.00

Jewelry box w/hinged lid, puffy egg crate mold, pink roses on creamy white ground, ormolu rims & feet, original lining, signed, 5" d...... 500.00

Jewelry box w/hinged lid, mushroom (or petticoat) mold, enameled cobalt blue & pink florals on creamy white ground, ormolu rims w/lock closure & ormolu feet, w/lining, signed, 5½" d., 6" h. 1,100.00

Letter holder, puffy Egg Crate mold, daisies decor, unsigned, 6 x 3 x 4½" 250.00

Memo spindle, blue forget-me-nots decor on domed white base, ormolu metal trim................ 465.00

Paperweight, 8-sided, blue forget-me-nots decor, ornate ormolu top, unsigned 350.00

Photo receiver, robin's egg blue w/baroque scrolls framing pink mums on all 4 sides, ormolu beaded rim, 6¼" l., 4¼" h. 335.00

Pin dish, scroll design, spray of blue flowers on 2 sides, ornate ormolu rim w/handles, 4 x 2½" 137.00

Pin tray, Helmschmied Swirl mold, purple floral decor, ormolu rim & handles 75.00

Ring dish, kittens playing in the grass on front & back, ormolu handles, signed, 3" d. 150.00

Salt & pepper shakers w/original pewter tops, Helmschmied Swirl mold, blue aster on alternating white & beige swirls, unsigned, 2¾" h., pr. 235.00

Salt & pepper shakers w/original pewter tops, bulbous shoulders, flared at footing, overall baroque except for reserve of pink asters on greenish blue ground, 4" h., pr............................ 165.00

Sugar sifter w/repousse top, Helmschmied Swirl mold, pink

rose buds on pale beige ground, 4" h. 295.00

Sweetmeat dish w/metal top & rim, Embossed Rococo scrolls, pastel floral decor, signed, 7½" 290.00

Syrup pitcher w/silverplate top & handle, Helmschmied Swirl mold, spray of pink wild roses on pale blue ground, unsigned 435.00

Tobacco jar, front & back medallions of lavender & blue Shasta daisies & "Tobacco" in pink lustre w/gold, ornately embossed hinged lid w/bouquet of same florals, metal shelf inside lid to hold moistener, signed, 5½" h.................. 475.00

Toothpick holder, pansy decor, footed ormolu base 325.00

Tooth powder jar w/original brass embossed lid, embossed blue forget-me-nots w/raised white dotted centers, signed 345.00

Vase, 9" h., dark green bold swirling & entwining lines, blue & pink blossoms on stark white ground, ormolu base, signed 385.00

Vase, 10¼" h., baroque scrolls, burgundy & pink floral beading on shaded yellow ground, ormolu foot, signed 325.00

Wave Crest Vase

Vase, 10½" h., baroque scrolls, pink to burgundy floral decor on shaded yellow ground, scrolled ormolu base, signed (ILLUS.) 475.00

Vase, 12" h., Wedgwood blue cartouche w/h.p. white florals & mauve cartouches against white ground, ornate brass feet & handles 950.00

Whisk broom holder, lavender, w/pink & lavender florals, satin lining, ornate ormolu frame for wall mounting 725.00

WEBB

Webb Cameo Vase

This glass is made by Thomas Webb & Sons, of Stourbridge, one of England's most prolific glasshouses. Numerous types of glass, including cameo, have been produced by this firm through the years. The company also devised various types of novelty and "art" glass during the late Victorian period. Also see PEACH BLOW.

Basket, gold thorn handle, red w/twenty-nine vertical air traps rising like dark silk ribbons, signed, 6½" w., 5¾" h. $310.00

Bowl, 3" d., 2½" h., tricornered top, gold prunus blossoms front & butterfly reverse on shaded brown satin ground, cream lining, gold trim 325.00

Bowl, 10½ x 7", 6¾" h., 4 applied amber reeded scroll feet, cream opaque w/transparent cranberry band around center & cranberry edging around ruffled top, enameled gold & silver butterfly & floral decor 495.00

Cameo mug, carved florals, leaves & stippling w/gold trim against ivory opaque ground, hallmarked silver bands & handle, 3½" d., 4" h. 895.00

Cameo vase, 2" h., 2½" d., carved white florals & foliage front & butterfly reverse against rose satin ground, white lining 658.00

Cameo vase, 4 5/8" h., 3" d., carved white florals & leaves & top & bottom bands against Peach Blow frosted ground 1,650.00

Cameo vase, 6" h., flattened ovoid, carved red flower-laden prunus branches pendant on overall gilt squiggle-patterned background against yellow ground, the flowers, leafage & butterfly further decorated w/copper & gilt highlights, ca. 1885, signed (ILLUS.) 3,850.00

Cameo vase, 6 7/8" h., 4 7/8" d., carved white to rose passion flow-

er & leaves front & large butterfly in flight reverse against vaseline-frosted ground w/overall acid-cut spider web network design 2,250.00

Cameo vase, 8" h., bulbous w/slender neck, carved white pendant cherry blossoms against strawberry red ground, ca. 1900 . . . . 1,045.00

Pitcher, 12" h., applied handle, raised enameled birds in nest & floral decor on opaque white shaded to blue satin, signed 235.00

Salt dip, enameled pink florals w/gold leaves & branches front & gold butterfly reverse on ivory ground, hallmarked silver rim, 2½" d., 1 5/8" h. 85.00

Scent bottle w/hallmarked silver screw-on dome cap, enameled gold prunus blossoms on shaded green to yellow satin ground, 2½" d., 3½" h. 325.00

Vase, 4½" h., 4" d., applied cream opaque handles w/gold trim, enameled gold prunus blossoms, branches & butterfly on cobalt blue ground 165.00

Vase, 7" h., cased, bright yellow satin w/enameled gold & brown dragonfly, flowers & foliage, white lining 250.00

Vase, 11" h., 4¾" d., squared shape w/dimpled sides, enameled white floral clusters w/yellow centers & branches on teal blue shaded to salmon pink satin ground, gold trim 450.00

Vase, 13 3/8" h., 5" d., shaded brown satin w/gold prunus blossoms & pine needles decor, cream lining 495.00

(End of Glass Section)

GRANITEWARE

This is a name given to metal (customarily iron) kitchenwares covered with an enamel coating. Featured at the 1876 Philadelphia Centennial Exposition, it became quite popular for it was lightweight, attractive, and easy to clean. Although it was made in huge quantities and is still produced, it has caught the attention of a younger generation of collectors and prices have steadily risen over the past five years. There continues to be a consistent demand for the wide variety of these utilitarian articles turned out earlier in this century and rare forms now command high prices. Also see FOOD MOLDS.

Baking pan, oval, grey mottled,
large........................... $22.00
Basin, blue & white marbleized..... 16.00
Basting spoon, grey mottled,
marked "L & G"................. 25.00
Bath tub, child's, grey mottled,
dated 1912 .... 110.00
Bed pan, robin's egg blue & white
mottled 22.00
Beer cooler, marked "Home Brew,"
used to cool beer in a well, 6
compartments for bottles, green
mottled 40.00
Berry bucket w/tin lid & bail handle,
child's, shamrock green & white
marbleized, 3½" h. 145.00

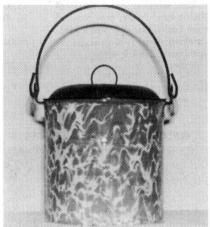

Graniteware Berry Bucket

Berry bucket w/tin lid & bail handle,
blue & white marbleized
(ILLUS.)....................... 58.00
Berry bucket w/lid & bail handle,
green & white marbleized,
7½" h........................ 54.00
Bowl, green & white marbleized,
8" d......................... 78.00
Bowl & plate, child's, yellow
w/brown trim, 2 pcs............ 18.00
Bread box, round, blue & white
marbleized 45.00
Bread pan, grey mottled, folded
edges 13.50
Bread riser w/tin lid, blue & white
marbleized 68.00
Butter bucket w/bail handle, cobalt
blue & white marbleized, 6" d. ... 35.00
Butter churn, turquoise & white
marbleized 285.00
Butter dish & cover w/pewter finial,
oval, grey mottled 100.00
Cake pan, child's, blue mottled..... 28.00
Cake pan, tube-type, cobalt blue &
white marbleized............... 22.00
Chamber pot, cov., turquoise blue &
white marbleized (ILLUS.) 85.00

Graniteware Chamber Pot

Coffee boiler, cov., Chrysolite, dark
green w/white veins, white
interior....................... 55.00
Coffee pot w/pewter lid, white
w/floral & birds decor, brass trim,
turned wood handle 130.00
Coffee pot, cov., gooseneck spout,
robin's egg blue, 6½" h.......... 65.00
Coffee pot & teapot, each w/pewter
lid, spout, handle & base, maroon
& white speckled, Manning-
Bowman & Co., pr. 300.00
Colander, wire bail handle, dark
brown & white marbleized, 9" d.,
4" h.......................... 36.00
Cream can w/tin lid & bail handle,
grey mottled, qt. 40.00
Creamer, white w/floral decor &
pewter trim.................... 75.00
Cup & saucer, child's, blue
mottled 20.00
Cuspidor, lady's, grey mottled 35.00
Custard cup, blue & white
marbleized 25.00
Dishpan, 2-handled, brown & white
marbleized, large 72.50
Dustpan, blue mottled 55.00
Egg poacher, 6-cup, grey
mottled 90.00
Food mold, ear of corn, grey
mottled 72.50
Frying pan w/pouring lip, grey
mottled, 7" d.................. 18.00
Funnel, canning-type, grey mottled,
3¾" d........................ 17.00
Grater, blue & white speckled...... 40.00
Kettle w/wire bail handle, chocolate
brown & white mottled, marked
"Majestic," large 65.00
Ladle, Chrysolite (dark green
w/white veins)................. 48.00
Ladyfinger pan, grey mottled....... 87.50
Liquid measure, grey mottled, gill
(4 oz.)....................... 78.00
Lunch bucket, child's, blue shaded .. 38.00
Lunch bucket, red & white mottled,
round 45.00
Milk cooling basin, handled, light
blue & white speckled, 13" d.,
2" h.......................... 22.00

Muffin pan, 6-cup, turk's turban,
grey mottled................... 50.00
Muffin pan, 12-cup, blue & white
speckled 120.00
Mug, cobalt blue & white
marbleized 22.00
Pie pan, brown & white
marbleized 35.00
Pie pan, child's, grey mottled 20.00
Pitcher, grey mottled, 8" h. 65.00
Pitcher, milk, Chrysolite 110.00
Plate, brown & white marbleized,
10" d...................... 42.00
Pudding mold, melon-ribbed, grey
mottled, marked "L & G" 65.00
Roaster, emerald green & white
marbleized, oval 55.00
Salt box, hanging-type, marked
"Salt," blue.................. 42.00
Sauce pan, blue & white marbleized,
9" d........................ 35.00
Skimmer, brown & white
marbleized 42.00
Skimmer, grey mottled ......15.00 to 25.00
Soap dish w/drain insert, hanging-
type, brown & white marbleized .. 130.00

Graniteware Soup Plate

Soup plate w/flange rim, grey mottled, 8½" d. (ILLUS.)............. 12.00
Spoon, cobalt blue & white
marbleized 14.00
Spooner, 2-handled, white w/fall
foliage decor, pewter rim &
bands 105.00
Spooner, turquoise blue & white
marbleized 175.00
Spoon rest, fish-shaped, grey
mottled 75.00
Sugar bowl, cov., ball-shaped, grey
mottled 180.00
Syrup pitcher w/original top, pewter
trim, grey mottled.............. 175.00
Tea kettle, red & white marbleized,
small 175.00
Teapot, cov., gooseneck spout,
Chrysolite 75.00
Trivet, "lacy heart" design, blue,
round ....55.00 to 65.00

Graniteware Utility Rack

Utility rack w/three containers
marked "Zand," "Soda" & "Zeep"
in black, white w/black trim,
4 pcs. (ILLUS.) ....60.00 to 75.00
Vegetable rack, hanging-type,
marked "Zwiebeln" (onions) in
black, white w/openwork front... 45.00
Wash basin, child's, grey mottled ... 20.00
Wash basin, brown & white marbleized, large 50.00
Washboard, blue & white
mottled ....50.00 to 75.00

GREENAWAY (Kate) ITEMS

Silver Bowl with Greenaway Decor

Numerous objects in pottery, porcelain, glass and other materials were made in or with the likenesses of the appealing children created by the famous 19th century English artist, Kate Greenaway. These are now eagerly sought along with the original Greenaway books.

Almanack for 1885 .... $40.00
Almanack for 1888, published by
George Routledge & Sons 65.00
Almanack for 1894 .... 55.00
Almanack for 1924 .... 25.00
Almanack for 1925 .... 35.00
Book, "A - Apple Pie," by Kate
Greenaway, w/illustrations 65.00
Book, "Mother Goose or The Old

Nursery Rhymes," illustrated by Kate Greenaway, published by Edmund Evans, London, 1881, 6¾ x 4¾" 55.00

Book, "The Pied Piper of Hamelin," by Robert Browning, illustrated by Kate Greenaway, published by Frederick Warne, London, ca. 1888 .... 60.00

Book, "Under the Window," illustrated by Kate Greenaway, published by George Routledge & Sons, 1878 (needs rebinding) 125.00

Bowl, sterling silver, shallow circular form, face of bowl chased w/flying bird & oak leaf & acorn branch overlapped w/scroll band showing young Greenaway girl seated on rail fence, ring foot, Gorham, 1881, 12" d. (ILLUS.) 1,210.00

Christmas card 35.00

Figure, bisque, 1¼" h. 28.00

Figures, bisque, "Rope Jumpers," marked Heubach, 9¼" h., pr. 600.00

Pickle castor, silverplate frame, Greenaway girl w/arms outstretched, square base, Tufts, w/glass insert 195.00

Picture frame, sterling silver & royal blue velvet, 2 embossed Greenaway girls looking out a window & grandfather clock striking eleven, ca. 1885, 6 x 5" 195.00

Print, 5 Greenaway girls pond fishing, framed, 16 x 20" 85.00

Prints, Greenaway boy & girl, pages from almanack, matted, 9 x 10½", pr. 25.00

Salt shaker, metal, figural Greenaway girl in coat, hat & muff (single) 40.00

Greenaway Figural Salt & Pepper

Salt & pepper shakers, china, figural Greenaway girl & boy, pr. (ILLUS.)....................... 145.00

GUTMANN ARTWORK

"The Reward"

This American artist, Bessie Pease Gutmann (1876-1960), is noted for her illustrations in baby's and children's books and for her published art prints which won acclaim not only in the United States, but in Canada, Europe, Japan and Australia as well. Often her subjects were her own children, nieces or nephews. The most famous of these prints, "A Little Bit of Heaven" and "Awakening" (depicting infants asleep and awake), were published in 1916 and 1918, respectively. Prints entitled "In Disgrace" and "The Reward" (depicting a child and puppy standing in the corner and a child sharing an ice cream cone with her puppy) became record sellers as a pair of matched prints during 1935-36.

Magazine, *Pictorial Review*, March 1913, "Our Alarm Clock" illustration on cover, 16 x 11" $125.00

Postcard, "Foster Mother" (The), 1911, girl feeding cat 15.00

Postcard, "His Majesty," 1913 ...... 15.00

Print, "A Little Bit of Heaven," infant asleep, 1916, 21 x 14", framed ... 58.00

Print, "An Anxious Moment," 1922, 21 x 14", framed 45.00

Print, "Awakening," 1918, infant awake, 21 x 14", framed........ 52.50

Print, "Blossom Time," 1917, 21 x 14", framed 98.00

Print, "Blue Bird," 1918, 21 x 14", framed 45.00

Print, "Bride" (The), 1909, 19 x 14", framed 110.00

Print, "Bubbles," 1923, 21 x 14", framed 95.00

Print, "Excuse My Back," nude toddler depicted as Cupid, 1911, 12 x 7", framed 40.00

Print, "Fairest of Flowers" (The), 1918, 21 x 14", framed.......... 135.00

Print, "First Dancing Lesson" (The),
  1923, 21 x 14", framed 78.00
Print, "Happy Dreams," 1939,
  21 x 14", framed 55.00
Print, "In Disgrace," 1935, 21 x 14",
  framed . . . . .40.00 to 80.00
Print, "In Slumberland," sleeping
  brown-haired baby beneath pink
  blanket, 21 x 14" 22.50
Print, "Kitty's Breakfast," child seat-
  ed on rug feeding kitty bowl of
  milk, 1941, 21 x 14", framed 35.00
Print, "Reward" (The), small child
  sharing ice cream cone w/puppy,
  1936, 21 x 14", framed (ILLUS.) . . .   55.00
Print, "Tommy," boy wearing blue
  feeding himself, 1931, 21 x 14",
  framed 50.00

HATPINS

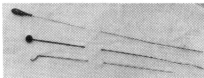

Assorted Hatpins

Amber glass, faceted, 1" sq. top . . . $15.00
Amber glass, set w/marcasite
  flowers 35.00
Amethyst glass 18.00
Black glass, set w/openwork twisted
  wire, 1 1/8" d. domed top,
  10¾" l. 24.00
Black glass (ILLUS. center) 5.00
Brass, openwork, set w/faceted am-
  ber glass stone, ¾" sq. top,
  7½" l. 18.00
Brass, Egyptian woman, 1¼ x 1"
  top, 9" l. 23.00
Brass filigree (ILLUS. top) 15.00
Cobalt blue glass w/silver deposit . .   75.00
Gold, 14k, pitch fork form, 28 rose
  diamonds 250.00
Gold, plain 15.00
Rhinestone-studded, diamond-
  shaped 26.00
Silverplate, lantern, 5" l. 15.00
Sterling silver, bust of Indian maid-
  en w/braided hair & 2 upright
  feathers & beads, ca. 1900, ¾ x
  1½" top, 8" l. 125.00
Sterling silver, flower form, 1¼ x 1"
  top, 8¼" l.   36.00
Sterling silver, golf club (ILLUS.
  bottom) 38.00

HOMER (Winslow) ENGRAVINGS

*Early training as an engraver and litho-
grapher enabled Winslow Homer (1836-1910)
to work as an illustrator for* Harper's Weekly *while still studying art at the National
Academy of Design in New York. The magazine sent young Homer off as a correspondent
to follow and sketch the Civil War battle skir-
mishes and many of his wartime drawings appeared in that publication. Subsequently his
illustrations were used by other publishers
and today collectors also seek out the genre
scenes of New England life and the seascape
and coastline scenes for which he eventually
became famous. Although some color lithographs of Homer's work do exist, the more
common black-and-white engravings are included in this listing.*

Army of the Potomac - A Sharp-
  Shooter on Picket Duty (The),
  1862 . . . .$110.00 to 150.00
Battle of Bunker Hill - Watching the
  Fight from Copp's Hill, in Boston
  (The), 1875 . . . .   95.00
Camping out in the Adirondack
  Mountains, 1874 . . . .   60.00
Chestnutting, 1870 . . . .   50.00
Gathering Wild Blackberries, 1880 . .   65.00
Green Apples, 1868 . . . .   50.00
News from the War, 1862 . . . .   35.00
On the Beach at Long Branch - The
  Children's Hour, 1874 . . . .   50.00
Our Next President, 1868 . . . .   75.00
Our Watering Places - The Empty
  Sleeve at Newport 45.00
Sea-Side Sketches - A Clam-Bake,
  1873 . . . . 140.00
Skating on the Ladies' Skating-Pond
  in the Central Park, New York,
  1860 . . . .   50.00
Songs of the War (The), 1861 . . . . . .   30.00
Strawberry Bed (The), 1868 . . . .   50.00
Swinging on a Birch Tree, 1867 . . . . .   50.00
Thanksgiving Day in the Army - Af-
  ter Dinner: The Wish-Bone, 1864 . .   55.00
Trapping in the Adirondacks, 1870 . .   60.00
War for the Union, 1862 - A Bayonet
  Charge (The), 1862 . . . .   40.00

HOOKED RUGS

*A true form of American folk art, hooked
rugs have caught the attention of numerous
collectors. It is believed this rug-making technique (pulling yarn or fabric strips through
a woven fabric background) originated in
America. Jute burlap (gunny-sacking) pro-*

vides the ideal background material and after this fabric was brought out around the 1850's, rug hooking became quite a vogue. It provided the opportunity to thriftily use up leftover burlap sacks and the remnants of discarded clothing to produce attractive floor coverings. Geometric and floral design rugs are the most common while animals, houses, figures, landscapes and ships are scarcer. Bold colorful, original designs are most appealing to collectors, but those hooked on stamped burlap patterns, even during the 20th century, are also avidly sought.

Bear & Rabbit Rug

Acorn design overall in shades of brown & green on grey ground within purple border, Pennsylvania Amish, ca. 1935, 41 x 25½" . .$125.00
Bear & rabbit, brown, grey & black, 32 x 25" (ILLUS.) 185.00
Dalmation dog, beige & brown spotted animal within scalloped oval beige surround, outer borders w/meandering rose & morning glory vine in tones of dark brown, yellow, green, blue, red & beige, Waldoboro, Maine, 1865-75, 54½ x 31" 4,400.00

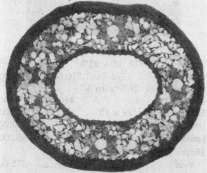

Floral & Fruit Wreath Rug

Floral & fruit oval wreath in variegated realistic shades of purple, red, yellow & green within brown

band on natural cream colored ground, late 19th/early 20th c., 118 x 95" (ILLUS.) 1,540.00
Goldfinch seated amidst branches on beige ground & "Goldfinch," black border, 36 x 18" 250.00
Horses, 2 grey animals w/black & red harness running on green grass w/brown fence & blue sky, Pennsylvania Amish, ca. 1925, 44 x 25" 200.00
Kittens (3) in a basket, bright green, red, brown, grey & blue, 40 x 25" 350.00

HORSE & BUGGY COLLECTIBLES

Silver Spurs

Bridle rosettes, Masonic emblem under convex glass, pr.......... $36.50
Buggy step, cast iron, "Key City Line" (single) 22.00
Buggy whip, carved ivory handle, inscribed "UI Hotel Boston" 125.00
Buggy whip, wooden handle carved w/dog's head 36.50
Buggy whip socket, cast iron......................15.00 to 30.00
Carriage lap robe, horse hide, red wool backing w/multicolored floral design, 84 x 72" 70.00
Carriage lap robe, wool, brown, gold, red & green floral design ... 225.00
Curry comb, wooden, hand-carved, ca. 1830, 4 x 6" 40.00
Harness racks, cast iron frame, pyramid shape w/curved wooden bars, 7 x 7 x 12", pr. 75.00
Horse bit, iron 14.00
Horse brass, standing harnessed work horse within pierced border, 3½ x 3½"........................ 30.00
Horse brush, leather back stamped "U.S.," marked "Hervert Brush Mfg. Co.," Civil War era 25.00
Horse hitching post, cast iron, model of horse's head on tapering fluted column w/two rings, panel w/molded lions' heads & inscription "M.D. Jones & Co. 52 Sudbury St. Boston," 72½" h. 1,210.00
Horse hoof pick & snow hammer, wrought iron, closed ring handle, 18th c., 9½" l. 39.00

Horse mane & tail comb, wrought
iron, embossed "R" on handle 55.00
Horse sweat scraper, hickory, hand-
carved, 2-handled, early 1800's ... 50.00
Lariat, woven horsehair, 25' l. 80.00
Riding crop, carved ivory handle.... 60.00
Riding crop, silver handle 45.00
Saddle, leather, McClellan Army-
type, 1917 .... 275.00
Saddle, leather, English-type,
w/brass stirrups 44.00
Spurs, brass, w/eagle medallions at
sides, original leather straps,
Mexican War era, pr............ 192.50
Spurs, silver, applied sprays of this-
tles, supports for rowels chased
w/foliage, w/matching buckles,
2nd quarter 19th c., 7¼" l., pr.
(ILLUS.)....................... 660.00
Spurs, wrought iron, pr. 60.00

Wooden Stirrup

Stirrup, wooden (ILLUS.) 14.00
Wagon jack, wrought iron & wood,
"Boston, Mass." 95.00
Wagon seat, ladderback w/turned
finials, worn brown paint, worn
splint seat, 34" l................ 360.00
Wagon wrench, cast iron, adjustable, marked "Joy," w/patent date
of 1898....................... 35.00

ICART PRINTS

Coursing II

*The works of Louis Icart, the successful
French artist whose working years spanned
the Art Nouveau and Art Deco movements,
first became popular in the United States
shortly after World War I. His limited edition etchings were much in vogue during
those years that the fashion trends were established in Paris. These prints were later
relegated to closet shelves and basements but
they have now re-entered the art market and
are avidly sought by collectors. Listed by
their American titles, those appearing below
have been sold within the past eighteen
months.*

Bathing Beauties, 1931,
17 x 24½" $1,430.00
Bird Seller, 1929, 14 x 19" oval 1,450.00
Chestnut Vendor, 1928, 14 x 19".... 715.00
Coach (The), 17½ x 21½"......... 550.00
Conchita, 1929, 14 x 21"...........1,050.00
Coursing II, 1929, 25 x 15½"
(ILLUS.) ....1,445.00 to 1,650.00
D'Artagnan, 1931, 14 x 21"....... 900.00
Hydrangeas, Lilacs, 1929, 21 x 17"
oval 605.00
Japanese Garden, 1931....135.00 to 165.00

Joy of Life

Joy of Life, 1929, 15 x 23½"
(ILLUS.) ....1,210.00 to 1,710.00
Kittens, 1925, 21½ x 16½"
oval ....440.00 to 775.00
Laziness, 1925, 19 x 15".......... 640.00
Leda, 1934, 31 x 21" 4,450.00
Louise, 1927, 13 x 20" 660.00
Masks (The), 1926, 15 x 18½"
oval 875.00
Meditation, 1928,
17 x 12"................600.00 to 815.00
Playfulness, 1922, 12 x 17" 605.00
Red Riding Hood, 1927, 14 x 21".... 500.00
Repose, 1933, 45 x 19" 3,300.00

Roses, 1933, 11 x 8½" 1,045.00
Speed, 1933,
  25 x 15½"...........1,045.00 to 1,980.00
Symphony in Blue, 1936,
  19½ x 23½".........1,160.00 to 1,870.00
Tea (The), 1926, 14½ x 18½"
  oval ....247.00 to 440.00
Thais, 1927, 20 x 16" oval 1,980.00
Thoroughbreds, 1938, 35 x
  18"..................750.00 to 1,255.00
Tosca, 1928, 13 x 21" cathedral 580.00
Youth, 1930, 15½ x
  24" ....1,540.00 to 1,980.00

ICE CREAM SCOOPS & SERVERS

Ice Cream Scoops

During the past decade, the ice cream scoop and ice cream server have become very popular with a growing number of collectors and prices have soared. While the nickel-plated brass scoop with a lever-operated blade that eases the ball-shaped scoop of ice cream from the server seems to be the most popular, there is also interest in the earlier cone-shaped tin scoops and in pewter or aluminum servers. Collectors can select a scoop that served up a small penny-size ice cream cone, a larger nickel-size cone, or a square slice for an ice cream sandwich.

"Arnold No. 50," 1927 patent $28.00
"Benedict Indestructo No. 30" 22.00
"Clewell's V. Clad Maker," conical
  bowl, steel w/tubular steel handle, ca. 1875, 8½" l. 35.00
"Dover Mfg. Co., Dover, N.H.,"
  nickel-plated brass w/wooden
  handle, 1924 patent, 11" l. 225.00
"Geer Clipper Disher," 1905
  patent ....125.00 to 190.00
"Gem Trojan No. 20," 1915 patent .. 35.00
"Gilchrist No. 20" 35.00
"Gilchrist No. 31," oval bowl (used
  for banana splits), nickel-plated
  brass w/wooden handle, 1915
  patent, 11½" l. 250.00
"Gilchrist No. 33," conical bowl,
  nickel-plated brass w/wooden
  handle, 1914 patent, 10½" l. 85.00
"Hamilton Beach No-Pak 31," round
  bowl w/hole cut in side,
  chromium-plated brass w/wooden
  handle, 1932 patent, 10" l. 75.00

"ICI PI" (Icy Pie) ice cream slice for
  ice cream sandwiches, nickel-
  plated brass w/wooden handle,
  ca. 1925, 10" l. ....110.00 to 150.00
"Jiffy Dispenser Co., Aurora, Ill.,"
  ice cream slice for ice cream
  sandwiches, nickel-plated brass
  w/wooden handle, 1925 patent,
  12½" l. 160.00
"Kingery Mfg. Co., Cincinnati,
  Ohio," conical bowl, nickel-plated
  brass w/wire squeeze-type
  handle, 1894 patent,
  8½" l. ....115.00 to 145.00
"Mayer Mfg. Corp., Chicago, Ill.,"
  ice cream slice for ice cream
  sandwiches, nickel-plated brass
  w/wooden handle, ca. 1925,
  12" l. ....125.00 to 150.00
"N & Co. Delmonico," conical bowl,
  brass, ca. 1900, 8" l. 65.00

ICE SKATES

Ice skating has long been popular as a sport and a means of transportation. The first skating club was formed in Edinburgh, Scotland in 1642. Ice skating was the major form of transportation in The Netherlands as the canals were frozen for so long each year. Pleasure skating was originally confined to long-distance racing but later became a contest to see who could inscribe the best design on ice. Skates have been made from such diverse materials as animal bone, walrus tusk and even corn stalks – a far cry from today's version.

Iron, heart-shaped pads, blades
  w/good curl, ca. 1860, pr. $90.00
Wooden platforms, racing-type
  w/long steel blades, marked
  "Batavus Heerenveen" & numbered, Holland, dated 1935, pr.... 30.00
Wooden platforms, racing-type
  w/long steel blades & brass face
  plates, marked "Union Hardware
  Co., the Donoghue Racing Skate,
  Torrington, Conn.," worn old red
  paint, 18" l., pr. (leather straps
  damaged) 65.00
Wooden platforms, metal blades
  w/short tight curl, brass fittings,
  leather straps, marked "Williams
  & Co.," dated 1853, pr. 130.00
Wooden platforms, steel blades
  w/short curl, brass fittings &
  leather straps, signed & w/patent
  date of 1850, pr. 130.00
Wooden platforms, wrought iron

curved blades, old worn orange
paint, 12" l., pr. 105.00
Wooden platforms, wrought iron
blades w/large curl & brass acorn
finials, 18th c., pr. 220.00

INDIAN RELICS

Silver Concha Belt

Blanket, Navajo, woven in homespun wool in natural tones &
black, analine tan, orange & red,
ca. 1930, 60 x 36" $425.00
Blanket, Navajo, woven in German-
town wool, serrated & cross design
in indigo blue, black, white &
tan on red ground, ca. 1880,
78 x 50" 2,550.00
Blanket, Navajo chief's, woven in
single strand homespun & ravelled
yarn w/a second phase pattern composed of 24 red bars against indigo
blue linear panels, natural ivory
& brown background stripe,
82 x 62" 3,300.00
Box, Micmac, quilled birch bark, ca.
1910, 2¾" d., 2¼" h. 60.00
Breast plate, Northern Plains, bone
w/leather dividers, cut green
beads at neck, blue trade beads &
brass bells at bottom, 45" l. 575.00
Canoe replica, Micmac or Penob-
scot, birch bark w/quilled floral
decor, ca. 1930, 15½ x 4½" 195.00
Concha belt, silver, turquoise &
leather, 10 oval silver sections,
each w/slender lines radiating
from an inset irregular turquoise,
on black leather strap, ca. 1950
(ILLUS.) 1,045.00
Cradleboard, miniature, Ute, green,
yellow, red & blue beading on
white ground, weasel claw fetish
& loom beaded amulet, w/bisque
doll, 16" l. 2,525.00
Hymnal, Choctaw, written in Choc-

taw, 1872, leather bound (some
loose pages).................... 275.00
Jar, Acoma, pottery, white, black &
orange fineline, checkerboard &
geometric designs, artist-signed,
8" d., 6½" h. 200.00
Leggings, Iroquois, leather, beaded
& fringed, w/matching belt,
1880's, 2 pcs. 400.00
Moccasins, Cheyenne, beaded hide,
pr............................ 265.00
Moccasins, Sioux, child's high-top
style, beaded hide, red, yellow,
blue & green beaded design on
white ground, sinew sewn, 5¾" l.
(bead damage & 1 heel fringe
missing) 205.00
Necklace & earrings, Navajo, silver
& turquoise, Squash Blossom
necklace w/horseshoe-shaped
pendant set w/three blue-green
spiderweb cabachon turquoise, 10
blossoms interspersed between
graduated silver beads, squash
blossoms form earrings, pendant
marked "Sterling," 1900-30, set ... 240.00
Pipe bag, Sioux, beaded & quilled
hide, 28" l. 625.00

Indian Plains Pipe Tomahawk

Pipe tomahawk, Northern Plains,
spontoon-style iron blade & bowl
combination head w/openwork
heart motif & curling flanges,
wooden handle decorated w/brass
tacks & file burn marks, stem
drilled for suspension, brass
covered mouthpiece, early 19th c.,
18" l. (ILLUS.) 3,740.00
Pouch, Cheyenne, beaded hide, geometric design in turquoise blue,
blue & white beading w/touches
of rose & red, yellow & red quill-
work base, 11" l. 275.00
Rattle, Arapaho, Peyote gourd
w/silver base & incised design,
leather-covered handle worked in
multicolor striped beading, horsehair crest, 15½" l. plus string
tassel 100.00
Rug, Navajo, Two Gray Hills area,
woven dark brown, black, grey,
medium brown & white,
37 x 21"...................... 400.00

Rug, Navajo, woven dark brown, red, medium brown & white, 1st quarter 20th c., 68½ x 48" 475.00

Saddle pad, Plains (probably Cheyenne), beaded hide, lazy stitched in dark blue, white & yellow w/pink hearts, 47 x 28" plus fringe 425.00

Shield, Plains, painted buffalo hide, double layer of hide painted w/yellow & black bird & blue stars, fur reverse, beaded blue jay feather dangles, ca. 1895, 23" d. 650.00

Shirt, Plains, buckskin, beadwork on yoke & lapel, 1890's 750.00

Tobacco pouch, Southern Plains Apache, beaded & fringed hide, geometric designs in green, rose, blue, red & white opaque & translucent beading on natural hide, 13" l. plus long beaded fringe 275.00

Vest, Plains, child's, beaded hide ... 225.00

IVORY

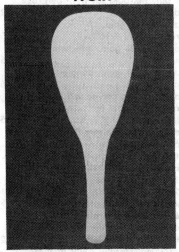

Carved Ivory Hand Mirror

Card case, overall intricately carved scene of people, trees, florals & buildings, 3 3/8 x 1¾" $130.00

Figure of an Immortal, face w/crinkled eyes & lips in a smile, moustache & beard slightly swept to one side, his loose robes gathered around him & holding a lingzhi stalk in the crook of his left arm, his peaked cap lacquered black & w/ribbons draped on his shoulders, Ming Dynasty, 4 1/8" h. 1,540.00

Figures, man & woman attired in formal robes, he carrying a sword & she a tasseled & ribboned sceptre, each on high octagonal stand, Chinese, 20" h., pr. 1,540.00

Figure group, young maiden holding basket of flowers in 1 hand & drapery of flowers on other arm, flanked by 2 playful putti, raised on an ivory & stained wooden base carved w/foliage, ca. 1885, 14¼" h. 3,300.00

Mirror, hand-type, reverse carved w/two fuchsias & long curving stems, obverse set w/rounded triangular mirror plate & carved w/slender stems, inscribed (Georges) de Feure, 10" l. (ILLUS.) 7,150.00

Pastry wheel, carved in the form of a sea horse w/ebony center band, 3-pronged horn flanked by triangular ears, eyes & nostrils inlaid w/ebony, forelegs grasping the crenulated wheel held in place w/silver pins, hub of wheel in the form of a 5-point star, ca. 1870, 8" l. 18,700.00

Pendant, carved in the form of 2 entwined dragons, 1½" w., 2¼" h., w/original silk cord...... 150.00

Spool holder, butter churn form, 1890's, 1¾ x 1" 84.00

Carved Ivory Table Screen

Table screen, pedestal & pediment carved w/lotus lappets & interlocking "kui" dragons, inset w/five later panels intricately carved in high relief w/scenes of ladies in garden settings, 18th-19th c., 16½" w., 13" h. (ILLUS.) 2,200.00

Tankard, barrel-shaped, carved w/male & female sea gods frolicking w/dolphins & mythical beasts, bell-form lid carved w/scrolling foliage, Continental, 19th c., 8½" h. 1,870.00

JADE

Large Jade Bowl

Bowl, elongated oval w/single handle carved & pierced as a chilong w/the head biting the rim, 2 further chilong along sides, tall foot incised w/classic scrolling design, pale grey, 6 3/8" h. $715.00

Bowl, rounded sides flaring to a slightly everted rim, dark green mottled w/black flecks, 18th c., 8¼" d. (ILLUS.) 2,750.00

Bracelet, 5 cabochon ovals set in silver elevated bezels circled w/beading, connected w/double twist loop chains, apple green, hallmarked & signed, Chinese 125.00

Brush pot, thick cylindrical sides supported on 4 ruyi-shaped feet, exterior incised w/scene of a scholar & his attendant traveling along a mountain path, details filled in w/gilt, pale celadon green w/two areas of brown mottling, 4¾" h. 550.00

Cups, scalloped rim continuing to form chrysanthemum petals, above a carved design of stylized flowers separated by branches of graduated leaves, low foot carved as a flowerhead w/double tier of petals, translucent apple green, 18th-19th c., 2 7/8" h., pr.......4,675.00

Dish, lily pad form, large pad w/curled edges forming the sides & supported by the stem naturalistically carved on the base & bound w/a ribbon, pale green, 9½" w. 1,980.00

Earrings, teardrop form w/gold mountings, pale green, pr........ 145.00

Figure of a boy kneeling on one knee, holding a bucket in one hand & a pelt in the other, creamy white, 1 7/8" h. 1,760.00

Incense burner, cov., squat ovoid, carved in relief w/panels of stylized interlocking phoenix, double oxen head & loose ring handles, conforming cover carved w/dragon finial, spinach green, whole raised on a conforming white jade stand pierced & carved w/floral scrolls, 19th c., 5½" h. 3,080.00

Model of a duck, seated w/wings

folded, head turned back over its body, lotus blossom clutched in its beak, creamy white, 2¾" l. 825.00

Vases, cov., upright form & rectangular section carved round the center w/a frieze of "taotie" masks, shoulders w/dragon's head loop handles suspending loose rings, Buddhist lion knop on cover, green w/slight mottling, 8½" h., pr. 1,320.00

JEWELRY (Victorian)

Hand-Painted Cuff Links

Bar pin, 14k gold, blue enamel, 2¼" l. $124.00

Bar pin, 14k gold set w/fifteen rose diamonds...................... 128.00

Bracelet, 14k gold, 13-link, ornate reticulation, 3/16" w. 150.00

Bracelets, 18k gold, intertwined snake, pr. 1,350.00

Bracelets, 18k gold, bangle-type, pr. 165.00

Brooch, cameo carved w/lady & cupid in a boat in 14k gold frame 250.00

Brooch, mosaic (Pietra Dura) spray of white jonquils, shaded violets, trailing buds & green leaves on black ground in 14k gold twisted & engraved frame, ca. 1860, 2 x 1½" 310.00

Chatelaine, silverplate, filigree work & "repousse" florals w/three drops (mirror, hinged perfume flask & ivory tablet) 225.00

Chatelaine, sterling silver w/three drops (perfume flask, pencil & ivory tablet) 325.00

Cuff links, 14k gold, engraved monogram within beaded border, 5/8" sq., pr. 75.00

Cuff links, lady's, porcelain w/gold finish metal fittings, h.p. green leafy spray on shaded pink ground, gold trim, pr. (ILLUS.) 45.00

Lavalier, gold-filled, large cabochon garnet w/two garnet set drops, 15½" chain 90.00

Locket, sterling silver, oval w/engraved floral motif, w/chain 38.00

Mourning brooch, h.p. scene of
woman at tomb & weeping willow
tree & "Rest in Peace" in black &
brown on ivory, in yellow gold
frame, lock of braided hair under
beveled glass reverse,
2¼ x 1 7/8" 350.00
Necklace, braided human hair
w/small compass pendant engraved "So Turns My Heart to
Thee," original box 125.00

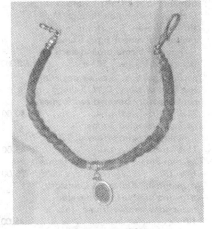

Hairwork Necklace

Necklace, braided human hair
w/gold-filled fittings, oval drop
w/woven hair center (ILLUS.) 95.00
Necklace, citrine quartz stones (16)
in pinchbeck mounts 325.00
Pin, 15k gold, shield-shaped
w/black enameled design & 2
gold mesh drops w/tasseled ends,
7/8" w. 189.00
Pin, gold-filled, horseshoe-shaped,
double row of rose cut garnets
(37), 1¼ x 1" 60.00
Pin, sterling silver set w/marcasites
in a design of entwined roses,
1¾" oval 50.00
Ring, lady's, 9k gold, 4 green garnet
doublets & 6 seed pearls, scroll-
carved sides 90.00
Ring, lady's, 9k rose gold scroll-
carved band set w/three round
blue sapphires 260.00
Ring, lady's, 14k gold set w/square-
cut lapis lazuli 450.00
Ring, lady's, 14k gold, large pearl
center surrounded by 8 smaller
pearls 155.00
Ring, lady's, 15k gold,
monogrammed oblong top, carved
sides 50.00
Ring, lady's, 18k gold, domed top
set w/fourteen blue-green opals .. 285.00
Watch chain, lady's, 14k gold,
w/two slides, the larger

enameled & set w/single pearl,
w/hinged swivel ring, 32" l. 625.00
Watch chain, lady's, 10k gold-filled,
heart-shaped slide, 50" l. 90.00
Watch chain, man's, braided human
hair w/gold-filled fittings, 12" l. .. 55.00
Wedding ring, 14k white gold w/two
rows of small diamonds, marked
"Cartier" 205.00

JUKE BOXES

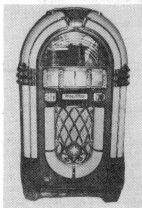

Wurlitzer Model 1015 Juke Box

AMI (Automatic Musical Instrument
Co.) Model A, 1946. .$1,850.00 to 3,000.00
AMI Model B, 1947 .....1,100.00 to 1,300.00
AMI "Continental," 1961 ...500.00 to 700.00
Capehart "Orchestrope" Model 28-G,
1928 ....2,500.00 to 2,950.00
Mills "Dancemaster,"
1926 ....550.00 to 750.00
Packard "Manhattan," 1946 ....1,800.00
Packard "Pla-Mor," 1946...........1,500.00
Ristaucrat, table-type, ca. 1950 ..... 500.00
Rock-Ola Model 39-A, table-type,
1939..........................1,095.00
Rock-Ola Model 1422,
1946 ....1,500.00 to 2,000.00
Rock-Ola Model 1426,
1947 ....1,600.00 to 2,500.00
Rock-Ola Model 1428, 1948 ....2,200.00
Rock-Ola "Monarch," 1938 .... 850.00
Seeburg Model S-146 (Trashcan),
1946...........................2,000.00
Seeburg Model S-148 (Trashcan),
1948...........................1,700.00
Seeburg Model 9800 (Hi-tone), early
1940's 800.00
Seeburg "Gem," 1938.............. 650.00
Seeburg "Plaza," 1939 .... 750.00
Seeburg "Symphonola," 1936 .... 850.00
Williams "Music Mite," table-type,
1951...........................1,500.00

Wurlitzer Model P-12, 1935
(restored) 1,900.00
Wurlitzer Model 41, table-type,
1940-41 . . . . .1,600.00 to 2,950.00
Wurlitzer Model 61, table-type,
1938-39. . . . . 975.00
Wurlitzer Model 412,
1937 . . . . .750.00 to 900.00
Wurlitzer Model 500,
1938-39 . . . . .1,600.00 to 3,000.00
Wurlitzer Model 780 (Wagon Wheel),
1941 . . . . .2,450.00 to 3,500.00
Wurlitzer Model 850 (Peacock),
1941 . . . . .8,200.00 to 9,800.00
Wurlitzer Model 1015, 1946-47
(ILLUS.) . . . . .7,425.00 to 7,920.00
Wurlitzer Model 1050,
1973 . . . . .3,875.00 to 4,800.00

KELLOGG PRINTS

Kellogg lithograph prints are not as well known as those of their rival firm, Currier and Ives, who issued far more titles and distributed them more widely. However, many collectors feel that Kellogg's work is superior in many repects. The four Hartford, Connecticut brothers involved in printmaking from about 1833 until 1875 were Jarvis G., Daniel W., Edmond B. and Elijah C. Kellogg. Their lithograph prints will be found variously signed: J.G. Kellogg, D.W. Kellogg, Kellogg & Hanmer, Kellogg & Thayer, E.B. & E.C. Kellogg and Kellogg & Bulkeley. Values of these prints are rising.

"The Angler," Kellogg & Comstock,
old beveled wood grain-painted
frame, 19½ x 15½" (damaged
margins) $85.00
"The Brave at Home, No. 1" & "The
Brave at Home, No. 3," framed,
17½ x 13½", pr. 110.00
"The Evening Prayer," old beveled
brown painted frame, 18½ x
13½" 35.00
"Expectation" & "The Children in the
Wood," Kellogg & Comstock,
framed, 16¾ x 13¾", pr. 80.00
"Father's Pride," young boy,
trimmed margins, matted, 14 x
10" 85.00
"Flock of Sheep," man on white
horse herding flock, original paint
decorated frame, 12 x 8" 150.00
"The Gardener's Pet," framed,
15 5/8 x 11 5/8" 22.50
"John Tyler," full-length silhouette,
E.B. & E.C. Kellogg, 1844,
framed 75.00

"Little Drummer Boy," red & black
painted frame, 16 x 12". 130.00
"Martin Van Buren," full-length silhouette, E.B. & E.C. Kellogg, 1844,
framed 75.00
"My Brother," beveled red & black
grain-painted frame, 16 3/8 x
12 3/8". 55.00
"Pope Pius IX," old relief-carved
cross-bar frame w/applied circles
at corners, 18¼ x 14¾" 25.00
Presidents of the United States -
George Washington through Martin Van Buren, 8 portraits in
mahogany veneer ogee frame
w/internal frame around each
portrait, 55¾" w., 38" h. 645.00
"The Prodigal Son," scenes depicting
the Biblical story, D.W. Kellogg, in
contemporary beveled red frames,
21½ x 16¾", set of 4 . . . . 140.00
"The Star Spangled Banner,"
trimmed margins, framed, 13½ x
11½" (stains) 45.00
"The Two Pets," original pine frame,
17 x 13". 75.00
"Washington," Kellogg & Comstock,
trimmed margins, old beveled
mahogany veneer frame, 16¼ x
12¼" 45.00

KEWPIE COLLECTIBLES

Rose O'Neill Kewpieville Scene

Rose O'Neill's Kewpies were so popular in their heyday that numerous objects depicting them were produced and are now collectible. The following represents a sampling.

Booklet, "The Jello Girl Entertains,"
Kewpies decor $20.00

Camera, Conley Camera Co. (Rochester, Minnesota), Kewpie No. 2, side-loading box-type 8.00

Candy container, papier mache, Kewpie emerging from egg 120.00

Cereal bowl, 6" d. plate & c/s, china, action Kewpies decor, signed Rose O'Neill, Royal Rudolstadt, 4 pcs. 275.00

Cup & saucer, china, 8 action Kewpies amidst green foliage, signed Rose O'Neill Wilson, Royal Rudolstadt 125.00

Dresser set: cov. powder jar, hatpin holder, footed pin dish, hair receiver & 10 x 7" tray; china, action Kewpies decor, Royal Rudolstadt, 5 pcs. 950.00

Feeding dish, china, action Kewpies decor, signed Rose O'Neill Wilson, Kewpie, Germany, marked Royal Rudolstadt, 7¾" d. 235.00

Figure, Kewpie sitting & holding a rose on rectangular base, bisque, 3 x 1¼" 95.00

Kewpie Traveler

Figure, Kewpie "Traveler," bisque, signed Rose O'Neill, 3½" h. (ILLUS.)........................ 200.00

Figure, Kewpie Confederate soldier, bisque, signed Rose O'Neill, 4" h. 400.00

Figures, Kewpie bride & groom, bisque, signed O'Neill, 4½" h., pr............................ 370.00

Figure, Kewpie standing, chalkware, 12" h. 45.00

Figure, Kewpie wearing sunsuit, composition, 13" h.............. 120.00

Flannel squares, Kewpies at various pursuits, assorted set of 6 .... 125.00

Handkerchief, "Sleigh Riding," signed Rose O'Neill, registered & dated 1915 (unused) 65.00

Letter opener, pewter, Kewpie in relief on handle................ 65.00

Mug, china, action Kewpies decor, signed Rose O'Neill, Royal Rudolstadt 125.00

Pin, sterling silver, Kewpie soldier,

farmer or carpenter, w/safety catch, each 00

Plate, china, 7 action Kewpies decor, gold trim, signed Rose O'Neill, Royal Rudolstadt, 6½" d. 130.00

Plate, 9 action Kewpies amidst green foliage, signed Rose O'Neill Wilson, Royal Rudolstadt, 7" d. ... 165.00

Postcard, "Easter Greetings," Kewpie w/chick & frog, signed Rose O'Neill 25.00

Scrapbook, action Kewpies playing in clouds on cover, signed Rose O'Neill, 8 x 11" 48.00

Tea set: cov. teapot, creamer, sugar bowl, 6 plates & 6 c/s; china action Kewpies decor, signed Rose O'Neill, Kewpie, Germany, 21 pcs. 1,100.00

Teaspoon, sterling silver, figural Kewpie at tip of handle, enameled color bust portrait of Rose O'Neill in bowl............ 125.00

Toothpick holder, silverplate, Kewpie standing beside basketweave holder 75.00

KITCHENWARES

"Betty Taplin" Beater Jar

Also see ADVERTISING ITEMS, BASKETS, BOTTLE OPENERS, BUTTER MOLDS & STAMPS, CANS & CONTAINERS, CLOCKS, COFFEE GRINDERS, COOKBOOKS, COOKIE CUTTERS, FIREPLACE & HEARTH ITEMS, FOOD MOLDS, FRUIT JARS, GRANITEWARE, ICE CREAM SCOOPS, METALS, SALESMAN'S SAMPLES, SCALES, SHAKER COLLECTIBLES and WOODENWARES.

Apple parer, cast iron, "Coons," 1915 patent, 36" l., 18" h. $210.00

Apple parer, cast iron, "Lockey & Howland Turntable," 1856 patent 42.50

Apple parer, cast iron, "Rival No. 296," dated 1899, hand-crank, approximately 35 lb., 32" l., 18" h. . . 195.00

Apple parer, cast iron, marked "Pat. 1868," 5-gear, hand-crank 50.00

Batter pitcher (or jug), utilitarian crockery, Wildflower patt., blue & white, w/wire bail handle & wooden grip 195.00

Bean slicer, table clamp-on model, cast iron, embossed "Alexanderwerck No. 1071, Germany," 12 x 6" 35.00

"Beaten Biscuit" board, cast iron base, marble slab table top w/nickeled iron rollers (like washing machine wringers) attached, "DeMuth Improved Dough Kneader & Beaten Biscuit Machine" 475.00

Beater jar, clear glass jar embossed "Betty Taplin" & marked beater w/red-painted wooden handle, 4 oz., overall 6½" h. (ILLUS.) 25.00

Biscuit cutter, rolling-type, tin w/wire handle, 19th c., 8¾" l. . . .   28.00

Bowl, utilitarian crockery, Wedding Ring patt., yellow & green, 5½" d. 35.00

Bowl, utilitarian crockery, Apricot patt., blue & white, 9" d., 4½" h. 70.00

Bowl, utilitarian crockery, Picket Fence patt., blue & white, 10" d. 70.00

Bowl, utilitarian crockery, Apricot patt., blue & white, w/wire bail handle 85.00

Bread & cake box, tin, cylinder-roll front, folding wire handles at sides, lettered "Cake" & "Bread" in gold, marked "Kreamer," 13½ x 11 x 12½" 95.00

Broom holder, wall-type, cast iron, 3 broomstick slots 70.00

Butter churn, "The Dazey Churn," embossed glass jar w/original gears, 2-qt.   67.50

Butter churn, wooden cylinder w/side crank handle, stave-constructed barrel on shoe-footed base w/oblong lift-lid, original yellow paint, 16" d., 18" l., overall 20" h. 175.00

Butter churn, pine cylinder churn w/cast iron crank fittings, worn stenciled label "Climax Churn," 33¾" h. 150.00

Butter churn, table-top cylinder churn w/iron hand-crank mecha-

nism & wooden paddles, grain-painted finish 225.00

Butter crock w/lid, utilitarian crockery, Apricot patt., blue & white . . 175.00

Butter crock w/lid, utilitarian crockery, Basketweave patt., blue & white 150.00

Butter crock w/lid, utilitarian crockery, Daisy patt., blue & white . . . . 120.00 to 145.00

Butter crock w/lid, utilitarian crockery, Daisy patt., yellow & green . .   80.00

Butter crock w/lid & bail handle, utilitarian crockery, Draped Window patt., blue & white, 2-lb. 125.00

Butter paddles, wooden, corrugated "Scotch Hands," factory-made, pr. 18.00

Butter working paddle, maple, hand-hewn, well-shaped bowl, scrolling handle, 10½" l. (w/some minor damage to front of bowl) . .   60.00

Cabbage (or slaw) cutting board, pine, 1-blade, 6¾" w., 19" l. 30.00

Cabbage (or slaw) cutting board, cherrywood, 2-blade, arched top pierced w/hand-grip, shaped bottom, 7" w., 16½" l. 65.00

Cake crock w/original lid, utilitarian crockery, 6 blue stripes & lettered "Cake" in blue on white, 13" d., 8" h. 350.00

Canister, cov., blown clear glass w/applied clear rings on body, pressed lid, 9½" h. 75.00

Can opener, cast iron, cow's head one end, wooden handle 65.00

Iron Wire Carpet Beater

Carpet beater, bent iron wire, triple loop forming heart, in wooden handle (ILLUS.) . . . . 16.50 to 30.00

Carpet beater, wicker, ornate 27.50

Charcoal iron, cast iron, w/lion's head finial 50.00

Cheese drainer, tin, round, center pierced w/concentric circles & star, wire ring handle for hanging at rim, ca. 1830, 14½" d., 5½" deep 250.00

Cheese sieve, bentwood round frame & side handles, woven

hickory splint sieve, 31" d. (old damage & age cracks) 250.00

Cherry pitter, single, cast iron, "Enterprise No. 1," 12" h. 27.50

Cherry pitter, cast iron, "New Standard, Mt. Joy, Pa.," clamp-on model .... 18.00 to 30.00

Coffee bean roaster, tin w/long wooden handle 22.50

Coffee pot & cover w/nipple-shaped finial, tapering cylinder w/braced handle & straight spout, tin, black japanned finish, 8-cup, 10" h. 140.00

Colander, tin, handled, 10" d. 15.00

Cookie board, carved cherrywood, double-faced, basket of flowers one side, tulip & leaves reverse, 18th c., 7 x 6" 495.00

Cookie board, carved wood, double-faced, full-length man one side & woman w/bird on shoulder reverse, 16½ x 6¼" 145.00

Cookie board, carved wood, peasant couple arm in arm, 12¾ x 7"..... 105.00

Cookie stamp, carved pine, pineapple, flat round, ca. 1800, 4" d. 120.00

Cream Whip

Cream whipper, "Whippit Cream & Egg Whip, Pat 1705639, Manuf. Duro Metal Products, Chicago" (ILLUS.) .... 10.00 to 18.00

Custard cup, utilitarian crockery, Fishscale patt., blue & white 75.00

Dipper, brass bowl w/well-shaped wrought iron handle, 9" l. 135.00

Dish cover (fly screen), dome-shaped wire mesh, 6¼" d. 39.00

Dough scraper, wrought iron, short hollow handle, 3½" w. .... 26.00 to 38.00

Drying rack, 3-tier, folding arms, legs on casters, original worn light green paint w/label "The Pease Clothes Tree," 68" h. 135.00

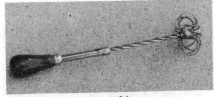

Egg Whip

Egg (or cream) whip, wire in wooden handle, marked "Made in

England, Prov. Pat. 8135" (ILLUS.) 6.00

Flatware: 6 knives & 6 forks; steel w/pewter-inlaid ebony handles, marked "Russell & Co.," 9½" l., set of 12 .... 50.00

Flour sifter, "Blood's Improved Flour Sifter," wooden frame w/screen & roller, w/patent of 1861 .... 130.00 to 150.00

"Hunter's Flour Sifter"

Flour sifter, "Hunter's Sifter," tin, Fred J. Meyer Mfg. Co., Covington, Kentucky (ILLUS.) 18.50

Fluting iron, cast iron, "Aug. 2, 1870" patent date, 2 pcs. 69.00

Food chopper, wooden handle, steel blade marked "Wm. Greaves & Sons," 5¾" w. 30.00

Food chopper, wooden handle, wrought steel semi-circular blade, 9" w. 30.00

Food chopper, hand-hewn wooden tapering bar handle, wrought steel blade, 18th c............... 85.00

Food grinder, cast iron, "Griswold No. 11," Puritan model 35.00

Food grinder, cast iron, "Universal," model made for Jewel Tea Co., w/three blades .... 15.00 to 22.00

French Roll Pan

French roll pan, cast iron, 12-compartment, "French Roll No. 11," 13 x 7¾" (ILLUS.) 35.00

Funnel, brass, rolled rim, brass, ca. 1830, 7 x 6" oval top 65.00

Funnel, wooden, 8" d., 5" h. 75.00

Gas iron, "Stuart Tailor," w/trivet,
1901 .... 90.00
Glove stretcher, wooden (single) ... 55.00
Grater, punch copper sheet on
board, triangular, w/hole for
hanging at top, 5½ x 3½ x 22" .. 150.00
Griddle pan w/bail handle, cast
iron, "Griswold," 11½" d......... 35.00

Hinged Griddle Pan

Griddle pan, hinged-type for pan-
cakes, cast iron, dated 1868,
17" l. (ILLUS.) 65.00
Ice cream freezer, wooden, stave
constructed exterior marked
"White Mountain," galvanized tin
inner compartment, 1923 patent,
2-qt. ....35.00 to 55.00
Ice shaver (or shredder), nickel-
plated steel, "Enterprise," w/pat-
ent of July 4, 1893 .... 40.00
Infant's food chopper (or grinder),
wall-type, cast iron w/crank handle, embossed "Baby" on tin
cup 22.00
Knife scouring box w/pumice
holder, hanging-type, pine, early
19th c. 130.00
Knife sharpener, counter-type, cast
iron w/small millstone & crank
handle 38.00
Lard press, cast iron w/wooden
handle, dated 1897 .... 42.00
Lemon squeezer, cast iron, hinged,
embossed "Boss" 24.00
Lemon squeezer, maple w/lignum
vitae inserts, hinged, oversized... 65.00
Meat tenderizer, cast iron, "Pat'd
Sept. 20, 1892," 2¾" w., 4" l. 16.00
Meat tenderizer, ironstone china
block w/waffled grid & wooden
handle, ca. 1890 .... 35.00
Milk cooling basin, utilitarian crockery, Diamond Point patt., off-
white fading to soft blue, 11" d.,
3½" h. 75.00
Muffin pan, cast iron, 8-cup "Filley
No. 5" 75.00
Muffin pan, cast iron, 8 almond-
shaped cups, marked "N. Waterman, Boston, Patent April 5,
1859," 14½ x 7" 40.00
Mug, utilitarian crockery, Boetie
patt., blue decal on white........ 42.50
Mug, utilitarian crockery, Cattail
patt., blue & white,
4½" h...................95.00 to 115.00

Nutmeg grater, tin, "The Boyer,"
1914 .... 33.00
Pan, cast iron, oblong w/invected
corners, cast design in base,
7½ x 5½"...................... 15.00
Pantry box & cover w/wire bail handle & wooden grip, bentwood
round, original green-painted finish, 19th c., 9½" d., 5½" h....... 155.00

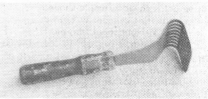

Pastry Blender or Masher

Pastry blender or masher, nickel-
plated steel & wood, 1915-40,
9½" l. (ILLUS.) 4.00
Pastry board w/rolling pin, tin,
pr............................. 170.00
Pastry wheel, copper w/tooled steel
shank & whale bone handle
w/brass trim, 7 3/8" l........... 225.00
Pastry wheel, maple, hand-carved .. 85.00
Pea skinner, wire slotted bowl,
turned wood handle, Dover
Stamping Co., 1870's 20.00
Pie cooling rack, twisted
wire ....25.00 to 40.00
Pie lifter, 2-tine wire prongs in
wooden handle ....25.00 to 38.00
Pie plate, utilitarian crockery, Star
patt., blue & white 75.00
Pineapple eye snip, cast iron,
scissor-shaped, 1880's, 5½" l. 10.00
Pitcher, utilitarian crockery, Alpine
patt., blue & white 285.00
Pitcher, utilitarian crockery, American Beauty Rose patt., blue &
white 200.00
Pitcher, utilitarian crockery, Avenue
of Trees patt., blue & white 210.00
Pitcher, utilitarian crockery, Bluebird
patt., blue & white ......215.00 to 275.00
Pitcher, utilitarian crockery, Butterfly patt., blue & white 185.00
Pitcher, utilitarian crockery, Castle
patt., blue & white .....140.00 to 195.00
Pitcher, utilitarian crockery, Cattail
patt., blue & white .....110.00 to 175.00
Pitcher, utilitarian crockery, Cosmos
patt., blue & white .....110.00 to 150.00
Pitcher, utilitarian crockery, Cow
patt., blue & white,
8" h....................130.00 to 195.00
Pitcher, utilitarian crockery, Cow
patt., yellow & green, 8 1/8" h. .. 95.00
Pitcher, utilitarian crockery, Dutch
Boy & Girl Kissing patt., blue &
white (ILLUS.) 140.00

Utilitarian Crockery Pitcher

Pitcher, utilitarian crockery, Flying
Bird patt., blue & white 185.00
Pitcher, utilitarian crockery, Grape
Trellis patt., brown 80.00
Pitcher, utilitarian crockery, Indian
Boy & Girl patt., blue & white 200.00
Pitcher, utilitarian crockery, Leaping
Deer patt., blue & white 195.00
Pitcher, utilitarian crockery, Love
Bird patt., blue & white 235.00
Pitcher, utilitarian crockery, Poinset-
tia patt., blue & white 185.00
Pitcher, utilitarian crockery, Swan
patt., blue & white 250.00
Polishing iron, cast iron, "Enterprise
No. 77," 5½" l. 35.00
Popover pan, cast iron, 11-cup,
"Griswold No. 10 949-B" 37.50
Pot scrubber, wire chain links, long
handle 18.00
Raisin seeder, cast iron, "Everett,"
1890's 30.00
Recipe box, oak, machine
dovetailing 10.00
Rolling pin, blown amber glass,
15" l. ....60.00 to 85.00
Rolling pin, blown aquamarine
glass, 17" l. 70.00
Rolling pin, blown cobalt blue glass,
16¼" l. 120.00
Rolling pin, ironstone china
w/wooden handles 125.00
Rolling pin, pressed clear glass,
"Roll-Rite," w/metal cap closure .. 12.50
Rolling pin, pressed custard glass,
w/tin sprinkler closure 125.00
Rolling pin, pressed milk white
glass, w/turned maple handles,
Cambridge Glass Co., dated
1921 .... 55.00
Rolling pin, tin w/wooden handles .. 85.00
Rolling pin, utilitarian crockery,
Wildflower patt., blue & white.... 185.00
Sad iron w/detachable handle,
"Colebrookdale" 30.00
Sad iron, "Enterprise," 2½" l. 30.00

Salt box, wall-type, pine, w/slant lid
on leather hinges, ca. 1820 ...... 295.00
Salt crock, wall-type, utilitarian
crockery w/wooden lid, Apricot
patt., blue & white 140.00
Salt crock, wall-type, utilitarian
crockery w/wooden lid, Eagle
patt., blue & white 255.00
Salt crock, wall-type, utilitarian
crockery, Good Luck patt., blue &
white 125.00
Salt crock, wall-type, utilitarian
crockery w/wooden lid, Waffle
patt., blue & white 92.50
Sausage grinder, wooden case
w/wrought iron fittings & crank,
old red paint, 20" h........45.00 to 65.00
Sausage stuffer, tin w/dovetailed
walnut frame & wrought iron
fittings, 24" l................... 105.00
Scrub board, pine frame w/mottled
brown Rockingham glaze corrugated insert, 12½" w., 22" l.
(worn glaze) 145.00
Scrub board, wooden frame w/em-
bossed soap saver top & brass
corrugated insert, "National" 20.00
Skillet, cast iron, "Griswold,"
11" d. 50.00
Sleeve iron, "Wapak," small 22.00
Spatula, brass blade & wrought iron
handle w/hook end, blade pierced
w/stylized initial design,
9 7/8" l......................... 170.00
Spatula, brass blade & shaped
wrought iron handle w/hook end,
10" l. 110.00
Spatula, pierced tin blade & turned
wood handle, 12 5/8" l.......... 70.00
Springerle board, carved maple, 8
designs, animals, flowers & fruit,
early 1800's, 8½ x 3½" oblong ... 130.00
Springerle roller, carved wood, 12
designs in squares on rolling surface, shaped long handles,
12" l. 75.00
Sugar devil (or fruit auger), cast
iron corkscrew form w/wooden
handle 140.00
Sugar nippers, wrought steel,
narrow-shaped tips, w/spring &
end catch intact, 9" l............ 100.00
Syllabub churn (or cream whip), tin,
cylinder w/perforated dasher that
works as egg beater or cream
whipper 85.00
"Taster" spoon, brass bowl & well-
shaped wrought iron handle,
10½" l. 165.00
"Taster" spoon, brass bowl &
wrought iron handle, 12" l. 80.00
Tea kettle, cov., cast iron, gooseneck spout, fixed overhead handle, 8" d. (ILLUS.) 85.00

Cast Iron Tea Kettle

Toaster, stove-top model, tin,
4-sided 20.00
Vegetable slicer, tin, hand-made
w/cut-out heart design in top 65.00
Waffle iron, cast iron, "Griswold
No. 1" 210.00
Waffle iron, cast iron, grid design
w/circle of 5 hearts, "Alfred An-
dresen & Co., Minneapolis,"
2-piece, 8" d. 45.00

KNIVES

Advertising Pocket Knife

Advertising, "Cities Service, Rich-
land Center, Wis.," pocket knife,
mother-of-pearl handle w/brass
bolsters $10.00
Advertising, "Northrup King Seeds,"
1-blade pocket knife, Kutmaster,
Utica, N.Y. 8.50
Advertising, "Purina," 3-blade pocket knife, red & white checkerboard handle, Kutmaster, Utica,
N.Y., 3 3/8" l. (ILLUS.) 15.00
Boker "Tree Brand" 2-blade pocket
knife, marked Solingen,
Germany 25.00
Bowie knife, stag handle, clippoint,
marked L.F. & C., 5½" l. blade,
10" l. overall, w/leather
scabbard 110.00
Case XX U.S.A. 1-blade "Sod
Buster" pocket knife, black com-
position handle, 1967-70,
No. 2138, 5 5/8" l. closed 30.00
Case Tested XX 1-blade pocket

knife, stag handle, pre-1940,
No. 5165, 5½" l. closed 135.00
Case Tested XX 3-blade pocket
knife, pearl handle, stainless steel
blades, pre-1950, No. 83088SS,
3 1/8" l. closed 135.00
Cattaraugus Cutlery Co., Camillus,
N.Y., 2-blade pocket knife, stag
handle 125.00
Coin silver 1-blade pocket knife,
textured handle, engraved blade,
3¼" l. 28.00
Fleam (lancet) knife, 3-blade in
brass case 38.00
Gold 10k, 2-blade pocket knife 65.00
Ivory 1-blade pocket knife, fish-
shaped, 2¼" l. 38.00
Ka-Bar 1-blade "Little Grizzly,"
pocket knife, stag handle w/dog's
head emblem, 5¼" l. closed 500.00
Ka-Bar 3-blade pocket knife, bone
handle, w/dog's head emblem ... 400.00
Landers, Frary & Clark pocket knife,
mother-of-pearl handle,
No. 72129 .... 15.00
Remington 1-blade "Barlow" pocket
knife, buffalo horn handle,
No. R1240, 5" l. closed.......... 140.00
Remington 3-blade "Stockman"
pocket knife, pyremite handle,
No. 3565, 4" l. closed........... 110.00
Saxonia Cutlery Co. 2-blade pocket
knife, mother-of-pearl handle,
Germany 30.00
Sterling silver 2-blade pocket knife,
Gorham Silver Co. 85.00
Valley Forge Cut. Co. 2-blade
pocket knife, nickel silver
handle ....225.00 to 290.00
Winchester 2-blade pocket knife,
stag handle, No. 2980, 3 5/8" l.
closed....................... 95.00

LEHN WARE

*Wooden items made and decorated by
Joseph Lehn, Lancaster County, Pennsylvania, command high prices. To supplement his
income from farming, Lehn began making
barrels for local gristmills in the mid-1850's
and, a few years later, began to turn small
wooden items as gifts for family and friends.
The popularity of the small wooden items led
him to begin to decorate these items for local stores in Lititz and New Euphrata, Pennsylvania. Today, these turned wooden bowls,
pails, boxes and covered, footed bowls, enhanced with hand-painted colorful stripes,
stylized borders, floral or fruit designs, almost*

*always on a salmon or dusty pink ground, will
seldom be found for under $200 unless there
is some damage to the piece.*

Lehn Ware Covered Jar

Goblet, turned wood, painted borders & large pink flower on
side $1,200.00
Jar, cov., turned wood, original
brown sponge-daubed decor on
yellow ground, 4½" h. 655.00
Jar, cov., turned wood, h.p. red,
black & green strawberry & floral
decor on salmon pink ground,
4 7/8" h. (ILLUS.) 450.00
Saffron box, cov., turned wood,
goblet-shaped, h.p. pink florals on
sides of bowl, painted borders &
finial 160.00
Spice or seed chest, 20-drawer,
shaped cornice above case w/five
rows of 4 drawers each, w/line
borders & porcelain pulls, molded
base, flattened ball feet, painted
& decorated 7,500.00

_____

LIGHTING DEVICES

*Also see CANDLESTICKS & CANDLE
HOLDERS, FAIRY LAMPS, CARNIVAL,
CUT and PATTERN GLASS.*

CHANDELIERS
Candle chandelier, brass, 12-light,
elaborate baluster- and ring-
turned central stem w/large ball
& ring pendant supporting 2 tiers
of 6 each (removable) candlearms
w/large drip plates below candle
nozzles, 18th-19th c., 26½" h. ..$5,500.00
Candle chandelier, brass, 6-light,
ring-turned stem supporting 6 scrolling (removable) candlearms
w/drip pans below bulbous candle
cups w/bulbous pendant below,
18th c., 27½" h. 6,050.00

Late 18th Century Candle Chandelier

Candle chandelier, ormolu & cut
glass, 12-light, 2 tiers of 6
lights each, the curved candle
branches attached to ormolu rings,
upper part w/crown, the whole
hung w/ropes of faceted cut glass
chains, prisms & teardrop pendants, late 18th c., 38" h.
(ILLUS.) 3,960.00
Chandelier, Daum Nancy signed,
domed shade, clear glass etched
w/radiating columns & random
ovals, on trumpet-shaped column
etched w/vertical bands,
15 7/8" d., 24" h...............3,850.00
Chandelier, Mission-style (Arts &
Crafts movement), hammered
copper frame suspending 8 Drape
patt. bisque shades, ca. 1915,
37" h. 395.00

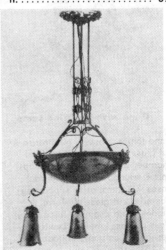

Muller Freres Chandelier

Chandelier, Muller Freres signed
cameo glass & wrought iron, shallow domical central shade in deep
orange-red overlaid in black & cut
w/three panels depicting hunters
w/wild boar & deer within strapwork
borders, 3 flaring outer shades in
conforming colors cut w/similar
scenes, all hung from a ribbed cylindrical support wrought w/rose
blossoms & leafage, ca. 1920,
35" d., 39" h. (ILLUS.) 5,500.00
Chandelier shade, Galle' signed
cameo glass, carved green &
brown flowering umbels against
pink-tinted matte white ground,
interior w/further pink sprays,
bronze mount cast as foliage,
w/matching rods & ceiling cap,
12¾" d. 9,900.00
Chandelier shade, Tiffany signed
leaded glass "Nasturtium" patt.
octagonal shade w/lower apron,
trellised flowering red & orange
nasturtiums amongst multi-hued
green leaves & vines on a streaked
purple, blue & green ground,
w/original chains, ceiling rod
& fixtures, 25" d. 41,800.00

LAMPS, MISCELLANEOUS

Gone-with-the-Wind Lamp

Argand lamps, double, gilt-bronze &
cut glass, central urn-form fluid
chamber above leaf-molded support & triangular dolphin-form
bases w/lateral arms supporting
frosted & cut glass pyriform,
shades, fluid chamber hung w/cut
glass prisms, labeled "Lewis &
Vernon & Company, Philadelphia,"
ca. 1835, 18½" h., pr...........2,530.00
Astral lamp, square stepped white

marble & gilded metal base, fluted column, triangular prisms hung
from font, floral cut frosted mushroom shaped shade, 19th c.,
30 1/8" h. (electrified & drilled) .. 935.00
Betty lamp, tin, w/pick & hanger,
ca. 1810, 4 x 6 x 7" 165.00
Camphene lamp, pewter, weighted
base, tall bulbous font, original
brass twin burner, overall 9" h. .. 295.00
Candle lamp, hanging-type, blue
glass w/enameled florals, brass
frame w/pull-down chain,
11½" h...................... 930.00
Fluid lamps, pewter, domed circular
foot, tapering stem, flaring cylindrical font, James H. Putnam,
Malden, Massachusetts, 1830-55,
7¾" h., pr.................... 660.00
Gone-with-the-Wind lamp, red satin
glass Grape & Leaf patt. ball-
shaped shade & base, original
slip-in brass font & burner,
25" h....................... 700.00
Gone-with-the-Wind lamp, opaline
glass ball-shaped shade & base
washed in pink shaded to burgundy w/enameled large owls decor,
original slip-in font, burner &
clear glass chimney, large 895.00
Gone-with-the-Wind lamp, blue
glass ball-shaped shade & brass-
footed glass base w/h.p. clusters
of red & yellow tea roses, original
slip-in font (ILLUS.) 750.00
Grease lamp, wrought iron triangular pan, hanging-type w/curved
ratchet for adjustment of pan angle, 7¼" h. plus twisted hanger .. 250.00
Kerosene hand lamp w/finger grip,
pressed glass, Aquarius patt.,
light green, 4½" h. 110.00
Kerosene hand lamp w/finger grip,
pressed glass, Banbury patt.,
green 70.00
Kerosene hand lamp w/finger grip,
pressed glass, Beaded Hearts
patt., clear w/frosted hearts 195.00
Kerosene hand lamp w/finger grip,
pressed glass, Beaded Hearts
patt., green 230.00
Kerosene hand lamp w/finger grip,
pressed glass, Coin Dot patt.,
blue opalescent 375.00
Kerosene hand lamp w/finger grip,
pressed glass, Diamond Sunburst
patt., cobalt blue.............. 175.00
Kerosene hand lamp w/finger grip,
pressed glass, Shield patt.,
clear 60.00
Kerosene hand lamp w/finger grip,
pressed glass, Snowflake patt.,
cranberry.................... 425.00
Kerosene table lamp, "Aladdin,"

pressed glass, Beehive patt.,
red 175.00
Kerosene table lamp, "Aladdin,"
pressed glass, Corinthian patt.,
green moonstone .... 65.00 to 85.00
Kerosene table lamp, "Aladdin,"
pressed glass, Corinthian patt.,
rose moonstone, w/burner &
chimney .... 95.00 to 125.00
Kerosene table lamp, "Aladdin,"
pressed glass, Lincoln Drape patt.,
clear 105.00
Kerosene table lamp, "Aladdin,"
pressed glass, Lincoln Drape patt.,
cobalt blue .... 350.00 to 425.00

Washington Drape Pattern Lamp

Kerosene table lamp w/stem, "Aladdin," pressed glass, Washington
Drape patt., clear, w/burner
(ILLUS.) 65.00
Kerosene table lamp w/stem,
pressed glass, Claude patt., cobalt
blue 185.00
Kerosene table lamp w/stem,
pressed glass, Feather Duster
patt., amber 135.00
Kerosene table lamp w/stem,
pressed glass, Inverted Thumbprint & Prism Stem patt., amber .. 85.00
Kerosene table lamp w/stem,
pressed glass, Moon & Star patt.,
sapphire blue base, frosted &
clear font 135.00
Kerosene table lamp w/stem,
pressed glass, Peacock Feather
patt., blue 175.00
Kerosene table lamp w/stem,
pressed glass, Peanut patt.,
green 145.00
Kerosene table lamp w/stem,
pressed glass, Sheldon Swirl patt.,
blue opalescent 290.00
Kerosene table lamp w/stem,
pressed glass, Snowflake patt.,
cranberry opalescent 295.00
Kerosene table lamp w/stem,
pressed glass, Three Face patt.,
clear w/frosted stem & base,
8½" h. 185.00
Kerosene table lamp w/two burners,
"Ripley Marriage (or Wedding)
Lamp," blue opaline glass double

fonts & center match holder,
milk white glass base, w/brass
connectors, collars & burners,
clear glass chimneys, "Ripley &
Co., Pat. Feb. 1st, 1870" on
base .... 1,050.00 to 1,850.00

HANDEL LAMPS (All Signed)

Handel Table Lamp

Desk lamp, cylindrical milk white
glass shade w/painted pond lilies,
patinated metal C-scroll support &
adjustable curving standard, early
20th c. 795.00
Table lamp, 17¾" d. reverse-
painted domical shade w/sunset
landscape, slender patinated
metal standard & base, early
20th c., 22½" h. (ILLUS.) 2,420.00
Table lamp, 17¾" d. reverse-
painted domical shade w/two
colorful parrots in flight amidst
blossoms & leafage against brilliant red ground, patinated metal
classically-molded standard w/cir-
cular base, early 20th c.,
25" h. 4,500.00
Table lamp, 18" d. reverse-painted
"chipped ice" domical shade w/a
Nile river scene of ruins & an
Egyptian village w/palm trees in
grey w/shades of green & tan
under a grey sky shading to pink,
patinated metal standard & base,
1914 .... 4,510.00

TIFFANY LAMPS (All Signed)

Candlestick lamp, "The Twilight,"
iridescent gold glass ruffled umbrella-type shade & swirl-ribbed
base, patent date of May 22, 1894,
14¾" h. (ILLUS.) 1,200.00

Tiffany Candlestick Lamp

Desk lamp, "turtleback," spherical shade set overall w/ogee green glass turtleback tiles, pivoting between bronze U-form arms above a waisted domical base, 1899-1920, 10¾" h. 7,425.00

Desk lamp, 7" d. ribbed hemispherical "Damescene" glass shade w/iridescent pale blue undulating bands on caramel ground, etched gilt-bronze base, 13 7/8" h. 1,870.00

Floor lamp, "Acorn," 24½" d. leaded glass domical shade w/lower band of mottled green-brown acorns on a green ground within radiating bands of deeply mottled green-brown glass, bronze standard & base w/lightly etched decor, 6' 2½" h. .7,700.00

Floor lamp, "Dragonfly," 22" d. leaded glass domical shade w/irregular lower border of 9 blue-bodied & red-eyed dragonflies on a white-streaked butterscotch ground w/amber "jewels," gilt-bronze base w/ribbed column supported by a platform cast w/stylized flowers, on 4 curved feet, 5' 2" h. 24,200.00

Floor lamp, "Laburnum," 26" d. leaded glass domical shade w/alternating clusters of lemon yellow, peach & pastel blue laburnum on olive green stalks w/emerald, olive & mustard-tinged green leaves against cornflower blue ground, gilt-bronze cylindrical standard applied w/vertical stringing continuing into the leaf-molded circular base, raised on 4 petal form feet, w/finial, ca. 1920, 6' 7" h. .45,100.00

Floor lamp, "Oriental Poppy," 26" d. leaded glass domical shade w/profusion of purple-centered multi-hued crimson, red & mauve poppies amidst bright mottled green leaves against a streaked turquoise blue-green sky, bronze cylindrical standard & leaf-molded circular base, pig-tail finial, 6' 7" h. 82,500.00

Floor lamp, "Swirling Leaf," 24" d. leaded glass domical shade w/beaded upper rim, central band of yellow-streaked green leaves on a green-streaked amber & yellow ground, bronze base w/ribbed column forming a band of spirals on flattened domed platform, 5' 9" h. (ball feet missing) 14,300.00

Lily lamp, 7-light, iridescent gold glass lily-form shades, bronze stems & lily pad base w/greenish brown patina, 21 3/8" h. 5,350.00

Lily lamp, 12-light, iridescent gold glass lily-form shades, bronze stems & lily pad base, 19½" h. .16,500.00

Lily lamp, 18-light, iridescent gold glass lily-form shades, bronze stems & lily pad base, 21¼" h. .33,000.00

Tiffany "Nautilus" Lamp

Nautilus lamp, original nautilus seashell shade supported by twin silvered-bronze arms continuing to a platformed foot cast w/stylized petals & inset w/a band of opalescent glass "jewels," 13½" h. (ILLUS.) 3,850.00

Table lamp, "Azalea," 19¼" d. leaded glass domical shade w/slightly waisted lower border w/overall rose, peach, red, salmon & dusty pink azalea blossoms, mottled & striated green leafage &

brown branches against striated &
mottled lavender, ochre & sky blue
ground, bronze 6-legged base conjoined by horizontal bands, on circular foot cast w/stellate device
at center, w/finial, 1899-1920,
29" h. .71,500.00

Tiffany "Black-Eyed Susan" Lamp

Table lamp, "Black-Eyed Susan,"
16" d. leaded glass domical shade
w/plum-centered yellow flowers
amidst green leaves on a white-
streaked ground, bronze base
w/tiered circular foot, 20½" h.
(ILLUS.) 9,350.00
Table lamp, "Crocus," 16" d. leaded
glass domical shade w/rippled
white, yellow & apricot crocuses
upon moss green stems on a
white-streaked green ground,
bronze mushroom base w/ribbed,
domed platform raised on 5 ball
feet, 23½" h. 7,700.00
Table lamp, "Dogwood," 18" d. lead-
ed glass shallow domical shade
w/pale mauve, rose & opalescent
dogwood blossoms w/pale avocado
green centers on striated deep
burgundy stems against pale
green, rose & brown partly "frac-
tured" ground, bronze cylindrical
standard cast w/vertical stringing
continuing into the leaf-molded
circular base, raised on 4 petal
form feet, 1899-1920, 23½" h. . .18,700.00
Table lamp, "Empire Jewel," 22" w.
leaded glass octagonal shade
w/eight triangular panels each
w/central stylized floral medallion
comprised of cabochons & colored
glass on a gunmetal grey ground
bordered by bands of cabochons,

bronze "Four Virtues" base,
26½" h. .8,250.00
Table lamp, "Geometric," 25¾" d.
leaded glass pagoda form shade
w/tiers of overlapping fishscale
tiles shading from grass green at
top to pale green opalescence at
lower rim, bronze reeded columnar
standard cast at neck & foot
w/American Indian patt., w/finial,
1899-1920, 30¾" h. 18,700.00
Table lamp, "Linenfold," 19" d. lead-
ed glass 12-sided conical shade
w/molded sage green panels,
bronze base, matching circular fin-
ial, 23½" h. 4,400.00
Table lamp, "Pansy," 16" d. leaded
glass hemispherical shade w/band
of bright yellow, purple, blue &
mauve pansy sprays amidst green
leaves on an emerald green
ground shading to white at the
upper rim, bronze base set w/cen-
tral band of gold turtleback tiles
& enclosing a fuel canister,
21 3/8" h. .15,400.00

Tiffany "Peacock" Table Lamp

Table lamp, "Peacock," 18" d. rippled leaded glass domical shade
w/radiating amber, yellow & green
peacock feathers w/turquoise & navy
blue "eyes" on mauve ground,
bronze base enclosing an electrified fuel canister, cast overall
w/peacock feathers, scalloped foot
inset w/iridescent glass "eyes,"
26½" h. (ILLUS.) . . .46,200.00 to 52,800.00
Table lamp, "Spider Web," 15" d.
leaded glass domical shade w/radi-
ating bands of streaked green
interspersed w/mauve panels,
bronze mushroom stem base,
18½" h. .8,250.00
Table lamp, "Tulip," 22" d. leaded
glass domical shade w/profusion

of burgundy & lavender tulips shading to pinkish red at the top amidst green leaves on a green ground, pierced adjustable bronze base, 27¼" h.................38,500.00

Table lamp, "Venetian," 13" d. leaded glass conial shade w/two graduated bands of brilliant blue, spring green & rose medallions w/medial band of geometric roundels in conforming colors, all within pale mottled green borders, gilt-bronze base cast as a Romanesque column w/scrolling leafage set w/two bands of green & blue glass bosses, w/finial, 1899-1920, 19½" h. 13,200.00

Table lamp, "Wisteria," 18" d. leaded glass domical shade w/irregular lower border, yellow-streaked white floral clusters amidst green leaves pendant from bronze openwork network of branches at the top, bronze tree form base, 26½" h. 49,500.00

MINIATURE LAMPS

Miniature Lamp

Numbers following our listing of lamps are those assigned to the various miniature lamps pictured in Frank R. & Ruth E. Smith's book, "Miniature Lamps," now often referred to as Smith's Book I.

Amber glass Bull's Eye patt. stem lamp, Nutmeg burner, clear glass chimney, advertised as "Daisy" in Butler Brothers "Our Drummer" 1912 catalogue, 5" h., No. 112.... 100.00

Apricot shaded to clear overshot glass tulip-molded base & shade, Nutmeg burner, clear glass chimney, 8½" h., No. 287 .... 650.00

Blue glass "Twinkle" & stars embossed on base, Nutmeg burner, ball-shaped shade embossed w/stars, 7" h., No. 432 .... 285.00

Blue Satin glass puffy Diamond Quilted patt. base & umbrella-type shade, Nutmeg burner, clear glass chimney, by Consolidated Lamp & Glass Co., Pittsburgh, ca. 1894, 8" h., No. 394 .... 475.00

Clear glass Fish-scale patt. stem lamp, Nutmeg burner, clear glass chimney, 5" h., No. 116......... 80.00

Clear glass Beaded Heart patt. stem lamp, Acorn burner, clear glass chimney, 5½" h., No. 109 .... 180.00

Clear glass ribbed base & ball-shaped shade, base embossed "Glow Night Lamp, No. 0262. Made in U.S.A. Pat. 5.5.08," w/glass wick holder, 6¼" h., No. 626 .... 95.00

Clear glass footed Block patt. base & globe-chimney w/h.p. blue & green florals, Acorn burner, advertised as "Mission" design in Butler Brothers "Our Drummer" 1912 catalogue, 6½" h., No. 192.. 60.00

Clear glass "Time & Light. Pride of America. Grand Vals Perfect Time Indicating Lamp" & time marks from 8 to 6, unmarked burner, white embossed Shell patt. shade, 6¾" h., No. 23 .... 160.00

Clear glass Daisy & Cube patt., Nutmeg burner, 8" h., No. 482 ...... 225.00

Cobalt blue glass base embossed "Little Buttercup" w/applied handle, Nutmeg burner, clear glass chimney, 2¾" h. base, No. 36 ....80.00 to 95.00

Frosted clear glass base & ball-shaped shade w/embossed scrolls, flowers & faint spiderweb, Nutmeg burner, clear glass chimney, 8¼" h., No. 292 .... 465.00

Green cased glass Florette patt. ball-shaped base & shade, Nutmeg burner, clear glass chimney, 7" h., No. 388 .... 525.00

Green Satin glass Drape patt. square base & globe-chimney shade, Nutmeg burner, clear glass chimney, 8½" h., No. 231 .... 310.00

Ice blue Satin glass base & rounded petal-molded ball-shaped shade, Nutmeg burner, clear glass chimney, 7" h., No. 385 .... 460.00

Milk white glass Hobnail patt. w/applied blue reeded handle, Hornet burner, clear glass chimney, 4" h. base, No. 43 .... 85.00

Milk white glass w/embossed Basket Weave patt. w/gold trim, Acorn burner, 6½" h., No. 277 ... 145.00

Milk white glass base and ball-shaped shade w/embossed & painted flowers & beading, sometimes called "Apple Blossom," Acorn burner, 7" h., No. 193 ..... 255.00

Milk white glass Block & Dot patt. footed base & ball-shaped shade, Acorn burner, clear glass chimney, 7½" h., No. 190....100.00 to 125.00

Milk white glass w/embossed beaded panels & boats, windmill &
lighthouse on base & vertical rows
of beading on globe-chimney
shade, Hornet burner, 7¾" h.,
No. 215 .... 325.00
Milk white glass embossed
w/orange-skin texture & design,
fired-on blue paint, Nutmeg burner, clear glass chimney, 8½" h.,
No. 272 (ILLUS.) 290.00
Milk white glass base & ball-shaped
shade, w/painting of angel &
clouds on base & praying child &
clouds on shade in pink, blue &
green, Nutmeg burner, clear glass
chimney, sometimes called "Prayer Lamp," 9" h., No. 323 .... 435.00
Milk white glass w/embossed
medallion & design w/gilt highlights on base & globe-chimney
shade, Hornet burner, 9½" h.,
No. 211 ....190.00 to 225.00
Milk white glass base & ball-shaped
shade w/embossed design &
painted house & windmill scenes
in shades of blue & green w/gold
trim, foreign burner, clear glass
chimney, marked "Amsterdam" on
bottom, 13¼" h., No. 331 .... 600.00
Nickel-plated wall lamp embossed
"Comet," filling spout on wall
reservoir w/slender tubing leading to burner, blue glass beehive
chimney-shade, sometimes called
"Beauty Lamp," 7¼" h., No. 78 ... 75.00
Pewter base w/embossed rococo
design, burner marked "Stellar.
E.M. & Co." (Edward Miller & Co.),
3½" h. base, No. 68 .... 85.00

Diamond Quilted Pattern Miniature Lamp

Pink mother-of-pearl Satin glass
Diamond Quilted patt. square base
w/applied shell feet & inverted-

type shade, foreign burner, 9" h.,
No. 594 (ILLUS.) 1,215.00
Red-painted clear glass base & ball-
shaped shade (resembling red satin glass) w/embossed flowers &
designs, Acorn burner, clear glass
chimney, 7¼" h., No. 135 .... 135.00
Red Satin glass Chrysanthemum &
Swirl patt. base & globe-chimney
shade, Hornet burner, 9" h.,
No. 213 .... 425.00
White opalescent glass melon-ribbed
base w/applied blue shell feet &
inverted-type shade, foreign burner, clear glass chimney, 7¼" h.,
No. 517 .... 945.00
White Satin glass w/embossed ribbing, painted pink, yellow &
green florals, Nutmeg burner,
clear glass chimney, 7½" h.,
No. 393 .... 285.00
Yellow glossy cased glass base &
rounded petal-molded ball-shaped
shade, Nutmeg burner, clear glass
chimney, 7" h., No. 385 .... 525.00

LANTERNS

Pierced Tin Candle Lantern

Barn lantern, tin, kerosene-type,
clear globe marked "Dietz D-Lite"
& "No. 2," 13¼" h. 45.00
Barn lantern, brass, kerosene-type,
"U.S. Brass Tubular" 65.00
Bicycle lantern, nickel-plated brass,
carbide-type, clear bull's-eye lens
w/red & green faceted glass insert at sides, "C.M. Hall Lamp
Co., Solar Model, Kenosha, Wis.,
U.S.A." 50.00
Candle lantern, copper, square
w/glass sides, ornate scalloped
finial vent, wooden handle,
9¾" h. 120.00
Candle lantern, tin, 2 sockets, origi-
nal black paint w/yellow striping,

stenciled label "Clark's Astronomical Lantern, Boston," 9½" h. 240.00

Candle lantern, pierced tin cylinder w/conical top & ring handle (so-called Paul Revere lantern), old dark finish, 13½" h. plus handle (ILLUS.) 145.00

Candle lantern, walnut, square w/four glass sides, conical pierced tin top & ring handle, crimped pan & socket, 16" h. (glued repair to frame) 625.00

Candle lantern, wooden frame w/glass sides, removable top attached to turned corner posts w/wooden nuts, remnants of old painted graining, 10" h. plus wire bail handle 150.00

Folding lantern, tin w/isinglass sides, "Stonebridge," dated 1908, 10" h. 65.00

Kerosene lantern, "Handy," cobalt blue globe, miniature 50.00

Kerosene lantern, corrugated brass base w/collared foot & original font marked "Holmes, Booth & Hayden, Waterbury, Ct.," blown clear glass spherical globe within wire guards, corrugated brass top w/vented dome & strap handle, 13½" h. plus handle 220.00

Miner's lantern, tin, 3-part, leather fitting for head, adapter w/brass plate for pole, 2 wire loop handles, adjustable reflector, hinged tin door, "Ferguson, N.Y.," 1878 .. 150.00

Miner's lantern, tin, coffee pot form w/straight spout at side & hook to attach to miner's cap, "George Anton, Mononhahela City, Washington Co., Pa." 45.00

Skater's lantern, lacy cast iron base, bulbous clear globe, pierced tin top & wire bail handle, 13½" h. ... 220.00

Skater's lantern, tin, clear glass pear-shaped globe & wire bail handle, 6½" h. plus handle 50.00

Skater's lantern, tin, cobalt blue globe & wire bail handle 105.00

Wall, exterior, kerosene-type, black painted metal square frame w/glass sides below pyramidal glass-sided top w/round metal finial, original burner & mercury reflector, stenciled label "C.T. Ham Mfg. Co's New No. 8 Tubular Square Lamp," ca. 1886, 24½" h. 175.00

(End of Lighting Devices Section)

LITHOPHANES

Lithophanes are pictorial panes of porcelain cast in molds, the layer of clay varying in thickness so that when light is transmitted through the panels, the picture is seen in highlights and shadows. Said to have been invented in France in the 1830's they were also made elsewhere. The panes are utilized in lamps, steins and also as scenic plaques.

Night lamp (or tea warmer), 4 scenic panels, 2 tinted & 2 all white, nickel-plated brass frame, original burner, 5" sq. $275.00

Panel, entitled "A Little Boy & His Dog," scene of boy wearing large hat & holding a sword w/his dog beside him, marked P.R. w/sickle & numbered, 4 5/8 x 3 7/8" 90.00

Panel, scene of man peering over a fence at a young girl drawing water at a well, marked P.R. w/sickle & numbered, 5 1/8 x 4¼" 125.00

Panel, scene of waves pounding against craggy shore & moon in sky, black border, marked P.R. w/sickle & numbered, 5 1/8 x 4¼" 125.00

Panel, entitled "Lady Trying on Shoes," scene of young woman holding a shoe as older man kneels to measure her foot, his wife watching from a curtained doorway, numbered, 6½ x 4½" .. 105.00

Panel, scene of grandmother teaching granddaughter to knit, marked P.P.M. & numbered, 8 x 6½" 160.00

Panel, scene of young Victorian girl & boy w/dog in a forest setting, in cobalt blue leaded glass frame, French, 9½ x 8" 175.00

Panel, scene of volcano & fishermen in boats on a lake, 8 x 6", on inlaid wood adjustable stand, overall 7" h. 250.00

LOCKS & KEYS

Box lock, wrought iron w/primitively tooled brass face plate, 6½" l. $16.00

Elbow lock, wrought iron, w/both handles, old worn white paint, 5¾ x 4½" (no keeper or key) 35.00

Key, jail skeleton-type, brass, ca. 1910, 7" l. 25.00

Key, folding-type, "Sergeant" 9.50

Padlock, brass, "Albion 6-Lever" 125.00

"Champion 6-Lever" Padlock

Padlock, brass, "Champion 6-Lever" (ILLUS.) 18.00
Padlock, brass, "Columbia 6-Lever" 25.00
Padlocks, brass, heart-shaped, "Corbin Cabinet Lock Co." & "Swift & Co.," w/keys, pr. 30.00
Padlock, brass, "Fordloc" 50.00
Padlock, brass, heart-shaped, "Fraim" & "U.S.B.I.A." 50.00
Padlock, brass, horseshoe-shaped, "Good Luck" & "Barnes Man'fg. Co., Pat'd June 24, 1879," 2 7/8", w/two keys...................... 65.00
Padlock, brass, "Harvard," 6-lever .. 37.50
Padlock, brass, "IXL," 6-lever 175.00
Padlock, brass, "Keen Kutter," small 275.00
Padlock, brass, "Magnolia Petroleum Co.," w/key 45.00
Padlock, brass, "E.C. Simmons - Keen Kutter".................... 35.00
Padlock, brass, "Simmons Wireless"...................... 100.00
Padlock, brass, heart-shaped, "Slaymaker" & "U.S. Int. Rev." 75.00
Padlock, brass, "Winchester 6-Lever" 70.00
Padlock, brass, "Western Union Telegraph Co.".................. 50.00
Padlock, brass, fish form, China, large............................. 35.00
Padlock, cast-iron w/brass fittings, "Eagle Lock Co., Terryville, Connecticut" 9.00

LORGNETTES, OPERA GLASSES & SPECTACLES

Lorgnette, 14k gold, pince-nez type $75.00
Lorgnette, 14k gold, short lacy design handle, push button to fold, 3½" 75.00
Lorgnette, 14k gold, 49" gold chain 375.00

Lorgnette, sterling silver, folding-type, ornate long chain 85.00
Lorgnette, sterling silver, hanging-type 52.00
Lorgnette, sterling silver, "repousse" Art Nouveau design, signed Unger Brothers...................... 135.00
Lorgnette, tortoise shell & silver metal 42.00
Opera glasses, brass, each eyepiece w/enameled portrait of beautiful woman, overall enameled garlands, tiny florals & leaves, enameled white hinged handle w/relief enameled silver stars & turquoise enameled relief portrait of beautiful woman center, ca. 1860, France 325.00
Opera glasses, mother-of-pearl, 4 h.p. portraits, marked "LeMaire Paris" 195.00

LeMaire, Paris Opera Glasses

Opera glasses, mother-of-pearl & brass, marked "LeMaire, France," w/case (ILLUS.) 65.00
Opera glasses, mother-of-pearl & brass, w/lorgnette-type handle, marked "L'Ing & Godghaux, 156 Rue de Rivoli, Paris," in (worn) plush bag 60.00
Pince nez, 14k gold, folding-type, w/chain & leather case 55.00
Pince nez, gutta percha frames, cobalt blue lenses 18.00
Spectacles, brass sliding frames, w/case......................... 25.00
Spectacles, coin silver frames, Church & Rogers, Hartford, Connecticut, ca. 1830 .... 95.00
Spectacles, coin silver frames, J. Hyde, New York & New Orleans, ca. 1815...................... 195.00
Spectacles, silverplate frames, folding-type w/chatelaine chain, ornate case 30.00
Spectacles, sterling silver frames, w/sterling case, signed "J. Peters, Phila.," 1821 .... 250.00

MAGAZINES

Craftsman Magazine

American Boy, 1924, December $8.50

American Builder, 1917, April, illustrations of house architecture of the day 7.50

American Druggist, 1884, full year bound 50.00

Arizona Highways, 1974, February, "Prehistoric Pottery of Arizona" article 10.00

Baseball Magazine, 1938, full year bound .... 200.00 to 300.00

Boy's Life, 1929, February, Norman Rockwell cover 20.00

Century Illustrated Monthly, 1886-87, November through April, Winslow Homer engravings of Civil War, 6 months bound 12.00

Click, 1938, February, Volume 1, No. 1 .... 5.00

Collier's, 1899, October 28, Jessie Wilcox Smith cover, Boer War article 12.50

Cosmopolitan, 1896, November, articles by Remington, Wells & Stevens 26.50

Country Gentleman, 1919, March 15, Norman Rockwell cover 20.00

Country Life in America, 1912-13, November through April, 6 months bound 50.00

Craftsman, 1912, August (ILLUS.) ... 28.00

Designer, 1910, February, lovely lady cover, Cream of Wheat ad & color fashion plates 16.50

Etude, 1905, October 7.00

Femina of Paris, 1901-30, including Vol. 1, Art Deco color covers by Erte, Benigni, Lepape & others, fashion designs, etc., 25 bound volumes, 293 issues 2,600.00

Field & Stream, 1911, April 13.00

Flair, 1950, February, Vol. 1, No. 1. .... 30.00

Fortune, 1933, February, Coca-Cola cigar label page 35.00

Harper's Weekly, 1861, full year bound 300.00

Inland Printer, 1899, June, Frank X. Leyendecker colorful lovely lady cover 25.00

Judge, 1903, November 21, color cartoon & double page on Lincoln & Teddy Roosevelt 18.50

Ladies' Home Journal, 1901, June, Maxfield Parrish cover 25.00

Ladies' Home Journal, 1912, August, Harrison Fisher cover, full page Cream of Wheat ad, color fashions 15.00

Ladies' World, 1912, August, Howard Chandler Christy cover 7.50

Liberty, 1947, January, Franklin Delano Roosevelt cover 20.00

Life, 1936, November 23, Vol. 1, No. 1, Fort Peck Dam cover 90.00

Life, 1937, November 8, Greta Garbo cover 25.00

Literary Digest, 1920, August 14, Norman Rockwell cover 25.00

Look, 1953, April 21, Lucille Ball, Desi Arnaz & family cover 25.00

McCall's, 1918, November, Howard Chandler Christy cover 6.50

Metropolitan, 1896, June 10.00

Modern Screen, 1955, June, Marilyn Monroe cover, James Dean picture & Elizabeth Taylor article 12.50

Motion Picture Classic, 1919, March, Theda Bara cover 25.00

Ms., 1972, July, Vol. 1, No. 1 .... 65.00

National Geographic, 1948, full year bound 22.00

Penthouse, 1969, September, Vol. 1, No. 1 .... 75.00

People's Popular Monthly, 1917, June, Norman Rockwell 2 boys licking ice cream paddles cover .. 25.00

Peterson's, 1872, full year bound ... 60.00

Photoplay, 1917, December, Billie Burke cover 39.50

Playboy, 1954, December, first Anniversary issue 80.00

Puck, 1889, January 23, double page color cartoon, political satire 14.00

Real Detective Tales, 1925, June 15.00

St. Nicholas, 1876, full year 45.00

Saturday Evening Post, 1903, April 18, Harrison Fisher woman in buggy cover 10.00

Saturday Evening Post, 1925, April 18, Norman Rockwell self-portrait cover 10.00

Science & Mechanics, 1932, May, Zeppelin article 8.50

Scribner's, 1890, January through June, 6 months bound 35.00

Silver Screen, 1949, full year 90.00
Special Detective, 1947, November.. 7.00
Sports Illustrated, 1954, August 16
   through September 20 (first 6
   issues) 300.00
Startling Detective, 1949, January... 7.00
Time, 1937, May 31, Dionne Quin-
   tuplets birthday cover 35.00
TV Guide, 1956, September 29,
   Jackie Gleason cover 20.00
Woman's Home Companion, 1901,
   March, Harrison Fisher cover 12.50
Young Ladies Journal, 1893, April... 5.00
Youth's Companion, 1890, full year
   bound 40.00

MARBLES

Two Sulphide Marbles

Bennington-type, mottled brown,
   1 5/8" d. $35.00
Clay, multicolored, Germany, set of
   75 .... 20.00
Glass, Akro Agate, w/bag & origi-
   nal box from 1920's, set of 50 .... 35.00
Glass, comic strip type, "Betty
   Boop" 45.00
Glass, comic strip type, "Emma" 35.00
Glass, comic strip type, "Koko" 35.00
Glass, comic strip type, "Skeezix" .. 40.00
Glass, "onionskin," overall slightly
   swirled blue & white, 4 lobes,
   1 5/8" d. 120.00
Glass, "onionskin," overall swirled
   red, white & blue, 2¼" d. 195.00
Glass, spatter, multicolored,
   polished, 1¼" d. 35.00
Glass, sulphide, w/bear, 1½" d. ... 190.00
Glass, sulphide, w/beaver 160.00
Glass, sulphide, w/child kneeling... 550.00
Glass, sulphide, w/clown standing,
   hands in his pockets, costume
   w/ruffled collar & baggy pants,
   blue hat w/white pom pom, black
   eyes, 2¼" d. 525.00
Glass, sulphide, w/dog, 1½" d. 155.00
Glass, sulphide, w/fish, 2" d. (ILLUS.
   left)........................... 150.00
Glass, sulphide, w/flying goose 425.00

Glass, sulphide, w/goat, 1¾" d..... 75.00
Glass, sulphide, w/heron, 1¾" d. .. 150.00
Glass, sulphide, w/rearing horse,
   2" d. (ILLUS. right) 350.00
Glass, sulphide, w/Labrador
   Retriever dog, 2½" d. 80.00
Glass, sulphide, w/mule, 1¾" d. ... 135.00
Glass, sulphide, w/poodle standing,
   1¾" d......................... 98.00
Glass, sulphide, w/prairie chicken,
   1¼" d......................... 325.00
Glass, sulphide, w/rabbit, 1½" d. .. 85.00
Glass, sulphide, w/squirrel eating
   nut, 1 7/8" d.................. 95.00
Glass, sulphide, w/Whippet dog,
   1½" d. 120.00
Glass, sulphide, w/wild boar,
   1½" d. 95.00
Glass, swirl, red, yellow, blue &
   green, 1½" d. 45.00
Glass, swirl, white solid swirl ribbon
   center w/red, white & blue outer
   swirls, bluish tinge to glass,
   1½" d. 50.00
Glass, swirl, w/divided core, 4 ribbons form the central core, 2 are
   red, white, blue, white, blue,
   white & red, remaining 2 are
   green, white, pink, yellow, pink,
   white & green, 4 groups consisting of 3 yellow threads each,
   2 3/16" d. 210.00
Glass, Vitro-Agate, "Cat Eyes," unused see-through bag w/Ameri-
   can flag atop, set of 60 .... 25.00

MATCH SAFES & CONTAINERS

Cast Iron Match Holder

Advertising container, wall-type, tin,
   "Ceresota Flour," little boy w/loaf
   of bread........................ $85.00
Advertising container, wall-type, tin,
   "Dr. Shoop's Health Coffee" 90.00

Advertising container, wall-type, cast iron, "Eclipse Stoves" 175.00

Advertising container, pocket-type, celluloid & metal, "Whitehead & Hoag," pretty girl w/low-cut gown one side, "Kanawha Coal & Cook Co., Cinn., Ohio" reverse, 1905 . . . 75.00

Advertising safe, pocket-type, celluloid, "San Felice Cigars," man smoking decor, w/case 78.00

Bisque container, table model, figural comical lady w/long nose w/fly on it, orange dress w/green base, 3" d., 4" h. 79.00

Brass container, table model, model of a bear chained to a post, finely detailed, original gilt, 3" h. 210.00

Brass container, table model, model of a Turkish shoe w/cigar cutter at heel, 3" 95.00

Cast iron container, table model, model of log cabin, roof lifts off, 3 x 4" 130.00

Cast iron container, wall-type, game pouch, dated 1870 (ILLUS.) 85.00

Cast iron container, wall-type, grape decor 35.00

Chrome safe, pocket-type, head of Spaniel dog center 40.00

Three-Dolphin Match Holder

Glass container, table model, pressed cylindrical jar on 3-dolphin base, amber (ILLUS.) 60.00

Glass container, table model, bucket-shaped, tab handles, blue opaline, 2 5/8" d., 2 7/8" h. 45.00

Glass container, table model, model of baby shoe, Daisy & Button patt., blue, w/striker, pat. Oct. 16, '86 . . . . 65.00

Redware container, wall-type, model of an acorn, original paint, 4½" d. 130.00

Silverplate container, table model, model of dog seated beside container, marked "Tufts" 28.00

Sterling silver safe, pocket-type, "F&P ADA" in relief above

wreath, "New York City, Feb. 11, 1898" below, scroll & leaf border 70.00

Tin safe, pocket-type, stenciled fruit & yellow & green striping on original reddish brown japanned ground, 2" l. 360.00

Wooden container, wall-type, basket-shaped pocket, openwork backplate carved w/bird & vines, 6" h. (minor edge damage & repair) 36.00

MEDICAL QUACKERY ITEMS

Numerous devices and contrivances offered last century and early in the present one as "cures" or palliatives for a host of ailments and subsequently found to be worthless, dangerous or at least unequal to their claims are now sought by some collectors. The following represents a sampling of items being collected.

Burnley's foot pads & hand grips, chromed metal, patent date of 1890, w/original cherrywood box $46.00

Dinshan Spectro-Chrome machine, colored light type, 1920's, 45" h. . . . 200.00

Electropathic medical apparatus, in oak box 40.00

Holder's Metallic Indicator, w/mahogany case 27.00

Marvel violet ray shock treatment machine, w/original case 25.00

Master violet ray kit, w/original box, 1920's 49.00

Radiant ozone generator, w/glass tubing, 18 x 8 x 8" 40.00

Renulife violet ray generator, controls mounted on marble interior slab, 1922 . . . . 67.50

Shelton's ultra violet shock machine, ca. 1920 . . . . 35.00

Violetta violet ray shock treatment machine, w/original case 25.00

METALS

Also see AUTOMOBILE ACCESSORIES, BANKS, BELLS, BOOKENDS, BOOTJACKS, BOTTLE OPENERS, BRONZES, CANDLESTICKS & CANDLE HOLDERS, CIGAR & TOBACCO CUT-

TERS, COFFEE GRINDERS, COOKIE CUTTERS, DOOR KNOCKERS, DOOR STOPS, FIREPLACE & HEARTH ITEMS, FOOD MOLDS, FOOT & BED WARMERS, FOOT SCRAPERS, FRAMES, HORSE & BUGGY COLLECTIBLES, JEWELRY, KITCHENWARES, LIGHTING DEVICES, LOCKS & KEYS, MATCH SAFES, NAPKIN RINGS, NAUTICAL GEAR, ROYCROFT ITEMS, SCALES, SOUVENIR SPOONS, TOOLS and WRITING ACCESSORIES.

ALUMINUM (Hammered-type 1920-50)

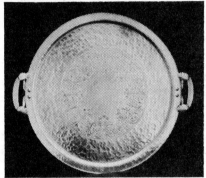

Aluminum Serving Tray

Bowl, fruit, 2-handled, fruits & florals in relief on hammered ground, 11" d. $12.00

Bread tray, Tulip patt., by Rodney Kent Co., 12½" oval 20.00

Candy dish, leaf-shaped 6.50

Casserole dish & cover (no Pyrex glass liner) 11.00

Cocktail set, shaker & 6 flared goblets, 7 pcs. 45.00

Creamer, cov. sugar bowl & tray, 3 pcs. 15.00

Ice bucket & cover, w/insert 25.00

"Lazy Susan" tray 20.00

Tray, florals on hammered ground, 11" sq. 16.50

Tray, Chrysanthemum patt., applied leaves on handles, 13" d. 16.00

Tray, world map w/wildlife animals of each continent, tubular handles, by Arthur Armour, 13 x 9" .. 14.00

Tray, 2-handled, by Canterbury Arts Co., 17 x 7½" 13.00

Tray, 2-handled, center ring of acorns & oak leaves on hammered ground, 18" d. (ILLUS.) 20.00

BRASS

Bird cage, dome top, on stand 80.00

Candle sconce, 3-light, elaborate punchwork backplate, w/attached drawer below, 18th c. 275.00

Candlewick trimmer & snuffer,

scissors-type, on tray w/beaded rim, 9 5/8" l. 50.00

Card holder, engraved Egyptian designs, Bradley & Hubbard 25.00

Clothes hook, slightly curved serrated arm w/star-shaped bracket & bird finial, overall 10¼" l. 75.00

Cyclist's cup, folding-type, dated 1897 .... 24.00

Doll's face mold, double-faced "Santa," overall 8" 50.00

Brass Jelly Kettle

Jelly kettle, spun brass w/wrought iron bail handle, 13¾" d., 6" h. (ILLUS.) 110.00

Kettle shelf, cabriole legs, 18th-19th c., 16½ x 12" 275.00

Letter rack, cherubs decor, Bradley & Hubbard, 8 x 5" 95.00

Motorman's coin changer, nickel-plated finish, large size, attached to leather 22.50

Pail, spun brass w/iron bail handle, stamped "The American Brass Kettle Manufacturers," 10½" d., 6¾" h. 65.00

Pail, spun brass w/iron bail handle, stamped "The Ansonia Brass Co., 1851," 12" d. 95.00

Pan, spun brass w/wrought iron rim handles, 20½" d., 7½" h. (some battering at bottom) 70.00

Sauce pan w/pouring lip, rolled hollow sheet iron handle, 18th c., 7" d., 3" h. 85.00

Stencil for barrels, w/numbers, letters, rotating placer & 2 space finders, 1868, 13" d. 88.00

Tankard w/hinged domed lid, shaped handle, baluster-shaped on circular base, w/"IL" touchmark on back near rim, England, 18th c., 7½" h. (ILLUS.) 2,750.00

"Taster" spoon, shaped handle w/hanging hook on end, signed "Schmidt," Pennsylvania, ca. 1830 .... 245.00

Tea kettle, cast, w/sliding lid 30.00

English Brass Tankard

Tobacco box w/hinged lid, engraved
railroad steam engine & tender,
swag borders, oval 270.00
Tripod, polished, 60" h. **145.00**

Brass Vase by Jean Dunand

Vase, hand-hammered lobed body
w/bands of elongated ovals,
signed Jean Dunand & dated,
11¾" h. (ILLUS.) 1,980.00
Watch holder, figural spread-winged
American eagle 135.00
**Weights, cast, bell-shaped, ¼, ½, 1
& 2 lbs., set of 4** **235.00**

BRONZE

Bill clip, Zodiac patt., signed Tiffany
Studios 115.00
Blotter, rocker-type, Zodiac patt.,
signed Tiffany Studios **90.00**
Blotter ends, Abalone patt., signed
Tiffany Studios, pr. 150.00
Blotter ends, American Indian patt.,
"dore" finish, signed Tiffany Stu-
dios & numbered, 19" l., pr. 250.00
Calendar frame, Bamboo patt.,
signed Tiffany Studios 45.00

Calendar frame, Zodiac patt., "dore"
finish, signed Tiffany Studios 150.00
Cigar box, Grapevine patt.,
w/green glass insets, cedar-lined,
signed Tiffany Studios 425.00
Cigar snuffer, figure of old gentle-
man w/cigar in mouth, his pixie
cap lifts up for snuffing 145.00
Desk set: large ink stand (lacking
glass liner), letter rack, stamp
box & pen tray; Zodiac patt.,
signed Tiffany Studios, New York,
4 pcs. 385.00
Desk set: clock, pr. blotter ends,
magnifying glass, paper clip, pen
tray, photograph frame & perpetual calendar; Pine Needle patt.,
filigreed bronze & glass, signed
Tiffany Studios & numbered,
8 pcs. 2,860.00
Desk set: pr. blotter ends, letter
clip, letter opener, utility box,
pen tray, ink stand, perpetual
calendar & paper rack; Adam
patt., signed Tiffany Studios,
New York, 9 pcs. 2,090.00
Desk set: letter rack, pen tray,
postal scale, double pen stand,
memoranda pad, ink stand, pr.
blotter ends, rocker blotter,
letter clip, ash tray & paper
knife; Venetian patt., "dore"
finish, signed Tiffany Studios,
12 pcs. 2,860.00
**Desk set: pr. bookends, thermom-
eter, 4 blotter corners, paperweight, rocker blotter, pen tray,
letter opener, postal scale, photograph frame, letter rack, ink
stand, perpetual calendar & utility
box; Abalone patt., signed Tiffany
Studios, New York, 17 pcs.** **3,520.00**

Monkey Finial

Finial, cast as a monkey seated,
brown patina, from a model by
Edouard Marcel Sandoz, France,
early 20th c., 4 5/8" h.
(ILLUS.) 1,100.00

Bronze Jardiniere

Jardiniere, cast w/bacchanalian
scenes & bacchus mask handles,
from a model by Gustave Joseph
Cheret, France, 19th c., stamped
"Copyright by E. Soleau, Paris,
1893" on base, 8" h. (ILLUS.) 880.00
Letter rack, Zodiac patt., dark pati-
na, signed Tiffany Studios 225.00
Magnifying glass, Zodiac patt.,
signed Tiffany Studios 225.00
Note pad holder, Zodiac patt.,
"dore" finish, signed Tiffany
Studios 175.00
Paper clip, Zodiac patt., signed
Tiffany Studios 125.00
Paper rack, Venetian patt., "dore"
finish, signed Tiffany Studios 325.00
Pen tray, Zodiac patt., dark patina,
signed Tiffany Studios ....85.00 to 135.00

Bronze Pitcher

Pitcher, vasiform, cast w/oak leaves
& acorns & w/handle in the form
of a nude figure, her legs in the
form of tree roots, golden brown
patina, after Henry Louis
Levasseur, ca. 1900, 12½" h.
(ILLUS.) 1,045.00

Planter, set w/band of irregular
segments of iridescent green turtle-back tiles, on 5 pad feet,
signed Tiffany Studios, 9¾" d. ...1,980.00
Plaque, pierced to hang, stork in relief against cattail ground, signed
Tiffany & Co., 11 x 6¼" 475.00
Spoon mold, 19th c., 2-pc. 95.00
Stamp box, American Indian patt.,
green & brown patina, signed
Tiffany Studios 175.00
Trays, "dore" finish, nested set
graduated from 3" to 5" d., each
signed Tiffany Studios & numbered, set of 3 .... 275.00
Vase, baluster-shaped, obverse &
reverse cast in low relief
w/ascending processions of nude
maidens & cherubs amongst flowing draperies, signed Tiffany
Studios, New York, w/handled
metal liner, 12¾" h. 1,320.00

COPPER

Copper Coffee Boiler

Ale shoe (ale warmer in the form of
a boot), w/long wooden handle,
1820's 200.00
Apple butter kettle, dovetail construction, wrought iron bail handle w/tulip-shaped terminals,
23" d., 14½" h. 190.00
Coffee boiler, cov., tapering cylinder, bail handle w/wooden grip &
domed lid attached to heavy
chain, applied handle at base,
13" h. (ILLUS.) 95.00
Desk set: 2-handled tray, chamberstick, stamp box & letter rack;
hand-hammered (Arts & Crafts
movement), signed w/three lines
within circle, 4 pcs. 125.00
Funnel, 5" l. 20.00
Measure, half-gallon 55.00
Pan, heavy, dovetail construction,
applied strap handle at rim,
10" d., 3¾" h. (ILLUS.) 90.00

Heavy Copper Pan

Pot, cov., dovetailed bottom, applied rim handles w/tulip ends ... 295.00

Sauce pan, dovetail construction, cast iron handle, stamped "D.H. & M. Co. NY," 10¼" d., 7" h. 80.00

Tea & coffee set: squat cov. teapot on stand, tall cov. coffee pot, cov. hot water pot, cov. sugar bowl, creamer, waste bowl & open handled tray; paneled bodies, wooden handles & finials, impressed Tiffany Studios, 7 pcs. 3,300.00

Tea kettle, cov., canted sides, dovetail construction, gooseneck spout, swing handle stamped "D.M. Smith," 5¾" h. plus handle (old repairs) 275.00

Tea kettle, cov., dovetail construction, gooseneck spout w/hinged flap, 7" h. plus swivel handle 105.00

Tea kettle, cov., dovetail construction, 3 small feet, gooseneck spout, brass finial on slightly domed lid, swing handle, 8½" h. 175.00

Tea kettle & cover on stand w/tray, burner & shield, tilts to pour, marked "Heinrich's" 110.00

Wash boiler & tin lid w/wooden handle grip, side handles also w/wooden grips, 22 x 13", 14" h. 70.00

IRON

Balustrade from Paris Metro

Baker's rack, hand-wrought, 5-shelf, grapevine decor at sides, ca. 1910, 78 x 60" 325.00

Balustrade (from the Paris Metro), cast w/ornate openwork floral & whiplash motif, designed by Hector Guimard, ca. 1900, unsigned, 29" h. (ILLUS.) 3,520.00

Bill holder, wall-type, cast, model of gloved hand w/spring clip 33.00

Calipers, hand-wrought, heart-shaped thumbscrew, 10¼" l. 12.50

Candle snuffer, hand-wrought, scissors-type, w/rat-tail curled handles, 18th c. 65.00

Candle stand, hand-wrought, central socket above 3 sockets on curved supports, twisted stem, tripod base w/penny feet, late 19th c., 59¼" h. 170.00

Clothes hooks, wall-type, hand-wrought, shaped back plate w/fold-down shaped hooks, worn dark green paint, 12" h., pr. 530.00

Coffee roaster, hand-wrought, skillet-like w/handle & handcrank, 9½" d. 40.00

Dough scraper, hand-wrought, punch-tooled initials on blade, 4½" l. 145.00

Flag standard, floor model, cast, marked "Annin & Co., N.Y." 15.00

Fork, hand-wrought, 2-tine, well-shaped handle w/simple tooling, 16" l. ....60.00 to 100.00

Garden urns, cast, flaring embossed rim, reeded standard, stepped square base, signed "M.D.J. & Co. Pat'd July 1, 1879," painted black, 16¾" d., 24" h., pr. 450.00

Kerosene lamp wall bracket, cast, lacy, 2-pc. 15.00

Mail box, cast, "Hubley" 30.00

Masonry tie-rod end, cast, 6-point star ....15.00 to 22.00

Model of an eagle, cast, well-detailed, 24" wingspan 190.00

Oven peel, hand-wrought, ram's horn handle ends, 42½" l. 85.00

Pipe tongs, hand-wrought, accordion-type, extends to 10½" l. 260.00

Porringer, cast, fan-like handle, worn white graniteware lining, 7½" across handle 45.00

Safe, cast, door opening to single drawer & open compartments, w/half-columns on all corners, baluster-shaped standard on 4 legs headed by Egyptian-style busts & ending in hoofed feet, painted w/floral bouquets & gilt-stenciled designs, ca. 1880, 42½" h. (ILLUS.) 2,200.00

Cast Iron Safe

Shelf brackets, cast, lacy,
3 x 4", pr. 22.00
Shooting gallery target, cast, model
of a duck 45.00
Skillet, hand-wrought, deep pan
w/long handle attached w/side
supports, 11½" d. pan, 20½" l.
handle 210.00
Snow bird, cast 38.00
Spatula, hand-wrought, broom-
shaped blade, well-shaped handle
w/hook end, 15" l. 55.00
Spoon, hand-wrought, straight han-
dle w/hook end, 5 3/8" l. 105.00

Cast Iron Strong Box

Strong box w/hinged lid, cast, studded strapwork design, locking
mechanism w/ten shooting bolts,
red-painted interior, Continental,
17th c., 33½" l., 18½" h.
(ILLUS.) 1,980.00
Sugar nippers, hand-wrought, sim-
ple tooling w/good details,
10½" l. 65.00
Tea kettle, cast, straight sides
w/sloping shoulder, gooseneck
spout, wrought iron handle,
7½" h. (minor chips on lid) 85.00

Wafer iron, cast grid w/tulip & waffle design, hand-wrought handles,
30½" l. 115.00

PEWTER

Pewter Cann

Basin, narrow reeded brim, William
& Samuel Yale, Meriden, Connect-
icut, 1813-20, 6¾" d. 319.00
Basin, molded brim, deep rounded
sides, Thomas Badger, Boston,
Massachusetts, ca. 1800, 8" d. . . , . . 467.50
Basin, single reed brim, Robert
Palethorp, Jr., Philadelphia, Penn-
sylvania, 1817-22, 10" d. 935.00
Beaker, flaring cylinder, 2 bands of
incised lines, Ashbil Griswold,
Meriden, Connecticut, 1807-35,
3" h. 190.00
Cann, tapering cylinder, scroll han-
dle w/bud terminal, Parks Boyd,
Philadelphia, Pennsylvania, 1795-
1819, 4½" h. (ILLUS.) 3,080.00
Chalice, tapering cylindrical cup,
baluster stem, domed & molded
foot, Timothy Brigden, Albany,
New York, 1816-19, 8 7/8" h. 6,600.00
Charger, English hallmarks, 18th c.,
20½" d. 495.00
Coffee pot, cov., baluster-shaped,
stepped domed lid, black-painted
wooden scroll handle, S-shaped
spout, flaring circular foot, Josiah
Danforth, Middletown, Connecti-
cut, 1825-37, 10½" h. 352.00
Coffee pot, cov., baluster-shaped,
S-scroll spout, spurred C-scroll
handle, domed lid w/wooden finial, Daniel Curtiss, ca. 1825,
10½" h. 242.00
Dish, deep, narrow rim w/single in-
cised line, Samuel Danforth, Hartford, Connecticut, 1795-1816,
13¼" d. 467.50
Flagon, flaring cylinder, domed lid &
knob finial, curved spout, S-scroll
handle, Oliver Trask, Beverly,
Massachusetts, 1832-39,
11½" h. 440.00

Flagon, lighthouse-shaped, stepped domed lid w/urn-shaped finial, double scroll handle w/scroll thumbpiece & bud terminal, curved spout, body w/raised mid-rib & flaring foot, Thomas D. Boardman, Hartford, Connecticut, 1804-60 & later, 13¼" h.................1,870.00

Measure, copper rim band at top, signed James Yates (England), 4¼" h., 1-cup................. 95.00

Measures, "Irish haystacks," 5 marked Austin & Sons, Cork, Ireland, one by the Austin shop & other by Munster Iron Works (successors to the Austin shop, 1850-75), assembled set of 7.....2,860.00

Pewter Mugs by Samuel Kilbourn

Mugs, Samuel Kilbourn, Baltimore, Maryland, early 19th c., 4" h., pr. (ILLUS.)....................1,320.00

Pitcher, cov., baluster-shaped, domed lid w/disc finial, curved spout, strap handle, Boardman & Hart, New York City, 1828-53, 7¾" h........................ 660.00

Pitcher, Daniel Curtiss, Albany, New York, ca. 1830, 8" h............ 715.00

Plate, David Melville, Newport, Rhode Island, 1776-93, 7¾" d..... 250.00

Plate, single reed brim, Gershom Jones, Providence, Rhode Island, 1774-1809, 7 7/8" d............. 440.00

Plate, Nathaniel Austin, Charlestown, Massachusetts, late 18th c., 8" d........................... 247.50

Plate, Richard Austin, Boston, Massachusetts, ca. 1800, 8½" d...... 302.00

Plate, lion touchmark & "London," 9" d........................... 115.00

Plate, Frederick Bassett, New York, late 18th c., 9" d.............. 522.00

Porringer, old English style handle, Edward Danforth, Hartford, Connecticut, 1790-1820, 4 1/8" d.....2,420.00

Porringer, flowered handle, William Calder, Providence, Rhode Island, 1817-56, 4¼" d................. 440.00

Porringer, tab handle, Thomas Melville, Newport, Rhode Island, 1770-90, 4¾" d. 1,650.00

Salt box, hanging-type, shaped crest w/engraved floral designs & "M.A.H., 1645," Continental,

9¼" h. (minor seam separation on back edge)................ 500.00

Saucer, single reed brim, Benjamin Harbeson or Benjamin Harbeson & Sons, Philadelphia or Lancaster, Pennsylvania, 1765-1800, 6" d..... 352.00

Spoon with Rat-tail Handle

Spoon, circular bowl & straight handle w/rat-tail, indistinct touchmark (possibly by Francis Bassett II, New York), 6½" l. (ILLUS.) 990.00

Tablespoons, heart design on back of bowl, Luther Boardman, 1825-50, set of 5............... 125.00

Teapot by Thomas Danforth Boardman

Teapot, cov., pyriform, domed lid, faceted scroll spout, spurred scroll handle, Thomas Danforth Boardman, Hartford, Connecticut, 1805-50, 7" h. (ILLUS.) 935.00

Teapot, cov., pyriform, domed conical lid w/conical finial, faceted scroll spout, scroll handle, William Calder, Providence, Rhode Island, 1817-56, 7"h 2,640.00

Teapot, cov., footed, bulbous body, domed lid w/acorn finial, gooseneck spout, Daniel Francis, Buffalo, New York, 1833-42, 7 3/8" h... 250.00

Teapot, cov., pyriform, conical lid, faceted scroll spout, scroll handle, Roswell Gleason, Dorchester, Massachusetts, ca. 1830, 7½" h... 495.00

Teapot, cov., tapering cylinder, domed lid w/finial, faceted scroll spout, double scroll handle, Morey & Ober, Boston, Massachusetts, 1852-55, 7½" h. 275.00

PLATED SILVER (Hollowware)

Victorian Plateau Mirror

Bowl, square, "repousse" florals on sides & Kate Greenaway-type girls w/dogs seated on rim, vaseline glass insert, Reed & Barton, Taunton, Massachusetts 350.00

Butter dish & cover w/recumbent cow finial, floral handles, bright-cut & chased decor, branch knife holder, Reed & Barton Co. 125.00

Candy dish, cherries decor, Pairpoint Corp., New Bedford, Massachusetts 45.00

Coffee urn, cylindrical, domed cover w/cast eagle finial supported by spiraled columns, molded conforming base, American, ca. 1876, 21" h. 143.00

Console set: 13" d. basket-tray w/overhead handle & pr. 10½" h. candlesticks; "repousse" Dutch scene, Barbour Silver Co., Hartford, Connecticut, 3 pcs. 120.00

Cracker jar & cover, w/floral bouquet finial, engraved "Crackers" on front, 5¾" d., 8" h. 115.00

Cup & saucer, bright-cut decor, James W. Tufts, Boston, Massachusetts 38.00

Entree server, double hinged blades w/thumb lever, ornate engraved & pierced top blade, Assyrian Head patt., Meriden Brittania Co., Meriden, Connnecticut, 10½" l.... 125.00

Pitcher w/ice lip, vintage design, ornate handle w/figural finial, Wilcox Silver Plate Co., Meriden, Connecticut : 75.00

Plate, pierced rim, Van Bergh Silver Plate Co., Rochester, New York, 10½" d. 28.00

Plateau mirror, double-beveled mirror plate engraved w/chain of rosettes within lacy framework, ornate feet, 12" d. (ILLUS.) 165.00

Punch bowl & tray, chased vintage decor at rims, 18" d. tray, 2 pcs. 125.00

Serving dish, cov., urn-shaped, elongated C-scroll handles, beaded borders, 9 3/8" h. 155.00

Soup tureen & cover w/vine finial surrounded by grape clusters, lobed slightly bombe form w/vintage rim, square pedestal base, w/insert, 12" d., 13" h. 425.00

Sugar bowl-spoonholder combina-

tion, 12 spoon slots, rococo pedestal base, handles & lid, Middletown Plate Co., Middletown, Connecticut 95.00

Tea & coffee service: cov. teapot, cov. coffee pot, sugar bowl, creamer, waste bowl & 28½" l. tray; heavily chased decor, ornate molded feet & handles, fruit & foliage finials, 6 pcs. 650.00

Tray, overall ornately chased scrollwork decor, on copper, English hallmarks, 25 x 15½" 95.00

Watch holder, model of an owl, Hartford Sterling Company, Philadelphia, Pennsylvania 135.00

PLATED SILVER (Flatware)
ALHAMBRA (Wm. Rogers Mfg. Co.)
Butter spreader 7.00
Dinner forks, set of 12 in original box 150.00
Gravy ladle...................... 18.00
Ice cream forks, set of 6 .... 70.00
Soup spoons, set of 6 in original box 75.00

ASSYRIAN (1847 Rogers Bros.)
Mustard ladle 15.00
Oyster fork 4.00
Pie server 20.00
Seafood fork..................... 5.00

AVON (1847 Rogers Bros.)
Chipped beef fork 12.00
Dinner fork, hollow handle......... 9.50
Jelly server 18.00
Salad serving fork................. 25.00
Seafood fork..................... 7.50

BERKSHIRE (1847 Rogers Bros.)
Carving set, 3 pcs. 125.00
Dinner knife, hollow handle 10.00
Gravy ladle...................... 15.00
Seafood fork..................... 12.00
Sugar tongs...................... 15.00
Tablespoon 7.50

BERWICK (Simpson, Hall, Miller & Co.)
Demitasse spoon 6.00
Fruit knife, hollow handle.......... 25.00
Gravy ladle...................... 23.50
Ice cream server 89.00
Youth set, 3 pcs. 79.00

CHARTER OAK (1847 Rogers Bros.)

Charter Oak Pattern Forks

Dinner fork (ILLUS. bottom) 17.00
Fruit spoon 19.00
Gravy ladle, gold washed bowl 35.00
Ice cream forks, set of 6 . . . . 69.00
Iced tea spoons, set of 6 . . . . 79.00
Luncheon fork (ILLUS. center) 15.00
Oyster ladle 149.00
Punch ladle, flat handle 395.00
Salad fork (ILLUS. top) 12.00
Sauce ladle 49.00
Soup ladle 149.00
Sugar spoon 12.50
Sugar tongs 59.00
Tomato server 129.00

DAFFODIL (1847 Rogers Bros.)
Carving set, large, 2 pcs. 60.00
Pickle fork 7.00
Salad serving fork & spoon 25.00
Sugar spoon 5.00
Tablespoon 6.00

EASTER LILY (Alvin Mfg. Co.)
Fruit knife, hollow handle 14.00
Grapefruit spoon 15.00
Gravy ladle 25.00
Meat fork 19.00
Salad fork 11.00
Tablespoon 9.50

FLEUR DE LUCE (Oneida Community)
Berry serving spoon 25.00
Ice cream fork 20.00
Oyster ladle 60.00
Seafood fork 12.00
Sugar tongs 24.50

GRENOBLE (William A. Rogers, Ltd.)
Carving set, 3 pcs. 135.00
Cold meat fork 39.00
Dinner fork 8.50
Dinner knife 20.00
Fruit spoon 16.00
Pastry fork 25.00
Pickle fork 29.50
Punch ladle 295.00
Salad fork 28.00
Sauce ladle 29.00
Seafood fork 20.00
Serving spoon, pierced bowl 22.50
Soup spoon, oval bowl 8.50
Sugar tongs, 3" l. 22.00
Teaspoon 6.50

SHEFFIELD PLATE
Candlesticks, baluster form shaft on
stepped circular base w/applied
decorative bands of flowers &
acanthus leaves, w/bell-form
clear glass hurricane shade
stencil-etched w/fruiting vines,
early 19th c., 20½" h., pr. 880.00
Entree dish, cover & hot water
warming stand, shaped rectangle

w/borders of gadrooning, C-
scrolls, flowers, grapes & shells &
detachable handle; warming stand
w/scrolling bracket handles
w/wooden stretchers, raised on 4
bun feet w/wooden bases, early
19th c., 12½" l. dish 412.50
Salver, flat-chased center w/rococo
cartouche & engraved armorials,
scroll & shell border, raised on 4
leaf-capped scroll supports, ca.
1830, 21" d. 715.00
Sauce tureens, cov., compressed ob-
long form w/gadroon border
raised on scrolled supports,
stepped domed lid, bracket form
handles w/oak leaves & acorns at
sides & on lid, early 19th c., 7¾"
across handles, pr. 467.50

Sheffield Soup Tureen

Soup tureen, cov., oval bombe form
raised on 4 foliate & shell decorated supports, bracket handles
w/foliate attachments, stepped
domed lid w/shell & foliate open
wreath handle above acanthus,
early 19th c., 13" l. (ILLUS.) 990.00
Soup tureen, cov., oval bombe form
raised on 4 foliate scroll feet,
reeded foliate handles, gadroon
border, domed cover w/matching
finial & engraved w/crest, ca.
1830, 15 7/8" l. over handles 1,320.00
Tea tray, 2-handled, shaped oblong
w/foliate scroll border & handles,
chased band of scrolling foliage &
flowers centering contemporary
armorials, on 4 pad feet, maker's
mark J.N., ca. 1840, overall
30 1/8" l. 880.00
Tea urn, cov., shallow melon form
w/forked & scrolled tendril handles, melon & leaf finial, square
base w/flower-flanked scroll feet,
ca. 1830, w/later monogram,
15¾" h. 990.00
Wine coolers, pail form w/upright
handles, applied w/shield on each
side, one engraved w/armorials &
other w/a crest, detachable rims

Sheffield Plate Wine Coolers

& liners, ca. 1800, 7¾" h., pr.
(ILLUS.) 2,640.00
Wine coolers, vase-shaped w/partly
fluted lower section, rising to 2
reeded bracket handles, everted
collar w/gadrooned band chased
w/acanthus & shells at intervals,
w/detachable liners, 8" h., pr. . . .1,320.00

**SILVER, AMERICAN, ENGLISH & OTHERS
(Hollowware)**

18th Century Silver Cake Basket

Beaker, tapering cylinder, body
"repousse" w/eagles amidst
rocaille scrolls & scalework,
w/monogram, Al'derman,
Moscow, 1766, 3" h. 440.00
Butter dishes, covers & stands,
George III, circular slightly
bombe form w/lobed lower
bodies, dishes & stands w/reeded
foliate scroll & shell borders,
domed covers w/matching lobed
decor & baluster finials, Rebecca
Emes & Edward Barnard, London,
1813, 7 3/8" d. stands, overall
5½" h., pr. .3,850.00
Cake basket, George III, shaped oval
on spreading foot w/ropework rim,
wirework sides applied w/grape-
vine, insects & sheaves of wheat,
center engraved w/contemporary
armorials, openwork swing handle
applied w/grapevine, Emrick Romer,
London, 1767, 14" l. (ILLUS.) 1,650.00

Cann, baluster form, double scroll
handle, molded rim & circular foot,
body engraved w/script monogram,
Samuel Minott, Boston, 1760-80,
5" h. 1,320.00
Caudle cup, cylindrical w/slightly
everted rim, rounded base chased
w/sloping gadroons, embossed
cable collar & reeded scroll strap
handles, John Coney, Boston,
1690-1710, 3" d. 22,000.00
Centerpiece bowl, monteith-type
notched rim applied w/flower-
heads, chased w/profuse flowers
above acanthus, matching domed
foot, Jacobi & Jenkins, Baltimore,
early 20th c., 10" d. 770.00
Coffee pot, cov., vase form w/in-
curved neck & pedestal base,
beaded borders, swan's neck
leaf-capped spout, reel-shaped
cover w/vase finial, scrolling
wooden handle, Christian Wilt-
berger, Philadelphia, ca. 1795,
15 1/8" h. 4,400.00
Creamer, helmet form, beaded rim
& pedestal base, reeded scroll
handle, bright-cut band of inter-
lacing floral & foliate swags, front
engraved w/monogram, Paul
Revere, Jr., Boston, 1790-1800,
6½" h. (foot repaired) 5,225.00
Dish ring, George II, reel-shaped,
pierced & chased w/a band of foliate strapwork enclosing shells
& paterae, base w/flat-chased
border of shells, flowers & leaves
on shaped matted ground, engraved w/later crests, John Hamilton,
Dublin, Ireland, ca. 1735, 7½"
rim d. 2,860.00
Entree dishes & covers, George IV,
rectangular w/incurved sides, gadroon borders w/acanthus-flanked
double-shells at the angles &
flowers in the centers, bases &
covers engraved one side w/a
crest, detachable foliate handles rising from lion's masks &
resting on a bed of overlapping
acanthus, Paul Storr, London, 1826,
13" l., pr. .13,200.00
Gravy ladle, twist handle, vermeil
shell bowl, Farrington & Hun-
newell, Boston, Massachusetts,
1838-85. . . . . 130.00
Ice tub, circular w/two pierced han-
dles, flaring sides chased to simulate wood-grained staves &
encircled by applied banding,
w/removable pierced strainer,
base stamped "Sterling," American, late 19th c., 7" d., 4" h.
(ILLUS.) 605.00

American Silver Ice Tub

Lemon strainer, George I, bowl
pierced in a simple flowerhead
design, 2 flat handles pierced in
foliate design, London, 1718,
6½" w. across handles 412.00
Marrow spoon, A. Gairdner, Edinburgh, Scotland, 1780's 235.00
Mint julep cups, slightly tapered
cylinder, molded borders, engraved w/foliate scroll monogram,
Asa Blanchard, Lexington, Ken-
tucky, 1810-20, 3 1/8" h., pr. 2,200.00
Pitcher, water, vase form, shell
form spout centered by water foliage terminating in a dolphin's
head, applied foliate C-scroll handle, neck engraved w/bands of
flowers & leaves, shoulders
w/repeating pinprick motif framing stylized foliage, engine-turned
body w/foliate cartouche enclosing presentation inscription,
Gorham & Co., Providence, Rhode
Island, ca. 1859, 9¼" h. 385.00
Platter, foliate scroll rim, wide border w/vacant foliate scroll cartouches, Bailey, Banks & Biddle,
Philadelphia, ca. 1900,
15 1/8" d. 715.00
Salver, reticulated Art Nouveau
style border, center engraved
w/butterflies & monogram, Leb-
kuecher & Co., Newark, New Jer-
sey, early 20th c., 10" d. 235.00

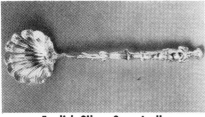

English Silver Soup Ladle

Soup ladle, William IV, handle cast
w/a female demi-figure, her
hands crossed over her chest, rising from shell & scrollwork above
treetrunk-form stem issuing a
spray of leaves at base (small
split at bottom of handle), shell-

shaped bowl, Edward Farrell, Lon-
on, 1831, 15¼" l. (ILLUS.) 1,870.00
Soup tureen, cover, stand & liner,
George III, partly lobed oval boat
form, ribbon-tied reeded rims &
leaf-capped loop handles, body
applied w/a band of virtruvian
scrolls & flowerheads on matted
ground, domed cover similarly decorated & w/floral basket finial,
stand w/domed center & scrolled
acanthus grips, removable liner
w/scrolled grips, cover, body &
stand engraved w/foliate scroll
monogram, Andrew Fogelbert &
Stephen Gilbert, London, 1788,
stand 21 7/8" l. 15,400.00
Sugar bowl, cov., inverted pear
shape, lower part spirally lobed
& fluted, domed cover similarly
chased & w/urn finial, pedestal
foot, all w/chased borders, engraved w/crest, Myer Myers, New
York, ca. 1770, 6" h. 38,500.00
Sugar tongs, shell-shaped grips,
bright-cut borders, shaped &
widened top w/monogram within
an oval flanked by bright-cut floral pendants, Paul Revere, Jr.,
Boston, ca. 1780, 5¾" l. 4,675.00
Tankard, tapered cylinder, molded
borders & girdle, domed cover
w/baluster & flame finial, partly
lobed scroll thumbpiece, scroll
handle engraved w/contemporary
monogram & 3 other sets of initials & terminating in circular
disc, John Coburn, Boston, ca.
1760, 9" h. 6,050.00
Tea & coffee service: cov. coffee
pot, cov. teapot, cov. sugar bowl,
creamer, waste bowl & kettle on
stand; Art Deco style paneled
bodies w/canted sides, Black,
Starr & Frost, New York,
6 pcs. 1,225.00
Tray, Victorian, 2-handled, beaded
rim, reeded & beaded handles,
engraved armorials surrounded by
band of strapwork enclosing fruit
& sprays of flowers, maker's mark
"T.S.," London, 1872, 28" oval....3,630.00
Vase, molded rim above "repousse"
& chased florals, molded footrim,
Gorham Mfg. Co., Providence,
Rhode Island, 1917, 12" h. 1,760.00
Wine glass coolers, George III,
partly lobed tub shape, engraved
w/contemporary armorials, 2 short
spouts cast & chased w/an anthemion on matted ground, egg &
dart rims, slightly spreading footrim, Benjamin Smith II, London,
1807, 4¾" h., pr. 12,100.00

STERLING SILVER (Flatware)
CACTUS (Georg Jensen)

Cactus Pattern

Cake server	225.00
Demitasse spoon	25.00
Egg spoon	44.00
Fruit knife	40.00
Salad serving set, ebony tips	195.00
Salt spoon	33.00
Tablespoon	80.00

CHRYSANTHEMUM (Tiffany & Co.)

Tiffany's Chrysanthemum Pattern

Berry spoon, kidney-shaped bowl	495.00
Butter spreader	42.00
Grapefruit spoon	60.00
Gravy ladle	195.00
Iced tea spoon	59.00

Luncheon fork	69.00
Luncheon knife	58.00
Soup ladle, fluted bowl	695.00
Sugar shell	65.00
Tablespoon	75.00

KING ALBERT (Whiting Mfg. Co.)

Dinner fork	37.50
Dinner knife	25.00
Ice cream spoon	22.00
Lemon fork	10.00
Luncheon fork	19.00
Luncheon knife	17.00
Serving spoon	34.00
Sugar tongs	18.00
Teaspoon	13.00
Tomato server	25.00

LA REINE (Reed & Barton)

Cheese scoop	85.00
Cucumber fork	110.00
Gravy ladle	88.00
Honey spoon	80.00
Jelly server	125.00
Luncheon fork	30.00
Olive spoon, pierced bowl	32.00
Soup ladle, gold-washed bowl	350.00
Teaspoon	13.00
Tomato server	110.00

OLYMPIAN (Tiffany & Co.)

Tiffany's Olympian Pattern

Asparagus tongs	525.00
Butter serving knife	180.00
Demitasse spoon	25.00
Dinner knife	95.00
Fish fork, 3-tine	90.00
Fish knife, silver blade	65.00
Gravy ladle, swirled bowl	265.00
Luncheon fork	30.00
Pie knife, serrated blade, 11¼" l.	550.00
Soup ladle, swirled bowl	950.00
Tomato server	395.00

PLYMOUTH (Gorham Mfg. Co.)

Cold meat fork	39.00
Demitasse spoon	10.00
Dinner fork	29.00
Dinner knife	16.00
Mustard ladle	65.00
Saratoga chip server	275.00
Serving fork, large, gold-washed tines	125.00
Soup ladle	250.00
Soup spoon, oval bowl	22.00

POMONA (Towle Mfg. Co.)

Berry spoon, bright-cut bowl	137.00
Butter serving knife	37.00
Ice cream fork	35.00
Ice cream slice, bright-cut blade	175.00
Lettuce fork	95.00
Pickle fork, long handle	59.00
Preserve spoon, bright-cut bowl	88.00
Teaspoon	15.00

REPOUSSE (Samuel Kirk & Sons)

Asparagus fork	200.00
Carving set, large	300.00
Fried egg server	125.00
Luncheon fork	25.00
Luncheon knife	20.00
Salad serving set, w/applied repousse edge	750.00
Stuffing spoon	365.00
Tomato server, w/applied repousse edge	350.00

ROCOCO (Dominick & Haff)

Cheese scoop	85.00
Fish serving knife	195.00
Grapefruit spoon	20.00
Gravy ladle, gold-washed bowl	60.00
Ice spoon, pierced bowl	185.00
Luncheon fork	42.50
Nut spoon	48.00
Soup ladle, large	345.00
Sugar sifter	80.00
Toast fork	110.00

WATTEAU (Wm. B. Durgin Co.)

Demitasse spoon	14.00
Dinner fork	32.00
Food pusher	55.00
Luncheon fork	26.00
Serving spoon	38.00
Strawberry fork, enameled	20.00
Teaspoon	12.00

WAVERLY (R. Wallace & Sons)

Asparagus tongs	115.00
Egg spoon	18.00
Fish fork	35.00
Luncheon fork	20.00
Luncheon knife	25.00
Pickle fork	13.00
Sardine fork	35.00
Serving spoon	45.00

Strawberry fork	20.00
Tea caddy spoon	50.00
Teaspoon	10.00

TIN & TOLE

Tin Candle Mold

Box, cov., tole, lid w/scene of 3-masted ship flying tricolor flag, 5½" oval ... 160.00

Candle box, hanging-type, tin, cylindrical w/hinged lid, backplate w/scalloped crest & hanging tabs, worn old dark paint, 10½" l. ... 195.00

Candle mold, tin, 12-tube, 2 rows of 6 each, tray top w/handle, oblong base, for half-size candles, 6¼" h. (ILLUS.) ... 255.00

Candle mold, tin, 36 tube, 4 rows of 9 each, double-earred handles, 9" h. (minor battering) ... 165.00

Candle sconce, tin, flaring reflector backplate w/rounded top, saucer pan w/sawtooth edge, overall 14¾" h. ... 275.00

Coal scuttle, tole, rounded rectangular body & conforming base painted w/gilt, blue, cream & brown flower sprays, foliate C-scrolls & cell-pattern on green ground, brass foliate scroll handles, Victorian, mid-19th c., 23" w., 22¾" h. ... 1,045.00

Tole Coffee Pots & Mug

Coffee pot w/flattened lid, tole, expanding straight-sided cylinder, applied strap handle, straight spout, free-hand red, yellow & green florals on dark ground, 8 5/8" h. (ILLUS. right) ... 2,050.00

Coffee pot w/slightly domed lid, tole, straight tapering sides, braced strap handle, gooseneck spout, free-hand stylized red, yellow & black florals on original brown ground, 10 5/8" h. (ILLUS. left) 3,700.00

Comb case, wall-type, tin (some rust) 10.00

Cottage cheese sieve, tin, heart-shaped w/ring handle & insert to press out water, 6¾ x 6¼" .... 145.00 to 185.00

Tole Document Box

Document box w/domed lid, tole, free-hand yellow-ochre brush strokes on lid & floral band on front & sides in shades of red, green & yellow-ochre w/black highlights, descended in the Upson family, Connecticut, ca. 1820, 9¼ x 5½", 6" h. (ILLUS.) 1,100.00

Dust pan, tin, Shaker style 35.00

Hanukkah light, tin, embossed w/Menorah & Hebrew inscription, 8 candle sockets, worn brown japanning, "Pat Aug 10, 1900," 10" l. 22.50

Lunch bucket, tin, 3-stack, dated 1884 .... 60.00

Mug, tin, stenciled "From Brother" .. 25.00

Mug, tole, free-hand colorful florals on dark ground, 4 3/8" h. (ILLUS. w/coffee pots) 950.00

Pitcher, water, tole, tapering cylinder w/flaring lip, braced strap handle, free-hand florals on light ground, 1920's 75.00

Syrup pitcher w/hinged lid, tole, straight-sided tapering cylinder, stenciled & pin-striped border on brown japanned finish, 4¾" h. ... 85.00

Tray, tole, commemorative of Oliver Hazard Perry's victory at Lake Erie, center w/oval painting of sea battle & oval portrait of Perry beneath, "I Have seen the Enemy and they are ours, Perry" & "Lake Erie," worn paint, 29½ x 23" (ILLUS.) 1,400.00

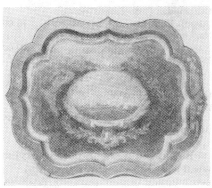

Lake Erie Sea Battle Tray

Umbrella stand, tole, red & gold repaint, 30" h. 65.00

Wash boiler w/cover, tin 85.00

(End of Metals Section)

MILITARY COLLECTIBLES

Civil War brass buttons, Naval officer's, from Commodore's uniform, back w/crown, London & initials, set of 6 .... $25.00

Civil War cap, Union officer's, blue Kepi-style 3" high crown w/gold twisted cord & gold wreath number 16 in center (moth hole in back) 225.00

Civil War fife, rosewood 90.00

Civil War map, showing the marches of General Sherman, ca. 1865, 47 x 30" 45.00

Civil War powder flask, copper, w/hands clasped below the American eagle w/flags & U.S. etc., embossed below, 8" l. 85.00

Civil War razor, ebony handle, incised "American Razor," Liberty cap, eagle & shield & "E Pluribus Unum" & "Geo. Wolstenholm & Sons" 55.00

Civil War scabbard, for Indian War trowel bayonet, "Pat. 1866 - U.S." 125.00

Civil War shaving mug, w/open side pocket, tin 57.00

Nazi dagger, Luftwaffe officer's, silver bullion strap & ball 220.00

Nazi helmet, fireman's, liner dated 1939 .... 75.00

Nazi helmet w/strap, metal, w/winged emblem on front & "Luftschutz," original liner, bluish black finish 85.00

Nazi medal, "Iron Cross" (no rib-
bon), 1939 . . . . 15.00
Nazi field radio, phone w/Zeppelin
terminal. 200.00
Nazi sword, Army officer's, lion's
head pommel, w/red stone
eyes 145.00
Nazi tunic, medical officer's 195.00
World War I belt & buckle,
German 18.00
World War I book, "U.S. Official Pic-
tures of the World War," em-
bossed cover, 1920 . . . . 30.00
World War I helmet, French, steel,
w/insignia 45.00
World War I helmet, U.S. Army,
doughboy-style, metal 18.50
World War I helmet, U.S. Medical
Corps 18.00
World War I holster, U.S. Army, pis-
tol size, leather 25.00
World War I trench flare pistol,
brass 100.00
World War I safari skirt, Army
Nurse Corps 35.00
World War I sword, German
officer's regimental, lion head
pommel 135.00
World War I camp telephone, U.S.
Army, 1917 . . . . 75.00
World War I uniform, U.S. Army
"doughboy" jacket, trousers, leg
wrappings & 3 different hats 70.00
World War II belt, U.S. Marine,
"Sam Browne" 40.00
World War II belt & buckle, German
police 35.00
World War II belt & buckle, Hitler
youth 25.00
World War II cartridge belt, British. . 15.00
World War II gas mask, German. . . . 25.00
World War II pilot's wings, sterling
silver 20.00
World War II field telephone,
German 110.00

Miscellaneous:
Binoculars, U.S. Navy, pre-World
War I, made in Germany 145.00
Ring, woman's, 10k gold, "Women's
Army Auxiliary Corps," ornate,
size 6 . . . . 60.00
Sword, U.S. Army, presentation
piece, engraved "1903, James H.
Rhodes & Co." 225.00
Sword, U.S. Naval officer's, ornate
30" etched blade, brass eagle
head pommel, brass & seed pearl
hilt, snakeskin scabbard w/brass
mounts, marked "W.H. Horst-
mann, Philadelphia" 300.00

MINIATURES (Paintings)

Miniature Portrait of Matilda Few

Bust portrait of a gentleman facing
right on ivory, long grey hair,
blue coat & yellow waistcoat, on
shaded blue field, gold locket
frame w/scalloped & bright-cut
border, reverse w/engraved
bright-cut border centering an engraved monogram, attributed to
William Verstille, ca. 1790,
1¾" oval $715.00
Bust portrait of blond boy w/blue
eyes on ivory, wearing coral bead
necklace over the lace collar of
his blue velvet jacket, signed
"Rinzi," 2½ x 3" oval 200.00
Bust portrait of Gouverneur Morris
facing right on ivory, w/wig &
black coat, shaded grey field,
signed "P.H." (Pierre Henri) 98",
2¾" oval 7,150.00
Bust portrait of Matilda Few (Mrs.
John C. Tillotson) facing left,
brown hair worn up with ringlets,
white dress w/shirred lace collar,
on olive green field, gold frame
w/inscription "Matilda Few, aged
21 years," in red leather case, by
Nathaniel Rogers, ca. 1820,
2 7/8" oval (ILLUS.) 3,080.00
Bust portrait of George Washington
facing right on ivory, in white powdered wig & black coat, shaded
brown field, signed "R.F. (Robert
Field) 1800," gold frame,
3" oval 2,860.00
Bust portrait of French officer on
ivory, crisp details & colors, early
19th century, artist-signed, original mahogany frame,
4½ x 5½" 65.00
Bust portrait of young man w/dark
hair on ivory, oval gilt frame, 6 x
5½" 155.00
Half-figure of a gentleman on ivory,
wearing blue coat, inscribed on
reverse w/name of subject, age &
date of death in Boston, in 18k

gold frame, American, early
19th c., 3" h. 418.00

Lovers scene on ivory, French
school, artist-signed, 3½" oval
within concaved black enamel
wood frame w/brass liner, overall
6 x 5¾" 195.00

Three-quarter portrait of a lady
w/curled black hair on ivory, a
band across her forehead, brown
eyes, wearing ring earrings, pearl
& ruby necklace & low-cut red
dress w/white lace trim against a
brown ground, Austrian School,
ca. 1840, neoclassical style gilt-
metal frame, 2¾" plus frame 192.00

MINIATURES (Replicas)

Miniature Pantry Box

Also see SALESMAN'S SAMPLES.

Blanket chest, Chippendale, carved
walnut, rectangular hinged molded top opening to well, case
w/molded base, bracket feet,
Pennsylvania, ca. 1760, 16" w.,
10½" deep, 12½" h. $990.00

Blanket chest, cherrywood, rectangular top lifting to well w/till,
turned feet, diamond inlaid es-
cutcheon, 24½" l. (one foot
replaced) 325.00

Box w/hinged domed lid, painted &
decorated pine, original polychrome painted scenes of houses
& trees around sides, wire staple
hinges, tin & wire hasp, 3½" l.... 250.00

Box, pantry, cov., circular w/fitted
lid, painted w/tole-like stylized
floral decor in the form of black
flowers & yellow leafage on bright
red ground, lid w/yellow crosshatching, Pennsylvania, ca. 1840,
3¼" d., 2¾" h. (ILLUS.) 3,850.00

Bucket, stave construction, wire bail

handle w/wooden grip, probably
Pease, 2" h. 40.00

Chest, Federal, inlaid mahogany,
rectangular top w/rope & line-
inlay centering an inlaid patera
opening to well w/tray over conforming case w/double-line & rope
inlay, on shaped skirt continuing
to bracket feet, Massachusetts,
ca. 1810, 10" w., 5" d., 5" h.
(interior tray of later date) 1,320.00

Chest of drawers, American Empire
country-style, pine, rectangular
top w/backboard above case
w/pr. set-back short drawers
above deep upper drawer & 3
slightly recessed long drawers
flanked by S-scroll pillars continuing to C-scroll feet, worn yellow
graining, 32 x 16", 34" h. 425.00

Chest of drawers, Classical, carved
mahogany & satinwood, rectangular top over 1 rounded projecting
long drawer flanked by
satinwood-veneered dies & 2
satinwood-veneered long drawers
centered by detached columns,
carved paw feet, American, ca.
1830, 12½" w., 7" deep, 11" h.... 990.00

Miniature Chest of Drawers

Chest of drawers, mahogany, rectangular top above four graduated
cockbeaded drawers w/turned
mushroom-shaped pulls, scalloped
skirt, bracket feet, early 19th c.,
14¾" w., 13¾" h., pr. (ILLUS. of
one)...........................1,870.00

Commode, Biedermeier, fruitwood,
rectangular ogee-molded well-fig-
ured top above conforming drawer &
2 recessed drawers, each mounted
w/lion's mask ring pulls, flanked
by ebonized disengaged columns,
on block feet, early 19th c.,
17¼ x 8½", 11½" h. 1,210.00

Compote, cut glass, relief diamond,

fans & bull's eyes, 16-point rayed
base, 3½" d., 2" h. 85.00

Firkin, cov., green w/yellow, yellow-green & black inner circles around outer edge, base w/carved initials "C. ?.," "Ann C. Wheeler" in yellow-ochre on lid, New England, 19th c., 2 1/8" d., 2½" h. (some paint wear to lid & minor damage to handle) .3,300.00

Mug, ironstone china, ornate handle, "gaudy," Oyster-type patt., 2" h. 45.00

Piano & matching chair, porcelain, pink & blue flowers in relief, crown within V mark, 3 x 5" 175.00

Pitcher, cobalt blue glass w/applied handle, blue, white & peach forget-me-nots w/overall lacy gold foliage decor, 1 7/8" d., 2½" h. 70.00

Pitcher, tankard, applied blue handle, cobalt blue glass overlay, w/enameled pink roses decor & gold bands, white lining, 1¼" d., 3¼" h. 65.00

Settee & chairs, porcelain, h.p. portrait on seat & back, brass backs, arms & legs, French, 2½" h., 3 pcs. 575.00

Stove, cast iron, "Crescent Stove," tin stove pipe 95.00

Tea kettle w/slightly domed cover, gooseneck spout, shaped flat handle, early 20th c., 3" h. 65.00

Trunk w/domed hinged lid fastened w/cotter pins, opening to deep well, top & sides painted w/compass drawn pinwheels in dark green against reddish brown ground, borders outlined w/dots, probably Southeastern Pennsylvania, 19th c., 19¾ x 11", 10" h. . . .   605.00

Vase, cut glass, bulbous base w/horizontal step-cutting alternating w/thumbprint, long narrow fluted diamond point neck, serrated & scalloped trim, 1" d., 3¾" h. 45.00

Vase, cut glass, thumbprint & line cutting at base, diamond-cut neck, fluted top & rim, 1¾" base d., 3¾" h. 75.00

Vases, ruby glass, enameled gold florals & scrolling within gold panels decor, 1½" d., 2 5/8" h., pr. 50.00

Wash set: bowl, pitcher, cov. toothbrush box, cov. soap dish & cov. potty; china, pink lustre w/gold trim, 5 pcs. 150.00

MOTHER-OF-PEARL FLATWARE

Serving Spoon

Mother-of-pearl refers to the lustrous pearly internal layer of certain mollusk shells. It was applied as a decoration to papier mache objects, fans, card cases and a variety of items or made into buttons and jewelry. Considered exceptionally fashionable throughout the 19th century, it was also used to form the handles of table silverware. While a variety of flatware pieces are available, fruit knives appear to be the most common form. Sometimes the ferrules, or metal rings used for securing the joint, are of sterling quality.

Bread fork . . . .$6.00 to   9.50
Bread knife, serrated blade 18.50
Butter serving knife, sterling silver ferrule, engraved blade, Landers, Frary & Clark 60.00
Butter spreader . . . . .6.00 to 15.00
Cake server, sterling silver ferrule 24.00
Dessert service: 6 each knives & forks; sterling silver ferrules w/ornate engraved scrollwork, 12 pcs. in original leatherette case . .   165.00
Dinner knife, carved handle, silverplate ferrule & blade, 10" l. 10.00
Dinner knives, sterling silver blades, Duhme & Co., Cincinnati, Ohio, 1839-87, set of 6 . . . .   140.00
Dinner knives, sterling silver ferrules, set of 6 . . . . .50.00 to 75.00
Dinner knives, ornate sterling silver ferrules, set of 12 . . . .   185.00
Fish set: serving spatula & 12 each forks, knives & butter spreaders; ornate sterling silver ferrules, 37 pcs. 148.00
Fruit knives, sterling silver ferrules, silverplate blades, "Keen Kutter," set of 4 . . . .   40.00
Fruit knives, "Sheffield," 6" l., set of 6 in original box 40.00
Fruit knives, sterling silver ferrules, set of 6 . . . .   55.00
Luncheon knives, sterling silver ferrules, set of 6 . . . .   45.00
Marmalade spoon 6.00
Nut picks, ornate sterling silver ferrules, set of 6 . . . .   95.00
Nut picks, embossed silverplate ferrules, set of 8 . . . .   38.00
Pickle fork 6.00

Salad serving fork, embossed sterling silver ferrule 25.00
Serving spoon, mother-of-pearl
bowl, metal handle, 9" l.
(ILLUS.)........................ 42.00

MUCHA (Alphonse) ARTWORK

Alphonse Mucha Advertising Poster

A leader in the Art Nouveau movement, Alphonse Maria Mucha was born in Moravia (now part of Czechoslovakia) in 1860. Displaying considerable artistic talent as a child, he began formal studies locally, later continuing his work in Munich and then Paris, where it became necessary for him to undertake commercial artwork. In 1894, the renowned actress Sarah Bernhardt commissioned Mucha to create a poster for her play "Gismonda" and this opportunity proved to be the turning point in his career. While continuing his association with Bernhardt, he began creating numerous advertising posters, packaging designs, book and magazine illustrations and "panneaux decoratifs" (decorative pictures).

Calendar, 1897, printed in colors on
4 separate sheets, "Chocolat Mas-
son/Chocolat Mexicain," framed,
12 3/8 x 5½" $1,210.00
Poster, "Gismonda, Bernhardt, American Tour," 1895, framed, 29½ x
77½" 4,180.00
Poster, "Job," cigarette paper advertisement, 1890, printed by F. Champenois, Paris, framed, 19 5/8 x
14¾" (ILLUS.) 2,750.00
Poster, "Job," cigarette paper advertisement, printed by F. Champenois, Paris, framed, 20¼ x
15 3/8" (horizontal creasing).....7,700.00
Poster, "Job," cigarette paper adver-

tisement, 1898, printed by F. Champenois, Paris, 58 3/8 x 38 5/8",
framed 8,800.00
Poster, "La Danse," 22¼ x 13¾"...2,200.00
Poster, "Lily," 1897, framed,
40¼ x 16 3/8" 1,600.00

Monaco Monte Carlo Poster

Poster, "Monaco Monte Carlo," 1897,
printed by F. Champenois, Paris,
framed, 41¼ x 27¾" (ILLUS.) 5,500.00
Print, "Flirt Biscuits," lithograph
printed in colors, 1899, framed,
23 x 10" 1,650.00
Print, "Salome," 1897, 16 x 12½" ... 605.00
Print, "Tete Byzantine-Blonde," lithograph in colors on paper, 13½ x
11 1/8", framed 1,760.00
Print, "Tete Byzantine-Brunette,"
lithograph in colors on paper,
13½ x 11 1/8", framed.........1,760.00

MUSIC BOXES

Baker-Troll & Co. (Swiss) cylinder
music box, 6-tune, double spring,
split comb, inlaid bird's eye maple
& ebonized wood case, 13" l. cylinder, 25 x 9½" case, 8" h......$1,430.00
Bremond (Swiss) cylinder music box,
4-tune, single comb, inlaid mahogany case, 8" l. cylinder 440.00
Bremond (Swiss) cylinder music box,
10-tune, rosewood veneer case
w/central medallion of musical &
floral motifs, ca. 1870, 13" cylinder, 22" w. (restored) 990.00
Conchon, F. (Swiss) cylinder music
box on stand, double spring drive,
rosewood veneer & ebonized wood,
on matching stand w/storage

Conchon Music Box on Stand

drawer, w/six 5-tune cylinders,
late 19th c., 39 x 20", 38" h.
(ILLUS.) 4,070.00

Gautschi Cylinder Music Box

Gautschi (Henry) and Sons (Philadelphia, Pennsylvania) cylinder
music box, 12-tune, w/drum &
bells, castanets struck by enameled bees, inlaid burl wood &
mother-of-pearl case on molded
ebonized base, brass side handles,
ca. 1860, 21½" l. cylinder, 36 x
14" case, 13½" h. (ILLUS.) 5,610.00
Junod (Swiss) "Sublime Harmonie"
cylinder music box, 10-tune, walnut
case w/fruitwood banding & central inlaid musical motif, late
19th c., 11" l. cylinder, 20" w.
(needs redampering) 1,320.00
Komet (Weissbach & Co., Leipzig,
Germany) disc music box, w/six-
teen 20¾" discs 3,750.00
Mermod Freres (Swiss) cylinder
music box, interchangeable cylinders, w/three 11" l. cylinders . . 2,800.00
Nicole Freres (Swiss) "Mandoline
Expressive" cylinder music box,

6-tune, burr walnut & rosewood
case w/fruitwood banding & central floral motif, late 19th c., 11" l.
cylinder, 21½" w. 1,760.00
Perfection (Perfection Music Box Co.,
Jersey City, New Jersey) disc
music box, oak case, 14" disc 2,200.00
Polyphon (Polyphon Musikwerke,
Leipzig, Germany) upright disc
music box, carved oak cabinet enclosed by 2 pair of doors applied
w/hanging game & fruiting vines,
carved paw feet, w/thirty 15½"
discs, 4' 9½" h. 1,650.00
Polyphon disc music box, Style 45,
double comb, 15½" disc 3,000.00
Regina (American subsidiary of Polyphon Musikwerks, Rahway, New
Jersey) disc music box, Style 10,
double comb (restored) 2,200.00
Regina "Sublima" disc music box,
Style 25, double comb, glazed
mahogany case w/storage cabinet
below, ca. 1900, w/eleven 20"
discs, 5' 10" h. 6,600.00

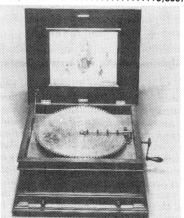

Regina Disc Music Box

Regina disc music box, table model,
single comb, start/stop switch,
crank-wound, mahogany case, ca.
1895, w/fifty-four 15" discs, 21" w.
(ILLUS.) 1,980.00
Regina disc music box w/automatic
changer, bow front mahogany
case, 15½" disc 9,000.00
Swiss interchangeable cylinder music
box, 8-tune, tune sheet to reverse
of lid, walnut case, front & lid
inlaid w/musical trophies within
banded borders, on ebonized stepped base fitted w/a drawer, late
19th c., w/four 13" l. cylinders,
34¼" l. 4,125.00

MUSICAL INSTRUMENTS

Packard Eastlake-style Organ

Autoharp, "Schmidt," 15-chord..... $100.00
Autoharp, "Zimmerman," 1890's 55.00
Banjo, bird's eye maple, 1928 ...... 48.00
Banjo-mandolin, "Orpheum"........ 140.00
Bassoon, "Cabart Paris"............ 850.00
Clarinet, boxwood w/ivory
   mounts........................ 125.00
Cornet, "Boosey & Hawkes," silver-
   plate (no case)................. 65.00
Fife, rosewood w/brass fittings,
   1850-70, 15" l. 85.00
Flute, "Gemeinhardt," student
   model, w/case.................. 150.00
French horn, brass, w/case 65.00
French horn, "Reynolds," piston
   valves, w/case & attachments 250.00
Guitar, "Gibson," flat-top, mahog-
   any w/tortoise shell line inlay &
   guard plate.................... 265.00
Guitar, "Martin D-35"............. 750.00
Harmonica, "Hohner - Chromonica
   III," inlaid wood, w/velvet-lined
   wooden case 30.00
Harmonica, "Hohner - Chromonica
   64," 4-octave, professional model,
   7" l. 35.00
Harmonica, "M. Hohner - Tucka-
   way," late 1920's, w/box 15.00
Mandolin, "M.E. Schoening" 75.00
Mandolin, "Dixon 'Tater Bug,"
   mother-of-pearl inlay 97.50
Melodeon, "Geo. A. Prince Co.,"
   rosewood case, 1848........... 1,750.00
Organ, "Estey," 1 manual, 13 stops,
   walnut case w/candle shelves,
   w/stool (restored) 1,200.00
Organ, "Melodigrand," curved sides
   (restored) 7,500.00

Organ, "Packard," walnut, ornate
   Eastlake-style case w/mirror
   above music rack, carpeted pe-
   dals, late 19th c., 52" w., 78" h.
   (ILLUS.)........................ 500.00
Piano, grand, "Hallet, Davis & Co.,"
   Boston, carved rosewood case,
   6' 7" l., w/matching chair,
   2 pcs. 5,000.00
Piano, grand, "Steinway & Sons,"
   lifting top painted w/18th century
   style landscape scene w/figures in
   subtle greenish brown tones, sides
   of similar style painted w/putti
   interlaced w/swags on a creme
   ground, raised on bulbous turned
   gilt & painted legs, ca. 1910, 8' l.,
   w/piano stool, 2 pcs. 11,000.00
Piano, square grand, "Charles Steiff
   No. 2395, Baltimore, Maryland,"
   rosewood, 1870-73, 82 x 42",
   39" h. 3,200.00

Carved Mahogany Pianoforte

Pianoforte, "James L. Hewitt & Co.,
   Boston," mahogany, line-inlaid oblong top w/hinged front opening to
   keyboard & gilt-stenciled name-
   board above apron w/two short drawers, on baluster- and ring-turned reeded &
   acanthus-carved legs on casters,
   67 x 26," 35" h. (ILLUS.) 1,650.00
Piccolo, ebonized wood, nickel-
   plated brass fittings, w/music
   book & instructions dated 1898 ... 50.00
Player piano, "Brenkerhoff," tiger
   oak 1,800.00
Player piano, upright, "Everette
   Orchestron," 1905 .... 5,000.00
Ukulele, "C.F. Martin Co.,"
   Nazareth, Pennsylvania 110.00
Violin, Alois Jais, Mittenwald, flame
   maple back & "mirror" spruce top,
   sharp line edge decor, original yellow to light brown varnished finish,
   signed "Jais 1867" on interior
   block 3,250.00
Violin, maple, hand-made, dated
   1860 .... 140.00
Zither, "Columbia No. 2," gilt trim,
   marked octaves 42.00

MUSICAL INSTRUMENTS, MECHANICAL

Nelson Wiggen Orchestrian

Accordion, "Accordeo Jazz," w/several "Accordion Boy" rolls $4,900.00

Band organ, "Wilhelm Bruder," plays 66 key Artizan rolls on duplex roll frame, facade repainted & gold leafed, w/customer trailer & mechanical bandmaster (unrestored) 18,500.00

Band organ, "DeCap," w/two large accordions & 6 percussion instruments 9,500.00

Band organ, "Gavioli," converted at Wurlitzer factory to play 165 Duplex rolls, deeply carved cabinet facade (restored) 19,000.00

Band organ, "North Tonawanda Style 158," w/drums, violins, trombones & trumpets, ornate painted cabinet 28,000.00

Calliope, "Tangley CA-43" (rebuilt) 9,800.00

Coin-operated piano, "Link Style 2-E," w/mandolin & xylophone attachments, 1920's 8,900.00

Coin-operated piano, "Peerless Style D," converted to play "A" rolls, colorful art glass panel (restored) 7,800.00

Orchestrion, "Hupfeld Helios Ic/31," overstrung piano w/mandolin effect & numerous other musical instrument attachments & effects, ornate inlaid wooden wall-sized cabinet w/three leaded glass panels 147,500.00

Orchestrion, "Nelson-Wiggen Style 5-X," oak cabinet, restored w/refinished cabinet (ILLUS.) . . . 18,000.00

Orchestrion, "Seeburg KT Special," tall wooden cabinet w/ornate leaded glass panel, ca. 1924 (restored) 19,500.00

Orchestrion, "Seeburg Style L," hardwood cabinet w/art glass front, w/three 10-tune type G or 4X rolls (restored) 39,750.00

Organ, "Orchestrelle Aeolian," Circassian walnut case, w/110 rolls, 66" l., 65" h. 4,800.00

Organ, "Orchestrelle Aeolian Style F," mahogany case, uses 116 note solo rolls or 58 note rolls (restored) 19,500.00

Reproducing piano, grand, "Chickering Ampico A," mahogany standard case, ca. 1918, restored w/refinished case 9,000.00

Reproducing piano, upright, "Seeburg X Expression," oak case, w/fifty rolls, restored w/refinished case 3,995.00

Reproducing piano, keyboardless, "Red Welte Mignon," oak case (unrestored) 4,500.00

Reproducing piano, grand, "Wurlitzer Apollo," w/over sixty rolls, 1927, 4' 10" l. 3,500.00

Mills "Violano Virtuoso"

Violano (violin player), "Mills Virtuoso," single violin w/piano & violin movements, unrefinished stained wood cabinet, ca. 1912, 43" l., 30" deep, 43" h. (ILLUS.) . . 7,425.00

NAPKIN RINGS

Baying Wolf Napkin Ring

Bird atop ring on footed
base . . . .$75.00 to 125.00
Birds (2) beside ring on floral cluster
base 135.00
Boy napping in front of ring,
Pairpoint 165.00
Boy on a dolphin supporting ring on
tail, flat oblong base, Meriden . . . 155.00
Branch w/pear & leaf against ring
on leaf base 65.00
Butterfly beside fan-engraved ring
on square base w/four ball feet,
Meriden . . . . .85.00 to 110.00
Cat seated beside ring, Babcock &
Co. 150.00
Cherub leading swan on ribbon-like
leash atop ring 250.00
Children (2) wearing pixie-type hats
seated & holding ring, Reed &
Barton 200.00
Dolphins (2) supporting ring
between tails 255.00
Eagle holding embossed ring be-
tween raised wings, knife rest on
base, Meriden 85.00
Goose standing beside ring 85.00
Greenaway boy on bench w/drum
forming ring 240.00
Greenaway girl pushing ring,
Barbour Bros. . . . . .150.00 to 175.00
Greenaway girls (2) climbing lad-
ders over ring . . . . .355.00 to 415.00
Hen standing beside ring . .150.00 to 195.00
Horse prancing & pulling engraved
ring on wheels, Meriden 125.00
Horse standing beside ring engraved
w/horse head, Pairpoint 200.00
Lion crouching w/ring on back, ob-
long base, dated 1887 . . . . 125.00
Little Red Riding Hood w/basket
beside ring 255.00
Monkey dressed as a man lolling on
grassy base before ring 265.00
Squirrel seated beside ring w/bird
atop on tree trunk base 225.00
Stag supporting ring on back,
Rogers Bros. 200.00

Victorian-style side chair w/ring on
seat 90.00
Wolf baying beside ring on footed
scrolled base, Barbour
(ILLUS.) . . . . .195.00 to 245.00

NAUTICAL GEAR

Brass Ship's Lantern

*The romantic lure of the sea, and of ships
in general, has opened up a new area of collector interest. Nautical gear, especially items
made of brass or with brass trim, is sought
out for its decorative appeal. Virtually all
items that can be associated with ships, along
with items used or made by sailors, are now
considered collectible for technological ad-
vances have rendered them obsolete. Listed
below are but a few of the numerous nautical items sold in recent months.*

Anchor light, "Perko," 24" h. $85.00
Bo's'n's whistle, silver, w/macrame
lanyard 36.00
Compensating binnacle compass,
brass, 7½" compass card contained within drum case w/gimble
mounts inscribed "Kelvin &
Wilfred O White Co., Los Angeles,
Boston, New York and Baltimore,"
within brass binnacle lid w/glass
window flanked by cast iron compensating spheres, tapering cylindrical case mounted w/inscribed
plaque, on spreading circular
base, E.S. Ritchie & Sons, Inc.,
Brookline, Mass., 52" h. 495.00
Float balls, green glass, within a
knotted rope frame w/attachment
loop, Japanese, 1st half 20th c.,
15" d., pr. 110.00

Harpoon, wrought iron, ca. 1850,
5" w. 25.00

Mast top, carved & decorated wood-
en crown, 13½" h. 2,100.00

Sailor's songbook, "Ships & Sailors,"
Zogbaum & Barnes, w/text & music, color & black & white illustrations, 15 x 11½", 124 pp. 45.00

Sailor's valentine, double hinged
octagon filled w/tiny shells in various colors arranged around central
heart & oval reserve "With Love,"
8 3/8" w. .1,300.00

Seaman's chest, walnut, dovetail
construction, brass strap hinges,
corner braces & end handles,
worn finish, 40½" l. 145.00

Ship's fog horn, brass, 4-hole flange
for mounting, 24½" h. 125.00

Ship's lantern, brass, pierced domed
chimney w/swing handle above
circular glass globe enclosing oil
lamp, lever stamped "P & A Mfg.
Co. Waterbury, Conn.," pierced
circular base w/tag inscribed
"Perkins Marine Lamp and Hard-
ware Corp.," 18" h. (ILLUS.) 522.50

Ship's log, whaling vessel "Canton,"
daily entries for voyage from New
Bedford, Massachusetts to Pacific
coast, July 1851 to March 25, 1853,
then becoming a day book,
w/whaling stamps, rebound 1,430.00

Ship's telegraph, brass, two 10" d.
dials & telegraph handles, mounted in a drum case on spreading
cylindrical base, Brelco, 55 Van-
dam St., New York, New York,
43¾" h. 330.00

Ship's wheel, mahogany & brass,
circular w/block- and baluster-
turned spokes & wood & iron pul-
ley, Brown Brothers & Co., Rose-
bank Ironworks, Edinburgh,
36" d. 265.00

Regimental Stein

Stein, regimental, pottery, "S.M.S.
Preussen, 1910-12," sailor w/stein
in hand seated astride keg
w/scene on front & back, 1 liter
(ILLUS.) 4,180.00

Telescope, leather & brass, 3-draw,
extends to 22½", pigskin case . . . 115.00

Telescope, mahogany & brass, 4-
draw, extends to 36" 235.00

NEEDLEWORK PICTURES

Needlework Picture

*Berlin wool work is embroidery with wool
on a canvas pattern, sometimes erroneously
referred to as tapestry, which was a popular
pastime of ladies of the 19th century. Wool
embroidery with glass beads worked in the
design became fashionable about 1850 and
this type is known as "German Embroidery."
Stool and book covers, panels for fire screens
and pictures are among the items available
to collectors today.*

Needlework embroidered on silk,
roses, bleeding hearts, pansy &
tiny blue star flowers, ca. 1860,
original walnut w/gold oval
frame, 11 x 9" $125.00

Needlework embroidered on linen,
depicting a 3-story white house
w/yellow roof, widow's walk &
black window, casement stitches
in yellow silk, w/enclosed rose
garden, pasture w/grazing cows
at left, trees at right, gentle-
men & ladies walking along a path
leading to a town w/steepled
church, white horse below & a

pond w/swan & flock of sheep,
one black sheep grazing in the
foreground, in green, blue,
white, pink, yellow & brown,
probably Newburyport, Massachusetts, late 18th-early 19th c.,
original frame, 17½ x 16¼"...101,750.00
Needlework embroidered on silk,
mourning picture depicting tomb
w/"V.A.O.D.," weeping woman &
child, matted & framed,
21½ x 19½"..................... 100.00
Needlework embroidered on silk,
Moses in the bullrushes, oval
eglomise matte & gilded frame,
23 x 18¾"..................... 185.00
Needlework embroidered & painted
on silk, depicting Liberty in the
form of a female w/painted body
& embroidered silk clothing, offering the contents of a beaker to an
embroidered eagle, w/Liberty cap
& American flag in background,
1790-1815, 23½ x 14"........... 330.00
Needlework embroidered on silk,
apple tree bearing apples
w/name & birth date of each
child, enclosed by floral vine
rising up from 2 urn-topped monuments, made by Lydia Adams Russell in 1809, recording her marriage to Edward Russell, birth
dates of their children & his death
date, worked in a variety of
stitches in silk yarn, 26¾ x 21¾"
(ILLUS.)....................5,500.00
Needlework embroidered on silk,
depicting 3 quail in a field, Japan,
narrow giltwood frame, 28½ x
22½"........................ 150.00
Needlework embroidered on silk,
maidens pleading w/Roman soldiers in a landscape, polychrome
silk & chenille thread, 19th c.,
framed, 31 x 24½"............. 605.00
Needlework embroidered on silk,
mourning picture depicting figure
at tomb inscribed "Sacred to the
Memory of Nelson"............. 308.00

OCCUPIED JAPAN

*American troops occupied the country of
Japan from September 2, 1945 until April 28,
1952, following World War II. All wares made
for export during this period were required
to be marked "Made in Occupied Japan."
Now these items, mostly small ceramic and
metal trifles of varying quality, are sought
out by a growing number of collectors.*

Crumber Set

Bowl w/underplate, lacquerware,
5" d........................... $15.00
Butter dish, china, model of
cottage....................... 39.00
Candy dish, metal frame & cover
w/cobalt blue glass insert, 6" d... 40.00
Character mug, china, General
MacArthur bust 75.00
Cigarette lighter, chrome w/mother-
of-pearl inserts on handle, model
of a gun...................... 18.00
Creamer & cov. sugar bowl, bees &
green leaves decor on beige
ground, large bee finial on lid.... 27.00
Crumber set, silver & gold finish pot
metal, scene of Statue of Liberty
& other New York City attractions,
6½ x 6½" tray & 7½" l. scraper
(ILLUS.)...................... 20.00
Figure of a lady w/tambourine, china, Delft blue garments, 5" h..... 22.50
Figure of a black shoe shine boy,
china, 6" h................... 45.00

Occupied Japan Bisque Figure

Figure of a boy beside rowboat,
bisque, pastel shades, Andrea "S"
mark, 10" l., 8½" h. (ILLUS.) 55.00
Figure group, Victorian lady & gen-

tleman on sleigh w/dog at side,
6" l., 5½" h................... 75.00

Lamps, china, figural Victorian lady
& gentleman, 6" h., pr.......... 90.00

Lemon dish, china, handled, h.p.
poppies decor, gold trim,
5¾" d....................... 10.00

Model of a cat w/kittens in shoe,
china, blue 8.00

Mug, china, barrel-shaped, grapes
decor on brown ground......... 10.00

Plaque, wall-type, bisque, Colonial
lady on swing, 7½ x 4½"....... 28.00

Plate, china, h.p. cottage landscape
scene, 9¼" d. 22.00

Salt & pepper shakers, model of
windmills, Delft blue, pr. 17.50

Toy, windup celluloid circus
elephant 65.00

Toy, windup celluloid monkey seated on tree stump & playing guitar,
head moves & hand strums,
wooden base, 7½" h. 65.00

Toy, windup tin boy on sled, celluloid head, original box........ 48.00

Toy, windup tin reindeer pulling
sleigh w/Santa, celluloid heads,
original box.................. 42.50

Wall pocket, china, Colonial lady in
balcony, 4 x 2¾"............. 15.00

Wall pocket, model of an owl,
6 x 6"...................... 10.00

Whimsey, china, lady's slipper, blue
floral decor.................. 10.00

PAPER COLLECTIBLES

Rockwell Magazine Advertisement

Also see ADVERTISING CARDS, ALMANACS, AUDUBON PRINTS, AUTOGRAPHS, AUTOMOBILE LITERATURE, BIG LITTLE BOOKS, CHILDREN'S BOOKS, COMIC BOOKS, COOKBOOKS, CURRIER & IVES PRINTS, FISHER GIRLS, FRACTURS, GIBSON ARTWORK, GUTMANN ARTWORK, HOMER ENGRAVINGS, ICART PRINTS, KELLOGG PRINTS, MAGAZINES, MUCHA ARTWORK, PAPER DOLLS, PARRISH ARTWORK, POSTCARDS, POSTERS, PRANG CHROMOLITHOGRAPHS, SCRAPBOOKS & ALBUMS, SHEET MUSIC and SILHOUETTES.

Bonds, "Western Maryland R.R.," engraved train scenes, $100, $500 &
$1000 denominations, 1858, set of
3 .... $60.00

Booklet, souvenir, "Madame Tus-
saud's Exhibition," ca. 1900 ...... 35.00

Booklet, souvenir, "Tournament of
Roses Parade," 1939, Shirley Temple as Grand Marshall.......... 25.00

Calendar, 1946, "Vargas Girl"
sketches 35.00

Calendar, 1947, "Petty Girl"
sketches, in original envelope 35.00

Calligraphic specimen, pen & ink
drawing of a black horse w/blue
polka dots & blue & red harness,
inscribed "Henry Adinger's horse,
made by Henry Hachenberger,
teacher, Feb. 22, 1829," red beveled frame w/green & white striping, 12½ x 10½"..............1,625.00

Calligraphic specimen, pen & ink
drawing of a bird, inscribed "Won
in Spelling by Irene Stauffer, Dec.
24, 1909," framed, 15 x 12¼" 50.00

Calligraphic specimen, pen & ink
drawing of a leaping deer, signed
in Spencerian script, framed, 29 x
23" 150.00

Circus broadside, "The Show of a
Century," "A.G. Kelly & Miller
Bros. 2nd Largest Wild Animal Circus," printed both sides,
30 x 11".................... 12.50

Circus magazine, "Ringling Bros.,
Barnum & Bailey," 1943 .... 20.00

Guide book, "New York Zoological
Park," 1939 .... 7.00

Magazine advertisement, "Lister-
ine," black & white illustration by
Norman Rockwell, from The Farm
Journal, December, 1929
(ILLUS.)..................... 10.00

Newspaper, "New York Times,"
1864, Abraham Lincoln inauguration front page................ 35.00

Newspaper, "Pittsburg Leader,"

1912, April 19, Titantic disaster,
complete paper 60.00
Newspaper, "Washington Daily
Morning Chronicle," 1865, April
15, Lincoln assassination story 65.00
Program, "Army-Navy Football
Game," 1938, Howard Chandler
Christy cover 10.00
Program, "Gone With The Wind,"
1939, w/color photographs 35.00
Program, "Hunchback of Notre
Dame," 1923, starring Lon
Chaney 50.00
Program, "Sonja Henie Hollywood
Ice Revue," 1949 .... 25.00
Program, "USC-UCLA Football
Game," 1946.................... 9.50
Ration book, World War II, w/folder
for book & tokens 10.00
View book, "King's Photographic
Views of N.Y." 45.00

PAPER DOLLS

Lion Coffee Paper Doll

Advertising, "Barbour's Flax
Threads," Dolls on Parade series,
w/outfit, 5½" h. $10.00
Advertising, "J.P. Coats," reversible,
5½" 10.00
Advertising, "Colgate Palmolive
Peet," Dionne Quintuplets "All
Aboard for Shut-Eye-Town,"
AP65E, 1937 ....75.00 to 100.00
Advertising, "Enterprise Coffee,"
Mother Goose 10.00
Advertising, "Hood's Sarsaparilla,"
w/sailor suit.................. 5.00
Advertising, "Lion Coffee," Aladdin
(ILLUS.)...................... 35.00

Advertising, "McLaughlin's Coffee,"
set of 8 including baseball player,
11 pieces of clothing & 4 animals,
pre-1900, 23 pcs. 85.00
Annette Funicello, uncut book, Whit-
man No. 1953, 1964 .... 20.00
Ann Sothern, uncut book, Saalfield
No. 2438, 1943 .... 45.00
"Barbie's Boutique," uncut book,
Whitman No. 1954, 1973 .... 20.00
Bette Davis, uncut book, Merrill
No. 4816, 1942 .... 58.00
Betty Bonnet's Christmas Party, un-
cut magazine sheet, Ladies' Home
Journal, 1916, December, Santa &
children wearing costumes, oak
frame 80.00
Betty Grable, uncut book, Merrill
No. 1558, 1951 .... 95.00
"Brady Bunch," uncut book, Whit-
man No. 4787, 1972 .... 20.00
Brenda Lee, uncut book, Lowe
No. 2785, 1961 .... 13.50
Charlie McCarthy, uncut book, Whit-
man No. 995, 1938 .... 35.00
Coronation (Queen Elizabeth), uncut
book, Saalfield No. 4312, 1953.... 25.00
Dennis the Menace, uncut book,
Whitman No. 1991, 1960 .... 10.00
Edd (Kookie) Byrnes, uncut book,
Whitman No. 2085, 1959 .... 25.00
Elizabeth Taylor, uncut book, Whit-
man No. 1951, 1955 .... 45.00
Esther Williams, uncut book, Merrill
No. 2553, 1953 .... 65.00
Gloria Jean, uncut book, Saalfield
No. 1664, 1941 .... 38.00
"Gone With the Wind," uncut book,
18 dolls, 106 outfits, Merrill
No. 3404, 1939 .... 150.00
Grace Kelly, uncut book, Whitman
No. 2609, 1956 .... 70.00
"Green Acres," Eva Gabor & Eddie
Albert w/plastic stands, uncut,
Whitman No. 4773, 1968, original
box 22.00
Hayley Mills in "The Moon Spin-
ners," uncut book, Whitman
No. 1960, 1964 .... 35.00
"I Love Lucy," Lucille Ball & Desi
Arnaz, uncut book, Whitman
No. 2101, 1953 .... 18.00
Jane Russell, uncut book, Saalfield
No. 2651, 1955 .... 36.00
Jane Withers, uncut book, Whitman
No. 989, 1940 .... 150.00
Judy Garland, uncut book, Whitman
No. 996, 1945 .... 225.00
"Julia," w/Diahann Carroll & cast
members, 4 stand-up figures, un-
cut book, Saalfield No. 6055,
1968 .... 12.00
Marilyn Monroe, uncut book, Saal-
field No. 4308, 1953 .... 125.00

Mary Martin, uncut book, Saalfield
No. 1539, 1942 .... 25.00
Patty Duke, uncut book, Whitman
No. 1991, 1965 .... 25.00
Rhonda Fleming, uncut book, Saalfield No. 5191, 1954 .... 30.00
Shirley Temple, uncut book, Saalfield No. 2112, 1934 .... 50.00
Tuck (Raphael), Bridal Party series,
"The Bridesmaid," No. 603A, ca.
1895 .... 85.00
White House (Pat & Tricia Nixon),
uncut book, Artcraft No. 4475,
1969 .... 17.00

PAPERWEIGHTS

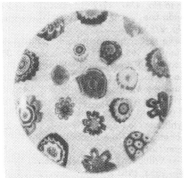

Clichy Chequer Paperweight

Baccarat, carpet ground weight, clear
w/brightly-colored assorted millefiori canes including silhouettes of
a stag, goat, dog, cockerel & a
butterfly, dated 1848, 3" d. $5,665.00
Baccarat, sulphide of John F. Kennedy, star-cut green ground 250.00
Baccarat, sulphide of LaFayette,
rose sand ground 250.00
Baccarat, sulphide of Thomas Paine,
green overlay.................. 125.00
Baccarat, sulphide of Pope Pius, red
ground, star-cut base 75.00
Baccarat, sulphide of Eleanor
Roosevelt, star-cut amethyst
base 85.00
Banford, bumble bee hovering over
blue & white flower w/bud
against green foliage, faceted,
2¼" d........................ 600.00
Clichy, chequer weight, clear glass
w/two circles of large brightly
colored assorted canes about a
central large pink & green rose,
divided by short lengths of white
latticinio, set on bed of horizontal
cable, 3 1/8" d. (ILLUS.).......... 950.00

Clichy, concentric millefiori weight,
ring of purple & white pastrymold
panes spaced by 5 lime green &
pink roses about a circle of lime
green & white canes enclosing a
cobalt blue, yellow & white central cane, set on an upset muslin
ground above a bed of horizontal
latticinio tubing, 2¼" d..........1,430.00
Clichy, spaced millefiori, 21 canes
including 2 roses 625.00
Lundberg Studio, iridescent blue &
yellow, 1974 .... 57.50
Millville, "Water Lily" weight on pedestal base, spherical, large flower
composed of 16 tuberous petals
about a yellow stamen center, surrounded by 4 opaque white &
green stiff upright leaves, on
spreading circular foot, 3" base d.,
4" h. 1,045.00
Perthshire, 1975 Christmas Rose
w/detailed petals & bud, No. 39
of 350........................ 190.00
St. Clair, lavender lilies in clear 125.00
St. Clair, sulphide of Lincoln, cobalt
blue & clear 75.00
St. Louis, "Pansy" weight, 2 large
deep purple petals above 3
smaller white petals w/purple
markings, growing from conjoined
green stalks w/two green leaves
& a deep purple bud, 2½" d...... 880.00
St. Louis overlay weight, encased
red & white overlay cut w/top & 6
circular side printies revealing a
concentric millefiori mushroom
weight, tuft composed of 7 rows
of assorted canes in shades of
salmon pink, cobalt blue, red,
lime green, white & ochre around
a central cane, dated 1953,
2½" d. 192.50
St. Louis, faceted garlanded sulphide weight, clear w/head &
shoulders of Louis Napoleon
Bonaparte w/a garland of alternating shaded ochre, blue & white
millefiori canes, cut w/top & 6
side windows, 3 1/8" d. 385.00
Snow-type weight, Snow Baby 75.00
Snow-type weight, telephone 45.00
Souvenir-type, photograph under
glass, Expo Building at fairgrounds, Springfield, Ill. 18.00
Val St. Lambert, sulphide of Dwight
Eisenhower, frosted, 4" w. 75.00
Whitefriars, 5 faceted windows
w/cutting between, mushroom
shape in green, white, red & 1
large cane center, 1972 .... 200.00

PAPIER MACHE

Various objects including decorative adjuncts were made of papier mache, which is a substance made of pulped paper mixed with glue and other materials or layers of paper glued and pressed and then molded.

Bust of Santa Claus, labeled
"Manufactured by M.H. Riddell,
Milwaukee, U.S.A.," 12¾" h. (old
worn paint & minor damage at
back) $255.00
Candy container, model of a comical
bull in seated position, w/spring
horns, paper candy cup at bottom,
Germany, 5" h. 75.00
Candy container, model of a turkey,
5" h. 80.00
Candy container, figure of Santa
Claus in white coat, w/red trim,
1930's, 10" h. 48.00
Candy container, model of a snowman, 10" h....................... 32.00
Candy container, model of a rabbit
w/felt ears & glass eyes, Ger-
many, 14" h....................... 135.00
Candy container, figure of an
English bobby (policeman),
15" h. 110.00
Candy container, model of chick on
egg, Germany 45.00
Figure of Santa Claus in red coat
w/white trim, ca. 1890, 3½" h.... 78.00
Figure of Father Christmas wearing
long red coat & blue pants, Germany, early 1900's, 5½" h........ 115.00
Figure of Father Christmas wearing
long golden yellow coat, 8½" h... 260.00
Milliner's model, flesh-colored face
w/painted features, curly dark
hair, 15" h. 250.00
Model of a rabbit w/revolving head
& glass eyes, carrying a carrot under each arm, dated 1909,
6½" h.......................... 115.00
Nodding figure candy container,
Santa Claus w/suit trimmed in
mica glitter, Germany, 10" h. 100.00
Nodding figures, Japanese boy &
girl, 5½" h., pr. 35.00
Plate, portrait of young black boy
w/large slice of watermelon,
12" d. (crazing & small rim
chips) 150.00
Pull toy, horse on wheels, 11" l..... 225.00
Pull toy, life-size model of a duck
on wheels 65.00
Tray, cast brass handles, h.p. scene
of pirates in a rocky ocean shore
setting, 12" d. 65.00

PARRISH (Maxfield) ARTWORK

During the 1920's and 1930's, Maxfield Parrish (1870-1966) was considered the most popular artist-illustrator in the United States. His illustrations graced the covers of the most noted magazines of the day-Scribner's, Century, Life, Harper's, Ladies' Home Journal and others. High quality art prints, copies of his original paintings usually in a range of sizes, graced the walls of homes and offices across the country. Today all Maxfield Parrish artwork, including magazine covers, advertisements and calendar art, is considered collectible but it is the fine art prints that command the most attention.

Book, "A Wonder Book of Tangle-
wood Tales," by Nathaniel Haw-
thorne, illustrated by Maxfield
Parrish, 1910................... $95.00
Book, "The Arabian Nights," illus-
trated by Maxfield Parrish,
1909 ....85.00 to 125.00
Book, "Dream Days," by Kenneth
Grahame, illustrated by Maxfield
Parrish, 1898.................. 70.00
Book, "The Golden Age," by Ken-
neth Grahame, illustrated by
Maxfield Parrish, 1899, 1st
edition 115.00
Book, "Italian Villas & Their
Gardens," by Edith Wharton, illus-
trated by Maxfield Parrish, 1904 .. 250.00
Book, "The Knave of Hearts," by
Louise Sanders, illustrated by
Maxfield Parrish, 1925, hard
bound.................500.00 to 750.00
Book, "Parrish - The Early Years,
1893-1930," by Paul Skeeters, col-
or illustrations by Maxfield
Parrish 200.00
Book, "Poems of Childhood," by
Eugene Field, illustrated by Max-
field Parrish, 1904, 1st
edition ....75.00 to 125.00
Calendar, 1921 or 1924, for Dodge,
in original box, each 60.00
Calendar, 1925, for Edison-Mazda,
entitled "Dreamlight" 290.00
Calendar, 1928, for Edison-Mazda,
entitled "Contentment" 310.00
Calendar, 1929, for Edison-Mazda,
entitled "Golden Hours" 245.00
Calendar, 1932, for Edison-Mazda,
entitled "Solitude"............. 150.00
Calendar, 1946, for Brown & Bigelow
Publishing Co., entitled "Valley of
Enchantment," 16 x 22" 55.00
Catalog, "Vose Galleries Parrish Art
Auctions," 1966, black & white
illustrations 45.00
Greeting card, "The Millpond,"
1940's 22.50

Jigsaw puzzle, "Jig of Jigs," in origi-
nal box 85.00
Magazine cover, "Collier's," March
3, 1906 .... 15.00
Print, "Canyons," 12 x 15" 115.00
Print, "Centaur," framed, 11 x 9" ... 65.00
Print, "Cleopatra," original ornate
frame, large 650.00
Print, "Dinkey Bird," original oak
frame, 11 x 16" 110.00
Print, "Egypt," framed, small 95.00
Print, "Eve Eating the Apple,"
framed, 11 x 14" 45.00
Print, "Harvest," original frame,
9 x 11" 95.00
Print, "Lute Players," 18 x 30" 450.00
Print, "Peaceful Valley,"
13½ x 17" 125.00
Print, "Pierrot's Serenade," Collier's
Publishing Co., 1908, 10 x 15" 50.00
Print, "Reveries," small, framed 75.00
Print, "Rubaiyat," w/verse, original
frame, 4 x 14" 155.00
Print, "The Sandman," 1905,
6½ x 9½" 25.00
Print, "Stars," original frame,
10½ x 6¾" 85.00
Print, "Twilight," 1937, 13½ x 17" .. 150.00
Print, "Wild Geese," original frame,
13½ x 16" .... 85.00 to 125.00
Print, "Wynken, Blynken & Nod,"
framed, 14 x 16" 155.00

PERFUME, SCENT & COLOGNE BOTTLES

*Decorative accessories from milady's bou-
doir have always been highly collectible and
in recent years there has been an especially
strong surge of interest in perfume bottles.
Our listings also include related containers
such as pocket bottles and vials, tabletop containers and atomizers. Most readily available are examples from the 19th through the
mid-20th century, but earlier examples do surface occasionally. The myriad varieties have
now been documented in several recent reference books which should further popularize
this collecting specialty.*

ATOMIZERS

Atomizer, sapphire blue glass, melon ribbed body covered w/tiny
heavy gold florals, leaves, swirls,
etc., original gold top & bulb, unmarked, possibly Moser, 4½" h. ...$245.00
Atomizer, orange glass w/Art Deco
black tear-drops outlined in gold,
DeVilbiss, 7" h. 65.00

Atomizer, turquoise green glass
w/gold decor, Art Deco style, unmarked DeVilbiss, 7" h. 95.00
Atomizer, cobalt blue glass w/large
enameled & faceted crystal stopper finial, Czechoslovakia, 1930's,
8" h. 85.00

DeVilbiss Atomizer

Atomizer, green glass w/gilded upper section & gilt enamel around
base, Art Deco style, DeVilbiss,
ca. 1930's, 8 5/8" h. (ILLUS.) 65.00
Atomizer, cranberry glass, paneled
body, silverplate plunger,
polished base, 9¼" h. 125.00

BOTTLES

Amber glass, Inverted Thumbprint
patt. w/light blue leaves & dark
blue, white, yellow & pink decor,
blue bubble stopper, 3" d.,
8" h. 103.00
Amethyst glass, w/etched animals &
buildings, 4" h. 70.00
Blue glass, w/overall enameled blue
& peach daisies & green & gold
leaves on sapphire blue body,
brass hinged cap w/chain,
1¼" w., 2¾" l. 115.00
Blue glass, w/enameled white
florals, bird, butterfly & bumble
bee decor, 3" h. 235.00
Blue glass, w/gold panels & lacy
gold scrolls on cobalt blue body,
gold trimmed handle & matching
ball stopper, 2 1/8" d., 4" h. 95.00
Blue glass, "Evening in Paris," cobalt blue vial w/tassel 15.00
Cased glass, pink w/gold bands
w/enameled gold florals &
garlands of flowers, original clear
ball stopper w/gold trim, 2½" d.,
4 1/8" h. 100.00
Cased glass, lemon yellow w/sand-
ed gold leaves & ribbon studded

w/red & green applied jewels,
clear ball stopper trimmed in
gold, 2 1/8" d., 5½" h. 94.00

China, shocking pink body w/white
florals & green leaves decor, gold
trim, matching stopper, 2 5/8" d.,
5 1/8" h. 125.00

Clear glass, w/ornate heavy relief
ormolu covering decorated w/lav-
ender quartz jewels & roses &
white enamel leaves, long
dauber, 1 3/8" w., 2 7/8" h. 38.00

Clear glass, w/silver overlay,
pyramid form, original stopper,
6¾" h. 85.00

Clear glass, paperweight-type, set
in brass filigree footed frame,
brass cap w/long crystal dauber,
7½" h. 125.00

Cranberry glass, squatty form,
matching bubble stopper, 2¼" d.,
3" h. 85.00

Cranberry glass, w/lavender & gold
branches, foliage & stylized colored florals, original clear ball
stopper w/gold trim, 2 1/8" d.,
4 1/8" h. 165.00

Cut glass, amber, cut panels & designs, matching stopper, 8½" h. ... 180.00

Cut glass, clear w/lavender fan
stopper, Morles sticker, 4½" h. ... 75.00

Cut glass, cranberry, lay-down type
w/ten cut panels, repousse silver
cap ends, one hinged, one screws
off 225.00

Cut glass, vaseline w/cut panels,
rayed base, faceted bubble stopper, 2 7/8" d., 7" h. 110.00

Czechoslovakian glass, overall filigree florals & mesh on white
enameled florals w/blue mirrored
faceted stones, jeweled screw-on
cap w/dauber, 1¾" d., 2½" h. 55.00

Czechoslovakian glass, clear, squat
round base w/graduated red dots
& 4½" h. clear feather stopper in
shape of 'question mark' 75.00

English cameo glass, round body
w/white florals & butterfly on
frosted vaseline ground,
hallmarked silver hinged cap, unsigned, 2½" d., 3 3/8" h. 795.00

English cameo glass, white florals &
butterfly on raisin ground, hallmarked silver hinged cap,
5¾" h. 1,350.00

Figural cat, blown clear glass body
w/blue head, Germany, 2" h. 30.00

Figural child, china, child seated in
yellow bag w/purple collar &
black hat, metal & cork stopper,
Germany, 2" d., 4¼" h. 40.00

Figural Kewpie, seated, porcelain,
Germany, 2¼" h. 55.00

Figural lady & parrot, china, blue,
white, black, yellow, green & orange decor, metal & cork stopper,
1¼ x 2", 3 3/8" h. 68.00

Mother-of-Pearl Perfume

Mother-of-pearl, flask-form w/flat-
tened ovoid mother-of-pearl body
w/scrolled metal top rim supporting metal neck & ribbed cap, fine
chain handle (ILLUS.) 65.00

Overlay glass, green cut to clear,
hallmarked silver rim band dated
1905, London, original cut stopper,
3 5/8" d., 8 3/8" h. 175.00

"Bohemian" Pattern Perfume Bottle

Pressed glass, "Bohemian" patt. in
ruby w/gold trim, U.S. Glass Co.,
ca. 1901, 9" h. (ILLUS.) 150.00

Rubina crystal glass, silverplate top
rim, cranberry cut stopper, 2" d.,
3¼" h. 110.00

Ruby glass, cylindrical form w/ster-
ling silver cap dated 1884, miniature size 90.00

St. Clair glass, paperweight-type,
clear w/pink, blue, yellow &
white flowers w/bubble centers
on green ground, St. Clair Glass
Works, Elwood, Indiana, 5½" h. ... 65.00
Sterling silver, head of man
w/beard & wearing helmet in
high relief on front, head of classic woman in high relief on reverse, hallmarked, w/chain
handle, 1¼" d. 55.00

PHONOGRAPHS

Columbia Graphophone

Berliner Trade-Mark Gramophone,
black metal horn $2,350.00
Columbia Type AB Graphophone
(ILLUS.)........................ 500.00
Columbia Type AO Graphophone,
oak case 450.00
Columbia Type AT Graphophone.... 225.00
Columbia "Regent" model, desk-
type 475.00
Edison Amberola 30 .... 450.00
Edison Amberola 50, oak case..... 250.00
Edison Concert Model A 1,750.00
Edison Fireside Model A 375.00
Edison Gem Model A 350.00
Edison Idelia, w/No. 11 cygnet
horn 800.00
Edison Standard Model C, oak
case 500.00
Edison Triumph Model, mahogany
case..........................2,250.00
Pathe, oak case, inside horn 210.00
Peter Pan, portable, box camera
form w/telescoping aluminum
horn 150.00
Thorens, portable, brown leather
case resembling folding camera,
Switzerland.................... 175.00
Victor III, oak horn 1,200.00
Victor IV, mahogany horn 1,200.00
Victor V, oak horn................1,045.00
Victor Model P.................. 525.00
Victor Monarch Special, wooden
horn ....1,150.00 to 1,300.00

PHOTOGRAPHIC ITEMS

Ambrotype of Village Scene

Albumen photograph, Civil War supply train, by A. Gardner,
framed $120.00
Albumen photograph, Sioux Indians
& teepee, by Carl Rau, 1897 ..... 70.00
Ambrotype, quarter plate (3¼ x
4½"), man w/dog, hand-colored &
framed 20.00
Ambrotype, half plate (4¼ x 5½"),
man playing violin, matted
w/case........................ 35.00
Ambrotype, half plate (4¼ x 5½"),
outdoor village scene of main
street w/churches & homes lining
both sides, signed "Sterling," attributed to McIntosh & Sterling,
New Hampshire, in full case
(ILLUS.)....................... 302.50
Booklet, "Lantern Slides, How To
Make & Color Them," Kodak,
36 pp.......................... 8.50
Cabinet photograph, experimental
automobile, 1900................ 22.00
Cabinet photograph, James G.
Blaine, Presidential nominee
1884 .... 22.00
Cabinet photograph, paddle wheel
ship "Tacoma" 25.00
Camera, Ansco, pat. date 1926,
wood w/brass 1:3.5 150 mm lens,
case & extra lens 295.00
Camera, Argus C-3 Matchmatic,
2-tone case, w/meter........... 19.50
Camera, Bell & Howell Filmo 75,
w/case........................ 90.00
Camera, Eastman Kodak No. 1A
Folding Pocket, R.R.-type lens 55.00
Camera, Eastman Kodak No. 2A Au-
tographic Jr., folding-type, original case, 1915-23.............. 92.00
Camera, Graflex Series D, w/bag
magazine...................... 90.00
Camera, Ilex No. 3, w/Universal
shutter & special case 75.00
Camera, Leica Model IIIF, Leitz El-
mar 1, 35 x 50 mm lens......... 400.00
Camera, Thornton Pickard Special,

3¼" plate, w/accessories & leather case.............................. 90.00

Camera, Voightlander Bessa I, w/leather case................... 45.00

Camera, Zeiss Contaflex 126, 2.8 lens, telephoto & wide angle lens, w/instruction booklet & case 200.00

Carte de visite, John Wilkes Booth, 1860's 65.00

Carte de visite, Indian "Medicine Bottle," by Whitney.............. 75.00

Carte de visite, Abraham Lincoln, by Warren, 1865 .... 125.00

Carte de visite, Tom Thumb & wife in wedding dress, published by E. & H.T. Anthony, 1863, "Compliments of Charles S. Stratton, Compliments of Lavinia Warren Stratton" 250.00

Carte de visite, Queen Victoria, w/wax seal, 1844 .... 25.00

Daguerreotype, sixth plate, lady holding open book, w/case 25.00

Daguereotype, half plate, California gold mining camp w/miners at work, hut in background, inscribed Dresser & Co. on plate 3,520.00

Daguerreotype, full plate, military officer standing w/sword & scroll inscribed "Gult of Manar" 1,980.00

Daguerreotype Case

Daguerreotype case, thermoplastic, Mary w/lamb (ILLUS.)............ 45.00

Daguerreotype case, thermoplastic, center picture of mother, child, cradle & dog, inside pictures of man & woman side by side, 6¼ x 3¾ x 1" 95.00

Glass negatives, scenes of Wisconsin logging operations, 8 x 10", set of 22 .... 330.00

Photograph, work-worn Kansas family (father, mother & 5 children) posed before sod house, ca. 1880, matted & framed, 11 x 16".. 55.00

Tintype, sixth plate, Civil War Confederate soldier w/gun in belt.... 75.00

Tintype, whole plate, bicycle, 1893.. 70.00

Tintype, child w/doll buggy w/china doll 20.00

Tintype, 3 girls holding tennis racquets, w/daguerreotype case 32.00

PIN CUSHION DOLLS

These china half figures were never intended to use as dolls, but rather to serve as ornamental tops to their functional pin cushion bases which were discreetly covered with silk and lace skirts. They were produced in a wide variety of forms and quality, all of which are now deemed collectible, and were especially popular during the first quarter of this century.

Bisque half figure of a lady w/arms away from body, black hair, pink hat w/blue bow at back, blue & rust small flowers at front, 2" d., 2¾" h........................ $53.00

Bisque half figure of a lady w/applied pink & yellow roses in her grey hair, arms away from body, 3" d., 4 7/8" h................. 150.00

Bisque half figure of a lady w/ornate coiffure, arms away from body w/detailed hands, heavy eyeliner, 3½" d., 5¼" h. 153.00

China half figure of a Colonial lady w/grey hair, one hand to laced bodice, Germany, 4" h............ 35.00

China half figure of a "flapper" w/right hand touching top of head & left hand touching side of neck, jet black hair w/pink band, blue bodice, impressed "Germany, 6102," 2¾" h. 85.00

China half figure of a girl w/hands on hips, sandy blonde hair, yellow bodice, impressed "Germany, 6099," 2¾" h................... 55.00

China half figure of a lady wearing a yellow hat, Germany, 3" h. 30.00

China half figure of a lady wearing a tan hat w/plume & holding fan, impressed "Germany, 5582," 3" h.......................... 65.00

China half figure of a lady w/flowers in her hair & at bosom, marked "Germany," 3¾" h....... 62.50

China half figure of a lady w/hands at bosom, green dress w/floral print, lavender sash & ribbons, lavender ribbon in blonde hair, 3" d., 4 3/8" h 130.00

China half figure of a lady w/one hand extended & other raised to pink rose in her grey hair, black ribbon at throat, Germany, 4½" h. 125.00

China half figure of a lady w/colorful feathers in her brunette hair, molded multicolored bodice w/ruffled collar, painted features, 4¾" h. 90.00

China half figure of a lady w/gold lustre cross on chain around her neck, molded pink & white bodice, pink ribbon & blue flowers in her grey hair, impressed "5266," 5" h. 135.00

China half figure of a nude "flapper" w/left elbow up & right hand touching shoulder, black bobbed hair banded in wide red fillet, impressed "Germany, 5882," 1¼" d., 2¾" h. 55.00

China half figure of a nude lady w/blue feathers in her grey hair, 5" h. 125.00

China half figure of a nude lady w/one hand to her bosom & other arm extended, ornately coiffured grey hair, marked "Made in Germany," 5½" h. 250.00

China half figure of Salome w/arms away from body, 4" h. 125.00

China half figure of a young girl wearing Dutch cap, arms away from body, Germany, 2¾" h. 85.00

Whisk broom doll, china half figure of a girl w/blonde hair, wearing low-cut pink dress. 30.00

Whisk broom doll, china half figure of a lady w/wide pink ribbon in her hair & whisk broom skirt, marked "Germany 8702". 65.00

PIPES

Lion's Head Meerschaum Pipe

Burl, carved fist as bowl, sapling stem, 3½" l. (damaged horn mouthpiece) $85.00

Meerschaum, carved lady's hand holding leaf & vine wrapped bowl, amber stem, w/case, 4 x 2¼". . . . 100.00

Meerschaum, carved w/mountain goat on bowl, amber stem, 4¼ x 2¼" 85.00

Meerschaum, carved head of a sultan w/jeweled turban as bowl, amber stem, 5½" l. 95.00

Meerschaum, carved Art Nouveau lady at front of bowl, golden amber stem, 6" l. 75.00

Meerschaum, carved w/hunter & dog standing on hind legs on bowl, w/case, 6" l. 200.00

Meerschaum, carved full-maned lion as bowl, amber mouthpiece, 6" l. (ILLUS.). 235.00

Meerschaum, carved "Old Salt" fisherman w/rain hat as bowl, w/case, 6" l. 375.00

Meerschaum, carved head of a bulldog as bowl, opening at neck, smoke escapes through mouth & ears, w/case, 6½" l. 575.00

Meerschaum, carved lady's hand holding ornate beer stein w/elf on handle as bowl, silver cap & beading, 8 x 2¾" 175.00

Meerschaum, carved Indians (2) w/rifles & hunting dog on bowl, original case, 12" l., 4½" h. 900.00

Meerschaum, carved boy w/top hat as bowl, amber stem, original case 450.00

Meerschaum, carved florals & gold inlay on bowl, amber stem. 150.00

Meerschaum, carved hand holding ear of corn as bowl, amber stem 375.00

Opium, bamboo stem w/ivory tips, 23½" l. (no bowl) 285.00

Porcelain, hand holding dog as bowl, original stem, 6" l. 125.00

Spatter glass, oval bowl on round base, 7" l. stem 75.00

Wooden, carved hand holding bowl 75.00

POLITICAL & CAMPAIGN ITEMS

Also see FRANKOMA POTTERY.

Admission ticket, "Republican National Convention 1928, Kansas City," w/envelope $35.00

Ash tray, Eisenhower (Dwight D.), chalkware, "I Like Ike," bust of elephant, red & grey, 4 x 3½" 28.00

Bandanna, 1888 campaign, Cleveland (Grover) & Thurman (Allen G.), red linen, "Our Candidates," pictures of Cleveland & Thurman, crossed brooms (2) & rooster, black, white & diamond border ... 195.00

Bandanna, 1900 campaign, Roosevelt (Theodore), Teddy on horseback w/drawn saber, 17 x 17½" 175.00

Bar pin, 1948 campaign, Dewey (Thomas E.), plastic, Dewey on bar, elephant suspended, 1¾ x 1¾" 7.00

Book, 1884 campaign, Blaine (James G.) & Logan (John), "Lives of Blaine & Logan," published by Condit Co., 1884 .... 22.00

Book, souvenir of inaugural ball, 1897, McKinley (William) & Hobart (Garret A.) 49.00

Bottle, whiskey, w/cap, 1953 Eisenhower Inauguration, "Souvenir/1953" on neck above white printed scene of U.S. Capitol & "Presidential Inauguration - MCMLIII - 1953," amber, 11¼" h. 22.50

Bracelet, 1965, Johnson (Lyndon B.) & Humphrey (Hubert H.), inaugural ball souvenir w/portraits, 1/10-10k gold 30.00

Bread plate, 1904 campaign, Roosevelt (Theodore), clear glass, bust profile of Roosevelt center, Teddy Bear border, 10½" l. 85.00

Button, jugate, 1896 campaign, McKinley (William B.) & Hobart (Garret), 1¼" d. 25.00

Button, jugate, 1904 campaign, Parker (Alton) & Davis (Henry) 32.00

Button, jugate, 1916 campaign, Hughes (Charles E.) & Fairbanks (Charles) 25.00

Button, 1960 campaign, Nixon (Richard M.) & Lodge (Henry C.), "I'm for Nixon & Lodge" 3.00

Button, jugate, 1964 campaign, Johnson (Lyndon B.) & Humphrey (Hubert H.), "Johnson & Humphrey Vote Democratic," 3 3/8" d. 6.00

Button, inauguration of George Washington, metal, "Long Live the President" & "GW" 550.00

Button, 1936 campaign, Landon (Alfred M.) & Knox (Frank) 10.00

Button, 1948 campaign, Truman (Harry), "Minnesota Truman Club," 2¼" d. 45.00

Button, 1960 campaign, Kennedy (John Fitzgerald), "The Man for the 60's," 2½" d. 10.00

Candle lantern, 1896 campaign, McKinley (William), clear glass

globe w/spring fastened wire frame, signed "R. Givens, Corpus Christi, Texas 1896" 95.00

Cane, 1888 campaign, Harrison (Benjamin), cast Brittania metal bust of Harrison as handle 85.00

Cane, 1896 campaign, Bryan (William J.), cast Brittania metal bust of Bryan above eagles, shield & "Free Coinage, Prosperity - 16 to 1" as handle 110.00

Clock, figural, Franklin D. Roosevelt "Man of the Hour," wind-up, animated, Roosevelt stands at ship's wheel, pot metal, 1930's, 15" h. .. 110.00

Cuff links, 1896 campaign, McKinley (William) & Hobart (Garret A.), pr............................. 70.00

Earrings, 1956 campaign, Eisenhower (Dwight), brass, "Ike," pr. 9.50

Ferrotype, 1864 campaign, McClellan (George), "McClellan" suspended from ribbon w/eagle on top 150.00

Inaugural medallion, Johnson (Lyndon Baines), bronze, 1965 .... 25.00

Inaugural program, Eisenhower (Dwight) & Nixon (Richard M.), 1957, Norman Rockwell cover 20.00

Teddy Roosevelt Pocket Knife

Knife, pocket-type, Roosevelt (Theodore), bust portrait center obverse, White House & Capitol reverse, gold finish metal w/steel blades, Germany, 3" l. (ILLUS.) ... 65.00

Lapel pin, 1920 campaign, Cox (James M.), rooster-shaped, pewter 20.00

Lapel pin, 1940 campaign, Willkie (Wendell), brass, figural elephant 12.00

Lapel stud, jugate, 1896 campaign, Bryan (William J.) & Sewell (Arthur), 7/8" d. 25.00

Mirror, pocket-type, 1912 campaign, Wilson (Woodrow)............... 125.00

Mourning ribbon, 1841, Harrison (W.H.), silk, 3 x 7" 50.00

Mourning ribbon, 1865, Lincoln (Abraham), silk, w/bust & black border, "ULA" 90.00

Pail, 1900 campaign, McKinley (William B.), glass pail, lid & wire bail handle, "Full Dinner Pail," (no cup), 5½" h..................... 195.00

Paperweight, memorial for James A. Garfield, 1881, bronze medallion embossed "James A. Garfield" on front, "Inaugurated President of The United States, March 4, 1881 - Assassinated July 2, 1881 - Died Sep. 10, 1881" reverse, 3" w. 95.00

Pencil, 1928 campaign, Hoover (Herbert), "Hoover for President," head of Hoover on pencil 30.00

Plate, 1908 campaign, Taft (William H.), milk white glass, eagles, flag & stars 85.00

Postcard, 1908 campaign, Taft (William), "Billy Possum" character representing Taft............... 12.00

Poster, 1928 campaign, Hoover (Herbert), "Herbert Hoover for President," w/portrait............... 15.00

Posters, 1904 campaign, Parker (Alton) & Davis (Henry), "Parker for President," "Davis for Vice President," edges torn, pr. 50.00

Poster, 1944 campaign, Roosevelt (Franklin D.) & Truman (Harry), 11 x 15"...................... 17.50

Razor, 1904 campaign, Roosevelt (Theodore) & Fairbanks (Charles W.), gold-washed 120.00

Ribbon, jugate, 1884 campaign, Cleveland (Grover) & Hendricks (Thomas), 5½" l................ 40.00

Ribbon, 1888 campaign, Harrison (Benjamin), photo in frame on ribbon 75.00

Sheet music, 1936 campaign, Roosevelt (Franklin Delano), "March on with Roosevelt" 28.00

Toby jug, 1928 campaign, Smith (Al), Syracuse China, limited edition of 961, 6½" h. 75.00

Hoover Toby Jug

Toby jug, 1928 campaign, Hoover (Herbert), Syracuse China, 6½" h. (ILLUS.)........................ 80.00

Token, 1864 campaign, McClellan (Gen. Geo. B.) & Pendleton (George H.), 2 ferrotype portraits...................... 45.00

Watch fob, 1904 campaign, Parker (Alton) & Davis (Henry) 28.00

Watch fob, 1920 campaign, Cox (James M.) & Roosevelt (Franklin D.), original strap 68.00

POSTCARDS

Advertising Postcard

Advertising, "Akron Oil Lamp," 1920's, pr. $12.00

Advertising, "Borden's," Elsie & her brand new twins, 1957 .... 22.50

Advertising, "Case Threshing Machine," men threshing in field 8.00

Advertising, "Doe-Wah-Jack (Dowagiac, Michigan) Round Oak Stoves," Indian scene, "The Hunter" 25.00

Advertising, "Globe-Wernicke Co." (ILLUS.)...................... 8.00

Advertising, "National Cash Registers," employees & factory, postmarked 1910 .... 22.00

Advertising, "Plymouth," Barney Oldfield, 1934 Chicago World Fair 10.00

Advertising, "Sleepy Eye Flour," set of 9..................500.00 to 700.00

Advertising, "Texaco," 1920's 7.00

Automobile race cars, 1908, set of 4........................... 40.00

Children series, "Little Breeches," fisherman, Ullman.............. 5.00

Christmas Greetings, Ellen Clapsad-

dle, Santa Claus in red coat, post-
marked 1907 . . . . .8.00 to 10.00

Christmas Greetings, Louis Prang,
frogs fighting w/ducks or geese,
each 20.00

Christmas Greetings, Raphael Tuck,
Santa Claus wearing blue velvet
suit carrying bag of toys, going by
lighted window 15.00

Christy (Howard Chandler), water
lilies . . . . .8.00 to 10.00

Commemorative, Hudson-Fulton
Celebration, 1909, set of 3 . . . . .   25.00

Coney Island, 1920, set of 13 . . . .   32.00

Corn Palace, Mitchell, South Dakota,
1907-60's, set of 25 . . . .   65.00

Disaster, Compton, California
earthquake 6.00

Easter Greetings, Ellen Clapsaddle,
mechanical, boy w/egg 17.50

Easter Greetings, Raphael Tuck, embossed rooster, eggs & chicks,
1900 . . . .   7.00

Ethnic work scene, black workers
hoeing rice field, South Carolina,
1910 . . . .   10.00

Halloween Greetings, embossed,
girl sitting on pumpkin & holding
mirror, "When Halloween has
come to pass may you see my
face in your looking glass," James
E. Pitts . . . . .6.00 to 8.00

Halloween Greetings, embossed
Jack-o-Lantern 15.00

Hold-to-light, Christmas Greetings,
Santa Claus in brown coat & pur-
ple pants, Milton Transparent
Christmas Series . . . . .70.00 to 80.00

Hold-to-light, Christmas Greetings,
Santa Claus w/two children by
Christmas tree 35.00

Hold-to-light, Easter Greetings, little
girl scolding rabbit w/chicks in
background 35.00

Hold-to-light, New Year Greetings . .   20.00

Hold-to-light, New York, London &
Boston scenes, set of 3 . . . .   60.00

Hotel Golfmore & golf course,
Grand Beach, Michigan, early
1900's, set of 11 . . . .   17.00

Human hair type, child 25.00

Indianapolis race, "Monroe Special,"
1920 . . . .   7.00

Indians, Navajos presenting baskets,
real photograph, early 1900's 18.00

Little Red Riding Hood, Ullman, set
of 6 . . . .   35.00

New Year Greetings, polar bear &
aeroplane, 1911 . . . .   15.00

New York City scenes, "New York
City by Night," early 1900's, set of
10 . . . .   16.00

Railroad depots, stations & bridges,
set of 70 . . . .   35.00

Real photo, midgets, "The Three Del
Rios" . . . . .12.00 to 15.00

St. Patrick's Day, flag, harp & 3
children 4.00

Ten Commandments series, Raphael
Tuck, set of 10 . . . .   150.00

World War I, troops, battles, towns,
etc., assorted set of 22 . . . .   50.00

World War II, Hitler shaking hands
w/Nazi youth group 25.00

POSTERS

"Automobile Club Belgique"

*Also see MUCHA ARTWORK, POLITI-
CAL & CAMPAIGN ITEMS and RAIL-
ROADIANA.*

Ammunition, "Remington UMC,"
cartridges below "Best Game and
Target Cartridges" across top
w/various scenes of animals from
around the world $192.50

Automobile, "Peerless Motor Car
Co.," copyrgt. 1903, "The Peerless
Girl VI," artwork by S. Crosby, 13
x 26" 85.00

Automobile race, "Automobile Club
Belgique, Course Bruxelles-SPA,"
Father Time driving early auto,
artwork by Georges Gaudy, 1898,
48 5/8 x 34 7/8" (ILLUS.) 1,210.00

Baking soda, "Arm & Hammer,"
birds, insects & migration informa-
tion, 1938, 42 x 20" 35.00

Carriages, "Davis Gould & Co.," early factory scene w/21 different
carriages, 17 x 25" 85.00

Cigarettes, "Old Gold," pictures
Stan Laurel & Oliver Hardy in
scene from their movie," Babes in
Toyland," 1934, 31 x 41" 300.00

Circus, "Al G. Barnes & Sells Floto
Combined Circus," presenting
"Old Mexico," colorful, 30 x 40" .. 100.00
Circus, "P.T. Barnum," depicting
General Tom Thumb & his wife,
Lavinia Warren, by Strobridge
Litho, ca. 1881 ....3,300.00
Dairy, "Sheffield Farms Dairy," cows
in stream, "Pure Milk Comes From
Healthy Cows," artwork by
Megaree, 24 x 18" 15.00
Gun powder, "Hercules Powder,"
entitled "Not This Trip Old Pal,"
original frame, 1942 .... 100.00

"Harper's July"

Magazine, "Harper's July," by Ed-
ward Penfield, 1896, 18½ x 13½"
(ILLUS.)........................ 330.00
Soap, "Babbits Soap," pictures "Little
Lord Fauntleroy," 1890's,
30 x 14"....................... 120.00
World War I, "And They Said We
Couldn't Fight," Victory Liberty
Loan, 41 x 30" 150.00
World War I, "Corn, The Food of a
Nation," bright colors showing
woman w/different corn products,
L. Harrison, 20 x 30" 45.00
World War I, Red Cross Nurse
banner, Harrison Fisher,
41½ x 8½".................... 30.00
World War I, "Sir Don't Waste While
Your Wife Saves (etc.)," man
w/cigar, having dinner in restau-
rant, C. Young, 21 x 28" 15.00
World War II, "A Careless Word, A
Needless Sinking," Marines in life
boat, 20 x 30" 60.00
World War II, airplane silhouettes
by Dept. of Navy Aeronautics, 3
views of black & white German,
Japanese & American planes,
18 x 24", set of 120 .... 150.00
World War II, American Junior Red
Cross, parade of people carrying

Red Cross flag, soaring eagle in
background, W.B. Humphrey,
23 x 15"...................... 65.00
World War II, "Even A Little Can
Help A Lot - Now," 20 x 14"...... 35.00
World War II, "Freedom of Speech,"
Norman Rockwell, 28½ x 40" 250.00

PRANG CHROMOLITHOGRAPHS

Set of Prang Cards

Book, "Butterflies & Moths in America & Europe," illustrated w/Prang
lithographs $65.00
Book, "Natural History Series for
Children," 1878, w/color lithographs, set of six, each volume .. 35.00
Card, Christmas, diagonal band
across center w/color scene of
snowflake fairies in vividly colored clothes jousting w/each other, L. Prang & Co., Boston, ca.
1884 .... 6.00
Cards, each w/a color scene of children representing the four seasons, L. Prang & Co., ca.
1885, set of 4 (ILLUS.)........... 20.00
Print, "Battle of Kennesaw Mountain," 1887, never framed, 17 x
23" 35.00
Print, "Psyche & Cupid," 20½ x
16½" 75.00
Print, bust of George Washington,
medallion style oval, black &
white, 2 x 2½", 2¾ x 4½" original bright metal frame 75.00

PYROGRAPHY

Glove Box with Charlie Chaplin

Pyrography is the process of producing designs on wood, leather or other materials by using heated tools or a fine flame. Commonly referred to as "burnt-wood" wares, creating these articles became a popular home craft earlier in this century after the invention of the platinum-pointed needle which could be safely heated. Prior to this a hot poker was used to scorch a design in the wood. But because of the accuracy the needle allowed, burning a design into wood became a hobby with many and companies issued kits with all the tools necessary to create the design on a pre-stamped soft wood box or article. A wide variety of designs were available including flowers, animals and scrolls. Women were popular subjects and the rights to Charles Dana Gibson's famous "Gibson Girl" were obtained by Thayer and Chandler Co. of Chicago who also sold items pre-stamped with the Sunbonnet Babies. Modest prices are still associated with burnt-wood wares unless the overall workmanship or design is exceptional.

Bowl, burnt squirrel on oak branch
& acorns decor $22.00
Box w/hinged lid, burnt cherries decor, 6" sq. 11.00
Box w/hinged lid, burnt strawberries & leaves, artist-signed & dated 1911, 6" sq., 2¾" h. 12.00
Box w/hinged lid, stamped poinsettias & leaves decor, w/original equipment & instruction booklet issued by Flemish Art Co., N.Y.C., 1907, 9¾ x 7 x 5" 85.00
Box w/hinged lid, 3-compartment, stamped floral design, 12" l. 35.00
Box w/hinged lid, burnt center medallion w/Indian girl & florals, 14 x 10" 24.00
Card box, book-shaped w/drawer,

burnt King & Queen of Spades decor, 3 7/8" l. 10.00
Cup rack w/hooks & slot, burnt grape clusters & leaves decor, dated 1912, 20" l. 30.00
Glove box w/hinged lid, burnt Charlie Chaplin figure on inside & outside of lid overall surface design & lettered "Gloves," 10 x 3½", 2" h. (ILLUS.) 45.00
Glove box w/hinged lid, burnt poinsettia decor, 10 x 4", 2¾" h. 25.00
Glove box w/hinged lid, burnt portrait of Art Nouveau woman within floral & grape clusters 24.00
Handkerchief box w/hinged lid, burnt Cleopatra-type woman on lid, 7 x 5", 1" h. 15.00
Handkerchief box w/hinged lid, burnt Gibson Girl decor 22.00
Hat rack, 2-prong, burnt scroll design 18.00
Photograph box w/hinged lid, burnt floral designs & "Photos" in ornate lettering, 15 x 7½" 24.00
Plaque, burnt portrait of lady, 9" d. 35.00
Plaque, burnt bust portrait of Daniel Webster, Eastlake-style frame, ca. 1880, 10¾ x 9" 82.50
Plaque, burnt portrait of Indian maiden, w/"jeweled" trim, 18 x 8" oval 40.00
Plaque, burnt scene of young girl guiding blind beggar beside country road, inscribed on back "The Blind Man of Gretna Green - This picture was burnt with a poker, Nov. 12, 1863 by Ball Hughes, Dorchester, Mass.," 19" w., 24" h. 82.50
Plaque, burnt grape clusters & ears of corn decor, 30 x 16" 65.00
Ribbon rack, burnt inscription "For a Neat Little Girl's Hair Ribbons" & 3 Victorian-type girls 30.00
Tie rack, Gibson Girl & beau on golf course, burnt & tinted scene, signed "Copyright C.D. Gibson, Life Publishing Co.," 20 x 12" 135.00
Towel rack w/attached towel bar, burnt scene of Dutch girls in various poses, signed & dated Dec. 25, 1909, 20 x 6" 50.00

RADIOS & ACCESSORIES

Early model radios, transmitting equipment and components are now being sought by a special group of collectors.

Emerson Bakelite Radio

Book, "Atwater Kent Radio Instruction Book," 1926, 3rd edition $10.00

Book, "Drakes' Radio Encyclopedia," 1928, Chicago 35.00

Book, "Radio Service Encyclopedia," 5th edition, 1946 .... 9.50

Catalogue, Badger Radio, Milwaukee, Wisconsin, 1925-26.......... 18.50

Catalogue, "Sylvania Tube Technical Manual," 1943, 275 pp. 4.00

Radio, Addison, black & white marbleized w/white columns & grill, bakelite case 325.00

Radio, American Bosch Model 28, w/Ambotone cone speaker 130.00

Radio, Atwater Kent Model 9, ca. 1923, breadboard case 550.00

Radio, Atwater Kent Model 10, 1923, breadboard case 485.00

Radio, Atwater Kent Model "L" w/horn speaker................. 65.00

Radio, Bendix, brown bakelite case 22.00

Radio, Buckingham, battery table model, 3-dial, walnut case, inside speaker 115.00

Radio, Centinental Deco, Model 1600 .... 75.00

Radio, Crosley Model 10-135 .... 45.00

Radio, Crosley Model 51SD, battery-type w/tubes, 1924 .... 80.00

Radio, Crosley, w/Musicone type D speaker 95.00

Radio, Crusader "Cathedral" model........................ 100.00

Radio, Delco Magnascope, wooden cabinet....................... 35.00

Radio, Echophone Model EC-1A, original box 85.00

Radio, Emerson, table model, rectangular amber bakelite case w/circular dial at right & cream & black horizontal grillwork at left, black bakelite handle at top, 9" h. (ILLUS.)..................... 495.00

Radio, FADA, rectangular w/rounded corners, amber bakelite case, 7" h. 242.00

Radio, Federal Model A-10, 5-tube..................... 125.00

Radio, Garod "RAF" 140.00

Radio, General Electric Model 81, 8-tube, 1934 .... 195.00

Radio, Geppert Kleertone, crystal dector replaced w/crystal diode, original label, ca. 1920 .... 60.00

Radio, Grebe Syncrophase, 1925 .... 350.00

Radio, Grundig Majestic 35.00

Radio, Hallicrafters Rec. Model 540, 54-42 MC, 9-tube 65.00

Radio, Kolster 6-tube w/speaker, 1926 .... 185.00

Radio, Majestic "Cathedral" Model 20 .... 100.00

Radio, Malone Lemmon Neutrodyne, battery-operated, w/ornately carved open speaker 110.00

Radio, Montgomery Ward, single tube w/large copper coil, 1914 ... 100.00

Radio, Motorola Model 5J11R, red bakelite case 30.00

Radio, National HRO, 4 sets of coils in box, HB power supply 250.00

Radio, Neutrowood, 6-tube, black metal case 125.00

Radio, Paragon Model RD5/10R 800.00

Radio, Philco, beehive limited edition, commemorating 100 years .. 145.00

Radio, Philco "Cathedral" Model 37-84, 1937, w/schematic design 85.00

Radio, RCA Model 14X 30.00

Radio, RCA "Radiola 17," w/100A speaker & 2 booklets 75.00

Radio, RCA "Radiola Model AR 812," 1924 .... 200.00

Radio, Sentinel w/S.W. receiver, table model, standard & short wave, 32-volt, 1931 .... 40.00

Radio, Spartan "Blue Mirror" table model..................... 990.00

Radio, Spencer "Pocket Radio," crystal set, original mailer, 1926 .... 13.00

Radio, Stewart-Warner Model 325, 5-tube, 1925 .... 85.00

Radio, Stromberg Carlson, table model, bakelite case, 1941 .... 38.00

Radio, Symplix "Cathedral" model .. 45.00

Radio, Trirdyne Super Model, 1920's 60.00

Radio, Wurlitzer Model 700, refinished cabinet 1,900.00

Radio, Zenith, robot-dial console model, 1930 .... 175.00

Radio, Zenith "Trans-Oceanic" portable model, 1954, w/case, wavemagnet & log 75.00

Radio receiver, Hammerlund Comet Pro American Airlines 120.00

Radio receiver, Western Coil & Electric Co., Radiodyne WC 15 Jr.,

style C, serial No. 2136,
w/phones, 1926 .... 125.00
Radio speaker, Acme double cone .. 55.00
Radio speaker, Midget Cone, 1929,
w/illustrated instructions &
paraphernalia................... 75.00
Radio tube, 80 .... 6.00

RAILROADIANA

"Missouri Pacific Lines" Plate

Also see the "Special Focus" at TOYS.

Ash tray, "St. Louis Southwestern
Railway - Cotton Belt Route," em-
bossed metal $10.00
Book, "Locomotive Dictionary Cy-
clopedia," 1919, 1284 pp. 106.00
Bouillon cup, "Union Pacific Rail-
road," Harriman Blue patt........ 15.00
Bowl, "Southern Pacific R.R.," Wild-
flower patt., 6" d............... 50.00
Broadside, "Bayline Seaboard &
Roanoke Railroad," colorful,
1880's 250.00
Butter pat, "Union Pacific R.R.," chi-
na, Winged Streamliner patt...... 25.00
Caboose backup whistle, "C & O
R.R." (Chesapeake & Ohio R.R.),
brass, Sherburne 55.00
Calendar, 1933, "Great Northern,"
Indian scene entitled "The Drum-
mers," by Winold Reiss 45.00
Chocolate pot, cov., "Atchison,
Topeka & Santa Fe R.R.," china,
California Poppy patt. 65.00
Coffee pot, cov., "Atchison, Topeka
& Santa Fe R.R.," silverplate,
Gorham, individual size.......... 55.00
Compote, "Pennsylvania Railroad,"
china, Mountain Laurel patt. 75.00
Conductor's hat, "N.P." (Northern
Pacific Railway), gold braid trim .. 80.00

Conductor's step stool, "A.T. & S.F.
RY" (Atchison, Topeka & Santa
Fe), steel, painted green, Morton,
18 x 13"...................... 175.00
Conductor's uniform, "Milwaukee
Road" (Chicago, Milwaukee, St.
Paul & Pacific), coat, vest & trou-
sers, 3 pcs................... 110.00
Coupon pass book, "Southern Rail-
way," 1913, 48 tickets 100.00
Creamer & sugar bowl, "Canadian
Pacific," silverplate, Morton-
Parker, pr. 60.00
Cup & saucer, "Southern Pacific,"
china, Prairie-Mountain Wildflow-
ers patt....................... 80.00
Cuspidor, "Pullman," nickel-plated
brass 60.00
Depot poster, "Northern Pacific -
North Coast Limited," scene
depicting Western rodeo parade,
by Edward Bremar, 1935,
28½ x 40".................... 47.50
Egg cup, double, "Chesapeake &
Ohio Railway," Buffalo Pottery ... 55.00
Fire extinguisher, "Chicago & Northwestern Ry.," glass tube w/blue
chemical, w/iron wall bracket,
18" h......................... 85.00
Hair receiver, "Pullman," brass, em-
bossed lid 65.00
Hatpin, "N.H.R.R." (New York &
New Haven), yellow button top,
8" l. 45.00
Lantern, "I.C.R.R." (Illinois Central),
amber globe w/etching, Adlake .. 65.00
Lantern, "Pere Marquette," red cast
globe w/flag logo 300.00
Lantern, "Wabash," bell bottom blue
globe w/etched logo 375.00
Letter opener, "N.P.R." (Northern
Pacific), brass, handle cast in the
form of a baked potato 50.00
Luncheon cloth, "Frisco" (St. Louis &
San Francisco), center logo, white
on white 32.00
Menu, "Great Norhtern Railway,"
Empire Builder, Indian pictured on
cover, 1930's 15.00
Menu holders, "I.C." (Illinois Cen-
tral), silverplate, w/pencil holder
at each side 45.00
Mug, railroad scene entitled "Fury,"
Staffordshire pottery, ca. 1850 .... 130.00
Mustard jar, "Atchison, Topeka &
Santa Fe," china, California Poppy
patt. 75.00
Oil can, "C.B. & Q." (Chicago,
Burlington & Quincy), 4-qt. 28.00
Padlock w/key, "C.R.I. & P. R.R."
(Chicago, Rock Island & Pacific),
brass 65.00
Padlock, "Great Northern Railway,"
cast iron 12.00

Pencil, "Rock Island Lines," mechanical, pearlized 15.00

Plate, "Chesapeake & Ohio," Charlottesville patt., 8" d. 150.00

Plate, "Missouri Pacific Lines," china, State Flowers patt. w/"The Sunshine Special" center, Syracuse China Co., 10½" d. (ILLUS.) 250.00

Plate, "Union Pacific RR," tin, lovely little girl in center w/children & bears throwing snowballs around edge, 1907 .... 85.00

Platter, "Baltimore & Ohio," Capitol patt., 15" oval 200.00

Lithographed Poster

Poster, "Exactitude," lithograph in colors on paper, by Pierre Fix-Masseau, 1932, France, 39½ x 24½" (ILLUS.) 2,860.00

Print, "Locomotive For Passengers With Outside Cylinders Built By The Lowell Machine Shope, 1852," lithograph printed in colors, Tappan & Bradford, framed, 32 3/8 x 20 5/8" 4,180.00

Screen, folding-type, 3-fold, oak & glass, each rectangular panel made up of 5 glass panes w/photographs of rice production on the Southern Pacific Sunset route, each panel 17¼" w., 74" h. 550.00

Switch key, "Baltimore & Ohio R.R.," brass 15.00

Token, "New Haven R.R.," aluminum, "Compliments of the Dining Service" 6.00

Transit w/tripod, "Chicago & Northwestern R.R.," brass, C.L. Berger & Sons No. 7977, 1910 .... 650.00

Water jug, "Rock Island R.R.," stoneware, 1-gal. 100.00

RAZORS

Straight Razors

Sterling Handled Straight Razor

Bakelite (green) handle, Keen Kutter blade $22.50

Bone handle, Sheffield blade, original papier-mache case, ca. 1860 .. 19.50

Celluloid (black) handle, "Keen Kutter" emblem on blade & handle, Simmons Hdwe. Co., made in Germany 25.00

Celluloid (gold) handle, "Gold Nugget," W.R. Case & Son, Bradford, Pennsylvania 37.00

Celluloid (ivory) handle, model of a bamboo stalk 15.00

Celluloid (ivory) handle, embossed deer in forest decor, blade marked "Oxford," Germany 25.00

Celluloid (ivory) handle, embossed Indian design 20.00

Celluloid (ivory) handle, embossed jockey on horseback jumping fence decor.................... 75.00

Celluloid (ivory) handle, embossed woman w/flowing hair decor 30.00

Celluloid (ivory) handle, blade stamped "W.R. Case & Sons" 22.00

Celluloid (ivory) handle, blade etched "Original Pipe Razor" 28.00

Celluloid (ivory) handle, blade engraved w/Theodore Roosevelt & General Batha 37.50

Celluloid (ivory) handle, Sheffield steel blade, set of 7 "Day of the Week" in felt lined box, Charles Clement, London, the set 250.00

Composition handle, marbleized brown, blade marked "W.R. Case & Sons," 5" l. 22.00

Copper handle, bust of Indian in full headdress both sides 38.00

Horn handle, embossed Art Nouveau lady decor front & reverse, blade marked "The Shapleigh Barbers" 35.00

Horn handle, auto etched on blade 30.00

Horn handle, embossed florals, eagle & sailboat decor, blade engraved "American Lines S.S. St. Louis, H. Boker Co.".............. 60.00

Sterling silver handle, Art Nouveau pattern w/raised scrolls across front & back, monogrammed in center open area, stamped, "Ster-

ling," blade etched in ribbon
"Wade & Butcher," Sheffield,
England, ca. 1900 (ILLUS.) 322.00
Wooden handle, grey & black origi-
nal paint, 33" l. 120.00

Safety Razors
Gillette "Bostonian" safety razor,
w/case 15.00
Gillette, pocket-type safety razor,
signed Kirry C. Gillette, dated
1902, w/sterling silver case 45.00
Gillette, travel-type safety razor,
brass handle & brass blade
holder, w/brass travel case w/flo-
ral decor on cover, velvet lined .. 16.00
Shurmack, lady's safety razor, round
head, 1930's, w/original box 14.00
Valet Autostrap safety razor,
w/case 18.50
Winchester safety razor w/blade,
new in box 95.00

ROYCROFT ITEMS

Roycroft Table Lamp

*Elbert Hubbard, eccentric entrepreneur of
the late 19th century, founded Roycroft Shops
and established a craft community in East
Aurora, New York in 1895. Individuals were
trained in the trades of bookbinding, leather
tooling and printing. Craft-style furniture in
the manner of Gustav Stickley and known as
"Aurora Colonial" furniture was produced.
A copper workshop, begun in 1908, turned out
numerous items. All of these, along with the
Buffalo Pottery china which was produced ex-
clusively for use at the Roycoft Inn and carries the Roycroft symbol, constitute a special
category associated with the Arts and Crafts
movement.*

Ash tray, hand-hammered copper,
octagonal, 4" $32.00
Book, "Elbert Hubbard of East Aurora," by Felix Shay, 1926,
w/illustrations 25.00
Book, "Elbert Hubbard's Scrapbook,"
by Elbert Hubbard II, hard cover,
1923 .... 20.00
Book, "Elbert Hubbard's Scrapbook,"
by Elbert Hubbard II, 1927........ 15.00
Book, "Elbert Hubbard's Scrapbook,"
by Elbert Hubbard II, 1928........ 25.00
Book, "Health & Wealth," by Elbert
Hubbard, soft suede leather cov-
er, 1908, 1st edition 9.95
Book, "Little Journeys," by Elbert
Hubbard, 1916, Wise Memorial
Edition, 14 vols., w/dust jackets .. 92.00
Book, "Little Journeys to the Homes
of Great Reformers," by Elbert
Hubbard, 1907 .... 9.00
Book, "Little Journeys to Homes of
Great Scientists," by Elbert Hub-
bard, 1905..................... 9.00
Book, "The Man of Sorrows," by El-
bert Hubbard, leather bound,
1904 .... 25.00
Books, "Elbert Hubbard Short Sto-
ries," 1920-21, 14 vols........... 200.00
Bookends, hand-hammered copper,
star pattern, 3" h., pr........... 40.00
Bookends, hand-hammered copper,
open, square, pr. 55.00
Bookends, hand-hammered copper,
poppies decor, pr................ 40.00
Calendar, hand-hammered copper,
perpetual-type 40.00
Candle holders, hand-hammerd copper, twist stem, pr. 300.00
Catalogue, 1909, leather items, pho-
tos, prices, 48 pp. 39.00
Compote, hand-hammered copper,
pedestal base.................. 75.00
Console set: bowl & pr. candlesticks; silverplate, 3 pcs.......... 240.00
Dish, hand-hammered copper w/rim
decor, 9¾" d. 70.00
Frame, hand-hammered copper,
4½ x 6½" 60.00
Inkwell & blotter, hand-hammered
copper, marked, 2 pcs. 80.00
Jug, stoneware, brown glaze, 6" ... 25.00
Lamp, hand-hammered & patinated
copper, domed shade w/flared rim,
trumpet-shaped base, ca. 1915,
13½" h. (ILLUS.) 1,430.00
Letter opener, hand-hammered
copper 15.00
Magazine, "The Fra," 1913, published by Elbert Hubbard, Roy-
crofter advertising.............. 8.00
Mug, handle w/cobalt blue accents,
incised rings on salt glaze
ground 65.00

Nut bowl w/spoon, silverplate, 2
pcs. 150.00
Storage box, cov., wood w/Roycroft
marked hardware, 23 x 12 x 10". . 460.00
Vase, bulbous, hand-thrown pottery,
4½" h. 75.00
Vase, hand-hammered copper,
5" h. 95.00
Vase, urn-shaped, hand-hammered
copper, 5" h. 160.00
Wall sconce, double, hand-
hammered copper, shooting star &
moon design, 5 x 8" 145.00

SALESMAN'S SAMPLES

*The traveling salesman or "drummer" has
all but disappeared from the American scene.
In the latter part of the 19th century and up
to the late 1930's they traveled the country
calling on potential customers to show them
small replicas of their products. Today these
small versions of kitchenwares, farm equipment, and even bath tubs, are of interest to
collectors and are available in a wide price
range.*

Armchair, oak, ladder back, rush
seat, 5 x 7½" $45.00
Baseball bat, wooden, "Hanna
Batrite, Athens, Ga." 10.00
Basin, graniteware, grey mottled . . . 35.00
Bath tub, porcelain, "Wilco Plumbing
& Heating Supply Co." 35.00
Billiard table, steel clad, ornate
legs, "Brunswick, Booth's Pat.,"
6 x 3", 2" h. 65.00
Boots, "Goodrich Hipress," pr. 8.00
Broom, "A. & P. Tea Co., Continen-
tal Broom Works" 10.00
Coffee pot, cov., "Revere Ware" 18.00
Commode, oak, harp back,
manufacturer's label on back 195.00
Cooking range, cast iron, "Charm,"
w/stoveplate lifter & utensils 285.00
Cooking range, cast iron, "Charter
Oak No. 103," dated 1881 . . . . . . 1,000.00
Cooking range, electric,
"Majestic" 1,375.00
Fire extinguisher, "Red Comet" 65.00
Food chopper, cast iron, "Rollman
Mfg. Co." 45.00
Furnace, "Pet Heating Furnace Mfg.
Fastco, Benton Harbor,
Michigan" 375.00
Hat, man's, "Adams," original box . . 12.00
Incinerator, "Kerner Incinerator,
Wisconsin" 110.00
Overshoe, rubber, "Wales,
Goodyear," 3" l. 10.00

Parlor stove, cast iron, potbelly-
type, "Spark" 225.00
Picnic table w/attached benches,
decorative wrought iron & wood,
patent number on ends, ca. 1900,
24" l. table 225.00
Pitch fork, cast iron & wood, "E. C.
Simmons - Keen Kutter" 250.00
Shade, glass, pulled feather design
w/green border on white, irides-
cent gold lining, "Quezal," 3" h. . . 190.00
Shoes, men's, "Nunn-Bush," pr.,
original box 15.00
Tray, cut glass, boat-shaped, hob-
stars, cane, star & fan, 2¼" w.,
4" l. 75.00
Typewriter, "R.C. Allen," w/movable
parts 50.00
Vacuum cleaner, "Hoover," 1933
Chicago World's Fair 185.00
Waffle iron, "Stover Jr." 150.00
Wash boiler, copper w/brass
handles 45.00
Washing machine w/wringer, metal,
battery-operated, "Rowley Tool &
Eng. Co., Green Lake, Wis." 115.00
Whet stone, "Pikes Selling Assoc.,
New Hampshire," fitted wooden
case 28.00

SCALES

Balance Scale

Advertising scale, "Purina," brass
front, "Cow Chow Makes More
Milk at Less Cost" $85.00
Advertising scale, "Wrigley's," tin &
brass 175.00
Apothecary scale, balance-type,
marble top, brass pans, w/five
weights, 1866 patent 250.00
Apothecary scale, oak & beveled
glass case, brass pans & weight,
1891 . . . . 335.00
Baby weighing scale, w/wicker bas-
ket, early 20th c. 25.00
Butter scale, balance-type, wooden,
square post w/beveled edges supporting balancing arm w/suspend-
ed wooden trays, on square
beveled base, attributed to the
Shakers, 24½" h. 65.00

Butter scale, balance-type, wooden, turned post w/acorn finial, cut-out heart on indicator, original yellow, blue & green paint......... 390.00

Candy scale, "Branford," 2-lb. 175.00

Candy scale, "Dayton No. 166," 1-lb. 185.00

Candy scale, calculating beam-type, iron w/nickel-plated brass scoop, "Pelouze, 1915" 42.00

Candy scale, w/brass scoop, "Standard Comp. Scale" 185.00

Coin-operated sidewalk scale, cast iron, "Mills," maroon & gold w/nickel trim, restored 800.00

Coin-operated sidewalk scale, cast iron, lollipop-type, "Mills Fat & Lean," 1-cent 750.00

Coin-operated sidewalk scale, white porcelain pedestal base w/brass platform, indicating chart in glass-faced housing, "Nat'l. Auto. Mach. Co., St. Paul, Minn.," 72" h....... 195.00

Compound lever balance scale, cast iron, w/removable brass pans, 27" l. (ILLUS.) 75.00

Countertop scale, fan-type, "IBM Style 251," 10-lb. 125.00

Countertop scale, "National Store Specialty, Lancaster, Pa.," 2-lb., 9" l., 10" h. (no scoop) 285.00

Railway Express Agency Scale

Countertop scale, cast iron, "Railway Express Agency," 2-sided glass covered face, 60-lb., 20" l., 11" h. (ILLUS.) 125.00

Countertop scale, white enamel, w/pan, "Toledo," 3-lb. 60.00

Egg grading scale, "Acme," 1924 patent 17.00

Egg grading scale, "Jiffy Way," red 13.50

Fur trader's hide scale, brass, "Winchester" 75.00

Gold scale, wooden & glass case, drawer w/ivory handle & name placard, "Christian Becker"....... 450.00

Grain scale, brass, "Winchester Howe No. 47".................. 250.00

Ice scale, "Gifford Wood Co.," 200-lb. 30.00

Jockey's weight scale, chair-type, cast iron & brass, circular brass

dial inscribed "Slater's Platform Machine," raised on a tapered support headed by a lotus leaf capital, terminating on a square platform base, England, late 19th c., 63" h. 440.00

Kitchen scale, Art Deco geometric design, red & cream 50.00

Kitchen scale, hanging-type, "Chatillon" 28.00

Kitchen scale, hanging-type, cast iron w/brass face plate, "Fray's Family Balance," 11" sq. pan 30.00

Peddlar's scale, cast iron, brass scoop, 3 iron weights, 1920's 40.00

Platform-type scale, "National," claw foot w/ornate round stand .. 750.00

Postal scale, "Columbian," dated 1908 .... 15.00

Postal scale, "Fairbanks," 1-lb. 30.00

Postal scale, platform-type, "Liberty Postal Scale," 4 x 5½ x 6" 28.00

Postal scale, "Triner Airmail Accuracy," 1949 .... 38.50

Postal scale, nickel-plated, "Victor," dated 1898, 4½" w., 4½" h. 28.00

Spring scale, "Chatillon," 50-lb...... 15.00

Spring scale, hanging-type, iron w/circular brass face, "Landers, Frary & Clark, New Britain, Conn., U.S.A.," 6" d.............. 55.00

Spring scale, iron w/brass face plate, "Lander's Improved Spring Balance," 8½" l. plus hooks...... 10.00

SCRAPBOOKS & ALBUMS

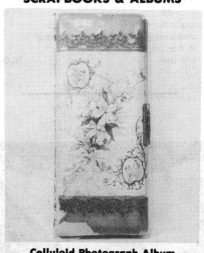

Celluloid Photograph Album

Album, musical-type, celluloid cover, soft pastel bust portrait of beautiful lady surrounded by flowers, ornate brass clasp $285.00

Album, photograph, creamy ivory celluloid cover w/florals center & portraits of lovely ladies within scrollwork, corner damage (ILLUS.)........................ 50.00

Album, photograph, celluloid cover w/portrait of lovely lady, plush back & spine.................... 40.00

Album, photograph, black leather cover w/embossed brass clasp, w/75 photographs.............. 70.00

Album, photograph, brown leather cover w/silver decorated clasp, w/50 photographs.............. 50.00

Album, photograph, plush cover w/diamond-shaped mirror insert, w/over 60 cartes de visite & tintypes, 1886 patent date 55.00

Scrapbook, w/80 trade cards & 20 calling cards, cover inscribed "1887 Christmas" 50.00

Scrapbook, w/over 90 greeting cards, calling cards & trade cards, ca. 1904 .... 60.00

Scrapbook, w/over 100 trade cards, calling cards, diecuts, etc., Victorian 89.00

Scrapbook, w/over 150 trade cards & Santa Claus diecuts, pre-1900... 40.00

Scrapbook, w/27 large pages of trade cards 85.00

Scrapbook, w/44 pages of newspaper clippings & photographs pertaining to Charles Lindbergh, the Sino-Japanese War, etc., 1932 .... 10.00

Scrapbook, w/letters & pamphlets written in German pertaining to Hitler, Goebbels & others, 1925-38........................ 75.00

Scrapbook, w/newspaper & magazine clippings & photos pertaining to Ronald Reagan & Jane Wyman........................ 50.00

SCRIMSHAW

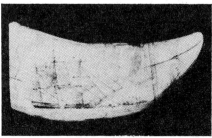

Susan's Tooth Scrimshaw

In recent years a flood of fine grade hard plastic scrimshaw reproductions have appeared on the market and the novice collector is urged to learn to distinguish these new items from the 19th century pieces.

Corset busk, whale bone, engraved overall w/ship, sunbursts, hex signs & "1767 Penn.," 18th c., 12" l. $220.00

Corset busk, pan bone, engraved house, rosettes, pr. of trees, plants, flower basket & branches, pierced heart design in end, 1830-40...................... 300.00

Paper cutter w/crown, ivory, young woman wearing dress, "G.D.," 2 hearts w/name, 19th c., 10½".... 100.00

Pipe tamp, whale bone, carved in the form of a lady's leg w/incised geometric designs, 2½" h. 135.00

Powder horn, engraved ship or sloop & primitive soldier w/gun, 18th c., 6" l. 150.00

Walrus tusk, obverse engraved w/figure of Liberty draped in American flag, hoisting a Phrygian cap above her head, above a fully-rigged whaling vessel & an American flag, reverse w/an American eagle grasping a sidewise United States shield in its talons & a banner inscribed "Union Forever" in its beak, above a hump-back whale, whole entwined w/floral vine, details picked out in red & blue, ca. 1870, 14" l. 825.00

Walrus tusk, engraved whaling ship, whales, birds, men in boats, 2 American flags, dated 1842, 23½" l. 2,000.00

Walrus tusk, engraved w/naval battle scene, Bonhomme Richard & Serapis Capts. John Paul Jones & Richard Pearson at War in 1779... 500.00

Whale's tooth, obverse engraved w/depiction of Confederate cruiser, inscribed "C.S.S. Sumter, R. Semmes, Esq., Commandg, Commnd, June 1, 1861, Disbanded April 9, 1862," reverse engraved w/another Confederate cruiser inscribed "CSS Alabama, R. Semmes Esq., Commnd Aug 24th 1862, Captured Jan 11, USS Halloras," base inscribed "290," 5¼" l. 1,650.00

Whale's tooth, engraved well-groomed gentleman, "Henry," one side & beautifully-gowned lady, "Emily," reverse, 1830-40, 6 1/8" l. 4,000.00

Whale's tooth, engraved Indian w/bow & arrow on one side, ca. 1840, 6 7/8" l. 950.00

Whale's tooth, "Susan's Tooth," engraved by Frederick Myrick w/the ship "Susan" cutting-in, her boats down, harpooning & lancing sperm whales & inscribed above the ship "The Susan on the coast of Japan," w/American eagle, shield & "E Pluribus Unum" banner above crossed American flags & anchor, banding inscription "Engraved by Fredk Myrick on board of the Susan, September 1, 1829," reverse engraved w/the ship Susan trying-out, her boats down after sperm whales below banner inscribed "The Susan on her homeward bound passage," tooth sides engraved w/"The ship Susan of Nantucket" & "Death to the living, long live the killers, Success to sailors wives & greasy luck to whalers," 7" l. (ILLUS.) 27,500.00

SEWING ADJUNCTS

Carved & Painted Wood Pin Cushion

Also see PIN CUSHION DOLLS.

Book, "The Sewing Book for Children's & Girls' Clothes," early 1900's $10.00
Buttonhole scissors, marked "Wolcott's, Boston, 1852" 25.00
Darner, blown blue glass 45.00
Darner, blown spatter glass, bulbous 3" d. head pulled into graceful twisted handle, red, pink, white & blue spatter in clear, Corning, New York, 1908, 7" l. ... 375.00
Darner, paperweight-type, lavender 5-petalled lily-type flower enclosed in clear glass, bubble center, green stem w/five elongated bubbles extending to end of handle, 6" l. 125.00
Darner, turned wood, egg shape w/handle...................... 7.00
Embroidery scissors, sterling silver,

repousse' handles w/beaded trim........................... 32.00
Eyelet punch, sterling silver, w/gauge 22.00
Garment cutter, 1895, in original box w/instruction booklet........ 45.00
Glove darner, sterling silver, attached top, 4 rows of beading, 4 5/8" l........................ 48.00
Needle case, celluloid, umbrella-shaped, ivory & black 46.00
Needle case, sterling silver, ornate, Victorian 100.00
Needle case, vegetable ivory, carved figural acorn w/screw-on ends, 3 7/8" l. 85.00
Pin cushion, beaded cloth, heart-shaped, intricate colorful design, Victorian 65.00
Pin cushion, bronze, figural lady holding spear, France, 19th c. 175.00
Pin cushion, green satin w/beige crochet overlay, heart-shaped, 7 x 5"........................ 24.00
Pin cushion, carved & painted wood, model of a high-button shoe w/shaped heel, painted in tones of light green, red, yellow & black w/decorative device on throat, opening w/green velvet cushion, ca. 1860, 3½" h. (ILLUS.)........ 495.00
Sewing bird, brass, clamp-on type, dated 1856 .... 175.00
Sewing bird, brass, single cushion at front of bird, "A. Gerould & Co." 220.00

Sewing Box with Pin Cushion Top

Sewing box, wooden, 1-drawer & turned post for pin cushion, 8½" h. (ILLUS.) 55.00
Sewing box, mahogany veneer & hardwood, 3-tier w/two drawers & thread compartment, pin cushion finial, early 20th c., 8½" h.... 105.00
Sewing box, pine, case w/two dovetailed drawers, applied ornaments & removable birds on corn-

ers, tiered top w/pins for spools of thread, pin cushion top w/bird finial, old red paint, 11" h........ 775.00

Tape measure, advertising, "Bell Telephone," celluloid, 1½" d. 40.00

Tape measure, advertising, "Hoover," model of a vacuum cleaner....................... 22.00

Tape measure, brass, model of a pig 75.00

Tape measure, celluloid, model of an alarm clock, marked Germany, 2" d........................... 65.00

Tape measure, celluloid, model of a fish, 4½" l.................... 40.00

Tape measure, china, figural Dutch Girl, Germany 24.00

Tape measure, metal, model of a cat playing w/brass ball, turn tail to retract tape into ball 75.00

Tape measure, metal, model of a shoe, embossed "Three Feet in One Shoe," 2¾" 65.00

Tape measure, silverplate, model of a fish 80.00

Tape measure, tin, model of an egg w/fly pull 30.00

Tatting shuttle, sterling silver, Art Nouveau design................ 70.00

Thimble, advertising, "Andrews Liver Salts," sterling silver, chased daisy band, dated 1926 .... 85.00

Thimble, 14k gold, beaded & floral band, crocheted holder, Victorian 110.00

Gold Thimble

Thimble, 14k gold, 8-sided band, alternating chased & plain panels (ILLUS.)....................... 95.00

Thimble, rose gold, "Simmons Bros. & Co." 100.00

Thimble, child's, sterling silver, chased scene of 3 houses in band, "Eva White" 32.00

Thimble, sterling silver, engraved house, trees & lake scene....... 35.00

Thimble, sterling silver, mother-of-pearl case.................... 90.00

Thimble case, blue Satin glass w/brass trim, egg-shaped, blue silk lining, w/ornate hanging loop, France, overall 8½" l....... 165.00

Thimble case, sterling silver w/reticulated hinged lid, embossed berries & vines, hallmarked 95.00

Thimble case, silverplate, Kate Greenaway type girl supporting holder, w/sterling silver thimble.. 125.00

Thread box, carved walnut, ivory eyelets, 3 sections 85.00

Thread caddy, cast iron, footed base w/saucer tray below revolving spool holder, grape decor on pin cushion 65.00

Thread caddy, silverplate, 8-spindle rotating-type, figural enameled cherub on post, pin cushion top, footed base, Tufts 395.00

SHAKER COLLECTIBLES

Group of Shaker Pantry Boxes

The Shakers, a religious sect founded by Ann Lee, first settled in this country at Watervliet, N.Y., near Albany, in 1774 and by 1880 there were nine settlements in America. Workmanship in Shaker crafts is an extension of their religious beliefs and features plain and simple designs reflecting a chaste elegance that is now much in demand though relatively few early items are available. Also see BASKETS and FURNITURE.

Apple peeler, circular ring blade, wood handle, 5¼" l. $30.00

Basket, cheese, w/support rails, miniature hexagonal weave, 9" d......................... 185.00

ısket, cov., handled, 10 x 9"...... 66.00

Basket, picnic, ash splint over reed, old white paint, 11" oval 125.00

Bonnet, cotton covered poplar, large brim 45.00

Bonnet carrying box, oval w/wide overlap, fitted cover w/two fingers, wide leather strap handle w/buckle at the top, 19th c., 16½ x 22", 13½" h. 605.00

Box, cov., palm leaf w/h.p. strawberries on lid, 3" w., 6½" l...... 98.00
Bucket, cov., wood, 4 finger lappets, copper tacks, wooden pins,
handled, 9½" d., 10" h. 195.00
Carrier, open, bentwood oval, 3-
finger lappet construction secured
w/copper tacks, bentwood handle, yellow ochre paint w/natural
finished handle, paper label
"Manufactured by the Canterbury
Shakers, East Canterbury, N.H.,"
date "1841" carved in, 9 x 6½"
oval 495.00
Coffee pot, cov., tin, Sabbathday
Lake, Maine, early 19th c., 4¾"
base d., 5¾" h................. 135.00
Firkin, cov., staved construction
w/four finger lappets w/copper
fasteners, wooden bail handle,
original putty colored paint,
9½" d., 9½" h. 220.00
Flour scoop, maple, half round back
w/wooden threaded turned handle, copper fasteners attach scoop
to back & handle, 3½ x 8 x 13" .. 49.00
Hearth broom, original paper label,
"Shaker Broom Geo. Salmon,"
37" l. 30.00
Lap board, pine, paper label "This
Shaker lap board was made by
Brother Delmer Wilson of Sabbathday Lake, Maine, Circa 1910,
signed, Sister R. Mildred Bankes,"
24 x 12¼"..................... 75.00
Maple syrup dispenser, tin, Enfield,
New Hampshire, 11½" l. 25.00
Pantry boxes, cov., bentwood oval,
pine & maple w/finger lappet construction, copper tacks, graduated
from 1¾ x 4 5/8" to 5 7/8 x 13½",
together w/circular ash sieve fastened w/copper pins, ca. 1850,
8 pcs. (ILLUS.) 3,575.00
Pantry box, bentwood oval, finger
lappet construction, wood pins,
copper nails, 3¾ x 2 3/16"....... 125.00
Pantry box, cov., bentwood oval,
single finger lappet construction
on lid & base, copper tacks, old
red paint, 8" l.................. 65.00
Pantry box, cov., bentwood round,
black metal band on lid, old red &
yellow paint, paper label on bottom inscribed "Lucy F. Willard,
Shaker Village, New Hampshire,"
11 5/8" d. 200.00
Pantry box, cov., bentwood oval, 4
finger lappet construction, box
painted light blue & cover banded
w/brilliant blue, 19th c., 12 x
8¼", 4¾" h...................... 715.00
Poster, "Shaker's Medical Prepara-
tions, Imperial Rose Balm, New

Lebanon, N.Y.," black printing on
yellow paper, framed, 17½ x 15"
(fading & stains) 110.00
Print, "Shakers near Lebanon,"
hand-colored lithograph, mahogany veneer beveled frame, 16½ x
12½" 625.00
Sewing basket, cov., woven splint in
cheese weave, nut brown patina,
round top, octagonal base, 10" d.,
2½" h......................... 150.00
Song book, Elder Eleazer Wright,
Watervliet, New York, in manu-
script composed during the years
1832-46, commencing at age 62,
w/an autobiography continuing
w/original verses, hymns, march-
ing songs, funeral hymn & songs
"received" from Mother Ann, written during visits to various Shaker
communities, New Lebanon,
Pleasant Hill, Shirley, full calf
binding, 4¾ x 7¼"............. 495.00
Spice boxes, 1 w/cover lap & body
lap in opposite directions, possibly
Harvard School, other smaller
w/two fingers, extra pins on top
& base, old finish on both,
19th c., 4¾ x 6¼" & 4 x 5¼",
pr............................. 192.50
Wire whisk w/turned wood handle,
10½" l. 50.00

SHAVING MUGS

FRATERNAL
American Legion $200.00
B.P.O.E. (Benevolent & Protective
Order of Elks), elk's head
emblem 175.00
F.O.E. (Fraternal Order of Eagles),
w/emblem & name.............. 215.00
I.O.O.F. (Independent Order of Odd
Fellows), w/emblem & name 175.00
Knights of Columbus, w/emblem &
name in gold 110.00
Knights of Pythias, red holly berries
w/green leaves decor & name in
gold 85.00
Masonic, emblem & floral decor,
w/name....................... 90.00
Modern Woodmen of America,
shield emblem & tools in wreath
of green leaves & red berries,
w/name in gold................ 140.00

GENERAL
China, decal of blue florals on white
ground, w/name in gold 35.00
China, pansies & long-stemmed

roses on white ground,
Germany 32.00

China, ironstone, Cable shape, all
white 25.00

China, ironstone, Chinese shape, all
white 90.00

China, ironstone, Moss Rose patt.,
John Maddock & Sons 27.50

China, Lenox Belleek, h.p. floral
decor 125.00

Limoges China Shaving Mug

China, Limoges, h.p. florals, gold
trim, Bawo & Dotter blank
w/American decoration (ILLUS.) .. 45.00

China, R.S. Prussia, carnation mold,
blue floral decor 165.00

China, R.S. Prussia, Flora portrait
decor on green lustre shaded to
white ground, gold trim 250.00

China, scuttle-type, Blue Onion
patt., marked "Union Shaving
Mug," 1870 patent date 58.00

China, scuttle-type, floral decor
w/gold ruffled edge 45.00

China, scuttle-type, h.p. florals,
marked "Union Shaving Mug, pat.
Sept. 20, 1870" 45.00

China, scuttle-type, Mastiff dog's
head w/red eyes & pointed teeth,
marked "Bavaria" 45.00

China, scuttle-type, roses decor,
gold trim, Germany 45.00

Hampshire pottery, scuttle-type,
relief-molded leaf spray, glossy
blue glaze w/gold trim 45.00

Silverplate, Art Nouveau style
woman w/flowing hair, "Derby
Silver Co." 95.00

Silverplate, milk glass insert, "Barth
Co." 22.00

OCCUPATIONAL

Automobile dealer, early auto 590.00

Baker, bakery wagon w/horse &
driver, w/name 425.00

Baseball player, player at bat &
florals, gilt trim, w/name 675.00

Boiler maker, large man w/sledge
hammer beside large boiler 375.00

Brewmaster, wooden vat, tools,
hops & barley 475.00

Butcher's Shaving Mug

Butcher, steer's head & crossed
knife & steel (ILLUS.) 200.00

Dry goods clerk, clerk in store
measuring cloth 475.00

Farmer, man plowing field w/two
horses, "K.T. & K. China" 120.00

Fireman, horse-drawn fire wagon,
Germany 195.00

Gambler, hand of cards decor (chip
under base) 250.00

Greengrocer, fruits & vegetables in
wagon w/horse & driver 375.00

Grocer, country store
scene .... 400.00 to 475.00

House painter, man on scaffolding
w/brush in hand, w/name 525.00

Hunter, man shooting at quail
w/Pointer dog at his side 325.00

Milkman, horse-drawn delivery
wagon & driver, w/name in
gold 200.00

Miner, "United Mine Workers of
America" clasped hands emblem,
pearlized finish .... 80.00 to 125.00

Musician, trumpet player,
w/name .... 200.00 to 275.00

Paperhanger, man brushing wall-
paper on ceiling 675.00

Railroad conductor, caboose,
w/name 350.00

Railroadman, "Brotherhood of
Locomotive Engineers," steam en-
gine & tender lettered "B. of L.F.
& E." 400.00

Sailor, anchor, woman w/American
flag & sailing ship in background 400.00

Telegrapher, hand operating telegraph key 335.00

Tinsmith, furnace & shears on
maroon ground, w/name in
gold 225.00

SHEET MUSIC

"Aren't You Glad You're You"

"America Today," 1917, Statue of
Liberty & Woodrow Wilson on
cover $20.00

"Aren't You Glad You're You," 1945,
Bing Crosby on cover (ILLUS.)..... 15.00

"As Time Goes By," Humphrey
Bogart & Ingrid Bergman on
cover 30.00

"A Warmin' Up in Dixie," blacks
dancing around campfire on cover
by E.T. Paull 40.00

"Blue Beads," beautiful Indian maid-
en on cover 7.00

"Charge of the Light Brigade," cover
by E.T. Paull 15.00

"Daddy Long Legs," Mary Pickford
on cover 5.00

"Dear Heart," Louis Armstrong on
cover 15.00

"Der Fuhrer's Face," 1942, Hitler
caricature on cover 20.00

"Don't Worry," Marty Robbins on
cover 5.00

"Dragnet Theme," 1953, Jack Webb
on cover 4.00

"Dream Train," 1928, Guy Lombardo
& train on cover 5.00

"Fire Drill," 1910, horse-drawn
steamer on way to fire on cover.. 15.00

"Follow the Fleet," 1936, Fred
Astaire & Ginger Rogers on
cover 8.00

"Four Horsemen of the Apocalypse,"
cover by E.T. Paull 45.00

"Gloria," 1960, theme from "Butterfield 8," Elizabeth Taylor on
cover 10.00

"Gold Mine in the Sky," 1937, Kate
Smith on cover................. 10.00

"Half As Much," Rosemary Clooney
on cover 5.00

"Hello My Dearie," 1917, Ralph
Kirchner Ziegfield Follies cover ... 20.00

"Hold Your Man," Clark Gable &
Jean Harlow on cover 15.00

"I Got Rhythm," Judy Garland &
Mickey Rooney on cover 20.00

"I'll Get By," Irene Dunne & Spencer
Tracy on cover 10.00

"I'm Putting All My Eggs In One Basket," Ginger Rogers & Fred
Astaire on cover 12.50

"I'm Wishing," Snow White on
cover 10.00

"In the Sweet Long Ago," 1916,
lovely lady wearing hoop skirt on
cover 5.00

"It's All New To Me," Shirley Temple
on cover 15.00

"Keep Away From Fellows Who
Own Automobiles," 1912, car on
cover 8.00

"Laughing Waters," Indian maiden
on cover 6.75

"The Little Red Schoolhouse," 1922,
schoolhouse, general store & post
office on cover 10.00

"Love Me Tender," 1956, Elvis Presley on cover 14.00

"Love Thy Neighbor," Bing Crosby &
Carol Lombard on cover 10.00

"Lucky Lindy," Spirit of St. Louis on
cover 20.00

"Maine Stein Song," 1930, Rudy
Vallee on cover 10.00

"Midnight Flyer," cover by E.T.
Paull 18.00

"My Pretty Firefly," Indian maiden
on cover 8.00

"The New Yorkers," 1930, Peter
Arno cartoon cover............. 20.00

"No Need to Worry," 1935, Gene
Autry on cover................. 10.00

"Oh Johnny," Andrews Sisters on
cover 4.00

"Old Spinning Wheel," Baby Rose
Marie on cover 4.50

"On The Good Ship Lollipop," 1934,
Shirley Temple on cover 14.00

"Over the Rainbow," Judy Garland
on cover 20.00

"Paper Doll," 1943, Frank Sinatra on
cover 10.00

"The Rainbow Schottisch," composed
by H. Kleber, w/colored lithographic view on cover by Sarony
& Major, 5 pp. 12.50

"Rock Me to Sleep Mother," ca.
1860, words by Florence Perry,
music by George R. Poulton, published by J. Church, Jr., Cincinnati, Ohio, 5 pp. 10.00

"Rum and Coca-Cola"

"Rum & Coca-Cola," Andrews Sisters
on cover (ILLUS.) 12.00
"Sadie Thompson's Song," Rita Hay-
worth on cover 10.00
"Sidewalks of New York," 1928, Al
Smith on cover 10.00
"Silver Haired Daddy of Mine,"
Gene Autry on cover 16.00
"Skippy," 1930, cartoon cover 25.00
"Sweetheart," 1939, Jeanette Mac-
Donald & Nelson Eddy on cover . . 6.00
"Sympathy," from The Firefly,
Jeanette MacDonald on cover 12.50
"Two Sleepy People," 1938, Bob
Hope on cover 10.00
"We Can Work It Out," 1964, Beatles
on cover 49.00
"You & I," Judy Garland on cover . . . 7.00
"You Gave Me Your Heart," Rudolph
Valentino on cover 30.00

SIGNS & SIGNBOARDS

*Also see BREWERIANA, COCA-COLA
ITEMS, POSTERS and the "Special Focus"
on WINE HISTORY & ADVERTISING.*

Ammunition, "Western," self-framed
tin, hunter w/two dogs in field . . . $370.00
Automobile parts, "Powell Muf-
flers," tin, devil's hand atop 1930
model automobile w/passengers
& "Carbon Monoxide Danger" 275.00
Automotive supplies, "Polarine Oil &
Greases for Motors," graniteware,
blue & white 135.00

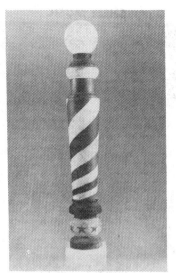

Wooden Barber Pole

Barber pole, turned & painted wood,
baluster-turned tapering column,
painted red, white & blue broad
spiraling stripes, w/metal collar
holding a milk white glass globe-
shade, probably Roanoke, Virginia,
ca. 1880, 78" h. (ILLUS.) 2,530.00
Bicycles, "Cleveland," embossed tin,
bicycle, ca. 1900 . . . . 245.00
Blacksmith, "J.E. Sheehan Horse
Shoeing," carved & painted wood,
horseshoe-shaped, rim, cleats &
lettering heightened w/gilding
on a black ground, top w/a rein-
forcing wrought iron band, Maine,
late 19th-early 20th c.,
27¼ x 21¼" 1,430.00
Boot maker, wooden, silhouette of
high boot w/Cuban heel, traces of
weathered red, white & black
paint, tin edging, wrought iron
hangers, 27½" h. 375.00
Boots, "Gold Seal Boots," self-
framed tin, large boot w/"Sold
Here," Standard Sign Co. 750.00
Bread, "Dexter's Bread," granite-
ware, "Don't Forget Dexter's
Mother's Bread," 24 x 18" 95.00
Candy, "Cartier's Chocolates," tin,
"The Cartier Idea, Eat Small
Pieces & Stay Trim," red box
w/bluebirds 125.00
Candy, "Towney's Chocolate," die-
cut cardboard lady eating chocolates beside Tiffany lamp, dated
1909 . . . . 325.00
Carpet sweeper, "Bissel Floor
Sweeper," cardboard, easel-type,
house in meadow & product on
bottom, white, pink & green,
1918 . . . . 135.00

"Grape-Nuts"

Cereal, "Grape-Nuts," self-framed
tin, schoolgirl starting her day
w/St. Bernard dog under watchful
eye of her mother, ca. 1910,
30½ x 20¼" (ILLUS.) 600.00
Champagne, "Korbel California
Champagne," self-framed tin, lady
w/grapes & bottle, Grand Pacific
Vintages, San Francisco, dated
1906 .... 375.00
Chocolate, "Walter Baker & Co.,"
self-framed tin, LaBelle Chocolatiere carrying tray of chocolate,
19¼ x 15¼" 540.00

"Murad" Sign

Cigarettes, "Murad," self-framed tin,
girl holding tray (ILLUS.) 950.00
Cigarettes, "Phillip Morris," embossed tin, Johnny holding cigarette pack 50.00

Cigars, "Randolph Macon," self-
framed tin, man, woman & show-
case w/boxes of cigars 1,700.00

"Munsingwear Underwear"

Clothing, "Munsingwear Underwear," self-framed tin, little girl
wearing underwear looking at
herself in mirror, 1910, 28 x 26"
(ILLUS.)........................ 295.00
Coffee, "McLaughlin's," lithographed
paper, sack of coffee w/two
hands clasped, ca. 1900 .... 65.00
Cotton, "Red Cross Cotton," paperboard, Negroes in field picking
cotton, 1894, framed, 33 x 24".... 235.00
Cream separator, "DeLaval," tin, 5
different pictures w/farm girl hug-
ging cow center, original frame,
41 x 30" 1,025.00
Dairy, "Metzger's Milk," graniteware, bottle-shaped w/baby's
face center, 3' h................. 575.00
Dime store, "F.W. Woolworth," reverse painting on glass, "Any
Item 10 Cents" 415.00
Fertilizer, "Virginia Carolina Fertilizer," lithographed cardboard,
farmer wearing straw hat & driving wagon filled w/colorful
vegetables down country lane,
1905 .... 82.50
Food product, "Beechnut Peanut Butter," lithographed cardboard, 3
children at table making peanut
butter sandwiches, pail & bread
on table, 1906, 36 x 24" 600.00
Food product, "Swift's Premium
Ham," self-framed tin, country
home, barn, ham & slab of bacon,
ca. 1915, round 200.00
Fountain pen, "Waterman's," self-

framed tin, 2 boys writing
w/pens 475.00
Furniture, "Globe-Wernicke Book-
cases," tin, couple filling
bookcase 200.00
Gum, "Clark's Teaberry Gum," tin,
colorful pack of gum 110.00
Gun powder, "Dupont," self-framed
tin, hunting dogs (2) & gun powder, 1903, 28 x 22" 680.00
Insurance, "Hartford Fire Insurance
Co.," tin, large stag, 22 x 19"
oval 140.00
Insurance, "New York Plate Glass
Insurance Co.," graniteware,
Brooklyn Bridge & Statue of Liber-
ty in background, 15 x 12" 290.00
Light bulbs, "Edison Mazda Lamp,"
tin, Maxfield Parrish illustration of
2 Robin Hoods w/light bulb 1,750.00
Mortician, hand-forged iron bracket
w/wooden die-cut gold leaf coffin,
ca. 1845 .... 275.00
Motorcycles, "Henderson," paper,
framed, 11 x 14" 100.00
Motor oil, "Atlantic Aviation Motor
Oil," tin, airplane pictured, wood-
en frame 100.00
Motor oil, "Texaco," graniteware,
"Free Crank Case Service," shows
oil can pouring oil.............. 170.00
Newspaper, "Baltimore Sun," embossed tin, "We Have the Sun De-
livered by Auto" 35.00
Optician, "American Optical Co.,"
paper, old man at country store
post office unwrapping new glasses, "Mail Order Specs," 1942,
framed, 20 x 25" 95.00
Optometrist, "Optometrist," reverse
painting on glass, eye-shaped,
oval 365.00
Organs, "Estey Co.," paper, 2-color
picture of organ, 1874, 28 x 22" .. 225.00
Paint, "Bay State," graniteware,
Pilgrim on outline of Massachusetts 125.00
Paint, "Carter White Lead Paint,"
die-cut paperboard, easel-type,
1923, colorful, 26 x 52½" 56.00
Paper, "Wissahiccon Paper Mills, 30
South Sixth St., Philadelphia, Pa.,"
lithographed paper, paper mill in
forest landscape setting,
24 x 19" 435.00
Patent medicine, "Abbey's Efferves-
cent Salt," die-cut cardboard, lady
holding glass, dated 1899 .... 125.00
Patent medicine, "Bromo Quinine,"
celluloid over tin, man pointing
finger, "For Colds & Grip"........ 165.00
Pawn broker, three gilt-copper balls
on wrought iron standard, overall
53" h. (ILLUS.) 325.00

Pawn Broker's Trade Sign

Peanuts, "Planters Peanuts," die-cut
of woman holding display for
bags of 5c peanuts 375.00
Pharmacy, "Prescriptions," reverse
painting on glass, Rx mortar &
pestle & "Compounded Exactly as
your Doctor Orders"............. 100.00
Phonographs, "Brunswick Phonographs & Records," self-framed
tin, lady listening to phonograph 975.00
Poison, "Rough on Rats," colorful
lithograph, children, adults, police, cat & dog chasing a rat
w/brooms, axes, irons, bottles,
clubs, etc., ca. 1890 .... 650.00
Poultry, "Tweddle Chicks! Order
Here!," embossed tin, hatched
chick, 19 x 27" 50.00
Radios, "Majestic," reverse painting
on glass, family scene around radio, ca. 1920, wooden frame,
18 x 15" 725.00
Railroad, "Chicago Northwestern,"
reverse painting on glass, "Safety
First," 23" sq. 350.00
Railway express, "American Express," embossed tin, 1904 ...... 175.00
Razor blades, "Eveready Radio Steel
Blades," lithographed tin, man
shaving 3¼' x 11" 185.00
Razors, "Gillette Safety Razor," die-
cut lithographed tin, man shaving,
Beach Co., 3 3/8 x 15".......... 875.00
Refrigerators, "Frigedaire," graniteware, "We Cool Our Milk with
Frigedaire - made only by General Motors," cow, 20 x 14" 188.00
Restaurant, iron, 4-tine eating fork
shape, ca. 1880, 21½" l. 250.00
Seafood, "Sealshipt Oyster Agency,"
graniteware, triangular, blue &
white 135.00
Sewing machine, "New Home Sewing Machine," lithographed paper,
living room scene, older woman
beside sewing machine, young
woman fitting pants on small
boy 345.00

Shoe polish, "Bixby's," tin, die-cut frog in tuxedo, spats & top hat holding can of Bixby's, large 750.00

Shoes, "Brown Shoe Co.," lithograph, Victorian lady 375.00

Soap, "Jap Rose Soap," paperboard, Japanese children giving doll a bath, 1910, framed, 39 x 23" 285.00

Soap, "Lava," hanging-type, cardboard, double-sided, children in river 30.00

Soft drink, "Alta Ginger Ale, San Francisco," self-framed tin 1,100.00

Soft drink, "Canada Dry," tin, bottle-shaped, dated 1925 .... 40.00

Soft drink, "Cleo Cola," tin, Cleopatra pictured 225.00

Soft drink, "Dr. Pepper," porcelain, "Good For Life," plaid decor, 27 x 11" 48.00

Soft drink, "Golden Spring Sarsaparilla," tin, bottle & flared glass, ca. 1905 .... 95.00

Sporting goods, "Paracord Black Knight Golf Balls," embossed tin, golfer wearing knickers.......... 145.00

Sporting goods, "Spalding," cardboard, 2 skaters, 1920, 14 x 22" .. 115.00

Stoneware, "Stoneware, The Best Food Container," self-framed tin, boy wearing high button shoes reaching in jar for donut, dog begging for bite................. 750.00

Stoves, "Front Rank Stoves," embossed tin, red, grey & black devils climbing out of stove 195.00

Stoves, "Round Oak," cardboard, street car sign w/couple, Indian & furnace 150.00

Suntan lotion, "Norwich Suntan Oil," tin, gentleman & lady at beach using oil, 1920's 80.00

Tailor, "Rose & Company, Merchant Tailors," metal, man in suit, "This Label Means Guaranteed Garments," book reading "Over 300 Samples to Select From," ca. 1900, 26½ x 18" 357.50

Tavern, "Rail Road House," carved & painted wood, painted in oil w/depiction of steam driven paddle wheeler gunboat in open seas, reverse w/steam locomotive, molded edge, W. Bursley, Barnstable, Massachusetts, mid-19th c., 28½ x 38½" planked rectangle 7,425.00

Tea, "Lyons Tea," porcelain, corner sign, colorful, "Lyons Tea Sold Here" 75.00

Telephone, "Bell of Canada Telephone Agency," graniteware, blue & white, 18 x 28" 325.00

Telephone, "Public Telephone,"

graniteware, blue & white w/arrow & emblem "The Bell System," 12¼ x 5¾" 75.00

Thread, "Clark's O.N.T.," paper & cardboard, lady holding spool of thread w/spools on table, 1880's 450.00

Tires, "Goodyear Motorcycle," porcelain, die-cut man on motorcycle 650.00

Tobacco, "British Navy Chewing Tobacco," cardboard, sailors & dog 85.00

Tobacco, "Bull Durham," paperboard, bullfighting scene, 1909, original wooden frame, 34 x 22".. 375.00

Tobacco, "Old English Curve Cut Pipe Tobacco," tin, man in red coat smoking long pipe 585.00

Prince Albert Tobacco Sign

Tobacco, "Prince Albert," self-framed tin, Prince Albert w/Indian (ILLUS.) 1,195.00

Transportation, "Yellow Cab," tin w/calendar holder, cab w/driver, 1920's 45.00

Varnish, "Voorhies Varnish," tin, figural die-cut of woman pointing to sign for varnish 4,500.00

Watches, "Elgin," paperboard, Father Time & watch, ca. 1910, wooden frame, 22 x 16" 160.00

Watches, "Rockford Watches," tin, shows time for 20 cities in the world, 1900, 23 x 17" 550.00

Whiskey, "Bauer," paperboard, cowboy, Indian & Chinaman rolling dice, 1870's, framed, 33 x 24" 650.00

Whiskey, "Belle of Anderson Sour Mash," reverse painting on glass, nudes at public bath, framed, 41 x 32" 1,275.00

Whiskey, "Green River Whiskey," self-framed tin, "She was bred in

Green River Whiskey Sign

Old Kentucky," black man & mule
(ILLUS.)........................ 650.00
Whiskey, "Old Darling," reverse
painting on glass, bourbon & rye,
Prestonville, Kentucky, ca. 1910,
original frame, 40 x 30" 550.00

"Paul Jones Whiskey"

Whiskey, "Paul Jones Pure Rye
Whiskey," self-framed tin, old
farmer pouring drink, 31 x 23"
(ILLUS.)........................ 250.00
Wine, "Virginia Dare Beverages,"
celluloid, lovely girl w/lettering
"Thanks for your Business" 50.00

SILHOUETTES

These cut-out paper portraits in profile were named after Etienne de Silhouette, Louis XV's unpopular minister of finance and an amateur profile cutter. As originally applied, the term was synonymous with cheapness, or anything reduced to its simplist state.

These substitutes for the more expensive oil paintings or miniatures were popular from about 1770 until 1860 when daguerreotype images replaced the vogue. Silhouettes may be either hollow-cut, with the head cut away leaving the white paper frame for mounting against a dark background, or the profile itself may be cut from black paper and pasted to a light background.

Bust portrait of a child, hollow-cut &
mounted on black, framed,
5 5/8" d. $85.00
Bust portraits of 2 children, hollow-
cut w/block-printed torsos, backs
inscribed "Ruth M. Johnson" &
"Anjanette Johnson," each in simple round pewter frame attributed
to Samuel Pierce, Greenfield,
Massachusetts, 3¼" d., pr. 475.00

"Peale's Museum" Silhouette

Bust portraits of a lady & gentleman, hollow-cut & mounted on
black paper, one impressed
"Peale's Museum" on white paper,
original frames, 5¼ x 6 3/8", pr.
(ILLUS. of one) 200.00
Bust portrait of a woman, hollow-
cut, back inscribed w/identity of
subject & history of portrait to
October 1900, turned wood frame,
5¼" warped d. 70.00
Bust portrait of a young woman,
hollow-cut, pen & ink detail,
arched gilt-edged mat & old
frame, 4 7/8 x 6" 250.00
Family group, full-length figures of
mother, father & child, cut & pasted on simple ink-washed background, original label on back
"Likenesses in profile - Executed
by Mons. Edouart," early black
reeded frame w/gilt liner,
20½ x 13½" 400.00
Gentleman wearing top hat & Prince
Albert type coat & carrying a

walking stick, full-length, cut &
pasted on paper w/a sepia-
washed background, inscribed
"Aug. Edouart fecit. New Orleans
Augt 1843," framed, 11 x 14¼". . . 485.00
Gentleman wearing a top hat in a
lithographed street scene background, full-length, cut & pasted,
cherrywood frame, 15½ x 12½".. 135.00
Lady & gentleman, full-length, cut &
pasted on paper w/simple ink
wash landscape background, inscribed "Chas. Fredk. Mayer" &
"Mary Mayer," signed by Auguste
Edouart, Baltimore, 1841, framed,
11¼ x 9 3/8" 825.00
Young man standing next to his dog
seated on a chair, full-length, cut
& pasted on paper against an ink
wash interior scene, w/ink inscription "Henry Hollingsworth
and Jasper," signed by Auguste
Edouart, 1843, framed,
11¼ x 9¼".................... 385.00

SNUFF BOTTLES & BOXES

*The habit of taking snuff (powdered tobac-
co meant for inhaling) began in 17th century
France and reached its peak during the 18th
century, spreading to England, elsewhere on
the Continent, and even to China, probably
introduced there by Spanish or Portuguese
traders. In Europe, tightly hinged porcelain
or metal boxes were considered desirable containers to house the aromatic snuff. Orientals
favored bottles of porcelain or glass, or carved
of agate, ivory or jade, often modeled in the
form of a human figure or fruit. By mid-19th
century the popularity of snuff declined and
consequently production of these exquisite
containers diminished.*

BOTTLES

Agate, supported on neatly finished
footrim, metallic stone encircled
by concentric band of white &
differing shades of grey & brown,
1820-80........................$880.00
Amber, ovoid, incised on front
w/prunus, mask & ring handles
on shoulders, rich honey color
cloudy suffusions, 1800-80..... 385.00
Carnelian, flattened ovoid, carved in
the form of melon w/trailing stalk
one side, rodent clambering up
reverse, orange, 1820-80 .... 550.00
Chalcedony, carved on front w/dark
layer depicting 2 squirrels clambering in search of grapes, reverse

w/small inclusion depicting fisherman in sampan, 1800-60........2,200.00
Cinnabar lacquer, ovoid, carved in
high relief on front w/attendant
leading horse & maiden, 2 further
maidens on reverse, all framed by
carved pine & rockwork 357.00
Enameled glass, double gourd form,
pale yellowish green ground
enameled w/Buddhist emblems
beneath tasselled collar on the
upper bulb 385.00
Hair crystal, double gourd form,
carved overall w/numerous aquatic creatures including fish, frogs &
shells, stone suffused w/almost
colorless rutile hairs............ 522.00
Jade, carved in the form of a rabbit,
white w/eyes set in coral,
1800-80 ....1,320.00
Peking Imperial yellow glass, carved
in the form of an elephant, the
Howdah cloth incised w/brocade
design beneath the ruyi head
collar on the back, rich egg-yoke
yellow tone, 1750-1830 ....2,750.00
Porcelain, bisque finish, molded one
side w/nine scholars seated
around table w/wine cups on top,
second group of 9 scholars on
reverse, one holding a qin, one
holding a fan, background studded
w/florettes, matching stopper,
Daoguang.....................4,675.00

BOXES

American Silver Snuff Box

Bird's eye maple, w/hinged lid,
3 3/8 x 2¾" 30.00
Brass, combination lock w/two dials
inscribed w/Roman numerals, 3 x
1¾" 45.00
Gold & enamel, oblong w/cut corners, cover w/oval plaque enameled w/courting couple in woodland setting, spandrels, sides &
base enameled w/translucent royal
blue over engine-turned ground,
borders w/opaque white enamel

stripes enclosing gold ribbon-
work, corners w/gold paillon urns,
Swiss, late 18th c., 3" l. 9,075.00
Horn, hinged lid w/tortoise shell in-
sert, 2¾" l. 40.00
Papier mache, round, painted scene
of young man reaching for miniature portrait held by young lady,
3½" d. (edge damage & repair) . . 100.00
Pewter, oval, hinged lid, marked
"Gerhardt," American, 2¾" l. 125.00
Silver, oval, channel-molded & rope-
molded sides, cover engraved
w/scene depicting Pyramus &
Thisbe by fountain, base engraved
w/three stylized cyphers surrounded by scrolling foliage within border of stylized leaves, Bartholo-
mew Schaats, New York, ca. 1720,
2 1/16" w., 2 7/8" l. (ILLUS.) 17,600.00
Silver w/"niello" decor, rectangular,
hinged lid w/scene of gentleman
traveling in open carriage, base
w/scene of courting people taking
refreshment, Russian, ca. 1825,
2¾" l. 660.00
Wooden, hand-carved model of a
heart, chamfered slide cover,
18th c. 150.00

SOAPSTONE

*This mineral used in producing all sorts of
soapstone wares has a greasy feel and has
been utilized, among other things, for carved
figure groups by the Chinese and others. It
also has been fashioned into utilitarian pieces.*

Figure of a Chinese fisherman,
laughing bearded man holding
fish suspended from pole &
w/basket & water birds at his
feet, China, early 20th c., 21" h. . . $330.00
Match holder, double, elaborate
carving 55.00
Model of a goat w/two kids at her
side, 5" h. 125.00
Salt dip, master size, carved Greek
Temple decor 27.50
Urn, carved w/figures, buildings,
florals & trees, large elephant
head handles, 7¼" d., 10¼" h.,
on wooden stand 150.00
Vase, carved ornate florals, variegated beige, tan & reddish brown,
marked "China," 6½" h. 85.00
Vase, bud, carved florals & foliage,
on wooden base, overall 7" h. . . . 40.00
Vase, bulbous, carved w/foliate
pomegranate tree one side, large

bird reverse, overall carved carp
& floral decor, 10" widest d.,
7" h. 95.00
Vase, double, carved w/two mon-
keys, birds & tree, 8¼ x 3½" 75.00

SOUVENIR SPOONS

Hudson-Fulton Celebration Spoon

Absecon lighthouse, Atlantic City,
New Jersey figural handle, plain
bowl $125.00
Alligator handle, Florida in bowl . . . 30.00
Art Nouveau nude woman handle,
Peoria in bowl 50.00
Bear figural handle, Yellowstone
National Park in bowl 30.00
Buffalo & full figure Indian handle,
Pan-American Exposition 1901 in
bowl 45.00
Buffalo Bill figural handle, Lookout
Mountain, Colorado in bowl 38.00
Buffalo, world globe & Pan Ameri-
can Exposition 1901 handle, Elec-
tricity Building in bowl 35.00
Catskill Mountains handle, kneeling
Indian in bowl 65.00
Cattails handle, Ft. Snelling, St.
Paul, Minnesota in bowl (demi-
tasse) 12.50
Chinook salmon handle, Mt. Rainier
& Seattle in bowl 35.00
Dehalve Maene, 1609 & New York
State seal on handle, Steamer
Clermont, 1807 & Hudson-Fulton
Celebration, 1909 in bowl, Tiffany
& Co. (ILLUS.) 90.00
General Houston & the Heroes
Monument handle, the Alamo in
bowl & back of handle 45.00
Graduate (girl) full figure handle,
plain bowl 48.00
Indian bust atop handle, Detroit har-
bor in bowl 32.00
Indian bust atop handle, Stanley
Park, Vancouver, B.C. in bowl
(demitasse) 18.50
Indian full figural handle, Banff,
Canada in bowl (demitasse) 19.00
Indian maiden on handle, Niagara
Falls in bowl 65.00
Indian chief w/full headdress han-

dle, University of Chicago in
bowl 39.00

Kansas City, Missouri handle, "Boss
of the Range" steer in bowl 32.00

Lily floral handle, San Luis Mission
in bowl (demitasse) 12.50

Masonic emblems handle, Pittsburgh
in bowl........................ 28.00

Milwaukee, Wisconsin handle, Pabst
Building in bowl................ 45.00

Miner full figure handle, Anaconda
mine, Butte, Montana in bowl 45.00

Miner holding bag of gold dust &
pick axe full figure handle, Gold-
en Gate, San Francisco in bowl,
Watson, Newell & Co. 50.00

Minnehaha Falls handle, Minneapolis, Minnesota in bowl 26.50

Mission San Gabriel 1771 handle,
Los Angeles in bowl 38.00

Mt. Hood atop handle, Portland,
Oregon & roses in bowl......... 55.00

New York City skyline handle, Luna
Park, Coney Island in bowl
(demitasse) 45.00

New York City skyline from North
River handle, Flatiron Building in
bowl 75.00

Niagara Falls handle, full figure
standing Indian in gold-washed
bowl (demitasse) 50.00

Niagara Falls w/enameled flags
handle, plain bowl, Gorham Co... 35.00

Pond lily floral handle, Wray,
Colorado in bowl............... 22.00

"Salem" witch & 3 pins handle, gold-
washed bowl, Daniel Low, Durgin
Co. (demitasse) 60.00

Salem witch, broom & cat handle,
plain bowl, Gorham Co.
(demitasse) 70.00

Santa Claus & chimney handle,
Merry Christmas in bowl 40.00

Statue of Liberty full figure handle,
Trinity Church in bowl 55.00

Teddy Roosevelt astride horse atop
handle, bust portrait in bowl 75.00

Woman at spinning wheel figural
handle, Home & Country in gold-
washed bowl 72.50

SPOOL, DYE & ALLIED CABINETS

Creamery supplies, "DeLaval," oak
case w/tin front w/embossed picture, holds 100 parts, 25 x 18"....$300.00

Dye, "Diamond," oak case
w/lithographed tin front depicting
the "Evolution of Woman"........ 575.00

Dye, "Diamond," oak case
w/lithographed tin front w/scene
of five children around hot air
balloon........................ 600.00

Dye, "Diamond," oak case
w/lithographed tin front w/scene
of mansion 550.00

Dye, "Putnam," tin w/lithographed
scene of Revolutionary War 145.00

Jeweler's supplies, 19-drawer, long
drawer across top, medium length
drawer center & 17 small drawers, porcelain knobs, molded top,
ca. 1860, 9½ x 9½ x 20" 225.00

Needles, "Boye," wooden, base-
drawer, round dispenser,
w/contents 75.00

Patent medicine, "Munyon's Pharmacy," wall-type, oak 450.00

Spool, "Best Six Cord," wooden,
2-drawer 255.00

"Clark's" Spool Cabinet

Spool, "Clark's," oak, 6-drawer
(ILLUS.)....................... 595.00

Spool, "Clark's," walnut, 6-drawer
w/ruby glass fronts 795.00

Spool, "Clark's O.N.T. Spool Cotton," oak, 6-drawer w/gold glass
fronts, brass drop pulls 695.00

Spool, "J. & P. Coats," cherry,
4-drawer 595.00

Spool, "J. & P. Coats," walnut finish,
3-drawer, countertop model, 19 x
17 x 6" 100.00

Spool, Richardson's Silk," wooden,
3-drawer 75.00

Spool, "Star Brand," metal,
4-drawer, w/glass panels, 16" l.,
14" w., 8" h.................... 45.00

Spool, "Star Twist," metal,
4-drawer 62.50

Thread, crochet, "Coats & Clark," tin
w/glass slant front 75.00

Watch parts, mainsprings, "American & American," oak, 3-drawer,
ornate trim, 15 x 9", 10" h. 225.00

STATUE OF LIBERTY COLLECTIBLES

"Liberty Enlightening the World" Figure

With the 1986 centennial celebration of Bartholdi's famous monument to Liberty the market was flooded with souvenir items representing "Lady Liberty." Interest in earlier souvenir items probably also peaked during the celebration but better quality pieces should continue to appreciate over the years.

Dye cabinet, "Dr. Morin Electric Dyes," lithographed tin, Statue of Liberty on door, Canadian $575.00

Figure, "Liberty Enlightening the World," white metal, classically draped figure w/right arm holding torch, black patina, stamped "American Committee Model/ Nov. 1878/ Feby 1879," 12" h. (ILLUS.) 3,190.00

Figure, "Liberty Enlightening the World," bronze, classically draped figure w/right arm holding torch, brown patina, inscribed "A Bartholdi" & "Thiebaut. Fres.," ca. 1885, 4' 5½" h. 148,500.00

"Liberty Bond," linen backed, by Macauley, 20 x 30" 185.00

Match holder, hanging-type, camphor glass, figure of Miss Liberty, dated 1876 .... 45.00

Paperweight, metal, figure of "Liberty Enlightening the World," advertising "Liberty Insurance Co.," pat. 1886, 7" h. 25.00

Pickle jar, clear glass w/brown stain, embossed figure of Statue of Liberty..................... 95.00

Reverse painting on glass, Statue of Liberty, oval frame painted to resemble tortoise-shell 125.00

Toothpick holder, amber glass, hand of Miss Liberty holding torch, 4¼" h........................ 475.00

STEAMSHIP MEMORABILIA

Liner "Aquitania" Tin Sign

The dawning of the age of world-wide airline travel brought about the decline of the luxury steamship liner for long-distance travel. Few large liners are still operating, but mementoes and souvenirs from their glamorous heyday are much sought-after today.

Advertising print, "Hamburg-American Lines," titled "The Development of Shipping," depicting ancient log dugout to steamship, shows 19 ships in all, framed, 29 x 40"......................$400.00

Ash tray, liner "Genova," smokestack-shaped............. 25.00

Ash tray, "Holland American Lines," Gouda Pottery 20.00

Bon bon spoon, liner "Queen Elizabeth I," silverplate w/engraved ship................... 14.00

Book, "The Blue Riband of the Atlantic," 1973, w/dust jacket 5.00

Book, pocket-type, "Diamond Jo Line Steamers, Mississippi River between St. Louis & St. Paul," 1890 .... 50.00

Bottle opener, liner "S.S. Vasari," sterling silver 20.00

Brooch, liner, "R.M.S. Mauretania," h.p. enameled ship, oval, ca. 1890 .... 42.00

Calendar tile, "Cunard Line," scene of Boston dock & ship, w/specs., 3½ x 4¾" 35.00

Call bell, liner "R.M.S. Alalunia," sterling silver 50.00

Canasta playing cards, double deck,

"Holland American Lines,"
in box......................... 15.00
Coffee & tea set: cov. coffee pot,
cov. teapot, creamer, sugar bowl
& demitasse c/s; "Furness Bermu-
da SS Line," china, Exotic Bird
patt., 6 pcs. 145.00
Compact, liner "R.M.S. Mauretania". 25.00
Creamer, "Great Northern Steamship Co.," china 55.00
Cup & saucer, "Dutch African Lines,"
china, straight sides, black medal-
lion of African map on white,
D.A.L. (Hutschenreuther, Selb,
Bavaria), 2¾" h. 15.00
Egg cup, "Luckenbach Line," china .. 26.00
Fork, liner "Norddeutscher Lloyd
Bremen" 15.00
Handbook, "Cunard Lines," maps &
pictures of old ships, hard bound,
1905, 179 pp. 37.50
Handkerchief, "American Line," red
& white 80.00
Keychain, liner "Queen Frederica" .. 45.00
Knife, pocket-type, 4-blade, commemorating "Kungsholm Cruise,"
Swedish American Lines, colorful
enameled flags, Swedish national
seal, etc., 3½" l., 1" w. 35.00
Letter opener, liner "Bremen,"
aluminum 4.00
Martini goblets, circular bowl impressed "CGT," raised on trumpet-
shaped base, by Ercuis for the
ocean liner Normandie, silver-
plate, ca. 1935, 4 3/8" h., set
of 6.......................... 330.00
Match safe, liner "Aquitania," ster-
ling silver 85.00
Menu, liner "R.M.S. Ivernia," Cunard
Lines, June 27, 1900 .... 20.00
Mirror, "Scandinavian-American
Steamship Line," colorful........ 35.00
Napkin holder, "Burns Philp Lines,"
silverplate.................... 27.00
Passenger list, "Steamship Graceline
- SS Santa Paula," 1936 .... 17.50
Plaque, "Mitsui Line," Noritake chi-
na blank, 10½" d. 110.00
Plate, "Georgian Bayline S.S.
South/North America," china, ship
scene on blue & white ground,
10" d. 30.00
Playing cards, "American Mail Line
Steamship," w/logo 25.00
Postcards, liner "Reliance," 1920's,
set of 6 .... 8.00
Print, liner "Aquitania," Cunard
Line, framed w/name plate on
frame, 12 x 19½" 75.00
Salt & pepper shakers, liner "M.S.
Europa," souvenir, pr. 17.50
Schedule, "Canadian Pacific Steam-
ship to Alaska," 1933 .... 7.00

Serving bowls, hemispherical body
impressed "CGT," raised on circular foot, twin spherical handles,
by Christofle for the ocean liner
Normandie, silverplate, ca. 1935,
10¼" d., set of 3............. 880.00
Shot glass, "United States Lines,"
etched eagle.................. 8.00
Sign, liner "Aquitania," tin, color
scene of liner at full steam, original black oak frame, 33 x 44"
(ILLUS.)....................... 350.00
Sign, "United States Line," plaster-
of-Paris, dome-shaped, high relief
half-globe w/dominant 2½" h.
ocean liner spanning sign, "We
Feature Heileman's Special Export
Beer," 11¼" d. 135.00
Stamp moistener, "Beckhard Line,"
china, model of a dog 25.00
Steering wheel, mahogany, turn-of-
the-century, 5' d............. 1,350.00
Teaspoon, "Alaska Steamship Co.,"
1915 .... 15.00
Tile, liner "Rotterdam," ceramic, liner pictured, Holland American
Line, 1908-40, 6 x 6"............ 125.00
Tip tray, "American Steamship
Lines"........................ 75.00
Toast rack, "Gelzerman Lines,"
silverplate.................... 100.00
Tureen, open, liner "Normandie,"
silverplate, galleried rim, 2 spherical handles, by Christofle, ca.
1935, 12½" l 550.00
Wine bucket, liner "Normandie,"
silverplate, cylindrical w/spherical
handles, by Christofle, ca. 1935,
8¼" d. 3,080.00

STEIFF TOYS

Navy Goat
*From a felt pin cushion in the shape of an
elephant, a world-famous toy company*

emerged. Margarete Steiff (1847-1909), a polio victim as a child and confined to a wheelchair, planned a career as a seamstress and opened a shop in the family home. However, her plans were dramatically changed when she made her first stuffed elephant in 1880. By 1886 she was producing stuffed felt monkeys, donkeys, horses and other animal forms. In 1893 an agent sold her toys at the Leipzig Fair. This venture was so successfull that a catalogue was printed and a salesman hired. Margarete's nephews and nieces became involved in the business, assisting in its management and the design of new items. Through the years, the Steiff Company has produced a varied line including felt or plush animals, Teddy Bears, gnomes, elves, felt dolls with celluloid heads, Kewpie dolls and even radiator caps with animals or dolls attached as decoration. Descendents of the original family members continue to be active in the management of the company still adhering to Margarete's motto "For our children, the best is just good enough."

Bear on wheels, "Fellow," dark brown mohair body w/hump, felt paws, glass eyes, metal wheels, 15" l., overall 11" h. $275.00

Bison, pull toy, brown mohair & felt, metal wheels, 1914, 10" (1 wheel replaced) 275.00

Cat, "Tom," black velvet body, mohair tail, glass eyes, sewn nose & mouth, 1960's, 5". 85.00

Cat, golden mohair, yellow-green glass eyes, holding ball between its paws, 17" l. 330.00

Cow, "Bessy," spotted mohair coat, felt horns, open mouth & udder, leather collar w/tin bell, 6" 65.00

Deer, "Bambi," velvet body, mohair chest & tail, sewn nose & mouth, 5½" 46.00

Dog, Cocker Spaniel, long & short mohair, jointed head, black sewn nose, felt mouth, w/squeaker, 6½" h. 60.00

Dog, Collie, long & short mohair, glass eyes, sewn nose, felt mouth, 20½" l., 10" h. 125.00

Dog, Dalmation, "Dally," black & white mohair, jointed head, sewn nose, felt mouth, 29" 650.00

Dog, Poodle, "Snobby," long & short mohair, jointed, glass eyes, ca. 1960, 8" 95.00

Doll, "Clownie," rubber head w/mohair wig, jointed felt body, cotton clothing, 1950's, 17" 200.00

Doll, elf, "Gucki," rubber face w/mohair beard, jointed felt body, felt clothing, 1950's, 7" h. . . . 55.00

Duck, Mallard, pull toy, felt & velvet, metal wheels, 8" 275.00

Fish, mohair, glass eyes, felt lips & mouth, 3½" 25.00

Frog, felt, 1940, 3" l., 4" h. 50.00

Giraffe, gold & orange mohair, long mohair tail, glass eyes, felt ears, w/squeaker, 1950's, 11" 85.00

Goat, mountain, grey mohair, glass eyes, felt horns, 1950's, 5" l., 6" h. 50.00

Goat, U.S. Navy mascot, plush, cream and blue coat (ILLUS.) . . . . 180.00 to 215.00

Gorilla, long mohair body, felt face, mouth, ears, paws & feet, jointed head, arms & legs, glass eyes, 5' 1" h. 500.00

Hamster, gold mohair body, felt mouth & paws, jointed head, glass eyes, 5". 50.00

Hedgehog, "Mecki," original clothes, 10½" 55.00

Hen, mohair body, felt face, comb & tail, felt-covered metal feet & legs, button eyes, 7" 55.00

Horse on wheels, spotted coat, original harness & saddle, 1950's, 26" l. 200.00

Koala bear, "Molly," grey & tan long & short mohair, jointed body, glass eyes, sewn nose & mouth, 1950's, 16". 135.00

Lamb, "Lamby," white mohair, glass eyes, sewn nose & mouth, ribbon w/bell around neck, 7" 55.00

Lion cub, gold mohair, jointed body, glass eyes, 1950's, 5". 50.00

Lion, yellow mohair, glass eyes, 5' l. plus 27" tail, 38" h. 2,800.00

Monkey, white mohair, felt face, hands & feet, green glass eyes, ca. 1905, 19". 695.00

Mouse, grey mohair, felt paws & ears, 3" 35.00

Ocelot, gold & black mohair, sewn nost & mouth, 1955, 6½ x 13" plus tail 150.00

Owl, "Wittie," mohair body w/felt wing tips, felt-covered metal legs & feet, 4" 35.00

Parrot, mohair, glass eyes, felt-covered metal feet, 5". 60.00

Polar bear, white mohair, swivel neck, jointed legs, button eyes, sewn nose & mouth, w/growling mechanism, 16" 600.00

Pony, white & brown mohair, felt ears, red vinyl saddle & bridle, 1950's, 5½". 85.00

Rabbit, tan mohair, jointed body, glass eyes, 1952, 16" 225.00

Raccoon, grey Dralon, felt paws, glass eyes, sewn nose & mouth, 8½" 55.00

Seal, "Floppy Robby," buff Dralon,

soft stuffing, sewn eyes, 1950's,
12" 65.00
Squirrel, "Perri," gold long & short
mohair, glass eyes, holding velvet
acorn, 7" 85.00
Stork, white & black felt, glass eyes,
felt-covered metal legs, 1898,
14" 350.00
Teddy bear, "Minky Zotty," platinum
mink plush, jointed glass eyes,
sewn nose, felt mouth, w/growl-
ing mechanism, 1970's, 11" 165.00
Teddy bear, "Zotty," tan curly mohair, jointed body, glass eyes,
sewn nose, felt mouth, 1950's,
11" 150.00
Tiger cub, seated, orange & black
mohair, jointed head, glass eyes,
4" 45.00
Turtle, mohair body, vinyl shell,
glass eyes, 1950's, 5" 65.00
Zebra, black & white felt,
1950's, 5" 40.00

STEINS

"Stag" & "Boar" Steins

Character, "Balloon," pottery, painted full color, pottery lid, marked
"1232 Germany," 1 liter $1,210.00
Character "Bismarck," porcelain, tan
& brown, marked "Musterschutz"
(copyright protection) on base, ca.
1900, ½ liter : 475.00
Character, "Boar," porcelain,
marked "Musterschutz" (copyright
protection), ½ liter (ILLUS.
right).......................... 4,520.00
Character, "Bowling Ball," porcelain,
inlaid porcelain lid, marked
"Musterschutz," ½ liter 325.00
Character, "Bison," porcelain, painted full colors, bisque glaze, inlaid
porcelain lid, marked "E. Bohne
Soehne," ½ liter 1,980.00

"Gentleman Rabbit" Character Stein

Character, "Gentleman Rabbit," porcelain, tan, brown & green,
marked "Musterschutz," ca. 1900,
½ liter (ILLUS.) 1,750.00
Character, "Hobo," pottery, painted
full color, inlaid pottery lid,
marked "723," ½ liter 605.00
Character, "Rhino," porcelain, painted grey, white & black, porcelain
lid, marked "Musterschutz" &
hash marks, ½ liter 1,265.00

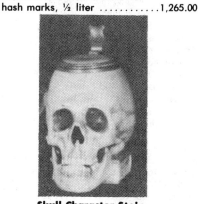

Skull Character Stein

Character, "Skull," porcelain, bone
color w/black trim, inlaid porcelain lid, 4 x 5½", 5¼" h.,
½ liter (ILLUS.) 298.00
Character, "Smoking Pig," porcelain,
pewter-rimmed bust-form lid, blue
& white, marked "Musterschutz,"
ca. 1900, ½ liter 600.00
Character, "Snowman," porcelain,
inlaid porcelain lid, marked
"Musterschutz," ½ liter 2,625.00
Character, "Stag," porcelain,
marked "Musterschutz," ½ liter,
(ILLUS. left) 3,850.00

Glass, amber, white enameled Mary Gregory-type boy, 3" h. 285.00

Glass, amber, encased in embossed pewter w/embossed pewter head & floral designs, large head below spout, hinged pewter lid, 7" d., 8¼" h. 550.00

Glass, blue opaline, blown, blue opaline inlaid lid, ½ liter 220.00

Glass, clear, enameled lamb, pewter lid, ca. 1840, ½ liter 797.00

Glass, green, enameled shield, armor & crown on front in red, blue, gold, white & grey, overall enameled floral-type designs in orange, white & blue, green applied handle, pewter lid & thumblift, 5½" d., 14¼" h. 495.00

Glass, ruby cut to clear, engraved dog in forest on front, applied ruby handle, inset glass top, pewter mounts, 3¼" d., 4¾" h. 302.00

Glass, presentation piece, ruby cut to clear, pewter lid engraved "Gegr 1828, Ritter, Franz Stingl," applied clear handle, 4" d., 5" h. 307.00

Mettlach, No. 171, relief-molded figures around body representing activities during months of the year, inlaid pewter lid, ¼ liter ... 150.00

Mettlach, No. 202, relief-molded group of singing men, inlaid pewter lid, ½ liter 250.00

Mettlach, No. 675, molded barrel shape, inlaid pewter lid, ¼ liter .. 75.00

Mettlach, No. 1028, oval cameo relief-molded panel of man carrying hay & walking w/woman on bark ground, inlaid pewter lid, ½ liter 190.00

Mettlach, No. 1054 (2262), printed-under-the-glaze scene of Gambrinus & his followers, pewter lid, 4.2 liter 1,100.00

Mettlach, No. 1109 (1909), printed-under-the-glaze, musicians, signed "Schlitt," pewter lid, 1 liter 350.00

Mettlach, No. 1395, etched French card symbols, inlaid pewter lid, ½ liter 465.00

Mettlach, No. 1467, 4 relief-molded panels: picking fruit, hunting, farming, weaving; inlaid lid, ½ liter 350.00

Mettlach, No. 1740, relief-molded floral design, inlaid pewter lid, ¼ liter .... 325.00 to 375.00

Mettlach, No. 1745, relief-molded leaves & scrolling design, inlaid pewter lid, ¼ liter 150.00

Mettlach, No. 1968, etched overall w/scene from Sleeping Beauty, inlaid lid, 7½" h. 495.00

Mettlach, No. 2001A, book stein for law, etched & glazed books, inlaid pewter lid, ½ liter 550.00

Mettlach, No. 2001C, book stein for scholars, etched & glazed books, inlaid pewter, ½ liter 550.00

Mettlach, No. 2024, Berlin stein, etched & glazed shield of Berlin, inlaid pewter lid, ½ liter 600.00

Mettlach No. 2038 & No. 3099

Mettlach, No. 2038, etched & relief-molded Town of Rodenstein, houses & towers on inlaid lid, 3.8 liter (ILLUS. left) 3,630.00

Mettlach, No. 2082, etched scene of William Tell shooting apple off his son's head, inlaid pewter lid, ½ liter 1,300.00

Mettlach, No. 2093, card stein, etched w/four playing cards around bulbous body, inlaid pewter lid, ½ liter .... 635.00 to 725.00

Siegfried Stein

Mettlach, No. 2394, etched scenes
from Siegfried's youth, inlaid pew-
ter lid, ½ liter (ILLUS.). 450.00
Mettlach, No. 2530, cameo relief-
molded boar hunt scene, signed
Stahl, inlaid pewter lid, ½ liter. . .   525.00
Mettlach, No. 2635, etched scene of
girl holding safety bicycle, inlaid
pewter lid, ½ liter 835.00
Mettlach, No. 2829, relief-molded &
etched scene of Rodenstein, inlaid
pewter lid, ½ liter. 1,800.00
Mettlach, No. 3099, etched scene of
Diogenes sitting in barrel, inlaid
lid, signed "Schlitt," 3 liter
(ILLUS. right) 2,200.00
Mettlach, No. 3200, etched scene of
Heidelberg, inlaid pewter lid,
½ liter. 475.00
Porcelain, h.p. Bavarian couple
dancing, musicians & other people
in background, lithophane bottom,
½ liter 185.00
Regimental, stoneware, "Bavarian 3
Fld. Artl. Regt., 1907-09, Munchen," 2 side scenes, roster, lion
thumblift, crown lid w/small cannon & 5 soldiers under glass,
½ liter 1,292.00
Regimental, porcelain, "Bavarian 12
Fld. Artl. Regt., 1902-04, Landau,"
4 side scenes, roster, lion
thumblift, inlaid porcelain lid,
½ liter 825.00
Regimental, stoneware, "Luftschiffer
Abteilung 1904-06, Munchen," 2 side
scenes of hot air balloons, roster,
lion thumblift, tschako helmet in
relief on lid, ½ liter 3,300.00
Regimental, porcelain, 177 Inft.,
Dresden, 1900-02, 2 s.s., roster,
pewter seated lion thumblift,
½ liter 270.00
Regimental, porcelain, "Jager zu
Pferde, Nr. 15," Strassburg,
1899-1902, 2 side scenes, roster,
eagle thumblift, ½ liter 1,225.00
Silver on copper, Baroque-style
relief-molded people & dogs
decor, Germany, 12½" h. 250.00

SUNBONNET BABY COLLECTIBLES

*Bertha L. Corbett, creator of these faceless
children, proved a figure did not need a face
to express character. Her pastel drawings appeared in "Sunbonnet Primer" by Eulalie Osgood Grover, published in 1900. Later Miss
Corbett did a series showing the babies at*

*work, one for each day of the week, and they
became so popular advertisers began using
them. Numerous objects including cards and
prints with illustrations of, or in the shape
of the Sunbonnet Babies are now being collected. Also see ROYAL BAYREUTH
CHINA.*

Sunbonnet Babies Print

Book, "The Overall Boys," by Eulalie
Osgood Grover, illustrated by Ber-
tha Corbett, 1905. . . . . $55.00
Book, "Sunbonnet Babies ABC
Book," by Eulalie Osgood Grover,
illustrated by Bertha Corbett,
1929 . . . .   40.00
Book, "Sunbonnet Babies Primer,"
by Eulalie Osgood Grover, illus-
trated by Bertha Corbett, 1923. . . .   65.00
Book, "Sunbonnet Babies & Overall
Boys," by Eulalie Osgood Grover,
illustrated by Bertha Corbett
Melcher 45.00
Book, "Sunbonnet Twins," by Eulalie
Osgood Grover, color illustrations
by Bertha Corbett, 1907 . . . .   55.00
Booklet, "At Work, At Play," verses
by Gunn, color & black & white il-
lustrations by Bertha Corbett,
1904, 16 pp.   80.00
Feeding dish, china, Sunbonnet Girl
& Overall Boy decor, "I Love
You". 175.00
Postcards, "Days of the Week"
series, set of 7. . . . . .45.00 to 75.00
Postcard, "Paying Toll," signed
Dorothy Dixon 10.00
Print, "Mending Day," by B.L. Cor-
bett, 8 x 6".   13.00
Print, "Wash Day," by B.L. Corbett,
1905, 8 x 6" (ILLUS.) . . . . . .25.00 to 35.00
Quilt top, Sunbonnet Babies decor,
soft brown & green on yellow
ground 65.00
Tea set: cov. teapot, creamer &
sugar bowl; china, Sunbonnet
Babies at various pursuits,
3 pcs. 110.00

Collecting Hiz Honor

Teddy Bear

by Sybill McFadden

After having been a child's toy for nearly a century, Teddy Bears are suddenly a hot item on adult collectors' lists. What is it about Teddy Bears that charms us so? Aside from the nostalgia carried over from childhood, it could be for as many reasons as there are collectors.

I would like to begin with definite guidelines on the how and why of Teddy Bear collecting, but personality is so intrinsic a part of bear collecting — yours and the bears' — that hard and fast rules are laid down only to be broken.

For instance, bears have a way of taking on a personality all their own. Without warning, one may adopt a hat, or an outsize necktie, or choose to sit on a bearskin rug. This is not our fault. They assume it! What's more, they stay forever like that. The manufacturer may have intended an entirely different sort of bear and sold him as such, but no one can predict what happens to a bear between the store and where he eventually winds up.

We shall try, in this article to be documentary and properly serious about the subject, but I warn you — bears are not always cooperative about being serious.

While doll collecting began more than 50 years ago, Teddy Bear collecting is fairly new. It started generating interest sporadically in about 1975, growing rapidly in the next ten years. The hobby was escalated along the way by such luminaries as the late famous actor and author, Englishman Peter Bull, whose respectful, albeit whimsical attitude toward his large collection of Teddy Bears resulted in nationwide TV interviews and talk shows in England and America, and another famous Englishman, Sir John Betjeman. This distinguished poet often paid tribute to his Teddy Bear companion for more than 60 years, the one and only Archibald Ormsby Gore.

Compared with the history of dolls, Teddy Bears are upstarts. Dolls have been found from the years B.C. in the graves of Egyptian children. Bear beginnings, on the other hand, are clouded. It all began in about 1903

with a conundrum very like "Which came first - the chicken or the egg?" With bears it is "Which came first - the Mitchom or the Steiff?"

Let me explain. In America Teddy got his name and being from an historical incident. It was the turn of the century when our then President Theodore Roosevelt, while hunting in Mississippi, refused to shoot a tired, bedraggled bear and her cub which his hunting dogs had brought to bay. His sportsmanlike act of compassion was publicized by the *Washington Post* in November of 1901, and the next day, newspaper cartoonist Clifford Berryman did a drawing of the scene showing the President, back turned with the butt of his gun on the ground, refusing to shoot the bear, and the caption "Drawing The Line In Mississippi" a double entendre because the President had gone to settle a boundary dispute between Mississippi and Louisiana.

It was shortly after the bear cartoon appeared that one Morris Mitchom who had a candy store in Brooklyn in which he also sold toys, asked the President for permission to name two toy bears his wife, Rose, had made for the shop, "Teddy's Bears". Permission was granted and in 1903 the Mitchom's introduced the first American toy bears known as "Teddy's Bears".

At the same time, however, over in Germany, a very similar type of toy bear appeared. A German artist, Margarete Steiff, who had been stricken with polio in childhood and was confined to a wheelchair, had since 1880 been originating and sewing toy animals of felt. Her first toy was an elephant. These were sold under the firm name, "Margarete Steiff GmbH". Eventually she was joined by her nephew, Richard Steiff, an artist. Richard was fond of bears and went often to the zoo to sketch them. Between them, they created a jointed toy bear of mohair. When it was exhibited in 1903 at the Leipzig Fair in Germany, an American toy buyer ordered 3,000 of these new Steiff bears for distribution in America. So which came first, the Mitchom or the Steiff? It appears they were created and released, a continent apart, at about the same time and in the same year, 1903.

By 1907 the name "Teddy Bear" was used on both continents, and the jointed bears became top sellers among all animal toys. Morris Mitchom then gave up the candy store and founded Ideal Novelty and Toy Co., which is today the giant Ideal Toy Corporation. So popular were Teddy Bears, both the Ideal and the Steiff, that people feared they would cause the demise of the doll entirely, and a Michigan minister warned that replacing dolls with toy bears would destroy the maternal instinct in little girls. On the same subject, the editor of a ladies' magazine of the day wrote:

"It is enough to make a perfect lady of a doll mad. The dear little girls who have always cried for dolls at Christmas are this year crying for Teddy Bears, and dolls are left on the shelf to cry the paint off their pretty cheeks because of neglect!"

Not to worry. Both dolls and Teddy Bears survived, and it has been this author's observation that as far as girls are concerned, they seem to divide into two camps — they are either doll lovers or Teddy Bear lovers — seldom both. An example of the latter is the testimony of an Englishwoman, Mrs. Freestone of the Isle of Wight. She said she preferred her bear to "any silly old doll. I had a dozen of them," she says, "But I never cared for them. I used to deck them out in beads and Teddy and I, as bandits, used to stalk them round the sofa and hold them up for ransom."

There are even a few bears who, we might say, have reached "Hall of Fame" just by dint of having been around a long time, or for one or another reasons. You may have some Hall of Fame candidates of your own. Mine would list four: Pooh Bear, Paddington, Smokey Bear and Misha.

Winnie-the-Pooh has been around so long we almost take him for granted. He was created in the early 1920's by the English author A.A. Milne for his small son, Christopher Robin. Pooh, as you must know, is the hero of three children's books, the first of which, *When We Were Very Young*, appeared in the United States in 1924. Two other Milne books followed, *Winnie The Pooh* and *The House At Pooh Corner*. Disney Productions made a Pooh Bear film in the 1960's, and since then toy Pooh Bears have been rampant. There are so many Disney-made Pooh Bears that it is possible youngsters today may even think Walt Disney created Pooh. There is little to criticize about the wonderful world of Disney, but their production of movies and toys from old Fairy Tales and classic children's books could be confusing, one might think, to children who are not aware of the proper origins of such characters.

The hilarious adventures of Paddington, a bear who captured hearts as easily as he caused calamities, is the subject of five other children's books by Michael Bond. Paddington who travelled from *Darkest Peru to London, England, via Paddington Station* wears a strange and wonderful hat, great coat and Wellington boots. He also wears a tag which says on one side "Please Look After This Bear. Thank You." The toy Paddington Bear is produced by Eden Toys, Inc.

In 1953 Ideal Corporation was given permission to make and sell "Smokey The Bear" as a toy. Smokey was invented by our National Wildlife Service to create awareness of forest fires. With each Smokey Bear, Ideal packed in the box a Junior Forest Ranger card. Some 16,000 youngsters applied to be Junior Rangers and Ideal was honored with a "Golden Smokey" award in 1967 for its contribution. Over a period of four years, Ideal came out with at least 4 versions of Smokey. One is a talking bear with an internal record which allows Smokey to make 10 statements in a low, growling voice.

Misha Bear has a proud history. He was produced by Dakin Company, of San Francisco, California to be the official Mascot of the 1980 Olympic Games being held that year in Moscow. However, when Russia invaded Afghanistan, the United States withdrew from the Olympics in protest, and Misha became a symbol of our country's stand against aggression. Unsold as an Olympic souvenir, he then became a collector's item and was never reproduced. A Misha Bear without his Olympic belt is greatly devalued. He should be wearing the belt with the five circles and the tag in his ear relating his history.

We are all aware of the comfort a Teddy Bear provides certain children, presenting itself for cuddling at bedtime, and cheerfully attending Sunday school and Kindergarten, going, nearly always without complaint, to the dentist and the doctor, as well as sharing happy occasions like birthdays and vacations, and if lost, proving itself inconsolable until found. Stemming then, from this nostalgia, perhaps we come full circle to the growing fad today among adults for collecting Teddy Bears.

Faced with this happy, accomplished fact, what then should we look for in putting together a collection? Today's collectors may find bears under three main categories: Antique, Modern and Artists' Bears. Some of us collect from each and mix them all together. Others of us prefer to collect "pure" — collecting only one category, or one type in one category.

ANTIQUE TEDDY BEARS
Prepare for a hunt. They are elusive and expensive. Remember with bears, "antique"

cannot be older than 1903. If unmarked, and they usually are, how can you tell an antique or early Teddy Bear? They are stuffed with straw or excelsior. The straw ones crackle when squeezed. Straw, however, was used for stuffing bears thru the 1950's so don't use that clue alone. They have shoe-button eyes — no glass eyes until the 1920's. The face is usually constructed with a protruding muzzle or snout. The nose or mouth is usually handsewn of black thread or yarn. They are constructed of good quality mohair or plush. This is not the same today and is a good clue when you familiarize yourself with the old plush and mohair. Humps on the back of some were common, but are not on all old bears. They are fully jointed with swivel necks. Long arms were common, but not on all. Most show wear, but it is misleading to take wear and tear as a criterion for obvious reasons — bears get lots of hard loving so that fairly recent one may *look* "old". Finally, find all the photos you can of documented early 1900's bears to acquaint yourself with the antique look.

MODERN TEDDY BEARS

Have fun! They are in stores and gift shops everywhere, dressed or undressed. Dressed bears are more a modern feature of today than in the early days of bears. The same advice for collectors of anything applies to bears — buy the best you can afford. With bears it would include quality construction with jointing of limbs and a swivel head. You may want separately constructed muzzles, but that's a preference. Since there are always interlopers, we can look for fringe-type bears

sneaking into collections. We call "fringe-types" polar bears, pandas and koalas, as well as two-faced teddies with dolls' faces on one side. All these have charms, too. Lastly — Restraint. Try to use it. There are so many bears available at so many prices, one is tempted to buy and buy. However, an accumulation does not a collection make!

ARTISTS' TEDDY BEARS

All of the above applies to this category. Here you should expect good construction. Some artists are highly original, some are excellent, some are poor. You will find your favorites. Most bears have personality — need I tell *you!* But does it have that indefinable presence and bearing (forgive, please!) that will keep you from tiring of it! Stick with quality. Be sure your artist's bear is signed and dated.

COLLECTOR HINT

One final suggestion: buy a notebook or box with file cards, and record each bear. Include all the information listed under the photos in this article, adding where and when purchased and original price, as well as any repair work done on the bear now or later.

Happy hunting, and may harmony reign forever in your Bear Den!

(Editor's Note: *Sybill McFadden, who displays a grouping of antique Teddy Bears in her Museum of Antique Dolls and Toys in Lakewood, New York, writes with the authority of 25 years of collecting, writing and lecturing in the doll and toy world.)*

"ANTIQUE BEARS" (1903 through 1950)

Listed by age, then size.

1905 Steiff Bear

Antique bear by Steiff, dark brown mohair straw-stuffed jointed body w/hump on back & extremely long arms, black shoe-button eyes & black thread-sewn nose & mouth, button in ear, ca. 1905, excellent condition (ILLUS.) $2,500.00

Antique bear by Steiff, buff-colored mohair straw-stuffed jointed body, black shoe-button eyes & black thread-sewn mouth, 1913, 10" 200.00

Antique bear by unknown maker, brown mohair straw-stuffed jointed body w/very long arms, 1915, 19" 375.00

Antique bear by unknown maker, "threadbare" mohair straw-stuffed body w/jointed arms & swivel head, shoe-button eyes, thread-sewn nose & mouth, wearing hand-knit navy blue pants &

1915 Teddy Bear by Unknown Maker

bowtie (probably not original
to the bear), ca. 1915, 13"
(ILLUS.)........................ 200.00

1918 "Doll-Face" Bear

Antique "doll-face" bear by unknown maker, beige mohair
straw-stuffed jointed body, molded celluloid face & hair, 1918, 8"
(ILLUS.)........................ 125.00

1920's Plush Bear

Antique bear by unknown maker,
beige plush straw-stuffed jointed
body w/swivel head, amber glass
eyes, velvet muzzle & paw pads,
wearing green leather collar,
1920, 7½" (ILLUS.)............... 70.00
Antique bear by Steiff, brown mohair straw-stuffed jointed body
w/long arms, black shoe-button
eyes & black thread-sewn nose &
mouth, 1920's, 16"............... 575.00

"Yes-No" Bear by Shuco

Antique "Yes-No" bear on wheels
by Shuco, bear moves head up or
down or sideways, glass eyes,
mounted on metal wheels, 1920's,
18" (ILLUS.) 1,200.00
Antique bear by unknown maker,
cinnamon mohair straw-stuffed
jointed body w/slightly curved
paws, 1930's, 10"............... 150.00
Antique bear by unknown maker,
white mohair straw-stuffed jointed
body w/hump on back & curving
paws, black glass eyes, w/growl-
er, 1930's, 19" 350.00

1935 Mohair Teddy Bear

Antique bear by unknown maker,
brown mohair straw-stuffed joint-

ed body, one brown glass eye &
other replaced w/brass button,
black thread-sewn nose & mouth,
ca. 1935, 20″ (ILLUS.) 250.00

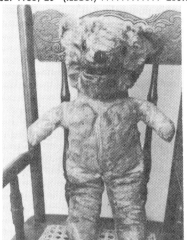

"Eating" Bear of 1937

Antique "Eating" bear by Common-
wealth Toy & Novelty Co., U.S.A.,
golden plush unjointed body,
metal-lined mouth opens as ring
in back is pulled (when fed, food
travels through metal tube & can
be removed through zipper open-
ing in back), 1937, 15″ (ILLUS.) . . . 500.00
Antique bear by unknown maker,
white mohair straw-stuffed body,
glass "googlie" eyes & "sweetie-
pie" expression on face, wearing
red polka-dotted polished cotton
pants w/suspenders, 1940's, 19″ . . 135.00
Antique bear by unknown maker,
silky yellow mohair straw-stuffed
jointed body w/swivel head, glass
eyes, 1940's, 20″ 225.00

MODERN TEDDY BEARS (1975 to present)

Listed by size.

Bear Issued for Strong Museum in 1982

Commemorative bear by Steiff, issued for opening of "Margaret W.
Strong Museum," gold synthetic
mohair jointed body w/swivel
head, plastic eyes, original Steiff
button on ear & original tags,
1982, 9″, w/original box (ILLUS.) . . 60.00

Queen Elizabeth Jubilee Bear

Commemorative bear by Nisbet
(England), issued for Silver Jubilee
of Queen Elizabeth II, nutmeg
brown mohair jointed body
w/swivel head, wearing white
satin overdress w/red coat-of-
arms, tagged on left foot, 1977,
10½″ (ILLUS.) 75.00

Bear in Striped Underwear

Bear with removable fur body suit,
acrylic plush bear wearing red &
white striped underwear beneath
his fur body suit, shoe-button
eyes & nose, 1977, hand-crocheted
hat not original to costume, 11½″
(ILLUS.) 45.00

Teddy Roosevelt with Spectacles

Teddy Roosevelt bear by H2W, Inc.,
brown synthetic plush unjointed
body, black plastic shoe-button
eyes, wearing wire-rimmed spectacles & Presidential tuxedo,
w/storybook "Colonel Teddy - The
Teddy Roosevelt Bear," 1980, 14"
(ILLUS.)........................ 50.00

Ideal's 75th Anniversary Bear

Commemorative bear by Ideal Toy
Company, 75th Anniversary issue,
grey-beige synthetic fur nylon-
stuffed unjointed body w/printed
paw pads, brown glass eyes,
1978, 15", original box w/history
of first Teddy Bear (ILLUS.)........ 60.00

"Wonder Bear" by Princess Soft Toy
Co., brown & beige plush unjointed body, black shoe-button eyes,
plush ball nose & thread-stitched
mouth, wearing blue T-shirt w/red

"Wonder Bear"

"W" on yellow ground & red cape,
ca. 1975, 16" (ILLUS.)........... 40.00

English Bear

English bear, beige dacron plush
jointed body, black shoe-button
eyes, original label "Made in
Hampshire, England," jacket &
honey bottle not original to bear,
1975, 17½" (ILLUS.)............. 75.00

"Ole Sorrowful" Bear

"Ole Sorrowful" bear, white acrylic plush unjointed body, large black shoe-button eyes & nose, yellow muzzle & paw pads, wearing original red satin ribbon, maker unknown, 1980, 18" (ILLUS.) 35.00

FAMOUS BEARS (or Hall of Fame Bears)

Listed in alphabetical order.

"Misha Bear"

"Misha Bear" by Dakin Co., San Francisco, California, official mascot of 1980 Moscow Olympics (never sold there since U.S.A. boycotted games due to Russian Invasion of Afghanistan), brown & beige plush body, glass eyes, wearing Olympic belt, 1980, 12" (ILLUS.) 50.00

Miniature Paddington Bears

Paddington English bears, beige flocked mohair unjointed bodies, each w/suitcase & original tags, hats & coats, 2" h. each (ILLUS. of 3) 5.00

Paddington bear by Eden Toys, Inc., honey beige synthetic plush body, black plastic shoe-button eyes, wearing blue hat, red great-coat, yellow Wellington boots, w/tag

Paddington Bear

"Darkest Peru to London via Paddington Station" one side & "Please look after this Bear - Thank You" reverse, 1975, 19" (ILLUS.) 60.00

Plastic Limited Edition "Smokey"

Smokey Bear, Limited Edition by R. Dakin Co., brown vinyl body w/jointed arms & swivel head w/yellow muzzle, wearing yellow plastic "Smokey" ranger hat, grey cloth trousers, w/silver finish metal shovel inscribed "Prevent Forest Fires," original tag, 1979, 8" (ILLUS.) 75.00

Smokey Bear by Ideal Toy Corp., cinnamon brown acrylic plush body w/yellow muzzle & paw pads, wearing "Smokey" belt buckle & "Smokey" ranger hat,

Smokey Bear by Ideal

in original box w/two brown bear cubs on stump & squirrel on tree limb marked "Official Smokey the Bear" & "Authorized by U.S. Dept. of Agriculture," 1967, 13" (ILLUS.)........................ 100.00

"Talking" Smokey Bear

Smokey "Talking" Bear by Knickerbocker Toy Co., cinnamon brown acrylic plush body w/yellow snout, black felt nose & red felt tongue, brown glass eyes, embossed badge "Smokey Ranger," cloth trousers & plastic belt, pull ring on side & bear repeats 10 recorded messages, missing "Smokey" ranger hat & belt buckle, 1960, 15" (ILLUS.) 125.00

TEDDY BEAR'S COUSINS

Listed in alphabetical order.

Koala & "Zotty" Bear by Steiff

Koala bear by Steiff, light tan mohair jointed body w/swivel head, glass eyes, button in ear & original tag, 1950's, 9" (ILLUS. left).... 200.00

"Polo" Bear

"Polo" bear by Russ Berrie Co., white plush polar bear w/cream muzzle, brown glass eyes, black plastic nose, holding American flag as symbol of Alaskan statehood, 1970, 10" h. seated (ILLUS.)........................ 40.00

"Zotty" bear by Steiff, brown mohair jointed body w/golden mohair chest & swivel head, original button in ear, 1950's, 9" (ILLUS. w/Koala bear at right).......... 200.00

ANIMATED BEARS

Animated "Drummer" bear, keywind Teddy bangs drum & turns

"Drummer" Bear

head, made in Germany, 1975, 7",
w/original box (ILLUS.) 50.00

"Knitting" Bear

Animated "Knitting" bear, key-wind
Teddy plys knitting needles &
green yarn while head moves up
& down, made in Germany, 1975,
7", w/original box (ILLUS.) 50.00

ARTIST'S BEARS

Listed by size.

"Doll-Face" Bear

Artist's "doll-face" bear, beige mohair body w/reproduction of
"A.M. *Googlie* No. 323" porcelain
face one side & Teddy Bear face
opposite, 1982, 10" (ILLUS.) 75.00

"Doll-Face" Bear

Artist's "doll-face" bear, white
wooly plush jointed body w/black
paw pads & swivel head
w/reproduction Kestner bisque
baby's face one side & bear's
face opposite, 1980, 14" (ILLUS.) .. 100.00

"Father Christmas" Bear

Artist's "Father Christmas" bear,
embroidered features & w/remov-
able white cotton beard, wearing
red robe (w/pillow stuffed beneath for added girth) & carrying
brown plush bag of toys, marked
"No. 1 by Pat Morrison," 1982, 15"
(ILLUS.)......................... 80.00

Artist's "faithful reproduction of antique bear," white plush jointed
body w/swivel head, black shoe-
button eyes, black thread-sewn

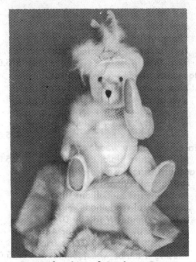

Reproduction of Antique Bear

nose, wearing rhinestone &
feather tiara & ropes of pearls,
seated on white bearskin rug, by
Dennis Heckert, 1985, 22"
(ILLUS.) 100.00

MINIATURE BEARS

Wagonload of Bears

Wagonload of miniature bears, pr.
3½" h. Steiffs ($30 each), 1¼" h.
yellow clay ceramic bear ($5),
1½" h. unjointed Paddington bear
w/suitcase ($5), 1½" h. unjointed
Koala bear ($5), pulled along by
4" wood-jointed bear (ILLUS.) 5.00

(End of Special Focus)

TELEPHONES

Candlestick-type, "Century Telephone Construction Co.," split
shaft model $475.00
Candlestick-type, "Kellogg Switch-

board and Supply Co.," oak box,
1901 . . . . 120.00
Candlestick-type, "North Electric
Co.," brass, tulip-style, oak
magneto box w/bells 150.00
Candlestick-type, "Stromberg Carl-
son," 'oil can' shaft, ca. 1898 . . . . . 700.00
Candlestick-type, "Western Electric,"
w/scissor-gate extension from
desk top bracket, ca. 1910 . . . . 75.00
Wall-type, "Ericsson Telephone Co.,"
all-steel 'fiddleback-style' case,
ca. 1907 . . . . 125.00
Wall-type, "Leich Electric Co.," oak
case, hand-crank 195.00
Wall-type, "Western Electric," wal-
nut 'fiddleback-style' case,
Type 301 . . . . 275.00
Wall-type, "Western Electric," brass
bells, wringer handle, w/original
magnetos, Erie Railroad tag on
back, brass frame sign on front
"Shortline 3" & lists departments,
pipe shop, blacksmiths, etc. probably from general store or RR
depot 300.00

TEXTILES

BATTENBURG LACE

Bedspread & pillow sham, three-
quarter bed size, pr. $110.00
Bedspread & pillow sham, draped
sides, light blue lining, double
bed size, pr. 265.00
Doily, floral motif, 4½" sq. 30.00
Doily, 12" d. 30.00
Doily, 14" d. 32.00
Pillow sham, embroidered red
horseshoe, florals & "Good Luck"
on linen, Battenburg lace border,
28 x 27" 29.00
Table centerpiece, octagonal linen
center, 5½" w. Battenburg lace
border, 17" w. 40.00
Table centerpiece, 21" sq. 44.00
Table centerpiece, 25" sq. 85.00
Table centerpiece, linen center, Battenburg lace vintage border,
33" d. 150.00
Table centerpiece, thread-
drawnwork center, 34" d. 45.00
Tablecloth, 54" d. 90.00
Tablecloth, 60" d. 140.00
Tablecloth, embroidered linen cen-
ter, Battenburg lace border,
68" d. 155.00
Tablecloth, linen center, Battenburg
lace vintage border, 72" d. 195.00

Tablecloth, 90" d. 750.00
Table runner, 4" w. linen center,
Battenburg lace border,
34 x 16½" 95.00
Table runner, 48 x 15" 115.00

BEDSPREADS

Crib-size, hand-crocheted white cotton filet, animal designs,
50 x 33" 135.00
Hand-crocheted creamy white cotton, Star & Popcorn patt.,
86 x 80" 65.00
Hand-crocheted white cotton, Queen
Anne's Lace patt., 100 x 84" 175.00
Hand-crocheted white cotton, 100 x
90" w/2" fringe 165.00
Hand-crocheted white cotton filet,
117 x 103" 150.00
Hand-crocheted white cotton, Irish
patt. w/solid blocks & rose motif,
fringed edge, full-size 250.00
Marseilles cotton fabric, white, full-
size 100.00
Trapunto-work, white stitching on
white marseilles cotton fabric,
76 x 72" 95.00

COVERLETS

Appliqued Wool Crib Coverlet

Calmanco (glazed wool w/a checkered warp), green central panel
flanked by brown panels, natural
heavy linen backing, 85 x 72" 700.00
Jacquard, single weave, 1-piece,
large compass stars alternating
w/floral medallions center, vintage & bird border, red, blue, olive green & natural white, signed
"W. in Mount Vernon, Knox County, Ohio by Jacob and Michail
Ardner 1851" in corners, 83 x 76"
(some wear & stains) 325.00
Jacquard, single weave, 1-piece,

red, blue, green & white floral design, corner w/partial label
"Pennsyl--, For--" (weaving er-
ror), other corner dated "1849,"
92 x 78" 375.00
Jacquard, single weave, 2-piece,
blue & white floral medallions,
side borders w/roses, bottom border w/eagles in the corners
w/"Liberty" & row of large 2-story
buildings, 82 x 68" 325.00
Jacquard, single weave, 2-piece,
blue & white plaid, 86 x 76" 265.00
Jacquard, single weave, 2-piece,
red, green & blue wool, white cotton, sunburst medallions alternating w/floral medallions, bird
border, signed "Made by D. L.
Myers, Bethel Township for Ann
Neff, 1838," 93 x 74" (some fringe
missing & minor wear) 325.00
Jacquard, double woven, 1-piece,
central repeated design of peacock in tree & eagle w/"Liberty,"
corners w/bust of Gen. Washington, blue & white, 80 x 69" 325.00
Jacquard, double woven, 1-piece,
patriotic theme, central reserve
w/floral medallion, 13-star flags,
liberty dollars, corners w/shield,
eagles w/banners, blue & white,
signed "Woven at Palmyra, N.Y.
by Ira Hadsell," corners marked
"Esther J. Rider 1856," 84 x 76"
(minor staining) 880.00
Jacquard, double woven, 1-piece,
red, blue & natural roses center,
bird & florals border, signed
"Columbia, N.A. 1838," 88 x 61" .. 750.00
Jacquard, double woven, 1-piece,
"Agriculture & Manufacturers are
the Foundation of our Independence July 4, 1827, Gnrl. Lafayette"
& "S. Harris," blue & white,
95 x 74" 475.00
Jacquard, double woven, 2-piece,
reversible, alternating rows of
rose sprigs & stylized floral
medallions, band of fruit trees
one end, sides w/double borders
of houses & monuments, 2 corners
w/state building & date 1847, blue
& white, 89 x 76" 660.00
Linsey-woolsey, glazed dark blue
panels (4) stitched together,
worked w/large floral vines,
leaves & florals, ground heightened w/diagonal line quilting,
putty-colored worsted reverse,
New England, late 18th c.,
88 x 88" 2,420.00
Overshot, 2-piece, brown & natural
optical design, 82 x 66" (minor
wear) 105.00

Overshot, 2-piece, 2 shades of blue,
red & white floral stripes, dated
1844, 92 x 80" 467.50

Wool, entwined letters "BABY" on
red center panel w/nursery rhyme
figures & representations on black
border, applied red scalloped felt
band at edge, New Hampshire,
late 19th c., 56 x 46" (ILLUS.) 1,100.00

QUILTS

Appliqued Crib Size Quilt

Crib-size, appliqued snowflakes,
stars & floral motifs along w/clus-
ters of grapes & cherries w/embroi-
dered stems centering large appliqued wreath w/presentation inscription, red & green calico
patches on white cotton field,
green sawtooth border, probably
Pennsylvania, dated February 8,
1860, 35 x 30" (ILLUS.) 1,430.00

Crib-size, pieced Bow Tie patt., lavender, blue, black & white cotton
quilted w/a central feather
wreath, diamonds & clamshells,
border worked in blue & white
bands, Amish, ca. 1930 .... 495.00

Crib-size, pieced Bow Tie patt.,
multicolored printed patches,
green calico border, 41 x 40"..... 125.00

Crib-size, pieced Flower Garden
patt., multicolored prints & pink,
scalloped edge, 41 x 29" 125.00

Crib-size, pieced Log Cabin patt.,
blue & white cotton patches
heightened w/leaf quilting,
57 x 47" 125.00

Crib-size, pieced Wild Goose Chase
patt., multicolored prints w/yel-
low calico & solid red patches,
38 x 37½" 200.00

Youth-size, pieced blue, green,
grey, white & black blocks within

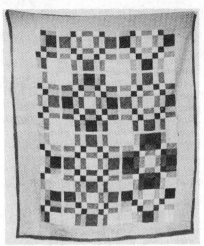

Amish Pieced Quilt

lavender border, machine-stitched
blue binding, Amish, Pennsylva-
nia, ca. 1930, 68 x 60" (ILLUS.) ... 650.00

Appliqued hearts, florals & foliage,
red & green patches on white cotton field, 84 x 83" 500.00

Appliqued Princess Feather patt.,
red & green patches on white cotton field, 90 x 77" 850.00

Appliqued & pieced stylized pots of
flowers within a zigzag border,
red, green & yellow patches on
white cotton field w/line quilting,
80 x 77" 335.00

Appliqued & pieced Basket of Flowers patt., red & light blue-green
patches, double diamond quilting,
green vine border, 83 x 70" 195.00

Appliqued & pieced Rose of Sharon
patt. variant, 9 wreath blocks
within a tulip & meandering vine
border, worked in red, green &
yellow on white ground, mid-
19th c., 94 x 94" 1,320.00

Pieced Bar patt., dark green & blue
calico patches w/line quilting,
backed w/deep red cotton,
90 x 80" 320.00

Pieced Bethlehem Stars patt., red &
white calico patches, corners
w/small double floral blossoms,
white cotton field w/scallop & leaf
quilting, probably Pennsylvania,
19th c., 84 x 84" 935.00

Pieced Bow Tie patt., aubergine-
bronze, jade green, royal blue,
lavender & black cotton & wool
flannel patches on field w/outline,
cable & diagonal line quilting,
Amish, Lagrange County, Indiana,
ca. 1925, 80 x 72" 4,125.00

Pieced Diamond in the Square patt., dark green, blue & red cotton patches quilted w/large central star, diamond cubes, feathers & a meandering grapevine, Amish, initialed MK, probably Pennsylvania, 19th c., 77 x 77" 3,410.00

Pieced Dresden Plate patt., multicolored patches on lavender cotton field, 95 x 78" 225.00

Pieced Economy Patch patt., blue, brown & red cotton print patches, narrow dark blue calico border, ca. 1840 .... 550.00

Pieced Flower Garden patt., colorful printed cotton flower petals w/solid color centers on white field, floral binding, 1930's 935.00

Pieced Flying Goose patt., purple, dark green, jade green, mauve, pink & salmon cotton patches on black cotton field w/sunflower & diagonal line quilting, Amish, Indiana, ca. 1920, 76 x 56" 4,070.00

Pieced Fringed Tulip patt., red, green & orange calico patches on white cotton field w/elaborate outline, feather & diagonal line quilting, whole within red & green swag & bud border, probably Pennsylvania, 19th c., 86 x 82" ... 302.00

Pieced Geometric patt., purple and white & red and white printed calico diamond & square patches, 19th c., 88 x 80" 467.00

Pieced Honeycomb patt., blue floral-printed cotton on solid mustard yellow, 1930's 825.00

Pieced Irish Chain patt., blue patches on white cotton field, blue scalloped border, 110 x 80".. 450.00

Pieced Lone Star patt., multicolored calico & solid patches w/compass star quilting in corners, 74 x 70".. 575.00

Pieced Maltese Cross patt., red, white & blue "linsey woolsey" patches w/concentric diamond quilting, late 19th c., 88 x 80" 715.00

Pieced Mariner's Compass patt., multicolored circular cotton "blocks" on rust-red calico ground, ca. 1850 .... 330.00

Pieced Nine Patch patt., rich dark prints on purple & white print ground, 78 x 64" 250.00

Pieced Pigs in a Blanket patt. in a Nine Patch patt. configuration, pink & blue calico w/brown & blue print, Bar patt. reverse in blue & pink calico w/two lavender stripes, Berks County, Pennsylvania, 80 x 80" 345.00

Pieced Pinwheel patt., goldenrod yellow & navy blue patches on dark brown ground, reverse in Bar patt. in red & pink calico, Mennonite, Lancaster County, Pennsylvania, 90 x 90" 395.00

Pieced Pin Wheels patt., maroon & blue-green patches on brown ground, meandering quilted floral border w/birds, Amish, Lancaster County, Pennsylvania, 86 x 86" ... 600.00

Pieced Star Pattern Quilt

Pieced Star patt., goldenrod, teal & reddish brown patches on white cotton w/floral quilting, 84 x 82" (ILLUS.) 2,100.00

Pieced Star of Bethlehem patt., red, green, blue & white calico patches, large central star surrounded by glazed brown, pink, green & white chintz, field w/conforming line & scallop quilting, 19th c., 108 x 101" 1,210.00

Sunburst Pattern Quilt

Pieced Sunburst patt., red, green, orange & black printed & solid

patches on white cotton field interspersed w/stars & floral buds &
heightened w/criss-cross & leaf
quilting, signed S.T., by her
Mother, dated 1860, probably Pennsylvania, 81 x 81" (ILLUS.) 1,320.00

Amish Quilt

Pieced Sunshine & Shadow patt.,
multicolored blocks within a blue
feather quilted border, Amish,
81 x 80" (ILLUS.) 1,150.00
Pieced Tree of Life patt. variant, red
& green cotton on white w/feath-
er wreath quilting between trees,
82 x 79"....................... 425.00
Pieced Trip Around the World patt.,
pink, blue, green, tan & yellow
printed & solid patches,
88 x 72"....................... 210.00
Pieced Turkey Track patt., blue &
multicolored calico on pink calico
ground, yellow calico border
stripe, blue & white homespun
fabric backing, Berks County,
Pennsylvania, 90 x 68".......... 350.00
Pieced Wedding Ring patt., multicolored print patches on white
cotton field, scalloped border,
88 x 78"....................... 230.00
Pieced Zigzag patt., alternating
black & maroon wool zigzags
within narrow maroon & black
borders & a wide maroon border,
black edge & backing, heightened
w/chain, diagonal line & square
quilting, Amish, Holmes County,
Ohio, ca. 1920, 79½ x 72" 550.00

SAMPLERS
Alphabets & numerals, stitched in 2
shades of green on homespun lin-
en fabric, signed "Frances Amelia
Parcelle, Age 13, 1851, Morris,
Otsego Co, N.Y.," framed,
10¼" sq. 235.00
Alphabet, verse & inscription over

floral bouquet in a basket flanked
by trees, 3-sided border of meandering green leaves & violet
grapes, vivid pink, red, green,
violet, pale yellow, rust & tan silk
stitches on linen, signed "Wrought
by Louisa S. Campbell aged 12
years 1824, born in Amherst,
Dec. 9, 18," central Massachusetts,
17 x 16¾" 2,740.00
Alphabets, numerals & row of
animals, birds & heart in shades
of red & green on homespun fabric, signed "Jean Page, aged 9,
1826," framed, 18¾ x 13½"...... 700.00
Alphabets & pot of foliage above
verse & names of the 6 members
of the Mason family, green, blue,
yellow, brown & black stitches on
homespun fabric, signed & dated
1846, framed, 21½" sq.......... 400.00
Alphabets & numerals w/various
decorative devices above 2 angels
holding wreath w/a crown over
stylized birds, trees & a reindeer
above Adam & Eve flanking a tree
wrapped w/a serpent, colorful
cotton stitches on linen, probably
English, late 18th-early 19th c.,
26 x 9¼" (stained) 352.00
Bands of bold flowers & cross-
stitched diamond motif, blue &
green silk stitches on linen,
Europe, late 17th c., 19 x 8"...... 605.00
Bands of stylized floral & figural
border motifs including crowned
mermaids, silk thread worked in
a variety of elaborate stitches
including raised & pulled lace-
work bottom panel, initialed "MT"
(probably Mary Tratt of Boston),
17th c., 22¾ x 7½"............2,750.00

Late 18th Century Sampler

House w/woman in front amidst
flowers, birds, trees & various

farm animals, initials "M D" at top
& "Jane Bell House Oswego Americ
(sic)" below within floral border,
pink, rose red & green woolen
stitches on natural cotton fabric,
by Jane Bell, Oswego, New York,
late 18th c., framed, 13¼ x 13"
(ILLUS.) 1,320.00
Map w/various districts outlined &
identified above inscription
"England and Wales" on homespun fabric, signed "Jane Perkins,
aged 11, 1798," giltwood frame,
25 x 23½" 325.00
Parrots (2), basket of flowers & 2
hearts, blue, green, brown, gold,
black & white stitches on homespun fabric, signed & dated 1810,
framed, 11¼ x 10 7/8" 375.00
Pious verse "The Feats of Death..."
above central floral basket surrounded by butterflies, birds &
trees within meandering strawberry vine border, shades of
brown, green, gold & grey
stitches on homespun fabric,
signed "Margaret Owens, A.D.
1834," framed, 13¼" sq. 425.00
Pious verse over scenic panel
depicting a seated stag flanked by
trees, birds & tiny dogs within a
vivid blue & red meandering tulip
& carnation border, worked in silk
in tiny cross-stitch on natural lin-
en, signed & dated 1825,
16¼ x 13" 660.00
Pious verse entitled "Resignation"
under a bold landscape panel
depicting a turreted castle flanked
by trees within border of flowering vines & under a cross-stitched
formal floral band, wool stitches
on coarse linen canvas, signed
"Margaret Smith aged 12 AD
1848," 18 x 17" 660.00
Pious verse above a rendering of
the school building, w/deep lawn
surrounded by birds, trees, animals
& carnation bouquets, scrolling
monogram "ABC" below, Westtown
School, Chester, Pennsylvania,
dated 1812 ....6,050.00
Stylized flowers, trees, birds &
animals, brown & green stitches
on homespun linen fabric, signed
"Thirza Hoar, Aged 11 years, June
the 21, 1839," beveled grain-
painted frame, 16½ x 13" 600.00

SHOW TOWELS

Embroidered red & blue single
florals on homespun fabric, signed
& dated 1786, 17" w., 52" l.
(stains & some wear) 125.00

Embroidered pink & blue stylized
florals on homespun fabric, drawn
& knotted fringe, signed & dated
1808, 15" w., 47" l. (colors
faded) 200.00
Embroidered red & blue stylized
florals & birds on homespun fabric, w/thread drawn-work panels
stitched w/florals & stars, 3 rows
of fringe, signed & dated 1838 in
embroidery & drawn-work, 17" w.,
53" l. 1,025.00
Embroidered red & blue stylized
stars, florals, dog, & bird on
homespun fabric, w/narrow bands
of cutwork, 2 rows of fringe,
signed & dated 1846, 19¼" w.,
55" l. (slight fading & hanging
tabs worn).................... 450.00
Embroidered stylized florals & "Ane
Kiehl 1840" in deep tones of maroon, tan, olive green & brown on
homespun fabric, 18¾" w.,
55½" l. 125.00
Embroidered red & blue stylized
birds & flowering trees on homespun fabric, fringed end, signed &
dated 1842, 17¾" w., 59" l. (some
wear & colors faded) 150.00
Embroidered red, blue & gold stylized pots of tulips & other flowers
& signed in red cross-stitch on
homespun fabric, woven & knot-
ted fringe, 18¼" w., 59½" l. 375.00
Embroidered red & blue stylized
pots of flowers, birds & "Elizabeth
Binkly is my name, Manheim
township is my dwelling place,
The Rose is red, the leves (sic) is
green" on homespun fabric,
w/thread drawn-work checkerboard design panel at bottom,
17" w., 61½" l. (colors slightly
faded) 375.00

STEVENGRAPHS

"The Present Time"

Bookmark, "Happy May Thy Birthday
Be" 45.00
Bookmark, "The Priceless Gem" 55.00

Picture, "Called to the Rescue -
Heroism at Sea" 140.00
Picture, "The First Point" 150.00
Picture, "The Good Old Days," Royal
Mail Coach .... 145.00 to 170.00
Picture, "The Present Time," original
frame, 9½ x 6½" (ILLUS.) 425.00
Picture, "Queen Victoria," framed .. 110.00
Picture, "Signing of the Declaration
of Independence" 395.00
Picture, race scene, "The
Start" .... 120.00 to 150.00

TOBACCO JARS

Pug Dog Tobacco Jar

Bisque, bust of a black lady
w/green, pink & white turban &
scarf & gold earrings, 3¾" d.,
5" h. $87.00
Bisque, bust of a black man smoking pipe, black hair, gold collar,
3½" d., 4½" h. 88.00
Bisque, bust of black man wearing
high pointed collar, Germany 200.00
Bisque, model of a monkey head
w/jaunty cap & eye glasses, light
brown w/gold trimmed eye glasses on chain, white collar & bowtie, glossy grey cap w/blue
stripes & red bill, yellow & brown
bee w/green wings cap finial,
4 5/8" d., 6" h. 175.00
Bisque, model of a skull wearing
golfing cap & sitting on a book ... 125.00
Glass, milk white decorated
w/hand-painted hunting dogs on
front, green & maroon background, metal top, Handel Ware .. 525.00
Jasper Ware, Indian chief on cover,
Indian regalia on front, raised
white on green ground 185.00

Majolica, bust of an American
Indian, 5" h. 135.00
Majolica, bust of a lady wearing fez,
w/cigar in mouth 100.00
Majolica, bust of monk, smiling
w/cigarette in mouth & smoke
curling, pink & light blue,
Germany 95.00
Majolica, model of a bear smoking
pipe, 6" h. 125.00
Majolica, model of seated pug dog
wearing collar (ILLUS.) ... 125.00 to 150.00
Majolica, barrel-shaped, embossed
figures of 3 Graces & scenery on
blue ground, signed "Wardle,"
6¾" h. 75.00
Majolica, square-shaped, Monk decor, pipe on lid 95.00
Pottery, bust of a black lady w/light
blue headdress & necklace,
3 3/8" d., 5¼" h. 110.00
Pottery, bust of a black man
w/straw hat w/blue band, gold
earrings, blue shirt, black hair,
4 5/8" d., 5 5/8" h. 130.00
Pottery, bust of an Oriental man
w/hat, black moustache & goatee,
hat lifts off as lid, 4¼" d.,
5½" h. 116.00
Pottery, bust of a seaman w/cap,
whiskers & sideburns, in navy outfit & sailor cap w/light band reading "H.M.S. Nelson," marked
"Made in Bohemia," 4 1/8" d.,
6" h. 130.00
Pottery, figure of a grinning gnome
on barrel, marked "JMI" & "No.
3388" 95.00
Stoneware, blue Edelweiss floral decor on grey pebbled ground, Star
of David lid & bail handle 210.00

TOOLS

Stanley No. 45 Plane Set

Butcher's meat hooks, iron, 49",
pr........................... $35.00

Butcher's rendering ladle, cast
iron......................... 35.00

Butcher's saw, "Keen Kutter"....... 40.00

Cabinetmaker's compass, hickory &
maple, mortised & pinned, hand-
forged iron thumbscrew, 18th c.,
24" l. 130.00

Cabinetmaker's panel gauge, tiger
maple & burl, heart-shaped hand-
forged iron thumbscrew, ca. 1800,
13½" l. 85.00

Cabinetmaker's scraper plane, metal, "Stanley No. 81"............. 42.00

Carpenter's ball pien hammer,
"Keen Kutter".................. 15.00

Carpenter's barn beam drill....... 65.00

Carpenter's block plane, "Keen Kutter K120"..................... 27.00

Carpenter's block plane, "Stanley
No. 9¼", indented finger grooves,
brass adjustments.............. 40.00

Carpenter's brace, brass & wood,
marked "H. Hawke, Sheffield".... 125.00

Carpenter's claw hammer, "Keen
Kutter"...................... 20.00

Carpenter's claw hammer,
"Winchester" 55.00

Carpenter's draw shave, brass fittings, "Jennings," 10" angled
handles 15.00

Carpenter's hand brace, "Nowles
1865" 30.00

Carpenter's level, cherry, copper
U.S. cents inset as washers at the
pivot end, ca. 1840 .... 150.00

Carpenter's level, wood & brass,
"Davis & Cook," patd. Dec. 1886.. 42.50

Carpenter's level, wood w/brass
trim, "Stanley No. 1872" 30.00

Carpenter's mitre box, laminated
maple, birch & oak, graduated
quadrant, "Stanley No. 115"...... 25.00

Carpenter's pipe wrench, "Winchester," 18".................. 60.00

Carpenter's plane, "Chaplin
No. 1210".................... 60.00

Carpenter's plane, "Fillister
No. 78" 20.00

Carpenter's plane, "Keen Kutter
K110" 20.00

Carpenter's plane, wooden, "Scioto
Works," 22" l. 10.00

Carpenter's plane, "Stanley 3"...... 15.00

Carpenter's plane, "Stanley,
No. 10½".................... 100.00

Carpenter's plane, "Stanley
No. 19"...................... 30.00

Carpenter's plane, "Stanley
No. 30"...................... 37.50

Carpenter's plane, "Stanley
No. 35" 35.00

Carpenter's plane, "Stanley No. 45,"
w/cutters..................... 80.00

Carpenter's combined plow & beading plane, "Stanley 45," original
box (ILLUS.).................. 175.00

Carpenter's plane, "Stanley
No. 85".....................1,150.00

Carpenter's plane, "Stanley
No. 444"..................... 675.00

Carpenter's plane, "Winchester
No. 3045".................... 75.00

Carpenter's plane, "Winchester
No. 9008" w/original Winchester
bit.......................... 40.00

Carpenter's plane, dark wood
hinged top, brass w/screw adjusts
& iron blade, "P. Shea" impressed
in wood & on brass, ca. 1860,
2" w., 7¾" l. 110.00

Carpenter's plumb bob, brass 10.00

Carpenter's ruler, folding-type,
ivory, "Stanley," 4-section,
12" l. 125.00

Carpenter's scissors, "Winchester
9014" 30.00

Carpenter's scissors, "Winchester
9045" 30.00

Carpenter's slick blade, "Greenlee,
USA," 3" w., 10" l............. 25.00

Carpenter's sliding trammel, points
mortised & pinned, 30" 30.00

Carpenter's wire center, "Winchester 6" 35.00

Coachmaker's biststock, metal,
w/thumblatch, marked "No. 5
H.O. White Bros.," ca. 1850,
10½" 85.00

Cooper's stave finisher, one brass
ferrule split, curved, 4½ x 7" 25.00

Furrier's buffalo hide shave, brass
ferrules, wood handles, 29" l. 60.00

Harness maker's vise, wooden,
portable-type, 1901............. 20.00

Lumberman's axe, "Winchester" 55.00

Lumberman's broad axe w/wooden
handle, 12" blade, 37" l. overall .. 45.00

Plumber's pipe wrench, "Keen
Kutter"...................... 30.00

Shoemaker's combination pliers &
hammer, marked "j.c.v. 7 s.
No. 3" 12.00

Surveyor's compass, signed "Spear,
Ireland," ca. 1800, 17" l. 850.00

Surveyor's steel tape, on reel
w/handle, "Champion," 100 foot.. 45.00

Surveyor's transit, "Berger,
No. 13142," w/case 275.00

Violin's maker's draw knife, miniature, brass, 1 x 3¾".............. 140.00

Wheelwright's traveler, iron w/brass
wheel, marked "N.Y., Ct" &
"Ans"....................... 180.00

American Tinplate Trains

Special Focus!

by Susan and Al Bagdade

Imagine a scene reinacted in countless living rooms across America: the first electric train set-up is being laid out by a proud, loving father to surprise and delight his son on Christmas morning. Picture the son's face when he encounters operating coal cars, milk loaders, billboards, stations, bridges, semaphores and gate keepers in a fantastic layout chugging around his Christmas tree. Despite the fact that transformers were so heavy that small boys could barely lift them, they could not wait to begin dumping coal, uncoupling cars or directing their trains to alternate tracks.

Memories of that first electric train stay with you for the rest of your life. Nostalgia appears to be the driving force behind the collecting of toy or tin plate trains. An irresistible desire to reproduce what was once yours as a child has inspired today's collectors who have the means to duplicate or enhance those early train sets for themselves and/or for their own children.

The earliest toy trains were pulled by a string without the benefit of motor or tracks. George W. Brown, a Connecticut toy maker, brought independent motion by introducing a keywind, clockwork motor about 1856, but still the train had no tracks. In the 1870's, toy engines powered by steam duplicated the power of real locomotives utilizing various fuels, but these were somewhat dangerous, occasionally leading to unexpected explosions.

Electric trains first became available in the United States about 1896 with battery power as the means of locomotion. As improvements were made, voltage requirements decreased and trains became safer to operate. For the first time, speed and direction could be controlled, along with operating switches and signals, from a central transformer.

Tinplate or toy trains differ from scale-model railroads since they were designed to be played with by children and were rugged in construction. They usually sacrificed authenticity for durability. Model railroading, on the other hand, reproduced everything in accurate scale. Tinplate collectors specialize by maker, by gauge and by period of manufacture.

Gauge is the measurement of a railroad track's width from the inside edge of one rail across to the edge of the other. A complete train set-up must all fall within the same scale range. The largest commercial size was *Gauge One* or *Standard Gauge* with *O-Gauge* being the most popular size. HO, N, TT and Z gauges, in descending order of size, fall more into the model-railroading category.

Many American toy train manufacturers had a significant impact on the marketplace. A brief summary of their histories relates the story of tinplate collecting.

Joshua Lionel Cowen was the most innovative marketer of toy trains in the world. His earliest trains were designed to help attract the customer's eye to merchandise in store windows during the holidays. He was well on his way when shoppers purchased his trains rather than the displayed merchandise. Cowen started his business in New York in 1900 and was soon producing toy trains as the Lionel Manufacturing Company; in 1902 he put out his first train catalog. This was modest in comparison to his elaborate full color "wish books" which were to become a tremendous merchandising device for Cowen and remembered by children everywhere. Fifty years after his first catalog, Lionel was the largest toy company in America.

"Play value" was the hallmark of Lionel trains. Trains and their accessories had to sustain a child's interest over long periods of time to be worthwhile. Lionel's first trains ran on two-rail tracks with a 2 7/8" wide gauge. By 1906 Lionel was using a three-rail track which became its standard.

Lionel has produced trains in a variety of gauges: 2 7/8 Gauge from 1900-1905; Standard Gauge, 1906-1930; O-Gauge, 1915 to present; O-27 Gauge, 1930 to present;

OO-Gauge, 1938-1942, and HO-Gauge, 1957-1967. There was competition for Lionel from various American train manufacturers and also from German toy makers. When World War I broke out, the German toys stopped coming to the United States, and the American manufacturers increased their share of the market.

During World War I, most of Lionel's efforts went into producing war goods. The company name was changed to The Lionel Corporation in 1918. In the following years Cowen became America's electric train king. 1920-29 was a decade of tremendous toy train innovation for Lionel. All sorts of accessories and switches worked automatically as the train passed by. Lionel catalogs became "the catalog" for children everywhere. Once they knew the name Lionel, they would never forget it.

After recovering from the Depression, the Lionel Corporation went full steam ahead producing new trains and inventions. Lionel based its trains on specific models of the real railroads, even working from actual blueprints. The Classic Period at Lionel, from 1923 to 1940, produced some of the most valuable and highly prized collectors' items. Action was increased in accessories and remote control provided a more sophisticated means of moving trains.

Train production at Lionel stopped for the World War II effort. The company did produce a cardboard train that "ran" on cardboard O-Gauge tracks to keep the boys of America happy. During the Golden Years at Lionel, after World War II until 1955, a tremendous variety of items were manufactured. Sheet metal locomotives were replaced by die-cast engines. Along with the trend towards realism came new devices that made toy trains more life-like.

The biggest success after the war was the locomotive that made real smoke which came out of the stack in time to the rhythmic turning of the locomotive drive wheels. Milk and cattle cars were the flashiest of Lionel's operating cars. All sorts of industries were featured in train layouts.

Magne-Traction, introduced in 1950, the 50th anniversary of the company, gave engines better traction on hills, additional pulling power and allowed them increased speeds.

During the mid and late 1950's, train sales declined dramatically along with the decline of the American railroads. Cowen's retirement, the development of television and discount stores as well as strikes added to the decline of the Lionel Corporation. Children of the times became interested in racing cars and airplanes instead of trains. Even the introduction of the Lionel HO line in 1957 could not save the company from losses. In the late 1950's, the family lost control of the company and by 1967 many of Lionel's products were discontinued. The firm was sold to General Mills in 1969. The manufacturing and sales of Lionel trains was handled by a subsidiary called "Fundimensions," located in Mt. Clemens, Michigan. Many of the original Lionel dies are still used today and, in addition, new engines and cars are sometimes created.

"Not just a toy, a tradition" is the slogan Fundimensions utilizes to establish its link to Lionel's long history. Today the Lionel company is owned by Richard Kughn who purchased the firm in 1985 when General Mills got out of the toy business.

The *Ives* company of Bridgeport, Connecticut, founded in 1868 by Edward Ives, was producing tin wind-up or clockwork trains by 1874 along with a diverse line of other toys. By the turn of the century Ives introduced an O-Gauge clockwork train. He manufactured electric trains beginning in 1910, but continued the popular clockwork trains too. Ives was an innovator and created a complete line of stations, tunnels and accessories for the trains. The firm's excellent lithography, fine details and durability contributed to the success of their line.

Ives electric trains were popular from their inception until they were later taken over. In 1928 Ives declared bankruptcy after which the firm was managed jointly by American Flyer and Lionel who supplied parts to Ives. Lionel marketed Ives trains in 1931 and 1932 after becoming sole owner of the company in 1929. The Ives line became incorporated into Lionel. This is known as the Lionel-Ives transition period.

American Flyer, the chief competitor to Lionel, was founded in 1907 by W.O. Coleman, Sr. and William Hafner, a manufacturer of toy wind-up automobiles. The clockwork trains they made were very successful. The firm introduced O-Gauge electrics in 1918 and became a leader in the industry. Standard Gauge was added in 1925.

A.C. Gilbert (of Erector Set fame) acquired American Flyer in 1938 and became a serious competitor for Lionel with each company having loyal supporters. After World War II, American Flyer marketed a realistic two-rail system in S-Gauge. Through the 1950's they produced many high quality trains and competed with Lionel over patents. With the lessening of public demand in the late 1950's and early 1960's, both American Flyer and Lionel were forced to diversify and cheapen their lines. After Gilbert died in 1961 there were troubled times. Lionel eventually purchased the remnants of American Flyer in 1967 and put a halt to all production of American Flyer trains. Some American Flyer trains were revived under Fundimensions (manufacturer of Lionel) in 1979.

In 1914 *William Hafner* of American Flyer fame, left Coleman and started making his own clockwork trains. He never made electrics.

Louis Marx first worked for the Strauss Toy Company and established himself as a toy maker in 1919. His toys dominated most dime store counters. Marx started selling Joy Line trains, produced by Girard Model Works under a commission sales agreement, in 1928 and continued through the mid-1930's. Eventually Marx acquired Girard and the Joy Line. The train line was then electrified.

The second series of Joy Line trains appeared with stamped steel shells in 1932. Marx ran the Girard Works as his train factory. Marx trains were inexpensive and durable, made to be played with by active children. Marx dominated the lower priced market as Lionel captured the higher priced one.

The late 1930's until World War II was the best period for Marx trains. They were sold under numerous tradenames for Sears, Penney's, Spiegel's, Montgomery Ward and Western Auto. After the war Marx went into train production in plastics. The company was sold to Quaker Oats in 1972, then to Dunbee-Combex-Marx in 1975. In 1980 they ceased operations.

Unique Art Manufacturing Company of Newark, New Jersey, made their first clockwork trains in 1949 and soon after introduced electric trains. Their main competition were the Marx trains, and with problems due to shortages caused by the Korean War, the company suspended production about 1952.

Dorfan manufactured trains for only ten years, starting in 1924, but were competitive with Ives, Lionel and American Flyer during that period. The company's origins go back to Nuremburg, Germany. When they set up shop in Newark, New Jersey in 1924 they produced both clockwork and electric trains. Despite the fact that they made a good product, the Depression took its toll on the firm and they stopped production in the mid-1930's.

About the Authors:
Susan and Al Bagdade's specialty is Quimper pottery. They write for several antiques newspapers and supply monthly columns for The Antique Trader, Antique Week *and* Hobbies Magazine. *They are advisors for several major price guides. Their first book,* Warman's English and Continental Pottery and Porcelain: An Illustrated Price Guide, *was published last summer. Since gathering data for this special section on tin plate trains, Al has put together a complete model railroad at home.*

Suggested Readings:
Greenberg, Bruce C., Greenberg's Price Guide to Lionel Trains: 1901-1942, *Sykesville,* Md: Greenberg Publishing Co., 3rd Edition, 1983;

Hollander, Ron, All Aboard!, *New York:* Workman Publishing, 1981;

Matzke, Eric, Greenberg's Guide to Marx Trains, *Sykesville, Md: Greenberg Publishing Co., 1978;*

McComas, Tom and Touhy, James, A Collector's Guide and History to Lionel Trains, Volumes I-VI, *TM Productions, 1975;*

O'Brien, Richard, American Premium Guide to Electric Trains, *Florence, Alabama: Books Americana, 1986.*

TINPLATE REPORT

Price and Condition:
Items found in this listing were gathered from a variety of sources including train shows, hobby shops, train magazines and price lists from dealers specializing in tinplate trains. Examples from the Charles Gasque Collection of tinplate auctioned at Christie's East in 1986 also are represented.

Condition is all-important in determining price and pieces found in this listing are good representative examples. Minor paint scratches and dents are to be expected due to the nature of the items. Restorations significantly affect the price and, conversely, pieces in mint or pristine condition command higher prices. All restorations are noted where applicable and should be recognized as such. Repainting and restoration if properly done are usually more acceptable to the collector than similar examples with missing parts, wrong parts or badly faded paint.

It is imperative that the serious collector understand what constitutes an original item, i.e., wheel configuration, paint color, coupling device, etc., to determine if the piece has been altered or restored in any way. Some items are so rare that any examples that surface may command stiff prices regardless of condition.

AMERICAN FLYER-GILBERT

Train Catalogs

1941-D1390	$25.00
1946-D1451	35.00
1948-D1507	40.00

1949 Toy Train Catalog

1949-D1536 (ILLUS.) 35.00
1952-D1677 .... 15.00
1956-D1866 .... 7.00
1958-D2047 .... 75.00
1959-D2115 .... 15.00

O GAUGE
Engines
401-Steam, w/3196 tender,
  ca. 1930 .... 44.00
420-Steam, 2-4-2 w/3199 tender, ca.
  1935 .... 77.00
423-Steam, 2-4-4 w/tender,
  ca. 1939 .... 220.00
435-Steam, 4-6-2 w/tender, "American Flyer Lines," ca. 1939 .... 275.00

#1093 Electric Engine

1093-Electric, green w/red trim, ca.
  1930 (ILLUS.) 125.00
3020-Electric, 4-4-4, dark green, ca.
  1920 .... 253.00
3309-Steam, 2-4-2 w/3199 tender,
  8-wheel, "American Flyer Lines,"
  ca. 1934 .... 100.00

American Flyer Cast-Iron Engine

Cast-iron, 0-4-0, keywind (ILLUS.) ... 25.00
"Champion," cast-iron, 0-4-0 w/121
  tender, ca. 1935 .... 22.00
"Hiawatha" w/tender, American
  Flyer 400.00

Passenger Cars
1106-Pullman, Union Pacific, green .. 11.00
1201-Pullman, red w/flashes 11.00
1202-Baggage Car, dark blue
  w/"American Flyer Electric
  Service" 11.00
Pullman, orange w/green roof,
  "Nationwide Lines" 83.00

Rolling Stock
476-Gondola Car, green 10.00
478-Box Car, white w/red roof 15.00

480-Tank Car, Shell, orange 15.00
484-Caboose, red w/white ends 10.00
1115-Automobile Car, yellow
  w/green roof 30.00
1116-Gondola Car, Burlington, red,
  4-wheel 10.00
3018-Dump Car, 8-wheel 20.00

Train Sets
#830-Engine-#9900, "Zephyr," key-
  wind, Coach, Observation, original box & track, ca. 1935 .... 396.00
#1333-"Explorer"-Engine-#3110,
  Baggage-#1204, Pullman-#1203,
  Observation-#1209, green, ca.
  1928 .... 110.00
#1711-Torpedo engine-#1686, 2-4-4
  w/tender, grey, Sand Car-#3207,
  Milk Car-#3212, "Borden's,"
  Caboose-#3211, original box, ca.
  1936 .... 220.00
"Broadway Limited"-Electric (2)-
  #3011, Baggage-#3011, Pullman
  (2)-#1206, "Broadway Limited,"
  Observation-#1207, Tuscan red
  w/brown roofs 209.00
Engine-#3680, Hudson w/tender,
  12-wheel, Pullman (3)-#1621-C,
  Observation-#1622-C, silver
  w/grey roofs, "New York Central
  Hudson Deluxe Passenger," ca.
  1938 .... 858.00
Engine-Steam, black cast-iron w/121
  tender, Baggage-#1205, "The
  Chicago, Milwaukee St. Paul Herald," Pullman (2)-#1206, "Seattle,"
  Observation-#1207, "Chicago," orange & black, 1920 .... 77.00

American Flyer Set with
"Golden State" Engine & Cars

"Golden State"-Engine-#3155, Club-
#3280, Pullman-#3281, Obser-
vation-#3282, green (ILLUS.) 350.00

S-GAUGE
Engines
15-Rectifier	25.00
282-Pacific, 4-6-2	40.00
283-Pacific, 4-6-2	40.00
290-Pacific, 4-6-2	35.00
293-Pacific, 4-6-2	45.00
300-Atlantic, 4-4-2 w/tender	20.00
301-Atlantic, 4-4-2, Reading	25.00
326-Steam, 4-6-4	125.00
334DC-Steam, 4-8-4 w/tender	165.00
336-Northern, 4-8-4	235.00
342AC-Switcher, 0-8-0	185.00

American Flyer #343 Switcher

343-Switcher, 0-8-0 w/tender (ILLUS.)	200.00
356-"Silver Bullet," 4-6-2	65.00
360-64 Diesel AB, Santa Fe	155.00
371-GP-7 Diesel, G. M., repaired	107.00
372-GP-7 Diesel, Union Pacific	165.00
374-75-GP-7 Diesel, T. & P.	295.00
470-1-3 Diesel, ABA	200.00
474-75-Rocket, chrome	175.00
474-75-Rocket, silver	200.00
477-78-"Silver Flash"-Diesel AB	175.00
481-"Silver Flash"-Diesel	195.00
21100-Atlantic, 4-4-2	35.00
21107-Steam, 4-4-2	50.00
21155-Switcher	250.00
21158-Dockside Switcher, blue	95.00

Passenger Cars
650R-Coach, New Haven, red	30.00
651G-Baggage, New Haven, green	20.00
661-Coach, American Flyer, chrome	40.00
718-Railway Express Car, red	25.00

Rolling Stock
605-Log Car	25.00
606-Wrecker Crane Car	25.00
607-Work & Boom Car	20.00
627-Girder Car, yellow	30.00
628-Log Car	18.00
629-Cattle Car, Missouri Pacific	12.00
630-Caboose	9.00
631-Gondola Car, T. & P., red	95.00
633-Box Car, B. & O., Tuscan red & white	20.00
635-Wrecker Crane Car	30.00
639-Cattle Car, Missouri Pacific	20.00
641-Gondola Car, Frisco	17.00

642-Reefer Car, brown	10.00
923-Reefer Car, Ill. Central	12.00
934-Floodlight Car, Southern Pacific	20.00
936-Depressed Center Car, Erie	15.00
938-Caboose, American Flyer	5.00

American Flyer #947 Reefer Car

947-Reefer Car, orange (ILLUS.)	20.00
973-Milk Car, Gilbert	75.00
24030-Box Car, M. K. T.	15.00
24316-Tank Car, Mobil	44.00
24323-Tank Car, Baker's Chocolate, repaired	100.00
24566-Auto Carrier Car w/5 auto load, Pikemaster	45.00
24631-Caboose, yellow	10.00

Train Sets
Baldwin Diesel-#355, C. & N. W., Reefer Car-#802, Ill. Central, Gondola Car-#804, Norfolk & Western, Caboose-#806	140.00
Engine-#293, Baggage-#951, Pullman-#952, Combine-#953, Observation-#954	395.00
Engine-#K335, 4-8-4, Union Pacific w/12-wheel tender, Baggage-#951, Combine-#953, "Niagara Falls," Pullman-#952, "Pike's Peak," Observation-#954, "Grand Canyon," green, ca. 1952	525.00
"Rocket"-Diesel-#474-75, Combine-#960, Vista Dome (2)-#962, Observation-#963, green stripe	475.00

Track
½ Curved-#703	0.25
½ Straight-#701	0.50
90-degree crossover	2.00
Curved-#702	0.35
Straight-#700	0.75
Switches, Electric-#720A, pr.	35.00
Switches, Manual-#26323-4, Pikemaster, pr.	8.00

STANDARD GAUGE
Engines

American Flyer-Ives #4694 Engine

4000-Electric, dark green 125.00

4039-"President's Special"-Electric,
0-4-0, restored 350.00

4670-Steam, 4-4-2 w/4671 tender ... 440.00

4694-Steam, w/"Golden State" tender, American Flyer-Ives
(ILLUS.)....................... 900.00

4696-Steam, 4-4-2 w/tender, "Gold-
en State," restored 1,200.00

Passenger Cars

4041-Pullman, "America," light
green 75.00

American Flyer #4042 Observation Car

4042-Observation, "Pleasant View,"
maroon (ILLUS.) 95.00

4151-Pullman, "America," green 55.00

4250-Club Car, "Lone Scout," green
w/red roof, ca. 1930 .... 44.00

Rolling Stock

4006-Hopper Car, Operating, red ... 600.00

4007-Hopper Car, maroon 40.00

4010-Tank Car, orange & dark
green 125.00

American Flyer #4017 Sand Car

4017-Sand Car, green (ILLUS.) 200.00

4021-Caboose 120.00

4022-Machinery Car, dark green 200.00

Train Sets

Engine-#4019, Baggage Car-#4040,
Pullman-#4041, "America,"
Observation-#4042, "Pleasant
View," maroon................. 400.00

Engine-#4643, Pullman,
Observation 575.00

Engine-#4680, w/4671 tender, Club
Car (2)-#4151, "Eagle,"
Observation-#4152, green w/red
roofs......................... 935.00

Engine-#4680, w/4671 tender, Club
Car-#4350, Pullman-#4351,
Observation-#4352, green w/red
roofs, ca. 1933 .... 1,320.00

"Lone Scout"-Engine-#4633, Club
Car-#4250, Pullman-#4251,
Observation-#4252, turquoise &
red litho..................... 700.00

Track

Curved-#4400 .... 1.00

Straight-#4401 .... 1.00

Switches, Electric-#4488, pr. 50.00

Train Accessories

Aircraft Beacon-#769.............. 35.00

Billboard, whistling-#2029, green ... 15.00

Billboard-#556, Ringling Bros....... 22.00

Bridge-#748 .... 75.00

Cattle Loader-#K771 w/#976 car 65.00

American Flyer #102 Central Station

Central Station-#102, orange base,
green roof (ILLUS.) 30.00

Crane, Electric Magnetic-#583 ...... 95.00

District School-#50................ 95.00

Eureka Diner-#275 .... 75.00

Factory-#162 .... 125.00

Freight Station w/crane-#612 .... 80.00

Log Loader, Operating-#751 .... 95.00

Oil Derrick-#773................. 50.00

Piggyback Loader w/car-#23830..... 75.00

Revolving Blinker-#769AB 25.00

American Flyer #108 Switch Tower

Switch Tower-#108, knife switches
(ILLUS.)...................... 100.00

Talking Station-#755 .... 75.00

DORFAN

O GAUGE

Engines

55-Steam, 0-4-0 w/tender, 4-wheel,
red w/black frame 65.00

Passenger Cars

498-Pullman, Boston, green w/peo-
ple, 8-wheel 17.50

5402-Coach, Jefferson, green 25.00

5402-Coach, Washington, red
(ILLUS.)...................... 20.00

Dorfan #5402 Coach

Rolling Stock

600-Gondola Car, cream & black.... 13.50
604-LRCX 84-Tank Car, Indian Refin-
ing Co., red 17.00
605-Hopper Car, grey w/black letters, 8-wheel 12.00
606-Caboose, bobber, Pennsylvania,
red w/yellow trim, orange roof,
4-wheel, hook coupler 55.00

Train Sets

Engine-#51, 0-4-0, red & gold,
Pullman-#498, "Boston," Pullman-
#498, "Atlanta," roof replaced,
Observation-#499............... 245.00
Engine-#99-100, orange, keywind,
Coaches (2), red & orange 200.00

STANDARD GAUGE
Engines

Cast-iron w/spoke wheels 450.00

Passenger Cars

771-Pullman, tan w/red roof 65.00
772-Pullman, tan w/red roof 65.00
773-Observation, tan w/red roof.... 65.00
789-Pullman, Mountain Brook, yellow & maroon 75.00

Rolling Stock

11701-Hopper Car, red............. 160.00
29325-Tank Car, light blue 160.00
121499-Box Car, Santa Fe, green.... 160.00
253761-Gondola Car, orange 160.00
486751-Caboose, brown 160.00

Train Sets

Engine-#51, Pullman (2), Observation, green w/yellow trim........ 400.00

HAFNER
Engines

109-Steam-black w/red stripe, keywind, w/1180 tender, C. &
N. W. 65.00
110-Steam, black w/red stripe, 3
domes, keywind, w/1190 tender,
red w/N.Y.C., ca. 1930 .... 100.00
1010-black & silver, keywind, w/box
tender, ca. 1930................ 11.00
1010-red & copper, smokestack, bell
& 2 domes, keywind, w/tender,
ca. 1935 .... 44.00

1110-green & gold litho, keywind,
w/1190 tender, red base & white
"Hafner," ca. 1934............. 66.00
2000-Steam, red, black & silver, keywind, w/tender 22.00
115041-Steam, yellow, blue & orange, keywind, w/78100 tender .. 30.00
"Century of Progress"-Steam, keywind, w/1180 tender, red & white
"Hafner," ca. 1933............. 77.00

Passenger Cars

Coach, "New York Flyer," black
base & roof, green & yellow sides,
red windows, "Made in America"
on sides...................... 132.00
Coach, "Sunshine Special-Rainbow,"
yellow w/red roof.............. 55.00

Hafner "Overland Flyer" Pullman Car

Pullman, "Overland Flyer," C. & N.
W. logo (ILLUS.)............... 75.00
Pullman, "Overland Flyer" 11.50

Rolling Stock

1010-Tank Car, "Hafner" 17.50
3057-Caboose, streamline 12.50
8000-Hopper Car, "Wyandotte," dark
green litho 8.00
41021-Caboose, orange litho, men in
windows 9.50
91746-Hopper Car, yellow & black
litho 8.00
91876-Hopper Car, silver litho 7.50
614333-Caboose, red, C. & N. W. ... 11.00

Train Sets

#29-Cast-iron engine, red w/red
stripe, keywind, w/1190 tender,
C. & N. W., Baggage-#97,
Pullman-#96, Observation-#98,
blue, gold & black, Union
Pacific 418.00
#602-Cast-iron engine, black w/red
stripe & gold trim, keywind,
w/tenders (2), Ill. Central, Coach,
red w/black roof, original box,
ca. 1915 .... 528.00
Cast-iron engine, black w/red
stripe, keywind, w/1181 tenders
(2), "Overland Flyer," Coach, yellow w/black roof, ca. 1915 ...... 165.00
"Century of Progress"-Engine-#1110,
green litho & gold trim, keywind,
w/1190 tender, green & red, "Hafner," Baggage, Coach, Obser-

vation, "Overland Flyer," cream &
red, original box 506.00
Diesel, streamline, keywind,
Coaches (3), Observation, copper
& green, 4-wheel, ca. 1937 . . . . 77.00
Diesel, streamline, blue & silver,
keywind, Coaches (3), silver, Observation, blue & silver, 4-wheel,
ca. 1937 . . . . 132.00

IVES

O GAUGE
Engines

Ives #3216 Electric Engine

5-Cast-iron, steam, 0-4-0 w/11
tender 85.00
17-Cast-iron, steam, 0-4-0 w/11 ten-
der, broken coupler 100.00
1116-Steam, w/11 tender 22.00
1118-Steam, w/25 tender, re-
wheeled, ca. 1915 . . . . 22.00
1125-Steam, w/17 tender, "Ives," ca.
1930 . . . . 230.00
3216-Electric, grey (ILLUS.) 100.00

Ives #3251 Electric Engine

3251-Electric, orange w/brown trim
(ILLUS.) 100.00
3252-Electric, maroon 110.00
Cast-iron, Steam, 0-4-0, keywind,
dated 1916, repainted 65.00

Passenger Cars
50-Baggage Car, red w/green roof . . 30.00

Ives #51 Chair Car

51-Chair Car, orange, ca. 1916
(ILLUS.) 40.00
51-Coach, Newark, yellow litho,
grey roof 75.00
60-Baggage Car, maroon & grey 30.00
62-Parlor Car, green w/dark green
roof, 8-wheel, auto coupler 25.00
68-Observation Car, dark green,
brass platform, lighted, 8-wheel,
auto couplers 39.50
70-Baggage Car, red w/yellow let-
ters & black roof 13.00
129-Pullman, "Saratoga," ca. 1920 . . 25.00
130-Buffet Car, ca. 1920 . . . . 25.00
135-Parlor Car, brown 13.00
136-Observation, brown 13.00
550-Baggage Car, red 22.00
1504-Pullman, red, cream doors,
blue roof, 4-wheel 22.50
1811-Pullman, light peacock litho
w/orange roof, 4-wheel 12.50

Rolling Stock
53-Box Car, Penn, grey 11.00
54-Gondola Car, grey & red 11.00
55-Cattle Car, white & green 11.00
63-Gondola Car, 4-wheel 10.00
63-Gondola Car, 8-wheel 25.00
65-Stock Car, 4-wheel 60.00
67-Caboose, 4-wheel 50.00
123-Lumber Car w/load, brown 11.00
124-Refrigerator Car 100.00

Train Sets
#30-Engine-#3251, red, Lumber Cars
(2)-#69, green, Lumber Car-#69,
brown, Tank Car-#66, Stock Car-
#69, Gravel Car-#128, Gravel Car-
#63, Lumber Car-#57 . . . . 220.00
"Blue Vagabond"-Engine-#1125,
0-4-0 w/17 tender, Baggage-#550,
Chair-#551, missing wheels,
Observation-#558, blue & cream,
ca. 1930 . . . . 395.00
Engine-#17, keywind, w/11 tender,
Baggage-#50, Chair Car-#51, Par-
lor Car-#52, olive, ca. 1920 . . . . . . 143.00
Engine-#17, keywind, w/11 tender,
Tank Car-#566, "Standard Oil
Company," Sand Car-#63, Box Car-
#64, "Atlantic Coast Lines," yellow
& grey, Caboose-#67, ca. 1927 . . . . 154.00
Engine-#116, w/11 tender, Baggage-
#550, Chair Car-#551, Parlor Car-
#552, green 285.00
Engine-#257, w/1663T tender,
8-wheel, Pullman (2)-#610,
Observation-#612, olive & red,
ca. 1932 . . . . 200.00
Engine-#3255, 0-4-0, Parlor Cars (2)-
#135, Observation-#136, 8-wheel,
tan 250.00
Engine-#3255R, Coaches (2), green . . 600.00
"Greyhound"-Engine-#3257, Pullman
(2)-#141, Observation-#142, grey . . 265.00

STANDARD GAUGE
Engines
1134-Steam, 4-4-2 w/40 tender, ca.
  1929 . . . . .1,650.00
3236-Electric, 0-4-0, tan, restored . . . 125.00
3241-Electric, dark green, ca. 1925 . . 750.00
3243R-Electric, orange 650.00

Passenger Cars
184-Club Car, olive, ca. 1927 . . . . 105.00
186-Observation, olive, ca. 1927 . . . . 105.00
187-Buffet Car, olive, ca. 1922 . . . . . . 50.00
189-Observation, olive, ca. 1922 . . . . 50.00
247-Combine, orange w/black roof,
  ca. 1930 . . . . 825.00

Rolling Stock
190-Tank Car, orange 125.00
191-Merchandise Car, brown 100.00
192-Box Car, olive sides, maroon
  roof 185.00
193-Stock Car, brown 125.00
195-Caboose, original box 125.00
199-Crane Car, green & red, ca.
  1930 . . . . 350.00

Train Sets
#1134R-"President Washington"-
  Engine & tender, Club Car-#184,
  Parlor Car-#185, Observation-#186,
  olive, ca. 1927 . . . . .2,310.00
"Black Diamond"-Engine-#3245,
  Diner-#240, Club Car-#241, Parlor
  Car-#242, Observation-#243 . . . . . .1,900.00
Engine-#1132, 0-4-0 w/tender, Club
  Car-#184, Coach-#185, Obser-
  vation-#186, red w/black roofs,
  ca. 1923 . . . . .1,320.00
Engine-#3235, Buffet-#184,
  Observation-#186, dark brown
  w/brass plates 200.00
Engine-#3242, Club Car-#184, Parlor
  Car-#185, Observation-#186, grey,
  ca. 1925 . . . . 242.00
Engine-#3243, orange w/black
  frame, restored, Buffet Car-
  #187-1, Parlor Car-#188-1,
  Observation-#189-1, orange, ca.
  1924 . . . . 660.00

Track
Straight 2.00
Train Accessories
Banjo Signal-#333 . . . . 34.00
Bell Signal-#332 . . . . 34.00
Crossing Sign-#68 . . . . 17.00
Freight Station-#115 . . . . 234.00
Semaphore-#1864 . . . . 34.00
Signal Tower-#1867 . . . . 325.00
Street Light-#306 . . . . 34.00
Telephone Pole-#86 . . . . 17.00
Union Station (2)-#116 w/platform
  cover-#121 .1,760.00
Warning Bell-#1884 . . . . 34.00
Water Tower-#89, orange 325.00

LIONEL
Train Accessories

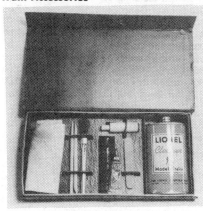

Lionel #927 Maintenance Kit

Maintenance Kit-#927 (ILLUS.) 10.00
Transformer, Type K, 150 watt 59.00
Transformer-#1033, 90 watt 39.00
Transformer-#ZW, 275 watt,
  rebuilt 149.00

Train Catalogs

Lionel 1950 Catalog

1937 . . . . 35.00
1939 . . . . 35.00
1946 . . . . 75.00
1947 . . . . 75.00
1950 (ILLUS.) 35.00
1951 . . . . 95.00
1952 . . . . 10.00
1955 . . . . 29.00

HO GAUGE
Engines
0058-Switcher, Rock Island 95.00
055P-Alco Diesel AB, Santa Fe 175.00
0581-Rectifier 125.00
0597-GP-7 Diesel, Northern Pacific . . 95.00
0647-Hudson, 4-6-4 w/12-wheel
  whistle tender 275.00

Passenger Cars
0708-Baggage, Penn 40.00
0709-Vista Dome, Penn 40.00
0710-Observation, Penn 40.00
0711-Pullman, Penn 80.00

Rolling Stock

0039-Track Cleaning Car	95.00
0050-Bumper Gang Car	95.00
0300-Lumber Car, Operating	35.00
0319-Helicopter Car, Operating	40.00
0333-Satellite Launcher	75.00
0337-Giraffe Car	75.00
0357-Cop & Hobo Car	95.00
0805-Radioactive Car	50.00
0807-Flat Car w/bulldozer	135.00

Track

Crossover-#0990	5.00
Curved, 18" long-#0998	5.00

Train Accessories

Engine House	125.00
Gateman-#0145	55.00
Missile Platform w/car-#0470	125.00
Radar Tower-#0197	125.00

O GAUGE
Engines

154-Electric, green	250.00
201-Switcher, 0-6-0, ca. 1940	2,500.00
204-Steam, 2-4-2 w/1689W tender, grey	125.00
224E-Steam, 2-6-2 w/2224W tender, ca. 1942	250.00
225E-Steam, 2-6-2 w/2235W tender, ca. 1940	375.00

Lionel #253 Electric Engine

253-Electric, 0-4-0, green (ILLUS.)	75.00
256-Electric, orange w/nickel trim	750.00
258E-Steam, 2-4-0 w/258T tender, ca. 1925, restored	195.00
259E-Steam, 2-4-2 w/2689W tender	85.00
260E-Steam, 2-4-2 w/260T tender, ca. 1932, restored	650.00
262E-Steam, 2-4-2 w/262T tender, ca. 1932, restored	295.00
385-Electric, 4-4-4, green, N. Y. C., ca. 1920	385.00
622-Diesel Switcher, A.T. & S.F.	295.00
746-Streamline, w/2046W tender, "Norfolk & Western"	1,430.00
763E-Hudson, 4-6-4 w/2263W tender, grey	1,050.00
1511-Commodore Vanderbilt type, keywind, red	100.00
2055-Hudson, 4-6-4 w/6026W tender, ca. 1955	200.00
2321-FM, Lackawanna w/red top	450.00
2322-FM, Virginian	600.00
2340-1-GG-1, Penn, Tuscan red, restored	395.00

Lionel #2343-F-3 Diesel Engines

2343-F-3 Diesel AA, Santa Fe (ILLUS.)	350.00
2351-Rectifier, Milwaukee	325.00

Passenger Cars

529-Pullman, olive w/orange trim, 4-wheel	20.00
530-Observation, olive & maroon	11.00
601-Pullman, N. Y. C., light green, 4-wheel, plain hook couplers	45.00
602-Baggage & Mail Car, U. S. Mail, 8-wheel	45.00

Lionel #607 Pullman Car

607-Pullman, peacock w/orange trim (ILLUS.)	25.00
611-Observation, silver & blue	28.00
630-Observation, red & cream	11.00
712-Observation, orange w/green trim	150.00
2436-Observation, Mooseheart, ca. 1958	58.00
2446-Observation, Summit, red	75.00
2530-Railway Express Car, aluminum	250.00
2614-Observation, State green, ca. 1940	250.00
3428-Mail Car, Operating	69.00
Pullman (2)-#610, Observation-#612, blue & aluminum, ca. 1935, restored	295.00
Pullman (2)-#613, Observation-#614, "Blue Comet," ca. 1934	795.00

Rolling Stock

651-Flat Car, green w/nickel trim	10.00
654-Tank Car, grey	100.00
655-Box Car, cream sides, maroon roof	55.00
656-Cattle Car, grey sides, red roof	90.00
657-Caboose, red w/ivory inserts	55.00
804-Tank Car, Lionel Tank Lines, 4-wheel, faded	48.00
815-Tank Car, pea green	75.00
2653-Hopper Car, Stephen Girard green	55.00

2810-Crane Car 80.00
2812-Gondola Car, green 75.00
2815-Tank Car, Shell 110.00
3356-Horse Car w/corral,
  Operating 125.00

Lionel #3464X Box Car

3464X-Box Car, Operating (ILLUS.) .. 35.00
3562-Barrel Car, Operating 49.00
3652-Gondola Car, Operating, yellow w/red letters 85.00
3672-Bosco Car, Operating 225.00
3859-Dump Car, Operating 35.00

Lionel #6457 Caboose

6457-Caboose, lighted (ILLUS.) 45.00
6460-Crane Car, Operating 49.00
6475-Heinz Pickle Car 40.00

Train Sets

#1536-"Mickey Mouse Circus"-
  Engine-Commodore Vanderbilt,
  red, keywind, w/tender, Stoker,
  Circus Car, Circus Dining Car, Cir-
  cus Band Car, no cardboard ac-
  cessories, ca. 1935 ....1,100.00
"Blue Comet"-Steam-#226E, 2-6-4,
  Pullman-#2613, Baggage-#2615, Ob-
  servation-#2614, original
  boxes 1,400.00
Burlington Diesel-#2328, Gondola
  Car-#6462, Hopper-#6456, Tank
  Car-#6465, Caboose-#6257 .... 185.00
"Congressional"-Engine-#2360-GG1,
  Tuscan red, Pullman-#2543, "Wil-
  liam Penn," Vista Dome-#2542,
  "Betsy Ross," Pullman-#2544,
  "Molly Pitcher," Observation-
  #2541, "Alexander Hamilton" 1,210.00
"Disney"-Diesel, U36B-#8773, Box
  Cars-#9660-9672, Caboose-#9183 .. 800.00
Engine-#250E-"Hiawatha," w/250W
  tender, Pullman-#782, Pullman-
  #783, Observation-#784, orange &
  grey, ca. 1938 ....1,650.00

Lionel Train Set with #258 Engine

Engine-#258, 2-4-2 w/1689T tender,
  Box Car-#655, yellow w/brown
  roof, Tank Car-#654, Sunoco, grey,
  Caboose-#657, red w/brown roof
  (ILLUS.)......................... 150.00
Engine-#763E-Hudson, grey,
  w/2263W tender, 12-wheel, Pullman (2)-#710, Observation-#712,
  blue & cream, 12-wheel, ca.
  1935.........................3,190.00
"Macy's Flying Yankee"-Power Car-
  #616E/616W, Coach (2)-#617,
  Observation-#618............... 575.00

Track

½ Curved 1.25
½ Straight....................... 1.25
45-degree crossing 7.95
90-degree crossing 6.95

Lionel Curved Track

Curved (ILLUS.)................... 0.70
Switches, Manual-pr., used........ 30.00
Uncoupling, Remote 11.95

Train Accessories

Automatic Gateman-#145 .... 22.00
Barrel Loader-#362 .... 79.00

Bascule Bridge-#313 .... 325.00
Block Signal-#153 .... 35.00
Coal Elevator, Operating-#97 .... 169.00
Crossing Gate-#077 .... 60.00
Crossing Signal-#154 .... 19.00
Culvert Unloader, Operating-#345 ... 325.00

Lionel #1045 Flagman

Flagman-#1045, red base (ILLUS.) ... 15.00
Freight Station-#356 .... 69.00
Ice Depot-#352 w/car 175.00
Lionel City Station-#134, green, tan
  & red 210.00

Lionel #438 Signal Tower

Signal Tower-#438 (ILLUS.) 125.00
Turntable-#375 .... 350.00

O-27 GAUGE
Engines
221-Steam, 2-6-4 w/221W tender, ca.
  1946, restored 195.00
239-"Scout" w/tender, Lionel Lines .. 50.00
628-Diesel Switcher, Northern
  Pacific 65.00
1110-"Scout," 2-4-2 .... 40.00

1615-Steam, 0-4-0 w/1615T tender,
  ca. 1955, restored 275.00
1655-Steam, 2-4-2 w/6654W tender .. 12.00
2036-Steam, 2-6-4 w/6466W tender .. 60.00
2046-Steam, 4-6-4 w/2046W tender .. 225.00
6220-Diesel Switcher, A.T. & S.F. ... 295.00

Passenger Cars
1865-Coach, West & Atlantic 15.00
2416-Observation, Santa Fe, blue
  stripe 75.00
2421-Pullman, Maplewood, silver ... 95.00
2436-Observation, Mooseheart 75.00

Rolling Stock

Lionel #6419 Wrecker Caboose

6357-Caboose, A.T. & S.F. 125.00
6419-Wrecker Caboose (ILLUS.) 20.00
6454-Box Car, Pennsylvania, ca.
  1948 .... 75.00
6465-Tank Car 10.00

Train Sets
Engine-#1666E w/1689T tender, Pullman (2)-#1630, Observation-#1631,
  blue w/grey roofs 165.00
"Scout"-Engine-#1110 w/1001T tender, Tank Car-#1005, Gondola
  Car-#1002, Box Car, Baby Ruth-
  #1004, Caboose-#1007 .... 68.00
"Streamliner"-Engine-#1700,
  Pullman-#1701, Observation-#1702,
  red & aluminum, restored 395.00

Track
½ Curved 0.60
½ Straight...................... 0.60
45-degree crossing 4.95
90-degree crossing 3.95

O-72 GAUGE
Track
Switches, Electric-#711, pr.,
  rebuilt 225.00

O-GAUGE SCALE
Engines
227-Switcher, 0-6-0 w/2227B tender, semi-scale 1,000.00
700E-Hudson, 4-6-4 w/700T tender ..2,750.00
773-Hudson, 4-6-4, ca. 1964 ....1,895.00

Rolling Stock
714K-Box Car, ca. 1940 .... 450.00
715-Tank Car, Shell, restored 395.00

716-Hopper Car 400.00
2954-Box Car, semi-scale 175.00
2955-Tank Car, Shell, semi-scale, ca.
    1940, restored 395.00
2955-Tank Car, Sunoco, semi-scale,
    ca. 1942, restored 395.00

OO GAUGE
Engines
5342-Hudson w/tender 300.00

Rolling Stock
0015-Tank Car 35.00
0017-Caboose, Penn 60.00
0027-Caboose, N. Y. C. 50.00
0045-Tank Car, Shell 70.00
0047-Caboose, N. Y. C. 60.00
0077-Caboose, N. Y. C. 60.00

Train Sets
Engine-Hudson-#5342, semi-scale,
    w/002 tender, Box Car-#0024,
    Hopper Car-#0016, Caboose-#0027,
    track 600.00

STANDARD GAUGE
Engines
5-Steam, 0-4-0, thin rim, ca. 1907 ..2,100.00
6-Steam, 4-4-0, thick rim, ca. 1923 . 950.00
7-Steam, w/tender, nickel & brass,
    late version, ca. 1924 ....1,650.00
8-Electric, 0-4-0, olive green 165.00
8E-Electric, 0-4-0, ca. 1932,
    restored 295.00

Lionel #10E Electric Engine

10E-Electric, 0-4-0, green, ca. 1932
    (ILLUS.) 250.00
53-Electric, 0-4-0, maroon, straight
    hook couplers, ca. 1912 ....1,720.00
318-Electric, green 200.00
380-Electric, 0-4-0, maroon 350.00
385-Steam, 2-4-2 w/385W tender,
    gunmetal w/nickel trim, 1936 ....1,250.00
400E-Steam, 4-4-4 w/400T tender ...1,800.00
402-Electric, Mojave, ca. 1923,
    restored 450.00
408E-Electric, dark green 900.00
1912-Electric, dark green square cab,
    "N.Y. Central Lines," ca. 1912 ....1,540.00

Passenger Cars
18-Parlor Car, green 200.00
29-Coach, N.Y.C., dark olive 400.00
31-Combo, dark olive, ca. 1920 ..... 66.00
36-Observation, dark olive, ca.
    1920 .... 68.00

337-Pullman, red 50.00
338-Observation, red 90.00
341-Observation, grey, ca. 1929 .... 110.00
425-Pullman, Stephan Girard, 2-tone
    green, repainted 400.00

Rolling Stock
12-Floodlight Car, ca. 1915,
    restored 150.00
13-Cattle Car, green 65.00
213-Stock Car, terra cotta & dark
    green 300.00
215-Tank Car, red 150.00

Lionel #217 Caboose

217-Caboose, orange & blue, ca.
    1932 (ILLUS.) 325.00
219-Derrick Car, yellow, red &
    green, ca. 1936, restored 250.00
220-Floodlight Car, green w/nickel-
    plated floodlights, ca. 1936,
    restored 395.00
511-Log Car, green w/nickel trim,
    ca. 1936, restored 95.00
513-Cattle Car, maroon & cream
    w/nickel trim 365.00
517-Caboose, red w/nickel trim, ca.
    1938, restored 125.00
520-Floodlight Car, green w/nickel-
    plated lights, ca. 1937, restored .. 250.00

Train Sets
"Bay States"-Engine-#318E w/Bild-A-
    Loco motor, Baggage-#310,
    Pullman-#309, Observation-#312,
    2-tone brown, track & transform-
    er, ca. 1930 .... 550.00
"Blue Comet"-Engine-#400E w/400T
    tender, Pullman-#420, Pullman-
    #421, Observation-#422, 2-tone
    blue w/nickel trim 5,000.00
Engine-#6-Steam, thick rimmed,
    w/tender, "N. Y. C. & H. R. R.,"
    Combine-#19, Coach-#18,
    Observation-#190, olive, ca.
    1918 .... 825.00
Engine-#318E, Mail-#310, Pullman-
    #309, Observation-#312 .... 500.00
Engine-#380E, Pullman-#18,
    Observation-#190, dark olive
    green 850.00
Engine-#408E, Combo-#419, Pullman-
    #418, Diner-#431, Observation-
    #490, apple green, ca. 1925 ......4,180.00
"States"-Engine-#381E, 4-4-4, Pullman-

#412, Pullman-#413, Pullman-#414,
Observation-#416, "States," green,
cast journals 12,100.00

Track
Crossover-#020X 10.00
Switches, Electric-#222, pr. 100.00
Switches, Manual-#210, pr. 100.00

Train Accessories
Barrel Set-#209, ca. 1930 .... 95.00
Bungalow, Illuminated-#184, ca.
1932 .... 75.00
Container Set-#205 .... 175.00
Crossing Gate, Operating-#77, ca.
1938 .... 95.00
Freight Shed, Illuminated-#155, ca.
1932 .... 350.00
Hellgate Bridge-#300.............. 850.00
Lamp Post-#57, ca. 1930 .... 125.00
Passenger Station-#122, ca. 1932,
restored...................... 175.00
Turntable-#200, ca. 1932 .... 395.00
Warning Signal-#69N 45.00

SUPER O GAUGE
Track
Curved-#31 .... 1.50
Straight-#32...................... 3.00
Switches, Electric-#112, pr.,
rebuilt 89.00

WINNER
Rolling Stock
1016-Tender, black w/orange side
panels 32.50
1515-Tank Car, Sunoco, missing
coupler....................... 20.00
1517-Caboose, N. Y. C., red
w/cream trim, brown roof 22.50

Train Sets
Engine-#1015-Steam, black w/orange
frame, w/1016 tender, "Winner
Lines," Pullman (2)-#1011, orange
w/green roofs, 4-wheel, ca.
1932 .... 55.00
Engine-#1035-Steam, w/1016 tender,
Box Car-#1514, Erie, Caboose-
#1517, N. Y. C. 160.00

Train Accessories
Station & transformer-#1012 .... 35.00
Station & transformer-#1017 .... 40.00

LIONEL-IVES
O GAUGE
Train Sets
Engine-#1651E, Lionel-Ives, Pullman
(2)-#1690, Observation-#1691, ma-
roon w/brown roofs, "Ives RR
Lines," ca. 1932 .... 210.00

O-27 GAUGE
Passenger Cars
1690-Pullman, red 35.00
1691-Observation, red 35.00

Rolling Stock
1514-Box Car, blue roof, pea green
doors, black base 35.00
1514-Box Car, turquoise roof, brown
doors, black base 35.00
1514-Box Car, turquoise roof, brown
doors, red base 30.00
1515-Tank Car, Sunoco, black base.. 30.00
1515-Tank Car, red base 20.00
1517-Caboose, black base 30.00
1517-Caboose, red base........... 40.00

Train Sets
Electric Engine-#1810, 0-4-0, Pullman
(2)-#1811 .... 225.00
Steam & Tender-#1506, 0-4-0, key-
wind, Observation (2)-#1812 ..... 200.00
Steam-#1661E, 2-4-0, Tank Car-
#1680, Ives, Gondola Car-#1677,
Ives, Box Car-#1682, Ives,
Caboose-#1682, Ives 225.00

STANDARD GAUGE
Passenger Cars
1766-Coach, red w/maroon roof 200.00
1767-Baggage Car, red w/maroon
roof, ca. 1940................. 200.00
1768-Observation, red w/maroon
roof, nickel journals 200.00

Train Sets
"Washington Special"-Engine-#385E,
2-4-2, grey w/copper trim, w/385T
tender, Baggage-#1767, Coach-
#1766, Observation-#1768, terra
cotta w/maroon roofs, copper
journals, ca. 1934..............1,980.00

MARX
Engines
99-F-3 Diesel AB, Rock Island 50.00
400-Steam, 0-4-0 w/N. Y. C.
tender 8.95
490-Steam, 0-4-0 w/N. Y. C. slope
tender, white stripe 7.50

Marx #495 Steam Engine

495-Steam, 0-4-0, Marlines w/951A
tender (ILLUS.) 19.00
588-Switcher, N. Y. C., black 15.00

Marx #597-C Engine

597-C-Commodore Vanderbilt w/500
tender, olive (ILLUS.) 159.00
897-Steam, 0-4-0, litho w/551 N. Y.
C. tender 45.00
1095-Diesel AA, Santa Fe, red &
grey 32.50
M10005-Freight, offset hook coupler,
cream & green 45.00

Passenger Cars

Marx #1 Baggage Car

1-Baggage Car, orange litho, 7" long
(ILLUS.) 30.00
246-Coach, Montclair, red w/black
litho trim, black & silver frame,
circular hook couplers 20.00
557-Coach, Montclair, red litho,
4-wheel 20.00
3197G-Observation, Santa Fe, litho
windows 17.50
10005-Coach, Los Angeles, green &
cream 17.50

Rolling Stock

256-Tank Car, Niacet, silver, 3/16"
scale 5.00
284-Tank Car-Allstate, dark blue triple dome, die-cast wheels 25.00
556-Caboose, Marx 2.00

Marx #1235 Caboose

1235-Caboose, Southern Pacific, Tuscan red & orange (ILLUS.) 4.00
2532-Tank Car, Cities Service, die-
cast wheels, 3/16" scale 4.50
6014-Box Car, Frisco 3.50
9100-Box Car, Union Pacific
Challenger, red & black, 3/16"
scale 15.00
28500-Gondola Car, Lehigh Valley,
4-wheel 5.00
34178-Box Car, Great Northern,
green 12.00
Dump Car, Erie, maroon, die-cast
wheels 5.00
Flat Car w/stakes, Erie, die-cast
wheels 7.50

Train Sets

#453-Engine, black plastic, keywind,
w/tender, Box Car, P. R. R., Hopper Car, Lehigh Valley, Caboose,
original box & track 44.00
#710-Diesel, Seaboard, keywind,
Pullman (2), "Bogata," Pullman,
"Montclair," original box &
track 121.00
#765-Diesel-AA, Union Pacific,
brown & yellow, keywind, Box
Car, B. & L. E., Gondola Car, C. R.
I. & P., Caboose, Union Pacific,
original box & track 110.00
"Army Train"-Engine-#500, 0-4-0,
w/500 tender, Machine Gun Car,
Ordnance Car, Searchlight Car,
Radio Car, Official Car,
4-wheel 285.00
Diesel AA, Southern Pacific, Box
Car, Gondola Car, Caboose, tin
litho 35.00
Engine-#1095 Diesel AA, Santa Fe,
Coach-#3152, Santa Fe, Vista
Dome-#3152, Santa Fe,
Observation-#3197, Santa Fe,
original box & transformer 99.00
Engine-#4000-Diesel AA, Seaboard,
green, yellow & red, keywind,
Tank Car-#553, Gondola Car-
#91257, Seaboard, Box Car-
#90171, Bessemer, Caboose-#956,
ca. 1958 .... 77.00
"Mercury-Blue"-Engine-#635, key-
wind, w/box tender, Coach,
"Montclair," Observation, blue,
ca. 1939 .... 396.00
"Mercury-Gray"-Engine-#635,
w/N.Y.C. tender, Baggage, U.S.
Mail, Passenger, Toledo, Observation, Detroit 99.00

Track
Switches, Electric-O-27, pr. 13.50

Train Accessories
Bell Signal, ringing 6.50
Block Signal, 2-light 6.50
Floodlight Tower-#416-A 50.00
Girard Whistling Station 30.00
Highway Flasher, plastic 5.00
Lift Bridge, hand crank, Ill.
Central 32.50
Semaphore-single arm, green base
& post 3.50
Street Lamp, double gooseneck 8.00
Unloading Platform, maroon 3.00
Water Tower, flat black 6.50

JOY LINE
Engines
104-Keywind, red cab & boiler, copper trim 60.00
105-Keywind, red body, black
frame 49.00

Passenger Cars

357-A-Coach, green w/orange
roof............................ 30.00
357-B-Coach, green w/red roof 19.00
357-D-Coach, green w/orange roof,
gold windows & numbers 35.00
458-C-Observation, green w/orange
roof, brass rails, red awning 30.00

Rolling Stock

351-B-Tender, embossed coal pile,
steps on front................... 45.00
351-C-Tender, embossed sides,
2-level deck 65.00

Joy Line #352-D Hopper Car

352-D-Hopper Car, red w/blue base
(ILLUS.)........................ 49.00

Train Sets

Engine-#102-B, keywind, cast-iron
w/351-A "Koal Kar" tender, Dump
Car-#354, Joy Lines & "Contrac-
tors," Box Car-#355, "Hobo Rest,"
Caboose-#356-"Eagle Eye," blue
frames, ca. 1927 .... 800.00
Engine-#102-B, keywind, cast-iron
w/351-C tender, Tank Car-#353,
"Everful," Gondola Car-#351-B,
"Venice," black frame, Caboose-
#352-B, "Eagle Eye," black
frame 400.00

O GAUGE
Train Sets

"Bunny Train"-Engine, pink w/blue
ribbon, keywind, Hopper Cars (3),
"Bunny Express," pink w/blue
bases.........................1,210.00
"Mickey Mouse Meteor Train"-Steam
engine, w/tender, Gondola Car,
Box Car, Caboose 572.00

UNIQUE
Engines

724-Steam, light & dark grey, blue,
yellow & black 43.00
742-Steam w/tender, keywind 50.00
1950-Steam w/tender 60.00
2000-Diesel AA, Rock Island........ 140.00

Rolling Stock

Caboose, red, yellow, black &
white 15.00
Hopper Car, orange, red & black
w/grey trim 12.00

Train Sets

#1951-Engine-#1950-steam, blue,
w/tender, Box Car-#3905, silver,
Hopper Car, orange, Caboose,
red, track & transformer 121.00
Engine-#742, blue & grey, keywind,
w/tender, Coach, "Garden City,"
Coach, "City of Joplin".......... 220.00
& original box 132.00
Engine-#742, w/tender, keywind,
Box Car-#100, Caboose-#105a..... 25.00

Unique Train Set

Engine-#1950, blue, w/tender, Hopper Car, orange, Box Car-#3905,
silver w/blue trim, Caboose,
orange (ILLUS.)................. 89.00
Engine-#1950, w/tender, Circus Animal Cars (2), "Jewel," Caboose,
track & transformer 264.00

Train Accessories

Control Tower, white, red & green .. 10.00

MISCELLANEOUS
AMERICAN MODEL
Passenger Cars

3160-Coach 72.00
3407-Railway Post Office 70.00
4170-Baggage Car 70.00
Pullman, "Dan River" 72.00
Vista Dome, "Georgia" 72.00

Rolling Stock

140449-Stock Car, "Atlantic Coast
Line"........................ 70.00

Train Sets

Engine-#8644-Diesel, red & silver,
Pullman-#3160, "Pennsylvania-City
of Pittsburgh," Diner, "Pennsylvania," Observation, "City of
Chicago" 170.00

BUDDY L
Train Sets

Engine, 2-4-2 w/tender, Tank Car,
black & yellow, Hopper Car,
black, Box Car, red, Cattle Car,
green, Gondola Car, Side Dump
Car, restored...................2,860.00

KUSAN
Engines

XT2167-Diesel, "U. S. Army," missing machine guns 37.50

Rolling Stock
1389-Flat Car, "U. S. Air Force" 11.00
2710-Caboose, yellow w/red, "Kusan
Line" 12.50
4111-Box Car, "Lost River" 8.50
5124-Box Car, dark green, "M. & St.
L.," 8-wheel 8.50

VOLTAMP
Engines
2100-Steam, 4-4-0 w/tender, B. & O.,
early 1900's 2,090.00
2210-"Royal Blue Limited,"
0-4-4-0, ca. 1911 .... 2,500.00

*For additional listings, see the December
1987 issue of The Price Guide to Antiques and
Collectors' Items.*

(End of Special Focus)

TRUNKS

Leather-covered Lady's Trunk

*These box-like portable containers are used
for transporting or storing personal possessions. There are many styles to choose from
since they have been made from the 16th century onward. Thousands arrived in this country with the immigrants and more were
turned out to accomodate the westward
movement of the population. The popular
dome-top trunk was designed to prevent water from accumulating on the top. Hinges,
locks and construction, along with condition
and age, greatly determine the values of older trunks.*

Dome-top, leather-covered wood
w/decorative brass studding &
bail handle, 16" l. (hasp
missing) $30.00
Dome-top, painted pine, original
dark green paint w/orange striping & yellow dots, original iron

hinges & end handles w/replaced
hasp & lock, 25" l. 67.50
Dome-top, painted & decorated pine
& poplar, dovetail construction,
original brownish red painted
graining in imitation of flame
grain mahogany w/inlay, initialed
"D.B." w/flourish, 26¾" l. 385.00
Dome-top, pine, dovetail construction, wrought iron bandings, end
handles, hasps & locks, 38½ x
23½ x 20" (refinished) 95.00
Immigrant-type, dovetailed pine
w/applied moldings forming 2
panels on front, worn original red
paint w/polychrome flowers on
pale blue ground in panels,
w/bear trap lock, strap hinges &
till, 39" w., 18¼" deep, 13¾" h.
(bottom boards old
replacements) 250.00
Immigrant-type, pine, dome top,
wrought iron bandings, hinges,
bear trap lock & twisted end handles, worn original brown finish
w/black & yellow painted initials
& "Anno 1744," 39½ x 20",
20¾" h. (repairs & some edge
damage) 125.00
Immigrant-type, pine, dovetailed
construction, truncated base,
domed lid, iron bound w/wrought
iron lock & strap hinges, green
paint w/black initials, 48½" l..... 70.00
Lady's, embossed leather covering
w/rows of brass studs, leather
straps & end handles, metal lock
& key, small (ILLUS.) 467.50
Storage, camphor wood, rectangular, dovetail construction, brass-
bound corners, shaped hasp, es-
cutcheon & carrying handles,
fitted interior, 39½ x 19¼",
17½" h........................ 550.00

UNIFORMS, COSTUMES & PERIOD
CLOTHING

*Recent interest in period clothing, uniforms
and accessories from the 18th and 19th centuries and from specific periods in the 20th
century, compelled us to add this category to
our compilation. While style and fabric play
an important role in the values of older garments of previous centuries, designer dresses of the 1920's and 30's, especially evening
gowns, are enhanced by the original label of
a noted couturier such as Worth, or Adrian.
Prices vary widely for these garments which*

*we list by type, with infant's and children's
apparel so designated.*

Robe, Dress & Coat by Fortuny

Apron, bib-style, calico, long $16.00
Apron, waist-type, white linen
w/tucks, long 10.00
Baseball uniform, "big league" style,
1923, complete w/underwear &
socks 150.00
Bath robe, man's, woven wool pais-
ley, ca. 1880 . . . . 68.00
Bed jacket, lady's, peach velour
w/large pearl buttons, Saks Fifth
Avenue label, 1940's 12.00
"Bloomer" dress, black serge, waist-
top w/braid trim & self-buttons,
full-pleated bloomers, 1880-1900 . . 55.00
Bloomers, lady's, peach crepe
w/satin backing, silk embroidery
& lace edging, 1920's 16.00
Blouse, lady's, Gibson Girl style,
white cotton w/Brussels lace &
embossed net inserts 25.00
Blouse, lady's, high neck, white cotton w/hand-crocheted Irish lace
trim, Edwardian, 1901-10 . . . . 75.00
Blouse, brown taffeta, leg-of-mutton
sleeves, Victorian 48.00
Bonnet, lady's, hand-crocheted black
cotton, intricate pattern, replaced
satin ribbon ties 5.00
Bonnet, Amish, dark brown cotton,
hand-quilted, 1890's 65.00
Camisole, white cotton w/Batten-
burg lace inserts 80.00
Camisole, white linen batiste,
numerous tucks & tiny buttons 15.00
Cape, lady's, three-quarter length,
flapper-style, black wool, pointed
hemline, 1930's 40.00
Capelet, elbow-length, black plush
w/Persian lamb fur trim,
Victorian 30.00
Christening bonnet, white linen ba-
tiste, ribbon latticework trim,
mother-of-pearl buttons,
Victorian 35.00

Christening gown, w/matching petticoat, white cotton w/crochet in-
serts, numerous tucks & lace trim,
Victorian, 1880's, 2 pcs. 95.00
Coat, baby's, pink silk, delicate em-
broidery, hand-sewn for Best &
Co., Paris, w/label 45.00
Coat, child's, mottled gold velvet,
w/matching brass-trimmed but-
tons, Victorian, 1890's 28.00
Coat, lady's, brown muskrat fur,
1940's 125.00
Coat, man's, bearskin fur 60.00
Coat, man's, coonskin fur 500.00
Coat, man's, grey wool gabardine,
Bogart-Casablanca style, 1940's . . . 40.00
Collar, hand-crocheted filet (for
deep neckline) 10.00
Collar, peach satin w/pearls & gold
threadwork, 1920's 20.00
"Cycling" dress, plaid cotton, bal-
loon sleeves, late Victorian,
1890's, 2-piece 125.00
Dress, child's, Amish, multicolored
cotton, together w/pinafore, cap
& shawl, 4 pcs. 65.00
Dress, lady's, designer-type, 3-piece
costume, brown wool crepe,
w/fitted jacket w/sheared beaver
sleeves & turban-type hat, 1937 . . 50.00
Dress, lady's, Edwardian, blue silk
gauze embroidered w/colored silk
& w/ecru lace trim, w/label of
Jeanne Hallee, ca. 1908 . . . . 715.00
Dress, lady's, Edwardian, purple silk
w/lace inserts, h.p. buttons &
cummerbund w/bow, early 1900's,
size 12-14 . . . . 60.00
Dress, lady's, flapper-style, black
chiffon w/overall beading & embroidered hemline & sleeves,
1920's 275.00
Dress, lady's, flapper-style, black
satin w/steel-cut beading, 1920's,
size 12-14 . . . . 75.00
Dress, lady's, Victorian, black &
white polka dot cotton, 2-piece
summer dress, 1890's 95.00
Evening coat, black velvet, knee-
length w/dolman sleeves, gilt-
printed in a bold scrolling foliate
pattern, pale green rolled edging,
cream charmeuse lining, w/"For-
tuny" label (ILLUS. right) 4,620.00
Evening coat, gold lame' & black
velvet, woven in an Art Deco pattern of linear & eliptical forms,
deep red velvet lining, late
1920's 660.00
Evening gown, "Delphos" style,
pleated amethyst silk, short laced
sleeves, opaque black & white
beaded trim, by Mariano Fortuny
(ILLUS. center) 1,650.00

Evening suit, man's, cut-away jacket, trousers, vest & bowtie,
1940's, medium size 60.00
Frock coat, man's, black wool 65.00
Gloves, child's, white kid, pr. 12.00
Gloves, lady's, white kid, opera
length, pr..................... 15.00
Hat, child's, Buster Brown type,
black velvet w/bow at back 10.00
Hat, lady's, black bugle beads forming widow's peak at front, green
velour winged sides trimmed
w/iridescent green bugle beads,
1930's-40's 35.00
Hat, lady's, white chiffon & satin,
wide brim, 1890's 35.00
Hat, lady's, black velvet w/wide
brim, fur band & single large cabbage rose at base of crown, ca.
1915 .... 50.00
Jacket, lady's, shirtwaist-type, mohair, 1890's, w/label "ABC Clocks
to the fashion born, man tailored
in the Celebrated workshop of
Worth" 48.00
Jacket, lady's, monkey fur, long
sleeves, round collarless neck, ca.
1940 .... 275.00
Kimono, silk, royal blue w/colorful
satin stitch embroidered Phoenix
Bird on flowered branch, embroidered sleeves & front, white silk
lining, 51" l. 100.00
Lounging pajamas, Oriental-style,
kimono sleeves, bright green &
blue embroidery on white,
1930's 35.00
Mittens, lady's, hooked wool, cream
w/green & pink leaves, ca. 1865,
pr........................... 120.00
Muff, child's, white curly lamb,
1920's 22.00
Muff, child's, white rabbit fur
w/kitty head, 7" 22.00
Muff, child's, brown seal,
Victorian 20.00
Night cap, lady's, white crocheted
cotton & net, w/satin ribbon &
rosettes 25.00
Nightgown, lady's, white cotton
w/embroidered yoke & cap
sleeves, pink ribbon trim,
ca. 1900 .... 25.00
Night shirt, man's, white w/Goose
Track embroidery, Victorian 25.00
Opera cape, lady's, blue silk & gilt
brocade, knee-length, full-cut
back gathered into a "hobble"
type hem, apple green lining,
mink collar & trim, ca. 1915 ...... 220.00
Overshoes, lady's, 4-buckle, black,
1930's-40's, pr. 30.00
Pajamas, lady's, peach satin 30.00
Pantaloons, girl's, white cotton

w/tucked details & lace trim, size
6 .... 16.00
Parasol, child's, black taffeta w/ruf-
fles, 18" d. 65.00
Parasol, blue lace, ivory handle 85.00
Petticoat, child's, white cotton
w/cutwork trim, Victorian........ 25.00
Petticoat, quilted blue, brown or
black cotton, each.............. 95.00
Riding (sidesaddle) ensemble,
lady's, black wool, 1900,
2-piece 125.00
Robe, seal brown velvet, knee-
length, gilt-printed w/foliate borders & medallions, pale gold charmeuse lining, w/"Fortuny" label
(ILLUS. left) 3,850.00

VENDING/GAMBLING MACHINES

Columbia "Standard"

Arcade, "Cail-O-Scope," Caille Bros.,
1904........................$1,250.00
Arcade, "Erie Digger," Erie Mfg.
Corp., 1924 .... 875.00
Arcade, "Grandfather's Clock," grip
tester, Exhibit Supply Co., ca.
1927 ....1,325.00
Arcade, "Princess Doraldina" fortune
teller, 1928 .... 7,500.00
Arcade, "Quartoscope," 1-cent, Mills
Novelty Co., Pat. Oct. 12, 1897 ..1,295.00
Chocolate vendor, "Wilbur's," cast
iron, patd. 1904 .... 600.00
Collar button vendor, 5-cent, Price
Collar Button Machine Co., ca.
1905 .... 550.00
Gambling, Baker's "Pacers" console
slot machine, 5-cent play, short
compact version (after World
War 2).......................12,000.00
Gambling, Bally's "Reliance" dice

counter-top slot machine, 5-cent
play, ca. 1936 ....3,600.00
Gambling, Buckley's "Bones" counter-
top dice slot machine, 5-cent play,
1936-39 ....3,500.00
Gambling, Caille's "Bull Frog" upright
slot machine, 1904 ....15,000.00
Gambling, Caille's "Four Reel Superior" counter-top slot machine,
5-cent play 1,500.00
Gambling, Columbia "Standard"
counter-top slot machine, 5-cent
play, ca. 1937 (ILLUS.) 700.00
Gambling, Jennings' "Duchess Vendor" counter-top slot machine,
10-cent play 1,100.00
Gambling, Mills' "Blue Front"
counter-top slot machine, 10-cent
play 1,300.00
Gambling, Mills' "Bursting Cherry"
counter-top slot machine, 5-cent
play, 1936 ....1,300.00
Gambling, Mills' "O.K." (Owl)
counter-top slot machine, 50-cent
play, 1924 ....1,350.00
Gambling, Mills' "Operators Bell"
counter-top slot machine, 5-cent
play, ca. 1911 ....3,690.00
Gambling, Mills' "Q.T." counter-top
slot machine, 1-cent play
(restored) 1,500.00
Gambling, Pace's "The Kitty"
counter-top slot machine, 10-cent
play 2,900.00
Gambling, Watling's "Rol-A-Top"
counter-top slot machine, w/cornu-
copia of fruit, etc., 5-cent play,
ca. 1935, 26" h. 3,500.00
Golf ball vendor, "Sportsman,"
Jennings, 1934-36 ....6,000.00
Gum "prize" vendor, "E-Z," w/hol-
low gumballs w/numbered papers
good for prizes or cash awards,
footed iron base, AsLee Novelty
Co., 5-cent play, ca. 1930 .... 475.00
Gum vendor, "Happy Jap," R.J.
White Mfg. Co., clockwork mech-
anism, 1902 ....3,700.00
Kissometer 750.00
Pinball machine, "World Series,"
Rock-Ola Mfg., counter model,
1933 .... 750.00
Stamp vendor, red, white & blue
stripes, silver stars, by Mills
Novelty Co. for the American
Vending Machine Co., 1915 ......1,000.00
Trade stimulator, "The Elk," Mills
Novelty, 1905 ....2,200.00
Trade stimulator, "Upright Perfec-
tion," nickel-trimmed polished
oak, Mills Novelty Co., 1901 .....1,000.00

WOODENWARES

Cookie Board

*The patina and mellow coloring, along with
the lightness and smoothness that come only
with age and wear, attract collectors to old
woodenwares. The earliest forms were the
simplest and the shapes of items whittled out
in the late 19th century varied little in form
from those turned out in the American colonies two centuries earlier. Burl is a growth,
or wart, on some trees in which the grain of
the wood is twisted and turned in a manner
which strengthens the fibers and causes a
beautiful pattern to be formed. Treenware is
simply a term for utilitarian items made from
"treen," another word for wood. While
maple was the primary wood used for these
items, they are also abundant in pine, ash,
oak, walnut, and other woods. "Lignum Vitae" is a West Indies species of wood that can
always be identified by the contrasting colors
of the dark heartwood and light sapwood and
by its heavy weight, which causes it to sink
in water. Also see BANKS, BUTTER
MOLDS, KITCHENWARES, LEHN
WARE and SHAKER COLLECTIBLES.*

Apple butter scoop, hand-hewn,
D-form handle, 11½" l. $175.00
**Apple tray, canted sides, original
brown-painted graining exterior,
yellow interior, 8 3/8 x 7½",
3 7/8" h. (edge damage)** 65.00
Apple tray, pine, scalloped rim,
canted sides, 13¼ x 9" 175.00
**Apple tray, walnut, dovetail con-
struction, canted sides,
26 x 16½"** 95.00
Barrel, straight tapering sides, stave
construction w/wooden bandings,
old worn blue paint, 20" h. 175.00
Boot last, 3-section w/mechanical
adjustment, w/extra section for
wider toe, overall 26½" h. 55.00
Bowl, burl sides w/inserted pine
bottom, 7" d., 3½" h. 215.00
Bowl, burl ash, good figuring, old
dark finish, 10½" d., 4" h. 250.00
Bowl, burl, excellent figuring, oval
w/canted sides, nut brown pati-

nated finish, 19¾ x 15",
7½" h. 2,300.00

Bowl, turned bird's eye maple, shallow, heavy rim w/turning lines on
exterior, old red paint, early
19th c., 9" d., 3 3/8" h. 165.00

Bowl, oblong, Norwegian rosemaaling interior decor, 19th c.,
20 x 12" 150.00

Bowls, factory-made, signed "Munis-
ing," 20th c., 9", 11" & 13" d.,
nested set of 3 .... 85.00

Box w/hinged domed lid, painted &
decorated, original red, white &
yellow designs on black ground,
brass bail handle & iron lock
w/brass hasp, 12" l. 900.00

Box w/lift-off lid, painted & decorated, square nail construction, black
& red-painted graining finish, Amish origins, 14" sq. 165.00

Bread (or pastry) board, pine, molded tray edge, 18½" sq.
(refinished) 57.00

Bucket & cover, stave construction
w/wire bandings & wire bail handle w/wooden grip, "alligatored"
white repaint, 14¼" d., 7" h. 125.00

Bullet mold (for round musket ball),
cherrywood, square w/pewter
lining & wooden pins, 18th c.,
2-pc. 160.00

Butter churn, dasher-type, tapering
cylinder, stave construction
w/bentwood bandings & one
stave continuing to form "piggin"
handle at side, w/dasher 350.00

Butter churn, dasher-type, tapering
cylinder, stave construction
w/bentwood bandings & one
stave continuing to form "piggin"
handle at side, w/dasher 165.00

Butter churn, floor model, pump-
type, painted, stenciled "E.H.
Funk's Champion Churn, Pat'd
Sept. 1888, Manuf'd at the Champion Churn Works, Toledo, Ohio"
in white on red, 2-gal. 175.00

Butter paddle, curly maple, flattened blade w/rounded end,
8½" l. 175.00

Butter scoop, burl, good figuring
throughout, hook at handle end,
New Jersey origins, 13" l........ 900.00

Cake board, square, carved spread-
winged American eagle & shield
flanked by flags, cannon & drum,
inscribed "Union Forever" in banner overhead, all within berry &
leaf surround, J. Conger, New
York State, 19th c., 13 x 11¾" ... 522.50

Candle box, wall-type, pine, arched
& scalloped backboard, ca. 1820 .. 230.00

Candle dipping rack, pine,
pumpkin paint ....
Canteen, keg-shaped, stav
struction w/wire bandin
bail handle w/wooden grip, potter collar on side opening w/cork,
traces of old blue paint, overall
10" h. 67.50

Carrier, bentwood round w/straight-
lapped seam, wire bail handle
w/wooden grip, 11" d., 6½" h.
(some edge damage) 45.00

Cheese box, cov., bentwood round
w/finger lappet in lid & 2 lappets
in base, 18th c., 12" d., 6½" h.... 175.00

Church collection box, painted finish, dovetail construction, boldly
turned handle, worn original red
paint, 19¾" l. w/handle 205.00

Cigar mold, 10-cigar, pine, stamped
"Cincinnati" & numbered, 2-pc.,
12" l. 35.00

Comb case, wall-type, w/mirror,
beaded edges.................. 45.00

Cookie board, carved w/six signs,
including birds & animals,
6¼ x 3½" (ILLUS.) 70.00

Cream skimmer, burl & tiger maple,
shell-shaped w/tab handle,
4 x 4½" 175.00

Cup, hand-hewn, well-shaped handle, thin sides, 2¾" h........... 175.00

Cutlery tray, curly maple & cherrywood, dovetail construction, scalloped sides, shaped center divider
pierced w/heart-shaped grip, old
refinishing w/good color,
14½ x 10½" 850.00

Cutlery tray, mahogany, dovetail
construction, center divider applied w/turned handle at top,
17½ x 10¾" 85.00

Document box w/flat hinged lid,
pine, molded edges, hinged lid
opening to well, top, front & back
painted to resemble tortoise shell,
ends w/grape & floral decor on
green ground w/yellow leafage &
outlining, 19th c., 13¼" oblong,
7½" h. 385.00

Dough trough on stand, poplar, box
w/canted sides & 2-board top on
cherrywood-finish stand w/turned
& splayed legs, 42 x 21½",
28½" h......................... 350.00

Drinking cup, 2-handled porringer-
style, interwined chain design,
dated May 14, 1846 .... 140.00

Dry fruit carrier, 1-qt. 32.50

Dry measure, bentwood round,
branded "Made by E.B. Frye &
Son, Wilton, N.H." & stenciled
"Dry 4 Qt. Measure," 9" d.,
5¼" h. 45.00

...ng rack, 2-section folding-type, walnut, reeded horizontal bars, tapering legs w/spade feet, each section 16 3/8" w., 30" h. 175.00

Egg carrier, w/interior tray & lid, marked "Gardner, 1889," 1-dozen 50.00

Egg crate, slat construction, w/wire bail handle, 12-dozen . . . . . . 15.00 to 25.00

Flour bin, painted & decorated, Norwegian-style rosemaaling decor 250.00

Turned Jars by Pease

Jar & cover, turned, attributed to Pease of Ohio, 4 7/8" h. (ILLUS. left) 196.00

Jar & cover w/bail handle & wooden grip, turned, attributed to Pease of Ohio, 9" d., 8½" h. (ILLUS. right) 200.00

Knife (sharpening) box, dovetail construction, pumice stone within nailed compartment, 15 x 8½" . . . 75.00

"Lefse" roller (corrugated rolling pin w/handles), 1-pc. 48.00

Lemon squeezer, w/lignum vitae insert 35.00

Mallet, burl head, turned wood handle 55.00

Mangling (or smoothing) board, full figure horse handle, painted free-hand florals on green ground, dated "1847" & w/initials, Swedish origins 475.00

Pantry box, cov., bentwood round, painted & decorated, lid w/flower & black leaves on red ground, 6" d. 95.00

Pipe box, hanging-type, curly maple, scrolling crest & shaped sides, one overlapping drawer w/early wide dovetailing, refinished w/soft brown stain, 20¾" h. 3,900.00

Rolling pin, pine, turned handles, 1-pc., 17½" l. 20.00

Rolling pin, maple w/some curl, button handles, 18" l. 45.00

Salt box, hanging-type, pine, scalloped top, slant sides, molded base, red & green trim, 5½ x 6½", 8" h. 85.00

Salt box, hanging-type, poplar, triangular crest w/circular hanging tab, hinged slant lid, original dark brown "alligatored" finish, 10½" w., 12" h. 300.00

Spoon, curved handle, oblong bowl, worn brown patina, 5¼" l. 25.00

Spoon rack, 2-tier, shaped backboard w/two racks held w/rosehead nails, single open compartment below, carved initials "A.H.," painted red, 19th c., 12½" w., 7" deep, 17½" h. 660.00

Sugar firkin w/lid, bentwood bandings secured by copper nails, wire bail handle w/wooden grip, original blue paint, 6¾" h. 325.00

Sugar Firkin

Sugar firkin w/lid, bentwood bandings & bentwood handle, redbrown patina, 12" h. (ILLUS.) 125.00

Toddy stick, turned tapering handle w/mushroom-shaped end, 1-pc., 10¾" l. 30.00

Trencher plate, birch, hand-hewn, 18th c., 19 x 10½" 150.00

Utensil rack, painted finish, stepped crest w/simple carving, 12 wrought iron hooks, old red paint, 20½" l. 100.00

Vinegar bucket, pine, stave construction, stenciled "Clear Vinegar" on side, iron wire bail handle 48.00

Wall box, open, walnut, high backplate, angled sides, low front, 4½" w., 10" h. 155.00

Wall shelf, walnut, half-round shelf, openwork Masonic & Eastern Star symbols on backplate, ca. 1870, 12" w., 6" deep, 23" h. 65.00

WORLD FAIR COLLECTIBLES

There has been great interest in collecting items produced for the great fairs and expositions held through the years. During the 1970's, there was particular interest in items produced for the 1876 Centennial Exhibition and now interest is focusing on those items associated with the 1893 Columbian Exposition. Listed below is a random sampling of prices asked for items produced for the various fairs.

1876 PHILADELPHIA CENTENNIAL

Stevengraph Bookmark

Ale glass, clear pressed glass,
paneled body, embossed stars
w/dates "1776" & "1876" $45.00
Bandanna, printed fabric, portraits
of George Washington & Ulysses
S. Grant flanking spread-winged
eagle, shield, flags & "Centennial"
at top, lower portion w/various
Fair buildings & "1776-1876,"
28¼ x 22¼" 110.00
Book, "Centennial Exhibiton - 100
Anniversary American Independence," by A.S. Barnes, illustrated
w/four-hundred engravings 12.50
Book, "Frank Leslie's Historical
Register" 50.00
Book, "The Great Centennial Exhibi-
tion," by Sandhurst, 1876 . . . . 25.00
Bookmark, woven silk by Thomas
Stevens, George Washington
above crossed flags & verse,
framed (ILLUS.) 150.00
Bust of Abraham Lincoln, frosted
glass, Gillinder & Sons . . . . : 225.00
Cup & saucer, china, flag & "1776"
on cup, "First Centennial of
American Independence 1776-
1876-Cincinnati" on saucer 85.00
Goblet, Liberty Bell patt. 55.00

Goblet, Washington Centennial
patt., 7" h. 45.00
Medallions, wooden, die-stamped
Main Building, Independence Hall,
Memorial Hall, George Washing-
ton, Alfred Goshorn & J.R.
Hawley, set of 6 in original
box 375.00
Whimsey, model of a lady's slipper,
clear glass, marked "Centennial
Exhibition - Gillinder & Sons,"
6" l. 35.00

1893 COLUMBIAN EXPOSITION

1893 Advertising Card

Advertising card, "Jersey Coffee,"
scene of Administration Building
w/greenery, Dayton Spice Mills
Co., Sole manufacturer, Dayton,
Ohio reverse (ILLUS.) 10.00
Bone dishes, china, transfer scene
of fair buildings viewed from the
lagoon, set of 6 . . . . 95.00
Book, "Official Guide to Columbian
Fair" 20.00
Creamer & open sugar bowl, china,
gold handles, shell decor w/gold
trim on cream ground, "Chicago
1893 Exhibition," Coalport, small,
pr. 150.00
Cup, vaseline glass, overlapping pe-
tals, "Libbey Glass Co. Toledo
Ohio - World's Fair 1893" 85.00
Model of the Santa Maria, mother-
of-pearl sail, 3¼" h. 24.00
Mug, relief-molded bust of Colum-
bus one side, Washington other . . 75.00
Paper cut-out, "Administration Building" model, heavy paperboard,
21 x 14" 65.00
Paperweight, "Algerian & Tunisian
Village, World's Fair, 1893," black
& white photograph under clear
glass 45.00
Picture, woven silk, "Administration
Building," 20" 22.00
Pincushion, pewter, model of lady's
heeled slipper, original cushion &
tiny pink satin rose, "World's Fair
Chicago 1893" on sole 75.00

Milk Glass Columbus Plate

Plate, milk white glass, bust portrait
of Columbus center w/"1492-
1893," openwork club border, gold
trim, 9¾" d. (ILLUS.) 45.00
Razor, straight, black handle, build-
ings engraved on blade, H. Baker
& Co. 35.00
Teaspoons, silverplate, bust of
Columbus on handle, building pictured in bowl, set of 6 in original
box .50.00 to 75.00
Tumbler, ruby-stained glass,
"World's Fair 1893" . . . . .50.00 to 60.00
Vase, cranberry glass, gold leaves &
berries w/central medallion of
white enameled Mary Gregory-
type girl, acid-etched "World's
Fair 1893" on base 225.00
World globe, tin w/iron stand,
"Chicago World's Fair 1893,"
4½" h. 38.00

1901 PAN-AMERICAN EXPOSITION

Silverplate Match Safe

Beer mug, stoneware pottery, "Compliments Burley & Co.," colorful
Continents decor 125.00
Cigarette case, hinged gold cover
w/grape leaves & sinuous vines in
relief, set w/diamonds & a central
grape cluster of sapphire & ame-

thyst cabochons, impressed Tiffany
& Co. & w/applied tag cast w/a
buffalo, 3" l. 2,640.00
Match safe, silverplate, nude wom-
an in relief (ILLUS.) 45.00
Picture, woven silk, Electric Tower
pictured, 10" w. 55.00
Teaspoon, demitasse, sterling silver,
Indian & buffalo handle, globe &
"Pan American-1901" engraved in
bowl 35.00
Tumbler, clear glass w/etched scene
of Manufacturing & Liberal Arts
Building, 3½" h. 30.00
View card, framed 30.00
Whiskey shot glass, clear glass
w/etched buffalo decor 20.00

1904 ST. LOUIS WORLD FAIR

Graniteware Mug

Book, "The Book of the Fair, St.
Louis," by Everett, 496 pp. 25.00
Book, "Official Photographic Views,
Art Edition," 302 pp. 48.00
Book, "Universal Exposition St.
Louis," black & white illustrations,
41 pp. 35.00
Change tray, metal, Uncle Sam &
Miss Liberty decor, 6 x 5" 32.50
Creamer, ruby-stained glass, clear
bottom w/Star of David, cranberry
top, 3¼" h. 125.00
Cup & saucer, demitasse, china,
"Agriculture Palace" decor,
marked "Made in Germany" 65.00
Handkerchief, silk, lithographed pic-
ture of Teddy Roosevelt, American
Eagle & "Louisiana Purchase," em-
broidered flowers around
edge . . . . .70.00 to 85.00
Jewelry box, leaded glass, "Cascade
Gardens" scene on lid 50.00
Letter opener, bronze, eagle
perched atop handle, 7¼" l. 80.00
Match safe, nickel-plated brass,
Lewis & Clark scene 65.00
Mirror, pocket-type, "Cascade
Gardens" 20.00
Model of a hatchet, clear glass, em-

bossed "St. Louis World Fair" &
engraved name 65.00
Mug, graniteware, Napoleon, Jeffer-
son, view of St. Louis & U.S. map
decor (ILLUS.) . . . . .60.00 to 70.00
Paperweight, "Palace of Liberal
Arts" scene under glass 28.00
Pinback button, multicolored fair
scene, 1¼" d. 22.50

Aluminum Pin Tray

Pin tray, aluminum, monument cen-
ter & bust portraits at corners,
4¾ x 3¼" (ILLUS.) 30.00
Plaque, Weller Art Pottery, portrait
of William B. McKinley, 4½" 310.00
Plate, china, Jefferson center, cobalt
blue transfer on white, Rowland &
Marsellus, 10" d. 80.00
Postcard, hold-to-light type, "Palace
of Education" 25.00
Reverse painting on glass, "Cascade
Gardens" scene, framed 36.00
Scarf, silk, "Festival Hall" & "Cas-
cade Gardens" scene on pink
ground, 20 x 20" 110.00
Sugar shell, sterling silver figural
mermaid w/shell handle, natural
shell bowl w/colorful Indian por-
trait & inscribed "1904 World's
Fair, St. Louis," 5½" l. 52.00
Teaspoon, demitasse, silverplate,
"U.S. Government Building" in
bowl, U.S. Silver Co. 20.00
Trade card, aluminum, "Cascade
Gardens" 19.00
Vase, china, "Missouri State Build-
ing" decal, 3½" h. 45.00
Watch fob, aluminum, embossed
bust portraits of Jefferson &
Napoleon 20.00

**1915 PANAMA-PACIFIC INTERNATIONAL
EXPOSITION**
Book, "Official Fair Guide" 9.00
Booklet, color illustrations, 9 x 6",
16 pp. 15.00
Bookmark, celluloid, advertising,
"Carnation Milk" 27.50
Pin, brass, "California" on bar, bear
below 45.00

Plate, glass, automobile & fair en-
trance scene, 7" d. 25.00
Print, overall view of Exposition,
night-illuminated frame, 27" w.,
6½" h. 42.50
Sugar spoon, silverplate, "Horticul-
ture Palace" in bowl 12.00
Tea set: 10½ x 8½" octagonal tray,
individual size cov. teapot, creamer, open sugar bowl & 5" d. lemon dish; china, Oliver Twist decor,
each piece marked "Panama Pacific International Expo 1915,"
Adams, 5 pcs. 200.00
Teaspoon, sterling silver, handle
w/American eagle on shield supporting maiden standing on world
globe & placing wreath of laurel
around rising sun's rays, original
box . . . . .50.00 to 65.00
Teaspoon, sterling silver, handle
w/bear on world globe finial,
"Official Souvenir P.P.I.E." 37.50

1933-34 CHICAGO WORLD FAIR
Ash tray, brass, embossed Sky Ride
& Fort Dearborn decor, 3½" sq. . . . 16.00
Badge, enameled Swastika, Wel-
tausstellung Zeppelin tag 35.00
Book, "Chicago & Its Two World's
Fairs," 102 pp. 15.00
Book, "Official Guide Book,"
194 pp. 13.00
Bottle, amber glass, impressed
building & 1934 . . . . 13.00
Box, diamond shape, orange bake-
lite w/black & silver flying ducks
decor, 7" 50.00
Cane, wooden, "Prosperity Cane" . . . 23.00
Cookbook, "Prudence Penny's Chica-
go World's Fair Recipe Book" 11.00
Creamer & sugar bowl, china, Art
Institute & Chicago Court House
decor, made for Marshall Field &
Co., 4½", pr. 150.00
Knife, pocket-type, 2-blade, handles
embossed "Century of Progress
1933," Camillus Cutlery 32.00
Model of baseball glove & ball, ce-
ramic, marked, "Chicago World's
Fair 1933" 15.00
Paperweight, Federal Building &
Goodyear Blimp decor 32.00
Paperweight, paper under glass,
view of Hall of Science 18.00
Photograph, marks location of all
exhibits, 60 x 11" 65.00
Pillow cover, scenes of fair 20.00
Pin tray, copper, center embossed
view of Chicago & Indians, rim
w/water, 3½" d. 8.00
Plate, china, "Travel Building"
scene, Pickard 14.00

Playing cards, original box 16.50

Postcard, "General Motors
Building" 4.00

Postcard, "50 Years Progress in
Burlington Locomotives" 15.00

Stein, ceramic, green glaze
w/figural nude handle 28.00

Tapestry, planes & dirigible scene,
24 x 45" 40.00

Token, "Lucky Penny," Indian & Ft.
Dearborn pictured, 2 3/8" d. 8.00

Toy wagon, "Radio Flyer," 2" w.,
4" l. 50.00

Tray, metal, white w/relief molded
scene of Hall of Science, 5 x 4" . . . 10.00

Viewer, "Foto Reel," metal, w/26
views on reel 35.00

Water jug, glass, embossed log cabin & teepee w/modern skyscraper
as "Century of Progress" 25.00

1939 GOLDEN GATE INTERNATIONAL EXPO

Bar pin, gold plated, filigree
w/white enamel circle logo cen-
ter, 1¾" w. 20.00

Compact, white enamel & gold,
original box 20.00

Token, aluminum, "Union Pacific" . . . 5.00

1939 NEW YORK WORLD FAIR

Ash tray, brass w/metal Trylon &
Perisphere 28.00

Ash tray, telescope disk-type, Py-
rex, Corning Glass Works 15.00

Bank, model of typewriter, advertis-
ing "Underwood" 45.00

Book, "Book of Nations," hard
bound, 189 pp. 15.00

Book, "Official Guide Book," first
edition 14.00
Perisphere on book-shaped 2-tier
base, Italian Pavilion, 4½" l.,
5½" h., pr. 125.00

Booklet, General Motors, Trylon &
Perisphere cover 8.00

Bottle, milk white glass, embossed
map of the world, "World's Fair
1939," 9" h. 16.00

Cigarette dispenser, model of a
mule 89.00

Coasters, glass w/Trylon &
Perisphere etching, original box,
set of 12 . . . . 75.00

Compact, Trylon & Perisphere
decor 20.00

Cookbook, "Sealtest Kitchens
Receipts, 1939" 14.00

Creamer, George Washington,
ivory, American Potters, 5" h. 25.00

Dagger, miniature, in original leath-
er case 10.00

Flag, Trylon & Perisphere pictured,
11½ x 7½" 15.00

Handkerchief, printed w/colorful
costumes of the world 15.00

License plate, 1940 New York 15.00

Map, greater New York City area,
auto routes & points of interest,
colorful 6.00

Pencil sharpener, Trylon &
Perisphere 15.00

Pin, goldtone, Trylon & Perisphere
w/figural "39" suspended 12.50

Pinback button, "The Ice Industry's
Peter & Penelope Rabbit," 2¼" . . . 14.00

Pitcher, figural George Washington,
marked "The American Potter -
Joint Exhibit of Capital & Labor,"
ivory gloss finish, 4½" h. 20.00

Plate, George Washington center
scene, Trylon & Perisphere & oth-
er scenes on border, 11" d. 45.00

Plates, commemorative, pink transfer, early New York scene series,
Wedgwood First Edition, set
of 12 . . . . 500.00

Salt & pepper shakers, models of
Trylon & Perisphere, cream &
pink, Lenox China, pr. 85.00

Scarf, multicolored, Hungary exhibit,
27" sq. 25.00

Stamps, scenes of attractions, set of
54 . . . . 22.00

Stereoscope viewer, hand-type,
w/Fair view cards, original box . . 39.00

Tapestry, Administration Building,
colorful, 19 x 18" 38.00

Teaspoon, silverplate, Trylon &
Perisphere medallion tip handle,
Wallace 11.00

Thermometer, wooden, Trylon &
Perisphere 15.00

Toby mug, bust of Washington, parian, "The American Potter" 20.00

Tumbler, glass, Trylon & Perisphere,
orange & red logo enameled
decor on clear 7.00

1962 SEATTLE WORLD FAIR

Book, "Official Guide Book, Seattle
World's Fair, 1962" 6.00

Bracelet, ID-type, gold finish metal,
w/fair emblem 7.50

Doll, original case 5.00

Knife, pocket-type, 2-blade 5.50

Plate, china, fair scenes, 4" d. 7.00

Poster, fair scenes 11.00

Slides, Lake Amusement Area
scenes, set of 10 . . . . 7.50

Tie clasp 3.00

1964-65 NEW YORK WORLD FAIR

Ash tray, advertising, "Sue Brett
Dresses" 4.00

Bank, dime register, metal, flat
square 10.00

Handkerchief, silk, fair scenes 7.00

Scarf, printed scenes of New York
City 12.00
Shoulder bag, child's, vinyl 12.00
Thermometer, wall-type on plaque .. 19.00
Tray, blue-colored aluminum, round,
large 8.00
View cards, set of 28 in original
box 14.00

WRITING ACCESSORIES

*Early writing accessories are popular col-
lectibles and offer a wide variety to select
from. A collection may be formed around any
one segment–pens, letter openers, lap desks
or ink wells–or the collection may revolve
around choice specimens of all types. Material, design and age usually determine the value. Pen collectors like the large fountain pens
developed in the 1920's but also look for pens
and mechanical pencils that are solid gold or
gold-plated. Also see METALS.*

FOUNTAIN & DIP PENS

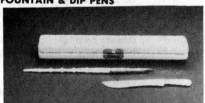

Mother-of-Pearl Pen Set

Dip pen, mother-of-pearl handle
w/gold ferrule, gold nib, original
hinged case $35.00
Dip pen, mother-of-pearl handle, together w/matching letter opener,
Madison & Buck Co., Chicago, in
original fabric covered case, early
20th c., 7" l. case (ILLUS.) 45.00
Conklin "50" fountain pen, chased
black hard rubber (some wear) ... 95.00
Conklin fountain pen, man's, gold-
filled, Gothic design (minor
wear) 175.00
Eastman pen w/mechanical pencil at
other end, red, green & grey mottled, lever fill 15.00
Montgomery Ward "Gold Bond"
fountain pen, ca. 1940, original
box 10.00
Moore "Red Ripple No. 2" fountain
pen, non-leakable 90.00
Parker "Blue Diamond Vacumatic"
fountain pen, green & black
stripe, 1940 .... 30.00
Parker "Duofold" fountain pen, lapis

lazuli blue, button filler, ribbon
ring, 1930 .... 25.00

Parker "Royal Challenger" Pen

Parker "Royal Challenger" fountain
pen, silver pearl & black, 1934
(ILLUS.) 30.00
Parker "No. 25½" fountain pen,
chased black hard rubber 135.00
Sears Roebuck "Diamond Medal"
fountain pen, 1930 .... 12.00
Sheaffer "Lifetime" fountain pen,
black, 1914 .... 60.00
Sheaffer "No. 3" fountain pen,
green, gold & black striped 16.00
Wahl-Eversharp "Gold Seal" fountain
pen, black & pearl, 1928 .... 50.00
Wahl-Eversharp fountain pen, lady's,
10k gold point 75.00
Waterman "Ideal" fountain pen,
black hard rubber, 1909 .... 85.00
Waterman "No. 7" fountain pen,
hexagonal barrel, black, eyedrop-
per fill, 1898, original box 65.00

INKWELLS & STANDS

Brass stand, Art Deco style, tray
holding 2 facet-cut clear glass
cov. wells, w/attached pen rest,
8½ x 6" 85.00
Bronze stand, oblong, obverse inset
w/panel of iridescent yellow-gold
mosaic tesserae, body & matching
cap cast w/interlacing swirls,
w/glass liner, signed Tiffany Studios, 3 1/16" w. 660.00
Cast iron stand, Art Nouveau style,
central cov. stamp compartment
flanked by 2 swirled glass wells,
signed Bradley & Hubbard 115.00
Cast iron well, head of man
w/pointed beard & hat 125.00
China well, clown's head, yellow,
purple & red, 5" h. 65.00
Pewter well, Art Deco style model
of a frog, signed Kayserzinn 475.00
Silver stand, capstan form, hinged
cover inset w/desk clock, w/glass
liner, Birmingham hallmarks for
1914, 8" d. 330.00
Silverplate stand, clear glass well,
pen wiper, & stamp box w/figural
bulldog stop, ornate, marked
Pairpoint 295.00

INDEX

*Denotes "Special Focus" section

ABC plates 1
Abingdon 96
Adams china 96
Advertising cards 3
Advertising items 4
Alcock, Samuel & Co. 97
Almanacs 21
Aluminum, metal 793
Art Deco 22
Art Nouveau 23
Audubon prints 25
Austrian china 98
Autographs 27
Automobile accessories 29
Automobile literature 30
Automobiles 30
Autumn Leaf 181
Aviation collectibles 31
Baby mementoes 31
Bakelite 33
Banks 33-43
  Mechanical 33
  Still 35
  Glass 41
  Pottery 42
  Tin 42
  Wooden 43
Barometers 43
Baseball memorabilia 44
Baskets 45
Battenburg lace 865
Bavarian china 99
Beaded & mesh bags 48
Bedspreads 866
Belleek china 100
Bells 49
Bennington ware 103
Berlin (KPM) porcelain 105
Bicycles 50
Big Little Books 51
Billiken collectibles 52
Biloxi (George Ohr) pottery ...106
Bisque 106
Blue Willow ware 107

Boch Freres pottery 109
Boehm porcelains 110
Bookends 53
Bookmarks 53
Bootjacks 54
Bottle openers 54
Bottles 55-74
  Barber 56
  Bitters 56
  Drug Store 59
  Figurals 60
  Flasks 61
  Inks 63
  Medicines 64
  Mineral Waters 67
  Nursing 68
  Peppersauces 68
  Pickle 69
  Poison 69
  Sodas & Sarsaparillas 69
  Whiskey & Other Spirits 71
Boy & Girl Scout items 74
Brass, metal 793
Breweriana 75
Bronze, metal 794
Bronzes, statuary 76
Brownie collectibles 78
Buffalo pottery 111
Buster Brown 79
Butter molds & stamps 79
Button hooks 80
Buttons 81
Calendar plates 81
California faience 113
Campaign items 824
Campbell Kid collectibles 82
Candlesticks & candle holders ...82
Candy containers 83
Canning jars 371
Cans & containers 87
Canton china 113
Capo di Monte china 114
Card cases 92
Carlton ware 115

Cash registers 93
Castors & castor sets 93
Catalina Island pottery 115
Cat collectibles 95
Caughley wares 116
Celadon wares 116
Celluloid 95
Ceramics (See also individual
  categories & potteries) 96-297
Chalkware 297
Chandeliers 781
Character collectibles 298
Chelsea porcelain 117
Children's books 307
Children's dishes 308
Children's mugs 310
China (See Ceramics & also
  individual types & factories)
Chinese Export porcelain 118
Christmas plates 323
Christmas tree lights 310
Christmas tree ornaments 311
Cigar & cigarette cases, holders &
  lighters 312
Cigar & tobacco cutters 313
Clarice Cliff designs 120
Clewell wares 121
Clews, J. & R., pottery 121
Clifton art pottery 121
Clocks 314
Cloisonne 317
Coalport china 122
Coca-Cola items 318
Coffee grinders 321
Comic books 322
Commemorative plates 323
Cookbooks 329
Cookie cutters 330
Copeland & Spode china 123
Copper, metal 795
Cordey 124
Coronation items 331
Country store collectibles 332
Coverlets 866

Cow creamers 333
Cowan pottery 124
Cup plates, ceramic 126
Currier & Ives prints 333
Davenport china 126
Decoys .335
Dedham pottery 126
Delft faience 127
Derby & Royal Crown Derby 128
Disney, Walt, collectibles 337
Doll furniture & accessories 342
Dolls 344-354
Door knockers 354
Door stops 355
Doulton & Royal Doulton 130
Dresden porcelain 137
Enamels 356
Epergnes 357
Eye cups 358
Faberge 358
Fairings & Goss & Crest items . . .138
Fairy lamps 359
Fans 360
Farm collectibles 361
Fiesta ware 138
Firearms 362
Fire fighting collectibles 362
Fireplace & hearth items 364
Fisher, Harrison, Girls 365
Flow Blue china 140
Flue covers 366
Food, candy & misc. molds 366
Foot & bed warmers 367
Foot scrapers 368
Fountain & dip pens 899
Fracturs 368
Frames .369
Frankenthal porcelain 151
Frankoma pottery 152
Fraternal Order collectibles 370
Frog mugs 153
Fruit jars 371
Fulper pottery 153
Furniture 372-436
    Armoires 387
    Beds .388
    Benches 390
    Bookcases 391
    Boxes 392
    Bureaus plat 393
    Cabinets 394
    Candlestands 395
    Chairs 396
    Chests & chests of drawers . . .402
    *Children's 372-386
    Commodes 406
    Cupboards 407
    Desks 410

    Garden & lawn 413
    Hall racks & trees 414
    Highboys 414
    Love seats, sofas & settees 415
    Lowboys 418
    Mirrors 418
    Parlor suites 419
    Screens 420
    Secretaries 421
    Sideboards 424
    Stands 426
    Stools 428
    Tables 429
    Whatnots & etageres 436
*Games 437-450
Geisha Girl wares 154
Gibson artwork 450
Gibson Girl plates 155
Glass 451-762
    Agata 451
    Akro Agate 451
    Albertine 451
    Alexandrite 452
    Amberina 452
    Animals 454
    Appliqued 456
    Art glass baskets 456
    Baccarat 457
    Blown three mold 458
    Bohemian 458
    Bread plates & trays 459
    Bride's baskets 460
    Bristol 461
    Burmese 461
    Cambridge, Ohio 463
    Carnival 465-521
        Acanthus, 465; Acorn, 465; Acorn
        Burrs, 465; Advertising & Souvenir
        Items, 466; Age Herald, 466; Apple
        Blossoms, 467; Apple Blossom Twigs,
        467; Apple Tree, 467; Australian,
        467; Autumn Acorns, 467; Basket,
        467; Basketweave Candy Dish, 467;
        Beaded Cable, 467; Beaded Shell,
        468; Beads & Bells, 468; Beauty Bud
        Vase, 468; Big Fish Bowl, 468; Birds
        & Cherries, 468; Bird with Grapes,
        468; Blackberry, 468; Blackberry
        Block, 469; Blackberry Bramble,
        469; Blackberry Spray, 469; Black-
        berry Wreath, 469; Blossom Time
        Compote, 469; Blueberry, 469; Bo
        Peep, 469; Bouquet, 469; Broken
        Arches, 469; Butterflies, 470; But-
        terfly & Berry, 470; Butterfly & Fern,
        470; Butterfly & Tulip, 470; Buzz
        Saw, 477; Captive Rose, 471; Car-
        nival Holly, 490; Carolina Dogwood,

        471; Caroline, 471; Chatelaine, 471;
        Checkerboard, 471; Cherry, 471;
        Cherry (Fenton), 471; Cherry (Millers-
        burg), 471; Cherry Chain, 472; Cherry
        Circles, 471; Christmas Compote,
        472; Chrysanthemum, 472; Circled
        Scroll, 472; Cobblestones Bowl, 473;
        Coin Dot, 473; Coin Spot, 473; Co-
        met, 473; Constellation, 473; Coral,
        473; Corn Bottle, 473; Corn Vase,
        473; Cornucopia, 474; Cosmos, 474;
        Cosmos & Cane, 474; Country Kitch-
        en, 474; Crab Claw, 474; Crackle,
        474; Crucifix, 474; Cut Arcs, 474;
        Dahlia, 474; Daisies & Drape Vase,
        475; Daisy & Lattice Band, 475;
        Daisy & Plume, 475; Daisy Basket,
        475; Daisy Block Rowboat, 475;
        Daisy Cut Bell, 475; Daisy Squares,
        475; Daisy Wreath, 475; Dandelion,
        475; Dandelion, Paneled, 476; Dia-
        mond & Rib Vase, 476; Diamond &
        Sunburst, 476; Diamond Concave,
        476; Diamond Lace, 476; Diamond
        Point Columns, 476; Diamond Ring,
        476; Diamonds, 476; Diving Dolphins
        Footed Bowl, 477; Dogwood Sprays,
        477; Dolphins Compote, 477; Dou-
        ble Dutch Bowl, 477; Double Star,
        477; Double Stem Rose, 477; Dra-
        gon & Lotus, 477; Dragon & Straw-
        berry Bowl, 478; Drapery, 478;
        Embroidered Mums, 478; Estate,
        478; Fan, 478; Fanciful, 478; Fan-
        tail, 478; Farmyard, 478; Fashion,
        478; Feather & Heart, 479;
        Feathered Serpent, 479; Feather
        Stitch Bowl, 479; Fentonia, 479;
        Fenton's Basket, 479; Fenton's Flow-
        ers, 480; Fern, 480; Field Flower,
        480; Field Thistle, 480; File & Fan,
        480; Finecut & Roses, 480; Fine Rib,
        480; Fisherman's Mug, 481; Fish-
        scale & Beads, 481; Fleur de Lis,
        481; Floral & Grape, 481; Floral &
        Wheat Compote, 481; Flowers &
        Beads, 481; Flowers & Frames, 481;
        Flute, 481; Flute & Cane, 482; Four
        Flowers, 507; Four Seventy Four,
        482; Frolicking Bears, 482; Frosted
        Block, 482; Fruit Salad, 482; Fruits
        & Flowers, 482; Garden Path, 483;
        Garland Rose Bowl, 483; Gay Nine-
        ties, 483; God & Home, 483; God-
        dess of Harvest, 483; Golden Harvest,
        483; Good Luck, 483; Grape & Ca-
        ble, 483; Grape & Gothic Arches,
        486; Grape & Lattice, 486; Grape Ar-

bor, 487; Grape Delight, 487; Grapevine Lattice, 487; Greek Key, 487; Hammered Bell, 488; Hanging Cherries, 471; Harvest Flower, 488; Hattie, 488; Headdress Bowl, 488; Heart & Vine, 488; Hearts & Flowers, 488; Heavy Grape (Dugan or Diamond Glass), 489; Heavy Grape (Imperial), 489; Heavy Iris, 489; Heron Mug, 489; Hobnail, 489; Hobstar, 489; Hobstar & Feather, 489; Hobstar Band, 490; Holly, 490; Holly Berries, 490; Holly Sprig, 490; Holly Star, 490; Holly Whirl, 490; Homestead, 491; Honeycomb, 491; Horseheads, 491; Horse Medallion, 491; Horseshoe Curve, 517; Illinois Soldier's & Sailor's Plate, 491; Illusion, 491; Imperial Grape, 491; Inverted Feather, 492; Inverted Strawberry, 492; Iris, 492; Iris, Heavy, 489; Jardiniere, 493; Jeweled Heart, 493; Kittens, 493; Lattice & Grape, 493; Lattice & Poinsettia, 493; Leaf & Bands, 493; Leaf & Flowers, 494; Leaf & Little Flowers, 494; Leaf Chain, 494; Leaf Rays Nappy, 494; Leaf Tiers, 494; Lily of the Valley, 494; Lion, 494; Little Barrel Perfume, 494; Little Fishes, 495; Little Flowers, 495; Little Stars Bowl, 495; Loganberry Vase, 495; Long Thumbprints, 495; Lotus & Grape, 495; Louisa, 495; Lustre Flute, 496; Lustre Rose, 496; Many Fruits, 496; Many Stars, 496; Maple Leaf, 496; Marilyn, 497; Mary Ann Vase, 497; Mayan, 497; Memphis, 497; Mikado, 497; Milady, 497; Millersburg Pipe Humidor, 507; Millersburg Trout & Fly, 517; Mirrored Lotus, 498; Mitered Ovals, 498; Morning Glory, 498; Multifruits & Flowers, 498; Nautilus, 498; Nesting Swan, 498; Night Stars, 498; Nippon, 498; Nu-Art, 498; Octagon, 498; Ohio Star, 499; Open Rose, 499; Orange Tree, 499; Orange Tree Orchard, 500; Orange Tree Scroll, 500; Oriental Poppy, 500; Palm Beach, 501; Paneled Dandelion, 476; Pansy, 501; Pansy Spray, 501; Panther, 501; Peach, 502; Peach & Pear Oval Fruit Bowl, 502; Peacock, Fluffy, 502; Peacock & Dahlia, 502; Peacock & Grape, 502; Peacock & Urn, 503; Peacock at Fountain, 504; Peacocks on Fence, 504; Peacock Strutting, 505; Peacock Tail, 505;

Perfection, 505; Persian Garden, 505; Persian Medallion, 506; Petal & Fan, 506; Petals, 506; Peter Rabbit, 506; Pillow & Sunburst, 507; Pineapple, 507; Pine Cone, 507; Pipe Humidor, 507; Plaid, 507; Plume Panels Vase, 507; Pods & Posies, 507; Poinsettia, 507; Poinsettia & Lattice, 507; Pond Lily, 507; Pony, 507; Poppy (Millersburg), 507; Poppy (Northwood), 507; Poppy Show, 508; Poppy Show Vase, 508; Primrose Bowl, 508; Princess Lamp, 508; Prisms, 508; Pulled Loop, 508; Question Marks, 508; Quill, 508; Raindrops, 508; Rambler Rose, 508; Ranger, 508; Raspberry, 508; Rays & Ribbons, 508; Ribbon Tie, 473; Ripple, 509; Rising Sun, 509; Robin, 509; Rococo Vase, 509; Rosalind, 509; Rose Columns Vase, 509; Rose Show, 509; Round Up, 509; Rustic Vase, 509; Sailboat, 509; Scale Band, 510; Scales, 510; Scotch Thistle Compote, 510; Scroll Embossed, 510; Seacoast Pin Tray, 510; Seaweed, 510; Shell, 510; Shell & Jewel, 510; Shell & Sand, 510; Singing Birds, 510; Single Flower, 511; Six Petals, 511; Ski Star, 511; Soda Gold, 511; Soutache, 511; Springtime, 511; Stag & Holly, 512; Star & File, 512; Star Fish, 512; Star Medallion, 512; Star of David, 512; Star of David & Bows, 513; Stippled Petals, 513; Stippled Rays, 513; Stork & Rushes, 513; Strawberry (Fenton), 513; Strawberry (Millersburg), 514; Strawberry (Northwood), 514; Strawberry Scroll, 514; Sunflower Bowl, 514; Sunflower Pin Tray, 514; Swan Pastel Novelties, 514; Swirl Hobnail, 514; Swirl Rib, 514; Target Vase, 515; Ten Mums, 515; Thin Rib Vase, 515; Thistle, 515; Thistle & Thorn, 515; Three Fruits, 515; Tiger Lily, 516; Tornado Vase, 516; Town Pump Novelty, 516; Tree Trunk Vase, 517; Trout & Fly, 517; Twins, 517; Two Flowers, 517; Two Fruits, 517; Victorian, 517; Vineyard, 517; Vintage, 518; Vintage Band, 518; Waffle Block, 518; Waterlily, 518; Waterlily & Cattails, 519; Whirling Leaves Bowl, 519; White Oak Tumblers, 519; Wide Panel, 519; Wild Rose, 519; Wild Strawberry, 519; Windflower, 519; Windmill,

520; Windmill & Mums, 472; Windmill Medallion, 520; Wine & Roses, 520; Wishbone, 520; Wishbone & Spades, 521; Wreath of Roses, 521; Wreathed Cherry, 521; Zig Zag, 521; Zippered Heart, 521; Zippered Loop Lamp, 521.

Chocolate **521**
Chrysanthemum Sprig, Blue . . .**523**
Coralene **523**
Cosmos **524**
Crackle **524**
Cranberry **525**
Crown Milano **526**
Cruets **527**
Cup plates **528**
Custard **529-535**

Argonaut Shell, 529; Beaded Circle, 529; Beaded Swag, 529; Carnelian, 530; Cherry & Scale, 530; Chrysanthemum Sprig, 530; Diamond with Peg, 530' Everglades, 530; Fan, 531; Fentonia, 530; Fluted Scrolls, 531; Fluted Scrolls with Flower Band, 533; Geneva, 531; Georgia Gem, 531; Grape & Cable, 533; Grape & Gothic Arches, 532; Grape & Thumbprint, 533; Intaglio, 532; Inverted Fan & Feather, 532; Ivorina Verde, 535; Jackson, 533; Little Gem, 531; Louis XV, 533; Maple Leaf, 533; Northwood Fan, 531; Northwood Grape, 533; Prayer Rug, 534; Punty Band, 534; Ribbed Drape, 534; Ring Band, 534; Victoria, 535; Winged Scroll, 535.

Cut **535-550**

Baskets, 536; Bottles, 536; Bowls, 536; Boxes, 537; Butter Dishes & Tubs, 537; Butter Pats, 537; Candlesticks & Candle Holders, 538; Carafes, 538; Celery Trays & Vases, 538; Champagnes, Cordials & Wines, 539; Cheese Dishes; 539; Compotes, 539; Creamers & Sugar Bowls, 540; Cruets, 540; Decanters, 540; Dishes, Miscellaneous, 541; Ferneries, 541; Goblets, 542; Ice Buckets & Tubs, 542; Jars & Jardinieres, 542; Lamps, 543; Miscellaneous Items, 543; Nappies, 545; Perfume & Cologne Bottles, 545; Pitchers, 545; Plates, 546; Punch Bowls, 547; Punch Cups, 547; Punch Sets, 547; Rose Bowls, 547; Salt & Pepper Shakers, 548; Salt Dips, 548; Spooners, 548; Syrup Pitchers & Jugs, 548;

Toothpick Holders, 548; Trays, 548; Tumblers, 549; Vases, 549; Water Sets, 550.
Cut Velvet **550**
Czechoslovakian **551**
D'Argental **551**
Daum Nancy **552**
Depression............. **553-591**
Adam, 553; American Sweetheart, 553; Block, 554; Bubble, 555; Cameo, 556; Cherry Blossom, 557; Cloverleaf, 558; Colonial, 559; Columbia, 560; Cube, 560; Daisy, 561; Diamond Quilted, 561; Diana, 562; Dogwood, 562; Doric, 563; Doric & Pansy, 564; English Hobnail, 564; Floral, 566; Florentine (Old), 566; Florentine, 567; Georgian, 569; Hobnail, 569; Holiday, 570; Homespun, 570; Iris, 570; Lace Edge, 571; Lorain, 572; Madrid, 572; Manhattan, 574; Mayfair, 574; Miss America, 576; Moderntone, 577; Moonstone, 577; Moroccan Amethyst, 577; Normandie, 578; Number 612, 578; Old Cafe, 578; Oyster & Pearl, 579; Parrot, 579; Patrician, 579; Petalware, 580; Pineapple & Floral, 581; Princess, 581; Queen Mary, 582; Raindrops, 583; Ribbon, 583; Ring, 583; Roulette, 584; Royal Lace, 584; Royal Ruby, 585; Sandwich, 586; Sharon, 586; Sierra, 587; Spiral, 588; Swirl, 588; Tea Room, 588; Twisted Optic, 589; Waterford, 589; Windsor Diamond, 590.

De Vez & Degue **591**
Duncan & Miller **592**
Durand **593**
Fenton **594**
Findlay Onyx & Floradine **594**
Fostoria **595**
Frances ware **595**
Fry **596**
Galle' **596**
Goofus **599**
Greentown **599**
Guttate................... **601**
Heisey.................... **601**
Historical & Commemorative ...**602**
Holly Amber **604**
Imperial **605**
Jack-in-pulpit vases **605**
Kelva **606**
Kew Blas **606**
Lalique................... **607**
Leaf Mold **609**
Leaf Umbrella **609**

Le Gras **609**
Le Verre Francais........... **610**
Libbey **610**
Loetz **611**
Lutz & Lutz-type **612**
Marble **612**
Mary Gregory **613**
McKee **614**
Mercury **615**
Milk White **615**
Millefiori **617**
Mont Joye **617**
Moser **617**
Mt. Washington **618**
Muller Freres **620**
Nailsea **620**
Nakara **621**
Napoli **621**
Nash..................... **622**
Opalescent **622-628**
Blown patterns **622-624**
Pressed patterns **624-628**
Opaline................... **628**
Orrefors **629**
Pairpoint **629**
Pate de Verre **630**
Pattern **632-734**
Actress, 632; Adonis, 632; Alabama, 632; Alaska, 633; Alexis, 707; Almond Thumbprint, 633; Amazon, 634; Amberette, 634; Apollo, 634; Argus, 635; Art, 635; Ashburton, 635; Atlanta, 688; Atlas, 636; Aurora, 636; Aztec, 636; Baby Face, 636; Baby Thumbprint, 659; Balder, 637; Baltimore Pear, 637; Bamboo, 643; Banded Beaded Grape Medallion, 637; Banded Buckle, 637; Banded Portland, 638; Banded Portland w/color, 705; Bar & Diamond, 686; Barberry, 638; Barley, 638; Barred Hobstar, 648; Barred Star, 719; Basketweave, 639; Beaded Band, 639; Beaded Bull's Eye with Drape, 632; Beaded Dewdrop, 734; Beaded Grape, 639; Beaded Grape Medallion, 639; Beaded Loop, 640; Beaded Medallion, 640; Beaded Mirror, 640; Beaded Tulip, 640; Bearded Head, 729; Bearded Man, 640; Bellflower, 640; Bigler, 641; Bird & Fern, 682; Bird & Strawberry, 641; Bird in Ring, 642; Bleeding Heart, 642; Block, 642; Block & Fan, 642; Block & Star, 729; Bluebird, 641; Bow Tie, 643; Brazilian, 643; Broken Column, 643; Bryce, 710; Buckle, 644; Buckle with Star, 644; Bull's Eye, 644;

Bull's Eye Variant, 723; Bull's Eye with Diamond Point, 644; Bull's Eye with Fleur de Lis, 645; Butterfly & Fan, 642; Button Arches, 645; Cabbage Leaf, 645; Cabbage Rose, 646; Cable, 646; Cable with Ring, 646; California, 639; Cameo, 649; Canadian, 646; Cane, 646; Cannon Ball, 636; Cape Cod, 647; Cardinal Bird, 647; Cathedral, 647; Ceres, 648; Chain, 648; Chain & Shield, 648; Chain with Star, 648; Chandelier, 648; Checkerboard, 648; Cherry Thumbprint, 699; Classic, 649; Classic Medallion, 649; Coin, 650 & 728; Collins, 652; Colonial, 649; Colorado, 649; Columbian Coin, 650; Comet, 650; Compact, 718; Cord & Tassel, 650; Cord Drapery, 651; Cordova, 651; Cord Rosette, 651; Corona, 721; Cottage, 651; Croesus, 652; Crowfoot, 652; Crown Jewel, 648; Crystal Ball, 636; Crystal Wedding, 652; Cupid & Venus, 653; Currant, 653; Currier & Ives, 653; Curtain, 654; Curtain Tie Back, 654; Cut Log, 655; Dahlia, 655; Daisy & Button, 655; Daisy & Button with Crossbars, 657; Daisy & Button with Narcissus, 658; Daisy & Button with Thumbprint Panels, 658; Daisy & Button with "V" Ornament, 658; Daisy in Panel, 728; Dakota, 659; Darby, 703; Dart, 659; Deer & Dog, 659; Deer & Pine Tree, 660; Delaware, 660; Dew & Raindrop, 661; Dewdrop, 661; Dewdrop with Star, 662; Dewey, 662; Diagonal Band, 662; Diagonal Band & Fan, 663; Diamond & Bull's Eye Band, 708; Diamond & Sunburst, 663; Diamond Bar, 686; Diamond Horseshoe, 636; Diamond Medallion, 663; Diamond Point, 664; Diamond Point with Panels, 679; Diamond Quilted, 664; Diamond Thumbprint, 665; Dinner Bell, 651; Doric, 668; Double Leaf & Dart, 687; Double Loop, 710; Double Wedding Ring, 665; Drapery, 665; Egg in Sand, 666; Egyptian, 666; Emerald Green Herringbone, 700; Empire Colonial, 649; English Hobnail Cross, 634; Esther, 666; Eureka, 667; Excelsior, 667; Eyewinker, 667; Feather, 668; Festoon, 668; Finecut, 669; Finecut & Block, 669; Finecut & Diamond, 663; Finecut & Feather, 668; Finecut & Panel, 670; Finecut

Band, 651; Fine Rib, 670; Fishscale, 670; Florida, 700; Florida Palm, 671; Flower Flange, 662; Flower Pot, 671; Flute, 671; Flying Robin, 682; Four Petal, 672; Four Petal Flower, 660; Frosted Circle, 672; Frosted Leaf, 672; Frosted Lion, 672; Frosted Ribbon, 673; Frosted Roman Key, 673; Frosted Stork, 673; Frosted Waffle, 679; Galloway, 674; Garfield Drape, 674; Georgia, 702; Giant Bull's Eye, 674; Goblets with Birds & Animals, 674; Goddess of Liberty, 648; Good Luck, 681; Gooseberry, 675; Gothic, 675; Grand, 663; Grape & Festoon, 675; Grape & Festoon with Shield, 675; Grasshopper, 676; Greek Key, 676; Guardian Angel, 653; Hairpin, 676; Halley's Comet, 676; Hamilton, 676; Hamilton with Leaf, 677; Hand, 677; Harp, 677; Heart with Thumbprint, 677; Hearts of Loch Laven, 718; Hercules Pillar, 678; Herringbone, 678; Herringbone Band, 678; Hickman, 678; Hidalgo, 679; Hinoto, 679; Hobnail, 679; Hobnail with Fan, 680; Hobnail with Thumbprint Base, 680; Honeycomb, 680; Horn of Plenty, 681; Horseshoe, 681; Huber, 682; Hummingbird, 682; Hundred Eye, 682; Illinois, 682; Indiana, 683; Indiana Swirl, 668; Inverted Fern, 683; Inverted Loops & Fans, 692; Iowa, 683; Irish Column, 643; Ivy in the Snow, 683; Jacob's Ladder, 684; Jewel & Dewdrop, 684; Jewel & Festoon, 684; Jewel Band, 685; Jeweled Moon & Star, 685; Job's Tears, 635; Jumbo, 685; Kamoni, 637; Kansas, 684; Kentucky, 686; King's Crown, 686; Klondike, 634; Kokomo, 686; Lacy Medallion, 649; Lattice, 686; Leaf, 691; Leaf & Dart, 687; Le Clede, 678; Liberty Bell, 687; Lily-of-the-Valley, 688; Lincoln Drape, 688; Lion, 688; Lion, Frosted, 672; Lion & Baboon, 689; Lion's Leg, 633; Locust, 676; Log Cabin, 689; Loop, 689; Loop & Dart, 689; Loop & Jewel, 684; Loop & Pillar, 693; Loop with Dewdrops, 690; Loop with Stippled Panels, 722; Loops & Drops, 697; Loops & Fans, 692; Magnet & Grape, 690; Maine, 692; Maltese, 684; Manhattan, 691; Maple Leaf, 691; Maryland, 692; Mascotte, 692; Massachusetts, 692; Melrose, 693; Michigan, 693; Mikado, 657; Miner-

va, 694; Minnesota, 694; Mirror, 674; Mirror, Early, 694; Missouri, 695; Monkey, 695; Moon & Stars, 695; Moon & Star with Waffle, 685; Morning Glory, 696; Nail, 696; Nailhead, 696; Neptune, 640; Nestor, 696; New England Pineapple, 696; New Jersey, 697; Notched Rib, 643; Oaken Bucket, 697; Oak Leaf Band, 697; Old Man of the Mountain, 729; Old Man of the Woods, 640; One Hundred One, 698; Open Rose, 698; Oregon (Beaded Loop), 640; Oregon (Skilton), 698; Owl in Fan, 701; Palm & Scroll, 695; Palmette, 698; Paneled Cane, 699; Paneled Cherry with Thumbprints, 699; Paneled Daisy, 699; Paneled Dewdrop, 699; Paneled Finecut, 670; Paneled Forget-Me-Not, 700; Paneled Grape, 700; Paneled Heather, 700; Paneled Herringbone, 700; Paneled Hobnail, 701; Paneled Jewel, 693; Paneled Star & Button, 716; Paneled Thistle, 701; Paneled Zipper, 683; Parrot, 701; Pavonia, 702; Peacock Feather, 702; Pennsylvania, Early, 677; Pennsylvania, Late, 637; Picket, 702; Pillar, 703; Pillar & Bull's Eye, 703; Pillar Variant, 678; Pillow Encircled, 703; Pillow & Sunburst, 703; Pineapple & Fan, 703; Pineapple Stem, 702; Pleat & Panel, 703; Pleat & Tuck, 632; Plume, 704; Pointed Thumbprint, 633; Polar Bear, 704; Popcorn, 704; Portland, 705; Portland Maiden Blush, 705; Portland with Diamond Point Band, 638; Post, 705; Potted Plant, 671; Powder & Shot, 706; Prayer Rug, 681; Pressed Leaf, 706; Primrose, 706; Princess Feather, 706; Priscilla, 707; Prism, 707; Prism with Diamond Point, 708; Psyche & Cupid, 708; Pygmy, 726; Red Block, 708; Reverse Torpedo, 708; Ribbed Grape, 708; Ribbed Ivy, 709; Ribbed Palm, 709; Ribbon, 709; Ribbon Candy, 710; Rising Sun, 710; Rochelle, 706; Roman Key, 673; Roman Rosette, 710; Rose in Snow, 711; Rose Sprig, 711; Rosette, 712; Royal Ivy, 712; Royal Oak, 713; Ruby Rosette, 703; Ruby Thumbprint, 714; Sandwich Loop, 676; Sandwich Star, 715; Sawtooth, 715; Sawtooth Band, 634; Scalloped Tape, 685; Sedan, 716; Seneca Loop, 689; Shell & Jewel,

716; Shell & Tassel, 716; Sheraton, 717; Shoshone, 717; Shovel, 718; Shrine, 718; Shuttle, 718; Skilton, 698; Smocking, 718; Snail, 718; Snakeskin & Dot, 719; Spartan, 719; Spirea Band, 719; Sprig, 719; Square Lion's Head, 688; Square Panes, 705; Star Rosetted, 720; States, 720; Stedman, 720; Stippled Chain, 720; Stippled Cherry, 720; Stippled Double Loop, 721; Stippled Flower Panels, 690; Stippled Forget-Me-Not, 721; Stippled Grape & Festoon, 721; Stippled Ivy, 721; Stippled Roman Key, 721; Sunk Honeycomb, 721; Swan, 721; Teardrop & Tassel, 722; Teasel, 722; Texas, 722; Texas Bull's Eye, 723; Thistle, 701; Thousand Eye, 723; Three Face, 724; Three Panel, 725; Thumbprint, Early, 725; Tong, 726; Torpedo, 726; Tree of Life - Pittsburgh, 726; Tree of Life - Portland, 727; Tulip with Sawtooth, 727; Turkey Track, 652; Two Panel, 728; U.S. Coin, 728; Valencia Waffle, 729; Victor, 716; Victoria, 729; Viking, 729; Virginia, 674; Waffle, 730; Waffle & Thumbprint, 730; Washboard, 632; Washington, Early, 730; Washington Centennial, 730; Wedding Bells, 731; Wedding Ring, 665; Westward Ho, 731; Wheat & Barley, 732; Wildflower, 732; Willow Oak, 733; Windflower, 734; Wisconsin, 734; Wooden Pail, 697; Zipper, 734; Zippered Block, 683.

Peach Blow 735
Peking 736
Peloton 737
Phoenix 738
Pigeon Blood 738
Pomona 738
Quezal 739
Rose Bowls 740
Royal Flemish 740
Rubina Crystal 741
Rubina Verde 741
Ruby 742
Sandwich 743
Satin & Mother-of-Pearl 744
Schneider 745
Shades, gas & electric 746
Silver overlay & silver deposit . . 746
Sinclaire 747
Smith Brothers 748
Spangled 749
Spatter 749

Steuben 750
Stevens & Williams 754
Stiegel & Stiegel-type 754
Stretch 755
Tiffany 755
Tortoise Shell 757
Vallerysthal................758
Val St. Lambert 758
Vaseline 759
Venetian 759
Verlys 759
Wave Crest 760
Webb 762
Goldscheider wares 155
Goss & Crest miniatures.......138
Gouda ware................156
Graniteware................762
Greenaway, Kate, collectibles ...764
Grueby pottery 157
Gutmann artwork 765
Hampshire pottery 157
Handel lamps 783
Hatpins 766
Haviland china 158
Historical & Commemorative
    china 159
Homer, Winslow, engravings 766
Hooked rugs 766
Horse & buggy collectibles.....767
Hound handled pitchers.......160
Hull pottery...............161
Hummel figurines 162
Hutschenreuther 165
Icart prints 768
Ice cream scoops 769
Ice skates 769
Imari ware 165
Indian relics 770
Ink wells & stands 899
Iron, metal 796
Ironstone china............166
Ivory 771
Jackfield pottery 180
Jade 772
Jasper ware...............180
Jewel Tea Autumn Leaf pattern ..181
Jewelry, Victorian 772
Jugtown pottery 182
Juke boxes 773
Kaufmann, Angelique, china 182
Kellogg prints 774
Kewpie items 774
Kitchenwares..............775
Knives 780
KPM porcelain 105
Lamps 782
Lanterns 787
Leeds ware 182

Lehn ware.................780
Lenox china 183
Lighting devices...........781-788
Limoges china.............184
Lithophanes...............788
Liverpool ware.............186
Lladro porcelain figures 187
Locks & keys 788
Longwy pottery 187
Lorgnettes, opera glasses &
    spectacles 789
Lotus ware 188
Lustre wares 188
Magazines................790
Majolica 190
Marblehead pottery.........193
Marbles 791
Martin Brothers pottery 193
Match safes & containers 791
McCoy pottery............193
Medical quackery items 792
Meissen porcelain..........194
Metals 792-805
Mettlach wares 197
Military collectibles 805
Miniature lamps 786
Miniatures, paintings 806
Miniatures, replicas 807
Mocha ware 198
Moorcroft pottery 199
Mother-of-Pearl flatware 808
Mucha, Alphonse, artwork 809
Music boxes 809
Musical instruments 811
Musical instruments,
    mechanical.............812
Napkin rings 813
Nautical gear 813
Needlework pictures 814
Newcomb College pottery 200
Niloak pottery 200
Nippon china 201
North Dakota School of Mines
    pottery 204
Nymphenburg porcelain 205
Occupied Japan items 815
Old Ivory china 205
Old Paris china 208
Old Sleepy Eye pottery.......206
Owens pottery............207
Paintings, miniatures 806
Pairpoint-Limoges china 207
Paper collectibles..........816
Paper dolls 817
Paperweights.............818
Papier mache 819
Parian ware 208
Paris & Old Paris china.......208

Parrish, Maxfield, artwork 819
Pate Sur Pate..............209
Paul Revere pottery 210
Pens, fountain & dip 899
Perfume bottles 820
Peters & Reed pottery 211
Pewabic pottery 211
Pewter, metal 797
Phoenix Bird china 212
Phonographs 822
Photographic items.........822
Pickard china 212
Pictorial souvenirs 214
Pin cushion dolls 823
Pipes 824
Pisgah Forest pottery 214
Political & campaign items 824
Porcelain (See Ceramics & also
    individual types & factories)
Postcards 826
Posters 827
Prang chromolithographs 828
Pratt wares 215
Pyrography 829
Quilts 867
Quimper ware 216
Radios & accessories 829
Railroadiana 831
Razors 832
Redware 217
Red Wing pottery 218
Ridgway china 219
Rockingham wares 220
Rookwood pottery 221
Rosemead pottery 224
Rose Medallion & Rose Canton ..224
Rosenthal porcelain 225
Roseville pottery 226
Royal Bayreuth china 249
Royal Copenhagen 253
Royal Doulton ware 130
Royal Dux ware 253
Royal Rudolstadt...........254
Royal Vienna porcelain 255
Royal Worcester porcelain 256
Roycroft items 833
R.S. Germany china 260
R.S. Prussia china 260
Salesman's samples 834
Samplers 869
Sarreguemines............257
Satsuma ware 258
Scales 834
Schlegelmilch porcelain 259
Scrapbooks & albums 835
Scrimshaw...............836
Sculpture, bronzes 76
Sevres porcelain 263

Sewing adjuncts 837
Shaker items 838
Shaving mugs 839
Shawnee pottery 265
Sheet music 841
Sheffield plate, metal 800
Shenandoah Valley pottery 265
Show towels 870
Signs & signboards 842
Silhouettes 846
Silver, American, English & others,
    metal .801
Silverplate, metal 799
Slipware .266
Snuff bottles & boxes 847
Soapstone 848
Souvenir spoons 848
Spatterware 267
Spongeware 268
Spool, dye & allied cabinets 849
Staffordshire figures 269

Stangl pottery birds 270
Statue of Liberty collectibles 850
Steamship memorabilia 850
Steiff toys 851
Steins 853
Stevengraphs 870
Stoneware 271
Sunbonnet Baby collectibles 855
*Tea Leaf Lustre Ironstone
    china 168-179
Teco pottery 274
*Teddy Bear collectibles 856-865
Telephones 865
Teplitz wares 275
Terra Cotta 275
Textiles 865-871
Tiffany lamps 783
Tiles 276
Tin & tole, metal 804
Tobacco cans 90
Tobacco jars 871

Toby mugs & jugs 277
Tools 871
*Toys 873-889
Trade cards 3
Trunks 889
Uniforms, costumes & period
    clothing 889
Van Briggle pottery 278
Vending & gambling machines . .891
Warwick china 278
Watt pottery 279
Wedgwood 279
Weller pottery 283
Whieldon-type wares 294
*Wine advertising 10-21
Woodenwares 892
Worcester porcelain 295
World Fair collectibles 895
Writing accessories 899
Yellowware 296
Zsolnay pottery 297

THE ANTIQUE TRADER WEEKLY

The leading publication of the antiques hobby for over thirty years. This tabloid sized newspaper has approximately 100 pages each week and is filled with advertisements for antiques and collectibles both for sale and wanted from around the nation. It also lists auction and show information plus news, feature stories and informative question and answer columns for the antique collector.

$22.00 per year (52 issues)
Sample copy $1.00
Your money back if not satisfied!

Send to:
THE ANTIQUE TRADER WEEKLY
P.O. Box 1050
Dubuque, Iowa 52001

Name_____

Address_____

City_____

State_____ Zip_____

Enclosed is $22.00. Please enter my subscription to **THE ANTIQUE TRADER WEEKLY** for one year.

Or charge my ( ) MasterCard, or ( ) Visa Card.

Card No._____

Expire Date_____

You can enter your order **FREE** by phone and charge one of the above credit cards. Have card handy.

Call **TOLL FREE 1-800-334-7165** except in Iowa, Alaska or Hawaii 1 (319) 588-2073.